MAJOR GENERAL JOSEPH KING FENNO MANSFIELD: A SOLDIER FROM BEGINNING TO END

BY

LAURENCE H. FREIHEIT

Camp Pope Publishing

2019

ISBN: 978-1-929919-88-8

Library of Congress Control Number: 2019937693

Camp Pope Publishing
P.O. Box 2232
Iowa City, Iowa 52244
www.camppope.com

Cover Illustrations:
Front cover: Mansfield photograph courtesy National Archives and Record Administration, colorized by RetouchRestore.
Back cover: Zachary Taylor at Walnut Springs, courtesy National Portrait Gallery, Smithsonian Institution.
Title page: Zachary Taylor at Walnut Springs, courtesy National Portrait Gallery, Smithsonian Institution.

Dedication

I dedicate this book to my wife, Terri, and to the memories of all Marines who served in the Pacific with my father, Private First Class Laurence W. Freiheit, in the 1930's on the *U.S.S. Houston*. And also to the Marines in the Marine Air Wings on the United States east coast, in Japan, and Chu Lai, Republic of Vietnam, who served with Sergeant Laurence H. Freiheit from 1962 to 1966, **Semper Fidelis**!

Contents

Preface

Courtesy the Middlesex County Connecticut Historical Society

MY INTEREST IN GENERAL JOSEPH KING FENNO MANSFIELD began as I learned more about the U.S. Civil War when I moved to Virginia in 1986. I was a Connecticut native prior to moving to the Washington, D.C., area, and so paid special attention to Connecticut units and especially general officers from the Nutmeg State. As I studied the pivotal Battle of Antietam during Confederate General Robert E. Lee's Maryland Campaign of September 1862, I was fascinated by the Connecticut general mortally wounded early on the morning of the 17th at the beginning of the Battle of Antietam.

I read most accounts of the battle which whetted my appetite to learn more about Connecticut participation and specifically about Mansfield. My fundamental fascination with the Maryland Campaign was sparked by Dr. Joseph L. Harsh's book, *Taken at the Flood: Robert E. Lee and Confederate Strategy in the Maryland Campaign*, which was an assigned text for a class at American Public University where I was pursuing my master's degree in military history.[1] His well-written analysis of the campaign is the exemplar of an American Civil War campaign study--every serious student of this campaign and the Battle of Antietam must read it. This campaign became the most important one of the war for me as I came to agree with many historians that it was the pivotal battle of the American Civil War, in addition to the most sanguinary day in United States history. Had the Union Army of the Potomac commander, Major General George B. McClellan lost and Lee continued north into Pennsylvania, the outcome of the Civil War would likely have been different. A more mundane reason is that Antietam is close to my home and the remainder of the area of the Maryland Campaign is within easy driving distance. I joined Save Historic Antietam Foundation (SHAF) specifically because it concentrates on this campaign and has done so well in preserving the Antietam battlefield. I also became a volunteer at the Newcomer House on the Antietam National Battlefield when this "witness" house opened to the public.

Mansfield spent his entire life from age 13 in the U.S. Army. This book will detail this life and will include every facet of his service to his country. To give the reader sufficient background for his adventures, I have supplied details to give historical context assuming that most readers are not experts in, for example, the early history of West Point Military Academy, the Mexican-American War, duties of Inspectors' General, etc. Thus, the patient reader who does take the time to read this book closely will come away with a fair understanding of much of the military history of the United States Army for the first half of the 19th century.

Doctor Thomas (Tom) G. Clemens, the leading Mansfield and Antietam scholar in the U.S., was very generous in allowing me access to his copies of hundreds of Antietam historian Ezra Carman's letters, and other materials, as well as patiently answering many questions. He also read this book in manuscript and provided many helpful suggestions. He has written the best short biography of Mansfield in a chapter of *Corps Commanders in Blue: Union Major Generals in the Civil War*, "'Too Bad, Poor Fellows.'"[2]

Debby Shapiro, retired director of the Middlesex County Historical Society, Middletown, Connecticut, opened her files containing thousands of items relating to Mansfield, his family, and Middletown. The Society headquarters is in General Mansfield's house. Without her patient help, this book would not be as detailed as it is. The U.S. Military Academy at West Point has a wonderful library and an invaluable Special Collections division holding much Mansfield material as well as related documents. The Director, Suzanne Christoff, allowed me full access to its records. Once I arrived, Susan Lintelmann, a fellow Nutmegger, was my liaison and spent time every day to ensure that I had materials I needed, plus cheerfully answered my questions.

This book could not have been written without the help of many contributors. Some came forward with details about various aspects of the campaign which saved me from tedious digging in obscure files while others read all or parts of the manuscript and offered comments and suggested sources. Tom Clemens, Steve French, and Terri Freiheit, read my entire draft and offered numerous suggestions. Others concentrated on particular chapters: Nick Picerno, Stephen Recker, Debby Shapiro, and Jim Rosebrock. Some commented on specific segments in the book, supplied materials, and helped clarify issues: Tom Shay, Dave Pelland, Tracy Evans, Paul Haggett, John Banks, Ron Coddington, Randy Buchman, Dan Vermilya, John Hoptak, Harry Smeltzer, and Don Caughey. Nicholas Picerno supplied many important illustrations for the Antietam chapter from his personal collection. Dave Pelland allowed use of his photographs of Mansfield monuments and cemetery markers. Fort Pulaski Park Ranger Michael Weinstein supplied much information about Mansfield's participation in the construction of Fort Pulaski near Savannah, Georgia, including Rogers W. Young extensive material about the fort. Brian Downey, "Antietam on the Web," (http://antietam.aotw.org) allowed use of information from his website which is the best single online source about Antietam and the Maryland Campaign. Also, the Virginia Historical Society supplied useful illustrations. Clark Kenyon at Camp Pope Publishing again supplied expertise and patience in bringing this book to press.

Almost all maps and illustrations are from the Library of Congress (LOC) or other Federal government sources such as the National Park Service (NPS). Hal Jespersen supplied an excellent custom-made map. The Battle of Antietam

---

[1] Harsh wrote a trilogy relating to Antietam and are required reading for all with a deep interest in the Maryland Campaign of 1862: Joseph L. Harsh, *Taken at the Flood: Robert E. Lee and Confederate Strategy and the Maryland Campaign of 1862* (Kent, OH: The Kent State University Press, 1999); *Confederate Tide Rising: Robert E. Lee and the Making of Southern Strategy, 1861 – 1862* (Kent, OH: The Kent State University Press, 1998); *Sounding the Shallows: A Confederate Companion for the Maryland Campaign of 1862* (Kent, OH: The Kent State University Press, 2000).

[2] Thomas G. Clemens, *Corps Commanders in Blue: Union Major Generals in the Civil War*, ed. by Ethan Rafuse "Too Bad, Poor Fellows'", Joseph K.F. Mansfield and the XII Corps at Antietam" (Baton Rouge, LA: Louisiana University Press, 2014).

Carman-Copes 1908 series of maps are also available from LOC as is the *Atlas to Accompany the Official Records of the Union and Confederate Armies (OA)*. Maps from government sources have been modified as needed to better display pertinent information. Quoted materials have usually been silently corrected to help the reader easily understand the original text. Military personnel biographical data is taken from George W. Cullum, *Biographical Register of the Officers and Graduates of the U.S. Military Academy at West Point, New York Since Its Establishment in 1802*; John H. Eicher and David J. Eicher, *Civil War High Commands*; and Francis B. Heitman, *Historical Register and Dictionary of the United States Army, from Its Organization, September 29, 1789, to March 2, 1902*. Abbreviation "MCHS" refers to the Middlesex County (Connecticut) Historical Society; "WPL" to the United States Military Academy Library Special Collections; "*ORA*" and "*ORN*" to the *Army and Navy Official Records of the War of the Rebellion*, *ORA* references are to Series 1, unless otherwise shown; "*OA*" is the *Official Military Atlas of the Civil War*, "NARA" is the National Archives and Records Administration; "USACMH" is the U.S. Army Center of Military History; and "RSOCE" is the Records Section, Office, Chief of Engineers.[3]

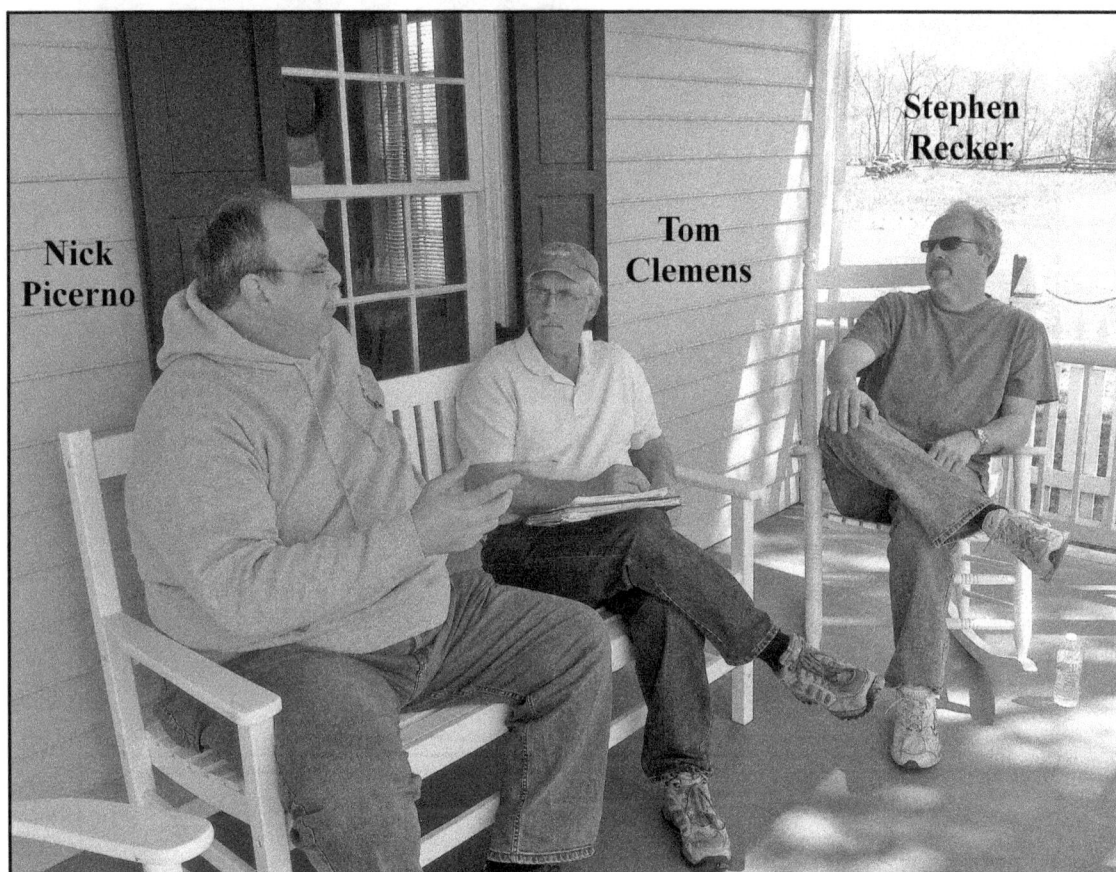

Historians Nick Picerno, Tom Clemens, and Stephen Recker gather on front porch of Newcomer House on the Antietam Battlefield with the author prior to a Mansfield driving tour. Photo by author April 2013.

No book is perfect and I take full responsibility for errors. Should any reader wish to bring them to my attention, please do so. You may send mail to me at PO BOX 613, BERKELEY SPRINGS, WV 25411, with the location of the error and its correction. Should a revised printing occur, I will fix errors and add relevant information.

Many thanks to those friends in Connecticut, Anne and Phil Forzley, who generously opened their home for the weeks I spent doing research in the Nutmeg State. Finally, without the love, support, and assistance of my wife, Terri, this book would never have been completed—my heartfelt thanks—"Go Huskies and Buckeyes."

---

[3] John H. and David J. Eicher, *Civil War High Commands* (Stanford, CA: Stanford University Press, 2001). Francis B. Heitman, *Historical Register and Dictionary of the United States Army, from Its Organization, September 29, 1789, to March 2, 1902*. vol. 1 (Washington, D.C.: Government Printing Office 1903. Reprint, University of Illinois Press, Urbana, IL: 1965). George W. Cullum, *Biographical Register of the Officers and Graduates of the U.S. Military Academy at West Point, N.Y. from Its Establishment, in 1802, to 1890* (Boston and New York: Houghton, Mifflin and Company, 1891).

MAJ.-GEN. JOS. K. MANSFIELD
Antietam, September 18, 1864.

This photograph of General Mansfield has been widely circulated in many sources since the 1911 book in which it was published: *The Photographic History of The Civil War*, vol. 10, 129, ed. by Francis Trevelyan Miller, New York, The Review of Reviews Co. This is not Mansfield for these reasons: his date of death was in 1862, not 1864; he never wore the rank of major general as that rank was posthumous; none of his photographs show the three-button major general button grouping on his frock coat, only two, and the hat shown in the full photograph is non regulation so it would be highly unlikely a major general would be wearing a non-regulation hat in a dress portrait in 1862; finally, most importantly, this is not his face when compared with the dozens of photographs of him extant. Debby Shapiro, the former Executive Director of the Middlesex County (Conn.) Historical Society, which houses a vast collection of Mansfield documents and images, is certain that this is not his picture. The intriguing question is who is this general? It is possible that this is a retouched photograph of Mansfield done for the *Photographic History* when the editors learned that there were no pictures of Mansfield as a major general. They could have decided to retouch an authentic photograph of Mansfield and in addition to adding stars to his epaulets and buttons to his coat, they tamed his mane of hair plus removed some of the careworn appearance of his face. If this is a retouched Mansfield photograph, where is the original? A less plausible explanation is that the editors decided to use this photograph knowing that it was not of Mansfield but thought it was close enough. An even more implausible possibility is that the editors used someone to impersonate Mansfield after a futile search for a photograph of him as a major general. Compare the photographs below with the one above and the differences are obvious. Clothing research and analysis by Tom Clemens from Frederick Todd, *American Military Equipage* (Providence, RI: Company of Military Historians, 1974) vol. 1, 61-65.

Mansfield as a colonel. Courtesy NARA.

Photograph of Mansfield taken in 1861 or 1862 at Union Photographic Gallery, Camp Butler, Newport News, Virginia, according to the photograph's back stamp. Note the two-button brigadier general frock coat. Courtesy LOC.

Chapter 1

Introduction

ONE OF THE MOST PROMINENT GENERALS FROM CONNECTICUT in the American Civil War, Major General Joseph King Fenno Mansfield, met his end at the most glorious moment in his long Army career: as a general leading his corps into battle at Sharpsburg, Maryland. He met his fate only days after assuming command of the XII Corps of the Army of the Potomac and leading it from the front. How did this veteran West Point-trained officer come to this abrupt end? This book will detail his life which began with a comfortable middle-class life in New Haven, Connecticut. He was born in 1803, the youngest of six children, son of Henry and Mary (Fenno) Mansfield. He entered West Point Military Academy in 1817 at age 13. He never knew his sea captain-father since his parents divorced in 1804 when he and his mother moved to Middletown, Connecticut. His father, Henry, died in 1805 in the West Indies, and his mother, Mary, of Middletown, died in 1825.

After graduating from West Point in 1822, second in his class of forty to his cousin, George Dutton, he was brevetted a second lieutenant in the Corps of Engineers 1 July 1822, to which the best and most promising were appointed, and simultaneously appointed a regular second lieutenant but, as was not unusual in the peace-time army, had to wait ten years to become a first lieutenant in March 1832. The year he was promoted to captain, 1838, he had further cause to celebrate as he married Louisa Mary Mather, who was from a wealthy New England family, and a neighbor from Middletown. With the exception of about five years, during which they resided in Brookline,

Massachusetts, their home remained in Middletown. When her parents died, their residence passed to Mansfield's wife so that she and her husband remained in Middletown making it their home. There they raised five children, and lived a simple life.[1] Their first son, Samuel, born a year later, was destined to follow his father into the Army as a career officer; he graduated from West Point, entered the Corps of Engineers, and briefly joined his father's staff. His father remained in the Corps of Engineers until 1853 when he was appointed a Regular Army colonel as an inspector general by Secretary of War Jefferson Davis. Davis, a Mexican War veteran and hero, had observed Mansfield's performance first hand during that war and was impressed by his bravery and dedication.[2]

Prior to the Mexican-American War, Mansfield had spent twenty years mainly in helping build forts, such as Fort Hamilton in New York Harbor, Fort Monroe on the Virginia peninsula, and Fort Pulaski in Savannah, Georgia, where he oversaw construction from 1831 until 1845.[3] While he was a superior, dedicated engineer, he was not known for his felicitous prose nor elocutionary prowess, but rather for his direct, sound and thorough writing and speech.[4]

In the Mexican-American War, Captain Mansfield was the chief engineer of Brigadier General Zachary Taylor's Army, responsible for doing field surveys and building field fortifications such as Fort Brown across the Rio Grande River from Matamoras, Mexico; he was brevetted major effective 9 May 1846, for gallantry and distinctive service helping defend that fort.[5] But his efforts there were not confined to mundane matters: he directly participated in assaults on Mexican positions most notably during the Battle of Monterrey, where he was far out in front designating points for attacking units. Both he and his companion topographical engineer officer were wounded, Mansfield sustaining a severe leg wound which kept him out of action for six weeks while his compatriot was mortally wounded. He remained on the battleground pointing out other avenues of approach for the attacking infantry units until his wounds forced him to leave the field the next day.[6] For this he was brevetted to lieutenant colonel for gallantry and meritorious service effective 23 September 1846. Finally, he recovered to participate in the Battle of Buena Vista for which he was brevetted colonel effective 23 February 1847, one of only a few to receive three such brevets during the war.[7]

Appointed by Secretary of War Jefferson Davis as an Inspector General in 1853 after a tour as a member of the Army Board of Engineers, he spent the years up to 1861 visiting, inspecting, and reporting on many posts west of the Mississippi to the Pacific Ocean and from the Mexican border to (and across) the Canadian border. He performed his duties well and managed to stay out of the internecine quarrels between the commanding general, Winfield Scott, and the Secretary of War, Davis. Mansfield was described "as an 'exceedingly energetic and productive inspector

---

[1]Joseph K.F. Mansfield and Joseph E. Johnston, *Texas & New Mexico on the Eve of the Civil War: The Mansfield & Johnston Inspections, 1859-1861*, Jerry Thompson, ed. (Albuquerque, NM: University of New Mexico Press, 2001), 4. Samuel later commanded the 24th Connecticut and led his regiment in the Port Hudson siege in 1863 where it was complemented by the commanding general, Nathaniel Banks; Blaikie Hines, *Civil War Volunteer Sons of Connecticut* (Thomaston, ME: American Patriot Press, 2002), 228-231. He remained in the army as an engineer and examined rivers and harbors on both coasts, retiring as a brigadier general in 1903, Mansfield and Johnston, "Conclusion," footnote 94.

[2]Mansfield and Johnston, 5. Mansfield's assigned area was west of the Mississippi (the Trans-Mississippi); Colonel Sylvester Churchill, the other inspector general, had the area east of the Mississippi. His jump from captain to colonel was unusual but clearly shows the esteem Davis held for Mansfield. Mansfield's Cullum number was 287, George W. Cullum, *Biographical Register of the Officers and Graduates of the U.S. Military Academy at West Point, New York Since Its Establishment in 1802*, suppl., vol. 5, 1900-1910, ed. Charles Braden (Saginaw, MI: Seemann & Peters, Printers, 1910), 883. Even though Mansfield was an inspector general, he was still on Army rolls in the Engineer Corps until he became a brigadier general in 1861.

[3]*Our Georgia History: The Capture of Fort Pulaski* (Woodstock, GA: Golden Ink, Inc., copyright 2001), http://www.ourgeorgiahistory.com/wars/Civil_War/ftpulaski.html; Internet; accessed 21 December 2006. Ironically, the engineer officer who preceded him was Robert E. Lee. Mansfield, obviously feeling an intense personal involvement in this project, even spent his own funds on its construction when government monies ran out.

[4]"General Mansfield, Phrenological Character and Biography," *American Phrenological Journal and Life Illustrated* 36, no. 5, (November 1862): 98; Mansfield and Johnston, 5. See also the almost 100 pages of his reports in Mansfield and Johnston which show that his prose was clear if not inspiring, typical of official reports, but more importantly, his reports show his excellent observational skills and abilities to analyze what he saw and suggest alternatives.

[5]Adrian G. Trass, *From the Golden Gate to Mexico City: The U.S. Topographical Engineers in the Mexican War, 1846-1848* (Washington, DC: GPO, 1993)120, 134; Mansfield and Johnston, 4.

[6]Trass, 135; 93-95; Mansfield and Johnston, 4, states that he was in hospital for months vice weeks and was forever scarred physically and psychologically by that severe wound; Rev. Jeremiah Taylor, *Memorial of Gen. J. K. F. Mansfield, United States Army, Who Fell in Battle at Sharpsburg, Md. Sept. 17, 1862* (Boston: Press of T.R. Marvin & Son, 1862), 32, states that he was hors-de-combat for five months. Mansfield in fact was treated in his own tent.

[7]Mansfield and Johnston, 5. The others were Robert E. Lee, Joseph Hooker, Joseph E. Johnston, Benjamin Huger, and Zealous B. Tower.

general'…was his own man, and managed to avoid the bitter political struggle by remaining constantly in the field." He was also noted for his diligence and sobriety helped by his religious convictions.[8]

Mansfield's role during the Maryland Campaign in September 1862 was regrettably brief given his long and distinguished forty-year military career. His participation in the Battle of Antietam was cut short only two days after he took command of the XII Corps in Major General George B. McClellan's Army of the Potomac.[9] Many of the officers Mansfield faced on that bloody day were his comrades during the Mexican-American War and after—even the commander of the Confederate Army at Antietam, General Robert E. Lee, was a fellow West Point graduate, engineer, and long-serving U.S. Army officer.[10]

What kind of a man was Mansfield? One learns several things from his letters--letters written to him and written by him--and comments made about him. Most obviously, he was a man of his times. He was religious, charitable, and devoted to his family, but had the typical white, male, middle class prejudices found in Victorian America. He was against slavery but did not believe that nonwhites were or would be the equal of whites. In the military, he strove to do his duty as best he could although fellow officers and subordinates sometimes found him "fussy" and "fond of meddling with his subordinates."[11] But no officer found him lacking in his zealous pursuit of his duty both during peacetime and especially during battle. And his enlisted subordinates universally described him in glowing terms. His writings and letters always show that officers and men who performed poorly due to alcohol received disapprobation even though Mansfield was not a teetotaler. Mansfield's focus was always on one's ability to perform military duties well but his Puritan background showed through when, in addition to alcohol abuse, he decried married officers who dallied with "ladies" during the Mexican-American War. Being a senior Army officer experienced in battle and well-educated, he did not suffer fools gladly, especially officers, but he was more sympathetic with enlisted men. He was one of the best, bravest, and most dedicated officers in the Old Army and, had he lived, would have been one of Lincoln's best generals.

---

[8] Mansfield and Johnston, 6; Taylor, 40, where he is described as making "his public profession of religion" in July, 1841. See also George T. Ness, Jr., *The Regular Army on the Eve of the Civil War* (Baltimore: Toomey Press, 1990), where he is described as "highly competent, [and] of strong religious convictions" (49).

[9] *ORA*, vol. 19, pt. 1, 157, pt. 2, 297.

[10] Richard Elliot Winslow III, *General John Sedgwick: The Story of a Union Corps Commander* (Novato, CA: Presidio Press, 1982), 43; *ORA*, pt. 2, 283.

[11] John Pope, *National Tribune,* 19 March 1891, "War Reminiscences."

Chapter 2

The Mansfield Family and Life in Connecticut

JOSEPH KING FENNO MANSFIELD CALLED MIDDLETOWN, CONNECTICUT, his home and often officially his "headquarters" or "post" for his entire life even though he spent years away from there during his Army service. He was born in New Haven, Connecticut, at 2 a.m. on Thursday, 22 December 1803, as the youngest child of six to Henry and Mary (Fenno) Mansfield, both of old and distinguished American colonist stock. His mother, Mary, was a Middletown native, and he moved there with her from New Haven in 1804 after his mother divorced, and grew up with her in her father's home.[1] His brother, John Fenno Mansfield, who became his guardian, died from an illness contracted after leading an infantry unit in Lower Canada in the War of 1812. In addition to this brother, John, he had earlier relatives who served in the colonial militia and in military service to the national government as will be seen below.[2] He was baptized in the First Church of Christ in Middletown 9 April 1806.[3]

---

[1] This house, called the Fenno House, was demolished in the 1920's, and is now the site of Spear Park.

[2] John died 12 September 1812. He had moved to Cincinnati early in life and raised a company of light infantry there. He commanded the company when it went to Detroit under command of Brigadier General William Hull and was ignominiously surrendered after the Battle of Fort Detroit 15-16 August 1812. Hull was court martialed and sentenced to death but President James Madison reduced his sentence to dismissal from the Army; William Hull, *Memoirs of the Campaign of the North Western Army of the United States, A.D. 1812* (Boston, MA: True & Greene, 1824), 169-170; H. Mansfield, *The Descendants of Richard and Gillian Mansfield Who Settled in New Haven, 1639 With Sketches of Some of the Most Distinguished.*

Mary's father and Mansfield's grandfather, Ephraim, was born in Boston in 1735, and arrived in Middletown at age 29. He married Mary King in 1765, a daughter of Captain Henry King and his wife, Mary Hamlin. Ephraim bought a half acre lot on the corner of Main Street and what would become William Street in Middletown and there built a large wooden house in 1764 for his family which was also used as a tavern. Their daughter, Mary, was the oldest of four children and was born on 3 April 1767. Mary's grandfather, Captain King, was the captain of a small colonial top-sail schooner, built for river and coastal use, sailing to Boston, Providence, and New York City. This type vessel carried farm goods to the cities and returned with finished goods primarily European imports. General Mansfield's paternal grandfather, Stephen, who lived in New Haven, was also a ship's captain, but of a sea-going vessel, who participated extensively in the West India trade. General Mansfield's father, Henry, became a captain like his father, inheriting his trade business. The West India trade flourished both from Middletown and New Haven sending lumber, meat, and grain to the islands and returning with sugar, rum, salt, and molasses. But with the beginning of the Revolutionary War trade was sharply curtailed.[4]

Middletown was settled first in 1650 by settlers from other Connecticut Colony towns. The city was incorporated in 1784 as part of Hartford County then it became part of Middlesex County which was incorporated in 1785. The city Mansfield came to know had progressed from a subsistence community which was always liable to Indian predations to a prosperous one. By the mid to late 1700's Middletown became a major port city with one-third of its population involved in maritime trading. Slaves were brought in by this commerce primarily from the Danish West Indies trade. But the War of 1812 took a toll on the city from which it did not recover with the exception of manufacturing which did thrive with many factories selling arms to the U.S. Government. Even though that business prospered for a time, after the War of 1812 much of the firearms business moved to other sites such as Hartford and New Haven, Connecticut, and Springfield, Massachusetts. Most of Mansfield's friends and acquaintances would have run businesses with which he would have been familiar. Joseph K.F. Mansfield would have known about steamships ported in Middletown as he frequently travelled from there to New York.[5]

The first of Joseph K.F. Mansfield's ancestors on his father's side to arrive in the American British Colonies was Richard Mansfield. Richard was the progenitor of most of the Mansfields in North America during its early history. He was born in Exeter, Devonshire, England, and arrived in Boston 30 November 1634. In 1639, he moved south and settled in Quinnipiac which later became known as New Haven in the future State of Connecticut. He had followed other groups which departed the Bay and Plymouth Colonies; one Puritan group left Massachusetts and started the New Haven Colony on the northern shore of Long Island Sound in 1637. He was apparently well-to-do as he wound up

---

Also, of Connections of Other Names (New Haven, CT: Hoggson & Robinson, Printers, 1885), 90; Joseph K. F. Mansfield and Joseph E. Johnston, *Texas and New Mexico on the Eve of the Civil War: The Mansfield & Johnston Inspections, 1859-1861*, ed. Jerry Thompson, (Albuquerque: University of New Mexico Press, 2001), 2. While most of this book contains documents written by Mansfield and Johnston, it also has much material written by the editor and has biographical information about Mansfield. Another excellent source of biographical information about Mansfield is contained in a chapter in *Corps Commanders in Blue: Union Major Generals in the Civil War*, ed. by Ethan S. Rafuse, "'Too Bad, Poor Fellows', Joseph K.F. Mansfield and the XII Corps at Antietam," Thomas G. Clemens (Baton Rouge, LA: Louisiana State University Press, 2014), 61-95.

[3] Azel Washburn Hazen, *A Brief History of the First Church of Christ in Middletown Connecticut for Two Centuries and a Half* (n.p., 1920); Mansfield's "official duties kept him away from Middletown a large part of the time, but whenever he was here he attended the Sunday and week-day services of the Church, always manifesting a genuine interest in its prosperity;" 88. In 1898, "The fine pulpit Bible, with its exquisite mark, was presented...by Miss Katharine Mather Mansfield, in memory of her mother, Mrs. Louisa Mather Mansfield, the widow of Gen. Joseph K. F. Mansfield;" 121. Mansfield and his family lived for about five years in Brookline, Massachusetts, after he returned from the Mexican-American War and was assigned to do engineering work on forts in Boston Harbor. He retained his wife's properties in Middletown and only lived in Brookline so that his family could be with him. Mansfield spent thousands of dollars improving the house and two lots in Brookline. Once he and his family moved away he rented the house out. Receipts and letters Courtesy of the Middlesex County Historical Society.

[4] Unpublished biography of Mary Fenno Mansfield, Courtesy of the Middlesex County Historical Society.

[5] Henry Whittemore, et al, eds., *History of Middlesex County, Connecticut, with Biographical Sketches of Its Prominent Men* (New York, NY: J.B. Beers and Company 1884), 60-100, passim. The islands in the Caribbean are named variously in contemporary reports and books as British or Danish Caribbean Islands and more particularly Frederickstead, St. Croix, West End, in the Virgin Islands. Britain and France were also involved from the 1600's into the 1800's. "The first British invasion and occupation of the Danish West Indies occurred during the French Revolutionary Wars when at the end of March 1801 a British fleet arrived at St. Thomas. The Danes accepted the Articles of Capitulation the British proposed and the British occupied the islands without a shot being fired. The British occupation lasted until April 1802, when the British returned the islands to Denmark. The second British invasion of the Danish West Indies took place during the Napoleonic Wars in December 1807 when a British fleet captured St. Thomas on 22 December and St. Croix on 25 December. The Danes did not resist and the invasion was bloodless. This British occupation of the Danish West Indies lasted until 20 November 1815, when Britain returned the islands to Denmark. On 17 January 1917, according to the Treaty of the Danish West Indies, the Danish government sold the islands to the United States for $25 million....Danish administration ended on 31 March 1917, when the United States took formal possession of the territory and renamed it the United States Virgin Islands." Courtesy Wikipedia.

owning 146 acres in and around New Haven. He had only two children with his wife Gillian: Joseph, born in 1636, and Moses, born in 1639. Richard died 10 January 1655, and Gillian died in 1669. Richard married Gillian in England before arriving in Boston. Richard's son, Moses, had a son, Jonathan, born in New Haven, 15 February, 1686, who would become Joseph K.F. Mansfield's paternal great grandfather. He was also well-to-do and was an ensign in a military company. Jonathan married Sarah Alling 1 June 1708 and had six children, one of which, Stephen, was Joseph K.F. Mansfield's grandfather. Stephen was born in New Haven 14 November 1716. On 31 December 1746, he married Hannah Beach and had eight children including Joseph K.F. Mansfield's father, Henry, all born in New Haven. Stephen died 15 July 1774 and Hannah died 20 September 1795. "He was an enterprising sea captain and engaged many years extensively in the West India trade. His home was on the northeast corner of Chapel and State streets and his store was adjacent to it. He and three others were appointed a committee for the improvement of common and undivided lands, for six pounds apiece, of land lying, east of his lot. He was a vestryman of Trinity Church in 1765 and later. He was a very prominent citizen in his day." Captain Stephen Mansfield was shown as a church warden in 1770 of the Trinity Parish.[6]

Joseph K.F. Mansfield's father, Henry, was born 1 February 1762, and participated in the West India trade for many years and lived in the West Indies most of the time where he died in 1805. General Mansfield's mother, Mary Fenno, was born 3 April 1767, the daughter of Ephraim Fenno of Middletown, Connecticut. Mary and Henry Mansfield married on 3 August 1785, when she was 18 years and 4 months old. She went to New Haven to live with her wealthy and socially prominent sea captain husband and joined him not only in his travels to and from the Virgin Islands but lived with him there. They had their first born son, Henry Stephen Mansfield, in New Haven, on 26 May 1786. This was certainly a happy event to counterbalance a sadder one when one of her younger brothers, John Fenno, who had followed her new husband to the West Indies, died in New Haven 2 September 1786 at age 17 from a disease he apparently contracted in the West Indies. After Henry and Mary had two more children, John Fenno and Mary Grace Caroline, Mary decided to move to St. Croix Island about 1799 not only to enjoy the more favorable climate but also because she had suspicions about her husband's fidelity. But despite possible marital problems, Henry and Mary had two more daughters in Fredrickstead, St. Croix, West End, in the Virgin Islands—Grace Totten and Hanna Fenno. Despite these joys, she found more sorrow as another of her brothers, Joseph King Fenno, who had followed his brother in the shipping trade, died 4 September 1800, at St. Croix, age 20. Very likely when her youngest son was born in New Haven in 1803, she named him after this brother: Joseph King Fenno Mansfield. She had left St. Croix just before his birth, returned to New Haven, and sued for divorce in the New Haven Superior Court in 1804. Divorce during this era was unusual and court records unfortunately for Mary portrayed for the public to read of her husband's scandalous behavior as he apparently had another family in St. Croix in addition to the one with Mary. Records stated that Henry about 1 January 1798 left her and then "lived in a State of Adultery with another woman and that the said Mansfield with the

---

[6] Mansfield, *Descendants*, 1-2; Ellery Bicknell Crane, *Historic homes and institutions and genealogical and personal memoirs of Worcester County, Massachusetts*, vol. 2 (Lewis Pub., 1907), 406. J.L. Rockey, et al, eds., *History of New Haven County, Connecticut*, vol. 1 (New York, NY: W.W. Preston & Co., 1892), 183, Sources differ regarding when Richard arrived in Boston—1634 or 1639. Crane, *Worcester*, shows 1639 as does Mansfield, *Descendants*, but *Encyclopedia of Connecticut Biography*, vol. 1 (Boston, MA: The American Historical Society, Inc., 1917), 85, shows 1634. Joseph K.F. Mansfield's uncles and aunts: "Hannah, born November 17, 1747, married, July 5, 1767, William Douglas; was prominent in the revolution, rising to the rank of colonel; born at Plainfield, Connecticut, January 27, 1742, and died May 28, 1777; she survived him forty-eight years, dying May 22, 1825. Stephen, born September, 1750, died August 25, 1751. Stephen, born July 31, 1753, died August 14, 1756. John, born April 11, 1756, died November 5, 1766. Jared, born May 23, 1759, married in New Haven, March 2, 1800, Elizabeth Phipps, daughter of David; graduate of Yale; master of Friends School in Philadelphia; appointed captain in the engineer corps and stationed at West Point; became surveyor general of the United States; professor at West Point fourteen years. Henry, born February 1, 1762.... Sarah, born 1765, married, 1784, James Sisson, of Newport, Rhode Island. Grace, born 1770, married, October 15, 1785, Peter Totten, and their son Joseph G. fought in the war of 1812 and attained the rank of general; he served also in the Mexican war;" Crane, 406-407. "Moses Mansfield, son of Richard Mansfield, was born in 1639. He was admitted a freeman May 1, 1660, and died October 3, 1703. He was a major in the military service of the colony, and that was the highest rank in the colonial troops, and Major Mansfield fought in King Philip's war. The town of Mansfield, Connecticut, was named in his honor. On the present site of the town he defeated the Indians in battle. He was a member of the general court or assembly forty-eight sessions....He married May 5, 1664, Mercy Glover, daughter of Henry Glover, an early settler and prominent man. He married (second) Abigail Yale, daughter of Thomas and Mary Yale. She was born May 5, 1660, died February 28, 1709, in her forty-ninth year....children: Abigail, born February 7, 1664, married John Atwater, September 13, 1682; Mercy, born April 2, 1667, married, 1691, John Thompson, son of John and grandson of the first settler, Anthony Thompson; Hannah, born March 11, 1669, married Gershom Brown, about 1795; Samuel, born December 31, 1671, graduated at Harvard College in 1690, followed John Davenport as teacher in charge of the Hopkins grammar school; Moses, born August 15, 1674, married Margaret Prout, daughter of John Prout, he was a leading citizen; Bathshua, born January 1, 1682, married, January 22, 1705, Joseph Chapman; Jonathan, born February 15, 1686;" Crane 406. Mansfields in New Haven were also involved in a brickmaking company and a wagon making firm, Rockey, 267-268. Mansfields there were also participants in the Revolutionary War and the War of 1812, Rockey, 271-272; Biography of Mary Fenno Mansfield Courtesy of the Middlesex County Historical Society.

various times and places and with divers persons since that time has committed the Crime of Adultery and particularly at St. Croix in the West Indies on or about the first day of January, 1798, and on or about the first day of July, 1799, and on or about the first day of March, 1802, committed the Crime of Adultery and for three years last past has lived and still doth live with a certain woman as his wife in a State of Adultery in the Island of St. Croix praying for a Bill of Divorce" which was granted Mary in 1804. Mary was a determined and likely strong woman to go through with this embarrassing public event but now had to return to Middletown with six children in tow as she had no resources for support in New Haven having severed her relationship with the Mansfields. Of these children, Joseph K.F. was the youngest at seven months and the oldest was Henry Stephen, age 18. Her father was now 70 and apparently did not run the Fenno tavern. Mary must have had some resources since she brought back from St. Croix a young slave named Venus. Venus had five children, one born in St. Croix in 1800, and the rest born in New Haven but there is no record of a father. With a total of 13 members, black and white in her household, Mary could not have been penniless and perhaps helped run the Fenno tavern. One source of income was recorded however when she sold the six-year-old slave George, to one Catherine Brooks, but he was to be free when he reached the age of 21. It is possible she sold or hired out others of the slave children to earn funds to support the household but at the least she benefited from their "free" help to support her family's life. One of her sons, Henry, an officer in a bank in Slatersville, R.I., likely gave his mother financial help as Middletown 1820 real estate records show that she settled with him upon her father's death concerning her father's house. More help for her arrived when one of her daughters, Grace Totten Parker, appeared, to live with her with the Parker family and stayed with her until her death in 14 January 1825. General Mansfield, while not in favor of slavery, joined the Office of the Colonization Society which shows him a member for life with the certificate date 18 May 1860. He never wrote about his mother's slaves or servants and nothing has been found to show that he personally owned or used slaves.[7]

---

[7] Biography of Mary Fenno Mansfield Courtesy of the Middlesex County Historical Society. The Parker family had three daughters, two of whom married Douglas brothers: Grace Caroline married William Douglas, Mary Adaline married Benjamin Douglas, the husbands being second cousins of their wives, since their grandmother was Hannah Mansfield Douglas of Northford, Connecticut. No evidence has been found which shows that General Mansfield or his wife or children owned any slaves. Certificate Courtesy of the Middlesex County Historical Society. Venus's children: Roselin or Rose born in St. Croix 12 April 1800; Dick, born in New Haven 4 December 1802; Jane Venus born in New Haven 1 October 1803; George born in Middletown 15 April 1806; and Margaret born in Middletown 21 December 1810; Mansfield's mother's journal, Courtesy of the Middlesex County Historical Society. Connecticut in 1774 passed a law to stopping the importation of slaves and in 1797 required that slaves born after 1784 would be free at age 21; slavery was abolished in 1848. Henry Stephen Mansfield, Jr., worked with his father in the scythe making business which in 1861 made some 30,000 swords for the U.S. Government. They were known as Mansfield & Lamb swords and were considered to be of very good quality. The company was located in Forestdale which was located on the Branch River, about one mile below Slatersville. "The first business engaged in here, of any importance, was that of the manufacture of scythes, by Newton Darling, about the year 1824. Mr. Darling had learned his trade of Col. Comstock Passmore, at Branch village. The water power cost Mr. Darling only one hundred dollars and the cost of sluice way, to be opened only when water ran over the dam. H.S. Mansfield afterwards joined Mr. Darling in the business. In 1839, Ansel Holman joined the firm. In 1841, Mr. Darling sold out his interest and the firm became Mansfield & Holman. It was afterwards Mansfield & Lamb, Estus Lamb having become a partner, and the firm owning the entire village. Prior to 1860 the annual product was 10,000 dozen of scythes; since, it has been about 8,000 dozen. During the war of the rebellion this firm furnished the government with thirty thousand sabres, officially declared to be equal to any manufactured in the country;" Thomas Steere, *History of the Town of Smithfield from Its Organization, in 1730-1 to Its Division, in 1871* (Providence, RI: E.L. Freeman & Co., 1881), 94-95.

Painting of the ship, *Mercury*, a similar type vessel that Mansfield's father would have sailed from New Haven to the West Indies. Courtesy of the Middlesex County Historical Society.

General Mansfield's mother, Mary, died 14 January 1825, at age 58.[8] Henry Mansfield, son of Stephen Mansfield, "built one of the finest residences of his day in New Haven on the east side of State Street, near Chapel Street....He made his home in the West Indies much of the time and died there in 1805. The last deed that he made is dated shortly before his death, May 10, 1805, at West End, Island of St. Croix, West Indies, to William McCracken and William McCracken, Jr., a quarter part of his pew in Trinity Church."[9] To summarize, Henry's and Mary's children were all born in New Haven except Grace and Hannah who were born in St. Croix:

1. Henry Stephen, born at New Haven, May 26, 1786.
2. John Fenno, born January 9, 1788, settled early at Cincinnati, Ohio; captain in war of 1812 [died unmarried, Cincinnati, Ohio, Sept. 12, 1812].
3. Mary Grace Caroline, born June 4, 1792, married David Wade, of Cincinnati, Ohio, distinguished as lawyer and jurist; she died April 16, 1825; was the mother of nine children.
4. Grace Totten, born February 13, 1799, in St. Croix, Frederickstead, West End, West Indies, (Danish territory), married Elias Parker, of New Haven; she died March 10, 1878, at Middletown, Connecticut, age 79.
5. Hannah Fenno, born in St. Croix, Frederickstead, West End, West Indies, (Danish territory) February 24, 1801, died unmarried at Middletown about 1872.

---

[8] Mansfield, *Descendants*, 45-46.
[9] Ellery Bicknell Crane, *Historic homes and institutions and genealogical and personal memoirs of Worcester County, Massachusetts*, vol. 2 (Lewis Pub., 1907), 407.

6. General Joseph King Fenno, born in New Haven, December 22, 1803, married, September 25, 1838, Louisa Maria Mather.[10]

Four of five of General Mansfield's children were born in Middletown, Connecticut:

Joseph K.F. Mansfield married Louisa Maria Mather 25 September 1838 in Middletown, and all five of their children, except Katherine, were born there:

1. Samuel Mather was born on 23 September 1839, and married Anna Baldwin Wright of Detroit, Michigan, on 16 April 1874. He died on 18 February 1928.
2. Mary Louisa, was born on 23 March 1841, and died 22 June 1863 at age 22, unmarried.
3. Joseph Totten, was born on 4 October 1843, and died as an infant 15 July 1844.
4. Henry Livingston was born on 31 March 1845, and married Adeline O. Carter on 29 August 1866. He died 14 January 1918.
5. Katharine Mather was born on 1 May 1850, in Brookline, Massachusetts, and married Walter Buckley Hubbard, son of Jeremiah Hubbard, 20 June 1899. She died 18 January 1918.[11]

Mansfield's wife, Louisa Maria Mather, was the eldest daughter of six girls of her parents, Samuel and Katherine (Livingston) Mather. Louisa Maria was born 14 June 1808, and died 22 February 1880. Samuel Mather, her father, was a 1792 graduate of Yale College and married Katherine in 1807. Katherine was the third daughter of Captain Abraham and Maria (Peoples) Livingston, of Stillwater, New York. Louisa's father and family moved to Middletown in the summer of 1815 from Troy, New York, to better educate his nine children--six daughters and three sons--and because the War of 1812 had impaired his mercantile business there, plus a fire had destroyed his store. Samuel and his family were originally from Lyme, Connecticut. His earliest ancestor, Rev. Richard Mather, had arrived in Boston in August 1635. His father, also named Samuel, was a shareholder and member of the first board of directors of the Connecticut Land Company. His son, Louisa's father, was also a shareholder of the Connecticut Land Company. After returning to Middletown in 1815, he retired from his shipping trade to devote himself to his family. He died in Middletown 6 April 1854 at the age of 84, noted as one of the wealthiest citizens of that town and of "excellent, exemplary character."[12]

Mansfield was educated in public schools and was remembered as one who was made to feel that he should depend upon himself, perhaps not unexpected in a family without a father.[13] When he entered at age thirteen into the U.S. Military Academy in October 1817, he was the youngest in his class.[14] Mansfield's family history likely helped fuel young Joseph's aspirations to military service. He had an uncle in the military service, Jared Mansfield, who not only supported his desires for martial endeavors, but helped obtain Joseph's admission to West Point. Major Moses Mansfield, Joseph K.F. Mansfield's great-great grandfather was a noted figure in Connecticut history: the town of Mansfield, Connecticut, was named in his honor for his military contributions especially in King Philip's War. During King Phillip's War in 1675-1676, he was lieutenant of the New Haven Company under Captain John Beard. He fought in the

---

[10] Ibid.

[11] Ellery Bicknell Crane, *Historic homes and institutions and genealogical and personal memoirs of Worcester County, Massachusetts*, vol. 2 (Lewis Pub., 1907), 406. Mansfield received a letter from his mother 28 Dec 1824 to which he attached a note: "The last letter I received from my Mother." She gave him advice to wear warm clothes, eat well, etc., and asked for a little money. She heard that he was doing well. "Heat the hollow of your feet every night before you go to bed." He also received a letter from his sister Mary Wade, from Cincinnati, Ohio, 3 Dec 1820, while he was at West Point: "Let no time pass unemployed—for time once lost can never be recalled." She says his "spelling has much improved, and you write a pleasing hand. There was but one word spelt wrong in your last letter as follows {douring} {during}." Letters courtesy WPL.

[12] Franklin Bowditch Dexter, *Biographical Sketches of the Graduates of Yale College with Annals of the College History*, vol. V, June, 1792-September, 1805 (New York, NY: Henry Holt and Company, 1911), 31-32. The Connecticut Land Company in which the Mathers were involved was formed in 1795 to purchase the greater part of the Western Reserve from the State of Connecticut as a land speculation. The Western Reserve was part of the original charter of Connecticut by King Charles II which gave lands to the west "to the South Sea on the West Part" but gave up claims to most of the land after the Revolution; the retained portion in the northeastern section became known as the Connecticut Western Reserve. In 1795, Connecticut sold to a group of investors for $1.2 million what was estimated to be 3,000,000 acres but turned out to be less due to faulty surveys. The company had difficulties in selling land to settlers and businesses and there were competing legal claims to the land. The company went bankrupt and dissolved in 1809. *The Western Reserve Historical Society, Tract No. 96, Oct. 1916, Annual Report for 1915-1916* (Cleveland, OH, 1916), 66-91, passim.

[13] [Rev. Jeremiah Taylor], *Memorial of Gen. J. K. F. Mansfield, United States Army, Who Fell in Battle at Sharpsburg, Md. Sept. 17, 1862*, (Boston: Press of T.R. Marvin & Son, 1862), 29. This 67-page book is apparently composed of addresses mostly by Reverend Taylor at Mansfield's funeral. It also contains two other shorter addresses as well as a newspaper obituary notice and a newspaper article reporting the funeral proceedings. There were four school districts within the City of Middletown, all incorporated in the Middletown City School Society; these districts were The North, North Middle, South Middle, and South; *History of Middlesex County*, 129.

[14] His age upon entry to West Point is 13; however, in *Memorial of Gen. Mansfield*, it is stated as 14, 29; other sources also incorrectly show his age as 14--he actually entered about two months prior to his 14th birthday.

Narragansett Campaign in Rhode Island in 1675. Following the war, he was named Captain of the New Haven train band in 1683 and was appointed Sergeant Major of New Haven County in 1694.[15]

Joseph K.F. Mansfield also contributed to building and maintaining a women's school in Middletown. He built the Middletown Female Seminary on Broad Street with Maria Payne in charge. A newspaper clipping dated 20 July 1860, "From Middletown," possibly from the *New York Times*, gave details about Mansfield's school. The article stated that the writer attended the first anniversary of Miss Payne's young ladies school. Miss Payne came to Middletown to take charge of a planned school from her post as a "preceptress at the seminary situated at Cooperstown, New York....After she arrived here, from some cause, the whole matter fell through. Nothing daunted, Miss Payne, with a courage worthy of a Mary Lyon, set herself to work to start a day school, which she did, in a room over a noisy store, on a stormy, gloomy morning, with one scholar. After a time, Col. Mansfield, of the U.S. Army, a wealthy and generous gentleman of this city, erected a fine, two-story brick building, and gave Miss Payne the use of it for her school, and yesterday she had the pleasure of graduating three young ladies, who have finished the course of three year's study, and of saying that she had a school of fifty, we might add, very fine ladies." The school was apparently a good one as the commencement address was given by the president of Wesleyan University. Another newspaper article titled "Young Ladies' Seminary," gave more details: "I was present on Friday last at the dedication of the new School House in Broad street, built by Col. Mansfield expressly for the Middletown Young Ladies Seminary. I was much gratified at the completeness of the building. On the first floor is a drawing room, a music room, a recitation room and a reception room. On the second floor is one large school room and a small recitation room attached. These rooms are all extremely well lighted and ventilated and warmed, and they are unexceptionable as to pleasantness. In the basement is a good well and pump, and a good cistern and an excellent furnace. The grounds around the building are well graded and drained, and ample for all purposes of recreation, and will be ornamented by handsome shrubbery, evergreens, etc. The location is quite central, and in an excellent neighborhood. In short, the building is just as it should be for the object so much desired in this city. The ceremonies of the occasion were quite interesting. An introductory prayer was made by the Rev. Mr. Lewis; a discourse by the Rev. Mr. Taylor; singing by Miss Payne's scholars; remarks by several gentlemen suitable to the occasion, and the concluding prayer by Rev. Mr. Hoyt. There will now be a choice of schools in this city, and parents will be enabled to educate their daughters without sending them out of town for that purpose....There is no doubt Miss Payne as the head of this school will make it what it should be, the first in the State with her assistants, in drawing, French and music...."[16] In a letter from Mansfield to Rev. Lathrop written from Middletown on 27 February 1856 he stated that he cannot contribute to the Female Seminary because of lack of funds but will "contribute something towards the erection of the buildings" when he obtains funds. In a letter to Mansfield 25 October 1861, a H.M. Colton wrote that he needed monies--$600 for the school. "He considered good education as of the highest importance to the honor, freedom and happiness of his country, and therefore exerted his influence to promote it. Such was his genius and enthusiastic love of education that he established a seminary for the education of young ladies in the higher branches of learning, and sustained it almost wholly with his own means, in Middletown." He might have also remembered stories from his mother about the girls' finishing schools she opened in September 1804 run from her home. Her newspaper advertisement stated that "She teaches what is commonly taught in schools, with the addition of drawing, painting, and lace-making, etc." Her school was not a success perhaps due to the scandal of her recent divorce.[17]

---

[15] Article from the November 2011 issue of the Mansfield Historical Society Newsletter, which named its sources: *The Colonial Records of Connecticut, 1678-1689 and 1689-1706* (Hartford: Case, Lockwood and Brainard, 1868) and Ellery Bicknell Crane, *Historic homes and institutions and genealogical and personal memoirs of Worcester County, Massachusetts*, Vol. 2 (Lewis Pub., 1907. A "train band" was a militia company established by the New Haven government in which males between 16 and 60 were required to serve. Its four squadrons were led by a captain, a lieutenant, and an ensign. It functioned to protect the town from Indians or other invaders and sometimes used for nonmilitary emergencies much as the modern National Guard is used today except in this case it was organized for New Haven only. If the newspaper articles are from Middletown, they would be from the *Middletown Sentinel and Witness, Middletown Democrat, Middletown News,* or *Middletown Constitution.*

[16] Newspaper clippings Courtesy of the Middlesex County Historical Society.

[17] Mansfield and Johnston, 2. Jared was a lieutenant colonel and professor of natural and experimental philosophy at West Point and later was Surveyor-General of the United States. Here, too, Jared described Joseph as "of 'fine bodily form & of superior mental endowments' and possessed a good understanding of 'Latin, French & German,' as well as a 'fine taste in painting, drawing & other minor arts.'" *Encyclopedia of Connecticut Biography*, vol. 1 (Boston, MA: The American Historical Society, Inc., 1917), 85. After Mansfield's mother's death on 14 January 1825, his aunt Elizabeth, Jared Mansfield's wife, wrote from West Point on 18 February 1825: "The only consolation you can feel at present must be that you have been a dutiful and affectionate son....You shall be as welcome to us as would have been your ever lamented brother." She wrote him again from West Point 20 February 1827 and mentioned his good qualities in asking about a Charles Drake: "he wants some of your good qualities: your silence, your love of truth and your industry." Letters courtesy WPL. Henry Franklin Andrews, *The Hamlin Family: A Genealogy of Capt. Giles Hamlin of*

Further information about the school was provided in the *History of Middlesex County*: "About 1850, Rev. Josiah Brewer, then residing in the house now occupied by Hon. Benjamin Douglas, on South Main Street, opened "The Middletown Female Seminary." The school was held in a brick building, then standing north of the residence, and it seems to have been a school of more than ordinary facilities for furnishing a complete education for young ladies. Some years later the school was moved to the Union Mills building, corner of Main and Union streets, and about 1856 was discontinued. Shortly afterward, a school of similar character was opened in the same place by Miss Maria Payne. This school was subsequently moved to a new brick building erected on Broad Street, near William, by General J. K. F. Mansfield. Miss Payne continued here, with excellent success, until 1868, when she gave up the control. The school was conducted a year or two by other parties, when it was discontinued."[18]

Middletown, Connecticut 1654-1900 (pub. by author: Exira, IA, 1900), 309. General Mansfield was described in this book: "He was a man of fine physique, a brave and fearless soldier; an accomplished officer, and strict disciplinarian; a gentleman of the old school; a big hearted man, gentle as a child, Ibid, 223. He was also described here as a "Congregationalist;" Whittemore, *History of Middlesex County*, 132. Mary Mansfield's school information Courtesy of the Middlesex County Historical Society.

[18] Whittemore, *History of Middlesex County*, 132.

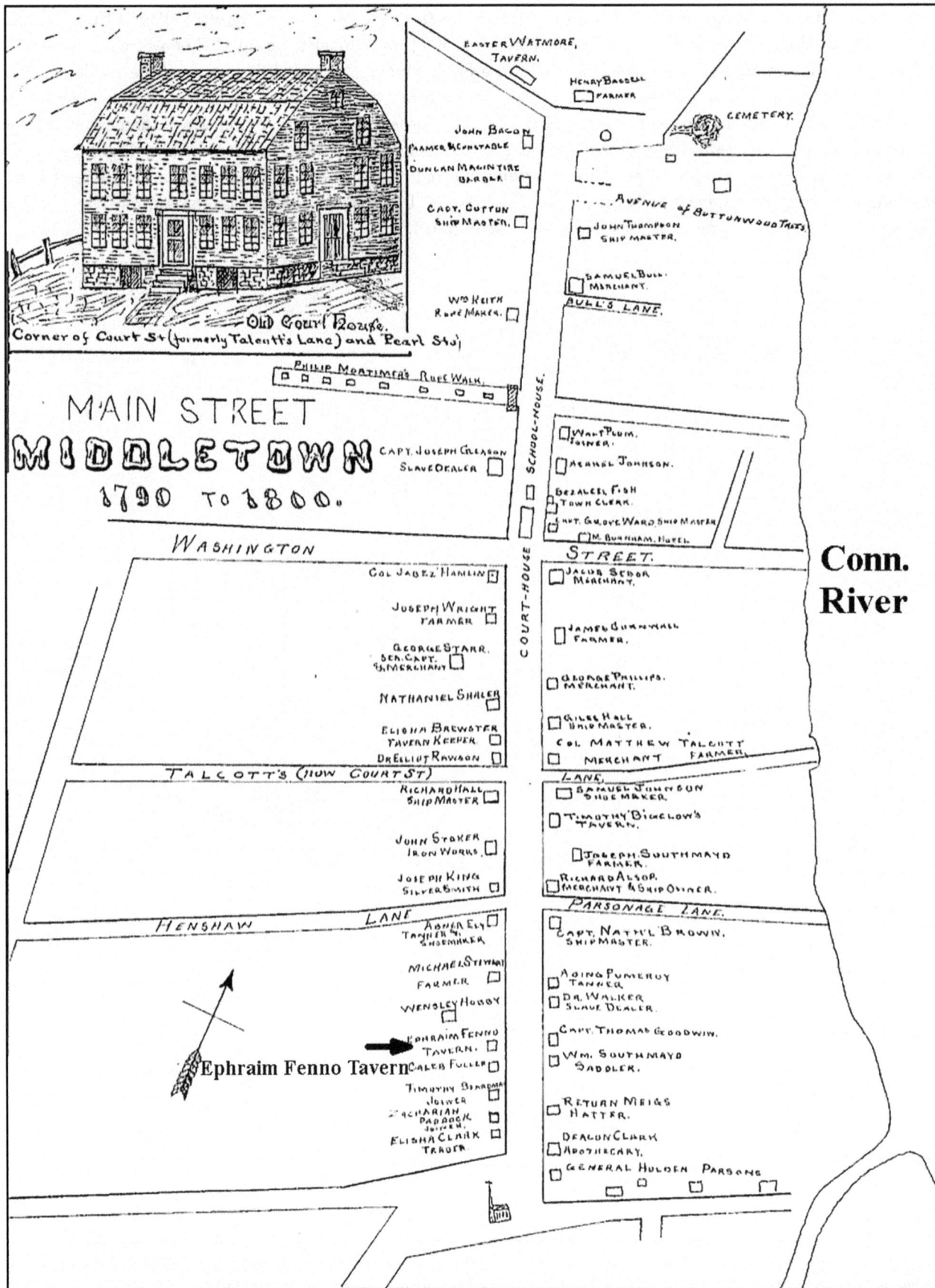

Middletown map of downtown 1790-1800 which shows the tavern owned by Ephraim Fenno, Joseph K.F. Mansfield's grandfather's house; Whittemore, *History of Middlesex County*, facing p. 85. William Street was built in the early 1800's and ran just below the Ephraim Fenno Tavern and the Captain Thomas Goodwin house.

Mansfield House c. 1910. The Chaffee House is to its left in this picture. Courtesy of the Middlesex County Historical Society. The house was built for Samuel Mather c. 1810-1817 and Joseph K.F. Mansfield's wife, Louisa, inherited it in 1854. General Mansfield never owned it however. Mansfield's youngest daughter, Katherine, inherited the house and she lived in it until her death in 1918. In 1959, the Middlesex County Historical Society purchased it from Mansfield's great granddaughter, Marietta Edgerton, saving the house. The house is an example of the Federal style and has served since 1959 as the Historical Society's headquarters.

Fenno family house on the corner of Main and William Streets, two houses south from Mansfield's later home. Joseph K.F. Mansfield and his mother moved here after they left New Haven and eventually he inherited it. Its large size explains how parts of three families could live there, the Mansfield's, their servants, and the Parker family. Note the dilapidated condition with missing shutters and weathered paint. Photograph taken after 1926 based on the billboard; *La Boheme* shown on the advertising poster was performed in 1926 in Middletown. This house is to the left of the Chaffee House shown below. Both of these houses were torn down in the 1920's and replaced by commercial structures; a park was constructed in the 1970's and the land is now owned by Middletown. Courtesy of the Middlesex County Historical Society.

Louis Chaffee House located between the Mansfield House and the Fenno House shown above, c. 1900, view from Main Street. Mansfield's later house is on the right and today survives as the Courtesy of the Middlesex County Historical Society. Chaffee was a grocer. Photo c. 1900, Courtesy of the Middlesex County Historical Society from William Vasiliou Collection.

This church was first named the North Church then the First Church of Christ Congregational at Main near Court Streets in Middletown in which Joseph Mansfield was baptized and where he attended services. Reverend Jeremiah Taylor, who delivered an address at Mansfield's funeral, was the pastor here, Hazen, *A Brief History of the First Church of Christ*, facing p. 58.

Modern view of Mansfield House looking west. Both the Chaffee and Fenno Houses are gone replaced by Spear Park below. Photograph by author April 2013.

Mansfield House looking north. Photograph by author April 2013.

William P. Spear Plaza at the corner of Main and William Streets was dedicated 2 July 1974, next to and west of the Mansfield House. William Street is at the top of the picture and the Mansfield House is not in view to the right. Below is the view north from the corner of William and Main Streets, Mansfield house in the right center. The Chaffee and Fenno Houses were torn down in the 1920's. Photographs by author April 2018.

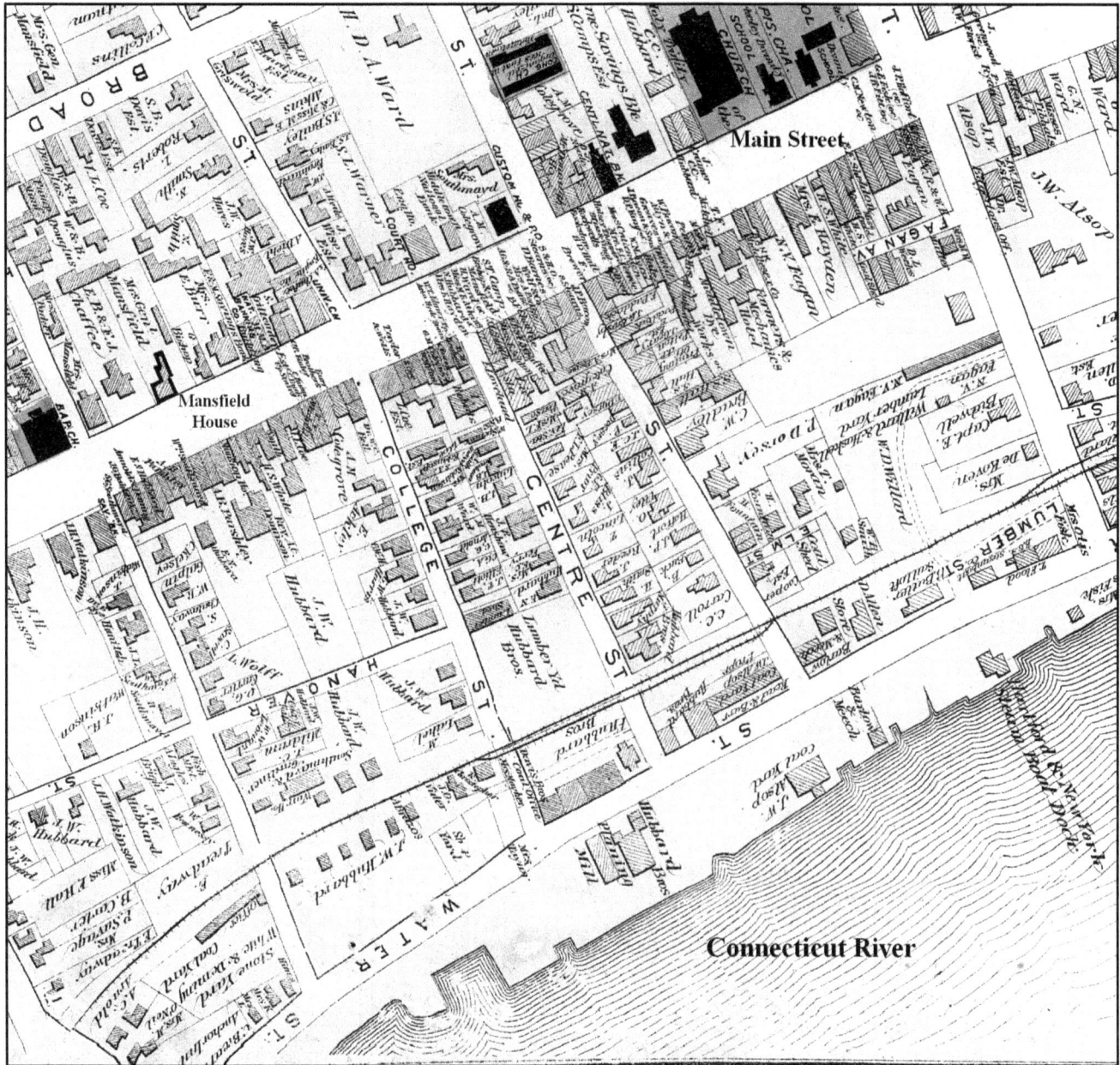

Map showing location of Mansfield House in Middletown, Connecticut. Note that the W.B Douglas Pump Company is to the rear of his house. At the time this map was drawn, his widow owned it as well as the house on the corner of Main and William Streets. The map also showed her name for a property with a house across Broad Street to the top left across from the T.L. Coe House. Scanned map of Middletown Mansfield's house in 1874, "County Atlas of Middlesex Connecticut" F.W. Beers & Co., NY, NY, 1874. Honorable Benjamin Douglas was a first cousin once removed of General Mansfield and escorted his body from Baltimore to Middletown. The Douglas Family and Mansfield's Family were close as relatives and business associates as was shown in a letter written by Benjamin Douglas on behalf of Mrs. Mansfield on 20 April 1859 to the Secretary of War. The Treasury Department was questioning Mansfield's military accounts and sent a letter to him in Middletown which his wife did not forward to him. Douglas suggested that Colonel Mansfield would attend to it on his return but the War Department should send any further inquiries to him. Letter Courtesy of the Middlesex County Historical Society.

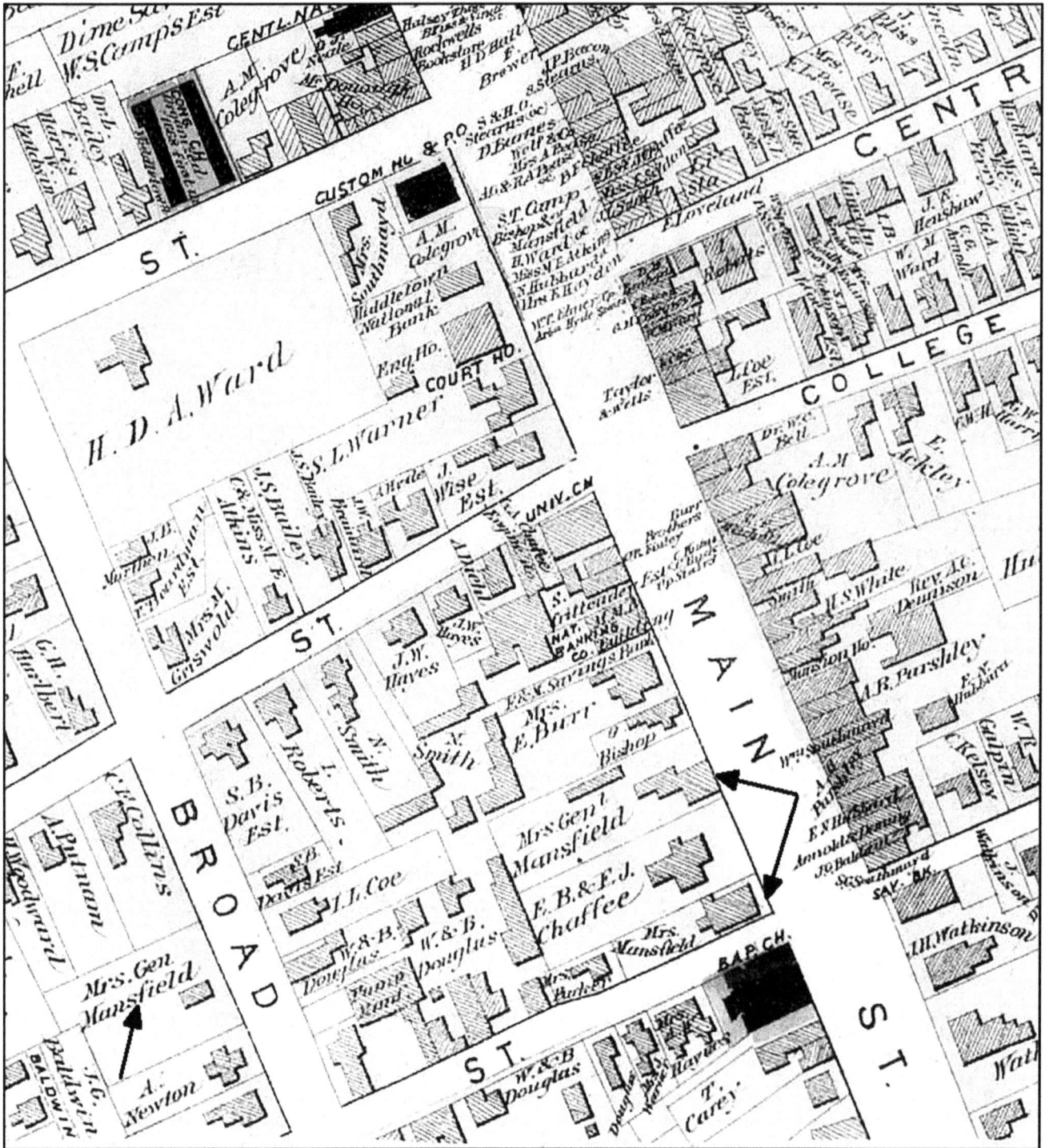

Note Mrs. Mansfield's name on three properties shown at arrows. Only the house on Main Street labelled "Mrs. Gen'l Mansfield remains—the Chaffee house and the "Mrs. Mansfield" house on the corner were removed in the 1920's. The house on Broad Street was first built by Colonel Mansfield as the ladies academy; "County Atlas of Middlesex Connecticut" F.W. Beers & Co., NY, NY, 1874. General Mansfield only owned his mother's house which is shown on the corner of Main and William Streets labelled "Mrs. Mansfield" house.

Bird's eye view of Middletown in 1877. The Mansfield House is the third north on Main Street from the corner of William Street, and the Mansfield School is the third building north on Broad Street from William Street. Number 22 on and near William Street show the Douglas Pump Works. Courtesy LOC.

Closer view of area around Mansfield House in 1877. Courtesy LOC.

Louisa Mather Mansfield

Louisa Mather Mansfield, Mansfield's wife, taken in her 60's, Courtesy of the Middlesex County Historical Society. Mansfield's wife's estate showed that three children, Samuel, Henry as administrator, and Katherine, divided total assets of $130,812.31 after subtracting debts of those three children from the estate of $51,213.89. Mansfield's Last Will dated 27 March 1852 written when he lived in Brookline, Massachusetts, distributed as follows: real property, his house and buildings in Middletown, to his two sisters, Hannah and Grace, who also receive $100 per year each to live on during their lifetimes; Grace to take care of "deranged sister Hannah." This sum may be increased by $50 if there is enough income and if necessary; Mansfield's wife, as executrix, would decide. Plus there would only be an increase if additional monies were not needed for his children. If Grace were unable to care for Hannah, Mansfield wished Hannah be cared for by "Margaret, a black woman, a faithful servant of my deceased mother during the life time of my deranged sister Hannah, provided my Executrix shall deem her able and competent to the task." His wife's inherited property is hers to do with as Mansfield would have had the right. She also had control and use of all his property, real and personal, to the support and benefit of herself and the children equally divided among his children when they have reached legal age. "Advances made to them will not be charged interest in the final accounting of his estate." His will was probated 10 November 1862. Documents courtesy WPL; copy of probated will Courtesy of the Middlesex County Historical Society. General Mansfield wrote a letter from Old Point Comfort to Joseph Taylor at the Middletown Almshouse dated 28 January 1829, and requested that his sister, Hannah, become a resident there at a cost to him of two dollars per week. He did this "with a great deal of reluctance" but required that she would be provided "with board and washing, a good room by herself and a [female] keeper who will be constantly in readiness to take proper care of her and treat her kindly." Letter Courtesy of the Middlesex County Historical Society.

Joseph K.F. Mansfield's son, Samuel, in 1862 at West Point, Courtesy of the Middlesex County Historical Society. Like his father, he spent his entire adult life in the U.S. Army. He was appointed a cadet 1 July 1858, and after graduation a second lieutenant of engineers 17 June 1862; colonel 24th Connecticut Volunteers 18 November 1862; first lieutenant engineers 3 March 1863; brevet captain 14 June 1863 for Port Hudson; mustered out of volunteer service 30 September 1863; captain engineers 15 August 1864; brevet major and lieutenant colonel 13 March 1865 for gallant and meritorious service during the war; major, engineers, 2 September 1874; lieutenant colonel 22 July 1888; colonel 5 July 1898; brigadier general 20 February 1903; retired 21 February 1903; died 18 February 1928, Boston, Massachusetts. He married Annie Baldwin Wright in St. Paul's Church, Detroit, Michigan, 16 April 1874.

Mansfield began his campaign to get his son, Samuel, admitted to West Point in 1856. He wrote to President Franklin Pierce from Middletown on 10 March 1856 and again on 29 January 1857 asking for Samuel to be appointed to West Point: "I should like very much indeed to receive an appointment of Cadet for my son, Samuel Mather Mansfield. He is between 16 & 17 years of age, and I think will do well at the Academy. As to his claims I can only say on his mother's side; his great grandfather Abram Livingston was with Genl. [Richard] Montgomery on the attack on Quebec and afterwards was faithful to the revolutionary cause throughout the war. On my own side his ancestors reached Boston in 1634, and Connecticut in 1639; and have performed distinguished services in the Indian Wars. My brother was captain of a volunteer company from Cincinnati in the War of 1812 and was the associate of Capt. [Thomas S.] Jesup, etc., and fell a victim to a fever he contracted in the field. An appointment at large conferred on my son will add to the obligations I am now under to you for favors conferred on myself." Mansfield continued his efforts on behalf of his son into the following year. He wrote to Secretary of War Jefferson Davis and General Joseph Totten 22 January 1857 from Middletown again requesting appointment of Samuel as a cadet. He sent another letter to Secretary of War William L. Marcy 28 January 1857: "You might lend me aid in this matter as it was under your administration of the War Department that I obtained three brevets without writing a letter speaking to anyone for them." Another letter went to Senator Isaac Toucey from Connecticut on 29 January asking for son's appointment: "I served through the whole Mexican War under Gen. Taylor and believe I did my duty; and on the score of politics I have always been a sound Democrat and lover of the great and glorious institutions we live under." But then on 20 February 1857 he received bad news from General Totten that Samuel was not appointed one of the 10 at large openings. Mansfield's entreaties on behalf of his son finally bore fruit as Samuel was admitted to West Point entering on 1 July 1858. A letter to Mansfield from W.W. Chapman from New York dated 17 March 1858 congratulated Mansfield on his son's admittance—"Our boys will be good friends." [19]

Mansfield's son, Henry L., with anchors on his collar showing that it was taken while he was in the Naval Academy. Courtesy WPL. He was admitted 29 September 1862 according to the *Official Register of the Officers and Acting Midshipmen of the United States Naval Academy*, 1862-1863, but resigned before graduation. Henry Livingston was born on 31 March 1845, and married Adeline O. Carter on 29 August 1866.

---

[19] NB: there is no record of a cadet Chapman graduating from West Point in the 1850's or 1860's; however there was a William Warren Chapman who graduated from West Point in 1837, and served with Mansfield in Mexico. Letters Courtesy of the Middlesex County Historical Society. Isaac Toucey was an attorney who was a prosecuting attorney of Hartford County, Connecticut, until 1835 when he was elected to the U.S. Congress. He served from 1835 to 1839, lost the election of 1838 and returned to his position as prosecuting attorney in 1842. In 1845, he ran for Governor of Connecticut and lost, but the Connecticut State Legislature appointed him to the position in 1846. He was defeated in an attempt at re-election. In 1848, President James K. Polk appointed Toucey the 20th Attorney General of the United States, a position he held until 1849. He returned to Connecticut and took a place in the Connecticut Senate in 1850, and then in the Connecticut House of Representatives in 1852. He was elected to the U.S. Senate and served from 12 May 1852, to 3 March 1857. President James Buchanan, who Toucey had served with in the Polk administration, appointed him U.S. Secretary of the Navy in his Cabinet in 1857. Toucey held that post until 1861 and the arrival of the Abraham Lincoln administration. Toucey was then replaced by one of his chief rivals in Connecticut, Gideon Welles. After 1861 he returned to his law practice. He died in 1869. Courtesy Wikipedia.

Henry later in life. Courtesy of the Middlesex County Historical Society. He became a civil engineer, was the secretary of the Middletown Gas Light Company, and in 1900, he was a director of the Middletown Savings Bank. He was a charter member of the Middlesex County Historical Society in Middletown, Connecticut. He died 14 January 1918. Courtesy of the Middlesex County Historical Society.

Katharine Mansfield.

Mansfield's youngest child, Katherine, was born 1 May 1850 in Brookline, Massachusetts, and died 18 January 1918. Courtesy of the Middlesex County Historical Society.

Office of the COLONIZATION SOCIETY

Washington May 18, 1860.

This certifies that Col. J. K. F. Mansfield, is a MEMBER for life, of the AMERICAN COLONIZATION SOCIETY.

LUX IN TENEBRIS

AM: COL: SOC: A.D. 1816.

R R Gurley
Secretary.

Henry Stone del. et sculp.

Jno H B Latrobe
President.

Mansfield's certificate for the American Colonization Society dated 18 May 1860, Courtesy of the Middlesex County Historical Society. This Society was founded in 1816 by Charles Fenton Mercer of Virginia. It supported the removal of free blacks from the United States to Africa for various reasons the most charitable of which was that they could not be assimilated into the white society and would always suffer discrimination so it would be best for them to leave the United States. These people saw this removal as a way to help the free blacks but slave owners in the South were not supportive of this plan since they saw that this could hurt chattel slavery. Mansfield, like President Lincoln, believed that due to the centuries of slavery in the United States that blacks would not survive and viewed this colonization as a humane way to help blacks return to their native lands and avoid troubles due to racism in the United States. Most blacks, free or slave, did not want to leave the United States which most viewed as their own country however, a few thousand did go to Africa most famously starting the country of Liberia. Many problems arose since most blacks did not want to go but the logistics of transporting millions of blacks to Africa would be impossible.

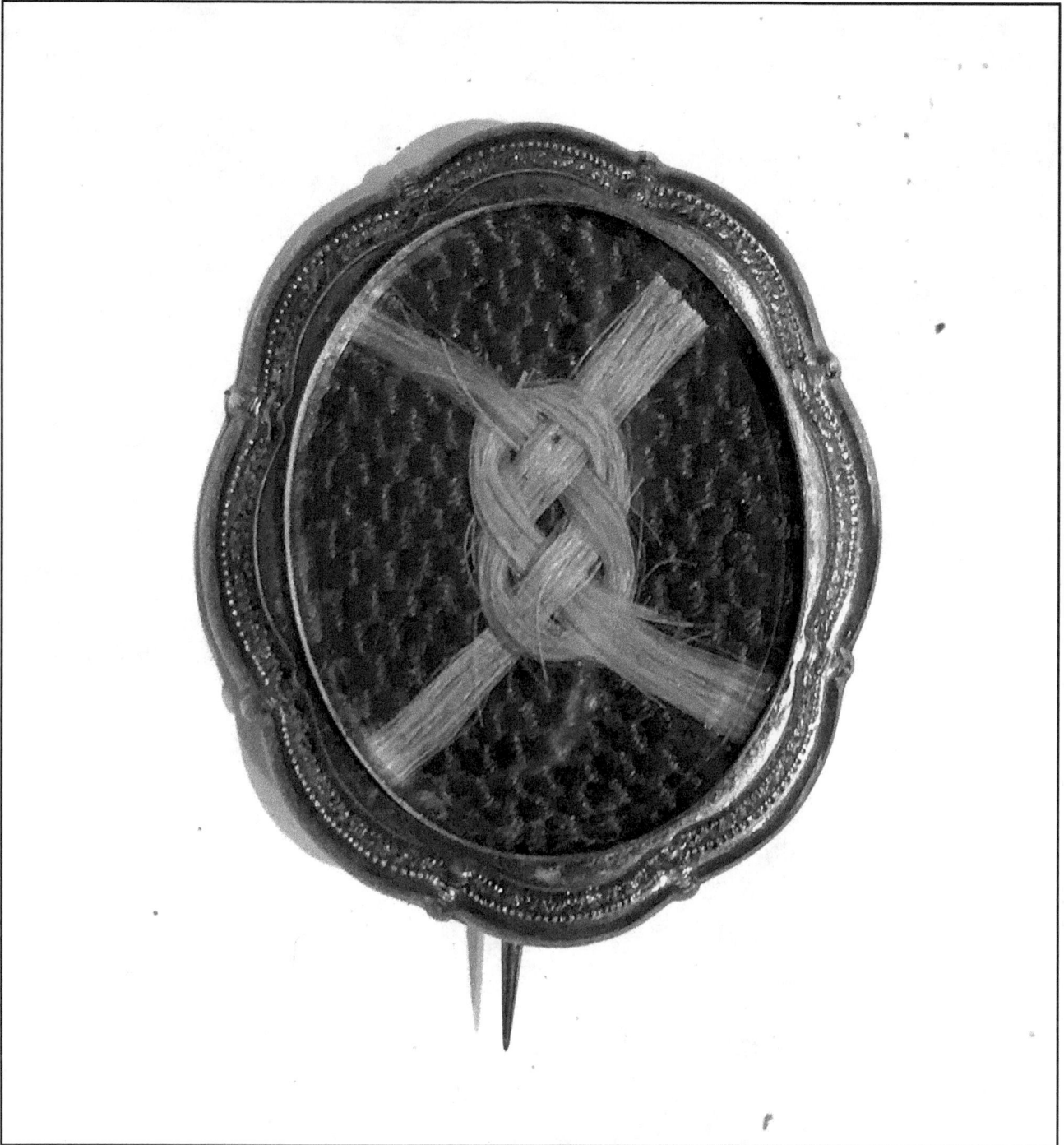

Brooch made from a lock of General Mansfield's hair. During the Victorian period, wearing hair jewelry was seen as a way of expressing one's love for the deceased as human hair does not decay. Courtesy of the Middlesex County Historical Society.

Religious books Mansfield likely carried with him during his U.S. Army career: upper left, *The Home Methodist*, upper right *J.K.F. Mansfield*, psalms and hymns, bottom, *Holy Bible*. Courtesy of the Middlesex County Historical Society.

Mansfield's cap, style of 1855, Courtesy of the Middlesex County Historical Society.

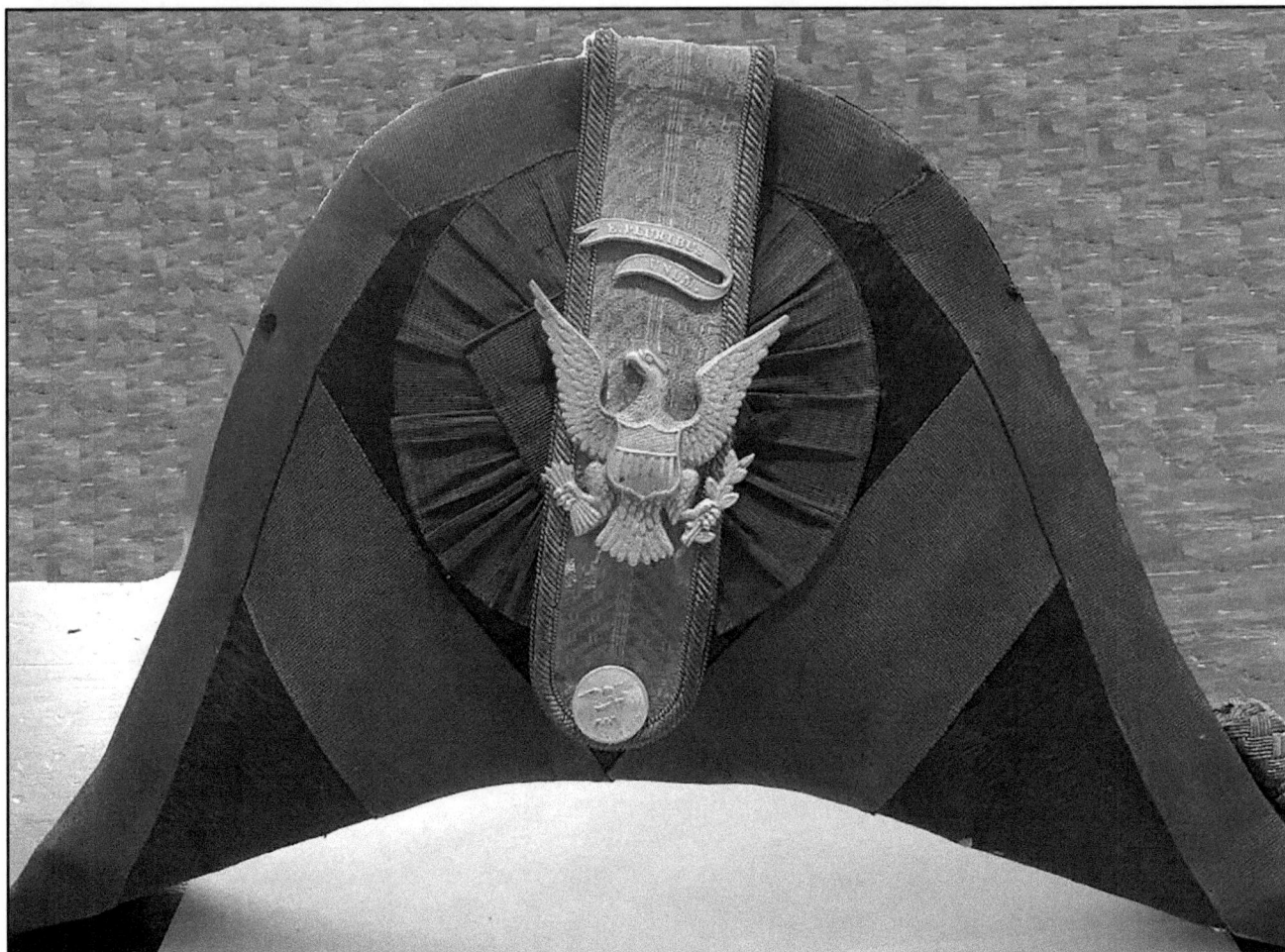

Mansfield's full dress hat, Courtesy of the Middlesex County Historical Society.

Attachment 1
Official Documents of Mansfield's Army Achievements

GENERAL MANSFIELD COLLECTION

The State Library is the recipient of a very unusual gift from the estate of Mrs. Katharine M. Hubbard, daughter of General Joseph K. F. Mansfield of Middletown, Conn., so renowned in the military history of our country. This gift consists of eleven folio parchments, all suitably framed, as follows:

Diploma from United States Military Academy, Corps of Engineers, July 4, 1822. This diploma is signed by the following: S. Thayer, Lt. Col., Supt.; Jared Mansfield, LL.D., Prof. Natural & Experimental Philosophy; D. B. Douglass, A.M., Prof. of Mathematics; Claudius Berard, Teacher of French; C. Crozet, Prof. of Engineering; W. J. Worth, Major U. S. A., Inst. of Tactics & Commander of Cadets; T. Gimbrede, Teacher of Drawing.

Commission appointing General Mansfield as 2d Lieutenant in the Corps of Engineers, to take effect July 1, 1822, signed at Washington, January 1, 1824, by James Monroe, President, and J. C. Calhoun, Secretary of War.

Commission as 1st Lieutenant in Corps of Engineers, to take effect March 1, 1832, signed at Washington, May 10, 1832, by Andrew Jackson, President, and Lew. Cass, Secretary of War. Countersigned by R. Jones, Adjutant-General.

Commission as Captain in Corps of Engineers, to take effect July 7, 1838, signed at Washington, July 10, 1838, by M. VanBuren, President, and J. R. Poinsett, Secretary of War.

Commission as Brevet Major, to take effect May 9, 1846, for gallant and distinguished services in the defense of Fort Brown, signed at Washington, August 13, 1846, by James K. Polk, President, and W. L. Marcy, Secretary of War.

Commission as Lieutenant-Colonel by Brevet, to take effect September 23, 1846, for gallant and meritorious conduct in the several conflicts at Monterey, signed at Washington, May 4, 1847, by James K. Polk, President, and W. L. Marcy, Secretary of War.

Commission as Colonel by Brevet, to take effect February 23, 1847, for gallant and meritorious conduct in the battle of Buena Vista, signed at Washington, May 12, 1848, by James K. Polk, President, and W. L. Marcy, Secretary of War.

Commission as Inspector-General with the rank of Colonel, to take effect May 28, 1853, signed at Washington, February 9, 1854, Franklin Pierce, President, and Jefferson Davis, Secretary of War.

Commission as Brigadier-General by Brevet, to take effect May 6, 1861, signed at Washington, May 9, 1862, by Abraham Lincoln, President, and Edwin M. Stanton, Secretary of War.

Commission as Brigadier-General, to take effect May 14, 1861, signed at Washington, September 9, 1861, by Abraham Lincoln, President, and Simon Cameron, Secretary of War.

Commission as Major-General of Volunteers, to take effect July 18, 1862, signed at Washington, March 12, 1863, by Abraham Lincoln, President, and Edwin M. Stanton, Secretary of War.

List of original documents of General Mansfield's Army promotions supplied by his daughter, Katherine M. Hubbard, to the Connecticut State Library. *Public Documents of the State of Connecticut*, vol. 4, pt. 1, 1918, Public Document No. 13, "Report of the State Librarian to the Governor for the Two Years Ended September 30, 1918" (Hartford, CT: State of Conn.), 33.

Attachment 2
Origin of the Name[20]

From all that can be gathered from Encyclopedias, and other sources, it would seem the name originated in Saxony. An educated German who has been in this country some ten years, by the name of Mansfeld, (he spells his name without the i) had taken much pains and interest to ascertain its origin years ago, and has at my request written several times to a gentleman in the city of Mansfeld, in Saxony, for information. Mr. Mansfeld writes, "It is clear to my mind that all the English Mansfields are of Saxon origin. The name Mansfield and Mansfeld means the same in both languages, viz. 'A Man in the field.' How the name originated in England after the Saxons mixed with the Normans, Danes, Celts and others is easily explained, no man in America for instance would call me Mansfeld, but Mansfield, in the same way no doubt many a German or Saxon name was changed in England, and this is done even now very often in the U. S. English speaking people make Hough out of the German Hoff. Herkhimer out of Herkheimer and hundreds of others which I observe myself in this country. "The shield on the Tower in the City of Mansfeld in Saxony shows the origin of the name, 'A man in the Field,' 'A Knight who first appeared as the Defender of his Country.' 'The noble Family of Mansfeld of Germany is very old, traces back almost to the time of Charlemagne;' and flourishes down to the present time; as the following extract will show, which is copied from the extended account of the great celebration of the unveiling of the Bronze Statue of Luther at Eisleben (adjacent to Mansfeld) on his four hundredth birth day, Nov. 10th, 1883. From the description of the long historical possession, we extract the following:

City Heralds

At the head of the procession walked several elegantly caparisoned horses. After them marched a herald with the emblems of the new German Empire. He was followed by a horseman with a kettle drum. The drummer was clothed in a suit of red and white, the colors of the city of Mansfeld. He was followed by twelve trumpeters. Then came, in blue and white colors, the herald of the city of Eisleben. The Burgomaster and his staff, with a crowd of citizens, welcomed the procession.

The House of Mansfeld

At the gates of the city they joined the procession. The color bearers of the Counts of Mansfeld came with some of the noblemen, bearing their coats of arms. They were followed by a large crowd of falconers and hunters on horseback and on foot. On a large horse rode the armour bearer of the house of the Counts of Mansfeld, followed by a splendid troop of noblemen of the Golden Aue. Then were seen the Counts von Mansfeld Albrecht and Gebhard themselves, with their wives, daughters and the young counts who were able to master horses. In this part of the procession were seen many garbs made out of brocade or Venetian mantles of silk or velvet suits and robes trimmed with real embroidery of Flanders.

The Renaissance

Herewith was given a true picture of the lustre and glory of the time of the Renaissance. So everything shows the immense wealth and opulence of the Counts of Mansfeld. With great favor also was welcomed the Prince Wolfgang of Anhalt, who rode on a vivacious battle horse. He was conducted by his banner bearers and marshals of his court, and he presented himself as a stately hero. As he likes very much the noble sport of hunting he was accompanied by many hunters.

---

[20] Quotation from H. Mansfield, *The Descendants of Richard and Gillian Mansfield Who Settled in New haven, 1639* (New Haven, CT: H. Mansfield, 1885), 166-167.

Attachment 3
Time Line[21]

1735	Ephraim Fenno born, Boston, Massachusetts
1738	Mary King born (mother)
1765	Ephraim Fenno and Mary King married
1767, April 3	Mary Fenno born
1771, January 14	Samuel Mather born, Lyme Connecticut
1785, August 3	Mary Fenno and Henry Mansfield married
1787, October 10	Catherine Livingston born, Stillwater, New York
1803, December 22	**Joseph King Fenno Mansfield born, New Haven, Connecticut**
1804	Mary Fenno and Henry Mansfield divorced; Mary and Joseph move to Middletown
1805	Henry Mansfield died, St. Croix, Virgin Islands
1807, September 12	Samuel Mather and Catherine Livingston married, Troy, New York
1808, June 14	Louisa Maria Mather born, Troy, New York
1825, January 14	Mary Fenno Mansfield died, Middletown, Connecticut
1838, September 25	**Louisa M. Mather married Joseph King Fenno Mansfield, Middletown, Connecticut**
1839, September 22	Samuel Mather Mansfield born, Middletown, Connecticut
1841, March 23	Mary Louisa Mansfield born, Middletown, Connecticut
1843, October 4	Joseph Totten Mansfield born, Middletown, Connecticut
1844, July 15	Joseph Totten Mansfield died, Middletown, Connecticut
1845, March 31	Henry Livingston Mansfield born, Middletown, Connecticut
1850, May 1	Katherine Mather Mansfield born, Brookline, Massachusetts
1854, April 6	Samuel Mather died, age 84, Middletown, Connecticut
1855, February 1	Catherine Livingston Mather died, age 67, Middletown, Connecticut
1855, May 31	Walter Bulkely Hubbard born
1862, September 18	**Joseph King Fenno Mansfield died, age 58, Sharpsburg, Maryland**
1863, June 22	Mary Louisa Mansfield died, Middletown, Connecticut
1870, May 21	Henry Cruger Edgerton born
1872, May 23	Ellie Burnham Mansfield born, Middletown, Connecticut
1875, May 3	Joseph Livingston Mansfield born
1876, June 30	Joseph Livingston Mansfield died
1877, May 29	Louise Mansfield born
1880, February 22	Louisa Mather Mansfield died, Middletown, Connecticut
1895, December 20	Ellie Burnham Mansfield married Henry Curger Edgerton
1897, December 5	Marietta Louise Edgerton born, Middletown, Connecticut
1908, April 3	Walter B. Hubbard Died
1918, January 14	Henry Livingston Mansfield died
1918, January 18	Katherine Mather Mansfield Hubbard died
1930	Henry Cruger Edgerton died
1940, February 7	Ellie Burnham Mansfield Edgerton died
1957, December 13	Louise Mansfield died
1959, May 25	Mansfield home deeded to the Middlesex County Historical Society by Marietta Edgerton
1977, September 29	Marietta Edgerton died

---

[21] Courtesy of the Middlesex County Historical Society.

Chapter 3

West Point 1817 to 1822

Cadet Mansfield left home late in September 1817. He must have felt some trepidation which tempered his anticipation of his new life at West Point. While he may not have realized that this trip as a 13-year-old would be the first of many he would make in the service of his country, the sense of adventure had to be foremost in his mind. He would have been concerned also that he could measure up to his ancestors who took part in the wars and military activities of the young country and he knew that his uncle, Professor Jared Mansfield, awaited him at his new home, The United States Military Academy at West Point, New York.[1]

The young boy probably took a coach on the Middletown, Durham, and New Haven Turnpike some 23 miles to the port at New Haven, Connecticut, and there boarded a steamer at the harbor's Long Wharf. His bumpy ride down the turnpike, gave him time to contemplate his future.[2] He knew he would not have to make a final decision to join the army until he graduated from West Point, but his options were limited. His family connections had pushed him in the direction of the Academy to give him an excellent, free, post-secondary education, and then a career in the army. His four-mile-ship ride out of New Haven harbor by the old Fort Hale and into Long Island Sound was the beginning of his

---

[1] Mansfield began his active "military service" upon becoming a cadet according to an opinion of the U.S. Attorney General 21 August 1819: "they are bound to perform military duty in such places, and on such service, as the Commander-in-Chief of the army of the United States shall order…the corps to which they are attached…is expressly recognized as a part of that military establishment….I come to the conclusion that the corps [of cadets] at West point form a part of the land forces of the United States, and have been constitutionally subjected by Congress to the Rules and Articles of War, and to trial by courts-martial," Edward C. Boynton, *History of West Point* (New York, NY: D. Van Nostrand, 1871), 220-221. The opinion was part of the Bliss affair in which Captain George Bliss, Commandant of Cadets, was accused by cadets of mistreatment. Mansfield and his cousin, Edward, were among the 179 cadets out of 200 who petitioned for Bliss's removal, R. Ernest Dupuy, *Where They Have Trod: The West Point Tradition in American Life* (New York, NY: Frederick A. Stokes Company, 1940), 147. The affair was finally settled with Bliss's replacement after much controversy including cadet petitions, resignations, courts-martial and Congressional hearings, George S. Pappas, *To The Point: The United States Military Academy, 1802-1902* (Westport, CT: Praeger Publishers, 1993), 123-126. In modern times, cadets are on active duty in the Armed Forces of the United States from the day they enter the Academy and are subject to military law; but time spent at the Academy does not count toward military active pay, retired pay and allowances, or years of service for retirement.

[2] It is improbable that he was able to take a steam boat from Middletown down the Connecticut River as none regularly ran until 1824, *History of Middlesex County, Connecticut with Biographical Sketches of Its Prominent Men* (New York, NY: J.B. Beers & Co., 1884, 37. The most likely road route would be on the Middletown, Durham, and New Haven Turnpike. No railroad was available until 1849, ibid., 38-39.

adventures which would eventually take him to most army posts in the east and eventually the majority west of the Mississippi River, and would include an eventful two-year sojourn in Old Mexico.[3]

The young Mansfield may also have been thinking about a letter he had received from his uncle, Jared, on 21 September 1817, which chastised Mansfield about his dilatory action in repairing to the Academy to begin his four years of study. His professor uncle was astonished that in Mansfield's last letter he is still "speaking of an appointment as a cadet when I informed you by every letter I wrote you that you were appointed. I have your confirmation or appointment in my hand. But if you are not here by the 30th of September you will lose all the advantages I have taken to obtain the commission for you. I say you must be here by the 30th at all hazards....Go to Mr. Lyon at New Haven whether you have clothes ___ ___or not. Go from there in the stage or steam boat whichever you may find the quickest to New York. Stop if you please at Mr. Reynolds Stage ___in Courtland [Cortland] Street....Take their advice for the first steam boat up North River....I shall know by your dispatch whether you have the ideas of a young leader??" Therefore it is very likely Mansfield did take the fastest method of transport available to avoid further angering his uncle. Mansfield took a steamer from New Haven steaming up the Hudson River to Haven's dock at Gee's Point, below the bluffs on which the Academy sat, arriving before 1 October 1817.[4] Jared had previously written glowing recommendations for Joseph to President James Monroe and Secretary of War John C. Calhoun describing him as of "'fine bodily form & of superior mental endowments' and possessed a good understanding of 'Latin, French & German,' as well as a 'fine taste in painting, drawing & other minor arts.'"[5]

---

[3] The first steamboat, the *Fulton*, arrived in New Haven harbor in March 1815, taking 11½ hours to make the trip from New York. This compared favorably with passage by stages of two days and by sailing packets of up to a week, J.L. Rockey, ed., *History of New Haven County, Connecticut*, vol. 1 (New York, NY: W.W. Preston & Co., 1892), 98, 133. As no record has been found of Mansfield's trip from Middletown to West Point, the most likely methods and routes are used.

[4] Benny Havens occupied a small building on Gee's Point where he built a dock where barges navigating the double bend in the river could tie up awaiting favorable winds to continue their trips. Apparently few cadets used his tavern there for frolic because it was too difficult to access it in the dark and Gridley's tavern was much closer, Pappas, 121. In 1824 after Haven's lease was cancelled, he moved to Buttermilk Falls and built a new tavern which, after Gridley's was closed, became the closest watering hole for cadets, Pappas, 160. There were four steamboats operating on the Hudson River at that time, the *Richmond*, the *Paragon*, the *Firefly*, and the *Chancellor Livingston*. They were slow so if the winds were favorable, a sailing sloop would be faster, John Hazlehurst Boneval Latrobe, *Reminiscences of West Point from September 1818 to March 1882* (East Saginaw, MI: Evening News, Printers and Binders, 1887), 1-3. Latrobe was a lawyer, civic leader, artist, author, and inventor in Baltimore, Maryland, and the son of architect Benjamin Henry Latrobe. Although born in Philadelphia in 1803, he and his family moved to Maryland in 1817 and returned there after he resigned from West Point in 1821; he was a member of the American Colonization Society and its president from 1853-1890, and president of Maryland Historical Society. Mansfield joined the American Colonization Society in 1860. *Register of the Officers and Cadets of the U.S. Military Academy June 1818* shows Mansfield was admitted 1 October 1817, so he likely arrived before that date as his acceptance letters show earlier dates below. Professor Jared Mansfield was an inveterate complainer as even his wife wrote that "It would be happy for me and for him if with his complaints he had lost the habit of complaining, but I fear it is an infirmity which time cannot remove," Pappas, 134-135.

[5] Joseph K.F. Mansfield and Joseph E. Johnston, *Texas & New Mexico on the Eve of the Civil War: The Mansfield & Johnston Inspections, 1859-1861*, Jerry Thompson, ed. (Albuquerque, NM: University of New Mexico Press, 2001), 2.

The President of the United States having been pleased to appoint *Joseph Mansfield*, a Cadet in the service of the United States, he is to be received as such, and entitled to all the consideration attached to said appointment.

Given at the WAR OFFICE of the UNITED STATES, this *first* day of *September*, in the year of our Lord one thousand eight hundred and *seventeen*, and in the *forty second* year of the Independence of said states.

Geo. Graham

acting   Secretary of War.

Mansfield's official West Point appointment. Courtesy of the Middlesex County Historical Society.

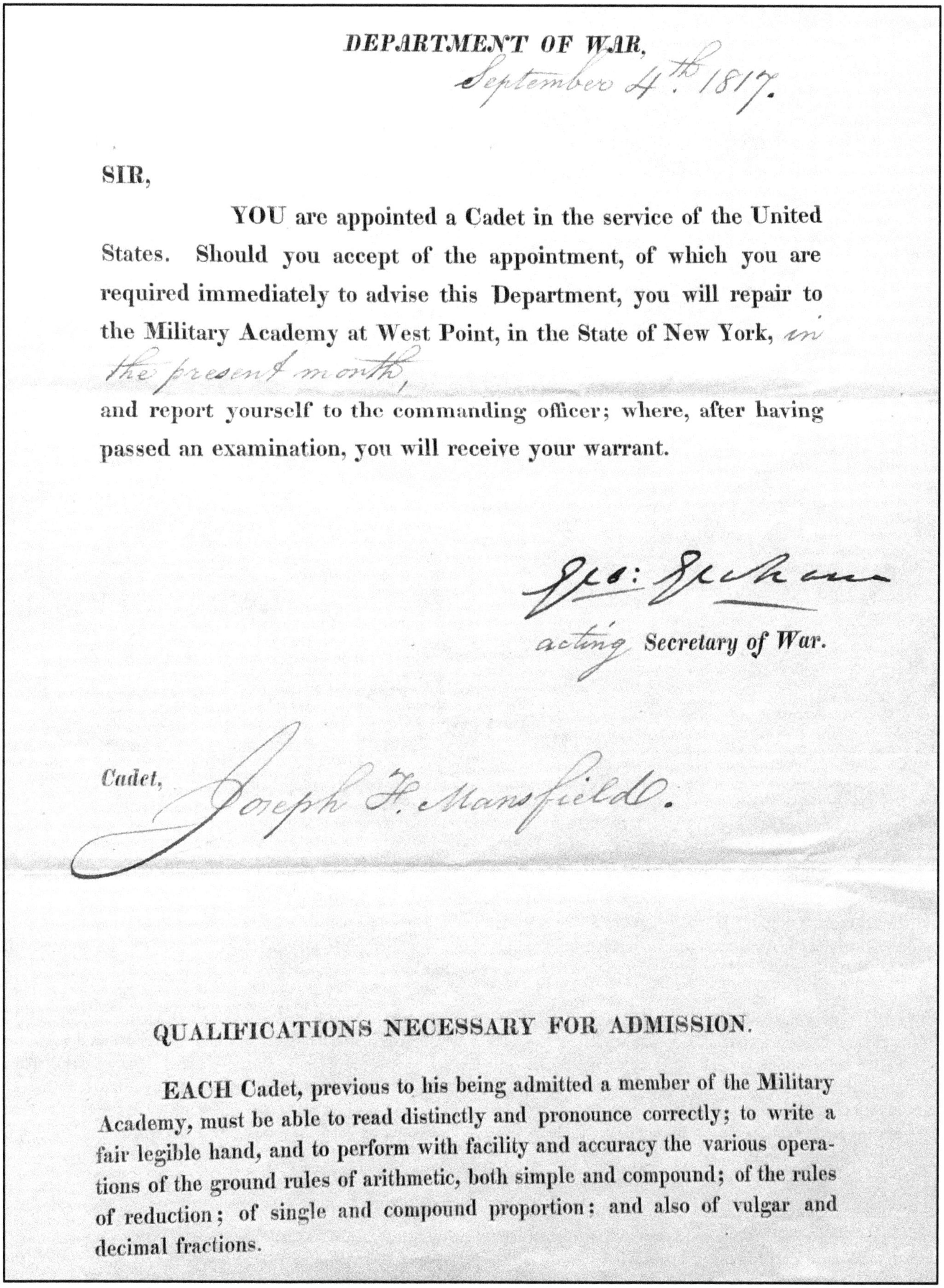

DEPARTMENT OF WAR,

September 4th 1817.

SIR,

YOU are appointed a Cadet in the service of the United States. Should you accept of the appointment, of which you are required immediately to advise this Department, you will repair to the Military Academy at West Point, in the State of New York, *in the present month,* and report yourself to the commanding officer; where, after having passed an examination, you will receive your warrant.

Geo: Graham

acting Secretary of War.

Cadet, *Joseph F. Mansfield.*

QUALIFICATIONS NECESSARY FOR ADMISSION.

EACH Cadet, previous to his being admitted a member of the Military Academy, must be able to read distinctly and pronounce correctly; to write a fair legible hand, and to perform with facility and accuracy the various operations of the ground rules of arithmetic, both simple and compound; of the rules of reduction; of single and compound proportion; and also of vulgar and decimal fractions.

West Point acceptance letter Mansfield received. Courtesy of the Middlesex County Historical Society.

Mansfield left little written record of his personal life at West Point. Fortunately, a member of his class of 1822, John H.B. Latrobe, did so, in his wonderfully detailed book, *West Point Reminiscences from September, 1818, to March, 1882*. Most of his experiences parallel Mansfield's. Latrobe, a resident of Maryland, knew Mansfield, wrote of him and other non-slave state classmates: "To say that there was no distinction between cadets from the slaveholding and non-slaveholding States respectively would not be true; but I can safely say that it did not affect personal intimacies. In my own case, the dearest friend I ever had was Mansfield, who fell at Antietam and was from Connecticut; another friend, Horace Bliss, was from New Hampshire; [Thompson B.] Wheelock was from Massachusetts; [George A.] McCall, distinguished in the late war, was from Pennsylvania....Sectional differences were unknown at West Point in 1818."[6]

Mansfield as an 1822 graduate would have been familiar with this depiction of his alma mater. It is a view of the Hudson River from above the banks facing west, opposite from the military academy. The side-wheel steamer is perhaps approaching the dock to its left. This is not the dock at Gee's Point which would have been to the left and around the bend. Artist W.G. Hall spent the summer of 1820 traversing 212 miles of the Hudson River's 315-mile course. Print published between 1821 and 1825. Courtesy LOC.

Latrobe boarded a sloop to sail to West Point from New York. His arrival at Gee's Point would have been similar to Mansfield's except that Mansfield's steamer may have been able to pull up to the public dock around the bend further north rather than copying Latrobe's much more exciting entrance at Gee's point. Latrobe's sail up the Hudson proved to be slower than the steamers due to unfavorable winds, but 24 hours after leaving New York City, he sighted his destination:

[A] promontory on our left, with a gray ruin [Fort Clinton] on a hill above it, dominated by high mountains beyond the wind had freshened, and the sloop was headed for Gee's Point; when the boat was lowered and hauled alongside, and I got into it with a sailor who took the helm and told me to jump ashore whenever we were close enough to a dock, that we were rapidly approaching in tow of the sloop — to permit my doing so. I jumped accordingly — my trunk was pitched after me....With Gee's Point I afterwards became familiar; but it was a rough spot, as I now recall it. There was a house near the dock, however, where I obtained a man to carry my trunk and be my guide to Gridley's, or "Grid's," as the place was commonly called, to which the "new cadets" went on their arrival.

---

[6] Latrobe did not graduate from the Academy: "I did not graduate with my class of 1822, I venture, as a piece of egotism, to insert the following extract from a letter from Colonel Thayer, dated January 23d, 1864: 'Forty-two years have not effaced from my memory the regret and disappointment I felt, when, near the close of 1821, your resignation was handed to me; for I had always counted upon you as a future officer of engineers. You were then at the head of your class, and without a rival.' ....My resignation was due to the death of my father, and family considerations only," Latrobe, 9, note.

A narrow, steep and ill-conditioned cart-road led to the plain above, with the east front of Fort Clinton on the right, and on the left, a precipice with trees wherever they found root among the rocks. On reaching the summit, the first objects I noticed, at some distance on the plain to the right, were several gray stone buildings, which I was told were the North Barracks, the South Barracks, the Academy and the Mess Hall. Our road lay along the edge of the plain for some distance to a gate, beyond which, and outside of the property of the United States, we came to Gridley's. This, as nearly as I can recollect, was a large two-storied wooden building, standing a few steps to the north of the road down the river. The house was crowded with newly appointed cadets, awaiting examination; and here I had my first experience of sleeping three in a bed.[7]

After reporting in to the Adjutant of the Post in his South Barracks office, Latrobe was taken to a room on the second floor of the east wing of the Academy building, where with half dozen others he was examined for "proficiency in the knowledge required to justify admission, before some members of the Academic staff….When my turn came…I was made to read a page, write some lines from dictation and answer some questions in Arithmetic…."[8]

Another cadet's account of his West Point arrival was similar to Latrobe's except that he arrived on a steamer in June 1819: "…we took the Albany steamboat. We were landed at the North [public] dock by a yawl towed by a long line from the steamer, which paid out the line till the yawl reached the dock at which the landing took place. Not more than two to four minutes was occupied in landing and receiving passengers, when the tow-line was hauled in by machinery on the steamer, carrying the embarking passengers."[9]

Sketch showing from the left, the North and South Barracks, the Academy, and the Mess Hall, with Wood's Monument in the center of the plain. Note the cadet's uniform—he is a cadet captain with standard wide "Cossack" pantaloons, the plume on his "bell crowned" leather hat is exaggerated; he has the flagpole at his back and the corps is marching across the plain in the center. The white pantaloons were made of white linen or cotton and were the usual summer uniform for cadets and in the Regular Army. Wood's Monument is a cenotaph erected by Major General Jacob Brown at his own expense in 1818 to the memory of Lieutenant Colonel Eleazer Derby Wood, class of 1806, killed in a sortie from Fort Erie, Canada, 17 September 1814. Thayer, who for a time was his roommate, described Wood: "He was every inch a soldier, cast in the mold of a hero. Had he lived in the time of the Crusades he would have figured among the foremost as apreux chevalier [a gallant and brave knight] and his moral character was without a blemish, or a defect as far as I ever knew."[10] Wood's monument is the oldest at West Point. It was originally located in front of the South Barracks, and then moved to the location shown above on a hillock on the northwest corner of the Plain. It was moved to the West Point Cemetery in 1885. Samuel E. Tillman, *The Centennial of the United States Military Academy at West Point, New York*, vol. 1, facing 508; Pappas, 123.

---

[7] Latrobe, 1-3. Joseph Mansfield's cousin, Edward Deering Mansfield, arrived with his father, Jared, on a sloop in 1812, sailing from New Haven. The trip took almost four days. Edward D. Mansfield, *Personal Memories, Social, Political, and Literary with Sketches of Many Noted People, 1803-1843* (Cincinnati, OH: Robert Clarke & Co., 1879) 58. Edward entered West Point as a cadet 1 August 1815 and graduated 1 July 1819 but declined an appointment as a second lieutenant of engineers.

[8] Latrobe, 3. It may be that as Mansfield arrived about a year earlier, he did not have to undergo this "entrance examination" as it was instituted by Captain Thayer in 1818, the incoming superintendent.

[9] George S. Greene, "Address," *Annual Reunion, June 11th, 1888*, Annual Report by the United States Military Academy Association of Graduates (East Saginaw, MI: Evening News, Printers and Binders, 1885), 11.

[10] Thayer Papers, courtesy West Point. http://digital-library.usma.edu/cdm/singleitem/collection/thayer/id/2/rec/2

contour interval
20 feet

Hudson River

Dock

Gee's Point

Storehouses

Barracks

Armory

Hospital

Tailor

Shoemaker

Chaplain

Commissary
Store

Mrs. Thompson's
house

Long
Barracks

**Fort
Clinton**

Officers'
Quarters

Old Academy
Officers' Quarters

Officers' Quarters,
Old Cadet Mess

pond

Cadet Mess 1815

Academy 1815

South Barracks 1815

North Barracks 1817
Quartermaster's Office

Fort Putnam

Officers'
Quarters
1817

Bake House
Laboratory

Gridley's
Tavern

U.S. Military
Academy
1818–1822

0   yards   400

Hal Jespersen

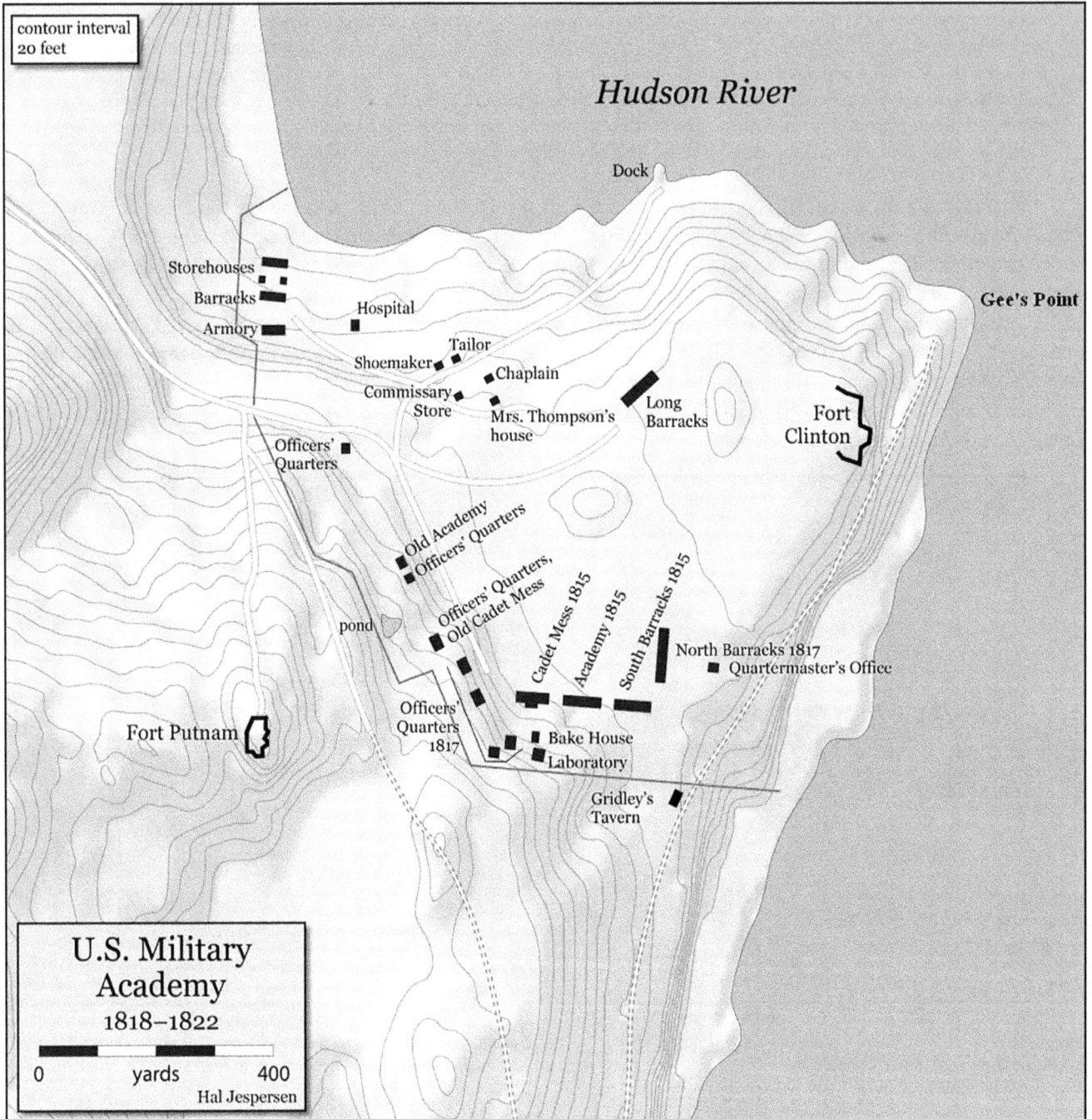

West Point when Mansfield attended. Map by Hal Jespersen.

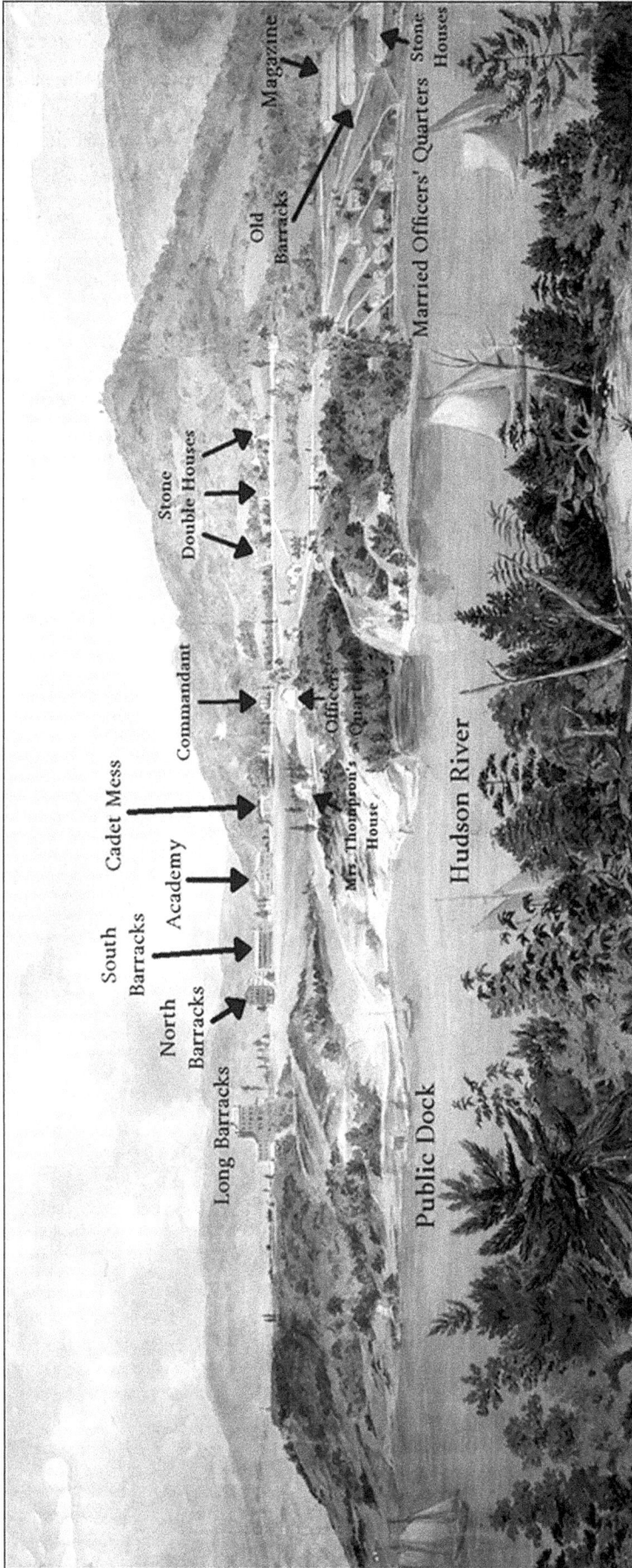

View of West Point c. 1820 from Constitution Island. Gee's (West) Point is out of sight to the left. Watercolor by John Rubens Smith, courtesy LOC.

Mansfield was fortunate since when he arrived as a 13-year-old in 1817, the oral examinations which the new Superintendent Major Sylvanus Thayer instituted in 1818 had not yet begun: "In its earliest years, the Academy did not have any specific entrance requirements. Some new cadets may not have even been able to read and write. The Academy first formalized its entrance requirements eight years earlier, and included the three major areas that would shape all future screening measures: physical, mental, and moral-ethical. A new cadet had to demonstrate that he was 'well-versed in the English language, in writing and arithmetic; [and] that he [was] of good moral character and of sound constitution.' Regardless of the requirements, the appointees were not formally screened until 1818, when all cadets had to take an oral entrance examination."[11] Latrobe passed this inquisition and joined 119 other cadets in the class of 1822. He was assigned to his room in the drafty South Barracks. He described his accommodations:

> The South Barracks consisted of three tiers of rooms, placed back to back, fronting north and south respectively, and opening on galleries, which abutted, at either end, on buildings containing offices and officers' quarters. The galleries were reached by a stairway in the centre of the building. At the end of the several galleries were large woodboxes for the use of the neighboring rooms. Each room was, perhaps, about eleven feet square; and, speaking only of mine, was furnished with three cots, that were nothing more than camp stools widened and lengthened to accommodate a person six feet tall. The head of my cot was in the recess on one side of the fire-place, and on the other side was Campbell Graham's; while Alfred's was at right angles to the latter and directly under the window. The door was opposite to the foot of my cot; and on the wall between it and the window was the rack for our three muskets and accoutrements. There was a shelf above the fire-place and shelves in the recesses over our heads as we lay in our cots. A table and three chairs, a pair of andirons and a fender completed the furniture of a room in which three tall men were "cabinned, cribbed, confined." I forgot where we kept our clothes—probably in our trunks under the cots. I often smile, when I remember our first winter's experience in the South Barracks, —as we sat with our feet on the fender around the fire, with the candle on the table behind us, or, on the mantelpiece, so called out of compliment to a narrow board on two brackets.[12]

THE SOUTH BARRACKS. (Looking Southwest.)
Erected, in 1815; Demolished, in 1849.

The South Barracks, the Academy building, and the two-story mess hall, were completed in 1815; the barracks was three stories high, containing 48, small, two-man rooms; the wings at each end contained small bachelor officer suites. The North Barracks was built in 1817 was four stories high and had 40 large, four-man rooms; Edward C. Boynton, *History of West Point, and Its Military Importance During the American Revolution: and the Origin and Progress of the United States Military Academy* (New York, NY: D. Van Nostrand, 1864), 254. Crackel, 95-97.

---

[11] Jeffrey S. Buchanan, C. McKenna, H. Raugh, "Institutional Survival: Evolution of the Admissions Process During the United States Military Academy's First Century," courtesy WPL; Samuel E. Tillman, *The Centennial of the United States Military Academy at West Point, New York*, vol. 1: Addresses and Histories, "The Academic History of the Military Academy, 1802-1902" (Washington, D. C.: Government Printing Office, 1904), 228-229. Thayer was the Superintendent of the Academy from 28 July 1817 to 1 July 1833. Thayer changed the prior Superintendent, Andrew Ellicott's, policy of admitting no one younger than 13 to admitting no one under 16, Thayer Papers, vols. 2 and 3 courtesy WPL.

[12] Latrobe, 4. Roommates he mentions are brothers Campbell and Alfred Graham. Alfred Graham is not listed in Cullum's Register as attending West Point so that brother may have been James D. Graham who had graduated in 1817 and was appointed to the military staff as Adjutant at the Academy 12 October 1817 to 10 February 1819, as a 3rd Lt. Only 40 of the 119 who began in the class graduated in the Class of 1822, "Register of Officers and Cadets, USMA, 1817–1822," courtesy WPL. The North and South Barracks, the Academy building and the Mess Hall were made of rough, gray granite with slate roofs. Cadets chose their own roommates who may not have been in the same class year. Cadets bought their own furniture and some slept on the floor.

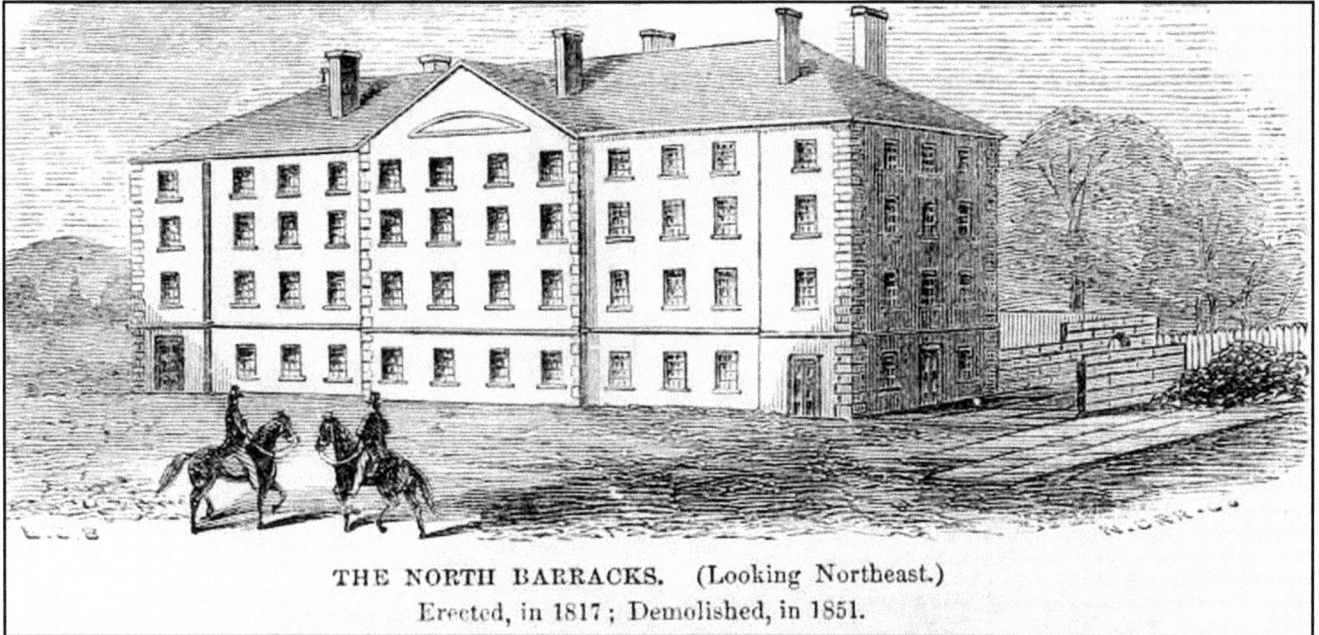

THE NORTH BARRACKS. (Looking Northeast.)
Erected, in 1817 ; Demolished, in 1851.

Boynton, *History of West Point*, 254.

The Long Barracks as it appeared in 1802. It was built in 1796 but after the two new barracks were finished in 1817, it housed enlisted men and families; it was destroyed by fire in 1827. Drawn by Colonel Walter Sturgill, courtesy WPL.

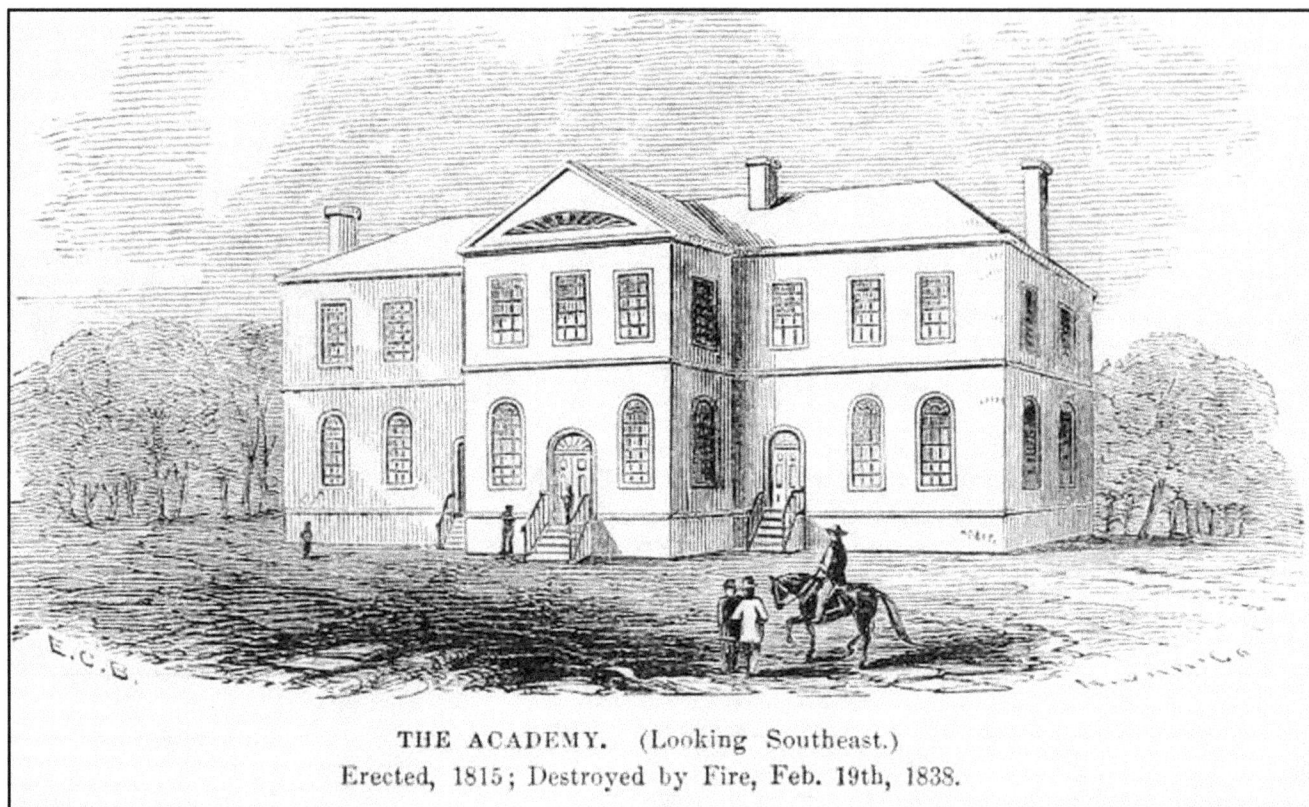

THE ACADEMY. (Looking Southeast.)
Erected, 1815; Destroyed by Fire, Feb. 19th, 1838.

The Academy building was built of stone; the ground floor in the center was the chapel and the library was in the room above it. West of the chapel was the chemical laboratory with the philosophical room above. Adjoining the chapel on the east was the engineering department with the Adjutant's Office in the room over it. The 1838 fire destroyed archives and records of the academy from 1802 to 1838, Augusta Blanche Berard, *Reminiscences of West Point in the Olden Time* (East Saginaw, MI: Evening News Printing and Binding House, 1886), 27; sketch by Boynton, *History of West Point*, 255.

Cadets' accommodations were austere and for most of the men more Spartan than those with which they were familiar at home. There was no running water so trips to the well near South Barracks were required and wood for stoves was carried in from the wood yard close to the barracks. Cadets devised a yoke to carry two buckets per trip and a bucket was always kept near the fireplace to quell the frequent blazes.[13] What furniture they had the cadets had to purchase from their $18 per month stipend. While standards of personal hygiene in the early 1800's differ from modern times, cadets made do with what were available—washbasins in their rooms. Baths were only available in the Hudson River:

> In the old time, our only bathtub was the Hudson River, and opportunity and inclination alone suggested the use of it. Those who could swim ventured into the river itself; those who could not swim resorted, when the tide served, that is to say when it made the water deep enough to keep one's feet from the grass and ooze, to a little bay between two rocky points to the west of the public dock. I remember it well, for there was a beach there, on which Sam. Ellis and I hauled, turned over, and caulked a leaky boat that we had bought from French John, whose sloop, with contraband matter on board for cadets who could pay for it, was almost always at anchor off the "flats." When not undergoing repairs, we kept the boat at Havens' dock, at Gee's Point. Well, this bay was our bathtub in 1818.[14]

Cadets' ingenuity at making do with what they could invent helped some who set up a "showerbath":

> But it would be ungrateful not to mention a contrivance that some of us got up, not far from the north gate, where a little stream crossed...the road to the cemetery. On the right of the road, where the bank descends precipitously, we set up a trestle, some six or eight feet high, on which rested one end of a trough, the other end resting on the bank, which in this way was made to receive the water of the stream to supply a sort of showerbath to one standing under the outer end of the trough. The

---

[13] Pappas, 114.
[14] Latrobe, 25-26.

contrivance was as simple as that which helped Phoebe Mayflower to fill her pitcher at the spring, in "Woodstock," and at certain times the supply of water was not much greater. Still, the spot was shady, and there is more than one pleasant memory connected with it. Without the means of ablution here described, our only resources were a washbasin and a toothbrush.

Nor did the nearness of the road interfere, practically, with the use of our showerbath without offense to public modesty. Few persons, in those days, passed that way. The cemetery was a savage spot, compared with what it has since been made.[15]

Cadets did not automatically receive their uniforms upon entering in September but drills commenced without them according to Latrobe. He described the uniform as it appeared in 1818:

The coat, as perfected by Wilton, padding and all, is identically the same; so are the trousers, with the exception of the black stripe on the outer seam. But we wore leather stocks, the shirt collar showing above them, instead of being turned over the collar of the coat. The cap, however, was a stiff leather cylindrical pot—for it deserved no better name— with a very narrow visor, the seam of the cylinder in front being concealed by a lozenge-shaped brass plate with the arms of the Corps of Engineers: Behind the plate was a socket for the whalebone on which were wound the feathers of the long black plume, which was held to be the crowning glory of a cadet's head-gear, especially when, in "loading by the twelve words of command," the word "prime" caused the plumes of the battalion to nod gracefully together. Each plume had a tulip-shaped holder; and, as if this was not weight enough to carry on one's head, there was a brass curb chain from the top of the cap on each side, and attached to the bottom of the lozenge. Such a cap was simply an abomination, and, rain or shine, we had nothing else to wear. The plume, however, might be removed when we were not on parade or guard. Cross-belts for cartridge-box and bayonet, and waist-belt completed the dress of a cadet in 1818.[16]

---

[15] Latrobe, 26. Phoebe Mayflower was a character from Sir Walter Scott's 1826 novel who was involved in an incident at a spring at which a contrivance was built so "that the water was collected, and, trickling along a wooden spout, dropped from a height of about two feet. A damsel was thereby enable to place her pitcher under the slowly dropping supply, and, without toil to herself, might wait till her vessel was filled," Walter Scott, *Woodstock; or, the Cavalier. A Tale of the Year Sixteen Hundred and Fifty-one* (London: Adam & Charles Black, 1897), 362.

[16] Latrobe, 13. The post tailor, Wilton, Latrobe further described: "Wilton was a genius in his way, who took a pride in his art, and did his best to fashion all the cadets on the same pattern; and, by judicious padding, to supply what was wanting, having regard to the build and soldierly appearance and carriage of the individual; he certainly accomplished, at times, wonders in this direction. It was to Wilton, I have always believed, that the chevron was made to assume its present form of curved lines, instead of the straight ones on an heraldic shield," 7.

Uniform c. 1820. Note trousers without shoe straps. Courtesy USMA.

Gray uniforms were adopted as a compliment to General Winfield Scott and his troops who wore gray rather than blue, as only gray was available due to shortage of uniforms during the War of 1812. Scott's troops, clothed in uniforms of gray, won a victory over the British at Chippewa 4 July 1814. The Superintendent before Thayer, Captain Alden Partridge, created this new uniform of "Cadet Gray."

Of the many changes Thayer instituted, his influence on uniforms was minimal. In September 1817, chevrons were first adopted:

> For the designation of rank, chevrons will be worn on the arms of the battalion officers and noncommissioned officers. The colonel shall wear three on each arm; the captain shall wear two on each arm; the adjutant one on each arm; the lieutenants one on the left arm; the sergeant major two on each arm; the sergeants one on each arm; and the corporals one on the left arm; those worn by the officers to be of gold lace and those by the noncommissioned officers yellow ribbon.[17]

He prescribed a few changes in November of the following year:

> The lineal rank of company officers will for the future be designated by chevrons of gold lace, edged with black cloth, borne upon the right arm, those of commissioned officers will subtend downward, and those of the noncommissioned officers upward. Captains will wear three, lieutenants and sergeants two, and corporals one. The first or orderly sergeant will add the interior bend or bar of a third chevron. The battalion staff will, in addition to the badges of their lineal rank, wear bars upon the left arm. The adjutant and sergeant-major will add the interior, and the quartermaster and quartermaster-sergeant the exterior bars of two chevrons corresponding to those of the right arm.[18]

Another change involved the cadets' chapeaux: "Between 1817 and 1820 the round hat with cockade gave place to a leather cap 7 inches high with full crown and drooping visor and plume…with a gilt diamond-shaped ornament bearing the letters "U.S." and a chin strap of gilt scales. An engraving of the date of 1820 shows the hat topped with a plume some 14 inches high of a single feather curled to the rear at the top."[19]

But the West Point Mansfield entered in October 1817 was still experiencing growing pains despite these directives. It was far from the premier engineering school in the western hemisphere but was beginning to show promise. Despite the 1816 rules, standards for admission or length of study were not enforced. Cadets ranged in age from 10 to 37 and attended between 6 months to 6 years.[20] General Alexander Macomb, then Chief Engineer of the Army, in a Report to the Department of War dated 30 March 1822, described the school: "The Military Academy may be considered as having been in its infancy until about the close of 1817, or beginning of 1818, prior to which there was but little system or regularity. Cadets were admitted without examination, and without the least regard to their age or qualifications, as required by the law of 1812. Hence the institution was filled with students who were more or less unfit for their situations. It is not surprising, therefore, that a large portion of them have been under the necessity of leaving the Academy without completing their education."[21]

---

[17] *The Centennial*, vol. 1, 512.

[18] Ibid.

[19] Ibid.

[20] "The Early Years," USMA Bicentennial, United States Military Academy.

[21] "Military Affairs," II, 381. Alexander Macomb joined the army in 1799 and became an engineer in 1802. He was promoted through the ranks to brigadier general in 1814 and retained as colonel and chief engineer in 1821. He was promoted to major general in 1828 and became the commander in chief of the army from 29 May 1828 to 25 June 1841. In 1814 he received a gold medal from Congress; he died in 1841 on active duty.

Etching of the Cadets Monument by John Rubens Smith done c. 1820 dedicated in 1818 to Cadet Vincent M. Lowe, who died as a result of a premature cannon discharge 1 January 1817. It has engraved on it also names of cadets and professors who died at the Academy in the 19th Century. The public dock in shown on the Hudson. Courtesy LOC.

Sylvanus Thayer Takes Command

Mansfield profited by beginning his studies the same year that the legendary superintendent, Sylvanus Thayer, took command as the fifth superintendent; it was also the year before oral examinations for admission were required. Thayer made West Point function as it should have:

> With the advent of Major Thayer as Superintendent there soon followed the organization of the Cadets into a battalion and a separation into classes and division of classes into sections, according to proficiency in studies, with transfers from one section to another; weekly class reports of daily progress, the system and scale of marking, which is still followed, and the publication of the annual register. He brought about the introduction of Boards of Visitors, which had been authorized by the academic regulations of 1816. The curriculum of studies was made definite, improved, and extended. Entrance examinations for candidates were made invariable; and semiannual examinations were established for the Cadets, commencing on the 1st of January and June yearly. These semiannual examinations were conducted before the entire Academic Board.[22]

Thayer became known as the "Father of the Military Academy" as under his command, the Academy regime became more regularized and organized. As importantly, he also instilled a spirit of order and professionalism in the Cadet Corps:

> The superintendent placed a "heavy stress upon the need for a total control of the student's activities." He believed that idleness was not conducive to instilling discipline. Thayer filled the cadet's entire day on a year-round basis, ending the three-

---

[22] Tillman, vol. 1, 230. Thayer served from 28 July 1817 to 1 July 1833.

month winter recess. To ferret out gambling activities and limit cadets' access to the nearby Gridley's Tavern, all of the students' money was kept by the college treasurer; the cadets were not allowed to bring or receive moneys from home. Thayer decreed that a cadet's final ranking would include a conduct grade, whose weight of importance would increase with progression from the first to the fourth year. Thayer required a battalion of cadets, making up most of the academy's student population...to make forced marches to Hudson, New York, Philadelphia, and Boston during the hottest month of the year and give performances of their precision drills. Thayer as well as the Board of Visitors was especially troubled by the mischief that cadets would get into because of the location of a tavern just outside the gates of the post and the relative proximity of the academy to "New York and other cities" where cadets could flock on vacations "to indulge in dissipation and to contract disease, vices and debts." To counteract these vices, Thayer instituted compulsory chapel attendance in 1818.[23]

Cadets' summers provided a welcome diversion despite the weather as the cadets marched away from their austere existence at the Academy under Thayer's orders; in 1821, the Corps was on the march from 20 July to the 26th of September.[24] See Attachment 7 below for recollections of that legendary 1821 march.

Colonel Sylvanus Thayer, the "Father of West Point." Courtesy USMA. See Attachment 5 below for his biography.

---

[23] Laurence M. Hauptman and Heriberto Dixon, "Cadet David Moniac: A Creek Indian's Schooling at West Point, 1817-1822," *Proceedings of the American Philosophical Society*, vol. 152 no. 3, September 2008, 322-348. In 1819, cadets made a 14-day march beginning 10 August by sloop to Cold Spring, through Poughkeepsie and up the Hudson, returning by boat to West Point. The Corps stayed three days in camp at Poughkeepsie with daily parades and drill thrilling the populace, Dupuy, 171. The corps marched to Philadelphia in 1820 after first moving by boat to Staten Island; Boston in 1821; and Goshen, New York, in 1822. Public relations was on Thayer's mind as a productive reason for the marches in addition to the obvious military and physical fitness aspects, Stephen E. Ambrose, *Duty, Honor Country: A History of West Point* (Baltimore, MD: The Johns Hopkins University Press, 1999), 81-82; Pappas, 146-147. Thayer stopped further marches as they interfered with or replaced the summer encampments on the Plain. There are no official records of the 1818 march during summer camp to Goshen, during which a Revolutionary War officer was buried with honor, nor of the march to Philadelphia in 1820. Most records were destroyed in the Academy Building fire in 1838, Dupuy 170-171.
[24] John H.B. Latrobe, "The March of the U.S. Corps of Cadets to Boston, Between the 20th of July and 26th September, 1821," *The Association of the Graduates of the Unites Dates Military Academy, Twentieth Annual Reunion, June 12th, 1885*, Annual Report by the United States Military Academy Association of Graduates (East Saginaw, MI: Evening News, Printers and Binders, 1885), 1-29. See Attachment 7 below.

Latrobe continued with his description of life for the class of 1822 and the buildings in which they lived and ate:

In 1818, the battalion was divided, when in winter quarters, into two companies of equal numbers, the tallest cadets occupying the South Barracks, and forming the first company, and the second company the North Barracks. This was changed in 1819, when I went into the North Barracks, to my great delight. A long corridor, running north and south, divided this building lengthwise; and at either end were broad stairways to the upper stories, or "stoops," so-called. On the first floor were the guard room and recitation rooms; and above these were the rooms occupied by the cadets. Each of these was some eighteen feet square, and was divided by a wooden partition, into two rooms of unequal size, the smaller one containing the cots of the occupants, one in each corner. In the larger were a table and four or five chairs, the gunrack with pegs above it for the accoutrements, and a large woodbox in a recess next the fireplace.

The two barracks were at right angles to each other, a space of about fifty feet intervening, through which many a cap and plume were carried toward the Hudson, when the owner attempted to cross the funnel thus formed, in a northwest gale. Prolonging the line of the South Barracks, west, was the Academy, so-called—a building with wings, containing in the centre, the chapel, over which was the library. The former, a long, narrow and high-ceilinged room, with bare whitewashed walls, was lighted by windows at each end. At the east end, were a platform and reading desk; on either side of which, were seats for the officials of the Academy and their families. The body of the hall was occupied by the cadets, seated on narrow benches, as close together as they could well be put, on either side of a centre aisle. Here, any general reading could be indulged in, in every row except the front one, without fear of detection. Both floors of the east wing were used by the Teacher of Drawing, and the Professor of Chemistry had as much as he wanted of the west wing.

Beyond the Academy, on the same line, and some seventy feet, or more, west of it, was the Mess Hall, a long, two-storied stone building, the west end of which was a hotel, where officers messed, and visitors generally were received; while the two stories of the east end contained the Mess Hall proper of the cadets. The west end of the building abutted upon a road, running north and south, on which were the houses of the Professors and the Superintendent. In front of the Mess Hall were the only trees worthy of the name on the Point—six elms...—under which the cadets constructed a mighty bower for their 4th of July celebrations....

THE MESS-HALL. (Looking Southwest.)
Erected, 1815; Demolished, 1852.

Boynton, *History of West Point*, 256.

Both floors of the east end of the Mess Hall were used for the cadets —the upper story being reached by a flight of steps on the south side. Nothing could have been plainer than the interior arrangement: — three or four long tables, with the commonest benches for seats, across which we had to stride to take our places. Tablecloths were unknown then, and, indeed, for a long time after. The food, however, was good, and there was plenty of it. The bread, I remember, was excellent, and we often surreptitiously took away with us in our high leather caps enough to have "a toast," with butter, obtained in the same way, in our rooms, at a later hour. Ah, these were merry days,—when we ate with our knives and two-pronged forks, on plain boards; and when the reply to the carver standing up at the head of the table when he asked a cadet what part of the roast or boiled beef he preferred, was "a big bit anywhere." Ah, I repeat, these were merry days, and the buttered toast, after "taps," was more enjoyed than many a feast which, later in life, it has been my fortune to partake of.

From my room in the South Barracks, I overlooked a large yard, enclosed by a high board fence. Between it and the river bank ran the road which I had passed on my way to Grid's; and within it were the barber and shoeblack premises, opposite to the east end of the North Barracks. The woodyard, too, was within this yard; and here, also, opposite to the Academy, was Mr. DeWitt's (the suttler's) store. The gun sheds mentioned by Mrs. Davies in her reminiscences I do not distinctly recall. Beyond the woodyard, the eye rested on the forest-clad mountains of the Hudson—the river itself unseen—which bounded the horizon.

The view from the north side of the South Barracks was very different. Immediately in the foreground was the plain of West Point, beyond which was seen the river, dividing the Crow's Nest on the one side from the giant mass of mountains above Cold Spring on the other, and forming, with Newburg in the distance and the still remoter range of the Shawangunk, a picture that is not surpassed in beauty in America. From this elevation, the plain seemed flat, except where broken by the remarkable depression called "Execution Hollow." To the left, or west side, of the plain, concealed by the elms already spoken of, was the residence of Professor Ellicott, fronting on the avenue running north and south; then came Professor Mansfield's; then the Superintendent's—the only double house in the row—and then the Chaplain's, the last on this part of the avenue, which then turned to the left and passed some stone houses, one of which was occupied by Mr. Berard, teacher of French, and the other by Mr. Gimbrede, teacher of drawing. Beyond these, the avenue terminated at the "North Gate;" although there was a road from thence, passing by the "German Flats" and leading over the mountain, to Cornwall.

From the bend in the avenue there was a road down the hill to the public dock. Of the houses to which it afforded access, I have a less distinct recollection than of those on the plain. The best remembered is Mrs. Thompson's, where, after my first year at the Point, I had my meals, as one of twelve cadets whom, as the widow of a revolutionary officer, Mrs. Thompson was permitted to board. Here we enjoyed the comforts and observances of a private family, at a table at which Mrs. Thompson and one or more of her daughters were always present [in a] low-browed yellow cottage, with its paling fence, enclosing a nicely-kept flower-bed or two....Another house, not far off, was Wilton's, the tailor....

The hospital, so-called, was down the hill; a mean frame building, utterly unworthy of the name given to it. Here I once saw a cadet on his death-bed, whose body the corps followed, a few days later, to be buried at the "German Flats."

Below Mrs. Thompson's, on the left of the road to the dock, was the shoemaker's, known as "George's," where buckwheat cakes might be had by cadets whom the rules of the Academy required should be in quarters. Ah, we had simple tastes in those days, when buttered toast and buckwheat cakes after "taps" were luxuries, all the more enjoyable because forbidden.

Returning now to the plain at the bend of the avenue, and following the outline eastwardly, we come to the flagstaff in its present position, with a battery close by, consisting of one twenty-four-pounder, one twelve-pounder, and four six-pounders; passing which, with "Execution Hollow" on the right, we come to the "Bombardier [Long] Barracks," so called, where the cadets were originally quartered, and now occupied by regular soldiers. This was a long, two-storied, yellow, wooden building, the upper story being reached by stairs on the outside, giving access to its several corridors....Beyond this was the ruin of Fort Clinton, on the northeast corner of the plain, turning southerly from which we fall into the road from Gee's Point. The river and south fronts of the fort were still in shape, but the other fronts were in a ruinous condition; and in advance of the west curtain was a deep hollow, now filled up....

The cadets were divided, when in winter quarters, into first and second companies, according to height. My height placed me in the first company, where I was twelfth from the right. This company, as already said, occupied, after my first year, the North Barracks, and carried a fourteen-pound musket, and the second company a light affair, like the muskets now carried by the entire corps....

It was quite a maneuver to get the company formed for drill in those days. After calling "one, two," and dividing the company into two platoons, the second platoon took one pace forward—number two having stepped behind number one, when, the rear rank of each platoon countermarching, and the second keeping on to the head of the company, and both facing to the front, it was found that the tallest were on the right and left respectively....[25]

---

[25] Latrobe, 4-12. Locations of privies or latrines were not noted but they must have existed near all buildings and residences. Chamber pots were likely under every bed also. In 1863, "Cadet Sinks" were constructed to replace those found in the barracks' basements and along the exterior barracks' wall, HABS West Point, 81. Room orderlies among other things emptied "slop water" from their rooms into large tubs in the halls of North Barracks or on the stoops of South Barracks; this likely included dirty water from washbasins and chamber pots, Pappas, 153. An 1800 drawing of the floor plan of the "Military Academy, cellar floor plan by Benjamin H. Latrobe, shows an exit labelled "Passage to the privies" but does not show privies within the cellar. Quarters were assigned by height putting taller cadets into the 1st Company, and shorter into the 2nd establishing the terms "flankers" and "runts," Pappas, 122. Turkey, chickens, and other comestibles were sometimes roasted in the fireplace but against regulations, Pappas, 152.

The West Point Board of Visitors in its 1826 report wrote of a "five-year" program of which Mansfield took advantage:

> In the last place, the undersigned would speak of the provision by which about one-seventh of those who are graduated in each class, are permitted to *remain five years* at the Academy. This, they conceive, is the only leniency in the existing rules of instruction, by which they can be safely qualified. Those Cadets who are unable to proceed in the course are cut off at the end of the probation; those who abuse the advantages offered them, are sent away as offences are committed; and those who grow gradually more idle, instead of more active, fall, at last, to the bottom of their class, and then resign or are removed. Still, there may well be a few, who, from youth, from sickness, or from unavoidable interruptions in their course, are unable, at once, to make good the claims and standing required from them. To these, one more year is both wisely and kindly given; and, in most cases, so improved, as to place them in, at least, a respectable standing among their competitors.[26]

George Catlin painting of West Point in 1828. Cadets engaged in artillery drill, Wood's Monument in foreground. Buildings from the left are the North Barracks, the South Barracks, the Academy, and the Mess Hall. Latrobe wrote that there was a battery of four six-pound guns near the flagstaff at which the second and third classes received artillery drill every morning before breakfast. Men substituted for horses as horses were not available for cadet use. Courtesy WPL.

Why did Mansfield choose to enter West Point? The most likely reason was that a free engineering education combined with a potential career, was hard to resist. Mansfield's father had died not leaving much of an estate so the lure of attending Yale College in New Haven, Connecticut, or any other expensive college, would have not been possible.[27] Lieutenant Colonel Jared Mansfield undoubtedly influenced Joseph as the professor was a leading early teacher at West Point and his son, Edward, Joseph's cousin, was a student there from 1815 to 1819, graduating second in his class. Joseph's grandfather Stephen, on his father's side, was a sea captain engaged in the West India trade. Joseph's father, Henry was also a sea captain who followed in his father's footsteps.[28]

---

[26] *Report of the Board of Visitors, on the United States Military Academy, at West Point, for 1826*, 4-5; courtesy WPL. http://digital-library.usma.edu/libmedia/archives/bov/V1826.PDF.

[27] While the tuition in 1817 was only $33 per year, associated costs such as room, board, books, etc., would have been costly, Brooks Mather Kelley, *Yale: A History* (New Haven, CT: Yale University Press, 1974), 143-144. One historian opined that "The army was the first major public sector employer under centralized national control in the United States, and...was psychologically attractive to men seeking occupational status and material security....Officers were accorded the status of gentlemen and the authority to command others....they received a fixed salary supplemented by a wide array of allowances for food, housing, and other necessities, and (barring outrageous misconduct) they never lost their jobs," Samuel J. Watson, "Manifest Destiny and Military Professionalism: Junior U.S. Army Officers' Attitudes Toward War with Mexico, 1844-1846," *The Southwestern Historical Quarterly*, vol. 99, July 1995 - April, 1996, 496.

[28] His cousin, Edward Deering Mansfield, was born in Connecticut but appointed to the Academy from New York. He declined his commission upon graduation. He received honorary degrees from Princeton and Marietta College, and was a lawyer and author. He was the author of several books and

Joseph also had a famous more distant relative, Major Moses Mansfield of New Haven, who was active in military service of the Connecticut Colony. During the bloody and destructive King Philip's War in 1675-1676, he was lieutenant of the New Haven company under Captain John Beard. He fought in the Narragansett Campaign in Rhode Island in 1675. Following the war, he was named captain of the New Haven train band in 1683 and was appointed Sergeant Major of New Haven County in 1694, the highest rank in the colonial militia. The Town of Mansfield, Connecticut, was named after him for defeating a body of Indians there in King Philip's War. Moses also was involved in civic life in New Haven as the Deputy from New Haven to the Connecticut General Court, and an Assistant in the colonial government of Connecticut from 1692-1703. He served as a member of the General Court or Assembly for forty-eight sessions. In addition, he was also judge of the probate court and the county court.[29]

Joseph had come from Puritan stock as noted above in Chapter 2. Given his family background it would not be possible for him to pursue a mundane trade and apparently he had no desire to pursue his father's profession as a sea captain. Joseph could be considered to have been of the "upper" class in society even though he was not wealthy. He would find men of similar background at West Point, although many did have wealthy families like Latrobe who commented on this aspect of West Point life:

> Then, again, the social class which furnished cadets for the Military Academy in the earlier days of the institution was different, in some respects, from what it now is [1887], so far as I have been able to judge from frequent visits, of late years, to West Point. There were more "gentlemen's sons" in the corps then, to use a term that is well understood, without intending any invidious application of it. Young men who had been accustomed to the amenities and observances of refined social life at home, when they met at West Point, were naturally drawn together, without regard to the first, second, third or fourth classes of the Academy. Brains and breeding, however, do not seem to have always gone together. There was W, for example, who, when he came from _ , promised, apparently, nothing remarkable of the latter, was always one of the "five" [highest ranking]; while X, who had enjoyed all its advantages, was one of the last of his class to graduate.[30]

Latrobe wrote again about this class distinction and "recreation" during his student days:

> I have no recollection of anything that could be called dissipation while I was a cadet. The worst that I can recall is the bowl of eggnog that, somehow or other, made its appearance about Christmas. That swearing was as common "as it was in the army in Flanders;" that we smoked cigars—and very miserable ones they were—without restraint, there can be no doubt; but that we drank whisky and got drunk, we did not; and I say it, at this late day, to the credit of my old comrades of the class of 1822. I do not pretend that we were saints; on the contrary; but the understanding was general, that we were gentlemen; and it was this feeling that it was pre-eminently the wish of Colonel Thayer, himself the noblest gentleman, to instill into those under his charge.[31]

Gridley's [North's] Tavern received an unfavorable review in the 1819 Report of Visitors: "There is one other expense which the Board of Visitors most earnestly recommend that Government would incur for the benefit of this Institution; they allude to the purchase of Mr. North's land adjoining the West Point Tract; they are assured and can readily conceive that the Tavern kept on this land within 100 Yards of the Cadet Barracks, & over which the Regulations of the Academy do not extend, has been productive of the very worst consequences to some of the Cadets, tho' the vigilant Superintendence of the Commanding Officer has, in a very great degree, diminished the evil, that it still

---

other works including *The Life and Military Services of Lieut. Gen. Winfield Scott*, and the *History of the Mexican War*; he was editor of the *Cincinnati Chronicle* for 12 years. He died in Ohio 1880 at age 79.

[29] Ellery Bicknell Crane, *Historic Homes and Institutions and Genealogical and Personal Memoirs of Worcester County, Massachusetts*, vol. 2 (New York, NY: The Lewis Publishing Company, 1907), 406; George Madison Bodge, *Soldiers in King Philip's War* (Leominster, MA: Rockwell and Churchill Press, 1896), 184; Mansfield Historical Society Newsletter, November 2011.

[30] Latrobe, 23. Thayer was concerned that his entrance examinations excluded many men who could not read or write well as they were not from well-to-do families which could afford to pay for education costs. He tried to resolve this starting in 1822 by requiring cadets to report during the second week in June for instruction in basic skills—mainly reading, writing and elementary mathematics, Pappas, 149-150.

[31] Latrobe, 28. Most of the cadets during this time were "members of 'respectable' and politically influential, if not necessarily affluent, families," William B. Skelton, *An American Profession of Arms: The Army Officer Corps, 1784-1861* (Lawrence, KS: University Press of Kansas, 1992), 140. Time and availability of recreation was limited, walking, hiking, and fishing were popular and in winter, cadets skated on a large pond near the Superintendent's house, Pappas, 115. Playing games like football were confined to an area near Fort Clinton. Cadet dances took place after the fencing master was allowed to give dancing lessons. Apparently few female dance partners were available so cadets usually danced with their roommates. Thayer also established an Amosophic Society, a literary and debating group open to all classes, and eliminated the rule against playing chess during free time, Pappas, 145, 153.

exists to too great an extent to render the Cost of removing it, an object of serious consideration."[32] Again in 1823, Gridley's Tavern was of concern to the Board of Visitors:

> Immediately adjoining the public ground at West Point, is a tract of land with several buildings on it, the property of a Mr. Gridley, who resides there and is licensed as an Inn-keeper. His proximity to the Public Building [West Point], and the easiness of access to his premises affords so strong an inducement to violate the orders of the Superintendent against his house; it is true the penalties are severe and certain disgrace awaits the detected offender; but as the Government have it in their power to remove this dangerous neighbour, it ought to be done; we have the divine injunction before us "Lead us not into temptation but deliver us from evil."[33]

It would be hard to believe however, that Latrobe's friend, Joseph Mansfield, would have partaken as freely as some of his classmates.

Joseph was not in the highest rungs of society since his family was not wealthy. This was noted by his aunt, Elizabeth Mansfield, Professor Jared Mansfield's wife: "...other wives [of instructors] were polite, [but] they were used to living in the high style.' They exhibited 'a set of manners very different from our acquaintances in New Haven...I see them seldom; tho I have been treated by them with the greatest attention. You know I was never no hand at visiting and I visit less now than ever.'"[34]

Latrobe's father wrote a letter to his father-in-law which described why he urged that his son attend West Point, sentiments to which Joseph Mansfield's family would have ascribed:

> We must now consider what part he is to act in the world. The reputation of the family on both sides forbids our looking to any profession but that of a gentleman for him. If he is to be a lawyer or a physician, he must receive a college education of three years at least. If a merchant, his time in any respectable counting-house will be extremely expensive to us. But as I am retrieving my affairs very rapidly, I am not in any doubt as to my being able to defray the expenses of his education, and I confess even now I could not have a more useful assistant in my office. But he ought to go from home, and that soon, and if it were otherwise desirable, I would much prefer to bring him up to any other profession. One of our most intimate friends here is Colonel [George] Bomford of the Ordnance....Colonel Bomford has filled his heart with the advantages of an education at West Point, and whatever else he may submit to be done with him, nothing will so well satisfy him as to go to West Point. The advantages which this career afford are:—
>
> First: His education will cost us nothing, and it will be of the very best kind. He will learn to speak French fluently, and become an excellent mathematician, draftsman and chemist.
>
> Second: His pay—$19.00 a month—will clothe him, and in fact $100.00 per annum will be ample additional allowance for other expenses. He can spend two months annually at home.
>
> Third: The severe military discipline he must undergo, the early hours and exercise among the mountains, appear necessary to his indolence and the development of his constitution.
>
> Fourth: As a preparatory education for civil department of his preference, he cannot possibly have a better.
>
> Fifth: In three years he is entitled to a Second Lieutenancy, and may then stay at West Point or be employed at some fortification which may then be in the course of construction. He may then at twenty-one or twenty-two, if I live so long, take my place and continue as an architect or civil engineer.
>
> The objection seems to me to be comprised in one, namely, a determined taste acquired at West Point for military life, yielding in our country neither profit nor honor.[35]

---

[32] Board of Visitors Report, 1819, 9.

[33] Board of Visitors Report, 1823, 87; courtesy WPL. http://digital-library.usma.edu/libmedia/archives/bov/V1823.PDF. Thayer in 1825 finally convinced Congress to purchase Gridley's property for $10,000 and his house became the cadet hospital. Benny Havens then became a legend supplying cadets with victuals and liquor for decades, Ambrose, *Duty, Honor, Country*, 164.

[34] Crackel, 86.

[35] John E. Semmes, *John H.B. Latrobe and His times, 1803-1891* (Baltimore, MD: The Waverly Press, 1917), 68-69. Monthly pay fixed by the law of 1802 was $16 per month and two rations per day altogether valued at $28, Chapter 9, Act of March 16, 1802, Sec. 26, Boynton, *History of West Point*, 245, 349. Skelton wrote that "it is likely that a significant portion of the antebellum regulars—perhaps more than a third of the total—entered the army mainly because it offered a free education and a modicum of economic security," 166. His comments about family fortunes are applicable to Mansfield's father's death, Skelton wrote "that the vaunted social mobility of the nineteenth century was not entirely upward and that the fluctuations of an expanding but unstable economy or the death of a key relative could throw middle- and upper-class families into decline or even poverty....Although paternal death did not inevitably bring poverty, it certainly increased the pressures on all but the wealthiest families and reduced the chances that the sons would receive higher education," 165.

Joseph, like many other highly-ranked cadets, was chosen as an instructor, in his case, as an assistant professor in the department of natural philosophy. Latrobe similarly was chosen—he wrote that he was "appointed Assistant Teacher of Drawing…and became entitled to ten dollars per month extra pay and to wear twice as many buttons on my coat as before, and was relieved from military duty."[36] Joseph would have appreciated that his academic efforts were similarly rewarded. Remuneration for teaching as a cadet assistance professor was instituted by Thayer after he complained to the War Department on 20 January 1818 as follows: "The present practice of employing Cadets as Assistant Professors is very objectionable --

1st Because, it is extremely difficult to find a sufficient number who are capable.

2nd Because, they perform with great reluctance a duty for which they receive no compensation & which deprives them, in a great measure, of the benefits of instruction in their own Classes.

3rd Because, being the equals & familiar companions of those whom they instruct, they are unable to inspire the respect so necessary to their duties.

4th From the frequent changes which it induces as a Cadet no sooner acquires the experience which is so valuable in the art of instructing, than he receives a commission & quits the unprofitable part of a Teacher without pay." Then on 15 April 1818, Thayer championed payment for cadet assistant professors: "It cannot be expected that Cadets who are directed to perform the Duties of assistants contrary to their wishes will, generally, Discharge them in a manner advantageous to the Institution & it is believed that no cadet of the Mil. Academy who is competent to the duty would willingly perform it without a reasonable compensation for his services….from an expectation that they would finally receive the reward due to their unremitted zeal & fidelity. Their long experience as teachers is highly valuable to the Institution & it is therefore very desirable that they should be retained."[37]

Mansfield's graduation class of forty in 1822 had several interesting classmates. They ranged from a Creek Indian (David Moniac), and future Mexican-American War participants, to Civil War generals:

> [F]ive future generals in the U.S. Army, two generals in the New Jersey militia, two high-ranking officers in the Confederate army, three college presidents, and at least five civil engineers and/or chief operating officers of railroads. At least ten of the forty graduates resigned their commissions or died before the outbreak of the Second Seminole War in 1835. Seventeen of the cadets served on the frontier, including three in Creek Country, ten in the Second Seminole War, and one in the Cherokee removal. Three in the class of 1822 died during the Second Seminole War….Among the most distinguished members of the class was David Hunter, who served in the Black Hawk War, Second Seminole War, and Civil War. Rising to the rank of major general, Hunter later served on the military commission for the trial of the conspirators in President Lincoln's assassination….[Mansfield's] cousin, George Dutton, who was first in the class but only achieved the rank of major before his death in 1857, later served as commander of federal harbor fortifications in New York City. Isaac Ridgeway Trimble…played a key role in the Confederate army in Stonewall Jackson's Shenandoah Valley operations in 1862, at the Second Battle of Bull Run, and as a major general at Gettysburg, where he lost a leg and was captured. Nicholas Trist, later the renowned diplomat who negotiated the Treaty of Guadalupe Hidalgo (1848), ending the Mexican War…dropped out of the academy [in 1821] before his graduation.[38]

---

[36] Latrobe, 31. The use of cadets as acting assistant professors began in 1815 and was considered an honorable distinction to be so chosen. Cadet instructors received an extra $10 per month, did not have to march to class, and were excused from some other routine duties. Later, they were allowed to wear three rows of 14 buttons on their dress coats vice the normal eight in a row, Pappas, 106-107.

[37] Thayer Papers, vol. 3, courtesy WPL. In his fifth year and final year, the *Register of the Officers and Cadets of the U.S. Military Academy, June, 1822*, shows that Mansfield was an "acting assistant professor of philosophy;" copy of register courtesy of Jim Rosebrock.

[38] Hauptman, "Cadet David Moniac," 336-337.

Roster of Graduates Class of 1822[39]

Class Rank/ Cullum No.	Name	State of Appt.	Date Appt.	Highest Rank U.S. Army	War Service	Age/Year of Death	Remarks
1/286	George Dutton	Conn.	7 Sept. 1818	Maj.	None	54; 1857	Cousin of J.K.F. Mansfield; died in service
2/287	Joseph K.F. Mansfield	Conn.	1 Oct. 1817	Maj. Gen.	Mex.-Am. War; Civil War	59; 1862	Nephew of Prof. Jared Mansfield. Died 18 Sept. 1862, Antietam
3/288	Charles G. Smith	Conn.	30 Sept. 1818	2nd Lt.	None	29; 1827	Died in service, Fort Moultrie, S.C.
4/289	Thomas R. Ingalls	N.Y.	21 Sept. 1818	2nd Lt.	None	66; 1864	Resigned 1829
5/290	Horace Bliss	N.H.	1 Oct. 1817	1st Lt.	None	76; 1878	Resigned 1836
6/291	William Cook	N.J.	7 Sept. 1818	1st Lt.	None	64; 1865	Resigned 1832; Maj. Gen. N.Y Militia 1848-1865
7/292	William Rose	N.Y.	24 June 1818	2nd Lt.	None	24; 1825	Died on active duty
8/293	Walter Gwynn	Va.	10 Sept. 1818	1st Lt.	Civil War (CSA)	80; 1882	Resigned 1832; CSA Brig. Gen.
9/294	Campbell Graham	Va.	1 Sept. 1817	Maj.	2nd Seminole War	67; 1866	Retired 1861 disability
10/295	Thompson B. Wheelock	Mass.	24 Sept. 1818	1st Lt.	2nd Seminole War	35; 1836	Died at Fort Micanopy, Fl.
11/296	James H. Cooke	N.C.	1 Sept. 1818	1st Lt.	None	29; 1833	Resigned 1833
12/297	William C. Young	N.Y.	21 Sept. 1818	2nd Lt.	None	1893	Resigned 1826
13/298	Augustus Canfield	N.J.	17 Sept. 1818	Capt.	None	53; 1854	Died in service
14/299	David H. Vinton	R.I.	1 Sept. 1818	Maj. Gen.	2nd Seminole War; Creek War; Mex.-Am. War; Civil War	70; 1873	Asst. QM Gen.; retired 1866
15/300	John J. Schuler	Penn.	7 Sept. 1818	2nd Lt.	None	85; 1888	Resigned 1828
16/301	John Pickell	N.Y.	2 Sept. 1818	Col.	Black Hawk War; 2nd Seminole War; Cherokee removal; Civil War	63; 1865	Resigned, sick, 1862
17/302	Isaac R. Trimble	Ky.	23 Nov. 1818	2nd Lt.	Civil War (CSA)	85; 1888	Resigned 1832; Maj. Gen. CSA
18/303	Henry H. Gird	N.Y.	14 Nov. 1818	2nd Lt.	None	44; 1845	Asst. Inst. USMA; Resigned 1829
19/304	Benjamin H. Wright	N.Y.	14 Sept. 1818	2nd Lt.	None	1881	Resigned 1823
20/305	William M. Boyce	Penn.	7 Sept. 1818	Capt.	Creek War	54; 1855	Resigned 1836
21/306	St. Clair Denny	Penn.	10 Sept. 1818	Maj.	2nd Seminole War	58; 1858	Died on active duty
22/307	Westwood Lacey	Va.	18 Sept. 1817	1st Lt.	Creek Country	26; 1829	Died Tallahassee, Fl.
23/308	Eustace Trenor	Vt.	1 Oct. 1817	Maj.	Creek Nation; Indian Terr.	44; 1847	Died in service
24/309	George Wright	Vt.	14 Sept. 1818	Brig. Gen.	2nd Seminole War; Mex.-Am. War; Civil War	62; 1865	Drowned in route to Dept. of Columbia
25/310	David Hunter	D.C.	14 Sept. 1818	Maj. Gen.	Black Hawk War; Mex.-Am. War; Civil	84; 1886	Lincoln Conspirators' trial; retired 1866

[39] Francis B. Heitman, *Historical Register and Dictionary of the United States Army, from Its Organization, September 29, 1789, to March 2, 1902.* vol. 1 (Washington, D.C.: Government Printing Office 1903. Reprint, University of Illinois Press, Urbana, IL: 1965), passim; Eicher, *Civil War High Commands*, passim; George W. Cullum, *Biographical Register of the Officers and Graduates of the U.S. Military Academy, at West Point, N.Y.*, vol. 1 (New York: NY: D. Van Nostrand, 1868), 220-239; Hauptman, "Cadet David Moniac," 344-347. Ranks shown include brevets.

					War		
26/311	George A. McCall	Penn.	1 Sept. 1818	Brig. Gen.	2nd Seminole War; Mex.-Am. War; Civil War	65; 1868	Resigned 1863
27/312	Albert Lincoln	Conn.	28 Sept. 1818	2nd Lt.	None	20; 1822	Died in service
28/313	Francis Lee	Penn.	2 Sept. 1818	Col.	2nd Seminole War; Mex.-Am. War	55; 1859	
29/314	James R. Stephenson	Va.	10 Sept. 1818	Capt.	2nd Seminole War	40; 1841	Died in service
30/315	John D. Hopson	Vt.	24 Sept. 1818	1st Lt.	None	31; 1829	Died in service
31/316	Thompson Morris	Oh.	1 Sept. 1817	Lt. Col.	2nd Seminole War; Mex.-Am. War	70;1870	Retired 1861 disability
32/317	John R. Wilcox	Oh.	31 Oct. 1818	2nd Lt.	None	39; 1839	Resigned 1824
33/318	Thomas Johnston	Penn.	30 Sept. 1818	1st Lt.	None	33; 1835	Dropped 1834
34/319	George W. Folger	Mass.	30 Sept. 1818	1st Lt.	None	46; 1845	Resigned 1826
35/320	Thomas McNamara	Va.	26 Sept. 1818	1st Lt.	None	1834	Resigned 1830
36/321	Aaron M. Wright	N.H.	30 Sept. 1818	2nd Lt.	None	Unk.	Dismissed from service 1826
37/322	John J. Abercrombie	Tenn.	7 Sept. 1817	Brig. Gen.	Black Hawk War; 2nd Seminole War; Mex.-Am. War; Civil War	79; 1877	
38/323	Samuel Wragg	S.C.	1 Sept. 1818	2nd Lt.	None	25; 1828	
39/324	David Moniac	Ala.	18 Sept. 1817	Maj.	2nd Seminole War	34; 1836	Killed 2nd Seminole War; Creek Indian
40/325	Henry Clark	Conn.	1 Sept. 1818	1st Lt.	None	30; 1830	Died on active duty

Mansfield did well at West Point despite a slow start necessitating repeating his second year making his a five year course vice four. In June of 1818 after one year, he was 16th in his Fourth (freshman) Class, First Section, out of 31, and had order of merit scores of 16 in mathematics and 3 in French (the lower number the better). The next year in June 1819, he was number 25 out of 28 in his Third (sophomore) Class. He was seventh in his repeated Third Class in 1820 while John Latrobe was fourth. In June 1821, Mansfield was in the Second (junior) Class and was ranked third, his friend John Latrobe was first and George Dutton, another Nutmegger and Mansfield's cousin, was second. In his final year in the First (senior) Class in 1822, Mansfield ranked second to George Dutton. Latrobe did not take his exam. Of the 40 men in the class of 1822, six, including Mansfield, began their studies in September or October of 1817 while the remaining 34 began in 1818. For his five years at the Academy, his uncle, Jared, was on the academic staff as the Professor of Natural and Experimental Philosophy and undoubtedly provided encouragement to Joseph when needed.[40]

The 18-year-old was ready to begin his career and was certainly eager to employ his newly learned talents as an engineer officer in the Army of the United States after going home for a well-earned leave. He would meet some of his classmates in the Mexican-American War as well as dozens of others who were in attendance during his five years at West Point. Unfortunately as will be seen, some later graduates would be officers with whom Mansfield would not be friends during the Civil War, as those far junior to him in years of service and rank would be promoted above him.

---

[40] *Register of the Officers and Cadets of the U.S. Military Academy June 1818; Catalogue of Cadets June 1819; Register of the Officers and Cadets of the U.S. Military Academy June 1820; Register of the Officers and Cadets of the U.S. Military Academy June 1821; Register of the Officers and Cadets of the U.S. Military Academy June 1822;* courtesy WPL. Records are not clear regarding in which courses he may have been deficient to make him a "turnback"—one required to repeat a year. Perhaps his admission at age 13 contributed to his five-year course; he was the youngest in all his classes. His sister, Mary Wade wrote from Cincinnati 3 December 1820 with suggestions for him, perhaps he had written a somewhat unhappy letter to her: ""Let no time pass unemployed—for time once lost can never be recalled." She says his "spelling has much improved, and you write a pleasing hand. There was but one word spelt wrong in your last letter as follows {douring} {during}," courtesy WPL.

Attachment 1
Early History of West Point

The United States Military Academy at West Point was established by an Act of Congress on 16 March 1802 after decades of recommendations beginning in October 1776. Prior to then, West Point was as an important defensive fortification from the time of the Revolutionary War. The area surrounding West Point was then considered a "no-man's land" between the British and Americans and was known for an abundance of loyalists. West Point is located approximately 50 miles north of New York City on the western bank of the Hudson River. The Academy's geographic location and geologic formations made it ideal for a military garrison because of the narrow curve in the river, creating a "west point" and the highlands, which rise up sharply from river level to 1,400 feet. After the Revolutionary War the Hudson Highlands remained largely unsettled. The area remained unruly as West Point Superintendent Sylvanus Thayer wrote in an 1819 letter to Secretary of War John C. Calhoun reporting the loss of arms and clothing from government stores due to "the gangs of thieves which infest the mountains about this place...." The U.S. Government acquired the original 1,770 acres of land for West Point from Stephen Moore for $11,085 on 10 September 1790. Prior to this purchase, the U.S. Government had an interest in this site. Only one month after the battles of Lexington and Concord in 1775, Congress passed an act providing for a military post on the Hudson Highlands. The combination of West Point and Constitution Island (then called Martelaer's Rock) would serve as an ideal defense against enemy ships having to navigate around this sharp west point in the river. A series of forts, and redoubts were built at West Point and on Constitution Island, and a "Great Chain" and boom were set between them--the chain was never challenged by British ships.[41]

The Act of 16 March 1802 which created the academy, named the instructors: Jonathan Williams, Major of Engineers and Superintendent of the Military Academy, April, 1802; William A. Barron, Captain Engineers, Teacher Mathematics, April, 1802; Jared Mansfield, Captain Engineers, Teacher Natural and Experimental Philosophy, May, 1802; James Wilton, First Lieutenant Engineers, Student; Alexander Macomb, First Lieutenant Engineers, Student; Joseph G. Swift, Second Lieutenant Engineers, Student; Simon M. Levi, Second Lieutenant Engineers, Student. "By the Act of 28 February 1803, there were added to the Academy, a teacher of French and a teacher of Drawing; but both positions were filled by Francis De Masson from July, 1803, until September, 1808, at which time Christian E. Zoeller was appointed teacher of Drawing. Upon the resignation of the latter, in April, 1810, De Masson again resumed the duties." Thus, at this early period, the Military Academy was recognized as a Scientific Institution for the education of the Corps of Engineers, and as such, its existence was not made contingent upon the presence or absence of cadets appointed in the army. By April 1808, 206 cadets were authorized but few were appointed: "No law attached them to the Military Academy; no provision existed for the reception or instruction of such a number at West Point, and to order them to their regiments without instruction was deemed useless.... In this embryonic condition the Military Academy furnished but seventy-one graduates during the first ten years of its existence, and was indeed appropriately compared to 'a foundling barely existing among the mountains, nurtured at a distance, out of sight of, and almost unknown to, its legitimate parents.'"[42]

Clearly the intent to instruct future officers in the army was not working well so on 29 April 1812, Congress passed an act providing details to ensure that the Military Academy would function as originally envisioned:

> That the Military Academy shall consist of the Corps of Engineers, and the following professors, in addition to the teachers of the French language and Drawing, already provided, viz.: one professor of Natural and Experimental Philosophy, with the pay and emoluments of lieutenant-colonel, if not an officer of the Corps, and, if taken from the Corps, then so much in addition to his pay and emoluments as shall equal those of a lieutenant-colonel; one professor of Mathematics, with the pay and emoluments of a major, if not an officer of the Corps, and, if taken from the Corps, then so much in addition to his pay and emoluments as shall equal those of a major; one professor of the art of Engineering in all its branches, with the pay and emoluments of a major, if not an officer of the Corps, and, if taken from the Corps, then so much in addition to his pay and emoluments as shall equal those of a major; each of the foregoing professors to have an assistant professor, which assistant professor shall be taken from the

---

[41] Historic American buildings Survey, HABS No. NY-5708, NPS, passim; Boynton, *History of West Point*, 11, 18-19, 176-180, 191; Wikipedia, "United States Military Academy."
[42] Boynton, 208-210.

most prominent characters of the officers or cadets, and receive the pay and emoluments of captains, and no other pay or emoluments while performing these duties. Provided, That nothing herein contained shall entitle the Academical Staff, as such, to any command in the army separate from the Academy.

That the cadets heretofore appointed in the service of the United States, whether of Artillery, Cavalry, Riflemen, or Infantry, or that may in future be appointed as hereinafter provided, shall at no time exceed two hundred and fifty; that they may be attached, at the discretion of the President of the United States, as students, to the Military Academy, and be subject to the established regulations thereof; that they shall be arranged into companies of non-commissioned officers and privates, according to the direction of the commandant of Engineers, and be officered from the said Corps, for the purpose of military instruction; that there shall be added to each company of cadets four musicians, and the said Corps shall be trained and taught all the duties of a private, non-commissioned officer, and officer; be encamped at least three months of each year, and taught all the duties incident to a regular camp; that the candidates for cadets be not under the age of fourteen, nor above the age of twenty-one years; that each cadet, previously to his appointment by the President of the United States, shall be well versed in reading, writing, and arithmetic, and that he shall sign articles, with the consent of his parent or guardian, by which he shall engage to serve five years, unless sooner discharged; and all such cadets shall be entitled to and receive the pay and emoluments now allowed by law to cadets in the Corps of Engineers.

That when any cadet shall receive a regular degree from the Academic Staff, after going through all the classes, he shall be considered as among the candidates for a commission in any Corps, according to the duties he may be judged competent to perform; and in case there shall not, at the time, be a vacancy in such Corps, he may be attached to it at the discretion of the President of the United States, by brevet of the lowest grade, as a supernumerary officer, with the usual pay and emoluments of such grade, until a vacancy shall happen....[43]

In 1816, rules were promulgated which required that no cadet should be promoted until after completing his course of studies, and receiving his diploma but apparently these rules were not implemented until 1818. But another series of regulations were put into effect which appointed a Board of Visitors consisting of "five competent gentlemen, who should attend at each general examination, and report thereon to the War Department through the Inspector. Of this Board the Superintendent was constituted the President." It was also provided that "annual and semi-annual examinations should be held in June and January, and that new Cadets should present themselves in the month of September, and be examined in spelling, reading, writing, and arithmetic."[44]

---

[43] Boynton, 210-211.
[44] Ibid., 214-215.

Attachment 2
Examination of Cadets by the Board of Visitors June 1826
By George Ticknor[45]

We went forthwith to the examination, which was extremely thorough. Thirteen young men were under the screw four hours, on a single branch, and never less than four on the floor, either drawing on the blackboard or answering questions every moment, so that each one had above an hour's work to go through; and, as I said, in a single branch. It was the lowest section of the upper class, but no mistake was made, except by one Cadet. Of course it was as nearly perfect as anything of the kind ever was. The manner, too, was quite remarkable. The young men do not rise when they answer; they are all addressed as Mr. So-and-so; and when the drum beat outside for one o'clock, Colonel Thayer adjourned the examination while a Cadet was speaking, so exactly is everything done here. We dined at Cozzens's, and the examination was continued in the afternoon till seven o'clock....

I delight exceedingly in the exactness with which everything is done here. The morning gun is fired exactly at sunrise...the first thing I hear is the full band, when, precisely at six, the maneuvering being over, the corps of Cadets begins its marching. I get up immediately....Breakfast precisely at seven; then we have all the newspapers, and, a little before eight o'clock, Thayer puts on his full-dress coat and sword, and when the bugle sounds we are always at Mr. Cozzens's, where Thayer takes off his hat and inquires if the President of the Board is ready to attend at the examination-room; if he is, the Commandant conducts him to it with great ceremony, followed by the Board. If he is not ready, Thayer goes without him; he waits for no man.

In the examination-room Thayer presides at one table, surrounded by the Academic Staff; General [Samuel] Houston at the other, surrounded by the Visitors. In front of the last table two enormous blackboards, eight feet by five, are placed on easels; and at each of these boards stand two Cadets, one answering questions or demonstrating, and the other three preparing the problems that are given to them. In this way, if an examination of sixteen young men lasts four hours on one subject, each of them will have had one hour's public examination on it; and the fact is, that each of the forty Cadets in the upper class will to-night will have had about five hours' personal examination. While the examination goes on, one person sits between the tables and asks questions, but other members of the Staff and of the Board join in the examination frequently, as their interest moves them. The young men have that composure which comes from thoroughness, and unite, to a remarkable degree, ease with respectful manners towards their teachers....

Thayer is a wonderful man. In the course of the fortnight I have been here, he has every morning been in his office doing business from six to seven o'clock; from seven to eight he breakfasts, generally with company; then goes to the examination-room, and for five complete hours never so much as rises from his chair. From one to three he has his dinner-party; from three to seven again unmoved in his chair, though he is neither stiff nor pretending about it. At seven he goes on parade; from half-past seven to eight does business with the Cadets, and from eight to nine, or even till eleven, he is liable to have meetings with the Academic Staff. Yet with all this labor, and the whole responsibility of the institution, the examination, and the accommodation of the Visitors, on his hands, he is always fresh, prompt, ready, and pleasant....I do not believe there are three persons in the country who could fill his place; and Totten said very well the other day, when somebody told him,—what is no doubt true, — that if Thayer were to resign, he would be the only man who could take his place,— "No: no man would be indiscreet enough to take the place after Thayer; it would be as bad as being President of the Royal Society, after Newton." ....

The examination, the exhibition of the institution, has gratified me beyond my expectations, and this feeling I believe I share with the rest of the Visitors. There is a thoroughness, promptness, and efficiency in the knowledge of the Cadets which I have never seen before, and which I did not expect to find here.

---

[45] George Ticknor, *Life, Letters, and Journals of George Ticknor*, vol. 1, ed. by George S. Hillard (Boston, MA: Houghton Mifflin Company, 1909), 372-376. George Ticknor was a Dartmouth classmate of Thayer and was asked by him to serve as a member of the Board of Visitors. He was the secretary for the 1826 Board. Ticknor was a scholar, author, and academic, and a professor at Harvard University in French and Spanish literatures and professor of belles-lettres. Even though this account is four years after Mansfield's graduation, the process was similar. Cozzens ran the mess hall for several years starting in 1821.

Attachment 3
Cadet Uniforms

Official sources were less personal and more detailed about the cadet uniform as shown in an order from the Office of the Adjutant and Inspector General describing the 1814 uniform:

A coatee of gray satinette, single-breasted, three rows of eight yellow gilt bullet buttons in front, and button holes of black silk cord in the herringbone form, with a festoon turned at the back end, a standing collar to rise as high as the tip of the ear; the cuffs 4 inches wide, the bottom of the breast and the hip buttons to range. On the collar one blind hole of cord, formed like that of the breast, 4 inches long, with a button on each side. Cord holes in the like form to proceed from three buttons placed lengthwise on the skirts, with three buttons down the pleats. The cuffs to be indented, with three buttons and cord holes lengthwise, on each sleeve, corresponding with the indentation of the cuff, in the center of which is inserted the lower button.

Vest.-—Gray cloth for winter, single breasted, yellow gilt bullet buttons, and trimmed with black silk lace. For summer, white vest, single breasted, with buttons but without trimmings.

Pantaloons.-—-Gray cloth for winter, trimmed down the side with black silk lace, and the Austrian knot in front; no buttons on the side or at the bottom, but made with under-straps. Russia sheeting or white jean for summer, without trimmings, the form the same as for winter.

The Jefferson shoe, rising above the ankle joint under the pantaloons.

Black silk stock. Common round hat. Cockade, black silk, with yellow eagle, to be worn at all times.

Sword—cut and thrust, yellow mounted, with a black gripe, in a frog belt of black morocco, and worn over the coat.

No dress resembling the military, without conforming to the regulation, will be worn on any occasion, excepting that when attached to corps Cadets will wear the uniform of the company officers, without epaulets.[46]

A report from the West Point Board of Visitors in 1820 is instructive filling in details about cadet uniforms especially the costs to the nascent centurions:

The clothing for the Cadets is for the most part uniform, and with conformity with regulation. The different articles are furnished by a storekeeper whose stock and the mode of manufacture are under the inspection of the officers of the Academy. The material is chosen and purchased by the quartermaster, and the profit allowed to the storekeeper is very reasonable. The coat, which is of gray cloth with black trimmings, is handsome and convenient. The present price is $16. It lasts on the average of eight months. The vest is of kerseymere of the same color. It costs $3.50, but it does not appear a favorite article of clothing, as not more than 100 are sold annually. Vests of white kerseymere are worn in common, and as they are much more becoming no good reason exists why they should not become the uniform. The pantaloons are also of gray kerseymere, and cost the Cadet $9.50. They are serviceable and becoming. These articles were formerly made of a very inferior material and cost much more than they do at present; besides a further reduction in the price may be fairly anticipated when a new contract for cloth is made.

For summer clothing they wear with the coat, vests of white Marseilles, which cost $2.50, and linen pantaloons, which cost $2.75. It may here be remarked that the pantaloons, both for summer and winter wear, have, in compliance with the present fashion, been shortened so as to leave an unsightly gap between them and the regulation shoe. For the encampment which has just commenced the corps have been directed to furnish themselves with a fatigue dress of low cost and excellent quality, which for the purpose will save much for the Cadets in the wear of their uniforms and in bills for washing. The uniform cap is showy and elegant, but heavy, and affords no shelter either from the sun or rain; with its trimmings it costs no less than $8, and is perhaps the most expensive part of their equipment. There is no halfdress cap, and the Cadets in consequence wear, except when on duty, common hats, which are very expensive to them. There are two sorts of shoes permitted by regulation and furnished them, one at the price of $3; the other of $4. They appear to be of good quality and very serviceable, but much too dear. There is no regulation for uniformity in any other species of clothing, nor any tariff of prices. These are, however, kept down in some measure by competition. The supply of all articles, except those of prime necessity, is under the immediate direction of the Superintendent.[47]

---

[46] *The Centennial*, vol. 1, 511.
[47] Ibid, 513.

Attachment 4
Professor Jared Mansfield[48]

Jared Mansfield was born in New Haven, Connecticut, 23 May 1759, the son of a sea captain, Stephen Mansfield. He was expelled in his senior year at Yale, but later reinstated and graduated in 1787. He was Rector of the Hopkins Grammar School, New Haven, from 1786-1795, and connected with an advanced school for both sexes in New Haven until 1802. Commissioned as a Captain of Engineers 3 May 1802, he served as Acting Professor of Mathematics at West Point from 1802-1803. In 1803, he was appointed Surveyor-General of the U.S. to survey Ohio and the Northwest Territory. On 7 Oct. 1812, he was appointed Professor of Natural and Experimental Philosophy at West Point, but because of the 1812 War was detailed to superintend fortifications at New London and Stonington, Connecticut. He resumed teaching at West Point and continued there until his resignation 31 August 1828. In 1801, he published *Essays, Mathematical and Physical.* The essays deal with problems in algebra, geometry, fluxions (calculus), and with nautical astronomy, giving practicable methods of finding time, latitude, and longitude from observations at sea. A chapter on gunnery dealt with fundamental problems of ballistics, and in it the importance of air resistance is pointed out, not only as a retarding force, but also its effect on the projectile. That effect, he showed, is a deviation of the projectile from its due course, what is known today as the gyroscopic phenomenon. Prior to his book, projectiles were treated without consideration of the effect of the medium through which they passed. He published a number of other papers on mathematical subjects. He died in New Haven, 3 February 1830, at age 71. Mansfield, Ohio, was named after him.

Latrobe described the distinguished professor: "My recollection of Colonel Mansfield, the Professor of Natural and Experimental Philosophy, is most distinct. I was a frequent visitor at his house, where I had the honor to be kindly noticed by his wife, one of the most intelligent and best-informed women that I ever knew. Colonel Mansfield, although a most competent instructor, was very near-sighted, and I am not prepared to say that this defect was not sometimes taken advantage of. I find, however, from a letter home, that it was this third year's course that gave me the most trouble, and required the hardest work to attain the head of the class for the year 1822, the graduating year of the class with which I entered the Academy."[49]

Professor Jared Mansfield. Painting by Thomas Sully, courtesy USMA.

---

[48] Edward D. Mansfield, 1-4, 64-66; West Point Thayer Papers, Bibliography, courtesy USMA. Natural and Experimental Philosophy included mechanics, physics, electricity, optics and astronomy, Pappas, 155-156.
[49] Latrobe, 3.

Attachment 5
Superintendent Sylvanus Thayer[50]

Thayer was born in Braintree, Massachusetts, the son of a farmer Nathaniel Thayer, and his wife Dorcas, 9 June 1785. In 1793, at the age of 8, Thayer was sent to live with his uncle Azariah Faxon and attend school in Washington, New Hampshire. In 1803 Thayer matriculated at Dartmouth College, graduating in 1807 as valedictorian of his class and received an appointment to West Point by President Thomas Jefferson. Thayer entered West Point 20 March 1807 and graduated after a single year on 23 February 1808, receiving his appointment to second lieutenant in the Corps of Engineers on that date. He performed various engineering duties and was promoted to first lieutenant 1 July 1812.

During the War of 1812, Thayer directed the fortification and defense of Norfolk, Virginia, and was promoted to major. In 1815, Thayer was provided $5,000 to travel to Europe, where he studied for two years at the French École Polytechnique. While traveling in Europe he amassed a collection of science and especially mathematics texts that began the library at West Point. In 1817, President James Monroe ordered Thayer to West Point to become superintendent of the Military Academy. Under his stewardship, the Academy became the nation's first college of engineering.

Thayer's time at West Point ended with his resignation in 1833, after a disagreement with President Andrew Jackson. He was elected an Associate Fellow of the American Academy of Arts and Sciences in 1834. Thayer returned to duty with the Army Corps of Engineers. Thayer spent the majority of the next 30 years as the chief engineer for the Boston area overseeing both Fort Warren and Fort Independence in Boston Harbor. Thayer retired from the U.S. Army on 1 June 1863 with the rank of colonel in the Corps of Engineers. On 21 April 1864, President Lincoln nominated Thayer for brevet brigadier general in the Regular Army from 31 May 1863. The U.S. Senate confirmed the award on 27 April 1864. He died 17 September 1872 and is buried in the West Point National Cemetery.

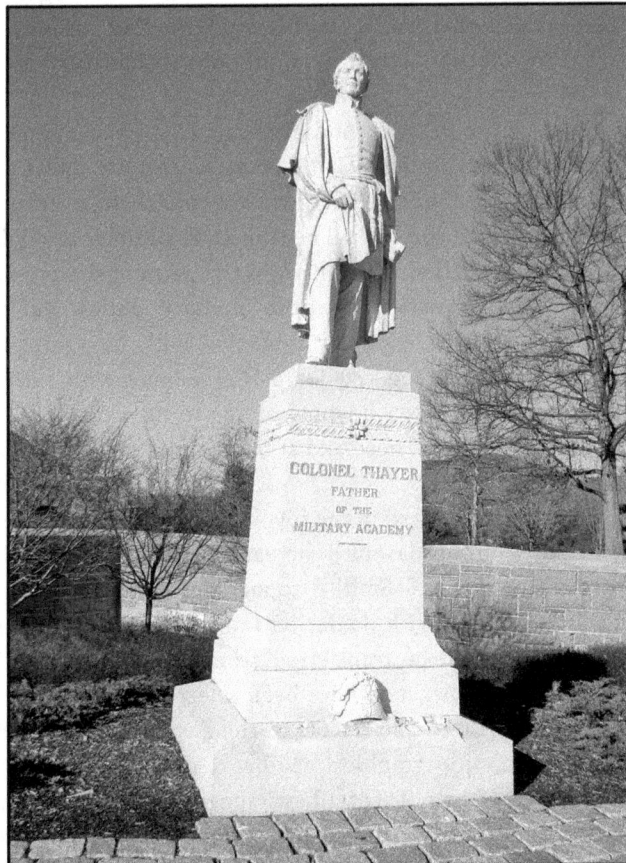

Colonel Sylvanus Thayer statue at West Point. Courtesy Wikipedia.

---

[50] Eicher, *High Commands*, 526; Ambrose, *Duty, Honor, Country*, 63-67.

Attachment 6
History of the Corps of Engineers to the Civil War[51]

The first formal establishment of a Corps of Engineers by resolution of Congress dates from March 11, 1779. Among other provisions were the following: "That the engineers in the service of the United States shall be formed in a corps and styled the Corps of Engineers, and shall take rank and enjoy the same rights, honors and privileges with the other troops in the Continental establishment. That a Commandant of the Corps of Engineers shall be appointed by Congress, to whom their orders or those of the Commander-in-Chief shall be addressed, and such Commandant shall render to the Commander-in-Chief, and to the Board of War, an account of every matter relative to his department." On the 11th of May following, Brigadier-General du Portail was appointed Commandant of the Corps of Engineers.

The services of this revolutionary corps, including its companies of sappers and miners to which reference will soon be made, were important and honorable; numbers of its officers were brevetted by Congress, and its chief, on November 16, 1781, was promoted to the grade of major-general, "in consideration of his meritorious services, and particularly of his distinguished conduct in the siege of York, in the State of Virginia." The names of one brigadier-general, six colonels, eight lieutenant-colonels, three majors and ten captains are preserved on the records, and unquestionably the list is incomplete. In November, 1783, the corps was disbanded.

The next need for the services of military engineers occurred at the period of threatened European complications during the administration of Pres. George Washington. On March 20, 1794, Congress authorized the President to fortify certain harbors on the coast, and there being no engineers in service he appointed temporarily several foreign-born gentlemen, a number of whom had served in the war, to direct the work. On May 9, 1794, Congress passed an act raising for a term of three years (subsequently extended) a corps of artillerists and engineers, to be incorporated with the Corps of Artillery then in service. The new organization was stationed at West Point, and preliminary steps were then taken for forming a military school there. By the Act of April 27, 1798, a second regiment of artillerists and engineers was authorized, on the same footing as the earlier corps. On July 16, 1798, four "teachers of the arts and sciences" were authorized for the instruction of this organization; which was only discontinued by the Act of March 16, 1802, fixing the new military establishment.

This latter act authorized the President to organize and establish a Corps of Engineers, not to exceed 1 colonel, 1 lieutenant-colonel, 2 majors, 4 captains, 4 first lieutenants, 4 second lieutenants, and 4 cadets. It was provided that the said corps "shall be stationed at West Point, in the State of New York, and shall constitute a Military Academy; and the engineers, assistant engineers, and cadets of said corps, shall be subject at all times to do duty in such places and on such service as the President of the United States shall direct." This was the germ of the present Corps of Engineers. Most of the officers were soon dispersed along the coast on various military duties, but the superintendence and the responsibility for the successful operation of the Academy remained with the Corps until July 13, 1866, when the institution passed to the army at large, having attained a standard of excellence which needs no eulogy here.

In the earlier period of its organization the duties now pertaining to the Corps of Engineers were divided between two different branches, sometimes under a common head and at other times separately commanded. Space will be saved by considering this subdivision here.

Although a somewhat similar organization existed in the revolutionary war, no officers with the special functions of topographical engineers were provided for our armies until the early part of the war of 1812, when Congress by Act of March 3, 1813, authorized as part of the General Staff, 8 topographical engineers with the brevet rank, pay and emoluments of majors of cavalry, and 8 assistants with the brevet rank, pay and emoluments of captains of infantry. The law authorized these officers to be appointed, or transferred from the line without prejudice to their rank and promotion therein, but the full number seems never to have been selected; and at the conclusion of peace all but two majors were mustered out of service under the requirements of the Act of March 3, 1815. By Act of April 24, 1816, however, the Corps was reestablished, three topographical engineers and two assistants (still attached to the General Staff) being provided for each division of the army. This staff assignment continued until, by general order dated July 2, 1818, the officers were "arranged to the Engineer's Department, and...made subject to the orders of the chief and commanding engineers." In the August following a separate topographical bureau was established in the War

---

[51] Adapted from Henry L. Abbot, "The Corps of Engineers," in *The Army of the United States, Historical Sketches of Staff and Line*, ed. by Theophilus F. Rodenbough and William L. Haskin (New York, NY: Maynard, Merrill, & Co., 1896), 111-125 passim. Only internal quotation marks are used.

Department, under the immediate direction of the Secretary of War and the chief engineer. The work of this branch of the Engineer Department soon increased, calling for an average detail of about twenty-five officers of the line of the army and the employment, under the Act of April 30, 1824, of a still larger number of civil engineers. On June 21, 1831, the topographical bureau was constituted by the Secretary of War a distinct bureau of the War Department; and by Act of July 5, 1838, an independent Corps of Topographical Engineers was created by Congress.

By the Regulations of 1841, issued shortly after this separation, the engineering duties of the War Department were divided between the Corps of Engineers and the Corps of Topographical Engineers upon the following basis:

> The duties of the Engineer Corps comprise reconnoitring and surveying for military purposes, the selection of sites, and formation of plans, projects, and estimates for military defenses of every kind; the construction and repair of fortifications and defensible works of every description, whether temporary or permanent, the planning, laying out, and superintending all military works, defensive or offensive, of troops in the field, camp, or cantonment; the planning and construction of military bridges; the planning, laying out, and superintending military trenches, parallels, saps, mines, and other works of military attack and siege; the planning and executing such works of river or harbor improvement, including sea-walls, breakwaters, and light-houses, as may be assigned to it by law, or by the President of the United States; the general direction and management of disbursements for the above works, including purchases of sites and materials, hiring workmen, and making contracts for supplies of materials or workmanship; the collection, arrangement, and preservation of all reports, memoirs, estimates, plans, drawings, and models, relating to the several duties above enumerated; and the superintendence and inspection of the Military Academy.
>
> The duties of the [Topographical Engineer] Corps shall consist, in surveys for the defense of the frontier, inland and Atlantic, and of positions for fortifications; in reconnaissances of the country through which an army has to pass, or in which it has to operate; in the examination of all routes of communication by land or by water, both for supplies and military movements; in the construction of military roads and permanent bridges connected with them, and, in the absence of an officer or officers of the Corps of Engineers, of military bridges, and of field-works, for the defense of encampments, fords, ferries, and bridges. For which purposes, officers of the Corps of Topographical Engineers shall always accompany armies in the field.

In the Regulations of 1857 and in subsequent editions, the duties of the two corps were defined jointly under a common heading, being practically a summation of those comprised in the Regulations of 1841 for both. In time of peace this modification of the Regulations introduced no change and no confusion, the Corps of Engineers retaining charge of the works for permanent defenses and of certain other public constructions, and the Corps of Topographical Engineers of the survey of the lakes, the exploration of the Western wilderness, and the demarcation of State and International boundaries,—while officers of both corps served upon works of river and harbor improvement, and upon the Coast Survey, the Light-house establishment and other special duties. At the outbreak of the Civil War however, it was soon discovered that engineer duties with armies in the field admitted of no advantageous division between different organizations. The officers were few in number, and the work was so onerous that practical consolidation on the staffs of commanding generals very soon resulted. Legal union, however, was desired by the officers themselves; and a petition to this effect, prepared by a joint committee representing both corps, was urgently favored by General McClellan, General Halleck and General Banks, and was approved by Mr. Stanton, the Secretary of War. A bill uniting the two corps was passed by the House of Representatives in 1862 and was favorably reported in the Senate, but received no action. Finally by Act of March 3, 1863, it was provided: "That the Corps of Topographical Engineers, as a distinct branch of the army, is hereby abolished, and from and after the passage of the Act, is merged into the Corps of Engineers which shall have the following organization: "That the general officer provided by the first section of this act shall be selected from the Corps of Engineers as therein established; and that officers of all lower grades shall take rank according to their respective dates of commission in the existing corps of engineers or corps of topographical engineers."

The Corps of Engineers, as thus established, and as at present constituted, becomes therefore the heir to the honorable record of both the original corps. The same Act of March 3, 1863, also inaugurated the present system of examinations for promotion in the army by providing that no engineer officer below the grade of field officer shall thereafter be promoted before having passed a satisfactory examination before a board of three engineers senior to him in rank; a like provision was also inserted for the Ordnance Department.

The Engineer Department.—Another organization should not be overlooked in tracing the history of the development of the service. The "Engineer Department" was established by order of the President shortly after the war of 1812, as a separate command with geographical limits coextensive with those of the United States and embracing the Corps of Engineers, and such officers of topographical engineers and other arms of service as might be attached thereto, and the Military Academy. Thus the chief engineer in early days exercised the functions of a department commander, being allowed an aide-de-camp, convening courts-martial, assigning officers to stations, granting leave of absence, and placing officers on "waiting orders." The headquarters which had been first established in New York, were transferred to Washington by order of the President on April 3, 1818. While this organization has nominally ceased to exist, its most essential functions are still vested in the chief of engineers as commandant of the Corps of Engineers.

The Board of Engineers.—On November 16, 1816, a "Board of Engineers for Fortifications" was constituted by the War Department to perform the following duties:

> It shall be the duties of the officers of this board to examine, in conjunction, all those positions where permanent works are or maybe proposed to be erected. They shall select the proper sites for, and form the plans of all new works. Where fortifications have been commenced or are finished, they shall report how far the sites for such fortifications have been judiciously selected, or whether or not the works are adequate to the defense of the prospective positions, and they shall propose such alterations or additions to them as may be deemed necessary.
>
> The report and plans adopted by the board, shall be submitted with…accurate estimates to the chief of the corps.
>
> The original reports and plans agreed upon by the board, as well as those reported by any member of it, shall be submitted by the Chief of the Corps of Engineers. with such remarks as he may deem proper, to the Secretary of War, for final adoption, and they shall be deposited in the secret bureau of the Department of War.

Under the Act of April 30, 1824, inaugurating works of internal improvement, a similar "Board of Engineers for Internal Improvement" was organized and continued until about the date of the segregation of the topographical engineers into a distinct bureau of the War Department; after which these functions seem to have devolved on special boards of greater or less permanency until, by authority of the Secretary of War, in an order issued on September 2, 1879, the functions of the "Board of Engineers for Fortifications," which had continued unchanged since 1816, were extended to include such works of river and harbor improvement, and other matters as may be referred to it by the chief of engineers. This organization, now officially designated "The Board of Engineers," continues to the present date.

Engineer Troops.—In view of the persistent efforts which have been made to class the engineer arm of service with the staff of the army, it should be noted that the Continental Congress established three companies of sappers and miners before it definitely constituted the Corps of Engineers. The dates of the resolutions effecting these objects are May 27, 1778, and March 11, 1779, respectively. Each of these three companies consisted of 1 captain, 3 lieutenants, 4 sergeants, 4 corporals and 60 privates. It appears that subsequently another company was added; for by the resolution of February 7, 1780, four captains were commissioned by name. The duties assigned were the following: "These companies to be instructed in the fabrication of field works, as far as relates to the manual and mechanical part. Their business shall be to instruct the fatigue parties to do their duty with celerity and exactness, to repair injuries done to the works by the enemy's fire, and to prosecute works in the face of it. The commissioned officers to be skilled in the necessary branches of mathematics; the non-commissioned officers to write a good hand."

These companies of sappers and miners were assigned to the command of Brigadier-General du Portail, [Louis Lebègue Duportail] the first commandant of the Corps of Engineers, and served throughout the war, being disbanded with that corps in November, 1783. It is interesting to note that David Bushnell, "the father of submarine mining" was appointed to this body of troops on the recommendation of Governor Trumbull of Connecticut; he signed one of the last returns (now on file in the archives of the Department of State) at West Point on June 4, 1783, as "Captain Commanding."

The two regiments of Artillerists and Engineers, formed before the reorganization of the army in 1802, each contained 992 enlisted men; of the privates 672 were designated sappers and miners and 160 artificers; the remaining 160 were non-commissioned officers and musicians.

After the reorganization of 1802 a few enlisted engineer soldiers [one artificer and eighteen privates] were authorized to be enlisted by Section 3, Act of February 28, 1803. By the Act of April 29, 1812, it was enacted that there be attached to the Corps of Engineers "either from the troops now in service or by new enlistments, as the President of the United States may direct, 4 sergeants, 4 corporals, 1 teacher of music, 4 musicians, 19 artificers, and 62 men, which non-commissioned officers, musicians, artificers, and men, together with the artificers and men already belonging to the Corps of Engineers, shall be formed into a company to be styled a company of bombardiers, sappers and miners, and be officered from the Corps of Engineers, according as the commanding officer of that corps may, with the approbation of the President of the United States, direct."

....

At the outbreak of the Mexican war, Congress, by the Act of May 16, 1846, created a company of engineer soldiers which were "entitled to the same provisions, allowances and benefits in every respect as are allowed to the other troops constituting the present peace establishment." It was to "compose a part of the Corps of Engineers, and be officered by officers of that corps as at present organized." Its functions included "all the duties of sappers, miners and pontoniers"; and it was also to "aid in giving practical instructions in these branches at the Military Academy." The enlisted organization comprised 10 sergeants, 10 corporals, 2 musicians, and 78 privates.

This company joined the column of General Taylor on October 11, 1846, but was soon transferred to that of General Scott, where it took a gallant and distinguished part in all the battles from Vera Cruz to the City of Mexico.

In 1853 a detachment of 25 men assisted on the survey of the Northern Pacific railroad; in 1858 the company took part in the Utah expedition; in 1858, 1859 and 1860 a detachment of 30 men served with the troops in Oregon and Washington territory, taking part in the Wallen expedition to Salt Lake, the joint occupation of San Juan Island, and performing other important services.

In the feverish excitement preceding the Civil War the company was ordered to Washington to guard public property, and at the inauguration of President Lincoln it was selected to form his immediate body guard when proceeding to the Capitol. It formed part of the second relief expedition to Fort Pickens, sailing from New York on April 8, and after spending the summer at that fort, putting the works in a state of defense, returned to Washington in October 1861.

By the Acts of August 3 and August 6, 1861, three additional companies of engineer soldiers and 1 company of topographical engineer soldiers were added to the military establishment. They were to have "the same pay and rations, clothing, and other allowances, and to be entitled to the same benefits in every respect as the company created by the Act for the organization of a company of sappers and miners and pontoniers, approved May 15, 1846." The old company and each of the new companies was to be composed of 10 sergeants, 10 corporals, 2 musicians, 64 privates of the first class, and 64 privates of the second class,—in all 150 men. During the war no legal battalion organization existed, although the companies were so organized in orders; but by the Act of July 28, 1866, this defect was remedied by the addition of a sergeant-major and a quartermaster-sergeant, and the recognition of the detail of officers of engineers to act as adjutant and quartermaster, the battalion thus comprising a total of 752 enlisted men, —its present legally authorized strength.

War Record of the Corps of Engineers.—Beside the military duties assigned to engineer troops, there are important professional functions which devolve upon engineer officers serving on the staff of generals commanding armies in the field; and in our service the command of volunteer troops, as well, has often devolved on officers of the Corps. In every war with a civilized power since the earliest history of our country these duties have been performed by them in a manner to merit and receive distinguished commendation; and in all these wars their blood has been shed on the field of honor. That this is no exaggeration is shown by the following list of officers who have been killed or mortally wounded in battle since the organization of the present Corps in 1802. All were graduates of the Military Academy:

Capt. and Bvt. Lieut. Col. E. D. Wood, Sept. 17, 1814, Sortie from Fort Erie, U. C.
Capt. W. G. Williams, Sept. 21, 1846, Monterey, Mexico.
1st. Lieut. and Bvt. Captain W. H. Warner, Sept. 26, 1849, by Indians near Pitt River, Cal.
Captain J. W. Gunnison, Oct. 26, 1853, by Indians near Sevier Lake, Utah.
Maj. Gen. I. I. Stevens, U. S. V., Sept. 1, 1862, Chantilly, Va.
Brig. Gen. J. K. F. Mansfield, U. S. A., Sept. 18, 1862, Antietam, Md.
1st. Lieut. and Bvt. Col. J. L. K. Smith, Oct. 12, 1862, Corinth, Miss.
1st. Lieut. and Bvt. Major O. G. Wagner, April 21, 1863, Siege of Yorktown, Va.
Major and Bvt. Major Gen. A. W. Whipple, May 7, 1863, Chancellorsville, Va.
Captain and Bvt. Col. C. E. Cross, June 5, 1863, Franklin's Crossing of Rappahannock River, Va.
1st Lieut. and Bvt. Col. P. H. O'Rourke, July 2, 1863, Gettysburg, Pa.
Captain and Bvt. Col. H. S. Putnam, July 18, 1863, Assault of Fort Wagner, S. C.
Captain and Bvt. Col. A. H. Dutton, June 5, 1864, Bermuda Hundred, Va.
Major and Bvt. Brig. Gen. J. St. C. Morton, June 17, 1864, Petersburg, Va.
Brig. Gen. U. S. A., J. B. McPherson, July 22, 1864, Atlanta, Ga.

1st Lieut. and Bvt. Maj. J. R. Meigs, Oct. 3, 1864, Harrisonburg, Va.

1st Lieut. Jacob E. Blake, Topographical Engineers, deserves to be mentioned in this list, although his death resulted from the accidental discharge of his own pistol on the field of Palo Alto after an act of the most conspicuous gallantry performed in the sight of both armies.

During the war with Mexico, 19 officers of the Corps of Engineers and 24 officers of the Corps of Topographical Engineers served actively in the field. One of them, Captain Williams, was killed, and sixteen wounds were divided among the others. Among those of this little band who subsequently, in the Civil War, reached high rank and distinction may be mentioned in order of seniority in their respective corps: Generals Mansfield, Robert E. Lee, Barnard, Beauregard, Isaac I. Stevens, Halleck, Tower, G. W. Smith, McClellan, Foster, Joseph E. Johnston, Emory, Fremont, Meade, Pope, Franklin, and T.J. Wood.

During the Civil War the officers of both Corps with few exceptions served with the armies in the field. Some were attached to the battalion, others were on the staffs of army and division commanders, and many held volunteer commissions in command of troops. This latter list would have been much larger at the beginning of the war had not the ground been taken at the War Department that their services in their own arm were too important to be spared in volunteer grades lower than that of brigadier general.

It is a matter of record that 33 officers, who either held or had held commissions in the Corps of Engineers, were appointed during this war general officers in command of troops. Of these, 3 became major-generals, and 3 brigadier-generals in the Regular Army; 15 were major-generals, and 12 were brigadier generals of volunteers; 8 of the 33 commanded armies; and 10, army corps. At least 8 general officers in the Confederate armies had been officers of our Corps of Engineers, and among them were General Robert E. Lee and General Joseph E. Johnston.

Attachment 7
Cadet March to Boston Summer 1821 by John H. B. Latrobe[52]

Mansfield was one of the members of this march; he was the Second Sergeant of the Fourth Company. This lengthy attachment is of interest as it describes one of the routine annual trials with which cadets had to comply and in this instance, of which Mansfield was a part. It also shows early 19th century New England and how it viewed the cadets.

According to previous arrangements made with the proprietors of the steamboats *Richmond* and *Fire-Fly*, they arrived at West Point on the 20th of July; the former at four, and the latter at two o'clock P.M. The left wing, together with the tents, baggage, etc., under command of Lieutenant Griswold, went on board the *Fire-Fly* immediately on her arrival, and proceeded to Albany, while the Commandant, with the right wing, remained to embark on board the *Richmond*, which reached the Point already crowded with passengers. The day was clear, and our having the band on board rendered the passage up the river delightful.

Saturday, 21st.—Reveille was beat at the usual hour, and we found we had overtaken the *Fire-Fly*, within a few miles of Albany, where we arrived in company at seven o'clock. The removal of the baggage and placing it in the wagons occupied considerable time, so that it was not until near nine that we disembarked, and were received by the independent uniform volunteer companies, under command of Major Williams, and escorted by them to our encampment; a spot noted from its having been the scene of the murder of Major Birdsall a few years since.

After having encamped, we were escorted to the Capitol, to partake of a collation prepared for us, and handsomely arranged in the great hall of the building; immediately opposite to the entrance was painted in large letters "The U.S. Corps of Cadets,"— this mark of attention was felt by those who noticed it and highly appreciated, as a testimony of regard from our fellow-citizens; we felt that we were soldiers, and the soldiers of a republic; and though many may laugh at this kind of enthusiasm, yet there are times, when, freed from the more disagreeable duties of our Profession and attentions are shown us as a body, that everyone in the heat of the moment will feel proud of himself and his fellows.

At three o'clock we returned to our encampment and relieved Captain Dunn's company, which had volunteered to do guard duty for us in our absence.

Sunday, 22d.—Having received invitations to attend divine worship at St. Peter's and the Dutch Reformed Church, we went in the morning to the former, and to the latter in the afternoon.

Monday, 23d.—In the morning, which was cloudy and disagreeable, we drilled at our encampment, and occupied the rest of the day in visiting the city and making preparations for our departure early on Tuesday morning. For the gratification of the inhabitants, the band performed in the evening at the capitol; when notwithstanding a drizzling rain, which had continued a great part of the day, an immense crowd had collected. Here the committee appointed by the Commandant, waited on that on the part of the citizens of Albany, to return thanks in behalf of their brother cadets, for the kindness and hospitality with which we had been received by the citizens during our short halt with them....

Tuesday, 24th.—At daylight the tents were struck, and we commenced our march through the city to the ferry, in a cold and disagreeable rain, which accompanied us with little intermission during the day, but which enabled the battalion to proceed farther than would otherwise have been to their power. We crossed the river to Greenbush, a small village on the opposite bank, and marched rapidly to the place intended to breakfast, four miles distant from the ferry. After remaining here two hours, we continued towards Lebanon, through a hilly country highly cultivated, and bearing every mark of the wealth of its inhabitants. Schodack, Union Village and Brainard's Bridge were the places we passed through this morning; and at half-past one we halted to dine, two miles beyond the last mentioned village, making the distance we had reached from the place of our encampment twenty-four miles. It was near four when we resumed our march, and when within two miles of Lebanon, the rain which had continued all day, poured down in torrents, nor did it cease until after we had pitched our tents.

Wednesday, 25th.—We remained at Lebanon and bathed in the water, for which the place is celebrated.

Lebanon, so deservedly celebrated for the beauty of its scenery, is situated near the head of a deep valley, in the highest possible state of cultivation. Even on the summits of the mountains around it, immense fields of grain are seen intermingled with the dark green foliage of the forest, and forming a scene more resembling an immense garden than a tract of country, including several counties, and terminated by the boundary line between New York and Massachusetts.

Thursday, 26th.—Having breakfasted at Lebanon, we started at nine o'clock for Lenox, a distance of twelve miles, and soon reached the Shaker's village (two and one-half miles), the neatness and regularity of which, together with the size and bright yellow color of the buildings, form one of the most pleasing objects seen from the valley. Conspicuously placed on the side of a mountain, and everything around them bearing marks of the greatest care and cultivation, it would seem that the beauty of the spot, and the certainty of support, would, exclusive of religious motives, be sufficient to induce many to enter a society and

---

[52] John H.B. Latrobe, "The March of the U.S. Corps of Cadets to Boston, Between the 20th of July and 26th September, 1821," *The Association of the Graduates of the Unites Dates Military Academy, Twentieth Annual Reunion, June 12th, 1885*, Annual Report by the United States Military Academy Association of Graduates (East Saginaw, MI: Evening News, Printers and Binders, 1885), 1-29.

embrace a religion, where, while living, they had no care for the morrow, and when dead were certain of a decent grave. Be this however as it may, during the hour's halt we made in the village, we had every kindness shown us, refreshments were largely distributed among the corps, and we left them, highly gratified with the entertainment received from a body, who, (on account of their religious principles) we had as little to expect as from any.

Our road, on leaving the village, crossed Mount Hancock, one of the Hoosack range, on which is the boundary line between New York and Massachusetts; and continued through a mountainous country, rivaling in some places the gloomy magnificence of Alpine scenery, and the contrast formed, when, on turning an angle in the road, Lenox, with its three steeples and houses of a brilliant white, appeared almost beneath our feet, was as striking as it was beautiful. From this spot we had a view as far as the eye could reach in the direction we were to proceed, and the endless succession of hills, among which the Becket Mountains were proudly conspicuous, gave us no favorable anticipation of the pleasure that would arise from the marching part of our expedition.

We entered Lenox at three o'clock, encamped—remained there that night.

Friday, 27th.—We marched on, after having a dress parade at nine in the morning. Two miles from the town we crossed the Housatonic, here a narrow, rapid stream, turning several mills and a factory, which formed quite a village on the road side. From this spot the country begins to be less thickly settled; the land is evidently worse, and the inhabitants look poorer than those a few miles back—this appearance increases as we approach, and continues until we pass the mountains.

At four o'clock we halted to dine, in a large field by the road, fifteen miles from Lenox, at the foot of the Becket Mountains, and remained there until near sundown, when we resumed the line of march for Chester Factory. It was the evening of a beautiful day; the heat, which was oppressive a few hours since, had moderated; the rest we had enjoyed, together with our dinner had refreshed us, and we started nearly all in good spirits.

We immediately entered the mountain defiles, where nothing was to be seen but precipices towering above you, scathed and blackened in many places to their very tops by fire, and nothing heard but the roar of the torrent, which is one of the sources of the Agawam, mingled with the hum of noises, as the battalion appeared and disappeared on the road which wound through this pass of the mountains. There was something in this evening's march which none of us will ever forget; all the enthusiastic feelings of youth were excited; what we had read in the fictions of romance or the facts of history, seemed here to be realized or experienced; and as the column almost ran down the gloomy defile, we wanted but the roar of artillery and the noise of action, to transport us in imagination to the confines of Italy, and make our peaceful march, the passage of the Alps. After marching five miles in this manner, we reached Chester Factory, a miserable spot among the hills, where no field could be found fit for us to encamp on, and our tents were pitched along the road side.

This place, during the late war, was quite a respectable village, owing to a large glass manufactory established here, which, together with the dwellings of the workmen, we saw deserted, and presenting the very picture of poverty. Since the conclusion of the war, when the factory fell through, the place has fallen off considerably, and everything appears as if it was going to ruin.

Saturday, 28th.—At daylight we struck our tents, and followed the course of the Agawam, which runs through a deep and narrow valley, having in many places scarcely width sufficient for the road, on its bank, we crossed and re-crossed the river several times, and at six o'clock arrived at Chester village, a pretty little spot at the entrance of the valley. Here we breakfasted, and after remaining an hour and a half, proceeded, still continuing with the Agawam towards Westfield.

From Chester village the country becomes more open, the land better, and everything bears the appearance of comfort and industry. The day was oppressively warm, the roads very dusty, owing to the long drought, and the march altogether fatiguing. Halting for a short time to rest under the shade on the bank of the river, the battalion were suffered to bathe, which enabled us to reach Westfield (twenty miles from the factory) with greater ease than otherwise would have been possible. We encamped on the green in the centre of the village, at three o'clock, and were indebted to the kindness of the ladies of Westfield for some additions to our late dinner, as agreeable as unexpected.

Sunday, 29th.—Between three and four in the morning we were on our road to Springfield (nine miles), which we reached near eight o'clock, and encamped on the square in front of the U.S. Armory.

Every country town or village, however small, (in Massachusetts), appears to have had for its principal aim, to build in the first place a church, and afterwards to paint it and all their houses white. This gives to all the towns in the New England States an air of neatness which we seldom meet with anywhere else, and which in no place is more conspicuous than in Springfield. In the afternoon the corps attended divine service in the chapel attached to the United States establishment here [Springfield Armory]. On Monday we visited the Armory, to the politeness of the superintendent of which we were indebted for much pleasure and more valuable information.

On Tuesday afternoon, after a short drill at our encampment, we marched under a national salute into the town, where refreshments were prepared for us, and at sundown returned to parade....

Wednesday, August 1st.—Understanding that for many miles on the road was one continued bed of sand, which, on account of the want of rain for the last two or three weeks, would be very fatiguing to march through in the heat of the day, the Commandant decided upon starting at eleven o'clock on the night of the 31st, hoping that the heavy dew would in some measure make amends for the want of rain. It was a fine star light evening, and everything was favorable for our march, which lay through a low country, where mosquitoes were so thick that it was impossible to stop for an instant without being covered with them; as to pantaloons, they were no sort of protection, and the only way to preserve a whole skin was to be continually in motion. After proceeding about nine miles, the road suddenly turning to the left, brought us to the bank of the Chickapee River, here a dark, sluggish stream, and which for three-fourths of a mile continues through one of the most lone, gloomy spots imaginable. On one side was the river separated only from the road by a line of trees, whose dark leaves made still blacker in appearance by the time of night, formed, by their branches uniting with those that projected from the hill which rose perpendicularly on our right, an arch excluding the little light we might otherwise have enjoyed.

Indeed, few of us had ever witnessed a more gloomy scene, and in the hands of the novelist, the stillness of the column as it marched through the glen, interrupted only by an occasional word of command, or the dull, heavy sound of the wagons and the voices of their drivers, would have been a subject on which he might well exert his powers of romantic description.

At five A. M. we reached Sodom, a few houses on the road side, where we breakfasted, and after remaining two hours, proceeded to Palmer, a small village five miles farther, which we reached by nine o'clock, making the distance from Springfield sixteen and a half miles. At Palmer we remained during the heat of the day, which was by far the warmest we had experienced on the road; and at four in the evening we proceeded over a hilly country, five miles to Thomas' tavern, which we reached, excessively fatigued, by sun down. This day was, without exception, the most oppressive of our march, as during the last five miles we were not able to procure a drop of water. We encamped on a delightful spot on the banks of the Chickapee, and completely refreshed ourselves by bathing and a good night's rest.

Thursday, 2d.—We marched at four in the morning of a fine day for Leicester, where we intended remaining the night. Two miles from Thomas' we passed through Western, a neat village, and by half-past six reached West Brookfield, where we breakfasted. The country here is filled with immense ponds, covering many acres of ground; and which, peeping here and there through the trees, add greatly to the beauty of scenery. The main post road from Albany to Boston, which we had been traveling, was in as good order and repair as it was possible, so that our baggage found but little difficulty in keeping up with the battalion; even in passing the mountains the road was excellent, and all to be complained of was the dust, which was unavoidable. Leaving West Brookfield, we passed through East Brookfield, prettily situated, two and a half miles from the former place—the country in a high state of cultivation, very hilly however, and the scenery the same. At eleven o'clock we reached Spencer, fifteen miles from where we last encamped—dined and remained there till four, when we started for Leicester, distant six miles, where we arrived without difficulty by sun down. The village is on the summit of a nigh hill, from whence you have a view of the surrounding country for many miles. We encamped on the green in front of the academy, which is said to be in a flourishing condition, and if a fine healthy situation can be of any advantage, nowhere is it enjoyed in a higher degree than at Leicester.

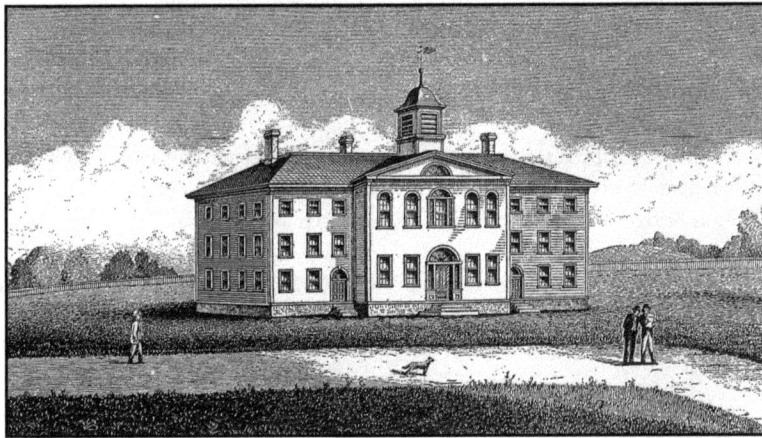

Leicester Academy, Leicester, Massachusetts, c. 1806. Courtesy Wikipedia.

Friday, 3d.—Early this morning we struck our tents, and proceeded rapidly towards Worcester. When within a few miles of the town, we were met by a committee of the inhabitants, who escorted us under a national salute to our encampment, which we reached by half-past six, and in the middle of which had been erected a staff, on which was waving a national flag.

At one o'clock the corps marched to an elegant collation prepared for them, and we enjoyed ourselves much to our satisfaction until three, when we returned to camp in a violent storm of wind and rain, the want of which had been so severely felt during the last days of our march.

....

Saturday, 4th.—At the usual hour we started on a beautiful road for Framingham. Half an hour's march brought us to the Worcester Long Pond, across which is a floating bridge. The scenery here is remarkably fine—the pond, with its dark green promontories over which the mists of the morning were yet hanging, together with the glittering of the rising sun upon our arms, formed a picture rarely if ever surpassed.

Six miles from Worcester we stopped to breakfast, near a large tavern, where a crowd of the neighboring inhabitants had collected to see us pass; and where, after remaining an hour and a half, we proceeded rapidly towards Framingham.

On the outskirts of the village we were met by the marshal of the day, with a large cavalcade of the inhabitants of the township, and a fine uniform volunteer company under command of Captain Hamilton.

....

We were escorted to our encampment under a national salute, and found tables set there on which it had been intended to have placed a substantial dinner; but our early arrival had prevented it, and they had only time to cover the long rows with plenty of lemonade, punch, etc.

Sunday, 5th.—We attended divine worship at the village church, on the green before which we were encamped, both morning and afternoon.

Monday, 6th. At daylight the tents were struck, and we were on the road to Boston. At eight and a half miles from Framingham we halted to breakfast, whence we proceeded rapidly to Roxbury, where we were met by the Norfolk Guards and escorted by them to our encampment on the hill above General Dearborn's, making the distance we had marched nineteen miles. We arrived at twelve o'clock, and at half-past one partook of an elegant collation, spread on tables under an immense marquee in the General's garden; and our long and dusty march in a hot sun, rendered the hospitality of our generous host highly acceptable. We were indebted to him during our short halt at Roxbury for many conveniences, the want of which we would otherwise have seriously felt, particularly water, which he had drawn in barrels to our encampment. Indeed, during our whole march, to no individual were we under greater obligations than to General Dearborn.

Tuesday, 7th.—After eight o'clock parade we commenced our march to the town of Boston, across the Neck. When within a short distance of the line we halted, and remained until informed that the municipal authorities had reached the place where they intended receiving us…[they] formed a cavalcade and escorted us to our encampment, through an immense concourse of people. As the battalion entered the Boston Common, a national salute was fired, under which we concluded our march to Boston; and surely never were troops, after a steady march of one hundred and seventy miles, in better spirits, or, from the gratifying reception this day given us, in better hopes as to the pleasure they would enjoy during their halt; nor can anyone say he was disappointed.

Boston

By half past ten everything was in order—tents pitched and sentinels posted. The situation of our camp was excellent, surrounded with undoubtedly the first buildings in Boston on three sides, and the other open towards the water. In front of us the Mall, with its rows of venerable trees, and the State House, rising proudly on the hill, just behind us. It would have been impossible to have selected another spot equally convenient as an encampment, and agreeable from the pleasing objects around it.

At one o'clock we partook of a substantial repast, which had been prepared for us at Concert Hall.

This day the Commandant received letters from Mr. Farnham, proprietor of the baths at Craigie's Bridge, and from the directors of the West Boston Bridge Company, inviting the corps to make free use of their bathing establishments during our halt in town.

Invitations were also received from Messrs. Shaw and Topliff, offering us the free use of the reading rooms of the Atheneum and Merchant's Hall, of which they were the respective proprietors.

Wednesday, 8th. Agreeably to a very polite invitation which we had received, we attended the Amphitheatre in the evening.

Thursday, 9th. Visited the New England Museum in the evening.

Friday, 10th ....We therefore started at nine, and arrived at the [Harvard] president's house a little after ten o'clock, from whence we were conducted by a procession of the officers and students of the institution to the University Hall, where we were welcomed to "academic ground" by the president.

The classes were then separated, and attended by the gentlemen of the college, visited the philosophical chamber and apparatus, the mineralogical collection, the chemical laboratory, the anatomical rooms, and the other parts of the establishment which it was thought would interest us. After this we drilled for an hour in the college yard, and at two o'clock sat down, together with the officers and students to a hospitable entertainment, which had been prepared for us in the Commons Hall.

In the afternoon we drilled at the Light Infantry, on the common, before the college, after which we returned to Boston in good time for parade.

Our visit to Cambridge was altogether one which we will not soon forget.

To give us a reception as a military body was nothing new; every town and village we had passed through had done it; but to be received as a scientific institution by one of the first colleges in the country, had something in it pleasing on account of its novelty, and gratifying to our pride as members of the Military Academy—and, as the long profession formed by the two institutions wound through the streets of Cambridge, we felt that though we were not, in the language of fulsome flattery, "the best hopes of the nation," yet still something was expected from us, in defence of our common country, and from them in the advancement of the happiness of their fellow citizens—our end the same, the benefit of community—we differ only in our means of obtaining it.

Saturday, 11th.—

To Major Worth, Commandant Corps Of Cadets:

Sir:

The selectmen of the town of Boston propose to present the Corps of United States Cadets, under your command, a stand of colors, on Saturday next, at twelve o'clock A. M., if that day and hour will suit your convenience.

Eliphalet Williams, Chairman.

Agreeably to the above note, the space allotted for such ceremonies was enclosed with chains on the sloping ground before the State House, and around it the inhabitants began to collect soon after breakfast; and at twelve o'clock the crowd was immense. The windows, roofs and balconies of the houses around were filled with spectators, forming as lively a scene as it was possible to be conceived. The day was remarkably fine, and had it been only a few centuries back, the cloudless sky and delightful air, together with the appearance of satisfaction manifested by the multitude about us, would have been regarded as a happy omen—a presage that the colors we this day received would be bravely defended, and that the eagle, the representative of the wild bird of our own native mountains, which for the first time waved over the battalion, would never be yielded while our graves could form it an intrenchment.

....

At twelve o'clock a procession was formed in front of the State House, consisting of several handsome volunteer companies, under command of Captain Brimmer, the board of selectmen, public officers, officers of the army and navy, and other invited guests, who entered the square, and formed a line on the highest part of the descent. The battalion then marched into the square, wheeled into line immediately opposite the board of selectmen. The ranks were opened, the officers took their posts in front; the battalion presented arms, and the Commandant and his staff then advanced to the chairman of the board, who delivered the following address to him, viz:

Sir:

Being called to reflect on the institutions of our country, we find much reason to rejoice that our origin was at a period in which the acts that contribute to the welfare of a nation, were, in general, well understood and highly appreciated.

With the history of other nations as lessons of experience and wisdom, our fathers devised the government, framed and endowed the institutions, which have for many years not merely upheld our nation in domestic tranquility and happiness, but shed a lustre on our history at home and abroad, in peace and in war, cheering to our thoughts, bearing joy and consolation to the firesides and bosoms of every friend to his country.

Among the institutions of our government, in which we have a pleasure and a national pride, is that of public schools for the education of our youth in military and naval tactics; and of these, none is held more highly in our estimation, than the one which has, at this time, done us the honor of a visit, and of which yon, sir, are one of the most respected instructors. With the thought that our national glory in arms may hereafter be confided to the skill and judgment of some one or more of these young gentlemen, we feel a lively interest—an anxious concern, in the improvement, character, and honor of every individual under your command; for, while we deprecate a state of war, and pray that we may be delivered from any hostile attempt, yet we are fully sensible that the true policy of our government is, and will be, in peace to prepare for war.

With this sentiment—with veneration for the institutions of our fathers—with particular and special approbation of the Military School under your charge—with sentiments of high respect for the general government, which has, and I trust will continue to foster and support this institution, to the honor of our country—and in conformity to the spirit of hospitality which the inhabitants of the town of Boston entertain towards you, and the pupils under your charge—in behalf of those inhabitants and in their name, I have the honor to present to you, and through you to the Military Academy at West Point, this stand of colors (here the colors were presented, and a national salute fired to them); may it long remain in that part of our country, hallowed to our feelings by the fortitude and patriotism which the immortal Washington there displayed in a time of peril and calamity, in opposing not only the powerful force of our open enemy, but in confounding the perfidy and treachery of his fellow officers in arms.

To which the Commandant, on behalf of the Corps of Cadets, returned the following answer:

Sir:

In accepting this splendid manifestation of the munificence of the citizens of Boston, of their good will towards and their approval of the conduct of the corps, which it is my good fortune, pride and honor to command. I feel entirely inadequate to the task of making to you, and to your fellow citizens, suitable acknowledgements. It cannot be doubted that this day and the interesting associations connected with it, will act as a powerful excitement to honorable exercise, whenever foreign aggressions shall compel the people to call them to the defence of our common country; and, that whether in peace or war, they will, by the transactions of this day, deem themselves doubly pledged to conduct themselves as becomes brave soldiers and good citizens.

That the sacred emblem of our country will never be tarnished by them individually, or collectively as a corps, I have no hesitation to pledge everything that is dear to a soldier; and this battalion flag, sir, will ever be their rallying point, whether in defence of their country's honor, or in pursuit of the science essential to successful war.

We particularly recognize on this occasion, the genuine expressions of attachment to the government and constitutions of our country generally, and an approval of every act calculated to consolidate its power and secure its defence. Such sentiments are the natural growth of a soil where the spirit of liberty first sprung into life.

Unable as I am to do justice to the occasion, I can only offer to you the cordial thanks of the superintendent, professors and teachers of the Military Academy, and more especially of this youthful corps; with the sincere assurance that the citizens of Boston shall never have occasion to reflect that their kindness and confidence have been misplaced.

[The colors thus presented to us are the productions of two rival artists, Penniman, who executed the battalion flag, and Curtis, who painted the national standard, and are done in their best style. The former (white) represents Minerva surrounded with her attributes. In the rear is seen a camp, near the figure the implements of war, together with the colors of the United States, and under the whole the motto, "*A Scientia ad Gloriam*," with the inscription, "Presented by the town of Boston."

The eagle is painted on a dark blue ground, with the same inscription as the first.]....

We returned at five o'clock to camp.

Sunday, 12th.—In the morning we attended divine worship at the Rev. Mr. Pierpont's, and at St. Paul's Church in the afternoon, at both of which Places the sermon was addressed entirely to us....

Monday, 13th.—This day being appointed for our review by the Governor, his marquee was pitched, and the same space enclosed as had been on Saturday. At twelve o'clock, the first and second classes, being detailed for the purpose, fired the Governor a national salute as he entered the square, accompanied by the officers of the militia in full uniform, and escorted by his guard, the Boston Independent Cadets, who did duty during the day at the marquee.

The battalion then passed with the usual ceremonies in review after which we were individually introduced to the Governor, and partook of refreshments provided for us on the spot.

The next day the Commandant received the following letter:

Commonwealth of Massachusetts

Governor Brooks is happy in the opportunity afforded him by the politeness of the Commandant, of expressing the high gratification he derived yesterday from reviewing and witnessing the perfect discipline of the United States Corps of Cadets, as displayed in their various exercises and evolutions in Boston. A perfect persuasion of the intelligence and scientific attainments of the individuals composing the corps, and of the relations they must hereafter maintain with the destinies of our country, associated with great tactical order and precision, imparted peculiar interest to the exhibition.

The institution of a national school for the advancement of philosophical and moral, as well as military improvement, is a measure that seems to be happily calculated to provide efficaciously for the national defence; whilst the friendships formed amongst the members of the same corps, who are engaged in the same honorable pursuit, who are taken from every section of the union, and are destined to be enrolled among the future guardians of our nation's interests and honor, must exert an auspicious and lasting influence on the harmony and integrity of the United States.

The Commandant, and the corps he with so much honor commands, may be assured that they will carry with them from Massachusetts, and into their future walks in life, the Governor's best wishes for their prosperity and happiness.

Medford, August 14th, 1821.

To a letter from the commanding officer, desiring that the corps might be allowed to pay their respects to President Adams, at any time when it would be most convenient to him, he received the following answer:

To Major Worth, Commandant Corps of Cadets:
    Dear Sir:

I have received the letter you have this day done me the honor to write. I congratulate you on your fortunate arrival in Boston, and shall be happy to receive a visit from you, and the U.S. Cadets, at any hour you will please to designate. Mr. Shaw will have the honor to deliver this, and to receive from you your commands.

I have the honor to be, with the highest esteem for the establishment at West Point, for its officers, and the young gentlemen, the cadets,

Yours, etc.,
John Adams.

Early on the morning of the fourteenth, we left our encampment for the ex-President's seat, at Quincy, and after marching nine miles through a finely cultivated and thickly settled country, reached there at nine o'clock. Having stacked our arms, we were formed in front of the house, when the following address was delivered to us by Mr. Adams:

My Young Fellow Citizens And Fellow Soldiers:

I rejoice that I live to see so line a collection of the future defenders of their country in pursuit of honor under the auspices of the national government.

A desire of distinction is implanted by nature in every human bosom; and the general sense of mankind in all ages and countries, cultivated and uncultivated, has excited, encouraged, and applauded this passion in military men, more than in any other order in society.

Military glory is esteemed the first and greatest of glories. As your profession is, at least, as solemn and sacred as any in human life, it behooves you seriously to consider—What is glory?

There is no real glory in this world or in any other, but such as arises from wisdom and benevolence. There can be no solid glory among men, but that which springs from equity and humanity—from the constant observance of prudence, temperance, justice and fortitude. Battles, victories and conquests, abstracted from their only justifiable object and end, which is justice and peace, are the glory of fraud, violence and usurpation. What was the glory of Alexander and Caesar? The glimmering which those "livid flames" in Milton "cast pale and dreadful"—or the "sudden blaze, which far round illumined hell."

Different, far different, is the glory of Washington and his faithful colleagues! Excited by no ambition of conquest, or avaricious desire of wealth—innated by no jealousy, envy, malice, or revenge—prompted only by the love of their country, by the purest patriotism and philanthropy, they persevered with invincible constancy in defence of their country— her fundamental laws—her natural, essential and unalienable rights and liberties, against the lawless and ruthless violence of tyranny and usurpation.

The biography of these immortal captains, and the history of their great actions, you will read and ruminate night and day. You need not investigate antiquity, or travel into foreign countries to find models of excellence in military commanders, without a stain of ambition or avarice, tyranny, cruelty, or oppression, towards friends or enemies.

In imitation of such great examples, in the most exalted transports of your military ardor, even in the day of battle, you will be constantly overawed by a conscious sense of the dignity of your character as men—as American citizens, and as Christians.

I congratulate you on the great advantages you possess for attaining eminence in letters and science as well as arms. These advantages are a precious deposit, which you ought to consider as a sacred trust—for which you are responsible to your country, and to a higher tribunal. These advantages, and the habits you have acquired, will qualify you for any course of life you may choose to pursue.

That I may not fatigue you with too many words, allow me to address every one of you in the language of a Roman dictator to his master of the horse, after a daring and dangerous exploit for the safety of his country —"Macte virtute esto."

John Adams.
....

In delivering his address our venerable host appeared to be considerably affected. The hand which forty-five years ago, pledged his life, his fortune, and his sacred honor, in support of the declaration we are bound to defend, now trembled with the infirmities of age; but as he proceeded, he grew warmer in his tone, and more energetic in his manner, and when he concluded, the stillness of all showed that we felt what he had uttered.

The hospitality of Mr. Adams had provided for us an excellent breakfast, placed under a large awning erected for the purpose; after partaking of which, at eleven o'clock, we proceeded to Milton Hill, the seat of Barney Smith, Esq., where the battalion had been invited to dine, and where a number of ladies and gentlemen had collected for the purpose of seeing us pass.

The elegant garden and extensive ground, together with the fine collection of paintings at Mr. Smith's, afforded us ample amusement until dinner, which was served in an immense bower, where everything was provided us that could render the repast agreeable.

At four o'clock we commenced our march back to Boston, which we reached at sun down.

Wednesday, 15th.—Nothing particular occurred.

Thursday, 16th....Cadet Corps invited to visit Charlestown....

In compliance with the...invitation we struck our tents on Boston Common at seven o'clock, and marched across the Charlestown bridge to our encampment on Bunker's Hill, where, on our arrival, a handsome address was delivered to the Commandant, and through him to the corps, by the committee of the inhabitants appointed for that purpose.

The place provided for us was a little to the left of Warren's monument, in front of the American intrenchments, and where the contest for them had been the warmest. The works were still visible; the rail fence was gone, but the exact spot where it stood was pointed out. A large potato field is on the ground up which the English grenadiers charged; and the neck where the slaughter was so great on account of the fire from the ship, and across which the Americans retreated, is now covered with houses.

The old intrenchments are scarcely visible—the parapet and ditch are almost on the same level, and little except the monument of wood (and it cannot last long) remains to tell the casual visitor, that here had been a battle; great, not on account of the numbers engaged, but as being the first hard struggle for independence.

....

While such enthusiasm existed in children, could England hope to subjugate America? They might! but it would have been over the dead bodies of two generations.

At one P.M. we marched into the town, where a handsome repast had been prepared for us.

Friday, 17th.—Visited the navy-yard, and through the politeness of Commodore Hull, who furnished the ship's barges, part of the battalion had an opportunity of visiting Fort Independence, in the harbor.

Saturday, 18th.— At daybreak everything was in readiness for the march. We left Charlestown and marched through Boston to Dedham (thirteen miles) where we intended breakfasting.

In leaving Boston, there were but few who did it without regret. The attention and hospitality shown us, both as a corps and individually, was such as we can never forget. The good will manifested by so large a portion of our fellow citizens, was an additional motive to the many who already had, for our exertions to deserve it. We had heard of the hospitality of the Bostonians, and from the accounts received as we approached their town, expected to be treated with kindness; but our reception surpassed our most sanguine expectations. Those who went prepossessed against the inhabitants, left there strongly prejudiced in their favor; and if anyone should, in our presence, speak lightly of them, we have only to say, "Go and visit them."

As passing visitors in mass, we could not help observing the manners of the children we everywhere met—they were convincing proofs that the numerous school houses we passed on the road were not without their use; and to see the boys and girls nodding and courtesying to us as we marched along, was a presage that the attentions which they as children thus showed to strangers, would, when men, grow into a hospitality honorable to themselves and the state in which they lived.

At eight o'clock we halted at Dedham, where a breakfast had been provided for us by the hospitality of the inhabitants. After remaining here three hours, we proceeded towards Walpole, eight miles farther, which we reached by two o'clock and encamped. Here the battalion was welcomed to the village (through the Commandant) by the minister, an aged man, who had lived there since the commencement of the revolution. This simple mark of kindness showed as much good will and hospitable feeling, as all the display made with the same view elsewhere.

Sunday, 19th.—Left Walpole early in the morning for Wrentham (eight miles), halted and encamped there at seven o'clock. Here an excellent breakfast was given us by the inhabitants. We attended divine worship at the village church, and at half-past five the tents were struck and we resumed our march towards Barrow's tavern, our halting place for the night. We passed, near sun down, through Attleboro, a pleasant village, in the immediate neighborhood of which there are nine cotton factories, and reached our place of encampment a little after dark.

Monday, 20th.—At daylight we were on the road to Providence. After marching four miles, we crossed the Massachusetts and Rhode Island line, at Pawtucket, a pretty manufacturing village on the Pawtuxet, where a breakfast was prepared for us. After remaining here two hours, we proceeded, accompanied by several gentlemen of that town to Providence; and, as we approached it, the cavalcade continued increasing, and at last formed a considerable escort.

On the outskirts of the town we were met by several volunteer companies, and escorted by them to the place provided for us.

....

The hospitality of the inhabitants showed itself to-day in making us a large present of claret, and indeed, during our halt in Providence, every attention was shown us that could conduce to our comfort.

In the evening the corps received a very polite invitation to attend the theatre, where the Boston company were then performing, and from whence we returned to camp, very highly gratified with our entertainment.

Tuesday, 21st.—At eleven o'clock we struck our tents and commenced our march towards New London. On our way through town we halted to partake of an elegant collation prepared for us in the State House, and which we left in high spirits at four o'clock for Warwick, or Green Factory. Providence is finely situated at the head of Narragansett bay. Its beautiful steeples, and the houses rising one above the other on the hill, presented a singular yet pleasing appearance; and the beauty of the town is only surpassed by the hospitality of its inhabitants.

We reached Green Factory, so called from an immense green cotton establishment, at sundown, and encamped for the night. On our way we passed through Natick, a small village on a creek of the same name, turning a number of cotton factories. These factories are, in one light, of service to the community in which they are situated, on account of the employment given to children who would otherwise be idle; but at the same time that it gives them employment, it destroys their health and renders them apparently unfit for any other employment than that of watching the innumerable revolutions of the spindles. Among all the children, boys and girls, at Green Factory, not one appeared even in tolerable health; and all those who were questioned, had either just recovered from sickness or were sick at the time.

Wednesday, 22d.—This morning when we started, the ground was covered with a heavy frost, which rendered the air so cold as to be quite inconvenient. The road this day was one which had not been opened more than two months. The country was miserably barren, and so sandy that it was with difficulty that the baggage could keep up with the battalion. At six miles from the factory we halted to breakfast, after which we proceeded to the city of Hopkinton, containing eighteen or twenty houses, where we dined. Two miles beyond the city we crossed the Rhode Island and Connecticut line, and reached Miner's Tavern (one mile further) by sundown. Here we encamped for the night.

The part of Rhode Island we passed through after leaving Providence was uncultivated and sterile, and to all appearance incapable of raising sufficient to support the few inhabitants scattered over the face of the country. Every stream, however, turned one or more cotton factories; and, as one of us was told, when observing that the land could produce but little. "If we can't raise grain on the land, we've cotton factories enough to buy it from others." And this is truly the case.

Thursday, 23d.—-This morning, like the preceding, was disagreeably cold. The moon was still shining when we started through a fine country on our last day's march; and this idea alone was sufficient to enable us to bear it. We were completely tired of everything like marching. Upwards of three hundred miles had shown us sufficient of its fatigue to make us all rejoice in the thought of steamboat carriage from New London to West Point.

By half-past six we reached our breakfasting place, a small spot at the head of the Mystick river, nine miles distant from our last encampment, and after remaining here two hours, continued on our road. At eleven o'clock we reached Groton, a village on the Thames, opposite to New London, where refreshments had been provided for us by the inhabitants.

The steamboat *Fulton*, in which we were to proceed to New Haven, carried us across the Thames, when we marched through the town to our encampment.

At one o'clock the corps attended a collation prepared for them. Indeed, this was the general, and undoubtedly the most acceptable way of testifying good will and approbation. To the hospitality of our fellow citizens, during our whole march through the New England states, we were indebted not only for gratification, but for substantial comforts; and though, on leaving the Military Academy, and mixing in the busy hum of society, objects of a far different nature may attract our attention, our march to Boston will always be remembered with pleasure, as a source of much gratification and instruction.

Friday, 24th.—At eight o'clock we struck our tents for the last time, marched to the steamboat wharf, and embarked on board the *Fulton* for New Haven. At twelve o'clock we met the steamship *Fulton*, on her passage to Providence, received and returned three cheers, and at sundown reached New Haven, where the *Connecticut* was waiting to take us to New York. The battalion disembarked and marched into the middle of the city—counter-marched, and came back again, when we started for New York, which we reached early in the morning of

Saturday, 25th.—We remained on board the *Chancellor*, which was to take us the remainder of our journey, until one o'clock, when we marched into the city, stacked our arms in the park, were shown through the City Hall, and at two partook of an excellent dinner, provided for us by the corporation; after which we proceeded on our return to West Point. At ten o'clock we came in sight of the barracks, which were illuminated for our return, when we gave three hearty cheers; soon after which we landed at the U.S. dock, and marched gaily up the hill, to the "Soldier's Return." The moment we were dismissed we began cheering, nor did many of us stop until we were once more in a *bed* and under cover of a *roof.*

In a march of upwards of three hundred miles, it would naturally be expected that much sickness would occur among those unaccustomed to the fatigues inseparable from the expedition, performed during the hottest months of summer. However, when we landed, there was not one case of serious indisposition amongst us. And here it would be ungrateful not to mention the name of Doctor Williams, of Albany, with the highest respect—volunteering to accompany us—his attention was unceasing, and many are indebted to his skill and care for the health they now enjoy. All the comfort that could possibly be procured in a camp, he endeavored to obtain, and his gentlemanlike deportment and kind attentions, will ever secure him our esteem.

Previous to the departure of the cadets from West Point, they were organized in the following manner:

Major W.J. Worth, First Regiment U. S. Artillery, Commandant.

Lieutenant H.W. Griswold, Assistant.
Lieutenant Z.J.D. Kinsley, Assistant.
Daniel D. Tompkins, Second Regiment U. S. Artillery, Disbursing Officer.
Doctor Platt Williams, Acting Surgeon.

BATTALION STAFF.
John C. Holland, Adjutant, South Carolina.
David Wallace, Quarter Master, Ohio.
Jonathan Prescott, First Topographical Engineer, Massachusetts.

John H.B. Latrobe, Second Topographical Engineer, Maryland.

Thompson B. Wheelock, Sergeant Major, Massachusetts.

James Grier, Commissary of Subsistence, New York.

W. Cook, Assistant Commissary of Subsistence, New Jersey.

E. Holmes, Assistant Commissary of Subsistence, Connecticut.

George Button, Quarter-Master Sergeant, Connecticut.

....

Fourth Company.

Jefferson Vail, Captain, Maryland.

John B. Scott, First Lieutenant, Connecticut.

Horace Bliss, Second Lieutenant, Connecticut.

James H. Coode, First Sergeant, North Carolina.

Joseph K. Mansfield, Second Sergeant, Connecticut.

Francis Lee, Third Sergeant, Pennsylvania.

Edmund B. Alexander, First Corporal, Kentucky.

T. Edwards, Second Corporal, Massachusetts.

Chapter 4

Engineer 1822 to 1845

LIEUTENANT MANSFIELD'S FIRST ASSIGNMENT WAS EXPECTED as he graduated second in his class which guaranteed him a posting as an engineer.[1] The corps which he joined dated from 1779 when Congress created the Corps of Engineers as a separate organization. Members fought during the Revolutionary War but were mustered out of service at its end. The Corps of Engineers as it is known today came into being on 16 March 1802, when President Thomas Jefferson was authorized by Congress to "organize and establish a Corps of Engineers...that the said Corps...shall be stationed at West Point in the State of New York and shall constitute a Military Academy." The West Point Military Academy became primarily an engineering school and was commanded by Army engineers.[2]

During Mansfield's military service, he participated in many activities in which his corps was involved, such as construction of coastal forts, surveys, repairs of seawalls, and even the National Road. The American West was mapped by the new Corps of Topographical Engineers, which was created in 1838, but it was returned to the Corps of Engineers

---

[1] Colonel Sylvanus Thayer recommended in 1818 that "Not more than two cadets 'distinguished in a remarkable degree for their scientific attainments' would be recommended for commissions in the Corps of Engineers; no other cadets would be considered for an Engineer commission," George S. Pappas, *To The Point: The United States Military Academy, 1802-1902* (Westport, CT: Praeger Publishers, 1993), 109-110. Upon graduation, the new officers were assigned by the Academy Academic Board.

[2] The U.S. Army Corps of Engineers: A Brief History, http://www.usace.Army.mil/About/History/BriefHistoryoftheCorps. *The U.S. Army Corps of Engineers: A History* (Washington, DC: Headquarters, U.S. Army Corps of Engineers, Office of History, Alexandria, Va., 2008), 1-8; Historic American buildings Survey, HABS No. NY-5708, NPS, passim; Edward C. Boynton, *History of West Point* (New York, NY: D. Van Nostrand, 1871), 11, 18-19, 176-180, 191; Wikipedia, "United States Military Academy" and "United States Army Corps of Engineers."

in 1863. The Corps of Engineers also constructed lighthouses, helped develop jetties and piers for harbors, built canals, lighthouses, and mapped navigation channels.[3]

Colonel Charles Gratiot, Chief Engineer, 24 May 1828 to 6 December 1838. Gratiot was born 29 August 1786, in St. Louis, Missouri. President Jefferson appointed him a cadet in 1804 and he graduated from the Military Academy in 1806 and was commissioned in the Corps of Engineers. He became a captain in 1808 and assisted in constructing fortifications in Charleston, South Carolina. He was commander of West Point in 1810-1811. He was Chief Engineer in the War of 1812. He served as Chief Engineer in Michigan Territory and superintending engineer, construction of Hampton Roads defenses. On 24 May 1828, he was appointed colonel of engineers, brevet brigadier general, and Chief Engineer. In March 1829, he became a brigadier general. He administered an expanding program of river, harbor, road, and fortification construction. In 1838, President Martin Van Buren dismissed him for failing to repay government funds. Courtesy LOC.

Mansfield spent time working on Fort Hamilton in New York Harbor from 1825 to 1828. Between 1825 and 1864, five Third System fortifications were constructed in New York City. They comprised Fort Hamilton at the Narrows, new Forts Richmond and Tompkins on Staten Island, Fort Schuyler at Throgs Neck, and Fort Totten at Willets Point. Fort Hamilton was the first Third System fortification built in New York City, and was named in honor of Alexander Hamilton, the Revolutionary War officer and first Secretary of the Treasury. Construction began on 26 April 1825 and was completed on 10 July 1831.[4]

---

[3] "The U.S. Army Corps of Engineers: A Brief History." The most famous road project, the National Road, was constructed between 1811 and 1841 at a cost of more than $6 million. The road extended from Cumberland, Maryland, across western Pennsylvania to Wheeling, Virginia, and then across the midsections of Ohio and Indiana to Vandalia, Illinois. Congress authorized the road in 1806, but in the following years there was unsatisfactory progress on the civilian-led project. In 1825, President John Quincy Adams turned the construction over to the War Department. The Engineer Corps applied the techniques of road construction developed in England by John McAdam, and it engaged in some innovative bridge building. At Brownsville, Pennsylvania, Captain Richard Delafield built the first bridge in the United States with a cast-iron superstructure, an 80-foot span that remains in use today. By 1840, Engineer Corps officers, including Mansfield, had overseen construction of 268 miles of macadamized surface. The following shows Mansfield's often overlapping assignments after his graduation from West Point up to his Mexican-American War tour:

     1822-1825 Assistant to the Board of Engineers at New York
     1825-1828 Assisted in construction of Fort Hamilton, New York
     1828-1830 Assisted in the construction of defenses of Hampton Roads, Virginia
     1830 Detached to survey Pasquotank River, North Carolina, and to take temporary charge of works in Charleston Harbor, South Carolina
     1830-1845 Superintending Engineer of the construction of Fort Pulaski, Savannah, Georgia
     1831-32 Charge of repairs of Cumberland Road (National Road), Maryland
     1833-1839 Charge of Savannah River Improvement
     1835-1839 Charge of inland navigation between the St. Mary's and St. John's Rivers, Florida
     1837-1838 Charge of Sullivan's Island Breakwater, South Carolina, and repairs of St. Augustine Seawall, Florida
     1838-1839 Charge of improvement of Brunswick Harbor, Georgia
     1842 May 8 to 1845 8 September, Member of the Board of Engineers for Atlantic Coast Defenses

[4] In the spring of 1828 Mansfield was ordered to Old Point Comfort and was for about one year principal assistant at Fort Monroe and one year principal assistant at Fort Calhoun at the Rip Raps. While at Old Point Comfort Mansfield was detached and made a reconnaissance of the Pasquotank River from the Canal in the Dismal Swamp to Elizabeth City in North Carolina, and surveyed the bars on there. In August 1830, he was ordered to

VIEW OF FORT HAMILTON, NEW YORK HARBOR.

Mansfield worked on Fort Hamilton early in his engineering career, 1825-1828. He would have been familiar with this view of the completed fort at the beginning of the Civil War as he often passed through New York City on his journeys to Washington, D.C., and to the west while he was inspector general. From "Gleason's Pictorial," courtesy U.S. Army.

Mansfield spent more time on his assignment to the construction of Fort Pulaski on Cockspur Island than any other single project—over 14 years—during his career, and it was his first sole command. His dedication and effort without recognition wore him out as shown in his letter to his wife on 20 August 1847, from his camp near Monterrey, Mexico, after he had joined Brigadier General Zachary Taylor's Army in 1845: "I am delighted to be clear of Fort Pulaski and never expect to see it again. Two weeks later on 1 September he wrote "I am rejoiced to be clear of Fort Pulaski and if I once get out of this country will never return to it again." The best part of my life has been wasted there." Again on 11 October he commented to his wife on his service at the fort: "I am rejoiced to be clear of Fort Pulaski and the Savannah Station. I will never again serve to be stationed south of the Potomac, nor be separated from my family; they must hereafter go where my station may chance to be till I quit the service. I prefer a civil life to this wild goose chase about the country....I look forward to something besides a mere captain of engineers. I have now a reputation of which I can build and I mean to improve the favors of God to do good."[5] Had he lived longer, he might have reflected on the fact that the "impregnable" fort on which he and others such as Robert E. Lee labored was taken by Union forces easily in April 1862 as will be seen. When he arrived at Savannah on 21 January 1831 from Charleston, South Carolina, on the schooner *Spy*, he did not foresee that most of his engineering career in the U.S. Army would be spent there. So by 1845, Mansfield was happy to be assigned to Taylor's Army in Texas not only to be rid of his tedious assignment on Cockspur

relieve Lieutenant Henry Brewerton at Charleston, South Carolina, when sick with the yellow fever and remained there to November when he returned to Old Point Comfort. While he was in charge at Fort Pulaski, was required to examine and report with Captain John H. Winder a plan for the western improvement of the Cape Fear River, North Carolina; letter in Cullum's handwriting with Mansfields military history later corrected by Mansfield, 18 Aug 1859 letter, courtesy WPL. The First System of Forts (also named the First System of Coastal Fortifications) was built from 1794 through 1808; surviving examples include Fort Mifflin near Philadelphia and Fort McHenry near Baltimore. The Second System of Forts was built from 1808 through 1816; surviving examples include Fort Moultrie near Charleston, S.C., and Fort Washington in Maryland on the Potomac River. The Third System of Forts was built from 1816 through 1867; surviving examples include Fort Pulaski and Fort Adams, Newport, R.I. Note that beginning and ending dates for these systems vary according to different authorities.

[5] His remarks may only show his fatigue and boredom during his inactive time in Mexico which was reflected in the pessimism pervading his letters in general during this period. Or perhaps that his slow promotions despite his hard work dispirited him as he saw others with less time in service promoted because of the war. Also likely is that his hard work and personal sacrifices at Fort Pulaski were, in his view, inadequately recognized; courtesy WPL.

Island, but to join an army which would likely face action which he had not seen in almost 30 years of service.[6] Rodgers W. Young, the primary historian of the building of Fort Pulaski and Mansfield's role there, clearly admired his labors in constructing Fort Pulaski when he described those efforts "as an enduring achievement of this strikingly capable native of the State of Connecticut. The construction of Fort Pulaski has been treated [by Young] as a glowing epoch in the life of Joseph K.F. Mansfield."[7]

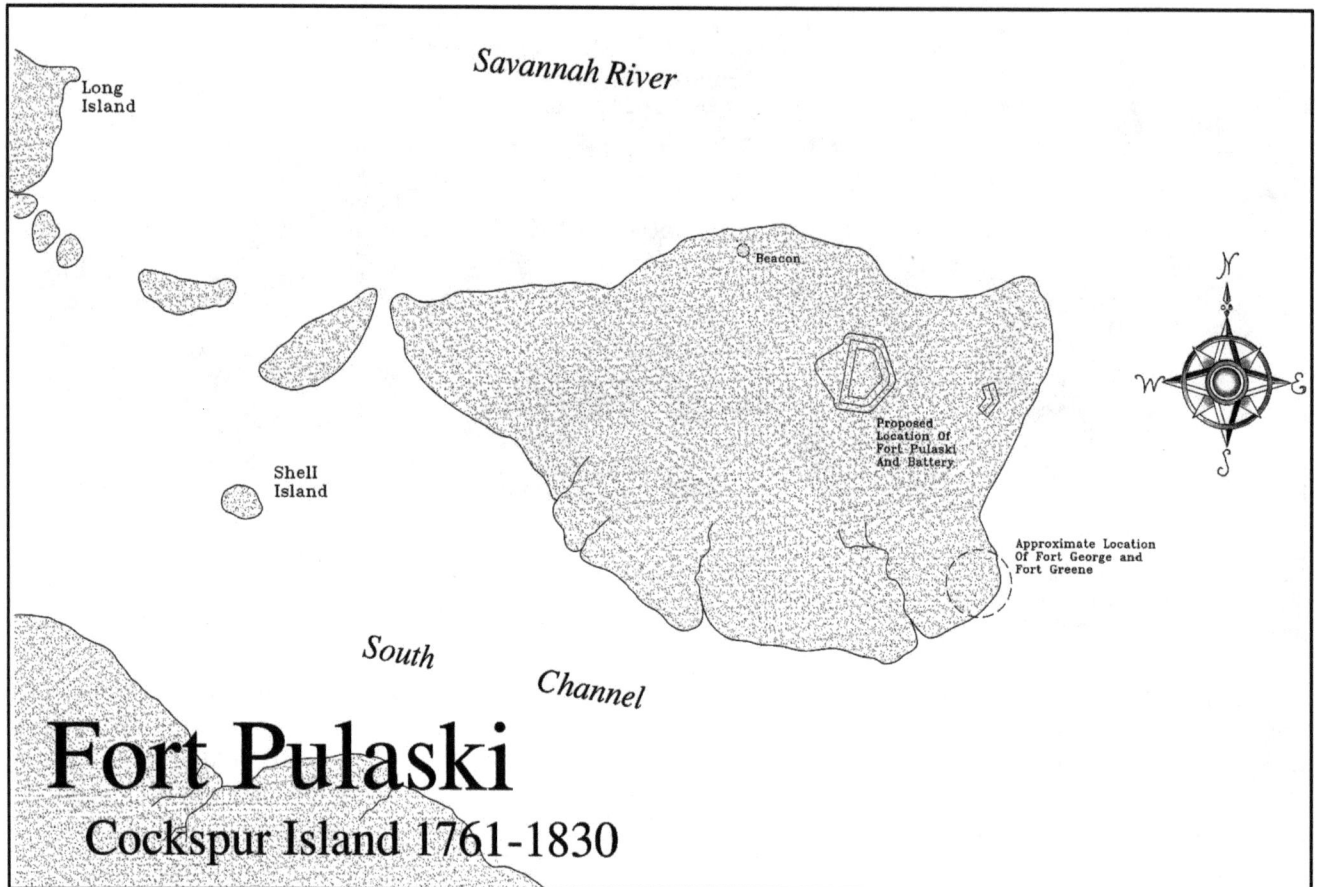

Fort Pulaski is located on Cockspur Island, at the mouth of the Savannah River, near the city of Savannah, in Chatham County, Georgia; it guarded the two entrances to the Savannah River to protect Savannah. Forts George and Greene were sites of the original British and Federal forts as the island was well-located for defending the entrances to the Savannah River. The first U.S. forts were later called the First System Forts which were simple and cheaply built mostly open works with earthen parapets. Cockspur Island is a one by one-half mile combination of mud flats and tidal marshes about 17 miles east of Savannah. To the north and south, the island is bordered by two channels of the Savannah River, and to the east by the Atlantic Ocean. Cockspur Island as pictured above was by the beginning of the 20th century joined on the west to Long Island thanks to materials dredged from the Savannah River. Dikes and ditches on the island, and sand and mud dredged from the Savannah riverbed, have changed the island's terrain since colonial days. Today, Cockspur is about forty percent dry land, and Fort Pulaski is the best preserved example of the Third System of Forts given its essentially unchanged appearance since its completion. Courtesy LOC and NPS (NPS, Historic American Buildings Survey (HABS) No. GA-2158, 1-2).

The first recorded visitors and residents to Cockspur Island were English. On 30 January 1733, six British ships which carried General James Edward Oglethorpe and a group of settlers sailed up the Savannah River and anchored at Cockspur Island. The fleet then went upriver a further 17 miles and established the small settlement of Savannah which

---

[6] Rogers W. Young, "Story of Gen. Mansfield, the Builder of Fort Pulaski During the Years 1831-45," *Savannah Morning News*, 3 February 1935. Young wrote extensively about the construction of Fort Pulaski and related matters; his research and writing are the most comprehensive available, and are heavily used in this chapter. His unpublished manuscripts which provide complete details from Engineering Department records were the sources for his published works and his written narrative is an essential source for this chapter: "A Connecticut Yankee on the Georgia Coast: The Engineering Epic of Fort Pulaski, 1821-1861;" subtitle: "Being The Story of the Trials and Triumphs of Lieutenant, later Captain, Joseph K.F. Mansfield, United States Corps of Engineers, in the building of Fort Pulaski, on Cockspur Island, Savannah River, Georgia" dated 1938 when Young was a member of the National Park Service, Branch of Historic Sites and Buildings. Manuscript copy supplied by Fort Pulaski Park Ranger Michael Weinstein, June 2014.

[7] Young, "Connecticut Yankee," i.

was the beginning of the State of Georgia. A later voyage to Cockspur Island in 1736 carried John Wesley, founder of American Methodism, who first recorded the visit of Europeans to the island. The British Crown granted most of Cockspur to Jonathan Bryan in 1759, but reserved 20 acres on the eastern side of the island. Here in 1761, British authorities constructed on the island's southeast point, Fort George (named for British King George II). It was a palisaded, 100 square foot square work which enclosed a 30-foot-tall log blockhouse designed to provide defense mainly against the Spanish not far away in St. Augustine, Florida. But by the 1770's, the structure yielded to the ravages of high winds and water; local colonists dismantled the structure in 1776 likely reusing whatever of value which could be salvaged. The island briefly served as a refuge of Loyalists abandoning Savannah during the Revolutionary War. In March 1776, British ships attacked Savannah capturing American boats anchored there.[8]

In 1794, the Federal government was deeply concerned with martial events in Europe and authorized coastal fortifications to defend Atlantic ports. Cockspur Island was chosen to protect the entrances to the Savannah River to guard the important port of Savannah. The site of the British fort was chosen as one of what came to be called the "First American System of Fortifications." The forts were not elaborate as monies for construction were limited: they were usually simple, open works with earthen and sand parapets. The new fort on Cockspur was built in 1794 and 1795, and named Fort Greene, after Revolutionary War hero General Nathaniel Greene. A guardhouse was built for the fort's garrison which arrived in 1800. The new fort was used as was its predecessor, mainly as a quarantine and inspection station; it had a cannon to warn incoming ships to stop for examination. But on the evening of 7 September 1804, a hurricane swept away the fort and half the soldiers stationed there.[9] At the end of 1808, the War Department decided to protect Savannah by building a masonry battery about three miles downriver from the city on the south bank, and at the end of the War of 1812, the six-gun battery there was named Fort Jackson.[10]

No further construction efforts were undertaken after Fort Greene was lost but in 1807, the Napoleonic Wars in Europe spurred President Thomas Jefferson and the U.S. Congress to action. It authorized what became known as the "Second American System of Fortifications." The Second System differed from the First System by greater use of modern concepts and the replacement of foreign engineers by American ones, many of them recent graduates of the United States Military Academy. This new system addressed weaknesses in the First System Forts which exposed gunners to enemy fire as they had mostly open tops and were poorly designed which allowed enfilading fire to wreak havoc along walls of gun batteries. A French engineer, the Marquis de Montalembert, in the late 1770's, designed fortresses to address these problems. A fort's gunners could be protected by placing most of them in covered casemates with walls having small openings for guns. Rows of casemates would be stacked in tiers permitting more guns to be mounted along shorter walls. These walls had to be strong so were built of masonry or stone, and were thick to withstand enemy cannon fire.[11]

While many of the planned Second System forts were not built or completed by the War of 1812, none were captured during the war with Britain. The British were thwarted in their attack on Baltimore, Maryland, by Fort McHenry, a Second System fort, although Washington, D.C., was captured and burned. Seeing that better protection was needed for coastal cities, Congress in 1816 appropriated $800,000 to provide an improved line of defense for coastal ports. President James Madison appointed a Board of Engineers for Fortifications which visited potential sites and prepared plans for new forts. The five-member board consisted of Brevet Brigadier General Simon Bernard, a French engineer under Napoleon, Brevet Brigadier General Joseph G. Swift, chief of engineers, Brevet Colonels William McRee, Joseph G. Totten, and Navy Captain Jessie Duncan Elliot.[12]

[8] HABS No. GA-2158, 2-3; *Fort Pulaski National Monument, Administrative History*, Cameron Binkley, ed. (Washington, DC: U.S. Government, National Park Service, 2003), 3-5; Young, "Connecticut Yankee," 1. A monument to Wesley was erected on Cockspur in 1950 by the Georgia Society of Colonial Dames. First visitors named the island "Peeper Island" thanks to the croaking of its many frogs making their homes on the marshy land.

[9] Ibid.; Ralston B. Lattimore, *Fort Pulaski National Monument, Georgia*; National Park Service Historical Handbook Series No. 18 (Washington, DC: GPO, 1954; reprint 1961), 2-3; Young, "Connecticut Yankee, 2." Totten gave the three systems of fortifications their formal names in his 1851 report to Congress, and designated the Third System's beginning date as 1816. Practically, there was a transition between the designs of the Second and Third systems incorporating features of both types. Ironically with the invention of rifled cannon in the 1840's, earthen forts proved superior to masonry forts as will be seen.

[10] Young, "Connecticut Yankee," 3. Fort Jackson suffered from neglect through the years as attention shifted to Fort Pulaski but it was expanded as will be noted later. It was named after James Jackson who fought for the American rebels during the Revolutionary War. He became a colonel and accepted the surrender of British forces in Savannah. He was later a member of the U.S. Congress and Governor of Georgia.

[11] J.E. Kaufmann, and H.W. Kaufmann, *Fortress America: The Forts that Defended America, 1600 to the Present* (Cambridge, MA: Da Capo Press, 2004), 148.

[12] Young, "Connecticut Yankee," 5-6.

The Board's original 1821 report suggested 50 sites on the Atlantic, Gulf of Mexico, and Pacific coasts, but by 1850 the board had identified nearly 115 sites for fortification. Eventually, forts were only constructed at 42 of these sites, with some additional sites containing towers or batteries. The main defensive works were large structures, based on a combination of the Montalembert concept, with many guns concentrated in tall thick masonry walls, and the Marquis de Vauban (Sébastien Le Prestre de Vauban) concept, with layers of low, protected, masonry walls. Construction was mostly overseen by officers of the U.S. Army's Corps of Engineers. Swift and McRee both considered Bernard's appointment to be an insult to American engineers and resigned from the army in protest. After they left the board, Bernard became its president but worked well with Totten who was bold enough to change some of Bernard's plans. Totten became senior engineer when Bernard returned to France in 1830 so Third System forts were mainly his creations; the Third System also became known as the "Totten System" given the amount of time and effort he invested. Totten became Chief Engineer on 7 December 1838, succeeding Colonel Charles Gratiot, while Mansfield was still engineer in charge of Fort Pulaski. After Bernard left and the Board was reconstituted, supervising engineers at each fort site became associate members when their sites were involved. Army engineers were found to be needed when problems arose with civilian contractors operating without direct military oversight. In anticipation of the Civil War, interest in fort construction was heightened and most Third System forts were quickly completed and armed by the Union government. Federal forts taken by the Confederacy were also improved by the Rebels but construction suffered due to lack of funds; slaves were used for labor but their masters still required compensation. Soon after the Civil War ended, major work on finishing the construction of Third System forts essentially ended. The reduction of Fort Pulaski showed that masonry walls were obsolete with the invention and use of rifled cannon, although in later years, the forts were improved and larger cannon added as the United States remained interested in protecting its coasts against attack.[13]

Fort Pulaski to be built on Cockspur Island was one of the Third System forts Bernard and Totten planned. Cockspur was recommended in February 1819 as the site to protect the river approaches to Savannah. Two years later in March 1821, after general surveys by Captain John Le Conte, who was personally supervised by Bernard, plans were begun. As this new fort was on the second prioritized group of forts to be built, it took over six years for the plans for the new fort on Cockspur to be finished; the plans were officially approved by the Board of Fortifications for Sea Coast Defense in September 1828.[14]

The first U.S. Army Engineer assigned to the construction of the new fort was Major Samuel Babcock, an 1808 graduate of West Point, and an experienced engineer as well as a War of 1812 veteran. He arrived 13 December 1828 after being assigned 1 August, and began work, probably happy to start in the cool, winter months, as his health was poor. His tasks were fundamental and had to be accomplished before actual work on the fort could begin. He began with detailed topographical surveys while overseeing the construction of temporary lodging for himself and workmen he had hired. He needed a dock as he knew materials needed for construction could not be found on the island so he had one commenced on the North Channel of the Savannah River. Of major importance on this swampy island were drainage ditches and embankments which were begun as were excavations for the fort site in February 1829.[15] Babcock soon found that the foundations for the fort would require pilings as the marshy soil was totally inadequate to support a

---

[13] Kaufmann, *Fortress America*, 205; John R. Weaver, II, *A Legacy in Brick and Stone: American Coastal Defense Forts of the Third System, 1816-1867* (McLean, VA: Redoubt Press, 2001), 3-5, 9, 13-17. Some of the 42 built were not completed or fully armed. Swift and McRee were both West Point graduates and received brevet promotions in the War of 1812; McRee resigned effective 31 March 1819, Swift 12 November 1818. Swift was one of the two first graduates of West Point in 1802; McRee graduated in 1805. The Board's 1821 report listed forts to be built/refurbished in three priorities-- Fort Pulaski was in the second priority group, Weaver, 8. Vauban's (1633-1707) designs included works ranged in depth with a system of trenches drawn in broken lines and interconnected by parallel fortifications encircling a city. Attackers must then take each trench one after another then negotiate artillery batteries controlling gaps in the trench lines. He designed his forts on high ground to control the surrounding land, to observe the enemy and help prevent plunging enemy fire. He designed thick walls reinforced by large volumes of fill reinforced by masonry. He included walls equipped with bastions to prevent flanking fire and protected by counterguards which were arrow-shaped detached works in front to help protect the fort against a direct attack. Vauban fortified over 160 locations for France; Paddy Griffith, *The Vauban Fortifications of France* (New York, NY: Osprey Publishing, 2006), passim.

[14] Rogers W. Young, *The Georgia Historical Quarterly*, vol. 20, no. 1, 1936, 41-42; Lattimore, 6. Young wrote that the survey was completed with General Bernard supervising; it was somewhat cursory in that he recommended a heavy brick fort, without pilings, which was unsuitable for the marshy island soil, "Connecticut Yankee," 10-11. Through efforts of a Georgia Congressman, Edward Tattnall, the Cockspur fort was raised to the first priority in 1826, Young, "Connecticut Yankee," 12-14.

[15] Young, *Georgia Historical Quarterly*, 42. Babcock graduated from West Point in less than two years meaning that his formal engineering education was limited compared to Mansfield's who spent five years at West Point. His poor health though was a major issue. Babcock was involved with Bernard and Totten in reviewing plans for the fort made by the Chief of Engineers.

heavy weight. He planned on using "piling or grillage or both" for the "wood work" of the foundation. The Engineer Department was surprised at this news and required further explanations from Babcock.[16]

A description of the proposed fort appeared on 31 December 1828, in a Savannah newspaper, with Babcock the likely source:

> It is to be…<u>Casemated</u>: the form of the work pentagonal, and will mount 136 guns, in three tiers; the two lower tiers are to be covered with bomb proof arches; the sally (or gateway) will be covered by a work called a <u>Demi-lune</u>; the whole will be surrounded by a ditch about 40 feet in width—in advance of the main work, is to be constructed an open battery, for mortars and howitzers. The permanent quarters for the troops will form that part of the main work, called the gorge—in the interior of the work will be located the furnace for heating shot—height of wall about 30 feet—a canal will connect the ditch of the work with the river, by which means it may be emptied and replenished at pleasure.[17]

Babcock had to deal with the problem of ownership of the island immediately upon his arrival. The 20 acre reserve on Cockspur Point where the two original forts were built was given by the British Crown to the State of Georgia which could be donated to the United States. But the remaining 150 acres of the western portion was granted in 1759 by the British Crown to Jonathan Bryan. Eventually it passed to the heirs of Georgia Governor Edward Telfair represented by Alexander Telfair. The United States finally bought this land for $5,000 on 15 March 1830, but it took another 15 years for the State of Georgia to cede its holdings on Cockspur Point.[18] Babcock left the island in June to avoid the extreme summer heat and arrived in Newcastle, Delaware, on 24 June 1829. He had left an overseer, William Kearney, and six workmen to maintain the ditches and secure government property.[19]

Beginning in late 1829, Babcock was assisted in this large project by a newly-graduated (July 1829) West Point engineer, Second Lieutenant Robert E. Lee, on his first tour of duty. The first order Lee ever received from the Engineer Department was 11 August 1829 which directed him to report to Babcock by the middle of November for duty at Cockspur Island. Lee, in the American Civil War, became the general commanding the best army in the Confederacy, the Army of Northern Virginia. Lee was Babcock's assistant engineer but he practically took over for Babcock as his superior was usually ill with fever and suffered greatly from the heat.[20]

Babcock's (and Mansfield's famous future) assistant, Lee, departed for Savannah by coastal steamer in late October 1829 and arrived at Georgia's principal port and largest city about 1 November. The young lieutenant, while waiting in Savannah for the return of Babcock from the north, passed several pleasant weeks since a classmate of his, Second Lieutenant John Mackay, was stationed at Oglethorpe Barracks in Savannah. Mackay's family welcomed Lee and he enjoyed all the pleasantness that the society of this quintessential southern city could offer.

Babcock finally returned to Savannah with his family on 23 December 1829. He learned that he had a new assistant, Lee, and that the overseer, Kearney, had drowned in October. Among Lee's highest priorities was constructing quarters for Babcock and himself as well as the laborers. Other priorities included construction of a wharf at the northern part of the island on the North Channel of the Savannah River and starting excavation of drainage systems and embankments on the marshy land. The temporary quarters were ready by early May 1830 so Lee and Babcock were able to live on Cockspur giving up the easy life in Savannah. Construction continued until early in July when Babcock and Lee took leave to return north avoiding the pestilential heat of the island. Babcock's doctors in Savannah had recommended in June 1830 that he leave the island "as soon as possible" to recover his health; he left in July 1830, resigned his commission on 22 December 1830, and returned home. He died 6 months later on 26 June 1831, in Connecticut. When Lee returned in November 1830, he found much of the work which he and Babcock accomplished undone by a recent storm, so Lee had to begin immediate repairs. Lee and a small crew of workmen began to repair the main embankment and reopen filled-in canals. Another storm raged in December but Lee's repairs proved adequate to prevent further damage. Lee, the new and inexperienced officer, undoubtedly wished for the arrival of a senior officer as Babcock left

---

[16] Young, "Connecticut Yankee," 19. Babcock wrote that 22 soil experiments showed that piling was necessary under most of the fort.

[17] Young, "Connecticut Yankee," 18. The newspaper was *The Daily Georgian*. This plan reflected the original plan drawn up by the Board of Engineers for Fortifications. The number of guns planned varied up to 172.

[18] Lattimore, 6.

[19] Young, "Connecticut Yankee," 21.

[20] Lattimore, 7; Young, 42; Douglas Southall Freeman, *R. E. Lee: A Biography*, vol. 1 (New York: Charles Scribner's Sons, 1936), 94; Rogers W. Young, "Robert E. Lee and Fort Pulaski," National Park Service Popular Study Series, History No. 11 (Washington, DC: U.S. Government Printing Office, 1941), 5-6; Records Section, Office, Chief of Engineers (RSOCE), file no. B1038, 2 July 1830.

affairs on the island in disorder. His hopes were answered when he received a letter from the Engineer Department 20 December 1830 informing him that Babcock had been replaced as superintendent by First Lieutenant Joseph K.F. Mansfield.[21]

Lieutenant Robert E. Lee as a young engineer officer in 1838 after he was Mansfield's assistant at Fort Pulaski in 1831. Courtesy Wikipedia.

1830-1831

The engineer officer who became the chief builder and the "Father of Fort Pulaski" arrived, likely not thinking that he would spend the majority of his time as an engineer officer in the army in what would become a 14-year assignment. While Lieutenant Mansfield was only a year older than Lee, he already had several years of experience in fort construction including Fort Hamilton, New York; Fort Johnson, Charleston, South Carolina; and Forts Monroe and Calhoun, Virginia. On 18 December 1830, the Engineering Department ordered Mansfield to take charge of the new fort's construction; he left Hampton Roads on the schooner *Cypress* stopping in Charleston, South Carolina, where he transferred to the schooner *Spy* arriving at Savannah. He finally hired a boat from Savannah to Cockspur Island, assuming command 21 January 1831. The Department's order instructed him to inventory the materials and public stores there with the help of Lieutenant Robert E. Lee, and report "the actual condition of the works."[22]

The capable and driven Nutmegger quickly found that despite the efforts of Babcock and Lee, much of what they accomplished was unacceptable. And importantly, Babcock left almost no written records of his actions on the island and those that were left were haphazard, so Mansfield wrote to Washington that he could "find no plans of what were the ideas of Major Babcock in relation to it [the works], and no plans as yet of what has actually been done." He wrote Chief Engineer Gratiot on 23 January that he ordered Lee to "make a Survey and Plan of the Island and the additions to it by Major Babcock, which with his zeal and industry will occupy but a few days and then the site and commencement of the body of the work will immediately be examined, fixed and take place."[23] And for the first time, Mansfield wrote

---

[21] Young, "Robert E. Lee," 1-10; Lattimore, 6-7; Freeman, 94-96; Young, "Connecticut Yankee," 22. No record has been found showing that Mansfield stayed with the Mackay's so likely he stayed in a hotel. During Mansfield's long stay at Cockspur, it is likely that he did visit Savannah perhaps combining business-related trips there with social functions. The island is "essentially a mud and marsh island, containing a few low sand ridges" presenting engineering challenges, Lattimore, 4; Young, "Robert E. Lee's First Tour of Army Duty Was on Fort Pulaski Project," *Savannah Morning News*, 2 December 1934. Babcock admitted in a 26 October letter to the Engineer Department that when he left in July he was too ill "to think of office matters" but would make his required reports when he returned to Cockspur; Young, 22.

[22] Young, Connecticut Yankee, 35-38. The Engineer Department order called his assignment "temporary." Young, "Story of Gen. Mansfield," *Savannah Morning News*, 3 February 1935; RSOCE, file no. M731, 23 December 1830; M739, 31 January 1831.

[23] Young, "Robert E. Lee's First Tour, *Savannah Morning News*, 2 December 1934.

that he would probably have to make changes in the original plans for the fort, asking the Department to approve his requests: "To build the work on a strong grillage and to alter the section and profile of the foundation accordingly and to execute that part of the Body of the work below the parade in brick which is on the plan represent in Stone." He opined that brick was cheaper, lighter in weight, more readily available, and adequate for the purpose. Then in February, he told Gratiot that because of what he found when he examined the soil on the island, he believed that the fort's site must be changed. The Department quickly ordered Mansfield on 1 February to make a complete examination of the soil and to report his findings to allow the Department to determine if changes were in fact needed. The foundation of the fort was critical as it supported the immense weight of the fort which had to last for many decades.[24]

Babcock's poor record keeping was also manifest in his accounts. Creditors assailed Mansfield who could find few, if any, records regarding contracts, payments, etc., among Babcock's records. Mansfield proposed, and the Department agreed, that he should start fresh on the first of February, so when a timber contractor asserted his right to payment, he was denied as Mansfield could find no evidence that such a contract ever existed; the Secretary of War, John W. Eaton, approved the young lieutenant's decision.[25] Mansfield also sent the paperwork for the title and deed for the island to the Department on 4 February as Babcock had neglected to do so. Mansfield was clearly making his presence felt and the Department had to be aware that it had made the correct decision by replacing Babcock with Mansfield.[26]

The new supervising engineer decided not to wait for authorization from the Department as he immediately began advertising for laborers in the *Savannah Georgian* newspaper on 26 January 1831, for "Fifty Stout Negro Laborers" and then two days later, for "one hundred white or black laborers by the year, month, or day." Next on 12 February, Mansfield advertised for oak and pine firewood to be delivered on the fort's wharf.[27] Of course Mansfield would let no contracts without permission from the Department but he obviously was seeking information on costs and availability so when the time came to actually restart work on the fort, he would be ready with data to support his requests.

Mansfield wasted no time in informing the Department about Cockspur's soil as on 16 and 26 February he reported that the soil by itself was inadequate to support the fort's foundation:

> 1st. That the Island is generally one complete deposit of mud from up the river. 2nd. That it is spiced throughout with small oyster beds that afford but little or no resistance in as much as they are not thick and seated on mud. 3rd. That occasionally very fine sand is mixed in with the mud but not uniformly as to quantity in strata but rather in patches and then in a small proportion to the mud. 4th. That a horizontal passed thro the high water level will cut off all the heterogeneous matter of which the ridge (which runs across the Island) is composed. 5th. That the mud of the Island when the water is empounded is hard, firm and more or less tenacious. 6th. That there is no such a stratum within a reasonable distance of the surface as a firm bed of sand.[28]

On 8 March 1831, Mansfield submitted his assessment of the Cockspur situation to the Department, and included a survey and topographic map of the island which Lee had finished. His survey showed the high water line, dikes completed, and drainage ditches. Lee also sketched the temporary quarters which included Mansfield's quarters, Lee's office and quarters, the overseer's and boatmen's quarters, and a stone house. There were also two barracks for laborers, a hurricane (storm) house located on slightly higher ground just west of the proposed fort location, and a bake house.

---

[24] Young opined that Babcock's poor performance was due to his age, poor health, "and his understaffed command;" Connecticut Yankee, 23. Also, the fort's site was mostly dictated by Bernard's plans. Young, "Story of Gen. Mansfield," *Savannah Morning News*, 3 February 1935. Grillage was necessary for use in soils with poor loadbearing capacity so loads could be spread over a wider area. Piles were driven in the soil until they reached a level determined to be adequate, then heavy planks were set side by side with no gaps on the piles then a second course of planks were set over the first laid at right angles; these could have wider gaps. This grillage and pile combination was a routine engineering response to building on poor ground and was first recommended by Babcock. That the fort's walls have survived for 180 years shows that Mansfield's engineering skills were excellent. For the walls of the fort, grillage was placed on piles while on other locations such as for pavement access at sluices, grillage was laid directly on excavated ground and no piles used. RSOCE, M1476, 4 June 1845. Grillage timbers measured one foot by one foot, while grillage planks were one foot wide and three inches thick. RSOCE, M742, 23 January 1831. His estimate for grillage materials for the fourth quarter of 1831 was 13,393 running yards of the one foot beams and 6,863 of the one foot by 3 inch planking.

[25] Young, "Connecticut Yankee, 39-44;" Young, "Story of Gen. Mansfield," *Savannah Morning News*, 3 February 1935; RSOCE, M731, 23 January 1831.

[26] Young, "Connecticut Yankee," 42; RSOCE, M747, 4 February 1831; M749, 1 February 1831.

[27] Young, "Story of Gen. Mansfield," *Savannah Morning News*, 3 February 1935. This shows that the North Dock was completed sufficiently to offload three boat loads of wood.

[28] Young, "Connecticut Yankee," 45; Young, "Story of Gen. Mansfield," *Savannah Morning News*, 3 February 1935; Young, "Story of Gen. Mansfield," *Savannah Morning News*, 3 February 1935; RSOCE, M758, 26 February 1831. Young notes that Mansfield's assessment of the soil conditions is similar to what exists in modern times, and that Mansfield's report supported Babcock that pilings would be required under the fort's foundations. As will be seen, Mansfield did eventually find a layer of sand under part of the fort site.

The bake house was certainly a welcomed addition. He also showed the boat house of the U.S. Revenue Department and the locations of the beacon, and north dock. These were built of wood frame construction about five feet above ground.[29]

But in this early March report, Mansfield found fault with most of what Babcock had accomplished. The dikes on the western side were "lost labor" and the sites of the boatmen's and laborer's quarters "injudiciously selected because of their exposure to northeast storms." The North Dock was faulty and was a wreck because it was built on mud, not pilings and the bath house was "an unauthorized expenditure of public money" as it was poorly constructed on piles which were not coppered. His most important criticism however, was that Babcock sited the fort poorly since it did not cover as well as it could both the North and South Channels of the Savannah River. Too, the site previously selected was on poorer soil. Perhaps Mansfield was not concerned with Babcock's reputation as the veteran engineer had by this time retired, or it may have been that Babcock's administration and engineering for Pulaski was remarkably poor, probably due to his ill health and age. A few days later, Mansfield wrote again supplying more details about Babcock's lack of any effective administration and his "curious method of doing business."[30]

The Engineer Department on 9 March commented on Mansfield's report which had concurred with Babcock's about the necessity for pilings under the foundations. Gratiot was not convinced yet of that need so he told Mansfield that he would send an engineer experienced in such soil conditions due to his Louisiana service—Captain Richard Delafield—who would arrive near the end of March to consult. The Department told Mansfield that after he conferred with Delafield, Mansfield should submit a report detailing the final opinion about the foundations and a comparative estimate of the costs. Delafield arrived late in March 1831 and began reviewing Mansfield's plans and examining the island. The Department meanwhile decided on 26 March to send Lee to Hampton Roads as work on Cockspur was likely to be suspended for the summer months. Lee, in a jovial manner, wrote to a lady friend, Catherine Mackay, on 13 April 1831 that "Capt. Delafield has arrived and is in high consultation about Foundations, Grillage, Piles and what not. And I have made them more little troublesome plans and worse calculations about weight, cost, etc., of Masonry, lime, sand and such stuff than I intend to do tomorrow, And that's the certain of it. Will you believe that they are still at it, and have just touched upon cranes, With "Lee give us a sketch of that?" But I happened to have my watch in my hand and seeing that it was ten minutes to 11 P.M. says: "Yes Capt. Tomorrow."[31] Lee likely was happy since he had learned on 26 March that he would be transferred to Hampton Roads even though Mansfield told Gratiot that he would require Lee's assistance for a short while as Captain Delafield and he were drawing up new plans. Lee finally finished his work and Mansfield, on 21 April, sent him to Old Point Comfort, Virginia, to report to Captain Andrew Talcott for duty.[32] Mansfield and his capable, but inexperienced assistant engineer, Lee, remained in the U.S. Army but did not serve together again. They were both at the Battle of Antietam 17 September 1862, where General Lee commanded the Army of Northern Virginia, and Brigadier General Mansfield, the XII Corps in the Army of the Potomac.

[29] Young, "Connecticut Yankee," 47; Young, "Cockspur Island Had Presented Problem in Building Fort Pulaski," Savannah Morning News, 17 February 1935, A5; Mansfield letter to General Charles Gratiot, 30 September 1831, NA; RSOCE M765, 8 March 1831; David P. Eldridge, "Brick Versus Earth: The Construction and Destruction of Confederate Seacoast Forts Pulaski and McAllister, Georgia," unpublished master's thesis, University of North Florida, 1996, 28, 33. Up to twenty-five hundred pilings were required to support each wall; it took four years alone to finish the foundation, 33, 35.

[30] Young, "Connecticut Yankee," 48-49; Young, "Mansfield and Lee Make Progress With Survey of New Fort on Cockspur," Savannah Morning News, 10 February 1935; RSOCE, M765, 8 March 1831. Young opined in this article that Mansfield's diatribe was usual as he "was prone to administer sharp reproof though, whenever or whenever he encountered inability or inefficiency."

[31] Young, "Robert E. Lee's First Tour, Savannah Morning News, 2 December 1934; RSOCE, M783 Mansfield to Gratiot 4 April 1831. A reader may dismiss Lee's apparent lack of desire to endure the late hour with his two, senior engineers, with his wish to impress his lady friend that he values writing to her more than being an amanuensis for Mansfield and Delafield. On the other hand, it may be that he was taking a more casual approach as he had already been informed that he would be transferred to Hampton Roads. In any event, it is unbecoming for such a junior officer to appear to shirk his duty due merely to the lateness of the hour.

[32] RSOCE, M795, 21 April 1831.

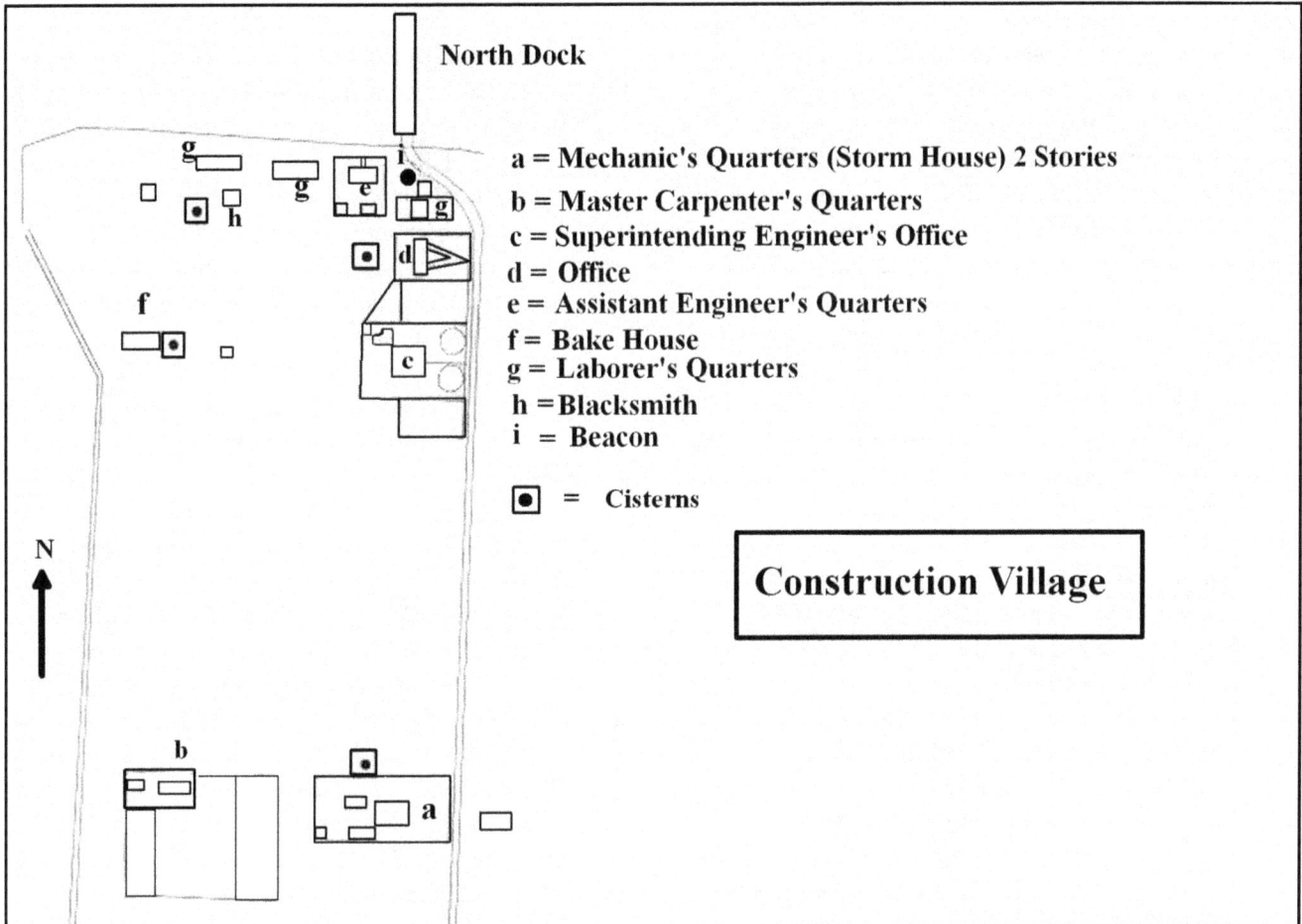

North Dock

a = Mechanic's Quarters (Storm House) 2 Stories
b = Master Carpenter's Quarters
c = Superintending Engineer's Office
d = Office
e = Assistant Engineer's Quarters
f = Bake House
g = Laborer's Quarters
h = Blacksmith
i = Beacon

◉ = Cisterns

Construction Village

Construction Village 1830-1831 adapted from Mansfield/Lee maps. The construction village as drawn by Mansfield in 1831 consisted of three laborers quarters, a bakehouse, a mechanics boarding house (storm house), master workman's (mechanic's) quarters, superintending engineers quarters, an office, assistant engineering quarters, a blacksmith shop, a stable, a customs/boatmen's house, and associated cisterns. The workmen's village and associated structures dating from the 1830's to 1840's are gone leaving only a few foundations, cisterns, and fireplaces, mostly covered and overgrown. Courtesy NPS.

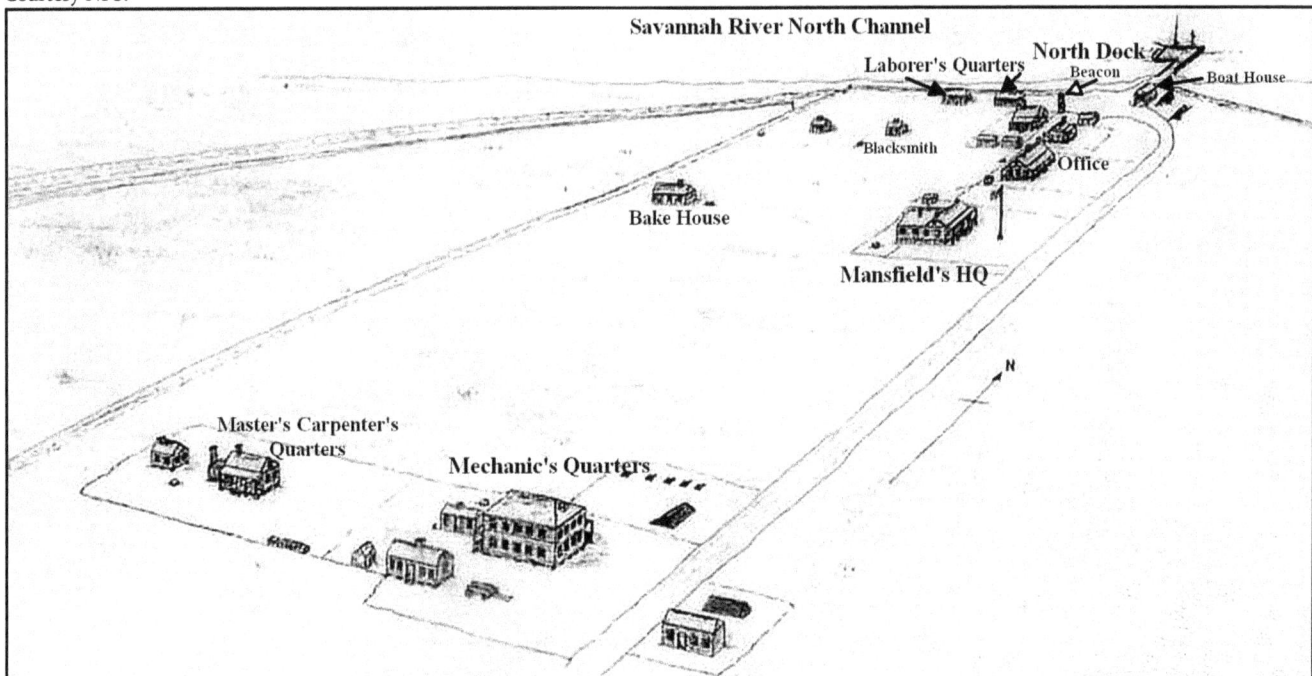

A sketch of the construction village as it would have appeared in the mid-1830's. Courtesy NPS.

Mansfield and Delafield continued their deliberations but Mansfield again decided that regardless of the outcome of their studies and the Department's decision, he would need building materials as it was unlikely that the Department would not continue the fort's construction. He sent two advertisements to the *Savannah Georgian* on 15 April soliciting bids for twenty thousand bushels of first quality, salt-free sand, and two million first quality, hard burnt brick. The total number of bricks used would eventually total about 10 million. The spring of 1831 was not an idle time even though Mansfield was deeply involved with Delafield and the new plans for the fort. Workmen built a new wharf on the South Channel opposite the fort site, a lime house, a blacksmith's shop, and a carpenter shop. Mansfield wisely considered a canal necessary so had laborers dig a 25-foot-wide, three-foot-deep ditch connecting the South Channel dock with the fort site. In 1832, it connected with a 15-foot-wide, three-foot-deep canal dug around the foundation excavation enabling materials such as brick to be easily transported from boats to the construction site.[33]

After Delafield returned to Washington with his report, the Department decided by May that the Board of Engineers must revise all of the fort's original plans. It ordered Mansfield to suspend work until the revision could be finished, and he was ordered to become a member of the Board for the revision. In addition, "you will repair to Newport R. Island, at which place the Board will meet, taking with you besides your own notes and drawings, the plan and memoir of the Board and the accompanying copy of Capt. Delafield's report." He received the Department's order on 11 May, and he immediately wrote a letter stating that he planned on leaving as soon as possible after June 2 and to arrive in Newport about 24 June.[34]

Mansfield's summer "vacation" proved to be anything but, as he had great difficulty in meeting with the Board of which he was a temporary member. The problem was that he was to confer with the two permanent members of the Board, Brigadier General Simon Bernard and Colonel Joseph G. Totten. Since Bernard was out of the country, Mansfield went to Newport to confer with his cousin Totten. But after he reached New York in the middle of June, he received news that Bernard was scheduled to return to Washington, D.C., so Mansfield was quickly ordered to Washington to meet with Bernard as the general was primarily responsible for the fort's original plans. Mansfield spent much of June and July waiting for Bernard but the Department finally told him on 16 July that Bernard would not be available as he decided to stay in France; Bernard had resigned from the U.S. Army 8 July 1831. The likely exasperated Mansfield repacked his paperwork and returned to Newport to meet with the remaining member of the Board, Totten. Finally, Mansfield was able to confer at length with the colonel to convince him of the necessity of revising the plans. He succeeded, so by 30 September Mansfield forwarded to the Department the revised plans, and told it he would remain in Newport a few more days, then journey to Middletown. In an uncharacteristically quick response, the Department on 4 October approved the revisions and informed Mansfield on the 6th that "You will accordingly proceed in its execution as early as practicable."[35]

Within a year from first arriving at Cockspur Island, Mansfield had moved the project from a state of confusion, inadequate planning, and poor implementation, to a point where he could begin to build a fort which would truly serve for many decades to defend Savannah, even though the advent of rifled cannon would lead to disaster early in the Civil War. The most important change to the original plan was Mansfield's insistence that due to poor soil conditions, pilings and grillage were clearly necessary as Babcock stated. Another change allowed the substitution of brick for stone for the foundation as well as the fort proper, and along with reducing the original three tiers to two, with a timber platform for the floor of the remaining bottom tier instead of earth. Thus the structure would be lighter but the reduction in the number of guns due to removal of the third tier required that the walls be lengthened so the total number of guns remained the same as in the original plan. A new, larger demilune surrounded by a moat would protect the drawbridge; the new total of guns would be 172 vice 143 which included those in the demilune. Mansfield also had his way in siting the new design at least by having his suggested change superimposed over the old one so most excavations already done

[33] Young, "Connecticut Yankee," 52, 55; Young, "Mansfield and Lee Make Progress With Survey of New Fort on Cockspur," *Savannah Morning News*, 10 February 1935; Young, "Cockspur Island Had Presented Problem in Building Fort Pulaski," *Savannah Morning News*, 17 February 1935; RSOCE, M943, 10 April 1832. The canal Babcock built from the North Channel dock to the fort site was abandoned when Mansfield built the South Channel wharf and a temporary canal to it. The old north canal was filled in in the early 1850's; Young, "Connecticut Yankee," 70-71.

[34] Young, "Connecticut Yankee," 56; Young, "Mansfield and Lee Make Progress With Survey of New Fort on Cockspur," *Savannah Morning News*, 10 February 1935; HABS No. GA-2158, 7; RSOCE, M809, 11 May 1831. Totten was at Newport supervising work on Fort Adams there.

[35] Young, "Connecticut Yankee," 57-59; Young, "Mansfield and Lee Make Progress With Survey of New Fort on Cockspur," *Savannah Morning News*, 10 February 1935; RSOCE, M822, 25 June 1831. Bernard informed Gratiot of his resignation 11 July 1831. Since Totten met with Mansfield in Newport, Rhode Island, the revised plans were "pre-approved."

could be used. The report gave a detailed estimate of $374,600 for the fort's completion which, as in virtually all Federal government projects even to the present day, was far too small as the actual total cost exceeded $1,000,000.[36]

Mansfield's life for the next 14 years fell into a routine of sorts: first, and most difficult, was obtaining funds from the Department (from Congressional appropriations) to continue construction during each fiscal year. Then, based on funding (or projected) funding, to plan the work which involved two main requirements: materials and workers. The second part of his routine was his travels north mainly during the summers months to avoid the heat, humidity, and malaria, as well as to negotiate contracts for materials. Spending time at his Middletown home "headquarters" attending to his private business and family was certainly a welcomed respite. During these months as well as other periods, he worked on various other engineering projects as the Department ordered. Thirdly, he spent much of his time in reporting the progress on Cockspur Island monthly, quarterly, and annually, and writing to the Engineer Department reporting on, and arguing about, various construction details. Both Mansfield and his first assistant engineer, Robert E. Lee, married during one of their summer "vacations" in the north.[37]

Mansfield's 2 October report to the Department for the year to 30 September 1831, written in Newport, reflected his hard work even though no fort construction had begun. The original plans for the fort had been revised and approved and infrastructure needed to begin actual work on the foundations was well along. Additionally, he had put the business of the fort's construction in order so that accounts, contracts, etc., were properly kept. Finally, he had obtained needed building materials in and around Savannah—brick, sand, timber, and lime—as well as hiring laborers, mainly negro slaves, but also a few white mechanics from the north, to work during the cooler months. He interrupted his return journey to Cockspur by a sojourn at his home in Middletown, Connecticut. He left for Cockspur late in October and arrived 7 November to begin work again.[38]

1831-1832

Mansfield was ready to begin building the fort's foundations so he advertised on 3 December 1831 for 900,000 feet of first quality timber and 50,000 feet three-inch plank. He also advertised on the 14th for an additional 100 white or black laborers to augment those on hand. Cooler months must involve heavier labor so he needed more help as soon as possible as the foundation was being dug. To his surprise as he laid out the site according to the new plans, he discovered a "large, firm bed of white sand" nine feet under most of the north wall site and under some of the southeast wall. This meant that he had a new engineering problem as this sand bed provided firmer support for the grillage and piles as compared to the mud and soft earth under other parts of the proposed foundations. He must make adjustments to ensure equal resistance for pilings so walls over both types of soils would be stable. Thousands of wooden piles were pounded through the Cockspur silt and mud into solid sand 60 to 70 feet deep. Mansfield used a manual pile driver to ensure that

---

[36] Young, "Connecticut Yankee," 59-60; Young, "Mansfield and Lee Make Progress With Survey of New Fort on Cockspur," *Savannah Morning News*, 10 February 1935; RG 77, Box 107, M976, from Eldridge, 35; Young, "The Construction of Fort Pulaski," 51. As will be seen, Mansfield had other suggestions one of which, bricking of the scarp and counterscarp, took years to convince the Engineer Department of the need. A scarp is the inner, fort side, of the moat, and the counterscarp the outer side. Mansfield was convinced that the soft sands required that both the scarp and counterscarp be bricked. See Attachment 1 for a glossary of terms.

[37] The first fiscal year for the U.S. Government started 1 January 1789 and ended on December 31, but Congress changed the beginning date of the fiscal year to 1 July in 1842, and finally to 1 October in 1977 where it remains today. Note that Mansfield sometimes submits a report he calls an "Annual Statement" which for 1842 shows "Expenditures 30 Sept. 1841 to 30 Sept. 1842" which shows that this year is often used for engineering reports even though it is not the official fiscal year; RSOCE, M896, 5 October 1842. Lee married Mary Custis on 30 June 1831, while he was stationed at Fort Monroe. He had courted Mary Custis during the summer of 1829 and he obtained permission to write to her before he left for Cockspur. She accepted his proposal with her father's consent in September 1830, while he was on summer leave. "The engineer superintending the construction of a fortification…is required to furnish to the engineer department the following stated reports, returns and estimates: an annual report of the progress of the operations during, and their condition at, the expiration of the year ending on the 30th September, comprising a statement…together with drawings illustrative, and a memoir explanatory, thereof; the memoir also to contain a narrative of the progress of the operations from their commencement, a review of the resources of the country adapted to the purposes of construction, a statement of contracts entered into within the year, and the character and resources of the contractors…a monthly report of the progress of operations, comprising a return of materials…a general quarterly return of property, shewing its condition at the commencement and expiration of the quarter, and tracing its alteration, from previous returns…a special quarterly return of the equipage and appurtenances of each vessel employed in the operations and belonging to the United States" and quarterly returns for provisions for the subsistence of persons employed, and a quarterly return for purchases and forage for horses, mules and oxen; *General Regulation for the Army of the United States, 1825*, 169.

[38] Young, "Connecticut Yankee," 61-62; Young, "Cockspur Island Had Presented Problem in Building Fort Pulaski," *Savannah Morning News*, 17 February 1935; RSOCE, M852, 2 October 1831.

the piles were well-set, and then he built a platform (grillage) of two levels of heavy beams each set at right angles to the other providing a level, sturdy platform for the ramparts (walls). The fort walls today demonstrate how well this fundamentally important part of the construction was done as they are in remarkably good condition.[39] The Department approved his changes for the foundations and on 10 April 1832, he submitted his plans for the remainder of the year. He planned on finishing the excavation for the foundation and a service canal around it and completing the entire grillage. He used a screw pump operated by horse power to keep water out of the foundations and placed the earth dug as a five-foot high dike around the foundation to protect it. Half the grillage on the north side had been laid and the piling for the southeast wall had been driven. Before all his plans were completed, he realized that the hot months were approaching so asked the Department on 2 June to allow him to suspend work from 1 July to 1 November. During this time, he would go north to buy building materials; when the Department approved he sailed north. But he found that the Department, always short of qualified engineers, found work for him for his summer "vacation" on the National Road.[40]

Mansfield began work 22 July 1832 on the National Road to oversee repairs east of the Ohio River. Chief of Engineers Gratiot, instructed him "to examine, make estimates and let contracts for overhauling the road, beginning with the worst sections."[41] Mansfield used the new system of road paving invented by Scotsman John Loudon McAdam. Its use in 1823 on the National Road was the first time that true macadam was used in the United States.[42]

The part of the road from Baltimore to Cumberland, Maryland, was generally known as the "National Pike" before the entire road from Baltimore to Vandalia, Illinois, was named the "National Road." The first National Road, authorized by President Thomas Jefferson in 1806, ran from Cumberland to Wheeling, Virginia; it was begun in 1811 and completed in 1818. Commercial banks supplied the funding for the Baltimore to Cumberland section so was called the "Bank Road." It was completed to Cumberland except for a few sections by 1820.[43]

When Mansfield arrived and looked at the road, he was shocked and dismayed. "The turnpike was in horrible condition, he wrote to Gratiot in August 1832, and 'every rod of it will require great repair. Some of it was impassable.'" Gratiot, in the Annual Report of the Corps of Engineers, 13 November 1832, wrote the following: "Lieutenant Mansfield, the officer who had temporary management of the affairs of this road, has done all that zeal, aided by sound judgment, could effect." By the end of 1835, the road was mostly finished east of the Ohio River. The Federal government spent over $900,000 to make it useable. On 5 October 1832, the Department ordered "him to turn over the property and funds in relation to the National Road to Captain Delafield and to proceed back to Savannah."[44]

---

[39] RSOCE, M943, 10 April 1831. The steam pile driver was not invented and put into use until the late 1840's so Mansfield could not have used this wonderful, labor-saving device. James Nasmyth, a Scottish engineer, demonstrated his new steam pile driver in 1845, while Otis Tufts of Cambridge, Massachusetts, had worked on a steam pile driver in the early 1840's; he did not patent it. Mansfield used his steam engines for pumping water and to power some tools. Mansfield spent $125 on a "pile engine" in 1836 in his report to the Department of expenditures prior to 30 September 1836. He never wrote about a steam powered driver, however, and always differentiates between a "pile engine" and "steam engine." "Engine" was used for devices which converted one form of energy to another, so in the case of the pile engine, it used human energy to lift a weight to drive a pile using the advantage of pulleys.

[40] Young, "Connecticut Yankee," 75; Young, "Cockspur Island Had Presented Problem in Building Fort Pulaski," *Savannah Morning News*, 17 February 1935; RSOCE, M943, 10 April 1832; RSOCE, M966, 2 June 1832.

[41] Harold Kanarek, *The Mid-Atlantic Engineers: A History of the Baltimore District, U.S. Army Corps of Engineers, 1774-1974* (Washington, DC: U.S. Government Printing Office, 1976), 15-16, 25.

[42] National Road workmen, some wearing goggles to protect their eyes, pounded stones (limestone, flint, or granite) into pieces with small hammers then inspectors passed each stone through rings assuring the correct size. It consisted of creating three layers of stones laid on a crowned sub grade with side ditches for drainage. The first two layers consisted of angular hand-broken aggregate, maximum size 3 inches, to a total depth of about 8 inches. The third layer was about 2 inches thick with a maximum aggregate size of 1 inch. Each layer would be compacted with a heavy cast-iron roller, causing the angular stones to lock together. The top layer, cemented with rainwater, became very hard and durable, albeit very dusty in dry weather. Gratiot suggested that the total stone covering be nine inches for rough sections but hauling good limestone from valleys and creek beds was costly as no good materials could be found close to the road; http://en.wikipedia.org/wiki/Macadam; Kanarek, 15.

[43] "One of the gaps was a 10-mile section between Hagerstown and Boonsboro, Maryland. A turnpike company was formed to close the gap, with the banks again buying the stock in exchange for another extension of their charters (to 1845). This section of the Bank Road has the distinction of being the first use in the United States of the principles of road building conceived by John Loudon McAdam, whose name gave the pavement its name. According to historian Albert Rose: The work consisted of resurfacing a former county road. This section was in a sad state of deterioration, in 1821, and in winter, stages required from 5 to 7 hours to cover the 10 mile distance. Contracts for reconstructing the road were advertised by William Lorman, the first president of the turnpike company, in September 1822. The superintendent of construction was John W. Davis of Allegany County, Maryland. The surfacing was completed in 1823." Federal Highway Administration website: http://www.fhwa.dot.gov/infrastructure/bankroad.cfm.

[44] Kanarek, 15-16, 17, 25. Captain Richard Delafield who succeeded Mansfield in October was also dismissed; Young, "Cockspur Island Had Presented Problem in Building Fort Pulaski," *Savannah Morning News*, 17 February 1935.

1832-1833

But the Department's orders were overtaken by the problems with the National Road's progress. Mansfield did not leave the north until late in December 1832 reaching Cockspur on 3 January 1833. He immediately resumed work on finishing the laying of the grillage and the piles on the southern foundation. On 20 March, Mansfield sent to the Department his plans for the rest of 1833. He had two main objectives: begin masonry work and "to drive the piles for the southern half of the work and to lay the grillage thereon and weigh down the same by deposits of brick to secure it against any accidental overflowing of the sea." He had already on 20 February 1833 advertised for one million bricks to be delivered by September 1833. On 21 March he already had four bids, the lowest from Henry McAlpin of Savannah at $11.50 per thousand ($11,500), for the well-known "Savannah Grey" brick which was an oversize sand and clay brick; McAlpin owned a large brickyard at his plantation, The Hermitage, about 2½ miles west of Savannah on the river. Mansfield forwarded a contract to the Department but requested permission to buy brick on the open market as this price could be had independent of a contract. This unprecedented request was denied.[45] The unnamed fort on Cockspur finally received its name, Fort Pulaski, on 18 April 1833.[46]

---

[45] Young, "Cockspur Island Had Presented Problem in Building Fort Pulaski," *Savannah Morning News*, 17 February 1935. Mansfield wrote that the grillage was to be placed on the piles. Sometimes, the wooden piles were placed on top of the grillage. Given Mansfield's descriptions, he used grillage on top of piles for the walls. "When timber grillage is used, it should be kept entirely below the lowest recorded water line or it will rot and allow the foundation to settle, but sound timber will last indefinitely if completely immersed in water. The advantages of timber grillage are that the timbers are easily laid and hold the tops of the piles in place....It also tends to distribute the pressure evenly over the piles, as the transverse strength of the timber assists in carrying the load over any single pile, which may not have the same bearing capacity as the others. Georgia pine makes excellent grillage;" Frank E. Kidder, *Building Construction and Superintendence*, vol. 1 (New York, NY: The William T. Comstock Company, 1920), 38-39, 68. Laying grillage first requires more digging but no pile driving.

[46] Young, "Connecticut Yankee," 78-80; RSOCE, M1133, 3 May 1833; Mansfield first used name "Pulaski." Count Casimir Pulaski was a Polish count and an experienced soldier in Europe. As a result of his bravery at the Battle of Brandywine, Congress made him a brigadier general in the Continental Army cavalry. He eventually wound up in Savannah and commanded the French and American cavalry. On 9 October 1779, while rallying fleeing French forces during a cavalry charge, Pulaski was mortally wounded by grapeshot. He died two days later aboard the privateer *Wasp*, and was buried at sea. Other accounts have him buried at Greenwich Plantation near Savannah; remains found at Monterey Square in Savannah were also alleged to be his but the actual location of his remains is in dispute. The Hermitage, a plantation just outside of Savannah, owned by McAlpin supplied from its furnace many bricks for the fort's construction.

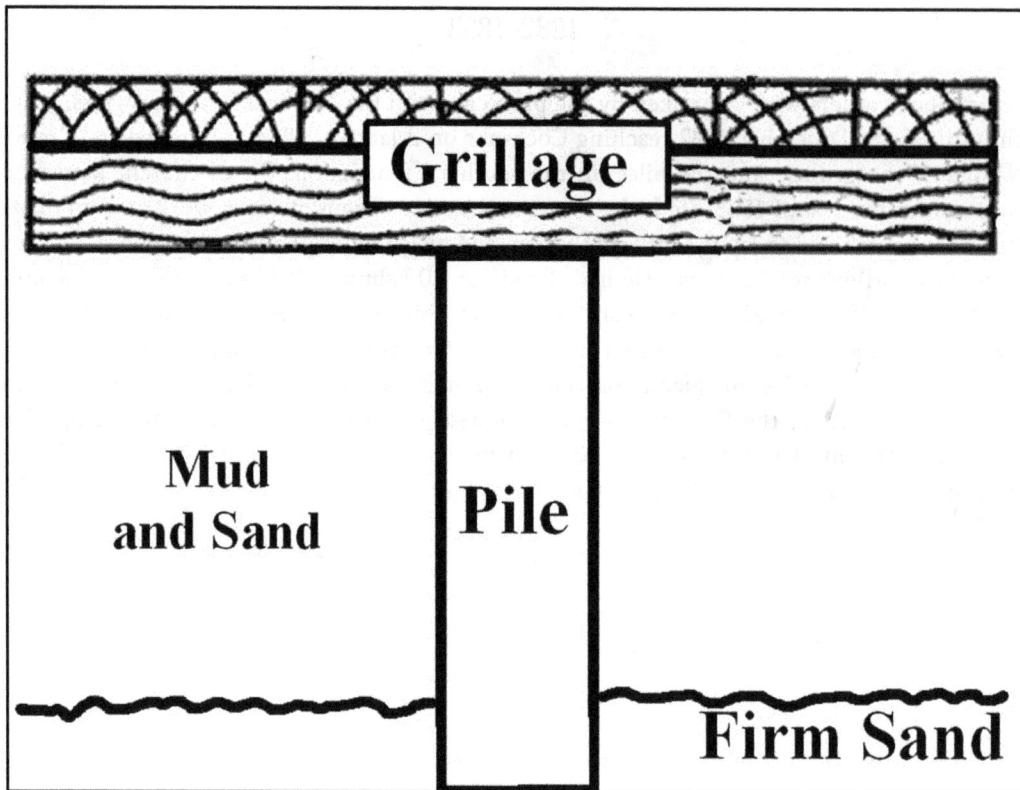

Diagram of grillage on a pile which Mansfield described. A few times Mansfield describes his carpenters "sharpening" piles so obviously they were driven into the earth.

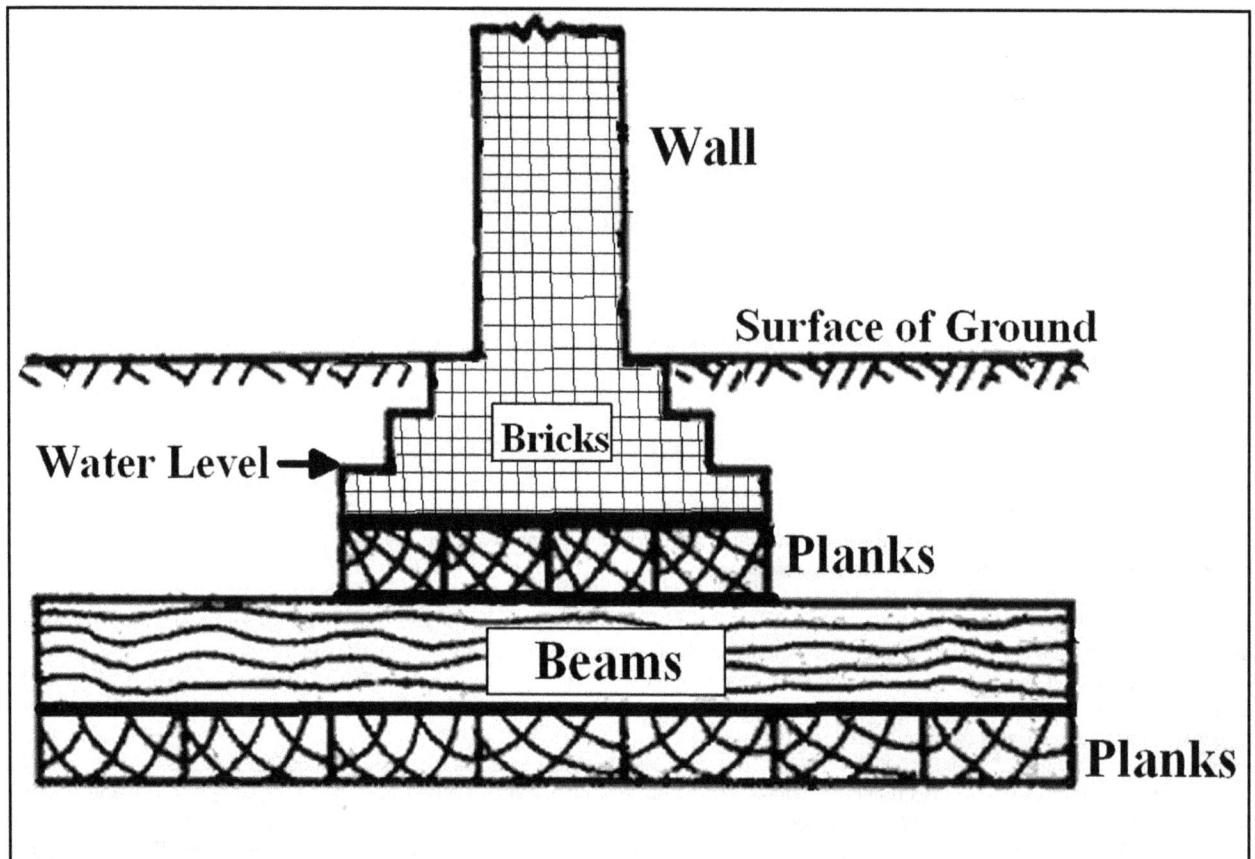

Diagram of a piling resting on grillage similar to what Mansfield may have used in some areas other than the main walls of the fort. To preserve the wood, the timbers had to remain covered by water. Adapted from Kidder, 53.

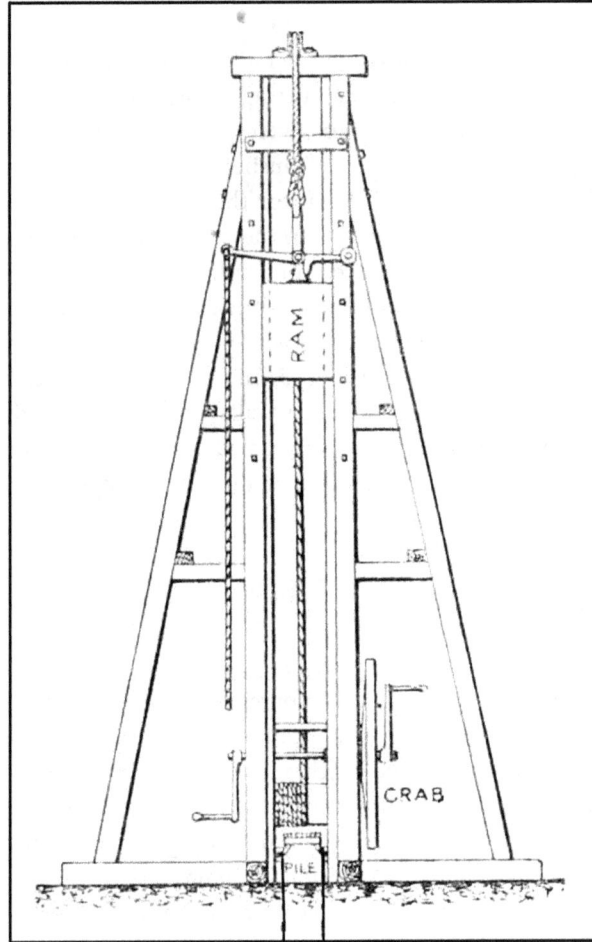

Pile driver operated by hand cranks. *Cassell's Cyclopaedia of Mechanics*, Paul N. Hasluck, ed. (New York, NY: Cassell and Company, 1900), 165.

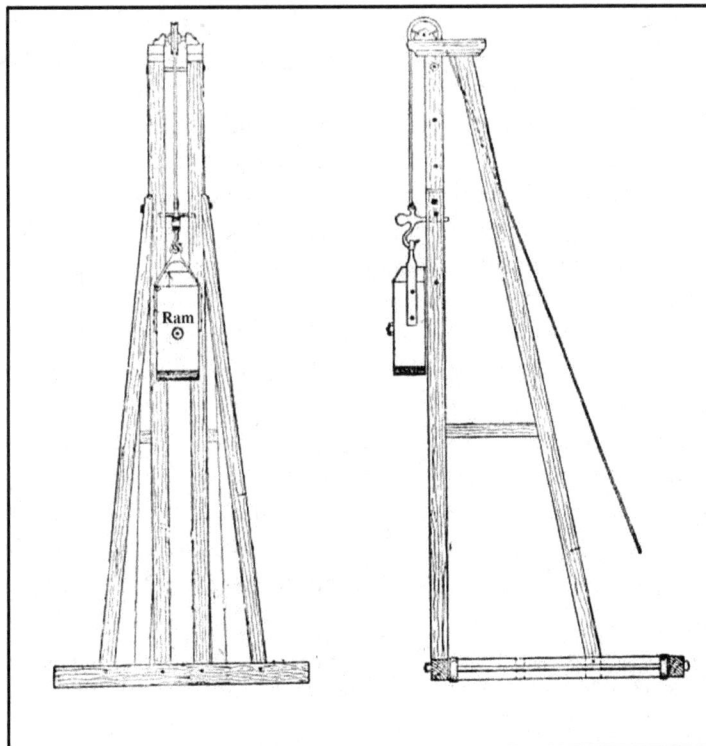

Pile driver operated by hand using one rope and a pulley. *Cassell's Cyclopaedia of Mechanics*, 316.

For the first time, bricks were laid for the north face and Mansfield hoped to finish the masonry work there by the end of the year. He needed more laborers so on 27 April 1833, he advertised for "Thirty Prime Negroes" to add to his force. This summer was unusual since construction lasted for most of the hot season. "Inability to retain skilled white northern labor for summer work, the necessity of conducting some project business in the North, departmental instructions, healthful considerations, and private business, were the main reasons for the summer suspensions which allowed Mansfield to take temporary refuge in the North." Mansfield on 1 June requested the Department to authorize a trip north to inspect building stone and let contracts for it for the next year. The Department agreed on 28 June as Mansfield had assured the Department that work could continue under the overseer at the fort. Before he left for the rest of the summer, he placed an advertisement for another one million bricks and two weeks later for 30 more "Prime Negroes" so he would be ready upon his return to continue the brick work. With this large labor force of Black workers who were thought to be better inured to summer heat than whites, work continued to 30 September 1833. But before Mansfield left he sent a memoir to the Department dated 5 July asking for additional funds for adding permanent masonry walls to the scarp and counterscarp since the earth walls would not be sufficiently strong. The Department took this added $50,000 expense under advisement and instructed Mansfield to submit this change with his annual report. He left for the north on 10 August, likely pleased to be on the schooner *DeKalb*, heading home via Old Point Comfort, to cooler climes.[47]

1833-1834

He returned 14 November having submitted his report to the Department in October for the year to 30 September 1833 from Middletown. It had been a busy year and much progress was made on the foundation: three pile drivers were in operation and 2,500 piles had been driven on the south front and the grillage of half the southeast front laid along with 2,470 cubic yards of foundation masonry on the north and northeast fronts. He also found bargains in New York City for lime and found good stone to purchase at Connecticut River towns such as Haddam and Chatham. He employed mules to provide power for the mortar mill redeploying them from operating the screw pump which kept water out of the foundation trenches. He added a small steam engine for the pump and used it also to power a lathe, saw, and a grindstone. On 16 November, he again advertised for 50 White or Black laborers followed in mid-December by an advertisement for a large order of Cypress lumber. And as the walls rose, he advertised for scaffolding poles in March and April 1834. Also at the end of March, he anticipated losing his white, northern, brick masons so he advertised for six good black masons. Then in mid-April, he asked for bids for one of the largest brick orders he made which totaled seven million bricks—three million to be delivered during calendar year 1834 and four million more by 31 December 1835.[48]

Mansfield in late spring 1834 began planning for his usual northern sojourn to escape the southern heat and purchase materials, so on 19 May he requested permission to be absent from mid-June to early November stating that work could continue again through the summer. Work at a reduced level could use up brick already delivered but the Department would not agree. Congress's current appropriation was running out and future funds were therefore uncertain so it ordered Mansfield on 7 June to suspend operations for the summer while authorizing his trip north. Mansfield demurred as he had to remain to settle accounts due to the suspension. Fortunately, Congress on 30 June made a new appropriation, so the Department told Mansfield on 2 July to submit his plans for the remainder of the calendar year 1834, showing how the funds would be spent. Mansfield did so about 10 days later; he reported that the foundations (pilings and grillage) were complete below the bottom of the moat and he anticipated the walls (ramparts) would all be built to five feet above ground level. He left Savannah 2 August on the ship *Celia* for New York. He was likely pleased at the work accomplished during his absence when he returned 27 October. He submitted his report and plans before the end of the month. It showed that by 30 September 1834, all of the pilings and grillage were done— 2,300 piles had been driven during the year and 5,530 cubic yards of masonry laid. In addition to this excellent progress, he reported that his materials procurement, locally and on his trip north, was fruitful: he obtained most of the required brick in Savannah, but also bought some in Baltimore, Maryland, Alexandria, D.C., and Charleston, South Carolina. He

---

[47] Young, "Connecticut Yankee," 86; Young, "Cockspur Island Had Presented Problem in Building Fort Pulaski," *Savannah Morning News*, 17 February 1935; RSOCE, 1190, 9 August 1833. Young commented that Mansfield should have ascertained the need for masonry for the scarp and counter scarp of the demilune moat and the fort scarp before this time.

[48] Young, "Connecticut Yankee," 87-88, 90; Young, "Pulaski's Construction Was Resumed With Vigor as Winter of 1833 Came," *Savannah Morning News*, 3 March 1935; RSOCE, M1218, 18 October 1833; RSOCE, M1230, 14 November 1833.

procured stone from the Connecticut River Valley and sand from the Savannah River 10 miles above the fort. It is noteworthy that he bought materials and obtained labor without contracts as the Department by now required contracts for only certain items. He returned to Fort Pulaski 27 October 1834.[49]

Work continued apace but Mansfield's good luck was about to run out. On 20 November, he reported to the Department that he was out of funds because he had not received the November credit. Almost as bad, he reported cholera had hit the island with several workmen stricken and a few deaths among the slave laborers. He decided to send most of them back to their masters and he was concerned that without funds he must also send the white laborers away. He certainly felt relief when he received the missing November funding in December and cholera had abated; Mansfield's year ended on positive notes.[50]

1835

Alas for the poor engineer-in-charge, 1835 would not be a good year on Cockspur Island. As usual, funding was a headache—on 1 January, Mansfield had $3,000 to spend on the fort's construction. As he fully believed that Congress would eventually appropriate funds, he decided on a bold course so he would not be forced to stop work and send laborers home: "Lt. Mansfield decided to assume the risk, and invite the project's creditors to continue their services after the exhaustion of the existing funds." But he did warn creditors in a circular dated 2 January "that the appropriation of last session of Congress...will be exhausted by the 10th instant...if you continue your services or those of your slaves on this work, or continue to furnish provisions or materials for the work after that time, you must do in anticipation of further appropriation by Congress, and at your own risk." Clearly his reputation for fair dealing and his honesty were factors which resulted in work continuing with no payments from the Treasury for his project. He was so confident of the forthcoming appropriations that he advertised in February for a house keeper for the Mechanic's Boarding House and then for 300 palmetto wharf logs to be delivered before 1 June. In late February, he advertised for 10 black masons. His hopes and plans were dashed since by 14 March he had received nothing from the Department concerning the expected appropriation—Congress had adjourned on 2 March without appropriating anything for his project! He wrote the Department only now informing it that he had written the 2 January circular and had continued working despite having no appropriated funds, so the project was now in debt several thousands of dollars. He had taken a calculated risk to avoid suspending work on his fort as he firmly believed Congress would continue funding the important fort, so he delayed telling the Department that he had issued the circular. Mansfield was now desperate to continue the work by only employing laborers who agreed to work in anticipation of wages, but the Department on 24 March ordered work suspended. Mansfield immediately began to put the project in order so after the work resumed when funding was at hand, the time and effort to restart would be minimized. He sold lime which could not be used and stopped the foundation pump so water which would refill the ditches would preserve the foundation; by the end of March 1835, work ended.[51]

Congress failed to appropriate funds for Fort Pulaski and indeed any other forts. There was a possibility of armed conflict with France leading Congress to suspend building of forts and rather arm those which could help defend American coasts. This imbroglio beginning in late 1834 resulted in the Engineering Department endeavoring to calculate how many cannon would be needed at various forts, completed or not, in event war began, so Mansfield on 24 February was ordered to submit a report on the classes of guns needed. He sent a report stating that instead of the 172 originally planned, all should be eliminated except for 66, as the remainder would be ineffective at the current stage of construction. Mansfield stayed on Cockspur after work on the fort essentially came to an end and was assigned other engineering duties which lasted into the early fall of 1835. The Department assigned him to be in charge of work improving navigation of the Savannah River from April to July. His assistant was Lieutenant John Mackay of the Topographical Engineers who was a Savannah native, an 1829 graduate of West Point, and Robert E. Lee's friend. Mackay was assigned to Mansfield specifically for this long-term project in December 1832. Then on 21 July 1835,

---

[49] Young, "Pulaski's Construction Was Resumed With Vigor as Winter of 1833 Came," *Savannah Morning News*, 3 March 1935; RSOCE, 1366, 16 May 1834; RSOCE, M1405, 1 August 1834; RSOCE, M1429, 20 October 1834.

[50] Young, "Connecticut Yankee," 96-97; Young, "Cholera Epidemic Was Controlled at Pulaski But Funds Had Depleted," *Savannah Morning News*, 17 March 1935; RSOCE, M1449, 25 November 1834.

[51] Young, "Connecticut Yankee," 101-103; Young, "Cholera Epidemic Was Controlled at Pulaski But Funds Had Depleted," *Savannah Morning News*, 17 March 1935; RSOCE, M1526, 14 March 1835.

Mansfield left Savannah sailing for North Carolina to inspect Fort Caswell on Oak Island at the mouth of the Cape Fear River. After he completed this task, he sailed north for Middletown not returning to Cockspur until 12 October 1835.[52]

Mansfield had other, less important duties assigned at which he only spent short periods. He was involved in improvements to waterways in Florida with the St. John's and St. Mary's Rivers. A canal was planned between the two rivers as part of a contemplated inland waterway and, by July 1830, ships could navigate between the rivers. In June 1835, Mansfield surveyed the project and recommended constructing a dredge boat and mud flats to deepen the channel at Amelia Dividings and the Sisters Dividings. He built the equipment and work began in December 1835 and continued until October 1836. Mansfield sent a letter of progress in 1836 reporting that he arranged for construction of a dredge boat to clear oyster beds in the area.[53]

After he returned to work on the fort on Cockspur 17 October 1835, he sent the Department his report for the year to 30 September. It showed that the foundation masonry was finished and the walls rising. His efforts to ensure that despite a long hiatus, work could restart quickly paid off as he reported that only a week would be needed to begin laying brick anew. He enumerated "disasters" which he and the fort endured including the cholera outbreak, storms which damaged most of his boats, and cold weather which damaged newly-laid masonry. Congress's failure to appropriate funds meant that the project was now $19,000 in debt and Mansfield asked the Department to secure funding from Congress to pay current debts and continue work for 1836. He received hopeful news from the Department on 28 October when it asked him the costs for preparing to restart the project so on 9 November he submitted his request for $5,500. Then the Department authorized him to buy brick from Alexandria, D.C. Believing that the Department was ready to continue funding he asked that the Department approve the construction of "a railway from the end of the [South] wharf to the canal" and the purchase of 10 railway cars as well as repair of the brick flats which carried brick to the canal around the walls. He also asked for permission to hire carpenters willing to work at their own risk if Congress did not make timely appropriations. His hopes to quickly restart were dashed as the Department could not authorize expenditures as Congress made no appropriations for almost nine months.[54]

Mansfield wrote from Fort Pulaski to his cousin, Edward Deering Mansfield. He said that he had been very busy and had turned down a job offer: "Last winter I had the situation of Chief Engineer of the Central Rail Road and Banking Company of Georgia pressed on me for three successive times but as often refused....It probably would have been worth $5,000 a year to me....My career in life thus far to me appears remarkable. Thus you see I do not yet love money well enough to go to rail roading in Georgia." He also commented on the impending (Second) Seminole War showing strong sympathy for the Seminoles: "I hope they will require no engineers. If I am to go into the field, it would be a satisfaction to risk my life where honor is to be gained and not in an unjust war on a few miserable savages, goaded to the fighting point, with a view to prise them from soil no rational man would live upon. Alas! My country, I blush for your principles of freedom, your justice and your honor!" He writes he isn't concerned about fighting savages but a different future war: "The time I fear is not far distant when the yells of the savages and the flourish of the scalping knife will be changed to the roar of cannon and the glitter of thousands of bayonets in deadly strife, father against son and brother against brother."[55] Apparently the time he spent in the southern states and acquaintanceships he made with southern soldiers and society during his many years in the U.S. Army showed him that eventually the differences inherent between the southern and northern sections of the United States would not be resolved peacefully. The following anecdote from an 1868 Connecticut military and civil history is probably exaggerated but is typical of what northern writers thought of southern chivalry in an age in which dueling was no longer accepted:

---

[52] Young, "Connecticut Yankee," 105-106. Young believed that Mansfield's 66 cannon represented a permanent reduction from the original 172, but this seems unlikely. Young, "Cholera Epidemic Was Controlled at Pulaski But Funds Had Depleted," *Savannah Morning News*, 17 March 1935.

[53] George E. Buker, *Sun, Sand and Water: A History of the Jacksonville District U.S. Army Corps of Engineers, 1821-1975* (Washington, DC: U.S. Government Printing Office, 1981), 31-32, 114. The Second Seminole War broke out in December 1835 and caused some excitement for U.S. Army troops in the state.

[54] Young, "Cholera Epidemic Was Controlled at Pulaski But Funds Had Depleted," *Savannah Morning News*, 17 March 1935.

[55] Letter 18 September 183?; courtesy WPL (likely written in the mid-1830's). Mansfield would spend time in Florida when he worked on river improvements. Problems with the Seminoles in Florida occurred off and on from 1814 to 1858. The Second Seminole War lasted from 1835 to 1842 and was also known as the Florida War. The letter also states that William Douglas was married to Mansfield's niece, Grace Parker, for about two years. William is doing well in business for himself "as machinist and manufactures steam engines, etc....Benjamin Douglas is also in Middletown and a machinist by trade. He no doubt will do well also." Mansfield's nephew Benjamin Douglas and his brother William ran the Steam Engine & Machine Manufactory, Iron and Brass Foundry, corner of William and Broad Streets, in Middletown.

Mansfield was always apt to administer a reproof and resent an insult promptly. He despised dueling, but never failed to defend his honor and himself. On one occasion, while building Fort Pulaski, he was invited to dine with a number of Southern gentlemen; and, while engaged in conversation, a hot-blooded Southern officer opposite took occasion to remark, in a tone of voice audible to all, "The Northerners are cowards, — men without any nerve." — "Do you intend that for me?" interrupted Mansfield. "I do, sir," replied the other, at the same time raising a glass of wine as if to hurl it in the face of this audacious Northerner. Mansfield seized a decanter, when the other returned the glass to the table. But Mansfield was now roused. "Bring in my pistols!" he ordered the servant. Pistols were instantly brought; and Mansfield rose, and presented one to his insolent! antagonist, saying, "Now we prove who is the coward." The other diners interfered, agreed that the insult was gross, and demanded that an ample retraction and apology should be made to Mansfield. The atonement was humbly offered, and amicable relations resumed.[56]

1836

The earlier difficulties with France continued and the Army commander, Major General Alexander Macomb, told Brigadier General Charles Gratiot to determine what was needed to make coastal defenses ready. The Department informed Mansfield 26 January 1836 that he could receive six cannon for the defense of Savannah before 31 March and to use them to arm Fort Jackson or Fort Pulaski as he saw fit. Likely Mansfield was thrilled at the prospect of action as he had seen none in his almost 20 years of service. He submitted plans on 30 January to assign the guns to Cockspur and to use the six guns in a temporary fort and block house on the parade (open plain between the walls). He asked twice for the guns in February but to no avail as the confrontation with France abated; the Department on 24 February told him that work to mount the cannon would not be needed as no guns were forthcoming. His disappointment must have made the next few months almost unbearable as no work was done from March through June 1836—Congress finally made a new appropriation in July so work could recommence.[57]

Congress, in its infinite wisdom, saw fit to make the largest, single appropriation in the fort's history on 4 July 1836, $170,000. Mansfield quickly sent his estimates for use of the funds for paying arrearages and to repair machinery to get ready to restart work. Because of the long period of inactivity on the fort starting in late March 1835, the canal which Mansfield had flooded to protect the foundations was now filled with silt and the excavation had mud and grass choking it. The flats used to haul brick were rotted and needed repair, machinery was rusted, and scaffolding rotten. So much work was needed to restart work and organize labor and materials, that Mansfield on 4 August, requested that the Department send him an assistant engineer immediately. The Department did so but not until November when it assigned Lieutenant Joseph Reid Anderson of Virginia. In the meantime, Mansfield continued to push ahead—on 19 July he advertised for 50 white or Black laborers—but realizing that because back payments were due slave owners, he assured creditors that payment of due bills would be paid quickly. To induce owners to lease slaves, on 4 August he advertised that "The wages to be paid for prime slaves...will be fixed at $14 per month and found [food and lodging]— the owner to lose runaway time only, and the Government to furnish physicians and medicine." Then, less than three weeks later, he reassessed his labor requirements and advertised for 10 Negro boys to augment his workers. Materials were also needed so he advertised late in August for joists and plank then a month later for five million bricks. Even though he wished to begin laying more masonry, work was needed to undo the ravages of nature during the long hiatus. He finally sent to the Department in mid-September his plan for continuing the fort's construction which had to begin with the cleaning out of the canals and foundation, and repairing of the brick-carrying flats and machinery. He stated that he wished to start in October on the masonry and to begin the construction of a large breakwater system and seawall on the northeast shore of the island as the construction village and North Dock needed more protection. He noted the need for more funds to repair the damage he already listed but also to "'revet with masonry the scarp and counterscarp" walls of the fort and demilune moats, and that part of the slopes of the canal to the moats.'" These changes would cost an additional $150,000 but were necessary changes in the 1831 mud wall plan because tidal action would erode the walls and fill in the moat. To make his point, he wrote that if these changes were not made, "in less than one year after the fort be finished one half the rampart of the Demi Lune will have slid into the ditch." This time the Department approved Mansfield's request for additional masonry work on 3 November and two days later, Secretary of

---

[56] Croffut and Morris, 284. This account has not been verified, but had it occurred, it was likely embellished to reflect well on the dead Connecticut Civil War hero.

[57] Young, "Cholera Epidemic Was Controlled at Pulaski But Funds Had Depleted," *Savannah Morning News*, 17 March 1935; RSOCE, M1645, 26 January 1836; RSOCE, M1648, 30 January 1836.

War Benjamin F. Butler, approved the change. On 24 September, he began advertising for five million bricks to continue construction.[58]

Mansfield had to be pleased and reinvigorated with this unconditional approval of these major changes to the original plan so he pushed ahead with construction resuming in mid-October after an almost 18-month lapse. On 15 October he advertised for additional brick masons to speed work which continued apace through June 1836. Finally, Mansfield's assistant, a recent West Point graduate, Lieutenant Joseph Reid Anderson, received orders on 11 November 1836, from the Department, to report to Mansfield "as early as practicable;" but he was unable to arrive at Cockspur until 10 December. Much to Mansfield's dismay, this, his second assistant in seven years, only lasted three months before requesting permission to resign from the service. Perhaps service on the remote, spare island, with much hard work soured the young graduate's outlook on military life. He departed 13 March 1837 after being granted leave by Mansfield to go to Washington. Even though he helped Mansfield for only a short time, given all that the senior engineer had to do, this respite was certainly welcome.[59]

1837-1838

By January 1837, Mansfield, although pleased with progress being made on the masonry and breakwaters, wanted to begin the revetment of the scarp and counterscarp walls. He urged the Department that he could begin preliminary work even without the Congressional appropriation but the Department was adhering strictly to the Secretary of War's admonition not to begin this new construction without appropriations. Mansfield and the Department were surely dismayed when the Congress adjourned on 3 March 1837 without appropriating any monies for any fort construction due to wrangling between the House and Senate—the 1837 fortification bill was not passed. But Mansfield this time, certainly instructed by the last failure of appropriations which held up work for many months, made extensive plans to not halt work. He had monies left over from the 1836 appropriation and he was able to add $90,000 in additional funds to be transferred from Fort Monroe. So on 3 April, he sought the Department's approval to continue working "'for 12 months from May 1, 1837, or until the unexpended balance of the present appropriation is spent.'" He would do this by starting on 1 May to confine most of the work to the masonry walls and by reducing the labor force to one inspector, two clerks, two white masons, four slave masons, two apprentice slave masons, and enough slave laborers to assist the masons. He urged the Department to approve this schedule to help avoid the losses incurred during the last long suspension so costs to restart would be mitigated. His argument that slowing down the work would be far better than stopping it won the day, and the Department approved. So on 8 April, he wrote the Department and told it that he would buy materials so work could continue during the early fall of 1837 and asked permission to go north in May. Mansfield had a capable superintendent to leave in charge for the summer and Mansfield reported that he planned to reduce the regular working force but add slave laborers. White laborers were likely the ones who would leave for the hot season and in any event, slave laborers were cheaper to hire and supposedly more inured to heat and humidity. He also desired to journey north to make purchases of stone. The Department approved his plans and he left in May to cooler climes for the first time in about two years. In route, he had to stop for a brief inspection of the Charleston Harbor forts as he had been put in general charge of them from 1836. On 4 May 1837 he submitted his accounts for fortifications in Charleston Harbor. This summer 1837 trip took him to New York, Rhode Island, and Connecticut, from June through part of September. From New York City on 16 June, he sent to the Department his plans for the summer's work at the fort for the third quarter of the Fiscal year: only masonry work on the walls would be done but materials such as brick and lumber for flooring would be bought. The Department had great good news for Mansfield on 31 July as it decided to assign him his third assistant engineer, Brevet Second Lieutenant Henry Washington Benham, a fellow Nutmegger, who graduated from West Point in July 1837. The two likely had a friendly journey together from Connecticut to the fort, reminiscing about West Point and Connecticut, with Mansfield enlightening Benham about

---

[58] Young, "Connecticut Yankee," 123126; Young, "Congress in July, 1836, Approves Appropriation For Work at Fort Pulaski," *Savannah Morning News*, 31 March 1935; RSOCE, M1728, 4 August 1836. The scarp wall is the inside wall or slope of the fort and demilune moat and the counter scarp wall is the outer or outside wall or slope of the moat, opposite the scarp wall. Therefore, the fort only needed the masonry counterscarp wall for the fort moat as the fort already had a masonry scarp wall, Young, "Connecticut Yankee," 115.

[59] Young, "Connecticut Yankee," 128-129; Young, "Congress in July, 1836, Approves Appropriation For Work at Fort Pulaski," *Savannah Morning News*, 31 March 1935; RSOCE, M1788, 8 December 1836.

construction of Fort Pulaski. They arrived there 29 September 1837. Neither could know that both would serve in the Mexican-American and Civil Wars and both be brevetted for their Mexican War service.[60]

In his 14 October 1837 annual report, Mansfield outlined the work accomplished during the year of which the most important was the work on the bricking of all of the walls. The important breakwater work on the northern part of the island was well underway and the mule-powered railway completed which hauled brick on flats to the canal around the fort. Earth had been moved to the fort's parade ground and the permanent dike system on the island commenced. As noted, Mansfield was wary of the continuity of appropriations by Congress so he husbanded funds whenever possible to transition funding gaps—at the end of September 1837, he had over $90,000 on hand to continue work until Congress could act to provide continuing monies. His concerns were justified as on 1 April 1838, Mansfield had no funds left to continue construction so he again, much to his dismay, was forced to suspend work from April through June. He wrote to the Department on 6 July that he proposed to sell government property to settle current debts and to pay workmen to maintain the construction activities until additional appropriations were authorized. On 7 July 1838, two pieces of news undoubtedly gave Mansfield great joy: Congress gave the fort $100,000, and he was promoted to captain.[61]

Mansfield wrote to the Department on 24 July 1838 giving his plans for the $100,000 for the next 12 months. The work would continue on wall construction all around the fort and related tasks such as roofing the arches of the casemates and loading the arches with earth. An item which did not appear in his report but had a very personal effect on him was his marriage to Louisa Maria Mather. On 21 August, he sailed north and after finishing some supply matters, journeyed to Middletown, Connecticut, and on 25 September 1838, was married to her by Rev. John Riley Crane in the First Church of Christ on Main Street. He enjoyed his stay in Middletown but eventually had to return to his post, only this time with his new bride; they arrived 12 November 1838. A week later he sent his report detailing work accomplished to 30 September 1838. Again, continuing work on the masonry of the walls was the main effort but work also included the necessary breakwater on the island's north shore. He had also improved transportation to and from Savannah by chartering a steamboat. The walls were from one-third to over one-half completed so for the newly-minted 35-year-old captain, 1838 was one of both professional and personal satisfaction.[62]

---

[60] Young, "Connecticut Yankee," 132-133; Young, "Congress in July, 1836, Approves Appropriation For Work at Fort Pulaski," *Savannah Morning News*, 31 March 1935. RSOCE, M1861, 3 April 1837; RSOCE, M1864, 8 April 1837; RSOCE, M1885, 4 May 1837; RSOCE, M1940, 30 September 1837. Mansfield would be brevetted three times in Mexico, from captain to colonel, Benham once to captain. During the Civil War, Benham was brevetted to colonel, brigadier general, and finally major general at the end of the war. But all might not have been well with Benham since Mansfield wrote to Louisa on 2 June 1838 that "I do not admire his [Benham's] principles or manners." Nothing is of record to show why he wrote this. Mansfield had a rocky courtship with his future wife as there was at least one other contender for her affections. Mansfield sent a series of letters to his future wife expressing his feelings about her in many ways, such as in his letter of 6 August 1837 when he wrote that he "would never marry a Lady who had been at any time engaged to another, or whose affections were at all interested in another." Her family was also of a higher station according to what he then wrote: "you have thereby escaped a connection with a family whatever may have been its origin, the branches of which in Middletown could probably never be a source of pleasure or satisfaction to you, but the reverse." He did wax romantic as in this 6 December 1857 to her which told her that your letter "has been kissed again and again, worn in my bosom, and placed under my pillow at night. Oh how I could kiss that dear lip of yours once more." There was another suitor, a doctor, and Mansfield laments that she permits him to call on her in her home. "I cannot reconcile it with my ideas of love for a Lady to receive the 'very frequent' visits of a gentleman when she is engaged to another, particularly so when she discovers she is not indifferent to him. It can only with difficulty be excused on the sense of a want of affection for the gentleman to whom the Lady is engaged. Then in his letter of 9 February 1838, after a lengthy exposition urging her happiness, he wrote that "Louisa you will never be happy with me!....it is my desire to act honorably towards you, and prevent future unhappiness....I now ask you hereafter to regard me as a Friend and Brother for I should never marry as I am now satisfied I ought not. Likely to make her jealous, he wrote that he planned on visiting St. Augustine "and take the opportunity to visit some of the amiable and excellent ladies." Letters courtesy of the Middlesex County Historical Society.

[61] Young, "Connecticut Yankee," 138-139; Young, "Vexatious Trials at End So Work On Fort Pulaski Is Pushed on Vigorously," *Savannah Morning News*, 7 April 1935; RSOCE, M105, 6 July 1838. Mansfield reported on 14 October 1837 that he had $226,773.76 total available for the fourth quarter of 1836 and the year 1837, RSOCE, M1965, 14 October 1837, and $92,867.79 remaining for the fourth quarter of 1837.

[62] Young, "Connecticut Yankee," 140; Young, "Vexatious Trials at End So Work On Fort Pulaski Is Pushed on Vigorously," *Savannah Morning News*, 7 April 1935; RSOCE, M200, 19 November 1838. He reported $118,357.30 expended in the year ending 30 September 1838, and that he had $77,427.78 available for the fourth quarter 1838 and 1839. Mansfield was baptized into this church 9 April 1806 and continued as a member until his death; Hazen, 88. Interesting description of a distant Mansfield Rhode Island relative who helped him in 1838 at the fort: "Henry Stephen Mansfield, son of Henry Stephen Mansfield, was born in Slatersville, town of Smithfield, Rhode Island, April 11, 1818. He was educated there in the public schools. At the age of twenty he went to live with his uncle, General Joseph K. F. Mansfield, at Charlestown, South Carolina, in the capacity of private secretary and bookkeeper. He assisted in the construction of Fort Pulaski, of which General Mansfield was the engineer in charge. After his return north he had charge of a hardware store in Worcester for a time, but not liking trade, he returned to his home in Slatersville, R.I., and was elected cashier of the bank to succeed his father, whose varied business interests caused him to withdraw from the management of the bank that he had founded;" Ellery Bicknell Crane, ed., *Historic Homes and Institutions and Genealogical and Personal Memoirs of Worcester County Massachusetts with a History of Worcester Society of Antiquity*, vol. 2 (New York, NY: The Lewis Publishing Company, 1907), 407.

This church was first named the North Church then the First Church of Christ Congregational at Main near Court Streets in Middletown in which Joseph Mansfield was baptized and where he attended services. Mansfield married Louisa here on 25 September 1838. Rev. Jeremiah Taylor, who delivered an address at Mansfield's funeral, was the pastor here, Azel Washburn Hazen, *A Brief History of the First Church of Christ in Middletown Connecticut for Two Centuries and a Half* (Middletown, CT: n.p., 1920), facing 58.

1839

Captain Mansfield hoped that 1839 would be another very successful year. But it was not to be so even though work progressed well: on 18 December 1838, the Department assigned his capable assistant engineer, Lieutenant Benham, to permanent duty at Fort Marion in St. Augustine, Florida; he arrived there on 12 January 1839. As had happened several times during his supervision of the fort's construction, Congress had not appropriated funding—Mansfield had less than $10,000 remaining—so he wrote the Department on 8 February that work would have to again be suspended at the end of April 1839 unless the annual appropriation was forthcoming. After wrangling between the House and Senate, they passed an appropriation bill 3 March giving Fort Pulaski a relatively small sum—$15,000. In April, he sent plans to the Department detailing how he would use the appropriation: continue the work on the walls and related items and finish the North Dock. The walls of the fort were sufficiently built to allow cannon to be mounted so the previous month on 6 March 1839, he had sent to the Department his request "to ship 'without delay,' thirty-six casemate seacoast guns and carriages complete, with four carronades and carriages 'to be immediately placed in battery for the defence of this position.'" He added that some guns from Fort Moultrie at Charleston, South Carolina, could also be sent if necessary. Mansfield was concerned as he read reports and newspaper articles concerning the dispute with England over the northeast boundaries of Maine and English New Brunswick since for decades the boundary line had been in contention.[63]

---

[63] Young, "Connecticut Yankee," 141-144. The Department placed Benham in charge of the detail of the duties and disbursements for the improvement of the Savannah River 24 November 1838, RSOCE, M220, 4 December 1838; RSOCE, M304, 6 March 1839. In 1838, the Maine legislature authorized $800,000 for military defense, and Congress gave the President authority to raise the militia with a $10,000,000 budget while Nova Scotia voted $100,000 to defend New Brunswick. Tempers on both sides escalated into early 1839 when Maine militia occupied the disputed lands. Congress authorized a force of 50,000 men and appropriated $10 million if foreign troops crossed into United States territory, and Maine committed several thousand militia. U.S. troops included the 1ˢᵗ U.S. Artillery and the Army constructed permanent Forts Kent and Fairfield. The British responded with its 11ᵗʰ Regiment and planned to build barracks across the St. John's River from the U.S. Fort Kent. This "Aroostook War" ended with the 1842 Webster-Ashburton Treaty of Washington which settled the Maine-Canada boundary as well as the boundary between Canada

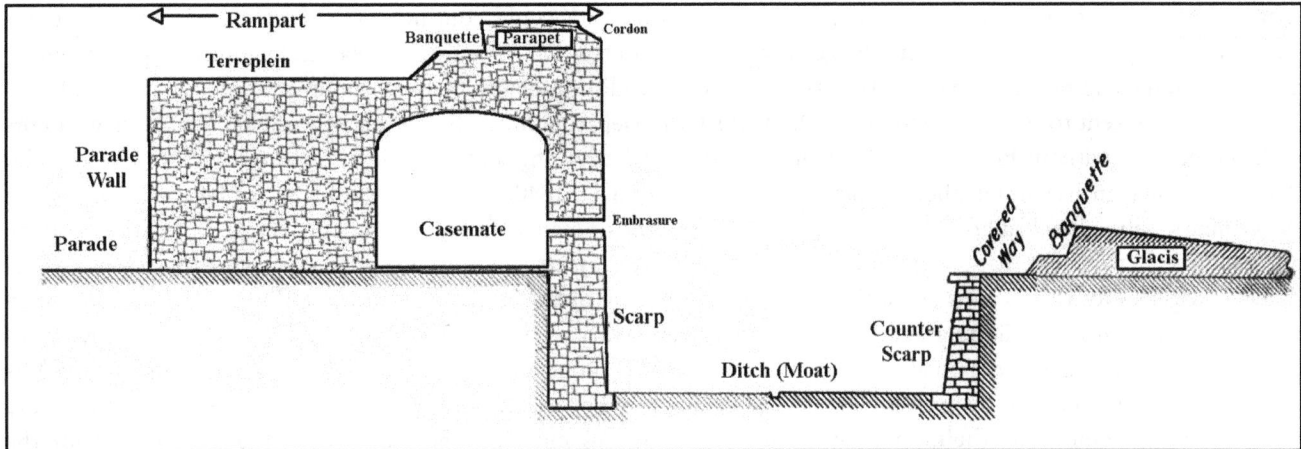

Adapted from U.S. Army Engineer School, William M. Black, "Pamphlet on The Evolution of the Art of Fortification" (Washington, DC: GPO, 1919), facing 58.

Other engineering duties kept Mansfield busy at sites away from Fort Pulaski from April 1839 through the end of September 1839. He made a brief trip to St. Augustine, Florida, in late May to investigate the expenditures on the seawall there, and then on 19 June 1839 he sailed for New York on the brig *Clinton*; undoubtedly his wife, Louisa, was happy to journey with him avoiding the hot season. He had a successful trip buying building materials in Connecticut and New York, and returned to Cockspur on 16 October 1839 alone. Later that month, he sent his report year to the Department; it showed great progress for the walls, roofing, floors, stairways, the breakwater, and the enlarged North Dock. Additionally, eight cisterns had been built and a sewer system started. Construction on the fort was progressing well as the foundations and walls were essentially completed and the masses of exterior brick masonry almost done. Interior work remained, along with a considerable amount of construction needed on the gorge face. Overall, an eventful year for Mansfield and Fort Pulaski.[64]

1839-1840

The last quarter of 1839 had brought some good news to Mansfield as another new assistant engineer, Lieutenant James Heyward Trapier, was assigned to Cockspur on 7 November 1839.[65] For the next few months, from late 1839 to early 1840, Mansfield was involved in planning for the installation of cannon even though the fort was not quite ready for their permanent installation. While plans and drawings were flying back and forth between Mansfield and the Department, work continued on all aspects needed for finishing the fort: the masonry was finished on the walls and the finished roofs were plastered, and casemate floors were installed and completely finished by the suspension of work early in May. This suspension was expected as Mansfield told the Department on 2 March 1840 that most monies would be gone by the end of the month. Even though the Department told him to continue work on a restricted basis for April, May, and June, by 16 April 1840, all masonry work was stopped and in early May remaining workers were all discharged except two white caretakers and two Negro boatmen.[66]

---

and New Hampshire, Michigan and Minnesota. This treaty awarded 7,015 square miles to the United States and 5,012 square miles to British control, courtesy Wikipedia.

[64] Young, "Connecticut Yankee," 148-149; Young, "Vexatious Trials at End So Work On Fort Pulaski Is Pushed on Vigorously," *Savannah Morning News*, 7 April 1935; RSOCE, M366, 18 June 1839.On 25 November 1841 Louisa wrote to him from Middletown recalling her visit to Fort Pulaski: "I often wish I was on the Island with you this winter, instead of keeping house here alone. I certainly never enjoyed myself or felt more happiness than I did, when there, although deprived of many of the comforts which I have here, but I trust we shall not long be separated, that soon you will have a settled place of abode with your family around you, where we can together raise and instruct our children." Letter courtesy of the Middlesex County Historical Society. In that letter she wrote that she was happy that Grace was taking care of him. Grace Totten was one of Mansfield's sisters who visited him at Fort Pulaski.

[65] An 1838 graduate of West Point, Lieutenant Trapier was a South Carolina native who would resign in 1848; in the Civil War, he became a Confederate brigadier general and died in 1866.

[66] Young, "Connecticut Yankee," 151.

But continued unsettled border tensions convinced the Department to send 20 guns to him. He planned on continuing work but on a somewhat reduced scale to ensure work could continue even if additional funds were not forthcoming, especially on areas where the guns would be mounted. On 7 April 1840, Mansfield requested permission to make his annual trip north to buy materials and visit home, and the Department consented, but only when the 20 guns which had been sent to him were mounted. On 3 April, the Department, realizing that Mansfield could manage affairs with the cannon without his assistant, Trapier was sent to Charleston, South Carolina, to become Captain Alexander Hamilton Bowman's assistant there; Trapier departed 18 April 1840. In early April 1840, Mansfield wrote the Department that he had had no replies from his inquiries to the ordnance office at Augusta, Georgia, but on 14 April, he informed the Department that the 20 guns were landing. Alas, they arrived with no carriages so were useless. Mansfield awaited carriages for the 20 guns and a sling cart to mount them onto the carriages so he could then start for home. In his letter to Totten 21 April, he asked for "discretionary authority as to how long I shall remain here." By now, most laborers were discharged and he had to advance $255.40 to the Ordnance Department for workers so the guns could be moved from the steamers to the South Dock. Finally, a Captain Edward Harding from the Augusta Arsenal arrived and the guns were mounted on their carriages and in the casemates but then they found that the iron wheels for the carriages would not fit. Iron carriages for the cannon had arrived but there was a delay getting them to the casemates from the wharf. Against all bureaucratic bungling, the guns were finally mounted and functioning, so Mansfield departed for the north 30 May 1840, on the Steamer *Southerner,* undoubtedly happy to be free from the cannon debacle and to return to his wife.[67]

---

[67] Young, "Connecticut Yankee," 151-156; Young, "Vexatious Trials at End So Work On Fort Pulaski Is Pushed on Vigorously," *Savannah Morning News*, 7 April 1935; Young, "Completion Of Work At Fort Pulaski Was Bright At End of 1839," *Savannah Morning News*, 14 April 1935; File No. M. 509, Records Section Office of Chief Engineers; RSOCE, M514, 25 April 1840; RSOCE, M523, 6 May 1840. Contemplating that work on a reduced scale would continue throughout the summer of 1839, he advertised on 7 May for "six half grown (negro) Boys." Mansfield did not mention powder or shot for the cannon and of course he had no troops to fire them anyway.

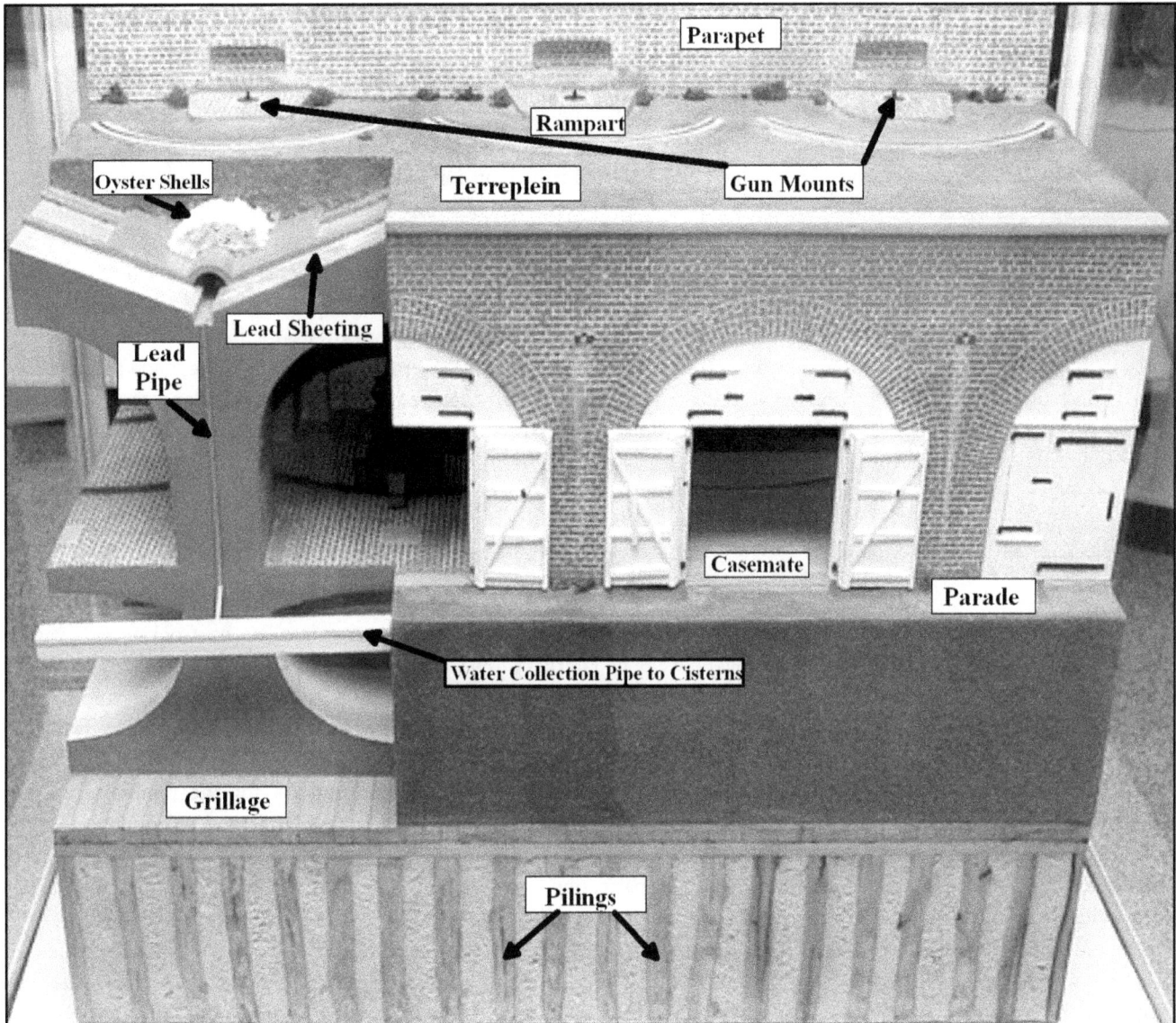

Mockup of fort's construction by NPS at Fort Pulaski Visitor's Center. Photograph by author, March 2014.

When he headed north, he knew that as usual, funding was of concern. For a few years, the U.S. economy was in turmoil because of problems revolving around the credit of the United States Bank and the Panic of 1837. Problems with the Treasury and state banks, expenses for the Seminole War in Florida, combined to produce large Federal deficits from 1837 to 1842. Appropriations for fort construction nationwide were restricted. No construction occurred on Cockspur from June through September 1840 while Mansfield was in the north. Finally on 21 July 1840, Congress agreed to appropriate $44,000 for Fort Pulaski but with restrictions—it could not be expended before 4 March 1841. Mansfield was authorized to work on credit to one quarter of the $44,000 ($11,000) between 1 January and April 1841. Eight weeks later on 17 October 1840, Mansfield submitted his plan for this amount from his temporary headquarters in Middletown and included a summary of accomplishments for the year ending 30 September 1840. Despite the near complete suspension starting in April 1840, much work had been accomplished including completing the masonry of the casemates and their wooden floors, and roofs finished ready for the lead to be laid on them, finishing and hanging the main door at the gorge, and finishing drains to the cisterns. The 20 cannon he had mounted were to be the only ones in the fort until the Civil War. Again, his accomplishments were noteworthy given the tasks he undertook and the limited and uncertain funding by Congress. Rogers Young wrote that Mansfield's successful efforts were "in the largest measure due to [his] untiring devotion to duty, his inspiring supervisory ability, and the depth of his technical engineering skill."[68]

From his temporary headquarters in Middletown, Mansfield had been planning during October 1840 for his return to Fort Pulaski. He knew based on past experience with long gaps in funding and work suspensions that significant monies would have to be spent to repair and replace equipment, and rebuild damaged structures. He had only the $11,000 sum available until 4 March 1841 and the Department had authorized him to reopen operations on credit for the last quarter of calendar year 1840—October through December, but only spending to the $11,000 limit. And he knew that the promised remaining $33,000 was not assured. Mansfield bravely notified the Department on 6 October 1840 that after "mature deliberation" he found it unwise to reopen construction at the fort at all during the Fiscal year 1841. Again, based on past work suspensions, he knew that extensive repairs would have to be made before any construction could restart and the $11,000 would be quickly used for those purposes after which, without more funding, work would again be stopped. Then after more funding was authorized, the repairs would have to be made again before actual construction could begin. So in his 6 October plan, he proposed that he remain in the north "and enter contracts for [stone for the] doors, windows, fireplace jambs, [and] gun carriage segments." Finally he asked that the Department make his Middletown location his "operations center" for his time in the north. The Department approved as it was unable to secure additional certain funding for the fort.[69]

1841

During the winter of 1840-1841, Mansfield remained in the north while two caretakers on Cockspur served as watchmen and made minor dike repairs. Mansfield on 12 February 1841 asked the Department to authorize $3,200 in April for "stone sills and lintels, marble fireplace jambs and mantles, window frames and sashes, front doors and frames, partition doors, loophole sashes, stone gun carriage segments, iron gun carriage tracks, and cast iron boxes and sheaves for the main drawbridge." He had good news as on 3 March, Congress appropriated $15,000 for the fort in addition to the prior $44,000 conditional appropriation. So in response to the Department's request for the remainder of the calendar year 1841, Mansfield submitted his estimate for using $26,200 between 1 April 1841 and 1 January 1842. He noted that his proposal did not reflect any military problems with the ongoing Maine-New Brunswick boundary dispute (finally resolved in October 1842). His report had two parts, one was repairs needed before full construction could begin then, what he planned for that construction. The repairs were the usual—repair of the north and south docks and the cranes on them, and the refurbishing of the flats which transported materials from the docks to the fort work site. An interesting addition to his request was for a pilot boat to be used as a tender for the island presumably easing travel not only around Cockspur but mainly to and from Savannah. His construction plan involved continuing prior work on the fort such as the lead roofs, iron tracks for the gun carriages, finishing casemate floors, and construction of the parapet wall on the terreplein. While the preliminary repair work was undertaken, Mansfield proposed that he remain in the north while those works continue under his overseer. The repair work was more extensive than he thought due to much rot and decay which had continued from April through September 1841. On 13 September he told the Department that he would leave for Pulaski between the "1st and 10th of October" and asked for funds to repair his quarters there as "they leak badly and are uncomfortable in bad weather." Mansfield remained in the north and continued to buy building materials for the fort including materials needed for the repairs. For $3,000, he also bought a small steamboat to use as his tender. When he returned in October, he would find that repairs were substantially completed so work on the fort could recommence.[70]

---

[68] Young, "Connecticut Yankee," 162; Young, "Completion of Work At Fort Pulaski Was Bright At End of 1839," *Savannah Morning News*, 14 April 1935.

[69] Young, "Fort Pulaski Awakens From Inactive Period To Repair Much Decay," *Savannah Morning News*, 2 June 1935.

[70] Young, "Connecticut Yankee," 178-182; Young, "Fort Pulaski Awakens From Inactive Period To Repair Much Decay," *Savannah Morning News*, 2 June 1935; RSOCE, M649, 18 March 1841; RSOCE, M720, 13 September 1841.

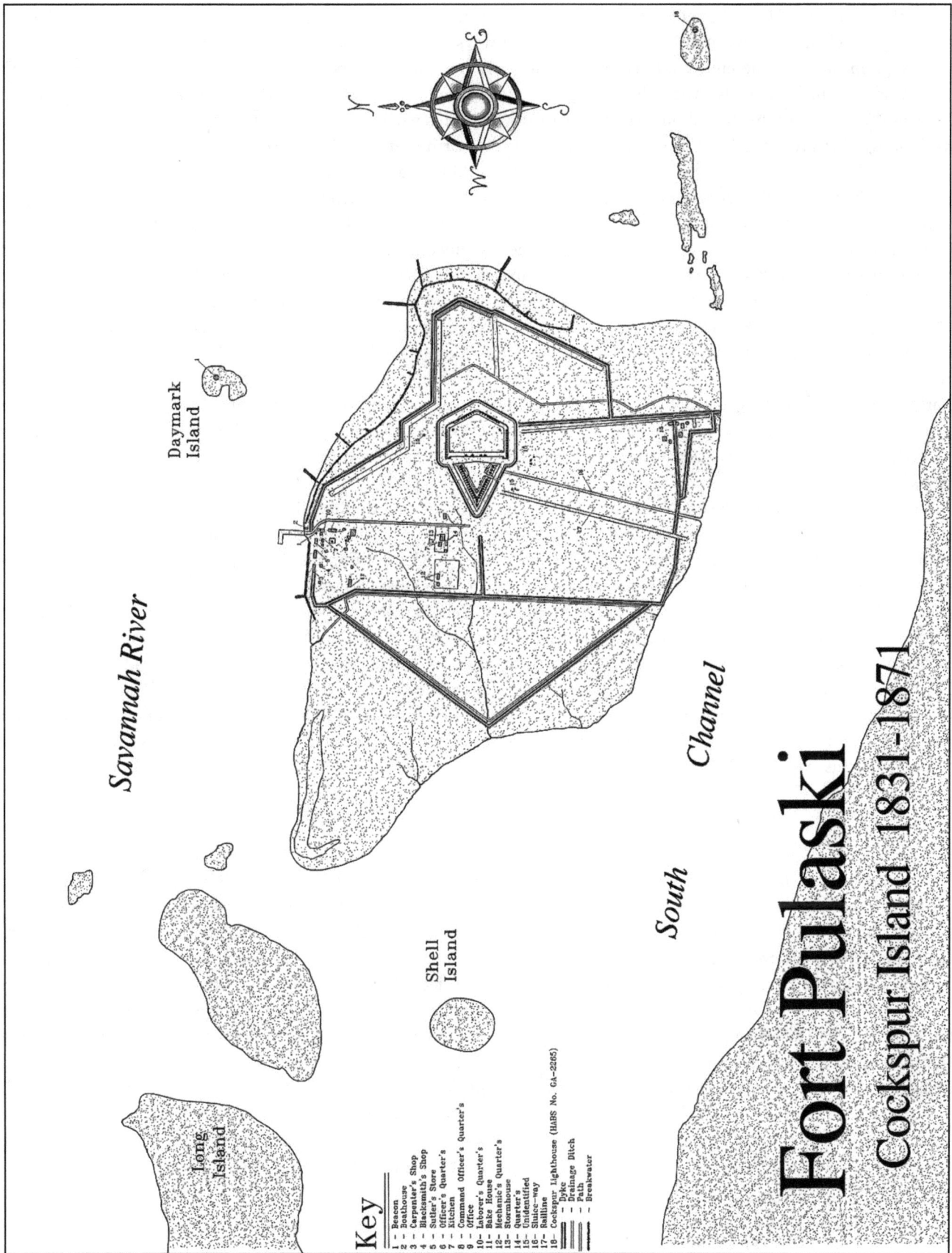

Key

1 — Beacon
2 — Boathouse
3 — Carpenter's Shop
4 — Blacksmith's Shop
5 — Sutler's Store
6 — Officer's Quarter's
7 — Kitchen
8 — Command Officer's Quarter's
9 — Office
10 — Laborer's Quarter's
11 — Bake House
12 — Mechanic's Quarter's
13 — Storehouse
14 — Quarter's
15 — Unidentified
16 — Sluice-way
17 — Railline
18 — Cockspur Lighthouse (HABS No. GA-2265)

▦ — Dyke
╎╎ — Drainage Ditch
╎╎ — Path
▦▦ — Breakwater

Fort Pulaski

Cockspur Island 1831–1871

This Third System Fort is a five-sided (truncated hexagon) brick structure, with 7½ foot-thick outer walls, and is approximately 350 feet long on each side. Opposite the western gorge face is a triangular demilune with sides approximately 400 feet long. The fort and its demilune are separated by a wet moat about 40 feet wide and 7 feet deep. Courtesy LOC and NPS.

On 14 October 1841, Mansfield left Middletown to return to the fort. He sent to the Department his report for the year 1841 which showed essentially that no construction work was accomplished. But the extensive repairs needed had been accomplished by the end of 30 September 1841, and he had made good use of his many months in the north purchasing building materials. At the beginning of October, he had the substantial sum of $94,000 to use starting in October 1841. So upon his arrival on 23 October, he dove into his work likely pleased that his plan for the cessation of work on the fort proved to be wise and his purchases in the north useful. He advertised on 25 October for 200 cords of firewood and also for 8,000 bushels of river sand. Then on 30 October, he advertised for 400,000 bricks by 31 March 1842 at the rate of 60,000 per month. Based on his experience with his laborers for the last 10 years, he asked the Department to approve a doctor for the fort and to purchase medicine as had been approved a few times in the past. The Department wanted details to support this request so he reminded it that prior to 1841 medical care had been provided mainly for slaves. Given that they did the hardest physical labor and were sometimes employed in the hot summer months, it is no surprise that they were more often injured and became sick requiring attention. He continued in his 14 December reply that the physician's salary averaged $45-$50 per month over the years and that for the 11-year period, $3,625.50 was spent for doctors and $671.17 for medicine. Even though a physician would not be needed regularly, medicine cost would remain especially for quinine used for treating malaria. He noted that sometime both he and his clerk administered the drug but that he usually did not discharge a worker who was temporarily ill as it was not humane to do so as he would have "no place to go" and that in any event there would be no one else readily available to replace him. He ended by telling the Department that if it did not pay for drugs, they "might have to come from his own funds."[71]

Work continued apace during November and at the end of the month, Mansfield restarted his discussions with the Department regarding the scarp and counterscarp walls of the fort and demilune. Even though the Department eventually agreed with Mansfield's proposal originally made in 1833, nothing had been done to start that work as the substantial funds needed for this were not available. On 25 November, he sent the Department his estimate for this work: $70,285.65. While he waited for the Department's decision, masons and carpenters continued work on the ramparts, casemates, and a sluice through the northwest dike to help drain the island. They also set iron carriage tracks for cannon mounts. Laborers worked on the eastern breakwater, permanent dike system, and the advanced battery. They also began the foundation for the hotshot furnace at the northeast corner of the parade ground. He asked the Department for plans for finishing the inside of the magazines and for complete information for the barbette gun mountings. Soon after receiving the mounting details, he requested that it send him the plates, pintles, and bolts for the 45 barbette guns. The calendar year ended with much being accomplished despite the long wait for funding.[72]

1842

Mansfield must have been happy with the pace of construction during the first half of 1842. The lead roofs were being laid over the casemates as detailed by instructions he received from the Department in December 1841. By 27 January, his plumbers had begun this task which was designed to provide good drinking water for the finished fort. Over the thinly plastered roofs was laid a tar pitch mixture, then one-eighth thick lead sheeting on top of which, in gutters, was placed oyster shells or coarse gravel about a foot deep. Next came several feet of well-packed sand then earth until the terreplein level was reached. Lead pipes carried the filtered water to large cisterns in the fort's foundations. The Department finally responded to Mansfield's repeated requests for a decision on his pet project—the revetting of the scarp and counterscarp walls. In a compromise plan, the Department on 18 January surely disappointed Mansfield as it only approved the scarp wall of the demilune. The Department's approval authorized him to begin this task at once and did tell him that his plan for the counterscarp might be approved in the future but if so, "it will be one of the last done" on the fort. However, no construction of even the demilune scarp was begun until 1843. With his large workforce and adequate budget, Mansfield was overworked. At the end of December 1841, he asked the Department to

---

[71] Young, "Connecticut Yankee," 182-187; Young, "Fort Pulaski Awakens From Inactive Period To Repair Much Decay," *Savannah Morning News*, 2 June 1935; RSOCE, M747, 26 October 1841; RSOCE, M768, 16 November 1841.

[72] Young, "Fort Pulaski Awakens From Inactive Period To Repair Much Decay," *Savannah Morning News*, 2 June 1935. Mansfield's December report included an interesting statistical exercise which showed the average number of workmen annually employed per month for eight months from 1835-1841 which reflected stoppages due to appropriation lapses (fractions rounded down): 1835, 25; 1836, 169; 1837, 128; 1838, 118; 1839, 99; 1840, 5; 1841, 6.

send him an assistant for 1842. The Department had no one to spare so on 18 January 1842 it offered to employ a civilian engineer for him. He suggested two names to the Department, a Mr. Bender or Mr. Anderson, but listed his requirements for anyone hired: "[It is] important that the man…have a knowledge of surveying, be free of laziness and of addiction to ardent spirits;" He could board with Mansfield for $15 to $25 per month and use a room formerly occupied by Lieutenant Trapier. Obviously Mansfield wanted a hard-working, sober assistant, who could do what was asked, when asked, without shirking.[73]

January 1842 also began with what could have been a calamity when the largest workmen's quarters burned to the ground on the afternoon of 7 January. This building, just west of the fort, was not rebuilt as remaining buildings adequately served. Fortunately, the men were at work so no one was hurt. Mansfield on 11 January requested that his temporary quarters built by Babcock needed repair as its piles were entirely rotted; he estimated the cost at $548.50 but later reduced it to $200.00. Work also was completed on 19 of 20 iron tracks for the guns he had received as well as the rest of the casement guns. He placed his guns as follows: three on the south front; two on the southeast front; seven on the east front; seven on the north front; and one in the northeast angle. Most heavily defended were the north and northeast walls as the deeper North Channel was more likely to be traversed by hostile vessels than the shallower South Channel. Ironically, when the fort was taken by Union troops during the Civil War, the Union cannons fired from the south from Tybee Island. Mansfield wrote that the 19 guns were fully operational and ready for use when needed. Masons, carpenters, and laborers were working hard from January through June finishing, among many other tasks, the terreplein walls, casemate roofing, setting steps, building a hot shot furnace at the northeast corner and beginning another at the southeast corner, building fireplaces in soldiers' quarters, and constructing permanent sluices through the northeast and southeast dikes. Work had progress sufficiently so that Mansfield on 18 February began advertising for 25,000 thousand bushels of oyster shells for March and April to finish the battery casemates up to the terreplein. Good news also arrived on 11 March when Mansfield's new assistant arrived, Mr. Edward Watts, who Mansfield put to work immediately drawing all work and temporary quarters on the island. Importantly, gun tracks and mounts were laid and fitted but his request to the Department for bolts, plates, and pintles for the barbette guns had gone unanswered.[74]

Obviously the Department was impressed with Mansfield's progress on the fort so that for the first time it was officially inspected in May by none other than his cousin, Chief Engineer Colonel Joseph G. Totten. Impressed by what he saw at the fort, when he returned to Washington, he instructed that the coping of the parapet wall be quickly done. Mansfield demurred, replying that it could not be done until the fall. But during the second quarter of the fiscal year, April through June, work slowed especially the middle of July due to heat and the Department's orders on the 14th that he should "lessen expenditures on the project." Construction had gone well but expenses for it had used up the large appropriations allowed so on 29 July 1842, the Department ordered Mansfield to suspend work except for existing contracts. After he received that order on 5 August, he pled with the Department to give him $25,000 so the "work would be in a good condition at the end of the fiscal year." Mansfield, much to his dismay, was again at the mercy of funding from Congress and the Department which forced him to lay off his recently-acquired assistant, Mr. Watts. Before he was discharged on 11 August, Watts had made a drawing of how the grillage had been accomplished on the fort and Mansfield submitted this requested drawing to the Department. Nature conspired to add to his misery during a ferocious thunderstorm on 19 August—a lightning bolt struck the limehouse at the South Wharf killing four workmen. Congress did not make an appropriation in 1842 so the Department ordered him to suspend work on 30 September. All workmen and laborers were gone by that date, and Mansfield again despaired for the future of his project after 11 years of hard work and many disappointments.[75] But Rogers Young, the fort's historian lauded Mansfield for his efforts and achievements: "Captain Mansfield had safely piloted the Fort Pulaski project through one of its most intensive working years. His influence and skill as an executive had been clearly evident in the year's successes….the greatest amount of detailed construction work ever completed…in any one year…had been finished [at] the end of the fiscal year 1841-1842."[76]

[73] Young, "Connecticut Yankee," 189-190, 197; Young, "Laying of Lead Roof Of Fort Pulaski Begun By Mansfield in 1842," *Savannah Morning News*, 9 June 1935; RSOCE, M816, 26 January 1842.

[74] Young, "Connecticut Yankee," 198-202; Young, "Laying of Lead Roof Of Fort Pulaski Begun By Mansfield in 1842," *Savannah Morning News*, 9 June 1935; RSOCE, M799, 7 January 1842; RSOCE, M804, 11 January 1842; RSOCE, M809, 19 January 1842.

[75] Young, "Laying of Lead Roof Of Fort Pulaski Begun By Mansfield in 1842," *Savannah Morning News*, 9 June 1935; RSOCE, M941, 22 August 1842.

[76] Young, "Connecticut Yankee," 202-206; Young, "Severe Storm of 1842 Had Little Effect on Fort Pulaski Structure," *Savannah Morning News*, 16 June 1935. Note that Congress changed the beginning date of the fiscal year to 1 July in 1842. November 5 letter courtesy of the Middlesex County Historical Society.

Again nature conspired to add to Mansfield's misery as on 5 October 1842, an extremely strong nor'easter battered the island for two days. He and a handful of men witnessed its fury which he described in his letter to Totten on 8 October: "[the waves] swept over all our dikes but one and breached them in several places...so as to require much repair....[but] the fort has sustained no damage as far as I can at present discover....in the whole course of my experience for the past 11 years I have been on this station [I have not] known so severe a storm." Amazingly, Mansfield's new assistant, Brevet Second Lieutenant Barton Stone Alexander, another newly-graduated West Point engineer, Mansfield's fifth assistant, arrived on 6 October to witness most of the storm.[77] Mansfield had 15 Negro laborers from Savannah repair the storm-damaged dikes and leaving repairs in charge of the overseer and Lieutenant Alexander, Mansfield left for home in mid-October. There, he wrote to the Department and requested "a leave of absence for a few months, while the work is suspended." But his valuable engineering skills could not be spared so the Department on 5 November appointed him to the Board of Engineers which reflected well on the esteem in which the Department held him. In that letter Mansfield was told that "you will without delay repair to this city for instructions and to enter upon the duties. This appointment will not relieve you from, nor interfere with, your duties as Engineer Officer in Charge of the construction of Fort Pulaski, and while you are necessarily absent from that work, engaged in the duties of the Board, you will continue to direct and control its operations through correspondence with your assistant at the work." From November until he returned to the fort in March 1843, he served on the board travelling as needed from his Middletown home. In a letter to Mansfield from the Department dated 5 December 1842, he was ordered to go to Boston as a member of Board of Engineers and join Colonel Thayer with a plan of Governors Island, Boston Harbor, and sketches for defense of that island, and after learning the necessary details return to Middletown and complete all plans to "prepare the project for execution." Meanwhile on Cockspur Island, his new assistant was involved in repairing the dikes and other storm damage plus he began a complete topographic survey of the island which would take three months to accomplish.[78]

1843

Mansfield remained in Middletown until he received a welcome order from the Department to return to Fort Pulaski as Congress had appropriated a total of $60,000 for the project on 3 March 1843; he left home on 22 March 1843 to begin was must have seemed to him another tedious trip. He finally reached Cockspur on 29 March eager "to commence operations on April 1 with a suitable force" after the six-month hiatus. On 3 April he sent the Department his ambitious plans to use the $60,000 which included excavation of a feeder canal from the South Channel which would bring water to the moats but firstly to drain water from around the fort so work could begin on the scarp wall of the demilune. He planned to use the excavated dirt to build a road 18 feet wide to the west paralleling the canal down to a small garrison wharf on the South Channel.[79] The scarp wall was the most important part of his plan for the year and was to be built first. Work in the fort was also planned such as completing the parapet walls, continuing finish carpentry in the gorge quarters, and constructing the portico along the gorge. The North Channel dock was to be repaired replacing rotting timbers with granite along its sides, and importantly, strengthening the dikes on the island. During May, work progressed well in all areas keeping masons, carpenters, and laborers very busy. Mansfield again agitated with the Department for its decision about construction of the counterscarp. On 22 May, he wrote the Department that without brick on that wall, the moat would fill up and as he was now constructing the scarp wall, doing the counterscarp at the same time would save time and money. Work continued during June progressing well inside and outside the fort: carpenters were laying floors in casemates, masons bricking the drains from the terreplein to the

[77] Young, "Connecticut Yankee," 208-209; RSOCE, M960, 8 October 1842. Alexander had a notable Civil War career including becoming a brevet major for First Bull Run, brevet lieutenant colonel for the siege of Yorktown, Virginia, aide-de-camp to General McClellan in September 1862, and brevet colonel and brigadier general in March 1865.

[78] Young, "Connecticut Yankee," 209-215; Young, "Severe Storm of 1842 Had Little Effect on Fort Pulaski Structure," *Savannah Morning News*, 16 June 1935; RSOCE, M980, 8 October 1842; RSOCE, M986, 22 October 1842; RSOCE, M994, 9 November 1842; letter to Mansfield 5 December 1842 courtesy of the Middlesex County Historical Society.

[79] Young, "Connecticut Yankee," 225-227. Young notes that Mansfield wrote that the road would be 180 feet to the west but upon restoration work on the fort in 1934, there was no evidence of a road 180 feet from the canal but only one 18 feet from it. He opines that Mansfield made a rare mistake or more likely his clerk did.

cisterns and plastering the two gorge cisterns with cement, and the laborers excavating the demilune scarp, and driving the pilings for it.[80]

Early June 1843 found Mansfield responding to the Department's questions about his plans. It questioned the need for a new wharf on the South Channel so Mansfield explained that while he did not plan on constructing the new wharf immediately it would be needed as the old one there was rotten and in a few years would be destroyed. He wrote that the North Channel Dock would be permanent however. He also rejected the Department's plan for the demilune scarp wall and wrote that he would probably increase its dimensions once he studied it further. On 12 June, he sent his plans for the counterscarp wall stating that it would cost $25,000. Three days later he notified the Department that Lieutenant Alexander had completed his topographic survey and asked if the scale of three miles to a foot was acceptable for the finished map. The Department on 7 July 1843 wrote that three feet to one mile is allowable—not three miles to one foot "as you have written." August found work progressing well on the demilune scarp wall—excavations continuing, pilings driven, grillage built, and placing of concrete on it. Carpenters continued finishing the interior of the fort in the officers' and soldiers' quarters.[81]

But the issues between Mansfield and the Department revolving around the design of the demilune scarp wall and the ongoing debate over the counterscarp wall continued during the summer of 1843. After Mansfield rejected the Department's design based on his soil studies, he went ahead with his own plans. On 19 August, he received the Department's revised plans but sent them back immediately writing that the plans "arrived too late to use as work on the foundations has progressed so far that the drastic changes called for cannot be made." Using the plan would have cost much more money to implement so the Department accepted Mansfield's revisions as it was too late to change the grillage; he was ordered to "add to the back of the wall the concrete [as] shown...." Mansfield accepted this change and had his assistant engineer, Alexander, draw up the revised plan and forwarded the new drawing to the Department on 19 September. This final revision for the scarp wall was accepted and was implemented. But still unresolved was the counterscarp wall. On 31 August, Mansfield received the Department's revised plan he had submitted on 12 June 1843. He studied this plan and determined that it needed revision as he believed he could build it much more cheaply so on 30 September, he sent his plan to the Department. On 25 October, after another exchange of plans and revisions, Mansfield finally had the Department's reply to his counterscarp plan—it would stay with its 22 August plan but with some of the modifications Mansfield suggested. At least some of Mansfield's arguments were of such importance that he prevailed.[82]

On 13 October 1843, Mansfield must have been comfortable with the progress of the fort's construction as he requested leave to go north. And he had remained on Cockspur during the summer so he was ready to see his family and conduct personal as well as Department business. He would leave his assistant in charge during his absence; Mansfield decided to stop in Washington, D.C., to visit the Engineer Department and personally deliver Alexander's island survey. Mansfield left Cockspur in early November and arrived in Washington on 8 November. He also left with the Department a memorandum with his questions about several construction issues with the fort and demilune. He left Middletown on 11 December and arrived on the island on 19 December. He soon received a reply at the end of the month from Colonel Totten giving detailed, lengthy answers to all of Mansfield's construction issues. Mansfield and Totten came to agreement on all open issues except for the width of the moat at the demilune: Mansfield insisted on 40 feet and Totten, 30. After exchanges of letters for two months, Totten on 4 March 1844 maintained his insistence on 30 feet. Mansfield perhaps was too insistent on what Totten saw as an unnecessary point of contention or perhaps was somewhat irritated at Mansfield's seemingly incessant revision of the Department's plans for the fort. Totten also

[80] Young, "Connecticut Yankee," 227-228; Young, "Severe Storm of 1842 Had Little Effect on Fort Pulaski Structure," *Savannah Morning News*, 16 June 1935; RSOCE, M1047, 22 March 1842. On 28 July he wrote the Department that total expenditures to 30 September 1842 on the fort including Babcock's totaled $777,747.93; RSOCE, M1123, 28 July 1843.

[81] Young, "Connecticut Yankee," 215-216; 229-230; Young, "Severe Storm of 1842 Had Little Effect on Fort Pulaski Structure," *Savannah Morning News*, 16 June 1935; RSOCE, M1094, 15 June 1843; RSOCE, M1103, 6 July 1843.

[82] Young, "Connecticut Yankee," 230-236; Young, "Fort Pulaski Project Continued Briskly in Third Quarter of 1843," *Savannah Morning News*, 23 June 1935; RSOCE, M1131, 19 August 1843. Mansfield estimated that the Department's plan would have increased the cost of the scarp wall by $1,983.25; RSOCE, M1140, 30 August 1843. In a report Mansfield made on 4 September 1843, he described full-time employees and of the eight described, three were from Connecticut, only one from Georgia (F.M. Stock—"Victualler", one from Florida, and three foreign born. The Nutmeggers were Ralph Dunning who was his clerk, Thomas E. Minor was his chief overseer, and Levi Mitchell was his master carpenter. The Floridian was Francis J. Cercopoly who was captain of the island's tender. He had been around since the beginning of the Cockspur construction under Babcock and was known to Lieutenant Robert E. Lee. Lee remembered Cercopoly when as a Confederate General he revisited Cockspur to inspect the fort 11 November 1861. Mansfield included the baker, Christopher Wagner, who was from Germany; the master mason, William Fludder from England, and the suboverseer, E. Harrington, from Ireland. Young, "Connecticut Yankee," 236-238.

rejected Mansfield's plan for toilets in the fort notifying him that they must be outside the fort! Historian Young noted that the moat around the fort was actually dug to a 48 foot width and the demilune moat to 30 feet--apparently Mansfield did not get his way after all. [83]

1844

Work continued progressing well on the fort for the first three months of the calendar year 1844 but Mansfield's dealings with the Engineer Department continued to be frequent and sometimes contentious over details. On 16 March the Department sent Mansfield a new demilune plan and told him to delay the construction of the demilune gateway until Colonel Totten sent him details for it. Totten also wanted Mansfield to send him detailed drawings of all the sluices. Mansfield disagreed with the Department's demilune plan requiring him to build the rampart terreplein 11 feet wide as he thought 10 was adequate and was in fact built to 10 feet. On 22 March 1844, the Department sent Mansfield the long awaited demilune drawbridge plans and told him that after the drawbridge was constructed, to send the Department drawings of it as built—perhaps to ensure that the headstrong engineer had followed Totten's orders. Mansfield quickly replied on 29 March that the drawbridge plans he received if followed exactly would be much more expensive to construct. He urged that earth walls would suffice in place of piles and grillage for holding up the masonry walls on each side of the passage from the parade to the piers of the drawbridge. This time the Department quickly agreed with his assessment and construction continued. On 10 May, Mansfield sent the demilune drawbridge plans as actually constructed to the Department via Captain John Mackay of the Topographical Engineers who was passing through on his way to Washington.[84]

The first six months of 1844 saw much progress on the fort even though during April, May, and June, the workforce was reduced from 80 on 1 April, to 17 on 11 June. The laborers worked on the excavations for the counterscarp wall and demilune moat, repairs to the North Dock, laying the foundations for the demilune hotshot furnace and the drawbridge, and filling in the parade of the demilune. Masons had much work to do also including plastering two gorge cisterns, fitting iron carriage tracks for the barbette battery, pointing of walls, and lathing and plastering officers' quarters. Carpenters also accomplished much such as casing doors and windows of the officers' quarters, fitting doors, windows, and mountings for the three casemates of the soldiers' quarters and constructing ventilators. Mansfield on 18 April wrote to the Department that he planned on stopping work between 1 and 15 June to buy iron for the drawbridge and for his health, and not return to the fort until 1 November. The Department was slow to respond so on 11 June he repeated his request and noted that his health was "bad." He supplemented his request by noting that work was suspended on 11 June and "good men will not work in the sickly seasons." Mansfield discharged the workers for the season; he left 14 June for the cooler north after receiving permission on 12 June. But the Department instructed him that he would resume active involvement with the Board of Engineers of which he remained a member. He left Lieutenant Alexander and eight laborers on the island to maintain and repair as needed what was already built. They spent July embanking the rear of the counterscarp wall among other things but even they were discharged by the end of July. Alexander requested leave to go north, Mansfield approved, and the Department agreed on 15 July. The Department ordered Alexander to report to Major John Lind Smith in New York Harbor and he left to do so on 27 July. But before he left, he prudently hired two laborers and one mechanic to remain on Cockspur to ensure the security of the place and maintain it.[85]

Meanwhile Mansfield, after his 10-day trip home to Middletown, arrived 24 June, found good news waiting when he arrived: Congress had appropriated $13,000 for his fort for the fiscal year 1 July 1844 through 30 June 1845. In response to the Department's request to supply it with a plan for its expenditure, Mansfield sent it on 19 July. He proposed primarily to complete the demilune moats, finish the scarp wall, build the draw and fixed bridges, bank the glacis and the demilune's parapet and rampart, and finish plastering the casemates. Then on 18 October 1844, he sent to

---

[83] Young, "Connecticut Yankee," 240-243; 246-248; Young, "Fort Pulaski Project Continued Briskly in Third Quarter of 1843," *Savannah Morning News*, 23 June 1935; RSOCE, M1177, 13 October 1843; RSOCE, M1191, 31 October 1843; RSOCE M1203, 8 December 1843; RSOCE, M1214, 20 December 1843; RSOCE, M1246 and M1249, 19 and 28 February 1844. Young, "Connecticut Yankee," 262, n. 61.

[84] Young, "Connecticut Yankee," 245-252; Young, "Lengthy Discussion On Construction Problems For Fort Pulaski in 1844," *Savannah Morning News*, 30 June 1935.

[85] Young, "Connecticut Yankee," 253-265; Young, "Lengthy Discussion On Construction Problems For Fort Pulaski in 1844," *Savannah Morning News*, 30 June 1935; RSOCE, M1286, 18 April 1844; RSOCE, M1312, 11 June 1844; RSOCE, M1329, 11 July 1844. The only "Maj. Smith" found in Heitman who was a major and engineer officer at that time was John Lind Smith.

the Department the tasks completed for the previous year which showed much accomplished as noted above. Unstated by Mansfield but noted by the fort's historian, Rogers Young, the year had been hard on him: "Correspondence with the Department over constructional problems, much of it of no great significance had measurably increased. The condition of his health had been none too good throughout the whole year. Though only forty-one, he had been laboriously engaged at Fort Pulaski, and at other projects along the malarial southern coast since 1828, and his constitution was beginning to give way. He had not allowed such circumstances to affect the work of the year." Mansfield was detained in the north for duty on the Board of Engineers in New York and Washington finally leaving for the fort 22 October. Prior to his departure on 19 October, he asked that Lieutenant Alexander be ordered to the fort by 1 November. Mansfield returned to the fort on 2 November and began work.[86]

Mansfield worked by himself in November as his assistant failed to appear. His paperwork fight with the Department continued as he asked several times for its plans for the main sluiceway but other work was accomplished by his one mason, three carpenters, and 68 laborers. While the mason was building the demilune shot furnace, the carpenters constructed the casemate quarters cupboard doors. But the laborers did much work such as excavating the moat and counterscarp foundation, grading the terreplein of the barbette battery, and embanking and grading the covert way and glacis of the north and northeast fronts. Mansfield finally received the long awaited sluiceway plans and he began at once his usual colloquy with the Department arguing for changes. On 20 December, Colonel Totten returned Mansfield's changes stating that it varied little from the Department's. Mansfield was not done so on 28 December he tried again, submitting explanatory information supporting his original request. Totten was tired of the exchanges with Mansfield so on 7 January 1845, he wrote that he would "not enter a discussion on points where there is a mere difference of opinion." Mansfield gave in perhaps seeing that his chief was not happy so on 17 January he wrote that he would construct the sluiceway according "to the plan furnished me by the Department." Alexander finally returned on 3 December 1844 so work during that month progressed well ending the year productively.[87]

1845

Other than the routine disagreements between Mansfield and the Department, January 1845 began well with his crew of some 60 men busily employed.[88] During the first quarter of the calendar year, much work was accomplished by laborers and masons who were completing the foundations of the main and demilune drawbridges and building the counterscarp wall. Masons also completed the demilune hotshot furnace. Carpenters helped by working on the grillage and piles for the counterscarp wall and the main sluiceway, and interior finishing details for the officers' and soldiers' quarters. But all this very productive and necessary work used up funds which Congress had appropriated and a new $17,000 amount approved on 3 March would only become available on 1 July. Consequently in late April, all funds were exhausted. Mansfield decided with the concurrence of the Department to continue work on credit from the Planters Bank of Savannah. On 1 May the project was over $800 in debt; he wrote the Department on 9 May that he would suspend operations at the end of May due to "lack of funds and the hot weather," the same reasons for work suspension he had given many times in the past. By the end of the month his workforce was down to 36 men and the project was more than $3,000 in debt.[89]

---

[86] Young, "Connecticut Yankee," 270; Young, "Lengthy Discussion On Construction Problems For Fort Pulaski in 1844," *Savannah Morning News*, 30 June 1935; RSOCE, M1362, 12 August 1844. Mansfield wrote that total expenditures on the fort totaled $800,591.16 as of 30 June 1844. On 3 December 1844, he requested permission to repair the temporary wooden quarters outside the fort as the roofs leak, and painting as required among other things; RSOCE, M1405, 3 December 1844. The Department in a 7 June 1844 letter to Mansfield agreed that he should suspend operations at Pulaski during hot months and work on Boston Harbor Governors Island defenses until about 1 November leaving a small force at Pulaski, letter courtesy of the Middlesex County Historical Society.

[87] Young, "Connecticut Yankee," 270-273; Young, "Lengthy Discussion On Construction Problems For Fort Pulaski in 1844," *Savannah Morning News*, 30 June 1935.

[88] A weather-related mishap occurred however in January due to extreme cold weather which sprung out part of the counterscarp wall near the drawbridge site necessitating rebuilding of that section. Young, "Mansfield's Active Supervision of Work at Fort Pulaski at End," *Savannah Morning News*, 7 July 1935.

[89] Young, "Connecticut Yankee," 276-277; Young, "Mansfield's Active Supervision of Work at Fort Pulaski at End," *Savannah Morning News*, 7 July 1935. Interesting that Mansfield and later his successor, Alexander, recorded that the carpenters worked on "sinks" (toilets) in the casemates for the soldiers' quarters so apparently Totten had relented in his views about outside latrines. Young notes that no evidence of sinks currently exists in other than the officers' quarters; Young, "Connecticut Yankee," 293, n. 37; 299.

Then in early June 1845 due to lack of funds, work ground to almost a complete halt. On 4 June he reported that "two casemates of the officers' quarters and five of the soldiers' were then complete, except for 'painting, locks to doors, and glazing to the lights over the doors.'" He also wrote that all work will be suspended around 15 June 1845 except for three or four laborers to maintain the works and embank the glacis. He added that "A summer's operations here would be superfluous as the fort can be occupied by troops should the state of the country require." Finally on 1 July, he reported that the "main sluice has been completed to the coping and water from the sea let into the ditches." Years of working on the fort under often hot and humid conditions, combined with the immense workload he had especially when he was without an assistant engineer, prompted Mansfield to ask the Department for a permanent change of station. The 44-year-old veteran engineer's health was not as strong as when he started the project 14 years earlier so he presented his case to his cousin, Colonel Totten, on 31 May:

> If there be a station at the North to which I can be ordered without injustice to another, I shall be pleased to change. I will merely remark that I have been at the South for 17 years; and 14 years of that time at this post where my duties comparatively have been laborious in the extreme. My constitution is now broken and my health to say the best of it poor. I have for several years been dissatisfied with this locality, but have supposed it a duty from which I could not be relieved without injury to the service till I had completed and secured the foundation of this fort which I had commenced. I believe this is now accomplished, and I must acknowledge my reluctance to continue on this station.
>
> I will observe here that the ditches of this fort are all excavated and the counterscarp completed to the coping and the sluice it is expected will be completed to its coping in a few days. The work here to be done, will of course, be above high water level. It will however require the Superintendence of an Engineer Officer for Two years to come to complete it, although on emergency it might receive a Garrison at once.[90]

Understanding that it would take some time for the Department to make a decision, on 10 June 1845 he requested leave from 1 July to 1 November to go home to Middletown and "recruit his health and attend to private business." Operations at the fort would be closed and the fort left under Alexander's charge. As there was unrest in Texas, he added that "the work is so far advanced as to be capable of defense in case of emergency." On 16 June 1845, the Department granted his leave request.[91]

During June, Mansfield was busy corresponding with the Department concerning the fort's cannon. First, the Department requested an inventory of what guns were at Pulaski. Mansfield replied that he had mounted 20, long, 32-pound casemate guns, with 1,000 shot, but no powder even though the two magazines at both ends of the gorge face were ready for powder. He then listed ordnance needed to complete arming the fort's casemates: 31 long, 32-pound guns and four carronades or howitzers for the flanks, with carriages, implements, shot and balls. Many more guns were needed for the fort and demilune: barbette—40 seacoast 24 pounders, 12 seacoast 8 inch howitzers, two eight inch siege howitzers, and four, 18 pounders; for the demilune—14 seacoast 32 pounders, 14 seacoast twenty-four pounders, and two coehorn mortars; for the advanced battery, one 13 inch and seven 10 inch seacoast mortars. He asked that the casemate guns be shipped immediately and the rest as soon as practicable. On 24 June, the Department told him that all of his requested guns had been requisitioned except for those he designated for the demilune as they could not be mounted yet. Even though he protested that he could build earthen walls to substitute for the breast-high walls there, his appeal was unproductive. At the end of June he wrote his final reports, the last of which requested that the Department ask the Department of the Treasury for a draft for the balance of $4,831.56 due the Planters Bank in Savannah "to make good an accommodation" made to him. He noted that it should be sent to him in Middletown, Connecticut, for which he sailed on 1 July 1845.[92]

His accomplishments cannot be exaggerated during his 14-year tour on Cockspur Island. The historian of the fort's construction, Rogers Young, summarized them: "The foundations of the fort and demilune had long been completed,

---

[90] Young, "Connecticut Yankee," 279-281; Young, "Mansfield's Active Supervision of Work at Fort Pulaski at End," *Savannah Morning News*, 7 July 1935; M1475, RSOCE, 31 May 1845.

[91] Young, "Mansfield's Active Supervision of Work at Fort Pulaski at End," *Savannah Morning News*, 7 July 1935; RSOCE, M1480, 10 June 1845.

[92] Young, "Connecticut Yankee," 282-284; Young, "Mansfield's Active Supervision of Work at Fort Pulaski at End," *Savannah Morning News*, 7 July 1935. Before he left, Mansfield did an inspection of Fort Jackson near Savannah as appropriations were available in 1845 to rehabilitate and repair the old, Second System work. Mansfield's successor, Lieutenant Alexander, took charge both of Forts Pulaski and Jackson; work continued on Fort Jackson until it was seized by the State of Georgia 3 January 1861; Georgia Historical Society, Old Fort Jackson, http://www.chsgeorgia.org/Old-Fort-Jackson.html. The total cannon Mansfield requested were 151 compared to the original 172 planned at the fort's beginning. Mansfield noted that his armament schedule followed the Department's of 21 March 1842 except he added one to the demilune and two for the barbette.

the massive walls of both works erected, much of the interior arrangement, finish, and trim of both works installed, the moats excavated and their sides revetted with masonry, necessary wharves built, and a drainage, dike and embankment system practically laid out on the island." Finishing details included installation of the drawbridges and portcullis, erection of a piazza along the gorge, and embanking of the barbette platform and the parades of the fort and demilune. The fort was declared finished on 3 April 1847 by Lieutenant Barton S. Alexander who succeeded Mansfield. Young provided a fitting assessment of Mansfield's efforts on the fort: "The fact that the Fort Pulaski project was so remarkably advanced on July 1, 1845, was due in the largest measure to the faithful and indefatigable devotion to duty, to the directing genius, and to the sound and practical engineering wisdom of Captain Mansfield."[93]

Mansfield had arrived home unwell and found his wife sick too, plus his personal business affairs were in disorder due to his long absences from home. But he received welcome news from the Department on 14 August—his orders relieving him from the supervision of construction at Fort Pulaski and detailing him for duty in Texas. On that day he replied:

> I have received the letters of the Department of the 11th with extracts of Special Orders 66 and 68 and orders for me to proceed to Aransas Bay Texas and report to Bt. Brig. Gen. Taylor for duty.
> I shall comply with the order as soon as practicable. My uniform must be altered and my wife is sick but I expect to leave here on Monday or Tuesday next and shall write the Department when I start. It is probable I shall take the route of the Ohio and Mississippi Rivers to New Orleans. And unless otherwise instructed probably shall not stop in Washington.[94]

Mansfield reported to Totten on 30 September 1845 that he had arrived at Corpus Christi 19 September 1845 for duty.[95] Other than his day at Antietam on 17 September 1862, his Mexican-American War duty would be the highlight of his long Army career.

Although it took two more years to finish the fort, once complete, it became fully functional to guard the entrance to the important Savannah River to protect the city except for being fully armed or garrisoned. The total cost from the time it was started to the beginning of the Civil War was over one million dollars for the 25,000,000-brick structure, 1,508 feet in circumference, with 32-foot-high walls, seven to eleven feet thick. It had two tiers of guns, one mounted in casemates and the other en barbette, and a seven-foot-deep, 35-40 foot wide moat. A two-mile long, six-foot-high dike protected the fort and construction village. The depth of the water in the Fort's moat was controlled by three tidal gates and the feeder canal to the river's South Branch. A causeway led from the Fort to the south wharf, with another path connecting the fort to the north dock and workmen's village. This village had grown since Mansfield and Lee's initial survey in 1831: in the early 1840s, there were about 20 structures in three areas, most located near the north dock. Northwest of the demilune were the mechanic's quarters, a storm house, and cisterns. The South Channel site had a stable, lime house, cement house, and two cisterns. Two outhouses were built in the mid-1840s just south of the fort's southwestern corner. But most of these wooden buildings in the three locations did not survive until the Civil War as a hurricane in 1854 and other strong storms either swept them away or severely damaged them. As the Civil War approached, Fort Pulaski was in poor condition with most of the moat filled with mud and grass and the 20 guns that Mansfield had mounted before his tour was finished in 1845 were all that were in the fort of the 146 planned for it.[96]

In 1860, the fort was not in condition to defend itself or Savannah. It had only a caretaker and ordnance sergeant stationed at the fort and the casemates in which the 20 cannon were mounted not only could not be manned but the carriages were so deteriorated so they could not be safely fired. Georgia seceded from the Union on 19 January 1861 and in February joined the Confederacy. But in what could be called a preemptive strike, Gov. Joseph E. Brown of Georgia on 2 January 1861, ordered Colonel Alexander R. Lawton, the commander of the 1st Georgia Volunteers in Savannah, "to take possession of Fort Pulaski...and to hold it against all persons....Immediately upon occupying the Fort, you will take measures to put it in a thorough state of defense." The next day, Lawton and 134 men landed from the steamer *Ida* at the fort and took possession, meeting no resistance. They found that the powder there was unusable as were the shells, and

---

[93] Young, "Connecticut Yankee," 288; Young, "Mansfield's Active Supervision of Work at Fort Pulaski at End," *Savannah Morning News*, 7 July 1935; Young, *The Georgia Historical Quarterly*, vol. 20, no. 1, 1936, 49-50.

[94] Young, "Connecticut Yankee," 289; RSOCE, M1505, 14 August 1845.

[95] Rodgers W. Young, vol. 2, 517.

[96] Young, "The Construction of Fort Pulaski," 48-50. NPS, Historic American Buildings Survey (HABS), "Addendum to Fort Pulaski," HABS No. GA-2158, Washington, D.C., 1, 9; Ralston B. Lattimore, *Fort Pulaski National Monument, Georgia*. Handbook Series No. 18 (Washington, DC: National Park Service, 1961), 10. Young, "Robert E. Lee and Fort Pulaski," 16.

the solid shot inadequate. Georgia troops immediately began needed repairs and arming the fort so by April 1862, the fort had a total of 48 guns. But this armament and repairs were inadequate when 36 Union guns located on Tybee Island began bombarding the fort on 10 April 1862. Despite General Robert E. Lee's pronouncement during his inspection of the fort on 11 November 1861 that "they [Union cannon] will make it very warm for you with shells from that point but they cannot breach at that distance" he did not consider the Yankee's effective use of rifled cannon. It is likely that Mansfield and all his fellow engineers would have agreed with Lee's assessment but after it was shown conclusively at Fort Pulaski that rifled cannon could breach masonry walls, at least a few would have contemplated altering current masonry forts and redesigning planned forts to prevent such rifled-cannon destruction. Colonel Charles H. Olmstead, commanding Confederate troops in the fort, surrendered unconditionally on 11 April, after 30 hours of bombardment with 5,275 shells. Two Connecticut regiments, the 6th and 7th Connecticut Volunteers, took part in the victory, but the 6th stationed on Jones's Island northeast of Fort Pulaski, did not fire as it was there to prevent reinforcements coming down the river while it manned its nine heavy guns. Troops of the 7th Connecticut had hauled 36 heavy guns 2½ miles across the swampy Tybee Island, where they were mounted at distances of up to 1¼ miles from their target. On the morning of April 10, a captain from Meriden, Oliver S. Sanford, touched off the first round. The shell carried a message to the defenders: "A nutmeg from Connecticut; can you furnish a grater?" Over 400 men of the 7th manned five of the six mortar batteries with its colonel, Alfred H. Terry, in immediate command. It served garrison duty after the fort's fall and helped in its repair.[97] The Union general commanding the district was none other than Brigadier General Henry Washington Benham who had been Mansfield's assistant 1837-1839. The fort became a Union military prison, then, in subsequent decades, the demilune was extensively remodeled. In 1899, construction began on Battery Horace Hambright near the North Dock. The steel and concrete battery contained three ammunition magazines and two gun emplacements. In the 1890's, the City of Savannah constructed a quarantine station on Cockspur and the Federal government constructed an extensive village which by 1928 contained over 20 buildings. On 15 October 1924, the fort became a monument by proclamation of President Calvin Coolidge. The National Park Service (NPS) took over Fort Pulaski 10 August 1933. The Civilian Conservation Corps arrived in 1934 and within two years rehabilitated the neglected fort and added visitor amenities. Fort Pulaski and Cockspur Island were again used by the military in World War II as a Naval Base but after the war military buildings were demolished by the early 1950's. The NPS constructed a visitor center which opened in 1964. Repairs and rehabilitation continue to ensure the structural integrity of the fort and to allow Cockspur Island and its famous fort to be appreciated by visitors.[98]

---

[97] Stephen Walkley, *History of the Seventh Connecticut Volunteer Infantry* (Hartford, CT: n.p., 1905), 38-46; Stephen R. Smith, et al, *Record of Service of Connecticut Men in the Army and Navy of the United States During the War of the Rebellion* (Hartford, CT: Press of The Case, Lockwood & Brainard Company, 1889), 257, 290; Niven, 142-145; Gillmore, "Siege and Capture of Fort Pulaski," B&L, vol. 2, 1-12.

[98] Quincy A. Gillmore, *Official Report to the United States Engineer Department, of the Siege and Reduction of Fort Pulaski, Georgia, February, March, and April, 1862* (New York, NY: D. Van Nostrand, 1862), 15-16, 38, 57, 58; *ORA*, vol. 6, 146. Charles C. Jones, Jr., "The Seizure and Reduction of Fort Pulaski," *The Magazine of American History Illustrated*, vol. 14, July 1885, 54-56; Charles H. Olmstead, "Fort Pulaski," *The Georgia Historical Quarterly*, vol. 1, no. 2, June 1917, 102; "Addendum to Fort Pulaski," HABS No. GA-2158, 12-15; Captain Francis S. Bartow became Fort Pulaski's new commander. By the time they left the fort in May 1861, the Georgia Volunteers had learned some military skills which were needed when they were ordered north to Virginia where they fought in the Battle of First Bull Run. Brigadier General Bartow died from wounds received while leading his men. The seemingly obvious lesson that Third System Forts were obsolete thanks to rifled cannon was not clear to all U.S. Army engineers after the end of the Civil War. The fact that the Union cannon, both rifled and smooth bore, were on land versus water greatly contributed to their efficacy as seacoast forts were designed to protect entrances to waterways leading to cities. Even later in the Civil War, armored Union ships never took well-defended coastal Rebel forts without aid from land forces. But Congress decided to retain masonry forts due to the expense of building new works or refitting current forts. In 1862 Totten "recommended keeping the current system of masonry forts, but either adding a dirt front or iron plating the casemates if they fell within range of potential land batteries" Totten also recommended adding a second tier of casemate guns replacing barbette cannon. "The damage done to the masonry scarps by the armored monitors, and occasionally by distant guns on land where such was possible, showed conclusively that the masonry scarp on sea fronts must in the future be dispensed with, as had been the case centuries before on land fronts. Consequently, beginning shortly after the Civil War, all the new batteries built for our seacoast defenses had earthen exterior slopes, and no additional masonry scarps were built," U.S. Army Engineer School, William M. Black, "Pamphlet on The Evolution of the Art of Fortification" (Washington, DC: GPO, 1919), 100. Experiments in 1869 with metal plates inside fort walls were unsatisfactory. Not until the Endicott Report in 1886 recommended new fort construction, did seacoast forts begin to move into the modern era ending the Totten System. The Endicott System improved fort defenses with their "one-tier works with dispersed batteries, built with reinforced concrete and padded with earth. The new forts utilized new technologies such as the 'disappearing' gun carriage, improved metals for casting weapons, smokeless powder, perfection of breech loading and indirect gun sights;" David P. Eldridge, "Brick Versus Earth: The Construction and Destruction of Confederate Seacoast Forts Pulaski and McAllister, Georgia" (1996), unpublished master's thesis dissertation, University of Florida, http://digitalcommons.unf.edu/etd/128, 63-73; Kaufman, 230-231; Weaver, 56-57; Lewis, 43-44.

The 48th New York Infantry band at Fort Pulaski in 1863 with northwest corner of fort in background. Note structures on top of walls constructed of sandbags built by Confederates to provide added protection against enemy fire on the open barbette. Courtesy LOC.

Another 1863 view of the 48th New York looking to the southeast wall showing the southeast hot shot furnace and south wall; the small structure to the left of center is in the east angle of the fort and served as a watch tower. Courtesy LOC.

Map of area in December 1864 for Major General William T. Sherman's operations which resulted in the capture of Savannah. *OA*, pl. 70. Courtesy LOC.

Modern photograph showing sally port on the gorge face which faces west. Courtesy Wikipedia.

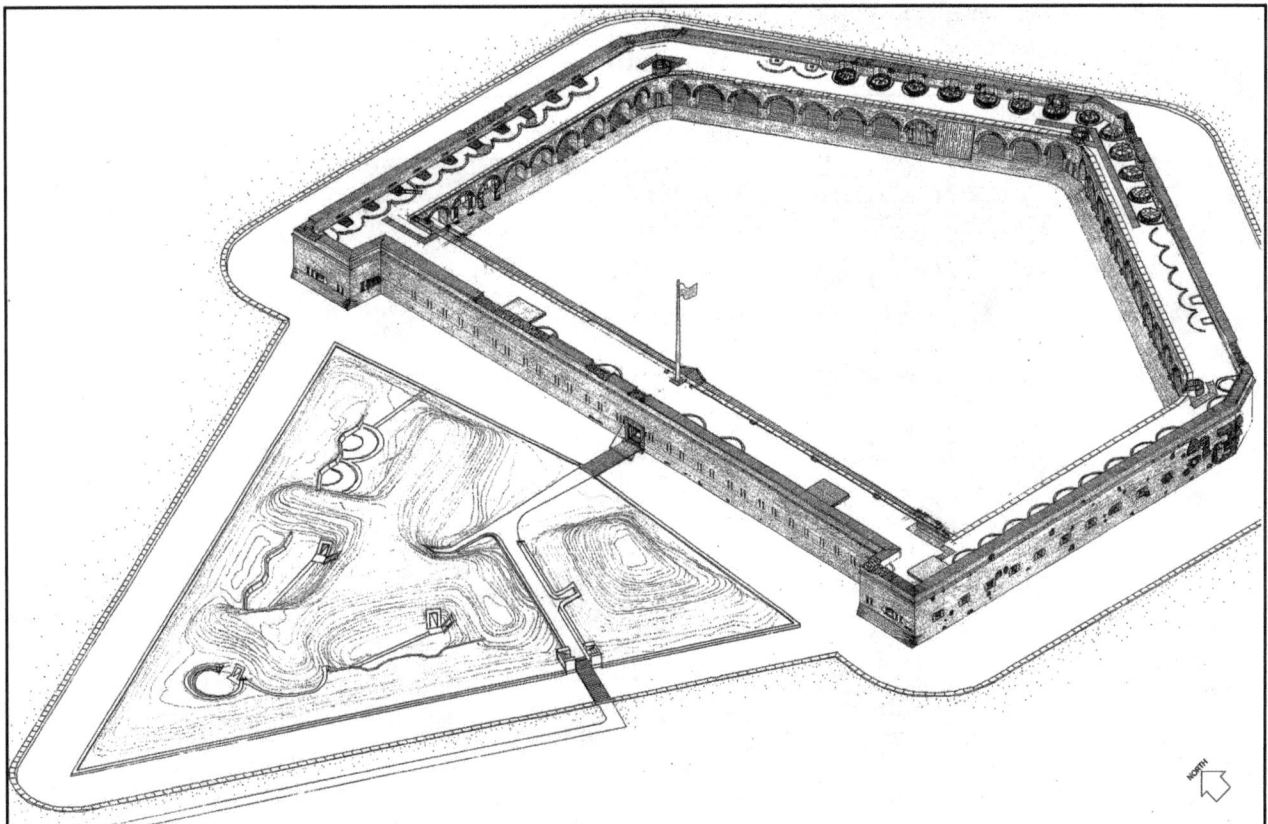

Modern sketch of Fort Pulaski showing damage from Union cannon on its south face. Courtesy LOC.

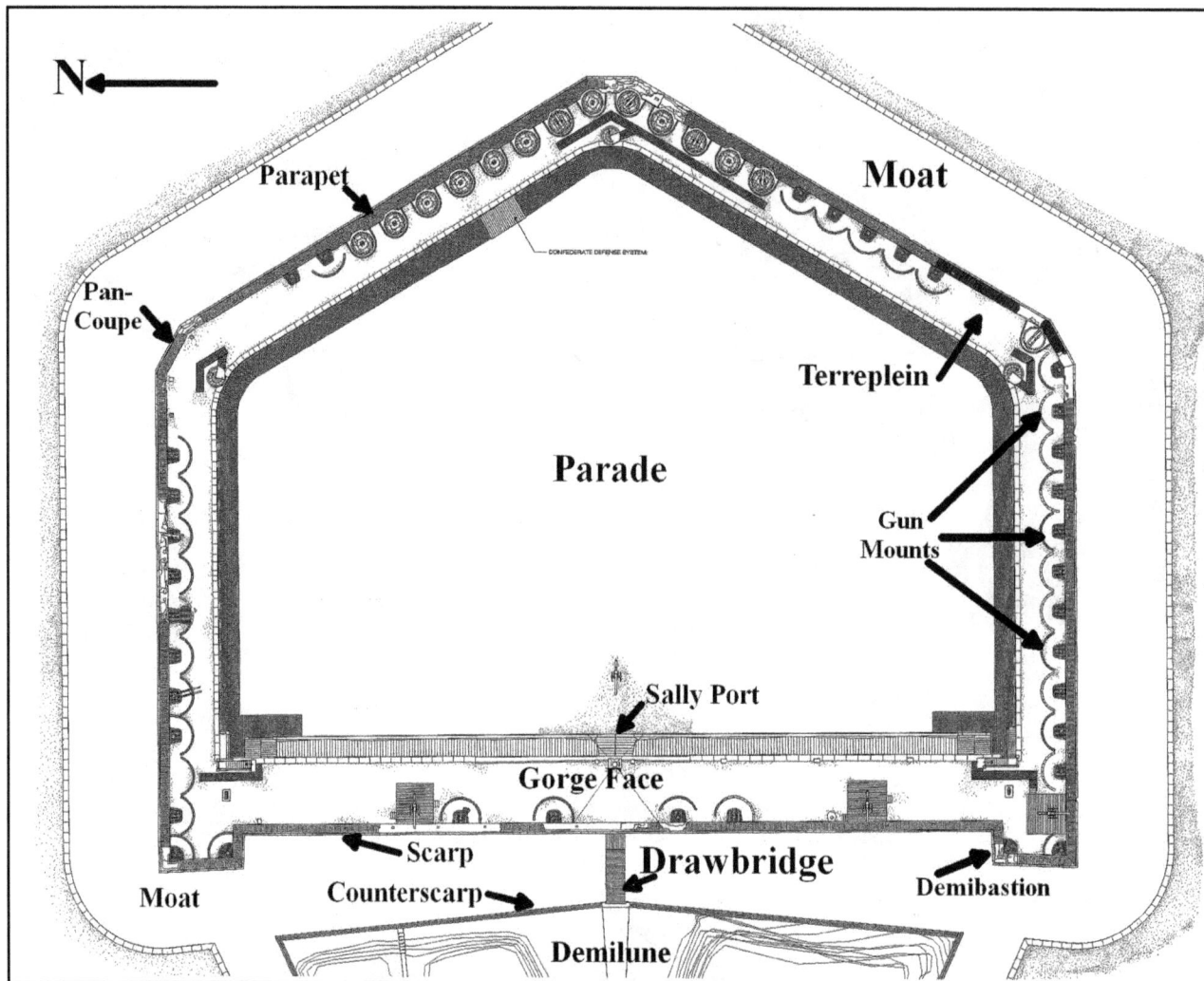

Modern drawing of top view showing elements of the fort. Courtesy NPS and LOC.

Photograph of a cistern which, among others, is all that remains of the construction village at Fort Pulaski. Given its location, it may have been near the Bake House. The square brick structure is possibly an oven. Photograph by author, March 2014.

Cockspur Island, North Dock, facing northwest. Note granite blocks still in place on the North Branch of the Savannah River. Large container ships use the channel on their journeys to dock in Savannah. Photograph by author, March 2014.

Detail of North Dock showing iron straps holding granite blocks together and mooring rings. Photograph by author, March 2014.

View facing south from south wall of fort. The South Channel of the Savannah River is today used only by small boats. Photo by author, April 2015.

Attachment 1
Glossary of Fortification Terms[99]

(A word in **bold** in a definition is a term defined elsewhere in this Glossary.)

Abatis: An obstacle made from trees driven into the earth that have been sharpened on the side facing the attacker, also known as fraises; also tree branches and brush which may be intertwined and used to obstruct and slow down the enemy advance.

Advanced Work: A work in advance of a fort, generally within range of the cannon of the day.

Angle of Traverse: The horizontal angle through which a gun can be rotated. The **pintle** location, the **embrasure** size, and the **carriage** design determine this angle.

Approaches: Trenches dug by an attacker, generally parallel to or at a slight angle to the walls of a fort. Also referred to as **parallels**. Approaches are used in the siege of a fort.

Banquette: An earthen or paved **platform** step behind the **parapet** which allows a soldier standing on it to fire over the crest of the **parapet**.

Banquette Slope: The earthen or paved slope leading from the banquet to the covered way or **terraplein**. Riflemen could use this slope for reloading their weapon while shielded from direct fire by the **parapet**.

Barbette: An earthen terrace or platform situated inside the **parapet** or a **rampart**, upon which cannon were mounted so that they could be fired over a **parapet** rather than through a gun port or **embrasure**. A **battery** mounted on the barbette is therefore a "battery en barbette."

Barbette Tier: The top tier of a fort where guns are mounted *en barbette* rather than *en casemate*.

Bastion: A projection from the wall of a fort with two walls and flanks forming an angle which allows soldiers within the bastion to provide protecting fire along the fort's walls. A full bastion has two faces and two flanks; a **demibastion** has one face and one flank.

Battery: 1. A structure, generally smaller than a fort and usually open-backed, designed to mount guns. A battery is generally constructed at a location that does not require a fort. 2. A group of guns or gun emplacements, either within a fort or in the **outworks** of a fort. 3. A group of guns, usually four or six, commanded by a single officer.

Blockhouse: A structure of heavy timber, masonry, or a combination of both. A blockhouse may be a stand-alone structure to guard a particular location, it may be used at a salient or along the **curtain** of a fort in lieu of a **bastion**, or it may be a central structure surrounded by an earthwork. A blockhouse often was a multistory structure with the second level having a larger trace than the first. The overlap would contain **machicolations** – openings to fire down on an attacker.

Bombproof: A structure protected from indirect or plunging fire; a place of refuge during a siege.

Breach: An opening created in a wall, most often during a siege. A breach is generally created by cannon fire or a mine.

---

[99] Note that several of these definitions may be applied to other chapters in this book especially posts which Mansfield inspected while he was an Inspector General. These definitions are primarily excerpted from *A Legacy in Brick and Stone: American Coastal Defense Forts of the Third System, 1816-1867*, 2nd ed., by John R. Weaver II (McGovern Publishing, Redoubt Press, McLean, VA: 2018), used with permission; H.L. Scott, *Military Dictionary* (New York, NY: D. Van Nostrand, 1861), passim; Kaufman, 403-405; Charles Stephenson, ed., *Castles: A History of Fortified Structures, Ancient, Medieval & Modern* (New York, NY: St. Martin's Griffin, 2011, 276-278; Richard P. Weinert, Jr., and Robert Arthur, *Defender of the Chesapeake: The Story of Fort Monroe*, third revised edition (Shippensburg, PA: White Mane Publishing Company, Inc., 1989), 337-340.

Breast-Height Wall: A revetment, generally masonry or wood, which protects defenders while allowing them to fire over the **parapet**. It may be used in **outworks** or the main work.

Breastwork: A breast-height wall that provides a defensive position.

Buttress: A projection from a wall to add strength and/or stabilize the wall. A buttress is generally triangular in shape.

Canister Shot: Containers fired by cannon which are filled with iron balls, usually ranging in size from three-fourths inch to two inches in diameter primarily used against troops. On firing, the canister splits open discharging the balls in a shotgun-like pattern.

Caponier: A small, vaulted **outwork** designed to provide flanking fire along a wall, generally located in the **ditch**. A caponier may or may not be attached to the **scarp** wall. Also, a defensive passageway, generally located in a **ditch** or closing a **ditch**. Caponiers had **loopholes**, **howitzer embrasures**, or both on at least one wall.

Carnot Wall: A detached **scarp**; a **scarp** wall which is separated from the **ramparts** of a fort, usually by a **chemin de ronde**. A Carnot wall was an infantry-defense device that was considered expendable in a siege.

Carronade: A short-barrel cannon used for flanking fire, similar to a **flank howitzer**. Carronades were originally designed for shipboard use, but were also used for antipersonnel missions in forts.

Carriage: A usually wooden structure designed to support a cannon when fired and to transport it. "Seacoast carriages are divided into barbette, casemate, and flank defense carriages, depending on where they are mounted in the fort."

Casemate: A vaulted, bombproof room of masonry construction, sometimes called a gunroom. It provides overhead protection to gunners, and allows tiers of guns to be stacked. Casemates may also provide firing positions for small arms, and may be used for quarters, kitchens, storage, and other sundry functions.

Castle: A tall fort. The term generally refers to a fort with multiple tiers of guns.

Chemin de Ronde: A pathway around the interior of the **scarp** wall of a detached-scarp fort, serving as a firing platform for riflemen.

Cheval-de-Frise: An obstruction consisting of pointed poles extending radially through a central axel. These were often used to block a breach in a wall, or as a barrier to a cavalry charge.

Citadel: A stronghold inside the **scarp** of a fort which serves as a defensive barracks and a last line of defense.

Coping: A sloped or beveled stone cap on top of a parapet to protect the masonry of the wall from rainwater.

Corbel: A block of stone in a corner of a fort which projects out from the wall to help support the weight of the structure.

Cordon: A masonry projection from the top of the **scarp** wall that helps prevent attackers from scaling the wall and protects the face of the **scarp** from drainage. It is called a **coping** when there is no exterior slope to protect.

Counterfort: A buttress on the earthen side of a wall, generally either the **scarp** or the **parade** wall, to increase its strength. A counterfort is generally hidden by earth.

Counterguard: A work with two faces forming a salient angle sometimes placed before a **bastion** or a **ravelin** as protection against attackers.

Counterscarp: The outer side of a ditch of a fortification facing the **ramparts** sometimes faced with stone to make entering and retreating from the **ditch** more difficult for attackers by making it a significant drop to the level of the ditch.

Counterscarp gallery: Casemated areas behind the **counterscarp** wall, allowing a cross-fire into the **ditch**. Counterscarp galleries generally contained **howitzers** at the corners, with **loopholes** in the remaining walls. Access is from the **ditch** or a tunnel under the **ditch**.

Covered way: A pathway or road running along the top of the **counterscarp**, provided with a protective embankment which formed the crest of the **glacis**. The embankment gave the soldiers standing in the covered way some protection from enemy fire, being high enough to obstruct the besiegers view. Also known as the covert way.

Coverface: An earthen, earth-and-masonry, or masonry **outwork** designed to protect the **scarp** of the fort from siege guns.

Crenel: An open-topped **embrasure** at the top of a wall. A crenel is defined by two adjacent **merlons**.

Crochets: Angled or curved paths around a traverse that spans a **covert way**, generally wide enough for only one soldier abreast to pass.

Crownwork: A very elaborate outwork consisting of two **demibastions** joined by **curtains** to a central **bastion**.

Curtain: A fort's wall; the portion of the **scarp** between **bastions**.

Defensive Barracks: A stronghold inside the **scarp** of a fort which serves as a barracks and a last line of defense. Also called a **citadel**.

Demibastion: A half-bastion; a **bastion** with only one **face** and one **flank**.

Demi-lune: A work in the shape of a half-moon which was used to defend the entrance of a fortification. Later, the demilune developed into a detached work called a **ravelin** which was situated within the line of the main **ditch** and was formed by two faces meeting in an outward angle, its purpose was mainly to cover the **curtain** it fronted and to prevent the flanks from being attacked from the side.

Detached work: An outwork which was separated from the main works, such as a **ravelin**, generally located outside of cannon range from the main work.

Ditch: A wide, deep trench excavated along the outer perimeter of a fort between the **scarp** and **counterscarp** wall which was used to impede the approach of an enemy toward the walls. The ditch could be filled with water or left dry. Usually called a "**moat**" when wet.

Drawbridge: A bridge which was used to provide access to a fortification, and when in the raised position it closed the entrance. Generally, a drawbridge was hinged at the bottom and free at the top, and could be drawn up to prevent and enemy gaining entry. The drawbridge usually spanned a **ditch** or **moat**, or the part of a **ditch** or **moat** between the fortification and a causeway.

Embrasure: An opening in the **parapet** or the fort's wall for firing guns through at an enemy protecting the gun crew. The embrasure was internally splayed to allow the gun to be swung through a greater arc increasing its field of fire. An open-topped embrasure, rare in the Third System, is also called a **crenel**.

En Barbette: The practice of mounting cannon on a platform (**barbette**) such that they fire over a wall rather than through an opening (**embrasure**) in that wall.

En Casemate: The practice of mounting cannon in a **casemate** such that they can fire through an **embrasure**.

Exterior Slope: The slope between the **cordon** and the **superior slope**. The exterior slope is usually the steepest slope on the exterior of the **parapet**. It is usually earthen, designed to absorb artillery fire.

Face: The side or sides of the fort which open onto the water, where the primary coastal guns will be located. On a **bastion**, the face is the wall of the **bastion** which is nearly parallel to the **curtain**.

Flank, or Cheek: The side. On a **bastion**, the flank is the portion which is most nearly perpendicular to the **curtain** of the fort. The flank of a **bastion** provided the primary fire along the **curtain**.

Flank Angle: The angle formed by the **curtain** and flank of a **bastion** or **demibastion**. Also called the curtain angle.

Flank Howitzer: A howitzer designed to fire the length of the **ditch**, usually from the flank of a **bastion**. A flank howitzer generally fired canister shot or grapeshot.

Flanking fire: Fire from the side. Enfilading fire.

Fortress: A fortification with a civilian population; a fortified city.

Fraises: A row of sharpened logs placed horizontally or angled downward. These were generally imbedded in an earthen **rampart** of a fort to inhibit escalade.

Gallery: A passageway, generally masonry or masonry revetted. A gallery differed from a **caponier** in that a gallery has no defensive mission and therefore has neither **loopholes** nor **embrasures**.

Glacis: The area outside the **ditch** which was scraped into a gentle slope running downwards from the covered way towards the open country and was kept deliberately free of any form of cover. The glacis brought an approaching assailing force into clear view from the **parapet** of a fortification under attack.

Gorge: The interior side or entrance of a **bastion** or other **outwork**, which is usually the interval between the two flanks of the work; the rear or any part of a work which is next to the body of the place at the **counterscarp** of the **ditch** where there is no rampart.

Grillage: A web of heavy planks used in soils with poor loadbearing capacity so loads could be spread over a wider area. Piles were driven in the soil until they reached a level determined to be adequate, then heavy planks were set side by side with no gaps on the piles then a second course of planks were set over the first laid at right angles; these could have wider gaps. At Cockspur, grillage timbers measured one foot by one foot, while grillage planks were one foot wide and three inches thick.

Guard Room: A room usually within the fort that guards the main **sally port**. A guard room generally has **loopholes** into the **sally port**, and often contains a cell for prisoners.

Hotshot Furnace: A furnace for heating shot. A masonry structure, it consisted of a fire chamber below rails on which the shot would travel. A loading mechanism sat at one end and an unloading mechanism at the other. Hot shot was used to set fire to wooden ships, sails, and rigging.

Howitzer: A short-barreled cannon. Flank howitzers generally were used for antipersonnel missions, firing canister shot. Seacoast howitzers (or siege howitzers) generally utilized a high angle of fire (between a gun and a mortar).

In Battery: A gun in firing position, i.e., at the front of the lower **carriage** with its muzzle at the throat of the **embrasure**.

Interior Crest: The highest point of the **parapet**. The top of the **superior slope**.

Interior Slope: The vertical or near-vertical slope from the crest of the **parapet** to the **banquette**, or the **terraplein** if there is no **banquette**. This slope is generally masonry or wood.

Loophole: A narrow opening in a wall which allows a rifle or musket to fire through it. Also called a rifle slit.

Magazine: The place for storage of powder inside a fort. The main (or storage) magazine would store the bulk of the powder, and day-use (or service) magazines would be secondary storage depots. Magazines were carefully designed to prevent sparks and to provide a dry atmosphere for the powder.

Masonry: Stone or brickwork of the wall.

Merlon: A rectangular projection from the top of a wall. **Crenels** and merlons alternate on a crenellated wall.

Moat: A wide and deep ditch filled with water which surrounded a fort.

Outworks: Works located within or beyond the **ditch**, i.e., works outside the **enceinte** of the fort.

Pan-coupé: A cut corner in a wall. A feature of an unbastioned fort, consisting of a wall that connects two **curtains**. It follows the trace of the **gorge** of a **bastion** in a bastioned fort, replacing a sharp **salient** with two broader **salients**.

Parade: The open area in the center of a fort, usually used for drilling troops, for barracks area, etc.

Parallel: Trenches dug by an attacker, generally parallel to or at a slight angle to the **curtains** of a fort. Also referred to as **approaches**. Parallels are used in the siege of a fort.

Parapet: A breastwork or wall used to protect the defenders on the **ramparts** of a fortification, either plain or provided with **embrasures**.

Pintle: The pin around which a gun carriage rotates. A front-pintle carriage for a gun mounted *en casemate* generally has the pintle at the narrowest part (throat) of the **embrasure**. A center-pintle carriage, sometimes used on a **barbette** emplacement, allows a full 360-degree traverse of the gun.

Portcullis: A heavy wooden or iron gate usually on the inner side of a **sally port** closed to prevent attackers from entering the fort but allows the defenders to fire at them. A portcullis generally opened vertically.

Postern : The "back door" of a fort. Posterns are secondary entrances leading through the **ramparts** and either into or over the **ditch**. A postern often connect to a **ravelin**, an exterior batteries, or another outwork.

Rampart: A thick wall of earth or masonry which was used for defense, excavated from the **ditch**, and either raised on the inside or outside of the **ditch** usually topped by a parapet.

Ravelin: An attached or detached pointed, triangular-shaped fortification with faces used to split attacking forces; also called a **demilune** when outside a fort giving protection to the **scarp** and/or providing additional **batteries**.

Revetment: A strong retaining wall constructed on the outside of a fortification's earthwork **rampart** and **parapet**, so as to prevent it falling into the **ditch**. The covering of an earthen **rampart** to prevent it from deteriorating, using such materials as stones or masonry.

Sally port: A small, heavily fortified gateway or gate, from the inner works to the outer works of a fortification used by defenders to launch sorties to attack besiegers usually located on the **gorge** wall.

Scarp: The side of the ditch next to the **parapet**; also known as the escarp.

Shell: A projectile fired from a cannon or mortar that has a hollow interior filled with explosives.

Ship-of-the-line, or **capital ship:** A large warship. A ship-of-the-line was generally a three-masted sailing ship with three of four decks of cannon. These large ships were the principal warships of a fleet prior to the use of ironclads.

Shot: A solid iron projectile fired from cannon. Shot had far more momentum than **shell**, but did its damage through momentum only.

Shoulder: The place on a **bastion** or **demibastions** where the **face** and the flank meet. The shoulder of a **bastion** is generally at its widest point.

Shoulder Angle: The angle formed by the face and flank of a **bastion** or **demibastion**.

Siege: The protracted taking of a fort, beginning with investment and continuing through the breaching and ultimate reduction of the work. By the time of the Third System, it was understood that ultimately no fort could hold out indefinitely to a siege.

Sole: The bottom of an **embrasure** or **loophole**.

Terreplein, also terraplein: The rear body of a **rampart**; the gun position on the top of a **rampart** located behind a **parapet**.

Throat: The narrowest part of an **embrasure** or the narrow portion between the flanks of a **bastion** nearest the **parade**.

Totten Embrasure: Four-inch thick cast iron reinforcement around an **embrasure** sometimes incorporating **Totten Shutters** developed by J. G. Totten.

Totten Shutters: Two-inch thick iron doors which had a self-closing mechanism to protect gunners. When the gunners ran out the gun, the door automatically opened and after firing, automatically closed when the gun recoiled. Some sources state that gas pressure from the gun firing opened the shutters.

Traverse: 1. An earthen or masonry-revetted earthen mound which breaks the open area of the **terraplein**, separating men and guns to eliminate enfilading fire and minimizing damage from exploding shells. Traverses also allow defense of portions of the **ramparts** when other portions have been stormed, and often house bombproofs and **magazines**. 2. The arc of stone on which the rear wheels of guns travel. The individual stones are generally referred to as traverse blocks. The iron rail that the wheels travel on is generally referred to as a traverse rail.

Attachment 2
Engineers and Assistant Engineers Assigned to Fort Pulaski to 1861
With Highest Civil War Rank[100]

Engineers

Maj. Samuel Babcock, 1 August 1828 - 18 December 1830; died 26 June 1831

1st Lt.; Capt. Joseph King Fenno Mansfield, 18 December 1830 - 11 August 1845; major general U.S.A.

1st Lt. Barton Stone Alexander, 1 September 1845 - 11 March 1848; brevet brigadier general U.S.A.

1st Lt. Isaac Ingalls Stevens, 11 March 1848 - 13 September 1848; major general U.S.A.

1st Lt. Jeremy Francis Gilmer, 13 September 1848 - 14 June 1858; major general C.S.A.

1st Lt. William Henry Chase Whiting, 14 June 1858 - 3 January 1861 (fort seized by Georgia State Troops); major general C.S.A.

Assistant Engineers

2nd Lt. Robert Edward Lee, 11 August 1829 - 21 April 1831; general C.S.A.

Bvt. 2nd Lt. Joseph Reid Anderson, 11 November 1836 - 13 March 1837; brigadier general C.S.A.

2nd Lt. Henry Washington Benham, 31 July 1837 - 12 January 1839; major general U.S.A.

1st Lt. James Heyward Trapier, 7 November 1839 - 8 April 1840; brigadier general C.S.A.

Mr. Edward Watts (civilian), 11 March 1842 - 11 August 1842

Bvt. 2nd Lt. Barton Stone Alexander, 26 July 1842 - 1 September 1845; brevet brigadier general U.S.A.

Bvt. 2nd Lt. George Washington Custis Lee, 10 March 1855 - November 1856; major general C.S.A.

---

[100] Young, "Connecticut Yankee," 319-320; Eicher, passim. Dates are those on official orders rather than dates of arrival or departure. Custis Lee was ordered to Fort Clinch, Fernandina, Florida, 30 January 1856, and relieved Gilmer at Fort Pulaski June to November 1856. Alexander did not report for duty until 6 October 1842.

Attachment 3
Army Chiefs of Engineers to 1866

Col. Richard Gridley, June 1775—April 1776

Col. Rufus Putnam, April 1776—December 1776

Maj. Gen. Louis Lebègue Duportail, 22 July 1777—10 October 1783

Lt. Col. Stephen Rochefontaine, 26 February 1795—7 May 1798

Lt. Col. Henry Burbeck, 7 May 1798—1 April 1802

Col. Jonathan Williams, 1 April 1802—20 June 1803; 19 April 1805-31 July 1812 (first Superintendent of West Point)

Col. Joseph Gardner Swift, 31 July 1812—12 November 1818

Col. Walker Keith Armistead, 12 November 1818—1 June 1821

Col. Alexander Macomb, 1 June 1821—24 May 1828

Col. Charles Gratiot, 24 May 1828—6 December 1838

Brig. Gen. Joseph Gilbert Totten, 6 December 1838—22 April 1864

Brig. Gen. Richard Delafield, 22 April 1864—8 August 1866

Attachment 4
Brigadier General Joseph Gilbert Totten[101]

Courtesy West Point Museum Art Collection, United States Military Academy.

Joseph Gilbert Totten was born on 17 April 1788, in New Haven, Connecticut, son of Peter G. Totten, and Grace Mansfield (Joseph K.F. Mansfield was Totten's cousin). Grace died a few years after her marriage, leaving two children, Joseph and a daughter, Susan Maria. After the death of Mrs. Totten, which occurred when Joseph was three years old, his father, having been appointed United States Consul at Santa Cruz, West Indies, took his post there, leaving his son under the care of his maternal uncle, Jared Mansfield. The boy continued to be a member of Jared Mansfield's family when Jared was appointed a captain of engineers and an instructor at West Point in 1802; Totten moved with the family and on 4 November 1802 was appointed a cadet. He was the 10th graduate from the academy at the time of his 1 July 1805 graduation when he was promoted to second lieutenant in the Corps of Engineers. He then served from 1805 to 1806 as secretary to Captain Jared Mansfield, who had been appointed by President Jefferson as Surveyor-General of Ohio and the Northwest Territory. Totten resigned from the army 31 March 1806, but remained as Jared's secretary from 1806 to 1808.

He was reappointed in the Army with the rank of second lieutenant in the Corps of Engineers on 23 February 1808. He was promoted to first lieutenant 23 July 1810 and captain 31 July 1812. He was in charge of construction at Forts Williams and Clinton under construction at New York City. He served at the outbreak of hostilities with Great Britain and was assigned to duty as Chief Engineer of the Army in the campaign of 1812, on the Niagara frontier, and took a conspicuous part in the Battle of Queenstown. He was subsequently Chief Engineer of the Army under the command of Major General Henry Dearborn in the campaign of 1813, and of the Army under Major General George Izard in the campaign of 1814 on Lake Champlain. On 6 June 1813, he was brevetted major for "meritorious services," and 11 September 1814, lieutenant colonel for "gallant conduct at the battle of Plattsburg."

Lieutenant Colonel Totten joined the distinguished French engineer, Simon Bernard, as a member of the Board of Engineers for planning the system for defense of the United States coast which, on 16 November 1816, consisted of Bernard as President, and Colonel William McRee. In 1817, Totten was relieved, and became Superintending Engineer of the Fort at Rouse's Point at Lake Champlain, New York, to 1819. Totten rejoined the Board of Engineers in 1819, and since later appointees, Brevet Brigadier General Joseph G. Swift and Brevet Colonel William McRee, had resigned, the permanent board consisted of Bernard and Totten alone. To these two fell the tasks of working out the fundamental

---

[101] John Gross Barnard, "Memoir of Joseph Gilbert Totten 1788-1864," *National Academy of Sciences Biographical Memoirs,* vol. 1 (Philadelphia, PA: Collins, Printer, 1877), 35-95, passim; John G. Barnard, *Eulogy on the Late Brevet Major-General Joseph G. Totten* (New York, NY: D. Van Nostrand, 1866), passim; George W. Cullum, *Biographical Register of the Officers and Graduates of the U.S. Military Academy at West Point, N.Y.,* vol. 1 (New York, NY: D. Van Nostrand, 1868), 94-96.

principles of coastal defenses and defining the projects of defense for U.S. seaports, although naval officers were associated with them whenever their examinations included positions for dockyards, naval depots, or other locations involving the Navy. The Board of Engineers drew up a series of reports which included a general summary of the principles which guided the board's deliberations. They defined the system of defense for the coast of the United States as follows: first, a navy; second, fortifications; third, interior communications by land and water; and fourth, a Regular Army and well-organized militia. In 1828, Totten took charge of the construction of Fort Adams, Newport harbor, and continued on this duty, making his residence in the town of Newport until 7 December 1838, the date of his appointment as Chief of the Corps of Engineers. He assumed control of the engineering operations of the army destined to invade the Mexican capital under General Winfield Scott, and directed the siege of Vera Cruz. For this successful service he was brevetted brigadier general, 29 March 1847, "for gallant and meritorious conduct." He tested methods for protecting the weakest part of the scarp, the embrasure, through which cannons fired. Embrasures in brick walls were protected by hardened brick or granite but Totten designed openings using four-inch thick cast iron around the embrasure. He also added Totten Shutters which were two-inch thick iron doors which had a self-closing mechanism to protect gunners. When the gunners ran out the gun, the door automatically opened and after firing, automatically closed. Salt air meant that the iron quickly rusted requiring much maintenance. It was first installed in a fort in 1857 so not used at Fort Pulaski.

He was a regent of the Smithsonian Institution from its founding 10 August 1846 to 22 April 1864; a member of the Lighthouse Board from its establishment in 1851 until 1858 and again in 1860-1864; and Corporator of the National Academy of Sciences 3 March 1863 to 22 April 1864. He continued as chief of engineers after the outbreak of the Civil War and was promoted to brigadier general in March 1863 when the Corps of Engineers and the Topographical Engineers merged. He was brevetted major general 21 April 1864, but he died the following day, 22 April, in Washington, D.C., at age 75. General Totten, the "Father of Fort Adams" and the primary designer of the Third System of Forts for the United States, had served well and faithfully for 62 years in the U.S. Army.

Chapter 5

The Mexican-American War
1845 to 1848

Captain Mansfield, as General Taylor's chief engineer, was a very happy man when he reported for duty with the Army of Occupation at Corpus Christi, Texas, on 19 September 1845. His health had improved after his sojourn in Middletown with his family, and his trip to Texas, mainly by water, was not exhausting interrupted only by the transitions from one mode of travel to another. Happy to have a new, war-time assignment, he could not know that in one year, his Mexican war experience would result in a serious leg wound in heavy fighting. However, given his noncombat career to that point, this change from his tedious service at Fort Pulaski, was welcomed. Mansfield knew about the long-term issues concerning the area of Mexican Texas, the establishment of the Republic of Texas in March 1836 after the Texas Revolution, and the annexation of Texas by the United States in March 1845. Mexico never recognized the independence of Texas in 1836 and refused overtures to sell parts of its northern territories to the United States. Sporadic fighting took place such as in March 1842 when a Mexican force captured San Antonio.[1]

This resentment by Mexico intensified when President John Tyler proposed the annexation of Texas. Mexico essentially declared war with the United States after Texas became officially the 28th state on 29 December 1845. "On the 7th of April [1845], the joint committee of the Mexican Congress to whom the memorial on the affairs of Texas had

---

[1] Mansfield's September arrival allowed him to miss Taylor's journey to Corpus Christi from New Orleans. Mansfield wrote to Colonel Totten, the Chief Engineer, on 14 Aug 1845 that he received letters with extracts of special orders 66 and 68 for Mansfield to proceed to Aransas Bay, Texas and report to Taylor for duty. But first his "uniforms must be altered and my wife is sick but I expect to leave here on Monday or Tuesday next....It is probable I shall take the route of the Ohio and Mississippi Rivers to New Orleans; letter courtesy WPL. His most likely route would have been via steamboat down the Connecticut River from Middletown to New York City, then by train to Baltimore. He next would have taken the B&O Railroad to Cumberland, Maryland, then by stagecoach on the National Road to Wheeling, Virginia, on the Ohio River to board another steamboat to Cincinnati, Ohio, then a series of steamboats down the Ohio River to the Mississippi River to New Orleans and then to Corpus Christi.

been referred, made a report, in which they asserted their right to Texas, and the duty to take up arms for its recovery; and made the most urgent appeals to the patriotism of the people to prevent its usurpation."[2] Tyler was a believer in "Manifest Destiney," a term coined by John L. O'Sullivan, editor of the *Democratic Review*: it must be "the fulfillment of our manifest destiny to overspread the continent allotted by Providence for the free development of our yearly multiplying millions." He added in reference to California that "The Anglo-Saxon foot is already on its borders. Already the advance guard of the irresistible army of Anglo-Saxon emigration has begun to pour down upon it, armed with the plough and the rifle, and marking its trail with schools and colleges, courts and representative halls, mills and meeting-houses."[3]

President Tyler's successor, James Knox Polk, was a Democrat who led the country to a complete victory over Mexico in the Mexican-American War. The Treaty of Guadalupe Hidalgo in 1848 added over one million square miles of territory to the United States, increasing it by a third. California, Nevada, Utah, most of Arizona, and parts of New Mexico, Colorado and Wyoming were included in the Mexican Cession. The treaty also recognized the annexation of Texas and American control over the territory between the Nueces River and the Rio Grande. Polk was less successful with Britain over the disputed Oregon Territory. Not wishing armed conflict with England and Mexico at the same time, Polk settled with Britain to place the Oregon boundary at the 49th parallel rather than parallel 54°40' north, the southern limit of Russian America, to the dismay of many in his own party.[4] Thus under Polk, much of the Far West was acquired for the United States expanding the nation into a continental power. Brigadier General Zachary Taylor began the vital military part of this expansionist saga in which Mansfield played an important role.

General Taylor had arrived at Corpus Christi, Texas, with his army on 25 July 1845 by land and by sea from his post at Fort Jesup, Louisiana. Taylor established and commanded Fort Jesup when it was built in 1822, 22 miles west of Natchitoches, Louisiana, near the confluence of the Red and Sabine Rivers. Initially called Cantonment Jesup, Taylor named it in honor of his friend, Major General Thomas Sidney Jesup. Taylor wrote that the fort is "upon a ridge which divides the waters of the Sabine from those of the Red River, and near the road leading from Natchitoches to the principal settlements in Texas; and not more than 18 miles upon a direct line from the Sabine River."[5]

---

[2] Nathan C. Brooks, *A Complete History of the Mexican War: Its Causes, Conduct, and Consequences; Comprising an Account of the Various Military and Naval Operations, from Its Commencement to the Treaty of Peace* (Philadelphia, PA: Grigg, Elliot & Co., 1851), 53-55.

[3] John O'Sullivan, "Annexation," *United States Magazine and Democratic Review 17,* no. 1 (July-August 1845): 5-10. Many Whigs did not support this expansionist philosophy as they rightly feared that it meant the extension of slavery in the new territories. Manifest Destiny was an outgrowth of "continentalism" as expressed by John Quincy Adams in 1812: "The whole continent of North America appears to be destined by Divine Providence to be peopled by one nation, speaking one language, professing one general system of religious and political principles, and accustomed to one general tenor of social usages and customs. For the common happiness of them all, for their peace and prosperity, I believe it is indispensable that they should be associated in one federal Union," Robert V. Remini, *John Quincy Adams* (New York, NY: Henry Holt and Company, 2002), 44. A part of the Manifest Destiny belief likely included the widespread, White, middleclass belief that the American Anglo-Saxon race was "separate, innately superior who were destined to bring good government, commercial prosperity and Christianity to the American continents and the world." This view also held that "inferior races were doomed to subordinate status or extinction." This was used to justify "the enslavement of the blacks and the expulsion and possible extermination of the Indians," Reginald Horsman, *Race and Manifest Destiny: The Origins of American Racial Anglo-Saxonism* (Cambridge, MA: Harvard University Press, 1981), 2-3.

[4] The Oregon Treaty between the United Kingdom and the United States was signed on 15 June 1846. The states of Washington, Oregon, and Idaho, and parts of the states of Montana and Wyoming, were later formed from the territory.

[5] Brainerd Dyer, *Zachary Taylor* (New York, NY: Barnes & Noble, Inc., 1967), 54. General Jesup was known as the "Father of the Modern Quartermaster Corps". He began his military career in 1808, served in the War of 1812, and was wounded at the Battle of Lundy's Lane. He was appointed temporary Adjutant General and Quartermaster General on 8 May 1818 by President James Monroe. Jesup assumed command of U.S. troops in Florida during the Second Seminole War (1837-1842) and was again wounded, but returned to his duty as Quartermaster General at the end of the war. During the Mexican-American War, he joined U.S. forces in Mexico overseeing supply requirements. He served as Quartermaster General for 42 years, and died on active duty 10 June 1860, in Washington, D.C.; http://www.floridamemory.com/collections/jesup/essay.php.

Brigadier General Zachary Taylor shown in his uniform which he rarely wore during the Mexican-American War. Courtesy LOC.

President James Knox Polk was the 11th President of the United States (1845–1849) who successfully led the country during the Mexican-American War. Courtesy Wikipedia.

Territories gained by the United States showing the 1819 Adams-Onis Treaty with Spain, the admission of Texas as the 28th state in December 1845, Oregon Treaty between the United Kingdom and the United States signed on 15 June 1846, and lands gained after the Mexican-American War in 1848 by the Treaty of Guadalupe Hidalgo. Courtesy Wikipedia from nationalatlas.gov.

Meanwhile the American government, believing that Texas would accept the terms of annexation, took precautionary measures for the protection of the country and the Republic of Texas. On 21 March 1845, General Taylor at Fort Jesup was ordered to hold his troops in readiness to march into Texas when notified to do so by the War Department. Then on 28 May, the Secretary of War clarified these instructions:

> I am directed by the President to cause the forces now under your command, and those which may be assigned to it, to be put into a position where they may most promptly and efficiently act in defence of Texas, in the event it shall become necessary or proper to employ them for that purpose. The information received by the Executive of the United States warrants the belief that Texas will shortly accede to the terms of annexation. As soon as the Texan Congress shall have given its consent to annexation, and a convention shall assemble and accept the terms offered in the resolutions of Congress, Texas will then be regarded by the executive government here so far a part of the United States as to be entitled from this government to defence and protection from foreign invasion and Indian incursions. The troops under your command will be placed and kept in readiness to perform this duty.[6]

Three weeks later on 15 June, the War Department sent a confidential letter to Taylor informing him in detail what he must do after Texas accepts annexation:

> You will forthwith make a forward movement with the troops under your command, and advance to the mouth of the Sabine, or to such other point on the Gulf of Mexico, or its navigable waters, as in your judgment may be most convenient for an embarkation at the proper time for the western frontier of Texas.
> ....The force under your immediate command, at and near Fort Jesup, to be put in motion on the receipt of these instructions, will be the 3rd and 4th regiments of infantry, and seven companies of the 2nd regiment of Dragoons. The two absent companies of the 4th infantry have been ordered to join their regiments. Artillery will be ordered from New Orleans.
> It is understood that suitable forage for cavalry cannot be obtained in the region which the troops are to occupy; if this be so, the Dragoons must leave their horses and serve as riflemen. But it is possible that horses of the country, accustomed to subsist on meagre forage, may be procured, if it be found necessary....
> The point of your ultimate destination is the western frontier of Texas, where you will select and occupy, on or near the Rio Grande del Norte, such a site as will consist with the health of the troops, and will be best adapted to repel invasion, and to protect what, in the event of annexation, will be our western border. You will limit yourself to the defence of the territory of Texas, unless Mexico should declare war against the United States.
> Your movement to the Gulf of Mexico, and your preparations to embark for the western frontier of Texas, are to be made without any delay; but you will not effect a landing on that frontier until you have yourself ascertained the due acceptance of Texas of the proffered terms of annexation, or until you receive directions from Mr. [Andrew Jackson] Donelson [American Charge d'Affaires in Texas].[7]

Taylor began his movement quickly: on 2 July the 4th Infantry left Fort Jesup and marched to steamers which left from Grand Ecore on the Red River, and arrived at New Orleans two days later after its 280 mile journey down the Red River and the Mississippi to the Crescent City; the 3rd Infantry followed on the 7th reaching New Orleans on the 10th. Taylor and his staff stayed behind at Fort Jesup to arrange for the overland departure of the Dragoons, finally joining his men in New Orleans on the 15th while the Dragoons rode overland south to Corpus Christi, Texas. The 3rd Artillery joined the Army of Occupation on the 19th, Lieutenant Braxton Bragg in command, from Charleston, South Carolina. Taylor was informed on 21 July that the Texas convention had accepted annexation so Taylor put his men in motion the following day from New Orleans--Taylor and his staff, along with the 3rd Infantry, embarking on the steamship *Alabama* which slipped its mooring on the morning of the 23rd. On the morning of the 26th of July they reached St. Joseph's Island, in Aransas Bay off Corpus Christi. Captain William S. Henry of the 3rd Infantry described the arrival on St. Joseph's finding rough seas and high wind:

> We made Aransas Bay...early on the morning of the 26th of July. Lieutenant [Daniel T.] C[handler] landed at nine o'clock, and on the top of one of the loftiest sand-hills erected a pole, from the top of which was unfurled the star-spangled banner....The

---

[6] Brooks, *A Complete History of the Mexican War*, 55-56. A U.S. Navy squadron commanded by Captain Robert Field Stockton was at the same time ordered to duty in the Gulf of Mexico to reinforce Commodore David Conner's Home Squadron which was being concentrated in Mexican waters. In October 1845 Stockton was ordered to the California coast to reinforce the Pacific Squadron where he took command participating in a blockade of the southern California coast and aiding U.S. forces in taking Mexican posts.

[7] Brooks, *A Complete History of the Mexican War*, 56-57.

company I commanded had the honor of landing first. The vessel, drawing too much water, could not cross the bar; it therefore became necessary for us to land in small boats. Seventy-five yards distant from the shore the men had to jump overboard into the roaring surf. They made a real frolic of it. Some old veteran camp-women took to the element as if they were born in it; while others, more delicately-nerved, preferred a man's back, and rode on shore....The landing of the troops' supplies was effected with great difficulty. On the 29th, two companies of the 3rd, one of which was mine, embarked on the steamer *Undine* for Corpus Christi. Aransas and Corpus Christi Bays are separated by a long flat of land. It was discovered that the *Undine* drew too much water to pass over it. We were forced to leave the steamboat, and cross the bay, a very rough one, in small boats. We landed on the main shore on the 31st of July.[8]

The camp at Corpus Christi was optimistically described as "healthy, easily supplied, and well situated to hold in observation the course of the Rio Grande from Matamoros to Laredo. While here, the troops were regularly practiced in the different evolutions and maneuvers of war, and reconnaissances were made with reference to an advance of the army towards the Rio Grande."[9] Taylor's 2nd Dragoons took over a month to reach Corpus Christi on horseback from Fort Jesup by way of San Antonio, then San Patricio, which was about 25 miles north of Taylor's camp. They arrived in camp 28 August led by Colonel David Emanuel Twiggs after their 500 mile ride from Fort Jesup. By August 1845, Taylor had reassembled his newly designated "Army of Occupation" at Corpus Christi.[10]

Both Taylor and the U.S. administration did not wish to alarm Mexico as negotiations were still in progress to try to settle issues peacefully, but Secretary of War William Marcy instructed him that he should "approach as near the western boundary of Texas (the Rio Grande) as circumstances will permit; having reference to reasonable security; to accommodations for putting your troops into winter huts, if deemed necessary; to the facility and certainty of procuring or receiving supplies; and to checking any attempted incursions by the Mexican forces or the Indian tribes."[11]

---

[8] William Seaton Henry, *Campaign Sketches of the War with Mexico* (New York, NY: Harper & Brothers, 1847), 10-12, 14-17. According to Colonel Hitchcock commanding the 3rd Infantry, they marched 16 miles from his camp near Fort Jesup to Natchitoches and the next day marched to the Red River embarking on two steamboats; Ethan Allen Hitchcock, *Fifty Years in Camp and Field: Diary of Major General Ethan Allen Hitchcock*, ed. by W.A. Croffut (New York, NY: G.P. Putnam's Sons, 1909), 192-193. Note that Hitchcock was a lieutenant colonel from 31 January 1842, and a brevet colonel 20 August 1847.

[9] Henry, *Campaign Sketches of the War with Mexico*, 15; Brooks, *A Complete History of the Mexican War*, 59. As will be seen, Brooks's description of Corpus Christi as "healthy" was an overstatement once winter began.

[10] Hitchcock, *Fifty Years in Camp and Field*, 196, 199. Even though Hitchcock wrote of him as a colonel, he was promoted to brigadier general 30 June 1846. Taylor changed the army's title on 6 August; K. Jack Bauer, *Zachary Taylor: Soldier, Planter, Statesman of the Old Southwest* (Baton Rouge, LA: Louisiana State University Press, 1985), 116-117. Taylor's army was first called a Corps of Observation by President Tyler in April 1844 which Taylor called his Army of Observation.

[11] Brooks, *A Complete History of the Mexican War*, 65. Marcy wrote this letter 16 October 1845.

Area of operations from Fort Jesup to Matamoros. Courtesy LOC.

Mansfield joined Taylor's camp at Corpus Christi 19 September 1845 finding the troops still settling in. By October, the army had some 4,000 men in camp, about half of the Regular Army's strength.[12] The camp at Corpus Christi became the army's home from 31 July 1845 to 11 March 1846 when it began its next march of 174 miles to the Rio Grande opposite Matamoros, Mexico.[13] Henry described the camp in wonderful detail and is valuable as a first-person description of the location as Mansfield would have found it although had he described it himself it would not have been in such poetic terms:

> The village of Corpus Christi, or *"Kinney's Ranch"* as it is generally called, is situated on the western shore of Corpus Christi Bay. The town consists of some twenty or thirty houses, partly situated on a shelf of land, elevated some six or eight feet above the water, about two hundred yards broad, and on a bluff which rises from the plain to the height of one hundred feet. The bay at this point is in the shape of a crescent, extending in a southeast direction to Padre Island, and northwest to the mouth of the Nueces. The bluff presents a beautiful aspect, the rise being sufficiently gentle to deprive it of all appearance of abruptness, clad with the mesquite-grass, and evergreen bushes scattered in clumps hither and yon in graceful confusion, looking, in its gentle undulations, as if its pleasing irregularities had been fashioned by the hand of man. The bluff and the plain presented, early on the morning after our arrival, quite a pastoral appearance. First came a large drove of cattle, driven by two Mexicans, mounted upon their mustang ponys; then followed at least five hundred goats and sheep, which, dispersing themselves in groups over hill and plain, added much to the beauty of the scene....From the top of the bluff the view that burst upon us was magnificent in the extreme. Far off to the east the scene was bounded by the white-caps of the beautiful bay; to the southeast Flower Bluffs stood out in bold relief; in the northeast the distant highlands of Maglone's Bluff were dimly visible; to the northwest, the land near the mouth of the Nueces; in the west, one unlimited plain presented itself, extending to the mountains, the home of the mustang and buffalo, the hunting ground of the bold Comanche and the fierce Lipan. The scene was charming, and the soft, refreshing seabreeze, cooling the atmosphere to the temperature of an October's day, made one exclaim, in the enthusiasm of the moment, "It is God's favored land—the Eden of America." When the enthusiasm subsided, it was not exactly *that,* but it certainly is very beautiful. The atmosphere is tempered by a constant breeze, and you hardly feel the heat.
>
> This place was first settled by Colonel H[enry]L[awrence] Kinney, in 1838, who, in conjunction with his partner, Mr. Aubrey, established a trading-post, to meet the immense traffic carried on by the Mexicans. It was the extreme frontier settlement. The incursions of the Indians were so frequent, and attended with so much danger, that he was forced to keep a regular company of men, at his own expense, to defend his "ranch." Its proximity to the Rio Grande made it the most convenient point for the contraband trade. This trade is carried on by Mexicans, who bring in immense droves of horses and mules, saddles and bridles, Mexican blankets and silver, and in return take back the common unbleached domestics and tobacco.[14]

In addition to the cool climate there was food in abundance including game, fish, turtles, and shellfish to add to rations of beef and mutton. Hunting also added sport for officers as they ranged far and wide to shoot geese, deer, cranes, snipe, ducks, turkeys, pelicans, and eagles. They saw herds of wild horses, antelope, and mules. Henry wrote of the success of one enjoyable hunt: "killed, ten deer, fifty-one geese, four bittern, two sand-hill crane, sixty-nine snipe, eighteen ducks, four curlew, three turkeys, and one panther."[15] There is no record of Mansfield participating in any

---

[12] During May 1846 opposite Matamoros, Taylor had an aggregate total of 3,554 present and absent: 20 in the general staff, 388 in the 2nd Dragoons, 344 in the 1st Artillery, 217 in the 2nd Artillery, 210 in the 3rd Artillery, 205 in the 4th Artillery, 464 in the 3rd Infantry, 383 in the 4th Infantry, 472 in the 5th Infantry, 418 in the 7th Infantry, and 433 in the 8th Infantry; House Ex. Doc. No. 24, Thirty-first Congress, first session, p. 8a table in Emory Upton, *Military Policy of the United States* (Washington, DC: Government Printing Office, 1904), 199. The U.S. Army's authorized strength was 8,613 but it had only 7,365 on the rolls at the beginning of the war scattered across the continent mainly on the coasts and on the western frontier in small units; Richard Bruce Winders, *Mr. Polk's Army: The American Military Experience in the Mexican War* (College Station, TX: Texas A&M University Press, 1997), 9. Of the authorized 8,613 officers and men authorized, probably only about 5,500 were available for duty; Donald S. Frazier, ed., *The United States and Mexico at War: Nineteenth-Century Expansionism and Conflict* (New York, NY: Simon & Schuster Macmillan, 1998), 24. In May 1846 Congress created a company of engineers and another mounted unit, the U.S. Mounted Rifles. These became part of the "Old Establishment" along with the infantry regiments, 1st through 8th, artillery 1st through 4th, and the 1st and 2nd Dragoons. During the Mexican-American War, 15,736 served with the Old Establishment while a total of 30,476 served in the Regular Army. Congress passed the "Ten Regiment Bill" on 11 February 1847 adding eight infantry regiments (9th through 16th), the 3rd Dragoons, and a regiment of Foot Riflemen and Voltigeurs. This "New Establishment" added 11,186 to the Regular Army although not all were organized in time to serve with Taylor or Scott; Frazier, *The United States and Mexico at War*, 24; Russell F. Weigley, *History of the United States Army* (New York, NY: Macmillan Publishing Co., Inc., 1967), 182-183. Weigley notes that about 15,000 men added to the Regulars volunteered in Mexico came mostly from volunteers. Compare Justin H. Smith, *The War with Mexico*, (New York, NY: The Macmillan Co., 1919), vol. 2, 511, n. 15, who shows total of 27,470 all types of Regulars who served during the war.

[13] Thomas Bangs Thorpe, *Our Army on the Rio Grande* (Philadelphia, PA: Carey and Hart, 1846), 11; Darwin Payne, "Camp Life in the Army of Occupation: Corpus Christi, July 1845 to March 1846," *The Southwestern Historical Quarterly*, vol. 73, no. 3, Jan. 1970, 326-342 passim.

[14] Henry, *Campaign Sketches of the War With Mexico*, 17-19. Others who wrote of this period also remarked about the sea breezes, Payne," 328.

[15] Henry, *Campaign Sketches of the War With Mexico*, 44.

hunting trips since as Taylor's chief engineer, he was more concerned with his duties.[16] No record has been found of Mansfield hunting at all. With the arrival of thousands of soldiers as customers, Kinney's Ranch, which became the village of Corpus Christi, provided much in the way of "necessities" and services for the troops. The village housed "lawyers, business 'agents,' hairdressers, photographers, sutlers, gamblers, whores, and plain hangers-on. The list included wives and sometimes children of the soldiers."[17] On the left near the village, the New Orleans volunteers camped for their brief stay while on the far right resided Twiggs's 2nd Dragoons; the 3rd, 4th, and 7th Infantry occupied the center, and the fearsome Texas Rangers stood picket on hills inland. "The whole line covered about a mile and a half, with a 300-yard fieldwork on the right, six feet thick."[18]

Lieutenant George Gordon Meade arrived on St. Joseph's Island on 12 September 1845 a few days before Mansfield arrived at Corpus Christi; Meade had a pleasant trip from New Orleans eventually ending at Taylor's camp:

> I arrived here two days ago, well, hearty, and in good spirits, having made the most delightful voyage from New Orleans I ever made; not at all sea-sick, pleasant company, cool breezes, and good fare....If you look on your map you will find the Aransas Pass laid down; I am there, just inside the open sea, on the point of the island to the north. This point is a large depot of provisions, having a bar to enter it, on which is only eight feet of water, consequently all large vessels anchor outside, are lightered by two steamers, and their contents forwarded to Corpus Christi (where is the main army) by two smaller steamers of light draft. I have been for the last two days getting my things ashore here, very much occupied, and am now going to join the army at Corpus Christi, twenty-five miles from here, on the right bank of the river Nueces, immediately at its mouth....I never was better in my life, and I can see at a glance that this point and Corpus Christi, of similar formation, are as delightful and as healthy spots as any in the world. It is a pure sand formation, surrounded by salt water and always having a fresh breeze, without mosquitoes, ticks, or any of the annoying vermin of the South. Nothing but the hot sun, from which, if you are shaded, you are cooler than at any place in the North.[19]

He also wrote about a steamship explosion which Mansfield fortunately missed arriving a few days later. The shallow-draft vessel, the 111-ton sidewheel steamship *Dayton*, was contracted to ferry men and goods from St. Joseph's Island to Taylor's camp; Taylor had used the ship on 23 July:

> A terrible disaster occurred yesterday [12 September], which I only mention to guard you against false rumors. The steamer *Dayton*, chartered by the Government in the commencement of the affair, the only one that could be procured, yesterday, on her return from Corpus Christi, where she had been discharged, owing to the arrival here of staunch and good boats to take her place, exploded, killing two officers, Lieutenant [Thaddeus] Higgins and Lieutenant [Benjamin A.] Berry, of the Fourth Infantry, and some eight or ten men, and badly wounding some three or four other officers, none of whom are dangerously hurt, but badly bruised.

Henry wrote of troop arrivals "Between the 13th and 24th of September:

> General [William Jenkins] Worth, with six companies of the 8th Infantry; Major [Samuel] Ringgold, with his company of Horse Artillery; two companies of the 8th, under Captain [Edmund Augustus] Ogden; also, Lieutenant [James] Duncan's company and battery. His horses have suffered very much, he having lost fourteen. Add to these Captain [Martin] Burke's command (artillery), and five companies of the 5th Infantry, under Captain [Ephraim Kirby] Smith. These latter-named troops have made a prompt and exceedingly rapid movement; they traveled *two thousand five hundred miles in twenty-one days*....The morning report of today gives the following as the strength of the command: two hundred and fifty-one officers, three thousand six hundred and seventy-one rank and file; grand aggregate, three thousand nine hundred and twenty-two. These are on the coast. The three companies of Dragoons in the interior number about one hundred and fifty. The following is the distribution of the forces: The 1st Brigade is on the right; it is composed of the 8th Infantry and twelve companies of Artillery, the whole commanded by Brevet Brigadier-general Worth. Next comes the Dragoons, commanded by General Twiggs. Then the 2nd Brigade, composed of the 5th and 7th Regiments of Infantry, commanded by Lieutenant-colonel [James Simmons] McIntosh. Then a command of four companies of Horse Artillery, under Major [John] Erving. Then the third Brigade, composed of the 3rd and 4th

---

[16] Payne 329.

[17] Edward J. Nichols, *Zach Taylor's Little Army* (Garden City, NY: Doubleday & Company, Inc., 1963), 23.

[18] Ibid, 22.

[19] George Gordon Meade, *The Life and Letters of George Gordon Meade*, ed. by George Meade (New York, NY: Charles Scribner's Sons, 1913), 26.

Infantry, commanded by Colonel [William] Whistler; and then two companies of [Louisiana] Volunteer Artillery, under the command of Major [Louis] Gally.[20]

On 9 October, Meade told his wife that she could "imagine how healthy a place this is, when we have, collected here, nearly four thousand men who have come from all parts of the country, and many from the upper Lakes, nearly all passing through New Orleans, and many detained there, and yet until this time there have been only two or three deaths from disease, though there have been several from accidents, such as blowing up of steamboats, strokes of lightning, drowning, etc. Nearly all have been affected by the diarrhea consequent upon the change of life and water, but these cases have all been mild, though many of the men are drunken, dissipated fellows who, you would suppose, would be carried off by any disease. We have here a fine breeze blowing constantly, which tempers the ardor of the sun; but at this season the sun begins to lose its powerful effect, and the middle of the day is the most agreeable part of it."[21]

By October however, some of the troops were growing restive as Hitchcock noted that "since the arrival of the 2nd Dragoons there have been several disgraceful brawls and quarrels, to say nothing of drunken frolics. The Dragoons have made themselves a public scandal. One captain has resigned to avoid trial, and two others have had a dirty brawl. Two others still are on trial for fighting over a low woman." Hitchcock's health was not good and he joined many of his men with diarrhea. "If I value either health or life I may feel it a duty to go away from this climate for a time altogether."[22]

The winter of 1845-1846 was much less pleasant than summer and early fall and the troops increasingly suffered from lack of proper clothing and tents as well as illnesses and boredom. Training which had begun with much enthusiasm during the fall almost stopped. And training was desperately needed as the regiments in camp had never before been assembled in one place as they had served in small units on the frontier. Colonel Ethan Allen Hitchcock, commander of the 3rd Infantry and an Old Army Regular, despaired for the army as he wrote that "among the senior officers, neither General Taylor nor Colonel [William] Whistler commanding the brigade could form them into line! Even Colonel Twiggs could put the troops into line only 'after a fashion' of his own. As for maneuvering, not one of them can move a step in it. Egotism or no egotism, I am the only field officer on the ground who could change a single position of the troops according to any but a militia mode."[23]

Historian Smith, not a Taylor admirer, described the conditions at the Corpus Christi camp:

Taylor, accustomed to frontier conditions, described his troops as healthy, remarkably well-behaved and very comfortable. But in reality the tents could scarcely keep out a heavy dew; for weeks together every article in many of them was thoroughly soaked; and much of the time water stood three or four feet deep in some. The weather oscillated sharply between sultry heat and piercing northers, so that one lay down gasping for breath and woke up freezing. As hardly enough wood could be obtained for the cooks, camp-fires were usually out of the question; and only brackish drinking water could be had. At one time nearly twenty per cent of the men were on the sick list, and half of the others more or less ill.[24]

Henry wrote of the changes in late fall and early winter in camp:

During the latter part of November and the month of December we had the most shocking weather imaginable; either cold "northers" or drenching rains, without intermission. Hast thou, dear reader, ever felt a norther? heard tell of one? No. Well, your northern cold is nothing to it. It comes "like a thief in the night," and all but steals your life. You go to bed, weather sultry and warm, bed-clothes disagreeable, tent open; before morning you hear a distant rumbling; the roaring increases, the norther comes. For several minutes you hear it careering in its wild course; when it reaches you it issues fresh from the snow-mountains, and with a severity which threatens to prostrate the camp. The change in one's feelings is like an instantaneous transit from the torrid to the frigid zone; blankets are in demand, and no one thinks of living without a good supply on hand. Ice has formed in pails several times, and one morning every tent had an ice covering; the sleet had frozen upon it, and the crackling of the canvas sounded like anything but music. We were forced to throw up embankments and plant chaparral to the north of our tents, to

---

[20] Henry, *Campaign Sketches*, 38-39. Smith and McIntosh were mortally wounded at the Battle of Molina del Ray 8 September 1847; William Hugh Robarts, *Mexican War Veterans: A Complete Roster* (Brentano's: Washington, DC, 1887), *passim*. Gally's two companies were sent home on 1 November as their three-month term of enlistment expired.

[21] Meade, 29. Dysentery and diarrhea were not uncommon due to lack of knowledge of the causes of them primary poor sewage disposal and of course no knowledge of the how such illnesses were caused by poor sanitary conditions.

[22] Hitchcock, 203-204.

[23] Hitchcock, 198-199. Hitchcock was the Old Army's curmudgeon.

[24] Justin H. Smith, *The War with Mexico* (New York, NY: The Macmillan Co., 1919), vol. 1, 143; References to this important work are to volume 1 unless otherwise noted. Payne," 332.

break the wind. The men, of course, suffer a great deal. The constant dampness and bad water have produced many serious cases of dysentery. The beauty of this climate is decidedly in the summer.[25]

Lieutenant Meade wrote on 9 December 1845 to his wife that he suffered from a regular attack of jaundice:

> I have been as yellow as an orange, and although not sick enough to keep my bed, yet I have felt very badly, and have been under the influence of medicine all the time. You cannot imagine the total want of comfort which one is subjected to here. It has been storming and raining incessantly for the last three weeks, and when one is taking medicine it is not very agreeable accompaniment to be sleeping in wet tents. The worst effect, however, of the disease, was upon my mind. It made me very low-spirited and gloomy, and for some days, combined with the bad weather, rendered me quite miserable. I am, however, now getting over it; all the uncomfortable sensations have left me, and my complexion is gradually clearing.[26]

But New Year's Day provided a respite as the weather, according to Hitchcock, was "mild and balmy. The day will go as other days—drinking, horse-racing, gambling, theatrical amusements. A ball is advertised for this evening in Corpus Christi. Colonel Kinney thinks there are 2,000 people here besides the army. They are nearly all adventurers....There are no ladies here, and very few women."[27]

Officers and men at the Corpus Christi camp were told of reports in newspapers that conditions there were bad so some wrote home trying to downplay more lurid aspects of the articles. Captain Ulysses S. Grant on 7 February 1846 reassured his inamorata Julia:

> The extract from some newspaper you send me is a gross exaggeration of the morals and health of Corpus Christi. I do not believe that there is a more healthy spot in the world. So much exposure in the winter season is of course attended with a good deal of sickness but not of a serious nature. The letter was written I believe by a soldier of the 3rd Infantry. As to the poisoning and robberies I believe they are entirely false. There has been several soldiers murdered since we have been here, but two of the number were shot by soldiers and there is no knowing that the others were not. Soldiers are a class of people who will drink and gamble let them be where they may, and they can always find houses to visit for these purposes. Upon the whole, Corpus Christi is just the same as any other place would be where there were so many troops.[28]

In addition to the 30 bars and other places in town for alcohol and female "refreshments," soldiers found time to read the newly-established local newspaper, the *Gazette*, and attend The Army Theater which opened on 8 January. "It was a capital building, capable of containing some eight hundred persons. The scenes were painted by officers of the army. A very clever company was engaged, and many an otherwise dreary evening was spent by many of us with infinite pleasure within its walls."[29] The *Gazette* wrote that the first performance would be "James Sheridan Knowles' *The Wife, a Tale of Mantua*. Following the play Mr. Wells would dance; then more singing and dancing would be topped off with the laughable farce 'Loan of a Lover.'"[30] Lieutenant Samuel G. French recalled that Lieutenant John B. Magruder "was a good theatrical manager" and the nightly entertainments welcomed.[31] Lieutenant James Longstreet wrote that army officers were cast members when professionals were unavailable:

> The officers...took both male and female characters. In farce and comedy we did well enough, and soon collected funds to pay for the building and incidental expenses. The house was filled every night. General Worth always encouraging us, General Taylor sometimes, and General Twiggs occasionally, we found ourselves in funds sufficient to send over to New Orleans for costumes, and concluded to try tragedy. The "Moor of Venice" [Shakespeare's Othello] was chosen, [Navy] Lieutenant Theorderic Porter to be the Moor, and Lieutenant U.S. Grant to be the daughter of Brabantio [Desdemona]. But after rehearsal Porter protested that male heroines could not support the character nor give sentiment to the hero, so we sent over to New

---

[25] Henry, *Campaign Sketches*, 45.

[26] Meade, 37.

[27] Hitchcock, 206-207. Note his tongue-in-cheek reference to lower class women in Corpus Christi and perhaps also to U.S. Army laundresses.

[28] Ulysses S. Grant, Image 57 of Ulysses S. Grant Papers: Series 1, General Correspondence and Related Material, 1844-1922; Subseries A, 1844-1883; 1844-1883 courtesy LOC. While no letters from Mansfield for this period have been found, it is likely that he too would have reassured his wife and family that things described by some in hometown newspapers were exaggerated.

[29] Henry, *Campaign Sketches*, 47.

[30] Nichols, 28. There were about 200 locations in total where thirsty soldiers could find alcohol such as "port, claret, and sherry wines, whisky, French brandy, or cider. They could visit a bar with no extra trimmings or they could partake at tenpin alleys, the theaters, or billiard halls," Payne, 337.

[31] Samuel G. French, *Two Wars: an Autobiography of Gen. Samuel G. French* (Nashville, TN: Confederate Veteran, 1901), 34.

Orleans and secured Mrs. Hart, who was popular with the garrisons in Florida. Then all went well, and life through the winter was gay.[32]

Lieutenant Abner Doubleday was amused at Magruder's management of the professional actors especially in relation to a star actress with whom Magruder apparently was smitten:

> Just before the first performance was to take place M. told me he was going over to inspect the dressing rooms to see that all was right there. He added, "You look surprised Sir! A man of my well known virtue and morality can go anywhere. All doors are open to him." I learned afterwards that he returned from his expedition in a damaged condition. His coat was nearly torn off his back and this face was seamed with scratches, so that evidently some slight misunderstanding had occurred.[33]

The Union Theatre was the second playhouse and had special attractions as it offered box seat patrons "'the choicest liquors, wines, Fruits and Segars, that can possibly be provided.'" Patrons in lower priced seats had a bar to procure alcohol as needed during shows and a restaurant purveying "oysters in any style, hot coffee and chocolate, beef, venison, turtle steak, wild game, turtle soup, and pastries."[34] Interesting those soldiers writing home rarely mentioned the many "refreshments" available but rather emphasizing the literary entertainments.

Lieutenant Meade wrote to his wife that he had been busy scouting south for Taylor. These expeditions were in addition to reports Old Zach received from his Mexican spy, Chapita. In 1845 and early 1846, Meade and other topographical engineers (Topogs) scouted up the Nueces River to San Patricio and down the coast along the Laguna Madre toward Point Isabel at the mouth of the Rio Grande. On 21 January 1846, Meade wrote that "I am ordered on another expedition and shall leave here immediately. It will be under the charge of Captain Mansfield, Corps of Engineers, and I shall return to my humble vocation of a sub. Like the former ones, it will also be a marine expedition, the object being to examine the Aransas Bay, a large body of water lying to the north of this place.[35] Meade wrote again on 26 January from the depot at St. Joseph's Island, bringing his wife up to date on his expedition led by Mansfield:

> We have reached this point on our expedition. We are about thirty miles from Corpus Christi, and shall leave here immediately, on our way up the coast along the inside passage. We will visit the little towns of Copano, Lamar, La Baca, Linnville, and Matagorda, in succession. You will see most of these places marked on the map I left with you, and thus can trace our route. We are fitted out for a month's expedition, though I trust to be back sooner.[36]

He followed with another letter on 18 February from Matagorda, Texas, writing that he had "been knocking about the bays between Corpus Christi and this place, making surveys, and visiting towns, and places where towns are to be." He said that the trip was "more agreeable than" he anticipated despite the "Northers" and rain. The town of 500 was a population "of a much better class" than expected as it was an old settlement, and he met several people from Philadelphia with whom he had delightful conservations.[37] He returned to camp at Corpus Christi on 2 March.

---

[32] James Longstreet, *From Manassas to Appomattox: Memoirs of the Civil War in America* (Philadelphia, PA: J.B. Lippincott Company, 1895), 20. Longstreet lost the role of Desdemona to Grant as Longstreet was apparently too overweight, Edward J. Nichols, 28.

[33] Abner Doubleday, *My Life in the Old Army: The Reminiscences of Abner Doubleday from the Collections of the New York Historical Society*, ed. by Joseph E. Chance (Fort Worth, TX: Texas Christian University Press, 1998), 47.

[34] Payne, 337-338.

[35] Meade, *The Life and Letters of George Gordon Meade*, 46; Holman Hamilton, *Zachary Taylor: Soldier of the Republic* (Indianapolis, IN: The Bobbs-Merrill Company, 1944), 166.

[36] Meade, *The Life and Letters of George Gordon Meade*, 46. Mansfield wrote to Cullum 18 Aug. 1859 that during the winter he made a survey and reconnoissance of the coast of Texas from Aransas Bay to Matagorda Bay with a view to a depot for the supply of the western ports of Texas and surveyed the harbors of Copano and Indianola and La Baca and made a reconnoissance of the various bars of the inland navigation along the coast. He made a report accompanied by a map, a duty which occupied 6 weeks with two assistants and two boats and crews; courtesy WPL. In a letter to Mansfield from the Engineer Department 12 May 1846, it informed him that it received a copy of Mansfield's report of the reconnaissance from Aransas Bay to Matagorda Bay and map; it sent him a copy of two reports on the defense of the coast of Texas; courtesy WPL and the Middlesex County Historical Society.

[37] Meade, *The Life and Letters of George Gordon Meade*, 48.

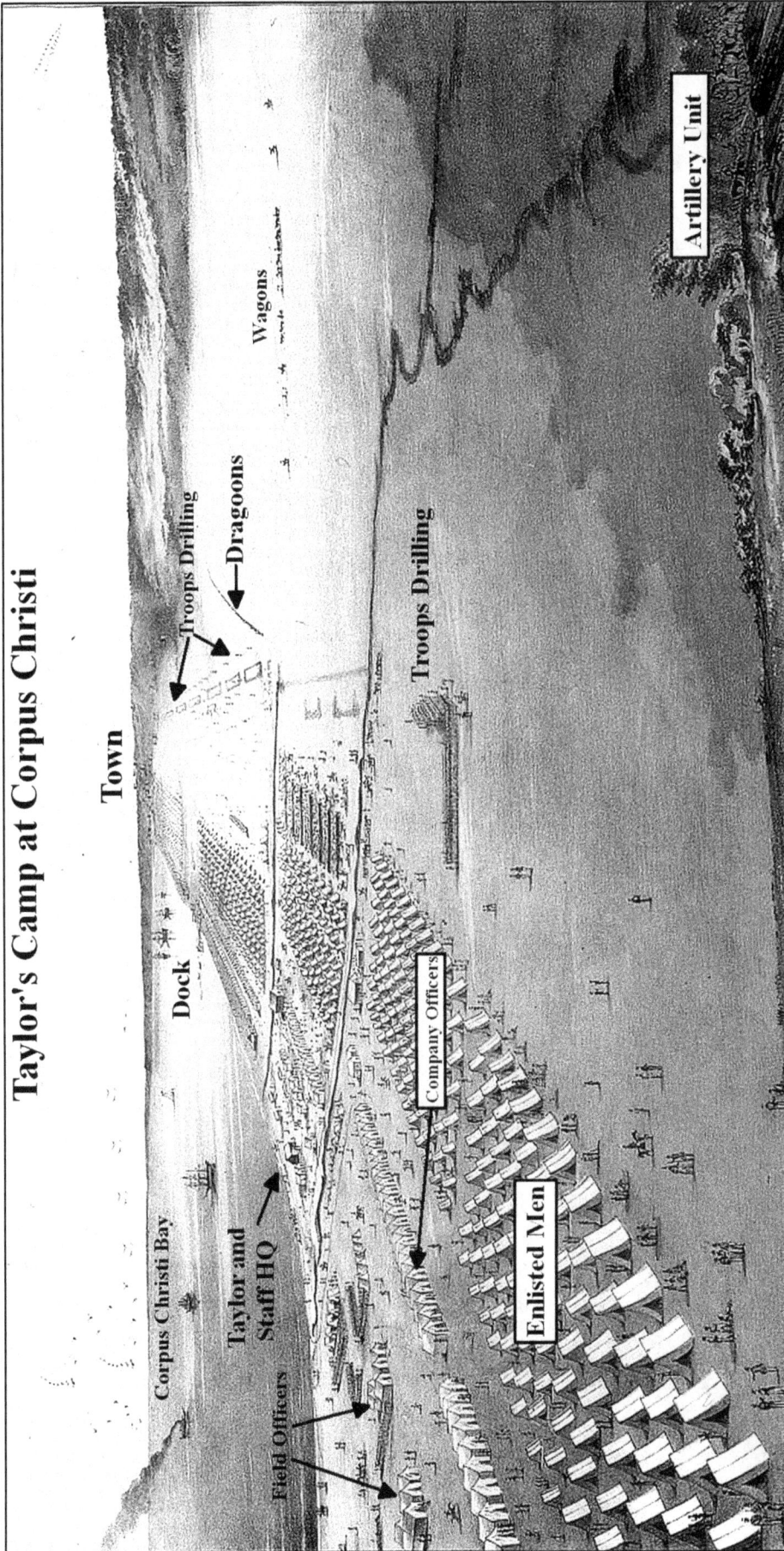

Taylor's Camp at Corpus Christi

Corpus Christi Bay

Town

Dock

Troops Drilling

Dragoons

Wagons

Artillery Unit

Troops Drilling

Taylor and Staff HQ

Company Officers

Enlisted Men

Field Officers

Taylor's camp near Corpus Christi, Texas, in 1845 looking south. Courtesy LOC.

Village of Corpus Christi showing Taylor's camp looking north. Henry, *Campaign Sketches of the War with Mexico*, frontispiece.

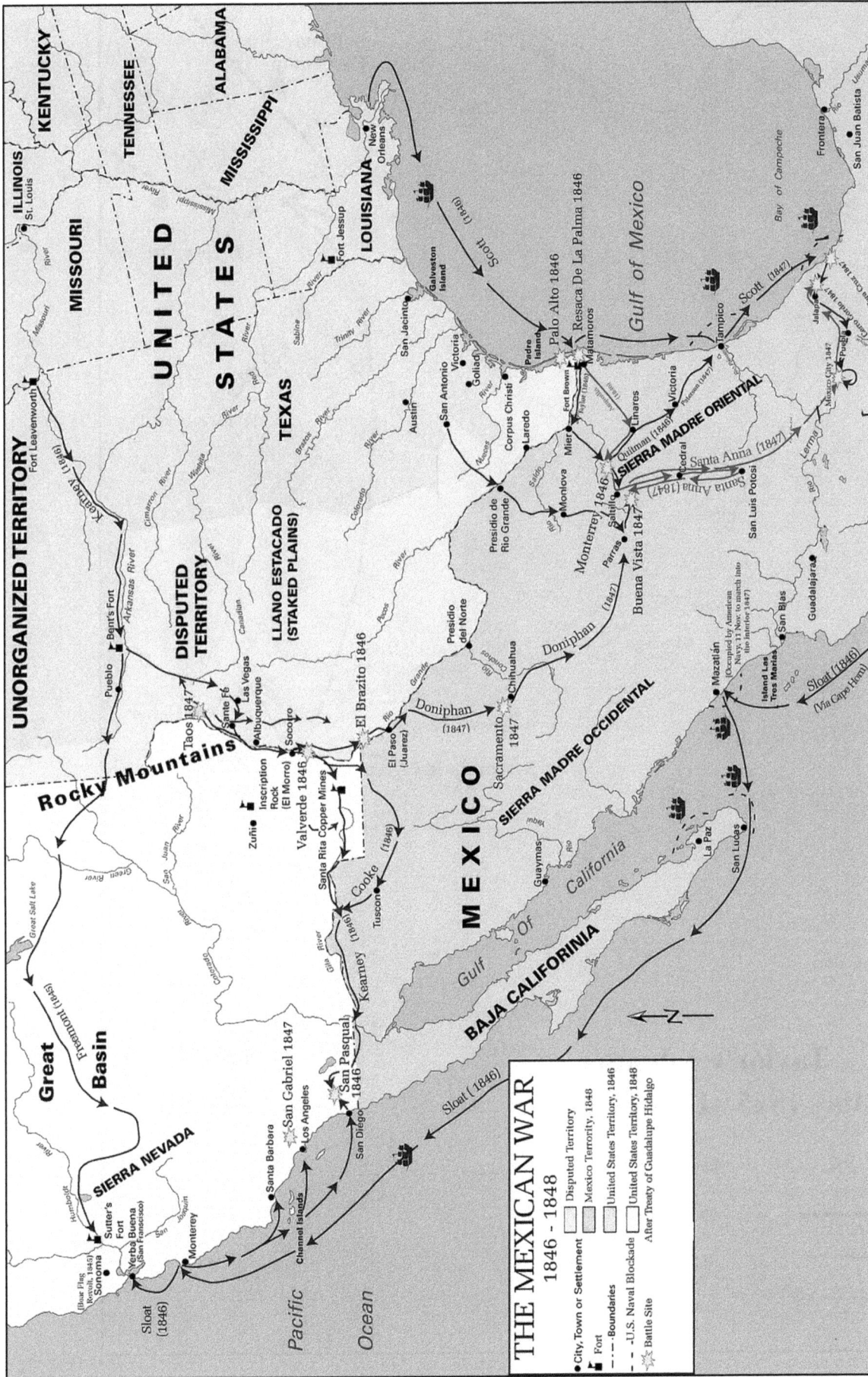

ILLINOIS
KENTUCKY
TENNESSEE
ALABAMA
MISSISSIPPI
MISSOURI
St. Louis
UNITED
STATES
LOUISIANA
New Orleans
Fort Jessup
TEXAS
Austin
San Antonio
Victoria
Goliad
Corpus Christi
Laredo
San Jacinto
Galveston Island
Pedro Island
Palo Alto 1846
Resaca De La Palma 1846
Matamoros
Fort Brown
Mier
Linares
Monterrey 1846
Monclova
Saltillo
Parras
Buena Vista 1847
Presidio de Rio Grande
Gulf of Mexico
Bay of Campeche
Frontera
San Juan Batista
Tampico
Scott (1847)
Scott (1846)
Cerralvo
SIERRA MADRE ORIENTAL
Santa Anna (1847)
Santa Anna (1847)
San Luis Potosi
Jalapa
Puebla
Mexico City 1847
Vera Cruz 1847
UNORGANIZED TERRITORY
Fort Leavenworth
Kearney (1845)
Bent's Fort
Pueblo
DISPUTED TERRITORY
Santa Fé
Las Vegas
Taos 1847
Albuquerque
Socorro
Inscription Rock (El Morro)
Zuñi
Valverde 1846
Santa Rita Copper Mines
El Brazito 1846
El Paso (Juarez)
Doniphan (1847)
Chihuahua
Doniphan (1847)
Sacramento 1847
Presidio del Norte
LLANO ESTACADO (STAKED PLAINS)
Rocky Mountains
Cooke (1846)
Kearney (1846)
Tuscon
MEXICO
SIERRA MADRE OCCIDENTAL
Guaymas
Gulf Of California
Mazatlán (Occupied by American Navy, 11 Nov. to march into the interior 1847)
Island Las Tres Marias
San Blas
Guadalajara
Sloat (1846) (Via Cape Horn)
La Paz
San Lucas
BAJA CALIFORNIA
Great Basin
SIERRA NEVADA
Fremont (1845)
San Gabriel 1847
Santa Barbara
Los Angeles
San Pasqual 1846
San Diego
Channel Islands
Monterey
Sutter's Fort
Yerba Buena (San Francisco)
Sonoma (Blue Flag Revolt, 1846)
Sloat (1846)
Pacific Ocean
Great Salt Lake
Green River
Humboldt

N

THE MEXICAN WAR
1846 - 1848
- City, Town or Settlement
■ Fort
--- Boundaries
--- U.S. Naval Blockade
☆ Battle Site

Disputed Territory
Mexico Territory, 1848
United States Territory, 1846
United States Territory, 1848
After Treaty of Guadalupe Hidalgo

Map showing all major actions during the war which demonstrates the vast expanse involved and the locations of major interest. Taylor's army was only a small albeit the first and an important factor in the drama. Courtesy USMA.

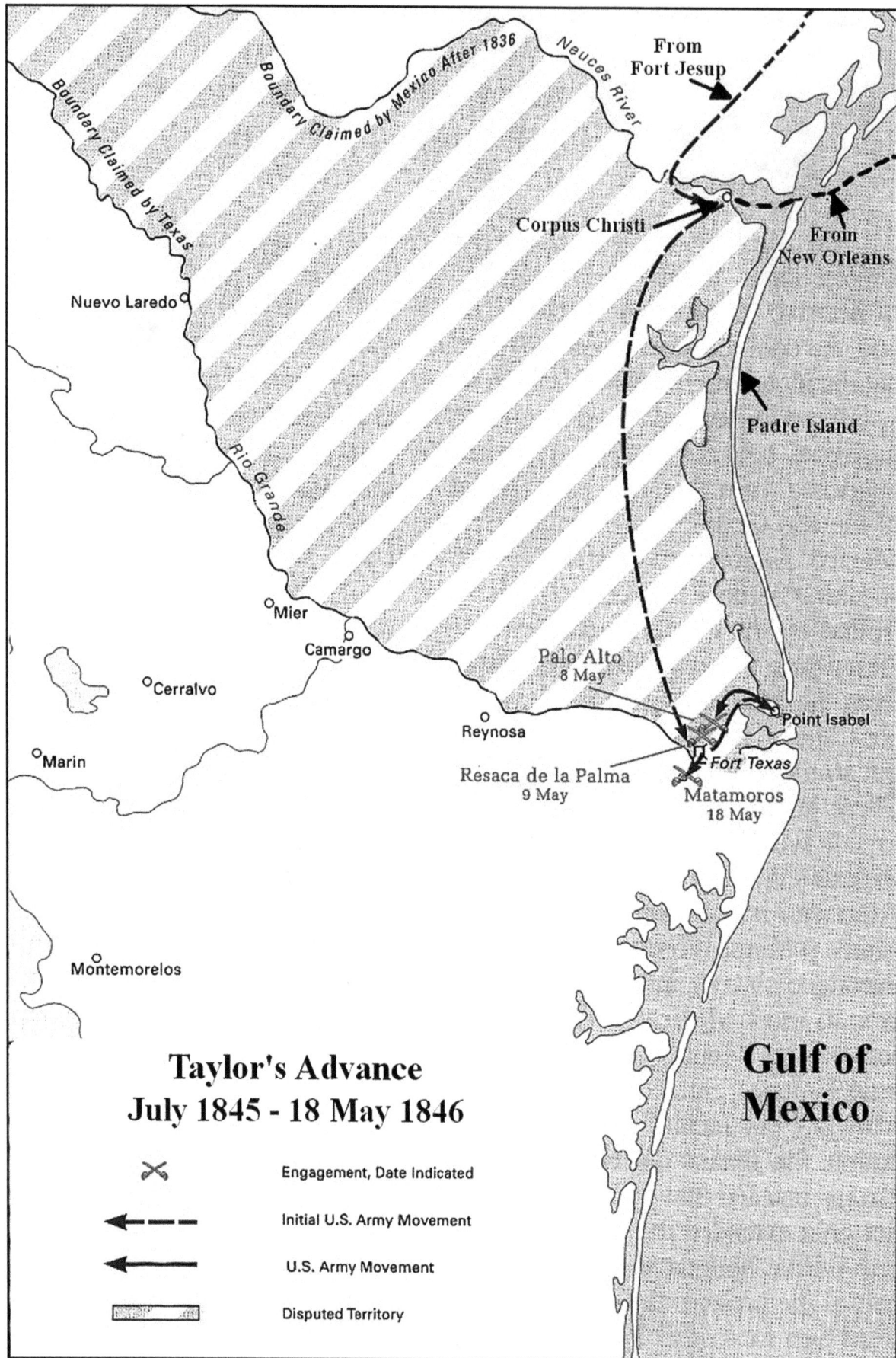

Boundary Claimed by Mexico After 1836

Neuces River

From Fort Jesup

Boundary Claimed by Texas

Corpus Christi

From New Orleans

Nuevo Laredo

Padre Island

Rio Grande

Mier

Palo Alto
8 May

Camargo

Point Isabel

Cerralvo

Reynosa

Marin

Resaca de la Palma
9 May

Fort Texas

Matamoros
18 May

Montemorelos

**Taylor's Advance
July 1845 - 18 May 1846**

Gulf of Mexico

Engagement, Date Indicated

Initial U.S. Army Movement

U.S. Army Movement

Disputed Territory

Taylor's route from Fort Jesup and New Orleans, to Corpus Christi and then Matamoros. Courtesy U.S. Army.

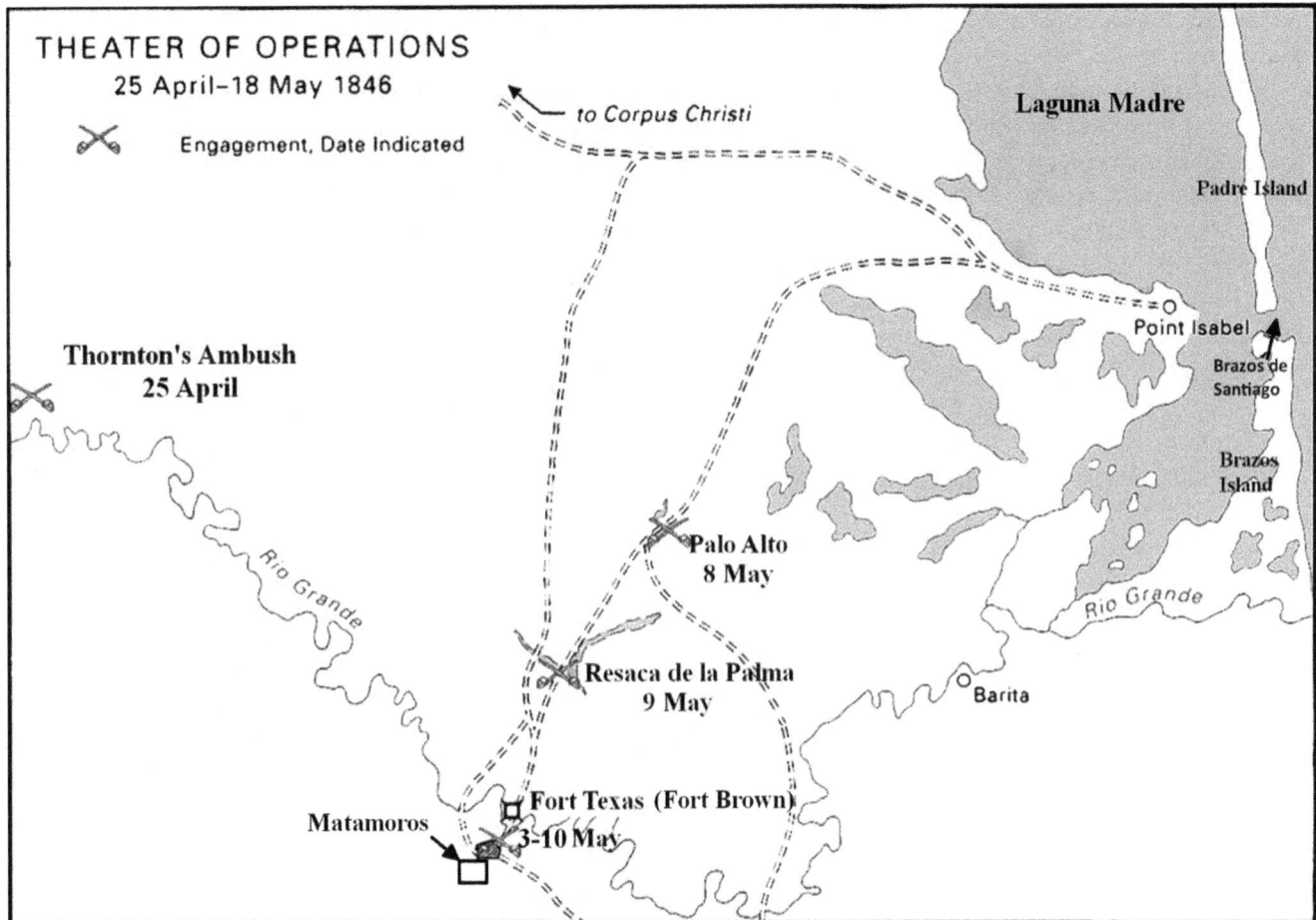

THEATER OF OPERATIONS
25 April–18 May 1846

Engagement, Date Indicated

to Corpus Christi

Laguna Madre

Padre Island

Point Isabel

Brazos de Santiago

Brazos Island

Thornton's Ambush
25 April

Rio Grande

Palo Alto
8 May

Resaca de la Palma
9 May

Barita

Rio Grande

Matamoros

Fort Texas (Fort Brown)
3–10 May

Detailed view of area of operations. Courtesy U.S. Army.

Polk's Mexico ambassador, John Slidell's mission to the Mexican government had failed so on 13 January 1846, Taylor was ordered to the Rio Grande. He received the order on 3 February and prepared his troops for the move. He began to move his stores and hospital back to St. Joseph's Island and had scouts examining the inland route to Point Isabel in addition to Mansfields' reconnoitering along the shores opposite Padre Island. Despite heavy winter rains, Taylor chose the inland route as warm weather rapidly dried the soggy ground; the more direct route closer to the coast to the Rio Grande was too muddy. The Quartermaster Department was unable to supply adequate animals to pull the 450 army wagons so wild mules were bought and broken to supplement the meagre number of horses and oxen available. A vanguard departed 4 March 1846 under Major William M. Graham composed of 100 men, two companies of the 4th Infantry, escorting a wagon train of 60 wagons carrying provisions. He was to set up a depot about one-third of the distance to the Rio Grande at Santa Gertrudis, about 40 miles from Corpus Christi.[38]

The army's almost 200-mile overland movement to the Rio Grande began at 10 a.m. on 8 March, on the old road from San Patricio to Matamoros, with Colonel David E. Twiggs in the van accompanied by Samuel Ringgold's Battery. Mansfield accompanied Twiggs. On 9 March, the 1st Brigade under Brigadier General William J. Worth departed with Lieutenant James Duncan's Battery in tow; on the 10th, the 2nd Brigade departed under command of Lieutenant Colonel James S. McIntosh, and finally on the 11th the 3rd Brigade marched under command of Colonel William Whistler with Bragg's Battery. Taylor and most of his staff also left on the 11th. The 307 wagons, 1,900 horses and mules, and 500 ox teams of the main supply train left after the last column just before Taylor and his staff. The brigades were to rendezvous

---

[38] Robert Thonoff's careful research described the exact route: "the army followed the west bank of the Nueces River approximately sixteen miles up to Barranca Blanca; turned westward to the crossing on the Agua Dulce; then followed the road to Matamoros southward across the Los Pintos, San Fernando, Santa Gertrudis, Escondido, and Bobido to Santa Rosa ponds. Beginning at Rancho Santa Rosa, the army gradually swung southeastward past several ranchos to Rancho El Sauz, then southward again to the crossing of the Arroyo Colorado and on the Rio Grande," Robert H. Thonhoff, "Taylor's Trail in Texas," *The Southwestern Historical Quarterly*, vol. 70, no. 1, July 1966, 15.

at the Little Colorado River about 30 miles north of the Rio Grande so that the unified force would be able to approach Matamoros together.[39]

Mansfield wrote to his wife on 9 March 1846 from Corpus Christi that he was sorry to hear about his bird dying as he raised it from the nest after its parents were killed by a cat, it was the only one to which he had taken a fancy. But pragmatic as always he gave direction about how to dispose of the cage—sell it or give it to a friend—as he does not want another bird. He also wrote that he hired a young discharged Irish soldier as a waiter at $20 month. He added that he and fellow engineer Lieutenant [Jeremiah Mason] Scarritt would march to the Rio Grande with the 1st Brigade: "company of horse artillery under Lieutenant Duncan, two companies of the 8th Infantry, a regiment of artillery....The Genl I suppose will soon be at the advance of the Army. We know not the manner we shall be received by the Mexicans. I trust however they will prefer negotiation to fighting."[40] He took time on the day he was to march off with his column to catch up the news with his wife as he knew that he would not be able to do any writing on his journey south. Taylor did catch up with Mansfield's column as predicted at the Little Colorado as Taylor planned.

For most of the soldiers, leaving Corpus Christi was a happy occasion as some were there for over seven months and camp life after such a long period was tedious and boring. Smith described the early days of the march:

> The weather was now fine, the road almost free from mud, and the breeze balmy. Frequently the blue lupine, the gay verbena, the saucy marigold and countless other bright flowers carpeted the ground. The cactus and the cochineal excited and gratified curiosity. Ducks and geese often flew up from the line of advance. Many rabbits and many deer scampered across the plain; and occasionally wolves, catamounts and panthers were frightened from cover. Wild horses would gaze for an instant at their cousins in bondage, and then gallop off, tossing their manes disdainfully; and once a herd of them, spaced as if to allow room for cannon, were taken for Mexican cavalry. Innumerable centipedes, tarantulas and rattlesnakes furnished a good deal of interest, if not of charm. The boundless prairie had somewhat the fascination of the sea; and occasionally, when a mirage conjured up a range of blue mountains — clothed with forests and reflected in lakes — that melted presently into the air, one had a sense of moving on enchanted ground.[41]

But not every day on the march was as delightful and undoubtedly as the days went on, tedium set in mixed with excitement as described by Henry after a day's march:

> The day was oppressively hot. As we were quietly marching along, some commotion was created at the head of the column. It was caused by some of the men killing two peccaries (wild hogs); one of them, after being shot, made for the column, and was knocked down by one of the men with the butt of his gun; and a mustang, taking it into his head to be a little restive, relieved himself of his load, a demure-looking camp-woman. After a march of sixteen miles, we encamped on the Nueces.[42]

Other descriptions of the country during early part of the march south through dry country were not as bucolic as Henry's as this description of the drier section attests:

---

[39] Smith, 144-146; Henry 52-53; Thonhoff, 7, n. 2, 10, 12; Meade, 50-51; Richard T. Marcum, "Fort Brown, Texas: The History of a Border Post," unpublished PhD dissertation, 1964, Texas Technological College, 10. Contrary to some historians, Taylor's route was well-planned using a path used for decades by Indians and early travelers; Thonhoff, 14. Note that in a letter to Cullum 1860, Mansfield wrote that he left on 8 March with Twiggs, not the 9th as he told his wife; letter courtesy WPL.

[40] Letter to wife 9 March 1846 courtesy WPL. Scarritt was an 1834 West Point graduate in the Corps of Engineers who was awarded a brevet to captain for his actions at Monterrey. Mansfield employed George Ormsby at Fort Pulaski who followed him to Corpus Christi and was employed by the quartermaster. Ormsby again entered in Mansfield's employment at Matamoros as his servant and remained more than a year and with him at Monterrey and the battle of Buena Vista. On 4 October 1846, Mansfield wrote from Monterrey that he is still confined to his tent due to his leg wound but can now sit up and read in addition to studying Spanish while eating delicious oranges and pomegranates. He commented that his waiter, George Ormsby, who served him at Fort Pulaski, "still holds on and I would not part with him on any account. I intend if I ever return to take him to Middletown with me where I hope he will find a good wife. He is sober and saving and industrious and young and would make a good match for Jane. I told him he must go to Connecticut with me and I would find him a good wife and he must settle down for life." Mansfield then got Ormsby out of Mexico and into a position with the quartermaster at New Orleans. Ormsby returned to Brazos and died of yellow fever 19 August 1848 while employed with the quartermaster. Mansfield was trying to give Ormsby's personal effects and monies to his legal heirs; 10 Nov 1848 letter from Mansfield to Rev. O'Neil in Savannah, GA; courtesy WPL, and letter to wife 4 October 1846, WPL. Mansfield gave more details about Ormsby in a 10 November 1848 letter to Rev. O'Neil at Savannah: Ormsby was employed by Mansfield at Fort Pulaski, and followed him to Corpus Christi and entered in Quartermaster Department employment but at Matamoros entered into Mansfield's private employ as his servant and remained with him more than a year; letter courtesy WPL. There is an undated letter from an attorney inquiring about some of Ormsby's personal property Mansfield had; letter courtesy WPL.

[41] Smith, *The War With Mexico,* 146-147.

[42] Henry, 53.

The march of the army was of the most toilsome and exhausting nature. The country over which they moved was sterile, and destitute of vegetation, except the wiry grass of the prairie; and its surface was varied only by slight elevations, never rising to the dignity of hills, and by occasional skirtings of stunted wood, in which the mesquite and prickly pear were predominant.

As they proceeded further south, the country became more desolate, till they entered the solitudes of a vast desert, where vegetation was suspended, and the weary soldier, encumbered with his burden, was ready to sink with exhaustion from the heat of a tropic sun and his toilsome progress over loose and burning sands like heated ashes, into which, at every step, the foot descended. At times, when faint with marching and fevered with thirst, the failing energies of nature were exhilarated by the appearance of blue mountains in the distance, beautiful lakes skirted with trees, and fields clothed with verdure—and the soldier forgot his suffering and toil in expectation of hospitable shade and refreshing streams; but as he advanced he either discovered that the mirage had spread a false verdure and beauty over barren sands, that mocked his sight, and then faded utterly away, or found the groves he had descried impenetrable thickets of thorn and cactus, that refused him shelter, and the glassy lakes pools of brine, which maddened the thirst they mocked.

Beyond this, and approaching the Arroyo [Little] Colorado, the country was much improved in appearance—the wood was increased in quantity and of better growth, and the soil changed from sand to a dark-colored clay, and covered with vegetation and flowers. The supply of fresh water, too, was abundant, and the troops in a measure forgot the hardships they had passed.[43]

On 12 March, Henry's column marched only eight miles due to the boggy nature of the ground as it had been a wet winter. Mansfield also experienced such conditions as his column was one day ahead although Mansfield certainly rode a horse. The next day Henry marched 11 miles as the roads were better plus good water holes were found. The beauty of the countryside the next day, 14 March, brought out Henry's descriptive powers:

Nothing could surpass, this morning, the magnificent mirage seen in the west. Far, far away in the distance appeared ranges of blue mountains, lakes fringed with trees, deep ravines, and farms with cultivated fields. The effect was exceedingly beautiful, and attracted universal attention. In conjunction with this curious scene appeared the phenomena of "converging rays." As the sun rose the fairy scene gradually disappeared, and when the advance sounded naught remained but the interminable vista of level prairies. The delusion was perfect; many unconsciously called the attention of the officers to what they really believed were mountains....Saw a herd of antelope, which dashed away to the verge of the horizon, and proudly looked at the passing column. An immense drove of mustangs made their appearance in the distant horizon; their forms, at first indistinct, became more apparent as they galloped toward us to gratify their curiosity.[44]

Mansfield would likely have not done much scouting as they were following those who left earlier; additionally, he was a senior engineer who, unlike Lieutenant Meade, probably would not have been "daily on duty with the advance guard, examining for the line of march, selecting and laying out positions for camps."[45] Mansfield had Lieutenant Scarritt as an assistant so he would have detailed him for menial duties. Colonel Kinney had apparently fastened a huge plowshare to one of his wagons to cut a furrow as a marker to allow following columns to ensure they were on the right trail. Taylor had contracted with Kinney at Corpus Christi to help furnish wagons, teamsters, and guides for the march south.[46]

Lieutenant French of the 3rd Artillery wrote of the effect the hot Mexican sun had while the troops were on the march with the benefit of the inadequate wheel caps:

The officers and men being in uniform, wearing caps, had their lips and noses nearly raw from the sun and winds, and could not put a cup of coffee to their lips until it was cold. I wore an immense sombrero, or Mexican straw hat. On the route I was often told: "When General Taylor comes up you will be put in arrest for wearing that hat." The army concentrated near the Arroyo Colorado, where the general commanding overtook us. I went over to call on him the next morning, and found him in front of his tent sitting on a camp stool eating breakfast. His table was the lid of the mess chest. His nose was white from the

---

[43] Nathan C. Brooks, *A Complete History of the Mexican War: Its Causes, Conduct, and Consequences*, 80-81. Mexican soldiers also burned some scrub brush which added soot and ashes to the marchers' misery, and for the leading troops, flames presented barriers, Smith, 147; Douglas A. Murphy, *Two Armies on the Rio Grande: The First Campaign of the US-Mexican War* (College Station, TX: Texas A&M University Press, 2015), 51.

[44] Henry, 53-54. The routes of the brigades varied before they reached the rendezvous at the Little Colorado River, Thonhoff, "Taylor's Trail in Texas,"

[45] Meade, 51. Note that Meade was a topographical engineer unlike Mansfield so Meade was more likely to be assigned these tasks even if engineers were present.

[46] Thonhoff, 11, 18. Thonhoff cites an undated newspaper article, "Taylor's Trail," found in the Nueces County Scrapbook, Archives, University of Texas Library, for the plowshare story. This furrow would have been most important travelling over dry, hard ground as the trail of preceding columns would have been obvious in muddy areas.

peeling off of the skin, and his lips raw. As I came up he saluted me with: "Good morning, lieutenant, good morning; sensible man to wear a hat." So I was commended instead of being censured for making myself comfortable. His coffee was in a tin cup, and his lips so sore that the heat of the tin was painful.[47]

[47] Samuel G. French, *Two Wars: an Autobiography of Gen. Samuel G. French* (Nashville, TN: Confederate Veteran, 1901), 42-43. French became a Confederate major general during the Civil War.

"The horseman in the foreground of this painting of a column of General Zachary Taylor's troops on the march in northern Mexico is a dragoon. The yellow band on his forage cap, in contradiction to regulations, was worn by many of the cavalrymen. His distinctive dark blue fatigue jacket laced with yellow is the same as that adopted in 1833. Beside the dragoon is a first lieutenant of infantry in the dark blue frock coat worn by most officers in this campaign. The lieutenant is wearing the regulation dark blue, waterproof, cloth forage cap, and his rank is indicated by the single silver bar on his shoulder strap to distinguish him from the second lieutenants, who wore no insignia on their shoulders/raps at this time. The light blue trousers with a white stripe down the side and the silver buttons on his coat proclaim his arm. In the background is a column of infantrymen in light blue fatigue jackets and trousers. These, with the dark blue forage cap, were the universal dress of the regular enlisted infantryman in this war," courtesy U.S. Army: http://www.history.army.mil/catalog/pubs/70/posters/70-1-1/70-1-1.html, from Wikimedia.

Enlisted infantry uniforms of the U.S. Army (left) and the Mexican Army, courtesy Wikipedia.

No Mexican Army resistance was met until the Little Colorado River was approached on 20 March. The Mexican commander decided to try to bluff the American troops that sufficient Mexicans were there to stop any crossings. Henry described the river and the Mexican ruse which resulted in Taylor's preparation for battle:

It is a beautiful stream, about one hundred yards broad, with bluff banks some twenty feet high, and bordered, for a depth of two to three miles on each side, with a dense growth of mesquite and prickly-pear (cactus). It is perfectly impenetrable, except in certain places; the water of the river is quite salt, arising from its coursing its way through immense salt plains.

When General Taylor, with his command, reached the bank, some twenty or thirty Mexicans presented themselves, and said that if his force attempted to cross, they would fire upon it; that such were their orders. Their troops were drawn up in order of battle upon the bank; the Mexican bugles sounded for some distance up and down the river, making out there was an immense force opposed to us. A fight appeared to be certain, and although our gallant fellows had made up their minds they would have to cross amid a shower of bullets, they were eager to advance. The men were employed cutting down the bank for the passage of the train. General Taylor, standing on the bank, told them that 'as soon as he cut down the bank he intended to cross, and that the first Mexican he saw after our men entered the water would be shot.' At this there was a regular scampering on their parts. The bank being prepared, the word "forward" was given, and our boys dashed into the river, which at that point was four feet deep. The batteries were drawn up to cover the passage; port fires lighted. Captain C.F. Smith, with a battalion of four companies of artillery, was selected as the "forlorn hope." General Worth and staff dashed in ahead of them, and led the way. Previous to the crossing, the adjutant-general of General [Francisco] Mejia, the commanding general at Matamoras, made his appearance, and handed to General Taylor a paper from Mejia, 'forbidding his crossing, stating that he would look upon it as a declaration of war,' and left, assuring the general he would be opposed, and that a fight was inevitable. No enemy showed themselves; no gun was fired. If they ever intended making a stand against us, here was the spot; they could have done us great damage, and rendered some desperate fighting necessary. The presumption is, there were very few men at the river, and they thought to frighten us away by the sounds of bugles and big threats. [48]

General Taylor reported the action at the Little Colorado which included Mansfield's role. Taylor likely chose Mansfield as his envoy since he was not only his senior engineer, but also a man he trusted given the 42-year-old Mansfield's almost 30 years in the U.S. Army:

The Arroyo [Little] Colorado is a salt river, or rather lagoon, nearly one hundred yards broad, and so deep as barely to be fordable. It would have formed a serious obstruction to our march had the enemy chosen to occupy its right bank, even with a small force. On the 19th, the advanced corps encamped within three miles of the ford, and a reconnoissance was pushed forward to the river. A party of irregular cavalry (rancheros) was discovered on the opposite bank, but threw no obstacle in the way of examining the ford. They, however, signified to the officer charged with the reconnoissance that it would be considered an act of hostility if we attempted to pass the river, and that we should, in that case, be treated as enemies. Under these circumstances, not knowing the amount of force that might be on the other bank, I deemed it prudent to make dispositions to pass the river under fire.… At an early hour on the 20th, the Cavalry and First Brigade of Infantry were in position at the ford, the batteries of field artillery being so placed as to sweep the opposite bank. While these dispositions were in progress, the party that had shown themselves the day before again made their appearance. I sent Captain Mansfield to communicate with the officer in command, who said that he had positive orders to fire upon us if we attempted to cross the river. Another party then made its appearance, and passed the river to communicate with me. One of them (who was represented as the adjutant-general of the Mexican troops) repeated substantially what had been sent before, viz.: that they had peremptory orders to fire upon us, and that it would be considered a declaration of war if we passed the river. He placed in my hands, at the same time, a proclamation of General Mejia, issued at Matamoros, a day or two previous, which I enclose. I informed the officer that I should immediately cross the river, and if any of his party showed themselves on the other bank after the passage commenced, they would receive the fire of our artillery. In the meantime, the Second Brigade (which had encamped some miles in my rear) came up and formed on the extreme right. The crossing was then commenced and executed in the order prescribed. Not a shot was fired; and a reconnoissance of cavalry, sent immediately forward, discovered the party which had occupied the bank retreating in the direction of Matamoros. Agreeably to my orders, they were not molested. The Cavalry and First and Second Brigades of Infantry,

---

[48] Henry, *Campaign Sketches of the War with Mexico,* 59-62; Smith, 147. The Mexicans at the stream were encountered on the 20th and Twiggs sent back to Taylor to come forward; he arrived the next day. Mejia, who first entered military service in 1811, was a senior Mexican Army commander who was stationed in Northern Mexico in the early 1840's. This capable commander, after failing to fool Taylor at the Little Colorado, returned to Matamoros but was succeeded as commander of the Army of the North by Generals Mariano Arista and Pedro de Ampudia. He went to Monterrey where, as second in command, he participated in the fortifying of the city and in the Battle of Monterrey in September 1846.

with a train of two hundred wagons, crossed over and encamped at this point, three miles distant, at an early hour in the afternoon.[49]

Before Taylor sent his men across, Mansfield went down to the riverbank, broke off a piece of river cane, and plumbed the depth at the ford finding that it was passable but very deep.[50]

Even though there was no fight, U.S. troops felt encouraged as the foe ran away rather than face them. The troops also were cheered by the demonstration by one of the laundresses known as the "Great Western" who accompanied the wagon train. She declared that "'if the General would give her a good pair of tongs, she would wade the river and whip every scoundrel that dare show himself.'"[51] On 22 March, about four miles south of Paso Real, the columns rested waiting for the wagon train bringing up the rear, as the oxen were slow. Here, Taylor decided to march to Point Isabel rather than Matamoros as he received information that Point Isabel was held by Mexican troops and there was information that Mexican General Pedro de Ampudia, Arista's replacement, was marching north with 5,000 men. Taylor wanted to ensure that he had a base of operations before he continued his march to the Rio Grande north of Matamoros, Mexico. Taylor marched about 14 miles on the 23rd in four columns abreast, about 400 yards apart, Dragoons on the right, the 1st and 2nd Brigades in the center, the 3rd Brigade on the left, baggage trains in the rear. Taylor believed that his next encounter with Mexican forces would not be as easy as his first at the Little Colorado and wanted to be ready to give battle.[52] Mansfield remained with General Taylor as the march continued.

The land through which the army now marched toward Point Isabel was pleasant according to Henry: "the land is much richer, and the country more picturesque. We passed many fresh-water ponds, in which were innumerable ducks and plover, so tame that you could hardly drive them away; started any number of hares (called jackass rabbits), and had no little amusement in witnessing some animated runs; their speed is wonderful; there are few dogs that can catch them....We marched through a wilderness of mesquite and acacia thickets, fragrant with the blossom of the latter; the grass was rich; the peavine, with its delicate blossom, abundant, and the country sufficiently rolling to relieve the eye. The air from the sea was delightful, and everything in nature appeared so happy that it was perfectly exhilarating."[53]

---

[49] Thomas Bangs Thorpe (pseud. Tom Owen), *The Taylor Anecdote Book: Anecdotes and Letters of Zachary Taylor* (New York: D. Appleton & Company, 1848), 83. The Arroya, Arroyo, or Little Colorado which was 30 miles north of the Rio Grande or Rio Bravo, was once the bed of that river some thousands of years earlier. The Rio Grande was constantly changing its course often leaving behind long, shallow ravines which the inhabitants called "resacas," Murphy, 75. During the rainy season, many of these became welcome waterholes.

[50] Murphy, 54.

[51] Thonhoff, 21-22. The legendary laundress, the six feet, two inch tall Sarah Borginnis, was the wife of a 7th Infantry soldier; Henshaw, 56-57, 201, n. 11.

[52] Murphy, 65.

[53] Hitchcock, 210-211; Henry, 60; Thonhoff, 17. The camp at Point Isabel was officially named "Fort Polk" 12 May 1846. "Point Isabel was connected to the mainland on the south and west, and was bounded on the north by the Laguna Madre, and on the east by the shallows of Brazos Bay. Just four miles across the bay lay Brazos Santiago, and fourteen miles south of Point Isabel, at the mouth of the Rio Grande, was Clarksville....Supplies were shipped from New Orleans by steamer, unloaded for the most part at Brazos Santiago (but also at Clarksville), and then transported overland by wagon train to Fort Brown," Marcum, 22-23.

Point Isabel from Brazos Santiago. Thorpe, facing 36. The inlet of Brazos Santiago had wharves on the lagoon side of Brazos Island where Taylor established a supply depot and where troops disembarked. Goods were offloaded at Brazos Santiago because the bars at the mouth of the Rio Grande were too shallow for large ships. Supplies for Matamoros were landed at the harbor on Brazos Island and then transported to Matamoros by oxcart.

On 24 March when he arrived at the junction of the road leading to Point Isabel, Taylor halted the army and ordered all the empty wagons started for that port to obtain supplies; he and the Dragoons escorted the wagons on the 10-mile trek. He had General Worth march the remainder of the army toward Matamoras--they advanced six miles on the 24th and five miles on the 25th camping at Palo Alto near the area which would later see the first major fight of the war. Worth encountered a friendly Mexican officer, Colonel Jose Maria Carvajal, who helpfully informed him that Mexican forces were concentrating in Matamoros. Mansfield reached Port Isabel with Taylor who tasked him to make plans for its defense as a depot for supplies. Mansfield, in half a day with the aid of two assistants, surveyed the area and staked out positions including a redoubt which was key to the port's defense. Taylor turned over Mansfield's report to fellow engineer Captain John Sanders. Taylor reached Point Isabel the same time as his supply ships he had sent there from Corpus Christi. Even though Mexican civilians at Point Isabel protested his "occupation" of their country, Taylor commenced fortifying the city for his supply base. Captain Sanders was in charge of constructing fortifications and Taylor assigned Major John Munroe as commander of the 450 men there including a squadron of Dragoons under Lieutenant Theodoric Porter.[54]

---

[54] Murphy 66-67. A "squadron" is two companies. Worth also encountered another Mexican who erroneously informed him that a force of 800 was going to attack his rear; Henry, *Campaign Sketches of the War with Mexico,* 65-66. Munroe had accompanied the transports down the coast along with two companies of troops. Both Munroe and Sanders were West Point graduates. Major Munroe had embarked for Brazos Santiago, accompanied by Captain Sanders of the Engineers, and the officers of the ordnance and the pay departments. With him were a siege train and a field battery which was shipped due to lack of horses. The movement to Brazos Santiago was covered by the revenue cutter *Woodbury* and brigs of war *Porpoise* and *Lawrence*. Taylor did his best not to inflame anti-American feeling among the Mexican populace: he told some citizens of Matamoros who were at Point Isabel with a large number of mules for sale that the United States, "in occupying the Rio Grande, has no motive of hostility towards Mexico, and that the army will, in no case, go beyond the river, unless hostilities should be commenced by the Mexicans themselves; that the Mexicans living on this side will not be disturbed in any way by the troops; that they will be protected in all their usages; and that everything which the army may need will be purchased from them at fair prices. I also stated that, until the matter should be finally adjusted between the two governments, the harbour of Brazos Santiago would be open to the free use of the Mexicans as heretofore. The same views were impressed upon the Mexican custom-house officer at Brazos Santiago by Captain [William J.] Hardee, who commanded the escort which covered the reconnoissance of Padre Island," Brooks, 77, 89; Henry Montgomery, *The Life of Major General Zachary Taylor* (Auburn, NY: J.C. Derby & Co., 1847), 91. Distance from Point Isabel to Matamoros by land, 27 miles, 90 miles by water; from Matamoros to Corpus Christi, by land 100 miles by the old road while 150 miles by the route

Taylor left the port on the 26th and returned to his army at Palo Alto on the afternoon of 27 March along with wagons filled with provisions. The next morning at 5 a.m., he marched his army the last nine miles toward the Rio Grande. While the march began again in the combat four-column formation, the dense undergrowth forced the men into a long column on the road. It arrived without incident across from Matamoros just before noon; the Dragoons were in the van followed by the 1st, 2nd, and 3rd Brigades, then the wagon train. Taylor met no resistance but two Dragoons who were scouting ahead were taken prisoner. Henry described his arrival at the river in his usual flowery style: "The far-famed and much-talked-about waters rolled beneath us, and the city of Matamoras rose like a fairy vision before our enraptured eyes. I was so agreeably disappointed, I was inclined to grant it more beauty than it probably possessed. When we arrived some two hundred persons were on the opposite bank. The Mexican colors were flying from the quarters of the commander, General Mejia; from the Place d'Artillerie; and from the quarters of the Sappers and Miners. Those were the prominent places pointed out to us upon our arrival." Smith also wrote of the army's arrival: "Rio Bravo, the 'Bold river of the North,' brown with mud, rolled swift and boiling at their feet; and in plain view about half a mile distant — black with crowded house-tops, gay with flags, and noisy with bugles and barking dogs — lay Matamoros. A rude pole was soon raised; to the music of our national airs the colors went up; and a small masked battery of field guns was planted near them." When Taylor arrived he had a total of 3,249 troops on hand. Henry elaborated on the flag raising ceremony: "Two hours after our arrival a flag-staff was erected, under the superintendence of Colonel [William G.] Belknap, and soon the flag of our country, a virgin one, was seen floating upon the banks of the Rio Grande, proclaiming in a silent but impressive manner that the 'area of freedom' was again extended. As it was hoisted the band of the 8th Infantry played the 'Star-spangled Banner,' and the field music 'Yankee Doodle.'" The view of this large Mexican city was enhanced for many American troops as unclothed Mexican ladies bathed frequently in the river and waved at the appreciative soldiers.[55]

After a short interval, a small boat arrived on the American side with two Mexican cavalry officers and an interpreter, the Mexican captain from the incident at the Little Colorado, Jean Louis Berlandier. General Worth told them he had a letter from General Taylor for General Mejia and that Worth wished to arrange a meeting. The Mexican army officers recrossed and returned, and told Worth that Mejia refused to meet with Worth since Mejia, as the Mexican commander, would only meet with Taylor but General Romulo Diaz de la Vega would meet with Worth across the river. Mejia along with a civilian representative, Licenciado Casares, two other officers and an interpreter met with Worth who, with Lieutenants Larkin Smith, John Magruder, George Deas, Edmund Blake, and an interpreter, Lieutenant Minor Knowlton, had crossed the river on the ferry. Worth had an open communication for General Mejia and a sealed letter for the civilian officials. General Vega refused Taylor's dispatch but the civilian accepted the other. Vega repeatedly refused to allow Worth to see the American Counsel in Matamoros while both sides assured the other that there was no state of war between their two countries. But Worth told Vega that the refusal to allow him to see the American counsel was a "belligerent act" and that any movement of armed Mexicans across the river would be considered an act of war.[56]

Taylor's army took up a defensive position, camped in a square with the wagons in the center, while Mansfield was scheduled to make a reconnaissance of the area so defensive positions could be begun in earnest. Mexican works were already visible on the opposite bank: a large redoubt named Fort Paredes, 600 yards west of the city on high ground at the main river ford, Anacuitas, which could hold 800 men; a smaller redoubt was built at the main ford, Paso Real, closer to the city near a breastwork which allowed fire to cover these two points; finally, a battery was built between the two redoubts in a small grove.[57] Captain Philip Norbourne Barbour of the 3rd Infantry wrote that the next day, the morning of 29 March, he saw that:

---

the army marched; from Matamoros to the mouth of the Rio Grande by the river is roughly 80 miles; in direct line, about 30 miles; from Point Isabel to New Orleans by sea 802 miles; from Matamoros eastward to the village of La Barita, 30 miles by land.

[55] Hitchcock, 216-117; Henry, 65; Smith, 148; 454, n. 21; Frost, 13; Nichols, 50, 52. The two dragoons were returned, unharmed, on 1 April at Matamoros, Barbour, 25.

[56] Murphy, 70-71; Cadmus M. Wilcox, *History of the Mexican War* (Washington, DC: The Church News Publishing Co., 1892), 40-41.

[57] Murphy, 89; Ramon Alcaraz, *The Other Side: Or, Notes for the History of the War Between Mexico and the United States,* trans. by Albert C. Ramsey (New York, John Wiley, 1850), 36. Within a few days of Taylor's arrival, the Mexican forces numbered about 3,000, Alcaraz, 37. General Mejia added to Fort Parades by extending trenches, bastions, and bombproofs 300 yards along the shore. He added several cannon to stop any crossing attempt at or near the ferry, Murphy 91; Barbour, 20.

a field work had been thrown up by the enemy during the night…and a 12 pounder placed in it and so pointed as to rake the front face of our Camp….Duncan's Battery, under mask, has been put in position so as to batter Mejia's quarters and the walls of the fort near them. These have been pointed out by Chipita, our guide….Our Engineers, Captain Mansfield and Lieut. Scarritt, having been engaged all today in reconnoitering, I suppose will present a plan of the Camp and entrenchments necessary so that we will commence the latter tomorrow.[58]

The engineers were ordered to find "'a defensive position for a permanent Camp,' and for the placement of batteries 'to command the town of Matamoros,'" so they spent the day conducting a "series of surveys, sightings, and measurements as the preliminary to designing the structure."[59] While Mansfield conducted his surveys, Taylor had temporary entrenchments dug. In addition to simple trenches and small earthworks scattered around the camp, Taylor, desiring a better effort, ordered Captain Allen Lowd "and his company of artillery to see to the construction of a redoubt near the broad point of the peninsula formed by the river bend. This structure, an arrow-shaped breastwork built of bundles of sticks, or fascines, and earth, was surrounded by a deep ditch and contained an underground magazine and bombproof areas….On April 6…Lowd mounted his four 18-pounder artillery pieces received two days earlier from Point Isabel, into the walls and trained them on the Mexican city."[60]

Taylor received Mansfield's report that day and ordered work to start on the fort the next morning. The location was near the Paso Real ferry on a bend in the river putting the river on three sides with two resacas to the north helping to block that flank. Putting the fort on this point would, however, allow converging fire to concentrate on the fort according to one of Taylor's engineers, Captain John Sanders. But Lieutenant George Meade said that "We have placed ourselves in so strong a position, and have such superiority in artillery, that it is impossible for them with any force to drive us from here; in addition to which we have a battery of heavy guns (four eighteen-pounders), erected so as to batter their town, and at the first gun we shall rattle them about their ears in such a manner as will soon silence their fire." It is not known whether Mansfield or Taylor chose the location for the fort but it is likely Mansfield presented to his general the site he thought best and Taylor accepted. Taylor had to trust his chief engineer's opinion as he knew of Mansfield's long experience in the field for over 20 years as an engineer on many diverse projects.[61] It was an earthen fort of 800 yards perimeter (two sides at 150 yards long and four sides at 125 yards), with six bastions, walls nine and one half feet high, a parapet of fifteen feet, and the whole surrounded by a ditch eight feet deep and twenty feet wide. It could hold 500 men and Taylor wrote that the fort "will enable a Brigade to maintain this position against any Mexican odds, and will leave me free to dispose of the other corps as considerations of health and convenience may render desirable."[62] "The First Brigade began the construction on 7 April but all brigades eventually were involved: "Week after week, from dawn until dusk, officers and enlisted men toiled side by side, as Mansfield and his engineers guided the process….Pressed to complete the job before the expected attack, U.S. soldiers received no exemptions from their shifts unless they were performing other essential duties."[63] Lieutenant Napoleon Dana wrote his wife that "For the last two days I have been constantly at work on our fort. About one thousand men work at it all the time….we went to work immediately after reveille and have been constantly at it ever since, and it has been a broiling hot day too."[64]

While work progressed on the temporary entrenchments and the fort, some of Taylor's soldiers appreciated the proximity of the Mexican city and desertions began on 31 March. Taylor gave instructions to his officers that deserters swimming the river to Mexico should be hailed, and if they did not return, they would be shot. On both the 4th and 5th

---

[58] Barbour, 20-21. Colonel James Duncan's breastwork contained two six-pounder field cannon and two 12-pounder howitzers, Murphy, 95.

[59] Lewis, 55; Murphy, 95.

[60] Murphy, 102-103.

[61] Murphy, 88-89; Philip Norbourne Barbour, *Journals of the Late Brevet Major Philip Norbourne Barbour and His Wife Martha Isabella Hopkins Barbour*, ed. by Rhoda van Bibber Tanner Doubleday (New York: G.P. Putnam's Sons, 1936), 18-20; Meade, vol. 1, 59. The fort was 50 miles upriver from the mouth of the Rio Grande but only 28 miles overland, Marcum, 20. Hitchcock and a few others questioned the location: "the bulk of his [Taylor's] force was in the vicinity of fort Brown, a set of textbook field works which he had built opposite Matamoros, on a site no textbook would have approved…it commanded nothing but a stretch of river, it was open to enfilade from three sides, and any competent enemy could have pinched it off from the rear," Bernard DeVoto, *The Year of Decision—1846* (Boston, MA: Houghton-Mifflin Co., 1943), 132. Hitchcock called it a "cul-de-sac", 217. The concern was that there was only one road from the fort leading to Point Isabel which could have allowed a Mexican force to shut that road and besiege the fort. Fortunately for Taylor, the enemy never successfully did so; Marcum, 21.

[62] Murphy, 104.

[63] Murphy 104. The fort was named officially Fort Brown after Brown was killed during the Mexican bombardment on 9 May 1846. Before then, it was informally called Fort Taylor or Fort Texas but it had no official name, Murphy, 108.

[64] Napoleon Jackson Tecumseh Dana, *MONTEREY IS OURS! The Mexican War Letters of Lieutenant Dana 1845-1847*, ed. by Robert H. Ferrell (Lexington, KY: The University Press of Kentucky, 1990), 46.

of April, men were shot and killed swimming across but over 60 were successful in following weeks. Deserters who took a cross country route usually met with death at the hands of Mexican bandits or neighboring ranchers. Most of the men deserting were foreigners from Ireland and Germany. Mexican commanders in Matamoros enticed American deserters who enlisted in the Mexican Army by granting them citizenship, paying higher wages than the U.S. Army, offering promotions and officer rank to some, and giving land grants. Attentions from young senoritas were also tempting. One deserter from the 5th Infantry, a former British soldier, John Riley, along with a company of 48 Irishmen, manned Mexican artillery during the Mexican siege of Fort Brown which is discussed below. Riley had been made a first lieutenant when he convinced General Ampudia he would form a company of deserters. His artillery company also fought Taylor later at the Battles of Monterrey and Buena Vista as will be seen.[65] Sentries shooting swimmers combined with drownings in the muddy river dramatically reduced attempts for the less motivated after the first two weeks. Taylor not only had to deal with deserters but also with Mexican irregular forces collectively named "rancheros." These horsemen continually harassed Taylor and acted as guerrillas and snipers preying on individuals and small groups. These rancheros did help unintentionally since American soldiers contemplating desertion were dissuaded after hearing reports about what rancheros did to men found outside of camp. Torture before death was not unusual based on what was seen when corpses were found. Lieutenant Meade wrote of their tactics: "hiding in the bushes whenever a force comes after them and seizing on all single individuals they find on the road."[66] The most egregious example of the rancheros' activities was the capture and murder of Colonel Truman Cross, the quartermaster general of Taylor's army. On 10 April, he left camp on a solitary ride but that evening failed to return to camp. Taylor ordered signal guns to be fired but without result, and numerous search parties found nothing. Taylor asked the new Mexican commander in Matamoros, General Pedro Ampudia if Cross was a prisoner but received assurances that that was not the case. On 21 April, Colonel Cross's fate was learned when a Mexican civilian reported to U.S. troops that he found a body in a thicket about three miles from camp. Cross's skull was crushed, his body stripped, and his corpse eaten by animals. His remains were brought back to camp and on 23 April he was awarded a full military funeral complete with a flag-draped, horse-drawn caisson, with his son walking behind, an honor guard, and three musket volleys, after which his body was laid at the foot of the fort's flagstaff. Taylor's men were outraged at Cross's murder.[67] An incident which involved a search party looking for Cross led to more American deaths.[68]

Lieutenant Theodoric Porter from the 4th Infantry led 10 men out on a scout on 19 April looking for Cross and the next morning, about 12 miles from Matamoros, fired at a horseman. Porter pursued and surprised a Mexican camp taking weapons, food and horses. Porter and his men left but were ambushed and due to a rain shower, had difficulty in using their firearms to defend themselves. Porter and one man were killed but the remaining nine solders straggled back to report the incident. Mexican sources reported that Porter and his soldier were only wounded but were stabbed to death by their captors; their bodies were not found. Cross's murder and those of Porter and the soldier further inflamed anti-Mexican feelings among Taylor's troops. Lieutenant Napoleon Dana wrote that on 5 June, two skeletons were brought to camp and were identified as Porter and the soldier. Dana further wrote that "We have vengeance to take on Mexico for more than one man's blood, and our boys are just in the humor for the business. They feel so indignant at the rascality of the brutes."[69]

Taylor did not feel justified in magnifying these incidents to ask President Polk to declare a state of war with Mexico as the Mexican generals firmly denied authorizing or condoning the murders of U.S. troops. In fact, after Colonel Cross went missing, Mexican officers had cautioned Taylor that rancheros and bandits abounded along the river and that they were uncontrolled by the Mexican Army.[70] Mexican General Ampudia ordered Taylor to move back to the

[65] Peter F. Stevens, *The Rogue's March: John Riley and the St. Patrick's Battalion, 1846-48* (Washington, DC: Potomac Books, Inc., 1999), Henry, *Campaign Sketches*, 72-73; Smith, 160; Alcaraz, The Other Side, 41-42; Murphy, 102; Hitchcock, 221; Barbour, 28-29. Black servants also deserted according to Barbour. Mexican ranchers were called "rancheros." This term covered men who ranged from land owners who organized troops to resist the Americans and sanctioned by the Mexican government to bandits who lay in ambush for an opportunity to kill unwary troops, Irving Levinson, *Wars Within War: Mexican Guerrillas, Domestic Elites, and the United States of America, 1846-1848* (Fort Worth, TX: Christian University Press, 2005), xvi. General Arista later offered privates 320 acres each, with more land for each higher rank, Frost, 211.
[66] Meade, vol. 1, 66; Stevens, 104; Murphy, 111.
[67] French, 46; Murphy, 117; Meade, vol. 1, 66; Barbour, 41.
[68] John Frost, *Pictorial History of Mexico and the Mexican War* (Philadelphia, PA: Charles Desilver, 1862), 196, 199. The original flagstaff erected when Taylor's troops arrived at Matamoros was close to the riverbank so after the bombardment by Mexican artillery began another was erected inside the fort, Henshaw, 62; Murphy, 229.
[69] Dana, *MONTEREY IS OURS!*, 48-49, 86-87. Porter was the son of the late Commodore David Porter and was admired by all, Lewis, 62-63.
[70] Murphy 118;

Hand-drawn map of area surrounding Fort Brown. Thorpe, *Our Army on the Rio Grande*, 50.

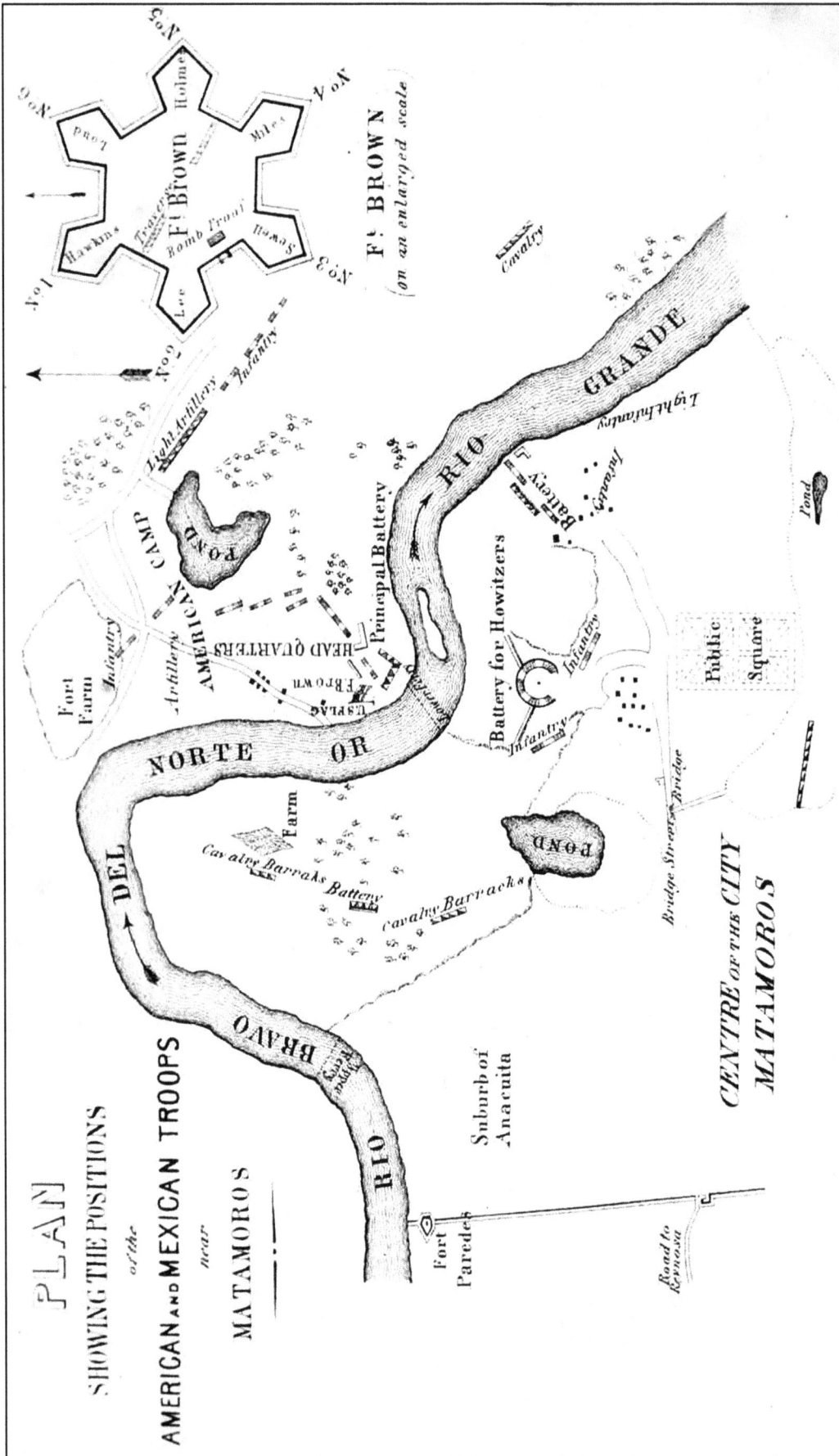

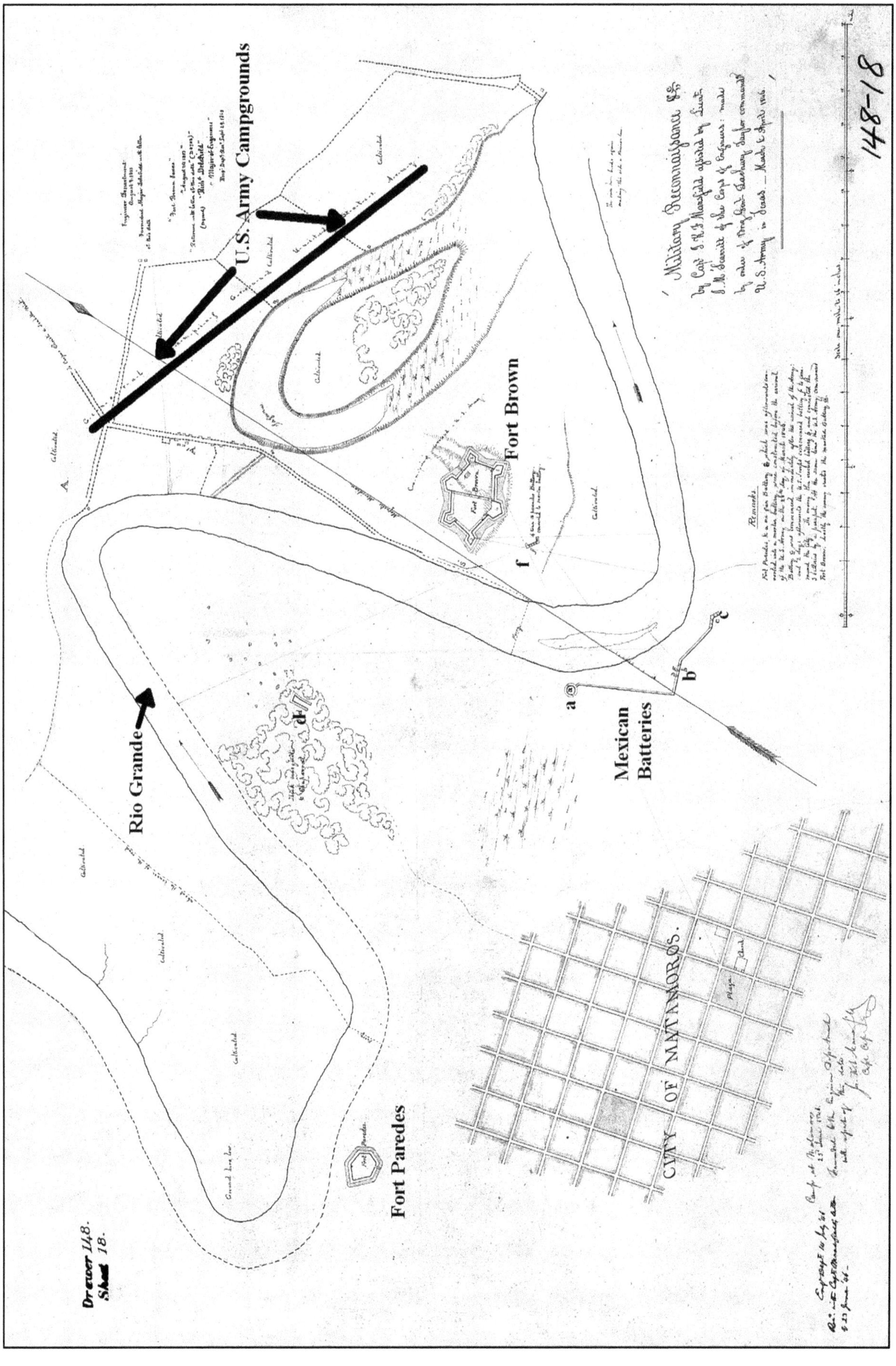

U.S. Army Campgrounds

Fort Brown

Rio Grande

Mexican Batteries

Fort Paredes

CITY OF MATAMOROS.

Drawer 148.
Sheet 18.

148-818

Mansfield's map of the area around Fort Brown showing part of Matamoros with author-added labels. His signature is in the lower left. Annotations include the following: "Camp at Matamoros 23 June 1846. Forwarded to the Engineer Department with report of this date. Military Reconnaissance etc. by Captain J.K.F. Mansfield assisted by Lieut. J.S. Scarrit of the Corps of Engineers made by order of Brig. General Zachery Taylor commanding U.S. Army in Texas, March and April 1846. Fort Paredes [upper left center] & a one gun battery which was afterwards converted into a mortar battery, were constructed before the arrival of the U.S. Army on the 26th day of March 1846. Battery c was commenced immediately after the arrival of the army and 2 days afterwards the U.S. troops commenced battery f to command the city. The enemy then erected battery b and connected the 3 batteries by a parapet. At the same time, the U.S. Army commenced Fort Brown. Lastly the enemy erected the masked battery d." Courtesy LOC.

Fort Taylor (Brown) during the siege likely showing Major Brown replying to Mexican artillery fire. United States troops were not dressed as neatly as portrayed in this lithograph. Courtesy LOC.

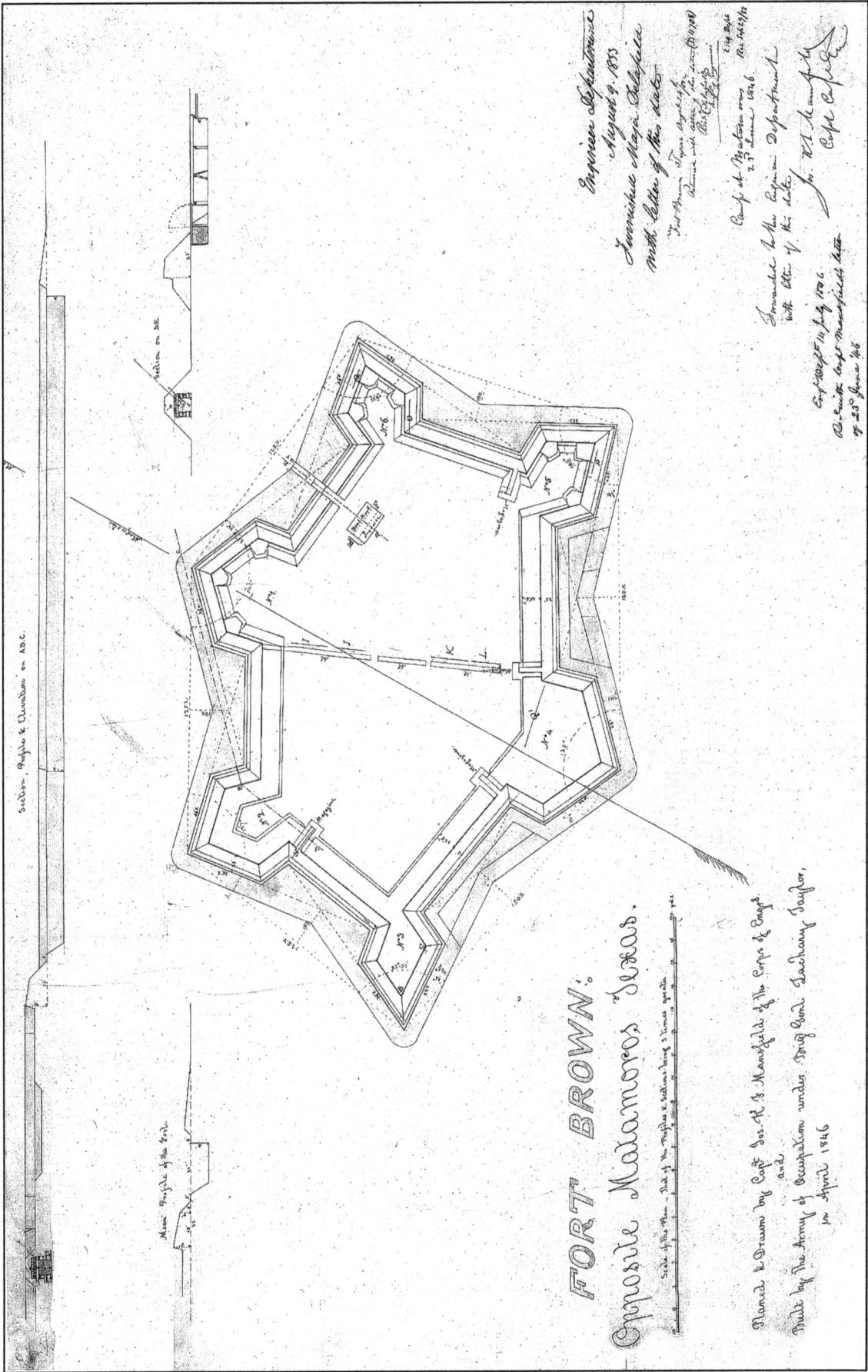

Mansfield's drawing of Fort Brown, signature in the lower right corner. Annotations include the following: "Planed & Drawn by Capt. Jos. K.F. Mansfield of the Corps of Enginrs. and Built by the Army of Occupation under Brigadier General Zachery Taylor in April 1846. Camp at Matamoros 23 June 1846. Forwarded to the Engineer Department with letter of this date." Courtesy LOC.

Matamoros before 1844. The main part of this port city was about a mile from the riverbank. After it surrendered on 17 May 1846, it remained under American control and served as a major supply base and rendezvous point for troops arriving from the U.S. The large sailing vessel in the center must have had a shallow draft as the entrance to the Rio Grande some 80 miles downstream was shallow only allowing steamboats and other shallow-draft vessels direct access to Matamoros and towns farther upriver. Larger vessels had to offload cargo and have it lightered up the river. George Winston Smith, and Charles B. Judah, *Chronicles of the Gringos: The U.S. Army in the Mexican War, 1846-1848; Accounts of Eyewitnesses & Combatants* (Albuquerque: University of New Mexico Press: 1968), 71-74; K. Jack Bauer, *The Mexican War 1846-1848* (Lincoln NE, Univ. of Nebraska Press, 1974), 81-88. John Philips and Alfred Rider, *Mexico Illustrated in Twenty-six Views* (London: E. Atchley, Library of Fine Arts, 1848), plate 26.

Fort Brown from the south bank of the Rio Grande, Henry, *Campaign Sketches*, facing pg. 103. The original flagstaff was outside the fort inside an early U.S. earthwork.

Matamoros from Fort Brown; Thorpe, *Our Army on the Rio Grande*, facing 128. The city was less than one mile, about 1000 yards, from the river bank. While estimates vary, it is about 90-100 miles by river to the Gulf of Mexico but only 35 airline miles.

Fort Brown interior showing the graves of Major Brown and Lieutenant Stevens at the foot of the flagstaff, Matamoros in the distance. Thorpe, *Our Army on the Rio Grande* (Philadelphia, PA: Carey and Hart, 1846), frontispiece. Colonel Cross was also buried here.

Mansfield performed well at Matamoros as this effusive praise describes:

> This indefatigable officer, [Mansfield] who so much distinguished himself at Monterrey and Buena Vista, showed his spirit and ability opposite Matamoras. He was, throughout the whole of the eventful period of the bombardment, the theme and admiration of both officers and men. He appeared to possess the power of ubiquity, for he was everywhere, encouraging the men and directing the fire from our batteries. While the enemy was pouring a galling fire into the fort, the balls rattling and bombs bursting all around him, this intrepid officer mounted the ramparts, and with the field-glass to his eye watched with the utmost *sang froid* the movements of the forces at Matamoras, and coolly praised their skill in gunnery, although his life was in imminent danger of being forfeited by the exposure. His object was to obtain a correct observation of their position, upon which he could direct the principal battery. As he closed his glass and descended, a smile that spoke more audibly than words brightened his countenance. The guns were promptly *ranged in the right line,* and the Mexican battery was immediately silenced.[78]

Lieutenant Meade wrote his wife that Mansfield "has gained for himself great credit for the design and execution of the work, and still more for his energy and bravery in its defence."[79] During the battle at the fort on the 7th, Mansfield and a party left the fort and levelled clumps of chaparral, a traverse, and some sheds from which Mexican sharpshooters had harassed American troops.[80] Lieutenant John Cory Henshaw of the 7th Infantry wrote that he was with Mansfield outside the fort and that "He is without doubt the soul of this little place and he is almost ubiquitous. He is without doubt of more service here than all the other officers put together."[81]

Taylor and his army remained on the north bank of the Rio Grande in the days after his return from Point Isabel. Mansfield took time to write to his wife from "Fort Taylor" during these relatively calm days. On 15 May, he lamented about Congress not passing the pontoon bridge train bill so Taylor only has three small captured boats to cross the army to take possession of Matamoros. He agreed with many Texans about the Mexican character: "I look upon the Mexican character as perfectly abominable and I have no sympathy for them. A party of the rascals not long since captured a few Texians in the prairie and cut their throats and threw them in the river….The dogs of war must now be let loose on such villains and the Texian Volunteers will be allowed full sweep and I hope they will do their work with every fellow caught with arms in his hands. For myself, I trust in a kind Providence and shall do my duty. Genl Taylor has notified me to accompany him and headquarters as soon as a march be commenced." But Mansfield also wrote about personal concerns as he described the loss of his animals: "My horse and mule were driven off by the enemy at the time of their attack on the fort. They two cost me 45 dollars. I have today purchased a horse for 100 dollars….I wish to know how much there is in the Middletown Bank to my credit." He cautions his wife about finances: "I trust soon if I live to have a place in Middletown and to spend the residue of my life in quiet. But time steals on us and if some steps are not soon taken we will not enjoy any such favors."[82]

Taylor did not immediately move on Matamoros due to the lack of pontoon boats which he had requested the previous September and the desire to build up his supplies and ammunition while awaiting reinforcements. On 12 May, Taylor was at Point Isabel conferring with Commodore Conner about investing Matamoros and opening up river navigation; he returned to Fort Brown on the 14th. The day after Taylor returned to Fort Brown, a party of U.S. troops swam across the river and brought back some boats to begin securing cross river transport for the army. On 17 May, perhaps becoming alarmed at seeing U.S. troops deploying along the river bank, the Mexican commander in Matamoros, General Mariano Arista, sent a delegation to Taylor suggesting an armistice; Taylor refused stating that he intended to take and occupy Matamoros. The delegation offered to surrender all public property, guns, ammunition, etc., if Taylor would not cross but Taylor was not moved. Taylor offered that Matamoros must surrender and all public property, ammunition, provisions, etc., must be given up. Then, Taylor would allow the Mexican Army to retreat. The Mexican delegation returned but no reply was received. The next day, the 18th, however, Mexican civilians crossed and told the Americans that the Mexican Army had fled. Civil authorities confirmed that the army was gone and Taylor began crossing troops at the upper ferry using the captured boats and then Mexican ferries; Dragoons swam their horses across.

---

[78] Tom Owen, *The Taylor Anecdote Book: Anecdotes and Letters of Zachary Taylor* (New York, D. Appleton & Company, 1847), 121.

[79] Meade, vol. 1, 76.

[80] John S. Jenkins, *History of the War Between the United States and Mexico* (New York, C.M. Saxton, 1859), 106; Thomas Bangs Thorpe, *Our Army on the Rio Grande*, 71.

[81] John Cory Henshaw, *Recollections of the War with Mexico*, ed. by Gary F. Kurutz (Univ. of Missouri Press, Columbia, MO., 2008), 58. Mansfield was one of the few officers Henshaw admired as Henshaw had a troubled Army career in Mexico and later.

[82] Letter to Louisa 15 May 1846 courtesy WPL.

United States troops quickly ran up the flag on the Mexican Fort Parades. The Mexican Army had left during the day and night of 17 May taking some artillery but leaving much military equipment and wounded behind in its haste to escape. Taylor and his staff made the army headquarters about a half mile from Matamoros having only a small guard in the city; he appointed General Twiggs in charge of the city who governed from his camp on the river bank. Taylor sent Colonel John Garland of the 4th Infantry with all U.S. cavalry and volunteers, some 250 horsemen, in pursuit of the fleeing Mexican troops but to no avail. Garland followed them some 60 miles skirmishing with the rear guard. He had two men wounded but killed two and wounded two of the enemy and captured 20.[83]

Mansfield wrote to Louisa on 18 May describing the capitulation by the delegation. He then went on to tell her about his visit that day: "The City of Matamoros is a dirty, mean Spanish place and the population of like character. I was astonished to get a good dinner at the Public Eating house and some good claret for 50 cents the bottle."[84]

Lithograph of General Taylor wearing his informal "uniform." Courtesy LOC.

---

[83] Henry, *Campaign Sketches*, 113; Thorpe, *Our Army on the Rio Grande*, 126-127. American forces remained in occupation of the city until August 1848 then used it for a forward operating base and staging area.

[84] 18 May 1846 letter courtesy of the Middlesex County Historical Society.

Drawing of Taylor's headquarter area tents near Matamoros showing how Mansfield was situated; Thorpe, *Our Army on the Rio Grande*, facing p. 125. His headquarters was placed to take advantage of shade.

Being free of these routine duties allowed Taylor to begin to manage the thousands of volunteers arriving from Louisiana, Alabama and Texas, who were encamped from Matamoros to the mouth of the Rio Grande on both river banks. Old Zach needed volunteers to pursue the Mexican Army deeper into Mexico as the Regular Army was inadequate: "In 1845, the line of the American Army consisted of only 14 regiments—2 of Dragoons, 4 of artillery, and 8 of infantry. The total authorized strength was 7,883 men. The actual strength at the end of that year was 5,300. ….About three-fourths of the line officers were graduates of West Point. The officers of the Adjutant-General's, Quartermaster's, and Ordnance departments and also those of the Engineer Corps and of the Topographical Engineers were nearly all graduates, but there were none among the general officers at that time."[85]

Unfortunately for the old general, he received too many volunteers: "the three-months men whom he had asked for and the six-months men whom General Edmund P. Gaines had bestowed on him—and not enough of anything else, especially steamboats. Until they arrived he was completely paralyzed."[86] Taylor needed volunteers if he were to continue deeper into Mexico as there was no sign that the Mexican government was willing to meet any U.S. demands. Taylor's ability to feed and sustain the thousands of volunteers he began to receive was going to be difficult. And as in virtually all wars fought by the U.S., the volunteers were needed to supplement the Regular Army once serious fighting began. Not only did Taylor have to sustain his newly arrived mostly raw troops, he had to try to instill some discipline and provide training when possible. Most Regular Army officers held volunteers in disdain but once volunteer units showed their mettle in battle, most of the critics gave them at least grudging compliments. Taylor's army had few volunteers initially and fought with Regulars for the first battles at Palo Alto on 8 May 1846 and Resaca de la Palma on 9 May 1846 as well as at Fort Brown. Of the total 73,532 volunteers the War Department raised during the war, several thousand never served in Mexico. Included also in this number are some 12,601 men who turned out in response to what was an illegal call by Brigadier General Edmund P. Gaines in May 1846 after the battles of Palo Alto and Resaca de la Palma. Gaines was the commander of the Department of the West, headquartered in New Orleans, and senior to Taylor, and had raised volunteers on his own without War Department authorization.[87]

---

[85] Samuel E. Tillman, *The Centennial of the United States Military Academy at West Point, New York*, vol. 1: Addresses and Histories, "The Academic History of the Military Academy, 1802-1902" (Washington, D. C.: Government Printing Office, 1904), 604.

[86] Henry, *Campaign Sketches*, 109-110; Henry, *The Story of the Mexican War*, 71-74; Hamilton, 193-195; Dana, *MONTEREY IS OURS!*, 77-79.

[87] Donald S. Frazier, ed., *The United States and Mexico at War* (New York, NY: Simon & Schuster Macmillan, 1998), 464-466.

Taylor had to deal with three volunteer categories: on 26 April 1846, he had made a call to the governors of the states of Texas and Louisiana for four regiments each—5,000 men from Louisiana and 2,000 from Texas; these troops under law could only be mustered for three months however. General Gaines's volunteers, although called up for 12 month's service, could also only be legally required to serve three months. On 13 May 1846 Congress authorized raising 50,000 volunteers to be enlisted for 12 months. The War Department ordered Taylor to muster out of service all volunteers who chose not to enlist for 12 months regardless of the number of months for which they originally enlisted. The 50,000 man call was extended nationwide from the Old Northwest states of Illinois, Indiana, and Ohio, to the Old Southwest states of Alabama, Kentucky, Mississippi, and Tennessee; only 18,210 men volunteered in total. Many of these volunteers were recent immigrants and were among the men who, with Taylor's regulars, fought at the upcoming Battle of Monterrey (September 21-23, 1846) and Buena Vista (February 22-23, 1847). Many of these earliest volunteers served on garrison or antiguerrilla duties with Taylor in northern Mexico and these unglamorous assignments meant that only 631 men reenlisted as "remustered" volunteers at the end of their 12-month enlistment. A few of these volunteer units were sent south to General Winfield Scott's army and caused problems as they refused to serve after their 12-month enlistments were up. President Polk and the Congress soon realized that the war was not going to be short and that the 12-month requirement had to be extended, so the 11 February 1847 Ten Regiment Bill specified that volunteers must serve the duration of the war. These new enlistees would also receive land warrants as a reward so this call got more native Americans versus the first call. This nationwide call garnered 33,596 men most of whom were assigned to the unpleasant garrison and antiguerrilla duties in Northern Mexico not combat assignments with Scott's army in its drive to Mexico City.[88]

[88] Henry, *Campaign Sketches of the War with Mexico*, 83; *History of the Mexican War*, 76-78; Tucker, 707-709; Frazier, *The United States and Mexico at War*, 464-466. Gaines, who was senior in rank to Taylor, was relieved from command on 2 June 1846, and eventually court martialed for his illegal actions. Gaines believed that he should lead the army into Mexico; Nichol's, *Zach Taylor's Little Army*, 21; Roswell Sabine Ripley, *The War with Mexico*, vol. 1 (New York, NY: Harper & Brothers, 1849), 151-152.

Satirical cartoon depicting volunteers flocking to the call. Courtesy LOC.

Most Regular Army officers did not appreciate the abilities of the volunteers but after witnessing some of the units perform in combat during Monterrey and at Buena Vista, opinions changed:

Meade charged them with losing all organization during the attack on the east end of Monterrey. They could not be depended on, he said. Behavior in the Baltimore Battalion seemed to bear him out, with so many of them taking off for camp at the first contact. Their casualties gave them away—23 (five killed) out of 230. But the Ohio regiment doubled those losses. Two West Pointers, Albert Johnston and Joe Hooker, had a lot to do with the better performance here. As staff officers serving under volunteer generals, they steadied the Ohioans. Volunteer regiments from Mississippi and Tennessee took the Teneria works, though only after the regulars under Captain Backus had softened Mexican resistance. Again casualties measured the effort: 52 for the Mississippi Rifles and a whopping 107 for the troops from Tennessee. These two regiments were a different breed of volunteers. Ex-West Pointer Davis had drilled his planters' sons, gentlemen farmers, and hunters almost into the ground. And he had armed them with the new Whitney rifle, the absolute best he could find. William B. Campbell's 1st Tennessee, with less class, gave nothing away in organization and morale. State rivalry added something to the performance of both regiments....The volunteers at Monterrey were 12-months men called by the national government to fight a war already begun....They were better material than the boys signed up in peacetime by states or cities to show off for three months on some local commons. Besides, the volunteers who marched out of Camargo [to Monterrey] in September [1846] had included only the pick of 15,000 or more who came south to the Rio Grande. Sickness, death, or refusal to re-enlist weeded out the other four fifths. This kind of screening at last gave the army citizen soldiers it could use. Fighting screened them further. If too many boys from Baltimore and Washington slunk off, most of the volunteers hung on up front. They needed help from professional officers and fought best alongside regulars. Competition worked here too—competition and example. By themselves the volunteers would have been useless, but for the first time America had a disciplined standing army, small as it was, and a trained officer corps to lead both kinds of troops. Taylor himself made the final difference in the over-all performance of his volunteers. His example was worth a hundred orders. The men took heart from the old man's easy contempt for enemy shells and bullets....To sum up, Monterrey produced the recipe for using citizens effectively in war:

(1) Call them up under national control.

(2) Enroll them for at least a year, or for the duration.

(3) Weed out the unfit....

(4) Drill them hard and often.

(5) Hold them under the strictest discipline.

(6) Weed out again.

(7) Fight them only alongside regulars led by professionals.

(8) Give them a natural leader whose presence is felt at the front.

For Taylor's purposes the government took care of national control and time of enlistment. Climate, sickness, and human frailty did the weeding. The general's own labors, character, and judgment, with help from the West Pointers, solved the training and leadership. That left number 5, the discipline problem. Old Zach could never be tough enough; few volunteer officers could be tough at all; there were too few West Pointers to go around; and pure citizen cussedness did the rest. Slack discipline also covered sanitation and camp policing, which in turn affected health. Unfortunately not all of the weeding took out the worst material. Good men, too, lay under sod at Camargo and on the banks and mouth of the Rio. Number 5 would continue to devil the U. S. Army for years.[89]

Meade wrote of his views of the volunteers based on what he saw in Mexico:

The volunteers have in this war, on the whole, behaved better than I had believed they would, and infinitely better than they did in the Florida war, under my own eye. Still, without a modification of the manner in which they are officered, they are almost useless in an offensive war. They are sufficiently well-drilled for practical purposes, and are, I believe, brave, and will fight as gallantly as any men, but they are a set of Goths and Vandals, without discipline, laying waste the country wherever we go, making us a terror to innocent people, and if there is any spirit or energy in the Mexicans, will finally rouse the people against us, who now are perfectly neutral. In addition to which, they add immensely to the expenses of the war. They cannot take any care of themselves; the hospitals are crowded with them, they die like sheep; they waste their provisions, requiring twice as much to supply them as regulars do. They plunder the poor inhabitants of everything they can lay their hands on, and shoot them when they remonstrate, and if one of their number happens to get into a drunken brawl and is killed, they run over the country, killing all the poor innocent people they find in their way, to avenge, as they say, the murder of their brother.

This is a true picture, and the cause is the utter incapacity of their officers to control them or command respect. The officers (many of whom are gentlemen and clever fellows) have no command over their men. They know they are in service for only twelve months; at the end of that time they will return to their homes, when these men will be their equals and their companions, as they had been before, and in consequence they dare not attempt to exercise any control over them. Then, for the most part, they are as ignorant of their duties as the men, and conscious of their ignorance, they feel they cannot have the command over their people that the regular officers do over their soldiers.[90]

On 8 June, Secretary of War Marcy wrote Taylor that he hoped the general could position bodies of troops along the Rio Grande and that Monterrey should be "taken and held. Much was left to the discretion of the general. His views upon future operations were requested....'Shall the campaign be conducted with the view of striking at the city of Mexico, or confined, so far as regards the forces under your immediate command, to the northern provinces of Mexico?'" General Scott sent his own letter to Taylor which, in addition to requesting his opinions, told him that one of the lines of march Taylor could choose "will, of course" be the high road to Mexico City. Old Zach wisely chose to only send one reply back to Washington on 2 July addressed to the adjutant general of the army. He primarily addressed his concerns with subsistence and transportation which would limit his army to 6,000 men with which he planned on marching to Monterrey. At Saltillo, south of Monterrey, he would know more about the topography and subsistence and decide if more men could be added to his force. But then he expressed his concern with the 1,000 mile distance to

[89] Nichol's, *Zach Taylor's Little Army*, 166-167.

[90] Meade, 162-163.

Mexico City and the lack of subsistence to pursue that line of advance: "Except in the case, deemed improbable, of the entire acquiescence, if not support, on the part of the Mexican people, I consider it impracticable to keep open so long a line of communication. It is therefore my opinion that our operations from this frontier should not look to the city of Mexico, but should be confined to cutting off the northern provinces an undertaking of comparative facility and assurance of success." Before Marcy received Taylor's reply, he sent another letter asking if beginning a campaign for Mexico City from the Rio Grande would not be practicable, should the main invasion be begun from the coast at Tampico or Vera Cruz. The main army would be transported to the landing site while a sufficient force would be left along the Rio Grande. Taylor on 1 August replied that his earlier reply about the infeasibility of the overland route south to Mexico City answered Marcy's question about that approach. Taylor also said that the practicality of a cordon across Mexico would depend on what he found as he entered Saltillo but he could not opine about the landing at Vera Cruz since he had no information to form a judgment. He did say that routes to Mexico City from Tampico "to be out of the question."[91]

While the administration in Washington contemplated its next moves in Mexico, Taylor proceeded to use his regulars and the arriving volunteers to clear the Rio Grande as he planned to use it as his primary line of communication from the Gulf of Mexico up to Camargo preparatory to his advance to Monterrey. Shallow draft steamers were finally on the way to Taylor in the middle of June to provide transport upriver as larger vessels could not clear the sand bars at the river's mouth. While awaiting these transports, Taylor sent a battalion marching up the river as far as Reynosa, and then a regiment to Camargo to use as a base of operations until Monterrey was secured. The land route all the way to Monterrey was not viable as it lacked drinking water. Fortunately for the Camargo-bound troops, the 7th Infantry, the Rio Grande rose so on 6 July the troops could use steamboats rather than marching the 120 miles. Unfortunately the distance by river was 240 miles. They passed Reynosa after 200 miles and 40 miles later entered the San Juan River traveling another three miles to Camargo. There Captain Dixon S. Miles summoned its alcalde and formally took possession of the town. No opposition was found as the Mexican Army had fallen back on the road to Monterrey. By 1 August, Taylor began moving most of his main body which now included regulars as well as some 12-month volunteers to Camargo, and on 4 August, Taylor moved with his headquarters to Camargo arriving on the 8th. Since there were insufficient boats to transport all the artillery and infantry, troops began to advance by the southern shore of the Rio Grande on 5 August although most volunteer troops arrived by steamers. "The road was in places deep with mud or covered with water; thick chaparral cut off the friendly breeze; the intense heat felled many a soldier, and thirst tormented all who retained their senses; but after a time the plan of moving by night lessened the suffering, and at last the painful march was achieved. The cavalry and wagons also proceeded in due course to the general rendezvous." A town a few miles upriver from the intersection with the San Juan, Mier, was occupied without resistance on 31 July.[92]

---

[91] Ripley, *The War with Mexico*, vol. 1, 157-166.

[92] Ripley, 170-172; Smith, *The War with Mexico*, 209-211. The distance by road from Matamoros to Monterrey is also estimated at 247 miles and from Camargo to Monterrey at 120 miles. Taylor's arrival was likely on the evening of the 7th vice 8th, Lewis, *Trailing Clouds of Glory*, 104.

Boundary Claimed by
Mexico After 1836

Corpus Christi

Boundary Claimed by Texas

Nuevo Laredo

Nadadores

Monclova

Bejan

Mier

Camargo

Cerralvo

Salinas

Reynosa

Fort Texas

Monterrey
20-23 Sep

Marin

Matamoros

Monterrey

Saltillo

Montemorelos

Agua Nueva

Hedionada

Linares

Mazapil

Matehula

TAYLOR'S ADVANCE

June–23 September 1846

Engagement, Date Indicated

U.S. Army Movement

Disputed Territory

ELEVATION IN METERS

0   1000 2000 3000 and Above

0   20   40   60   80   100   150

Miles

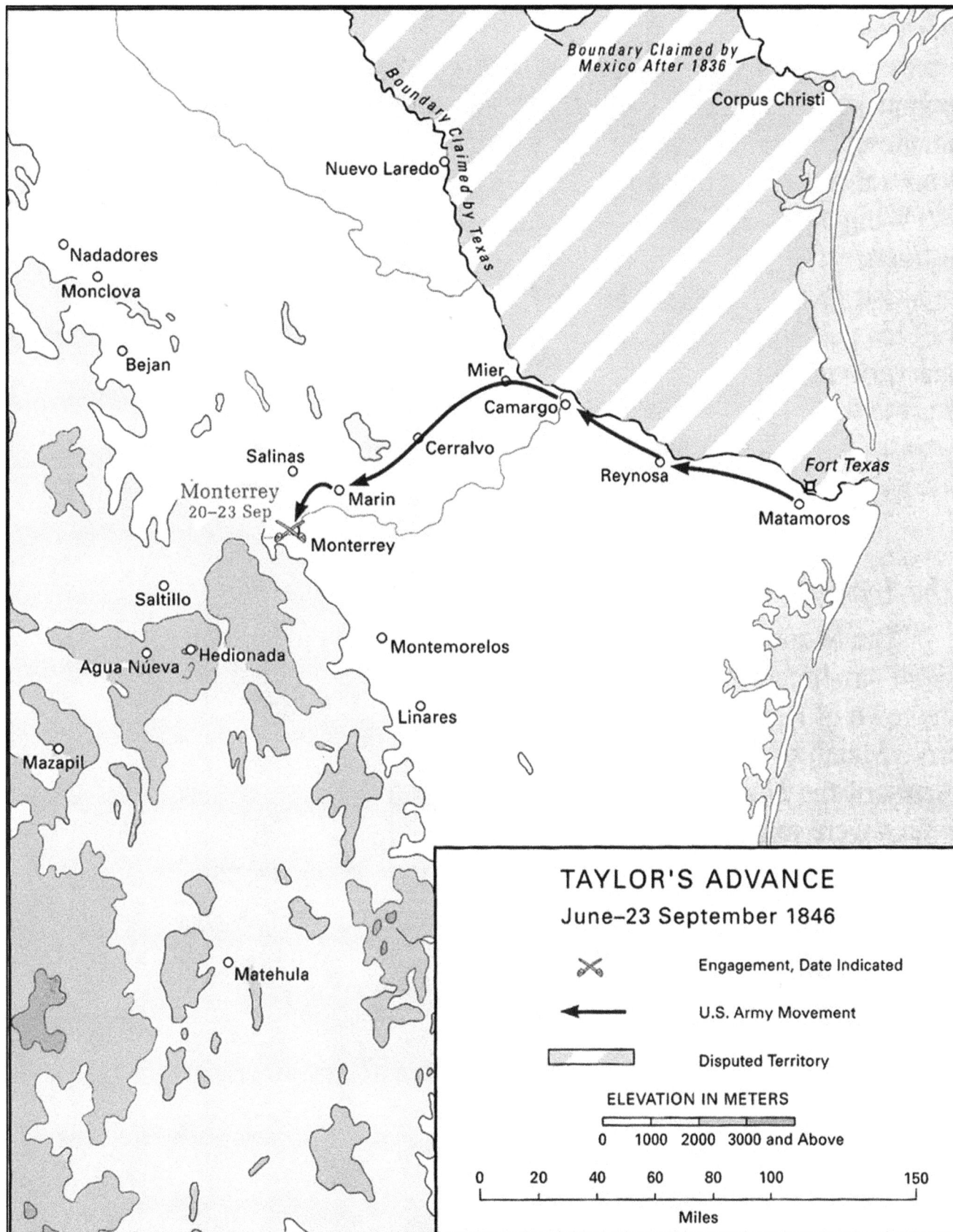

Spellings of towns and geographical locations often differ in American and Mexican sources, e.g., "Cerralvo" is sometimes shown as "Seralvo." "Monterrey" versus "Monterey" is used as it was the spelling most often used during the war and to differentiate it from Monterey, California. Courtesy U.S. Army.

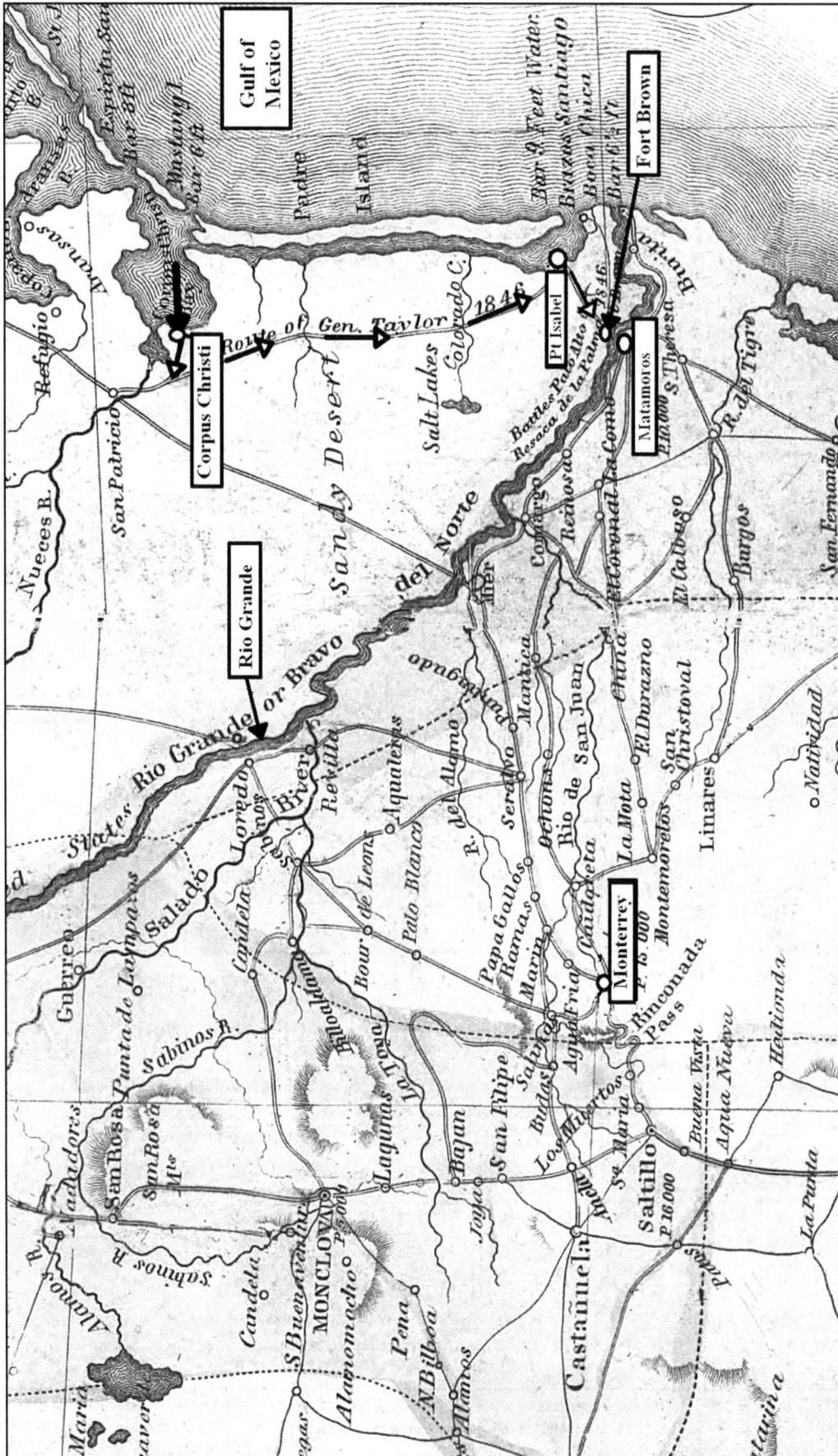

Area of operations for Taylor during his move up the Rio Grande to Camargo. Courtesy LOC.

Mansfield wrote to Louisa from the camp at Matamoros 10 July 1846, and after discussing finances and instructing his wife to solicit her father's advice about investing part of the monies in the bank, he wrote: "It is of no use to me to have my money laying idle and paying interest" so he advises paying his mortgages. He also said that he plans on paying her "wants" by orders on the Douglas's, his friends, who were also relatives by marriages to his nieces. The Rio Grande rose so they had to move camp, and he wrote that the army is now 10 to 15,000 strong but are awaiting steamers to move the army to Camargo preparatory to moving toward Monterrey. Camargo to Monterrey is about 200 miles he reports. He wrote that he is glad General Scott is not coming to Mexico as he is "certainly deficient in common sense and our whole army are surprised at his letters and folly. He has but few friends in this quarter now." Apparently he thinks Scott, as a possible Whig candidate, is repugnant as he is a "mere military chieftain." Mansfield also does not believe that Taylor would be a suitable candidate either: "General Taylor is certainly a kind and good hearted man, but no statesman at all." Mansfield appears to perhaps be homesick for his wife and family: "A little time may set all thing right and we may once more embrace each other and spend our remaining days in happiness and peace."[93]

Captain Mansfield received good news from the Engineering Department on 13 Aug. 1846: "the grateful task which this Dept. now performs in announcing to you that for gallant and distinguished service rendered with the Army of Occupation on the Rio Grande, the government has conferred upon you the brevet rank of major in the Army of the United States, to date from the 9th of May 1846. This mark of approbation will, I am sure be doubly enhanced in your estimation when you are informed that, in conferring it upon you, the government has done nothing more than what would appear from the unanimous voice of your brother officers and from the general sentiment of the country at large to have been due to your valuable services and intrepid conduct in the defense of Fort Brown—as sentiment in which this Department begs leave most heartily to concur." On 5 Aug. 1846, H. Chase wrote to Colonel Joseph G. Totten, chief engineer of the army about Mansfield: "I have conversed with a great many officers of the Army from the Rio Grande who all testified to the solid judgment, untiring zeal and personal bravery of Mansfield....It is a great happiness to convey to you what I have heard others say of your gallant and accomplished brother officer."[94]

Mansfield wrote again to Louisa on 12 August 1846 from the "Camp at Camargo." He arrived on the 8th after a four-day passage on the steamer *Natchez Eagle* instead of two and a half days due to an accident to the ship's rudder. Taylor and most of his staff were on the steamboat. Mansfield was happy to make this trip by boat as he wrote that weather was exceptionally hot so he bought a white, broad-brimmed hat to help keep the sun off his head and neck. He cogitated that peace may come after only one or two more battles which he anticipates at Monterrey and then Saltillo. He reiterated his desire that the war end: "I shall rejoice when this war is at an end and I am honorably clear of it and I would say the army too. I do not look in the war as just at all and the people of the U.S. should have an end put to it as soon as possible. The best course for the U.S. would be to take possession of all the country to the Rio Grande and the

---

[93] Mansfield letter to Louisa 10 July 1846 courtesy of the Middlesex County Historical Society. His letters usually contain religious references to God and His Will. Most ask his wife to write more often. Many say not to believe half of the newspaper reports and rely on official accounts only--letters written to newspapers are very suspect. He often mentions that her "allowance" is enclosed. He also discusses financial matters in every letter. Obviously money is tight in the Mansfield family and he shows concern that she uses it wisely. His letters later in the war always say how he hates the war and wants to get out of it. Mansfield in a letter 29 January 1857 asked a Connecticut congressman to appoint his son, Samuel, to West Point, and wrote "and on the score of politics I have always been a sound Democrat and lover of the great and glorious institutions we live under," letter to Senator Isaac Tracey, courtesy of the Middlesex County Historical Society. William Douglas born 19 April 1812, "In 1832, he came to Middletown and commenced the manufacture of steam engines and other machinery in connection with W. H. Guild, under the firm name of Guild & Douglas. This firm built all the brass and iron work for Fort Pulaski, at Savannah. He continued in this business for about six years, and during this period he received the first patent for pumps, which was granted on the 20th of August 1835....In connection with his brother Benjamin, he [William] commenced, in 1839, the manufacture of pumps and hydraulic rams....On the 12th of April 1835, he married Grace, daughter of Elias and Grace Totten Mansfield Parker, and niece of Major General Joseph K. Mansfield." Benjamin Douglas, William's brother, "In 1839, he joined his brother William, who was previously one of the firm of Guild & Douglas. For three years they carried on the business of an ordinary foundry and machine shop.... On April 3rd 1838, he married Mary Adeline, daughter of Elias and Grace Totten Mansfield Parker, and a niece of Major General Joseph K. Mansfield;" No author, *History of Middlesex County, Connecticut, with Biographical sketches of Its Prominent Men* (New York, NY: J.B. Beers & Co., 1884), 163-164.

[94] Letters 13 Aug. 1846 and 5 Aug. 1846 courtesy WPL. Officers' ranks usually include brevets effective dates awarded so from 13 August "Major Mansfield" will be shown, not "Brevet Major Mansfield." H. Chase is unidentified; he is possibly Daniel H. Chase who was a representative from Middletown to the Connecticut General Assembly in 1852 and 1853 and ran a school there.

whole of upper California—establish posts along the line and hold it as indemnity for the past. They would never attempt or be able to force the line and in the meantime our citizens would fill up the country and secure it permanently. A conquest of Mexico would produce no good and be attended with immense expense and loss of life." He commented on his living expenses observing that only meat is cheap but everything else from paying for washing clothes to buying eggs is expensive, additionally, there are no vegetables to be had at any price but he did find some wild greens. There is only cornbread to be bought from the Mexican women who "work harder than the men" but he seems to find them brave as many remain with their men on the firing line. He is amused that whenever two women are together one is always picking bugs out of the other's hair. He observed that they are ugly apparently since they bear children early, growing old and haggard quickly. He wrote that he hopes to get a good horse from a volunteer as they are selling theirs before their terms of enlistment are up. And he is spending time studying Spanish and jokes that by the time he reaches Mexico City he will "be quite a Spanish scholar." Again he wrote of missing his family: "Oh that all this may be over soon and I be released from such a life—it is now about a year since I left Middletown.[95]

Then on 16 August, he again wrote but chastised his wife as he often did for not writing more often but thinks that her letters are likely in the mail. He is very exercised that she has not paid the installments on his life insurance and instructs her in detail about what she must do. He wrote that he was insured at sea and to and from Mexico and against death in battle. He spent most of the rest of the letter instructing her about their finances and investments to "ensure the wisdom [of] the investments" and finally asked for a complete accounting from her. He then spent a few words about the heat and dust which are severe but he wrote that "I am now quite a philosopher and take things very easy." Based on his many concerns about the family's finances and minute instructions to his wife about all aspects of financial and family life in Connecticut, it is unlikely that his wife was convinced of his new, more relaxed attitude. He concluded by adding that the army now has 14 steamers and expected six more soon. And as will be seen in his later letters, his taking things easy does not extend to being easy on Mrs. Mansfield.[96]

Taylor made two divisions of regular troops soon after he arrived at Camargo under commands of Generals David E. Twiggs and William J. Worth; on 19 August the movement on Monterrey commenced. On that day Worth's first brigade marched from Mier to establish a depot at Cerralvo, about 60 miles away, almost half way between Camargo and Monterrey. Taylor left with some 6,000 troops about half of which were volunteers. Cerralvo was occupied without opposition on 25 August, and the establishment of the depot was begun. On the 24th, Butler's second brigade moved from Camargo, and advanced as far as Puntagudo, twelve miles from Cerralvo, quickly followed by its trains. Twiggs's troops marched by brigades subsequently, each having under its escort a train of provisions. In short order, Regular Army troops gathered near Cerralvo. Lastly came the volunteers which were formed into a division of four regiments under command of Major General William Orlando Butler of Kentucky with Brigadier Generals Thomas L. Hamer appointed from Ohio and John A. Quitman appointed from Mississippi as his brigade commanders. Taylor also created a second volunteer division, the "Texas Division," under Texas governor, Major General James Pinckney Henderson, composed of the 1st and 2nd Regiments of Texas Mounted Volunteers, led by Colonel John C. Hays and Colonel George T. Wood. On 5 September Taylor's headquarters moved out for Cerralvo. By 15 September, with the exception of the Texas contingent, which had marched by a more southerly route, all of Taylor's troops were concentrated near Cerralvo. Taylor's order of 11 September left two companies of the Mississippi Regiment in Cerralvo as a garrison and to guard "All sick and disabled men, unfit for the march…under charge of a medical officer." The advance of Taylor's army to Marin was led by all the army's pioneers "consolidated into one party…on the route to Merine [Marin], for the purpose of repairing the roads and rendering it practicable for artillery and wagons….This pioneer party will be covered by a squadron of Dragoons and Captain McCulloch's company of Rangers. Two officers of Topographical Engineers, to be detailed by Captain [William G.] Williams, will accompany the party for the purpose of examining the route."[97]

[95] Letter 12 August 1846 courtesy WPL.
[96] Letter 16 August 1846 courtesy WPL.
[97] Ripley, *The War with Mexico*, 173-174; Smith, *The War with Mexico*, 228-230; Nichols, 141-142; Thorpe, *Our Army at Monterey*, 38-39. Compare troop numbers and organization below n. 103. Note that "Cerralvo" is variously spelled as "Ceralvo" and "Seralvo."

Grand Plaza at Camargo, Henry, *Sketches*, facing page 153.

Map showing routes from Camargo to Monterrey and to Saltillo. Copied from a map taken from General Arista at the Battle of Resaca de la Palma 9 May 1846. Courtesy LOC.

The army's next movement was southwest to Marin about 24 miles northeast of Monterrey. On 18 September the army again moved toward Monterrey with the 1st Division in the van behind the advance guard. After spending the night at San Francisco, the army set out on the 19th now with the newly arrived Texas troops. Taylor entered the San Juan Valley and finally saw Monterrey in the distance some 1,500 yards away. Mexican artillery welcomed Taylor and his party which included Mansfield, the rest of Taylor's staff, and Captain Benjamin McCulloch with 20 Texians from his company, with 12 pound cannon balls from the "Black Fort," somewhat diminishing the beauty of the scene. Monterrey was located on the main road from the Rio Grande to Mexico City which road then went south to Saltillo and San Luis Potosi. Taylor decided to make camp about three miles from Monterrey "at Walnut Grove (Basque de San Domingo), an extensive and beautiful group of pecans and live-oaks, watered by large, pure springs, where pleasure parties of well-to-do Mexicans were accustomed to enjoy themselves." The area was used as a park by the Mexican populace and had brush cleared over some 100 acres.[98]

S. Compton Smith, who was a volunteer surgeon in Taylor's army, wrote the following delightful description of Taylor's Walnut Springs Camp:

> The spot the General had selected on which to erect his city of tents, was the most desirable to be found on this portion of our line…. and commanded its principal approach.
>
> It was an extensive park of magnificent live-oaks, mingled with a great variety of other trees, many the peculiar growth of this particular locality.
>
> In the centre of this delightful grove there bubbled up, from a large basin, several large springs of the coldest and purest crystal, from whence flowed as many joyous streamlets, conveying the grateful element to every part of the encampment. The deep shade of those oaks, which grew the most luxuriantly near these springs, and whose roots were covered with thick mosses, made this a favorite place of resort in the sultry hours of midday….
>
> To this spot, also, would come the rancheros, who had learned that the Americanos del Norte were not the cannibals their priests had at first taught them to believe; but were Buenos Cristianos as well as themselves. Here would they assemble, and display their stock-in-trade, consisting usually of carne seco [dried meat] and carne fresco [fresh meat], leche de cabro [goat milk]), chile con carne, tamales, frijoles, tortillas, pan de maize, and other eatables, with puros [cigars]), blankets, saddles, etc. These articles found ready purchasers among our men, often at most unreasonable prices; for soldiers, as well as sailors, spend their money, freely….
>
> We were on the best terms with the people of the surrounding villages, who, as another means of lightening our purses, would frequently get up fandangos [lively dances], and invite our men to join them. These invitations were rarely slighted; for, officers as well as privates readily availed themselves of the amusements they furnished.
>
> All the senoritas of the neighboring ranchos would be assembled on these occasions to grace the party. Arrayed in their holiday dresses, they were very pretty. Their forms are models of womanly beauty, and their motions in the dance are free and graceful as the waving of forest boughs.[99]

Historian Joseph E. Chance gave more details for this bucolic park and the cemetery constructed after the Battle of Monterrey:

> This site, wooded with stately oak and pecan trees and watered by several springs, continued to be used as the principal camp for U.S. soldiers at Monterrey for the remainder of the war….
>
> The cemetery of the 3d Infantry was located at Walnut Springs. Surrounded by a wall of neatly dressed limestone blocks four feet high and adorned by a rectangular pillar [ornamental column] surmounted by a cross, the cemetery became the final resting site of many of the officers slain in the attack on Monterrey. The remains of Major William W. Lear, Bvt. Major Lewis

[98] Ripley, *The War with Mexico*, 173-174; Smith, *The War with Mexico*, 228-230; Edward J. Nichols, *Zach Taylor's Little Army*, 141-142; Spurlin, 75-76. The first division of Regulars was composed of units of the 3rd Brigade (Dragoons, Ridgley's and Bragg's mobile artillery batteries, the 3rd and 4th Infantry Regiments, and Captain William Shivors's Texas Volunteer Company) and the 4th Brigade (1st Infantry Regiment, and the Baltimore Battalion of Volunteers); the 2nd Division had the 1st Brigade (Duncan's light artillery company, the Artillery Battalion and the 8th Infantry Regiment), the 2nd Brigade (5th and 7th Infantry Regiments, Captain Albert Blanchard's Louisiana Volunteer Company, and William Mackall's mobile artillery battery). A heavy battery of 24-pound howitzers operated as an independent company. Butler's volunteer division Hamer's Brigade had the 1st Kentucky and 1st Ohio Infantry Regiments white Quitman's Brigade had the 1st Tennessee and the Mississippi Rifles. Unfortunately in some volunteer units, a quarter to a half of the men became ill, Lewis, *Trailing Clouds of Glory*, 107-109. When the volunteers left Camargo, "only 370 of 795 Georgians would answer roll call; only 324 of 754 Alabamians; 317 of 588 in the 2nd Tennessee. Almost every volunteer regiment listed a third to a half sick. An estimated 1,500 died," Nichols, 128.

[99] S. Compton Smith, *Chile Con Carne; Or, The Camp and the Field* (New York, NY: Miller & Curtis, 1857), 98-101. Married soldiers writing home about these dances usually downplayed the beauty of the Mexican senoritas. Smith may have been a volunteer as his name does not appear as officially attached to Taylor's army.

Nelson Morris, Captain George P. Field, Captain Philip Nordbourne Barbour, 1st Lieut. Douglas Simms Irwin, 2nd Lieut. Robert Hazlitt of the 3rd Infantry, and 2nd Lieut. Rankin Dilworth of the 1st Infantry were interred within these walls. The mortal remains of Brig. General Thomas L. Hamer were temporarily buried at the site and later moved to Ohio for reburial....[100]

The City of Monterrey provided its 10,000 residents with a beautiful location in a valley on the north bank of the San Juan River:

> In the rear [of the city], and around it, rise the mountain-ridges of the Sierra Madre....and under the ridges of hills, runs the river San Juan. On the east, or on the left of the road approaching from Marin, the river makes a turn, so as nearly to cover that flank. The road to Cardereita [Santa Catarina] thence crosses the river. On the opposite side the right, as the army approached, lay the road to Saltillo, up the valley of San Juan. In front, the road from Ceralvo and Marin entered the town. On the heights, in rear of the town and beyond the river, works were erected which commanded the valley and the approaches from the north. Above the Saltillo road was a height upon which was the Bishop's Palace, and near it other heights, all fortified. In front of the city was the Cathedral Fort, or citadel, [Black Fort] which was regularly fortified, and about two thousand yards in front and below the Bishop's Palace. The opposite side of the city, to the left, as the Americans approached, were forts also erected, and there were barricades in the streets of the city.[101]

The Mexican commander, General Pedro de Ampudia, had over 10,000 regular and militia troops to defend the city against Taylor's army. Ampudia also had 42 cannon in the city and at various forts and strong points within and around the city:

> The defensive works around the city had accumulated during the period of American inactivity succeeding the battles of the 8th and 9th of May [Palo Alto and Resaca de la Palma] and the occupation of Matamoras, and, although they were in great degree irregular, they had a formidable strength. Directly to the north of the town, at the junction of three roads, that from the east by Marin, and two from Pesqueria Grande and Monclova, was the citadel, a square bastioned work, with dry ditches and embrasures for thirty-four guns. It, however, mounted but ten or twelve of all calibers, from fours to eighteens. Within it, the walls of an unfinished Cathedral rose some thirty feet from the ground, and were of sufficient strength to protect troops from any distant fire. Around the top of these walls was placed a parapet of fascines, which afforded a good position whence musketry could he delivered against an assaulting force. The ditches of the citadel were not completely finished in front of the curtains, nor were they at any place more than twelve feet wide.
>
> The distance from this work to the closely-built part of the town was about one thousand yards, but within that the space was filled with squares containing gardens inclosed by hedges and irrigating ditches, and built up with scattered huts. From a point south of the citadel a branch of the Rio San Juan ran through the suburb in a southeasterly direction, and emptied into that rivulet beyond the town. Its banks were in many places steep and difficult, and deep irrigating ditches extended for much of its length along the northern side. The branch was crossed at a point near the middle of its course through the suburb by the bridge of La Purisima, which was defended by a strong tete du pont. Two breastworks along its southern bank opposed the passage of the lower part of the stream.
>
> The southeastern front of the town was defended by a system of lunettes, well arranged for flanking purposes, and with ground between them almost impracticable, on account of the hedges and bramble by which it was covered. Fort Teneria, the most advanced of these, covered by its fire the roads from Marin and Cadereyita [Cadareta or Caidareta], and mounted four guns. Fort El Diablo, to its southwest, mounted three, and a third, still further toward the rivulet, four. Each of these commanded the lunettes more advanced, and the system terminated in a lunette having a high command, and covering the fords across the river.
>
> The approaches to all of the fortifications on the southeastern front of the city were so masked by shrubbery that accurate reconnaissance was exceedingly difficult. From the most southern lunette a line of barricades extended along the northern bank of the San Juan for many squares, and, turning at right angles, encircled the strongest buildings, and connected with the tete du pont of La Purisima. Each barricade was strongly and regularly constructed, with embrasures for one or more guns, and the tops of the neighboring houses were covered by parapets of sand-bags. The streets leading to the west were barricaded beyond the main line, and the Campo Santo, a strong stone inclosure in the Plaza de la Capilla, which was traversed by these streets, was prepared for defense. The walls had been fortified to resist cannon shot, and were plentifully crenelled for musketry, with embrasures for guns at the angles.

---

[100] Joseph E. Chance, "Walnut Springs in Donald S. Frazier, ed., *The United States and Mexico at War: Nineteenth-Century Expansionism and Conflict* (New York, NY: Macmillan Reference USA, 1998), 469.

[101] Edward D. Mansfield, *The Mexican War: A History of Its Origin* (New York, NY: A.S. Barnes and Co., 1873), 58. The river to the south of the city is often named as the Santa Catarina River which branches off from the San Juan River to the north of the city. The main road to Saltillo heads south to San Luis Potosi and eventually to Mexico City.

Immediately beyond the town and to the north of the main road to Saltillo lay the Loma d'Independencia. Half way up the acclivity were the massive ruins of the Obispado, which had been fortified with a view of covering a retreat from the city, if it should be necessary. Its battlements were furnished with a sand-bag parapet, and the city front was covered by a priest-cap work, with platforms for four guns in barbette. A branch road turned to the southwest as the main road left the city, and, crossing the San Juan, traversed a range of hills which lay along the southern bank of the river. At the summit lay Fort Soldado, a rudely-constructed square redoubt. The hills extended northwest to the river, where they were terminated by the Loma de Federacion, the steep declivity of which reached to its banks, and to the southeast beyond the town to the main chain of the Sierra. Between the citadel and the Obispado a system of redoubts had been commenced, but not completed. The ground in that direction, however, was difficult, on account of the many hedges and irrigating ditches by which it was traversed.[102]

The buildings of the city itself as U.S. troops would soon find gave the defenders the advantage as "Every principal street was barricaded with strong works of masonry; cannon on the most of them; the whole number of pieces of artillery in and around Monterrey was about 50. Besides these fortifications, another great item of strength consisted in the manner in which the houses of the city were built; of close construction to each other; one high story; flat stone roof, with parapet walls of the same material around them, and with interior courts and gardens, presenting a naked view in the street, of continuous bare walls, of few door, and still more few windows; which, where so placed, were guarded by perpendicular iron bars."[103]

---

[102] Ripley, *The War with Mexico*, 195-198. Exact numbers of Mexican troops in and around the city are not known, one Mexican civilian told Taylor that there were 9,000 total in the city, 6,000 rancheros and 3,000 regulars, Henry, *Campaign Sketches of the War with Mexico*, 186. Smith wrote that on 10 September, the Mexican commander, General Mejia had 7,303 troops, 230. This last figure is the generally accepted number. Mexican troops included some Irish U.S. Army deserters, the San Patricios. Gaspar de Zúñiga Acevedo y Fonseca, 5th Count of Monterrey, was a Spanish Viceroy of New Spain (Mexico). Monterrey was named in honor of the viceroy's wife. Mejia was in command until superseded by Ampudia.

[103] George C. Furber, *The Twelve Months Volunteer or, Journal of a Private in the Tennessee Regiment of Cavalry* (Cincinnati, OH: J.A. & U.P. James, 1849), 97.

Taylor's 3 September 1846 order of battle:

1st Division, Brig. Gen. David E. Twiggs
        2nd Dragoons, Maj. Charles A. May, 4 cos., 250 men
        Ridgeley's and Webster's Batteries, 110 men
        1st, 3rd, and 4th Inf. Regiments, and Bragg's Battery, 1,320 men
        Baltimore Battalion, 400 men
Total 2,080

2nd Division, Brig. Gen. William J. Worth.
        Duncan's and Taylor's Batteries, 100 men
        5th, 7th, 8th, Inf. Regiments, 1,500 men
        Blanchard's Louisiana Volunteers, 80 men
        Texas Rangers, 2 companies, 100 men
Total 1,780

3rd Division, (Volunteers) Maj. Gen. William O. Butler
        1st Ohio Regiment, Col. Alexander M. Mitchell, 540 men
        1st Kentucky, Col. Stephen Ormsby, 540 men
        1st Tennessee, Col. William B. Campbell, 540 men
        Mississippi Regiment, Col. Jefferson Davis 690 men
        Texas Regiment, Col. John C. Hays 500 men
Total 2,810

Total of the army, 6,670 effectives. Mansfield, *The Mexican War*, 57. Taylor had about 9,000 men scattered at posts from the Gulf of Mexico upriver to Camargo. On one of his scouts on the 19th, Mansfield was accompanied by Captain John Sanders and Lieutenant Jeremiah M. Scarrit, fellow engineers; Furber, *The Twelve Month Volunteer*, 99.

A general view to the north with U.S. troops marching on Monterrey, shown in the middle distance. Sierra Madre Mountains surround the city. General Taylor in the left foreground. Lithograph by Carl Nebel, courtesy Wikipedia.

Taylor's Walnut Spring's Camp in the foreground and Monterrey in the middle distance. Note the rugged terrain of the Sierra Madre Mountains surrounding the city. Mitre Mountain in the center background likely named after a Catholic bishop's chapeau. The Black Fort is in the lower center flying a large U.S. flag. The path to its left is the route of attack on the city on the 21st. The Teneria Fort is to the far left flying the smaller flag. Frost, *Pictorial History of Mexico and the Mexican War*, 278.

Painting done in 1847 by William Garl Browne, Jr., depicting Taylor and some of his staff and other notable officers in camp at Walnut Springs near Monterrey, begun sometime after 19 September 1846, when Taylor chose this campsite. See more details about this painting and the artist below in Attachment 1. Taylor is third from left and Mansfield is fifth from the left, see Attachment 1 for names of others. "Zachary Taylor at Walnut Springs," by William Garl Browne Jr., 1847, Oil on canvas mounted on wood, courtesy National Portrait Gallery, Smithsonian Institution.[104]

[104] Letters courtesy of WPL. Browne apparently was looking to make more money painting officers in addition to the group scene. Mansfield wrote to his wife that his portrait was painted but no further information about it has been found.

Detail of above painting showing officers near Mansfield; "Zachary Taylor at Walnut Springs," by William Garl Browne Jr., 1847, Oil on canvas mounted on wood, courtesy National Portrait Gallery, Smithsonian Institution.

Mansfield without facial hair. It may have been taken just after he became an Inspector General in 1853 as he likely grew facial hair during his many arduous trips in the west, and he is shown as a colonel. He would be about 50 years old. Courtesy of the Middlesex County Historical Society, retouched by retouchrestore.com.[105]

The Mexican Army was obviously not going to give up Monterrey without a fight and was very unlikely to leave its fortified positions and attack Taylor on open ground. Taylor began his strategic planning by sending out scouting parties. On 19 September at 2 p.m., Mansfield rode to within 200 yards of the Black Fort to examine the work and environs, escorted by Lieutenant Walter P. Lane and 20 troopers from Captain Christopher B. Acklin's Texas Mounted Rifle Volunteers company. "They were almost within musket range, and [Lane] scattered his men for safety while he and Mansfield dismounted to use their glasses. The engineer suggested that all the Rangers should be dismounted, so that the gunners could not tell the officers from the privates. Lane informed him haughtily they were paid a big sum to be officers and the risk came with it." Later at 4 p.m. Mansfield was in charge of a reconnoitering party with a company of Texas Rangers under Captain Robert Addison Gillespie. His mission was to scout the main road to Saltillo to learn if it could be secured thereby cutting off the main line of communication for Monterrey's garrison. The party rode within 500 yards of Monterrey and came under enemy cannon fire. The uninhibited Texians challenged each other so see how close they could get to the Mexican batteries. "The daredevil mounted riflemen took turns riding rapidly around the walls of the city while the enemy attempted to unseat them. 'A cheer would ring from the citadel as a well-aimed shot would produce some confusion among the Texans.'" Whenever the mounted volunteers regained their composure, they lambasted the artillerymen with a string of profane words. None of the madcap Texans were injured in the episode." Mansfield returned at 10 p.m. with five prisoners and reported that he was fired on by grape about 500 yards from the enemy's works but posited that the Saltillo Road could be taken and held and the works above the Bishop's Palace could be taken. Based on this report and others, Taylor decided to send General Worth and his division to secure the road and take the Bishop's Palace and Independence Hill if practicable, then attack the city from the west. Taylor supplemented Wool's command with Colonel Hays's regiment and Captains McCullough's and Gillespie's Texas Rangers. Wool's command of some 2,700 left on the 20th while Taylor made a demonstration in the plain in front of the city to cover Wool's movements.[106]

Mansfield the next day may also have been involved with the fun-loving Texas Dragoons when he rode to take another look at the Bishop's Palace escorted by Acklin's boys:

> They could not get a decent view of the fortification from the ground, without being hit by artillery fire, so the enterprising Rangers found a large mesquite tree and managed to get Mansfield up in the top. He had a good view with field glasses and began making notes. It will never be known if one of the Rangers saw, or thought he saw, enemy troops. There is a good chance that one of the Rangers had a fine sense of horseplay and came riding toward the tree, shouting that lancers were coming.
>
> The escort began mounting and riding about. Poor Mansfield, thinking he was abandoned, started climbing down and slipped and fell to the ground. He was not injured, other than to his dignity. Lane did not speculate about the validity of the alarm, other than to say they could not find any lancers.[107]

Another description of Mansfield's adventures on that day shows that Mansfield was certainly busy:

> Before the attack on Monterrey had come to close quarters—that is, while Generals Taylor and Worth were taking their positions—there was a Mexican battery of three or four guns which it was expedient to examine somewhat closely. To this end Major Mansfield, taking with him half a dozen Dragoons as an escort, rode within cannon-ball distance of the battery, where he placed his men in a little hollow that afforded some safety, and rode forward himself about a hundred yards nearer. Then rapidly dismounting and adjusting his glass he took a quick survey of the position, from which a gun was fired directly at him. The moment he saw the smoke, down he dropped upon the ground—the ball passed, in an instant he was up again and using his glass; another gun, down he dropped again—and so he continued, alternately dropping and starting up to look, until he had satisfied himself, when he mounted and rode off.[108]

Major Philip Nordbourne Barbour who was killed on the assault of the city on the 21st wrote in his last letter to his wife that: "The first intelligence I hear this morning [20 September] was that Major Mansfield had crept up to a battery

[106] Henry, *Campaign Sketches of the War with Mexico*, 192-193. The author, William S. Henry, was a captain in the 3rd Infantry and received a brevet to major for Monterrey; he wrote first-hand of this part of the Monterrey battle. Captain William G. Williams of the Topographical Engineers scouted the eastern fortifications with Captain Ridgely's men from the 2nd Texas; Wilkins, 83-84; Lewis, 128. Spurlin, 75-76.

[107] Wilkins, 86-87.

[108] Thomas Bangs Thorpe, *The Taylor Anecdote Book: Anecdotes and Letters of Zachary Taylor* (New York, NY: D. Appleton & Company, 1848), 60. Bangs in his preface wrote that his stories came from personal observation or from reliable sources; however some seem to be somewhat florid.

on a height beyond the city and ascertained its exact strength and the nature of the ground about it. An act of skill and daring combined for which I sincerely hope he may be rewarded by another brevet."[109]

Worth arrived in position to the west of Monterrey and was ready to begin his assault on the 21st. He wrote Taylor that he would first assault the two heights southwest of the Palace before storming the height directly west of it. Again Taylor sent units out into the plain to distract the Mexicans from Wool's attacks. Mansfield was near the city scouting locations of forts and strongpoints supported by the 1st Division. This division was commanded by Colonel Garland as General Twiggs was ill. Taylor had told Mansfield to order the troops to action if he thought the works could be carried. Mansfield's reconnoitering party which included Captain William G. Williams, Lieutenant John Pope, and Colonel Henry Kinney, was first supported by Co. C, 3rd Infantry, commanded by Captain George P. Field. Mansfield designated the point of attack and led the attackers. "Taylor gave Lieutenant Colonel Garland this verbal order, written down by one of Garland's aides: 'Colonel lead the head of your column off to the left, keeping well out of reach of the enemy's Shot, and if you think (or you find) you can take any of them little Forts down there with the bay'net you better do it but consult with Major Mansfield, you'll find him down there.' Garland then advanced with the First and Third regiments and the Washington-Baltimore Battalion, about 800 men, and made his way forward a considerable distance over broken and obstructed ground. He soon came in sight of Mansfield, and before long that officer galloped back to meet him. Garland no doubt communicated Taylor's orders at this time; and Mansfield, supported by some skirmishers, then went forward again."[110]

Another account adds details to the Mansfield-Garland interaction:

> The quarry-holes, the chaparral, the strong hedges, and the tall waving corn that clustered so abundantly in the suburbs of the town, made it impossible to see anything ahead; but Colonel Garland proceeded on, and finding Major Mansfield, reported to him that he had a force at hand to attack wherever he should direct. Captains Hazlitt and Field, each with companies of the Third, were first detached from the main body to protect Lieut. Pope, while making a reconnoissance of the Mexican cavalry, that continually threatened the engineers. A brief consultation was then held between the commander of the troops and Major Mansfield, when the latter advised an immediate advance into the city. Colonel Kinney, who was with the Major, suggested the hazard of the experiment, with the then limited knowledge of the enemy's force, and of the strength of the defences of the place. Major Mansfield, as he cast his eye along the glittering arms of his fellow soldiers, said—that he thought the enemy would run the moment that our troops were seen. Accordingly, with Colonel Kinney by his side, he moved toward the town.[111]

Lieutenant Napoleon Jackson Tecumseh Dana wrote of Mansfield at Monterrey: "These reconnaissances were conducted by Major Mansfield of the engineers and Captain Williams of the topographical corps. Both were indefatigable in this all-important and dangerous duty. They were out under fire all the time, and one night they kept out alone, creeping up in the dark to ascertain the most practical methods of forcing the enemy's positions with least loss....That Mansfield is one of the most noble specimens of gallantry and heroism and chivalry I have ever met with. He is unacquainted with a feeling of fear and is persevering to death. After he was wounded, he tied a handkerchief round his leg and led the murderous charge on the enemy's works where the First and Third Divisions suffered so severely."[112]

Captain William S. Henry of the 3rd Infantry also described the action:

> For five hundred yards we advanced across a plain under fire of the two batteries. We rushed into the streets. Unfortunately, we did not turn soon enough to the left, and had advanced but a short distance when we came suddenly upon an unknown battery, which opened its deadly fire upon us. From all its embrasures, from every house, from every yard, showers of balls were hurled upon us. Being in utter ignorance of our locality, we had to stand and take it; our men, covering themselves as well as they could, dealt death and destruction on every side; there was no resisting the deadly, concealed fire, which appeared to come from every direction. On every side we were cut down. Major Barbour was the first officer who was shot down; he fell, cheering his men. He was killed by an escopet [musket] ball passing through his heart. He never spoke....

---

[109] Barbour, 18-20.

[110] Smith, *The War with Mexico*, 250-251. Captain Electus Backus of the 1st Inf. wrote that Garland's force was as follows: 1st Inf. 187 men; 3rd Inf. 296 men, total regulars 483. The Baltimore and Washington Battalion had 334, total of 817. Backus received a brevet to major for Monterrey; Electus Backus, "A Brief Sketch of the Battle of Monterrey," The Historical Magazine, 10, July 1866, 208-211.

[111] Thomas Bangs Thorpe, *Our Army at Monterey* (Philadelphia, PA: Carey and Hart, 1947), 50.

[112] Napoleon Jackson Tecumseh Dana, *MONTEREY IS OURS!*, 125.

We retired into the next street, under cover of some walls and houses. Into this street the body of Major Barbour was carried. Here were lying the dead, wounded, and dying. Captain Williams, of the topographical corps, lay on one side of the street, wounded; the gallant Major Mansfield, wounded in the leg, still pressed on with unabated ardor, cheering the men, and pointing out places of attack. It was in this street I saw the gallant Colonel Watson, followed by a few of his men (some of them were persuading him to retire). Never shall I forget the animated expression of his countenance when, in taking a drink from the canteen of one of his men, he exclaimed, "Never, boys! never will I yield an inch! I have too much Irish blood in me to give up!" A short time after this exclamation he was a corpse. Lieutenant Bragg's battery arrived about this time. He reached the street into which we had retired, but it was impossible for him to do anything. Finding the struggle at this point hopeless, our force originally having been deemed only sufficient to carry battery No. 1, without any expectation of finding some two or three others raking us, we were ordered to retire in order, with the view of attacking the battery at a more salient point. In the meantime. Captain Backus, of the 1st Infantry, succeeded in stationing himself, with some fifty men, in a tan-yard, which was about one hundred and thirty yards in the rear of battery No. 1, and nearer the town; in this yard was a shed, facing battery No. 1: its roof was flat, encompassed by a wall about two feet high, which was an excellent breast-work for his men. About twenty yards to the southwest of the battery was a large building, with very thick walls, used as a distillery. On the top of this building sand-bag embrasures had been constructed, and it was occupied by the enemy. The gorge of battery No. 1 was open toward the shed. Captain Backus, with his men, drove the enemy from the distillery with considerable loss. About this time he received information that we had been ordered to retire. Our firing having ceased, he was about withdrawing, when he again heard firing in front of the battery, and at the same time all the guns of the battery opened in the direction of the fire. This was the advance of two companies of 4th Infantry, about ninety strong, upon whom the fire of the enemy's batteries were concentrated, and actually mowed them down. It was actually ninety men advancing to storm a work defended by five hundred! It was here the gallant [Captain Charles] Hoskins and [Lieutenant James S.] Woods fell, bravely cheering their men, and the generous Graham was wounded. Backus determined to retain his position; reposted his men on the roof of the shed, and shot down the enemy at their guns, firing through the open gorge of the work.[113]

Captain Electus Backus of the 1st Regiment talked with Mansfield during the attack: "Major Mansfield, Lieutenant Scarritt and Lieutenant Pope were in front, with Mr. Kinney as a guide, ready to commence the reconnaissance and Captain Field's company of the 3rd Inf. was deployed as skirmishers, to protect the engineers....Major Mansfield sent Mr. Kinney back to Colonel Garland, and requested him 'to change his point of direction more to the right." The Baltimore Battalion could not perform this maneuver and "broke into fragments" with most eventually retreating back to camp. The Regulars continued but by the time the 1st Infantry had reached the town, Captain Backus had only about 88 men left. With them he took possession of the Tannery, on his right was Fort Diablo about 250 yards to his south. After fire from the distillery had been silenced and Mexican troops driven off, Mansfield passed the east corner of the Tannery where Backus was standing. Mansfield's "efforts to obtain a closer observation were frustrated, for as often as he raised his spyglass, just so often were Mexican muskets presented towards him, by Mexicans behind the adjacent building. At length, he turned back, and seeing me on the roof, asked me where he could find Colonel Garland, and I understood him to say, 'he should advise him to retire.' I replied, I was sorry to hear him say to, as I thought we could carry Battery No. 1, before us. He said, 'we had not men enough,' and passed on towards Colonel Garland, but receiving a ball in his leg he stopped to tie it up with his handkerchief." From this account, Mansfield was wounded sometime between 10 and 11 a.m. near the tannery. Backus began to retreat but heard a report that a party of Mexican troops were coming up the street he was on so he and about 15 of his men attacked them sending them fleeing and his men retook the tannery. About 1 p.m., Taylor ordered Garland with the remnants of the 1st, 3rd, and 4th Infantry along with Captain Randolph Ridgely's Battery, to assault the Purisima bridgehead. Ridgely's and Bragg's Batteries and the infantry fired at the barricades but with little effect on its stone walls. At sunset, the troops fell back to Battery No. 1 ending the day's battle.[114]

---

[113] Henry, 194-197. Henry received a brevet to major for his actions at Monterrey. After meeting with Garland and advancing into the city, Mansfield was on foot, Smith, 251. Taylor's "diversion" turned out to be bloodier than all of General Worth's efforts west of the city. About 14 percent of the American force at the city, 394, were casualties, including 11 West Point graduates killed, Christopher D. Dishman, *A Perfect Gibraltar: The Battle for Monterrey, Mexico, 1846* (Norman, OK: University of Oklahoma Press, 2010), 141-142. This book is the best book extant for the Battle of Monterrey. The 11 West Point graduates killed in one day remains the largest number in its history.

[114] Backus, 208-212 passim.

Street fight in Monterrey showing the close quarters and Mexican troops firing from rooftops. Mansfield would have been in an area like this when he was wounded. Frost, *Pictorial History*, 317.

Monterrey, fighting in the streets of the city on the third day of the battler. Notice Mexican troops and irregulars shooting from balconies, windows, and rooftops here and in the illustration above. A hard fight for the U.S. troops. Courtesy LOC.

BATTLE OF MONTEREY
DETAILED PLAN

G Garland
H Henderson
Q Quitman
1 Redoubt abandoned early Sept. 21
2
3
4 } Redoubts
5
6
7 Building used by Backus
8 Stone Tannery

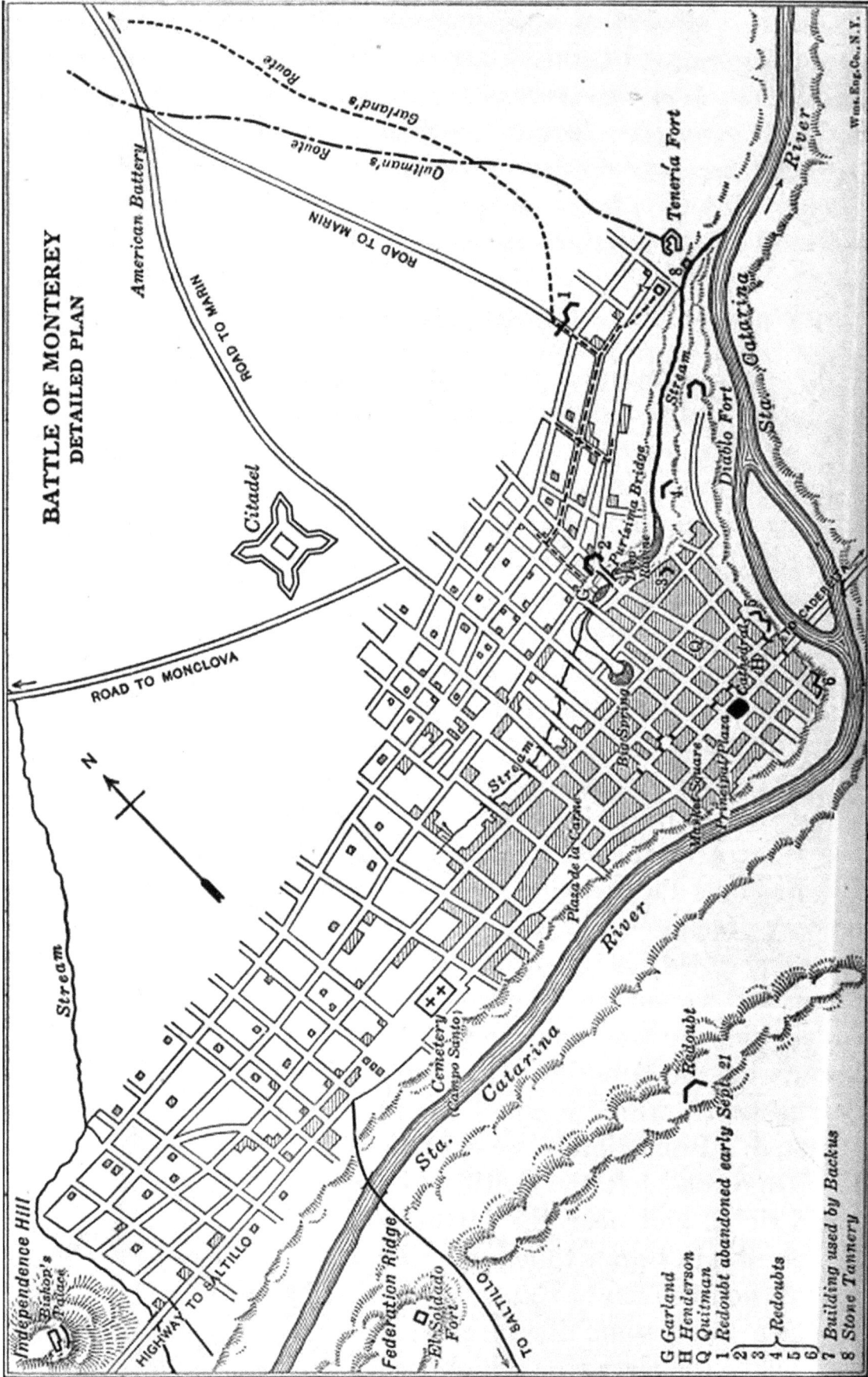

Taylor ordered Mansfield to act as a guide to direct Garland's troops into the city. Mansfield was likely wounded near letter "G" in the vicinity of the Purisima Bridge which spanned the Ojo de Agua Canal and was defended by 300 infantry and artillery; the Citadel was also known as the Black Fort which described its 30-foot high stone walls with four hundred Mexican troops and thirty guns. The Teneria Fort was in an old tannery building housing 200 troops; Smith, 240. Backus was near Mansfield when he was shot which would be near number "7," and the tannery at no. 8, near the Teneria Fort; Backus, 208–212 passim

The seriously wounded Mansfield had witnessed the carnage and saw futility of continuing the attack in the streets, so based on what he saw, he wisely decided to retreat. "General Butler, with the First Ohio, Hamer's Brigade, felt his way gradually into the suburbs of the town, assailed at every step by heavy fire in front and flank, and meeting Major Mansfield, who had directed the move made by Garland, was informed by him that it had failed, and advised the withdrawal of his command. General Butler reported this to the commanding general, who ordered a retrograde movement, and it was commenced but immediately countermanded, Quitman's success having been just then reported. The direction of General Hamer's brigade was instantly changed and Monterrey entered by another route, which, after exposure to a heavy artillery fire, brought it confronting the enemy's second work. General Butler, regarding it as a strong position, resolved to attempt to carry it by assault."[115]

While Garland's men were fighting for their lives in and near the city, General Worth on the right flank executed successful attacks often against superior numbers in well-fortified positions: Colonel Thomas Childs carried Independence Hill, Captain Charles F. Smith carried Federation Hill, and General Persifore Smith carried Fort Soldado. By the end of the 21st, Worth had secured most of the Mexican strongpoints west of the city and held the main road to Saltillo sustaining light casualties; however, Taylor had only a foothold in the city after heavy losses after his "diversion" turned into a full scale assault. On the 22nd, the Bishop's Palace fell to Colonel Childs and Worth consolidated his positions to the west; Worth's assignment to secure the Saltillo Road and the heights west of the city was accomplished—he was now ready to attack the city. There was little activity on the bloody battleground in the city on the 22nd. Taylor solidified the small gains he made in the city mainly at Fort Teneria while his men gathered their strength for the next day's fight.

On the 23rd, Taylor's pincer movement on the city commenced in earnest as Worth moved in from the west and the rest of the U.S. troops reopened their attacks before the city. Mansfield could not leave his tent due to his wound. Mexican troops withdrew into the city to make a stand hoping to repeat their success on the 21st against Taylor's assault into the city. "The American assault began again early on the morning of the 23rd with General Worth moving in from the west and Taylor's remaining troops advancing from the east. The pincer movement was designed to force Mexican resistance toward the center of the city and into the main plaza. The American infantry, however, had learned a valuable lesson from their experience on 21 September. Instead of advancing up the narrow streets where they were exposed to sniper fire and fortified batteries, they began smashing holes through houses and walls to by-pass enemy defenses. They used battering rams, picks, axes, sledge hammers, and occasionally 8-inch artillery shells. The new tactic worked well and cost fewer casualties, but the process was tedious." Worth heard the firing in the city about 10 a.m. on the morning of the 23rd so he formed his division in two attack columns and hurried along the two main streets toward the main plaza. As Taylor's troops on the 21st found, the city buildings themselves proved difficult:

> heavy masonry walls crossed the streets in every direction, pierced with embrasures and defended by cross batteries. But the work went steadily on, the inhabitants retiring towards the eastern extremity of the city. The assault had hardly begun before the firing ceased in that direction. The strength of the place was a constant theme of remark and admiration. It seemed as if the defences could have held out against any number of troops, and that preparations had been made never to yield. But the possession of the commanding heights had paralyzed opposition, and no serious resistance was met with, until near the principal buildings about the main plaza. Here a raking fire opened from the barricades, and every further attempt to advance was met by showers of balls of every kind, and our troops were forced to seek the protection of the houses. Soon they broke into the buildings, got into the gardens, broke down walls, and finally appeared on the house-tops. Now, upon an equality with the enemy, the galling fire so long received was returned. The deadly effect was soon perceivable, in the retreat of the Mexicans, many of whom threw themselves, in the agony of death or in despair, headlong from the parapets to the streets below. Darkness

---

[115] Wilcox, 94-95. Taylor's 22 September official report lists Mansfield as "slightly wounded." Henry described his ride into the surrendered city on the 26th: "After riding over the city and examining minutely its defenses, my only astonishment is how they could yield it. It is a perfect Gibraltar. At the eastern extremity, where so many of our brave fellows fell, my wonder is that any escaped;" Henry, *Campaign Sketches of the War with Mexico*, 218. Here is an article from a newspaper which was very complementary to Mansfield but likely embellished: "An incident at the Battle of Monterrey-- While Colonel Davis, with his command, was hotly engaged with the enemy, exposed to their direct fire, a man in a long gray surtout suddenly rode up, and, dismounting, placed himself in the middle of the street. There, in face of the enemy, amidst the thickest of the fire, he coolly drew from a case, suspended about his person, a spy-glass, with which, having adjusted it to a proper focus, he proceeded to reconnoiter the Mexican battery. Having satisfied himself as to the information he sought, he shut up the glass, returned it to its case, and, approaching Col. Davis, said to him: 'Sir, the enemy has but two pieces, and by making a detour to the right you can take them in flank?' 'And who the devil are you?' 'I, sir, am Major Mansfield, of the corps of engineers.' 'All right! Come on boys!' responded the colonel. The battery was soon carried." Newspaper clipping courtesy of the Middlesex County Historical Society. Mansfield wrote his wife that he dismounted at the beginning of the battle on the 21st so this account is suspect. Also, Mansfield never wrote that he ever wore a surtout--a long overcoat.

began to set in, when it was discovered that the division was within a square of the main plaza, the Texians in the advance, having been in the van all day, destroying the enemy with their unerring rifles, or filling them with terror by their war cry. Hostilities ceased, with the occupation of all the large buildings that towered over those about the plaza; upon the roof of one of which were carried, with infinite labor, two howitzers and a six pounder, ready at a moment's warning to throw down the walls that masked them from the enemy, and pour a continued fire into the solid masses of human beings that had been congregated in the great square of the city.[116]

While there was hard fighting on the 23rd it did not compare to the slaughter two days earlier. Taylor accompanied his troops into the city lending his authority: "General Taylor was in town with his staff, on foot, walking about, perfectly regardless of danger. He was very imprudent in the exposure of his person. He crossed the street in which there was such a terrible fire in a walk, and by every chance should have been shot. I ran across with some of my men, and reminded him how much he was exposing himself, to which he replied, 'Take that ax and knock in that door.'"[117] The Mexican commander, General Ampudia, had his headquarters in the square and saw firsthand that his situation was hopeless so on the evening of the 23rd he sent his letter to Taylor proposing surrender. Taylor received this letter early on the 24th and proposed terms which were more harsh than Ampudia had proposed. Ampudia requested a meeting with Taylor and at this noon meeting, they reached no agreement but they did agree to appoint a commission of three men on each side to arrange terms of surrender. Taylor appointed General Worth, General Henderson of Texas, and Colonel Jefferson Davis, of the First Mississippi Volunteers. After much discussion over the terms, the formal surrender was agreed upon and signed on the 25th:

> Article 1. As the legitimate result of the operation before the place, and the present position of the contending armies, it is agreed that the city, the fortifications, cannon, the munitions of war, and all other public property, with the under mentioned exceptions, be surrendered to the commanding general of the United States forces now at Monterrey.
> Art. 2. That the Mexican forces be allowed to retain the following arms, to wit: The commissioned officers their side arms; the infantry their arms and accoutrements; the cavalry their arms and accoutrements; the artillery, one field battery, not to exceed six pieces, with twenty-one rounds of ammunition.
> Art. 3. That the Mexican armed force retire within seven days from this date beyond the line formed by the pass of the Rinconada, the city of Linares, and San Fernando de Presas.
> Art. 4. That the citadel of Monterrey be evacuated by the Mexican and occupied by the American forces tomorrow morning, at 10 o'clock.
> Art. 5. To avoid collisions, and for mutual convenience, that the troops of the United States will not occupy the city until the Mexican forces have withdrawn, except for hospital and storage purposes.
> Art. 6. That the forces of the United States will not advance beyond the line specified in the third article before the expiration of eight weeks, or until the orders of the respective governments can be received.
> Art. 7. That the public property to be delivered shall be turned over and received by officers appointed by the commanding generals of the two armies.
> Art. 8. That all doubts, as to the meaning of any of the preceding articles, shall be solved by an equitable construction, and on principles of liberality to the retiring army.
> Art. 9. That the Mexican flag, when struck at the citadel, may be saluted by its own battery.[118]

These generous terms of surrender met with controversy when received in Washington. And the loss of 12 officers and 108 men killed, and 31 officers, and 337 men wounded, added fuel to the criticism of Taylor's liberal surrender terms. Congress's resolution of thanks contained a proviso censuring him for the terms of surrender. President Polk believed that Taylor exceeded his authority by granting such terms but Taylor's defenders asserted that given the worn out condition of his army, his actions were proper. Secretary of War "Marcy...directed on October 13 that it should be terminated, explaining that it stood in the way of prosecuting the war vigorously and forcing Mexico to seek peace. As by its terms the agreement was subject to the approval of the respective governments, no difficulty stood in the way of cancelling it; and on November 5 Taylor notified Mexican President Santa Anna, that since the Washington authorities disapproved of the armistice, he should consider himself at liberty to resume offensive operations on the fifteenth, since

---

[116] Stephen A. Carney, "Gateway South, The Campaign for Monterrey," in *The U.S. Army Campaigns of the Mexican War Series*, U.S. Army Center of Military History, Pub. 73-1, 29; Thorpe, *Our Army at Monterey*, 79-80.

[117] Henry, *Campaign Sketches of the War with Mexico*, 207.

[118] Thorpe, *Our Army at Monterey*, 154-155. Taylor appointed Worth as governor of Monterrey. Note that the official version is dated the 24th even though all parties did not sign until the 25th.

by that date he reckoned that his dispatch would reach San Luis Potosi....The termination of the armistice enabled Taylor to occupy Saltillo, upon which his eye had long been fixed.[119]

Taylor's direction of the three-day fight at Monterrey received mixed reviews. His pincer movement in which he sent General Worth to the west was viewed as wise given that he could not conduct a siege since he could not completely surround the city. But his diversion on the 21st and its subsequent change to an attack was seen as imprudent. Taylor knew little about the fortifications within the city and what he did know from reconnaissances and maps drawn by Meade was not shared with his second in command Butler—"Butler stated officially that when he attacked city he knew nothing about the locality." Henry wrote that they were "in utter ignorance of our locality" during the attack with his 3rd Infantry. Smith opined that waiting for Mansfield to complete a full reconnaissance of that area of the city could not have happened since Mansfield "would not have lived to finish it." Smith also stated that Taylor "should have kept out of the street fighting." United States artillery as at the earlier Battles of Resaca de la Palma and Palo Alto did well enough but the streets of the city proved difficult as Lieutenant French noted on the 23rd as he maneuvered his 12-pound howitzer:

> I turned my gun to the left, into a street leading into the plaza. To my astonishment, one block distant was a stone barricade behind which were troops, and the houses on either side covered with armed men. They were evidently surprised, and did not fire at us. We were permitted to unlimber the gun, and move the horses back into the main street. I politely waved my hand at the men at the barricade, which should read I shook my fist at them, and gave the command to load. Instantly the muskets were leveled over the barricade and pointed down from the house tops, and a volley fired at us that rattled like hail on the stones. My pony received a ricochet musket ball that struck the shoulder blade, ran up over the withers, and was stopped by the girth on the other side. I dismounted, and turned back to the gun. The two men at the muzzle were shot. One poor fellow put his hands to his side and quietly said, "Lieutenant. I am shot." and tried to stop the flow of blood. I had the gun run back into the street by which we entered the city. I now resorted to a device once practiced by a mob in the city of Philadelphia: two long ropes were made fast to the end of the trail, one rope was held by men on the lower side of the barricaded street, and the other by the men above. The gun was now loaded, and leveled in safety, then pushed out, and pulled by the ropes until it pointed at the barricade, and then fired. The recoil sent the gun back, and the rope brought it around the corner to be reloaded. In this manner the gun was worked for two hours, and with all this protection, four out of the five gunners were killed or wounded."[120]

John Pope in a tribute to Mansfield in 1891 wrote of his bravery and zeal:

> I first saw him in action at the storming of Monterrey. He was the Chief Engineer on General Taylor's staff, and I was one of the junior officers under him. We led the advance of the column which attacked and carried some of the fortifications on the lower part of the city. Of course Mansfield was wounded, shot through the calf of the leg; but he had it bound up, and the next I saw of him he was stretched out in a partly-reclining position behind a piece of artillery of Webster's battery, within open sight of the enemy's intrenchments, not 200 yards distant, and from which A TERRIFIC FIRE FROM ARTILLERY and small-arms was being poured upon the spot until the dust and dirt were flying in every direction. The place was too hot even for the gunners, and this one gun was served in person by Lieut. J.L. Donaldson, the First Lieutenant of the battery, who seemed as careless of his life as Mansfield. The latter was unable to walk on his wounded leg but was lying in the midst of this tremendous fire, in which it seemed impossible to live, with his field-glass to his eye, directing Donaldson where to aim his gun. Absolutely he seemed as unconscious of danger or as indifferent to it as if he had been walking the streets of Washington. I saw him again in battle under somewhat different circumstances at Buena Vista. Although still on General Taylor's staff, he did not go back with the General that night to Saltillo, but remained on the field with General Wool to help him select positions and post the troops for the next day's work. When we rode up on the plateau in the midst of a lost battle, as I have described, one of the first men I saw was General Mansfield. He rode a gray horse, which made him very conspicuous, and was charging furiously back and forth across the field, trying to rally the broken columns, but without success. He was beside himself with shame and humiliation, and the tears poured down his face. He was not tranquilized until the effects from Bragg's and Sherman's batteries became apparent.

---

[119] Smith, *The War with Mexico*, 258, 260-264. Ampudia reported losses of 29 officers and 338 men killed and wounded, very likely his losses were much higher--in a later report numbers increased to 438 total casualties. Smith estimated Taylor's losses at about 800, Smith, *The War With Mexico*, 506; Dishman, *A Perfect Gibraltar*, 199. It is possible that U.S. losses exceeded Mexican losses given that the Mexican forces were fighting behind cover.

[120] Smith, *The War With Mexico*, 499; Henry, *Campaign Sketches of the War with Mexico,* 194; French, 65-66. French also noted Taylor's presence: "Gen. Taylor and staff came down the street on foot, and very imprudently he passed the cross street, escaping the many shots fired at him. There he was, almost alone. He tried to enter the store on the corner. The door being locked, he and the Mexican within had a confab, but, not understanding what was said, he called to Col. Kinney, the interpreter: 'Come over here.' The Colonel said and went over at double-quick, and made the owner open the door. The store was empty;" French 66.

Mansfield had a keen military eye and most excellent military judgment, but he never afterward had the opportunity to exhibit them until the civil war, and he was killed, as it was almost certain he would be, in the first battle in which he was engaged.[121]

The only benefit of Taylor's imprudent attack on the 21st according to Smith was that his troops' bravery bordering on recklessness dismayed the Mexican commander, Ampudia, but that result was not one of Taylor's goals. Had Ampudia followed up Taylor's futile attack with a counterattack using his lancers, the day would have gone much worse for the U.S. Army.[122] The bloody result of the attacks in the streets showed that blindly rushing into a fortified city could not succeed despite the bravery and ardor of the troops. The attacks on the 23rd from the west were more successful in large part due to the Texans demonstrating how to fight in a city. They had learned much by fighting in Mier during the war between Texas and Mexico. Using tools such as pickaxes and crowbars, the Texans showed the regulars how to cut holes in walls to avoid attacking down streets and to use ladders to gain the rooftops to fire down at the enemy in the street or on nearby rooftops. One obvious lesson imparted was to avoid charging down open streets but rather to use cover. This new style of warfare was learned by paying a large price on the 21st as Mansfield personally learned.[123]

---

[121] John Pope, *National Tribune,* 19 March 1891, "War Reminiscences." Pope may have been overly kind and generous in his reminiscences 30 years after Mansfield's death. And he did not know of Mansfield's remarks to Louisa about Pope's conduct in Mexico. Mansfield wrote Louisa about his horse at Buena Vista: "My own horse, a powerful grey, was completely fagged out and the day after the battle could just move along. But he behaved admirably. The blare of cannon and discharge of arms never troubled him and he moved without opposition in any direction;" 28 February 1847 letter courtesy of the Middlesex County Historical Society.

[122] Smith, n. 10, 501, "Taylor had no reason to suppose that operations so badly planned, so ineffective and so costly would have that effect [on Ampudia]; they were wasteful; and they demoralized his own men".

[123] Dishman, *A Perfect Gibraltar,* 175-176. Mansfield made use of maps Meade had drawn to supplement his own reconnaissances, Adrian G. Trass, *From the Golden Gate to Mexico City: The U.S. Army Topographical Engineers in the Mexican War 1846-1848,* CMH Pub. 70-10 (Washington, DC: US GPO, 1993), 134.

Monterey

Mitre Mountain

Taylor's Walnut Springs Camp

Roads to Marin

Grand or Main Plaza

Citadel or Black Fort

Road to Monclova

Santa Catarina River

Bishop's Palace

Highway to Saltillo

Sketch of the City of Monterrey looking north by Stephen G. Hill of the 1st Ohio. Courtesy LOC.

Taylor's men entering into Monterrey's main plaza after the Mexican Army retreated. Thorpe, *Our Army at Monterey*, frontispiece.

Main or Grand Plaza in Monterrey looking west, October 1846 by Major Daniel P. Whiting, 7th Infantry. The tallest mountains are part of the Sierra Madre Mountain Range, the mountain to the upper right is Mitre Mountain. Fort Soldado is in the distance in the upper left center as a white block and the Bishop's Palace is to its right in the right center; at the peak of the hill to the right of the Bishop's Palace is Independence Hill taken on the 22nd as was the Bishop's Palace. Fort Soldado was taken on the 21st as was Federation Hill, the hill just to the right of Fort Soldado. The valley in the upper right center is the pass leading to Saltillo captured on the 21st. Courtesy LOC.

Mansfield was finally placed on his horse and he rode back to his tent on the 22nd as he at last became incapacitated by his wound. He wrote to Cullum that he kept the field until he saw the U.S. flag go up at the Bishop's Palace. He was able to write to his wife on 25 September 1846, and his first sentence carried alarming news: "I am now on my back having been wounded by a musket shot through the calf of my leg in the storming of a battery that took place on the 21st. The city is now in our possession having been given up today....I shall not probably be able to stand on my leg for 3 or 4 days yet. It has been exceedingly painful but is easier. I was fortunate in getting no worse wound. Many of our officers were killed. Among them Captain Lewis [Nelson] Morris [3rd Inf.] who married a relative of your mother." Perhaps to give her some better news he talked about more pleasant subjects: he found this city and the area much nicer than previous camps and found oranges, limes, lemons, peaches, apples, grapes, etc., along with canals meriting comment. But his wound obviously bothered him: "I am not in a condition to write to you a long letter....say to my sister I am out of danger for the present." His servant would have taken care of him as Mansfield was confined to his cot.[124]

This letter and the several he wrote to his wife up to the next battle at Buena Vista on 22-23 February 1847, may be divided into two broad categories, martial and nonmartial—he gave news on the progress of his wound and about the battle itself, and discussed a few of the officers, including Taylor, giving his experiences with them. He also expressed his opinions about the quality of volunteers, and perhaps quoting camp gossip, the course of the war, and his feelings about it and the Mexican people. His nonwar comments concern primarily his family and finances in which he dispensed advice about his wife's and children's health and finances.

Mansfield talked about his wound in almost every letter following this one obviously to ensure his wife that he is recovering. "I am still on my back and only able to write with paper in my lap. The pain however of my wound is subsiding fast and I expect in 6 days to walk on my leg and ride as usual." He asks that if Mrs. Totten [wife of Colonel Joseph G. Totten, chief engineer of the Army] wrote again, reply to her that "she must have me ordered home as soon as hostilities cease. I cannot get away before unless my bones should hereafter get broken in a future occasion. There is nobody here can take my place." His wound, although painful, was not grave as no bones were broken. Taylor in an official 22 September report listing officer casualties wrote that Mansfield was "slightly wounded" which made sense as Mansfield was able to stay in the street fight for a full day after he was shot. It took about two weeks before he could sit up in his cot so his wound although not serious, was far from a trifle. He discussed his wound again in a later letter: Dr. Barrett's views [likely a doctor in Connecticut his wife consulted] as to wounds are correct—the bone was not touched—but by night the tourniquet on my leg to keep it from bleeding and the excitement occasioned by using it so much inflamed the wound and I was obliged to be lifted on a horse to go to camp. While nothing has been found to show the exact time he was taken back to his tent, it is likely that he stayed near Monterrey through the evening of the 21st. Taylor wrote in his official report that Mansfield, "though wounded on the 21st, remained on duty during that and the following day, until confined by his wound to camp." Mansfield wrote Louisa that "I shall accompany him [Taylor] if my wound be well enough and I suppose it will be although it heals very slowly. Tell your father that the ball passed through the fleshy part of the calf of my leg and made two round holes through my pantaloons and two through my drawers. It went with such velocity that I only felt it and it was an hour before it lamed me. My sock and shoe was full of blood when a physician put a tourniquet around just above my knee to prevent bleeding too much. I suppose the man that fired at me could not be more than 40 or 50 yards off and from one of the stone buildings." In another update he wrote that "My wound is getting on very slowly. I fear I shall not be out of my tent for 10 days yet. I apply nothing to it but lint and cold water to keep down the inflammation. Indeed there is nothing better for any wound or bruise than to keep the bandages moist constantly to reduce inflammation." In his 25-27 October letter he wrote Louisa that he is "now able to walk about slowly and limp a little but shall in a few days I hope walk as usual. I was on my back just one month. Wounds heal very slowly here...the doctors say the climate is bad for wounds. An early November update: "I am now walking about and shall be able to mount my horse in a few days. I am however weak from so long confinement to my tent. Yet my appetite is tolerably good. It is now just two months since the battle and I am not yet able to use my leg except just about my tent. It does not heal at the orifices—there is yet some considerable inflammation but no material pain. It is however getting better every day yet very slowly." It took him about a month

---

[124] Letter 5 September 1846 courtesy WPL. Mansfield and Taylor both wrote that he did not quit the field until the 22nd, see note 125 below.

after he was wounded to be able to walk. He gave her good news also: "Yesterday afternoon [2 November] I took a walk of over a mile slowly through the volunteer camp."[125]

He went on to describe his role in the battle: "Peculiar circumstances obliged me to take a more conspicuous and active part in the storming of this city than I had any wish or desire for. But I was not my own master in this matter. I was compelled to dismount from my horse and accordingly left my pistols in my holsters and went into the battle for the city going foremost with nothing but my sword by my side and spy glass in my hand. The thought of being shot never entered my head and it is wonderful how I escaped." He commented about a letter published in the *Matamoras American Flag* newspaper exaggerating General William Worth's actions at Monterrey which made him a hero, but more importantly to Mansfield, the letter also demeaned him: "It represents the performances of my duties in an improper and false light—all that I did was strictly in obedience to my orders and I am not accountable for anything but the faithful performance of them....From my peculiar position as chief of the engineers here I am necessarily more frequently brought forward than I could desire." Apparently there was some speculation that the directions Mansfield gave to Garland in the ill-fated attack into the city streets on the 21st were unwise. Mr. Kinney witnessed the conversation between Mansfield and Garland and believed that Garland's attack "with the then limited knowledge of the enemy's force, and of the strength of the defences of the place," was improvident. Mansfield wrote that he expected "that Garland's men would, by taking cover 'among the stone buildings,' be able to protect themselves while seeking to 'attain the gorge of the redoubt.'"[126] But Mansfield knew almost nothing about the strength and exact location of the city's defenses as he was not privy to information learned from deserters and of course had not been able to penetrate deeper into the city. Given what he knew and saw, it is difficult to fault his actions and clearly everyone who saw him witnessed his bravery. In hindsight, Mansfield might have suggested to Garland that his troops not expose themselves in the streets which were raked with Mexican musket and artillery fire but Mansfield could not make such a comment since Garland was the infantry officer in command and Mansfield was merely reconnoitering for him. Neither Garland nor Mansfield had ever participated in street fighting tactics nor had the U.S. Army since the War of 1812.[127]

---

[125] Letters to Louisa 25 September, 29 September, 4 October, 10-12 October, 25-27 October, 1-3 November, 22-24 November, 29 November 1846, courtesy WPL. Mansfield wrote that he was on his back the night of the 22nd. There is no record of exactly what he did the evening of the 21st. Mansfield corrected Cullum's military history about him concerning this wounding—he "kept the field until night and on the next day although lame till Gen. Worth's division had stormed the Bishop's Palace and he reported the American flag flying from its top [about 4 p.m.] when he retired unable to stand longer and was confined two months," annotated Cullum notes courtesy WPL.

[126] Lewis, *Trailing Clouds of Glory*, 143. Lewis opined that although Mansfield was "a top-notch engineer, had little reconnaissance experience" perhaps comparing him to veteran topographical engineers. Lewis wrote that Taylor needed Captain George A. McCall who had done well at Palo Alto and Resaca de la Palma but who was not at Monterrey. Lewis also mentioned Captain Charles F. Smith who was with McCall at Resaca de la Palma but Smith was with Worth at the attack on the city's left flank. Taylor used the best men available, and in this case it was Mansfield, his chief engineer—wishing, in hindsight, for better scouts is a vain exercise in the author's opinion.

[127] Letters to Louisa 25 September, 29 September, 4 October, 10-12 October, 25-27 October, 1-3 November, 22-24 November, 29 November 1846, courtesy WPL. In his 4 February 1847 letter to Louisa he expressed his dislike of General Butler: "Genl. Butler was left at Monterrey still making a fuss about his wound. He is not popular here. In his official report he has misrepresented me. I don't think him well calculated for an important a rank as he holds," letter courtesy of the Middlesex County Historical Society.

Mansfield's 1840 Dragoon sabre manufactured by the Ames Manufacturing Company and sword belt; courtesy of the Middlesex County Historical Society.

He filled in more details about the circumstances of his wounding by talking about the death of Major [William W.] Lear [3rd Infantry]: "Major Lear who was wounded in the storming of the city died yesterday and will be buried today. He was shot the instant after a ball passed through my leg and close by me. I saw him fall and thought at first he was dead but as I looked at him he made an effort to rise and as good luck would have it, one of our soldiers was just conducting along 3 Mexican prisoners and as there people almost always have a blanket on their arm I made them spread it on the ground and lay him on and carry him out to camp. Our own soldiers will rarely put down their muskets in such cases to take out any wounded men or officers. The newspaper reports are not correct. I dismounted when within 500 yards of the enemy's battery and left my horse as I could not enter the suburbs mounted. Besides, the firing and the cannon balls as [they] whizzed by would [have] rendered them troublesome to manage. I foresaw this and all of us in the advance dismounted. We had something else to do besides managing uneasy horses. If I had been mounted in the streets I most certainly would have been killed. There are a vast number of newspaper accounts of our battle that are not at all true. I know not how I escaped as I was among the first to approach the enemy and I believe the very first to enter the suburbs."[128]

He noted that "Genl Taylor has been very kind and attentive in visiting me since I have been confined and well may he be—for no man in this army has done more for his service than I have as I will one day inform you. He is extremely anxious the war should be closed and there is now a prospect at least that it will be before long. I have got as many honors and run into as many dangers as I ought. I look upon the honors as empty baubles, and most gladly wish I never have joined this army if I could have avoided it....I told Genl Taylor today I was sick of it and he says he is so himself and is anxious to retire as soon as possible."[129] Taylor obviously was concerned about Mansfield's recovery since he is "visited daily by Genl. Taylor who has established a great interest in me and been very friendly disposed from the time of the battles of the 8th and 9th May." Mansfield was not present at these two battles, Resaca de la Palma and Palo Alto, so

---

[128] Letters to Louisa 25 September, 29 September, 4 October, 10-12 October, 25-27 October, 1-3 November, 22-24 November, 29 November 1846, courtesy WPL.
[129] Letter 29 September 1846 courtesy WPL.

perhaps he means that his important role in designing and then holding Fort Brown permitted Taylor to be absent and win those battles. Mansfield again commented on how he wished to be home and away from this war and said that Taylor is ready for peace, too. But he wrote that the general is ordering up troops and supplies and preparing if necessary to pursue the war. Mansfield said that Taylor is needed: "If anything should happen to him there is nobody here fit to command and we would be in a state of chaos." In his report of the battle, Taylor commended Mansfield: "From the officers of my personal staff, and of the engineers, topographical engineers, and ordnance, associated with me, I have derived valuable and efficient assistance during the operations....I must express my particular obligations to Brevet-Major Mansfield and Lieutenant [Jeremiah M.] Scarritt, corps of engineers. They both rendered most important services in reconnoitring the enemy's positions, conducting troops in attack, and strengthening the works captured from the enemy. Major Mansfield, though wounded on the 21st, remained on duty during that and the following day, until confined by his wound to camp;" In one of this later letters he again expresses his like of Taylor: "Genl. Taylor has been very kind and attentive in calling to see [me] every day since I have been on my back. He is a man of good heart and just and honorable, with as few vices as could be expected of a man situated as he is and raised as he has been. He mentioned camp talk that Taylor may be replaced by General Butler because of Taylor's paroling of the Mexican Army at Monterrey, but asserted that he had nothing to do with that as he was already wounded and on his back the night of the 22nd. He does say that he was "astonished" that Taylor had done so. He again wished to be gone from Mexico: "If this war is to continue I shall embrace the first opportunity to get out of this country honorably and not to my disadvantage."[130] He happily reported to his wife that now his mailing address has changed since he has received a brevet promotion to major: "Bvt. Major J.K.F. Mansfield, U.S. Army in Mexico, c/o U.S. Quarter Master New Orleans."[131]

Like many regulars, the topic of volunteer troops was of interest as was the condition of Taylor's regular troops. He lamented that a continuation of the war will cost the U.S. much more plus "We have a deficiency of troops already particularly of the regular force which is fast dwindling down as to numbers to insignificance. The soldiers will none of them reenlist as their time expires but they seek other employment. The 1st, 3rd, 4th, 5th, and 7th Regiments of Infantry will not average over 200 men each, while as they should be from 800 to 1,000 strong each....Our volunteers are brave and good marksmen but in other aspects like a herd of cattle for they have no discipline and cannot maneuver in the field. Genl Taylor himself has expected too much from a few men and begins to open his eyes. Again he commented about the volunteers: "Our volunteers begin to think there is not so much _fun_ after all in facing the enemy and being shot down. And many are endeavoring to get off in various ways. The disabled and sick can go but our Genl. cannot spare the service of a single able bodied man." He commented again about the volunteers: "Many of our volunteers have been murdered and in return many Mexicans have been shot by them. A party actually went out of camp a few days since, as it was said, Mexican hunting and shooting in retaliation. Genl Taylor has recently ordered a Kentucky Regiment to the rear in disgrace on this account yet I suppose they will beg off....About 30 desertions from our ranks have taken place in Monterrey. The enemy give them 40 dollars and a horse. They are principally the foreign Germans and English who enter into the Mexican Army. The Alcalde's son and two other were put in irons the other day for enticing our men to desert. And the Genl told him he would hang him, if he caught him at it."[132]

Two Regular Army officers also gained Mansfield's negative attention, Captain Randolph Ridgely of the 3rd Artillery and Brigadier General William J. Worth. He details the death of Captain Ridgely who fell with his horse while riding on the cobblestone streets of Monterrey after the battle and fractured his skull. "He was a distinguished officer on the battlefield but it was not permitted him to be shot." But he then commented on the officer's life "in Savannah and St. Augustine by his disgraceful intrigues. He leaves an amiable young lady, his wife and an infant, to lament his loss—she however had a handsome property of her own which if Captain R[idgely] should chance to live will be dissipated and wasted." He finishes his story about Captain Ridgely's condition in a subsequent letter telling her that he died never regaining consciousness. Mansfield said it was for the best as Ridgely "gambled and dissipated and wasted his wife's property and had nothing but his pay besides. He was such a character that he would eventually be dismissed from the service. He was a gallant soldier and that is all that can be said in his favor." Compare Mansfield's opinions with those of

---

[130] Letter 25-27 October 1846 courtesy WPL. Kinney's reservations noted in Thorpe, _Our Army at Monterey_, 50. Lieutenant Scarritt was brevetted captain for Monterrey and Mansfield lieutenant colonel. As already noted, Mansfield and Taylor wrote that he kept the field until the 23rd.

[131] Letter 29 September 1846 courtesy WPL. Cullum noted that Mansfield was laid up to 3 December 1846, Mansfield's notes to Cullum 5 June 1860, courtesy WPL; No Author, _The Mexican War and Its Heroes: Being a Complete History of the Mexican War_ (Philadelphia, PA: J.B. Lippincott & Co., 1860), 47-48.

[132] Letter 29 September 1846 courtesy WPL. Cullum noted that Mansfield was laid up to 3 December 1846, Mansfield's notes to Cullum 5 June 1860, courtesy WPL.

other officers. Captain Henry wrote of Ridgely that "His dauntless courage and reckless exposure of person, combined with the most perfect coolness and judgment in the hottest fire, won golden opinions for him from all. Those who knew him in the social circle can well appreciate his loss. A bright star is extinguished! He will never return to pluck fresh honors for, and add new luster to, the gallantry and chivalry of the service." Mansfield perhaps was one of a few who knew about Ridgely's more unsavory affairs or Mansfield was a bit of a Puritan-like prude. Mansfield obviously knew of Ridgely's character from personal observation or from trusted officers. Other officers like Lieutenant Meade had nothing but good things to say of Ridgley: "He commanded Ringgold's battery on the 9th [of May], and gallantly drove it up within two hundred yards of the Mexican artillery, unlimbered his pieces, and returned their fire, all in the face of their eight pieces of artillery. In our recent operations he was equally distinguished for his cool and undaunted bravery, and it seems hard, after passing with so much credit through these three affairs, he should finally die the inglorious death that threatens him."[133]

General Worth, like Ridgely, was a good fighter but not of good character off the battlefield. Mansfield commented about a letter published in the *Matamoras American Flag* newspaper exaggerating General Worth's actions at Monterrey which made him a hero. "I look upon Genl. Worth as a very insincere, intriguing and selfish man who cares for nothing but his own aggrandizement. I would not trust him out of [my] sight." In a later letter he again expresses his dislike of General Worth ending with "His smiles can never deceive me. Some letter writers are endeavoring to make a great hero of Genl. Worth and they entirely over do the matter. We here know the merits of every man." He again told her that the newspaper reports of Worth's part in the battle were greatly exaggerated and that the number of casualties shown for Taylor's troops will attest to where the hard fighting took place. Worth was also viewed by other officers as vain and pompous. Lieutenant Dana wrote that "I believe he does not lack much of being a little cracked. He is very much inclined to make a noise about nothing and a fuss out of trifles." But Taylor chose Worth for the flanking movement at Monterrey based on his military experience and judgment. Ulysses S. Grant also thought that Worth was a good fighter but "He was nervous, impatient and restless on the march, or when important or responsible duty confronted him." As Worth was not a West Pointer, perhaps its graduates, who were Regular Army officers, had a more jaundiced view of him, but Meade and others did not, as Meade wrote that Worth treated him "with all possible courtesy and kindness, and I hope I shall remain with him so long as he is in the advance." Colonel Ethan A. Hitchcock confided to his diary about a transfer to a post away from Worth: "Now, thank God, I am separated from Colonel Worth, I care less about the promotion than I do for its effect....Worth will never give an immediate subordinate any authority and permit him to move in anything without his special leave. No officer near him is or can be anything but a cipher unless he will quarrel all the time."[134] Mansfield complained about Taylor's inspector general, Colonel George Croghan, "that he is publicly drunk and has to be carried to his quarters and is a nuisance to the army." He also expressed disdain for some other officers he had served with: "There are some officers in our army that are worthless in consequence of their early habits and their effeminate manner in which they have been raised in our southern states to be waited on all their lives."[135] Mansfield, as his letters show, was a no nonsense, professional officer who was not one to overindulge in alcohol or female companionship despite his long separation from Louisa. He obviously also believes that he is doing an excellent job as Taylor's chief engineer and that Old Zach could not do without him. Perhaps a bit of braggadocio on his part or, as Old Zach's senior engineer and a friend, he is accurate?

The nonmartial parts of his letters talk about the health of his wife and children along with advice on his children's upbringing. Finances for this captain are of concern as his brevet promotions do not increase his pay. He again wrote to his wife on 29 September 1846 a few days after his wound instructing his wife on how to treat one of his children, Henry, by not giving him too much arrow root as it would "impair the firmness of his constitution. Let him have a leg of a chicken or a spare rib or a bone of meat and a cold potato." He worried that she will coddle him but Mansfield believed this diet will help "make himself rugged. I want none of your delicate children in my family. They must all grow up rugged and accustomed to hard work." He wrote that he approved "of all your arrangements as to stock and

---

[133] Letters to Louisa 25 September, 29 September, 4 October, 10-12 October, 25-27 October, 1-3 November, 22-24 November, 29 November 1846, courtesy WPL; Henry, *Campaign Sketches*, 234-235; Meade, *Life and Letters*, vol. 1, 149.

[134] Richard Dalzell Gamble, "Garrison Life at Frontier Military Posts, 1830-1860," unpub. PhD thesis, The University of Oklahoma, Norman, OK, 1956, 48-4, from Grant Foreman, ed., *A Traveler in Indian Territory - The Journal of Ethan Allen Hitchcock* (Cedar Rapids, IA: Torch Press, 1930), 180.

[135] Letter 4 October 1846 courtesy WPL; Dana, *Monterrey Is Ours*, 116; Lewis, *Trailing Clouds of Glory*, 129; Ulysses S. Grant, *Personal Memoirs* (New York, NY: The Modern Library, 1999), 60; Meade, 125. In Mansfield's 1 September 1847 letter he again wrote about Croghan--the inspector general is "a beastly drunkard....He is often carried in a wagon from Monterrey too drunk to ride and has to be carried into his tent. Other officers must take on his duties for days at a time as he is often drunk." Perhaps Mansfield is envious of southern officers who had come from well-to-do families?

payments and think you have acted wisely." The following week's letter updated Louisa. Mansfield is still concerned with the health of his children and instructed his wife again on what to feed Henry. He said that dysentery prevails in Middletown because in the fall people eat too much fruit! He shipped some wine to her and told her to use it is needed for sickness, as he only takes water, coffee and tea and "feel all the better for it." He advised her to exercise and "not be seated in your chair all day. Take Mary by the hand and Samuel and take every day in the middle of the afternoon a long walk. It will benefit you all." He also chastised her for not properly sealing her letters to him—is it her neglect? He again advised care in the children's diet emphasizing mush and milk, plainly cooked meat, but no jellies and "no stimulants of any kind." In a subsequent letter he again advised milk—apparently a cure-all in his opinion--treat Henry's illness [with] "a little milk and let nature take its course." In a later letter he warned against too much milk—poor Louisa, how much is too much? As usual, he cautioned her about Samuel's schooling and clothing: "I wish him to be a man and not a fashionable fool! Fine clothes and smooth skin and white hands will not make him respectable. These things he can obtain whenever by his merit and earnings he is entitled to wear them." His final order to her: "I hope I am not now writing in vain! See to it." He again expressed his love for them and found pleasure that his "children progress and promise to be good members of society hereafter." He ended his 22-24 November letter by asking that Samuel write something in his wife's letters even "if it be but one line." His PPS tells her also that "Your letters are not full and are hurriedly written." He again extolled the virtues of a simple diet in his next letter as "there is nothing like good mush and milk. I have it here sometimes—I take my horses corn and grind it in a corn milk and my man makes it very nice." He reminded her that all he needs is "his little family about me" but then chides her that the children should be "healthy and strong and rugged. You must feed them on coarse food and clothe them with coarse and strong clothes and let them rough it....There is nothing so good for anybody as hard work. Only don't over strain children by anything they are not able to accomplish with ease." He closed one of his letters by asking her to "tell Samuel and Mary to be good children...tell them always to remember their father in their prayers. I have got a hard row to hoe."[136]

On 4 October 1846, Mansfield, still confined to his cot, wrote to his wife and he proudly noted that Taylor's official report would be published in the papers with the particulars of the battle. He noted that he is still confined to his tent but can now sit up and read in addition to studying Spanish while eating delicious oranges and pomegranates. He commented that his waiter, George Ormsby, who served him at Fort Pulaski, "still holds on and I would not part with him on any account." He again wrote about Ormsby on 4 April 1847 said that his 'servant George went into the woods for an hour and came back with a fine deer he had shot so you see I am in luck for fresh meat. He has learned to make flour puddings and I get along quite well....We have abundance of eggs and bread and coffee and salt and pepper and tough beef." Mansfield again commented on how he wished to be home and away from this war and said that Taylor is ready for peace, too. But he wrote that the general is ordering up troops and supplies and preparing if necessary to pursue the war.[137]

Mansfield wrote that General Santa Anna is reported to be in San Luis Potosi with about 8,000 troops but he said that is 270 miles away, so it is doubtful there will be an attack. He again hoped for an armistice in December noting that the Mexican congress will assemble and "the sense of the nation known as to peace or war." Every step we advance into the enemy's country we meet with stronger resistance and our own line of communication becomes lengthened and weakened. We can obtain nothing to eat in this country for our army but corn and fresh beef. Thus we have to bring

---

[136] Letters 29 September 1846, 4 October 1846, 10-12 October 1846, 1-3 November 1846, 22-24 November 1846, 29 Nov. 1846, 25 April 1847, courtesy WPL. Later he wrote to her that he does take some wine. His seemingly unending detailed instructions to Louisa about domestic matters in Middletown finally resulted in her rebelling although this letter was not found. He wrote on 10 August 1847 that even though he has given her sufficient exposure to his views on certain points, "hereafter as you do not appear to view what I say in the light it is meant I shall leave you to choose your own course in future." He continues that he cares too much for the welfare of others and that he "frequently I have met with but a very poor return. I am learning wisdom every day," letter courtesy WPL. Brevet pay as well as precedence of rank has always been an issue in the army with arcane rules. Brevet pay was probably not allowed for Mansfield as he was an engineer officer; see James B. Fry, *The History and Legal Effect of Brevets in the Armies of Great Britain and the United States from Their Origin in 1692 to the Present Time* (New York, NY: D. Van Nostrand, 1877), "no brevet pay is allowed to officers in the engineers, topographical engineers, ordnance or in any staff department. Nor does it appear to me necessary to rest this decision upon a strict or narrow interpretation of the word 'command' in the act of 1818, because staff officers are excluded from brevet pay while serving in their particular corps in like manner as from the exercise of their brevet rank, and are to do duty, take rank, and receive pay according to the commissions by which they are mustered," 195. This excerpt was taken from a letter sent by the Secretary of War, George W. Crawford, to the Chairman of the Committee on Military Affairs, House of Representatives, 26 June 1850. Mansfield did not give up on pursuing brevet pay for some of his service as he apparently requested brevet pay 5 March 1856 in a letter to the chairman on the Committee of Military Affairs seeking brevet pay while in command as Chief of the Engineer Department, reply letter to Mansfield 10 March 1856 from chairman, letter courtesy WPL.

[137] Letters 4 October 1846, 4 April 1847, courtesy WPL.

from the U.S. almost everything we get and it can be done cheaper than we can purchase things here." In his 25-27 October letter Mansfield stated that he does not believe Santa Anna will accomplish much for Mexicans and formulated a plan to set the border between Mexico and the U.S. "at the parallel of 32 degrees from the Pacific to the Rio Grande and down that river to the Gulf and occupy the country by military posts. Then continue the blockade the ports of Mexico." He, like others in the army and government, hoped that Mexico would give up fighting and sell parts of northern Mexico to the U.S., so Mansfield was suggesting where the dividing line should be.[138]

In his next letter he again wrote of his proposition for a border between the two countries but then continued his soon to be proven correct appraisal of the war situation that "We cannot with success and advantage to this country, advance further into Mexico." This comment is based on the long supply line Taylor or Scott would need to transport supplies south from Monterrey to eventually attack Mexico City. He told his wife to keep all newspaper articles which mention his name as "I shall if I live at a future day want to refer to them." He asked her to "Tell your father I shall rejoice when this war will be over and am as anxious as he to be honorably out of it. It is no part of my taste or wishes to engage in battles or bloodshed. It is my misfortune and with God's will may an end soon be put to it!" After repeating camp rumors about Santa Anna and a December armistice when the Mexican congress meets, He gave her good news also: "Yesterday afternoon [2 November] I took a walk of over a mile slowly through the volunteer camp. I called on General Quitman. He commands a brigade under General Butler. His income is $30,000 per annum and a gentleman educated. What could induce such a man to come here and make himself a mark for the [?] vagabond Mexican to shoot at him?"[139]

In his 22-24 November letter, Mansfield wrote that he is happy to read that Henry is better and read Samuel's writings. He again expressed his love for them and found pleasure that his "children progress and promise to be good members of society hereafter." He said that he looks forward to rejoining them all: "I am truly sick of the life I lead. We have been too much separated and it has been my lot from youth to struggle with adversity. The empty distinction that is acquired in the field of battle has no value in my estimation....There are individuals of large fortune and abundant means, volunteered to fight the battles of their country for conquest, not for patriotism. I can readily conceive how men can fight to defend their firesides and their homes, but alas, for those who come for empty fame. I am one of those who could not escape the task, but it was none of my own seeking. Circumstances have controlled my career that I could not avoid." He reported that Taylor has not returned from Saltillo after he took possession of it but he is expected shortly. He repeated his belief in the location of the border he has proposed in his letters twice. His wife may have asked about his going home on sick leave but he wrote that "the idea of going home on a short sick leave 2,500 miles and that too at my own expense is beyond consideration." Apparently his assistant, Lieutenant Jerimiah M. Scarritt, left for home on sick leave so Mansfield "is now alone. Yet I have written for two assistants and hope soon to see one of them." He told his wife about a camp rumor that Colonel Totten [Chief Engineer of the U.S. Army and Mansfield's cousin] was coming out to join in an expedition on Vera Cruz. "If so, I hope I shall be relieved, particularly as he will supersede me in command here. This I shall insist on and carry out if possible." He updated Taylor's return from Saltillo on the 24th after taking possession of it. He commented wryly about a "New Jersey Yankee" who has a large cotton factory near Saltillo "going full blast." And he said that he finds such men in every province of the country. He began another diatribe against General Scott's apparent ambitions for president stating that there must be civilians better qualified. He also wrote that he sent to [?] in Washington his views of the war and a small map. The man may be a congressman from Connecticut as he then said that "I hope that Congress will endeavor to bring about a peace before the 4th March."[140] She apparently asked again about his visiting home as he wrote in his next letter: "In regard to my coming home I alone can judge of the propriety of such a movement. I trust that peace will soon be established ....at any rate I can only say I have no desire to remain in such a war as this except as a necessary duty and the consequence of my peculiar situation." He said she should have no fear of him in another battle as Santa Anna is 200 miles away in San Luis Potosi and that he would have to come with 15,000 troops to expect to succeed. He did not expect a Mexican attack nor that Taylor's army will advance but he does think Taylor will eventually advance to occupy Linares and Victoria. "I shall accompany him if my wound be well enough and I suppose it will be although it heals very slowly. She must have written about her teeth

---

[138] Letters 10-12 and 25-27 October 1846 courtesy WPL. Although army supplied food is limited, Mansfield details in his other letters the abundance of fruit and vegetables along with game.

[139] Letter 25-27 Oct 1846, 1-3 November 1846, courtesy WPL. Mansfield is interested in Quitman's wealth as he is later with Taylor's. He then wonders why someone who does not have a financial need to be in the war would volunteer.

[140] Letters 22-24 November, 29 November 1846, courtesy WPL. Scarritt received a brevet to captain for Monterrey and then major for Chapultepec.

as he told her to get them "filled without delay." He then commented about the comforts of home and Louisa's physiognomy: "I suppose you will be quite fat and fleshy before I get home with your good living and many comforts about you." He closed with his assessment of current realities: "If we have not peace before two months we shall have to make a conquest of Mexico."[141] In his 4 February 1847 letter to Louisa, Mansfield expresses his love for his children and wife: "Tell Samuel and Mary as soon as I can get a little rest I will write them a letter. But now I can only send them a kiss each, which I will delegate you to give them. My constant thoughts and hopes are on you and my dear children and I trust in God's mercy as he has been good to me thus far in life he will soon restore me to the arms of those I love." He also discussed finances and tells her to pay the $50 he sent toward the mortgage on the house and that the monies he previously sent were to be paid to the mortgage also. But he did write that he had enclosed a $25 draft on the Douglas's "to be applied as you think proper for the family."[142]

Wool was ordered by the administration to use his command as part of President Polk's plan to separately attack the northern region of Mexico to the west of Taylor's area of operations to help convince the Mexican government to sue for peace. Wool originally had 2,940 troops of which only 500 were Regulars. Wool's units rendezvoused at San Antonio (Antonio de Bexar), Texas, and were ready to head south by the end of August 1846. They marched to Santa Rosa but the topography forced them to head toward Saltillo. On 29 October the column reached Coahuila where it remained for a month. Unsure how to proceed, Wool wrote to Taylor who replied that Wool should head toward Saltillo and halt at Parras. Wool finally joined Worth near Saltillo in December. On 16 November 1846 Taylor moved south to Saltillo unopposed, accompanied by two squadrons of the 2nd Dragoons. Wool moved south from Saltillo, the capital of the State of Coahuila, on 21 December to Agua Nueva based on rumors of an approaching Mexican force.[143]

---

[141] Letter 29 November 1846, courtesy WPL. He was laid up on his cot until 3 December.

[142] Letter to Louisa 4 February 1847. In his 8 February 1847 letter he said that he is sorry she is out of funds despite him sending her drafts in prior letters on the Douglas's. He wrote that a dollar a day should be sufficient for her allowance "with the other advantages you possess of house and garden." But in this letter he relented and sent her another draft on the Douglas's for $28. "The money I have sent to be applied to the mortgage on the house you live in must be religiously applied to that purpose and no other." He also included a $50 dollar treasury note to apply toward the mortgage as he "may not have again so good an opportunity." Letter courtesy of the Middlesex County Historical Society.

[143] Smith, *The War with Mexico*, 264-266; Mansfield, *The Mexican War*, 84-90; Horatio O. Ladd, *History of the War with Mexico* (New York, NY: Dodd, Mead & Company, 1883), 183-188. Taylor also took possession of Monclova, Linares, Victoria, and Tampico. Taylor estimated his total effective strength at less than 12,000 on 15 October.

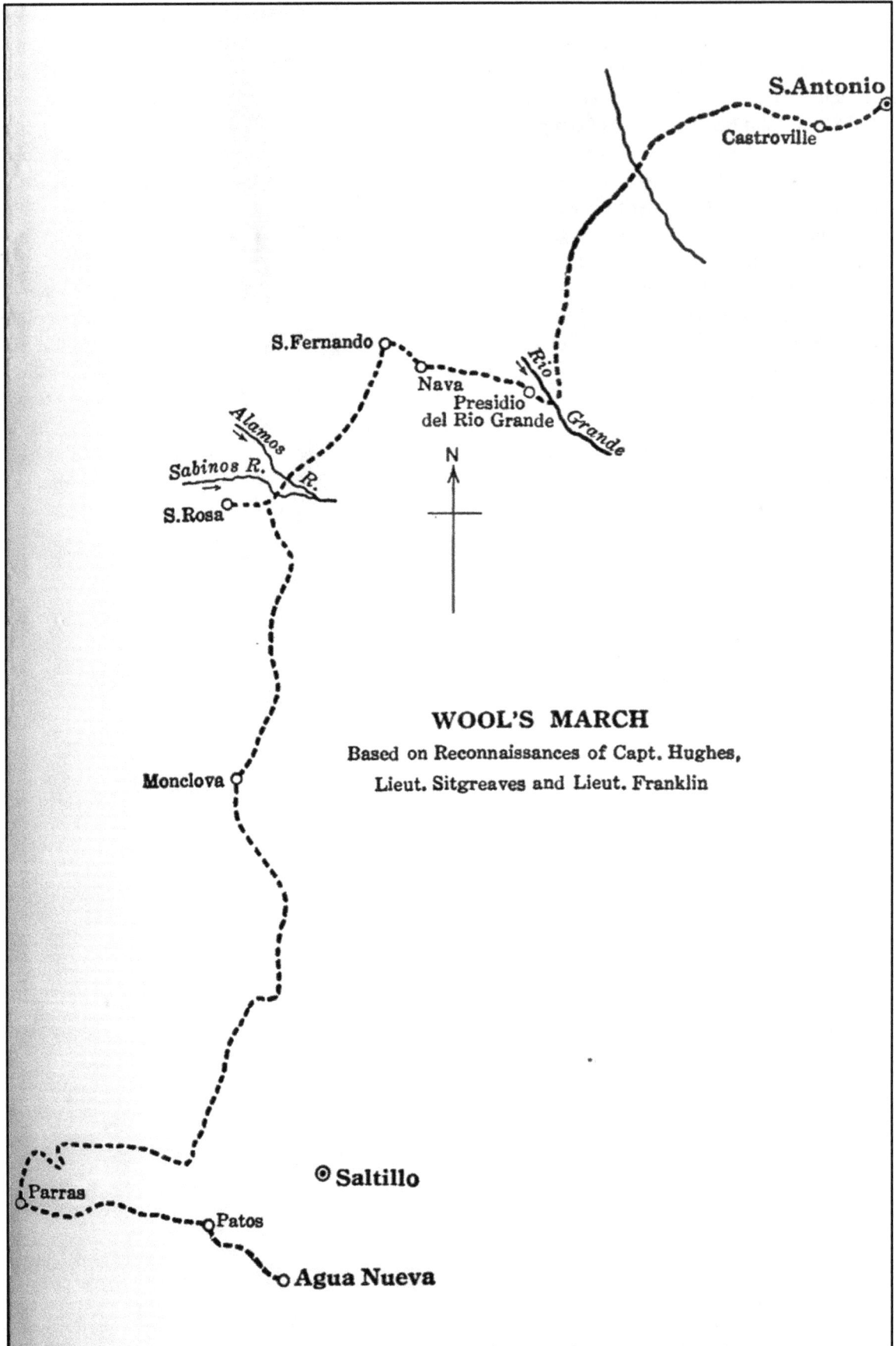

General Wool's 900 mile journey from San Antonio, Texas, 25 September to 21 December 1846 to join Taylor near Saltillo. Smith, *The War with Mexico*, 271.

President Polk realized that he had to use military force to convince the Mexican government to give in to American demands. Scott and his new army would land at Vera Cruz and fight its way to Mexico City. Polk had to call up nine volunteer regiments (6,750 men) for the duration of the war. Polk picked General Scott over Taylor as Taylor was perceived as not a friend of the administration, to open this new front. He finally chose Scott as any other commander would have engendered a political fight—Polk appointed Scott to command on 18 November 1846. Scott proposed on 21 November to take about 5,000 of Taylor's Regulars, 6,000 of his volunteers, and the first 4,000 of the new regiments Polk called up. Scott wanted to leave enough troops to allow Taylor to defend Monterrey and his line of communication down to Matamoros and the Gulf. Taylor on 10 December broke up the temporary Field Division sending the Georgia, Mississippi and 1st Tennessee Regiments to General Quitman and the Ohio and Kentucky Regiments to General Butler; General Twiggs's 1st Division of Regulars was reorganized and on 13 and 14 December this division and Quitman's Brigade marched to Victoria. Taylor marched with them having left Butler in command at Monterrey. At Montemorelos the column met the 2nd Infantry and the 2nd Tennessee giving a total of some 3,500 men. But Santa Anna heard about Taylor's march so decided to attack Saltillo and Monterrey with 13,000 men and 12 cannon while Taylor was absent. Fortunately, Worth heard intelligence of this Mexican movement and Taylor took his Regulars and reversed marched on 18 December for Saltillo. Two days later, Taylor learned that Santa Anna had turned back so Taylor turned and headed back to Victoria. On 4 January 1847, Taylor and his Regulars marched into Victoria six days after Quitman occupied it; Mansfield was with him. On 12 January, Mansfield inspected sappers at Victoria. General Patterson had set out on the 28th of November, to march south from Matamoros with the two Illinois regiments and the regiment of Tennessee horse, about 1,500 men, for Victoria, reaching there on 4 January. Scott ordered Taylor "to concentrate in Tampico all the troops of Patterson, Quitman and Twiggs except an escort for himself and, if necessary, a garrison for Victoria, and then return to Monterrey....Scott further explained that Taylor would have to act 'for a time' on a 'strict defensive.'" Taylor was furious and let it be known that he and his remaining troops were in serious danger. He viewed these actions as an intrigue against him but according to Smith, Taylor may have been engaging in a bit of "electioneering melodrama....[which resulted in the] overthrow of the Democratic party and the accession of Taylor to the Presidential chair." Mansfield wrote that "Before the army marched to Victoria to embark at Tampico he directed the fortifications to hold the City of Monterrey, abandoning all the main works and retaining the Black Fort with instruction to his assistant Captain [William D.] Fraser how to modify and strengthen it to stand a siege as it commanded the whole city. [He also] Directed a survey of the city and surroundings by his assistant, Captain [Jeremiah M.] Scarritt."[144]

---

[144] Smith, *The War with Mexico*, 354-362. General Gideon Pillow was Patterson's second in command. Scott ordered on 3 January the following troop dispositions: "place at the mouth of the Rio Grande about 4,000 regular infantry under Worth, 4,000 volunteer infantry, 500 regular cavalry, the best 500 volunteer cavalry and two field batteries deducting, however, from these numbers the troops then at Victoria, except an escort for Taylor, all those at Tampico except about 500 for a garrison, and one volunteer regiment at Matamoros. Scott added that he hoped eight new volunteer regiments would be at the Brazos by the end of January, and that three or four of these would remain in northern Mexico," Smith, 362. Mansfield wrote to Captain George W. Cullum 18 August 1859 supplementing/correcting Cullum re Mansfield's military history, courtesy WPL. Fraser received a brevet to major for Mexico and Scarritt a brevet to captain for Monterrey and major for Chapultepec.

U.S. and Mexican troop movements from March 1846 to February 1847. Courtesy USMA from LOC.

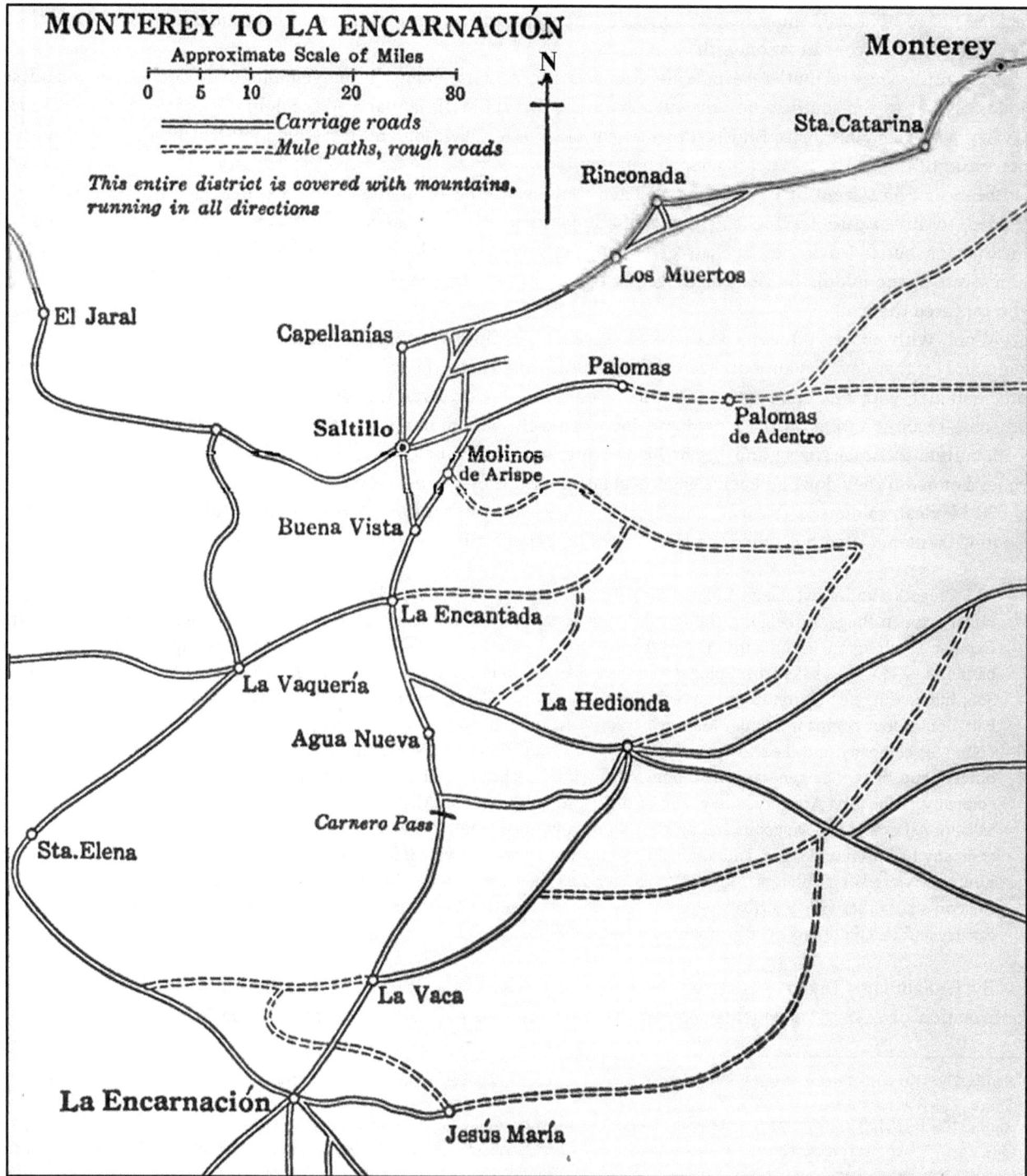

MONTEREY TO LA ENCARNACIÓN
Approximate Scale of Miles

Carriage roads
Mule paths, rough roads

This entire district is covered with mountains,
running in all directions

Taylor's Area of operations from Monterrey to La Encarnacion, Smith, *The War with Mexico*, 382.

Taylor on 12 January ordered his regular infantry and Patterson's troops to march for Tampico and then on the 14th Taylor ordered Quitman's Brigade to follow Patterson. Thus some 4,733 men were on the move toward Tampico to add to Scott's army. Scott arrived on 19 February greeting his fledgling army but left the next day to sail to his next rendezvous, the Lobos Islands, with a safe anchorage about 60 miles southeast of Tampico. There Scott began to put together his army for his attack on Vera Cruz and eventual march to Mexico City. Taylor, escorted by a squadron of Dragoons, the Mississippi Regiment, and two field batteries, left Victoria on 16 January and reached Monterrey eight days later. Despite the orders of the administration and Scott, Taylor, still smarting from the diminution of his army, decided not to hold at Monterrey but to march back south to Saltillo with most of his remaining army. Thus the stage was set for a direct confrontation with General Santa Anna.[145]

At Saltillo General Butler became nervous hearing rumors about the movements of Mexican troops and seeing clouds of dust to the south so he sent out a scouting party. On 19 January, Major John P. Gaines of the 1st Kentucky Cavalry with Captain Cassius M. Clay, Lieutenant George R. Davidson and forty men left Saltillo but found nothing of interest until the 21st at La Encarnacion. There the troopers met 50 Arkansas Cavalry under Major Solon Borland who had been sent on a scout by General Wool. Then they heard of a small enemy force at El Salado so the combined party decided to investigate leaving the night of 22 January. Unfortunately they found nothing and returned to La Encarnacion but failed to post pickets given the rainy weather. This proved to be a mistake as they awoke to find themselves in the middle of Mexican Brigadier General Jose Vincente Minon's cavalry brigade of some 1,200 troopers who captured them all.[146]

Wool, with about 700 men, occupied an advance position near Saltillo on 2 February; Mansfield joined Wool's command on that day. Taylor marched south of Saltillo and camped near Agua Nueva on the 5th and by the 14th he had some 650 men with him and about 4,000 with Wool a mile away. Even though he did little scouting, Taylor's engineers did some reconnoitering on their own and found that the mountains were passable. Mansfield marched with Wool's headquarters to Aqua Nueva and began his reconnoitering. Taylor determined to meet the enemy there: "'Let them come; damned if they don't go back a good deal faster than they came.'" Santa Anna was assembling his forces with over 15,000 Mexican soldiers at Encarnacion some 40 miles south of Saltillo on 18 February ready to meet Taylor's force of about 4,700 men.[147] Smith detailed the U.S. "forces in action" at Buena Vista, units and numbers:

> Dragoons under Bvt. Lieut. Colonel May (First [Dragoons], 133; Second [Dragoons], 76), [total] 209; Third Artillery (Co. C under Captain Bragg, three guns, the fourth being at Saltillo; Co. E under Captain Sherman, four guns), 150; Fourth Artillery, Captain Washington, eight guns, 117; Arkansas horse, Colonel Yell, 479; First Kentucky (two squadrons of cavalry and a battalion of mounted riflemen), Colonel Marshall, 330; Second Kentucky, Colonel McKee, 571; First Mississippi, Colonel Davis, 368; Indiana Brigade (Second regt. under Colonel Bowles and Third under Colonel Lane), General Lane, 1,253, including a rifle battalion of four companies under Major Gorman; First Illinois, Colonel Hardin, 580; Second Illinois, Colonel Bissell, 573; Texas volunteer company (attached to Second Illinois), Captain Conner, 61; Major McCulloch's Texan scouts, 27. The figures include officers and men. The general staff numbered forty-one. Three hundred and sixty-four of the men were on the sick list. A company of the First Artillery, a few men of the Third Artillery, two Mississippi companies and four Illinois companies were at Saltillo. All except the Dragoons and artillery were volunteers. Only the artillery, Dragoons, Mississippi regiment, and Conner's company had been under fire, and some of these men were raw recruits; but Colonel Davis and all the field officers of the Second Kentucky were West Pointers. Mostly Wool's men had been well trained. McCulloch's company probably served under May. All the corps not otherwise described were infantry. In the volunteer horse certain companies appear to have been regarded as true cavalry and certain others as only mounted infantry.[148]

By 19 February, Taylor was alerted by his cavalry scouts who learned that Santa Anna was near and on the 21st confirmation of enemy movements showed that they intended to turn his flank at Agua Nueva; the American army

---

[145] Smith, *The War with Mexico*, 364-369. Of the 4,733 there were about 1,400 regulars and 3,000 volunteers.

[146] Smith, *The War with Mexico*, 372-375.

[147] Smith, *The War with Mexico*, 372-375. At Buena Vista, Taylor had the following Regular Army troops: three companies of artillery: Capt. Braxton Bragg's Co. C, 3rd Artillery; Capt. Thomas W. Sherman's Co. E, 3rd Artillery; and Capt. John M. Washington's Co. B, 4th Artillery) and two squadrons of dragoons, Capt. Enoch Steen's and Lt. Col. Charles A. May's squadrons of the 1st and 2nd Dragoons. Taylor had the following volunteers: Brig. Gen. Joseph Lane's Indiana Brigade (Col. William A. Bowles's 2nd Indiana Infantry and Col. James H. Lane's 3rd Indiana Infantry); Col. John Hardin's 1st Illinois Infantry; Col. William Bissell's 2nd Illinois Infantry (Capt. P. Edward Conner's Texas Volunteer Company attached); Col. Humphrey Marshall's 1st Kentucky (mounted and dismounted troops); and Col. William McKee's 2nd Kentucky Infantry. Col. Archibald Yell's Arkansas Cavalry regiment and Capt. Benjamin McCulloch's mounted Texas Rangers was the volunteer cavalry. Yell was killed on 23 Feb. After the battle McCulloch was promoted to major of U.S. Volunteers in recognition of his bravery. Strength of regular units going into the battle and casualties: 3rd Artillery, two companies: 150/20; 4th Artillery, one company: 117/28; 1st Dragoons, two companies, 133/9; 2nd Dragoons, two companies: 76/2; total regulars 476 with eight killed and 53 wounded. Strength of volunteer units going into the battle and casualties: Col. Yell's Arkansas Reg.: 479/42; Col. Marshall's 1st Kentucky Mounted Reg.: 330/50; Col. McKee's 2nd Kentucky Foot Reg.: 571/87; Col. Hardin's 1st Illinois Foot Reg.: 580/45; Col. Bissell's 2nd Illinois Foot Reg.: 573/115; Capt. Conner's Texas Co.: 61/16; Col. Bowles's 2nd Indiana Foot Reg.: 627/102; Col. Lane's 3rd Indiana Foot Reg.: 626/49; Col. Davis's 1st Mississippi Foot Reg.: 368/98; Total 4,215/605; James Henry Carleton, *The Battle of Buena Vista with the Operations of the Army of Occupation for One Month* (New York, NY: Harper and Brothers, 1848), 212. Carleton was a captain in the 1st Dragoons and was brevetted major for Buena Vista.

[148] Smith, *The War with Mexico*, 555-556. Compare Carleton's data above. A "squadron" is two companies. "Cavalry" fights on horseback, "dragoons" can fight mounted or on foot, and "mounted infantry" only fights on foot using horses for mobility.

retreated hastily to Buena Vista. Colonel Archibald Yell with his mounted Arkansas regiment was left behind to guard the army's stores until they could be carried back to Buena Vista. The 2nd Kentucky and some guns were detached at La Encantada in support, and the 1st Illinois under Colonel John J. Hardin was posted at La Angostura. About midnight Yell's pickets at Carnero Pass were driven in so the stores at Agua Nueva were destroyed and some wagons abandoned while a wagon train raced back to the village of Buena Vista. By the next morning all except Hardin's command and the advanced pickets were at Buena Vista. Taylor entrusted to Wool the disposition of the troops.[149] Smith commented favorably on Wool's dispositions: "Wool recommended it near the end of December and is entitled to the credit of the choice. The author [Smith] visited the ground twice, and found that a good route for infantry and cavalry ran from La Encantada behind the hills west of Buena Vista valley, and entered this valley north of La Angostura. Apparently it could have been made practicable for cannon easily, and could have been used effectively by either general for a feint at least. Engineer Mansfield had a picket guard it during the afternoon and night of February 22."[150]

Santa Anna on 22 February entered Agua Nueva on the heels of the precipitate U.S. retreat. He thought that he could harry the rear of the fleeing Americans and perhaps damage them so he rushed ahead with some 2,500 cavalry and assorted infantry battalions and swept away American pickets at La Encantada. He sent General Minon with his 2,000 cavalry to get in rear of the enemy in front of Buena Vista. Later on the 22nd Santa Anna sent mounted men to the west of Minon to ensure that escaping Americans would be trapped between his two mounted forces described by Captain Carleton of the 1st Dragoons: "a thousand mounted rancheros, armed with lances and machetes, who had been collected at Monclova, Buenaventura, and Parras, and were commanded by Colonel Miguel Blanco and Colonel Aguierra, were also sent from Patos, by a mule-path leading through the mountains, into the same valley. While, therefore, General Minon was to hover about the east side of the road leading from Saltillo to Monterrey, along which, it was supposed, we should soon be flying in great confusion, Colonels Blanco and Aguierra were to occupy the small town of Capellania on the west, likewise to await our retreat, and to assist in cutting us up without quarter."[151] "Wool who was still near Saltillo now knew Santa Anna was an imminent threat so he alerted his troops and sent a section of Captain John Macrae Washington's battery toward La Angostura. But Santa Anna gave up an excellent chance to damage the U.S. troops when he stopped his advance upon sighting the American position at La Angostura and decided to wait for his infantry to catch up. Santa Anna next sent his chief medical officer, Dr. Pedro Vanderlinden, to Taylor with a surrender demand: "You are surrounded by twenty thousand men, and cannot, in any human probability, avoid suffering a rout and being cut to pieces with your troops. But, as you deserve from me consideration and particular esteem, I wish to save you from a catastrophe; and for that purpose I give you this notice, in order that you may surrender at discretion, under the assurance that you will be treated with the consideration belonging to the Mexican character. To this end, you will be granted an hour's time to make up your mind, to commence from the moment when a flag of truce arrives in your camp."[152] Taylor had rejoined Wool and "As he rode along our lines, he was everywhere received with the most enthusiastic cheers; and the sound of each wild hurrah could be distinctly heard by those of the Mexican army who had already arrived on their ground."[153] The Mexican general realized that the battlefield favored the defender so an American surrender or retreat was highly desired. Taylor wrote back "I beg leave to say that I decline acceding to your request." The American center was on a spur where Hardin's men hastily constructed a breastwork during the night, with Captain Washington's battery on the road below, protected with a ditch and a parapet. Near this point and just north of it, Wool stationed most of the 4,759 U.S. troops, "placing near the mountain under Colonel [Humphrey] Marshall the Kentucky and Arkansas horse [on foot] and Major [Willis A.] Gorman's rifle battalion (four companies) of the Indiana foot....the main body of the Mexican forces formed two lines with heavy reserves behind them and cavalry in the rear, while Mexican artillery was planted on the road and also on the high ground east of it; and General Minon's brigade, the duty of which was to cut off the American retreat, showed itself early in the day at the rear of Buena Vista." Santa Anna saw an opportunity to outflank the American left so he sent General Pedro de Ampudia with a large force of infantry to seize a portion of high ground at the foot of the mountain. Colonel Marshall joined in a race with the Mexican troops to get to the summit and try to outflank the enemy but the Mexican troops beat him and took away that option. Taylor placed the 2nd Kentucky under West Point graduate Colonel William R. McKee, two guns under Captain

---

[149] Smith, *The War with Mexico*, 382-383. Carleton, *The Battle of Buena Vista*, 24-25.

[150] Smith, *The War With Mexico*, 555.

[151] Carleton, *The Battle of Buena Vista*, 43-44.

[152] Carleton, *ibid.*, 37.

[153] Carleton, *ibid.*, 35.

Braxton Bragg, and a detachment of horse on the opposite side of the valley to support a section of Captain Washington's guns and Colonel William A. Bowles's 2nd Indiana on the opposite side of the valley. Santa Anna did not press forward so Taylor returned to Saltillo escorted by the Colonel Jefferson Davis's Mississippi Regiment and Colonel May's squadron of the 2nd Dragoons. At Saltillo, Taylor arranged the defense of the town by William Barton Warren's and Lucien B. Webster's commands leaving one 6-pounder from Captain Bragg's Battery and two companies of Colonel Davis's riflemen under Captain Rogers. During the night, Colonel Marshall's Kentucky troops retreated down the mountain. Mexican forces held all the gains they made with light losses on both sides--four Americans wounded and an estimated 300 Mexican casualties.[154]

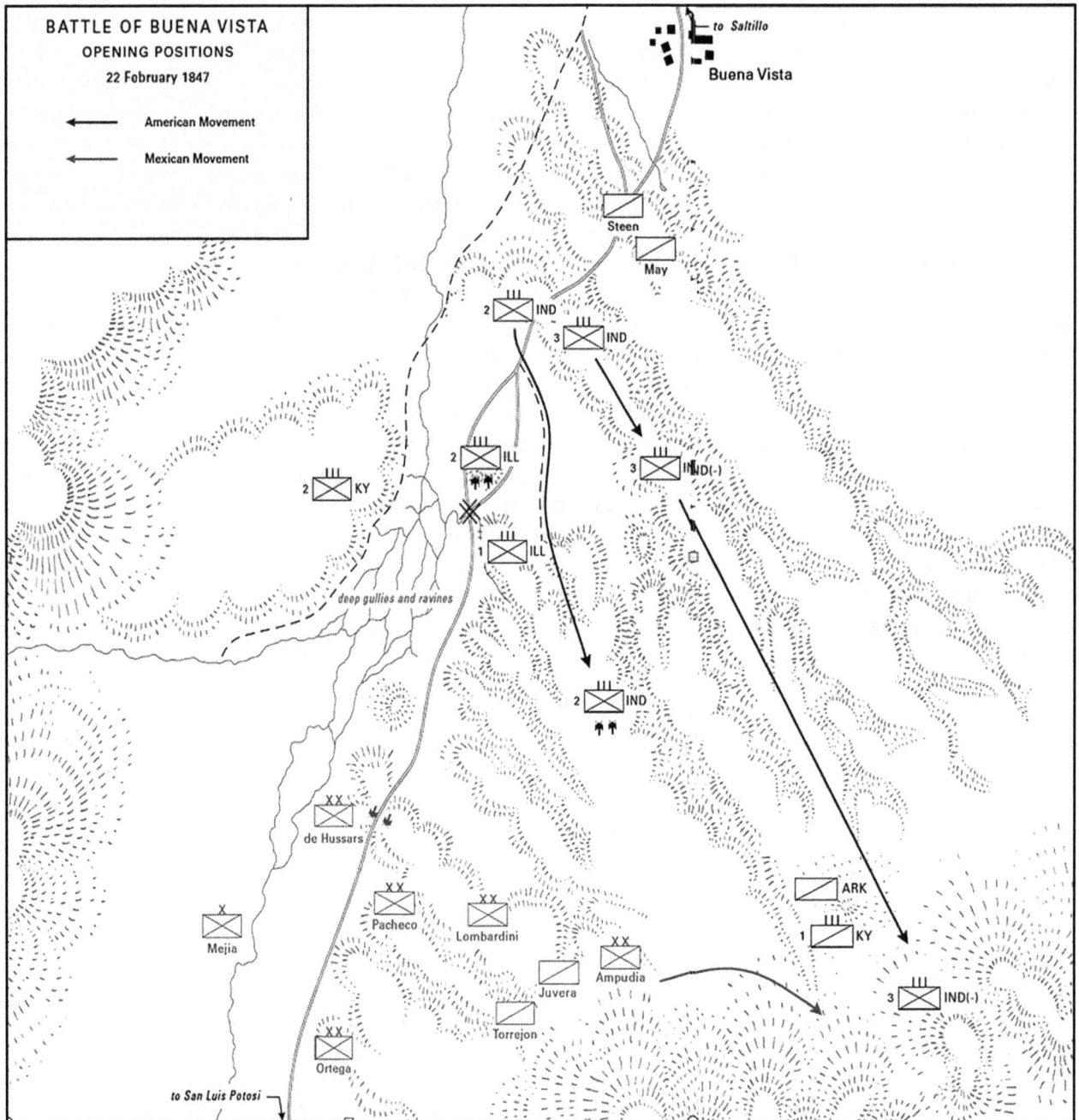

Buena Vista on the first day, 22 February 1847. Courtesy USACMH, USA.

[154] Smith, *The War with Mexico*, 384-388. Colonel John Selden Roane commanded four companies of the Arkansas Mounted Volunteers. Of Taylor's volunteers, only Colonel Jefferson Davis, Taylor's son-in-law, and his 1st Mississippi Rifles had experienced combat at Monterrey. Santa Anna's army contained at least 17,000 troops including 20 guns and several siege guns in wagons, 4,338 cavalry plus 2,000 under General Minon, Carleton, *The Battle of Buena Vista*, 22, 42. Other data show that Santa Anna had 20,653, at Encarnacion just before the battle, Alcaraz, *The Other Side*, 98.

Based on what the Americans viewed on the morning of the 23rd, they knew they were going to have a serious fight on their hands--they saw thousands of Mexican troops arrayed against them resplendent in brightly-colored uniforms: "The men were all in full dress, the horses were gayly caparisoned, and the arms of both cavalry and infantry shone bright as silver. Every regiment, corps, and squadron had its standards, colors, and guidons unfurled; and, while the infantry marched steadily onward with a most perfectly marked and cadenced step, the cavalry moved with the regularity and precision it would have observed in an ordinary field review."[155] Colonel Marshall's troops aided by Major Xerxes A. Trail and two companies of the 2nd Illinois and a company of Conner's Texas regiment had a fight with General Ampudia's men back on the mountain. Santa Anna sent a strong column down the main road but Captain Washington's guns stopped it. Seeing this, Santa Anna attacked the American left with a strong force composed of cavalry and infantry supported by a battery of artillery. General Lane attempted to relieve the heavily engaged 2nd Indiana and Captain John Paul Jones O'Brien's three guns by having them advance but Colonel Bowles did not follow O'Brien instead retreated taking four companies of Arkansas troopers with him. O'Brien had to withdraw in haste leaving one gun and firing his other two by prolonges. Unfortunately Colonel William Bissell's 2nd Illinois was outflanked by the attacking Mexican troops and had to retreat. Colonel Marshall's troops also had to retreat and took loses as it retreated three miles back to Buena Vista where, along with other fleeing Americans, helped repulse a Mexican cavalry attack by lancers. Other U.S. troops had seen the Mexican successes on the left so Colonel McKee and Captain Bragg, who were not attacked, came from the other side of the valley to help, as did four of Hardin's companies along with a just-arrived squadron of Captain Enoch Steen's 1st Dragoons. With the combined American artillery of Bragg, O'Brien, and Thomas W. Sherman, U.S. positions other than on the left were held which meant that the American rear was exposed from that left flank. Taylor and his escort arrived about 9 a.m. and the Mississippi Regiment, with help from the 3rd Indiana and one of Bragg's guns, forced the Mexican attack back despite well-directed Mexican artillery fire from the American deserters of the San Patricio Company. But the danger remained that Mexican troops on the destroyed American left flank would attack north and either take the American force from the rear or attack U.S. supplies at Saltillo.[156]

About noon a Mexican Cavalry Brigade with infantry attempted to take the Saltillo Road but the Mississippians and Indiana troops stopped the Mexican cavalry by first firing at close range and then attacking the troopers on their horses by seizing their reins and using their Bowie Knives. Sherman's howitzer came up and aided this winning effort repelling the Mexican attack. Dragoons and Bragg's artillery helped repel this Mexican attack on the Mexican left and American artillery on a nearby plateau added to the Mexican carnage. A little after noon, Mexican General Minon moved his 1,500 lancers out of Palomas Pass and rode toward Saltillo behind the American lines at Buena Vista. Taylor had left behind two companies of Mississippi infantry to help defend Saltillo before he rode forward. The Mississippians along with one 6-pounder commanded by Captain William Shover, two 24-pounders under Captain Lucien B. Webster and some 100 mounted teamsters and American civilians held Minon at bay inflicting 63 casualties while suffering none. Major William Barton Warren of the 1st Illinois was in overall command which included four of his companies at Saltillo during the attack. Meanwhile Mexican officers engaged in a ruse and rode up to find Taylor. General Wool at about 1 p.m. carried a white flag to find out Santa Anna's intentions about the reason for the white flag carried by the Mexican officers. He did not locate the Mexican commander and then saw that the Mexican artillery continued to fire so Wool returned. Santa Anna succeeded in delaying American attacks allowing his troops to regroup. Santa Anna still wanted to attack the American force in the rear so he gathered his troops for another attack. Taylor decided to finally rout the Mexican force so sent Colonel Hardin and his six companies in an attack. Colonel Bissell, 2nd Illinois, and Colonel McKee, 2nd Kentucky, saw that Hardin's force was overmatched against the enemy so joined him and moved forward. Unfortunately the Mexican corps of General Francisco Perez emerged from cover and despite heroic effort by American troops and artillery the three U.S. regiments retreated down toward the main road where Hardin was killed along with McKee. Washington's guns saved the retreating troops as they held back the attacking Mexican lancers; U.S. troops made their way to La Angostura. Meanwhile, another Mexican force attacked the American center which was stripped of troops except for O'Brien's guns. He delayed the Mexican attack losing most of his men in the fight. The American center and Taylor were saved as Bragg and Sherman arrived with their guns from the north and along with the Indiana

---

[155] Carleton, *The Battle of Buena Vista*, 56-57.
[156] Smith, *The War with Mexico*, 389-392. Firing by prolonge meant that ropes were used to retreat with the artillery pieces as they were fired allowing continuous fire during the retreat.

and Mississippi regiments, stopped the Mexican attack--the infantry charged the Mexican flank and rear while canister tore bloody gaps in the Mexican lines. At five o'clock the Mexican troops retreated and for a while U.S. artillery continued to pound the troops and the guns of the San Patricio battery but at dark the battle ended—Taylor had won.[157]

While Taylor held the field, his losses were severe and were it not for the bravery of most of his officers and men, and his wonderfully effective artillery, the outcome could have been a disaster for his army. As it was, he lost 673 soldiers killed and wounded and some 1,500 to 1,800 of his army had fled to safety in the rear. Taylor ordered some of his best troops, Davis's Mississippi Regiment, back to Saltillo for rest replacing them at the front with fresh troops from there. He also called up the Kentucky Mounted Volunteers and four guns from Rinconada Pass in case Santa Anna decided to renew the fighting. Santa Anna probably lost some 1,800 killed and wounded with 294 captured, with about 4,000 of his men fleeing during the fighting. The Mexican commander knew that his troops could not fight another battle with Taylor so, soon after dark, marched south toward Agua Nueva. The next morning when the American troops could see that there was not going to be another battle but rather the Mexican army was gone, "A joyous murmur ran from group to group. Soon it was confirmed; it swelled to a shout; hard-featured, battle-worn men became boys again; and Taylor and Wool threw themselves, with moist eyes, into each other's arms." Taylor's adjutant, Major William Bliss, rode to Agua Nueva proposing an exchange of prisoners and an end of hostilities—Santa Anna demurred to the second proposal. But after Bliss returned, Santa Anna held a council of war and decided upon retreat which commenced on 26 February 1847. Taylor rested his army for three days but on the 27th he reoccupied Agua Nueva, then on 1 March, a detachment took La Encarnacion against no opposition. Taylor now found that his rear was threatened as Santa Anna's aggressive actions motivated Mexicans to attack the American army's long supply lines. Taylor returned to Monterrey to see what he could do to defend his lines of communication from bandits but had only limited success. Regardless, Americans cheered his victory over Santa Anna after most of his best troops were commandeered by Scott, and despite Polk's anger at disobeying orders not to journey further south than Monterrey, the Battle of Buena Vista ensured that Old Rough and Ready would be the next president of the United States.[158]

---

[157] Smith, *The War with Mexico*, 392-395; Lavender, *Climax at Buena Vista*, 196-197; Carleton, *The Battle of Buena Vista*, 119-123. The San Patricio Battery under its commander Captain John O'Reilly did good work for the Mexican Army during the battle suffering one third casualties and causing concern with its 16- and 24-pounder guns. Taylor, angry at the destructive fire of the deserter battery, pointed at the green flag and ordered Lieutenant Rucker of the 1st Dragoons to "Take that damned battery," but he failed, Samuel E. Chamberlain, *My Confession* (New York, NY: Harper and Brothers, 1956), 124.
[158] Smith, *The War with Mexico*, 397-400.

BATTLE OF BUENA VISTA
23 February 1847

Mexican Attack and Initial
American Reactions

NOTE: Following the defeat of Blanco's column,
Santa Anna made repeated efforts to turn
the American left. Although his cavalry
succeeded in this, its unwillingness to
charge home made it relatively harmless.
On the American side, the battle was won
by the courage and initiative of lower unit
commanders and the effectiveness and
mobility of the artillery.

SALTILLO

TAYLOR
(4,700)

BUENA VISTA

Miñon
(1,500)

Only a small part of these
two mounted regiments could
be rallied.

Miss.

May

2 Ky.

3 Ind.

LA ANGOSTURA

1 Ill. (-)

Ravines in this area had
sheer sides, 5 to 50 feet
high.

Texas

1 Dragoons

Blanco

2 Ill. (-)

Mejia

Ark. (-)

Pacheco

Ky.

2 Ind.

Ortega

Lombardini

Torrejon

Juvera

Riflemen

Andrade

Ampudia

SANTA ANNA
(15,000)

Remained in this
area throughout
battle.

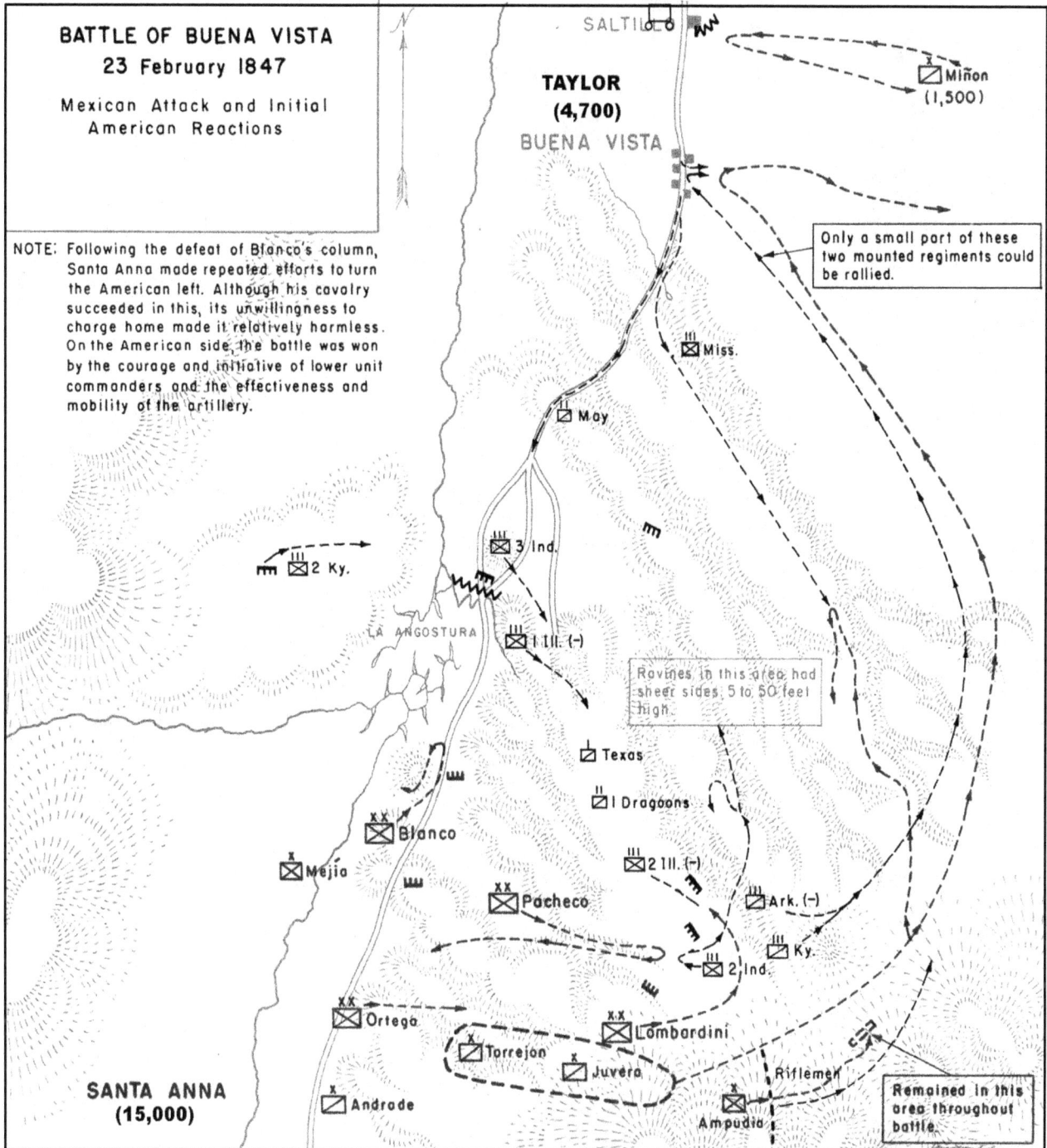

Battle map for 23 February 1847, the second day. Courtesy USMA from LOC.

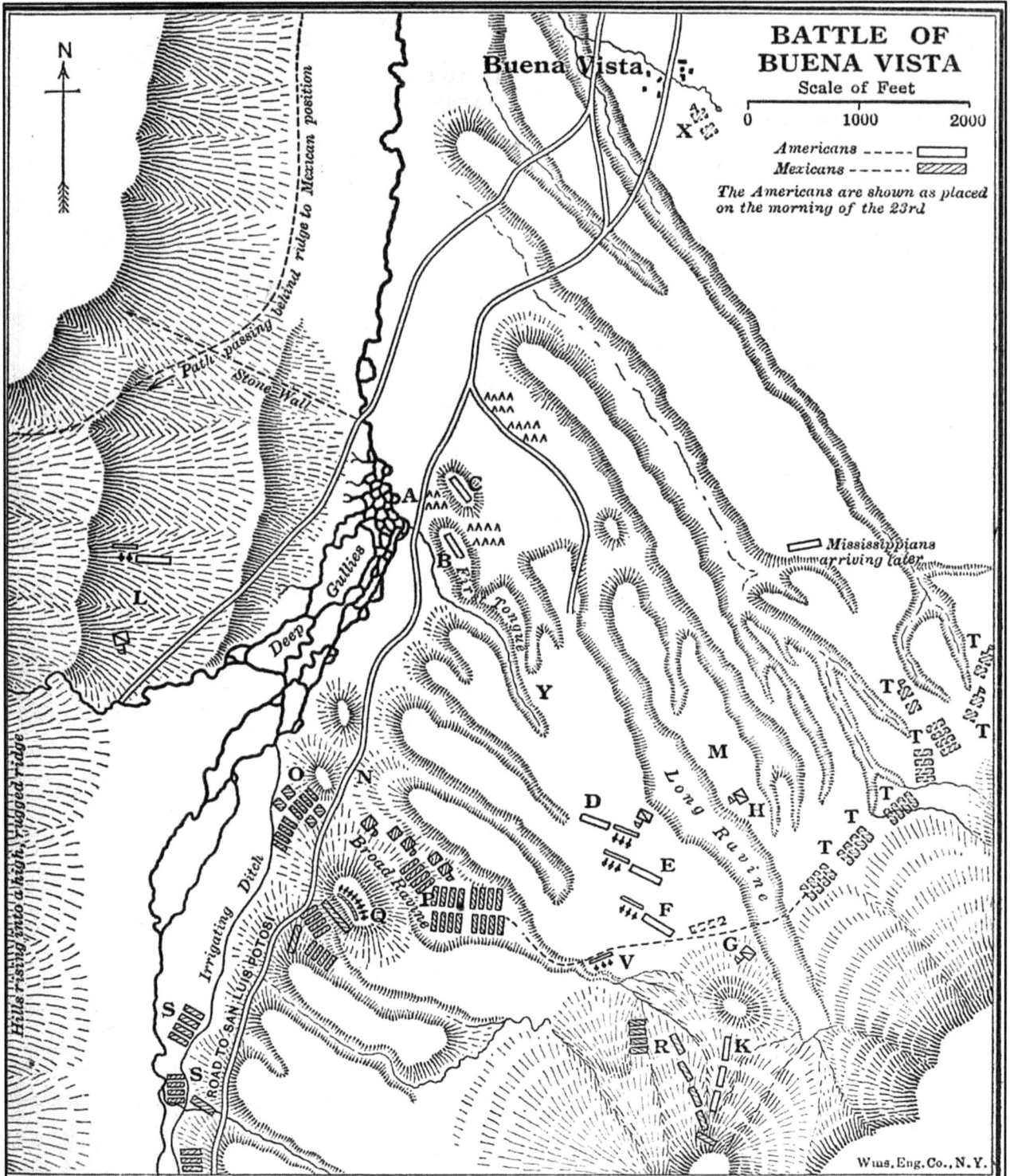

BATTLE OF
BUENA VISTA
Scale of Feet

The Americans are shown as placed
on the morning of the 23rd

A La Angostura, Washington's Battery and
   two companies 1st Illinois Vols.
B Six companies 1st Illinois Regt.
C 3rd Indiana Regt.
D 2nd Kentucky Regt. and Sherman's Battery (later position)
E 2nd Illinois Regt. and 1st Section Bragg's Battery
F 2nd Indiana Regt. and three pieces Washington's Battery
G Kentucky Horse Regt. and one squadron 2nd Dragoons
H Arkansas Horse Regt. and one squadron 1st Dragoons
K Dismounted Cavalry, etc.
L 2nd Kentucky Regt., Bragg's Artillery and
   detachment of Horse (early position)

M 2nd Indiana partly rallied here after retreating
N Heaviest Mexican cannon
O Blanco's Column
P Column to force American left
Q Battery
R Light Troops
S Reserve
T Columns turning American left
V Mexican Battery
X Cavalry from head of Column T, attacking Buena Vista
Y Taylor and Staff

Buena Vista battlefield with U.S. positions on the morning of 23 September 1847. Smith, *The War With Mexico*, 387.

Battle of Buena Vista on the second day showing General Taylor and his staff in the center foreground with guns under Captain O'Brien and Bragg rushing to hold off attacking Mexican Infantry, painting by Carl Nebel, courtesy LOC.

Print of the action on the 23rd looking south from the American side, based on sketch by Taylor's aide-de-camp, Major Eaton, courtesy LOC.

Mexican Lancers attacking U.S. infantry. During the battle, witnesses reported that surrendered and wounded Americans were often lanced. *Heroes of the War*, 59; David Lavender, *Climax at Buena Vista: The Decisive Battle of the Mexican-American War* (Philadelphia, PA: University of Pennsylvania Press, 2003), 210; Carleton, *The Battle of Buena Vista*, 111.

Wool, to whom Mansfield was attached, wrote to Taylor of the engineer's actions: "Though belonging to the staff of the major-general commanding, yet the very important and valuable services of Major Mansfield, to whom I am greatly indebted for the aid I received from his untiring exertions, activity, and extensive information, as well as for his gallant bearing during the days and nights of the 21st, 22nd, 23rd and 24th, give me the privilege of expressing to the commanding general my entire admiration of this accomplished officer's conduct."[159] Taylor commended Mansfield for Buena Vista and had him brevetted colonel for his actions: "Major Mansfield was employed before and during the engagement in making reconnaissances, and on the field was very active in bringing information and in conveying my orders to different points." The Dragoon Carleton was effusive in praising Mansfield: "The services, during the battle, of Major Mansfield, of the Corps of Engineers, were just such as would be expected from an officer who enjoys the reputation throughout the army of being qualified in every respect to command a hundred thousand men." He also praised Lieutenant Benham among many other officers: "Lieutenant Benham, of the same corps, was always in advanced positions, and consequently always in danger. He performed his duties with great credit, and had the honor to be wounded."[160]

Lieutenant Henry W. Benham was Mansfield's assistant and was brevetted to captain for his actions but unlike Mansfield, was wounded at Buena Vista. Some 25 years later, he wrote a 27 page article about his experiences at the battle from which the following excerpts are taken:

> I reached the head-quarter camp at Agua Nueva [20 miles south of Saltillo] in the first week in February, and joined the staff as the assistant to the other military engineer, Bvt. Major Mansfield....On the morning of the 22nd February....[Taylor] desired the engineers [Mansfield and Benham] to go both together (remarking, 'two heads were better than one') to Wool's camp, and call for Rucker's squadron of Dragoons...and that they should then proceed to reconnoitre the passes south of our late camp, towards Encarnacion. That journey we were saved...for starting from camp from half-past seven to eight, A.M., Major Mansfield and myself rode leisurely along, reconnoitring, taking the bearings, etc., and sketching the obstacles, cross-gullies, and hills on our route, till, on nearing the hacienda of Buena Vista [five miles south of Saltillo], about nine, A.M., we met a dragoon on a gallop with dispatches in hand, who called out to us, 'The enemy are in sight.' We sprung our horses forward by the side of

---

[159] *The Mexican War and Its Heroes*, 155.

[160] Ibid., 258. Note that Mansfield was brevetted to lieutenant colonel for Monterrey in May 1847.

Wool's camp on our left, then aroused and in great alarm....we were brought up at about 800 yards farther by finding some 1,800 of the Mexican cavalry already up, and forming a line to their right, within a half mile of us.

I would say now, that we were perfectly astonished that such a body of troops could have approached so near without our men being in a position to meet them; and we were surprised that the news should have been dispatched to General Taylor, as we personally witnessed, only some fifteen minutes previously.[161]

Benham opined that had the Mexican cavalry commander not hesitated but attacked Wool's camp, they would have slaughtered the unprepared American volunteers and then galloped on to do the same to the remainder of the American forces at Saltillo. Benham then described in detail the broken terrain on which the battle would take place and the positioning of U.S. forces. He also thought that the high altitude, some 6,000 feet, made exertion difficult, as well as that the clear air distorted estimation of distance:

[On the 22nd] Major Mansfield gave me his directions to remain there, [on a high ridge on the American right flank] and report to the general in the rear the numbers and kinds of troops of the enemy, as they came up and formed in front; adding personal requests, in case he fell, even showing me the peculiarities of his teeth to recognize him even in decay, as he stated, for he seemed to have anticipated the death upon the battle-field which fell to his lot some fifteen years later. He then mounted and rode to the rear to assist in organizing and arranging the troops to meet the attack. I remained at that position until nightfall, with a small infantry picket, and counted the regiments as they came up as far as possible, and the pieces of artillery, etc., and sent the news in by Dragoons....some 40 pieces of artillery were reported, with some eighteen to twenty bodies of infantry, mostly regiments, and sixteen regiments of brilliantly uniformed cavalry, drawn up in two lines on dress parade that afternoon.[162]

After detailing the Mexican forces and bemoaning the apparently overmatched numbers of U.S. forces including some poorly disciplined American volunteers, he related a story Mansfield told him about controlling raw troops newly under fire:

[There is] little danger from the fire of artillery, if you watch the pieces and have cover; an incident precisely such as occurred to Major Mansfield at the Battle of Monterrey, which he had told but a day or two before. While there with his glass, reconnoitring the 'Black Fort' near that city, with a picket of Texans to guard him, he looked, as he said, 'directly into the muzzles of three guns' pointed at him, and ordered his party to keep down, or leave him, that they might not draw this fire. As they did not heed him in their anxiety to see what was going on, he found a little hollow he could drop into, and continued his observations; until his party at length brought upon them the fire of each of these three guns in succession; the major dropping under cover each time and immediately rising. After this, he was left unmolested, while he found his guard more obedient. Precisely the same thing occurred at this lookout on the afternoon of the 22nd.[163]

Benham ended his recount of the actions on the 22nd by making a comment probably about Mansfield although he did not write his name: "A proposition was made by an engineer officer who knew the ground, through General Wool to General Taylor, for a night attack, with the offer to guide it from our front, along the road, 'after midnight and the setting of the moon;' but he declined, from the fear of the confusion incident to such assaults in the darkness." Benham and Mansfield were the only two engineers in the vicinity and Benham was on his ridge so Mansfield was the one who made the suggestion not acted on by Taylor." Certainly Mansfield did not lack for aggression and willingness to lead an attack.[164]

---

[161] Henry W. Benham, "Recollections of Mexico and the Battle of Buena Vista, Feb. 22 and 23, 1847," in *Old and New*, June and July, 1871 (Boston, MA), 1-27, passim.

[162] Ibid.

[163] Ibid.

[164] Benham, 1-27, passim. Mansfield was scouting for Worth as Brooks wrote of one such incident: "Major Mansfield, of the engineers, about nine o'clock came with the intelligence that Pacheco's division, which had moved along screened from sight, was coming up the ravine with the evident design of gaining the plateau by way of the ridge adjoining the third principal gorge, which scalloped the plateau. At this time General Wool was at La Angostura, having gone thither to give some directions about the defences in that quarter. General Lane, therefore, the next in command, ordered Lieutenant O'Brien, with his three pieces of artillery, and the 2nd Indiana regiment, to take position just beyond the head of the third gorge, and repel the enemy," N.C. Brooks, 214. Compare this account with Lavender: "Brevet Major Joseph Mansfield of the engineers galloped up to the headquarters marquee on the northwest corner of the plateau with word that Pacheco's division was massing in the upper ravine, ready to charge against the left. Wool sent Inspector General Sylvester Churchill to warn Gen. Lane, who was busy watching Ampudia on the mountain and Lombardini across the ravine....He then sent Mansfield riding wildly across the gullies to McKee with orders to bring his Kentuckians to the plateau and help Bissell. Though no specific orders went to Braxton Bragg, stationed on the right with McKee, he and Mansfield decided that Bragg should bring his guns into the fray,

Benham, the next day at about 7 a.m., saw General Santa Anna and his staff some 400 yards away: "I noticed their horses, with their showy trappings, and several large and beautiful greyhounds gamboling round them." Then the enemy infantry columns marched to the attack after an ineffectual artillery barrage while Benham rode to join General Taylor to report the Mexican movements. Benham saw Washington's Battery stop the enemy attack adding "That the horse of Santa Anna was killed under him in this charge." He met Taylor and his staff as they rode up from Saltillo "when Captain Bragg rode up with the exclamation, 'General, they are too strong for me, they are six pieces to my two!' Upon this General Taylor authorized him to withdraw to a safer place. As he turned to join his battery he saw me, and, grasping my hand, cried out,' I give you joy. I shed a tear for you just now. I thought I saw you dead.'" Taylor had apparently just seen Captain [George] Lincoln killed and thought it was Benham.[165]

After discussing the battle, and two instances of volunteers not doing as well as Taylor expected, Benham wrote about a controversy and how Mansfield counselled restraint. The controversy revolved around who gave the order for the final charge which proved to be a near disaster for American troops. Taylor and other commanders saw an apparent withdrawal by Mexican troops so a charge was ordered, likely by Taylor. The American charge was made by Harden's and Bissell's Illinois Regiments and McKee's Kentucky Regiment, about 1,500 men according to Benham. They were supported by three of Captain O'Brien's guns. These troops were not aware of some five to seven thousand Mexican troops who appeared to come up out of the ground from a defilade less than 80 yards away and flanked the American attackers. The surprised U.S. troops fled with the Mexicans in hot pursuit; the Americans ran into a large force of Mexican lancers and the slaughter began. Lancers and Mexican infantry shot or lanced wounded and surrendering Americans. Fortunately the batteries of Bragg and Sherman came up and helped save some of the fleeing Americans. It was at this time that the famous remark supposedly made by Taylor to Bragg—"A little more grape, Captain Bragg" was born but Benham wrote that it was more likely "Give 'em hell, Bragg" after Bragg told Taylor that "I have no support; they will take my pieces." Taylor replied "They will take them anyhow, fire away." Bragg's and Sherman's relentless and accurate fire saved the day for Taylor preventing further penetration by the Mexican troops and more slaughter of Americans. Hard fighting by Colonel Davis and his Mississippi Regiment also greatly contributed to the stopping of the Mexicans. Taylor denied giving the order for the fatal charge but Captain Robert H. Chilton of the 1st Dragoons who was an extra aide to Taylor and the one who gave it said, and Mansfield agreed, that Taylor ordered it. Benton wrote that "The careful major [Mansfield] cautioned him [Chilton], as a young captain, not to insist upon this against the General's denial. I cannot doubt that the good old General did really issue this order while in the excitement of the moment; possibly it did not rest upon his mind; it was an order that, but for the opportune arrival of our artillery, would have insured our destruction. Mansfield urged Chilton not to insist upon this against Taylor's denial.[166]

As the fighting seemed to be winding down, Benham and others saw a Mexican heavy battery and a few thousand infantry which appeared to be preparing for an attack which could have been devastating given the condition of the American lines. Benham gathered up some broken troops to defend against this but fortunately the Mexican force did not attack. During this time Wool desired to break up this possible Mexican move so he ordered May and "his Dragoons and the spy company, some two hundred and thirty in all, to attack that heavy force, when Mansfield rushed up to him, and urged him to revoke the order, 'if he would not destroy us, as we had no support for such a charge, if they were driven back.' The general then countermanded it." Again there was controversy about this order but the bearer of the order, Addicks told that he delivered it and Benham heard Wool tell Jefferson Davis who was wounded in hospital that he had given it. "I told the actual facts to Davis soon after, receiving a caution as to the impolicy of truth-telling always. And a former Texan surgeon, Irvine, in the spy company, told me that he heard it delivered, and that, turning to his companions, he said, 'Goodbye boys,' with the feeling that this was to be the last of all of them."[167]

---

although this meant a long detour to find a spot where he could take his caissons across the gullies," David Lavender, *Climax at Buena Vista: The Decisive Battle of the Mexican-American War* (Philadelphia, PA: University of Pennsylvania Press, 2003), 189. Note that O'Brien was a captain assistant quartermaster 18 Jan. 1847, and received a brevet to major for Buena Vista.

[165] Benham, 14, 23.

[166] Henry W. Benham, "Recollections of Mexico and the Battle of Buena Vista, Feb. 22 and 23, 1847," in *Old and New*, June and July, 1871(Boston, MA), 24; Lavender, 210; Carleton, *The Battle of Buena Vista*, 111. There are several versions of the Bragg/Taylor exchange (if there was one), another popular one has Taylor asking Bragg "What are you using, Captain, grape or canister? Canister, General. Single or double? Single. Well, double shot your guns and give 'em hell;" Bauer, *Zachary Taylor*, 204-205. Chilton was an 1837 West Point graduate who was brevetted to major for Buena Vista. He resigned in 1861 and became a Confederate brigadier general; he died in 1879.

[167] Benham, 24. Addicks was likely Mr. Thomas H. Addicks from San Antonio, Texas, a civilian and former Texan officer who served Taylor as an interpreter. Irvine may be James Thomas Patton Irvine or Josephus Somerville Irvine.

A few days after the battle, Mansfield wrote his wife on the 26th from the camp at Saltillo and gave her a summary of Buena Vista. He told her that he has "come safely out of a tremendous battle. The greatest ever fought in America in my opinion. We have whipped Santa Anna with an army of 20,000 men, whereas our force all told amounted to only 5,000. All volunteers except 4 companies of artillery, 4 companies of Dragoons and the commanding officers and staff of the army. The volunteers fought generally like blood hounds." As Santa Anna threatened the Americans at several locations at some distance, the Saltillo camp broke up at 12 o'clock on the 20th into the mountain passes. Wool established himself at Buena Vista 6 miles from Saltillo while Taylor remained at his headquarters at Saltillo where they made a redoubt to command the city. On the morning of the 21st, the engineers were all ordered to reconnoiter. Mansfield "with Lieutenant Benham proceeded to General Wool's camp and were to reconnoiter the strange positions at that place and for 5 miles in his advance but we had hardly reached the camp when notified the enemy were advancing in force close upon us. General Wool then requested me ride in advance and reconnoiter…and my noble horse soon carried me in advance to a table land on slope of the mountain from which I could see the strength of the enemy and the positions he took up. All day both parties were preparing for the struggle. And about 8 o'clock of the morning of the 22nd was commenced a terrible battle that lasted till dark." The Mexican army was forced to fight on a table land as American artillery had the road covered. Enemy forces were routed with American units chasing down pieces of the enemy in ravines and gullies. He wrote that "There were no mistakes made and the battle raged all day till dark….The enemy must have lost at least 3,000 killed and wounded. Our killed I suppose may not much exceed 200 and our wounded about 450….General Taylor's clothes were cut into rags but he was not wounded nor am I. We have lost valuable officers….In the night, Santa Anna retreated to Aqua Nueva and we were truly glad of it in our fatigue and worn out condition."[168]

About two months later, Mansfield wrote a more detailed letter to an unknown officer friend which did become public when it was published in the Niles National Register:

BATTLE OF BUENA VISTA

Through the kindness of a friend, we have been furnished with the following extracts from a private letter written by Lieutenant Colonel Mansfield, of the corps of engineers to a brother officer in this city, giving a brief and hastily written description of the 22nd and 23rd of February.

Eighteen miles south of Saltillo, at camp U.S. army, Agua Nueva, March 1, 1847.

Dear Captain-We are just recovering from the fatigues of a tremendous battle, fought by this little army on the 22nd and 23rd at Buena Vista, a place about eleven miles in our rear and seven miles this side of Saltillo.

We had previously been on this very ground from the 6th to the 20th February, reconnoitring the positions, roads, and &c. and ascertaining where the enemy was, and his numbers. We found Santa Anna was at Encarnacion, thirty miles in our advance, with twenty thousand troops of infantry and artillery, and that on our left was General Minon, at Matehula, say twenty five miles off, with three thousand cavalry and lancers.

On the 21st at noon, we broke up our camp, and fell back to a good position at Buena Vista, to await the enemy. On the 22nd he came in sight-his advance a heavy body of lancers and cavalry, followed by large bodies of infantry, and about eighteen pieces of artillery. A skirmish took place in the afternoon and the enemy gained the mountain side on our left. On our right of the road commenced steep ascents to the tops of the spurs of the mountain, which united and formed a beautiful table land for a battle ground, say one mile east and west by half a mile north and south. There were other spurs on the same side, stretching along the road north and south of us, with deep gullies between, many of them impassable, but none of them forming a table land like this.

A ditch and parapet were immediately thrown across the road, and Washington's artillery placed there, supported by two companies of volunteers behind another parapet.

On the morning of the 23rd the enemy made a rush with his infantry and lancers to possess the table land, the key to the whole position; and at the same time a column of infantry and cavalry advanced on the road towards Washington's battery. A

---

[168] Letter 26 February 1847 courtesy WPL. Other less florid reports state that Taylor had only a few holes in his clothing. Note that he was very politic with his wife in case his "private" letter to her reached other eyes as mistakes were in fact made as Benham related, and about 1,500 or more volunteers fled. Louisa evidently wrote Mansfield that she hoped he would be able to visit home in the spring; he wished for the same as he was "sick of the scene of blood--the dead—and the dying—with the first opportunity I hope to leave and my I never witness another battle or be instrumental in one. Honors to me are empty and I look on them with indifference. All I ask is a fair name without spot or blemish." He continues that if he deserves a brevet for Monterrey, he deserves one more for Buena Vista since he "had more to do with the success of this than either of the others [Monterrey and Fort Brown]. And I feel more satisfaction with myself for it. It was a hard day for us all but a glorious one to the little army that beat back four times its own numbers." Letter courtesy of the Middlesex County Historical Society.

terrible fight ensued. Our left was forced back off the table land, and rallied under the bank; but our centre charged with a tremendous fire of horse artillery, (eight pieces) and volunteers, and hurled them back against the mountain and broke their centre, so that large bodies of infantry saved themselves by moving into the ravines and on the spurs of the mountains to the rear of our left where we sent regiments and artillery to fight them and drive them back across the same ground on our extreme left over which they had been forced. If we had had but one single full regiment of regulars in reserve we could have charged their battery on our extreme left and taken four or five thousand prisoners. As it was, we could only hold our own against such odds.

At the close of the day, they made another charge and rush, in great force, to possess the table land and were again repulsed with great slaughter, and with much loss on our part. Night put an end to the scene, and under the cover of darkness the enemy retreated to this place, (Agua Nueva), where our light troops followed them the next morning.

It was a beautiful battle-not a mistake made the whole day; but every man perfectly exhausted at night. Our loss about 264 killed and 450 wounded. The enemy's loss about 2,500 killed and wounded, and 3,000 missing.

It is said that Santa Anna is in full retreat to Salado and San Luis [Potosi], with his army dispirited and disorganized. He is said to have lost many officers of high rank. You will in due time get correct accounts. Nothing could exceed the gallant bearing of our horse artillery and Dragoons, nor the bravery and good conduct of the volunteers as a body. Not a regular infantry soldier was in this fight.

We have lost most valuable officers. Captain [George] Lincoln was killed in the first charge. Colonel [William R.] McKee and Lieut. Colonel [Henry] Clay, of the Kentucky regiment, and Colonel [John J.] Hardin were killed, besides others, in the second charge of the enemy. We lost three pieces of cannon, which we had not the men to recover. Our men actually sunk to the ground from excessive exhaustion.

It has ever been the misfortune of our brave old General to be obliged to fight the enemy with inferior numbers. This, his last battle, has done him more credit than any of his previous ones. His case was not so desperate at Palo Alto, for there he had the best of regular infantry.

I had almost forgotten to speak of our corps. We endeavored to do our duty. Lieut. Benham behaved well, and was slightly wounded. As for myself, I was more fortunate than at Monterrey, and escaped unhurt. The old General, however, was made ragged by the balls passing through his clothes.

Yours &c.
JOS. K. F. MANSFIELD[169]

Wool described the forces involved at Buena Vista: "The United States troops, commanded by Major-General Taylor, amounted to only four thousand six hundred and ten, including officers. The forces under the command of General Santa Anna amounted to twenty-two thousand. Some of the Mexican officers taken prisoners stated the number to be twenty-four thousand, exclusive of artillery. This number, I presume, included General Minon's cavalry, reported to be from two to three thousand. The army is represented to be in a disorganized state, and that the losses in killed and wounded, and by desertion, exceed six thousand men. The dead, the dying, and the wounded in a starving condition, everywhere to be seen on its route, bespeak a hurried retreat and extreme distress."[170] Taylor in his official report wrote that "the American force upon the field numbered 4,425 bayonets and sabers, exclusive of officers, and fifteen light field guns. In the achievement of the victory and the effects which have been narrated, the loss was 267 killed, 456 wounded, 23 missing, and three [of our] guns captured."[171]

Historian Smith found that Taylor substantially contributed to the winning of the battle while having little to do directing it since Wool was in command:

It was an extraordinary battle. On the part of the Americans it began in flight and ended in success. Marred by mistakes and failures, it exhibited even more strikingly both skill and moral grandeur. Taylor seems to have had but little to do with directing it, and that little seems to have been poor work; but he did more than engineer success he created it. Huddled rather than mounted, a great part of the time, on Old Whitey, with arms folded and one leg unconcernedly thrown across the pommel of his saddle, the conspicuous target of the Mexican artillery yet utterly unmoved even when his clothes were pierced, he was a fountain of courage and energy. In other words, the victory of Buena Vista was due primarily to Taylor's prestige, valor and gift

[169] Niles' National Register, NNR 72.099-100, April 17, 1847; Mansfield's account of the Battle of Buena Vista. Captain (Bvt. Maj./Bvt. Lt. Col.) George A. McCall had received letters from Mansfield previously so this may have been written to him, but at this time McCall was not nor had ever been in the Engineer Department, so when Mansfield wrote "our corps" McCall could not be the recipient unless Mansfield meant "our West Point Corps." At the time of this letter he was an assistant adjutant general to Taylor. He was in Mansfield's West Point class of 1822; George Archibald McCall, *Letters from the Frontiers* (Philadelphia, PA: J.B. Lippincott & Co., 1868), 465-466. McCall was an Inspector General from 10 June 1850 to 29 April 1853.
[170] *The Mexican War and Its Heros*, 156.
[171] Ripley, *The War With Mexico*, 427.

of inspiring confidence.... Wool, who commanded on our left, played the role of the fearless professional soldier that he was. Many other officers and certain corps exhibited a heroism of the noblest quality. Our artillery was beyond praise for both daring and skill. As Wool said in his report, the army could not have stood for "a single hour" without it; and the batteries served indispensably, moreover, as rallying-points for the infantry. The lancers, cantering over the plain and finishing the American wounded, gave great assistance by exasperating and warning our men.[172]

The Mexican Army began its retreat during the night of the 23rd so it was not in sight on the morning of the 24th as American scouts pushed forward. Taylor with Wool and his staff rode forward to La Encantada with a dragoon escort where Taylor sent Major Bliss to Agua Nueva with a proposal to exchange prisoners. Prisoners were exchanged including those Santa Anna took at Encarnacion and Palomas Pass.

On the 27th, General Taylor moved his force again in advance to Agua Nueva. The road from Buena Vista to that point was strewed with dead and dying Mexicans, and numerous wounded were found in the ruins of the hacienda. These, as well as those left upon the battlefield, were transported to Saltillo and treated by American surgeons. Nothing prevented General Taylor from beating up Santa Anna's headquarters on the morning of the 27th but the jaded state of the dragoon horses, and the want of water on the route. But, having cared for the wounded, on the 1st of March he dispatched Colonel Belknap, with all the cavalry, two pieces of artillery, and a regiment of infantry, in wagons, to Encarnacion, for the purpose of cutting up the Mexican rear guard, reported as being still at that point. The command left Agua Nueva at three o'clock in the afternoon, and made the distance in the night. The same appearances of hurried and disordered retreat were visible which had been met with on the route to Agua Nueva. Multitudes of dead and dying, from wounds, fatigue, and hunger, encumbered the road; and, upon arriving at Encarnacion, that hacienda was found unoccupied, except by a small party of the enemy, and 220 wounded men in an almost utter state of destitution. The party of Mexican cavalry endeavored to escape, but were all captured and made prisoners. Belknap returned to Agua Nueva on the afternoon of the 2nd; and, having informed General Taylor of the state of the Mexican wounded, with characteristic humanity, he sent thither a quantity of provision, and caused such as could be transported to be moved to Saltillo.[173]

But after the battle, Taylor's forces encountered trouble further north. Mexican cavalry, irregulars, and rancheros successfully attacked wagon trains. "Mexican generals [Jose] Urrea and [Manuel] Romero, with their corps of cavalry, reached the American line of communications through the Tula pass, Victoria, and Montemorelos." On 24 February, the Mexican guerilla leader Urrea "made his appearance near Ramos, and cut up an upward-bound train, killed some forty or fifty wagoners, captured the weak escort, and in the afternoon appeared before Marin, where his troops skirmished with the American garrison." Further Mexican Army and guerilla activities occurred behind Taylor:

A detachment from Monterrey having arrived and re-enforced the garrison [at Marin], Lieutenant-colonel [William] Irvin abandoned Marin, and marched on the 25th, without further communication with [Colonel George W.] Morgan, who arrived the same afternoon, and quartered for the night in the town. Irvin continued his march without interruption, but on the following morning Morgan fell in with Urrea at Agua Frio. A continual skirmish ensued for some miles along the road, as far as San Francisco. The Mexican cavalry hovered about the column, threatening an attack for the whole distance. To oppose it, Morgan disposed his troops in square, with his wagons in the center, and in this order, without a close encounter with the enemy, he reached San Francisco. From that point he sent forward an officer to communicate with Irvin, who was by this time near Monterrey. Irvin returned with two field pieces, which, when he came in sight of the enemy, then in advance of Morgan's position, were at once opened, and the Mexican cavalry fell back immediately to the rear. Immediately after, a heavy fire of escopetas [muskets] was opened upon Morgan's command, which killed one captain and four soldiers and wagoners. Irvin's troops were then moved to the right, and, from a general discharge from the whole force, Urrea fled. The column continued its march to Monterrey without molestation.

On the 7th of March Urrea was at Cerralvo, and near that place fell upon an empty train of one hundred and fifty wagons, which had been sent to the rear immediately after the battle of Buena Vista, under the escort of six companies of infantry and two guns, commanded by Major [Luther] Giddings. Urrea's force at once attacked it, killed two privates, cut the train, burned forty wagons, killed fifteen teamsters, and, having surrounded the rear guard some two miles from the advance, he summoned it to surrender; but the captain in command was, singularly enough, allowed an hour to communicate with his chief in the advance. The reply was, of course, a refusal, and immediately after it had been dispatched a re-enforcement was sent to the rear.

---

[172] Smith, *The War With Mexico*, 395-396. Smith noted Taylor's losses and the rout of some volunteers: "In killed and wounded Taylor had lost 673 officers and men, and in spite of his personal influence 1,500 or 1,800 appear to have quit the field," 396. Smith also noted Santa Anna's losses: "Probably not less than 1,800 of his men had been killed or wounded; 294 had been captured ; and he was probably not far from the mark when he said that more than 4,000 had left him during the battle," 397.

[173] Ripley, *The War With Mexico*, 423-427.

The Mexicans gave up the attempt to consummate their success and enforce the summons. The whole command, with the remaining wagons, was concentrated in the advance, and on the following morning entered Cerralvo without opposition. There it met an advancing convoy, from which it was supplied with ammunition, and proceeded on to Camargo.[174]

Taylor had to stop these depredations of his supply trains and reopen his lines of communication. On 8 March he departed Saltillo with cavalry and light artillery and on the 15th, sent Colonel Marshall and his Kentucky cavalry and an artillery piece on the road to Marin. On his way, Marshall heard of "Urrea in the vicinity of Marin, near Curtis's convoy, Marshall joined with his escort, and, as Urrea fell back before his advance, effected a junction with Curtis, who was sent to Monterrey. Taylor, with the cavalry and artillery, pushed on after the enemy, who fled before him to Montemorelos, and thence to Victoria, through the pass of Tula, and out of the valley of the Rio Grande....Communications being thus re-established, operations upon the northern line were thenceforth confined to simple occupation, and active war in that quarter was at an end."[175]

The Battle of Buena Vista won for Taylor the admiration of the American public even though he disobeyed orders Scott and Polk had given him to not venture further south from Monterrey. Before the public heard of Taylor's victory, it was informed that Taylor's army was surrounded and destroyed near Saltillo. An Ohio volunteer colonel at Camargo, Colonel Samuel Ryan Curtis, in March, urgently requested 50,000 more troops to retake the Rio Grande Valley from Mexican forces so when the joyous news of Taylor's victory at Buena Vista against Santa Anna's overwhelming odds Taylor's fame was assured. "The tidings of his failure, exaggerated of course into news of a brilliant and overwhelming triumph won by a general robbed of his troops, caused a tremendous rebound. Polk, holding that only Taylor's blundering and violation of orders had created the peril, and that his brave men had rescued him from it, would not permit a general salute in the army; but the nation saluted, and the General's nomination for the Presidency became inevitable."[176]

Taylor had already given up most of his regulars to Scott and now the 12-month terms of enlistment for many of his volunteer units were expiring. By summer he gained some new regular units: five companies of the 3rd Dragoons, under Colonel Edward G.W. Butler; 10th Regiment of Infantry, Colonel Robert E. Temple; 13th Regiment of Infantry, Colonel Robert M. Echols; 16th Regiment of Infantry, Colonel John W. Tibbatts. Taylor added newly raised volunteer units to his roster: one regiment of infantry from Indiana, and one from Ohio; one battalion (five companies) from New Jersey; one battalion of five companies from Delaware and Maryland; one battalion of five companies from Alabama; one company of foot from Florida; four companies of horse from Illinois, Ohio, and Alabama; two companies of foot from Virginia, and one from North Carolina. These, with the addition of the Massachusetts, North Carolina, Mississippi, Virginia, and Texas regiments, were presumed to have given General Taylor a force of ten thousand men. "When the new levies shall have all reported, deducting for contingencies, his force will probably amount to eight thousand. The volunteer regiments were pressed forward to relieve those whose term of service had nearly expired. A camp of instruction was formed at Mier for the new levies, under the command of General Enos D. Hopping."[177] Both regular and volunteer units were slow to arrive as Taylor wrote in a letter to his friend, Dr. R.C. Wood on 20 July 1847: "I understand from private letters received here that a battalion called out from Alabama could not be raised which was to form part of my command nor have I heard anything from the Jersey & Maryland Battalions which were to form a portion of my forces also; nor do we know here what progress has or is making to fill the ranks of one of the new regiments the 13 which has been assigned to me. I am however making every arrangement for a forward movement, & shall advance on San Luis Potosi as soon as all the reinforcement expected reach the country, unless otherwise directed."[178] In his remaining letters while in Mexico, Taylor did not again discuss manpower problems so given that he was not campaigning but rather only manning strong points along the coast and the Rio Grande as well as maintaining his lines of communication, the strength of his army was adequate.

Mansfield remained with Taylor in or near Monterrey, primarily in the army camp at Walnut Springs, until they both left for the United States in the fall of 1847. As Mansfield had fewer duties to perform because Taylor and his army were stationary, he was able to write home regularly with most letters sent to his wife, Louisa. As usual, he was full of

---

[174] Ripley, *The War With Mexico*, 429-430. The supply train attack at Ramos became known as the "Ramos Massacre."

[175] Ibid, 430.

[176] Ripley, *The War With Mexico*, 431; Smith, *The War With Mexico*, 399-400.

[177] Henry, *Campaign Sketches of the War With Mexico*, 329-330. Hopping died 1 Sept. 1847.

[178] Zachary Taylor, *Letters of Zachary Taylor from the Battlefields of the Mexican War*, ed. William K. Bixby (Rochester, NY: The Genesee Press, 1908), 119. Dr. Robert Crooke Wood was a U.S. Army surgeon and a son-in-law to Taylor having married his daughter, Ann Mackall.

advice, counsel and criticism for his wife and children but as will be seen, his wife eventually had enough of his "advice" so he tempered it somewhat after she spoke up. His letters will be summarized and divided generally into martial and nonmartial topics. Not surprisingly, with little to occupy his time, Mansfield had thoughts of home and ruminated on his life and army career. Not being a drinker or one enamored of parties, time passed slowly for him. He freely commented on the activities of fellow officers who engaged in what he deemed unacceptable behavior with "ladies" or with alcohol. He also reminded his wife about what he considered proper conduct for her and his children, evidently he heard of a single gentleman who called on her unchaperoned? Finances were always a concern. He certainly appears to be a frugal New Englander but when he was promoted from captain to colonel in 1853 as an inspector general, his financial worries lessened. But now, his salary and income from business investments were barely enough to keep him and his family in a relatively comfortable life. These letters and those already seen reveal his personality traits and social status providing a window into his worldview.[179]

In his 1 March 1847 letter to Louisa from Monterrey, Mansfield included praise for his son, Samuel, for including comments in his mother's letters and that he has heard such good things about him. He assures him of his love however, he gave a stern warning: "I could never love you if I thought you told any untruth and did not mind your mother." Mansfield said that he wanted him to take care of his sister Mary and his brother Henry and asked him also to plant a little garden and show him the flowers when he returned home. He sent his love in his 4 April letter for his family and wrote that his "greatest wish and desire now is to join you my family as soon as this unfortunate war will admit."[180]

Food, medicine, health and weather are frequent topics in his letters. Corn and onions are abundant as is grass but everything else must come from the U.S. and therefore is expensive. In a July letter, he praised plain and simple food but not too much milk, as it is not healthy and too costly. Note in his earlier letters he extolled the virtues of milk so perhaps it is just milk in excess especially if it is expensive which evokes mention. He added that "if the children don't like plain food let them go hungry until they do. A cold potato soup and a crust of bread will not hurt them." He related that his expenses are $50-$60 dollars month. In his 25 April 1847 missive he is happy with the spring weather and his situation and hopes for a healthy summer. He did not describe in detail the delightful camp at Walnut Grove perhaps wishing to downplay its charming sylvan character. He described some troops who are fond of spirits but wrote that "For myself I drink claret and water, and lemon syrup and water, and have as heretofore set my face against all strong liquors." He was not a teetotaler but there is never any record or report of him being fond of alcohol or being drunk. He described some volunteer officers from Kentucky who appeared to love their drinks and he opined with tongue in cheek that "Kentucky is a great state for whiskey drinkers. It is wonderful our old Genl. [Taylor] happens to be a sober man from that state." He told of a promising young 1st Mississippi Volunteer officer who was half drunk and resisted the guard in the city. He was shot and his leg amputated. He not only holds John Barleycorn evil but also finds the troops are involved in all "species of vice" although he does not go into detail perhaps to spare his wife further description of "this disgusting subject." He apparently is referring to "ladies of the night" plying their trade in Monterrey. Mansfield continued his study of Spanish but finds few with whom to converse except in the shops in town. He had to increase his servant's wages to $25 and hopes Ormsby will remain with him as long as he remains in the country. He has had to spend monies on uniforms and also a better horse but he entreats his wife to "live plain and have no rich food given to our children as it is the worst thing you can do for them. It will heat up the blood and gives an artificial taste that will terminate in high living and dissipation as they grow up." Mansfield is ever the Puritan it seems. But as he closed his

179 Virtually all of Mansfield's letters are written to his wife, Louisa, and most are copies of his original letters. The author's research at the West Point Research Library and the Middlesex County Historical Society revealed few original letters—those with his seal. Apparently he kept copies of most letters he wrote while replies to his letters are missing. As will be seen in later chapters of this book, when his children grew older, he wrote to them directly. Underlining is as found in Mansfield's letters. Mansfield's worldview is mostly similar to other white, middleclass, native-born Americans: "'racist,' 'sexist,' 'anti-Catholic,' and 'nativist,'" so when judged by 21st Century standards he, and others of his status and class, would not be considered politically correct; William H. Goetzmann's Forward to Samuel Chamberlain's *My Confession: Recollections of a Rogue* (Austin, TX: Texas State Historical Assoc., 1996), ix. In his 28 February 1847 letter Mansfield wrote much to Louisa about finances: "I am sorry you are out of money but I have sent you letters enough with orders for money, beside some to pay up my mortgage." He describes the dividends he receives for his East Boston property if he ever decides to sell them he wrote that they will be worth "thousands." But Mansfield does not want to buy any more East Boston stock but rather pay off his mortgage on the Smith house. He states that he will have nothing to do with his sister's debts and neither should Louisa but if he dies, Louisa "should pay all those debts and give his sister the annuity he has designated in his will;" letter 28 February 1847 courtesy of the Middlesex County Historical Society.

180 1 March and 4 April 1847 letters to Louisa, courtesy WPL. Mansfield's Puritan bent was recognized in his eulogy: "It has been said he was of the Puritan stock. Nothing is more true. All the elements and unfoldings of his being evinced him to be worthy of such a lineage. Had he lived in England in the days of the protectorate, the Puritan cause would have had no firmer friend; its great leader no braver soldier"; H. Mansfield, *The Descendants of Richard and Gillian Mansfield Who Settled in New Haven, 1639* (New Haven, CT: Hoggson & Robinson, 1885), 94.

letter, he revealed that not all his thoughts are devoted to moral and religious topics: "It will take a great deal to separate me again from you. I live in hope and the only pleasure I enjoy is the anticipation of pressing you all once more to my heart. I trust that you will be as full and fat and plump as a pumpkin by the time I return.[181]

In his 2 May 1847 letter he talked about Mrs. David Hunter, the paymaster's wife, the only woman in camp, perhaps to allay Louisa's fears that there are nubile nymphs frolicking about the camp but more likely to dissuade her from travelling to Mexico to be with him. In June he attended a party given by the paymaster, Major David Hunter, and his wife. "General [Caleb] Cushing and his mustaches attended." It is rare to read of any sort of humor, however subtle, in his letters so it is refreshing to see it here. Apparently General Worth was involved in some depravity, "guess ladies and he a grandfather." Again Mansfield wrote that he is "truly sick of the war and tired of its evils." He said Taylor will leave Mexico by the end of the year regardless to give her hope that he will not be there until the war is over. His wife apparently asked for sketches but he somewhat brusquely said that "I have no time for such things now. There are other matters of greater importance than mere pictures, however pleasant and agreeable it may be sometimes to make them and for you too." While other officers, especially those educated at West Point, sometimes included sketches in letters home, there is no record of Mansfield so doing. He did write her that he would make her a sketch of some houses in Monterrey if he had time to supplement his description of the town and its buildings.[182]

He again talked of poor reporting in newspapers but said that if his wife saw his name it would only be "in a respectful manner." He said that "I have never thirsted for notoriety in any way being content with simply doing my duty to my country and exerting myself that my name and character may be above slander or reproach and that my children may never have cause to blush when their father is spoken of." By "poor" he likely meant both inaccurate and also sensational reports which are factually challenged. He described a ride to the camp of the 1st Indiana Regiment and was appalled and astonished that they were violating the Sabbath, even "card playing!" "There is no order or discipline in their camps and I doubt not that on the very first fire they would run from the enemy. I hold that no set of men that are void of moral principles can be truly brave." His wife must also have mentioned a party she attended as he warned her not to neglect the young and innocent "that some party might be attended." Is this again an example of Mansfield as the Puritan or merely jealous that his wife is having fun while he is at war abstaining from frivolity? His mention that she is neglecting their children to do so seems a bit cruel. But in his 9 May 1847 letter he again pined for her: "When my Dear Mag shall we meet again—I am longing for the period of my return. It will take a great deal to separate me from you again." And again on 23 May he wrote at length and very movingly about how much he missed his wife and children and wished to be with them again in Middletown. "It is really trying beyond measure to be separated as I have been from you all for nearly two years and at present in no immediate prospect of a return. Truly a military profession is anything but an agreeable one and I look on newcomers to this field with perfect astonishment." He closed with another admonishment somewhat surprising after his earlier loving remarks: "Take good care of them [his children] and train them up in the way they should go, and you shall have your reward, and enjoy the love of your husband. If you love me you will keep my commandments." One might wonder if he thinks too many compliments will turn her head but it is interesting to note that he always sees himself as the *pater familias*.[183]

Mansfield again in his 21 June 1847 letter to Louisa spoke of many money orders involving Mr. William Douglas in Middletown—finances are usually on his mind. And he chastised her for a 14-day gap between her letters to him and continued to complain that she allowed Samuel to be truant even though she said he was a good boy. He said that if Samuel has bad principles it is solely her fault and goes on at length how he hates liars. "She must do her duty!" He

---

[181] 4 February, 4 and 25 April, 2 and 23 May, 4 July 1847 letters to Louisa, courtesy WPL. Mansfield as well as other officers when writing about the physiognomy of their spouses prefer them plump or at least for certain portions of their anatomy. Svelte ladies are not the Victorian fashion.

[182] 2 May, 27-30 June 1847 letters to Louisa, courtesy WPL. Drawing classes were part of the West Point curriculum. Brigadier General Caleb Cushing "served in the Army during the Mexican War first as colonel of the 1st Massachusetts Volunteer Regiment, of which he was placed in command on January 15, 1847. He was promoted to brigadier general of volunteers on April 14 of the same year. He did not see combat during this conflict, and entered Mexico City with his reserve battalion several months after that city had been pacified. He was discharged from the Army on July 20, 1848"; courtesy Wikipedia. Unfortunately no photographs have been found showing Cushing "and his mustaches."

[183] 9 and 23 May, 4 July 1847 letters, courtesy WPL. "The *pater familias* was the head of a Roman family and was the oldest living male in a household. He had complete control of all family members even as to life and death but those extreme measures were rarely carried out and were limited by law. In Victorian America, the father was still the head of the household and for most families had control of all of the family's activities especially financial and legal although women were gaining more of a role in family life as the 19th century progressed. "Fathers had powerful claims, both legal and customary, on their children's labor until they reached maturity….American families worked as patriarchal units, governed by their male heads. Men's work, and men's decisions about work, were primary"; Jack Larkin, *The Reshaping of Everyday Life 1790-1840* (New York, NY: Harper & Row, 1988), 14, 17.

cautioned her to not have unaccompanied male visitors, even relatives. In a July letter he again discussed bills with his usual refrain about living within their means and not setting standards by their well-to-do friends. Then he warned her again about male visitors. Interesting to speculate about how he learned of this—perhaps from a friend or family member in Middletown, or Louisa mentioned this in a letter? He admonished her to not associate with a certain Mr. Parsons due to his reputation. "For myself I only ask to go home and live in my plank house and enjoy the happiness of a respectable and well-regulated family. Good principles and sound morals are better for a family than riches and luxury." In his 11 July letter he criticized her last letter—hastily written, paper not filled up—appears as if "you wanted to get rid of the task as soon as possible" plus it was not clearly addressed which is embarrassing to him as other officers see the addressee. He cannot understand why her weekly letter should be hastily written when she has a whole week to do so: "It is an index of a want of system in your time….You have too much time and it hangs heavy in your hands." Instead of spending a few hours at the school, she should more wisely cultivate her time in a more acceptable manner for a lady such as by practicing her music. He cannot understand why with only three children to take care of and with a nurse to help she cannot better manage her time. She is thin because she does not exercise which would help her appetite for plain wholesome food. People must work and exert themselves in this life also to prepare for the next; handsome drapes, parties, eating ice creams, drinking wines and rich cakes will not advance anybody in respectability. When he returns to Middletown he will "make it obligatory on you to make the most of your time, and devote it to the raising of those children in a proper manner." One might imagine that this notice was less than pleasing to his wife. But he praises Louisa next in his 25 July letter telling her that her current letter was better than the last. Again he brought up her visiting with bachelors—perhaps he is a bit jealous or does not want rumors to circulate to embarrass him; Mr. Parsons is mentioned again as a single man who is one, for "their own selfish gratifications and not out of any particular respect, would visit….In short, no gentleman would call and pressure to obtrude his visits on a married lady situated as you are. At all events a lady must never receive such visits unless it be her wish, for nothing is easier than to send word always you are engaged; and let that be a standing order to your servant." He wrote that he is sorry to have to tell her this but she does not "appear to have good judgment in such matters" and in his opinion "situated as you are such visits are extremely indelicate: and I am surprised your mother has not given you a hint on this point." Her Uncle Thomas would not think much of such visits either. He wrote that if she had not brought up this subject he would not have been concerned—it is not a wanton attack on her since she brought it up. But he has done his duty in telling her what she should do now she knows her duty. This being Sunday he has read the Bible. He is not interested in a new, bigger house as the one they have is entirely adequate. Wealthy acquaintances may spend their money on luxuries but it would be better to apply his means to rent small houses to people who are not able to live in their own. Two years since they parted "ask yourself in what you have improved in that time during the many moments of leisure at your disposal"—has her music improved, studied history, read truly instructive books? He said he has studied Spanish and things in his profession and learned something of the world in Mexico. He doesn't want her or her father to speak about him and his acts. "I wish my friends to let me alone. It is quite enough for you so far as I am concerned, to rest your bosom on mine and be satisfied. The time may not be far distant when I shall again clasp you to my heart and mingle with you the tears of joy and gladness."[184]

In his 3 August letter he revealed that Lieutenant Alexander told him that Lieutenant Green and his lady from Middletown are at the Fort Hamilton House and that he was told that Mansfield's wife and some of her friends were coming there for the sea breezes. "This is too ridiculous to be believed." Mary is just as well in Middletown as anywhere else with proper exercise. If she gets worse, he will "come home if it does cost a little money." He tells her that Mary should sleep with only a low pillow other she will injure her chest and make her crooked. In a September letter he is happy she decided not to attend a large party as her time is better spent "keeping a good home and attending to your own household and domestic affairs." Long section from him in that letter discussing attentive husbands and wives as she apparently wrote that "I like attentive husbands." This set him off into a tirade that "good and attentive wives make attentive husbands." He then tells her he expects that her piano playing has improved and she has become "a first rate performer on the piano….I trust I shall never more have to sit still and hear a piece of music murdered….There is nothing I so much delight in as a well-played piece." He said that if he passes through New York City on his return home he will bring her some new music. "I have never yet enjoyed properly the advantages of a married life and I look to the future for my share of them." He warned her that "the children Samuel and Mary must never be permitted to sleep together nor with any other children or person. I have conversed with several of my army friends, the doctors, and

---

[184] 7 August, September 1847 letters, courtesy WPL.

they all say it is of the utmost importance to keep them clear of bad habits. And it is important you should know how your children conduct themselves in every particular."[185]

Louisa apparently had had enough of his sometimes unkind advice about not only how to conduct the raising of their children, but also her personal life with Mansfield implying that her conduct was unseemly. In his 10 August letter he replies to her feedback on his "suggestions" as he wrote that even though he has given her sufficient exposure to his views on certain points, "hereafter as you do not appear to view what I say in the light it is meant I shall leave you to choose your own course in future." He continued that he cares too much for the welfare of others and that he "frequently I have met with but a very poor return. I am learning wisdom every day." He appeared to be attempting to apologize for his unkind remarks and opinions. In any event, he continued with what he deemed necessary rules for bringing up their children: medical advice for Mary—"she must have more exercise…strong chicken soup and shoes without stockings and let her play outdoors." She must grow up strong so she can marry well. Her schooling can wait. Then he repeated his warning about sleeping accommodations: "By no means allow her sleep with any children or with anybody but have her sleep in her room or the front chamber. This is of the utmost importance and the like may be said for Samuel."[186]

Money, debt, banking, and payments are a frequent theme in most of his letters as has been already seen. He also speculated about his professional future and is worried since after the war he will still be only a captain even though brevetted to colonel. The Secretary of War hasn't awarded him brevet pay. "I do not think he treats me well. But it is and ever has been my lot to beat the bush while another catches the bird." He hoped to be stationed at New York or

---

[185] 27-30 June, 7 August, September 1847 letters, courtesy WPL. Unmarried persons sometimes slept in the same bed in the late 18th and early 19th centuries but usually only when the mixed couples were betrothed. Up to one third of brides were pregnant as a result, Larkin, 193-195. William Douglas was Mansfield's cousin. Mrs. Colonel William (Hannah) Douglas, the mother of William Douglas, Jr., was the sister of Colonel Jared Mansfield, Joseph Mansfield's uncle. Lieutenant Alexander may have been Captain Edmund Brooke Alexander of the 3rd Infantry. Fort Hamilton is located in the southwestern corner of the New York City borough of Brooklyn. Lieutenant Green's identity remains unknown. Mansfield wrote to his cousin, Edward Deering Mansfield on 18 September 1830 regarding the Douglas family: "William Douglas has been married to my niece Grace Parker for about two years. William is doing well he is in business for himself as machinist and manufactures steam engines, etc….Benjamin Douglas is also in Middletown and a machinist by trade. He no doubt will do well also," letter courtesy WPL. There was a Parsons family with male members in and around Middletown but the identity of the specific man who visited Louisa is unknown. There was a Samuel Parsons who was described "as the richest man in Durham," a town near Middletown, which is the only possibility after a search through the *History of Middlesex County*, 280, 317.

[186] 10 August 1847, courtesy WPL. Letters to spouses from three other West Point graduates, Lieutenant Napoleon Jackson Tecumseh Dana, Major Philip Norbourne Barbour, and Major Edmund Brooke Alexander are more sentimental and contain few admonitions, e.g., Dana's 11 May 46 letter to his wife from Fort Brown "You may rest assured that I await on every word in them [your letters]….you get along so bravely, my beloved Sue, that I cannot give you too much praise." If the world would have us alone, to live and love together, I would be entirely contented….let me enjoin you to provide yourself with everything you deserve. Get another servant if you wish it, and anything which would add to your comfort or pleasure, do not fail to provide….I would see yourself nicely and prettily fixed and having all which you can afford….I will be pleased with anything which may tend to make you contented or happy or which may amuse you….Make no apologies about asking for it [money] or about how you want to spend it." "You have no idea…how rejoiced my heart was at the receipt of your last five letters. I sat down and studied them all over and have it to do again." "You must be plump and round and fat by the time I meet you again. I will want to see a pretty rosy face and a nice round plump pair of ____ ____." "I have often wanted to press you some flowers….I collected some sea beans and shells at St. Joseph's Island for you." When there is a gap in her letters: "[19 May 1846] (Fort Brown) I fear, dearest one, that you are not well, that your continual anxiety and the news of our bombardment have made you sick at last." Philip Nordbourne Barbour wrote a poem to his wife, Martha Isabella Hopkins Barbour, 22 April 1846 near Matamoros; 3rd stanza:

"I would not linger, for when mem'ry flies
Back to the scenes of all our fondest joys,
Imagination pictures to my view
All the endearments I enjoyed with you."

Edmund Brooke Alexander 1847 letters to his wife: "My Dear Pet, use what money you need. Thank you for writing. Keep in good cheer and sometimes put a little curl behind your ear, dress pretty and be lively as though you were looking for your husband….[Even when he has not heard from her for a while he does not criticize her] "God bless you my dear Pet—I have not had a letter for some time from you….Keep in good cheer—eat hearty….I have read & reread them with so much interest….Pet don't want for money….I do want you to get for yourself what you want, and for dear little Eddy dress her as a fond and doting Pa would be proud to see her….I received another of your truly interesting and affectionate letters…."God knows I would most willingly give everything I have to be with you, my last thoughts at night & first in waking up are of my dear wife…your dear picture is always at my side….I hope you have not wanted for money…get what you wish dear for yourself, Eddy & the boys;" Dana letters 11 and 19 May 1846; Barbour letter 22 April 1846; Alexander letters 9 February, 19, 26, 29 April and 16 September 1847, courtesy WPL. One may speculate that these three officers were younger and perhaps better off financially than Mansfield and were not married as long thus drawing out the differences in the tone of their communications with their spouses. Mansfield in 1846 was 43 years old, Dana 24, Barbour 33, while Alexander was one year older than Mansfield at 44. Perhaps they were less Puritan-like than the New England born Mansfield. Dana was born in Maine, Barbour in Kentucky, and Alexander in Virginia.

Boston at war's end "I however do not calculate to remain many years in the service if I can do without it." "I am delighted to be clear of Fort Pulaski and never expect to see it again. The best part of my life has been wasted there." Lieutenant Alexander wrote that officers are talking about him for the next Superintendent at West Point but he hopes that Captain Henry Brewerton will remain there. If he is sent it will be only for a few years for "I shall eventually resign if I live through this war." "I understand they have laid out a city on the American side opposite Matamoros and called it Mansfield after me." These rumors about West Point and the Texas city proved to be unfounded but it is noteworthy that he did not dissemble modesty by dismissing them as accolades which he did not deserve. He spent more monies for uniforms but said that he will not have enough to pay his waiter, George Ormsby—he is trying to pay all his bills, debts, and mortgages apparently to spare Louisa financial problems if he dies. He owed his servant Ormsby about $300 and the U.S. government $3,500. "Takes all of his pay to live." He cannot live on his salary as he and his servant consume it all so he must also depend on dividends. He told her to ensure mortgages are properly recorded and released and that the insurances have not run out. He also approved a $5 gift to their church but she should have asked how the debt was incurred which required special gifts—better to give it to the poor. His Fourth of July dinner cost $13.50 and he didn't want to spend the money but had to as others did. He does not like debts so in case he dies her finances can go to supporting the children. He gives her an order "on [William?] Douglas for one year's interest of the debt he owes me independent of the [Douglas Steam Engine & Machine Manufactory, Iron and Brass Foundry] Company." This she will apply to the mortgage. He is very impatient with his brother's [Henry's] financial dealings: "I doubt if I could treat him politely when we meet. I now expect to have the whole burden of my sisters on my shoulders as long as they live—I am glad it is in my power to support them in a plain way."[187]

Now that Mansfield had more time on his hands, he socialized more with his cohorts and had more contact with Mexican civilians even though from his letters he never seemed to be a convivial man. Their 4th of July dinner went well and took place in Arista's Palace. He described that after festivities at Arista's palace, they stopped at the large farm of Senor Villarreal where they were served excellent food on plates made of massively heavy silver. They also attended a large fandango a few miles away. He did not approve of the familiarity of the men and women in public and the way masters mingled with common people. Most were not white and ugly. Again, he demonstrated his dislike of Mexico: "The country, population, religion and government appear to be worthless. It would seem as if the curse of God was upon them. Irrigation gives excellent corn crops and sugar cane does well also. Peasant women dress poorly and are normally barefooted. Houses don't have chairs but use cushions. Young children are naked and dirty head to toe. No moral principles govern any class. Religion is a mere form and a license for all evil." In a letter written 29 September 1846 he again lamented about the illiterate Mexicans noting that many priests are illiterate and that they have no bishops. Priests charge 50 to 250 to marry a couple so most go unmarried. Peasants always in debt to masters due to low pay "and are no better off than our southern negroes." He heard reports that Scott is fighting his way into Mexico City but Mansfield has "no further ambition for battle." He is concerned about a peace: "They [Mexicans] are a treacherous and degenerate race as far as I can see. There is nothing good in the whole land. Their government like their individual character is worthless." He didn't like to eat food Mexicans prepare: "They are the dirtiest beasts I have ever seen. In this respect worse than our Southern negroes."[188] On 6 July Taylor and staff took a pleasure tour 30 miles to General Arista's hacienda—large—200 laborers; on return stopped at the hacienda of Senor Villarreal and had an 8 course dinner--had "2 fandangos and a tour of Salinas." Females dress modestly and are fond of dancing and have features of their class with the Indian and European. "I shall be glad to bid adieu to this 'copper colored' country. What a degenerate race! When out of it I shall never again return. I have had my share of this abominable war."[189]

Mansfield remarked to his wife in his 15-17 August 1847 letter that it was two years ago today when he left home for Texas. Many changes in the army none more so than to Taylor—colonel to major general with pay of $7,000 year. "And I suppose that he owes his rank and success more to my opinions before the battle of Palo Alto and Resaca than to

---

[187] 29 September 1846; 6, 11, 12, July; 3, 10, 20 August; 1 September 1847; letters courtesy WPL. Note that brevet rank for staff officers does not award extra pay, therefore Mansfield even though brevetted to major, lieutenant colonel, and colonel in Mexico was paid as a captain. Arista's Palace was near Monterrey at the base of the hill on which the Bishop's Palace stood.

[188] 7 Sept. 1847, courtesy WPL. Robert Anderson, *An Artillery Officer in The Mexican War, 1846-7: Letters of Robert Anderson, Captain 3rd Artillery, U.S.A.* (New York, NY: G.P. Putnam's Sons, 1911), 21. Robert Anderson: "You have a right to expect from me some remarks upon the Mexicans, but as yet I have seen nothing of them except of the lower class, who differ very little in social position from our slaves. They work for us, unload our vessels, assist in throwing up embankments to the fortifications around Tampico, etc.; in fact, they seem to evince no dissatisfaction at our presence."

[189] 29 September 1846; 6 July, 20 August 1847. Most U.S. soldiers expressed similar remarks concerning the Mexican populace and reflected the general attitude of Americans toward Mexicans.

any other circumstance." But Mansfield was not at either battle it is difficult to understand how his opinions helped unless he was referring in general to conversations he had with Taylor about maintaining a supply line and ensuring that Mexican troops are not in the American rear. He wanted to leave military life before many years certainly at the first favorable opportunity. "My Brevets give me nothing but honorable distinctions. There is no pay attached to them and our corps is so circumstanced that there is no chance of my being a full major for 10 or 12 years. And then the gain will be small. I cannot endure such a sacrifice of life. My only ambition now is to live a respectable life and lay my bones in Middletown in that little plot I have already prepared." Taylor isn't extravagant and is satisfied and content with bacon and greens. Taylor is worth about $200,000 and has $15,000 from his plantation. He saves about $5,000 from his pay. His brother Joseph P. Taylor is drawing a colonel's pay and is a money-making man with a large property. "He made a show of duty here for a few months but his health soon took him off home again....Genl. Taylor is connected with Senator [John J.] Crittenden and Judge [John] McLean of Ohio." It is unclear whether Mansfield is a bit jealous of Taylor's wealth and success or is just reporting it to Louisa for comparison with his or for her edification. Taylor had a son educated at Yale and not yet in business and Mansfield continued on about how some like him have their fortunes made already unlike himself. Mansfield said it took him 25 years of service to accumulate $16,000 dollars of his $20,000 estate." His letter to Louisa 3 October 47 again lamented his time away from home but here he wrote of his business interests: "Too much of my time has been consumed in distant duties where I cannot attend to my private business." I am rejoiced to be clear of Fort Pulaski and the Savannah Station I will never again serve to be stationed south of the Potomac, nor be separated from my family they must hereafter go where my station may chance to be till I quit the service. I prefer a civil life to this wild goose chase about the country....I look forward to something besides a mere captain of engineers. I have now a reputation of which I can build and I mean to improve the favors of God to do good." The following month he repeated his dislike of Fort Pulaski: I am rejoiced to be clear of Fort Pulaski and if I once get out of this country will never return to it again."[190]

On 1 September 1847 he sent her his brevet commission to major but will "keep his for Lieutenant Colonel....I shall expect another of Bvt. Colonel for Buena Vista if they brevet any of the officers for that battle." He wrote that she should buy coal now when it is cheap. "It will be cold weather when we meet if God in his Mercy will grant me that privilege once more. You must get plenty of flesh on your bones to keep me warm and I shall require much playing on the piano from you so you had best prepare. The happiness of being with you all once more is too great to think of where I am now for fear of disappointment." Mansfield wrote Louisa on 21 September 1847, the anniversary of his leg wound. "At that very hour on year ago I was in the suburbs of Monterrey amid the whistling of balls and the deafening discharge of cannon and musketry. Passing by regardless of the dead and wounded on the work of destruction. Oh how awful is war and all its consequences! How demoralizing to the community! When will man learn wisdom and be regenerate." They now spend their time amusing themselves reading Spanish, newspapers, visiting Monterrey and adjacent ranches and awaiting mail. He is unsure about peace as he doesn't believe the Mexican government is honest. "I have no sympathy for such a people and such a government. It is an illustration of the government of Military chieftains combined with a corrupt clergy interested in the establishment of monarchical government. Nothing can be more corrupt than the Catholic Religion as existed in this country....The want of schools and the freedom of the press is the great evil we have to contend with."[191]

His more martial letters discussed primarily Taylor, Scott, and other officers in Mexico, as well as the progress of the war on other fronts since Taylor's army was not active. Mansfield also freely criticized officers who have a penchant for liquor and women, especially those officers who are married. Discussions like these, if they were to be made public, would be extremely embarrassing to him so he warned Louisa more than once to ensure that they are kept private: "This [letter 21 June 1847] is for your eyes only. I do not wish my letter thrown carelessly on the table or mantle piece where anybody can take them up and read them. They are designed for your eye only and contain matter that you should not

---

[190] 15-17 August; 11 Oct. 1847, letters courtesy WPL. He wrote three times during this period, 20 Aug. 1847, 1 Sept. 1847, and 11 Oct. 1847, about his relief "to be clear of Fort Pulaski." Letters courtesy WPL. During this era, it was not unusual for army officers to have civilian business pursuits to supplement their meager army pay. Joseph Pannill Taylor served as a commissary general and died as a Union brigadier general 29 June 1864. His nephew, Richard Taylor, was a Confederate lieutenant general in the Civil War. Annual pay for a major general in 1845 was $6,006 including double rations; for a captain of engineers, $1,378; officers pay included "pay proper, servants' pay and clothing, and commutation of subsistence and forage;" Thomas H.S. Hamersly, *Complete Army Register of the United States for 100 Years (1789 to 1879)* (Washington, DC: T.H.S. Hamersly, 1881), 190-193.
[191] Letters 1 and 27 September 1847, courtesy WPL.

explore in that way. I burn your letter as soon as answered. <u>Lock</u> up mine." On 25 July he again tells her to "keep my letters properly locked up."[192]

On 4 April 1847 he wrote Louisa that "I trust that General Scott will progress rapidly with the troops under his command and that an end will soon be put to this war and that we may once more meet never to part." He ensured his wife again on 25 April 1847 that there is little danger that they will be attacked and that General Scott will "'Conquer a Peace.'" He again praised Taylor: "Our old Genl is strictly moral and in his individual character is simplicity of living. I presume [he] will stand comparison with the best of men." Then on 9 May "We have now in the field two victorious Generals both candidates for the Presidency. It is a pity our population are so military as to be worshipers of the sword." He now has completely changed his views from his previous letters about Mexican desires for peace writing that "These deluded people will never I fear think of peace till their Capitol is taken from them. They must now be forced to treat. There appears to me to be no other way of bringing it about. General Taylor's troops are so few and the time for the volunteers to leave the country so near at hand that he can do nothing more at present but held his own. But unless other troops arrive as his present force leaves the country he cannot hold our present conquests." Mansfield was wrong in his estimation about Taylor being not able to hold what he held after the Battle of Buena Vista; Taylor was never attacked by any large Mexican force but was harassed only by bandits and rancheros. He described the beautiful springtime in Monterrey which is mostly deserted save for troops and traders. He deplored the actions of some American troops, apparently volunteers, who shot 20 Mexicans in cold blood in retaliation for what some Mexican troops did during the Battle of Buena Vista as well as depredations by Mexican bandits. He related how Colonel Clay lay on the ground with a broken leg and was lanced and killed, then robbed. "Genl. Wool in his report complements me but Genl. Taylor is rather sparing of his compliments. I have hitherto shown myself independent of anybody's favor and intend to maintain it. But hope to be always correct in my duty and intercourse." He likely is referring to reports of his actions at Monterrey but in fairness to Taylor, Mansfield was with Wool most of the battle and Wool did complement Mansfield fairly. Mansfield wrote on 23 May that Taylor said he will advance by the end of June if Scott does not make peace but fears that the green volunteers would not do well. Mansfield asserted that Taylor has done well because of the trained officers and men he had fighting with him. He believed Taylor is not a good manager: "I do not think he manages as systematically as might be done. Nothing but bulldog courage and fighting could have carried him through some of his battles." Mansfield wanted the abominable war to end soon and being chief of engineers for Taylor not easy. Taylor told him the general would likely go home in November. Mansfield wrote to his cousin, Edward Mansfield, in Cincinnati: "My life has been too hard and laborious—I have been obliged to overcome so many difficulties in life that I begin to tire." Most of the old volunteers had gone and only 1st and 2nd Illinois have come. In an interesting reversal of some of the feelings of disdain for General Scott he wrote that he is happy to learn of his successes and hoped for a peace. Mansfield wanted to go home and now that that event depends on Scott's success in central Mexico, Scott as a martial leader was important. Mansfield wrote on 5 June 1847 that Taylor cannot advance until more men arrive and are trained say by 1 September. On 21 June 1847 Mansfield reported a Virginia regiment which arrived as did a Massachusetts one but "all these troops are as green as grass and if Genl. Taylor advances with them to San Luis he may never return to run for President." Yellow fever was reported in Vera Cruz but apparently none at Mansfield's camp at Walnut Grove near Monterrey. Taylor greatly disliked Scott, Secretary Marcy and Polk—Mansfield withheld his opinions. "I have frequently expressed an opposite opinion to his [Taylor's] and it was my views he follows which gave him the battles of Palo Alto and Resaca, as I shall tell you so." Mansfield never clarified what advice he gave Taylor for those battles. Conjecture might be that he told Old Zach of the qualities of the flying artillery and the abilities of West Point officers. By 11 July 1847 Mansfield began to realize that Taylor cannot advance for lack of troops, all new ones being sent to Scott. Taylor said that he will apply for leave of absence in September and leave in November. Taylor received many letters on the presidency and he would make a better one than Scott Mansfield wrote; Mansfield is a Democrat while Scott and Taylor were Whigs. Taylor confided in him but Mansfield "always speaks his opinions to him honestly and care not if he be pleased. I cannot play the hypocrite and flatterer. However he has always benefitted by what I have said to him." Then he wrote Louisa in a letter dated 15-17 August 1847 "I think of all our generals that Genl. Taylor is the only one that has a good moral character and who is disposed in the generally long run to act honestly. I would not trust Scott, Worth or Twiggs out of sight. They are rotten indeed."[193]

---

[192] 4, 25 April; 21 June; 25 July 1847, letters courtesy WPL. Since he burned her letters and she apparently kept no copies, hers are missing.
[193] 10 July 1846; 4, 25 April; 9 May; June ; 15-17; 11, 25 July; August 1847 letters courtesy WPL.

Mansfield supplied more military news on 10 August 1847: "A guerilla party between here [Monterrey] and Camargo of about 500 men under General Antonio Canales was attacked by Captain Henry W. Baylor and his Texas Rangers but was whipped. Texans lost all their horses and 4-5 men and had to travel on foot 80 miles to camp." Official reports show for this fight that 27 Texans were ambushed by 300 guerrillas. On a personal note on 20 August, he wrote that "I cannot bear the idea of parting with my horses—particularly Squirrel (my grey). He has been through all General Taylor's battles, and I know him so well....I am the best mounted officer, as to good horses, at General Taylor's headquarters. I never move a mile except on horseback." A shocking event in his next letter told Louisa that morale in Taylor's quiescent army was not perfect and how the event affected Mansfield: "Everything in life is so uncertain. And how miraculous are the escapes of many. Last night we were aroused by a heavy discharge. It appears that some rascal of Major [Braxton] Bragg's company had placed a loaded shell close by his tent just where his bed was and set fire to a slow match. It exploded and the pieces passed through his tent in several places and through the blanket he had covered over him and left him uninjured. It is wonderful he was not killed. In no battle was his life so much exposed as on this occasion. This was undoubtedly the act of some one or two of his soldiers who owed him a grudge." Lieutenant Benham, Mansfield's assistant engineer, applied to go to Vera Cruz apparently to join Scott's army but was refused "as we have not officers enough now of our corps if anything should chance to be done here." He again wrote that he is sick of this war and demoralization. "Almost every day some man or soldier is shot either in a drunken frolic or by Mexican Robbers. Colonel [George] Croghan the inspector general is "a beastly drunkard." He is often carried in a wagon from Monterrey too drunk to ride and has to be carried into his tent. Other officers must take on his duties for days at a time as he is often drunk. Again, some married officers are involved in depraved activities as he tells her in his 27 October 1847 letter. He reported that the topographical engineers "have recently been engaged in some dirty business in Monterrey and it may be something may appear in the newspapers. He hoped their corps is reported not his. Taylor ordered Captain [Brevet Major Thomas B.] Linnard of the Topographical Engineers to Saltillo and Lieutenant [Brevet Captain John] Pope under arrest.[194]

In his 24-26 August letter to Louisa, he wrote that he applied to Taylor for a leave of absence but Taylor asked him to "wait a while till matters are a little more settled." Taylor obviously valued Mansfield's services and besides Taylor had few engineer officers with his army. Mansfield hoped that if there is a peace he can get orders to save travelling at his own expense. If not, he will travel at his own expense on leave and never return: "I have done my share." He then wrote of rumors that Scott has taken Mexico City which would mean that his chances for a home leave improved if true. Mansfield will not leave however until after the sickly season in New Orleans at the close of October. And Taylor will not let him go home until he hears about Scott's success. "But I would willingly run the gauntlet of the yellow fever in New Orleans to get you once more in my arms surrounded by my Dear Children." In his letter 14 September 1847 to Major William Bliss, A.A.G., he asked Taylor for two months leave of absence and authorization to apply for extension at Washington, D.C. Mansfield wrote that he was making a map of that part of Mexico and would give a copy to General Wool who is expected from Saltillo about 1 November 1847. On 11 October 1847 Mansfield wrote that Taylor would "move down to Matamoros by the next train say between the 1st and 10th of next month and he will accompany him." Then Taylor will allow Mansfield to continue home with an authorized two months leave on his own (Taylor's) account and then Mansfield must get an extension at Washington. He told her he will arrive about the end of December. "A cold time, but I trust a warm reception from you." He planned on having enough time to accomplish army matters. He will leave with Taylor on 8 November for Matamoros. Should "arrive there about 20 November, weather is cooler so the

---

[194] Spurlin, 120; 10, 20, 24-26 August; 1 Sept.; 27 Oct. 1847 letters courtesy WPL. Interesting that most of the officers Mansfield complained about had at least very good combat records as they had received brevets while under Taylor's command. Colonel Croghan did not and died in the cholera epidemic of 1849, which also took the life of former President of the United States James K. Polk. Linnard died in 1851 at age 40, while Pope died at 70 in 1892 after a somewhat checkered career in the army, most infamously in command of the Union Army at Second Bull Run in August 1862. Bragg wrote about this attempt in a letter dated 26 August 1847: "An attempt was made about two, A.M., night before last, to assassinate me in my bed. I have no clue to the perpetrator, and can suggest no reason for the act. My escape without injury is regarded as almost miraculous. As exaggerated accounts will probably reach the press, the truth may interest you. A twelve pound shell, heavily charged, was placed within two feet of my bed, just outside of my tent, and exploded by a slow match; the fragments literally riddling my tent and bedding, pieces passing above and below me, some through a blanket spread over me, and yet I was not touched. I was not aware that I had an enemy in the world, and at times feel disposed to believe now that it may have been intended as a practical joke, by some fool ignorant of the effect of shells thus exploded. Be that as it may, my escape was almost miraculous, and I prefer not repeating the joke," *General Taylor and His Staff* (Philadelphia, PA: Grigg, Elliot & Co., 1848), 255. On 8 February Mansfield wrote Louisa that he expected Benham to join him as his assistant, Captain Frazer was left in Monterrey to work on the fort there. Mansfield said that General Scott was taking Colonel Totten, Major Smith, Captain Lew, Captain Swift and the company of Sappers and Miners and Captain Sanders with him on ship to Vera Cruz, letter courtesy of the Middlesex County Historical Society.

yellow fever there may be abated….Do you think you can keep me warm if I get home in the middle of winter? You will have to hug me pretty close at all events." He decided to leave this army early in October to pass thru New Orleans in order to pass through in a healthy season. He has done his share and isn't ambitious to do more in the war—and "this army will not advance." On his way home, He planned on visiting New Orleans and probably Pensacola and Mobile and ascend the Mississippi and visit St. Louis, Cincinnati, Cleveland, Pittsburg and through Washington. "This will satisfy my curiosity as to our great west, and I shall then have no desire to travel in that direction. I have seen our southern Atlantic states to my heart's content and care no more about seeing them. Of course I shall be content to settle down and enjoy the blessings of domestic happenings in our little plank house, and attend to the rearing of our children. He said he will visit his land in East Boston and determine what to do with it—perhaps keep it as the railroad would make it more valuable. Taylor wrote to Dr. Robert Crooke Wood on 27 October "I have fixed on the 8th of November for leaving here for Matamoros, & expect to reach there by the 18th where I intend to await the action of the department on my application for permission to leave the country; & if acted on immediately I expect to hear the result from the 20th to the 25th & if favorable I will sail on the first good vessel that leaves the Brazos for N. Orleans, & hope to reach that place early in December, if not by the first."[195]

Mansfield wrote Louisa from the St. Charles Hotel in New Orleans on 28 November 1847; he left Taylor at Matamoros on the 18th of November and proceeded to the Brazos after staying one night in Matamoros. He left the Brazos on the 20th in a schooner which encountered head winds all the way across the Gulf to La Balize. He then anchored off La Balize on the mouth of the Mississippi River. Next, they were towed for 24 hours up the river about 100 miles to New Orleans which he described as a "large, splendid city….but the hotel was crowded with officers leaving the war going home." He wrote that he would spend one day in the city sightseeing and on business and take a steamer upriver to Cincinnati, spending two days in Cincinnati and two in Washington DC, and one or two in New York City. On his way out of Mexico he visited Fort Brown which was still in good order and recalled the scenes from there during the battle remembering gallant fellows "now no more."[196]

With his departure, Mansfield would never visit Mexico again but as an inspector general he would see many of the U.S. military posts west of the Mississippi for the eight years of that tour of duty. The areas of the U.S. southwest he inspected were part of Mexico up until the 2 February 1848 Treaty of Guadalupe Hidalgo ended the 26-month war and specified its major consequence: adding about one million square miles of land to the U.S.: California, Nevada, Utah, most of Arizona, and parts of New Mexico, Colorado and Wyoming were included in the Mexican Cession. The treaty also recognized the annexation of Texas and American control over the territory between the Nueces River and the Rio Grande. The U.S. agreed to pay $15 million compensation for the physical damage of the war. Also, the United States assumed $3.25 million of debt owed by the Mexican government to U.S. citizens. Mansfield had spent his time only with Taylor and therefore heard just rumors about the progress of Scott's march to take Mexico City starting from Vera Cruz and U.S. actions in securing California and activities in Santa Fe. As seen in his letters above, he was tired of the war and more than ready to be home. The next chapter will show that he did decide to remain in the army despite all his protestations and his promotion to colonel in 1853, when he became an inspector general, ensured that he would spend the rest of his life in uniform.[197]

---

[195] Taylor, *Letters of Zachary Taylor*, 145.

[196] 15-17, 24-26 Aug.; 11, 27; 1, 7, 14 Sept.; 11, 27 Oct.; 28 Nov. 1847, letters courtesy WPL. His hopes to leave the army and get a well-paying civilian job came to nothing as he remained in the army as a captain until he was promoted to colonel as an inspector general in 1853. It is ironic that he said that he had had enough of travel given that his new job as inspector general involved his travel thousands of miles visiting most U.S. installations west of the Mississippi and not being able to take his family with him. Most of the letters in *Letters of Zachary Taylor*, were written to Dr. Robert Crooke Wood. Brazos Santiago Pass is a narrow passageway extending inward from the Gulf. The pass lies between Brazos Island and Padre Island. La Balize, Louisiana, was an old French fort and settlement near the mouth of the Mississippi River, which was home to river pilots and fishermen.

[197] Stephen A. Carney, U.S. Army Center of Military History, "The Occupation of Mexico, May 1846-July 1848, 2; Wikipedia, "Mexican–American War."

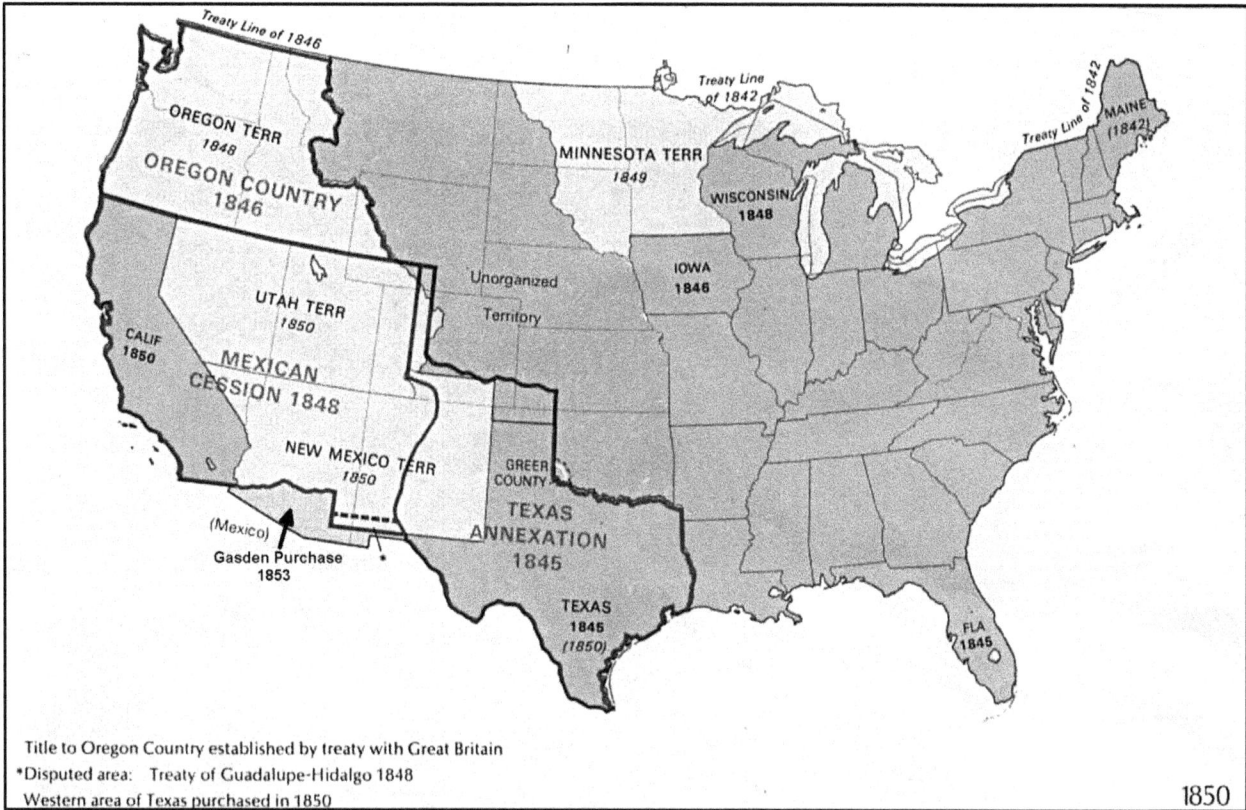

Title to Oregon Country established by treaty with Great Britain
*Disputed area: Treaty of Guadalupe-Hidalgo 1848
Western area of Texas purchased in 1850

1850

Territory gained from Mexico, about 1,000,000 square miles. In the 1848 Treaty of Guadalupe Hidalgo, Mexico gave up all claims for Texas. The Gadsden Purchase of 1853 gave the U.S. another 30,000 square miles. Courtesy Wikipedia.

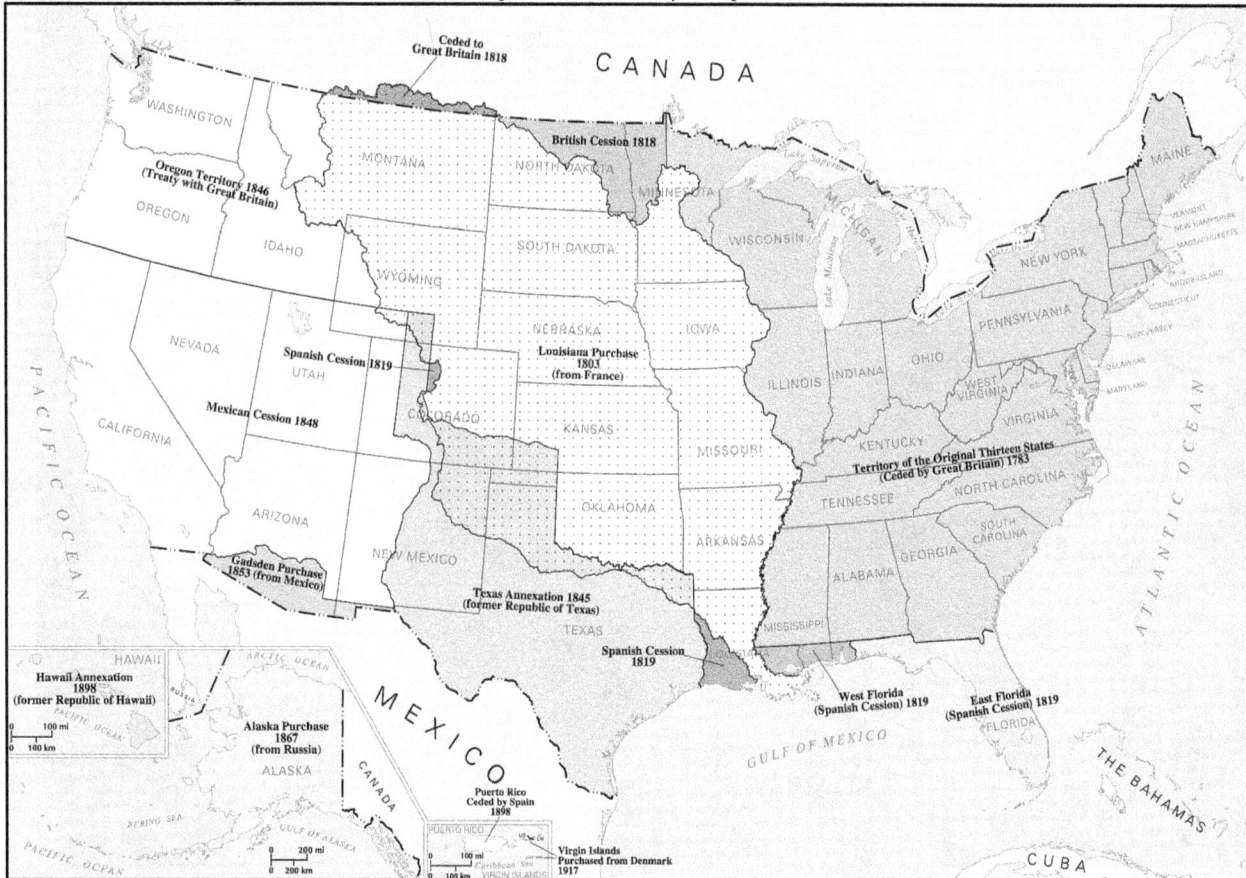

Wikipedia from *National Atlas of the United States.*

Attachment 1
Painting of Taylor's Camp at Walnut Springs, Monterrey, Mexico

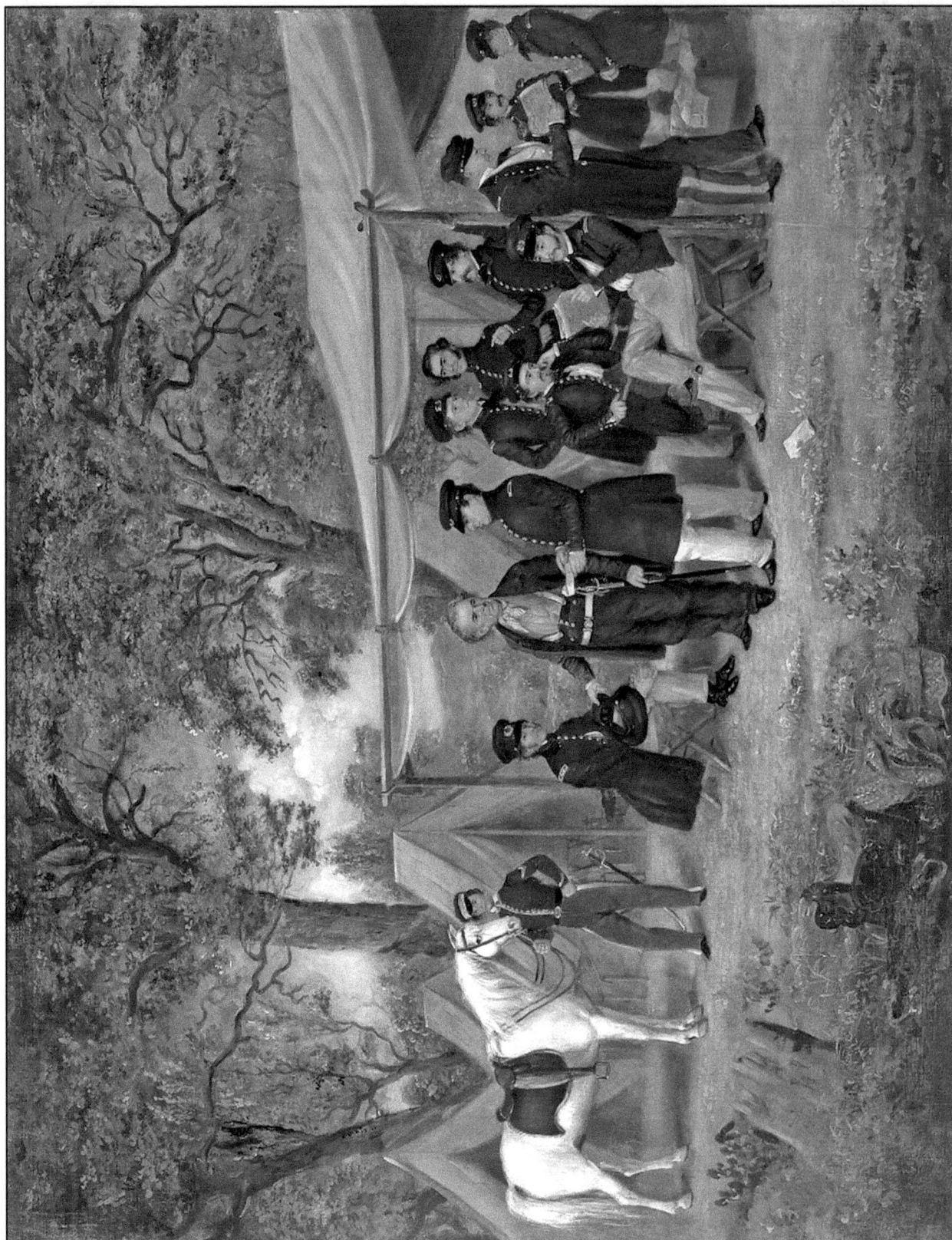

Taylor is third from left, Mansfield is fifth from the left, Captain Braxton Bragg, 3rd Artillery, standing on Mansfield's left with Colonel Albert C. Ramsey standing to his left; Major William Wallace Smith Bliss, Assistant Adjutant General and Taylor's most trusted aide given the sobriquet "Perfect Bliss" due to his notable abilities, standing on Taylor's immediate left; Chief Quartermaster Colonel Henry Whiting seated on Taylor's immediate right; Captain Joseph Horace Eaton, Chief Paymaster, fourth from left, seated in front of Mansfield; Lieutenant Robert Selden Garnett, 4th Artillery, seated fourth from right reading a newspaper, next to Eaton; Captain Thomas B. Linnard is standing second from the right; Surgeon Presley H. Craig is at the far right; "Old Whitey," Taylor's favorite horse, is being held by Taylor's orderly Bingham; Bingham was captured at Buena Vista. Bliss was Taylor's son-in-law. Detail below identifying officers near Mansfield. In the Civil War, Bragg and Garnett became Confederate generals. Eaton received brevets for Monterrey and Buena Vista and was a Union brigadier general in the civil war. Ramsey was directly appointed as colonel of the 11th Infantry in the Mexican-American War. "Zachary Taylor at Walnut Springs," by William Garl Browne Jr., 1847, Oil on canvas mounted on wood, courtesy National Portrait Gallery, Smithsonian Institution.

This 30 by 36 inch painting was commissioned by Robert H. Gallaher, editor of *The Richmond Daily Republican*, who thought Taylor would be a good Whig candidate. William Garl Browne, Jr., who had a studio in Richmond at the time, spent months painting the general and his staff. It was shown nationwide when it was done.

Garnett is reading aloud a copy of *The New York Herald*.[198] Browne's oil painting is in the Smithsonian National Portrait Gallery in Washington, D.C., while prints were made and widely distributed.

Taylor wrote about paintings made by Browne and Jesse Atwood in a letter to Dr. Wood 13 July 1847: "Without being decided fine, I imagine the likenesses painted of me by Mr. Atwood are tolerable; the one which has been just finished by a Mr. Browne from Richmond is said by those who understand or are judges of such matters to be a much better painting; Mr. B. has nearly completed a group of officers, myself & staff in addition to several others, which I imagine will be considered a good painting by connoisseurs; he is now engaged in making a painting describing the battle ground of Buena Vista; it is uncertain when he will complete them, but I suppose for the most part will do so in 8 or ten days, when he will return from whence he came, stopping a short time in N. Orleans, where they may be exhibited, if so you no doubt will examine them with Ann & can then judge as to the merits of both."[199]

Mansfield wrote at least four times to Louisa about the artist and the painting, once from the camp near Monterrey 5 June 1847 telling her that the artist, Atwood, has painted two portraits of Taylor and another (presumably Browne) arrived to do all of his staff—"you must not be surprised to see me painted." Again on 27-30 June 1847: "Browne the painter made a handsome group to be engraved of the headquarter officers." Then on 10 August 1847 he wrote her that Mr. Browne has done an excellent portrait of him and Mansfield told him to send it to Louisa and she would pay him for it if Mansfield dies--cost $100. But Browne wanted to keep it to use it to paint Mansfield in a battle scene; and finally on 15-17 August 1847 that Mr. Browne left with the portraits and two Frenchmen are there taking the bust of Taylor.

[198] Dyer, 250; see also Zachary Taylor, 32. General Taylor wrote on 11 August 1846 of his brother's poor health: "Col. Taylor will visit Fort Polk or Brazos before he come up, & I hope will be able to take the field with us but I think it very doubtful if his health will permit," 39. His brother apparently spent little time at General Taylor's headquarters as the general noted on 10 September 1846: "Col. Taylor is still absent, when he left us at Camargo he expected to join us before we got to Monterrey, this I think doubtful," 56. On 28 September, Colonel Taylor was "on his way from Camargo to this place [Monterrey] with funds for his department escorted by a detachment from the 2nd Infantry," 62. Colonel Taylor, the general wrote on 26 November, was "just recovering from a severe attack of sickness" so had difficulty bearing the bad news of his children's illness, 70. On 13 December, the general wrote that his brother "left here [Monterrey] about two weeks since in quite feeble health, I feel very uneasy about him," 80. Finally on 30 May 1847, the general noted that his brother had been ordered out of Mexico and should arrive in New Orleans soon, 104. Taylor's brother, who was chief officer of the Commissary Department until the middle of 1847 when poor health forced his return to the United States, was rarely at the general's camp but mostly in the rear pushing up supplies to the army from Matamoros or Point Isabel which is why Eaton is usually mentioned as commissary chief. Army regulations at this time required that troops be clean-shaven although in Mexico this rule was rarely enforced: "The hair is to be short, or what is generally termed cropped; the whiskers not to extend below the lower tip of the ear, and in a line thence with the curve of the mouth; moustaches will not be worn, (except by cavalry regiments,) by officers or men on any pretense whatever;" Winders, 107.
[199] Zachary Taylor, 113. A flyer was printed to announce a showing of Browne's painting in Washington, D.C., at the Odd Fellows' Hall, 27 and 28 September 1847. An outline of the subjects identifies them and included a testimonial from Gen. Taylor as to its accuracy: List of Officers in the United States, Army in Texas. General Staff--Brigadier Gen. Z. Taylor, commanding; Capt. W.S.S. Bliss, assistant adjutant general; 1st Lieut, J.H. Eaton, 3rd Infantry, aide-de-camp; Lieut. Col. M.M. Payne, 4th Artillery, inspector-general "army of occupation;" Colonel T. Cross, Ass't. Q.M. Gen., (killed;) Major C. Thomas. Qr. Master, (Point Isabel;) Major S. McKee, do. do. do.; Assistant Quarter Master, Capt. G.H. Crossman, Capt. E.S. Sibley, Capt. E.A. Ogden, Capt. W.S. Ketchum; Commissary of Subsistence, Capt. G.C. Waggaman; Surgeon P.H. Craig, medical director; Surgeon N.S. Jarvis; Assistant do., B.M. Byrne, (St. Josephs;) Assistant do., J.R. Conrad; Paymasters, St. Clair Denny, Lloyd J. Beall, Roger S. Dix. Engineers- Capt. J.K. Mansfield, Capt. John Sanders, 1st Lieut, J.M. Scarritt. Topographical Engineers- Capt. T.J. Cram, 1st Lieut. J.E. Blake, 2nd Lieut. George Meade. This list is not accurate, the caption to the picture above is the best identification which can be made. Atwood was an itinerant portrait painter from Philadelphia who visited Taylor at Walnut Grove. He later exhibited Taylor's portrait in New Orleans for a fee.

William Garl Browne, Jr. was born 10 October 1823 in England, and died 28 July 1894 in Buffalo, New York, where he was visiting his sister from his home in Virginia. His public exhibition of a series of portraits of Taylor and his staff in 1847 met with acclaim as accurate depictions of the men. Browne chose to spend most of his career in the South and painted some 2,000 works during his 50 year career, most of which were portraits.

Attachment 2
Major General Zachary Taylor

Taylor was born 24 November 1784 in Orange County, Virginia, into a prominent family of planters who migrated westward from there to Kentucky in his youth. He was commissioned as an officer in the U.S. Army in 1808 and made a name for himself as a captain in the War of 1812. He climbed the ranks establishing military forts along the Mississippi River and entered the Black Hawk War as a colonel in 1832. His success in the Second Seminole War attracted national attention and earned him the nickname "Rough and Ready."[200]

Taylor spent two and a half years fighting Seminoles in Florida, and three years in command of the Second Military District of the United States in 1841 (which included Louisiana, Arkansas, and the Indian Territory), headquartered at Fort Smith, Arkansas. Taylor next took command of the First Department in 1844, to which Louisiana had become a part in 1842; he established his headquarters at his old post, Fort Jesup, taking command on 17 June 1844.[201]

Brigadier General Zachary Taylor, known as "Old Zach" or "Rough and Ready," was a leader who engendered radically different emotions in his men, and historians to this date are divided over his martial abilities. Justin Smith who wrote the standard history of the Mexican-American War first published in 1919 was not a Taylor admirer and his influence clouded the judgment of some later historians such as Nathaniel W. Stephenson in his *Texas and the War with Mexico*, and William A. Ganoe in his *History of the United States Army*.[202] Smith summed up what he saw as Taylor's strong and weak points:

> Personally Taylor possessed a strong character, a very strong character, neither exhausted by self-indulgence nor weakened by refinement and study. He was every inch a man, with a great heart, a mighty will, a profound belief in himself, and a profound belief in human nature. The makings of a hero lay in him, and to a large extent the making had been done. He was gifted, too, with solid common sense, not a little shrewdness and ambition, a thorough knowledge of men—the sort of men that he knew at all—a military eye, and a cool, resourceful intelligence that was always at work in its own rather ponderous fashion. The sharp gray eyes and the contraction of his brows that made the upper part of his face look severe were tempered by the benignity of the lower part; and the occasional glimmer of a twinkle betokened humor.

Smith then went overboard as he adopted the viewpoint of some of Taylor's detractors such as Colonel Ethan Allen Hitchcock and Lieutenant Roswell Sabin Ripley:

> On the other hand, everything about him suggested the backwoodsman. His thick-set and rather corpulent body, mounted on remarkably short legs, typified barbaric-strength. In speech he was rough and ungrammatical, in dress unkempt and even dirty, and in every external of his profession unmilitary. He never had seen a real battle nor even a real army. Ignorance and lack of mental discipline made him proud of his natural powers and self-mastered attainments, and he saw very distinctly the weaknesses of school-taught and book-taught men. West Pointers, trim in person and in mind but inferior to him in strength, practical sense and familiarity with men and things, he felt strongly inclined to belittle; and this feeling went so far that he despised, or at any rate frequently seemed to despise, knowledge itself. He could not, however, fail to recognize on occasions the professional superiority of his trained officers, and no doubt found himself unable now and then to defend his opinions. In such cases, being by temperament extremely firm, he naturally took refuge in obstinacy; and sometimes he appears to have been positively mulish, holding to his own view after he must have seen its incorrectness.[203]

But Taylor was admired by virtually all of the officers who served in his army in Texas and Mexico, other than Hitchcock who admired few in the army other than himself, and Ripley who only fought with Taylor at Monterrey.

On 29 June 1846 Taylor was promoted to full major general (brevet from 28 May) and on 18 July received the thanks of Congress.[204] Old Rough and Ready was always dressed in simple clothes and did not appear to be a general officer. He wore a variety of hats which he used to keep the hot Mexican sun from scorching his head. Thorpe wrote that he met General Taylor:

---

[200] "Zachary Taylor," courtesy Wikipedia.

[201] Hamilton, 157. The fort was built there to protect the United States' border with Spain when the Louisiana Purchase Treaty of 1803 failed to clearly define the western boundary of Louisiana, which was also the western border of the United States.

[202] Nathaniel W. Stephenson, *Texas and the War with Mexico: A Chronicle of the Winning of the Southwest* (New Haven, CT: Yale University Press, 1921); William A. Ganoe, *History of the United States Army* (New York, NY: D. Appleton and Company, 1924).

[203] Smith, *The War With Mexico*, 140-141.

[204] Hamilton, *Zachary Taylor: Soldier of the Republic*, 198.

About a mile above the city of Matamoros, a little distance from the banks of the Rio Grande, are to be seen…some stunted and ill-shaped trees, which bend their gnarled and almost leafless limbs over a group of three or four small tents, only different from those of the common soldier in their rear, in this, that they are heterogeneously disposed of for shade, instead of being in a line, regardless of all else than military precision. The plain about is dotted over with thousands of tents, before many of which are artillery, and groups of men and soldiers; and over some wave in triumphant folds our national flag, giving promise of more importance and pomp, than the little knot to which we have particularly alluded. We wended our way on towards…the headquarters of the commanding general of a triumphant American army.

Not the slightest token was visible, to mark one tent in the group from another; there were no sentinels, nor any military parade present; a chubby sunburnt child, "belonging to the camp," was playing nearby in the grass, temporarily arrested in its wanderings by some insect of unusual size, that was delving in the dust. We presented ourselves at the opening of one of the tents, before which was standing a dragoon's horse, much used by hard service. Upon a camp stool at our left sat General ____ in busy conversation with a hearty-looking old gentleman, who was dressed in Attakapas pantaloons [linen trousers], and a linen roundabout, and was remarkable for a bright flashing eye, a high forehead, a farmer look, and a "rough and ready" appearance, it is hardly necessary for us to say, that this personage was General Taylor, the commanding hero of two of the most remarkable battles on record, and the man who, by his firmness and decision of character, has shed lustre upon the American arms.

There was no pomp about his tent; a couple of rough blue chests served for his table, on which were strewn in masterly confusion, a variety of official-looking documents; a quiet-looking citizen-dressed personage made his appearance, upon hearing the significant call of "Ben," bearing on a tin salver a couple of black bottles and shining tumblers, arranged around an earthen pitcher of Rio Grande water. These refreshments were deposited upon a stool, and "we helped ourselves," by invitation. We bore to the general a complimentary gift from some of his fellow-citizens of New Orleans, which he declined receiving for the present, giving at the same time a short, but "hard sense" lecture, on the impropriety of naming children and places after men before they were dead, or of his receiving a present for his services, "before the campaign, so far as he was concerned, was finished."[205]

After debarking from his steamboat ride upriver from Matamoros to Camargo, Major Luther Giddings of the 1st Ohio Volunteers described his meeting with General Taylor:

Passing on through some narrow streets and lanes, and between gardens surrounded by mud walls, on the top of which grew many varieties of the luxuriant cactus plant, we arrived in a few minutes at a little grassy lot just without the town, in the center of which were pitched three soiled and ragged tents. A small guard of Dragoons was posted nearby. The spot was remarkably quiet, being removed from the noise and bustle of both the camp and village. Under an awning in front of the tents, sat a solitary man, dressed in linen coat and trowsers, twirling a straw hat between his fingers, and apparently conversing with or dictating to someone within. The first glance assured us that it was the old hero, with whose name and fame the country was then ringing; and as we approached, we recognized the mahogany complexion, piercing eye, iron-grey hair, and stout frame, which we had been told distinguished the commanding general. As he arose to greet us, I was struck with the benevolent expression of his face, and the affability of his manner. He was invested with no silly pomp or ceremony. There was no ice to break in approaching him; but the natural grace and kindness of his reception at once placed us at ease, and during the time he gave us audience, our respect and admiration for the sturdy old republican general momentarily increased. His first question was concerning the health of the men, about which he seemed extremely solicitous; and he expressed his anxiety to hasten his army forward into a more salubrious region.

He conversed with a stammering voice. But if slow of speech, no man could be more prompt in action than Old Rough and Ready.[206]

Second Lieutenant Lew Wallace of the 1st Indiana Infantry in his autobiography provided another first-hand description of his encounter with Taylor at his Walnut Springs headquarters near Monterrey:

Moving forward with lengthening steps, and drawing nearer and nearer, we strained our eyes to catch every point in the surroundings of the hero. A tall white flag-staff was the first thing observable. A flag floated from it high up, but the flag was dingy and worn. That was a disappointment. Next, back of the staff, fifteen or twenty steps, perhaps, we noticed two marquees one in rear of the other, a fly before the first answering for a porch; and they, too, were dingy and discolored. Under the fly there were a few campstools, a small table, also dirty, and a deal bench, long and straight-backed. No orderlies in trim dress uniforms; not even a sentinel stiffly stalking a beat suggested state thereabout. These His quarters?

---

[205] Thorpe, *Our Army on the Rio Grande*, 161-162.
[206] Luther Giddings, *Sketches of the Campaign in Northern Mexico in Eighteen Hundred Forty-Six and Seven* (New York, NY: George P. Putnam & Co., 1853), 71-72.

Presently, without halting, we broke into column of companies—quickly and without a break we did it, and then advanced intervals and alignment perfected. Where was He?

Now the head of the column was passing the dingy flag on the tall pole. One by one in quick succession the companies reached the prescribed saluting distance. Officers glanced to the right. *Their swords remained at carry*. So, also, the color-bearer swept by, his nose, like his flag, mutinously in the air. And all there asked themselves, anxiously, Where is He?

It came my turn to salute from my place behind the rear rank. I readjusted the sword-grip in my hand, and looked for the reviewing officer out of the corner of my eye first, then broadly. Leaning lazily against the butt of the white pole, I saw a man of low stature, dressed in a blouse unbuttoned and so faded it could not be said to have been of any color, a limp-bosomed shirt certainly not white, a hang-down collar without a tie of any kind, trousers once light blue now stripeless, rough marching shoes, foxy from long wear—such the dress of the man. He also wore a slouch wool hat drawn down low over a face unshaven, and dull and expressionless as the wooden Indian's habitually on duty in front of tobacco-shops. I did not salute him, but, like all who had preceded me, and all who came after me, passed on wondering, Where can He be?

Looking backward once, I noticed Colonel [James P.] Drake riding to the man with the slouch hat. There is reason to think he stopped with him and dismounted. Still I plodded on grumbling to myself, "he is treating us shabbily, as usual."

That evening, when the good colonel's tent was pitched, I went to see him, unable to contain my indignation.

"Colonel," I said, "did General Taylor tell you that he would review us as we marched past his quarters?" "Yes. I sent the adjutant to notify him of our coming. Didn't you see him?" "No, sir, or I would have saluted." The colonel's face sobered as he said, "Nobody saluted." "Why, there was nobody to salute." "Yes there was." "Who?" "*The man leaning against the flagstaff.*" "That General Taylor? I took him to be a teamster."[207]

Many junior officers liked Taylor's unassuming, informal appearance:

Any kind of head covering, from local sombrero to oilcloth cap; any kind of coat that suited the weather, linen or wool, of accidental color and cut. His pantaloons lacked the regulation stripe; loose socks showed his calves; and any boots would do. Everyone who saw the general remembered his costumes. Did he affect his dress to bother the shine-button, torso-tight men from the Point? Probably not; he had cheated on regulations for years. Out on the country's fringes who cared? Taylor simply wore what a man over sixty felt good in. He put on his finery just twice, once for a grand review at Corpus that never came off, and once for Commodore David Conner. Zach knew the Navy—all spit, more spit, polish, and braid; and he came aboard turned out in his best. But Conner had heard about Taylor too, and as host he showed up in mufti to save embarrassment. After that reverse in roles, Taylor put fancy garb aside for all time.[208]

In November 1848, Taylor, the Whig candidate over Scott, was elected President, receiving 163 electoral votes out of 290, and was inaugurated on 5 March 1849. Taylor resigned from the army 31 January 1849 and died at Washington, on 9 July 1850.

---

[207] Lew Wallace, *Lew Wallace: An Autobiography* (New York, NY: Harper & Brothers, 1906), vol. 1, 152-154.

[208] Nichols, 30-31. Grant adopted Taylor's informal uniform style as well as his pithy, direct orders and unassuming demeanor; Grant, 47, 48, 67-68.

Attachment 3
Timetable of Events[209]

1845
March 1: President John Tyler signs official proposal of Texas statehood
    4: James Knox Polk becomes president, desires acquisition of California and New Mexico

July 4: Texas legislators consent to statehood; Taylor proceeds to Corpus Christi, Texas
    25: Taylor and his army arrive in Corpus Christi, Texas

Sept. 19: Mansfield arrives in Corpus Christi, Texas

Nov. 10: President Polk orders John Slidell to Mexico to offer $30 million for California

Dec. 20: Slidell offer rejected by Mexican President José Joaquín de Herrera
    29: Texas became the 28th state; Mexico breaks diplomatic relations with U.S.

1846
Jan. 2: General Mariano Paredes y Arrillaga becomes President of Mexico
    13: Taylor ordered to the Rio Grande River

Mar. 8: Taylor marches south from Corpus Christi
    21: Slidell finally rejected by Mexican President Mariano Paredes y Arrillaga
    25: Taylor and HQ reached Point Isabel and on 26-27 **Mansfield's** plan for the fortifications completed
    28: Taylor reaches the Rio Grande River across from Matamoros
    29: Reconnaissance after enemy commenced his batteries on the opposite shore; U.S. fortifications commenced

Apr. 25: Mexican cavalry attack U.S. Army Captain Seth Thornton's cavalry detachment at Carricitos

May 1 Taylor marches to Point Isabel
    3-9: Mexican troops lay siege to Fort Texas; 6 May: Major Brown's leg shot off while standing next to **Mansfield**
    8: Battle of Palo Alto
    9: Battle of Resaca de la Palma
    13: U.S. Congress declares war with Mexico
    16: U.S. Navy ordered to blockade Mexican ports
    17: Taylor crosses Rio Grande and occupies Matamoros

June 5: Kearny's march to Santa Fe begins

July 7: Mexican Congress declares war on the U.S.; Monterey, California, occupied
    14: Camargo occupied by Taylor

Aug. 4: Paredes overthrown; Taylor's HQ ascended Rio Grande in the steamer *Eagle Natchez*
    8: HQ reached Camargo and marched for Monterrey
    13: Los Angeles, California, occupied by U.S. Navy
    16: General Santa Anna lands at Vera Cruz
    18: Kearny occupies Santa Fe
    19: Taylor advances toward Mier

Sept. 14: General Antonio Lopez de Santa Anna enters Mexico City

---

[209] Smith, *The War With Mexico*, vol. 2, xix-xxi. Added are Mansfield's notes to Cullum 5 June 1860, courtesy WPL.

19: Taylor and **Mansfield** arrived at Monterrey, reconnaissance began at 2 p.m.
20-24: Operations at Monterrey, Mexico; 21 Sept. Mansfield made forced reconnaissance and wounded
22-23: Insurrection in California precipitated
23: General Wool begins advance from San Antonio

Oct. 8: Santa Anna arrives at San Luis Potosi
24: San Juan Bautista captured by Perry
29: Wool occupies Monclova

Nov. 15: Commodore David Conner captures Tampico
16: Taylor occupies Saltillo
18: Polk appoints General Winfield Scott to command the Vera Cruz expedition

Dec. 3: Mansfield leaves his tent after convalescing from 21 Sept. wounding
5: Wool occupies Parras de la Fuente
6: Kearny's fight at San Pasqual
15: Mansfield marched with HQ to Victoria
25: Doniphan's skirmish at El Brazito
26: Taylor arrives at Brazos de Santiago
27: Scott reaches Brazos
29: Victoria occupied

1847
Jan. 3: Scott orders troops from Taylor
8: Fight at the San Gabriel, CA
9: Fight near Los Angeles, CA
28: Santa Anna begins his march against Taylor

Feb. 5: Taylor places himself at Agua Nueva
19: Scott reaches Tampico
22-23: Battle of Buena Vista
28: Battle of Sacramento, CA

Mar. 9: Scott lands unopposed near Vera Cruz
29: Vera Cruz occupied
30: Operations in Lower California opened

Apr. 8: Scott's advance from Vera Cruz begins
18: Battle of Cerro Gordo
19: Jalapa occupied

May 15. Worth enters Puebla

June 6. Trist opens negotiations through the British legation
16: San Juan Bautista again taken

Aug. 7. The advance from Puebla begins
20: Battles of Contreras and Churubusco
24-7 Sept.: Armistice

Sept. 8: Battle of Molino del Rey
13: Battle of Chapultepec
14: Mexico City occupied

22: Manuel de la Peña y Peña assumes the Presidency

Oct. 20: Trist reopens negotiations

Nov. 18: Mansfield departed Matamoros
    28: Mansfield reached New Orleans

1848
Feb. 2: Treaty of Guadalupe Hidalgo signed

Mar. 10: Armistice ratified

May 30: Mexican Congress ratifies treaty

July 15: Last U.S. forces leave Mexico from Veracruz

Chapter 6

Engineer 1848 to 1853

AFTER READING LETTERS MANSFIELD WROTE during the Mexican-American War, it would appear that he would soon resign from the U.S. Army and return to civilian life as an engineer. Many West Point graduates had followed this path, with George B. McClellan the most famous example. During his tour of duty in Mexico, Captain Mansfield wrote to his wife, Louisa, several times of his feelings that he could not stay in the Army as these excerpts from his Mexican-American War letters show: "I shall rejoice when this war is at an end and I am honorably clear of it and I would say the Army too." "I told Genl Taylor today I was sick of it [the Army] and he says he is so himself and is anxious to retire as soon as possible." Mansfield hoped to be stationed at New York or Boston at war's end to be near his family in Middletown, Connecticut. "I however do not calculate to remain many years in the service if I can do without it." "I am delighted to be clear of Fort Pulaski and never expect to see it again. The best part of my life has been wasted there." "I shall eventually resign if I live through this war." His words show that he wants to leave military life before many years at the first favorable opportunity. "My Brevets give me nothing but honorable distinctions. There is no pay attached to them and our corps is so circumstanced that there is no chance of my being a full major for 10 or 12 years. And then the gain will be small. I cannot endure such a sacrifice of life. My only ambition now is to live a respectable life and lay my bones in Middletown in that little plot I have already prepared." "Too much of my time has been consumed in distant duties where I cannot attend to my private business." "I am rejoiced to be clear of Fort Pulaski and the Savannah Station I will never again serve to be stationed south of the Potomac, nor be separated from my family, they must hereafter go where my station may chance to be till I quit the service. I prefer a civil life to this wild goose chase about the country....I look forward to something besides a mere captain of engineers."[1]

But Mansfield did decide to remain in the Army as a captain of engineers. Perhaps the late 1847 to late 1848 recession, during which business activity declined almost 20%, helped his decision.[2] As seen, he wrote Louisa that he wanted to be stationed in Boston or New York and he was so assigned. He became a member of the Board of Engineers for Atlantic Coast Defenses effective 13 March 1848 to 11 April 1853, and for Pacific Coast Defenses, from 11 April 1853 to 28 May 1853. He was also Superintending Engineer of the construction of Fort Winthrop, Boston Harbor, Massachusetts, from 1848-1853, and involved in the improvement of the James and Appomattox Rivers, Virginia, and

---

[1] Letters 12 August, 29 September 1846; 6, 11, 12, July; 3, 10, 15-17, 20 August; 1 Sept., 11 Oct. 1847; letters courtesy WPL. His family did accompany him to Boston while he was an engineer but did not travel with him after he became an inspector general.

[2] This U.S. recession coincided with the British Panic of 1847, "a minor British banking crisis associated with the end of the 1840's railway industry boom and the failure of many non-banks;" courtesy Wikipedia. Mansfield's business interests however may have been doing well enough since he was able to supervise them personally after his return from Mexico.

survey of the Rappahannock River in 1852-1853.[3] He obviously weighed his prospects outside of the Army and chose not to resign. He was able to gain assignments near his Middletown, Connecticut, home so he was able to spend more time with his family and to look after his business interests in his home state and those he had near Boston. Mansfield wrote from Boston 18 April 1849 to Joseph Fay, Engineer, Savannah and Macon Railroad, declining to have his name put forward to its board by him: "It is true I have nothing more to gain, even if gain were my real motive in remaining. For I am so wedded to the Army that I could not quit it at any time I pleased without hesitation....The time for me to quit the Army is not yet at hand."[4] It must be assumed that once he weighed all his options, and given his requirements to prefer to remain near his family, he decided to stay in the U.S. Army.

On 14 January 1848, Mansfield penned a letter to his cousin, Colonel Joseph G. Totten, from his Middletown, Connecticut, "headquarters," to request a 90 day extension to his leave of absence of 60 days previously granted by General Taylor which would have ended on 18 January 1848. Totten approved and forwarded Mansfield's request to Secretary of War William L. Marcy who approved it on 19 January.[5] Mansfield began his duty as chief engineer for Fort Winthrop's construction in orders from the Engineer Department early in 1848. On 14 July 1848 Mansfield wrote Chief Engineer Totten from Boston and asked that "the Department will relieve me from duty as a member of the Board of Engineers, and assign another officer to this duty without delay." He made this request because he believed that he was not "able to do as severe duty as formerly." His Mexican-American War service combined with his leg wound took a toll on him and he needed fewer duties at least in the near term.[6]

---

[3] George W. Cullum, *Biographical Register of the Officers and Graduates of the U.S. Military Academy at West Point, N.Y.* vol. 1 (Boston, MA: Houghton, Mifflin and Company, 1891), 276-277. "On 16 November 1816, a Board of Engineers for Fortifications was constituted by the War Department to perform the following duties: It shall be the duties of the officers of this board to examine, in conjunction, all those positions where permanent works are or maybe proposed to be erected. They shall select the proper sites for, and form the plans of, all new works. Where fortifications have been commenced or are finished, they shall report how far the sites for such fortifications have been judiciously selected, or whether or not the works are adequate to the defense of the prospective positions, and they shall propose such alterations or additions to them as may be deemed necessary....The report and plans adopted by the board, shall be submitted with...accurate estimates to the chief of the corps....The original reports and plans agreed upon by the board, as well as those reported by any member of it, shall be submitted by the Chief of the Corps of Engineers. with such remarks as he may deem proper, to the Secretary of War, for final adoption, and they shall be deposited in the secret bureau of the Department of War....Under the Act of April 30, 1824, inaugurating works of internal improvement, a similar 'Board of Engineers for Internal Improvement' was organized and continued until about the date of the segregation of the topographical engineers into a distinct bureau of the War Department; after which these functions seem to have devolved on special boards of greater or less permanency until, by authority of the Secretary of War, in an order issued on September 2, 1879, the functions of the Board of Engineers for Fortifications, which had continued unchanged since 1816, were extended to include such works of river and harbor improvement, and other matters as may be referred to it by the chief of engineers. This organization, was designated The Board of Engineers;" Henry L. Abbot, "The Corps of Engineers" in Theophilus F. Rodenbough and William L. Haskin, eds., *The Army of the United States Historical Sketches of Staff and Line* (New York, NY: Maynard, Merrill & Co., 1896), 115. Mansfield also wrote that in 1849 as one of the Board of Engineers he examined all the harbors and inlets of Florida; Mansfield's corrections to Cullum's Mansfield history 18 Aug. 1859, courtesy WPL. River improvements were periodically done to ensure that river travel for commerce was safe up to the fall lines—inland limit to which ships can navigate from the mouth of a river. Obstructions such as snags and sand bars had to be cleared for boat travel. On 30 August 1852 the Congress appropriated $45,000 "for the improvement of the James, and Appomattox Rivers, below the cities of Richmond and Petersburg;" and also $3,000 "for a survey of the Rappahannock River, Virginia;" *Laws of the United States Relating to the Improvement of Rivers and Harbors from August 11, 1790, to March 4, 1907*, vol. 1 (Washington, DC: GPO, 1907), 119, 122.

[4] Letter courtesy of the Middlesex County Historical Society. On 12 April 1849 Mansfield wrote Taylor asking for a favor for his nephew, Joseph Wade, to receive a position in the government. Letter courtesy of the Middlesex County Historical Society.

[5] Letters courtesy of the Middlesex County Historical Society. Extended leaves were not unusual in the Army at that time, e.g., Colonel Joseph E. Johnston of the Topographical Engineers asked for and was granted in 1852 a year's leave; Craig L. Symonds, *Joseph E. Johnston: A Civil War Biography* (New York, NY: W.W. Norton & Company, 1992), 75. 1847 Army Regulations spoke to officers' leaves: "The commander of a geographical military department is authorized to grant leaves of absence to officers serving in the department under his command, for a period not exceeding twenty days. Generals commanding geographical divisions may grant leaves of absence for a period of sixty days. All applications for leave of absence, for a time exceeding that above specified, will be addressed, through the proper channels of communication, to the General Commanding-in-Chief, at the headquarters of the Army. If the applicant be an officer of the general staff, or an officer not serving in the line, leave will not be granted before the application shall have been referred, by the Adjutant-General, to the chief of the staff department to which the officer belongs;" *General Regulations for the Army of the United States, 1847* (Washington, DC: J. and G.S. Gideon, 1847), 46.

[6] Letter courtesy of the Middlesex County Historical Society.

Epaulette showing Mansfield's rank as a lieutenant colonel with the Engineers' castle. Because it appears tarnished, is likely a lieutenant colonel's rank woven of silver thread. He would have had this made sometime during the Mexican-American War after he was brevetted a lieutenant colonel for the Battle of Monterrey in September 1846 and before the Battle of Buena Vista in February 1847 when he was brevetted to colonel. He never held the full rank of major, lieutenant colonel, or colonel, in the engineers but would have worn insignia of those three brevet ranks. Courtesy of the Middlesex County Historical Society.

One of two images of Mansfield found without a beard. He is shown with captain's bars so the photograph was taken between 1838 and 1853. It was likely taken after the Mexican-American War given his somewhat careworn appearance. It was not taken before the Mexican-American War as photographs were rare before 1848. While it appears to be Mansfield, its provenance has not been confirmed. Courtesy of the Middlesex County Historical Society.

President Zachary Taylor in 1849. Taylor was the 12ᵗʰ President, born 24 November 1784 and died in office 9 July 1850. His term began 4 March 1849; he was succeeded by his Vice President Millard Fillmore. Photograph by Mathew Brady courtesy LOC.

Brigadier General Henry Washington Benham taken after the Civil War. Courtesy LOC. Benham was a fellow Nutmegger born in Cheshire, Connecticut. He graduated first in his class from West Point in 1837. Mansfield wrote to Pres. Taylor 20 January 1849 asking that Captain Benham receive another brevet for Buena Vista as Benham was not satisfied with what he received. He was brevetted to captain during the Mexican-American War and was wounded at Buena Vista, and to colonel, brigadier general and major general during the Civil War. He retired as a colonel in 1882 and died in 1884.

Secretary of State William L. Marcy. Courtesy LOC. He was in office from 7 March 1853 to 6 March 1857 under Presidents Franklin Pierce and James Buchanan. He was Secretary of War from 6 March 1845 to 4 March 1849 under President James K. Polk.

President Millard Fillmore, 13th President of the United States, in office from 9 July 1850 to 4 March 1853, courtesy LOC.

President Franklin Pierce, 14th President of the United States, served from 4 March 1853 to 4 March 1857. He was appointed a colonel in command of the 9th Infantry Regiment in February 1847 and was promoted to brigadier general in March. He was injured during the Battle of Contreras in General Scott's army. He resigned from the Army in 1848. Courtesy LOC.

President James Buchanan, 15th President of the United States, served from 4 March 1857 to 4 March 1861. Courtesy LOC.

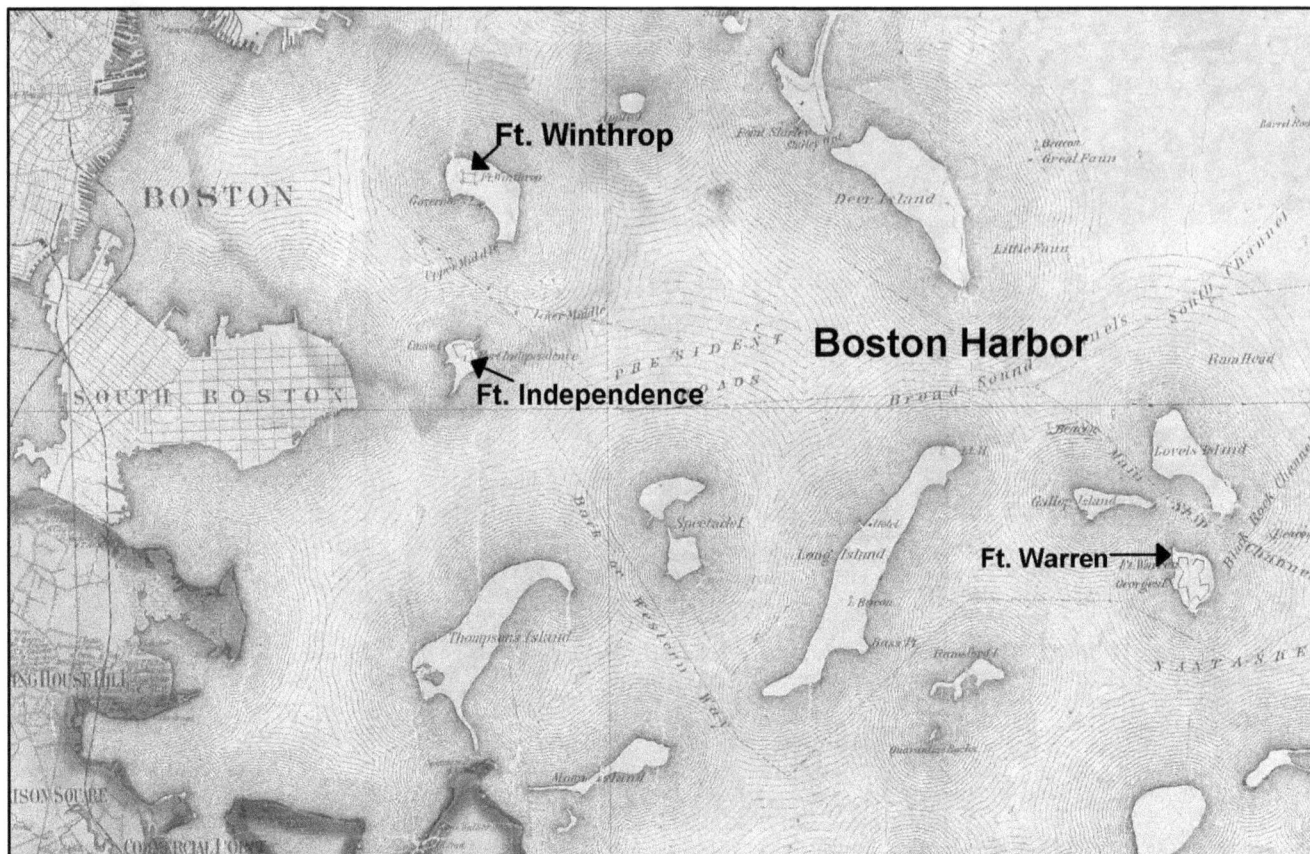

Boston Harbor forts, Fort Winthrop on which Mansfield worked on Governor's Island; Fort Independence on Castle Island, and Fort Warren on George's Island. Mansfield first became associated with Fort Winthrop in 1842 while he was still chief engineer for Fort Pulaski. Governor's Island and Fort Winthrop no longer exist as Logan International Airport took the location for expansion; Fort Independence is now connected to Boston and the fort can be toured; Fort Warren is also open for tours but is accessible only by boat. Map courtesy LOC.

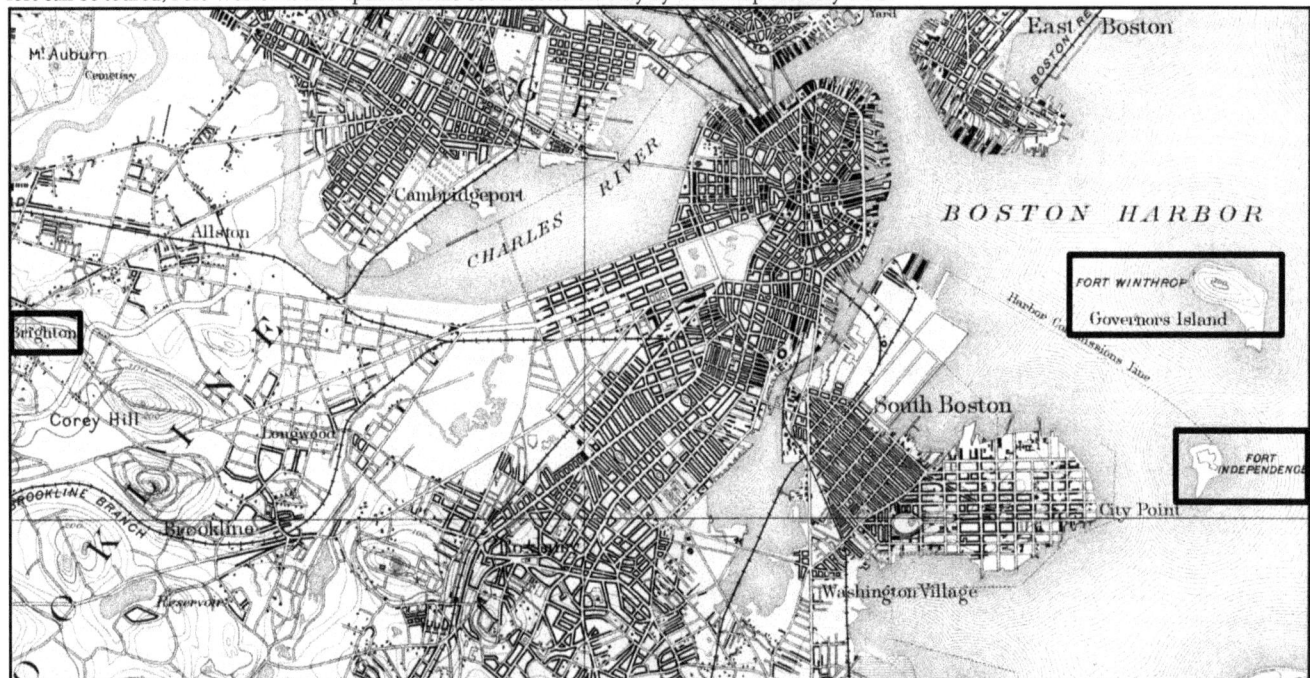

Map of harbor showing Fort Winthrop, Fort Independence, and Brookline, where Mansfield and his family lived while he worked on Fort Winthrop; 1893 map courtesy USGS.

View of Boston Harbor with a white box showing Brookline where Mansfield and his family lived while he was employed on Fort Independence and Fort Winthrop. Bird's-eye view, oriented with north to the right, c. 1905, courtesy LOC.

Mansfield's property in Brookline with his annotations written in for two lots on Vernon Place which became Vernon Street. One of the lots Mansfield bought was owned by Charles and Mary Wild. Lot 39 Mansfield bought from William Wilson; this lot had a house on it. Mansfield paid two thirds of the price of $2,466.45 and Dr. Edward A. Wild paid the remaining one third. The road between lots 38 and 39 was called Harvard Place; and Thomas Griggs granted Mansfield and Wild a right of way over it for $1 a year. Vernon Place on the south was later named Marion Street. The deed required the new owners to allow the current tenants four months to move from the sale date of 6 March 1852. It is not clear why Mansfield only paid two thirds and Dr. Wild one third unless Wild wanted to help his apparent relatives who owned the lot. Courtesy of the Middlesex County Historical Society.

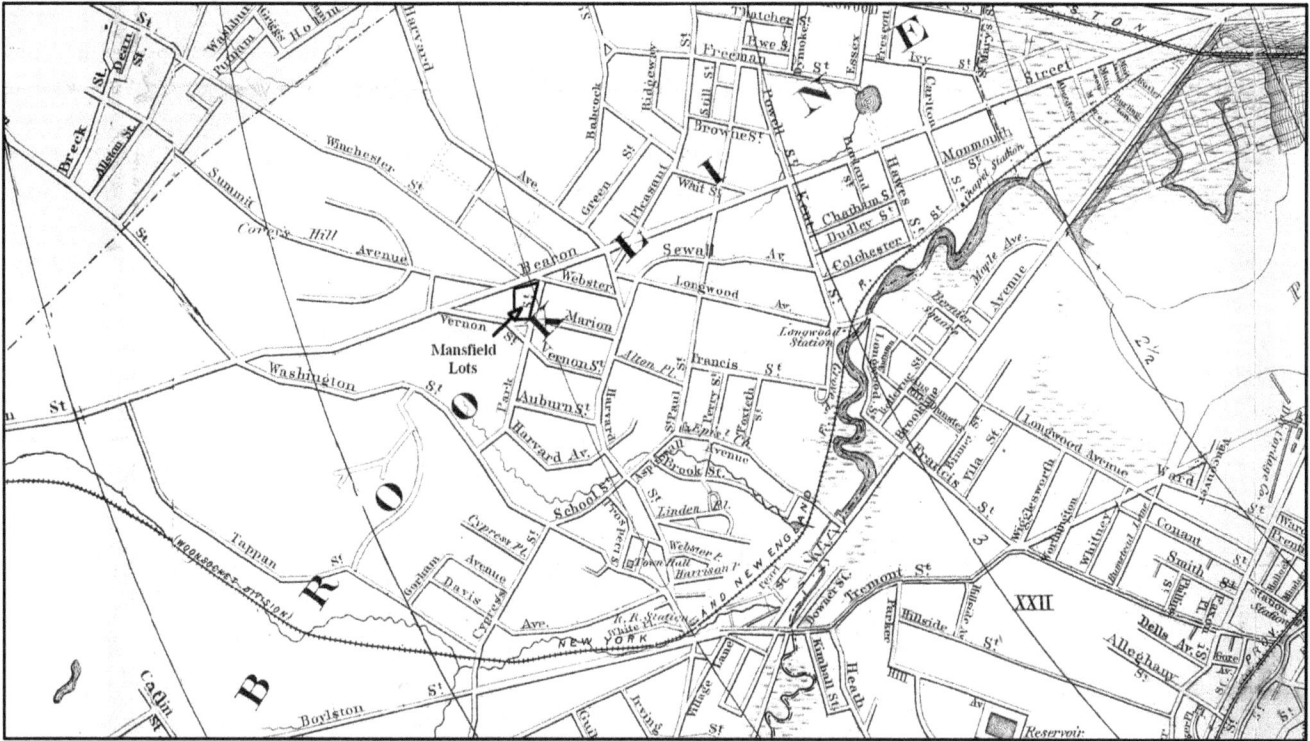

Location of Mansfield lots on 1883 Boston map, courtesy LOC.

Mansfieldw was well aware of the various forts in and near Boston due to his experience as an East Coast engineer before the Mexican-American War. He also visited his cousin Totten in the 1830's at Fort Adams in Newport, Rhode Island. Fort Pulaski on which he spent many years of work in Georgia was a Third System fort designed to defend vulnerable and important coastal cities like Savannah and Boston. Unlike Fort Pulaski which was constructed of brick, New England forts were built of the abundant granite found in the northeast. Long before Mansfield arrived on the scene, Totten began work in Boston Harbor on 23 May 1808 on a demilune (semicircular outer) battery on Governor's Island and began on the fortress at the summit of the hill near there which was named Fort Warren. In 1846 construction began on a new Third System stone fort to supplement these earth works and the original Fort Warren first constructed on Governor's Island. The new fort included a three-story citadel with musket loopholes and 16 guns in a rooftop battery on top of the center of the star fort, and rebuilding of the West Head and Southeast batteries with seven guns each. Mansfield took over supervision from Major Sylvanus Thayer in 1848. Thayer was in charge of building a new fort to which the name "Fort Warren" was transferred. Construction on the new Fort Warren on George's Island began in 1837.[7] Another Boston Harbor fort, Fort Independence on Castle Island, just southeast of Fort Winthrop, was constructed from 1836 to 1848 when construction stalled due to lack of funding; it was finally completed and regarrisoned in 1851. This reconstruction of an older Second System fort was designed to guard the inner harbor with 79 guns. The original fort on Castle Island was the oldest one in the United States begun in 1634.[8]

---

[7] The future Fort Warren, a pentagonal granite fort, was designed to take 300 guns. Thayer was the superintendent of West Point from 1817 to 1833. He was president of the Board of Engineers from 1838 until 1857 and was in charge of much of the engineering work from Boston north. Fort Warren was not complete when the American Civil War broke out but served during the war as a prison for Confederate officers and government officials including civil officers from Maryland and Northern political prisoners, most noteworthy of which were Confederate diplomats James M. Mason and John Slidell. Confederate military officers held included Richard S. Ewell, Isaac R. Trimble, John Gregg, Adam Johnson, Simon Bolivar Buckner, Sr., and Lloyd Tilghman. High-ranking civilians held included Confederate Vice President Alexander H. Stephens and Confederate Postmaster General John Henninger Reagan. "Fort Warren was designed to hold over 200 42-pdr, 32-pdr, and 24-pdr cannons, a number of flanking howitzers to defend the fort, and more than a dozen heavy 10-inch mortars." Kaufmann, *Fortress America*, 209. Fort Warren guarded the two main shipping channels to Boston.

[8] Aubrey Parkman, *Army Engineers in New England: The Military and Civil Work of the Corps of Engineers in New England 1775-1975* (Waltham, MA: U.S. Army Corps of Engineers, New England Division, 1978), 18-20; Robert B. Roberts, An *Encyclopedia of Historic Forts: The Military, Pioneer, and Trading Posts of the United States* (New York, NY: Macmillan Publishing Company, 1988), 402-403, 411, 413; John R. Weaver, II, *A Legacy in Brick and Stone: American Coastal Defense Forts of the Third System, 1816-1867* (Missoula, MT: Pictorial Histories Publishing Co., 2001), 83-89.

Mansfield liked his new assignment as chief engineer for Fort Winthrop because he was able to move his family from Middletown, Connecticut, to Brookline, just west of Boston and an easy commute to Fort Winthrop. Also his new fort construction assignment was unlike Fort Pulaski in that he did not have to start from scratch since there was an earlier fort there--the original Fort Warren. That name was transferred in 1834 to the new fort being built on George's Island. The name Fort Winthrop was the name of the original tower built on Governor's Island. Fort Winthrop consisted of the old tower and four external batteries. It complemented Fort Independence across the main shipping channel.[9]

Mansfield had already visited Governor's Island while operations were suspended at Fort Pulaski for the summer months. On 5 December 1842, the Engineer Department ordered him to go to Boston as a member of Board of Engineers to join Colonel Thayer with a plan of Governor's Island in Boston Harbor and sketches for the defense of that island. And after learning the necessary details he was to return to Middletown and complete all plans etc., to "prepare the project for execution." Colonel Thayer wrote to Mansfield on 20 January 1843 "My Dear Joseph" that he was going to look at Mansfield's drawings for a redoubt on Governor's Island. And on 7 June 1844, the Engineer Department replied to Mansfield agreeing with him that he should suspend operations at Pulaski during hot months and work on Boston Harbor Governor's Island defenses until about 1 November leaving a small force at Pulaski. Mansfield's letter to Major John L. Smith, Senior Member of the Board of Engineers, on 3 Oct 1844 informing him that plans for Boston Harbor which tasks were assigned to him in 1842 were done and ready for "final action and disposal." At Fort Winthrop, all of the many logistical problems he faced constructing Fort Pulaski were absent or greatly reduced: there was no "sickly season" so work could progress throughout the summer with no fear of Yellow Fever; skilled workmen were readily at hand as were required supplies and materials; unskilled immigrant labor was also abundant as Boston was a major center of immigrant flow from Europe; communication with Army headquarters in Washington, D.C., was quicker aided by telegraph; transportation to and from Governor's Island was easily obtained; and the threat of catastrophic flooding from hurricanes was somewhat diminished. In short, other than occasional severe winter weather and somewhat higher wages required, Mansfield had a much easier time doing his work in Boston Harbor than what he experienced for those many years on Cockspur Island, Georgia. The most important benefit for him was being with his family and secondarily being better able to manage his business and financial affairs. But as we will see, he decided to seek the post of an inspector general which would require much travel and time away from home. He likely knew that even though he would be away from home for many months, between inspection tours he would be able to be with his family as his "headquarters" would be in Middletown. He also knew that if he remained in the engineer department, promotion to major would take years and to lieutenant colonel many more years so jumping ranks from captain to colonel with the concomitant perquisites--most importantly pay--the pecuniary benefits to him and his family outweighed the months away from home.[10] See Attachment below for a first-person description of a visit to Fort Winthrop and Governor's Island in the late 1800's (supplemented by later sources) which also gives an excellent history of the place.

---

[9] Mansfield wrote a 2½ page letter to President Taylor from Boston 1 Dec. 1848 congratulating and praising his "old Commander" on his election to the presidency; he wrote that his family is in Brookline. His niece, E.B. Hammond, wrote to him from Worcester, Massachusetts, 16 April 53. She visited Smithfield, R.I. to see his brother, Henry, and learned Mansfield is going to California in June. She stated that it was too bad he must leave his beautiful home in Brookline but she wants him to stop in Worcester to visit before he leaves. She also wrote that all the reports she has received from the boys in California (see Chapter 7) are good. Perhaps Mansfield saw them when he inspected posts there when he became an Inspector General. Mansfield received an inquiry from Deacon Thomas Griggs on 6 April 57 about buying a lot in Brookline adjacent to his home there; letters courtesy of the Middlesex County Historical Society. Mansfield apparently rented out his Brookline house from 1 May 1853 for $400 per year. It is not known if he did so but there is no mention of Brookline property in Last Will dated 27 March 1852. His earlier letters mentioned land in East Boston but that land was not this Brookline house. Brookline is west of Boston Harbor and was annexed by Boston. East Boston is to the northeast of Boston on Boston Harbor; Brookline is not on Boston Harbor but is adjacent to the Charles River. Worcester, Massachusetts, is about 40 airline miles west of Boston. Charles Pope on 13 February 1857 wrote to Mansfield about two deeds for land Mansfield sold to him. Mansfield notes that the total cost of the Wilson lot to me" to date $1,846.59. Other notes by him show the "Cost of Settlement of Purchase of Estate from William Wilson apparently in 1852. It showed a balance due and settled by Mansfield of $1,693.19, 19 March 1852. On 28 March 1865, Mansfield's wife, Louisa, as Executrix, sold the Brookline property which included a dwelling house, stables and other structures, to Lewis Clark for $15,000. While Mansfield and his family lived in Brookline, he rented his house in Middletown to John Wyse for $600 per year as long as he made improvements and repairs to it, and if the roof needed repair to have Benjamin Douglas hire a roofer; letters courtesy of the Middlesex County Historical Society.

[10] Letters courtesy of the Middlesex County Historical Society. When he was promoted to colonel as an inspector general, he was third in seniority on the list of engineer officers for promotion to major.

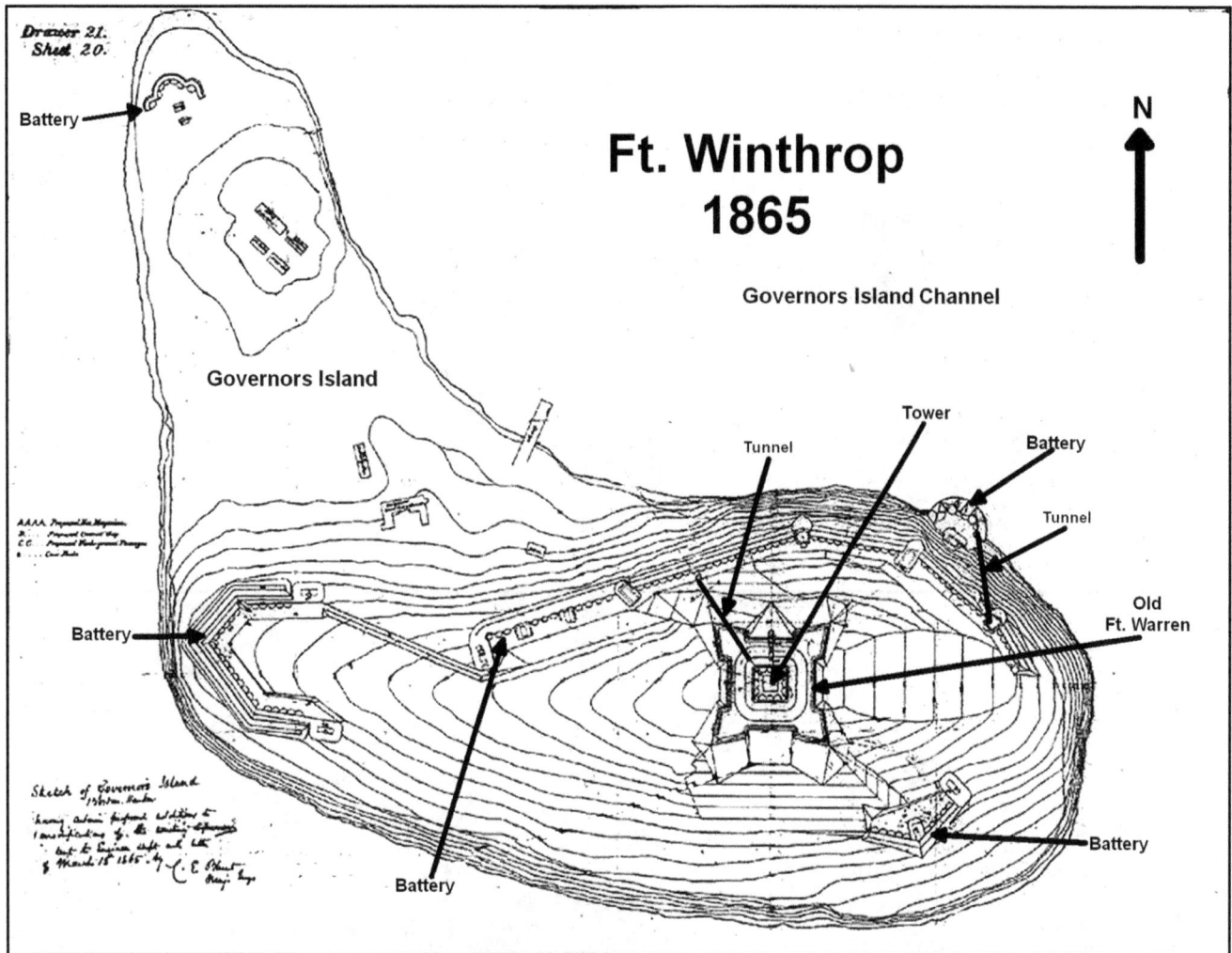

Map of Fort Winthrop in 1865, courtesy NARA. The tower is in the center of the old square earthen battery. There are four external batteries and two tunnels. The long ravelin runs almost two-thirds of the way across the island. Each face of the square tower measured 138 feet.[11]

Fort Winthrop from Boston Harbor; sketch from Edwin M. Bacon, *Boston Illustrated* (Boston, MA: Houghton, Mifflin and Co., 1886), 123.

---

[11] Weaver, 88-89; Gerald W. Butler, *The Guns of Boston Harbor* (n.p.: 1ˢᵗ Books Library, 1999), 20-23).

Fort Independence sketch from Edwin M. Bacon, *Boston Illustrated* (Boston, MA: Houghton, Mifflin and Co., 1886), 123.

Fort Warren sketch from Edwin M. Bacon, *Boston Illustrated* (Boston, MA: Houghton, Mifflin and Co., 1886), 124.

Mansfield was next assigned to execute improvements of the James and Appomattox Rivers below the cities of Richmond and Petersburg and the survey of the Rappahannock and Appomattox Rivers in a 7 October 1852 letter from Alexander Dallas Bache, superintendent Coast Survey. Mansfield noted that "it affords me pleasure to be associated with yourself in this business." Mansfield wrote in a 5 November 1852 to P. Sanger a civil engineer in the Navy Department, asking for the plans of dredging machine for James and Appomattox rivers. They had worked together on the dry dock at Brooklyn, years before, probably before Mansfield began work at Fort Pulaski and was stationed in New York City. Work went well on this assignment as on 21 November 1852, Mansfield wrote to Totten two letters with completion reports for the Rappahannock, Appomattox and James Rivers projects.[12]

---

[12] Letters courtesy of the Middlesex County Historical Society. An interesting letter Mansfield wrote to a Thomas W. McCance [?] shows Mansfield's concern with appearance if not actual attempt at bribery. On 24 January 1853, he instructed McCance concerning the $6 he paid for Mansfield's hotel bill at the Richmond Exchange Hotel: "If your committee on the river were military men I should certainly have you court martialed for meddling with my account at the Exchange Hotel." Mansfield sent $6 to McCance to square the account. Even though Mansfield previously accepted a favor he cannot now as "things have now taken a settled and business course and I cannot with propriety accept a continuation of such favors." While it is not clear that Mansfield was the object of a bribe of any sort, it is at least an indication that he wishes to prevent any gossip about his accepting favors. Letter courtesy of the Middlesex County Historical Society. Mansfield also took the time to update his will on 27 March 1852: Real property--his house in Middletown to his two sisters, Hannah and Grace, and they also get $100 each per year to live on during their lifetimes; Grace to take care of deranged sister Hannah. May be increased another $50 if there is enough income from his estate and the increase is necessary. Mansfield's wife, as executrix, will decide. There would only be an increase if the extra sums were not needed for his children. His wife's inherited property is hers to do with as Mansfield himself would have had the right. She also has control and use of all his property real and personal to the support and benefit of herself and the children equally divided between his children when reached legal age. Advances to them will not be charged interest in the final accounting of his estate. Copy of will courtesy of the Middlesex County Historical Society.

Alexander Dallas Bach graduated from the United States Military Academy 1825, first in his class, he was an assistant professor of engineering there then he was in charge of the construction of Fort Adams in Newport, Rhode Island. He resigned from the U.S. Army in 1829. After serving as a professor at the University of Pennsylvania, president of Girard College, and president of Central High School of Philadelphia, he was appointed superintendent of the United States Coast Survey in 1843 and served 24 years until his death in 1867. Courtesy Wikipedia.

Mansfield was in Washington, D.C., on 28 March 1853 and wrote to Totten that he would journey to San Francisco to be in general supervision of San Francisco and the construction of Fort Point but requested pay at his brevet rank (colonel) while on this duty. He again wrote to Totten 21 April 1853 from Boston about his orders to San Francisco to "enter upon the construction of a fort on Fort Point." He wrote that the cost of the project would be $500,000 to begin. Mansfield's assistant, "Lt. [William Henry Chase] Whiting must take out with him his instruments...and confer with me before he leaves."[13]

Mansfield's mission to the west coast to begin to fortify the San Francisco area built upon earlier efforts by a Joint Commission for Defense of Pacific Coast. In 1849, three army and three navy officers constituted the commission and assembled at San Francisco harbor. After some fits and starts, the commission decided in March 1850 that strong works near Fort Point on the south side of the channel and Lime Point on the north side were needed. In its final 1 November 1850 report the commission wrote that among other things San Francisco was of primary importance for military purposes on the West Coast. Totten next established a Board of Engineers for the Pacific Coast in June 1851 which

---

[13] Letters courtesy of the Middlesex County Historical Society. Brevet Lieutenant Colonel James Louis Mason was to be in charge of constructing Fort Point but he died on 5 September 1853. Mason was an 1836 West Point graduate and served on General Scott's staff. He was brevetted to major for his conduct at the Battles of Contreras and Churubusco, to lieutenant colonel for Molino del Rey. He was seriously wounded there and was incapacitated for three years; he died in 1853 at age thirty six. Whiting became a major general in the Confederate States Army and died on 10 March 1865 while a Union prisoner of war at Fort Columbus in New York City.

began planning works for areas near San Francisco and submitted estimates to Washington. In February 1853, Secretary of War Charles Magill Conrad submitted costs for the works planned to the U.S. Senate ranging from $1.9 to $3.5 million dollars. Congress appropriated $500,000 for fiscal year 1854 so Totten decided to select engineers to supervise the construction—of the five engineers on the board, he chose Mansfield to be the senior engineer for all the works and to directly supervise the construction of Fort Point. But before Mansfield left for this new assignment, he was chosen as an inspector general so Totten chose Lieutenant Colonel James L. Mason as his replacement. Unfortunately Mason contracted Yellow Fever on his journey across Panama from the east coast and died on 5 September 1853; in late 1853, Captain John G. Barnard replaced him. In 1854, Mansfield did visit San Francisco but as an inspector general. Like his preceding engineer officers, he reported that "At least two hundred guns should occupy Fort Point. The Government reservation for the purpose consists of that point of land to the northward called Fort Point extending southward about three miles to include the presidio. This is all sufficient and none too much…. [Fort Point was] the key to the whole Pacific Coast in a military point of view, and it should receive untiring exertions."[14]

---

[14] Joseph K.F. Mansfield, *Mansfield on the Condition of the Western Forts, 1853-4*, Robert W. Frazer, ed. (Norman, OK: University of Oklahoma Press, 1963), 121-122; Erwin N. Thompson, "Historic Resource Study, Seacoast Fortifications, San Francisco Harbor, Golden Gate National Recreation Area, California" (NPS, Dept. of the Interior, 1979), 20-28. John Gross Barnard was an 1833 West Point graduate at age 18 and superintendent there from 31 May 1855 to 8 September 1856. He received a brevet to major during the Mexican-American War and three brevets up to major general during the Civil War after serving in many engineering duties including Engineer of the Army of the Potomac. He was an author and a co-founder of the National Academy of Sciences. He retired from the Army in 1881 and died in 1882.

Attachment
Governor's Island-- Fort Winthrop[15]

The first known of this island is that on 5 July 1631, it was appropriated to public benefits and uses. On April 3, 1632, Conant's Island, as it was then called, probably for Roger Conant, a prominent colonist, was granted by the colony to John Winthrop, the Governor of Massachusetts Bay, for the term of his life, for the sum of forty shillings, and a yearly rent of twelve pence. The name was then changed to Governor's Island. Governor Winthrop agreed to plant a vineyard and orchard. In consideration of this the Court granted that the lease should be renewed to his heirs for twenty-one years for the yearly tribute of one-fifth of the fruits and profits. This lease could be renewed from time to time to the heirs, unless they should let the land go to waste, when it should be appropriated again by the State....

The island, which has an area of seventy-two acres, was not fortified at the time of the War for Independence. On 18 May 1808, the United States purchased from James Winthrop, for the sum of $15,000, the summit of the island where the keep [fortress] now stands, and a strip of land running down to the half-moon battery, six acres; also, one acre at the south end of the island, where the brick fort stands. The purchase comprised seven acres in all, which included the necessary roads.

Between 1808 and 1812, an earth fort was constructed on the summit; the half moon and south-point batteries were built at the same time, and the name Fort Warren was given to the whole. In 1812 the earth works along the water's edge were constructed. In 1834 the name of the fortification was changed from Fort Warren to Fort Winthrop, the name Warren being given to the fortifications on George's Island.

The construction of the present Fort Winthrop began about 1846. On the 25th of February of that year, Captain James H. Bigelow, Corps of Engineers, and wife, deeded to the United States, only, in consideration of the sum of one dollar, all that part of Governor's Island which had not been purchased from James Winthrop in 1808. Between 1846 and 1860, the north, east, and south batteries were commenced, and from 1860 to 1861 these batteries were enlarged and extended; and from 1865 to 1875 the ten-inch guns were replaced by fifteen-inch guns, and traverses constructed. The work of construction on the fort was stopped in 1875 and the fort was in caretaker status with only an Ordnance Sergeant for maintenance until the Spanish-American War in 1898. Following a magazine explosion in 1902, the fort was abandoned in 1905. Governor's Island was separated from other harbor islands and the mainland by extensive mudflats but was joined to the mainland in 1946 and became part Logan International Airport. There are no traces left of Fort Winthrop.

The Engineer Corps expended on the various works, from 1846 to 1875, about $700,000; and this sum does not include the cost of armament, guns, carriages, etc., furnished by the Ordnance Department. Major (afterwards General) Sylvanus Thayer, Corps of Engineers, was in charge of construction from 1847 to 1848. Colonel Joseph K. F. Mansfield, Corps of Engineers, was in charge from 1848 to 1853. Other eminent officers of the Corps of Engineers who have had charge of this work at various times; include Generals John Gray Foster, Henry Washington Benham, and George Henry Thomas. It has been in charge of Lieutenant Colonel Samuel Mansfield, Corps of Engineers, a son of General Mansfield, for over six years.

The old Fort Warren was an enclosed "star fort," built of stone, brick, and sod, with brick barracks for seventy men, and a cellar under it 65 feet by 20 feet for provisions, etc. It had also a brick officers' quarters, magazine, and guardhouse. The Fort Warren battery was on the south side of Governor's Island, and built of brick, stone, and sod, with a brick guardhouse for fifteen men, and a brick magazine. The battery was to mount fifteen cannon, and to have a block house in its rear.

---

[15] "The Bostonian, An Illustrated Monthly Magazine of Local Interest," vol. II, April-Sept. 1895 (n/a, The Bostonian Publishing Company, 1895), 498-500. The quoted material from "The Bostonian" is supplemented from Wikipedia, "Fort Winthrop."

Chapter 7

Inspector General 1853 to 1861

Department of New Mexico 1853 (10 inspections)
Department of the Pacific 1854 (22 inspections)
Department of Texas 1856 (16 inspections)
Utah Army and Forts Leavenworth and Randall 1857
Department of California and Department of Oregon 1858-1859 (25 inspections)
Department of Texas 1860-1861 (17 inspections)[1]

---

[1] Joseph K.F. Mansfield, *Mansfield on the Condition of the Western Forts 1853-1854*, Robert W. Frazer, ed. (Norman, OK: University of Oklahoma Press), xxix.

CAPTAIN MANSFIELD'S BRAVERY AND MILITARY SKILLS were noticed by all who saw him during the Mexican-American War but most importantly, by Colonel Jefferson Davis, a future Secretary of War in the Pierce administration. Davis was the colonel of the 1st Regiment of Mississippi Volunteers during that war who later became President of the Confederate States of America.[2] Mansfield kept in contact with his acquaintances from the Mexican-American War, writing to Secretary of War Davis among others to ask for favors such as getting his sons and other relatives into service academies and most importantly for himself and his U.S. Army career. On 29 April 1853, he penned a "private" letter from Boston to Davis. He wrote that the Inspector General, "Colonel [George A.] McCall, had resigned, and if you think I am qualified for the position, and have not a preference for another, I shall be happy to receive such an appointment at your hands. I suppose there will be many applicants for the office. I have served in the Army since 1st July 1822—two years with the Board of Engineers as an assistant—three years at the fortifications N.Y. Harbour—two years at Old Point Comfort and the Rip Raps—fifteen years in building Fort Pulaski at the mouth of the Savannah River and have at intervals been in charge of the fortifications at Charleston Harbour and on the National Road, and harbor and river improvements prior to the Mexican War. In the field under General Taylor, I built Fort Brown and on other occasions had the good fortune to serve him faithfully of which you are as well acquainted as anyone." He wrote other letters asking for help to Connecticut's Governor Thomas H. Seymour, and a prominent engineer in Hartford, Connecticut, Edwin Stearns. Mansfield's long service in the Army and excellent performance in the Mexican-American War stood him in good stead with those who knew him there, as well as politicians and others in Connecticut who knew him for his sterling character as well.[3] What is clear is that Mansfield knew if he stayed in the Corps of Engineers, it would be unlikely that he would ever reach the grade of colonel and most likely that since he was 50 years old in 1853 he would still have at least 20 years before health would force him to leave the Army as there was no retirement option available. Therefore, the best he could realistically hope for as an Army engineer was to become a lieutenant colonel so the chance to be promoted three grades from captain to colonel was too much to ignore. His brevet promotions to colonel for his Mexican-American War service which allowed him to be called "colonel" gave him no extra pay. Mansfield decided that this was his best option although accepting this position would require that he spend more time away from his family and business interests. But, as a senior Army staff officer for the first time in his long career, Mansfield at least would be better able to control time spent on his inspection duties and could schedule extended time with his family in Middletown between his travels, making Middletown his "headquarters" and his "post." He certainly discussed with his wife the requirements and responsibilities that this new position would exact on him and his family, the first of which would be to move them back to Middletown from Boston. The time he spent with them since he returned from the

---

[2] Jefferson Finis Davis was born 3 June 1808 in Fairview, KY. He was an 1828 graduate of West Point, but resigned from the U.S. Army in 1835. On 18 July 1846, he became colonel of the 1st Mississippi Volunteer Regiment (1st Mississippi Rifles) and mustered out on 12 July 1847. He met Colonel Zachary Taylor at Fort Crawford, Michigan Territory, in 1829, and married Taylor's daughter, Sarah Knox, 17 June 1835, against her father's wishes. Sarah died at the age of 21 on 15 September 15 1835, after just three months of marriage and Davis became seriously ill. He married Varina Banks Howell 26 February 1845. He was elected to the U.S. House of Representatives in 1845 as a Mississippi representative but resigned his House seat in early June 1846 and raised a volunteer regiment. The regiment became known as the Mississippi Rifles because it was the first to be fully armed with the M1841 Mississippi Rifle which proved its worth in the war. In September, Davis participated in the Battle of Monterrey during which he led a brave charge on the La Teneria Fort. On 23 February 1847, Davis and his regiment fought well at the Battle of Buena Vista taking a crucial role in Taylor's victory where his 370 men faced some 4,000 Mexican troops. He was seriously wounded in the foot and was carried to safety by Captain Robert H. Chilton. In recognition of Davis's bravery and initiative, Taylor reportedly said, "My daughter, sir, was a better judge of men than I was." On May 17, President Polk offered Davis a federal commission as a brigadier general and command of a brigade of militia. Davis declined the appointment. He was elected a U.S. Senator in 1847 and chairman of the Committee on Military Affairs on 3 December 1849. He resigned in September 1851 to run for governor of Mississippi but lost by a slim margin. Franklin Pierce won the presidential election and made Davis his Secretary of War in 1853. He had the size of the Regular Army increased and did the same for Army pay. Congress added four regiments which increased the Army's size from about 11,000 to about 15,000. Davis also introduced the Mississippi Rifle that he used successfully during the Mexican-American War. When the Pierce administration ended in 1857, Davis lost his position so he ran for the Senate again and was reelected entering 4 March 1857. On 21 January 1861, the day Davis called "the saddest day of my life," he delivered a farewell address to the Senate, resigned, and returned to Mississippi. He was President of the Confederate States of America 22 February 1862 to 10 May 1865. Holman Hamilton, *The Three Kentucky Presidents: Lincoln, Taylor, Davis* (Lexington, KY: The Univ. Press of Kentucky, 1978), 13-15; Ethan S. Rafuse, "Jefferson Finis Davis," in *The Encyclopedia of the Mexican-American War*, ed. by Spencer C. Tucker (Santa Barbara, CA: ABC-CLIO, 2013), 189-190.

[3] Letters 29 April and 1 June 1853, courtesy of the Middlesex County Historical Society. "Brevet Colonel Joseph K.F. Mansfield, captain in the Corps of Engineers, to be inspector-general with the rank of colonel, vice McCall, resigned, to date from May 28, 1853." From Executive Journal 11 Jan. 1854 Journal of the Executive Proceedings of the Senate of the United States, vol. 9, By United States Congress, Senate, pg. 189; document courtesy of the Middlesex County Historical Society.

Mexican-American War was valuable and any misunderstandings between himself and his wife during his absence in Mexico were ameliorated. He likely told her that he would be able to spend more time at their Middletown home as it would become his official post between inspections, and the added benefits to which he would become eligible, due to his senior rank, would have pleased her. Regardless, Mansfield deeply desired this position and would have found few material impediments to interfere with his application.[4]

---

[4] 1857 Army Regulations detailed when brevet pay could be allowed: "Officers having brevet commissions are entitled to their brevet pay and emoluments token on duty and having a command according to their brevet rank, and at no other time. (Act April 16, 1818.) Officers are on duty and have a command according to their brevet rank only when assigned to their brevet rank by the President with the appropriate actual command composed of different corps, or when serving on detachments composed of different corps, with such appropriate command. But in the regiment, troop, or company to which officers belong, they do duty and draw pay according to the commissions by which they are mustered in their own corps;" *Regulations for the Army of the United States, 1857* (New York, NY: Harper & Brothers), 285. There was no retirement system in place until 1861 when Congress authorized a voluntary retirement system for officers. "The Act of August 3, 1861, authorized the voluntary retirement, at the discretion of the President, of regular officers of all branches of service after 40 years of duty. The Act of December 21, 1861, permitted the involuntary retirement of Navy officers after 45 years of service or at age 62 while the Act of July 17, 1862, permitted the same for Army and Marine Corps officers [45 years' service or age 62]," Bruce R. Breth, *An Historical Analysis and Comparison of the Military Retirement System and the Federal Employee Retirement System*, unpublished master's thesis, Naval Postgraduate School, Monterey, CA, 1998, 38. His jump from a regular captain to full colonel was rare during the middle 1800's up to the Civil War.

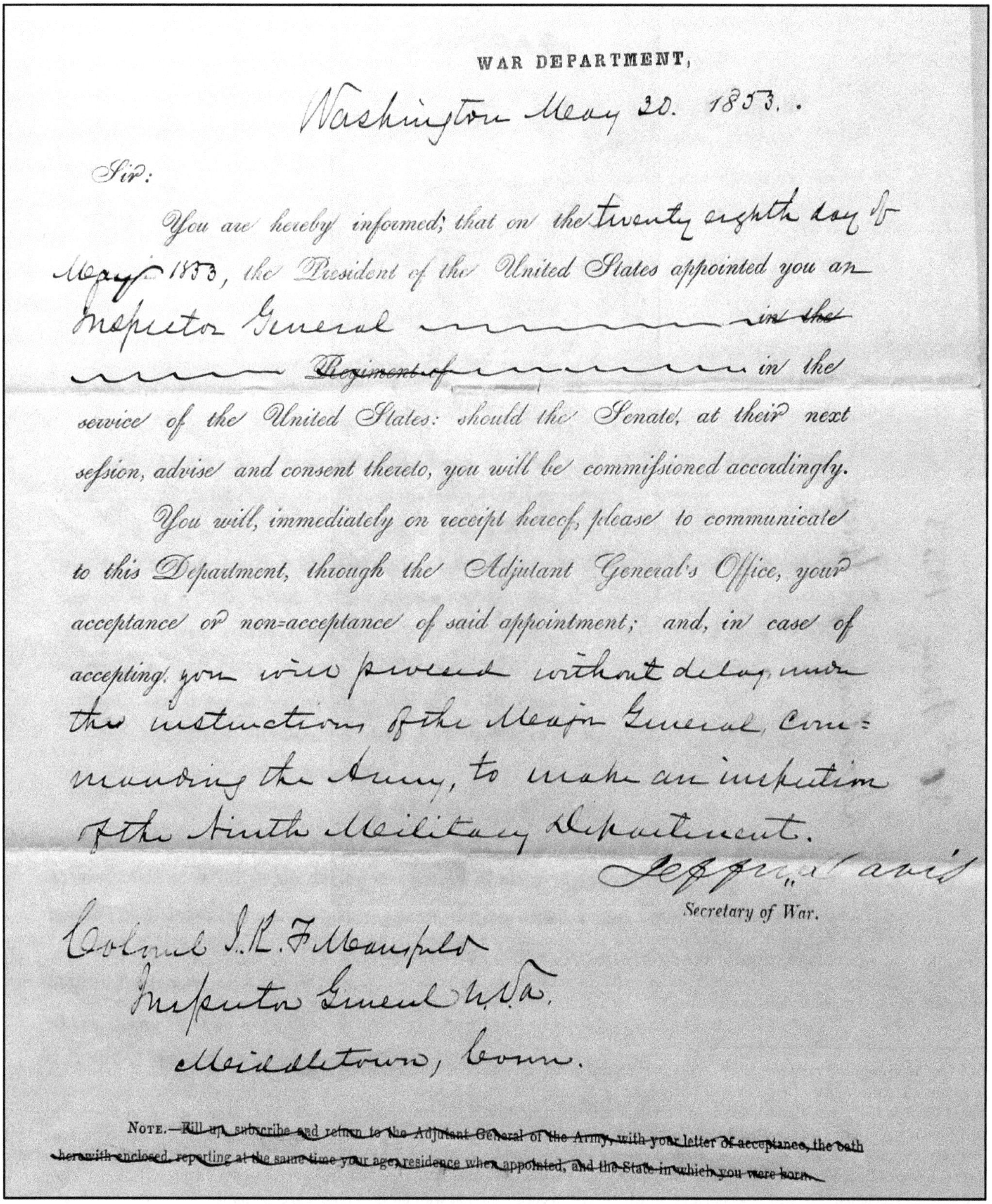

WAR DEPARTMENT,

Washington May 20. 1853.

Sir:

You are hereby informed; that on the twenty eighth day of May, 1853, the President of the United States appointed you an Inspector General in the Regiment of in the service of the United States: should the Senate, at their next session, advise and consent thereto, you will be commissioned accordingly.

You will, immediately on receipt hereof, please to communicate to this Department, through the Adjutant General's Office, your acceptance or non=acceptance of said appointment; and, in case of accepting, you will proceed without delay, under the instructions of the Major General, Commanding the Army, to make an inspection of the Ninth Military Department.

Jeff. Davis

Secretary of War.

Colonel J. K. F. Mansfield
Inspector General U. S. A.
Middletown, Conn.

NOTE.—Fill up, subscribe and return to the Adjutant General of the Army, with your letter of acceptance, the oath herewith enclosed, reporting at the same time your age, residence when appointed, and the State in which you were born.

An original copy of Mansfield's appointment as an Inspector General from the 28th day of May 1853. The 9th Military Department at this time was New Mexico. Courtesy of the Middlesex County Historical Society.

Colonel Mansfield as he appeared when the Civil War began and before he was promoted to brigadier general. This is how he would have appeared to Colonel Oliver O. Howard which prompted this description on his meeting Mansfield in 1861: "I reported at an early hour on June 8th to Colonel Joseph K. F. Mansfield, Inspector General of the Army, commanding the Department of Washington. He was already frosted with age and long service. Probably from his own Christian character no officer of the Army then could have inspired me with more reverence than he. At that time Mansfield appeared troubled and almost crushed by an overwhelming amount of detail thrust upon him."[5] Photograph courtesy of NARA.

---

[5] Oliver Otis Howard, *Autobiography of Oliver Otis Howard*, vol. 1 (New York, NY: The Baker & Taylor Company, 1907), 132. Mansfield was placed in command of the Military Department of Washington on 27 April 1861 in War Department G.O. 12, and promoted to brigadier general effective 14 May 1861. The 1847 Army Regulations stated: "The hair to be short, or what is generally termed cropped; the whiskers not to extend below the lower tip of the ear, and a line thence with the curve of the mouth; mustaches will not be worn, (except by cavalry regiments,) by officers or men on any pretense whatever;" *General Regulations for the Army of the United States, 1847* (Washington, DC: J. and G.S. Gideon, 1847), 215. Officers and men did not closely adhere to the facial hair regulations during the Mexican-American War. However, General Order 35 of 6 July 1848 stated that the hair and whisker regulation "The non-observance of [which] (tolerated during the war with Mexico) is no longer permitted. It is enjoined upon all officers to observe and enforce the regulation." General Orders No. 2 dated 6 January 1853 amended paragraph 218 of the Regulations of 1851: "The beard to be worn at the pleasure of the individual, but when worn to be kept short and neatly trimmed." The 1857 edition of the General Regulations provided for officers: "The hair to be short; the beard to be worn at the pleasure of the individual, but when worn to be kept short and neatly trimmed." This liberalization of hair and facial hair rules allowed Mansfield to spend less time on grooming during his months-long arduous inspections tours in the west. It is likely that Mansfield did try to adhere to other 1857 War Department Regulations which required that "Where conveniences for bathing are to be had, the men should bathe once a week. The feet to be washed at least twice a week. The hair kept short, and beard neatly trimmed;" *Regulations for the Army of the United States, 1857* (New York, NY: Harper & Brothers), 13, 456; Richard Dalzell Gamble, "Garrison Life at Frontier Military Posts, 1830-1860, "unpublished Ph.D. Dissertation Univ. of Oklahoma, 1956, 303.

Franklin Pierce, 14th President of the United States c. 1855. Courtesy LOC. He was in office from 4 March 1853 to 4 March 1857.

Colonel George A. McCall, Mansfield's predecessor as Inspector General and whose resignation allowed Mansfield to gain the post. Photograph taken c. 1860, courtesy LOC.[6]

---

[6] "In 1851 [McCall] was ordered to make a tour of inspection of the posts on the Pacific coast in California and Oregon. Having completed that tour, and returning to Philadelphia, he remained waiting orders till April 1853. During that time his health had become much impaired, the result of long exposure in malarious regions; and at the time the order was received, he was too feeble to undertake the arduous journey required of him." He wrote to the adjutant general from Philadelphia on 22 April 1853 as follows: "I had the honor to receive, yesterday, Special Orders, No. 11, directing me to make an inspection of the 9th Military Department, and I immediately acknowledge the receipt of the Order. I have now to state that I am not in such health as to undertake this important duty with the prospect of discharging it to my own satisfaction or the best interests of the service, I therefore, respectfully tender the resignation of my commission of Inspector General, U.S.A., and request it may be laid before the President of the U.S. for his acceptance. The regret I might entertain in offering my resignation at this juncture is removed by the conviction that the office will be filled by one more competent." In his cover letter to this resignation McCall wrote that "I am not prompted to this step by any sudden feeling; I am sincere in the reasons I give, and have had it lately in contemplation to leave the service, on account of my health. For some years past I have labored under the effects of neuralgia, and I suffer greatly when exposed. The service must now be principally upon the extreme western frontier, and to perform it properly requires a man to be active and hardy. This I am not. I, therefor, do not desire to retain an office, the duties of which I am unable to discharge to my own satisfaction." He received the following reply from the headquarters of the Army 23 April 1853: "Dear Sir: The General-in-Chief [General Winfield Scott] has desired me to express to you his sense of the loss the Army will sustain by your withdrawal from it. I cannot better do so than by quoting the language used by him, in forwarding the tender of your commission, as Inspector-General of the Army, to the Secretary of War: 'Herewith I forward for your consideration Colonel McCall's tender of his commission as Inspector-General of the Army. If the tender be accepted, the public service will lose a highly valuable and distinguished officer.' 'Happy in being the medium of communicating the above expression by its Chief of the sentiments of the Army, I have the honor to be, your obedient servant, Schuyler Hamilton, Captain by Bt. A.D.C.' The resignation was accepted in compliance with the reiterated request of Colonel McCall. Thus terminated his connection with the service in which the better part of his

Mansfield wrote several letters on 1 June 1853 as he feverishly prepared for his new Army career. He penned a letter to Colonel Samuel Cooper, Adjutant General in Washington, D.C., from his home in Middletown: "I have the honor to acknowledge the receipt of the letter of the Hon. The Secretary of War informing me that the President of the U.S. appointed me an Inspector General in the service of the U.S. from the 28th day of May 1853. Accordingly I take the pleasure in accepting the same and in stating to the Hon. The Secretary of War that I appreciate highly the distinction he has bestowed on me in the selection to so important an office." Mansfield also wrote to Lieutenant Colonel Lorenzo Thomas, Assistant Adjutant General, to report his promotion and that he is in Middletown having brought his family there from Brookline preparatory to going to San Francisco as previously ordered. He also wrote to Colonel McCall to take advantage of the knowledge of the outgoing Inspector General, asking him for practical advice and instructions as Mansfield must make an inspection tour of the 9th Department--New Mexico. Would he need a "full dress uniform? How to get there from Independence, Missouri--by himself or with troops—need private arms beyond a Colt revolver— can he obtain an outfit at Independence in servants and horses, etc.?" In two more letters five days later, he wrote to Davis "Your friendly feelings and partiality to me who has fought side by side with you for our country is all the merit I claim." He also told him that he would leave New York by the middle of the month via the Erie Railroad and Chicago as the quickest way to reach Independence and Fort Leavenworth. He also composed another letter to President Pierce thanking him for the appointment. One can sense his excitement and pleasure in receiving this appointment and his anxiety to undertake his mission soon and to learn from his predecessor practical wisdom for his first inspection. But his joy must have been somewhat tempered with the knowledge that he must again leave his family for extended periods and this time with no summer breaks as he had during his tour constructing Fort Pulaski. But he realized that between his tours he would be able to spend months with his family living with them in his home town as his "post" since there was no official post for an inspector general. Also, he was within easy commuting distance from the station of the General-in-Chief of the Army in New York City, Lieutenant General Winfield Scott. On balance, he dove into his new life with eagles on his shoulders and renewed zeal believing that he would likely end his career as a senior army colonel and with the perquisites attaching to that rank.[7]

---

life had been passed." George A. McCall, *Letters from the Frontier* (Philadelphia, PA: J.B. Lippincott & Co., 1868), 530-537; letters courtesy NARA. McCall became a major general of Pennsylvania Volunteers in 1861 and resigned in 1863. He died in 1868.

[7] Three letters written on 1 June, and two on 6 June 1853, courtesy of the Middlesex County Historical Society and NARA. Mansfield's 3 June letter from Middletown to Thomas noted that he would proceed on his inspection tour "immediately after my uniform can be made which will occupy three or four days." Obviously his old engineer's captain's togs would not do; letter courtesy NARA.

3

MIDDLETOWN, CONNECTICUT,
June 2d, 1853.

Bvt. Brig. Gen'l. Jos. G. TOTTEN,
　　Chief Engineer.

SIR:—My appointment of Inspector General in the army, necessarily severs me from the Corps of Engineers, and deprives me of that interesting association with the officers of the Corps in the performance of duty, which I have always regarded as one of great satisfaction. I feel pleasure in saying, that without exception, I have never had the least personal or official misunderstanding with any officer of the Corps, and that I now take leave of them as a body with feelings of great respect for them as gentlemen of the highest scientific talents and attainments, and they have my most hearty good wishes for their success: and I trust they all of them feel as I do, that it is an honor to belong to the Corps of Engineers.

But, sir, with respect to yourself, I feel I owe to you, as the distinguished head of the Corps, a duty of thanks and gratitude for the official kindness and forbearance you have invariably extended to me at all times. And it gives me pleasure at this time, as I am severed from your immediate command, and can now do so with propriety, to make this acknowledgment to you.

To the whole Corps, I am under obligations for the courtesy they have invariably extended to me in the course of my official duties. Words are inadequate to express my feelings in separating from the Corps of Engineers, of which I have been a member for over thirty years— you have my best wishes for the honor and prosperity of the Corps and its individual members.

With great respect,
I have the honor to be,
Your obedient servant,
JOSEPH K. F. MANSFIELD,
Colonel and Inspector General.

———

Col. J. K. F. MANSFIELD,
　　Inspector General.

ENGINEER DEPARTMENT,
Washington, *June 6th,* 1853.

SIR: I have the honor to acknowledge the receipt of your letter of the 2d instant; in which, while taking leave of the Officers of the Corps of Engineers on your appointment as

Copy of Mansfield's resignation from the Corps of Engineers printed by that Department along with General Totten's reply. Courtesy of the Middlesex County Historical Society.

4

Inspector General, you express your hearty good wishes for their success; your great respect for them as gentlemen of the highest scientific attainments, and your trust that they all feel as you do, " that it is an honor to belong to the Corps of Engineers."

As the senior officer replying, in what I am sure is the feeling of the whole Corps, to these expressions of good feeling, I have to say, that while we greatly regret the loss of an officer who has contributed so much to exalt the reputation of the Corps by high scientific attainments, great experience in the multifarious duties of an Engineer, and distinguished military services in the face of the enemy—we are much gratified by the public recognition of these merits and services; and cannot but feel proud that, while there were so many officers of the different arms of the service, prominent by very distinguished merits, the selection should have fallen on one of our own comrades.

Many of us, moreover, have by personal association, in some cases running through many years, and always of the most friendly nature, acquired a personal interest in your welfare, and professional success, causing them to look on your promotion with unfeigned satisfaction.

For my own part, as Chief of the Corps, while I participate with sincerity and warmth in all these sentiments and feelings, I cannot but add that my regrets at the separation are very great, for I must often in the future, as I do at this moment, feel the want, for important operations, of the assistance of an officer possessing so much experience and talent, and so prompt and energetic in the execution of every duty.

I am certain that you will continue to render important services to your country: may they, like your past services, redound to your own honor; and happiness and prosperity attend all your private relations.

I am with great respect,

Your obedient servant,

J. G. TOTTEN,

Bvt. Brig. Gen'l,

and Col. Engineers.

General Totten was Mansfield's cousin. Courtesy of the Middlesex County Historical Society.

Adjutant General Lorenzo Thomas here shown as a brigadier general taken c. 1860, courtesy LOC.[8] Mansfield addressed virtually all of his inspection reports to him and sent all of his monthly and most other reports to Adjutant General Samuel Cooper. The Adjutant General's Office was the official contact point for Mansfield with the U.S. Army.

Samuel Cooper, photograph taken before the Civil War. Courtesy LOC.[9]

---

[8] Thomas was an 1823 West Point graduate and was brevetted to lieutenant colonel for his actions at Monterrey, Mexico. He was chief of staff for Major General Winfield Scott from 1853 to 1861 and colonel (7 March 1861) and brigadier general as the Adjutant General of the U.S. Army until his retirement 22 February 1869. On 3 August 1861, he was confirmed as a brigadier general in the Regular Army and brevetted to major general from 14 July 1866.

Mansfield spent the next eight years of his Army career inspecting Army posts west of the Mississippi River as well as inspecting recruits in several locations around the United States mainly in the East. Having spent over two years in Texas and Mexico, he was familiar with the southwest and also with the types of Army enlisted men and officers he would later encounter. As will be seen, most of the officers with whom he interacted during his western experiences were those he met during the Mexican-American War or during his long Army service beginning at West Point. His inspections showed that enlisted men were troubled with the same issues he saw firsthand in Mexico and most of his inspections listed desertions and recruiting problems he found similar to this infantry regiment: "When the 10th Infantry began recruiting in 1855, of the first 500 men who enlisted in the new regiment, 66 were born in New England, 149 were from the West and Midwest, and 285 were foreign-born. The regimental history notes that 55 percent of the recruits deserted before completing their enlistments."[10] One of the few literate enlisted soldiers, Eugene Bandel, wrote that "The greater part of the Army consists of men who either do not care to work, or who, because of being addicted to drink, cannot find employment."[11] Another enlisted man, Augustus Meyers, related what he experienced at Carlisle Barracks in 1855:

A company of soldiers, after they have served together for some months, become like a large family. My own company was a fair sample. We soon knew each other's good points, failings and weaknesses. It took but a short time for the company to separate itself into two parties; the larger of which contained the men who kept themselves clean, and took some pride in soldiering. The other contingent, happily small in numbers, were often slovenly, disorderly, and sometimes vicious. They were given to quarrelling, and occasional fighting. Though they banded together, they were not able to create much trouble while in the quarters, as they were so largely outnumbered. It became necessary sometimes to teach one of them a severe lesson, and I remember one case wherein a man of filthy habits was taken to the creek by his comrades, stripped and washed with soap and sand until his skin was raw.[12]

The famous raconteur dragoon, Samuel Chamberlain, also described those with whom he served during this era:

Soldiers of the Army may be divided into three classes. First, 'Dead Beats,' men who can never be trusted, they are dirty and careless, never ready for duty, in the guard house or on the sick report most of the time. This class is hated by their comrades, and despised by the officers. Second, the 'old soldiers,' men who do their duty in a quiet mechanical sort of a way, always on the hand in camp, never in the guard house, never known to get drunk or spend their money, they are disliked by the men who suspect them of being tale bearers to the officers; they are often made Corporals, but rarely Sergeants, being jumped by the Third Class, the 'Dare Devils.' These men are first in a fight, frolic or for duty with uniforms fitting like a glove and faultlessly clean, arms, horses, and accoutrements always in inspection condition, faithful in the discharge of every duty, but when off duty no

---

[9] Cooper was an 1815 West Point graduate. In 1838, he was appointed assistant adjutant general of the Army. In the Second Seminole War of 1841–42, he was chief of staff for Colonel William J. Worth, and after hostilities ended he returned to staff duty in Washington from 1842 to 1845. He received a brevet promotion to colonel on 30 May 1848, for his service as Adjutant General in Washington during the Mexican-American War, and was promoted to the permanent rank of colonel in the Regular Army and appointed the Army's Adjutant General on 15 July 1852. He also served very briefly as acting U.S. Secretary of War in 1857. He resigned 7 March 1861 joining the Confederacy and was appointed a brigadier general on 16 March 1861 serving as both Adjutant General and Inspector General of the Confederate Army. On 16 May 1861, he was promoted to full general in the Confederate Army and became its senior general. He died in 1876.

[10] Clayton R. Newell, *The Regular Army before the Civil War 1845-1860* (Washington, DC: The Center of Military History, 1975), 36. Low salaries helped contribute to soldiers' dissatisfaction in the Army so when opportunities for better fortune were found such as in the gold fields, desertions increased. "In 1830 a private received five dollars a month, plus clothing, food, and medical care. In 1838 his salary was raised to six dollars a month, and to eight dollars a month after two years' service. By 1860 the regular Army private earned monthly between eleven and twelve dollars, the higher pay being the amount for dragoon and artillery personnel. During the same period, corporals' wages increased from seven to nine, and later to twelve dollars, sergeants', from eight to thirteen to seventeen, and sergeant majors', from ten to seventeen to twenty-one dollars a month. Musicians, blacksmiths, and artillery artificers received proportionately higher increases to their respective salaries, which usually were in the range between private and sergeant. Ordinarily, officers and men were paid every second month. However, if the paymaster had to travel a great distance between departmental headquarters and the many isolated posts, six or more months often elapsed between pay periods," Gamble, 53-54. The many criticisms found in Mansfield's letters to his wife written in Mexico detailing how she should manage their family, its health, finances, etc., and his minute reviews of posts he inspected led credence to the thought that he was someone who indeed paid attention to even small details fitting to one with engineering training. In any event, this attention to detail and honest criticisms, both good and bad, stood him in good stead in his new career. Perhaps with this new official outlet, his wife was spared excessive micromanagement.

[11] Eugene Bandel, *Frontier Life in the Army, 1854-1861*, ed. by Ralph B. Bieber (Glendale, CA: The Arthur H. Clark Company, 1932), 110, 114;

[12] Augustus Meyers, *Ten Years in the Ranks U.S. Army* (New York, NY: The Sterling Press, 1914), 43.

camp can hold them. They often turn up in the guard house, but never in the Hospital; they are the 'orderlies' of the regiment, the pride of the officers and the admiration of their companions. I was considered a fair representative of the third order.[13]

But Chamberlain generally thought well of his officers: "Our officers were all graduates of West Point, and at the worst, were gentlemen of intelligence and education, often harsh and tyrannical, yet they took pride in having their men well clothed, and fed, in making them contented and reconciled to their lot."[14] While most company and many field grade officers were West Point graduates, the senior officers were not. In the middle 1850's about 73 per cent of the officers were West Pointers but generals such as Scott, John E. Wool, and Daniel E. Twiggs were not but had decades of service some starting in the War of 1812. Dissatisfaction in the officer ranks increased in 1855 after four new regiments were formed as about half of the officer billets were filled by political appointment. Secretary of War Davis probably did this to curry political favor to be allowed to pass legislation through Congress required to authorize the formation of these new units. Service on the frontier was usually harsh and boring so many officers as well as enlisted soldiers found comfort in alcohol with many becoming alcoholics. Slow promotion and low pay added to the low morale of numerous officers, many of whom resigned to pursue more lucrative civilian pursuits. With no retirement system in place until 1861, superannuated officers who had difficulty performing their duties abounded.[15] Even though the officer corps was small, 1,032 total authorized in 1855, that corps was never fully harmonious given the strict seniority promotion regime, and contained several quarreling factions such as infantry versus mounted, line against staff, and North against South. This last factor became more exacerbated as the decade of the 1850's wore on. Also given that the authorized numbers of officers at a post were rarely present, remaining officers often had to perform the duties of two or more slots. "Jealous of prerogatives, quick to prefer charges for the most trivial offenses real or imagined, eternally quarreling over precedence, from general-in-chief down, the officers engaged in prodigies of disputation and decreed that a large share of one's service be spent on court-martial duty." As a senior army officer and an inspector general, Mansfield spent much time on court martial boards.[16]

The U.S. Army posts Mansfield would inspect during his peripatetic years would become familiar to him as he visited most of them more than once. As was seen in the last chapter, the U.S. Army greatly expanded to fight the war over a great geographical distance although major battles were concentrated in northern and central Mexico with Taylor's and Scott's armies. Congress strengthened the Regular Army and also called up thousands of volunteers, but at the end of the war in November 1848, disbanded the volunteers and reduced the Regular Army strength to 929 officers and 9,106 enlisted men somewhat larger than it was when the war began in May 1846, (637 officers and 5,925 enlisted) and down from the grand total of 42,587 regulars who served during the war. The Army had eight infantry, four artillery, and three mounted regiments to garrison the west, as the artillery regiments remained mostly on the east coast. At the end of the war, Army units were disbursed as follows: "The 1st, 2nd, 3rd, and 4th Infantry initially went to Louisiana, the 5th deployed to Arkansas and Indian Territory, while the 6th, 7th, and 8th, Infantry traveled to Jefferson Barracks, Missouri. The 1st and 2nd Artillery went to Governor's Island, New York, while the 3rd and 4th assembled at Fort Monroe, Virginia. The Regiment of Mounted Riflemen went to Fort Leavenworth and the two dragoon regiments remained in the southwest to patrol the Mexican border along the Rio Grande. From these locations the regiments further broke down and dispersed in small detachments to bring security to America's long coast and expansive frontier."[17] The large increase in the size of the territory gained by the United States following the end of the war meant that the U.S. Army had to send its forces further west to cover areas from the Rio Grande River in southern Texas to the border with Canada and to the Pacific Ocean while still maintaining coastal defenses in the east. Settlers needed protection from hostile Indians and travelers heading west required safe resting points along migration trails such as the

---

[13] Samuel Chamberlain, *My Confession: Recollections of a Rogue*, ed. by William H. Goetzmann (Austin, TX: Texas State Historical Association, 1996), 215. Chamberlain wrote a breathtaking history of his time in the Army and the West, much of which is probably true, and is a must read for anyone interested in the U.S. Army during this time.

[14] Chamberlain, *My Confession: Recollections of a Rogue*, 116.

[15] Robert M. Utley, *Frontiersmen in Blue: The United States Army and the Indian, 1848-1865* (New York, NY: The Macmillan Company, 1967), 31-34. Of the 116 civil appointees, 66 were veterans of the Mexican-American War or West Point dropouts.

[16] Durwood Ball, *Army Regulars on the Western Frontier, 1848-1861* (Norman, OK: University of Oklahoma Press, 2001), xxii-xxiii. A law passed 17 June 1850 allowed the President to increase the number of privates to 74 in each company serving on the frontier which was done in 1855 raising the legal enlisted strength to 16,822. Utley, *Frontiersmen in Blue*, 22, 34-35. Utley notes that Southerners were more numerous in the officer corps so Northerners bore the brunt of bias. Prior to the uniform 74 men per company, cavalry and dragoon companies had 50 privates, Mounted Rifles 64, infantry 42 if heavy, 64 if light.

[17] Smith, *The War with Mexico*, vol. 2, 511, n. 15; Newell, 23.

Santa Fe and Oregon Trails. In 1850, the U.S. Army had an aggregate strength of 10,763, while in 1855; it had 15,752 with an upper limit of 18,318 as the President was authorized to expand the size of companies in the western territories. Authorized strength however, was always higher than aggregate strength. Plus, desertion, discharge, and death gave an annual turnover rate of about 28 per cent so that, combined with the actual strength being 18 per cent below authorized strength, many frontier posts were barely able to perform their required functions—Mansfield would often comment upon this during his inspections. Data in 1850 also show "there were 2,109 officers and men stationed at 33 posts east of the Mississippi and 6,385 officers and men at 67 posts west of the Mississippi. By 1860, the preponderance of troops located in the western frontier area was even more pronounced. Out of an actual strength of 16,006, the Adjutant General reported 929 men and officers stationed in the Department of the East and 13,143 in the Departments of the West, Texas, New Mexico, Utah, Oregon, and California. "On the frontier any regiment could theoretically number nearly 900. In fact, 1 or 2 officers and 30 to 40 men per company, or 300 to 400 per regiment, was the usual average."[18]

> Military garrisons were placed at strategic points in advance of farmers and cattlemen to act as the "cutting edge" of civilization….[and] had the multifold task of keeping the Indians and whites from clashing. This mission meant that the Army was policing the frontier to prevent renegade whites, unlicensed traders, and impatient farmers from taking advantage of those tribes who had made treaty agreements with the United States in regard to relocation in the West. At the same time it was the duty of the military to keep the Indian within his prescribed area, to forestall intertribal warfare, and to attempt to prevent Indian ravages on white settlements behind or in advance of treaty boundaries. There being no effective civil government to cope with the transgressions of Indian and white, the Army frequently acted as disciplinarian on the frontier. Punitive expeditions were as common as exploratory and patrolling maneuvers during the pre-Civil War period….military posts also were established along the Oregon and Santa Fe trails as havens for immigrant parties traveling to the West Coast. The Army posts provided supply depots, a protection against hostile Indians, a resting place for the tired, and a sanatorium for the sick and dying. These posts, initially established as wayside inns, later assumed the same roles as their eastern predecessors in upholding the Indian restriction policies of the federal government."[19]

Mansfield's reports followed a general outline guided by the requirements given him by General Scott's orders such as he received from his commanding general on 18 March 1854 and 12 March 1856: "to 'exhibit the true state and conditions of the commands,' as well as the location of the several posts, and stations, the object they were designed to accomplish, and to what extent thus far the purposes in view have been attained, their distances from each other, the practicability of the routes leading to them, the nature of the country in which they are situated, and to what extent it may be relied on in obtaining supplies; specifying also the nearest settlements, and the number of population capable of bearing arms; what Indian tribes reside in the vicinity, and the number of warriors they could bring into the field, and such other general information as in a military view may be deemed important to be communicated."[20] This instruction was a distillation of Army Regulations in force for decades. Mansfield also sent monthly reports to the Army Adjutant General which gave a summary of his tasks for that month and sometimes a preview of what he planned for the following month. He invariably called his Middletown home his "post" and sometimes reported that he was there "awaiting orders" and reported no accomplishments. He even occasionally forgot to send a report so caught up in following months. Mansfield also sent interim reports to the Adjutant General's Office during his inspections and a lengthy final report after he returned to Middletown. His rough drafts of his inspections which he retained in his personal files and all final reports included sketches of the posts he inspected. His retained rough drafts show that some

---

[18] Erna Risch, *Quartermaster Support of the Army: A History of the Corps, 1775-1939* (Washington, DC: Department of the Army, 1962) 301. This total distribution figure of 14,072 does not include men at depots, the Military Academy, recruit rendezvous, and en route. Heitman, *Historical Register*, vol. 2, 282, 626; troops engaged in Mexico: 30,954 Regulars and 73,776 Volunteers. Utley, *Frontiersmen in Blue*, 18-19, 22. Utley notes that in June 1853, the authorized strength of the Army was 13,821 but the actual size was 10,417; even worse on the frontier, of the 8,342 officers and men stationed there, only 6,918 were at their posts.

[19] Newell, 22-53 *passim*. Authorized Army strength at the beginning of the Mexican-American War was 12,540, increased during the war to 31,000, then at the end of the war down to 10,320. The number of troops in service was always less than the number authorized; Gamble, 3-4, 6, 8.

[20] Letter courtesy of the Middlesex County Historical Society. See full letter below in Attachment 2. Martin Lalor Crimmins, "Colonel J.K.F. Mansfield's Report of the Inspection of the Department of Texas in 1856," *The Southwestern Historical Quarterly*, vol. 42, July 1938-April 1939, 125, 378 Texas State Historical Association. Austin, Texas. (texashistory.unt.edu/ark:/67531/metapth101107/: accessed April 10, 2017), University of North Texas Libraries, The Portal to Texas History, texashistory.unt.edu; crediting Texas State Historical Association. 122-148, 215-256, 351-387, passim.

of the post diagrams were not done by him but all of those in his final reports were. He obviously used accurate drawings given to him while he visited posts as bases for his own sketches.[21]

Mansfield and other Inspector Generals were required to submit to the Adjutant General monthly reports. This copy was sent to Mansfield on 14 June 1853 as he was unaware of this requirement of his new job. Courtesy of the Middlesex County Historical Society.

[21] See, e.g., his reports to the Adjutant General for 1855-1856, RG 94, NARA. His 19 and 22 June 1855 letters to Colonel Samuel Cooper, the Adjutant General, serve as examples of his occasional omissions: "I have accidentally omitted my personal report for the month of May last—I have now the honor to report that during that month I was permitted to remain in this City at my post till such time as the Commanding Gen'l or the Secretary of War should require my services." "As I have omitted accidentally my personal report for April last I have now the honor to state that during that month I was permitted to remain here at my post [in Middletown]."

GENERAL ORDERS, } **HEAD QUARTERS OF THE ARMY,**
ADJUTANT GENERAL's OFFICE,
No. 7. } *Washington, March 15, 1853.*

1. With the assent of the PRESIDENT, the General Head Quarters of the Army, after the 31st of the present month, will be re-established in the city of New York, as immediately prior to November 1, 1850.

2. Lieutenant Colonel Lorenzo Thomas, First Assistant Adjutant General, is announced as Chief of the Staff, and all communications will be addressed to him. Brevet Captain Irvin McDowell, of the same branch of the Staff, will also be on duty at General Head Quarters.

3. Muster rolls, Returns and Inventories, enjoined by the 13th, 19th, 94th and 95th of the Rules and Articles of War, and by the General Regulations for the Army, will, as at present, be forwarded to the Adjutant General's Office, Washington. Officers on leave of absence and on detached service, will make the prescribed reports in like manner, and also to General Head Quarters, New York. Certificates of disability and for pension will be forwarded for decision to General Head Quarters, whence after being finally disposed of they will be transmitted to the Adjutant General's Office.

4. Commanders of Divisions, Departments and Posts, will make monthly returns to the Chief of the Staff, commencing with the month of April next.

5. The recruiting service will be conducted by the Adjutant General under the direction of the Secretary of War.

BY COMMAND OF MAJOR GENERAL SCOTT :

Adjutant General.

Army requirements for reports, copy found in Mansfield's records. Courtesy of the Middlesex County Historical Society.

Monthly report requirement the Engineer Department sent to Mansfield 24 February 1853. Courtesy of the Middlesex County Historical Society.

Regulations published in 1825 show early inspection requirements:

The commander of each department shall, as often as he may be required by the War Department, or general-in-chief, make tours of inspection and review, embracing the military posts within the department.

The objects of these tours, will be: to ascertain, critically, the state of the several bodies of troops under the heads of discipline, police, instruction, service, and administration within the command; to ascertain whether the several branches of the administrative departments of the staff under his command, be well executed; to point out, on the spot, all defects or irregularities to be brought to trial, and to give such other orders as may be bound necessary, in order to correct promptly all defects or neglects observed.

The inspectors-general are under the direction of the general-in-chief of the Army. Whenever they commence a tour of inspection, they will communicate information thereof to the general commanding the department then to be inspected, together with the probable time of arrival at each post; and immediately on the inspection of a military post, the inspector will make a confidential report to the commanding general of the department, of any defects, irregularities, or abuses; which he may discover at the time of his inspections, in order to their being immediately remedied or corrected. Copies of these reports will, on the termination of the tour, be forwarded to the general-in-chief. The reports of the inspectors will be considered strictly confidential, so far as they relate to the character and habits of officers. In other respects, they will be subject, under the discretion of the general-in-chief, to be communicated to the commands affected by them, with a view to the correction of abuses.

The generals commanding departments will inspect in person, at least once in two years, all the military posts and forces assigned to their commands, and will report to the general-in-chief such facts, connected with the condition of the departments, as they may judge necessary.

The field officers of artillery will inspect their regiments, respectively, under the orders of the commanders of departments, making such reports of the inspections as may be required at department headquarters. Each company of artillery ought to be so inspected once in six months.[22]

In a history of the organization of the Army, Fayette Robinson described the duties of an Inspector General in 1848: "to make inspections of the personnel and materiel of the Army, to report on the condition and efficiency of the other staff corps, and to inquire into the discipline and drill of the forces. They may report on anything—the character, moral and physical, of officers, nature of defences, health of posts, and the countless minutiae which make up the sum of the service. Their reports being the result of individual examination, are of course only valuable as such, in proportion to the estimate placed on the character and standing of the inspectors-general."[23] Regulations of the U.S. Army in 1857 again detailed inspectors' duties:

Inspection reports will show the discipline of the troops; their instruction in all military exercises and duties: the state of their arms, clothing, equipments, and accoutrements of all kinds; of their kitchens and messes; of the barracks and quarters at the post; of the guard-house, prisons, hospital, bake-house, magazines, store-houses, and stores of every description; of the stables and horses; the condition of the post school; the management and application of the post and company funds; the state of the post, and regimental, and company books, papers, and files; the zeal and ability of the officers in command of troops; the capacity of the officers conducting the administrative and staff services, the fidelity and economy of their disbursements; the condition of all public property, and the amount of money in the hands of each disbursing officer; the regularity of issues and payments; the mode of enforcing discipline by courts-martial, and by the authority of the officers; the propriety and legality of all punishments inflicted; and any information whatsoever, concerning the service in any matter or particular that may merit notice, or aid to correct defects or introduce improvements.

Inspectors are required particularly to report if any officer is of intemperate habits, or unfit for active service by infirmity or any other cause.

When military stores or other Army supplies are reported to the War Department as unsuitable to the service, a proper inspection or survey of them shall be made by an Inspector-General, or such suitable officer or officers as the Secretary of War may appoint for that purpose. Separate inventories of the stores, according to the disposition to be made of them, shall accompany the inspection report: as of articles to be repaired, to be broken up, to be sold, of no use or value, and to be dropped, &c, &c. The inspection report and inventories shall show the exact condition of the different articles.[24]

---

[22] *General Regulations for the Army; or, Military Institutes* (Washington, DC: Davis & Force, 1825), 61, 367.

[23] Fayette Robinson, *An Account of the Organization of the Army of the United States*, vol. 1 (Philadelphia, PA: E.H. Butler, 1848), 39.

[24] *Regulations for the Army of the United States, 1857* (New York, NY: Harper & Brothers), 63, 119. These 1857 regulations for inspectors were essentially unchanged from the 1855 version, David A. Clary and Joseph W.A. Whitehorne, *The Inspectors Generals of the United States Army 1777-1903* (Washington, DC: U.S. Government Printing Office, 1987), 201. The 1847 Regulations were more detailed and it is likely that Mansfield had a copy of them for reference; see Attachment 2 below. Army General Regulations were published in 1821, 1825, 1835, 1841, 1847, and 1857. Later editions of the regulations which do not specifically supersede earlier articles in the Regulations appear to add to them and subsume the earlier ones. Post funds were detailed in the 1857 Army Regulations: "A Post Fund shall be raised at each post by a tax on the sutler, not to exceed 10 cents a month for every officer and soldier of the command, according to the average in each month to be ascertained by the Council, and from the saving on the flour ration, ordinarily 33 per cent, by baking the soldiers' bread at a post bakery. Provided, that when want of vegetables or other reasons make it

Robinson touched on a sore point in the Army Inspector General saga—to whom does an Inspector General report, i.e., is he under the General of the Army, Scott, or under the War Department, therefore under the Secretary of War? Scott had made his headquarters in New York City and after Taylor won the presidency he again became Commanding General of the Army. After his unsuccessful run for President in 1852, Scott returned to New York City in command of the Army and remained there until the Civil War. But Scott had an unhappy time when Jefferson Davis was Secretary of War as they feuded over lines of authority and subordination. In the Mexican-American War, each of the four armies sent under Generals Scott, Taylor, Wool, and Kearney, had an officer detailed as Inspector General and the officer so detailed was almost always made chief of staff of that Army.[25] In 1849, the two Army Inspector Generals were ordered to report to the Army commander. In 1850, one inspector, General George A. McCall, conducted an inspection of New Mexico and adjacent lands and prepared two special reports for Davis. "Inspector General McCall was in 1850 the agent of the Secretary of War, not of the Commanding General. His reports were intended for the Secretary, and were addressed to the Adjutant General. The latter circumstance was symbolic of Scott's declining control over the Army, but it was not new. During the 1840's, after Macomb's death, the reports of inspectors general increasingly were addressed to the Adjutant General, the old tradition of confidential reports directly to the Commanding General fading away....One of the results of this shift of power was that the inspectors became separated more and more from the Commanding General. Instructions for the inspectors general began to come through the Adjutant General, 'by order of the Secretary of War,' Scott was effectively excluded from much influence over inspectors' activities. After he returned to Washington in 1850, Scott made one last, feeble attempt to reclaim his inspectors general, at the same time that the Secretary wanted the inspectorate revitalized."[26]

The schism between the War Department and the Commanding General continued despite a new inspector arrangement in which Scott assigned Brigadier General Sylvester Churchill to inspect the Eastern Division, Colonel George A. McCall the new Pacific Division, and Major Samuel Cooper the Western Division. But two months later this system was changed to require the three inspectors to rotate the examination of the three departments "after which they will report in person to the General-in-Chief for further instructions." This new arrangement did not help Scott reassert control of the inspectors as "Churchill and McCall moved at their own pace, largely doing the Secretary's bidding while Cooper was devoted to the interests of the Adjutant General."[27] Cooper never completed his inspection and resigned from the Army in 1861 to become the adjutant and Inspector General of the Confederate Army while McCall did inspect Department No. 9 in 1850; he resigned in April 1853, thus opening the way for Mansfield. Mansfield managed to keep both his old Army friend, Davis, happy, and not antagonize Scott by spending much time in the field on inspections and as little time in Washington, D.C., and New York City, as possible. Mansfield's senior counterpart, Churchill, inspected east of the Mississippi River. It is likely that since Mansfield was a friend of Davis and was appointed by him, Scott was somewhat suspicious of his loyalties but Mansfield proved to be judicious in his dealings with the War Department and the General of the Army. All of his letters to the Adjutant General or the Assistant Adjutant General refer to inspections of departments, recruits, or posts, ordered by the General of the Army, and since New York was usually on Mansfield's route to inspections west of the Mississippi River, he had many opportunities to visit Scott and his staff at the New York Headquarters. Mansfield wrote a monthly personal report to the Adjutant

necessary, the commanding officer may order the flour saved, or any part of it, issued to the men, after paying expenses of baking....The following are the objects of expenditure of the post fund: 1st. Expenses of the bake-house; 2nd. expenses of the soldiers' children at the post school....The distributions from the post or regimental fund, and the savings from the company rations, constitute the Company Fund, to be disbursed by the captain for the benefit of the enlisted men of the company, pursuant to resolves of the Company Council, consisting of all the company officers present;" *Regulations for the Army of the United States, 1857*, 26, 27.

[25] Robinson, *An Account of the Organization of the Army*, 40; Clary, *The Inspectors General*, 176-177; Franklin Hunter Churchill, *Sketch of the Life of Bvt. Brig. General Sylvester Churchill, Inspector General U.S. Army* (New York, NY: Willis McDonald & Co., 1888), 54-56. Colonel George Croghan was the inspector general for Taylor and as has been seen, a worthless drunkard according to Mansfield—Croghan narrowly avoided a court martial in 1845 for mismanagement of funds among other things; Colonel Churchill was the other inspector general and had been with Wool then Taylor and participated in the Battle of Buena Vista where his horse was wounded four or five times by musket balls; he received the brevet rank of brigadier general for Buena Vista conferred May 1848; Colonel Ethan A. Hitchcock was inspector under Scott. In California, the smaller sizes of American units precluded assigning inspectors; Lieutenant Colonel John C. Fremont had Marine Lieutenant Archibald H. Gillespie as his adjutant and Major General Stephen Watts Kearny had Captain Henry S. Turner; Dale L. Walker, *Bear Flag Rising: The Conquest of California, 1846* (New York, NY: Forge Books, 1999), 67, 219. No formal inspectors were named for any of the California units given their small sizes and relatively informal organization.

[26] Clary, 187.

[27] Ibid., 188.

General giving an outline of his activities for that month. His senior counterpart, Churchill, also sent in monthly reports to the Adjutant General. Mansfield took opportunities to visit the War Department whenever he passed through Washington, D.C. He did an excellent job for the several years he had the position satisfying both masters without angering either. Mansfield, as an Old Army career veteran, knew that despite any personal feelings he might have concerning his superiors in the Army and in the Capitol, he had, at least, to appear cooperative to all.[28]

Brigadier General Sylvester Churchill was the senior Inspector General over Mansfield; he inspected posts mostly east of the Mississippi River. Photograph courtesy LOC.[29]

Colonel George Croghan; courtesy Wikipedia.[30]

---

[28] Mansfield's final inspection reports for each of his inspection tours were sent to General Scott with summaries sometimes sent to Department Commanders and the Adjutant General. Churchill in his 1 May 1853 letter to General Scott suggested that Churchill "inspect the eastern Division or all on and east of the Mississippi River, the north western posts first thence east and south. This may be done, I think, within a year." Churchill received an affirmative reply on 23 May 1853 in which he was ordered to inspect the posts on and east of the Mississippi River and wrote on the 24th that he would leave if possible later that week via Pittsburg, Newport Barracks, and St. Louis. Letters courtesy NARA. Secretary of War Davis also sought information outside of the normal Inspector General route so "He dispatched Bvt. Captain Edward R.S. Canby, assistant adjutant general, on 30 November 1853 to make "minute" inspections of arsenals, depots, and military posts on the Arkansas and Red rivers. Canby began at Little Rock Arsenal, then gradually extended his tour along the Gulf Coast to Florida, visiting twenty-nine places by July 1854. The experience exhausted Canby, making him so ill that it took almost a year for him to submit a 150-page report." Scott also did some traveling on his own in the east rather than tasking Inspector Generals; Clary, 192-193.

[29] At the outbreak of the War of 1812, Churchill was appointed a 1st lieutenant, 3rd U.S. Artillery, on 12 March 1812, and was promoted to captain on 15 August 1813. He transferred to the 1st Artillery on 1 June 1821, promoted to major, 3rd Artillery, on 6 April 1835, and colonel and Inspector General on 25 June 1841. He received the rank of brevet brigadier general from 23 February 1847, in recognition of his services under General John E. Wool at the Battle of Buena Vista during the Mexican–American War. At the beginning of the Civil War, he had been Inspector General of the Army for 20 years. He retired 25 September 1861, due to ill health, and was succeeded by Colonel Randolph B. Marcy. He died 7 December 1862.

Mansfield, as a new Inspector General, was described by historians as one of the best the department ever had—energetic and enthusiastic:

> Mansfield was a fitting successor to George Croghan. Although he lacked Croghan's literary gifts and sense of controlled outrage when something affronted his sensibilities, he compensated with his greater diligence and sobriety. His reports were readable enough, and highly informative. They combined travelogue, inspection, and commentary--a running narrative of his journey with comments on the countryside, punctuated with reports of the condition of posts and garrisons, followed by remarks on subjects of general interest to the Army command. Mansfield's typical inspection of a post included a head count (those present, absent, sick, those in the guardhouse, and so on) then characterized in general terms the discipline and instruction of the command, arms and equipment, condition of buildings, medical services, the funds remaining for subsistence and quartermaster operations, the fort's environment, and the abilities of the officers (whom he usually commended). Engineer that he was, Mansfield included detailed plats of the posts that he inspected, and--with apparently no objections from former fellow engineers--he gave careful attention to coastal fortification construction projects supervised by the Corps of Engineers. His emphasis was always on military readiness: whether the post was properly located, what the proximate dangers were, what the garrison should be--and so on....Despite their best efforts, Mansfield and Churchill could not inspect the whole Army all the time. Scott, however, made the best of the situation. He traveled a lot on his own, and he managed to enforce the orders of 1849 and 1850 that the inspectors general addressed their annual reports to him, although Mansfield made some inspections on behalf of department commanders.[31]

A review of Mansfield's drafts of his inspection reports held in the Mansfield collection by the Middlesex County Historical Society shows that in many post inspections, he included in his draft report files, original written reports such as from commanding officers showing a complete breakdown of officers and men assigned to the commands, Quartermaster reports, etc. Mansfield summarized these reports in his final documents which he sent to the Adjutant General. His draft reports show many corrections which are almost never found in his official submitted documents. However, few post files contain original rosters or other similar documents so it is likely Mansfield did not request them but rather kept them if they were given him. He may have also requested specific reports to help him resolve issues. Several of his inspection files he retained for himself include, in addition to his notes, meteorological data for some posts which in one case for Fort Tejon, included a list of "shocks" or earthquakes which were quite numerous, sometimes several per month. When his final reports are not available there are no introductory summaries normally found in his finished products.[32]

A noted historian of the American Southwest, Robert W. Frazer, who wrote of Mansfield's inspections in 1853-1854, penned the following:

> His "inspection reports cannot be termed models of composition, yet they contain much valuable detail regarding problems and conditions in the departments inspected. Though they are concerned primarily with matters deemed to be of interest to the military, they also have much to say, even if indirectly, of the socio-economic conditions of civilian life. They are straightforward accounts, as inspection reports usually are, containing little that is deliberately imaginative or colorful. Nevertheless, here and there is a touch which would seem to indicate that Mansfield took pleasure in the performance of his duties. Invariably he found something of beauty in the settings of the more isolated posts, such as Forts Defiance, Yuma, and Dalles. Rarely does he fail to mention a snow-capped peak, whether on the horizon or near at hand. His private "digressions" into the mining districts of California give further evidence of a healthy curiosity about the region which he traversed. Mansfield's attitude toward the Indians, whether labeled wild, friendly, or civilized, reflects some understanding of their needs and sympathy with their plight. Mansfield is critical of certain characteristics of the Spanish-American population in New

---

[30] Croghan was born in 1791 in Louisville, Kentucky, graduated from the College of William and Mary in 1810 and joined the Army. He fought at the Battle of Tippecanoe in 1811. For his defense during the Battle of Fort Stephenson, Ohio, during the War of 1812, he was brevetted to lieutenant colonel. He resigned from the Army in 1817 and served as a postmaster in New Orleans. In 1825, he became one of two Army inspector generals. He was presented with the Congressional Gold Medal in 1835 for his actions at Fort Stephenson. During the Mexican-American War, he was the inspector general under General Zachary Taylor. Mansfield disliked him and called him a "beastly drunkard." He died in New Orleans, Louisiana, in the cholera epidemic of 1849, which also took the life of former President of the United States James K. Polk." Courtesy Wikipedia.

[31] Clary, *The Inspectors Generals*, 192.

[32] Future researchers may find it interesting to compare Mansfield's final inspection reports to his draft reports to determine if changes he made were mere grammatical corrections or were for political reasons. Mansfield, as an Old Army career soldier, would not want to make enemies among senior officers. Mansfield's 1857 to 1859 Utah Army and Department of West inspections and the Departments of Oregon and California have not previously been published making that fertile ground for future authors.

Mexico, notably of their lack of education their prejudices, and their unsuitableness for military service. Here again, he avoids the wholesale condemnation of this segment of the population in which so many visitors from the "states," both military and civilian, indulged. If Mansfield's observations were not always accurate, they, at least, represent the opinions generally prevailing at the time.[33]

A second historian who edited and published Mansfield's inspection reports of Texas in 1860-1861, Jerry Thompson, lauded Mansfield's efforts and tireless exertions in the Lone Star State describing his travels starting from San Antonio:

> At 8 A.M. on October 8, 1859, in a spring wagon pulled by four mules, the fifty-five-year-old Mansfield departed San Antonio on the El Paso Road….Among those accompanying the Inspector General were an Irish-born servant, a ten-year veteran of the Texas frontier Army, and an escort of ten men and a sergeant. The ponderous caravan consisted of three canvas-covered wagons carrying provisions, including tents, two hams, flour, hard bread, coffee, sugar, and tea for the men and corn for the six mules needed to pull each wagon….[he was] often on the road from sunrise to sunset, traveling up to twenty-five miles a day. At one of the many forts, he would take detailed notes in a small leather notebook and draw rough sketches of the post and the environs. [He] would then ride on to places such as Dead Man's Hole, Escondido Creek, Howard Spring, California Spring, or Noria de los Federales, where he would compile his official report and draw a more complete plat based on his preliminary sketches. At these isolated watering holes, he was able to escape the distractions and politics of post life and complete his reports with a greater measure of objectivity. In his inspection reports that were sent to Adjutant General Samuel Cooper, Mansfield not only recorded the efficiency of post sutlers and officers but made several pleas for improving the circumstances of individual veterans. He always emphasized military readiness, noting soldiers who were present, absent, and even those who were in the guardhouse. In addition, he offered detailed recommendations for specific congressional funding projects, carefully noting the costs of leasing land and buildings at both department headquarters in San Antonio and various posts.[34]

Middlesex County Historical Society has seven of Mansfield's leather bound journals dated from 1854 to 1859 which combine diary, journal, and travelogue. On page one of his notebook labelled "1" he wrote at the top of it "Journal" and on the inside of the front cover: "Colonel J.K.F. Mansfield, U.S. Army. Please return this if you find it. 6th May at the Oriental House [Hotel]" and wrote similar requests inside two of the others. They are of two sizes: four and three quarters inches by seven inches closed, and four and three quarters inch to five inches tall. They contain hand drawn maps, sketches, and notes on locations, including posts he visited, but only two post plats, Fort Orford and San Diego. They are usually written in pencil rather than ink which indicate that he was taking quick notes as he was examining the post, its books, troops, buildings, etc. The journals also show distances travelled and expenses he paid which helped him when he made travel expense claims. His journal from 1858 – 1859 appears to be water soaked; it may be the one he had when his belongings were dumped in the river when his canoes capsized in Oregon. From reviewing his journals, rough drafts of his inspection reports, and his final, submitted reports, Mansfield clearly made notes first in his journals either while he was on site at a post, on a steamship, etc. Then once he had some time, he added to his notes at the first opportunity perhaps later that day or as historian Thompson posited, once he left a post and was on the road to the next. He wrote in his journal on 15 April 1859 that he was "at San Francisco writing up reports." Mansfield occasionally sent interim reports to a department head of the department he was inspecting at that general's request plus Mansfield also sent in interim reports to the Adjutant General's Office. When Mansfield returned to Middletown, he then used these notes as well as reports he was given at a post such as rosters, meteorological data, diagrams of a post drawn by others,

---

[33] Mansfield, *Mansfield on the Condition of the Western Forts 1853-1854*, xxix-xxx. Frazer not only examined and wrote about Mansfield's inspections in this book, but wrote and edited other important books about topics pertaining to the southwest such as *Forts and Supplies: The Role of the Army in the Economy of the Southwest 1846-1861* (Albuquerque, NM: University of New Mexico Press, 1983), and *Forts of the West: Military Forts and Presidios and Posts Commonly Called Forts West of the Mississippi River to 1898* (Norman, OK: University of Oklahoma Press, 1975).

[34] Joseph K.F. Mansfield and Joseph E. Johnston, Jerry Thompson, ed., *Texas and New Mexico on the Eve of the Civil War: The Mansfield and Johnston Inspections 1859-1861* (Albuquerque, NM: University of New Mexico Press, 2001), 9. In addition to Frazer's and Thompson's books, there are two other published accounts of Mansfield's inspections but with little editorial comment: one of his inspections of the Department of Texas in 1856: Martin Lalor Crimmins, "Colonel J.K.F. Mansfield's Report of the Inspection of the Department of Texas in 1856," *The Southwestern Historical Quarterly*, vol. 42, July 1938-April 1939; and Mansfield's inspection of Fort Townsend in December 1858 in an article edited by Jesse S. Douglas, "Colonel Joseph K.F. Mansfield Visits Fort Townsend, 1858," in *Readings in Pacific Northwest History, Washington, 1790-1895*, ed. Charles Marvin Gates (Seattle, WA: The University Bookstore, 1941), 157-163. A "War Department's amendment to the regulations in 1858 permitted inspectors general to take one servant on their tours, with the government compensating for the servant's transportation costs;" Clary, *The Inspector's General*, 201. Note that on p. 85 of Frazer's book, top of the page, "[San Luis]" should be changed to "Las Flores]". Both of these books are available at very reasonable prices and should be read for those interested in this period of history in the west and in Mansfield's details about the posts and related geography.

etc., to compose rough drafts for his personal files which the Middlesex County Historical Society also houses. These rough drafts can be difficult to read given that he wrote hastily and made many corrections and additions before he wrote a clean, final copy to send to the Adjutant Generals' Office. His final reports also have introductory summaries as noted in his earlier inspection tours but are missing for his 1858 and 1859 Pacific inspection tours. Mansfield's duties were not confined to inspecting far flung Army posts as he was ordered to inspect recruits and their transports while he was in Middletown between inspection tours. His inspections were often in New York City but sometimes in Newport, Rhode Island, or even in Virginia. He also sat on court martial boards in the East. In some of his rough drafts Mansfield does not make clear which of the days he spent at a post were dedicated to actually inspecting and which were spent in resting and recuperating, or awaiting transport to his next post. Most post inspections required him to spend days travelling among the posts but when possible these travel days are not included as his "inspection" days.[35]

---

[35] Journals and rough drafts courtesy of the Middlesex County Historical Society. Final copies of his reports are found in the National Archives. NARA does not have Mansfield's rough drafts or journals, and the Middlesex County Historical Society does not have his final reports. His journal for 1858-1860 shows that he and his family went on two vacations as they apparently accompanied him to West Point and also stayed with him at the Astor House in New York City in August 1859, and then in August 1860 he and his family journeyed to Boston and the White Mountains in New Hampshire. "Officers who travel under orders, without troops or military-stores, beyond the range of their appropriate daily duties, not less than 10 miles, shall be allowed ten cents per mile, or if they prefer it, the actual cost of their transportation for the whole journey, provided they shall have travelled by the shortest mail route, and in the accustomed or other manner. Staff officers, such as Inspectors-General, Paymasters, etc., who travel under the general authority of the regulations, are to be considered as travelling under orders. A general or field-officer, when travelling on duty, without troops, will be entitled to transportation for *one* servant, at the rate of eight cents per mile, on certifying that the servant actually accompanied him on his journey;" *General Regulation for the Army of the United States, 1841*, 191; but if there was no mail route, "by the shortest practicable route;" 192. "An officer who travels not less than ten miles without troops, escort, or military stores, and under special order in the case from a superior, or a summons to attend a military court, shall receive ten cents mileage, or, if he prefer it, the actual cost of his transportation and of the transportation of his allowance of baggage for the whole journey, provided he has traveled in the customary reasonable manner. Mileage will not be allowed where the travel is by government conveyances, which will be furnished in case of necessity;" *General Regulation for the Army of the United States, 1857*, 128.

Mansfield's journals in which he kept notes and sketches of his travels and inspections as well as for some personal vacations. Courtesy of the Middlesex County Historical Society.

This Book belongs to Col. J.K.F. Mansfield
Inspector Gen. U.S. Army. The finder
will please forward it by Mail
To him at San Francisco California
& receive a Suitable Consideration.

Inside front cover of one of his journals. Courtesy of the Middlesex County Historical Society.

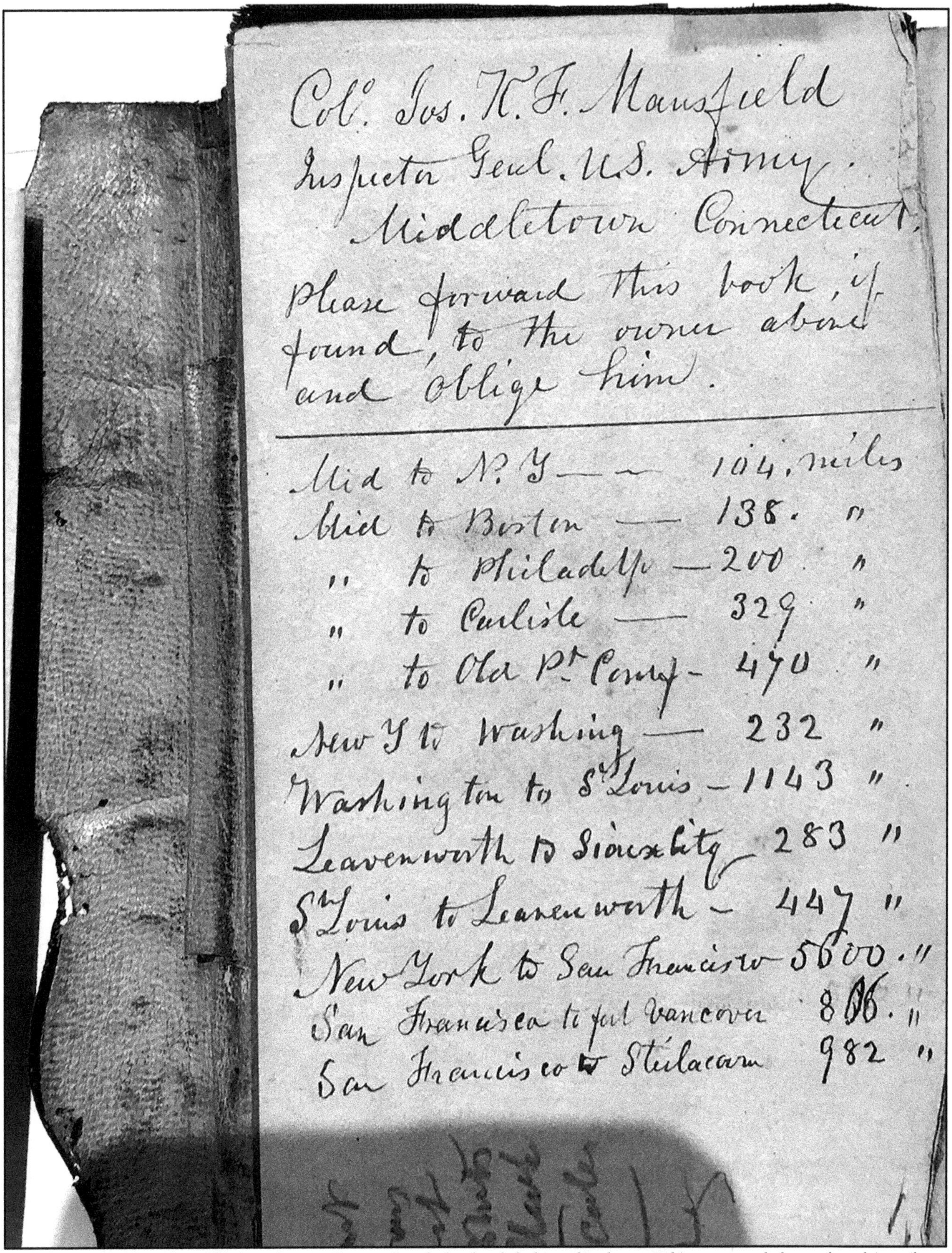

Col. Jos. K. F. Mansfield
Inspector Genl. U.S. Army.
    Middletown Connecticut.
Please forward this book, if
found, to the owner above
and oblige him.

Mid to N.Y ——— 104. miles
Mid to Boston —— 138.   "
  "   to Philadelp —200.   "
  "   to Carlisle ——— 329   "
  "   to Old Pt Comf- 470   "
New Y to Washing —— 232   "
Washington to St Louis — 1143 ".
Leavenworth to Sioux City 283 "
St Louis to Leavenworth — 447 "
New York to San Francisco 5600. "
San Francisca to ft Vancouver 806. "
San Francisco to Steilacom 982 "

Inside front cover of another of his journals; note distances he calculated to help him when he wrote his reports and also used to claim mileage payments. Note the total mileage from New York City to San Francisco, 5,600, which included crossing Panama. Courtesy of the Middlesex County Historical Society.

A sketch of Yo-ja-se-ho from one of his journals which he did not send in with his reports or show his wife. Courtesy of the Middlesex County Historical Society.

Indian moccasins Mansfield brought back home from one of his inspection trips west. Courtesy of the Middlesex County Historical Society.

Mansfield's drafting set and measuring tape. Courtesy of the Middlesex County Historical Society.

Much of the information found on the many hundreds of pages of Mansfield's inspections show routine data so the many details he reported will not be repeated for every post. Rather, a chronological review of them interspersed with interesting or important details will be presented with his letters home intertwined to add personal interest. Reports of posts he inspected which have not been published will be shown in more detail due to their rarity. Samples of his handwritten notes and sketches will be included below. A letter he wrote to Adjutant General Cooper on 19 September 1853 from Fort Defiance is shown in Attachment 3 below. He explained that he sent this letter in advance of his inspection report so the Secretary of War could include Mansfield's recommendations in his next report to Congress about road improvements and renewal of the law which allowed an additional one dollar per day per diem for officers and of an increase of half pay to enlisted men in this department. Unlike in other departments, the increase was needed because of the very high cost of shipping goods over long distances. During this period, the Army Quartermaster Department struggled with increased costs to support new posts and forts west of the Mississippi River. Mansfield often documented in his reports the benefits of improved roads and proposed railroad lines evident to him as he traversed thousands of miles in the vast expanses of the west.

**FRONTIER POSTS
AND LINES OF COMMUNICATION**

* Old Frontier Stations now abandoned
o Old Frontier Stations still occupied
● New Frontier Stations
▬▬ ▬▬ Extreme Limit of Line of Frontier Stations in 1845
••••••••• Lines of Land Transportation
～～～～ Lines of River Transportation
▬▬▬▬ Lines of Ocean Transportation
━━━━ Boundary Lines
═══ Lines of Land Transportation anterior to War with Mexico

SCALE OF MILES
0   50 100   200   300

Reproduced from QMG's Report, 1851

Posts and lines of communication in the 1851 Quartermaster General's report. Fort Leavenworth was one of the starting points for the Santa Fe and Oregon Trails and was the headquarters for troops serving along the Santa Fe Trail. For West Coast inspections, Mansfield would have taken a steamship from New York to Panama, and then crossed the Panama Isthmus from Chagres on mule back and canoe. He may also have taken the route through Nicaragua not Panama. The railroad across the Isthmus was not completed until 1855. On the Pacific side he would board another steamship for San Francisco. Goods were transported across the isthmus by human porters and mules. The Cruces Road was begun in the 1520's to cross the isthmus at its narrowest point. The road was originally almost completely paved, with basaltic cobble stones spanning an average width of eight feet, but it was not kept in good repair which resulted in a difficult and dangerous journey. During the 1849 Gold Rush in California, the activity on the Las Cruces Road increased due to large number of 49ers' in route to the gold fields. They would go by mail steamship from New Orleans, New York, or Savannah, to the town of Chagres, at the mouth of the Chagres River. From Chagres they would take Cayucos, (hand-carved wooden canoes) which used poling and/or paddling up the river to the town of Cruces, some 20 miles away. In Cruces, they would have to wait, to rent or purchase mules and hire guides to make the trip to Panama; they also had the option of walking. At best, this trip could be completed in 4 days; but generally took much longer with some trips taking several weeks. Besides the problems with Yellow Fever, Malaria, and Chagres Fever, the traveler had to contend with bandits and the swarms of mosquitoes, snakes and insects. In one of his diaries, Mansfield described taking various boats and also walking miles around rapids.[36]

---

[36] Erna Risch, *Quartermaster Support of the Army: A History of the Corps, 1775-1939* (Washington, DC: Department of the Army, 1962), 305, 307. See Hubert H. Bancroft, *History of California*, vol. 6 (San Francisco, CA: The History Company, 1888), 128-140 *passim*. Diary courtesy of the Middlesex County Historical Society.

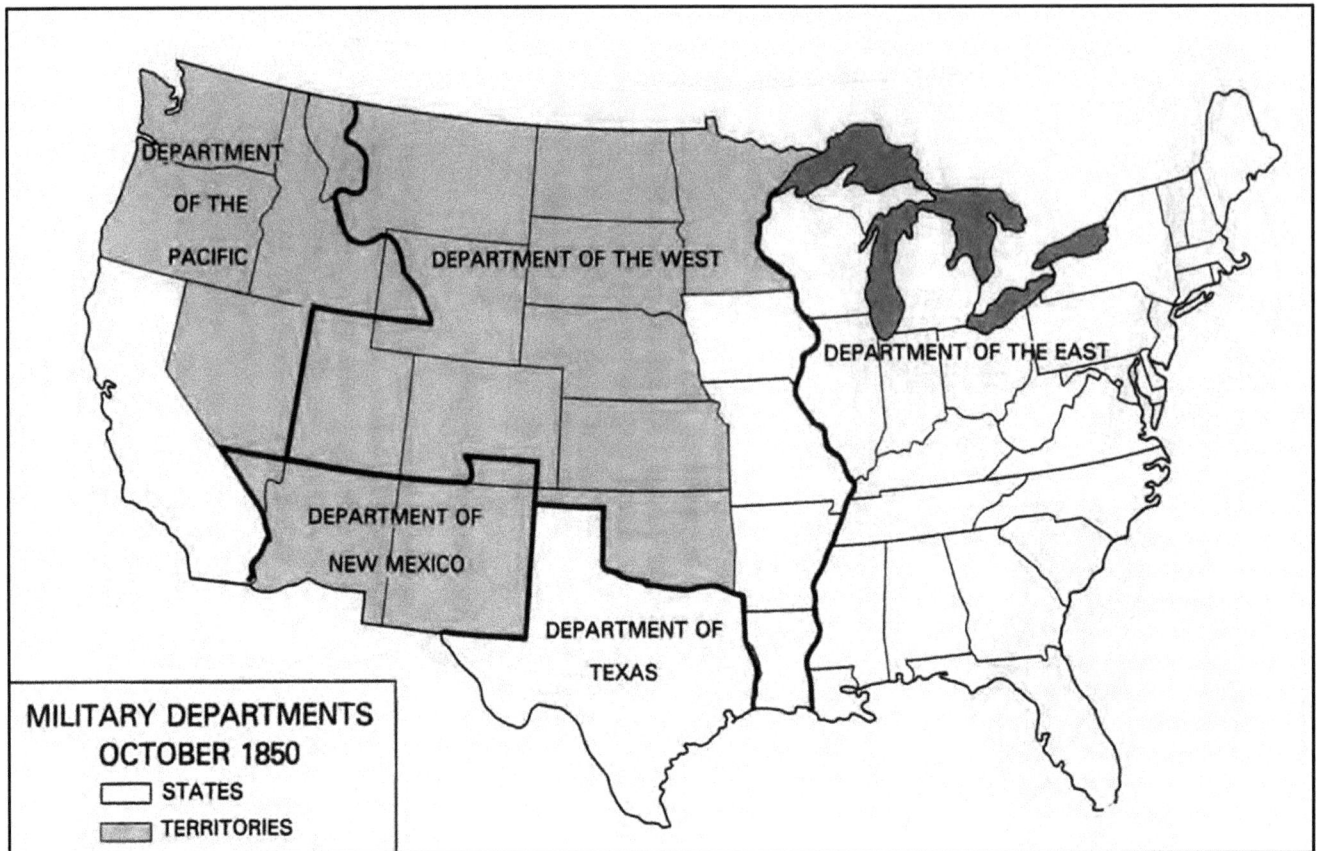

Military Departments in 1850. Courtesy USACMH.

1853 Department of New Mexico

Fort Union	1–6 August 1853
Cantonment Burgwin	11–13 August 1853
Fort Massachusetts	18–21 August 1853
Fort Marcy at Santé Fe	27–31 August 1853
Albuquerque	3–8 September 1853
Fort Defiance	15–20 September 1853
Los Lunas	25–27 September 1853
Fort Conrad	30 September–4 October 1853
Fort Webster	10–13 October 1853
Fort Fillmore	17–29 October 1853

During his years of traveling thousands of miles as an Inspector General, he grew a beard and let his hair grow. He also likely adapted his travel uniform to a more practical and comfortable one during his many weeks on horseback, a wagon, or canoe. But it is not likely that he wore practical clothing to the extent a soldier on escort duty with a surveying party in Kansas described: "Every man is wearing a broad-brimmed hat, each of a different color: white trousers of rough material; a woolen shirt of red, green, blue, or brown--in short, of any and every color, usually open in front and worn like a coat; the shoes (we still have shoes, though who knows how soon we may have to wear moccasins) with the uppers slashed wherever they might chafe in marching." Historian Robert M. Utley explained clothing worn in the field in the West at this time:

> The ornate uniforms prescribed by the regulations yielded to less military, more functional attire. Picturing himself on the Texas frontier in 1855, Captain E. Kirby Smith of the 2nd Cavalry wrote that "corduroy pants; a hickory or blue flannel shirt, cut down in front, studded with pockets and worn outside; a slouched hat and long beard, cavalry boots worn over the pants, knife and revolver belted to the side and a double barrel gun across the pommel, complete the costume as truly serviceable as it is unmilitary.[37]

And since the Army did not at this time issue cold weather gear, soldiers had to purchase their own or manufacture it. "For example, In the Mormon expedition described below, most of the soldiers on the sick report were rendered unfit for duty by frostbitten feet. Soldiers who stood guard or marched in snow shod only in leather bootees were soon incapacitated....the soldiers made for themselves out of 'old blankets, skins, pieces of old canvas and cast-off clothing, anything that necessity prompted them to invent for protection from the bitter cold.'"[38] One soldier stationed at Fort Pierre, Nebraska Territory in 1855, wrote that "I possessed three buffalo robes, two deer skins and some wolf skins. With these and four blankets, we had a warm bed on the coldest nights....Most of the soldiers made their own fur clothing, such as caps, mittens, coats and boots, and produced some curious looking objects. One of them made for himself a complete outfit of boots, pantaloons, jacket and cap of buffalo skin with the hair outside. He presented a weird picture when dressed in them and was given the name of 'Standing Buffalo'....We were permitted to wear anything we pleased on or off duty, except at inspection or muster."[39] Fortunately for Mansfield, he could purchase needed clothing and equipment plus schedule his inspections so that he could usually avoid the worst weather. And he learned from McCall or others that he would not need his full dress uniform! It is unlikely that the veteran colonel adopted casual dress except while travelling between posts as his duty was as an inspector. So while he was involved in inspecting posts he certainly was in complete, proper uniform as he noted defects in uniform wear among the troops.

Mansfield wrote to his wife, Louisa, from on board the Steamer *Sonora*, 360 miles up the Missouri River, 23 June 1853, on his way to Fort Leavenworth. He met an old acquaintance in St. Louis, Colonel Joseph Eaton, who congratulated him on his appointment as Inspector General. Eaton told him a story about his son being promised that

---

[37] Robert M. Utley, *Frontiersmen in Blue: The United States Army and the Indian, 1848-1865* (New York, NY: The Macmillan Company, 1967), 24.

[38] Eugene Bandel, *Frontier Life in the Army*, 1854-1861, ed. Ralph P. Bieber (Glendale, CA: The Arthur H. Clarke Co., 1932), 221- 222.

[39] Myer, *Ten Years in the Ranks*, 94.

position by General Scott and President Pierce. Mansfield detailed to Louisa his slow trip up the full river. He was happy that he had no debts and $80 in his pocket to pay his servant and also buy a mule to add to the horse he purchased in St. Louis. He noted that it was 480 miles by water to Fort Leavenworth from St. Louis on the Missouri River. He supplies his usual advice that Louisa must "train up" her children and "must be firm and have no play until the lessons are all got....Let all pleasure and parties and visits go to the Evil one, who is their patron saint, and do your duty in hope and one day you will reap your reward." He then wrote her from Fort Leavenworth later in June that he met old friends and is fitted out with a wagon for baggage and four mounted riflemen as escort. He told her that he had sent two orders on railroad companies to pay stock dividends to Louisa but were those orders still attached to his letter? Finances are still an important item of discussion but perhaps less so now that he would soon be receiving pay at his new rank of colonel. While he travelled on his inspection duties, he received pay for miles travelled, rations, etc., but usually his expenses exceeded his remunerations so in most of his letters to Louisa, he discussed bills she should pay and often talked of his high expenses and cautioned her to ensure that she was frugal as she may not have the benefit of his income should he not live. "My children cannot expect their father to last many years longer, and then they will feel the importance of being able to work. Your income if I am out of the way will not begin to support you and the children except they be able to help themselves."[40] The tone of his post Mexican-American War letters to his wife was more gentle but he still gave advice about raising his children and detailed instructions about matters relating to his business and properties. Perhaps age mellowed the old colonel combined with the years he spent with his family after the war during which he found that his wife did acceptably well on her own.

---

[40] Letters courtesy WPL and of the Middlesex County Historical Society. Joseph Eaton was an 1835 graduate of West Point and received two brevets during the Mexican-American War to major and lieutenant colonel. He resigned in 1856 but rejoined in 1861 receiving three brevets during the Civil War to brigadier general. He retired from the Army in 1881 and died in 1896. Mansfield wrote to Thomas from St. Louis on 18 June 1853 that he arrived there on the 16th "via Chicago and the Illinois River. I have been detained to the present time in procuring horse and servant and horse furniture, etc. I shall leave this afternoon on the Steamer *Sonora* for Fort Leavenworth, thence across the country." Letters courtesy NARA.

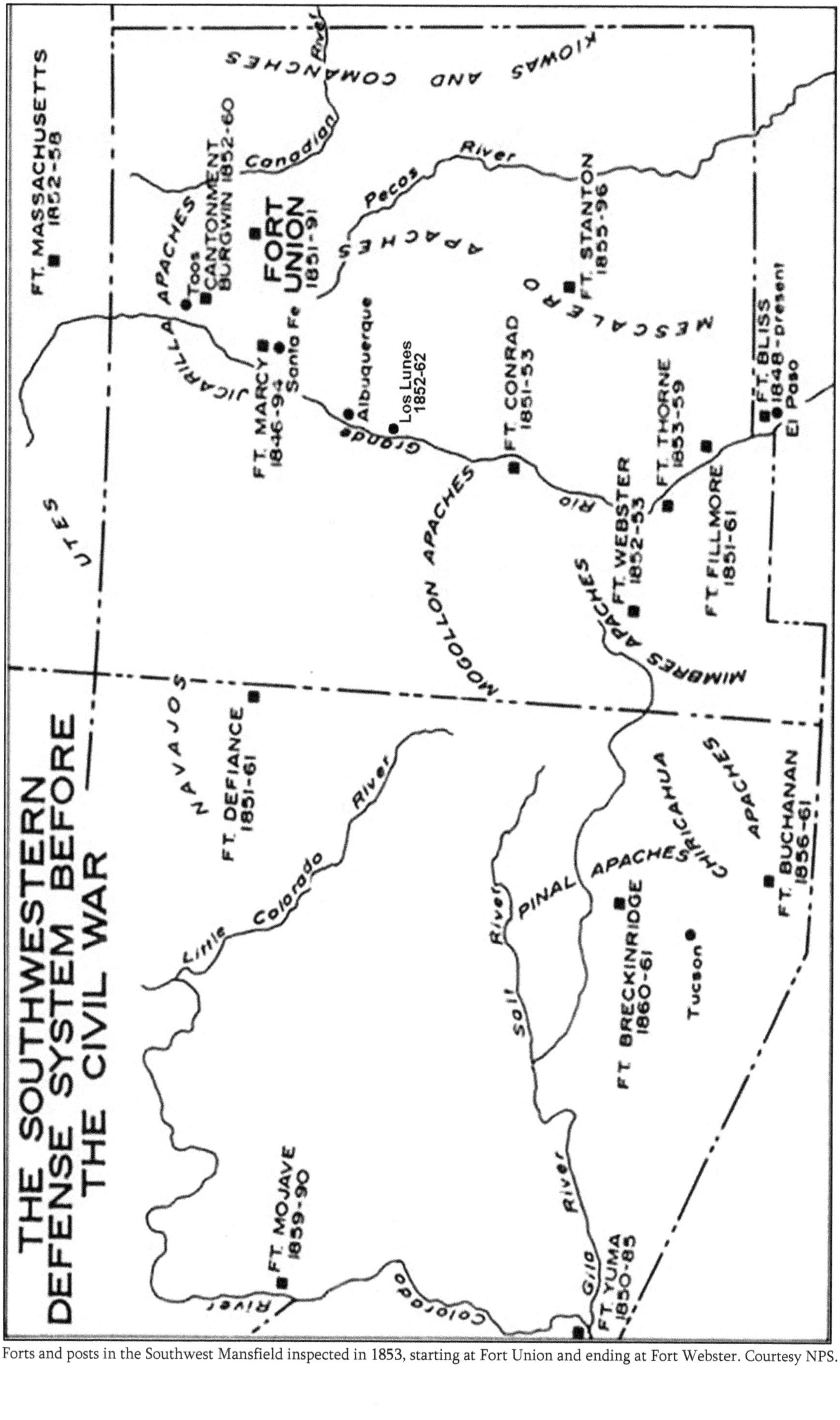

THE SOUTHWESTERN DEFENSE SYSTEM BEFORE THE CIVIL WAR

FT. MASSACHUSETTS 1852-58

UTES

NAVAJOS

FT. MOJAVE 1859-90

FT. YUMA 1850-85

Colorado River

Gila River

Little Colorado River

FT. DEFIANCE 1851-61

Salt River

PINAL APACHES

FT. BRECKINRIDGE 1860-61

Tucson

CHIRICAHUA

APACHES

FT. BUCHANAN 1856-61

JICARILLA APACHES

Taos

CANTONMENT BURGWIN 1852-60

FT. MARCY 1846-94

Santa Fe

Albuquerque

Los Lunes 1852-62

Rio Grande

MOGOLLON APACHES

APACHES

FT. WEBSTER 1852-53

MIMBRES

FORT UNION 1851-91

Canadian River

Pecos River

APACHES

FT. CONRAD 1851-53

MESCALERO

FT. STANTON 1855-96

FT. THORNE 1853-59

FT. FILLMORE 1851-61

FT. BLISS 1848-present

El Paso

KIOWAS AND COMANCHES

Forts and posts in the Southwest Mansfield inspected in 1853, starting at Fort Union and ending at Fort Webster. Courtesy NPS.

U.S. Troops going to Mexico in 1847 on the Santa Fe Trail by Frederick Remington, from Henry Inman, *The Old Santa Fe Trail: The Story of a Great Highway* (Topeka, KS: Crane & Company, 1916), facing p. 109. The Army used the Cimarron Cutoff on the Santa Fe Trail in the mid to late 1850's; there were two cutoffs from that route to the old Fort Union, one at Rock Crossing of the Canadian River which provided a ford with a natural stone floor, and the Wagon Mound Crossing farther south. That latter crossing made for a shorter march to the fort so was more frequently used; it was probably the one Mansfield used. See Robert M. Utley, *Fort Union and the Santa Fe Trail* (El Paso, TX: Texas Western Press, 1989), 3; and William E. Brown, *The Santa Fe Trail* (St. Louis, MO: The Patrice Press, 1988), 142-145. Mansfield apparently described the Mountain Branch of the Santa Fe Trail as a road to Fort Union's farm, Frazier, sketch following 112. Both the old and new Forts Union had branches from both routes of the Santa Fe Trail during the life of the fort from 1851 to 1891; it was the largest U.S. military fort in the southwest; David Dary, *The Santa Fe Trail: Its History, Legends, and Lore* (New York, NY: Alfred A. Knopf, 2000), 317.

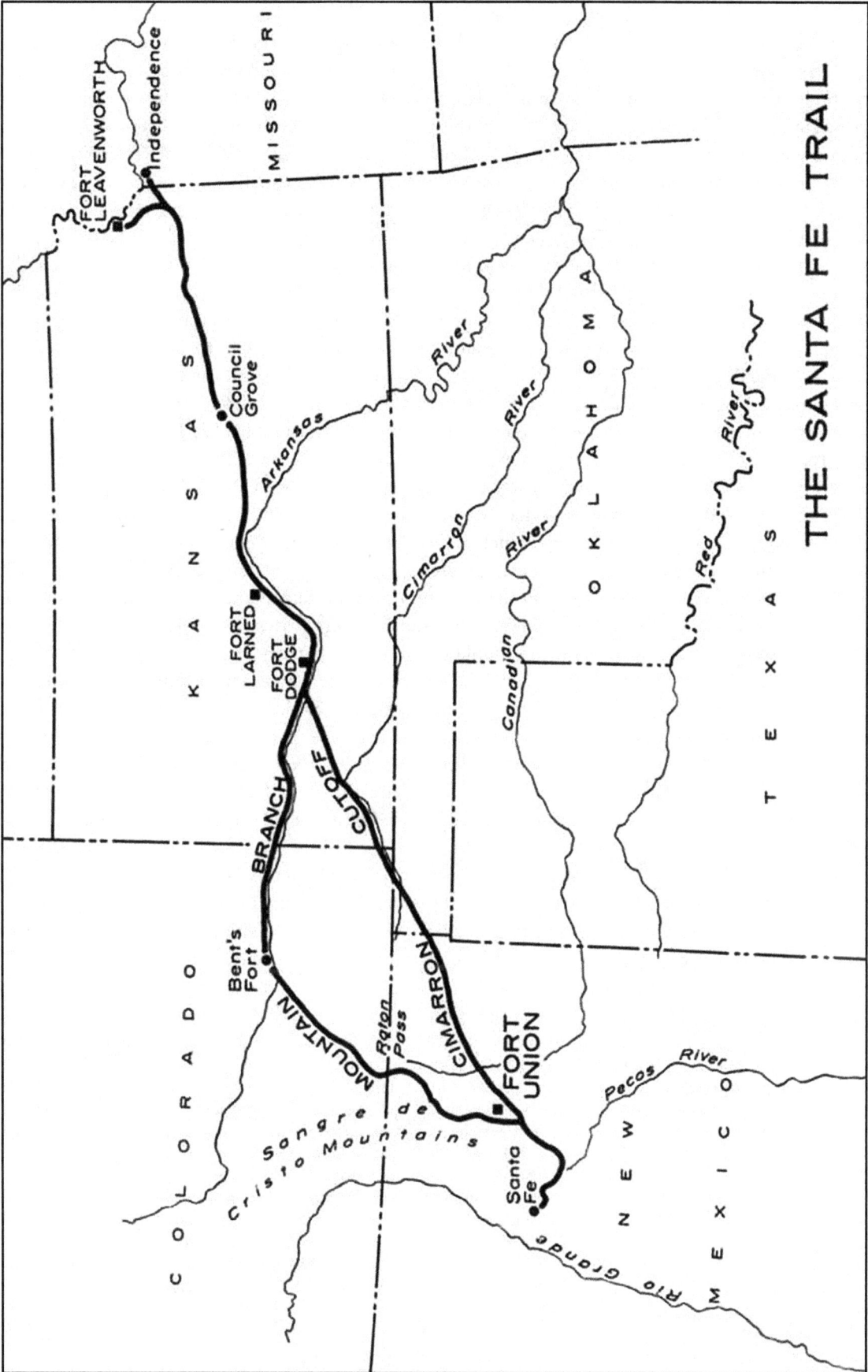

Main routes of the Santa Fe Trail. The earlier Cimarron Cutoff route had a spur which joined with Fort Union from the southwest. Wagon wheel tracks are visible today at Fort Union, the first fort Mansfield inspected during his Inspector General career. Courtesy NPS.

Mansfield's first inspection trip was obviously a learning experience for the novice inspector. But he quickly discovered what was needed as his trip took him to places he had never visited before and on a mission with which he was unfamiliar. But as an Old Army veteran well acquainted with Army policy, Mansfield was not overwhelmed. Most of the officers he met on his tours were known to him either personally or by reputation and since almost all were West Point graduates, he had much in common with them. Given the uniformity of his reports, he knew what he was expected to examine and which aspects were most important for Secretary of War Davis and General Scott. But his first trip to his inaugural inspection, Fort Union, was easy compared to many which would follow over the next eight years—Mansfield journeyed from Fort Leavenworth accompanied by Brigadier General Garland for most of the route and arrived on 31 July 1853. Mansfield wrote to Thomas on 29 June 1853 from Camp at Council Grove, 118 miles from Fort Leavenworth: he arrived there "last evening, in company with General Garland, having overtaken him 71 miles this side of Fort Leavenworth [on 26 June] and that the command will probably move forward tomorrow morning." Garland and Mansfield were partners during the Mexican-American War in the bloody attack on Monterrey 23 September 1846 during which Mansfield was wounded. The new inspector was fortunate to fall in with the new Department commander, Garland, since he was in command of a wagon train heading to Fort Union. Major Electus Backus was in command of the troops of the column, and the 51 six-mule team baggage and commissary wagons were under command of Quartermaster Captain Langdon C. Easton. Mansfield noted favorably that Backus "conducted it with strictly military propriety to the comfort and convenience of the whole" and Easton's management of the wagon train was "systematically and well conducted." He further reported that Assistant Surgeon David C. DeLeon "cheerfully attended to his duties" although he was himself sick. The doctor attended to 361 cases plus officers' families and servants losing none. Mansfield recommended that on long marches such as this there should be two doctors assigned. He further suggested that due to heavy rains and the subsequent illnesses, marches should not be started from Fort Leavenworth before 20 June to take advantage also of the new grass near the beginning point and the newly growing grass as the wagon train entered New Mexico Territory. As was seen in his comments in letters written from Mexico, Mansfield was a moral person and after he commented on the roads which would be excellent when dry and too heavy (muddy) when wet, he wrote that "I must here remark as to the profanity of the citizen teamsters as a general thing. If there be any thing shocking to the moral sense, it is the awful and hearty swearing bestowed by them on their mules. On the most trifling occasion, the whole vocabulary of 'billingsgate' [coarsely abusive language] is poured out to the annoyance of every person within hearing. I have no doubt this evil can be corrected by making it a matter of sufficient importance to be noticed by wagon masters and others in authority." To help remedy the need for these profane civilians, he recommended that "at least three soldiers in each company in the service be instructed wherever practicable to drive teams, to be ready at hand on emergencies."[41]

Mansfield had left New York City on 10 June and arrived at Fort Leavenworth on the 24th; he left there on the 25th and on the 26th overtook Garland at Wakamipi Creek. On the 28th they reached Council Grove "where we found the command of recruits and horses, etc., encamped awaiting the arrival of General Garland 118 miles from Fort Leavenworth....For the month of July we continued our march across the prairies—reached Fort Atkinson on the 14th

---

[41] On 1 June 1853 Mansfield received a letter from the Secretary of War which directed him to "inspect any troops that you may find in the vicinity of El Paso, Texas, although they do not form a portion of the troops assigned to the 9th Military Department. A detachment of recruits will leave Fort Leavenworth about the 15th of this month for New Mexico, which offers a favorable opportunity for proceeding to that country, if you can make your arrangements to reach Fort Leavenworth in season to join that command." Letter courtesy of the Middlesex County Historical Society. Also on 1 June Mansfield received a letter from Army Headquarters containing Special Orders no. 35 directing him to "immediately proceed to make a minute inspection of the 9th Military Department after which he will report to these Head Quarters." Letter courtesy of the Middlesex County Historical Society; Mansfield, *Mansfield on the Condition of the Western Forts 1853-1854*, 30-32; Leo E. Oliva, *Fort Union and the Frontier Army in the Southwest* (Southwest Cultural Resources Center Professional Papers No. 41 (National Park Service, Department of the Interior, 1993) 205. Even though Mansfield made his inspections starting during the late summer, many of the posts were in high desert, e.g., Fort Union at 6,700 feet so the climate was dry and not hot: "the average annual temperature at the monument is 49.2 Fahrenheit. July has the highest monthly temperature at 69.7 Fahrenheit, and December the lowest at 33.1 Fahrenheit. Precipitation measures 18.01 inches per year;" Liping Zhu, "Fort Union National Monument: An Administrative History" (NPS, Santa Fe, NM, 1992), ch. 1. Fort Union was established 26 July 1851 and abandoned 21 February 1891. In addition to any specific instructions from Secretary of War Davis or General Scott, he would have reviewed the *General Regulations for the Army of the United States, 1847*, pertaining to inspections and he may have carried a copy of specific requirements from those regulations and later versions promulgated in 1855 and 1857 so he would have known what he was expected to report in addition to special requests from General Scott or the Secretary of War. See Attachment 2 below for requirements found in the 1847 Regulations. Captain Langdon Cheves Easton was an 1838 West Point graduate and from 1847 spent the remainder of his Army career as a quartermaster. During the Civil War, he was promoted to colonel and brevetted to major general at the end of the war. He retired in 1881 and died in 1884. Backus was an 1824 graduate of West Point and received a brevet to major for Monterrey, Mexico. He became a colonel in the Union Army in 1862 but died 7 June 1862 of disease. Letters courtesy NARA.

and on the 20th crossed the Arkansas River…entered the 9th Department, and finally reached Fort Union on the evening of the 31st." Mansfield took time during his journey with Garland to write his wife, Louisa, from his "Camp at Pawnee Creek 290 miles from Fort Leavenworth." He described the country through which they marched: "Our march has been uninterruptedly over an extensive prairie and we have seen no game and but a few Antelope and wolves and rabbits which the dogs generally gave chase to. We have seen a few Indians and Squaws and Papooses….We travel from 12 to 22 miles per day according to the facilities of getting wood and water and grass. The water is quite indifferent and often quite muddy and dirty. It is quite remarkable we have seen no Buffalo, as thousands have been seen on this route by several officers now with us….It will take us two or three days yet to reach Fort Atkinson which is on the Arkansas at the crossing. At this rate it will take us till August to reach [Fort Union]."[42]

His final report for this and most later inspection tours followed a general outline usually beginning with a review of the physical aspects of the department touching on climate, crops, natural resources, religion, routes of travel, and population. Population data was important as one of the primary roles of forts was to protect civilians from Indians especially along trade routes. Thus he discussed which groups of Indians were civilized posing no threat to others and those who were "wild" or uncivilized who attack and murder sometimes retreating into Mexico out of U.S. military reach. The other group Mansfield discussed was the Mexican "who speaks the Spanish language, being a cross with the Spanish and Indian." They were farmers and herdsmen, mainly uneducated, located mostly along the Rio Grande valley. He opined that the "American race" is small because there is not much to attract settlers as the land is not good for farming and the long distances to large markets. He mentions several times that a railroad line would enhance American settlement and allow the resources of the territory to be explored. This southern railroad route would not only open up the territory for exploitation but also then continue on to the Pacific Coast. He added that the boundary line between Texas and the New Mexico Territory on the east and south needed to be surveyed as jurisdictional issues were extant. Mansfield would not live to see any transcontinental railroad built but boundary line disputes were addressed sooner. The Gadsden Purchase was a 29,670-square-mile region of southern Arizona and southwestern New Mexico that the United States purchased by treaty that took effect on 8 June 1854. The purchase was a necessary prerequisite for a southern transcontinental railroad route which had been discussed since 1845. The transcontinental route would be able to connect with an El Paso, Texas, to San Diego, California, line. The problem with the location of the U.S.-Mexican border stemmed from the Treaty of Guadalupe Hidalgo in 1848 which ended the Mexican–American War, but left issues affecting both sides to be resolved. The treaty provided for a joint survey commission, made up of a surveyor and commissioner from each country, which would determine the location of the final boundary line. The treaty specified that the Rio Grande Boundary would veer west eight miles north of El Paso. The disputed territory involved a few thousand square miles and about 3,000 residents. The Mesilla Valley on the Rio Grande consisted of flat desert land measuring about 50 miles north to south, by 200 miles east to west and was essential for the construction of a transcontinental railroad using a southern route. Plus cross border raids by Indians had to be addressed as part of the treaty. The Gadsden Purchase was a compromise among political factions in the U.S. and caused much dissent in Mexico but it resolved the issue of the border location, until the course of the Rio Grande shifted later in the century and forced the U.S. Army to more efforts to control cross border raids by Indians. As will be seen, it did so by establishing forts such as Fort Buchanan in June 1857 south of the Gila River at the head of the Sonoita Creek Valley.[43]

---

[42] Letters courtesy of the Middlesex County Historical Society. Fort Atkinson was established by Lieutenant Colonel Edwin Vose Sumner on 8 August 1850 on Walnut Creek where the Santa Fe Trail crossed the Arkansas River. Named in honor of Colonel Henry Atkinson, it was permanently abandoned in October 1854.

[43] Mansfield, *Mansfield on the Condition of the Western Forts 1853-1854*, 3-13, *passim*; Wikipedia, "Gadsden Purchase."

Colonel John Garland, one of Mansfield's friends. He was born in Virginia 15 November 1793 and served in the War of 1812 and the Seminole Wars. He was brevetted to major for 10 years in grade, and to colonel and brigadier general during the Mexican-American War. He was wounded at Chapultepec; he died in June 1861. Courtesy LOC.

Mansfield next detailed the locations of the posts in the territory examining their utility in protecting civilian travelers and the U.S. Mail after which he explained where more forts are needed. Mansfield found that Fort Union was well-sited and important but an improvement was needed to build a wagon road to Cantonment Burgwin some 50 miles to the north. Cantonment Burgwin was also well-located and "should not be dispensed with." Fort Massachusetts was about 105 miles from Burgwin but was not in a suitable location Mansfield decided. The fort was abandoned in 1858 and replaced by Fort Garland six miles to the south. Fort Marcy he found was "the only real fort in the Territory and is located at Santa Fe…about one thousand yards to the northeast of the plaza, and commands the city perfectly." It was about 100 miles from Fort Union and a desirable location but the road to Las Vegas needed improvement. Sixty five miles north was Albuquerque and was well-located for the headquarters of the commanding general of the department. Fort Defiance was 200 miles from Albuquerque which he found to be the "most beautiful and interesting post as a whole in New Mexico" although one of the roads from it to Albuquerque needed improvement. Los Lunas he described as "merely a temporary station" for dragoons which location "can be changed up or down the river at will, to a view to...thwarting...the movements of the Indians." Fort Conrad, 88 miles south of Las Lunes, he wrote should be moved 10 miles south; it was abandoned in 1854 based on Mansfield's recommendation replaced by Fort Craig. Fort Webster, like Fort Conrad, was in a poor location and should be on the Gila River with a view to having a "chain of posts that must eventually be extended across to the Pacific." The fort was abandoned in 1853 and its garrison transferred to Fort Thorn; Fort Thorn, established as Cantonment Garland, was begun on 24 December 1853. Fort Fillmore was well-sited, located 42 miles north of El Paso, serving its purpose of operating against Apaches. He recommended new posts to be located near El Paso, and three along the 674 mile route from El Paso to Fort Clark on the Mora River. These new locations would not only protect travelers from Indians but also allow sites where U.S. Mail contractors could have mules placed improving mail service. Three forts were established at the locations he suggested: Forts Quitman (1858), Davis (1854), and Lancaster (1855). Thus the novice inspector's suggestions were closely followed by the War Department and were a credit to his martial and engineering skills.[44]

---

[44] Mansfield, *Mansfield on the Condition of the Western Forts 1853-1854*, 13-29, *passim*.

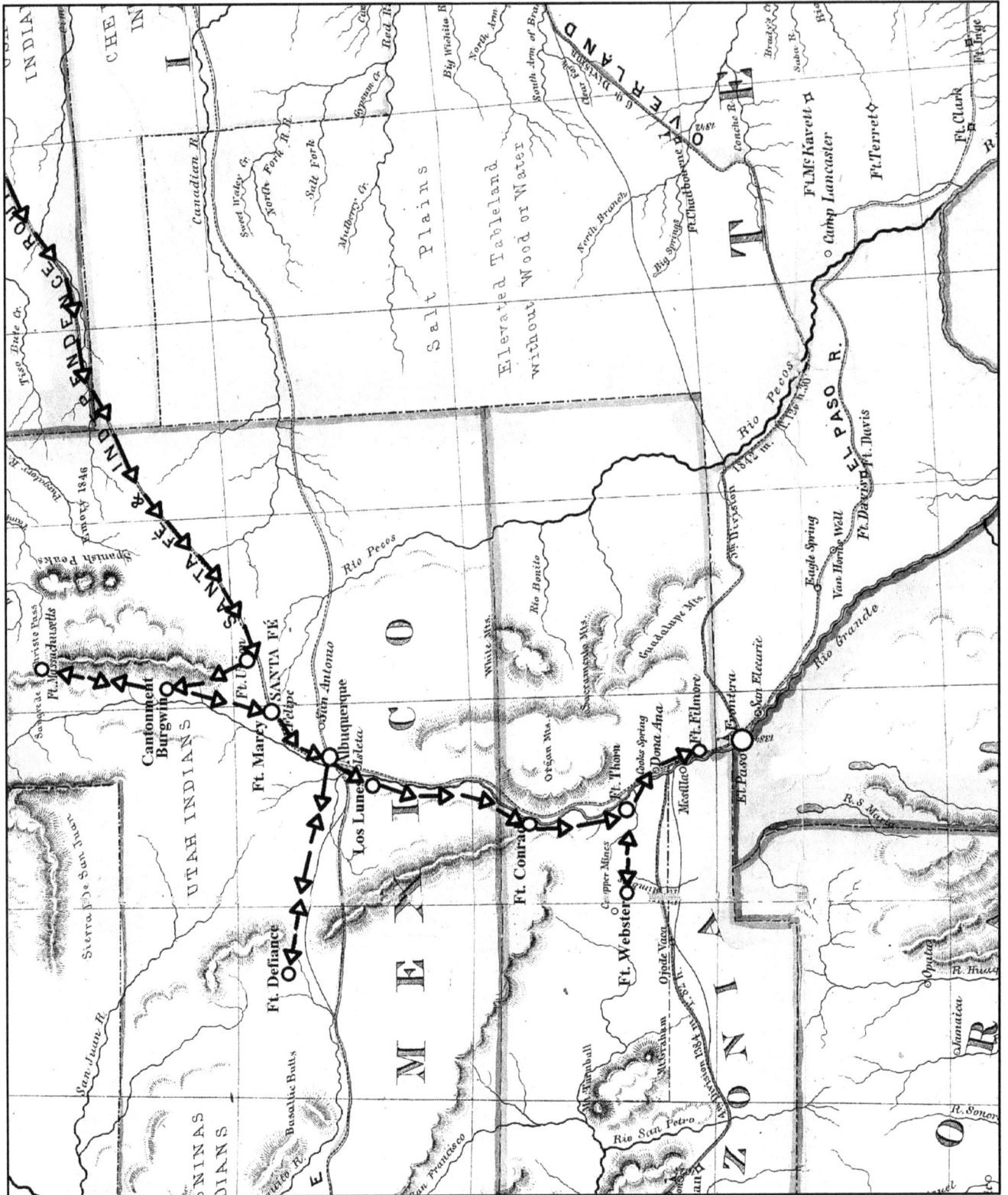

Map of Mansfield's first inspection tour of New Mexico Territory in 1853. He journeyed from Fort Leavenworth on the Santa Fe Trail, here approximated by the Santa Fe and Independence Railroad Route to Fort Union, then to Cantonment Burgwin, Fort Massachusetts, Fort Marcy at Santa Fe, Fort Defiance, Los Lunas, Fort Conrad, Fort Webster, and Fort Fillmore. He ended at El Paso and returned home to his "post" at Middletown, Connecticut, riding "from the westward of Victoria, Texas through Indianola" to take a steamship to New Orleans; after stopping in Washington, D.C., and Army Headquarters in New York City, he reached Middletown on 17 December 1853; letter courtesy of the Middlesex County Historical Society. Map of railroad routes in 1859 courtesy LOC.

Fort Union 1-6 August 1853

Mansfield found Fort Union to be satisfactory leading one historian of Fort Union to write that he was positive in his "informative but uncritical overview of the first Fort Union perhaps, because this was his first inspection duty in New Mexico. As he proceeded through the rest of the department, he became more critical in his judgment of conditions and of Sumner."[45] His friend Garland had just taken over command of the Department so that also may have been a factor in his going easy on the inspection. Mansfield reported as follows:

> Found this post in a high state of discipline and every department of it in good order and highly creditable to the gallant and distinguished officer, Colonel [Horace] Brooks, in command. The artillery, infantry, and dragoon companies were found in excellent efficient order. Of course they were all in the old uniform such as the Government had provided—their arms and equipments in excellent serviceable condition although much worn, and the arms and equipments and clothing in particular charge of the commanders of companies in a good state of preservation. The quarters occupied by the respective companies were in a good state of police, and the comfort of the troops studied in all the details....The horses of the dragoons well provided with safe and good accommodations. It was necessary to condemn 8 horses and 5 ponies....The Mexican pony is wholly unfit for the dragoon service.[46]

The quarters and structures Mansfield reported "in a good state of police" became, in a few years, rundown: "The roofs of the company quarters were 'in such a bad state as not to afford protection from the weather'....the buildings of Fort Union were in such a state of decay that it would be easier to build a new post than to repair the old one....One of the company quarters was torn down because it was in danger of collapsing on its inhabitants."[47] Did the novice inspector not look carefully at the fort's buildings or was his report correct? It is probable that he did report what he saw but he did not document the poor construction of unseasoned, unhewn, and unbarked pine logs which meant that the buildings would not last. And harsh winters with strong winds and heavy snows contributed to the deterioration.

The units at the post--dragoons, infantry, and artillery--participated in "a very handsome battalion drill, taking them through all the changes of position....[and] the artillery drill with a mountain howitzer battery of four pieces...closed with...a very complete drill at the rifle." But he was critical of the dearth of officers at the fort: "I must here call the attention to the fact of there being but one officer to a company at this post. The consequence is that heavy duty is thrown upon a few, and posts are left or detachments sent off without a commissioned officer." The lack of a sufficient number of officers was common at almost all of the posts Mansfield would visit while he was an Inspector General. But he approved of a garden the troops cultivated so that they had fresh vegetables which were required since they could not be bought in the vicinity. However, a large farm 25 miles away received scrutiny. The Army had hired a civilian to be in charge of the farm with a detachment of troops to cultivate it. Mansfield recommended that the civilian should be removed and supervision be placed under the direction of the quartermaster and that the soldier detachment receive normal extra duty funds as the farm should be operated not to earn money but as a place to pasture horses and cattle. He noted that 39 soldiers were employed on extra-duty for 18 cents per day, performing tasks such as artificer, carpenter, blacksmith, wheelwright, sawyer, hay cutter, and other unspecified jobs. He approved this use of soldiers: "the system of employing soldiers is an excellent one, when the officer in charge is active and energetic. It prepares them for every description of duty in the field and as teamsters in particular; more reliance can be placed on them, and a more perfect control had over them. Care should be had to change the laborers where practicable as often as once in twelve days to give all the men an opportunity and to keep them well instructed in their military duties proper. It is a great advantage to the soldier, as well as officer to be engaged habitually at some occupation that will improve his physical ability." Mansfield knew that idle soldiers on an isolated post could easily find unwholesome diversions. And as he reports in virtually every post inspection, bread is important, here, he found "a good bakery." He was critical of his finding that the troops had not been paid for five months—"there seems to be no good reason for so much delay." Lack

---

[45] Oliva, 205. Mansfield inspected the first Fort Union built 26 July 1851, the second fort was built in 1861 of earth as an eight-pointed star with quarters in the demilune one mile east of the first; the third and final one was built in 1863 near the star fort. On 1 April 1894, the fort reverted to the original land grant owners.

[46] Mansfield, *Mansfield on the Condition of the Western Forts 1853-1854*, 33; "police" meaning clean and in good order. Colonel Horace Brooks was an 1835 West Point graduate brevetted to first lieutenant in 1835 for actions against the Florida Indians and to major and lieutenant colonel for his actions during the Mexican-American War. He was brevetted to brigadier general at the end of the Civil War and retired in 1877, dying in 1894.

[47] Oliva, 210, 212.

of timely troop payments were common among remote posts and a point on which he would often comment. Another sore point was the quality of a few troops: "more care should be taken in the enlistment of men…I observed one ignorant German who could not understand English when spoken to; such men are not fit for this service." He also recommended that time of the extra duty enlisted men in the ordnance depot should not be applied to haying, driving teams, and taking care of mules. This force would then be ample for the whole Territory at repairs of arms and making cartridges, etc." While this last recommendation would seem to differ from his earlier view of keeping soldiers busy, it may be that he learned that in fact maintenance and repair of arms and related tasks could have been better although this is not found in his report. Overall, his assessment of Fort Union was very favorable.[48]

The extremely high cost of shipping food to western posts led the War Department on 8 January 1851 to order large scale farming on military posts thus reducing the costs for shipping and to make a profit from the sales of the produce; soldiers would share in the profits. The Department also thought that civilians would be drawn to the areas of posts and begin their own farming industries further reducing shipping costs but as Mansfield and other inspectors found this scheme almost always worked poorly. This farm experiment lasted only three years as it was discontinued in War Department General Orders in 1854:

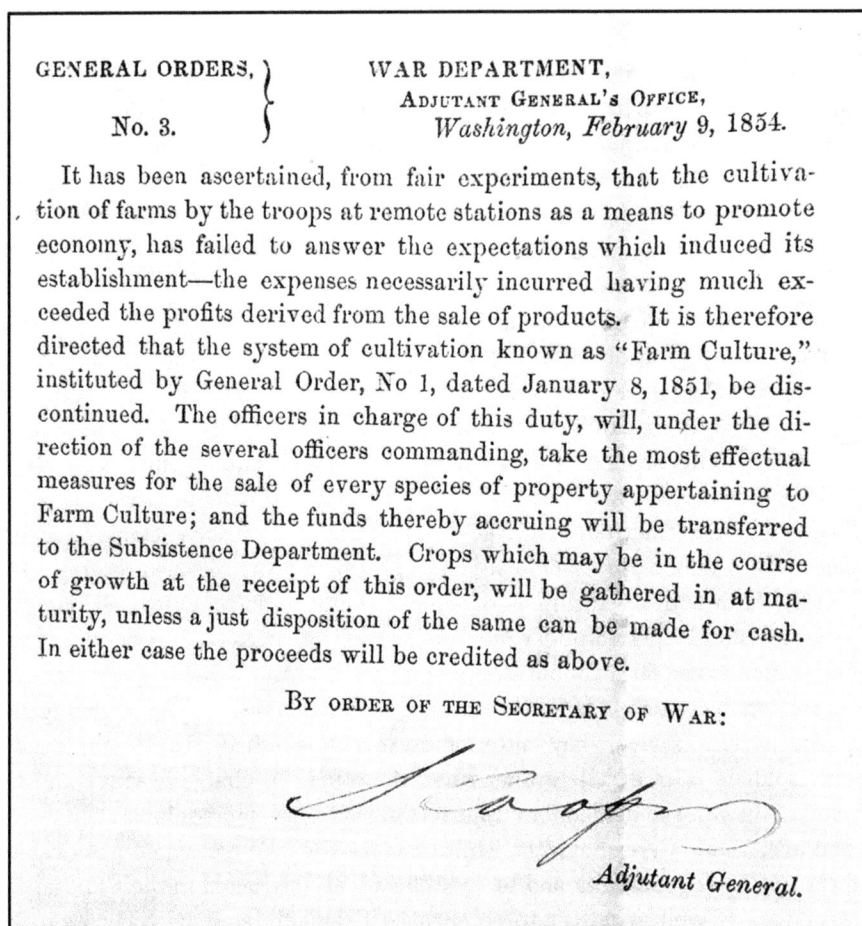

GENERAL ORDERS, }   WAR DEPARTMENT,
No. 3.   }   ADJUTANT GENERAL'S OFFICE,
                 Washington, February 9, 1854.

It has been ascertained, from fair experiments, that the cultivation of farms by the troops at remote stations as a means to promote economy, has failed to answer the expectations which induced its establishment—the expenses necessarily incurred having much exceeded the profits derived from the sale of products. It is therefore directed that the system of cultivation known as "Farm Culture," instituted by General Order, No 1, dated January 8, 1851, be discontinued. The officers in charge of this duty, will, under the direction of the several officers commanding, take the most effectual measures for the sale of every species of property appertaining to Farm Culture; and the funds thereby accruing will be transferred to the Subsistence Department. Crops which may be in the course of growth at the receipt of this order, will be gathered in at maturity, unless a just disposition of the same can be made for cash. In either case the proceeds will be credited as above.

BY ORDER OF THE SECRETARY OF WAR:

Adjutant General.

Courtesy of the Middlesex County Historical Society.

---

[48] Mansfield, *Mansfield on the Condition of the Western Forts 1853-1854*, 33-38. Fresh vegetables were needed to ward off scurvy. A visitor to the fort in 1854 found it a pleasant site: "Fort Union, a hundred and ten miles from Santa Fe, is situated in the pleasant valley of the Moro. It is an open post, without either stockades or breastworks of any kind, and, barring the officers and soldiers who are seen about, it has much more the appearance of a quiet frontier village than that of a military station. It is laid out with broad and straight streets crossing each other at right angles. The huts are built of pine logs, obtained from the neighboring mountains, and the quarters of both officers and men wore a neat and comfortable appearance;" Davis, *El Gringo*, 51. The forts Mansfield visited on this inspection tour were mostly of the open type. Regulations in 1847 showed the following recruit requirements: "All free white male persons, above the age of 18, and under 35 years, being at least 5 feet 3 inches high, who are effective, able bodied, sober, free from disease, and who have a competent knowledge of the English language, may be enlisted. *General Regulations for the Army of the United States, 1847*, 134; Clary, *The Inspector Generals*, 184-185.

First Fort Union c. 1856; view toward the southeast from the bluffs. The cluster in the left foreground depicts an infantry company in formation. Sketch by Captain Joseph Horace Eaton of the 3rd Infantry, from William Watts Hart Davis, *El Gringo: New Mexico and Her People* (New York: Harper, 1857), 49. Lieutenant Colonel Edwin V. Sumner, 1st Dragoons, established Fort Union in 1851; Captain Edmond Brooke Alexander, 3rd Infantry, served as post commander.[49]

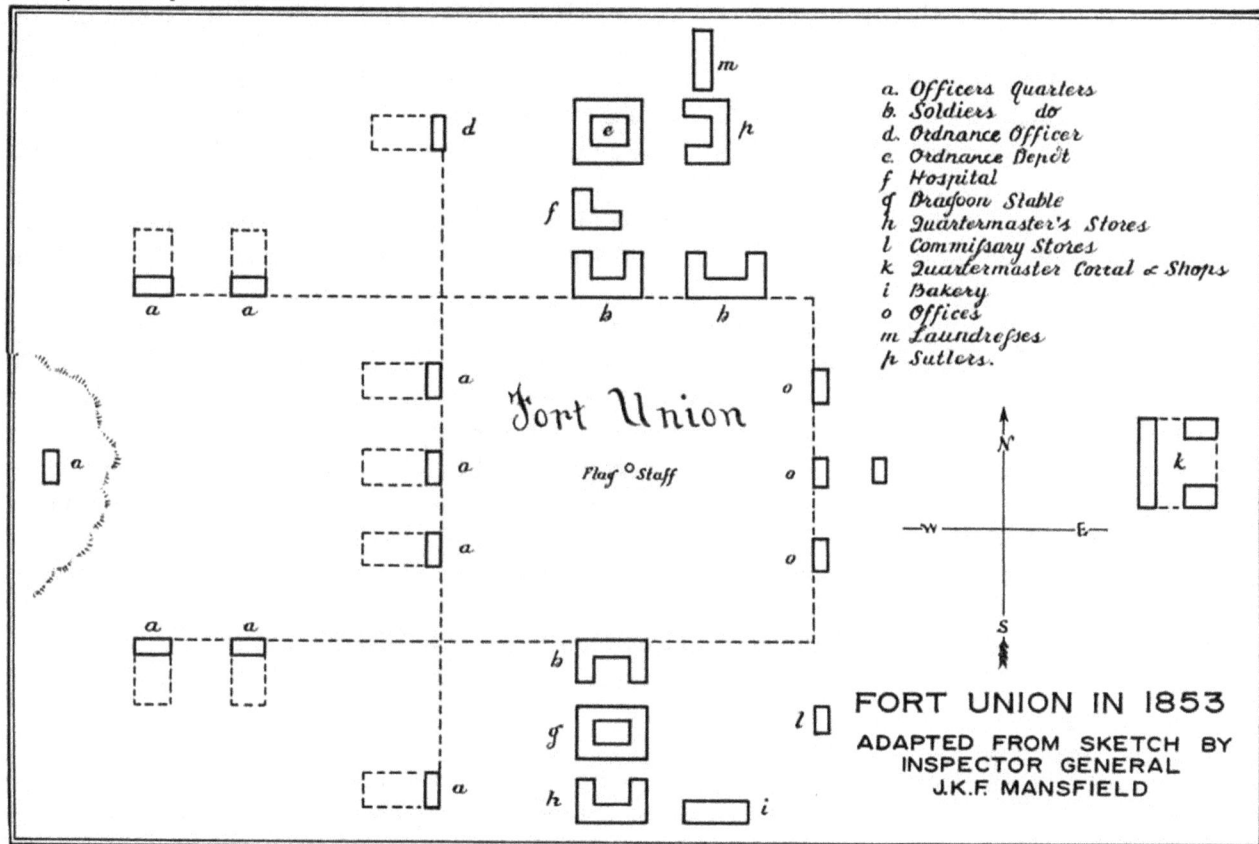

Mansfield sketched every post he visited to include with his inspection reports; this is adapted from his Fort Union inspection. Courtesy NPS.

[49] Captain Edmond Brooke Alexander was an 1823 West Point graduate and received brevets to major and lieutenant colonel for his actions during the Mexican-American War. He received a brevet to brigadier general at the end of the Civil War and retired in 1869, dying in 1888.

Cantonment Burgwin 11–13 August 1853

His next stop was at a much smaller post, Cantonment Burgwin, to the northwest of Fort Union. It took six days to make the trip. Mansfield wrote to his wife on 14 August 1853 to give her a short status report from "Cantonment Burgwin 10 miles south from Taos on the road to Santa Fe." He had completed his inspection of Fort Union and left there on the 6th. He and fellow West Point graduate, "Lieutenant John W. Alley, with some recruits and a wagon, crossed the mountains directly to this valley of some 7,000 inhabitants, but no schools. Inspection completed at Burgwin and …will leave that day and reach Taos at night. Next day to Fort Massachusetts, about 100 miles, which will take four days. [He] will stay there four days and return to Santa Fe about 1 September. Lieutenant Robert Ransom, Jr., of the 1st Dragoons in charge of Cantonment Burgwin fed us well—vegetables and fresh meat."[50] Perhaps helped by this excellent gastronomic treatment, Mansfield found little to be upset with during his three days at this small post.

He found only 41 soldiers present of 75 assigned to the post after subtracting those on detached duty and on leave. He reported that "This post is in good discipline and police, and the comforts of the troops, both sick and well, cared for. The quarters and store houses are good and [there is] a safe and commodious corral for the horses and mules, and a good garden is cultivated.…The troops are well instructed in the drill, and the arms and equipments in good serviceable condition although much worn and the uniform of course old, no other having been provided.…There is a good bakery here." He found only a few topics to criticize—deficiency in mule and horse shoes, and poor quality of recruits but this time added to the usual men who could not understand English, there was one who was near sighted and one left handed. He opined that the "left handed man was awkward in the ranks." And as at Fort Union, he learned that the troops had not been paid for five months.[51]

Corporal James Augustus Bennett, in the 1st Dragoons, stationed at Cantonment Burgwin when Mansfield inspected it, described the post he saw in 1852: "The buildings are built of mud brick in a hollow square, leaving in the center what is called a 'parade ground' where the military parades are held every morning. One side of the square is used as officer's quarters; the opposite side as a guard house, commissary department, offices, etc. The other two sides are soldiers' barracks. There is a flag staff in the center from which the stars and stripes flash and wave in the breeze. Out of this square are to be found a hospital, dragoon stables, yard, etc. Buildings are all of one story with flat roofs, having a parapet on the top of the outer walls. There are no windows on the outside of the square and only port holes in the parapet through which one may look or shoot."[52]

Quality of recruits was a persistent problem throughout the Army as it was very difficult to obtain good volunteers for such low pay and difficult working conditions: "'The material offered in time of peace…is not of the most desirable character, consisting principally of newly arrived immigrants, of those broken down by bad habits and dissipation, the idle, and the improvident.'" "Immigrants outnumbered native Americans more than two to one. Ireland supplied more than half the foreign element, Germany about a fifth." Desertion was a constant problem especially on the Pacific Coast after gold was discovered: "In 1856, with the Army expanded to more than fifteen thousand, 3,223 men deserted." The training of the recruits sent to Western Posts was often either inadequate or nonexistent. "General Scott complained in 1857, 'Incessant calls for reinforcements received from the frontiers compel us, habitually, to forward recruits without the instruction that should precede service in the field, and on joining their regiments, perhaps in the act of pursuing an enemy, it is long before the deficiency can be supplied.' The result was that the replacements…often could not handle a weapon or, if cavalry, stay in the saddle."[53] On-the-job training at the Western posts was difficult due to "the chronic shortage of officers on line duty, the dispersed condition of the regiments, and the constant employment of men on fatigue labor…Sporadic target practice and daily dismounted drill helped a little." Mansfield often commented on the

---

[50] Letter courtesy WPL. Alley was an 1850 West Point graduate and became a captain during the Civil War; he was dismissed in 1863. Ransom too was an 1850 graduate and also entered the Civil War as a captain but resigned in 1861 becoming a major general in the Confederate Army. Located about 10 miles south of Taos on a tributary of the Rio Grande, Burgwin was established 14 August 1852 to safeguard the Taos Valley. Captain John Henry K. Burgwin was an 1830 West Point graduate and mortally wounded in a battle at Pueblo de Taos, New Mexico dying on 7 February 1847. Cantonment Burgwin was abandoned 18 May 1860.

[51] Mansfield, *Mansfield on the Condition of the Western Forts 1853-1854*, 39-41.

[52] James A. Bennett, *Forts and Forays: A Dragoon in New Mexico, 1850-1856*, ed. by Clinton E. Brooks and Frank D. Reeve (Albuquerque, NM: The University of New Mexico Press, 1948), 40. Corporal Bennett helped build the post.

[53] Utley, *Frontiersmen in Blue*, 39-40.

lack of officers to conduct training and the lack of training new recruits received before they were sent to their new posts.[54]

Fort Massachusetts 18–21 August 1853

Fort Massachusetts was about 100 miles away from Burgwin and 85 miles north of Taos; the journey took five days. It was then in the New Mexico Territory, but today it is in the state of Colorado. Mansfield began his inspection on 18 August of this slightly larger post consisting of Company F of the 1st Dragoons, and Company H of the 3rd Infantry. "This command was in a good state of discipline. The arms and equipment of the dragoons and infantry in good serviceable order although much worn and a deficiency of spurs....The quarters occupied by the troops were abundant and good. The comfort of the troops, both well and sick, cared for. A good bakery exists...and the supplies of food good....A large corral well calculated for horses, mules, and cattle...has been built and a garden made for the use of the troops and an effort made at farming which, owing to the seasons and other causes, has not been successful." As at the first two posts he inspected, the soldiers had not been paid for more than five months, obviously the Paymaster had not made his rounds to these remote forts. Unlike earlier posts, he reported that the "troops have been little instructed in the drill for the past year, in consequence of the constant labor within the year in building the post. The whole command is entitled to great credit for the work they have done in so short a time." He also commented that all food supplies must come from a great distance which explains why many are deficient. A similar problem concerns goods shipped in from Fort Union forcing the troops to buy clothing from the sutler at high prices; he blamed the "Government" for this problem which caused problems for the soldiers as the sutler's prices "are exorbitant and much beyond the ability of the soldier to pay." His concern for the rank and file is noteworthy as many officers did not view hardships on enlisted men with much sympathy.[55]

---

[54] Ibid., 41-42.

[55] Mansfield, *Mansfield on the Condition of the Western Forts 1853-1854*, 40-41. Fort Massachusetts was established on 22 June 1852 and abandoned on 24 June 1858 due to its unhealthy location; it was replaced by Fort Garland. He wrote that the fort must be relocated: "It is seated at the foot of the White Mountain which is perpetually snow topped; and on Utah Creek at the mouth of a ravine out of which the creek flows a cool limpid stream. There is an abundance of wood and in the summer the grazing is good, but the warm season is short, and it is doubtful if corn will ripen here. The nearest settlement is 30 miles to the southward on the Culebra River where there are about 25 families engaged in the planting of corn and wheat. The design of this post was to keep the Utah Indians in check and it is calculated for Dragoons and Infantry. The buildings are good and suitable as well as abundant. They are, however, placed too near the spur of the mountain for good defense against an enterprising enemy. All supplies for this post come from the settlements at the south as far as Taos Valley, and Fort Union which may be called 165 miles distant. In winter the snow falls here to the depth of four feet....My impressions are that this post would have been better located on the Culebra River, the most northern settlement in New Mexico, where access could be had to the Troops by the population of the Valley, without the hazard of being cut off by the Indians. The home of the Utah Indians is here, and particularly in the west of the Rio Grande del Norte. A post is therefore necessary in this quarter, and this Valley may before long be a good route of communication with the States in the summer season, and it probably is the best route of communicating between New Mexico and the Great Salt Lake and Northern California;" Mansfield, *Mansfield on the Condition of the Western Forts 1853-1854*, 17-19, *passim*.

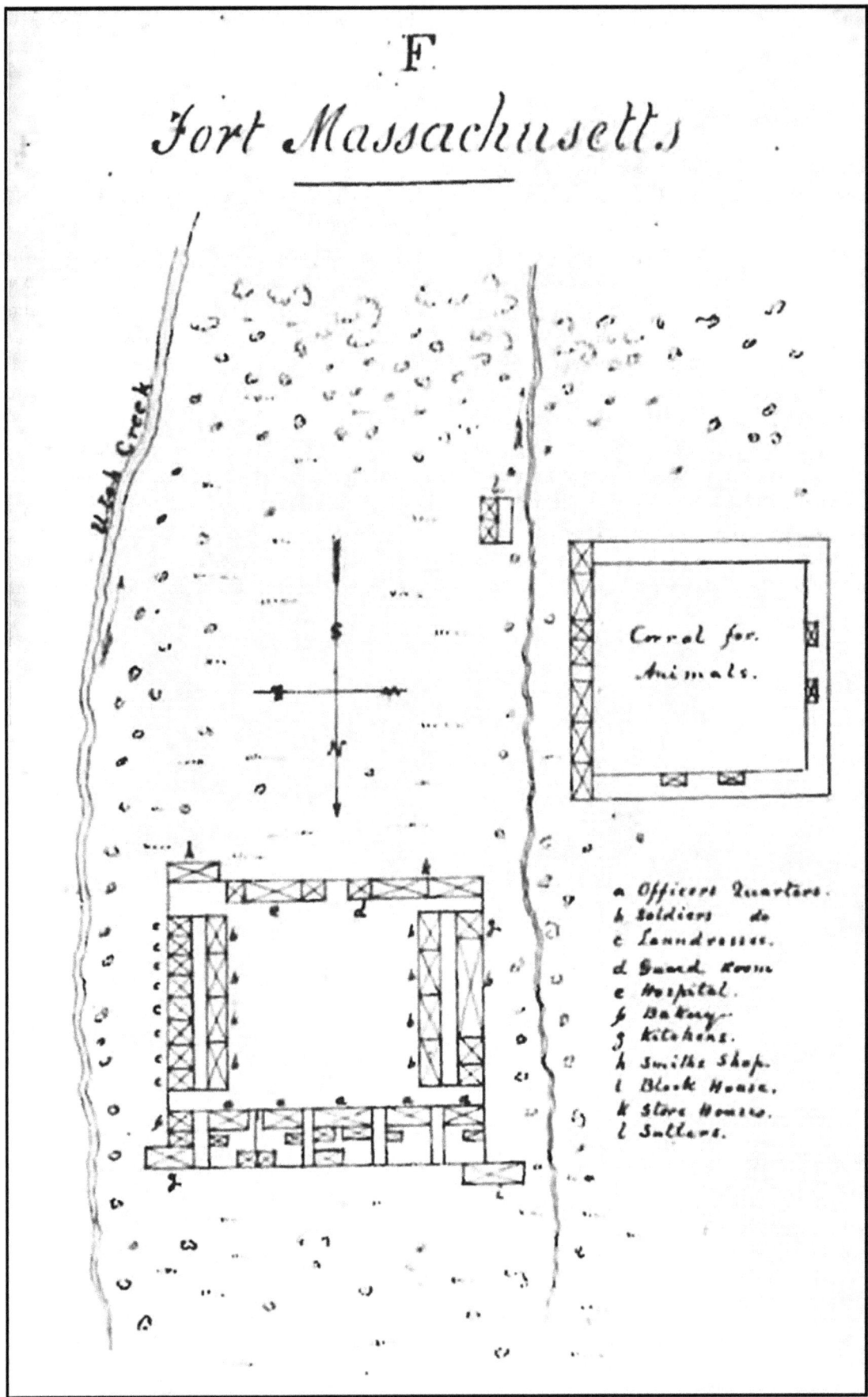

Mansfield's sketch of Fort Massachusetts which accompanied his report. Courtesy NARA.

Lithograph of Fort Massachusetts by J.M. Stanley from a sketch by Richard H. Kern published in Lieutenant E.G. Beckwith's report on Captain J.W. Gunnison's expedition; Senate, 33rd Congress, 2nd Session, Ex. Doc. 78, "Reports of Explorations and Surveys to Ascertain the Most Practicable and Economical Route for a Railroad from the Mississippi River to the Pacific Ocean, 1853-1854," vol. 2 (Washington, DC: Beverley Tucker, Printer, 1855), 38. Kern and Gunnison were killed by Indians while on this survey. His depiction is an idealized version of this wooden fort. Mount Blanca is in the distance.

Fort Massachusetts as it appeared in 1852; model located at the Fort Garland Museum in Fort Garland, Colorado; sutler store on the lower left outside the fort; view is facing north. Fort Garland, established on 24 June 1858, replaced Fort Massachusetts which was six miles to the north. It is one of the very few stockade forts Mansfield inspected. Courtesy Wikipedia.

Fort Marcy at Santé Fe 27–31 August 1853

Six days after he left Fort Massachusetts on 21 August 1853, he arrived at Fort Marcy at Santa Fe for his next inspection. Fort Marcy was adjacent to the Palace of the Governors in Santa Fe. About 1,000 yards away was an earthwork which commanded Santa Fe.[56] The post was in Santa Fe and was manned by Company G, 3rd Infantry. He found "This company...in a high state of discipline, arms and equipments in the best serviceable order, and the rank and file extremely well instructed....The quarters were in a good state of police and the public property in a good state of preservation in suitable store houses—except some field pieces and carriages, which required the attention of the Ordnance Department....A good garden is attached to the post, and other supplies good and abundant except solders' shoes." Mansfield found the commanding officer, Major William Thomas Harbaugh Brooks, "peculiarly well qualified for this post."[57]

Mansfield, while in Santa Fe, also inspected the paymaster's office, which consisted of Major Francis A. Cunningham and Major Cary Harrison Fry. Mansfield was not happy with a $1,294.50 loan to the Topographical Engineers, Captain John Pope, among other loans to others, on orders of Colonel Sumner, the Department commander. "The loan to the Topographical Department not being indispensable to the transportation of supplies and the subsistence

---

[56] Fort Marcy was established 23 August 1846 and was the first Army post established in New Mexico. It was deactivated 23 Aug. 1867 but a post was established in Santa Fe. Fort Marcy was reactivated in 1875 and again abandoned in 1891, reactivated, then permanently abandoned 10 Oct. 1894. Robert B. Roberts, *Encyclopedia of Historic Forts: The Military, Pioneer, and Trading Posts of the United States* (New York, NY: Macmillan Publishing Company, 1988), 527.

[57] Mansfield, *Mansfield on the Condition of the Western Forts 1853-1854*, 41-42. Brooks, an 1841 West Point graduate, did not do well in the Union Army during the Civil War although being brevetted to captain and major during the Mexican-American War: he was appointed a major general of volunteers 10 June 1863 which appointment was revoked 18 April 1864 as a result of the cabal against Major General Ambrose E. Burnside. He resigned from voluntary and regular service 14 July 1864 and died in 1870.

of the troops seems entirely too irregular for a time of peace." As has been noted, the first posts he inspected were over five months in arrears for pay so that was a sore point for him. It is likely that he questioned the men about this situation. He found that Cunningham paid posts north of Santa Fe—Forts Union, Cantonment Burgwin, and Massachusetts, and Fry the posts south, Albuquerque, Fort Defiance, and Los Lunas, etc. He finished his report by noting that while the post in Santa Fe may be convenient for the paymasters, "it is inconvenient to obtain suitable escorts and transportation in the performance of their duties." This may help explain why some posts were in arrears for pay.[58]

SANTA FÉ.

A sketch of Santa Fe in the 1850's with the fort in the far right distance at the flag. In 1854, William Watts Hart Davis described the city and the Palace adjacent to which the 3rd Infantry had its barracks: "The population, according to the census of 1850, was between four and five thousand, and may be set down about the same at this time, but this number includes all the little settlements along the river up to the foot of the mountains. It is laid out with considerable regularity in the manner of all Spanish-built towns. In the centre is a public square or plaza, some two or three acres in extent, from the four corners of which lead the main streets, at right angles to each other. The streets are of medium width and wholly unpaved; and but for the shelter afforded by the portales (the side-walks) in the rainy season, they would become almost impassable for foot-passengers. In the middle of the Plaza stands a flag-staff, erected by the military authorities some years ago, from the top of which the star-spangled banner daily waves to the breeze. The houses are built of adobes, or mud bricks dried in the sun, and are but one story in height; and there are only two two-story houses in the place, neither of which was erected by the Mexicans. The walls are much thicker than those of a stone or brick house, and, being of a drier material, they are cooler in summer and warmer in winter than the former....The government palace, a long, low mud building, extends the entire north side of the Plaza, and is occupied by the officers of the territorial government, and is also made use of for purposes of legislation. Nearby, and on the street that leads out at the northeast corner of the square, is the court-house, where the United States, District, and Supreme Courts hold their sessions. On the south side, and opposite the palace, stands the old Mexican Military Chapel;" Davis, *El Gringo*, 161, 164-166.

---

[58] Cunningham was a volunteer paymaster entering service in 1847 and retired 27 Aug. 1863 dying in 1864; Fry, an 1834 West Point graduate, remained a paymaster and was a brevet brigadier general 15 Oct. 1867. Mansfield, *Mansfield on the Condition of the Western Forts 1853-1854*, 42-43. Paymasters in the West often had difficulty in making regular rounds. One enlisted man wrote that when the paymaster visited his regiment, the troops were paid for eight months; Augustus Meyers, *Ten Years in the Ranks*, U.S. Army (New York, NY: The Sterling Press, 1914), 135.

PLAZA OF ALBUQUERQUE.

The main plaza of Albuquerque, New Mexico. El Gringo, 344.

Albuquerque 3–8 September 1853

Mansfield left Santa Fe on 31 August and began his inspection of Albuquerque on 3 September 1853. This post was the headquarters of the Department commander, Brigadier General John Garland, Mansfield's old friend from Monterrey. The inspector found much to criticize here starting with the usual understaffing of men and especially officers in the resident company, Company H, 2ⁿᵈ Dragoons. Of the 80 on the rolls, only 60 were present for duty of which five were sick and two confined. "The men and horses required instruction and training. There was no farrier to this company and the horses unshod and not in a fit condition to move off at an hour's notice after Indians. In short, the company required a complement of officers, and much attention, and accordingly has subsequently been ordered by General Garland to Fort Union for that purpose, and Brevet Major [James Henry] Carleton's company ordered to take its place." He also found that "The quarters for the soldiers and the public stores were quite indifferent and insufficient for the post." He wrote that since the location of the post is convenient as a depot "an effort should be made to lease land at a nominal rent and erect buildings in this vicinity that would remove the troops from the close contact with the citizens and afford a better state of discipline." One might read between the lines that being "in close contact" with the populace for the soldiers provided easy access to liquor and female entertainment. Mansfield noted that a 30 acre farm failed and that the post garden mostly did too. Lieutenant [Kenner] Garrard who was in charge was not faulted by Mansfield however: "Lieutenant Garrard deserves credit for his great exertions here, but there was too much for any one officer to perform, and more than should ever be expected of an officer."[59] It is noteworthy that Mansfield was not averse to reporting problems at Garland's headquarters and also for not blaming a young officer who he found was doing the best he could under impossible circumstances.

Mansfield wrote his wife from Albuquerque 7-8 September 1853 and in addition to his usual finance and children recommendations he told her about the adobe houses which have carpets on the dirt floors. He was staying at the headquarters of General Garland, having arrived on the evening of the first of the month. His horse stepped in a hole and rolled over on him--the horse was not injured however, Mansfield was bruised. He planned on starting on the 8ᵗʰ

---

[59] Mansfield, *Mansfield on the Condition of the Western Forts 1853-1854*, 43-46. Garrard was an 1851 West Point graduate and received several brevets during the Civil War the last being to major general of volunteers in 1864. He resigned in 1866 and died in 1879. Carleton was appointed a second lieutenant directly in 1839 and brevetted to major during the Mexican-American War. During the Civil War he was brevetted from lieutenant colonel to major general. He became governor of the New Mexico Territory and an author. He died in 1873.

for Fort Defiance with Major Cary Harrison Fry the paymaster, with a 20 man escort. He then hoped to return on the 27th and go to Fort Conrad.[60]

Fort Defiance 15–20 September 1853

One week after he left Santa Fe, he began inspecting Fort Defiance on the 15th of September. Today the fort's location is in the state of Arizona just over the New Mexico state line.[61] This was a larger post as it had two companies of the 3rd Infantry, Companies B and F, and Company B of the 2nd Artillery; the post was commanded by Major Henry Lane Kendrick. This larger post merited an assistant surgeon, chaplain, and a schoolmaster. Mansfield found nothing to complain about as the "post was in a high state of discipline, and every department of it unexceptionable and highly creditable to the distinguished officer, Major Kendrick....The drills at the artillery and heavy and light infantry showed that the instruction of the troops was not lost sight of notwithstanding the great labor that had been performed in erecting quarters, etc., in this locality where everything had to be originated." He also found the quarters for officer and enlisted as well as store houses good. But he did find that the soldiers were forced to buy expensive shoes and socks from the sutler as the quartermaster had none. He found an excellent garden, well-irrigated, which accounted for its success but the farm that was attempted had failed. Soldiers had not been paid for six months. He noted that there was no school at the fort so he implicitly questioned the need for the schoolmaster. He finally reported that Indians are freely admitted into the post and are friendly; they have a building into which they must stay if any do not leave before nightfall. These Navahos who could field 1,000 warriors sometime commit depredations of the civilians but apparently not on soldiers or their families.[62]

Fort Defiance in Canyon Bonito, the first military post in Arizona; 1873 oil painting by Brigadier General Seth Eastman, about 20 years after Mansfield inspected it; U.S. Senate, courtesy Wikipedia.

---

[60] Letter courtesy of the Middlesex County Historical Society.

[61] Fort Defiance was established 18 September 1851 by Colonel Edwin Vose Sumner in Canyon Bonita due to large numbers of aggressive Navahos. It was abandoned 25 April 1861; Roberts, *Encyclopedia of Historic Forts*, 37.

[62] Mansfield, *Mansfield on the Condition of the Western Forts 1853-1854*, 46-48. Kendrick was an 1835 graduate of West Point who returned there in 1857 to become a professor and remained there until his retirement in 1880. Mansfield wrote to Adjutant General Colonel Samuel Cooper that he was at Fort Defiance 19 September 1853, and had just completed inspection of the post; he would leave for Los Lunas the next day; letter courtesy WPL. Company B of the 2nd Artillery did not have guns and served as infantry.

Los Lunas 25–27 September 1853

Five days after he departed Fort Defiance, he arrived at Los Lunas 25 September 1853. This small post contained Company G of the 1ˢᵗ Dragoons commanded by Captain Richard Stoddert Ewell. Ewell was the only officer present for duty as the two others were absent. While Mansfield found the horse equipments "much worn" the arms and other equipments were in good order. "The company was well instructed and drilled handsomely. The quarters were good and all the public property in a good state of preservation." As at Fort Defiance, solders were forced to purchase their own shoes and socks from sutlers at high prices. But other supplies such as corn, beans, flour, beef and mutton are "readily obtained." He also reported there was a "good garden" and that Ewell had been successful with a small farm using irrigation.[63]

Fort Conrad 30 September–4 October 1853

In only three days after leaving Los Lunas, he arrived at Fort Conrad on 30 September to inspect the post under command of Lieutenant Colonel Daniel T. Chandler. Chandler commanded Company I of the 3ʳᵈ Infantry and Captain William Steele commanded Company K of the 2ⁿᵈ Dragoons. Mansfield reported that the post "was in a good state of discipline" and the arms "in good serviceable order"; the companies were well drilled but he saw "indications in both companies of the want of sufficient number of commissioned officers on duty." He had noted that the infantry company was drilled by its first sergeant. Here, for the first time on his inspection tour, he found "The quarters of both officers and soldiers are falling to pieces. The timbers had rotted away—some of the troops were in tents….and the public store houses worthless." Fortunately the garden was doing well but the farm "proved a failure" due to excessive costs to use the private land. Given the problems he found, he "recommended that it [the fort] be broken up and another substituted."[64]

---

[63] Mansfield, *Mansfield on the Condition of the Western Forts 1853-1854*, 48-49. Ewell graduated from West Point in 1840 and resigned 7 May 1861 becoming a lieutenant general in the Confederate Army; he died in 1872. Los Lunas, 22 miles south of Albuquerque, was established 3 January 1852. It was abandoned and reoccupied several times and finally abandoned in October 1862.

[64] Mansfield, *Mansfield on the Condition of the Western Forts 1853-1854*, 49-51. Chandler entered the Army from civilian life in 1838 as a captain in the Mexican-American War receiving brevets to major and lieutenant colonel. He resigned 24 Dec. 1862 and became a lieutenant colonel in the Confederate Army; he died in 1877. Steele was an 1840 West Point graduate and was brevetted to captain for his actions during the Mexican-American War; he resigned 30 May 1861 and became a brigadier general in the Confederate Army; he died in 1885. Fort Conrad was located on the west bank of the Rio Grande near Valverde and established 8 September 1851. It was abandoned 31 March 1854 and replaced by Fort Craig 10 miles to the south.

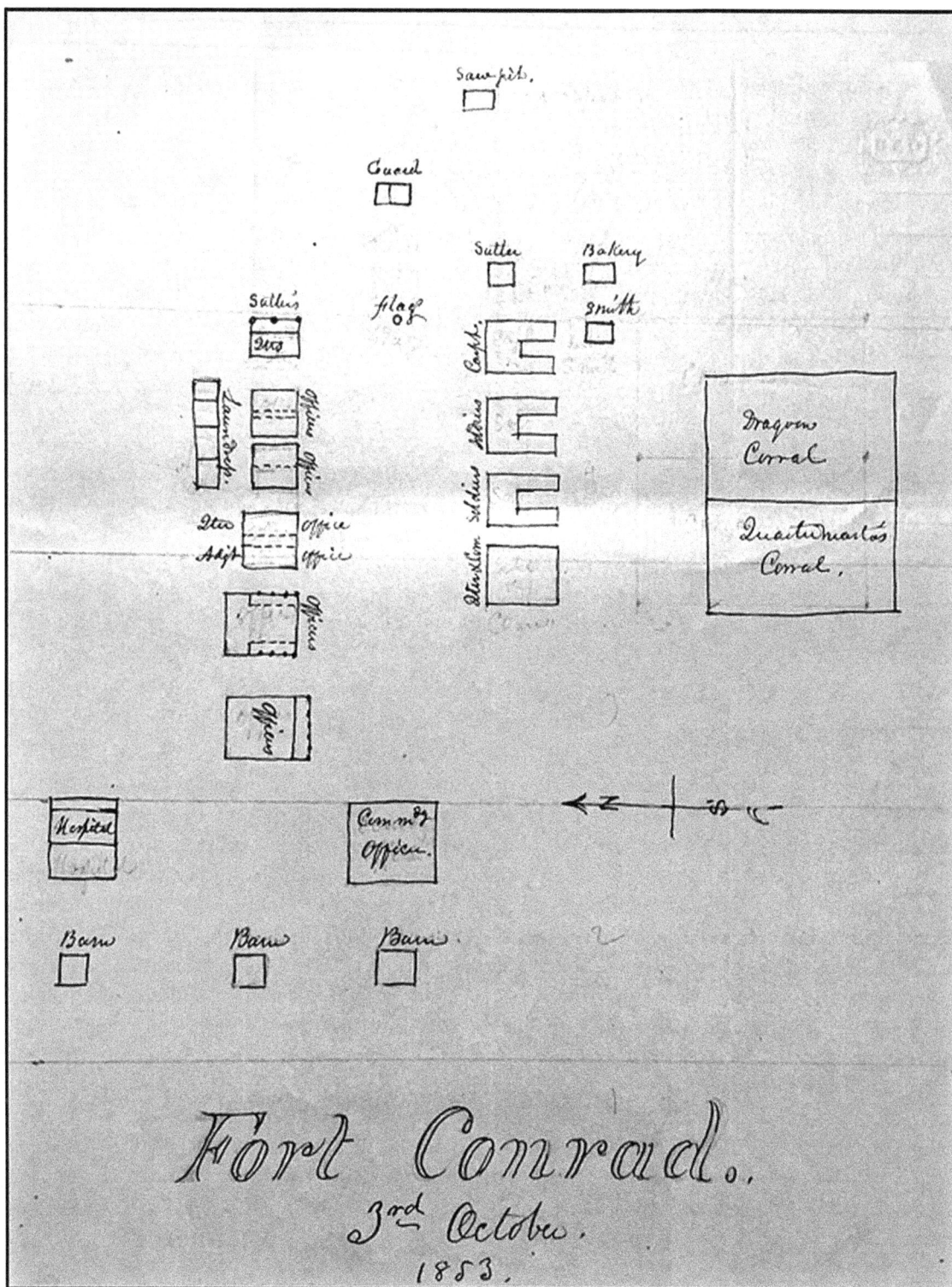

Mansfield's sketch of Fort Conrad; courtesy of the Middlesex County Historical Society.

Fort Webster 10–13 October 1853

Mansfield arrived at Fort Webster to begin his inspection on 10 October. This post had three companies—Company H of the 1st Dragoons under command of the post commander, Major Enoch Steen, Company K of the 3rd Infantry under Major Israel Bush Richardson, and Company E of the 2nd Dragoons commanded by Captain Reuben Philander Campbell. Mansfield found that the post "was in a good state of discipline" under the "experienced and gallant officer Major Steen."

Mansfield had known Steen in the Mexican-American War where Steen was brevetted to major but perhaps more importantly to the inspector was that he learned "most of the men of his own company had joined the Temperance Society." Up to this time, Mansfield had not commented on the universal problem of drunkenness at frontier posts but in some future inspections he would find time to mention the problem of alcohol and troops confined for its abuse. The inspector found "their arms and equipments in good serviceable order," although the "horse equipments were much worn. The muskets of Major Richardson's company were quite old, and there was a great deficiency of pistols in Company E, 2nd Dragoons, and many sword knots wanted. These troops, considering the hard labor they had to perform in moving and erecting quarters within the year, were well instructed." Mansfield found sympathy for Lieutenant William Duncan Smith who suffered greatly from kidney stones, called "gravel." "The quarters and buildings of the command were in a good state of police, but quite indifferent and insufficient, the post not having been completed. Major Richardson's company were in tents….supplies were abundant with the exception of horse shoes and horse shoe nails and horse brushes and curry combs. A good garden was cultivated and a corn and oats farm planted which looked well….There is a post bakery." Like the last post he inspected, Fort Webster, he recommended that it be moved to the Gila River.[65]

Mansfield wrote to his wife from Fort Webster 12 October 1853 telling her that he completed his inspection and that tomorrow he would begin his journey to Fort Fillmore on the Rio Grande del Norte. He added that he left Fort Conrad on the 4th and travelled three days down the west side of the Rio del Norte and then 2 1/2 days to Fort Webster. The last two days he travelled with General Garland who he overtook on his way from Fort Fillmore to Fort Webster. Mansfield had an escort of two Dragoons. He anticipated five days travel to Fort Fillmore which would probably be the last post to inspect. He thought he would leave Fort Fillmore for San Antonio about 1 November traveling 600 miles at 25 miles a day taking 24 days, so he cannot reach home until the middle of December and he would have to stop in Washington, D.C.[66]

Fort Fillmore 17–29 October 1853

The last inspection on this tour for Mansfield was Fort Fillmore; he began his inspection on 17 October 1853 four days after leaving Fort Webster. This was the largest of the posts as it had four companies so it also took the longest to complete—11 days. The post was commanded by Major Electus Backus of the 3rd Infantry; four companies at this post were Companies A, C and E, 3rd Infantry, and Company D, 2nd Dragoons. Mansfield praised Backus fulsomely likely because he knew him from the Battle of Monterey in Mexico: "This post is in a high state of discipline in every respect, and the commanding officer, Major Backus, enjoys the high respect of his whole command, [to] which his distinguished services in the field, combined with his individual character entitle him; and he is peculiarly well fitted for the command where so much discretion, as well as firmness, is necessary, within two miles of a Mexican population directly on the opposite side of the river, at Mesilla, and the nearest post at this time to El Paso." The troops under Backus's command "were well instructed in view of the great labor they have performed in building this post. Major Backus took the infantry through the battalion drill handsomely and the companies afterwards went through the company drills under their respective commanders creditably." But Mansfield was concerned that the dragoons were commanded by an infantry officer, as the three dragoon officers assigned were on detached service. Mansfield was pleased with "the quarters for this post for both officers and men" finding them "the best in the Territory." And all the public property "is in a good state of preservation" and there is a "good hospital and magazine and store houses." He was also happy with the garden and bakery.[67]

---

[65] Steen entered from civilian life in 1832 becoming a lieutenant colonel in 1861 and retired in 1863. Richardson was an 1841 graduate of West Point; he became a major general of volunteers 4 July 1862 and died of wounds received at the Battle of Antietam 17 September 1862. Campbell was an 1840 West Point graduate and resigned 11 May 1861 becoming colonel of the 7th North Carolina Infantry in the Civil War. He was killed 27 June 1862 at the Battle of Gaines's Mill. Smith resigned 28 January 1861 and became a brigadier general in the Confederate Army; he died 4 October 1862 of yellow fever. The Fort Webster Mansfield inspected was the second one on the site, established 9 September 1852 on the Rio Mimbres. Based on Mansfield's recommendation that it should be moved to the Gila River, the fort was abandoned 20 December 1853 and its garrison moved to Fort Thorn, so no fort was built on the Gila River. Webster was named after Secretary of State Daniel Webster.

[66] Letter courtesy WPL.

[67] Fort Fillmore was established on 23 Sept. 1851 by Lieutenant Colonel Dixon S. Miles. It was on the east bank of the Rio Grande about 40 miles above El Paso. It was named after President Millard Fillmore. It was given up to Confederates in July 1861 when Federal troops evacuated it and retreated to Fort Stanton. Confederate troops abandoned the fort when Union troops approached 8 July 1862 then on 10 October 1862 Union troops withdrew and

Mansfield took time to write to General Garland from Fort Fillmore on 26 October 1853 telling him that he completed inspection of Garland's Department and that he would start for El Paso Friday where he will await mail and his escort from this post. He included some suggestions for the commander: "I would recommend a more full use of the ball cartridge at the target as indispensable to accuracy of fire in battle at long as well as short distances....I have generally found the supplies at posts deficient in soldiers' shoes, coffee, horse shoes and horseshoe nails."[68] Note that in the copy of the letter below in Attachment 3 in September he had written to Adjutant General Cooper with recommendations regarding road improvements and additional pay for soldiers to ensure that Secretary of War Davis could get these budget items presented to Congress.

In addition to these letters, his summary of his inspection tour was comprehensive spelling out his recommendations based on what he saw at the posts. After reviewing the numbers of officers and men and arms, the only deficiency he found was in the number of dragoon horses as they "are quite limited, being but 383 horses to 483 rank and file." The men at the posts he visited had only the "old uniform." The old uniform to which he referred was the one worn during the Mexican-American War although as noted in the Mexican-American War chapter above, troops including officers often wore was comfortable despite regulations. Even though the Secretary of War in 1850 decreed a new, more practical uniform, in regulations of 1851, that order was quickly rescinded because the Quartermaster Department had more than a million dollars' worth of the old uniform on hand at the Schuylkill Arsenal in Philadelphia so the Secretary soon directed that the old uniform would be issued until that supply ran out.[69] Among other things, the new uniform replaced the shorter jacket called a coatee with a longer frock coat. The coatee was single breasted for privates with nine buttons in front, and lace on the collar. Troops continued to wear the forage cap for fatigue duty. Mansfield detailed the shortcomings of the old uniform mainly due to poor choices of sizes forcing troops to pay "from one and a half to three dollars to have his clothes altered. Also some sizes of shoes were in short supply." When Mansfield inspected troops at a post, they would have worn their dress uniform not their undress uniform. He also reported that the current knapsack did not do well in the western climate as the painted canvas and gum elastic wrought havoc on the men's clothes and should be replaced by a plain canvas sack made in one piece. He also noted briefly that gum elastic "in any shape but the water bucket meets with general objection in this climate." He commented on wagon wheels again for the climate in the desert that the tire should be thicker to help prevent its movement on the trail. Another of Mansfield's suggestions however was not adopted—Mansfield supplied four drawings and much text concerning tents. He reviewed in detail current Army tents and then found that a tent designed by Major Henry Lane Kendrick of the 2nd Artillery Regiment was best. Just a few years later, Major Henry Hopkins Sibley invented and patented in 1856 a conical tent supported by a central pole that telescoped down into the supporting tripod making it easier to pack and store. The tripod usually was built over a fire pit for cooking and heat. It required no guy ropes, being held down by twenty-four pegs around the base. The use of a cowl over the central pole allowed for ventilation and for the escape of smoke. Sibley probably got his ideas from accompanying Captain John C. Fremont on his expeditions. Mansfield was not familiar with Sibley's tent but with the then current Army style bell tents on which Sibley's design was a marked improvement. The Army used about 44,000 Sibley tents during the Civil War.[70]

---

the fort was not reoccupied; Roberts, *Encyclopedia of Historic Forts*, 524-525. Mansfield, *Mansfield on the Condition of the Western Forts 1853-1854*, 54-57.

[68] Letter courtesy WPL.

[69] Risch, *Quartermaster Support of the Army*, 302.

[70] Mansfield, *Mansfield on the Condition of the Western Forts 1853-1854*, 58-60. Randolph B. Marcy, *The Prairie Traveler: A Hand-Book for Overland Expeditions* (New York, NY: Harper & Brothers, 1861), 142-144. Kendrick was an 1835 graduate of West Point and became a professor there in 1857. Sibley was an 1838 graduate of West Point but resigned from the Army in 1861 to become a Confederate brigadier general. Marcy was an 1832 West Point graduate and became a U.S. Army Inspector General 9 August 1861. The painted knapsack was not changed and in 1855, a two-bag, canvas knapsack, painted in the same manner as the haversack, began replacing the box knapsack; David Cole, "Survey of U.S. Army Uniforms, Weapons and Accoutrements," http://www.history.Army.mil/html/museums/uniforms/survey_uwa.pdf, accessed 1 May 2017, 22.

Army uniforms prior to 1855 changes. During the Mexican-American War, the white cotton uniform was not issued so the men either suffered wearing wool or purchased their own cooler outfits. These uniforms would be the "old uniform" to which Mansfield referred. "The horseman in the foreground of this painting of a column of General Zachary Taylor's troops on the march in northern Mexico is a dragoon. The yellow band on his forage cap, in contradiction to regulations, was worn by many of the cavalrymen. His distinctive dark blue fatigue jacket laced with yellow is the same as that adopted in 1833. Beside the dragoon is a first lieutenant of infantry in the dark blue frock coat worn by most officers in this this campaign. The lieutenant is wearing the regulation dark blue, waterproof, cloth forage cap, and his rank is indicated by the single silver bar on his shoulder strap to distinguish him from the second lieutenants, who wore no insignia on their shoulder straps at this time. The light blue trousers with a white stripe down the side and the silver buttons on his coat proclaim his arm. In the background is a column of infantrymen in light blue fatigue jackets and trousers. These, with the dark blue forage cap, were the universal dress of the regular enlisted infantryman in this war." Courtesy USACMH.

"A battery of light artillery in 1855, a first sergeant of the light artillery is shown in the left foreground in the new jacket issued for the mounted troops in 1854, with the...piping denoting the light artillery. His grade is indicated by the three bars and lozenge...on his sleeve and by the...sergeant's sash. The red pompon on his cap and the red stripe at the base of the crown show his arm -- artillery -- and the letter on his cap, his battery. In the right foreground is a quartermaster officer in the blue frock coat prescribed in 1851 for all officers. The buff welting on his trousers and the ornament on the front of his cap (U.S.) identify him as a general staff officer, and his pompon-- the lower two-thirds buff and the upper third light or Saxony blue -- indicates he is an officer of the Quartermaster Corps. In the background is a battery of light artillery." These would be the "new uniforms" to which Mansfield referred. Courtesy USACMH.

Mansfield continued to report on items which he found needed correction. He found the rations too small for coffee, sugar, and salt—they should be increased about one-third. He also found that the ration of fresh beef too small in the territory because the men worked hard. He wrote that the troops would like more salted provisions and that the "supplies of bacon and ham are excellent." He found no salt pork available. Packing of bacon received much attention in his report because the way it was packed in the warm climate "forces the grease out to waste; and here where butter and lard are scarce is a great disadvantage." Cheaper flour was now available in the territory obviating the need to import from the states.[71] As has been seen Mansfield usually found the small post gardens beneficial for the troops' vegetable supply but he never favorably commented on the large farms established to sell their products. In his summary, he said that they were a failure. One reason was that soldiers were not trained as farmers and that the system of dividing the profits from farming among the enlisted men results in exciting "the cupidity of the soldier, to the neglect of other duties." He correctly observed that the aims of the soldier must be to spend their time training in their duties versus farming especially for gain—"the instruction of the troops in every branch of military duties in New Mexico, and the protection of the population against Indians, and the building of their own quarters and making their gardens will…occupy all their time, and leave them but little recreation." Mansfield previously complained about the pay for troops stationed on the frontier in New Mexico Territory. The long distances over which goods must be shipped made costs for nonmilitary items "100 to 400 percent higher than in the States." He again recommended that "that the law giving to the officers and soldiers stationed [here]…additional pay, and which expired by limitation in March last, be renewed." The small additional pay expired 1 March 1852 and was not renewed. On 4 August 1854 all troops received an increase in pay and those employed on extra duty west of the Rocky Mountains were recommended for a daily increase.[72]

He next addressed weapons and their use. Mansfield was clear that the musketoon was "almost worthless" and that there is nothing better at the time other than the carbine and Sharps rifle. He said that the Dragoons had a variety of long arms in addition to the majority musketoons—Sharps rifles, Harpers Ferry rifles, and carbines. In passing he wrote that contrary to the belief of some, horses and mules should have all four feet shod. He also determined that since there is little call for the use of artillery against the Indians, that artillery soldiers should become thoroughly familiar with infantry drills. As combat experienced officers knew, Mansfield recommended that the soldier must know how to accurately fire his rifle so practice is required. Sufficient numbers of officers are required to be on duty to ensure that this practice is undertaken and to supervise the drill of the troops. The officers who are actually present for duty are overworked, burdened with multiple duties which shortchange the time allowed for military drills. Mansfield earnestly believed that the primary duty of the soldier is to learn the skills he will need for combat and anything which detracts from that must be changed.[73]

---

[71] Mansfield, *Mansfield on the Condition of the Western Forts 1853-1854*, 61-62.

[72] Mansfield, *Mansfield on the Condition of the Western Forts 1853-1854*, 63-65. Army Regulations of 1857 supported Mansfield: "Although the necessities of the service may require soldiers to be ordered on working-parties as a duty, commanding officers are to bear in mind that fitness for military service by instruction and discipline is the object for which the Army is kept on foot, and that they are not to employ the troops when not in the field, and especially the mounted troops, in labors that interfere with their military duties and exercises, except in case of immediate necessity, which shall be forthwith reported for the orders of the War Department;" *Regulations for the Army of the United States, 1857*, 114. This regulation in the 1847 regulations was similar: "Troops, when not in the field, are not to be employed in any work not strictly military, which can be done by hire, or by contract with individuals not belonging to the Army, unless by special authority of the War Department. Instruction in all military duties, and efficiency for active service, being of paramount consideration, the labor which soldiers may occasionally be required to perform, will not be allowed to interfere with either; nor will any of the stated inspections enjoined by the regulations be omitted;" *General Regulations for the Army of the United States, 1847*, 117. Transportation costs for the Army in 1850 had grown 1,500 percent from 1844 even though the size of the Army grew only 50 percent; Clary, *The Inspectors General*, 183-184. This explains why Mansfield was looking at ways to reduce costs at posts such as improving roads to decrease shipping costs.

[73] Mansfield, *Mansfield on the Condition of the Western Forts 1853-1854*, 65-67. The Springfield Model 1847 Musketoon was a shortened version of the Springfield Model 1842 standard infantry musket. Carried by Dragoons in a muzzle-down position, the cartridge often unseated. It also had a tremendous kick when fired and had poor accuracy—smooth bore musketoons had no sights. The .52 caliber Hall-North Carbine was first issued to the Dragoons in 1833 and was the first percussion weapon and the first breech loading weapon adopted by any government; Cole, "Survey of U.S. Army Uniforms, Weapons and Accoutrements," 18. The Sharps Model 1852 carbine is referred to as the "Slant Breech" or "Sloping Breech" model which was a single-shot breech-loading weapon with a pellet priming mechanical system. The "Sharps primes" or pellets, used on Sharps carbines and rifles, were little discs of copper containing the priming mixture. The mechanism threw one of these discs between the nipple and the hammer during the fall of the hammer. The Sharps was easily loaded by lever to drop its breech block and expose its breech for inserting a combustible linen cartridge. It became the most popular long arm of the Dragoons before the Civil War. Mansfield saw other carbines likely including the Hall-North Carbine.

He had suggestions for carrying the mail among posts and for U.S. Mail also. A regular service "to leave Santa Fe for El Paso and return…once a week, under the direction of the Post Office Department…and in due time, a line of stages would be established."[74] While seeming to intrude on U.S. Mail prerogatives, he was trying to find ways to ensure regular mail service to the many Army posts with less need of Dragoon protection among the posts, cities and with the States.[75]

His twelve point recapitulation summarized his individual post reports and the letter he sent to the Secretary of War on 19 September 1853:

First, appropriations are recommended for the following military roads: from Fort Union over the Moro Mountain to Cantonment Burgwin of $2,000; from Cantonment Burgwin to Fort Massachusetts on six hills, impassible for loaded wagons between the Rivers Hondo and Colorado, $6,000; from Cantonment Burgwin to La Joya on the road to Santa Fe over the mountain is precipitous and impassible for loaded wagons, $4,000; from Fort Union to Santa Fe direct, $2,000; from Albuquerque to Fort Defiance, $1,000; from Fort Conrad following the Rio Grande del Norte to Fort Fillmore, $1,000.

Second, the southern boundary line between the county of El Paso, Texas, and New Mexico recommended to be immediately established by monuments.

Third, a weekly mail recommended to be established between Santa Fe and El Paso.

Fourth, one or two sound moral mechanics recommended to be stationed in each of the Pueblos Indian Villages to teach them.

Fifth, three or four new posts recommended to be established in Texas on the mail route between El Paso and San Antonio in addition to a post at El Paso.

Sixth, the boxing of bacon in a particular manner deemed indispensable to prevent wastage.

Seventh, a limit is recommended to the number of the French bell tents—and attention called to the cut of soldiers' clothes.

Eighth, the officers' and soldiers' pay for New Mexico and the county of El Paso, Texas recommended to be increased.

Ninth, the armament of dragoons with musketoons recommended to be changed.

Tenth, farming by troops regarded unfavorably.

Eleventh, the enlisting of near sighted men and men that cannot understand English are unfavorable.

Twelfth, more officers with a company recommended to be kept at their posts.[76]

On 2 March 1854 from Middletown, Connecticut, Mansfield wrote to Colonel Lorenzo Thomas and forwarded his final report of the inspection of Military Department of New Mexico. He noted that he devoted all his time to it except for 10 days court marital duty at West Point. Thus the novice Inspector General finished his first assignment obviously learning much and not being timid in stating his recommendations to his superiors. His most obvious concerns were for the military preparedness of the posts and for the welfare of the enlisted men so that they would best be able to perform as soldiers. His next inspection tour on the West Coast would prove more adventurous and tedious for the now experienced inspector.[77]

---

[74] Mansfield, *Mansfield on the Condition of the Western Forts 1853-1854*, 67-68.

[75] Soldiers referred to the United States as the "States" since they were stationed outside of the states of the United States.

[76] Mansfield, *Mansfield on the Condition of the Western Forts 1853-1854*, 68-70. On 22 October 1853 Mansfield wrote Thomas from Fort Fillmore, New Mexico, that he arrived there on the 17th of October "having left Fort Webster on the 13th. I shall probably leave here about the 1st Nov. after the arrival of the mail from the states, and proceed via El Paso and San Antonio to Head Quarters." Letter courtesy NARA.

[77] Letter courtesy WPL and NARA. On 2 March in his monthly report for February he noted that he had "been engaged continually and laboriously all the month of February last in writing out and completing my report of the inspection of the late 9th Military Department of New Mexico. It consists of 100 pages and will by this mail be transmitted to the Head Quarters of the Army;" courtesy of the Middlesex County Historical Society. The next day, he sent instructions to Captain Irvin McDowell, Assistant Adjutant General in New York, concerning how to unbind his report to be more easily read: "take a knife and split off the sticks and draw tight the string and tie again….I have labored hard in writing it out from my notes." 3 March 1854 letter courtesy NARA. He followed up on 7 March and asked for an acknowledgment of receipt by Army Headquarters in New York of the package containing his report: "The roll was about 2 ½ inches in diameter and 15 inches long done up with yellow enveloping paper and red sealing wax." Letter courtesy NARA. He admitted in his 18 March letter that he had not known that he had the franking (free posting) privilege because he had "been so constantly engaged under my new appointment…that I have hitherto had no leisure to inform myself—I trust I shall be better prepared to perform my duty hereafter. When I next visit N.Y. I will reimburse the postage on my documents hitherto paid in consequence of my own fault." Letter courtesy NARA.

1854 Department of The Pacific

Fort Point	5–6 May 1854
Alcatrazes Island	5–6 May 1854
Presidio of San Francisco	10 May 1854
Monterey	18–21 May 1854
Sub Depot of New San Diego	25–28 May 1854
Old San Diego	27 May 1854
Mission of San Diego	26–27 May 1854
Fort Yuma	5–7 June 18543
Tejon Reservation	22–24 June 1854
Fort Miller	28–30 June 1854
Benicia Quartermaster's Depot	7 July 1854
Benicia Arsenal	7 July 1854
Benicia Barracks	8 July 1854
Benicia Subsistence Depot	8 July 1854
Fort Reading	18–21 July 1854
Fort Humboldt	27–29 July 1854
Fort Jones	4–8 August 1854
Fort Lane	10–12 August 1854
Fort Vancouver	21–23 August 1854
Fort Dalles	26–31 August 1854
Fort Steilacoom	8–15 September 1854
Fort Orford	27 September 1854

Mansfield wrote again to Lieutenant Colonel Lorenzo Thomas, Assistant Adjutant General, from Middletown on 16 March 1854 that he received timely notice to inspect the Department of the Pacific so he could make arrangements to leave his family. He again reported to Thomas 22 March that he received Special Order 45 dated 18 March 1854 to make an inspection of the Department of the Pacific. The guidelines were the same as he received for his inspection of the New Mexico Territory.[78] He planned on sailing on the first steamer for San Francisco; Mansfield would also report to General Scott at his headquarters in New York City.[79] After visiting Scott's headquarters, he sailed from New York on 5 April via the Nicaragua Route north of the Isthmus of Panama and reached San Francisco on 4 May 1854. He wrote Thomas that "I shall proceed tomorrow [15 May 1854] to posts south of this which will occupy me probably till about the 1 July."[80]

Arriving at San Francisco, he reported to the veteran Department commander, Major General John Ellis Wool, where he learned that Wool would detail officers to accompany Mansfield given the vast territory he had to cover: Wool's Aide-de-Camp, Lieutenant Tredwell Moore, of the 2nd Infantry would accompany him south of San Francisco, and Lieutenant George Henry Mendell, of the Topographical Engineers, north of that city. Wool, on 12 May 1854, gave Mansfield a detailed letter and described what he wished Mansfield would inspect on his tour and which also reflected

---

[78] See Attachment 4 below.

[79] Letters courtesy WPL and of the Middlesex County Historical Society. His order also required him to report to Army headquarters after his inspection was completed.

[80] Letter 14 May 1854 courtesy NARA. The Nicaragua route was a rival to the Panama route and was financed by Cornelius Vanderbilt. "It had the advantage of flexibility, as its timetable and routes were not set by government contract....[it] also had the advantage of proximity to the United States and, hence, required less coal—no small matter, given that the wooden-hulled side-wheelers of the era crushed forty tons or more of coal per day....Less coal in a ship's bunkers meant more cargo tonnage for freight and passengers;" Jay Sexton, "Steam Transport, Sovereignty, and Empire in North America, circa 1850-1885," *The Journal of the Civil War Era*, vol. 7, no. 4, Dec. 2017 (Chapel Hill, NC: Univ. of North Carolina Press, 2017), 630-631.

Wool's ideas for his department, see Attachment 5 below for a copy of this letter and Wool's Special Order to his Department which accorded Mansfield every courtesy. Before he arrived in San Francisco, he wrote his wife from on board the steamer *Southern Light* outlining his tour itinerary telling her that he crossed the Caribbean Sea 13 April 1854; he had left New York at 3 p.m. on the 5th. He was seasick for two days on this leg of the trip. In Kingston, Jamaica, he noted free blacks there were well-dressed, educated, and he saw fine churches and houses. He then boarded another ship and went back to sea on what he described as a "smaller Pacific boat….cross the peninsula (through Nicaragua) and maybe reach San Francisco on the 1st of May, then finish his inspections in California in May and June and next travel to Oregon in July and August. After he was done, [he] probably would return across Nicaragua or less likely over the Rockies." On 19 April 1854 from San Guar del Sud, a coastal town on the Pacific Ocean, in southwest Nicaragua, Mansfield wrote to his wife that he "Arrived today, in Pacific Hotel. On river from San Juan del Norte to its source Lake Nicaragua and the Passage across the lake was Virgin Bay to here 14 miles on mule back over the Cordilleras Mt. His carpet bag was his pillow. Slept in the Nicaragua Hotel at the Castillo Rapids. 12 remaining days on the Pacific." His ship put into Acapulco for water and coal. He had his handkerchief stolen from his pocket and had no clean clothes. "I shall never at my age make many more such trips—I feel it is too hard for me and I ought to be able to live without such hardships." Clearly his trips to the Pacific Coast through Panama or Nicaragua were tedious and unhealthy but these routes were the common ones used to the West Coast. A railroad added in 1855 across the Isthmus of Panama would help ease this leg of the trip for him in the future.[81]

Benicia Arsenal, California, located next to Suisun Bay in Benicia, California c. 1850. Mansfield inspected the post in 1854 and again in 1859. The post was first occupied on 9 April 1849, when two companies of the 2nd Infantry Regiment set up camp and established Benicia Barracks, which also housed the 3rd Artillery Regiment. In 1851, at the urging of General Persifor F. Smith, the first Ordnance Supply Depot in the West was established in Benicia. Established by 2nd Lieutenant (Brevet Captain) Charles P. Stone, Ordnance Department, on 19 Aug 1851 for the storage and issuance of military materials; it was the first Ordnance Supply Depot in the West. In 1852, it was designated Benicia Arsenal. Notable military personnel who were stationed there during this time included Ulysses Grant, Edward Ord, and Joseph Hooker. The grounds of the Benicia Arsenal are also famous for stabling the Army's one and only Camel Corps. The short-lived Camel Corps, promoted by Secretary of War Jefferson Davis, was disbanded in 1863, but the Camel Barns, built in 1855, survive. Courtesy California State Military Department, http://www.militarymuseum.org/Benicia.html

---

[81] Letters courtesy WPL. Moore was an 1847 West Point graduate who received four brevets during the Civil War the last to brigadier general. He remained in the Army as a lieutenant colonel dying in 1876.

His inspection tour of the Department of the Pacific would take five months versus the three it took for his New Mexico Territory inspection due to its vast geographical expanse. Plus he spent almost two months to make the round trip journey to California and back versus the few weeks to get to and from New Mexico. Perhaps the journeys themselves in the State of California and the Territories of Oregon and Washington (current States of Oregon and Washington) merited Mansfield's describing in great detail the paths he took, recording the miles he travelled and the sights he saw. Certainly the country he visited in California and the northwest merited comment both in his official reports and his letters home. He even took two side excursions which he called "digressions" during which he visited gold fields. It may be that when he visited General Scott in New York prior to his departure, the general requested these side trips as well as more extensive comments on the routes Mansfield would take, populations he would encounter, and the details about the country. Mansfield's first digression was as follows:

> At Shroder's Tavern on the Merced River....took a mule and proceeded alone through the mining regions via Quartzburg and Mount Ophia to Mariposa, thence across the mountains via Simpsonville, the crossing of the Merced, Coultersville, Maxwell's Creek, Black Gulch, Quartz Mountain Gulch, Mockasin Creek, the ferry across Tuolumne River to Sonora. Thence to Columbia and thence by stage via James Town and the ferry of the Stanislaus River to Stockton. Throughout this whole route there is a large American population. The miners are engaged along the rivers and in the gulches and in spots the farmer is occupying the ground, and the saw mills and grist mills are supplying rapidly the wants of the people....From Stockton I proceeded to Benicia by steamer, and thence to San Francisco.[82]

His second side trip began at Marysville north of Sacramento where he "proceeded by stage via Bear Creek and Rough and Ready to Grass Valley and Nevada, the middle mining country, and thence to Marysville at the junction of the Yuba and Feather rivers, whence by stage up the Sacramento Valley to Fort Reading", 130 miles; It would have been unlikely that Mansfield would have made and reported on these digressions without General Scott's permission. Also Scott or possibly Jefferson Davis could have wanted first-hand information about mining activities or, if the investigations were solely for Mansfield's benefit, perhaps he like other Army officers might have been contemplating engaging in some mining related business.[83] On these side excursions as well as for his entire trip he faithfully recorded distances travelled by horse or boat as well as the settlements and Indians he saw and included comments on the natural and cultivated vegetation.

Next, before Mansfield began his detailed accounts of inspections of each post, he penned an extensive almost travelogue description of "Climate, Harbours, Rivers, Country and Productions, Resources and Necessity of Military Posts, Indians, etc." As in his report of the routes he took, these observations were likely done at the verbal requests of General Scott or perhaps Secretary Davis because much of this area was not as heavily explored and travelled as was the New Mexico Territory. And certainly many parts of the Department of the Pacific were much more fertile than the mostly desert southwest. Mansfield noted the large variety of climates from the temperate and rainy northwest coast, to dry and hot interior locations as in southern California. He found the mountains noteworthy: "the perpetually snowcapped Sierra, and the magnificent snow topped mounts, Shasta, Jefferson, Hood, Adams, St. Helens, and Rainier."[84]

The best harbor on the west coast he found was San Francisco "which is perfectly landlocked against all winds and capacious enough for any navy and commerce that can possibly be required on this coast, and from its local position seems designed by nature and adapted for the supply of the whole country inland of the state of California." San Diego harbor was also good but much smaller; other locations were only suitable for beach landings but some locations further north especially the Columbia River provided access inland; the Columbia "is broad and deep, and capable of floating

---

[82] Mansfield, *Mansfield on the Condition of the Western Forts 1853-1854*, 86-87. There is a letter to Mansfield 26 November 1852 which noted that his nephew, Joseph, stopped in to visit Mansfield on his way to the mines in California. Apparently Mansfield lent money to Joseph for a quartz crushing machine. Mansfield had not heard from him for months and neither had this letter writer, John Kenneth[?]. Mansfield received a letter dated 8 May 1854 from his nephew, Jared, who wrote from Columbia, California. Jared invited him to visit so he could be shown the mining in the area and the camp Jared spoke about. Jared said that William and he had an interest in the company which supplied water to the camp. Then Jared supplied directions: "To come up here, you take the steamboat to Stockton and then the stage to Tourna where you will take another stage to Columbia and put up at Clark's Hotel." Jared described the place "as the most prosperous camp in the southern mines." Letters courtesy of the Middlesex County Historical Society.

[83] Mansfield, *Mansfield on the Condition of the Western Forts 1853-1854*, 86-87.

[84] Ibid., 91-92.

the largest ships of the navy, and as beautiful as it is grand." He then commented on rivers finding the Colorado River being the primary route of drainage west of the Rocky Mountains which he estimated was navigable 150 miles up to the Grand Canyon by small steamers. Among other rivers, he again mentioned the Columbia River navigable 140 miles from its mouth, then portage five miles, then by steamboat 40 miles to The Dalles."[85]

Comments followed on "Soil, productions, timber, minerals, metals and ores" which help explain his diversions mentioned above to mining areas. He found not surprisingly that the valleys of the Department had generally good soil although irrigation was essential in the country south of Monterey, California. Overall he wrote that "Although the extent of productive soil is comparatively limited, yet the produce of only the best part of it is, and will be, more than sufficient for the supply of all the population that will occupy this department....fruits...grow in great luxuriance, [and]...will in two or three years make the fruits one of the best and cheapest articles of consumption." Fish were abundant on the coast especially salmon and cod in Puget Sound. Timber was abundant throughout the department also and he cited especially pine, fir, redwood, and cedar but found that the types of oak were not good quality for "the arts and shipbuilding, and it is believed to be generally only fit for firewood." He also mentioned that there were some pockets of coal available in the northwest but opined that more would be found. Additionally he found that there was abundant building stone although the quality of the granite was not as good as that found in the Atlantic States. Gold finds were scattered throughout the Department with mercury found near San Jose. All of his comments concerning natural resources showed that this large department had more than enough resources for further development and population growth.[86]

Population took up the largest part of his "travelogue" section which he divided into five classes: "first, Indians or aboriginals which he subdivided into "partly civilized or friendly and the uncivilized or unfriendly: second, the native Californians, descendants of the Spanish and a cross with the Spanish and Indian; third, the Canadian (Oregon Trapper) and the cross with the Indian; fourth, the Chinese; and fifth, the American or Anglo Saxon race so called." Not surprisingly, most of his population discussion was spent on Indians describing their locations, methods of sustenance and whether or not they were threats to others but in any event, "This whole race are fast disappearing before the white man by disease and other causes." The native Californians were found primarily south of San Francisco "but are quite limited as to numbers and seem to be generally contented with the raising of stock and a few vegetables." The least numerous were the Canadians found only in Oregon and Washington Territories. Mansfield observed that the Chinese were found only in California "scattered over the whole trading and mining country....[and] next to the Americans, are decidedly the most numerous and probably will increase faster than the Americans by immigration hereafter." Americans were the most populous "and rule the country without opposition by their superiority in every respect....[they] occupy and control all that part of the department west of the Sierra Nevada and Cascade Mountains, notwithstanding the heterogeneous population scattered among them."[87] Mansfield, as with virtually all native-born Americans, held the white native race as the measure against which all others were measured.

The final category in his preliminary report was the "Necessity of military posts and their location" as a separate item from the post visits themselves. He determined the reason for military posts were to protect civilians from unfriendly Indians so posts were needed along the line of demarcation of unfriendly Indians and along emigrant trails. He reviewed the 15 locations in the department: New San Diego, Mission of San Diego, Fort Yuma, Fort Miller, Fort Reading, Fort Jones, Fort Lane, Fort Vancouver, Fort Dalles, Fort Steilacoom, Fort Orford, Fort Humboldt, Benicia, Monterey, and San Francisco.

New San Diego was established in 1850 and the Army had a depot there for commissary and quartermasters stores to supply area posts, but no troops. It was located three miles south of Old San Diego as the channel was closer to the shore but Mansfield recommended that it be dispensed with once Fort Yuma could be supplied by water as that location was better sited to supply posts in the area. The building could then be moved to the Mission of San Diego so that place could hold more supplies. The Mission of San Diego was about six miles from Old San Diego on the San Diego River and

---

[85] Ibid., 92-94. Frazer comments that Mansfield's estimate for the Colorado River was too short by half although exploration on the river at this time was just beginning, n. 20.

[86] Mansfield, *Mansfield on the Condition of the Western Forts 1853-1854*, 95-96. Jared was in Columbia which was a gold mining boom town located in the Sierra Nevada foothills, in Tuolumne County, California. It was founded in 1850 when gold was found in the vicinity, and was known as the "Gem of the Southern Mines." Mansfield visited Jared there as Mansfield noted in his 20 August 1854 letter. Letter courtesy of the Middlesex County Historical Society.

[87] Mansfield, *Mansfield on the Condition of the Western Forts 1853-1854*, 97-103.

nine miles from New San Diego on the extreme southern boundary of California. He found this post to be necessary unlike New San Diego. The distance from the Mission of San Diego to Fort Yuma was about 220 miles. Fort Yuma in Mansfield's opinion should become the primary location for supplies to posts in the area as it was on the Colorado River. This location allows small steamers to navigate up from the Gulf of California permitting supplies to be shipped by water directly from San Francisco, a great savings in time and monies. Fort Miller, on the south bank of the San Joaquin River was well-located, 286 miles from Los Angeles and 583 from Fort Yuma; he recommended that it be retained. Fort Reading located on a tributary about a mile and a half from the Sacramento River was not well located and Mansfield suggested that it be moved eastward to provide better protection for emigrants. In 1856, the garrison was withdrawn and Fort Crook was established to the east in line with Mansfield's recommendation. Fort Jones was 120 miles from Fort Reading and was an important post although he said that its supplies should come from San Francisco "over the wagon road through Fort Lane" instead of via Shasta City and Fort Reading.[88]

Fort Lane in the southern part of the Oregon Territory was in an excellent location south of the Rogue River 84 miles northwest of Fort Jones and 140 miles from Scottsburg in the Oregon Territory. Scottsburg was 25 miles from the mouth of the Umpqua River with a direct water link to San Francisco. Since Scottsburg should supply posts in northern California and southern Oregon Territory, the military road from Fort Lane should be improved and continued to Scottsburg. Fort Vancouver was an essential post located on the north bank of the Columbia River 100 miles above its mouth. While he considered that it would have been better sited below the mouth of the Willamette River, it still was in direct communication with San Francisco and was an important supply depot for posts in Washington Territory and northern Oregon Territory. He suggested a wagon road to Fort Steilacoom and a second along the Columbia River to Fort Dalles. He also recommended that a fort be built "soon" at the mouth of the Columbia River, but forts on both sides of the river were not started until the Civil War. Fort Dalles was on the south bank of the Columbia River at The Dalles; it was 40 miles downriver to the rapids through the Cascade Mountains, a five mile portage, and then 50 miles further downriver by steamer to Fort Vancouver. He found this post to be important as one in a link of posts which should be established on the emigrant trail through the mountains. The only fort established in Oregon Territory east of Fort Dalles was Fort Henrietta in 1855 but only to serve during the 1855 Indian uprising. Fort Steilacoom is two miles from Puget Sound and 170 miles from Fort Vancouver on the Cowlitz River supplied through Fort Vancouver. This important post needed roads constructed to Fort Vancouver and Fort Dalles as Fort Steilacoom had excellent access to Puget Sound and then San Francisco. Port Orford on the Pacific coast had no harbor and served only to protect a few inhabitants nearby. Mansfield wrote that "It has no military merit;" it was abandoned in 1856. Fort Humboldt is on Humboldt Bay with good water access by steamer and with a tugboat to bring in vessels. He found the post to be "important now and should be maintained for some time yet to come, if not always, for the defense of this bay." Benicia "is of great importance as a depot of supplies generally and arsenal...being about 30 miles from San Francisco on the water communication between that city and the interior of the country...secure against direct attacks by sea...and should be maintained permanently." Monterey Mansfield found was only occupied by a storekeeper with a magazine, arms and some heavy guns which he recommended be sent to the arsenal at Benicia eliminating the post as it had "no military importance;" it was evacuated in 1856 but the government retained the land. San Francisco he determined was "a very important point and should be permanently and strongly fortified against any attempt on the part of an enemy in command of the sea entering this harbor. At least two hundred guns should occupy Fort Point....I look upon this point as the key to the whole Pacific Coast in a military point of view, and it should receive untiring exertions."[89]

He ended this section by recommending new posts at the Tejon Indian Reservation and on the Snake River about 350 miles east of Fort Dalles. Fort Boise was built on this second location in 1863. He also recommended a post at Billingham Bay near the northern Washington Territory boundary. Fort Bellingham was established there in 1856. He finally wrote that "a chain of posts across from Fort Yuma...to El Paso...a distance of 600 miles [is needed but]....A reconnaissance...would certainly be necessary." This route would sometimes follow Lieutenant Colonel Philip St. George Cooke's route taken when he led the Mormon Battalion; it became known as Cooke's Wagon Road. Only two forts along the route Mansfield suggested were constructed before the Civil War, Forts Buchanan and Breckenridge, in

---

[88] Mansfield, *Mansfield on the Condition of the Western Forts 1853-1854*, 105-122, *passim*.
[89] Mansfield, *Mansfield on the Condition of the Western Forts 1853-1854*, 105-122, *passim*.

New Mexico. Mansfield reported that at Fort Yuma he talked with Andrew B. Gray, a surveyor, who recommended locations for forts. Gray had been exploring potential railroad routes along the southern boundary of the United States.[90]

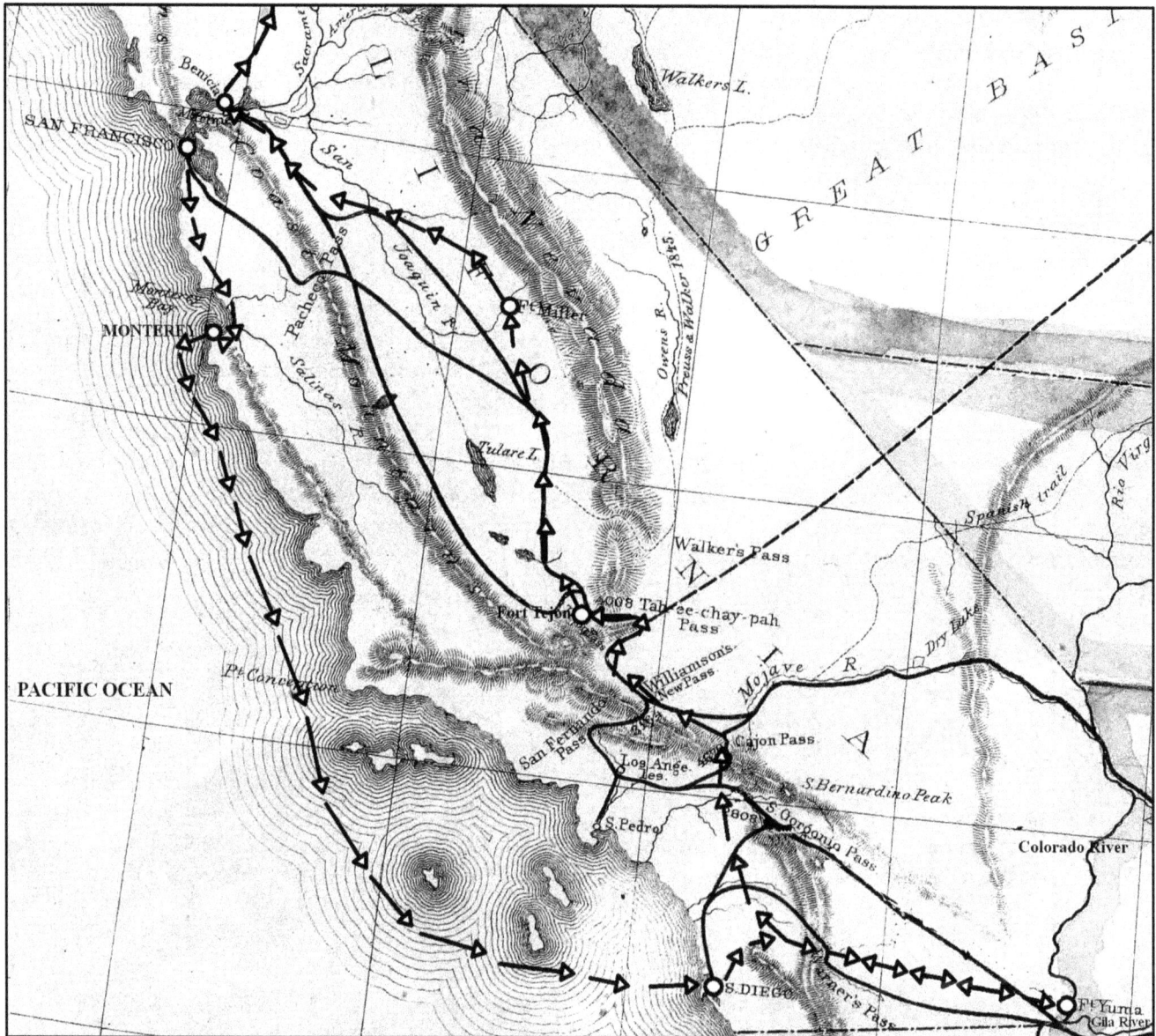

Map of the southern part of Mansfield's 1854 Pacific Department tour, from his arrival point in San Francisco, Fort Point, Alcatrazes Island, Presidio of San Francisco, Monterey, Sub Depot of New San Diego, Old San Diego, Mission of San Diego, Fort Yuma, Tejon Reservation, Fort Miller, Benicia Quartermaster's Depot, Benicia Arsenal, Benicia Barracks, and Benicia Subsistence Depot; he then headed north to Fort Reading. Dark lines without arrows show proposed rail routes. Detail from 1855 Warren map of western U.S. railroad routes, courtesy LOC.

Mansfield began his inspections at the Headquarters of the Department at San Francisco consuming 11 days from 4 through 15 May 1854. The commander of the department, Major General John E. Wool, moved his headquarters to Benicia after Mansfield finished. The several departments of the command, Adjutant General's, Quartermaster's, Subsistence, Pay, and Medical he found to be in good order with records properly kept. All departments having funds on

---

[90] Mansfield, *Mansfield on the Condition of the Western Forts 1853-1854*, 123-125, *passim*. The Mormon Battalion was a religiously-based unit which served from July 1846 to July 1847 during the Mexican–American War. The battalion was a volunteer unit of 550 men led by Mormon company officers but commanded by regular U.S. Army officers. The battalion made a trek of almost 2,000 miles from Council Bluffs, Iowa, to San Diego, California, over which trail others followed, opening a southern wagon route to California. Cooke's Wagon Trail did not go through El Paso however. After the Gadsden Purchase in 1857, the Pacific Wagon Road was begun. It was a military road built between El Paso and Fort Yuma to the ferries on the Colorado River across from Fort Yuma. The Pacific Wagon Road shortened the route Cooke had taken. Fort Bliss near El Paso, Texas, was reestablished 11 January 1854 near the trail to El Paso; Fort Lowell was near Tucson, Arizona, but was originally in Tucson, established 20 May 1862.

hand had deposited some of them in private banks despite regulations of 7 March 1854 requiring them to be held by assistant treasurers of the Treasury Department. Officers in charge of these funds were in the process of transferring the funds to comply with the new regulations so were not faulted by him. Mansfield recommended that a steamer be purchased instead of a private contractor to supply Fort Yuma. He also recommended that the pay officer who was in charge of paying the posts of Fort Humboldt, Vancouver, Steilacoom, Dalles and Fort Orford be stationed at Fort Vancouver so that he could more quickly handle pay matters for these posts instead of working out of San Francisco. He found a topographical engineer, Lieutenant Robert S. Williamson, in San Francisco, who had been surveying a southern route for a railroad under the orders of the Secretary of War. Williamson had finished his survey and was completing his written report. Mansfield was satisfied with what he found and he then moved on to Fort Point.[91]

Fort Point 5–6 May 1854

He spent two days at Fort Point, 5-6 May, the post to which he was assigned before his appointment as an Inspector General. Captain James L. Mason was appointed after Mansfield but was unable to take the post as he died after contracting a fever crossing the Isthmus of Panama. Major John. G. Barnard replaced him and work continued. When he examined the site, Mansfield found that workmen's quarters had been finished and a wharf nearly done. He found however, that the site for the battery was not yet chosen "and as this is a matter of much importance, it should be well studied by the Board of Engineers. My own impressions are that 200 guns at least should be the armament of a suitable and efficient battery." He finally noted that the engineers had not yet found good building stone and that a source of good brick would be needed for arching. Before the fort was far along, engineers imported granite from China but then decided to manufacture their own brick to finish the fort.[92]

Alcatrazes Island 5–6 May 1854

Close by Fort Point was Alcatrazes (Alcatraz) Island which he inspected on 5-6 May. He wrote that this site is second in importance to Fort Point. The engineer in charge, Major Zealous B. Tower, began in the summer of 1853, and had temporary quarters built for workers, and "excavations made, masonry commenced." Good stone and bricks were issues as at Fort Point. Tower and his assistant, Lieutenant Frederick E. Prime, Mansfield found to be doing well but had to quarter in San Francisco as their quarters on the island had not yet been built.[93] Mansfield must have felt at home inspecting these last two sites with his fellow engineers and West Point graduates. Lieutenants Whiting and Alexander assisted Major Tower at Fort Point, while Lieutenant Prime served under him on Alcatraz.

Presidio of San Francisco 10 May 1854

His next stop on 10 May was the Presidio of San Francisco, three miles from San Francisco, where he found several problems. The first one was that the post commander, fellow Nutmegger Captain John H. Lendrum, was the only line

[91] Mansfield, *Mansfield on the Condition of the Western Forts 1853-1854*, 125-132. The issue with Army funds in private banks Mansfield found at all the posts he visited in the department on this tour. Robert Stockton Williamson graduated from West Point in 1848 and became a lieutenant in the Topographical Engineers. He received two brevets during the Civil War ending as a lieutenant colonel. He remained in the Army and retired in 1882 as a lieutenant colonel; he died in 1882.

[92] Mansfield, *Mansfield on the Condition of the Western Forts 1853-1854*, 132-133. Mansfield in his conclusion to his inspection tour recommended "that 200 heavy sea coast guns and mortars be shipped to Benecia Arsenal as soon as convenient, and suitable field batteries, to prepare that department to resist any sudden and unlooked for collision with Great Britain or France. Either of these powers could land an Army on that coast, which should be met in the field to save the country," Frazer, 183. At this time there were no transcontinental railroads although Mansfield and many others had urged that they be built so having a good defense in place was necessary as sending men and material across the continent or by sea would have taken much time. Fort Point was first occupied in 1861 and deactivated in 1914. It was the only Third System style fort built west of the Mississippi River.

[93] Mansfield, *Mansfield on the Condition of the Western Forts 1853-1854*, 134-135. Construction on Alcatraz began in 1853 and ended in 1858 with the arrival of the first garrison. The Army used it for military prisoners in 1868 until 1933 when it became a federal prison until it closed in 1963. Major Tower was an 1841 graduate of West Point and received three brevets during the Mexican-American War to major. During the Civil War he received five brevets to major general of volunteers and died in 1900. Frederick Edward Prime was an 1850 West Point graduate brevetted four times during the Civil War to brigadier general; he died in 1900.

officer present as two others were absent. Mansfield reported that "Captain Lendrum is an ambitious and meritorious young officer, but the duty of commander of post and of company and acting commissary, and the instruction of troops cannot be performed by one officer to the advantage of the service." Also he found that as the company was made up of mostly recruits, infantry drill was poor and skirmish drill absent. Lendrum selected some "old soldiers" who handsomely performed artillery drill with two guns. The men were housed in a "miserable adobe building…but were kept in good police and order. And the quarters for the officers not much better. A temporary barrack for the soldiers has been subsequently erected by order of General Wool. A remodeling and rebuilding of this post and quarters will be necessary at a future day when they will be required for troops to man the fortifications." The storehouses for arms and clothing as well as the hospital were also in poor condition. Ten long, 32-pounder guns required overhauling and four 6-pounder pieces required painting. The post garden was in bad condition but there was sufficient land to expand it. This first post visit perhaps was a surprise for Mansfield since it had several problems despite its proximity to the department headquarters in San Francisco. That Wool soon began addressing the housing issue shows that Mansfield's reports had an effect. He then rode overland south to Monterey.[94]

Monterey 18–21 May 1854

The post of Monterey, 120 miles south of San Francisco by land but less by water, was next on his list with his inspection lasting from 18 to 21 May 1864. As noted above, he found that "The place possesses no military merit, and I would recommend that all the stores and supplies now here, in a precarious state as to safety, be shipped to Benicia…and the post left in the hands of the collector." He then boarded a steamer and sailed south to San Diego.[95]

Sub Depot of New San Diego 25–28 May 1854
Old San Diego 27 May 1854
Mission of San Diego 26–27 May 1854

Mansfield inspected posts in and around San Diego from 25-28 May: Sub Depot of New San Diego, Old San Diego, and the Mission of San Diego. The Mission of San Diego was the only post with soldiers as the Sub Depot had only a quartermaster, paymaster, and commissary of subsistence. The Sub Depot's departments he found in excellent order with good buildings. The site had neither water nor grass and most supplies had to come from San Francisco. As seen above, Mansfield recommended that the post be removed once Fort Yuma could be supplied by water but he wrote that it should not be done until the Fort Yuma route be proven. Old San Diego he inspected on 27 May but it served as only a location for Lieutenant George H. Derby of the topographical engineers who had been working on improving the course of the San Diego River into False Bay (Mission Bay). The Mission of San Diego had two permanent companies assigned: 1st Artillery, Company I, commanded by Lieutenant Colonel John B. Magruder and 3rd Artillery, Company F, commanded by Captain Henry S. Burton who was also post commander as Magruder was on leave of absence seeking an assignment in Europe. While the discipline of the command and the arms and equipments in good order, the quarters were not; he described them as "worthless." Company I lived in "miserable old adobe buildings while Company F lived in tents. Captain Burton and his men were working on converting the old mission church into quarters but most of the other buildings "being merely ruins, should be leveled, and other buildings prepared and erected for store house, etc.....This is a beautiful locality on an eminence above the bottom lands of the river, is healthy, and there is a fine garden and olive grove attached to it, with abundant water in the bed of the river."[96]

---

[94] Mansfield, *Mansfield on the Condition of the Western Forts 1853-1854*, 135-137. The Presidio dated back to Spanish arrival in 1776 which established a mission. U.S. Marines landed a detachment and took the fort in 1846 which was next occupied by a regiment of New York Volunteers. In 1994 it was transferred to the National Park Service. John H. Lendrum was a rare company grade officer which Mansfield encountered who was not a West Point alumnus. He was brevetted twice during the Mexican-American War to captain and died in 1861.

[95] Ibid., 137-138.

[96] Mansfield, *Mansfield on the Condition of the Western Forts 1853-1854*, 138-145. San Diego was established as a Presidio in 1774 and was occupied by the United States in 1846 and was active until 1920. George Hasket Derby was an 1846 West Point graduate and received one brevet during the Mexican-American War to first lieutenant. He died in 1861 as a captain. John Bankhead (Prince John) Magruder was an 1830 graduate of West Point and was brevetted twice during the Mexican-American War to lieutenant colonel; he was also wounded at Chapultepec, Mexico. He resigned in 1861 and joined the Confederate Army becoming a major general. He fled to Mexico after the war but returned in 1867. He died in 1871. Magruder never did a European tour for the Army.

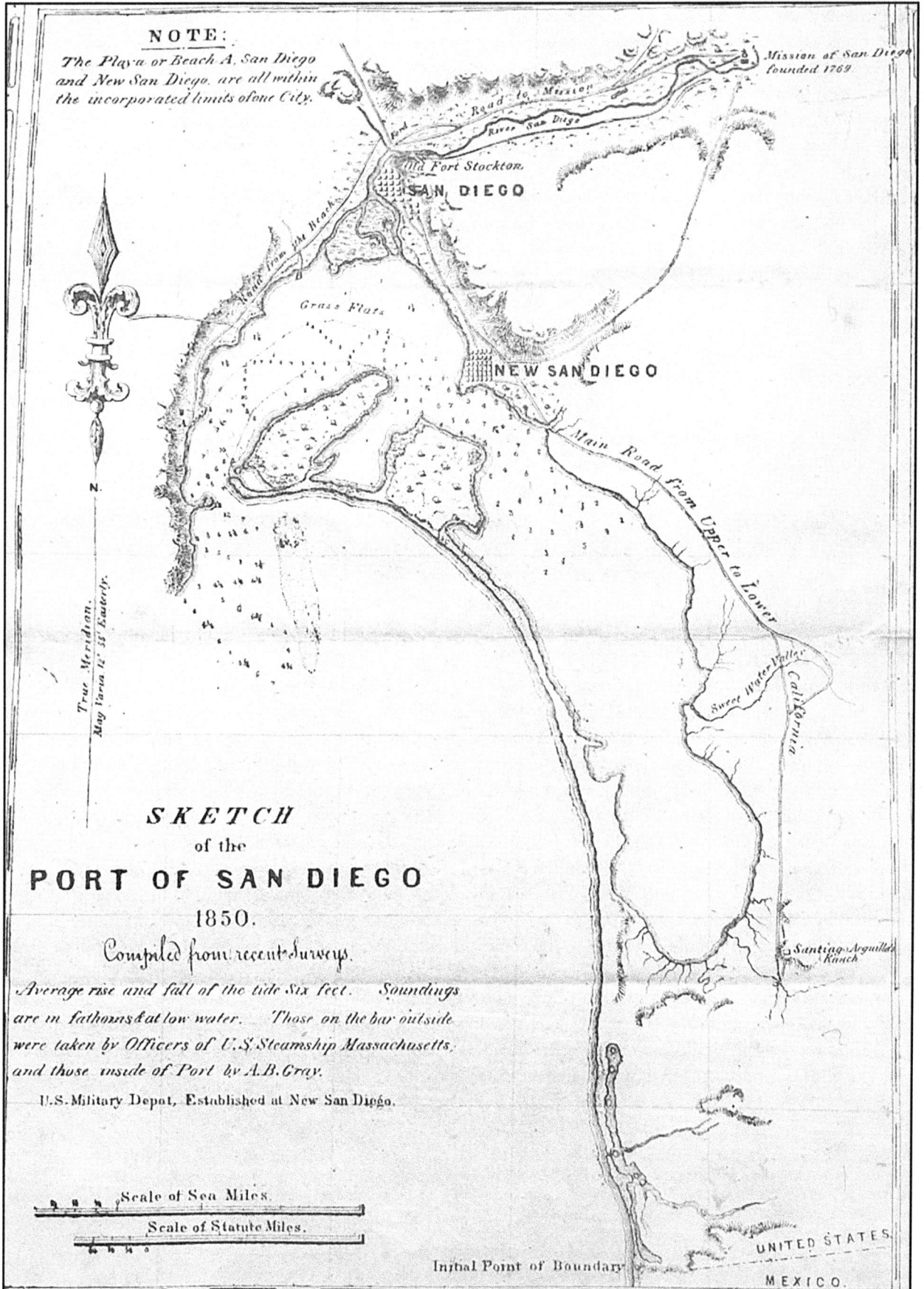

Sketch dated 1850 found in Mansfield's papers; it is likely that he obtained this map before his inspection of the Pacific coast. Courtesy of the Middlesex County Historical Society.

Sketch of Mission of San Diego, United States, War Department, "Reports of Explorations and Surveys, to Ascertain the Most Practicable and Economical Route for a Railroad from the Mississippi River to the Pacific Ocean," vol. 5, 1855, p. 41.

Fort Yuma 5–7 June 1854

After a tedious overland journey he arrived at his most southern post visit, Fort Yuma, for his inspection lasting from 5 to 7 June 1864. This post, established by and under the command of Major Samuel P. Heintzelman, was garrisoned by his Company D of the 2nd Infantry, and detachments from the Mission at San Diego of Company I, 1st Artillery, and Company F of the 3rd Artillery. Mansfield's 7 June 1854 letter informed Thomas that he arrived at Fort Yuma on the 5th and that he planned on "leaving there on the 7th for Fort Miller, overland via Tejon Pass." Mansfield liked the location and site of the post:[97]

> Fort Yuma is beautifully situated on an eminence about 80 feet high directly opposite the junction of the Gila with the Colorado, and at the crossing of the Colorado by emigrant trail from El Paso on the Rio Grande, and affords protection to emigrants, and is one link in a chain of posts that should be established on the route to El Paso. It is well selected and should be maintained. It is 220 miles from San Diego, 275 miles from Los Angeles, and 600 miles on Cook's Route to El Paso via the Pima Villages, which are 185 miles distant. It is 150 miles from the mouth of the Colorado, about 150 miles below the big Canon [Grand Canyon]....It has a commanding and extensive view, with Pilot Knob in the distance lifting its head above the horizon for a beacon. It was once a mission station but destroyed by the Indians. The water of the Colorado, a very rapid stream, is good for drinking, and it is navigable for small steamers to the Gulf of California, and supplies are being furnished that way direct from San Francisco which no doubt will result in a great saving of expense over the transportation across the desert 100 miles with bad water and no grass, 120 miles over steep mountains and bad roads in wagons exposed to the hazard and suffering consequent to such trips. This mode of supplying will undoubtedly eventuate in making this post a sub depot for the supply of such posts as will probably be established on the route to El Paso. And here I would remark I shall again refer to this subject under the head of posts recommended and endeavour to designate localities, sites, or positions which would open this route to monthly mail and stage across the country to San Diego or Los Angeles. The Gila is not at all seasons a running stream, and the water is not good, and stands at times in pools in its bed. There are two ferries, one just below the fort and the other at the point of rocks within six miles of this post....There is good grazing, abundance of wood, and a garden for vegetables no doubt can be established here by irrigation."[98]

Mansfield found the arms and equipment all in good order and Heintzelman put his troops through a "handsome battalion drill and some target firing." Mansfield did find fault with the powder being piled in the center of the parade covered by a tarpaulin as there was no magazine. The men's and officers' quarters were constructed of willows and "were worthless." Based on Mansfield's findings, Wool directed that quarters be constructed. The post's supplies came in

---

[97] Letter courtesy NARA.
[98] Mansfield, *Mansfield on the Condition of the Western Forts 1853-1854*, 146.

by land from San Diego or by water from San Francisco. The post garden was poor due to bad soil and lack of water but efforts to improve it continued. Heintzelman had constructed a pump using mule power to get water up from the Colorado River to a reservoir at the post. Mansfield did get complaints about insufficient coffee and sugar but too much salt meat and too few vegetables. Mansfield requested an appropriation of $10,000 for repairs to the road to San Diego writing that the amount would also help emigrants using it. The route was one used as a primary southern route from El Paso to Southern California also. Mansfield found much to like about this post and its location as an important one on the Southern Trail. Mansfield's main concern was the long overland distance from San Diego through the desert.[99]

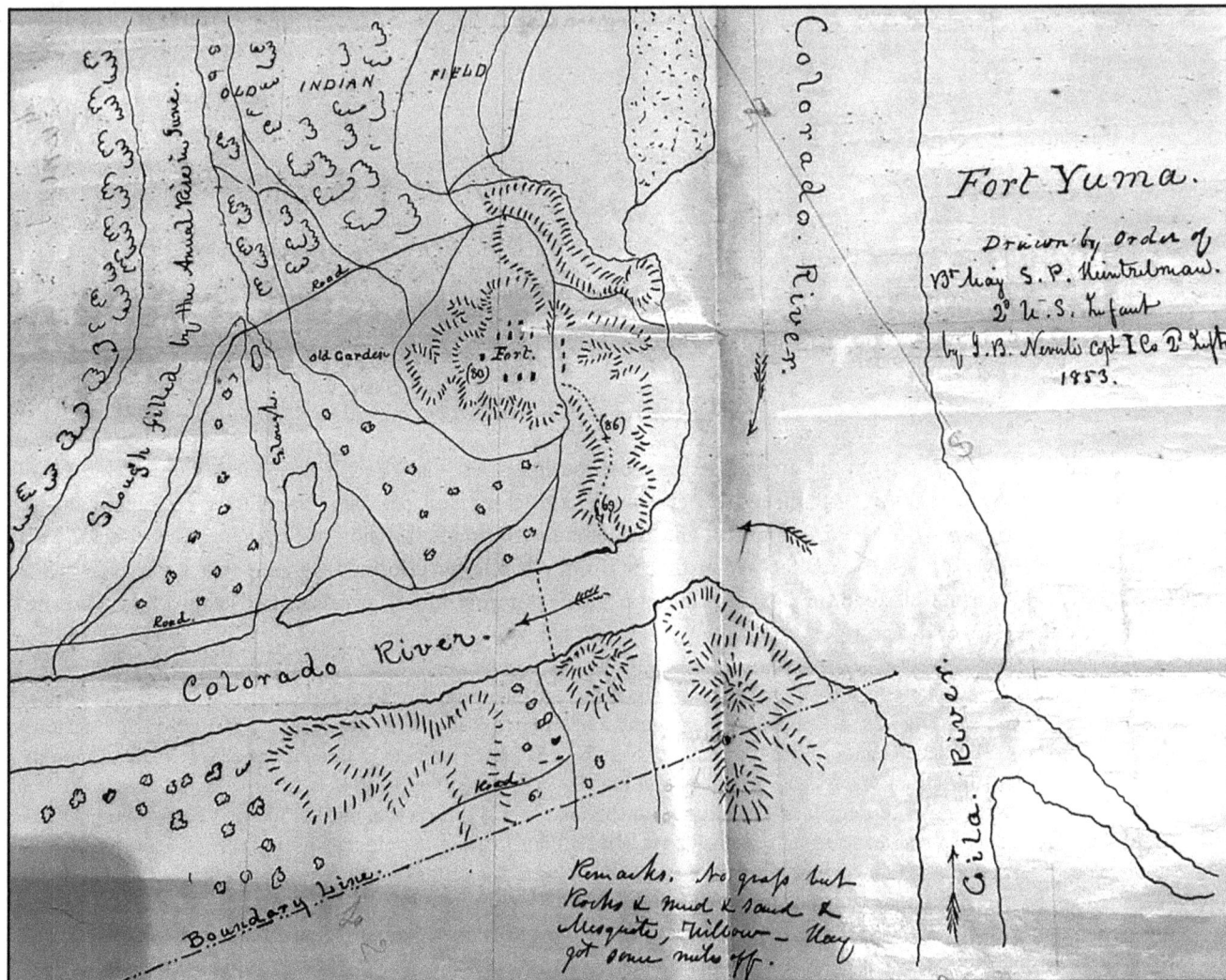

Sketch of Fort Yuma done in 1853 found in Mansfield's papers, drawn by Captain Neverli of the 2nd Infantry. No officer by this name has been found. Courtesy of the Middlesex County Historical Society.

[99] Mansfield, *Mansfield on the Condition of the Western Forts 1853-1854*, 146-148. Fort Yuma became a stop on the Butterfield Overland Mail Route (1857-1861) and the El Paso-Fort Yuma Stage Line. Colonel McCall inspected this post in 1852. Fort Yuma was first established on 27 November 1850 in the bottoms near the Colorado River, less than a mile below the mouth of the Gila River. In March 1851 the post was moved to the Colorado's west bank on land which had been occupied by Camp Calhoun, named for John C. Calhoun, a former vice president of the U.S., Secretary of War, state senator and representative and secretary of state, established on 2 October 1849 for the boundary survey party led by Lieutenant Amiel W. Whipple of the Topographical Engineers. Fort Yuma protected the southern emigrant travel route to California and confronted Yuma Indians in the area. Heintzelman established the post originally named Camp Independence. In March 1851 the post was moved to its permanent site, and became Camp Yuma. A year later the post was designated Fort Yuma. In 1851 it was abandoned without authority but was re-occupied by Heintzelman on 29 February 1852. It was permanently abandoned 16 May 1883. Whipple, an 1841 West Point graduate, died 7 May 1863 as a brevet Union major general after being wounded at the Battle of Chancellorsville. Samuel Peter Heintzelman was an 1826 West Point graduate and received one brevet to major during the Mexican-American War and two during the Civil War to major general and retired in that rank in 1869; he died in 1880.

Tejon Reservation 22–24 June 1854

From Fort Yuma, Mansfield rode two weeks to the northwest to arrive at Tejon Reservation which he inspected from 22 to 24 June. He found a detachment of 12 soldiers, commanded by Lieutenant Thomas F. Castor, temporarily stationed there with the Indian Agent, Edward F. Beale. The troops were from Company A, 1st Dragoons, assigned by General Wool to establish a post at a point in the Tejon Pass where the Coast Range meets the Sierra Nevada. While they had adequate uniforms, arms and equipments in serviceable condition, and horses and horse equipments in good order, they were mostly recruits so they could not perform any drills.[100]

Fort Miller 28–30 June 1854

Four days after leaving the Tejon Reservation, Mansfield arrived at Fort Miller some 150-160 river miles above Stockton on the south side of the San Joaquin River in the foothills of the Sierra Nevadas; Lieutenant Thomas F. Castor in command. His two day inspection, 28 to 30 June 1864, of this two company post, found no major problems. Company G of the 2nd Infantry was at the post and Company A of the 1st Dragoons was temporarily there on its way to establish a post on the Tejon Reservation. As Company A was composed of mainly new recruits, their drilling was poor and horse equipments dirty; horses "were old and generally worn out…and not properly shod." He did note however that the company had just marched from Benicia and had not had time to clean up. He found a good bakery and garden; quarters were good but buildings under canvas not acceptable. And as at many posts, the ration of coffee and sugar was too small. Having soldiers permanently living in tents or under canvas roofs was never acceptable for Mansfield and he always commented unfavorably on these whenever found during his visits.[101]

---

[100] Mansfield, *Mansfield on the Condition of the Western Forts 1853-1854*, 149. Tejon Reservation was established 10 August 1854 and in 1858 became a station on the Butterfield Overland route. The site was selected by Navy Lieutenant Beale who became superintendent of Indian affairs in California in 1853. It was permanently abandoned 11 September 1854; Frazer, *Forts of the West*, 32. The Butterfield Overland Mail Route was a stagecoach service from 1857 to 1861. It carried passengers and U.S. Mail from two eastern termini, Memphis, Tennessee, and St. Louis, Missouri, to San Francisco, California. The routes from each eastern terminus met at Fort Smith, Arkansas, and then continued through Indian Territory, Texas, New Mexico, Arizona, Baja California, and California ending in San Francisco. The total distance was about 2,800 miles which took about 600 hours to traverse. The Butterfield Overland Stage Company employed more than 800 people, had 139 relay stations, 1,800 head of stock and 250 Concord Stagecoaches in service at one time; LeRoy Reuben Hafen, *The Overland Mail, 1849-1869: Promoter of Settlement, Precursor of Railroads* (Norman, OK: University of Oklahoma Press, 2004), 94-96. Fort Tejon was established by Lieutenant Thomas F. Castor, 1st Dragoons, to replace Fort Miller. It was permanently abandoned 11 September 1864.

[101] Mansfield, *Mansfield on the Condition of the Western Forts 1853-1854*, 150-153. Thomas Foster Castor was an 1846 West Point graduate and died 8 Sept. 1855. The site of Fort Miller is now under Millerton Lake. It was established on 26 May 1851 by soldiers of the 2nd Infantry and named for Major Albert S. Miller of the 2nd Infantry. The post was intermittently garrisoned until 1 December 1864. It was first inspected by Colonel McCall in 1852, who wrote that it was located in the wrong place and should be moved to higher ground for healthier air. But, he felt the post was important and should be garrisoned by two or three companies.

Sketch of Fort Miller by C.F. Otto Skobel who was stationed there in 1864; courtesy California Military Museum website, http://www.militarymuseum.org/FtMiller.html, accessed 20 June 2017.

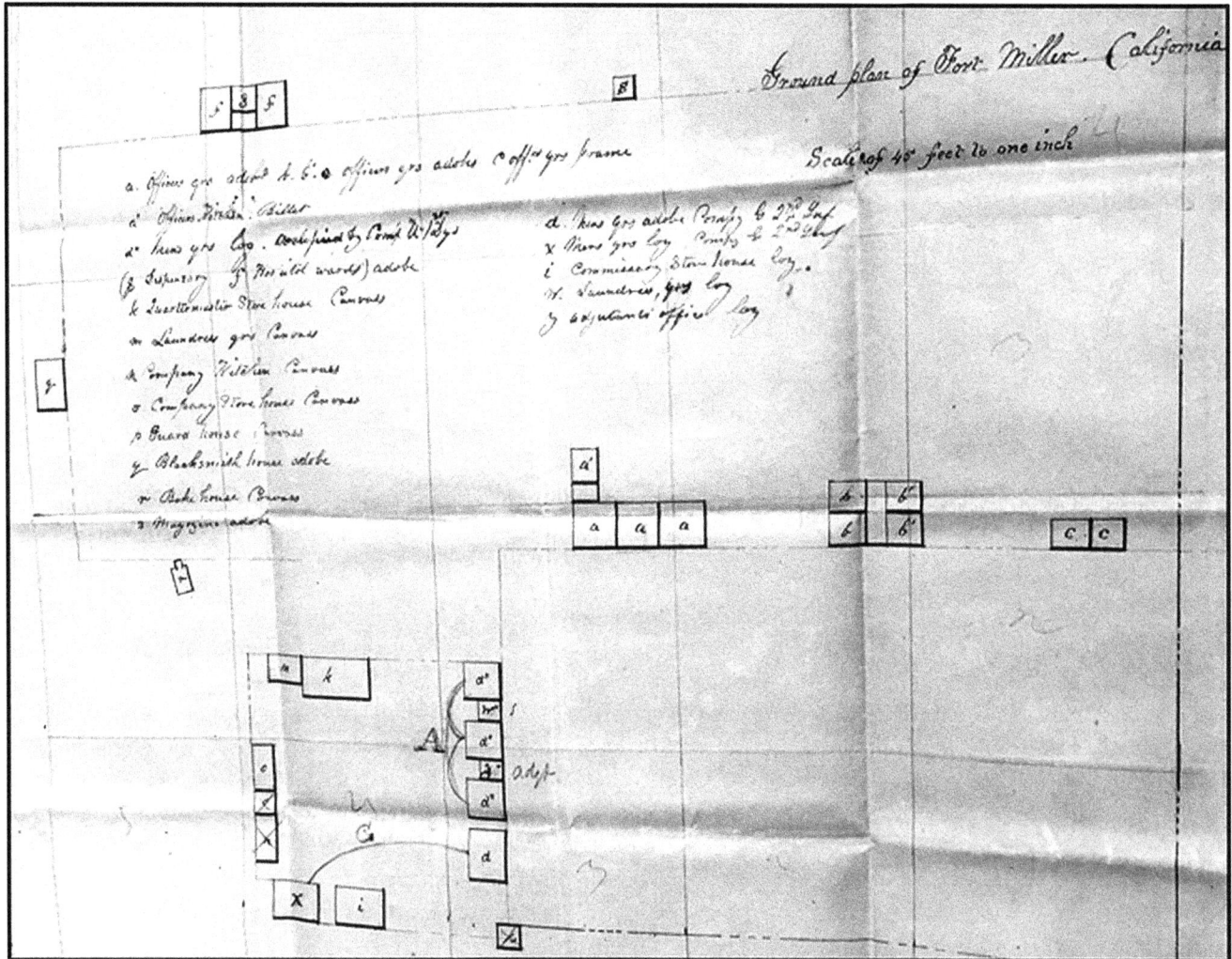

Sketch of Fort Miller found in Mansfield's papers, courtesy of the Middlesex County Historical Society.

Benicia Quartermaster's Depot 7 July 1854
Benicia Arsenal 7 July 1854
Benicia Barracks 8 July 1854
Benicia Subsistence Depot 8 July 1854

Next on his inspection list were Benicia Arsenal, Barracks, Subsistence Depot, and Quartermasters Depot, all of which he inspected on 7-8 July 1854. In command at Benicia Barracks was Lieutenant Colonel George Nauman of the 3rd Artillery. Only Company B of the regiment under Captain Edward O.C. Ord was present. The post was in very good order and had a garden attached. "The Government reservation here is ample for all purposes of troops, arsenal and depots that will be required in this quarter of this department." Benicia Arsenal was established by and in command of Captain Charles P. Stone. The arsenal he found in good order with a new store house under construction but a new magazine was also needed. This post had a good garden. The Benicia Subsistence Depot was in charge of Lieutenant John Hamilton of the 3rd Artillery. Mansfield found the post to be in order with the supplies well-stored and abundant. He suggested that more supplies be obtained on the West Coast as they will be less expensive than being shipped from the East. The Depot was in charge of Captain Robert E. Clary and Mansfield found all "in excellent order" with ample buildings and no deficiencies; Clary had built a wharf and had three ships under charter to supply posts along the Pacific Coast.[102]

---

[102] Mansfield, *Mansfield on the Condition of the Western Forts 1853-1854*, 153-158. Nauman was an 1823 graduate of West Point and earned two brevets in the Mexican-American War; he died on 11 Aug. 1863, while he was colonel of the 5th U.S. Artillery. Ord was an 1839 graduate of West

Benicia viewed from the west, United States War Department, "Reports of Explorations and Surveys, to Ascertain the Most Practicable and Economical Route for a Railroad from the Mississippi River to the Pacific Ocean, 1855," vol. 5, frontispiece.

Fort Reading 18–21 July 1854

Mansfield had a long ride north to Fort Reading which he inspected on 18-21 July. He wrote a letter from there to his wife on 20 July 1854 and told her that he reached Sacramento on the 12th at night and the next night hurt his leg in a large fire—but he would be better in a few days. With him was Major Zealous Bates Tower of the engineers and Lieutenant George H. Mendell. They started for Grass Valley which they reached at dark and on the 15th went to Nevada and the 16th started for Marysville; on the 17th Major Tower went back by steamer to San Francisco and Mansfield and Lieutenant Mendell, who would accompany him to Oregon, took a stage for Fort Reading which they reached on the 18th. "Leave tomorrow for Fort Humboldt on the coast west of here about 150 miles over the coast range. Take Lieutenant [William McEntire] Dye and 6 men for escort. Then to Fort Jones and into Oregon all the way by land to the Columbia River. Saw gold mining regions. Return from Vancouver directly to San Francisco by steamer. Colonel George Wright 4th Infantry is in command here, a classmate he had not seen for 32 years. [Mansfield stayed in his quarters during his visit.] His family is in Syracuse, New York, he has not seen them for several years." Mansfield recorded that he would probably not leave for home before 1 October 1854.[103]

Point and was brevetted four times in the Civil War to major general; he died 22 July 1883. Stone was an 1845 West Point graduate and received two brevets during the Mexican-American War. As a brigadier general of volunteers, he resigned 13 September 1864. Hamilton was an 1847 West Point graduate and received three brevets during the Civil War; he attained the rank of colonel in the Regular Army and died on 15 July 1900. Clary was an 1828 West Point graduate and was brevetted twice during the Civil War the last to brigadier general. He died 19 January 1890. On 30 April 1849, Lieutenant Colonel Silas Casey of the 2nd Infantry established the post at Point Benicia, becoming Benecia Barracks, 43 miles northeast of San Francisco. On 15 August 1851 Captain Charles P. Stone arrived to establish a new arsenal near the barracks site. Quartermaster's and Commissary Depots were also near the barracks site. The Arsenal had employed a sailing brig and a schooner to move supplies between the San Diego Barracks and the barracks at Puget Sound and a sloop to move supplies to Stockton, San Francisco and Sacramento. The Arsenal and Barracks closed in 1964.

[103] Letter courtesy WPL. On 20 July, Mansfield wrote Thomas from Fort Reading that he arrived there on the 18th "having completed the inspections of the posts south of this; and traversed the country from Fort Yuma here by land. I shall leave here tomorrow for Humboldt by land; thence expect to visit Fort Jones, and Fort Lane, and Port Orford and continue by land northward to the several posts in Oregon." Letter courtesy NARA. Mansfield also wrote a letter to Adjutant General Lorenzo Thomas 25 July 1854 from Fort Reading telling him that he arrived at Reading on 18th and that he completed inspecting forts south of there. Letter courtesy WPL.

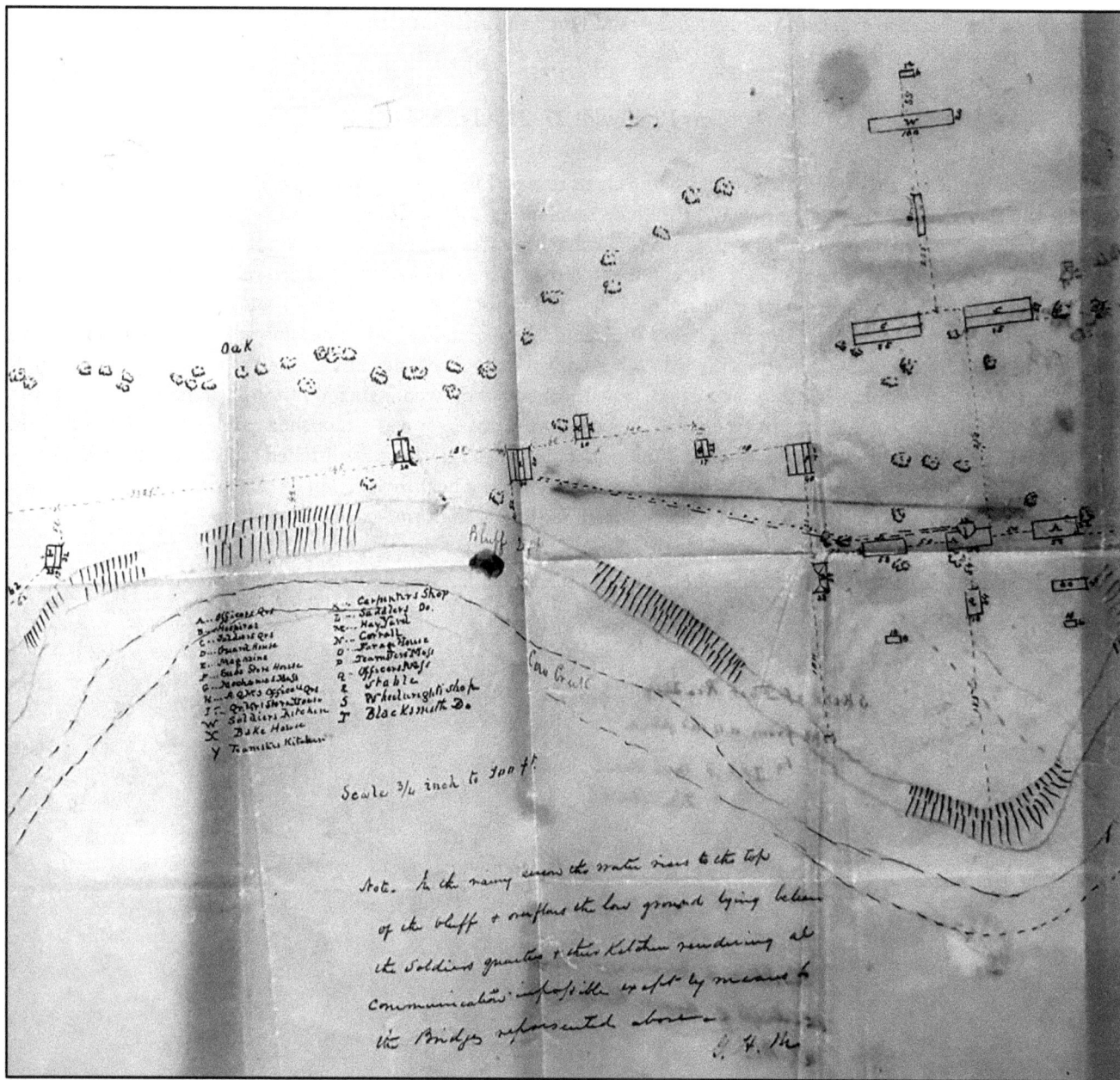

Sketch of Fort Reading found in Mansfield's papers. His note reads "In the rainy season the water rises to the top of the bluff and overflows the low ground lying between the soldier's quarters and their kitchen rendering all communication impossible except by means of the bridges represented above." Courtesy of the Middlesex County Historical Society.

Lieutenant Colonel George Wright was in command of Fort Reading as well as of northern California and southern Oregon; Forts Jones and Lane were under his authority. At the post were Company D, 3rd Artillery and Company D, 4th Infantry. Mansfield found that the troops were in good discipline and well-instructed but there was only one drummer boy present—more musicians were required. "Colonel Wright gave a handsome battalion drill....The command was...in perfect order and efficient....the books and quarters in excellent order but in some degree limited as to kitchens for the men." The quarters were also excellent with a good bakery and an excellent garden. Mansfield did find something unusual here—the troops of the companies were in the "new uniform." While the medical department was well run, it was too small because of the large number of sick men due to the poor location of the post apparently due to the marshes around Cow Creek near the post. And during the hot season temperatures reached 107 degrees. Mansfield judged that the post was not in the best location, but with all the effort and monies spent it had to stay. On 25 July 1854 he wrote to Thomas from Fort Reading and told him that he arrived there on 18 July "having completed the inspections of the posts south of this and traversed the country from Fort Yuma...to here by land. I shall leave here tomorrow for

Humboldt by land, thence expect to visit Forts Jones and Fort Lane and Fort Orford and continue by land northward to the several posts in Oregon"[104]

Fort Humboldt 27–29 July 1854

Mansfield had a long, 175 mile ride to the Pacific Coast to next inspect Fort Humboldt, also a two-company post, on the 27th through the 29th of July. Fellow West Pointer Lieutenant Colonel Robert C. Buchanan commanded the post consisting of Companies B and F of the 4th Infantry. Mansfield found all in good order except that the enlisted quarters could only comfortably hold one company. He commented that the troops had constructed their quarters and they and their commander, Buchanan, deserved much credit. The troops also had a good garden and bakery and drilled well except as skirmishers. "This post is important now and should be maintained for some time yet to come, if not always, for the defense of this bay--particularly as the troops here on an emergency may be regarded as a reserve that a steamer could transport to any point along the coast. There is abundant lumber, wood, grazing, fresh beef, potatoes, and barley here. All other supplies come from San Francisco." The comfort of the men was diminished as Mansfield noted that the white flannel shirts shrank badly but the colored did not. This shows again that he listened to all complaints no matter how trivial concerning the enlisted troops. He also commented on the healthy location of this post compared to others. "Both companies appeared in excellent and efficient order, in the old uniform, except a bugler and one drummer at the post."[105]

Officer inspecting troops at Fort Humboldt perhaps representing Captain U.S. Grant while he was stationed there in 1854 although uniforms appear to be Civil War era. Grant did not enjoy his time here and resigned from the Army 31 July 1854. Al Sondag painting courtesy LOC.

---

[104] Mansfield, *Mansfield on the Condition of the Western Forts 1853-1854*, 159-162; Journal No. 4, courtesy of the Middlesex County Historical Society. Wright was a classmate of Mansfield, graduating in 1822 from West Point. He received four brevets during his career, one for the Seminole War, two for the Mexican-American War, and one during the Civil War. He became a brigadier general of volunteers during the Civil War and died from drowning 30 July 1865. Fort Reading was established on 26 May 1852 on the west side of Cow Creek about two miles from its joining the Sacramento River. It was named for Major Pierson B. Reading, paymaster of the California Volunteers during the Mexican War. Colonel McCall had inspected the post in 1852. It was intermittently occupied and finally abandoned 6 April 1870.

[105] Mansfield, *Mansfield on the Condition of the Western Forts 1853-1854*, 162-165; Mansfield Journal No. 4, courtesy of the Middlesex County Historical Society. Fort Humboldt was established on 30 January 1853 by Lieutenant Colonel Robert C. Buchanan of the 4th Infantry, situated on a 35-foot-high bluff overlooking Humboldt Bay. It provided protection for the nearby citizens from Indians and served also as a supply depot for other posts in northern California. Captain Ulysses S. Grant served there in 1854. In 1866 the garrison, except for one company of artillery was withdrawn, and the post then became a sub depot. On 14 September 1867 the post was completely abandoned. Robert Christie Buchanan was an 1830 West Point graduate and received two brevets during the Mexican-American War to lieutenant colonel, and three brevets during the Civil War to major general. He retired in 1870 as a colonel in the Regular Army and died in 1878.

Fort Jones 4–8 August 1854

Fort Jones was next for Mansfield as he rode northeast from Humboldt; Lieutenant John C. Bonnycastle was in command. His 4th through 8th August inspection of this small, one company post, Company E, 4th Infantry, found all in good order except for skirmisher drill, with the troops in adequate log quarters and a good garden and bakery. There was no musician. "There is abundant grazing, wood, water, tillable land for gardens, oats, barley, wheat, and vegetables in the immediate vicinity, and grist mill and saw mill convenient. All other supplies have been heretofore received via Shasta City and Fort Reading, but in my opinion should hereafter come from San Francisco, over the wagon road thro' Fort Lane to Scottsburg, 224 miles.... The officers and soldier's quarters, and storeroom, and hospital, and stable, were of logs, and erected by the men. Of course quite indifferent, but such as other people enjoy and sufficient for the present."[106]

---

[106] Mansfield, *Mansfield on the Condition of the Western Forts 1853-1854*, 167-170. Fort Jones was established on 16 October 1852 as a 640-acre post situated on the east side of the Scott River Valley in Siskiyou County, about 16 miles west of Yreka. The post was established by Major Edward H. Fitzgerald, with Companies A and E, 1st Dragoons, to protect the mining town from Indians. The Fort was named for Major General Roger Jones, Adjutant General of the Army, who died on 15 July 1852. It was last garrisoned in 1864. The post was commanded by Lieutenant John C. Bonnycastle of the 4th Infantry, who attended but did not graduate from West Point; the Virginia native resigned in 1861 and died in 1884.

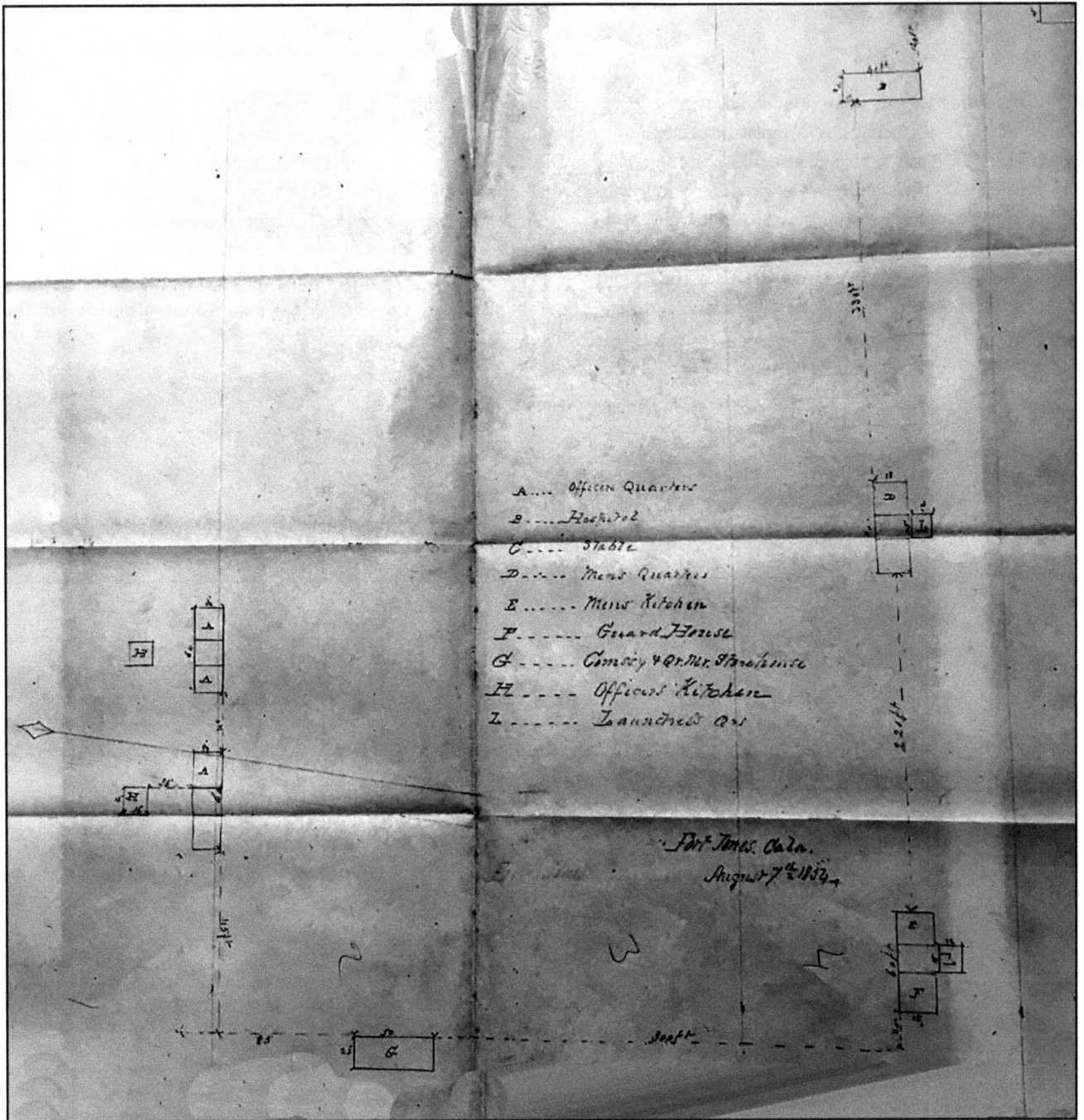

Sketch of Fort Jones 7 August 1854. Courtesy of the Middlesex County Historical Society.

Fort Lane 10–12 August 1854

Mansfield continued north to Fort Lane, commanded by Captain Andrew J. Smith, another West Point graduate, which contained Companies C and E, 1st Dragoons. Mansfield wrote about the heavy desertions by recruits apparently to try to obtain their fortunes in the gold diggings. This high rate was the worst he would encounter. As at previous posts, he found all in good order and the post "well commanded" but here there was a shortage of pistols. He again complained about the musketoon as "a worthless arm for mounted men, or the service." He wrote that "They should be turned in and Sharps' Carbine Rifle substituted." The post ordnance consisted of one mountain and one field howitzer, both brass. Drill demonstrations went well except that the new recruits "had not yet been taught the charge, nor the sword exercise on horseback, nor as skirmishers." Log buildings constructed by the men served as quarters and storehouses; there was a good garden but plagued by grasshoppers. This was one of the few times he did not comment on a post's bakery. He also noted that "the horses' feet however, were not in a very good condition and some of them wanted shoes and were badly shod. Each company had a farrier but that of Company C is not very good."[107]

Fort Vancouver 21–23 August 1854

He continued his journey in Oregon Territory now making a very long ride north to Fort Vancouver on the Columbia River for his inspection from 21 to 23 August. This was one of the oldest posts in the northwest established in 1848 but its location was problematical since the post's 640 acres partially overlaid land and buildings owned by the Hudson Bay Company which erected its fort in 1824. This large, three-company post 124 miles from the river's mouth was commanded by Lieutenant Colonel Benjamin L.E. Bonneville and was the headquarters of the 4th Infantry Regiment. It housed Companies G and H of the 4th Infantry and Company L of the 3rd Artillery. Mansfield reported everything as good especially the drills of the infantry and artillery; troops in the new uniform. Quarters, while ample, were made of logs which he again found defective as they were difficult to heat in winter plus they did not last long. "The logs are constantly changing by shrinking and expanding and rotting and settling, and it would be better to put up entirely new buildings of plank." Store houses and the hospital in buildings rented from the Hudson Bay Company were inferior but he saw a good bakery and garden. He also wrote that the quartermaster had spent over $50,000 dollars to pay for a Pacific Coast survey for a railway from the Mississippi River to Puget Sound. Captain Ulysses S. Grant previously had spent a similar amount for this purpose. Overall, Mansfield was pleased with what he found at Fort Vancouver.[108]

---

[107] Mansfield, *Mansfield on the Condition of the Western Forts 1853-1854*, 167-169; Journal No. 4, courtesy of the Middlesex County Historical Society. Fort Lane was constructed and occupied by two companies of the 1st U.S. Dragoons commanded by Captain Andrew Jackson Smith to protect settlers and Indians from each other. It was named for Brigadier General Joseph Lane who was the first territorial governor of Oregon. It was abandoned 17 September 1856. Smith was an 1838 West Point graduate and received three brevets during the Civil War to major general. He retired as a colonel in 1889 and died in 1897. Note that Mansfield called the guns he saw on his inspections "brass" when they were in reality bronze according to cannon authority Tom Clemens. Cannon barrels which Mansfield saw were made of either bronze or steel, never brass.

[108] Mansfield, *Mansfield on the Condition of the Western Forts 1853-1854*, 170-174; Journal No. 4, courtesy of the Middlesex County Historical Society. The post was established as Columbia Barracks in 1849 and renamed Fort Vancouver 13 July 1853. Vancouver Arsenal was located here in 1859. It was retired in 1947. Captain George Vancouver was a British explorer as the post was originally constructed by the British Hudson's Bay Company. Parisian born Benjamin Louis Eulalie Bonneville was an 1815 West Point graduate and was wounded and brevetted to lieutenant colonel during the Mexican-American War and to brigadier general during the Civil War after he retired in 1861; he died in 1878.

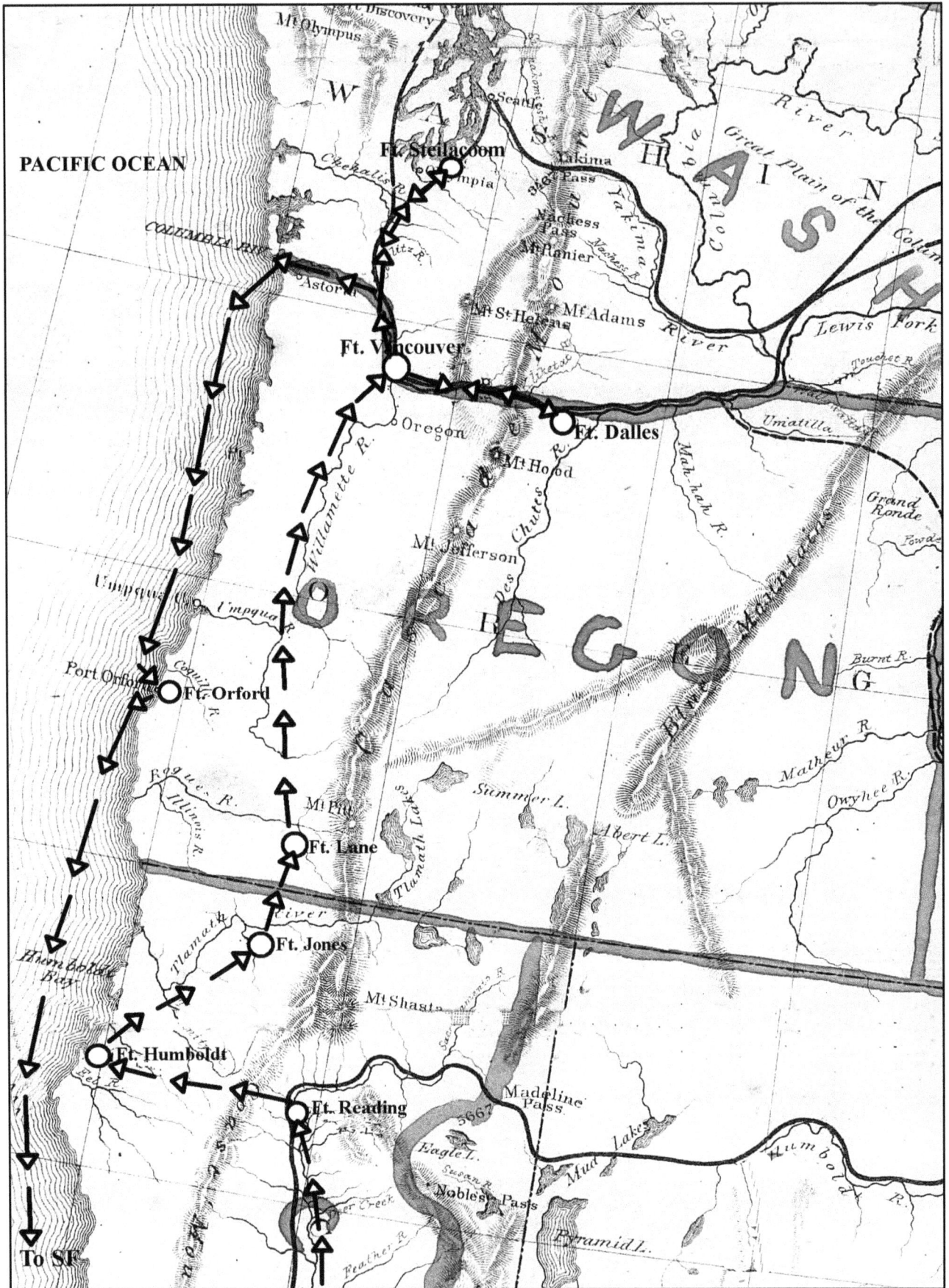

Mansfield's route from Fort Reading to Fort Humboldt, Fort Jones, Fort Lane, Fort Vancouver, Fort Dalles, Fort Steilacoom, Port Orford, then back to San Francisco. Detail of map from LOC.

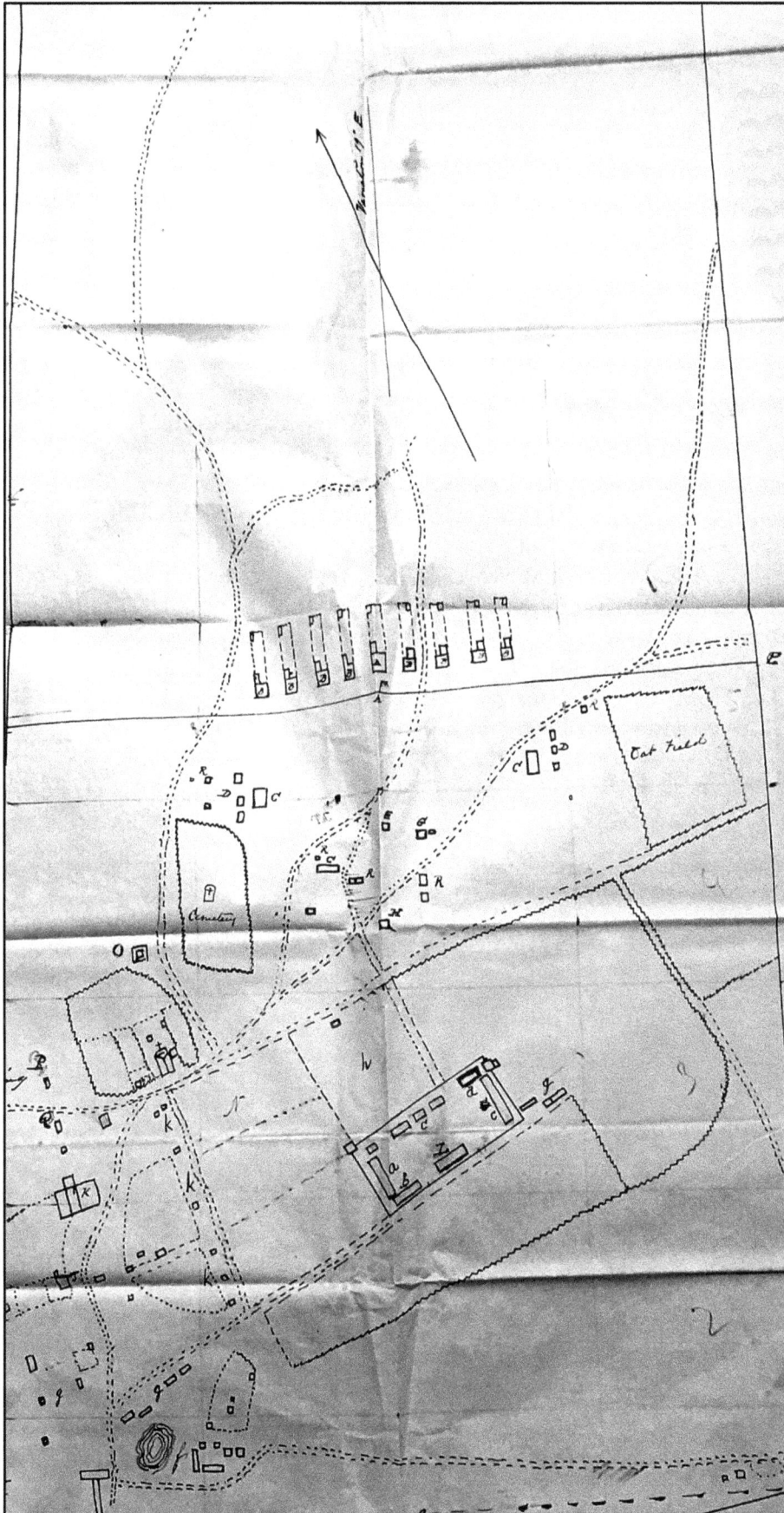

Legend:
A: Commanding Off. Qtrs.
B: Officers' Qtrs.
C: Soldiers' Qtrs.
D: Soldiers' Kitchen
E: Magazine
H: Hospital
K: Corral
J: Qtr. Master's House
L: Qtr. Master's Storehouse rented from H.B.C.)
N: Garrison Garden
O: Sutler's Store
P: Blacksmith's Shop
Q: Carpenter's Shop
R: Laundresses' Qtrs.

Hudson Bay Company
a: Store
b: Lumber Room
c: Dwellings
e: Superintendent's House
g: Old Buildings—worthless
h: Garden
k: Houses of employees

Sketch of Fort Vancouver found in Mansfield's files, drawn by Lieutenant Colonel Benjamin L.E. Bonneville of the 4th Infantry in 1854, showing U.S. and Hudson Bay Company (HBC) buildings. Courtesy of the Middlesex County Historical Society.

Mansfield took time to write home from Fort Vancouver on 26 August 1854, to update his wife and family of his adventures and plans: "Washington Territory 95 miles up the Columbia River…In Colonel Benjamin L.E. Bonneville's quarters and finished inspection of the post. Leave tomorrow up the Columbia in a steamer to the Cascades then by land about 5 miles and then by steamer again to The Dalles some 40 miles. Then down the river to here and down the river and up the Cowlitz River and over land to Puget Sound and Fort Steilacoom and my last inspection then return and take steamer for San Francisco stopping at Fort Orford for the final inspection. After writing from Fort Jones we travelled on mules northward over the Siskiyou Mountains to Fort Lane on the Rogue River in Oregon then northward along the Willamette Valley to Corvallis, Salem then Oregon City, Portland back to Fort Vancouver on the 21st."[109]

Fort Dalles 26–31 August 1854

Next he journeyed upriver to Fort Dalles in the current state of Oregon; this inspection took Mansfield six days from 26 to 31 August. This 640 acre, two-company post--Companies K and J, 4th Infantry--was established by the Mounted Rifles on the south bank of the Columbia River in 1850 on the former site of an 1820 Northwest Company trading post. Major Gabriel J. Rains commanded the post. It was about 95 miles up the Columbia River, east of Fort Vancouver; 45 miles by steamer to the Cascade Falls then a five mile portage over the falls, then 45 more miles by steamer. There was no hospital but there were plans to convert officers' quarters to one and build new officers' quarters. All was in good order except for the quarters and other buildings which were badly arranged and in generally poor condition. Rains had plans for new buildings which would alleviate all problems however. The bakery, garden, ice house, and sawmill were good and Rains was complemented by Mansfield as being "indefatigable in his efforts at improvement." Mansfield did not have the troops drill as a large detachment was away protecting emigrants; it had left the morning of 28 August after reports were received that a party of emigrants had been attacked about 300 miles east of the post with eight men murdered and four women and five children captured. There was one field six pounder which needed paint. Mansfield recommended that "Military roads to Fort Vancouver and Fort Steilacoom should be opened, in order to strengthen each post and develop the country."[110]

---

[109] Letter courtesy WPL.

[110] Mansfield, *Mansfield on the Condition of the Western Forts 1853-1854*, 175-179; Journal No. 4, courtesy of the Middlesex County Historical Society. Gabriel James Rains was an 1827 West Point graduate and was wounded in the Seminole Wars in Florida in 1840 receiving a brevet to major. He resigned as a lieutenant colonel in 1861 becoming a Confederate brigadier general and died in 1881. The Indian attack was the Ward Massacre 20 August 1854 during which 20 members of an emigrant wagon train were attacked by Shoshone Indians and slaughtered. The fight was initiated when the emigrants shot and killed an Indian who had stolen one of their horses. "Soon after, the entire party was ambushed by Snake and Shoshone Native Americans. The wagon train leader, Alexander Ward, fell dead in the first few minutes, and with careful speed and defense tactics, the men of the Ward Party reached out to protect the women and children and hold off the ambushers. Their defense turned out to be quite futile, as most were killed before sundown while the women were sexually tortured and killed. Children were held over a large, blazing fire and were burned to death." Two seriously wounded survivors feigned death and crawled for several days until they reached Fort Hall. https://www.theclio.com/web/entry?id=23713, accessed 1 Sept. 2018.

1853 sketch of Fort Dalles shown at right center. "Railroad Survey", vol. 12 facing p. 154

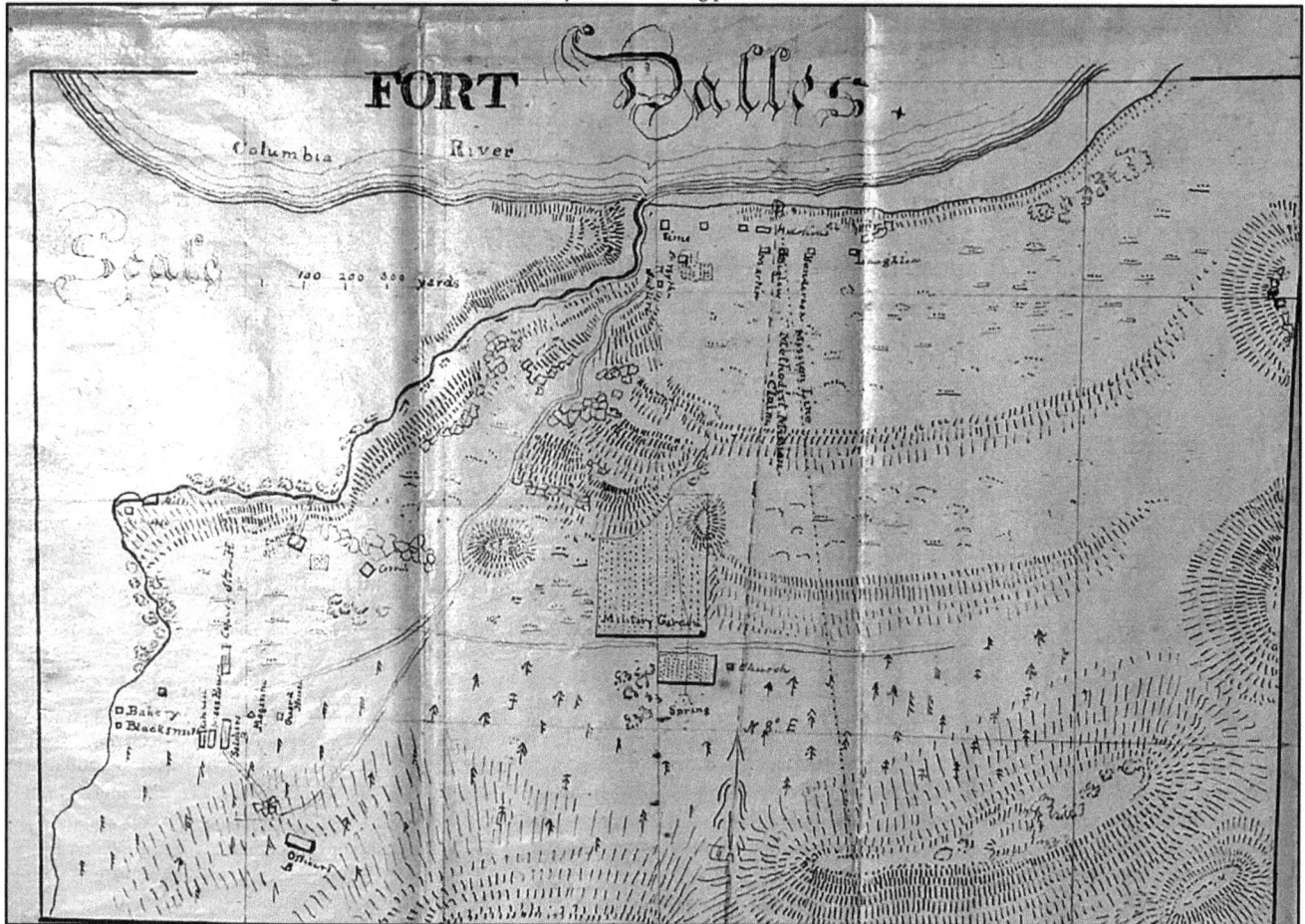

Sketch of Fort Dalles found in Mansfield's papers, courtesy of the Middlesex County Historical Society. This map is on paper unlike the rest of Mansfield's draft report plus it does not closely resemble his writing. The name "J.W. Adams" appears at the map's bottom; he was a 1st Dragoons officer.

Fort Steilacoom 8–15 September 1854

Mansfield then began his trip downriver on his longer journey to Fort Steilacoom. He stopped at Fort Vancouver and wrote again to his wife from there on 3 Sept 1854: "Reached here on the north bank of the Columbia River 6 miles above the mouth of the Willamette River 100 miles from the ocean last evening [2 Sept.] on my return from Fort Dalles which is 100 miles up this river. Saw Major [Gabriel J.] Rains and family there; Fort Brown acquaintance. Then took a steamer up river to Fort Dalles; pleasant. Great scenery; foot of Cascade rapids disembarked and stayed at a tavern for the night." He slept on a bench next morning and got an Indian to carry his baggage and walked five miles over the rapids to "where we took a miserable little iron steamer with no seats to sit down on and here our troubles commenced. We had a hard, deep river, and high mountains on either side and perpendicular rocks with the current running rapidly and the wind howling a gale (as it does here all summer) up against the current, thereby raising a high sea and our little iron shell was accordingly wet and difficult to manage." They ran aground 50 feet from shore but arrived safely. Mansfield was cold and wet and was sick for five days at Fort Dalles with fever. His return was better at the Cascade Rapids "got into an Indian canoe with 4 Indians and glided down over the rapids beautifully. Tomorrow start for Puget Sound and take steamer and descend this river about 30 miles and ascend the Cowlitz River to the head of navigation and there take Indian canoes and finally mules or horses to Olympia, the seat of Governor of Washington Territory, then to Steilacoom. That is the last post except Port Orford." He hoped to reach San Francisco before 1 October to take a steamer for home.[111]

Mansfield finally arrived at Fort Steilacoom and accomplished his inspection there from 8 to 15 September 1854. Fort Steilacoom was established in 1849 near the Steilacoom River about a mile east of Puget Sound. It was built by the U.S. Army on land claimed by the Hudson Bay Company in response to Indian depredations by the Nisqually tribe. The post was commanded by fellow West Pointer Captain David A. Russell who was also commander of Company A of the 4th Infantry located there. Company C of the 4th Infantry commanded by Captain David R. Jones, another West Point graduate, was stationed there too. Mansfield also noted that there were eight Indians under arrest for murder. All that Mansfield examined was in fine order except that he noted the buildings were of log construction which was inferior. But he wrote in his journal: "Barn and Smith's shop and carpentry shop and bakery "all indifferent." A good garden was about five miles away and there was a "beautiful plateau" near it—"I would recommend that a Military Reserve be made there at once the post removed to it." He did not report on the soldiers' drilling. The Indian Agent on the post represented to Mansfield that the Indians were not as friendly as those further south. Mansfield opined that supplies which now come from San Francisco by steamer should be carried instead by a permanent mail steamer to this sound.[112]

Fort Orford 27 September 1854

Fort Orford was Mansfield's final inspection on this tour which he did in one day, 27 September, at this small post on the Pacific Coast in Oregon Territory. Commanded by Lieutenant August V. Kautz of the 4th Infantry, it was located at the town of Port Orford on Trichenor Bay. Enlisted troops were from Company M of the 3rd Artillery. Mansfield arrived by boat after his last inspection likely a welcome change from horse and mule back, wagon, and canoe. There was only one officer, one surgeon, and 24 men there and one post howitzer--Mansfield found all in excellent order but the quarters "worthless." He recommended that the post "be abandoned as soon as it will be safe to do so" as it was of "doubtful utility." Due to his recommendation, the post was abandoned 22 August 1856.[113]

---

[111] Letter courtesy WPL.

[112] Mansfield, *Mansfield on the Condition of the Western Forts 1853-1854*, 179-181; Journal No. 4, courtesy of the Middlesex County Historical Society. Ironically, Mansfield and the two captains, Russell and Jones, were all killed or died during the Civil War, and all three fought in the Battle of Antietam. Captain David Allen Russell graduated from West Point in 1845, fought in the Mexican-American War receiving a brevet, and was killed on 19 September 1864, at the Battle of Third Winchester, brevetted posthumously to a major general in the Union Army. Captain David Rumph Jones graduated from West Point in 1846, was also a Mexican-American War veteran receiving a brevet, and became a Confederate major general during the Civil War; he died 16 January 1863 due to a heart condition. Fort Steilacoom was decommissioned as a military post in 1868. Mansfield usually wrote "Port Orford" not "Fort Orford" in his reports.

[113] Mansfield, *Mansfield on the Condition of the Western Forts 1853-1854*, 182; Journal No. 4, courtesy of the Middlesex County Historical Society. August Valentine Kautz served in the Mexican-American War as a private in the 1st Ohio Infantry. He then entered West Point graduating in 1852. He served at Fort Steilacoom where he was wounded twice during Indian Wars in 1855 and 1856. He was brevetted five times to a Union major general for his actions during the Civil War. He retired as a brigadier general in 1891 and died in 1895.

Mansfield finished his final 1 March 1855 report written from his "post" in Middletown, Connecticut, with conclusions first containing recommendations for numbers of troops required to man posts and where new posts should be established. He recommended that a one-company post be established at Bellingham Bay in Washington Territory near the Puget Sound. Two years later, Fort Bellingham was established in 1856 by 9th Infantry troops commanded by Captain George E. Pickett to protect nearby mining activities. As already noted Mansfield recommended posts be established toward El Paso and over the Rocky Mountains. He remarked on the requirement for more musicians at the posts—"There was a great deficiency of musicians for companies." And again he voiced his highly unfavorable opinion of the musketoon as not "fit for any arm of the service." He was a little less concerned with the lack of horses for the dragoons as he believed that supplies will be forthcoming in the area. He deplored the lack of target firing and no drill at the bayonet exercise; and "drill as skirmishers generally was indifferent." He then segued into six "Remarks for Immediate Consideration." He first referred to the San Juan Island dispute regarding the boundary line among islands on the Canadian (then British) border. This long standing dispute was not settled until 1872 and involved Lieutenant George E. Pickett in the bloodless 1859 "Pig War" concerning which country had sovereignty over the San Juan Islands. Mansfield's second recommendation was to employ "a steamer revenue cutter…on Puget Sound…to act in concert with the troops and keep up a communication with the mouth of the Columbia River." Number three was his opinion that "fortifications at the mouth of the Columbia River should be immediately commenced" to deny entrance to the river. His advice was followed but not "immediately" as Fort Canby (originally Fort Cape Disappointment) on the Washington side on the north bank of the entrance to the Columbia River was established in 1864, and Fort Stevens on the south side completed in 1865. Interestingly, Fort Stevens was shelled by the Japanese in 1942 but guns at the fort and other forts were not large enough to reach the enemy submarine so it received no return fire. Mansfield would have been pleased that his assessment of the importance of the sites was correct. His fourth remark was that mail routes were needed from Fort Vancouver to Cascade City and a second from Stockton to Millerton near Fort Miller. His next recommendation concerned military road construction or repair: improvements on the road from Rogue River to Myrtle Creek, construction of a road from Fort Vancouver to Fort Dalles, from Fort Dalles to Fort Steilacoom, from Fort Steilacoom to Fort Vancouver, and repair of the road from San Diego to Fort Yuma. Most of these projects were eventually completed. His final recommendation was one that had been talked about by others for years including Secretary of War Davis—a railroad across the Rockies. Progress was made but the first transcontinental railroad of almost 2,000 miles was not finished until 1869.[114]

While Mansfield was on his inspection tour, he wrote three letters to Major General Wool, the Pacific Department Commander, dated 7 June, 1 July and 29 September 1854. He used these as a summary of important items with which Wool would be concerned and which the commander could address. Wool had requested these summaries rather than waiting some months for Mansfield's final report. The first was from Fort Yuma basically recounting what he had written in his official report about the three sites in and near San Diego and Fort Yuma. Similarly on 1 July, he wrote Wool from the Mercede River east of Snellings summarizing his visits of Fort Miller and the Tejon Reservation. His final letter of 29 September was a lengthy one as it covered the 12 posts he inspected after Fort Miller. As in his two earlier letters, he summarizes his inspections of the posts but the main difference in this letter is that Mansfield goes into more descriptive detail about his travels to these posts thus giving contemporary readers some insight into the perils involved on the frontier. Some examples follow: "From Fort Reading we took mules and packs and proceeded over the mountains via Shasta City, Weaverville, Trinity River, Mad River, to Union at the head of Humboldt Bay. Then a steamer conveyed us to Bucksport (Fort Humboldt), a distance of 185 miles from Fort Reading and most of it an extremely difficult mule trail over and along the sides of mountains." He then headed for Fort Jones by a succession of rivers and over "Scotts Mountain into Scotts Valley, a distance of 138 miles." It is not clear if he was on the rivers using canoes or boats or as in his earlier trip was on mule back and traversed them. It may be the latter as he then wrote "we proceeded over a good wagon road via Yreka, across Klamath River, over the Siskiyou Mountain and Jacksonville 84 miles to Fort Lane." He

---

[114] Mansfield, *Mansfield on the Condition of the Western Forts 1853-1854*, 14. Fort Bellingham was abandoned in 1860. Frazer, 185-186. "In 1856 the Select Committee on the Pacific Railroad and Telegraph of the U.S. House of Representatives published a report recommending support for a proposed Pacific railroad bill: The necessity that now exists for constructing lines of railroad and telegraphic communication between the Atlantic and Pacific coasts of this continent is no longer a question for argument; it is conceded by everyone. In order to maintain our present position on the Pacific, we must have some more speedy and direct means of intercourse than is at present afforded by the route through the possessions of a foreign power," courtesy Wikipedia, "First Transcontinental Railroad". One of the possible routes, the southern, surveyors found, should be through land owned by Mexico so in 1853 the U.S. appropriated $10 million for what became known as the Gadsden Purchase completed in 1854.

then traversed 285 miles to Fort Vancouver "over a good wagon road almost the entire distance" over several rivers and creeks and the towns of Corvallis, Salem, Oregon City, and Portland. He next reached Fort Dalles some 95 miles mostly by steamers and one, five-mile portage. His return from Fort Dalles took him again through Fort Vancouver then 160 miles to Fort Steilacoom via the Cowlitz River and Olympia. His detailed travelogue stopped, other than his mention of taking a steamer to department headquarters. He took steamers down the coast once he finished his inspection at Fort Steilacoom.[115]

Mansfield wrote to Adjutant General Samuel Cooper from Middletown 25 October 1854 notifying him that he arrived in Middletown having left San Francisco on 30 September via the Panama Mail Route and that he would complete his report of the inspection of the Pacific Department. As a follow-up to his report, the Adjutant General's Office wrote to him on 17 November 1854 to seek his opinion about supplementing troop strength in the Department of the Pacific. Six companies of the 6th Regiment were put under orders to go to the Department of the Pacific and were to leave Jefferson Barracks, Missouri, "in January next. They are destined for active service in Oregon....The Secretary of War desires that you will please report with as little delay as practicable whether this command can be comfortably quartered for a few months, at the posts in Oregon and Washington Territories." Mansfield must have answered favorably as the 6th Regiment moved west in its grand march to the Pacific a few years later. "The movement began on 18 March 1858, and it arrived at camp near Benicia Barracks on 15 November, having marched some 1017 miles. From Benicia Barracks the Sixth was distributed among different posts and stations in the Department of the Pacific. By January, 1859, the headquarters and Companies F and H were at the Presidio, A at Benicia Barracks, B at Fort Humboldt, C and I at Benicia Depot, D at Fort Weller, Cal., E and K at Camp Banning near San Bernardino, Cal., and G at New San Diego, Cal. In January, 1860, the headquarters and Companies A and H were at Benicia Barracks, B at Fort Humboldt, C, E and F, at Fort Yuma, D at Fort Bragg, and G, I and K, at New San Diego."[116]

1855

Mansfield used his Middletown home as his base as he completed his report of his 1854 Pacific inspection. Secretary of War Davis had Mansfield on his mind again in 1855 but the Inspector General could not do what Davis asked. Davis, in his confidential letter to Mansfield 23 March 1855, wrote "If you are in condition for a tour of many miles and many months and beyond seas, I would be glad to see you at your earliest convenience. I have seen your letter to the Adj. Genl, and if such service as I have indicated would embarrass you, have no hesitation in declining it, as any consideration of my personal wishes." Two days later, Mansfield in his confidential reply responded from Middletown: "Your esteemed favor of the 23rd came to hand last evening. It will afford me at all times great pleasure to perform any duty I am qualified for, but I am not at this time, although in as good health as I have enjoyed since the Mexican War, at liberty conscientiously and of duty to my family to say I am in a condition to leave immediately without great personal inconvenience and sacrifice. Nor shall I be before about the 1st of June. My family for the last 18 months have been residing at much inconvenience in a small house not large enough and since the death of my mother-in-law we are refitting her house for ourselves and I am now in the midst of that business, and so far advanced that I cannot suspend it nor can any person manage it for me. When my family are settled I shall be able to perform any duty you will desire. If you had issued an order without previously consulting me in this way I of course at all sacrifice would have obeyed instantly. It is proper in this case you should know how far I am qualified for any duty abroad. As to foreign languages, at one time I understood the French and could speak it some, but I have become rusty in that, and I can say the same of the Spanish. These languages would soon be familiar to me by a little attention to them. I know no other languages at all. Under the foregoing circumstances I have thought of my duty not to visit Washington as your letter would seem to imply immediate movement unless I hear from you again."[117]

---

[115] Mansfield, *Mansfield on the Condition of the Western Forts 1853-1854*, 186-197.

[116] Letter courtesy WPL. Sixth Regiment history from USACMH, "The most important U.S. [steam company] service established in the mid-nineteenth century was the 'Panama Route', which connected New York and San Francisco via an overland crossing in Panama. It was principally operated on the Pacific side by the federally subsidized Pacific Mail Steamship Company and on the Atlantic by the federally subsidized U.S. Mail Steamship Company. The isthmian crossing was dramatically improved in 1855 with the opening of the world's first transcontinental railroad, the forty-seven-mile Wall Street-owned (and unsubsidized) Panama Railroad;" Sexton, 629.

[117] Letter from Davis 23 March 1855 and draft letter from Mansfield 27 March 1855, courtesy of the Middlesex County Historical Society.

Davis was interested in the Crimean War which had begun in October 1853 which pitted the Russian Empire against an alliance of France, Britain, the Ottoman Empire, and Sardinia. It ended with the Treaty of Paris on 30 March 1856. It was of interest to U.S. military officers as it employed novel technologies as railways, steamships, explosive naval shells, and telegraphs, and the use of trenches and blind artillery fire. Total casualties were over 400,000 including 143,000 killed and 80,000 wounded. Davis had previously sent officers to Prussia, France, and Great Britain to examine changes in cavalry and infantry tactics especially those caused by the use of rifled weapons. He dispatched this second military commission to Europe—the Delafield Commission. He considered five U.S. Military Academy graduates and all commissioned in the engineer branch: Colonel Joseph K.F. Mansfield, Lieutenant Colonel Robert E. Lee, Major Richard Delafield, Major Alfred Mordecai, and Captain George B. McClellan. Mansfield and Lieutenant Colonel Lee declined but the remaining officers accepted. On 5 April 1855, Davis met with them in Washington and gave them his charge. He told them that he had selected them for a study of modern war and armies in Europe and issued a detailed list of military subjects that they were to pursue dealing with organization, technology, logistics, equipment, fortifications, and even the use of camels for transport. Each member had a specific field to observe and write about: Delafield on engineering matters, Mordecai on ordnance and artillery, and McClellan on cavalry. McClellan finished his report in January 1857, Mordecai in March 1858, and Delafield in November 1860. These lengthy reports were widely distributed and closely studied by Army officers and the administration.[118]

Secretary of War Jefferson Davis about age 45 in 1853 when Mansfield would have seen him in Washington, DC. Courtesy Wikipedia.

---

[118] Matthew Moten, *The Delafield Commission and the American Military Profession* (College Station, TX: Texas A&M University Press, 2000), 86-107, *passim*, 217, 336; Lester W. Grau, "The Delafield Commission: Forerunner of the Foreign Area Officers Program," in "The FAO Journal," vol. XIV, no. 4, Dec. 2011, 6-14. One tangible result of McClellan's Delafield Commission report was the development and use of the "McClellan Saddle" in the U.S. Army from the Civil War well into the 20th Century.

Secretary of War John B. Floyd was in the Buchanan administration from 6 March 1857, successor to Jefferson Davis. Floyd resigned 29 December 1860 and in 1861 became a brigadier general in the Confederate Army despite having no military experience. He was responsible for the ignominious surrender of Confederate forces at Fort Donelson and was relieved of command by Confederate President Davis on 11 March 1862; he died on 26 Aug. 1863.

Brevet Lieutenant General Winfield Scott portrait done in 1855, courtesy Wikipedia.

The Delafield Commission; 1855 Daguerreotype photo of Major Albert Mordecai, Russian Lieutenant Colonel Obrezkov, Major Richard Delafield, and Captain George McClellan, Courtesy USACMH.

Mansfield wrote from Middletown on 5 January 1855 in his monthly report to Adjutant General Cooper for December 1854 that it was spent "completing my report of my inspection of the Pacific Department—I have found it quite laborious, & shall not probably have it in much before the close of this month, of which I will notify you." Then on 1 February he updated Cooper: "for the month of January 1855, I have been engaged in compiling my report of my inspection of the Pacific Department, and it is now about completed in the rough, but it will take me some days to transcribe it & hand it in to the Commanding General." On 5 March he wrote Cooper with his February 1855 monthly report: "I have been engaged in compiling & transcribing my report of my inspection of the Pacific Department, and have just completed the same & shall hand it in to the Commanding Gen'l tomorrow morning." He then continued with a request that the "Department will afford me a little rest if it can be done without injury to the service. During my absence in the Pacific Department my wife's Father died & since my return she has lost her Mother & my family are in consequence thrown into a little confusion & I am desirous of an opportunity to prepare myself for further duty." He wrote on 6 March that he handed in to the "Commanding General my report of the result of my inspection of the Pacific Department made agreeably to Special Orders No. 45 dated 18 March 1854."[119]

On 1 April Mansfield reported that "I have been resting here [Middletown] & preparing myself for further duty." Next on 8 June 1855 he wrote Assistant Adjutant General Lorenzo Thomas with details on his inspection of recruits on Governor's Island who were bound for Jefferson Barracks. The 214 men included infantry, cavalry and artillery recruits who "were of good size, and young, and generally healthy, & made up of 38 Americans, 8 English, 98 Irish, 10 Scotch, 4 French, 5 Prussians, 45 Germans, 3 Swiss, 1 Pole and 2 Danes." They had adequate clothing and good rations. Transportation was also good. He did note that the soldiers' pantaloons and socks needed more sizes as they did not fit well especially the socks which came in only one size. Soldiers were forced to pay for tailoring of their uniforms which was a hardship on them. He again on 18 June reported on an inspection he completed for recruits on Governor's Island bound for Corpus Christi. The 411 men had 23 women as laundresses. The transportation the Quartermaster chartered for them was good with ample accommodations but while their uniform issue was good they were not in the new

---

[119] Letters courtesy of the Middlesex County Historical Society.

uniform coat. "They however were a fine healthy looking set of men" which nationalities he then detailed. He ended with an apology for not reporting to headquarters in New York due to inadequate time. On 19 June 1855 he tardily submitted his personal report for the month of May writing that he "was permitted to remain in this City at my post till such time as the Commanding Gen'l or the Secretary of War should require my services." A few days later on 22 June he realized that he had not submitted his April report so did so, again writing that he remained at his Middletown post. Then on 25 June 1855 he reported to Thomas that he inspected 156 troops at Governor's Island who were being sent to Old Point Comfort. Their clothing was adequate and in this relatively brief report with no nationality list he determined that their transportation was "safe & suitable" with nothing wanting. Mansfield in his June monthly report wrote on 2 July 1855 that he "made inspection of three detachments of recruits & their transports, etc., from Governors Island—one for Jefferson Barracks, one for Corpus Christi & one for Old Point Comfort." He detailed this inspection of recruits for Old Point Comfort in his 25 June 1855 letter to Assistant Adjutant General Lorenzo Thomas reporting a total of 156 men "in good health & supplied with sufficient clothing & cooked rations for the voyage." And as he did for most such inspections he broke down not only the rank of recruit but also the national origin. Here, he found "22 Americans, 4 English, 2 Scotch, 80 Irish, 1 Welch, 6 French, 1 Swiss, 5 Prussians, and 35 Germans. He also examined their clothing and equipment remarking on deficiencies as he found. He lastly commented on the transportation for the recruits, usually a ship of some kind as to its seaworthiness and ability to contain the men as well as the costs for the transportation.[120]

He wrote his July 1855 monthly report on the 31st of that month that he was at his post ready to perform any duties and that he received "notice of the intention of the Gen'l in Chief to order me on an inspection of the Department of Texas next December and I have also received an order [S.O. no. 134] to a Court martial at Fort Leavenworth in September next." On 20 August Mansfield wrote to Cooper and asked that the Secretary of War make changes to the regulations to allow payment of transportation for a servant as Mansfield did not take one to the Pacific inspection even though he had one in New Mexico but "kept two most of the time." He wanted to be reimbursed for transportation of servants given the large areas of land he was required to traverse since the expansion of the United States after the Mexican-American War. Mansfield's August report written on 1 September from Middletown stated that he was at his post and expected to receive orders to leave for Fort Leavenworth on 10 September. Mansfield wrote Cooper from Fort Leavenworth on 20 September and reported that he arrived on that day and that he was in Middletown "at my station till the 12th, when I took my departure for this place...for the trial of Brevet Lieutenant Colonel [William Reading] Montgomery & others. I started at that early day apprehensive of a low state of the Missouri, & consequent detention but fortunately reached here on the 20th in company with several members of the court...thus closed my occupation for September." He also wrote that "Colonel Sumner took up his line of march this morning with 8 companies and a commissary and ordnance etc., train of about 21 wagons and a drove of beef cattle of 90 head. The command appeared in excellent order and condition." Mansfield's October report was sent 1 November from Fort Riley, Kansas Territory. Mansfield was at Fort Leavenworth involved with the trial of Lieutenant Colonel Montgomery which was adjourned, then the court was ordered to Fort Riley for the trial of Assistant Surgeon James Simons. Mansfield arrived there 29 October and the court met on the 30th then adjourned. Mansfield was uncertain how long the trial would last. On 23 November Mansfield wrote to Thomas from St. Louis, Missouri, that the General in Chief had ordered him to inspect recruits at Jefferson Barracks but when he arrived he found none. Finally they arrived and he inspected a total of 121 men in good condition. He did write that there were problems with a few men: "about ten...were too delicate for strong & useful soldiers, and two...who did not sufficiently understand English when spoken to, and two indifferent Frenchmen...who were physically and in other respects, worthless: would make good soldiers under suitable training." He also wrote that transportation on the rivers must be adequate to allow men to sleep inside rather than on the decks to prevent illness. "This unhealthful passage humbles the character of the soldiers also to be thrown into bad company sleeping on deck....The soldier sees his officer enjoying a comfortable cabin & apparently unconcerned as to the

---

[120] Letters 5 January, 1 February, 25 June and 2 July 1855 to Samuel Cooper and Lorenzo Thomas, NARA, RG 94, Letters received by the Adjutant General. His 22 June letter reported that Mansfield remained during April 1855 at his Middletown post; NARA, RG 94, Letters received by the Adjutant General. All of his monthly summary letters were written to the Adjutant General, while reports of his recruit inspections were written to Assistant Adjutant General Thomas. Mansfield's 18 June 1855 letter concerned his inspection of 411 recruits at Governors Island bound for Corpus Christi. A review of his draft reports of inspections revealed that sometimes he wrote down a list of names of the men he inspected but apparently he did not submit that list with his reports to the Adjutant General. More rarely found are lists of subsistence stores transported on ships he inspected. Army General Order No. 5 assigned Brevet Colonel J.E. Johnston "to duty as Acting Inspector General of the Army, according to his brevet rank."

comforts of his men, and in this way unkind and secret feelings of dislike to a ruinous degree, and the pride of service destroyed."[121]

Back in his Middletown post, Mansfield wrote Cooper and submitted his November monthly report which showed that he was at Fort Riley on general court martial duties then when the court adjourned on the 12th he was on the road to Fort Leavenworth. From the 16th to the 20th he was descending the Missouri River then on the 21st and 22nd he inspected recruits at Jefferson Barracks as ordered by General-in-Chief Scott. Then from the 22nd to the 30th he was on route from St. Louis to Middletown. General Scott sent Mansfield a telegram on 6 December 1855 that he must immediately go to New York to inspect the steamship which was chartered to transport the 9th Infantry. Mansfield did so and reported the results of his inspection on 11 December 1855 of the steamship *St. Louis* which was chartered to take the 9th Infantry to the Isthmus of Darien (Isthmus of Panama). It was a "new ship built in 1854 and apparently strong." It had accommodations for 30 officers, 760 men and 40 laundresses with everyone having a berth. He found all in excellent order: "I unhesitatingly state that I have seen nothing in this steamship that would leave a doubt in my mind as to her seaworthiness and accordingly report her suitable in that respect for the object so far as her size will permit." Mansfield on 13 December asked Cooper for copies of the Statutes at Large for the 1st and 2nd sessions of the 33rd Congress to prepare for his inspection of Texas department in January 1856.[122]

Fort Leavenworth barracks c. 1858, courtesy Wikipedia from LOC.

---

[121] Letters 31 July 1855; 20 August; 1, 10, 20 September; 1, 29 October; 1, 23 November, to Samuel Cooper and Lorenzo Thomas, NARA, RG 94, Letters received by the Adjutant General.

[122] All letters from NARA, RG 94, Letters received by the Adjutant General. Mansfield sent a telegram from Middletown on 6 December 1855 to Adjutant General Irvin McDowell at the headquarters of the Army 11th Street, 6th Avenue: "I shall be in New York tonight at the Astor House." Courtesy NARA.

Fort Leavenworth date unknown, note steamer on Missouri River to the center right. Courtesy NPS.

On 1 January 1856, Mansfield submitted his December report in which he said that he was preparing for his Texas inspection and had inspected the steamer *St. Louis*, but he also found himself in a quarrel over rank. This happened after he was ordered to report on 7 January for general court martial duty for Lieutenant Newton C. Givens at Carlisle Barracks. While he wrote Cooper on 10 January that the court will adjourn shortly, the question of his rank precedence over another member of the court, Brevet Colonel Charles Augustus May was an issue. They both had the same date of brevet promotion to colonel, 23 February 1847. Mansfield asserted that the next lower rank, excluding this brevet to colonel, must prevail. Since May's was to brevet lieutenant colonel 9 May 1846, Mansfield's promotion to full colonel in May 1853 obviously prevailed in his opinion. It is likely it did so as nothing further has been found to show Mansfield was incorrect. On 1 February 1856 Mansfield wrote his January report that he attended a general court martial in Carlisle Barracks from the 4th to the 12th including travel time and he expected to leave for New York on 2 February to inspect 382 recruits who would leave on the 5th for the Pacific Department. On 15 February he received orders to report to attend a general court martial at West Point on 21 February. While in New York Mansfield wrote to Thomas on 29 February that he inspected 134 "fine looking" recruits and transport bound for Florida. His 1 March monthly report fleshed out his activities for February: on the 2nd, he inspected 392 recruits and transport in New York and returned to Middletown on the 6th and remained there until the 15th. He was supposed to inspect recruits for Florida in New York but could not as their ship was not available until the 29th so on the 20th he went to West Point to attend the court martial. He then returned to New York on the 28th and inspected the recruits and ship on the 29th. An interesting sidelight concerned the hand writing of the judge advocate at the West Point court martial. The adjutant general had received complaints about the apparent difficulty in reading the recorder's scrawl and Mansfield agreed but wrote that the judge advocate had not received other complaints and that otherwise he was "highly talented."[123]

On 5 February 1856 Mansfield was in New York and submitted to Thomas his report of his inspection of 382 recruits and transport destined for the Pacific Department. As usual most were Irish, 157, and Americans, 96, with Germans third at 84. In his tally, Mansfield also recorded one East Indian. He found the men "apparently healthy and youthful and athletic and I doubt not will make good soldiers." They were well supplied and dressed. He next inspected the steamer *Illinois* and found it an "excellent ship", a "first class vessel", and "well and amply found for the trip in every essential particular." He concluded by lauding the Navy Ration as it "relieves the soldier, on this, to him, unnatural element, of a deal of care and trouble and affords him great comfort and relaxation at a time he needs it most." On 17 March 1856 he requested "authority to prolong my stay here [in Middletown] till near the close of this month as the duties in Texas will occupy several months and I wish to make some arrangements for my children's schooling before my departure."[124]

---

[123] NARA, RG 94, Letters received by the Adjutant General. Squabbles over brevet rank were troublesome and frequent as noted above in the Mexican-American War chapter, 5.

[124] Letters courtesy NARA.

1856 Department of Texas 31 March–5 September

Galveston	18–19 April 1856
Indianola	21–22 April 1856
Corpus Christi	24–26 April 1856
Fort Brown	2–8 May 1856
Ringgold Barracks	12–14 May 1856
Fort McIntosh	19–23 May 1856
Fort Duncan (Eagle Pass)	28–30 May 1856
Fort Clark	1–3 June 1856
Fort (Camp) Lancaster	9–11 June 1856
Fort Davis	16–20 June 1856
San Antonio (Department HQ)	4–14 July 1856
Fort Mason	17–19 July 1856
Fort McKavett	20–22 July 1856
Fort Chadbourne	27–28 July 1856
Camp Cooper	31 July–1, 2, 3 August 1856
Fort Belknap	4–6 August 1856

While 1855 was not filled with many months away from home on far away inspections, 1856 put Mansfield again into the field, this time to the Department of Texas. Ten years before he had explored the coast of Texas from Corpus Christi down to near the mouth of the Rio Grande as was seen in the previous chapter during his Mexican-American War experience. His two years in Texas and Northern Mexico meant that he was aware of many parts of the country to which he was ordered and one of the posts he was to inspect, Fort Brown, he had intimate knowledge. And three years before in 1853, he inspected posts near Texas so he was well aware of the climate and country he would encounter.[125]

On 14 March 1856 Mansfield wrote to Cooper and reported that he had just received orders from Army headquarters "to proceed to the Department of Texas and make a minute inspection thereof." In a postscript Mansfield asked for a copy of the new Army Regulations. In his companion letter on 14 March to Thomas, Mansfield reported that he received Special Orders No. 15 of the 12th to inspect the Department of Texas and "in a few days [I] shall be able to leave, and will report at Headquarters as I pass thru New York." Mansfield wrote on 31 March to Cooper from Middletown and sent his March report. On the 13th he received orders from the Commanding General to inspect the Department of Texas but he asked permission to remain at home to the end of March "to make some private arrangement." On the 26th he received orders to inspect recruits at Newport, Rhode Island Barracks, on his way to Texas; he left on 31 March for Texas and wrote that "shall report in person as I pass through Washington."[126]

Lieutenant General Scott required Mansfield "to make a minute inspection of the Department of Texas "to 'exhibit the true state and conditions of the commands,' as well as the location of the several posts, and stations, the object they were designed to accomplish, and to what extent thus far the purposes in view have been attained, their distances from each other, the practicability of the routes leading to them, the nature of the country in which they are situated, and to what extent it may be relied on in obtaining supplies; specifying also the nearest settlements, and the number of population capable of bearing arms; what Indian tribes reside in the vicinity, and the number of warriors they could bring into the field, and such other general information as in a military view may be deemed important to be communicated.'"[127]

Mansfield was on duty on this inspection from 31 March to 5 September 1856 and sent his final report to Scott on 27 December 1856 from Middletown, Connecticut. He added his travel time to the actual inspection dates thus spending over five months his inspection of 16 posts. As seen in the map below, this time his travel was easier eliminating the

---

[125] The new Fort Brown he would visit was not the one he designed and built for General Zachary Taylor.

[126] Letters courtesy NARA.

[127] Martin Lalor Crimmins, "Colonel J.K.F. Mansfield's Report of the Inspection of the Department of Texas in 1856," *The Southwestern Historical Quarterly*, vol. 42, July 1938-April 1939, 125. These requirements are similar to his previous inspection requirements, shown above.

weeks required crossing Panama to the Pacific Coast; he took a steamboat from New Orleans to Indianola, Texas. Unlike his New Mexico Territory inspection but similar to his Pacific Coast inspections, he did use rivers for easier transport but he did not write of any adventures similar to the water perils he endured in Oregon and Washington. He took the usual route down the Connecticut River by steamboat to New York City, then by rail to Baltimore, then to Cumberland, Maryland, traveling by coach to another steamer on the Ohio River, then down the Mississippi River to New Orleans. From Cairo, Illinois, on the Ohio River, Mansfield wrote to his wife on 8 April 1856 that he went down the Ohio in the steamer *Tecumseh*, and travelled down river reaching Louisville, Kentucky, and went into a canal. He stayed in a house where the Kentucky Giant lived. Mansfield saw him and said he was seven feet, eight inches tall. On his ride overland from Corpus Christi he must have reminisced about his journey along the same route in 1847 with the now deceased General Taylor. Mansfield also wrote to Thomas in an undated letter in April 1856 from the steamer *Tecumseh* on the Ohio River that he inspected recruits at Newport Barracks on the 25th on his way to Texas. On the 5th he reached Newport Barracks and inspected 40 recruits; he found two or three "rather young for the service" but all were well supplied to reach San Antonio. He noted that he was informed that it was difficult to keep a recruit properly supplied due to much selling of clothes in the neighborhood. He found the recruits "good looking men" and the steamer "unexceptionable in all respects." All embarked on the 5th "and are now at Cairo [Illinois] on the way and myself on board and shall probably reach New Orleans before the close of the month."[128]

Before Mansfield left on his Texas inspection, he took the time on 21 March to write a lengthy commentary "on the subject of ball cartridge firing" concerning an Army circular he received on 15 March 1856. He wrote that the soldier in battle fires his weapon in two ways, fire by volley at command, and "independent file firing which always affords the soldier an opportunity to direct his piece at the object designed to kill, and this is the practice desirable, in as much as a good shot independently, necessarily qualifies the soldier to hit his object readily and fire well by volley." Mansfield left the problems of "scientific principles' such as "time, distance, and winds" to officers. He posits that the object of shooting is "the destruction of an enemy before he can reach you." To accomplish this "it is necessary to be kept constantly in practice. A soldier should be as prompt in shooting an object at say 300 yards as he is at going through the manual and should aim and fire as readily and with as much confidence as he goes through the manual." Mansfield recommended weekly practice with the musket with five rounds "commencing with short ranges and in squads under the direction of the officers until every soldier be a good shot at distances varying from 30 to 700 yards according to the arm of service.....the most proficient [soldiers] should be put forward into advanced squads and others into squads according to their progress." Then once the soldier becomes proficient at this weekly practice he would be excused and only be required to practice monthly. Once squads became skilled in monthly firing, then it need be held only every other month. The only inducement to acquiring shooting skills could be that the "names of the best shot of each squad [be] read out on parade." As will be seen, during Mansfield's post inspections, he usually required the men to fire at targets six feet tall by 22 inches wide generally at 100 yards, and recorded the troops' performance. He found that the troops who were the best target shooters had the most practice, not a surprise to him certainly.[129]

His final report for this Texas inspection tour was similar in format to his two earlier except that he added latitude and longitude data for the posts. He began with an overview of the Department of Texas which "comprises the whole of the State of Texas with the exception of the posts in El Paso County which are attached to the Department of New Mexico." He then discussed the population who were "principally planters and farmers" and he commented that "raising stock" was better fitted than anything else" as the "want of seasonable rains...is a great drawback to the further progress of population toward the Territory of New Mexico." He found that the population was scattered due to the dry

---

[128] The Department commander, Colonel Albert Sydney Johnston, wrote to Mansfield on 10 April 1856 informing him that he would authorize him an escort of two NCO's and 10 privates from the Mounted Riflemen to accompany him from Corpus Christi, and "It will be reinforced or replaced at his [Mansfield's] discretion at any post on his route." On the reverse of a letter to Mansfield from Lieutenant Edward Treacy confirming the escort was written the following inventory: "1 teamster, 1 wagon and 6 mules, 1 tent, 12 horses, 12 revolvers, 6 days for San Antonio, rations to 28 inclusive of April." 12 April letter courtesy of the Middlesex County Historical Society. Next Mansfield wrote to Lorenzo Thomas from Indianola on 22 April 1856 that he arrived yesterday in "Steamer *Louisiana* with 40 recruits under Major [Theophilus H.] Holmes for Fort Clark and will go to Corpus Christi today in the Mail Boat...The Camels have not yet arrived but the quartermaster has a shed and enclosure almost ready for them;" letters courtesy NARA and of the Middlesex County Historical Society. On 24 April Colonel W.W. Chapman wrote to Mansfield and Captain Marcy inviting them to stay with him "at my house during your stay here [Corpus Christi]." Letter courtesy of the Middlesex County Historical Society. Theophilus Hunter Holmes was an 1829 West Point graduate who was brevetted to major during the Mexican-American War. He resigned in 1861 and became a Confederate lieutenant general. He died in 1880.

[129] Letter courtesy NARA.

conditions. He went on to discuss the Indian population stating that "there are nominally no wild Indians. But there are two reservations for friendly Indians made by the State of Texas, one of 8 square leagues [95 square miles] about 15 miles below Fort Belkamp…occupied by five friendly tribes….I visited these tribes…and I have reason to believe they are friendly and well disposed." He also described the "other reservation located on the Clear Fork of the Brazos" of 4 square leagues which consisted of 509 Comanches. He wrote that "they are the wildest of all the friendly tribes" so Camp Cooper was established near their reservation. Mansfield then described "other Indians, wild, inhuman and thievish, numbering 500 to 800 souls" not yet under government control. "All Indians in this Department are treated as enemies unless they show a pass from the Indian Agent." He noted that "the State of Texas set aside another reservation to settle the remaining wild Indians and this "should be done at once." He reported that on the northern border of Texas there are three bands of Indians who send "war parties to commit depredations on both the frontiers of Texas, and New Mexico." On the southern border of Texas along the Rio Grande, he stated "that smuggling is carried on, and bandits of both Indians and Mexicans commit at times depredations." Americans along the river are mostly traders and cannot be relied on to assist the U.S. Government "to preserve order and enforce the laws, and repel the attacks of Bandits, and assist the revenue officers…and to prevent revolutionary parties in armed bodies from crossing into Mexico and then again taking refuge on our own soil."[130]

Mansfield next reviewed each post discussing the "Necessity of the Military Posts and the Suitableness of the Same." He began by stating "that the troops of the Army are indispensable in this Department to protect the peaceable inhabitants, and preserve our neutrality in all revolutionary movements in Mexico for some years to come." He first listed the posts and their types—headquarters, depots, and posts for troops, including temporary camps. He next reviewed each one commenting on their utility: San Antonio, the Department headquarters, was well-located with good roads to other posts. The Indianola Depot was indispensable as it had a good harbor and free navigation to U.S. ports. It also had good "inland water communication with Corpus Christi and with the Town of Matagorda." Indianola readily supplied all posts beyond San Antonio. On the other hand, the Corpus Christi Depot "does not seem of importance." As he knew from his Mexican-American War travels, access to the depot some 30 miles from the coast was solely by lightering due to the bar at the mouth of the bay. It only supplied two posts which could be better supplied by steamer. He concluded that the post was unnecessary. The depot at Brazos Santiago he found indispensable as it is accessible to all vessels coming from the United States and only about nine miles from the mouth of the Rio Grande. Posts at Fort Brown, Ringgold Barracks, Fort McIntosh, Fort Duncan, Fort Clark, Camp Lancaster, and Fort Davis, he determined were also indispensable. Additionally, Forts McKavett, Chadbourne, Belknap and Camp Cooper "constituted a chain across the country which I regard as indispensable for years to come, as protection to the citizens of Texas against the inroads of the savage Indians; and well situated to throw out scouts in pursuit of depredators." Fort Mason however, he regarded "temporary till the Troops there stationed be required in another quarter." Finally, he again recommended as he did in his inspection report of New Mexico in 1853 that a new fort be established about 90 miles below El Paso as "A post here would add very much to the security of the traveler, and no doubt aid the ready transmission of the mail."[131]

---

[130] Crimmins, 125-128.
[131] Crimmins, 128-132. "Lightering" is the practice of loading/unloading ships using large, flat-bottomed boats.

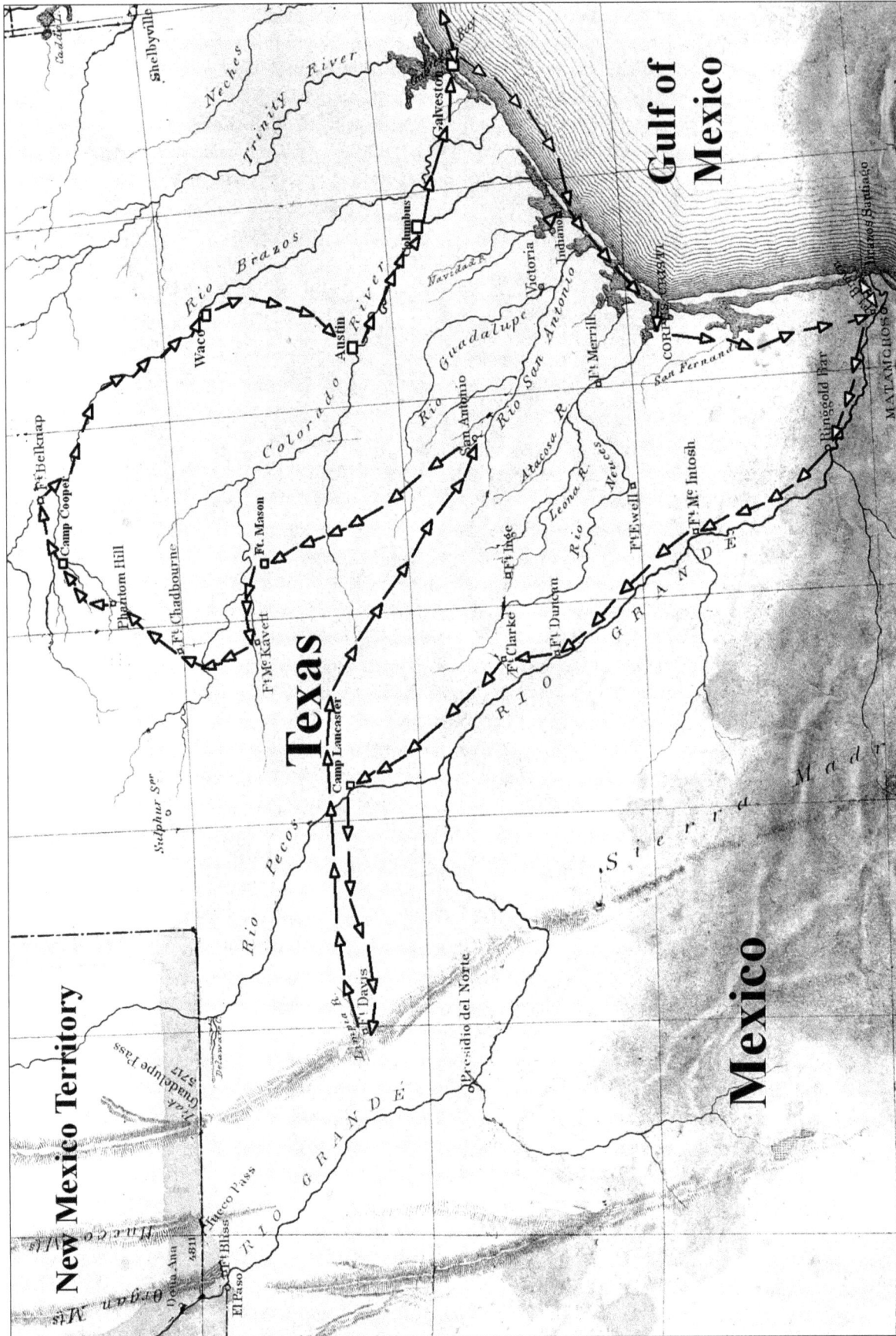

Mansfield began his Texas inspection from Indianola, and then "took the inland water route to Corpus Christi; thence across the prairie to Fort Brown, and followed up the Rio Grande to Fort Duncan [stopping at Ringgold Barracks, Fort McIntosh, and Fort Ewell]; and thence via Forts Clark and Lancaster to Fort Davis." He then rode to San Antonio "thence to Fort Mason, and the western posts [Fort McKavett, Fort Chadbourne, Camp Cooper, and Fort Belkamp]. I then passed down the Brazos [River] to Waco, and struck over to Austin; and thence down the Colorado [River] to Columbus; and thence to Galveston where I took steamer to New Orleans." SHQ 132–133. Map courtesy LOC. Mansfield's started inspecting at Galveston.

Galveston 18–19 April 1856

On 18 and 19 April 1856, Mansfield began his inspection tour at the port of Galveston where his steamship landed on its journey from New Orleans. There he found fellow Engineer, Lieutenant Walter H. Stevens, in charge of building a lighthouse at Aransas Inlet, and Sabine Pass, and repairing a light at Brazos Santiago. Stevens was also placing a beacon to mark the entrance to Galveston Bay and another beacon on a wreck. The busy lieutenant was also in charge of the 9th Light House District and several forts. Mansfield was not able to inspect all of the works and posts because of his steamer's short stay so could only review the engineer's papers. He found Stevens "active, industrious and talented, and is respected by the community here."[132]

Indianola 21–22 April 1856

Mansfield remained on the Gulf Coast as he sailed south and next inspected the depot at Indianola on the 21st and 22nd of April. He noted that the post is 10 miles from San Antonio and 90 water miles from Corpus Christi. He wrote that during the Mexican-American War he surveyed the coast in the area and found that this was a good location for a supply point as it is accessible from U.S. ports. "I regard it as the *principal* and *most important* depot on the Coast of Texas, and it cannot be dispensed with for years to come." He said that there will likely be a railroad completed between here and San Antonio within two years decreasing the cost of transporting goods to the Department headquarters. Captain William K. Van Bokkelen was in charge of the depot and Mansfield found all in order including a large shed which was being built to receive a shipment of camels. Despite the efforts and monies to build the camel shed, higher authority decided to send the beasts to San Antonio where there was better grazing. Mansfield planned on leaving Indianola on the 22nd on the U.S. Mail Boat for Corpus Christi.[133]

Corpus Christi 24–26 April 1856

Mansfield's next stop down the coast was Corpus Christi for three days from the 24th to the 26th of April. He found Major William W. Chapman in charge of this depot. As he already noted he found that this post was not needed. In addition to being a bad location due to the difficulty of getting supplies there from the Gulf of Mexico across the Aransas Bar, Mansfield wrote that it "is no place for a paymaster…to be stationed. It is difficult to get his funds here safely. There are no troops to guard them, and his escorts have to be sent 150 miles on the back track to him, before he can move to pay off." Otherwise books and papers were in order.[134] Mansfield wrote Cooper on 26 April from Corpus Christi, Texas, that he had left Indianola on 22 April "in the Quartermaster's mail boat….the camels had not then arrived, nor had they been heard from. The quartermaster had a shed and enclosure nearly prepared for them." He stated that he would leave Corpus Christi today [20th] "for Brownsville thence expect to proceed via the forts on the Rio Grande to the interior."[135]

---

[132] Crimmins, 143-144. Walter Husted Stevens was an 1848 West Point graduate and was dismissed from the Army in 1861 becoming a Confederate brigadier general; he died in 1867. Mansfield sent his April report to Cooper from Fort Brown on 2 May: 1st to 5th "travelling from my station [Middletown] via Washington City to New Port Barracks where I inspected 40 recruits for Texas. From the 6th to the 13th in descending the Ohio and Mississippi Rivers; from the 14th to the 18th in New Orleans awaiting steamer; from the 18th to the 20th going to and inspecting Galveston and next inspecting the operations of Lieutenant Stevens of the Engineer Corps in Indianola, then to and inspecting from 23rd to the 26th Corpus Christi. Then from the 27th to the end of the month going to Fort Brown arriving 2 May."

[133] Crimmins, 144-146; emphases in the original. William Kemble Van Bokkelen was an 1843 West Point graduate brevetted to first lieutenant during the Mexican-American War; he was cashiered from the service on 8 May 1861 and died in 1907. Letter 22 April 1856 courtesy NARA.

[134] Crimmins, 146-148. William Warren Chapman was an 1837 West Point graduate and received a brevet to major for Buena Vista during the Mexican-American War; he died in 1859 while in service. Mansfield wrote to Samuel Cooper from Corpus Christi on 26 April 1856 that he would leave that day for Brownsville then via the forts and up the Rio Grande to the interior; letter courtesy of the Middlesex County Historical Society. On 22 April 1856, Mansfield wrote Thomas from Indianola that he arrived there on the 21st on the steamer *Louisiana* along with Major Holmes and 45 recruits. He wrote that he would leave for Corpus Christi that day, the 22nd, in the next mail boat. Letter courtesy NARA.

[135] Letter courtesy of the Middlesex County Historical Society.

Fort Brown 2–8 May 1856

Memories must have flooded in as his next visit was to the fort he designed and helped build almost 10 years earlier—Fort Brown. This new Fort Brown however was not the one he remembered as it was entirely different and not on the site of the original. His inspection lasted from 2 May to 8 May. Here he found three companies of the 4th Artillery: K, M, and Light Company B, totaling 7 officers and 87 men, commanded by Major Giles Porter. While the companies drilled well, Mansfield found that equipments especially in the Light Company were in poor condition and the brick stable "too dangerous to keep horses in." He recommended that the Light Company be removed as the ground is "either very dusty or muddy." Additionally there were few Indians in the country and the Mexicans across the Rio Grande in Matamoros are friendly. Records were in good order as were the company drills. He found as he likely remembered from his experience here that "This post is not considered healthy the whole year through. There has been yellow fever here, and in 1853 fifty seven died of that disease." But he did praise the store houses and quarters as "all sufficient and probably the best in Texas." As part of his Fort Brown inspection, he also inspected the post at Brazos Santiago about 40 miles away which he would also have well remembered from his Mexican-American War tour. There he found "a new & good wharf & abundant store houses" with all in good order. Also in good order was a brick magazine containing large numbers of guns, ammunition and powder.[136] From Brownsville on 4 May, Mansfield wrote Cooper that he arrived 2 May and "yesterday the anniversary of the first guns[?] fired from Fort Brown I inspected the troops….all the companies…need recruits very much." The Light Company had only 63 men and not all suitable while Company M had 21 enlisted and Company K, 32.[137]

Ringgold Barracks 12–14 May 1856

From Fort Brown, he journeyed up the Rio Grande by steamboat to Ringgold Barracks which he inspected from 12 to 14 May. This large post under the command of Colonel Carlos A. Wait consisted of Companies B, C, E, G, and K of the 5th Infantry, Company C of the Mounted Rifles, and Company D of the 4th Artillery. B and E Companies had 64 men on a scout led by Captain Caleb Chase Sibley and Lieutenant Edmund Freeman of G Company, 5th Infantry; and C Company had 50 men scouting with Lieutenant Colonel Benjamin S. Roberts and Lieutenant James Wright. The total number of officers assigned to the post was 10 with 380 enlisted men. Mansfield found the command "in a good state of discipline & in fine order." Mansfield only observed three companies in drill as the rest were on a scout while Company K had just returned the night before. He reported that after he left Ringgold Barracks heading northwest, he encountered E Company at Saline about 30 miles above Ringgold, B Company at Las Lajas about 55 miles from Ringgold, and C Company some 70 miles above Ringgold. In the field they appeared to Mansfield to be "efficient and in good discipline." He reported that the men had not been drilled at target firing and bayonet drill but all else was in good order. For the artillery he recommended that a shed be built for it as it was stored only under tarpaulins. Also two company's quarters were limited and miserable as they were partially under canvas and company kitchens were in the open air. But he found that the officers' and noncommissioned officers' were in very good condition compared with the enlisted men's. He also found that the magazine needed repair and that there was too much powder stored some of which should be moved to San Antonio. He also recommended that the guns be removed from the carriages to save wear on them and to store the tubes on other available materials. He found that the doctors were performing well but "This is decidedly a sickly post" so that the men should remain in residence for no more than three years. He found 61 men on the sick list. He determined that an ambulance should be added to the hospital equipment. The post bakery was good as were the library and the gardens that three companies cultivated. The post should be a chaplain post vice Fort Brown and a school would be of benefit. Mansfield also noted that the post sutler was not allowed to sell "spirituous liquors." Mansfield recommended that the quartermaster set up a bank for enlisted men to allow them a place to save money rather that spend it on dissipation. His most important recommendation was that the "number of troops be reduced to one Company of Artillery and one Company of Mounted Infantry, that is to say infantry with saddle mules at

---

[136] Crimmins, 215-220. Major Giles Porter was an 1818 West point graduate and retired in 1861; he died in 1878. Mansfield wrote to Samuel Cooper from Brownsville on 4 May 1856 that he arrived on the 2nd and "all companies need recruits. Light company B has 64 enlisted not all suitable. Company K—32;" letter courtesy of the Middlesex County Historical Society.

[137] Letter courtesy of the Middlesex County Historical Society.

hand ready to mount for a scout after Indians on short notice." This smaller force could more easily be relieved every two years before it became so debilitated to be useless.[138]

Fort McIntosh 19–23 May 1856

His next stop upriver was at Fort McIntosh on the Rio Grande which he inspected from 19 to 23 May. He arrived on horseback as the Rio Grande was not navigable far above Ringgold Barracks. Here he found seven companies under the command of Lieutenant Colonel Daniel Ruggles: Companies D and E of the Mounted Rifles; Company F, 1st Artillery; and Companies A, D, F, and H, 5th Infantry. The aggregate strength of the command was 13 officers and 431 men, the largest post Mansfield would inspect on his Texas tour. Mansfield found the battalion drill good but the rifle companies drilled indifferently and only one third hitting a target at 100 yards during target firing. The 5th Infantry companies drilled well as did the Artillery Company. Company D of the Mounted Rifles had just returned from a 700 mile scout after a band of Lipan Indians, so their horses were hors-de-combat with sore backs. Company E of the Mounted Rifles had on inspection 21 mounted and 17 on foot. Both of these companies suffered from lack of good quarters as they lived in tents and there was no shade for the horses. Mansfield noted that "The thermometer stood at 99 degrees. The suffering of both men and horse was great, yet with quiet submission looking forward to a change for the better....The equipment of these two Mounted Rifle Companies, very much worn and a large part of it worn out." On the other hand, he found Company F, 1st Artillery "in excellent order." The company's camp was just outside of a small field fort built under direction of Major Richard Delafield of the Corps of Engineers and all of the guns and magazine were in excellent order under "Captain [Samuel] Jones who is a highly meritorious and ambitious officer." Mansfield noted that the officers' quarters were "quite limited" and that two officers were building quarters at their own expense yet he opined that it is more important to have the enlisted men in buildings instead of tents "before further buildings be erected for officers." He also wrote that "There is a sutler at this post, and as at other posts is permitted to sell ardent spirits. The regulations forbid the sutler to sell ardent spirits, but the disregard of it is excused on the ground that others would hover around in the vicinity of a post and sell liquor to the men and that it was better for them to obtain it of the sutler. The regulation should either be rescinded or enforced. Beer, cheap wine or cider would be a very good substitute for strong drink and no doubt satisfy all the wants of the men who have been brought up to drink habitually." He found a good bakery but no gardens due to the lack of water so the men "suffer very much from scurvy." He recommended that due to this reason among others which included sickness and no hostile Indians in the vicinity, "no more troops should be kept in this locality than just sufficient to pursue depredators whenever they make their appearance. And I think 3 companies, one of Artillery, one of Cavalry, and one of Infantry mounted on mules ...sufficient."[139]

---

[138] Crimmins, 220-228. Army General Order no. 9 of 23 June 1857 Allowed a liquor ration: "When from excessive fatigue or exposure, the commanding officer may deem it necessary, he may direct the issue of whiskey to the enlisted men of his command, not to exceed a gill per man for each day." A gill is about a quarter of a pint. Colonel Carlos Adolphus Wait, unlike most officers Mansfield encountered, entered Army service directly from civilian life in 1820. He was brevetted to lieutenant colonel and colonel during the Mexican-American War and to brigadier general for long and faithful service in the Army (This promotion to general was not issued.). He was wounded in Mexico and captured by Confederates in 1861; he retired in 1864 and died in 1866. Of the officers he encountered at this post, two would become famous during the Civil War: Lieutenant Colonel Benjamin Stone Roberts and Lieutenant Stephen Dill Lee. Stone was an 1835 West Point graduate and received two brevets during the Mexican-American War to major and lieutenant colonel. During the Civil War he received brevets to colonel, brigadier general, and major general. He became a professor of military science at Yale University and retired from the Army in 1870; he died in 1875. Lee was an 1850 West Point graduate who resigned in 1861 to join the South Carolina Militia. During his eventful career in the Confederate Army, he was promoted to the rank of lieutenant general (temporary). He was wounded twice and captured once and became president of Mississippi A&M College; he died in 1908. A third officer also gained fame in the Civil War, William Woods Averell. He was an 1855 West Point graduate, and brevetted during the Civil War to major, lieutenant colonel, colonel, brigadier general, and major general. He resigned from the Army in 1865 and died in 1900.

[139] Crimmins, 230-239. General Order 47 of 21 September 1849 added to the General Regulations: "Sutlers are not allowed to keep ardent spirits, or other intoxicating drinks, under penalty of losing their situations." General Order No. 7, 11 April 1859, reiterated the regulation about sutlers and spirits: "Instances have come to notice of a departure from the strict meaning of the 208th paragraph of the Regulations, which forbids sutlers to 'keep ardent spirits, or other intoxicating drinks;' but as they may have arisen from misapprehension, the Department has requested a postponement of legal proceedings against such cases, as violations of an act of Congress, until the intention of the regulation should be more fully explained. It is therefore made known, that the prohibition referred to is absolute and admits of no exception; and a violation of it not only subjects the offender to the penalty which the regulation prescribes, but also, within the Indian country, renders him amenable to the act of Congress of the 30th June, 1834, regulating intercourse with the Indian tribes." Lieutenant Colonel Daniel Ruggles was a Massachusetts native who graduated from West Point in 1833. He was brevetted twice during the Mexican-American War to lieutenant colonel but resigned in 1861 becoming a Confederate brigadier general. He died in 1897. Ruggles's successor in command, Captain Randolph Barnes Marcy, was at the post but had not yet taken over due to Mansfield's arrival. Marcy was an 1832 West Point graduate who became the father-in-law of George B. McClellan. During the Civil War, he was brevetted to brigadier and then

Fort Duncan (Eagle Pass) 28–30 May 1856

Off he rode again northwest to visit Fort Duncan also on the Rio Grande which he inspected from the 28th to 30th May. Here he found Lieutenant Colonel Andrew Porter in command of five companies: Companies B and F of the Mounted Rifles; Company C, 1st Artillery; and Companies B and G of the 1st Infantry. The post had seven officers and 349 men on the rolls. Mansfield found the companies and the post "in a good state of discipline" and wrote that Porter was "highly respected and a good commander" but as at other posts, that there was a dearth of officers—six present for five companies. He also reported that the three foot companies drilled "tolerably well" and that target shooting was "much better" than at Fort McIntosh. He was concerned that the horses of the Mounted Rifles had no shade and that much of the equipment was in poor condition "the result of the requisitions for supply not being met." The men were quartered under thatched roofs. The Artillery Company was also under thatched roofs but the quarters were neat. The two companies of the 1st Infantry were in tents and hackales. The hospital and magazine were made of stone but the hospital's kitchen was in a "worthless building." The bakery was good despite a poor oven but Mansfield did not write of a garden—likely due to the hot and dry climate it was impractical. Officers built stone quarters with their own funds. He recommended that since Indians were seldom seen that the force at the post be reduced to three companies—one artillery and two infantry one of which should be mounted on mules. Mansfield's final recommendation was that due to the very hot summer weather, "a light jacket of strong material suitable to wash, be substituted for the soldier's uniform coat at all the posts of this department.[140]

Fort Clark 1–3 June 1856

He then departed and rode to Fort Clark which he inspected for the first three days of June. Here he found Lieutenant Colonel John B. Magruder commanding Light Company I of the 1st Artillery, and Cos. H and I of the Mounted Rifles, totaling six officers and 240 men on the books. Mansfield wrote that many of the troops "were recruits" and the rifle companies were uninstructed so he did not have them drill or fire at targets; many of the "old soldiers" were either on a scout or serving as an escort to the Inspector General (Mansfield). The Artillery Company contained many recruits so even though it was neat, its drill was indifferent; the men were quartered in poor hackales. Colonel Magruder requested that this company which was dismounted in 1851 by order of the Secretary of War Conrad, be remounted. The two Mounted Rifle companies were quartered in "miserable hackales but their horses at least were under shade trees. The hospital was in a log building but a new stone structure was ready for occupancy. Mansfield noted that a good hospital was needed as this post was on the routes from Forts Duncan and San Antonio so travelers would find it helpful. The stone magazine's construction was suspended due to orders but he suggested that it be completed. The post bakery was good and gardens have been planted on the bottomlands. He recommended that officers' quarters be built by the men. He also found that the portable Turnley Houses he found "in a pile" be "sent to some post where stone is not abundant. There is an excellent quarry here and it would be better to put up stone

---

major general. He retired from the Army in 1881 and died in 1887. Captain Samuel Jones, an 1841 West Point graduate, resigned in 1861 becoming a Confederate major general; he died in 1887. Fort McIntosh was a U.S. Army base in Laredo, Webb County, Texas, that existed from 1849 to 1946. Fort McIntosh was established on 3 March 1849 by the 1st Infantry commanded by Lieutenant Egbert Ludovickus Viele to guard Texas at an important crossing point on the Rio Grande. Originally named Camp Crawford, it was renamed Fort McIntosh in 1850 in honor of Colonel James Simmons McIntosh who was mortally wounded at the Battle of Molino del Rey during the Mexican–American War. After the Civil War it was occupied by the Army until it was deactivated in 1946. On 23 May Mansfield wrote to Thomas from Fort McIntosh that he arrived at this post on the 19th and will likely leave on the morrow for Fort Duncan. Letter courtesy NARA.

[140] Crimmins, 240-245. Colonel Porter left West Point after one year as a cadet and resigned from the Army. He reentered during the Mexican-American War and was brevetted twice to lieutenant colonel. During the Civil War he became a brigadier general of volunteers and resigned from the Army in 1864; he died in 1872. "Hackales" ("hackles") an adaptation of "what the Army called hackadales. These were wood frames with canvas sides and roofs;" Ray Miller, *Texas Forts: A History and Guide* (Houston, TX: Cordovan Press, 1985), 88. Fort Duncan was established on 27 March 1849 by Captain Sidney Burbank with Companies A, B, and F 1st Infantry. It was named Fort Duncan for Colonel James Duncan who was brevetted three times during the Mexican-American War to colonel. He died in 1849. It was abandoned initially by Union troops at the beginning of the Civil War and occupied by Confederate volunteers and Texas Rangers. Reoccupied by Federal troops in 1868 the post remained in service until 1883. Mansfield reported to Thomas in his 23 May letter that he arrived at Fort McIntosh on the 19th and would probably leave on the 24th for Fort Duncan. Letter courtesy NARA.

buildings which the soldiers could readily do with but little aid from the department." He found the post to be "healthy and with great harmony among the officers."[141]

The Turnley Houses were a type of prefabricated building which Mansfield did not find useful. He saw these buildings again at Fort Lancaster in his 1860 inspection there. He described them as a "failure" being replaced by adobe buildings. Captain Parmenas Taylor Turnley, West Point class of 1846, completed the design of these structures in November 1854. He wrote that he wished to "devise some kind of convenient and portable shelter, inexpensive, yet superior to the tent. My design consisted of two sizes of cottage, one 30x15 feet, with a movable partition…and another size 40x18 feet….One of the smaller cottages, completed, weighed about 2,000 pounds….the larger one weighed about 3,000 pounds, and could also be transported on one wagon. When unloaded at the place required, it took three men about three hours to erect one, and one additional hour to put on the roof." He convinced the quartermaster-general to "construct twenty of the smaller and ten of the larger" which he had done in Cincinnati. But instead of shipping them to Texas it sent them to Fort Pierre on the upper Missouri River. Apparently some made their way to Texas which Mansfield saw. It is likely that the huts were not well set up by untrained men so they appeared unusable to Mansfield. Turnley constructed two, parallel to one another at Fort Pierre, and lived there comfortably with his wife.[142]

---

[141] Crimmins, 245-251. Major Joseph H. LaMotte established the post in June 1852 with Companies C and E of the 1st Infantry and a detachment of the Mounted Rifles. Initially named Fort Riley after retired General Bennett C. Riley, Riley asked that it be renamed instead for Major John B. Clark who was killed during the Mexican-American War in 1847. The post saw long service but was finally closed in 1946.

[142] Mansfield, *Texas & New Mexico on the Eve of the Civil War: The Mansfield & Johnston Inspections, 1859-1861* (Albuquerque, NM: Univ. of New Mexico Press, 2001), 119. Parmenas Taylor Turnley, Reminiscences of Parmenas Taylor Turnley: *From the Cradle to Three-Score and Ten* (Chicago, IL: Donohue & Henneberry, 1892), 127-129, 169; Thompson 225 n. 47.

Fort Clark

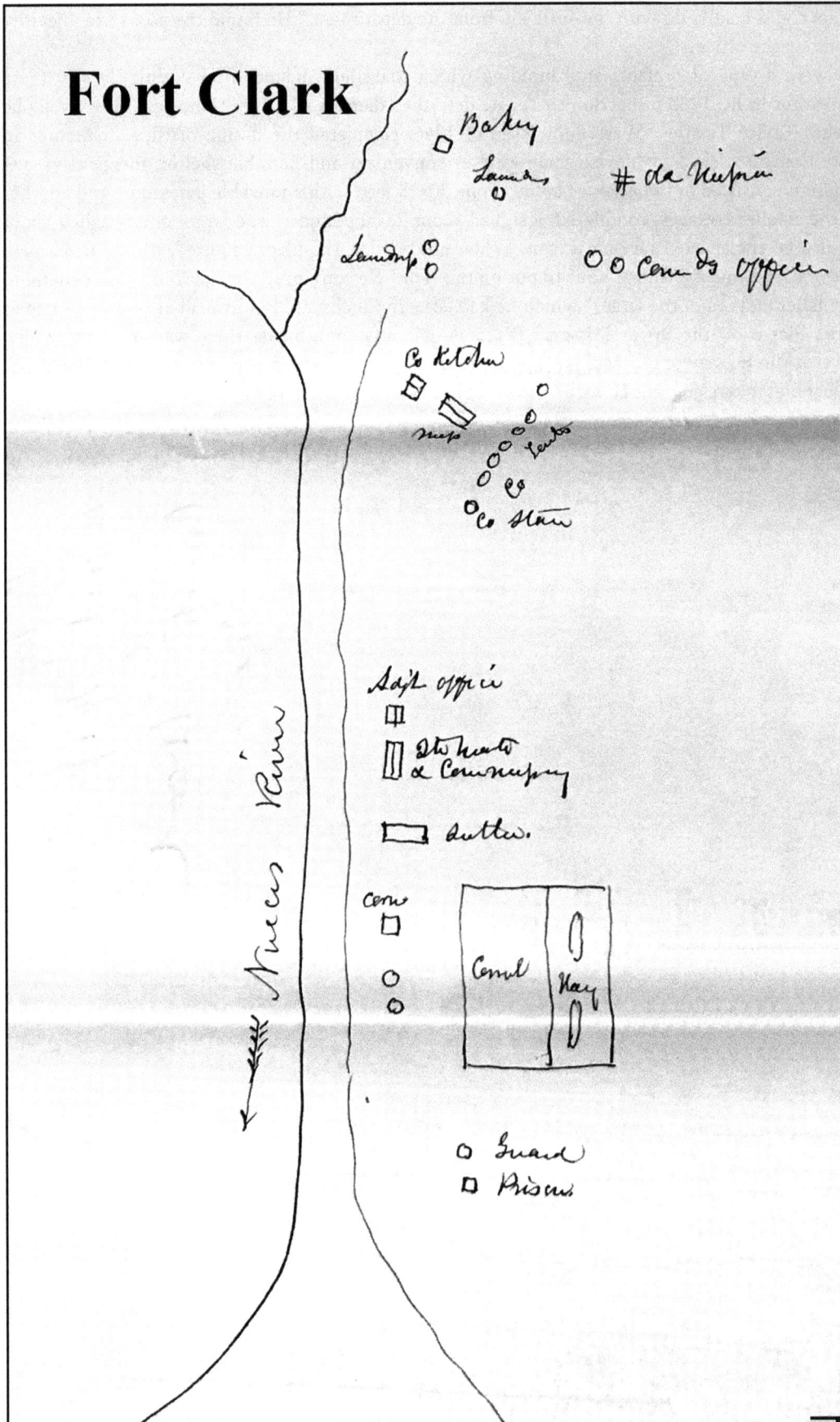

Mansfield's rough sketch of Fort Clark. Courtesy of the Middlesex County Historical Society.

Fort Lancaster in 1861; *Harpers Weekly* 23 March 1861.

Fort (Camp) Lancaster 9–11 June 1856

Mansfield again rode northwest to Camp Lancaster further up the Rio Grande which he inspected on 9 through 11 June. This small post had just two companies of the 1st Infantry and was commanded by Captain Robert S. Granger. Total on the books for the companies was three officers and 150 men and Mansfield found both companies in "excellent order," well-quartered in Turnley portable buildings. As at other posts, the lack of officers on duty affected the quality of the drill although he found that the drill was well done even though about half of the men were recruits. He suggested that "There should be at least 2 Officers present to a Company at all times, to insure proper & efficient instruction to the men....They could not drill as skirmishers, as so many of the men were recruits. Nor could they drill at the bayonet. I dispensed with Target firing for the same reason. All the officers at this post were active, industrious and willing, but the labour of instructing inferior recruits, by the Captain of a Company at the squad drill is great & most of it should fall on subalterns [junior officers—lieutenants]. The non-commissioned officers, in most instances, are not properly qualified. Add to this the labour of building a post in such a locality." Mansfield commented unfavorably on the large number of men in the guardhouse for drunkenness: "I presume the great error is in enlisting confirmed drunkards who desire nothing better than to get drunk & lay in the guardhouse." He also commented on one prisoner who was in the guardhouse for a year awaiting trial which was "hard on the man." Mansfield noted that the post had a "good bakery despite being in a hackale and covered with a canvas" but the gardens would have trouble due to the dry climate. He wrote that "marauding parties of Apaches & Mescaleros...commit depredations & murders [and are] always concealed & difficult to find." He then recounted his personal experience with them after he left Fort Lancaster. Mansfield met Captain Lindsay who was on a scout from his post at Fort Lancaster. On the night after that meeting, Mansfield recalled that a large cow and cattle train bound for New Mexico had passed him and was attacked. When he came up to the train he found it disorganized with one man killed and another wounded so he detached five men from his escort from Camp Lancaster to help them back to Camp Lancaster. In his summation for the Camp, he wrote that it "is well located, being about ½ way between forts Davis and Clark" and the two companies are adequate if they have their officers but "one of them should be mounted on mules...so as to be able to trail Indians after they had committed depredations and follow them up and particularly at this place would the new rifled musket be available, for Indians when running must be reached at a long range, up the mountains etc. or not at all."[143]

---

[143] Crimmins, 251-256. Captain Robert Seamen Granger was an 1838 West Point graduate who was brevetted to major general during the Civil War. He retired from the Army in 1873 as a colonel and died in 1894. Captain Stephen Carpenter established Camp Lancaster on 20 August 1855 with Companies H and K, 1st Infantry. It was redesignated a "fort" in 1856. It may have been named after Captain Carpenter's West Point classmate, Job Roberts Hamilton Lancaster who was killed by lightening in 1841. Camp Lancaster initially used tents then wood frames covered with canvas (hackadales or jacales) followed by Turnley Portable Cottages. Finally more permanent buildings were constructed of stone and adobe. Occupied by Confederate troops during the Civil War, Federal troops reoccupied it after the war and occupied intermittently until it was permanently abandoned by 1874.

Fort Davis 16–20 June 1856

After his encounter with the cattle train, he continued on riding west with the remainder of his escort inspecting Fort Davis from the 16th through the 20th of June. The fort is located 162 miles from Fort Clark and 210 from Fort Bliss in a box canyon. Criticizing the location Mansfield opined that "I look upon all posts in this Indian country, commanded by hills, difficult of access as injudicious; enabling the enemy to choose his time to pick off any man at will. This is a locality for marauding Indians as they cross the country into Mexico and to intercept trains and travelers. They have been known to drive off Government animals in broad daylight and run them over the mountains in spite of the Troops." It is interesting to note that troops on mules cannot catch the Indians but previously Mansfield recommended mules for infantry at posts such as this. This was a much larger post with six companies of the 8th Infantry (A, C, D, F, G, and H) under command of Lieutenant Colonel Washington Seawell. The command totaled eight officers and 415 men. Mansfield noted that on inspection most men lacked caps and some pantaloons but all companies had good discipline, with neat uniforms, and quartered in hackales and tents. However he did note that Company A had no officers present since the senior officers were on assignment and 2nd Lieutenant Zenas R. Bliss who was in command was away on a scout. Mansfield reported that the companies performed well at battalion drill and then the companies drilled independently as skirmishers. Target firing followed but no bayonet drill since the companies never drilled with them. Company D did the best with hitting one out of three targets (33%) even with a musket firing buck and ball cartridges. The post had a good bakery and a partially successful garden depending on rain and a spring. He noted that the post sells supplies to travelers. Mansfield proposed that the post be moved to a location suggested by Colonel Seawell. On 13 July 1856, Mansfield wrote Thomas from San Antonio that he arrived there from Fort Clark and would leave on the 14th for Forts Mason, McKavett, Chadbourne and Belkamp. He also believed that it "will probably take me till the 1st September before I shall be able to leave this Department."[144]

---

[144] Crimmins, 351-357. Fort Davis was established in October 1854 under orders of Major General Persifor Frazer Smith by Colonel Seawell on the San Antonio-El Paso Road located in a box canyon near Limpia Creek on the eastern side of the Davis Mountains and named after Jefferson Davis, who was then the Secretary of War. Lieutenant Colonel Washington Seawell was an 1825 West Point graduate who retired as a colonel in 1862 but continued as a recruiting and enrollment officer through the Civil War. He was awarded a brevet to major for action against the Florida Indians and brigadier general for long and faithful service in the Army. He died in 1888. Lieutenant Zenas Randall Bliss was an 1854 West Point graduate who remained in the Army after the Civil War attaining the rank of major general when he retired in 1897. He was brevetted to major and lieutenant colonel during the Civil War, was a POW, and was awarded the Medal of Honor in 1898 for his actions at the Battle of Fredericksburg 13 December 1862. He died in 1900. Letter courtesy NARA. Mansfield wrote his June monthly report to Cooper on 1 July from a "camp on the Nueces River 32 miles from Fort Clark." On 1 June he reached Fort Clark and finished his inspection there on the 4th and then he was in route westbound. On the 9th he arrived at Camp Lancaster near the Pecos River and finished there on the 12th then was in route to Fort Davis on the 16th, finishing there on the 20th then eastwards to San Antonio. On the 30th he was at Fort Clark and expected to be in San Antonio on the 4th [of July] then journey to the other posts.

Sketch of Fort Davis shown in the lower right distance, *Harper's Weekly,* 16 March 1861, 172. This post was the headquarters of the 8ᵗʰ Infantry and located on the San Antonio and San Diego mail route built in a box canyon. Mansfield criticized its location. It is about 500 miles from San Antonio.

San Antonio (Department Headquarters) 4–14 July 1856

Mansfield then visited the Department Headquarters at San Antonio. During his 10-day visit from 4 to 14 July, he found most of what he examined to be excellent order. He praised the current Department commander, Colonel Albert Sidney Johnston, and his headquarters staff. Mansfield examined all the departments at headquarters: Adjutant General's, Quartermaster's, Commissary, Medical, Ordnance, and Pay, finding all in good and proper order. He did however, find a few items which deserved mention. As he found during his inspection of the Department of New Mexico, spoiled food shipped into the Department was a concern as within a one-year time span, 10 percent of the pork, eight percent of the bacon, 13 percent of the flour, and 21 percent of the bread was condemned. The total condemned was 206 barrels of pork, 23,861 pounds of bacon, 703 barrels of flour, and 60,762 pounds of bread. Not only did the spoilage reduce the amount of food available to be shipped to the posts, the large cost of shipping was an important factor as the spoilage was not usually found until the barrels or boxes were opened at the final destination. Mansfield's opinion was that the foods were not good when they were sent and not spoiled at the posts. He witnessed the opening of 10 barrels of flour at Fort Lancaster of which six or eight were not good. His solution was to inspect all items before they were shipped out from the Department depots to save the cost of transporting useless goods. Further, the items should be marked with the time and place of purchase, and the person who bought the item as well as the time received at a post, and the depot from which received. He added that the rations of coffee and sugar should be increased. In his review of the Medical Department, he agreed with the surgeon that in addition to an increase in the coffee and sugar ration, antiscorbutics should be added to the soldiers' diet to prevent the many cases of scurvy. Mansfield found that the climate was too dry to grow vegetables at the posts. Mansfield was pleased with what he found at the San Antonio Department Headquarters.[145]

He must have been at least somewhat amused by something else he found in San Antonio—camels. The possible use of camels as beasts of burden in the arid southwest was a topic with which Secretary Davis was very interested so Mansfield spent some time in describing what he found with these dromedaries. Mansfield wrote that "Major Henry C. Wayne was in San Antonio in charge of a drove of Camels of 34 in number, as follows: 1 Tunis Camel, a mule; Bactrian Camels, mules; 1 male Booghdee Camel, a mule; 4 Arabian male Camels of burden; 14 Arabian female Camels of burden; 1 Arabian male calf camel; 1 male Senaar Dromedary; 1 female Muscat dromedary; 2 male Siout dromedaries; 4 female Siout dromedaries; 1 male Mt. Sanai dromedary; and 1 female and 1 male calves." Major Wayne employed nine civilians to help with the animals including a clerk, an interpreter, three Arabians, two Turks, and two Americans. The camels were kept at a ranch about 12 miles from San Antonio. Mansfield "inspected these animals, and have no doubt they were designed by the Creator for beasts of burden; but it is impossible to say at this time, before a fair experiment, whether they will be found the best means of transportation for great thoroughfares. They drink once in two days and can carry burden from three to nine hundred pounds, and as their cost of keeping is less than a horse or mule, I doubt not that individuals who live off the frequented routes will find them very convenient and profitable. The hump on the back and the pacing of them as they crouch on the ground makes it very easy to keep in the saddle and to load them." A very favorable report perhaps because Mansfield knew that this was a pet project of Davis.[146]

Mansfield next reported on the 2nd Cavalry which the Department commander, Colonel Albert Sidney Johnston, led. The regiment had 610 men and 474 serviceable horses dispersed into five squadrons located at various posts and other locations. The inspector urged that the regiment "should be filled up with recruits, and the necessary horses furnished, as it is the only mounted regiment in the Department."[147]

Fort Mason 17–19 July 1856

From San Antonio, Mansfield rode 110 miles northwest to Fort Mason which he inspected from 17 to 19 July. Fort Mason was established on 6 July 1851 by Major Hamilton W. Merrill and two companies of the 2nd Dragoons. It was named for Dragoon Lieutenant George T. Mason who was killed in 1846 near Fort Brown during the Mexican-American War. It was abandoned in January 1854 until March 1855 then it was again garrisoned until May 1855, then again abandoned. Finally on 19 January 1856 the post was re-occupied by Colonel Albert Sidney Johnston with three squadrons of the 2nd Cavalry. Johnston was promoted to command of the Department of Texas so the post command devolved upon Captain Edmund Kirby Smith, then Lieutenant Colonel William Joseph Hardee, and finally to Major George Henry Thomas. Second in command of the 2nd Cavalry was Lieutenant Colonel Robert Edward Lee. The fort was permanently abandoned by Federal forces in 1869. Mansfield found Major George H. Thomas in command of the post with three companies of the 2nd Cavalry which Mansfield noted would soon be reduced to two. Total men assigned to the post in the three companies were four officers and 85 men. Mansfield was only able to inspect Company C, as Companies B and G were out on a scout after Indians with Colonel Robert E. Lee. Company C Mansfield "found neat in men and horses" but all its property was packed in preparation for its move to Fort Clark. Company drill was good

---

[145] Crimmins, 133-140. The City of San Antonio was one of the oldest Spanish settlements in Texas having being first settled in 1690. In 1836 the Battle of the Alamo took place at an old Spanish church in San Antonio pitting a small force of Texans against a large Mexican army under General Santa Anna which resulted in the defenders being wiped out. The U.S. annexed Texas in 1845 and by 1860 San Antonio had grown to 15,000 people.

[146] Crimmins, 141-142. Davis was not afraid to try experiments but the use of camels in the desert southwest failed. Davis sent Major Henry C. Wayne to the Middle East to purchase camels in 1855. In 1856, 34 camels arrived in Texas then in the next year 41 more were imported. The new arrivals joined the others at the new camel station, Camp Verde, Texas. They proved very useful more so than mules in the desert, sure-footed and could survive on little water but they proved impracticable. They reportedly frightened horses, mules, and teamsters, even while they could have been an added mode of transport, it is likely that because they were the brainchildren of Davis who became the Confederate President, Union officers and Lincoln's administration took a jaundiced view of the camels no matter their true value. The experiment ended at the end of the Civil War when the 66 camels which could be found were sold in 1866, after an earlier auction held in 1864; Wikipedia, "United States Camel Corps;" Forrest Bryant Johnson, *The Last Camel Charge: The Untold Story of America's Desert Military Experiment* (New York, NY: Berkley Caliber, 2012), 88-112 *passim*; Vince Hawkins, "The U.S. Army's 'Camel Corps' Experiment,'" 16 July 2014, National Museum of the United States Army, https://Armyhistory.org/the-u-s-Armys-camel-corps-experiment/. Mansfield wrote Thomas from San Antonio on 13 July that he arrived there on the 4th from Fort Clark and would leave tomorrow [14 July] for Forts Mason, McKavett, Chadbourne and Belknap. He thought it would take until 1 September before he would be able to leave the department. Letter courtesy NARA.

[147] Crimmins, 142-143.

except for the charge since it was not trained for it while target firing at 100 yards with the new musketoon had only one hit in six (17%), a poor showing. He found the post's buildings sufficient including a bakery but the garden was destroyed because of a drought. He judged the post well located with good water, wood and grazing. Indians consisted of only a few marauding parties which destroy property.[148]

---

[148] Crimmins, 357-361. In January 1857 Mansfield wrote to Secretary of War Davis that "I saw Colonel Lee at Camp Cooper in the clear fork of the Brazos about 40 miles from Fort Belkamp. Of course he was separate from his family and alone. He will make a good cavalry officer if he remains in the service." He also opined that it was a bad idea of Congress to establish a southern military academy in Tennessee; letter courtesy of the Middlesex County Historical Society.

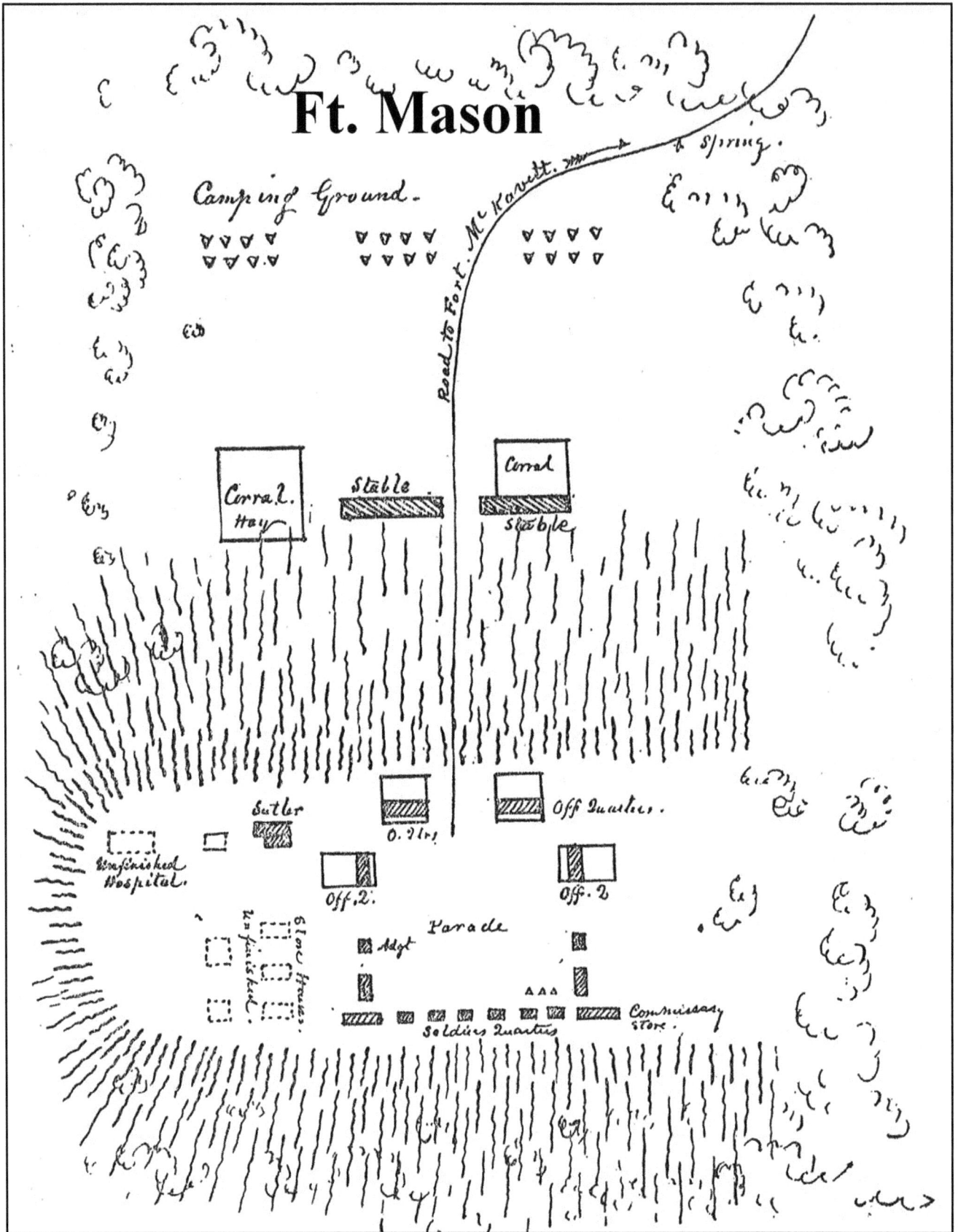

Mansfield's sketch of Fort Mason, courtesy NARA.

Fort McKavett 20–22 July 1856

Fort McKavett, headquarters of the 1st Infantry, Mansfield inspected on 20 through 22 July. At this small post with only Companies C and E of the 1st Infantry commanded by an old West Point classmate, Lieutenant Colonel Henry Bainbridge, Mansfield found an aggregate of five officers and 162 enlisted men. Mansfield found both companies in very good order and quartered in stone buildings with shingles. The bakery however, while producing good bread, was housed in an unsuitable canvas building. At drill Mansfield found both companies "performed tolerably well" although containing many recruits; the companies had not learned skirmisher drill and fired poorly at targets hitting only one out of six (17%). Mansfield recommended that the shoulder scales be abolished and replaced by "some stout and ornamental cloth…which would take the wear of the musket on the shoulder…and would not hinder the free use of the arm so essential in firing and the bayonet exercise." He determined that the post was "important and should be maintained" and the two companies were sufficient especially if they had some mules "on hand to mount men occasionally." The garden was poor due to lack of rain hence cases of scurvy appeared. Overall Mansfield found that the post was "in good discipline and well commanded by Colonel Bainbridge."[149]

---

[149] Crimmins, 361-365. Fort McKavett was established 14 March 1852 originally called Camp San Saba. It was named after Captain Henry McKavett of the 8th Infantry who was killed in 1846 in the Mexican-American War Battle of Monterrey. Five companies of the 8th Infantry were assigned to the post and they began building permanent buildings using local limestone for foundations and mortar with logs used for construction. Mansfield found all quarters and other buildings made of stone during his inspection however. It was permanently abandoned in 1883. Lieutenant Colonel Henry Bainbridge had begun West Point with Mansfield in 1817 but graduated one year before Mansfield in 1821 spending only four years rather than the five Mansfield required to graduate. Bainbridge received two brevets during the Mexican-American War to major and lieutenant colonel and died 31 May 1857 in a steamship fire in Galveston Bay, Texas.

Ft. McKavett

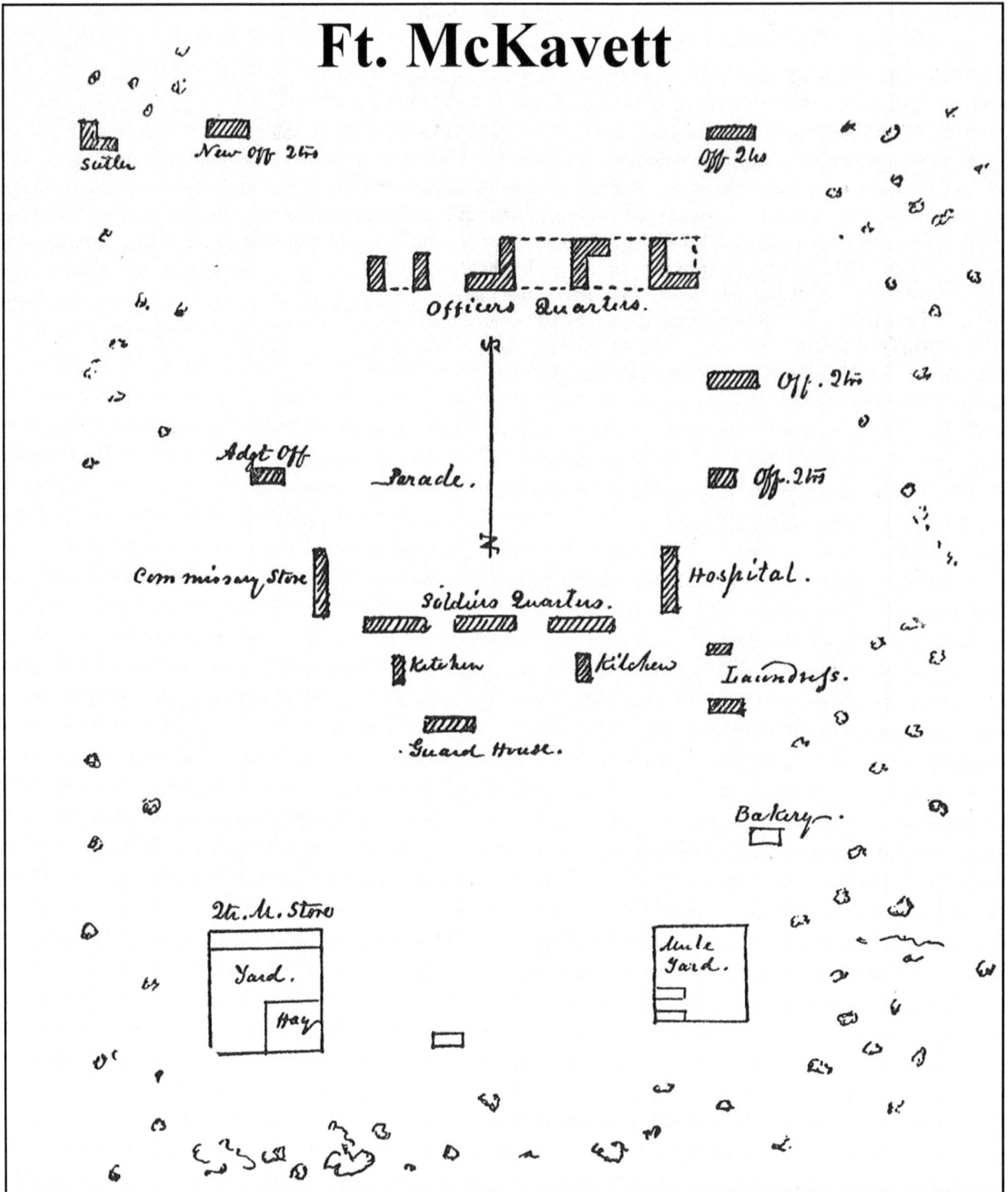

Mansfield's sketch of Fort McKavett, courtesy NARA.

Fort Chadbourne 27–28 July 1856

Mansfield was off again riding north to spend two days at another small post, Fort Chadbourne, which he inspected on 27 and 28 July. Here he found Lieutenant Andrew G. Miller in temporary command of two more companies of the 1st Infantry: D and F; aggregate at the post, 20 officers and 160 enlisted men. As he had noted in his reports of his other inspections, lack of officers was found here as only one of 20 on the books was present. As at Fort McKavett, the buildings were made of stone for the most part but with some canvas roofs but he did note that several other buildings, while adequate, were made of logs also with canvas roofs. Battalion drill showed that the companies did not know skirmisher drill or the bayonet exercise plus Company D hit only one of eight (13%) shots during target shooting, while Company F did better at one of four (25%). There was a good bakery but a poor garden due to lack of rain. He determined that Lieutenant Miller was "a very promising officer" and that the discipline on the post was good. Mansfield stated that here and at some other posts, lumber is scarce, so coffins are "made of pieces of commissary and ordnance boxes and chests." Later in his letter to Colonel Albert Sydney Johnston briefly summarizing his inspection tour, Mansfield wrote that "There is no lumber for coffins and at each of these posts an Officer has been buried in a box made up of gun chests and old bacon boxes and in two instances I was witness to the same description of coffins."[150]

Camp Cooper 31 July – 1–3 August 1856

Camp Cooper to the northeast of Fort Chadbourne was Mansfield's next stop which he inspected from 31 July to 3 August. Here he found four companies: Companies E and K of the 2nd Cavalry, and Companies A and I of the 1st Infantry; the post commander was Lieutenant Colonel Robert E. Lee, a fellow engineer and West Point graduate. Mansfield likely enjoyed talking with a fellow West Pointer, engineer, and Mexican-American War veteran, but certainly had no thoughts that this officer would be in command of the Army he would face on the fateful day at Antietam in September 1862. Aggregate at the post was eight officers and 174 men who included Captain George Stoneman who would lead the Union Cavalry Division at Antietam in 1862. All buildings consisted of tents and the horses on picket ropes but appeared well-grazed and groomed. Mansfield reported that the horses were too young for cavalry service—four to six years old but should be six to eight years. Cavalry drilled at the platoon level well as far as they were instructed but they had not yet learned the complete platoon and squadron drills. The two infantry companies drilled as one due to small sizes and did well. Target firing at 100 yards showed Company E of the cavalry one out of four (25%) and Company K one of three (33%), while Company A of the infantry made one of six (17%) and Company I, one of three (33%). Mansfield thought highly of Lee's command reporting that "The post is very well commanded by Colonel Lee and in good discipline….[but] It labors under the disadvantage of being an open camp in winter and poor water in summer and dry seasons which cut off the crops of summer vegetables." He recommended that once the Indians are settled, the troops at this post should be relocated at Fort Belknap where there are better accommodations. But it turned out that the troops from Fort Belknap were instead relocated to Camp Cooper.[151]

Fort Belknap 4–6 August 1856

Mansfield again rode northeast to Fort Belknap, the furthest north on his tour; he inspected it from 4 to 6 August. Major Gabriel R. Paul commanded Companies A and I of the 7th Infantry with an aggregate of 147 men. Both companies were quartered in stone buildings and were in excellent order. The two companies accomplished the battalion drill but not as skirmishers nor at the bayonet drill. Target firing for both was one hit out of four (25%). There was a good bakery and a large garden which should prove to be productive. Mansfield found the post a good one: "Major Paul has this

---

[150] Crimmins, 365-369, 378. Mansfield noted also that this post had 18 commanders in less than four years. First Lieutenant Andrew Galbraith Miller was an 1848 West Point graduate who became a colonel of the 1st Maryland Cavalry in 1861 and resigned in 1862; he died in 1865. Fort Chadbourne was established 28 October 1852 by Captain John Beardsley and units of the 8th Infantry. It was named in honor of Lieutenant Theodore Chadbourne from the 8th Infantry who was killed in 1846 at the Battle of Resaca de la Palma. It housed a station on the Butterfield Overland Mail Line in 1858. The fort surrendered to Confederate troops in 1861 but was reoccupied in 1865 then abandoned in 1867 to be sporadically reoccupied during the Kiowa and Comanche campaigns. On 1 August 1856 he wrote his July monthly report from Camp Cooper. From July 1 through July 4 he was travelling from Fort Clark to San Antonio; from the 4th to the 13th he inspected there the Department Headquarters. From the 13th to the 18th he travelled to and inspected Fort Mason, and from the 18th to the 23rd, Fort McKavett. Next on the 23rd through the 28th he travelled to and inspected Fort Chadbourne and on the 28th to the 31st he rode to Camp Cooper and planned on staying there a short time apparently to rest after he inspects the post. Monthly report courtesy of the Middlesex County Historical Society.

[151] Crimmins, 369-373. Camp Cooper, established by Lieutenant Colonel William J. Hardee with three companies of the 2nd Cavalry on 3 January 1856, was named for United States Army Adjutant General Samuel Cooper. The post was built to watch over a nearby Indian reservation. It was permanently abandoned at the beginning of the Civil War. Lieutenant Colonel Robert Edward Lee was an 1829 West Point graduate and was brevetted three times to colonel during the Mexican-American War. He resigned from the U.S. Army in 1861 eventually becoming commander of the Confederate Army of Northern Virginia; he died in 1870.

command in good discipline, and has made great and necessary improvements. The quarters of the officers have been built of stone in a new spot and well laid out and officer and men comfortably arranged; and well calculated for two Companies."[152]

In his summary of his inspection tour written to Colonel Albert Sydney Johnston on 18 August 1856, he highlighted a few of his concerns and opinions: "In the course of my inspection I have found the posts in a good state of discipline; and at some of them the troops instructed in every branch of the arm to which they belong. But it is my opinion that the excessive labor in Extra Duty, and on scouts, have prevented that progress in instruction which the officers in command of the different posts have been anxious to bring about. I have also to remark that the Troops have been extremely exposed to the burning sun on the Rio Grande, for instance at McIntosh and Duncan, where they have not been allowed by their own labor to cut posts and make shades and elevate their tents, in as much as the population on that river expect pay for all trees and stakes cut, and your predecessor prohibited any expenditure for the temporary accommodation of the Troops. Horses of the mounted men have been much exposed without shades." As Mansfield knew and experienced, horses as well as troops can suffer from sunburn.[153]

On 6 September 1856, Mansfield sent to Cooper his August report. On the 1st and 2nd of August he inspected Camp Cooper and on the 4th to the 6th travelling to and inspecting Fort Belkamp; on the 7th travelling to the Indian Reservation and visiting Indians there. The remainder of the month he spent travelling to Cairo, Illinois, on the Ohio River in route back east. He reported to the General-in-chief on September 5th when he reached New York but then wrote that "I am now quite unwell but hope to be able to commence the compilation of my report on Monday. His September report written on 5 October from Middletown showed that he spent the first five days of the month getting to Middletown from Texas and the "residue of the month I have been unwell a few days and occupied with the compilation of my report of the inspection of the Department of Texas." Then on 30 October Mansfield wrote to Thomas from Middletown that he was ordered to inspect troops on the 19th of the month—seven detachments of recruits for the 1st and 4th Artillery and five companies of the another five companies of the 4th Artillery and their transport before their departure for Columbus, Ohio. He also inspected 40 recruits for Fort Moultrie on the 5th and on the 15th 135 recruits at Fort Independence in Boston. He reached there on the 17th and inspected transport for the recruits. He found all in good order although he did not see them drill as there was insufficient time.[154]

After Mansfield arrived in Middletown he was ordered to inspect several detachments of recruits and transport for the 1st and 4th Artillery before they left for Columbus and to inspect five companies of the 4th Artillery before they left Fort Independence. In his letter of 30 October 1856 to Thomas, he reported that on the 7th he inspected 80 recruits for Fort Moultrie who were 'fine looking men well provided" with clothing, equipment, and rations. Then on the 8th, Mansfield inspected artillery recruits were also fine looking and well supplied. Next on the 15th he inspected 135 recruits of the 4th Artillery at Fort Independence who "were fine looking men and well provided" and had a neat appearance. From the fort, he went to Boston reaching there on the 17th and on the 18th and inspected the transport for companies which had not yet arrived. The transport was to take five companies to Charlotte Harbour. The five companies finally arrived so Mansfield inspected them on the 20th at Fort Independence; they were "fine in every particular except muskets. It was too late to change them as the ship was laying in the stream." Apparently the men did not have rifled muskets which they should have so Mansfield wrote that they should get them at their destination. He noted that there was no time for drills but for the lack of rifled muskets and the practice with the ball cartridge, most of what he found was good. He ended this report noting that it would have been sent sooner but "in Boston I had an operation performed

---

[152] Crimmins, 373-376. Major Gabriel Rene Paul was an 1834 West Point graduate who received a brevet to major during the Mexican-American War and to brigadier general for his service at the Battle of Gettysburg; he died in 1886. Fort Belknap was established in June 1851 by Captain Carter L. Stevenson at a point chosen by Colonel William G. Belknap, and then was moved two miles for a better water source. The fort was abandoned in 1857 due to poor water supply and the troops transferred to Camp Cooper but was occupied by Confederate troops during the Civil War. U.S. Army troops briefly reoccupied the fort in 1867 but it was finally closed later that year replaced by Forts Griffin and Richardson; Roberts, *Encyclopedia of Historic Forts*, 751-752.

[153] Crimmins, 378. On 6 October 1856 Mansfield wrote to Major Electus Backus from Middletown that he would inspect recruits on the 7th at Fort Columbus, New York. Backus may have been on recruiting duty at this time otherwise it is unclear why he would be involved in asking Mansfield to perform this duty. On a personal note, Mansfield noted that he had a $15 surgery on his eye on 21 October 1856 by Dr. John H. Dix in Boston; letters courtesy of the Middlesex County Historical Society. Dr. Dix was a member of the American Ophthalmological Society and practiced in Boston, Massachusetts; he was born in 1813 and died in 1884. In his 10 October 1856 letter to Thomas Mansfield recommended arming "the troops about to start from Forts Independence and Monroe for Florida with the new pattern rifled musket. If this could be done, it would put that arm at once in trial, and test its qualities in the field, and would be suitable to commence the practice of ball cartridges with." Letter courtesy NARA.

[154] NARA, RG 94, Letters received by the Adjutant General.

on my eye which prevented my writing for several days." On 5 November 1856 Mansfield sent his October report from Middletown. He had been compiling his report for his Texas inspection until he was ordered to go to Columbus to inspect recruits for the 1st and 4th Artillery bound for Forts Moultrie and Monroe. He returned to Middletown on the 8th and then on the 15th was again sent to inspect recruits at Fort Columbus bound for the 4th Artillery at Fort Independence. On the 18th Mansfield journeyed to Fort Independence and inspected the five companies of the 4th Artillery and their transport to convey them to Charlotte Harbour. He returned to Middletown on the 23rd. He again wrote about his eye surgery in Boston but said that "it is now almost entirely well and as soon as practicable complete the compilation of my report of the inspection of the department of Texas which will occupy me at least two weeks if not more."[155]

Perhaps becoming frustrated with interruptions while he was trying to finish his report, he wrote to Cooper on 12 November that "I have to request I may not be ordered on any duty till my report of the inspection of the Department of Texas be completed of which I will duly notify you." In his November report sent to Cooper on 5 December 1856, he wrote that he had spent the month compiling his inspection report but "part of the time I have been unwell. It is all ready to be copied and I shall complete it soon after my return from Philadelphia where I have been ordered to inspect transport and recruits for Indianola on the 10th instant." On 18 December 1856 Mansfield wrote Thomas from Middletown reporting on his inspection of recruits and transport bound for Indianola from Philadelphia. He journeyed there on 12 December and inspected the ship which he found to be excellent with ample supplies on board. On the 16th he inspected 248 recruits who "were quickly inspected by my me and went on board the ship immediately....These recruits were well found with everything necessary to their comfort and were an excellent set of men as to height and personal appearance and I am happy to relay they are entirely free from the influence of intoxicating liquor." He ended his report with some bad personal news: "I would have inspected these recruits at Carlisle but my little son was dangerously ill at that time and I deferred my departure to the latest day. I wrote Colonel May in case I did not reach Carlisle by the time for them to be dispatched that I would do my inspection in Philadelphia." On 31 December 1856 Mansfield sent Cooper his December report stating that he had spent the month completing his Texas inspection report "which I handed in to the Commanding General on the 28th instant." He also noted his trip to Philadelphia from the 12th to the 17th to inspect transport and recruits for Indianola, and from the 28th to the 30th in New York inspecting transport and recruits for Florida.[156]

Thus Mansfield concluded his 1856 inspection tour during which he spent over five months inspecting 16 posts. He sent his final report to Lorenzo Thomas from Middletown 27 December 1856. In his December 1856 monthly report he wrote on the 31st, he said that he had "been engaged at completing my report of the inspection of the Department of Texas which I handed in to the Commanding General on the 28th." He wrote that he had also been to Philadelphia from the 12th to 17th to inspect transport and recruits for Indianola, and from the 28th to the 30th in New York inspecting transport and recruits for Florida. His journeys of hundreds of miles during the hottest months mostly in the desert country of Texas had to be less than pleasant but he registered no complaints other than requesting additional time to complete his report because of his illness. He continued his efforts stressing that the officers and men at the various posts primary mission was their military duties and readiness. Anything which diminished that was addressed ranging from poor equipment and uniforms to lack of vegetables to prevent scurvy and adequate shelter from the sun for both horses and men. Adequate quarters for troops was always a concern for Mansfield over shelter for arms, cannon, and ammunition. Concerns with the poor quality of recruits remained along with spoiled food which he attributed to lack of care of the purchasing officials rather than spoilage in route to the posts or at the posts. He was concerned with drunkenness and desertion and usually recorded numbers of desertions and reasons as he saw them. Numbers of officers actually on duty with their men versus those on the books he emphasized caused poor troop performance as noncommissioned officers could not adequately replace them. He always complemented the commanding officers at the forts and camps and gave special mention to those who made efforts to better accommodate their men by building more

---

[155] NARA, RG 94, Letters received by the Adjutant General.

[156] NARA, RG 94, Letters received by the Adjutant General. Fort Columbus was located on Governors Island in Upper New York Bay. It began life when the island was first fortified during the Revolutionary War and was first named Fort Jay. Fort Jay was rebuilt and enlarged and was renamed Fort Columbus in 1808. It was renamed Fort Jay in 1904 and is still in use albeit by the Coast Guard as the Army left in 1966.

substantial quarters. Many of these officers he would meet again, some as enemies, within a few years beginning in 1861 and some he would face across battlefields in Virginia and Maryland ending with his death at Antietam.[157]

1857–1858 Utah Army and the Mormon War

Mansfield travelled west in 1857 to inspect recruits destined for several units of the Army gathering at Fort Leavenworth prior to their marching to Utah to a possible confrontation with Mormon militia. Mansfield sent a letter to Major Irvin McDowell, Assistant Adjutant General, at Army headquarters in Washington, D.C., on 29 January 1857 from Middletown, acknowledging that he was ordered to inspect recruits for the Army of Utah, and then the forts in the Department of the West which he had begun last year. On 28 February he reported that he planned on leaving Middletown on 3 March to inspect recruits and transport which were leaving for California. Then on 30 June he wrote to Thomas that on 28 June he journeyed to Fort Columbus, New York, and there inspected 130 recruits for the 10th Infantry. He found them in good order and supplied adequately to reach Fort Leavenworth via the Erie Railroad except for a change of shoes. Next on 6 July 1857, Mansfield wrote, still in Middletown, that he had received orders requiring him to "proceed immediately to the Department of the West and inspect in Missouri, Kansas, and Nebraska, etc." He also wrote that he had received instructions on 3 July to inspect General William S. Harney's command which was gathering at Fort Leavenworth. In another letter dated 6 July, he reported his inspection of 4 July of 106 recruits for the 5th Infantry to leave New York. They "were physically unexceptionable and were well provided with clothing and shoes all sufficient to reach Fort Leavenworth." He ended after giving the usual nationality breakdown that he "observed that two or three of them did not understand English promptly when spoken to. I regard this defect as quite important."[158]

On 11 July Mansfield wrote again to Thomas this time from St. Louis and reported that he reached there on the 10th and on the morning of the 11th he visited the Quartermaster, Commissary and Ordnance Departments. He reported that "so far as relates to the command for Utah that one year's supplies for 2,500 men have been forwarded by Major [George G.] Waggaman and in addition 3 months supplies for the same force to be used on the route. The Quartermasters supplies have all been forwarded with the exception of about 193 horses….I shall leave here this afternoon via railroad and steamer for Fort Leavenworth." He noted that shortages for requisitions would probably reach Fort Leavenworth before the end of the month to be ready before the troops leave.[159]

---

[157] NARA, RG 94, Letter received by the Adjutant General. His second 31 December letter detailed his inspection of 294 recruits for the 4th Artillery and 5th Infantry and their transport ship. The ship was "very well found for accommodation, convenience and safety of men." He found "the recruits…fine looking men as a body and well provided" and gave the customary nationality breakdown, here the majority were Irish—120, and Americans 85, composing the largest groups. Letter courtesy NARA.

[158] Letters courtesy NARA. The troops were originally to be led by Harney but affairs in "Bleeding Kansas" forced Harney to remain behind. The troop nationality breakdown was typical, for example, for the Fort Leavenworth group: "36 Americans, 2 English, 56 Irish, 3 scotch, 22 Germans, 5 Prussians, 2 Swiss, 2 Italian, 2 British-American." Mansfield requested 12 months leave of absence on 10 June 1858 but his request was denied by the Secretary of War then, perhaps in response to this request, he was ordered by telegraph on 28 June to report immediately to the Secretary of War in Washington from Middletown apparently to receive his orders to travel to Fort Leavenworth. Letter courtesy of the Middlesex County Historical Society.

[159] Letters courtesy NARA and of the Middlesex County Historical Society. On 15 April he received orders of the 11th to inspect recruits so he inquired of the respective commanders to learn when the recruits would be ready for him. Letter courtesy NARA. Mansfield was still in Middletown as he sent a letter to Secretary of the Navy Isaac Toucey on 27 March 1857 requesting that his nephew, Joseph Wade of Ohio, be appointed a purser in the Navy; letter courtesy of the Middlesex County Historical Society. His 6 July 1857 letter reported his inspection of 106 recruits destined for the 5th Infantry on 4 July in New York. He noted that "about half of these recruits have never been drilled at all" plus he wrote that "two or three of them did not understand English….I regard this defect as quite important." Letter courtesy NARA. Major George G. Waggaman was an 1835 West Point graduate who was brevetted to major during the Mexican-American War. He resigned in 1861 and died in 1884. The Department of the West was created 31 October 1853 from a consolidation of the 7th Military District headquartered at Fort Smith, Arkansas, and parts of Military Departments 5, 6, 8, and 9. It existed to 3 July 1861. It consisted of the country west of the Mississippi River and east of the Rocky Mountains, except Texas south of the 33rd degree north latitude and New Mexico. On 28 February 1857 there was a change which transferred the northern part of Texas to the Department of Texas. Next on 1 January 1858 Utah Territory was transferred to the Department of Utah, and then on 27 March 1858 it changed to consist of the country west of the Mississippi River and east of the Rocky Mountains except Utah, Texas, and New Mexico, and so much of the line of communication as passes through the Territory of Nebraska. Minor changes occurred until 3 July 1861 when the Department of the West was merged into the Western Department. On 4 June 1857 Mansfield wrote to Lieutenant Colonel George W. Lay, Acting Assistant Adjutant General that he is available to serve at a general court martial at Fort Monroe, then on the 6th he replied to orders to so report; he would leave by steamer on the 10th for Fort Monroe. Then in his 9 June letter he asked if the Commanding General wished him to inspect the fort since he would already be there. Finally on 22 June Mansfield had apparently received orders to inspect Fort Monroe while he was there but Mansfield suggested that that not be done since that post's new commander, Colonel Brown, had been only in command a short time so Mansfield opined that he should have "time to get his command arranged to his mind." Letters courtesy NARA. Army General Order 12 of 30 June 1857 order "The 2nd Dragoons, 5th Infantry, and 10th Infantry, as

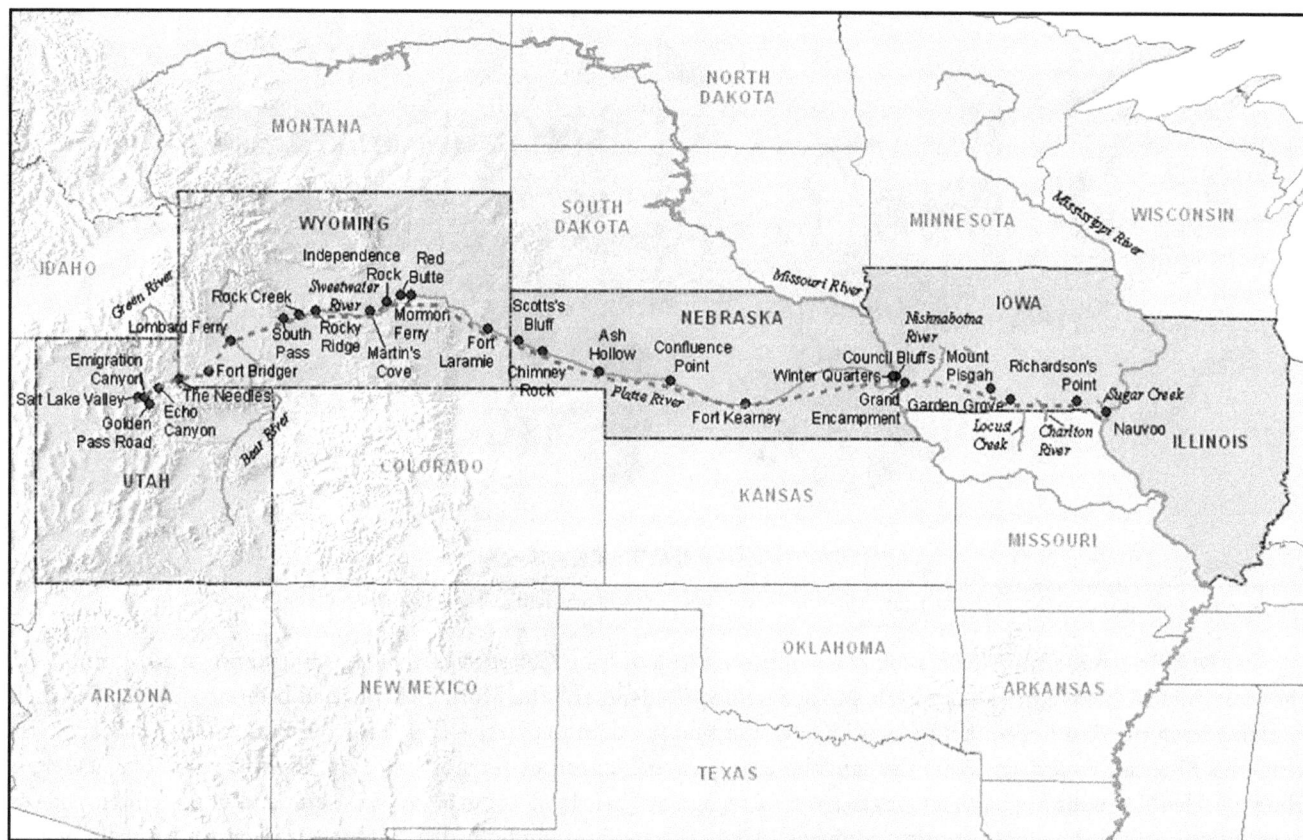

The Mormon Trail from Nauvoo, Illinois to Salt Lake City, Utah, which approximates the route followed by Army troops leaving Fort Leavenworth marching to Salt Lake City. Courtesy Wikipedia.

Finally on 15 July, Mansfield wrote Thomas that he had reached Fort Leavenworth and launched into a discourse upon hearing that Fort Kearney "is to be abandoned or broken up. Under my instructions that post cannot for some time be inspected by me and of course I cannot express an opinion at this time of the importance of that position as a military post in connection with the defence of the frontier and of travelers to Oregon and California. My information is that it should be preserved and maintained for some time to come....It is a very important post" but he confessed that he did not know the grounds which prompted the late Secretary of War to order it broken up. Mansfield also wrote that "The order for the 10th Infantry is out to march on the 17th. I understand on the requisition of Governor [Robert John] Walker the 2nd Dragoons move tomorrow for Lawrence [Kansas]. The 5th Infantry are now here in camp under Colonel [Carlos A.] Wait but the men not healthy, having suffered in Florida for want of vegetables. I know not what object the government has in view at Lawrence, unless it be to prevent the organization of a city government there."[160]

---

they assemble at Fort Leavenworth, will be prepared, with the battery of the 4th Artillery now at that post, to march to, and establish a post at, or near, the Salt Lake City, Territory of Utah. Brevet Brigadier General Harney will command the whole force...but will...retain his present command of the troops in Kansas. On the 1st of January next after the Territory of Utah shall have been entered by the troops, it will constitute a new and separate military department, to be styled the Department of Utah...." Copy of General Order courtesy of the Middlesex County Historical Society.

[160] Letter courtesy NARA. Fort Kearney No. 2 also known as Fort Childs, Fort Gillette, and Fort Mitchell, was located on the south bank of the Platte River established in May 1848 by two companies of Mounted Riflemen under Lieutenant Colonel Ludwell E. Powell of the Oregon Battalion. First known as Fort Childs to honor Major Thomas Childs it became officially Fort Kearney 30 December 1848. It was also known as New Fort Kearney as there was an earlier Fort Kearney on the west bank of the Missouri River near Nebraska City established in May 1846 which was permanently abandoned in May 1848. The newer Fort Kearny also had two supporting earthworks, known as Forts Gillette and Fort Mitchell. It was abandoned on 17 May 1871. Governor Walker was appointed governor of Kansas Territory on 27 May 1857 by President James Buchanan, but resigned 15 December 1857.

OLD FORT KEARNY

Fort Kearney when it was on the line of the Pony Express in 1860 to 1861, by William Henry Jackson, courtesy Wikipedia.

In 1847, Brigham Young led his followers of the Church of Jesus Christ of Latter-day Saints, known as Mormons, to the valley of the Great Salt Lake in Utah. Mexico owned the land and the Mormons who had been hounded out of their settlements in the East hoped that in Utah they would find freedom to practice their religion. But after the United States won the Mexican-American War, the land became part of American territory as part of the Treaty of Guadalupe Hidalgo. The Mormons hoped that Congress would recognize their land as the State of Deseret and not be under Federal control but instead the administration confirmed Utah as a territory and decided to replace Governor Brigham Young with Alfred Cumming. During the 1856 presidential election, polygamy was an issue and after his inauguration in March 1857, the new president, James Buchanan, ordered the Army into Utah's Great Salt Lake Valley. General Winfield Scott decided that an escort of "'not less than 2,500 men'" would accompany him to ensure that there was no trouble for the new governor. Most Americans viewed the Mormons with suspicion because of their unusual religious tenets. United States Army troops began gathering at Fort Leavenworth in May 1857 but none left for Utah Territory until 18 July.

Alfred Cumming, President Buchanan's choice for governor of Utah Territory from 12 April 1858-17 May 1861. Courtesy Wikipedia.

Brigham Young photograph by Charles Roscoe Savage, c. 1855. He was the second president of The Church of Jesus Christ of Latter-day Saints (Mormon Church) from 1847 until his death in 1877. He founded Salt Lake City and he served as the first governor of the Utah Territory from 3 February 1851 to 12 April 1858. Courtesy Wikipedia.

Colonel Edmund B. Alexander led the first troops dispatched to Utah. "About the end of May orders were given that a force, consisting of the 5th and 10th Infantry, the 2nd Dragoons, and a battery of the 4th Artillery, should assemble as soon as possible at Fort Leavenworth. Several reinforcements were sent forward during the year, and in June 1858 there were more than six thousand troops in Utah, or en route for that territory." Mansfield journeyed to Fort Leavenworth arriving on 13 July 1857 to inspect troops gathering there. Brigadier General William S. Harney was the commander of the troops but he was ordered back to Kansas to address issues arising from fighting between proslavery and free soil advocates. He retained the 2nd Dragoons to help maintain the peace in "Bloody Kansas." On 19 July 1857 Mansfield wrote from Leavenworth that the 10th Infantry marched on the 18th and "probably made 3 miles to Salt Creek." He inspected Phelps Battery on the 18th and said that "it will march this afternoon and probably make 3 miles." He also inspected the 5th Infantry on the 19th and believed that it would march on the 20th. The Dragoons remained at Lawrence under the Governor's direction but Captain Reno with "his Artillery Park of 4 guns 12 pdrs. and 2 howitzers 32 pdrs. are here [Fort Leavenworth]." He also referenced his orders: "I have to state that I see at present no difficulty in the way of complying therewith in all respects unless the lateness of the season, and the want of escort to reach Fort Laramie should make it impracticable for me to reach that place. In that event as it is on the route to Utah, it could well be inspected at that time an inspection, a year or two hence, may be necessary in Utah. I therefore have to request of the Commanding General some discretion relative to that point. As soon as the 5th Infantry will have marched I will make out my report relative to the three commands." On the 20th Mansfield again wrote that Phelps's Battery left on the afternoon of the 19th but the 5th Infantry had to defer its departure as Mansfield was not able to inspect it soon enough to allow it to march. He noted that "The regiment is much reduced by desertion, and many sick, and two of the officers sick with the scurvy. The General has ordered vegetables for this Regiment." Mansfield did not feel that the regiment was ready to march until the 40 recruits arrived and a full complement of officers was on site. Also on 20 July, Mansfield composed a letter which concerned the Medical Director of the Army of Utah, Surgeon W. Mills. The problem concerned an invoice for 336 boxes of supplies and other medical stores. An accurate inventory was required so that medical personnel would know which box had needed supplies to avoid opening many, looking for specific items. Mansfield opined that the Quartermaster should be furnished with a complete inventory so that boxes needed could be sent when required without requiring the presence of the medical officer. On 23 July Mansfield wrote that the 5th Infantry left Fort Leavenworth on 23 July and like other departing units he wrote that it "probably made about 3 miles." He also wrote that the 40 recruits arrived "and will probably join the march with Captain Reno of the ordnance with the pack Battery, etc. A telegraph dispatch dated 17th from the Secretary of War reached General Kearney requiring him to remain here with the 2nd Dragoons and Phelps's Battery till further orders. Phelps's Battery had previously marched and I trust it will be permitted to proceed."[161]

Colonel Edmund Brooke Alexander was an 1823 West Point graduate and likely knew Mansfield at the Academy as Mansfield had graduated in 1822. He was brevetted to major and lieutenant colonel during the Mexican-American War and during the Civil War he served at Fort Laramie and then in St. Louis as Acting Assistant Provost Marshal General, Superintendent of Volunteer Recruiting Service, and Chief Mustering and Disbursing Officer for the State of Missouri. He was brevetted to brigadier general during the Civil War and retired from the Army in 1868; he died in 1888; courtesy Wikipedia.

---

161 Letters courtesy NARA.

Mansfield's second letter to Thomas on the 24th reported his inspection of the 10th Infantry of the Army of Utah on the 17th and it marched on the 18th at 5 p.m. He inspected eight companies and staff with Colonel Edmund B. Alexander in command. He discussed each company and listed numbers present and aggregate then gave the total for the regiment present: Field and Staff: five officers and 15 enlisted men; eight companies with 18 officers and 585 enlisted men; total of 23 officers and 601 enlisted. "Of the 48 men absent without leave 7/8 may be put down as deserted." He also reviewed arms and equipment finding a deficiency in bayonets to be remedied. He determined that "The Regiment is well armed and equipped and found in every aspect essential to the march to Utah." He also detailed the 88 six-mule wagons for the regiment which carried among other things 25 days rations sufficient to reach Fort Kearney. There were also two ambulances and one travelling forge with four horses each; about 35 head of cattle accompanied the train. He noted that many recruits in the ranks "had not been instructed at all, and of course at this particular time under such circumstances, when men were falling from the excessive heat, no drill was attempted. And I can say nothing as to the proficiency of the Regiment. I will however remark that I dislike the rifle and sword bayonet, and trust it will eventually give place to the new model musket." He also found that there were 40 prisoners at the guard tent and that the regiment's books and records were in good order. After detailing desertions in 1855 and 1856 by company (491 total in the last three years for all companies), he noted that when the regiment marched, "Lieutenant Colonel and Brevet Colonel Charles F. [Ferguson] Smith was ordered by Genl. Harney to remain at these Headquarters till further order for reasons I am not acquainted with." Mansfield saw no problem with the regiment reaching Fort Kearny and then be resupplied at Fort Laramie sufficient "to reach Salt Lake some 600 miles further." In his 25 July letter he reported that he forwarded his inspection of Phelps's Battery and that on the 26th he would mail his inspection report of the 5th Infantry. He also noted that about seven companies of the 2nd Dragoons were at Lawrence, Kansas, camped under Lieutenant Colonel Cooke along with the Governor. "I trust there will be no trouble with the citizens."[162]

OLD FORT LARAMIE.

Fort Laramie when it was on the line of the Pony Express in 1860 to 1861, by William Henry Jackson, courtesy Wikipedia

Mansfield sent to Thomas on 25 July 1857 his full report of his 18 July inspection of "the Light Company B, 4th Artillery, commanded by Captain J.W. [John Wolcott] Phelps which marched as part of the Army of Utah on the next day the 19th instant at 6 p.m." The company had an aggregate of three officers and 70 men "after leaving 3 sick with broken and bruised limbs in the hospital at Fort Leavenworth. Twenty seven of these men are new recruits." There were 58 men fit for duty. Mansfield noted that there was no farrier but rather a citizen was employed. The battery had four six pounder brass guns; two 12 pounder howitzers, with six caissons, two battery wagons, one travelling forge—all new and complete—with new harness and implements." He found adequate ammunition and that the men of the battery

---

[162] Letters courtesy NARA. In his first 24 July letter he enclosed his inspection report of the 10th Infantry and said that he would forward those for Phelps's Battery and the 5th Infantry when he wrote them.

were well supplied. As with his prior inspection of the infantry, he found the troops with 25 days rations sufficient to reach Fort Laramie, then resupplied sufficient to reach Salt Lake City. He found no foreseen issues which would prevent the company from a successful march. The company's train of 16 wagons and one ambulance was followed by a drove of 10 beef cattle. He was not able to drill the company due to the limited time and the large number of new recruits but he did note that there were insufficient officers and he strongly urged that two lieutenants be detailed "immediately" to march to the company "in time to go on with the General or the Governor. The 38 recruits for the battery are needed and they would leave with Captain Reno to join it when the battery reached its destination." He ended the letter with a comment on uniforms: "I have to remark in justice to the recruits, that they should be sent from the depot with the uniform of the Corps for which they are designed or in fatigue dress—those last sent to this battery were subjected to the expense of a change."[163]

His letter of the 26th informed Thomas that he included the inspection report of the 5th Infantry which departed Fort Leavenworth on the 23rd accompanied by the paymaster and the medical director. He also reported that the park of artillery is expected to leave on the 27th and he will forward his report of that inspection. Mansfield's letter dated 25 July gave Thomas details of the inspection of the 5th Infantry on the 22nd of July 1857; Mansfield noted that it marched the next day. [Mansfield corrected these dates in his 31 July letter to Thomas: Mansfield inspected the 5th Infantry on the 21st and it marched on the 22nd of July.] Brevet Colonel Wait commanded the regiment as Colonel Gustavus Loomis was absent in command of the Department of Florida. After noting the structure of the staff, and the officers and men present or not, he described in detail similar compositions of the 10 Companies A, B, C, D, E, F, G, H, I, and K: total available of 17 officers and 521 enlisted men and an assistant surgeon; the Field and Staff had three officers and 17 enlisted men. He noted 125 men absent without leave "7/8 may be regarded as deserters." The troops were armed with rifled muskets and new equipments, 82 for each company, with 20 rounds of ammunition per man with 2,000 rounds in bulk to each company. He noted that the rifle was fired with caps or the Maynard primer but he opined that "the gun is a little too light for such weight of ball, and therefore unless held properly might hurt [the shooter]...by the recoil. In other respects it is far superior to the rifle with the sword bayonet." He also reported that "This Regiment was well supplied with everything essential to the service, and comfort of the men" which included tools, clothing, tents, cooking items, but given the weight of items for each man, some 30 pounds, they were carried in the baggage wagons. "The Regiment was well and amply supplied with all the necessaries to a long march" which included 25 days rations corn for each animal which would allow the column to reach "Fort Kearney where it will be replenished with 25 days further supplies to Fort Laramie thence it will receive suitable supplies already forwarded to that point, in concert with the other divisions of the Army of Utah to Salt Lake City. I can see no obstacle to its reaching its destination before severe cold weather." He also reported that the paymaster marched with the regiment carrying almost $350,000. He noted that the transportation of the command was ample with "5 wagons...allowed for the field and staff and band; 4 to each company; 2 to the Hospital; 10 to the transportation of the sick with 2 ambulances." The train consisted of 109 wagons with six mules each and two ambulances and a travelling forge of four mules each followed by a drove of cattle. He also noted that the regiment had 71 sick men, 11 of which had severe scurvy; they were ordered left in the Fort Leavenworth Hospital. "I will here remark that on the arrival of this Regiment at this post, Genl. Harney ordered vegetables to be issued to it, and it takes with it, 6,000 rations of mixed desiccated cabbage, carrots, turnips and potatoes, and 2,500 rations of desiccated potatoes." He found that the regiment had "a good band." Mansfield wrote that "No attempt whatever was made to drill, the number of new recruits, and the want of time in the preparation for the march forbid it. I must remark here, there is a want of officers to the Regiment only one field officer—and with 7 companies but one available officer to each. This does not promise a very rapid progress in drills, and instruction. The duties of the officers present with so many recruits and so few old soldiers are excessive. The Regiment must suffer under such circumstances."[164]

The very busy Mansfield next wrote on the 27th July 1857 to Thomas from Fort Leavenworth with his report of the inspection of the "Park of Artillery under Captain Reno of the ordnance which has taken up its line of march for Salt

---

[163] Letters courtesy NARA.
[164] Letters courtesy NARA. Men available in the aggregate was the total number of men present for duty, and others on the rolls but not present for duty which included men detached on other assignments, absent sick, absent without leave, confined, etc. Mansfield in his "aggregate" numbers included all enlisted men available for duty or not but only officers present available for duty. Colonel Gustavus Loomis was a long-serving officer having graduated from West Point in 1811. He received a brevet promotion to brigadier general in 1865 for long and faithful service in the Army. He retired in June 1863 and died in 1872.

Lake City. The 7 Companies of the 2nd Dragoons are still in camp near Lawrence, and as far as I can learn all is peaceable in that quarter. Governor Walker is encamped with them. I shall immediately commence the inspections of forts in this Department. I shall take the first opportunity to go to Fort Randall as it is difficult of access. I have not yet inspected this post [Fort Leavenworth] and do not know that I shall for the present." In his second letter dated the 27th, he reported "to the General in Chief, that today the last detachment of the Army of Utah marched under the orders of 1st Lieutenant and Brevet Captain J.L. Reno of the ordnance." Reno had the "command of the Park of Artillery and ordnance supplies which consisted of 4 brass 12 pounder guns and 2 brass 32 pounder howitzers with 6 corresponding caissons, 1 battery wagon, 1 travelling forge with 474 rounds of fixed assorted ammunition in the caissons. And in wagons 20,000 elongated ball cartridges for muskets of 69 caliber; 10,000 elongated ball cartridges of caliber 58, and 30,000 of caliber 54; 25,000 Sharps rifle carbine cartridges; 30,000 Colts Dragoon pistols; 20,000 Colts navy size pistols; 300,000 Maynard primers; 5,000 friction tubes; 11 Sharps Carbines; 48 Colts Navy size pistols...." After numbering further ammunition and other ordnance items he wrote "I believe there is nothing in the Ordnance Department of this Army that will be found deficient." Captain Reno's force consisted of 37 recruits, 11 enlisted men of the Ordnance Corps, citizen drivers furnished by the Quartermaster Department, and 97 horses. Reno was accompanied by a post surgeon with required equipment. Reno's wagon train consisted "of 12 wagons with ordnance supplies; 3 with camp equipage; 1 with hospital supplies, each of 6 mules and 1 ambulance for the sick of 4 mules. Lieutenant J.[ohn] Green, 2nd Dragoons, was ordered to march with him, and take 58 recruits and 65 horses, etc., to Companies E and H of the 2nd Dragoons at Fort Laramie, and he successfully left today with 57 recruits and 65 horses, etc., with 3 wagons with forage and 3 with camp equipage and baggage." Mansfield found Reno, an 1842 West Point graduate, twice brevetted during the Mexican-American War, an excellent officer: "Captain Reno has shown great energy and activity since he has been assigned to this Army, and I doubt not that he will conduct the pack of Artillery...safely to its destination." Military store keeper S.U. Montgomery also marched with Reno and a wagon was assigned to him. Reno's whole command had 39 wagons of six mules each and one ambulance of four mules followed by a drove of 12 head of cattle. He finally noted that Captain John H. Dickerson, Assistant Quartermaster, was appointed by General Kearney to duty with the Army of Utah and had marched accompanied by Captain Henry Francis Clark, Commissary of Subsistence. Dickerson took with him stragglers of the 5th and 10th Regiments and when they overtake the 5th Infantry which already left, the two officers will get an escort and continue on to Fort Kearney so they took seven, six-mule wagons with extra horses and mules. He closed his letter and stated that he finished his inspection of the Army of Utah: "I can see no obstacle to the detachments reaching their final destination, Salt Lake City, before very cold weather. The distance from Fort Leavenworth to Fort Kearney is about 294 miles; from Kearney to Laramie about 330 miles; from Laramie to Fort Bridger 397 miles; from Fort Bridger to Salt Lake City 113 miles; in the aggregate say 1,150 miles which will probably require 85 days...till about the close of October next." He further wrote that General Harney's guide, Captain Bridger, told him that the cold at Salt Lake City is not severe and that snow seldom exceeded 12 inches and melted quickly so that animals could graze. It being a farming region so wheat, potatoes, and oats grow without irrigation. He finished his letter by saying that he did not know when General Harney would leave Fort Leavenworth because he was awaiting orders from the Secretary of War.[165]

On 28 July 1857 Mansfield wrote General Harney from Fort Leavenworth summarizing his inspection of "the 4 Divisions of the Army of Utah under your command which have marched. My inspection has been chiefly with a view to their armament and outfit and efficiency, rather than uniform, drill and instruction." Mansfield then wrote that he would confine his remarks to a "few leading facts." He first discussed the Quartermaster Department which forwarded via Fort Laramie eight months supplies for 2,500 men "which is equivalent to one year's supply for 1,600 men." He noted that probably another 2,500 rations will also be sent to Fort Laramie "thus showing ample supplies of rations." He next wrote that "the 10th Infantry marched on the 18th instant with a field and staff of 5 officers and 16 men and eight companies of 18 officers and 601 men." He then reviewed their arms and the regimental wagon train with an ending note that "the Regiment was well supplied with clothes for the march." He next reviewed Phelps's Battery with

---

[165] Letters courtesy NARA. Fort Bridger located on Blacks Fork of the Green River, Wyoming, was originally built by Jim Bridger as a trading post in 1842. After he abandoned it the Mormons rebuilt it in 1855 and then burned it in 1857 at the start of the Mormon War. Colonel Albert S. Johnston designated it as an Army post on 7 June 1858, when he left it for Salt Lake City. It became an important post on the Overland Trail and a supply depot for the Army. It was finally abandoned on 6 November 1890. Captain John H. Dickerson was an 1847 West Point graduate and received a brevet promotion to major in 1865. He resigned in 1864 and died in 1872. Captain Henry Francis Clark was an 1843 West Point graduate and was brevetted to captain during the Mexican-American War and to colonel, brigadier general and major general during the Civil War. He retired in 1884 and died in 1887.

marched on the 19th "with 3 officers and 70 men, 1 assistant surgeon and 100 horses, 4 guns, 2 howitzers, 6 caissons, 2 battery wagons, 1 travelling forge of 6 horses each, with 556 rounds of assorted shot in the caissons and well supplied with clothes, etc., for the march." After reviewing the command's train he summarized: "In the aggregate 16 wagons, 1 ambulance and a drove of 10 beef cattle." Next was the 5th Infantry which marched on the 22nd with a "field and staff of 3 officers and 17 men and of 10 companies, 14 officers and 504 men available." As with the 10th Infantry, he reviewed their arms and ammunition and detailed the regiment's train which consisted of 47 wagons for baggage, 10 for transportation of sick, 30 for subsistence for 25 days, 10 with forage for animals, 10 with Quartermaster's supplies, 2 with Paymasters money and baggage, 2 ambulances, 1 travelling forge, in the aggregate 109 wagons of six mules each and two ambulances and one travelling forge of four mules each and a drove of 30 head of cattle. Mansfield then reviewed Captain Reno's ordnance park which marched on the 26th with four brass 12 pounders and two brass 32 pounder howitzers with six caissons, one battery wagon, one travelling forge, with suitable ordnance supplies. "The force consisted of 37 recruits..., 11 enlisted ordnance men, 14 citizen drivers from the Quartermaster's Department and he had 97 horses." Reno's train was accompanied by 57 recruits and 65 horses for the 2nd Dragoons at Fort Laramie. The train consisted of 39 wagons and 12 beef cattle. Finally, Captain Dickenson, Assistant Quartermaster and Captain Clark, Commissary, left on the 27th accompanied by a train of six wagons, two extra horses and three extra mules. "Total force of the Army of Utah exclusive of the 2nd Dragoons and sundry staff officer at date: 45 officers, 1,256 available enlisted men, 259 wagons of 6 mules each, 5 ambulances, 2 travelling forges, besides those of the batteries and 197 horses to the artillery. As to the instruction of the troops in their respective arms, I must say I fear they are very deficient. There are many recruits that do not know how to handle their guns properly, and there is a decided deficiency of officers, particularly of the 5th infantry and Phelps Battery. To 7 companies of the 5th Infantry there was but one officer to the company available; to 2 others but 2 officers and but one company with 3 officers when Captain [Thomas H.] Neill will have joined; 5 companies out of the 10 were commanded by 3 first lieutenants and 2 by 2nd lieutenants. Your command will labor under great disadvantage, if brought into action before properly instructed and drilled to the use of their arms and maneuvering in the field."[166]

Mansfield wrote a specific letter concerning desertions to Thomas on 29 July. This situation merited a detailed explanation of desertions which take place "in bringing recruits from the east to this post [Fort Leavenworth]." Mansfield detailed specific numbers lost usually starting at the beginning of the trip but the majority at the various landings on the Missouri River, e.g., "Captain D.L.F. Jones 4th Inf. Lost 22 by desertions—4 at St. Louis, and 18 on the Missouri River at the different landings. Captain Duncan of the Rifles lost 7 on the Missouri River." And he wrote that they continued to desert after reaching Fort Leavenworth because of the proximity of towns above and below Fort Leavenworth as well as the many steamers on the river. Mansfield recommended that before recruits left the recruiting depot, that they be "made good soldiers before leaving, and then not paid off till they reach their destination, and are made acquainted with the service, there would be much less desertion. The recruits are tampered with by the deck hands of the steamers, and the service misrepresented; and they take every opportunity to jump ashore just as the boats leave the landings....This is all the result of a want of suitable training, before leaving the depots in consequence of the want of time to make soldiers of them. The 10th and 5th Infantry and Phillips Battery and Reno's Park of Artillery left with many raw recruits, some did not know how to handle their guns, and I doubt not never fired a musket with a ball cartridge, which should be one of the first things taught them at the depot." In his 3 August 1857 letter to Thomas, he noted that he enclosed a copy of his inspection of the Army of Utah which he had sent to General Harney on the 28th. He included notice that orders were sent to four companies of the 1st Cavalry and four of the 6th Infantry in the field to rendezvous at Fort Laramie and then march to Utah. He concluded by informing the Assistant Adjutant General that he would "probably leave tomorrow on the Steamer *Omaha* as she comes along for Fort Randall."[167]

---

[166] Letters courtesy NARA.

[167] Letters courtesy NARA. Mansfield's letter to General Harney of the 28th gave details for each unit that Mansfield had previously inspected as noted in his letters above to Thomas. He told Harney that these inspections were done with the view of the troop's readiness for duty rather than for "uniform, drill, and instruction." He concentrated on "their armament and outfit and efficiency." In summary, the Army of Utah, exclusive of the 2nd Dragoons and sundry staff officers was composed of 45 officers and 1,256 men available for duty with 259 wagons of six mules each, five ambulance, two travelling forges, besides those of the batteries and 197 horses to the artillery. Captain De Lancey Floyd-Jones was an 1846 West Point graduate who was brevetted to first lieutenant during the Mexican-American War, and lieutenant colonel, colonel, and brigadier general during the Civil War. He retired as a colonel in 1879 and died in 1902. War Department General Order No. 12 of 29 August 1857 assigned Colonel Johnston of the 2nd Cavalry to command the Utah expedition since it was "deemed inadvisable to detach Brevet Brigadier General Harney from service in Kansas....Harney will...detach six companies of the 2nd Dragoons to escort the civil officers of Utah on their mission, and remain attached to the

The first detachment of the Utah Expedition left Fort Leavenworth on 18 July 1857 "with 500 men, 97 wagons, and 600 hundred animals under the command of Colonel Edmund B. Alexander, the elderly commander of the 10th Infantry." Unfortunately this force had no dragoons. The Mormons readied for this Federal force by sending Mormon troopers to harry the column under these orders: "On ascertaining the locality or route of the troops, proceed at once to annoy them in every possible way. Use every exertion to stampede their animals and set fire to their trains. Burn the whole country before them and on their flanks. Keep them from sleeping, by night surprises; blockade the road by felling trees or destroying the river fords where you can. Watch for opportunities to set fire to the grass on their windward, so as, if possible, to envelop their trains. Leave no grass before them that can be burned. Keep your men concealed as much as possible, and guard against surprise." So even though the U.S. troops supposedly had "two thousand head of beef cattle, together with a huge and unwieldy convoy...sent in advance, the trains being larger than in ordinary warfare would have been required for a force of ten thousand troops" many of the supplies never reached the troops due to Mormon raids or severe winter weather.[168]

On 8 September, Captain Stewart Van Vliet arrived in Salt Lake City from Kansas, less his small escort which remained outside the city. He had orders to "purchase forage and lumber and to assure the Mormons that the troops would not molest or interfere with them." He then journeyed east to meet the advance of the Utah Army and told it that while the Mormons did not want war, they would burn crops and farms and the route through Echo Canyon would be difficult. The total strength of the Mormon militia, the Nauvoo Legion, was estimated at 5,000 men. Harney was needed again in Kansas and was replaced by Colonel Alexander until Colonel Albert Sidney Johnston, then at Fort Leavenworth, could arrive. Alexander received a letter from the Mormon Militia commander, General Daniel H. Wells, which stated that U.S. armed forces were forbidden from entering Utah Territory and he and U.S. forces must withdraw. If they stayed they must surrender their arms and ammunition and would not be molested. Alexander replied that he would give the letter to Johnston when he arrived but his troops would remain. Meanwhile Mormon forces intercepted and burned three Army wagon trains of some 75 wagons. Faced with the probability of armed conflict with the Mormons and an unseasonable blizzard, Colonel Alexander retreated as he had only sufficient fodder and provisions for 14 days. Alexander, after a council of war, determined to march to Fort Hall on Beaver Head Mountain. His troops began marching on 11 October in heavy snow making only three miles a day. Finally Alexander received a dispatch from Johnston instructing him to meet him and his cavalry at Fontenell Creek but then changed that to near the junction of Ham and Black Forks.[169]

All the forces met on 4 November with the welcomed supply trains Johnston had with his force. The War Department ordered Alexander replaced by Colonel Albert S. Johnston, commander of the 2nd Cavalry, to command the expedition. It was too late to continue the campaign and he decided to winter over at Fort Bridger, Utah, some 35 miles away, and begin again in the spring. Hundreds of cattle, mules and horses died during this trek during which temperature plunged well below zero and many men suffered frostbite. The 35 mile trip took 15 days. During this march, Colonel Phillip St. George Cooke arrived on the 19th with 500 troopers from the 2nd Dragoons. When the tired and cold column arrived at Fort Bridger they found that the fort had been burned by Mormon troops and all provisions gone. Johnston divided the troops between Fort Bridger, and a new camp named Camp Scott in a sheltered location near a stream to the northeast; the cattle were sent to winter over to the southeast at Henry's Fork with Colonel Cooke and six dragoon companies. The new territorial governor, Alfred E. Cumming, arrived at the fort, and conferred with Johnston. But before a spring offensive could commence in earnest, peace commissioners sent by President Buchanan arrived in Utah and reached a settlement with Mormon leaders. Buchanan was convinced to stop the war, and on the 6 April signed a proclamation promising amnesty to all who returned their allegiance to the United States: "I offer now a free and full pardon to all who will submit themselves to the authority of the government." Meanwhile some 3,000 additional troops had arrived at Fort Leavenworth: the 6th and 7th Infantry, 1st Cavalry, and two batteries of artillery. The

---

command of Colonel Johnston. The companies so detached will, if possible, be carried to at least sixty privates each, by transfers from the remaining companies." General Order courtesy of the Middlesex County Historical Society.

[168] Hubert Howe Bancroft, *The Works of Hubert Howe Bancroft: the History of Utah*, vol. 26 (San Francisco, CA: The History Company, 1889), 497-498, 511-525 *passim*. Mansfield's arrival noted by Captain John Wolcott Phelps, 4th Artillery; "Diary of Captain Phelps," *Mormon Resistance: A Documentary Account of the Utah Expedition, 1857-1858*, ed. by Leroy R. Hafen and Ann W. Hafen (Lincoln, NE: University of Nebraska Press, 2005), 93. Phelps was an 1836 West Point graduate but resigned from the Army in 1859. He became the colonel of the 1st Vermont Infantry and resigned as a brigadier general in 1862; he died in 1882. David L. Bigler and Will Bagley, *The Mormon Rebellion: America's First Civil War, 1857-1858* (Norman OK: University of Oklahoma Press, 2011), 132. NARA, RG 94, Letter received by the Adjutant General.

[169] Bancroft, vol. 26, 505-506, 515-517; 530, 538; Newell, 5-36.

Mormon War turned out to be a fizzle; the only U.S. losses were due to weather and illness as no major battles between U.S. forces and the Mormon Militia took place. On 26 June 1858, the U.S. Army of Utah entered the valley of the Great Salt Lake. The largest loss of life happened during a Mormon Militia massacre of California-bound settlers during which 120 men, women, and children were killed in what became known as the Mountain Meadows massacre. Historian Bancroft writing from primarily the Mormon perspective saw the "war" as a waste: "The Utah war was an ill-advised measure on the part of the United States government. In this, as in other crises, from the time when the latter-day saints mustered six members until now when they counted nearly sixty thousand, the Mormons, hated as they were by their fellow-men, won the respect and almost the esteem of a large portion of the gentile world. The Utah war cost several hundred lives, and at least $15,000,000, at a time in the nation's history when men and money could least be spared, and accomplished practically nothing, save that it exposed the president and his cabinet to much well-deserved ridicule."[170]

Fort Randall 13–27 August 1856

Mansfield arrived at Fort Randall on 13 August 1857 "via Sioux City and the east side of the [Missouri] River" as he wrote in his 14 August letter to Thomas. Fort Randall was on the right bank of the Missouri River about a quarter mile from it at a point where the river crosses the Nebraska line. He informed Thomas that he would be there at least a week and "then shall take the first opportunity to return to Fort Leavenworth" which he anticipated reaching at the end of August. On the 27th of August he told Thomas in a letter he wrote from Sioux City, Iowa, that he finished his inspection of Fort Randall and would "continue my journey of return to Fort Leavenworth…by stage; as there is no boat now here." [171]

Mansfield returned to Fort Leavenworth on 2 September, finished his report of his inspection of Fort Randall, and included it in his 4 September letter to Thomas and noted that he had been occupied with this inspection one day shy of a month. He noted that he had received discretionary orders to inspect Fort Laramie and he wrote that "I shall not probably reach that post this season." He added that he would inspect troops there which are preparing to leave the post and that the "The Governor of Utah is at Leavenworth and expecting to move soon." Mansfield left Fort Leavenworth on 3 August and reached Sioux City via the Missouri River on the steamer *Omaha* on the 8th. He arrived at Fort Randall on the August 14th from Sioux City. His included inspection of Fort Randall noted that it "is 150 miles by land above Sioux City through the Indian Country on the east side of the river occupied by the Yanktons. I was accordingly obliged at Sioux City to hire a two horse wagon and driver and obtain an Indian Guide to convey me to the fort which occupied me on the road from the 10th to the 14th. He found that the fort was "in a beautiful prominent position…on the east bank of the river…[on] a plateau some 80 feet above the river." Cottonwood trees near the fort supplied timber for the construction of troop quarters. Saw and grist mills were near the river but a small garden attempted by one of the companies failed. Other gardens only produced a few potatoes as he wrote that the chief difficulty for gardens "in this region are the grasshoppers, which swarm about the middle of August and destroy almost every vegetable." He urged that the fort commander be ordered to "mark out" two islands with abundant cedar trees to enable use of this valuable wood on the post. The cedar islands would also furnish ample hay and pasturage. He also suggested that a light draft boat be obtained to use to travel down to St. Louis which could be travelled in 10 or 12 days. He lauded the site of the post: "I do not know that a more eligible position could have been selected beyond the nearest white settlements."[172]

He reported that the only Indians in the vicinity were the Yanktons "who occupy the Big Sioux Reservation." Mansfield spoke with the chief, Black Bear, who complained that whites were stealing wood and the U.S. agents keep presents meant for his tribe and use them to "buy their women for wives." The chief wanted men to instruct his people "how to plant and build houses, and I must earnestly recommend it be done." Fort Randall Mansfield wrote was established by orders of General Harney of the 2nd Dragoons 10 July 1856 and Captain Nelson H. Davis of the 2nd Infantry reached the new post from Fort Pierre with Companies C and I on 4 August 1856 followed during the rest of the year and the next by remaining companies. Colonel Francis Lee of the 2nd Infantry was left finally at the new post with six companies after the breaking up of Forts Pierre and Lookout. On 20 August 1856 the troops labored to cut

---

[170] Bancroft, vol. 26, 505-506, 515-517; 530, 538; Newell, 5-36. Mansfield wrote a letter to his daughter, Mary, from Fort Leavenworth on 13 September 1857, that her "lessons MUST be kept up" and that he hopes she will be straight (erect) as her sister Katie by using shoulder straps and laying straight. She should also clean her room and help with breakfast but don't allow anyone to clean her room. Letter courtesy WPL.
[171] Letters courtesy NARA.
[172] Letters courtesy NARA.

timber and erect buildings "before the exceedingly cold weather." Citizens employed by the Quartermaster put up the hospital, surgeon's quarters, and the enclosure for commissary supplies. Mansfield believed that the men would be comfortably quartered before the winter. Colonel Francis Lee commanded the 2nd Infantry at the post. The Field and Staff had an aggregate of two line officers and 19 enlisted men. Company A was commanded by Captain Christopher S. Lovell with an aggregate of two officers and 57 men available present. Company B was commanded by Captain Nathaniel Lyon who was on leave; in his stead was Lieutenant Thomas W. Sweeney with an aggregate of one officer and 43 men present. Captain William M. Gardner was in command of Company D in aggregate two officers and 38 men present for duty. Company G was commanded by Major [__] had in aggregate two officers and 48 men. Company H was commanded by Captain J. May absent sick; Lieutenant William F. Lee was in command of the aggregate of one officer and 34 men. Company I led by Captain Delozier Davidson had Lieutenant T. W. Sweeny in command with two officers and 31 men available present. "The whole available force therefore is 10 officers of the line and 267 enlisted men present—to which add 40 enlisted men on detached service." All companies were armed with the rifle and sword bayonet except for Company H which had the old smooth barrel musket but Mansfield noted that rifled muskets sufficient for two companies were awaiting shipment at Sioux City.[173]

Next in his report, Mansfield began his description of the inspection of each company first listing the type of rifle and ammunition then any equipment which he condemned. Company A "was perfectly and neatly equipped for the field in every respect." Even though all of the enlisted men and laundresses were housed in tents, they "in the course of 20 days will all be in good and comfortable log buildings now being erected." All company books were in "excellent order." Company B he found neatly equipped for the field in every respect." As with Company A, all were in tents "but in a few days will be in good log buildings now being completed. He noted however that the company "books, etc., not very neat." Company D was also in tents with log buildings under construction; company books "in order." Company G was also "neatly equipped for the field in every respect." All were in tents as with the other companies, including officers, awaiting "comfortable log buildings; books were in order." Company H was also "neatly equipped for the field in every respect—I think this the neatest company of the command....books in excellent order." Company I was housed in "good log buildings with soldiers ample room and kitchen also of logs—all neat and comfortable." Books were in order. Noncommissioned Staff of 13 are in comfortable log buildings and "The Band is a very good one." The command and staff are in comfortable log buildings except for the Quartermaster who is in a tent awaiting completion of his log quarters. Regiment and Post books are in good order. But Mansfield found that "Desertions have been great owing first to the worthless character of many recruits, and to the excessive labour of hutting themselves, and to the high price of labor on the upper Missouri. At Sioux City laborers get from 2 to 3 dollars per day and mechanics from 4 to 6. The men have been well governed by Colonel Lee since he has been in command."[174]

Colonel Lee commanded the companies for Mansfield's review and inspection. He found them neat and of "good countenances" and looked healthy. The companies were in excellent order with full equipment but were not able to drill in battalion order "as Colonel Lee informed me they have not for over a year drilled in the battalion in consequence of the great labor the men have had to perform in their hutting themselves, etc. and the snow and extreme cold weather in winter. The Companies however were drilled at the Company drill and as skirmishers and did indifferently for the reason there had been no time to instruct them, and it must be so till the command is thoroughly housed—only one drill parade a week and the usual guard mounting daily. I dispensed with target firing as they had not practiced. The discipline of the post is good, and harmony prevails among the officers." Mansfield charitably and perhaps realistically wrote that Colonel Lee expects "next summer to be able to undertake the drill and carry them through thoroughly. In winter little can be expected, and I would suggest that an order be issued to all the posts for the officers to learn the bayonet exercise at that season, preparatory to instructing the soldiers in warm weather." He noted 11 prisoners in the guardhouse. As he already mentioned, all gardens attempted failed "except for a few things" due mainly to grasshoppers.

---

[173] Letters courtesy NARA. Fort Randall was established on a site selected by Colonel William S. Harney, 2nd Dragoons, on 10 July 1856 according to Mansfield's report, however, Frazer, in *Forts of the West* wrote that it was established by Harney's order on 26 June 1856 by Lieutenant George H. Paige, 136-137. Randall in *Encyclopedia of Historic Forts*, 732, wrote that it was established by Captain Nelson H. Davis of the 2nd Infantry on 4 August 1856 agreeing with Mansfield. It was named after Lieutenant Colonel Daniel D. Randall, Deputy Paymaster General of the Army. It replaced Fort Pierre, abandoned 16 May 1857, to keep the peace among local Indian tribes and settlers. Fort Lookout was abandoned 17 June 1857 also replaced by Fort Randall to which point some of its material was sent; Frazer, 136. The post was officially abandoned on 7 December 1892. Colonel Francis Lee was an 1822 West Point graduate and a classmate of Mansfield. He was brevetted twice during the Mexican-American War to lieutenant colonel and colonel. He died in 1859.

[174] Letters courtesy NARA.

He found the amount of ordnance large apparently since it was collected from two posts, Forts Pierre and Lookout, which were broken up and the ordnance sent to this new post. The post had four 12 pounder mountain howitzers, "in good order" along with copious ammunition and firearms. The hospital department was in good order waiting rehousing in a new log building; there were few ill men and medical supplies were ample but he decided that only one hospital steward was needed so the other should be transferred. Apparently this was a healthy post. The Subsistence Department was well conducted with all books and records neatly kept in good order. As noted regarding ordnance, there was an abundant supply of food due to the consolidation of two forts into this new one. Mansfield wrote that the excess would certainly spoil so he would contact the Chief Commissary of Subsistence at St. Louis to remove excess food. The Quartermaster's Department had ample supplies again due to the consolidation of the two older forts. He found a steam saw and a working grist mill employed in hutting. Timber and hay were in ample supply at reasonable prices and there was good grazing. Stables were not yet built so the animals were temporarily housed in the deserted Dragoon huts. He noted an item of serious concern for the post: "A disease prevails among the horses and mules which causes them to shed their hoofs and hair on the mane and tail and no cause has yet been satisfactorily given for it." He discussed at length some problems with an officer selling government horses improperly but in the end believed that the officer did not intentionally do wrong and should be allowed to explain the matter and fix it. Mansfield found that Major Gaines of the Pay Department had only been able to pay two companies six months' pay and four for four months which he found too long an interval but it was not the fault of the paymaster but rather that he was required to get funds from Fort Leavenworth. While there, Major Gaines was ordered to pay at Fort Riley then had to go to St. Louis for more funds. From there he travelled to Washington, D.C., to renew bonds. Based on this pay debacle, Mansfield suggested that Fort Randall's paymaster would be better located at Fort Leavenworth from where his funds must come then he could visit Fort Randall and pay every two months. Paymaster funds were correct. Mansfield then repeated suggestions he made before in his inspection of the Department of Texas that the Army should establish a soldiers' savings bank to encourage savings and help prevent their pay being spent for unsavory things such as liquor and female companionship.[175]

---

[175] Letters courtesy NARA.

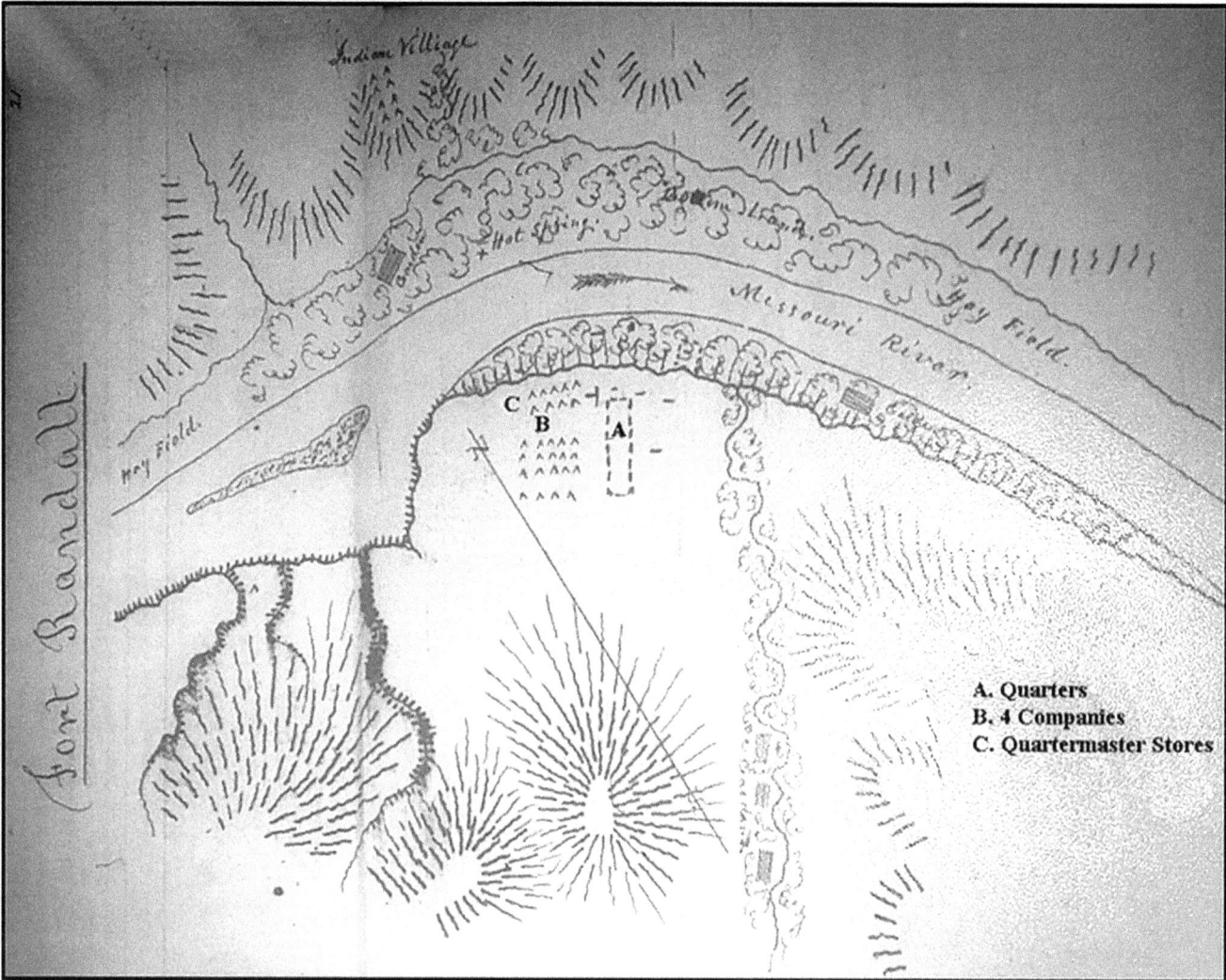

Mansfield's drawing of Fort Randall submitted with his inspection report with author's additions; courtesy NARA.

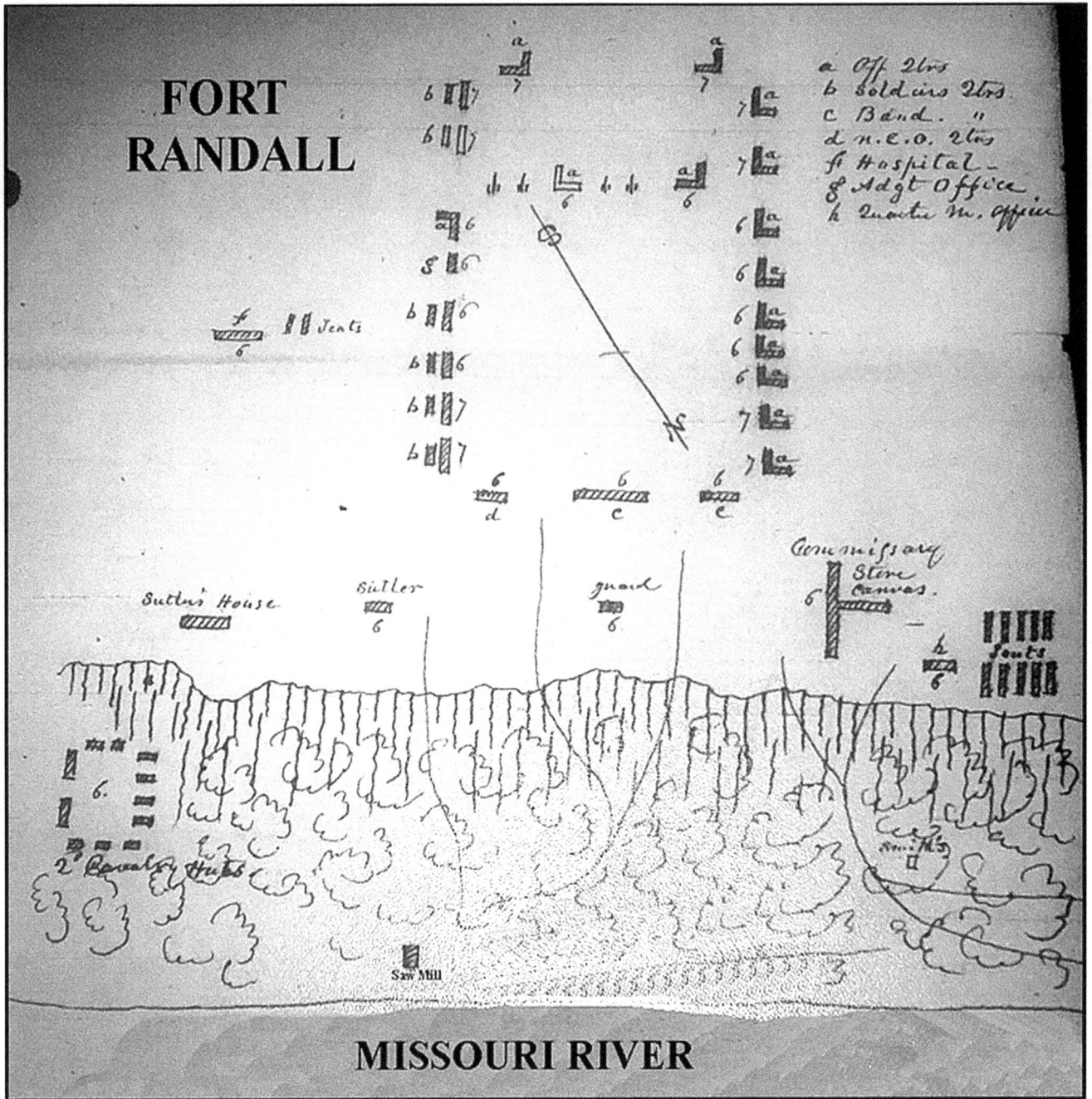

Mansfield's detailed drawing of Fort Randall from another perspective and submitted with his inspection report. Note 2nd Dragoon huts on the lower left; courtesy NARA.

Mansfield was kept busy as he reported in his 10 September 1857 letter to Thomas from Fort Leavenworth that on the 8th he inspected recruits assembled at the fort which were there under order of Lieutenant Colonel Daniel T. Chandler; the next day the recruits marched for New Mexico. The men were divided into two divisions, one for the Mounted Rifles and the infantry for the 3rd and 8th Regiments, and were accompanied by others bound for New Mexico including a surgeon. He reported that the men were "well supplied with the necessary clothes and their arms were taken in bulk till they reach about 100 miles, when they will be distributed." One division under "Brevet Major [James Henry] Carleton was divided into 3 Companies, the 1st rifle company composed of 66 enlisted men present inclusive of 2 buglers, 49 horses, 6 tents, and organized with suitable noncommissioned officers." The 2nd was commanded by a future Civil War notable, Lieutenant William Woods Averell, also a rifle company with 62 enlisted men present inclusive of two buglers, 49 horses, six tents, and organized with suitable noncommissioned officers. The 3rd was again a rifle company with 68 enlisted men including two buglers, 48 horses, six tents, and organized with suitable noncommissioned officers. The Division under Major Horace Brooks was divided into four companies: the 1st composed of 64 men, five tents; the 2nd contained 65 men, five tents; the 3rd with 65 men, five tents; and the 4th composed of 64 men, five tents. "These companies were all organized with suitable noncommissioned officers but no musicians. The aggregate force is 456 enlisted men, 7 laundresses, 2 physicians, and 10 officers of the line." Mansfield also wrote that Colonel Chambliss has $100,000 for the Pay Department. He also listed the transportation for the march with "12 wagons for the sick and 25 wagons for 6 teams of 5,500 pounds each and nine ox team wagons of 4,000 pounds each. The Commissary had 60 days' supply for 550 men" and he added that four officers took "their families with them in private carriages." He ended his report by writing that "My inspection was more with a view to the manner the men were to move and their organization than anything else. There were some desertions on the route to this place, and some after they had reached here." Still at Fort Leavenworth on 15 September, Mansfield wrote to Thomas that on 14 September he received a telegram ordering him to proceed to Washington, D.C., and report to the War Department; Mansfield said he would leave on the 16th. He also reported that he would inspect the six companies of the 2nd Dragoons who would probably march in two days under the command of Colonel Johnston.[176]

On 4 September 1857, Mansfield received an order by telegraph from the Adjutant General's office at the direction of the Secretary of War to "repair to Washington and report to the War Department for further instructions." But then on 7 September 1857 Mansfield received an order from General Harney to "inspect the different Departments at this Post [Fort Leavenworth] while awaiting an opportunity to proceed to Fort Kearney." Mansfield wrote to Thomas on 23 September 1857 from Washington City and reported that he arrived there that day "at 11 a.m. having left Fort Leavenworth on the afternoon of the 17th instant and Leavenworth City on the morning of the 18th instant. Colonel Johnston accompanied by Acting Adj. General Porter left Fort Leavenworth in route for Utah on the evening of the 17th instant and the 6 companies under Colonel Cooke left on that day and the succeeding day." Mansfield wrote that he inspected the troops and would send in his report "tomorrow." Mansfield ended by stating that he was in Washington under War Department orders but "at present do not know the nature of the duty I am to perform." But on the 25th, he received another order to instead report to the General-in-Chief of the Army since the employment envisioned in the original order on the 4th did not require his immediate attention.[177]

Mansfield's 24 September 1857 report he wrote from Washington, D.C., showed that he had completed his inspection of the Army of Utah before he left Fort Leavenworth on 17 September. He noted that he had previously inspected the "Books and Records of the Army previous to their being turned over to Colonel A.S. Johnston and the 6 companies of the 2nd Dragoons which will escort the Governor of Utah to his destination, and afford a detachment which will escort Colonel Johnston by forced marches, to overtake the Troops which left in July last, at some point beyond Laramie. It will probably take Colonel Johnston 35 days to overtake this command, whereas the troops with the Governor will not probably reach Salt Lake City before the 1st of December, if not obstructed by snow." Mansfield also wrote that General Harney had received orders on September 8 "that the six companies of the 2nd Dragoons were to go to Utah, and the command of the Army transferred to Colonel A.S. Johnston, 2nd Cavalry; and that the 4 companies of the 1st Cavalry, and 4 companies of the 6th Infantry, and 4 companies of the 6th Infantry were to be recalled from that army and expresses were accordingly dispatched by General Harney. The 6 Companies 2nd Dragoons reached Fort Leavenworth on the 11th instant, and were to be immediately after transfers, refitting and arming, and inspections, turned over to the order of Colonel Johnston, who had previously arrived with Asst. Adj. General Porter."[178]

Mansfield had to quickly inspect the six 2nd Dragoon companies and finally did on the 11th. The companies were commanded by Colonel Philip St. George Cooke "and numbered 387 enlisted men and 14 officers and 1 assistant surgeon." Mansfield supplied an accounting of the compositions of the field and staff and then the six companies reviewing commanders, noncommissioned officers and men along with arms, equipment, and horses. He also noted the locations and duties of those officers and men absent. Arms included Colt's pistols and rifles, Sharp's carbine rifles. Company A had 44 men for duty with an aggregate of 68 men and two officers; Company B had 40 fit for duty with an

---

[176] Letters courtesy NARA.

[177] Letters 4 and 25 September 1857, NARA RG 94, Letters sent from the Adjutant General's Office. Letter 7 September 1857 courtesy of the Middlesex County Historical Society. On 8 September General Harney issued an order to six companies of the 2nd Dragoons to remain under the command of General Johnston and would escort the civil officers of Utah on their mission; Lieutenant Colonel Philip St. Cooke and Major M.S. Howe would be in command. Finally on 11 September, the War Department placed General Johnston in command of the Army of Utah. Letters courtesy of the Middlesex County Historical Society. Letters NARA RG 94, Letters sent from the Adjutant General's Office.

[178] Letters courtesy NARA.

aggregate of 57 men and one officer; Company C had 54 fit for duty with an aggregate of 65 men and two officers; Company F had 52 fit for duty and an aggregate of 68 men and two officers; Company G had 58 men fit for duty and an aggregate of 68 men and one officer; Company I had 52 men for duty and an aggregate of 64 men and two officers. "These companies were in undress and marching costume, and were inspected in the least practicable time, on account of the weather, and the little time that was allowed them to turn in superfluous articles, and arms and unserviceable horses, etc., and prepare for the march. Of course I confined my inspection to this outfit and the condition of the horses, and men, and supplies, for the march and service. The men were healthy and the horses good, and arms and supplies of all kinds good, and everything needful for the march supplied." He also reported that the Medical Department was well supplied with equipment and wagons. But he again complained about the insufficient numbers of officers: "It is to be regretted so few officers were with the Companies and two companies of one officer each and those young lieutenants. I do not think it possible to keep up the service properly with so few officers at their companies, and this too on war service. There seems to be a want of ambition on the part of <u>some</u> officers to join their companies on perilous and hard service, and it argues badly for the future state of discipline. As to the instruction of these men in their various arms, I can say nothing, for I know nothing of their qualifications. There was no time, nor opportunity to test them." He also noted that about half of the companies had the old style books "not well adapted to the service." Colonel Johnston's escort "consisted of 40 men and 1 sergeant and two corporals under Lieutenant Charles H. Tyler of the 2nd Dragoons and all dismounted to ride in spring wagons armed with Sharps rifle carbine and colts pistols and 100 rounds the man of each arm and supplied with all needful requisites for the march….The column will move at an average of 35 miles per day whereas the 6 companies will only be able to average 20 miles per day." Mansfield determined that "every requisite has been prepared by General Harney to complete the outfit for a successful command."[179]

Next on 25 September he wrote Thomas and enclosed his "report of the inspection of the 6 companies of the 2nd Dragoons before they marched on the 17th and 18th. He added that "I shall soon make a report of the inspection of the Department of Fort Leavenworth which I had completed before I received order to repair to this post." On 23 October 1857 he wrote to McDowell to report his inspection of recruits at Fort Columbus and transport for them to the Pacific Department. He arrived the morning of the 19th and that afternoon inspected the steamer *Nathan Light*. While his inspection found no issues, he learned that since the ship had struck a coral reef on its way to New York, it would not sail until it was "hauled and examined before she could be pronounced seaworthy." That ship was replaced by the *St. Louis* so Mansfield inspected that ship too. He found it unexceptionable and safe and it sailed immediately. The ship was contracted to carry 220 men and five officers with servants. He saw that the quarters for the troops "good and ample with a good mattress in each." Mansfield commended the Quartermaster method of furnishing rations at the same time with transportation as it "is a very great advantage and comfort to the soldiers and I would always recommend it on board these regular steamers where other than soldiers are passengers." This meant that the Subsistence Department must pay to the Quartermaster Department monies. Mansfield wrote that "I feel it my duty to urge on the Commanding General a regulation to that end to take effect from the commencement of the current fiscal year. This would relieve the Quartermaster's Department of an inappropriate charge." At Fort Columbus Mansfield inspected a total of 213 recruits; he found then "good looking men and with the exception of some 3 or 4 not prepossessing in appearance will probably make good soldiers. I however am of the opinion that more attention should be had to the personal appearance of a recruit in addition to his physical soundness." The recruits had "all the essentials of clothing, etc., for their comfort but there was no uniformity of dress. The fatigue jacket and uniform coat were side by side in the ranks. But they were neat and in good discipline."[180]

Mansfield was kept busy with recruit and transport inspection as he wrote to Assistant Adjutant General McDowell from New York City on 4 December 1857 and reported his inspection of the steamer *William Nelson* which was contracted to take up to six officers and 410 men to New Orleans. He found all in good order with adequate berthing and "ample arrangements for cooking, etc." He estimated that the voyage would take 30 days and there was ample water aboard. On 2 December Mansfield inspected 413 recruits at Fort Columbus who were bound for Texas. "These recruits were all sound looking men and well found with all that is requisite to take them to their respective posts." Mansfield learned that there were 30 days supplies on board and that the assistant surgeon scheduled to sail had ample medical supplies. Then on 8 December 1857 Mansfield in Middletown wrote to McDowell with his report of the inspection of

---

[179] Letters courtesy NARA.
[180] Letters courtesy NARA.

the "Steamer *Nathan Light* which was contracted to take 170 recruits and 2 officers and Laundresses and Servants" to Benicia, California. He found the ship unexceptionable with adequate quarters and rations "for the quartering and feeding of all in case of delay at Panama." He also inspected 170 recruits at Fort Columbus "and found them also unexceptionable and well found in every respect." After the usual recitation of nationalities of recruits, he closed with the following: "This report would have been forwarded yesterday but for extreme indisposition by a hard cold from which I am now rapidly recovering."[181]

Drawing of 2ⁿᵈ Dragoons on the Utah Expedition by E. Forbes; T.F. Rodenbough, *From Everglade to Canon with the Second Dragoons* (New York, NY: D. Van Nostrand, 1875), faces p. 175. Note the officer riding a mule.

As Mansfield found during some of his inspections, good cavalry weapons were a problem for troopers. And as an Army inspector, Mansfield was approached by inventors who thought that his interest in their inventions would help promote them with the Army. One case was the North and Savage Revolving Rifle manufactured by a Middletown company. Likely Mansfield was approached by Henry S. North and given some of their firearms. Apparently Mansfield sold a revolving rifle to Captain William R. Bradfute of the 2ⁿᵈ Cavalry in 1857. The cavalry officer gave it a poor review in a letter to Mansfield on 26 March 1857 from his Camp on Grape Creek: "I think it is the most worthless arm that I ever saw in its present form or rather as when I received it from you. It has to be kept in a perfect state of cleanliness or it doesn't shoot but an improvement can be made probably that might make it useful to a certain extent but it is too complicated an arm ever to be useful to an Army, too easy to get out of order, will not shoot over sixty yards with any certainty and in damp wet weather it is a surplus weight that ought to be dispensed with." However Mansfield wrote a memorandum dated 25 Feb. 1858 that the six chamber revolving rifle by H.S. North of Middletown was a "Very superior arm" and North's revolving pistol was good too. Perhaps Mansfield's hometown loyalty affected his judgment or it may have been that heavy field use highlighted its shortcomings. Unlike the U.S. Model 1843 Hall-North Breech-Loading Percussion Carbine which was manufactured by North from 1844 until 1853 with 10,500 produced, the revolving rifle was not a success and was not adapted by the Army.[182]

---

[181] Letters courtesy NARA.

[182] Letter and memorandum courtesy of the Middlesex County Historical Society. See discussion of U.S. Model 1843 Hall-North Percussion Carbine: https://www.newmarketarms.com/rare-model-1843-hallnorth-percussion-carbine-1847-p-1142.html; accessed 10 October 2017. Letters courtesy of the Middlesex County Historical Society.

Mansfield also responded when asked by anyone about the curriculum at West Point that among other things, the course of study should be four years. Congressman Samuel Arnold wrote to Mansfield on 25 March 1858 from Washington, D.C., mentioning that, and added: "I feel gratified however with having had the honor of introducing you to the President, and shall feel much pleasure in rendering you any future services which it may be in my power to afford." In 1860, Mansfield wrote further about this topic in two letters written from Middletown: On 25 July 1860, he suggested to the committee established by Congress to examine the West Point course of study that four years is enough, five years means that more officers will be appointed from civilian life to fill vacancies and those appointments are done by favoritism. The Mexican War showed how well West Point graduates did: "there was no failure in the undertaking of any military operation or expedition during the war, resulting from a want of education the graduate" except for the Spanish language. He further suggested that from the first two years, "delete all English studies of Belles Lettres, grammar, practical ethics compositions. Devote 2 years to math, French, military drills fencing and gymnastics." And an entrance exam was necessary. The next day, 26 July 1860, he added: "I would here recommend that the young graduate in the line be sent to the school of practice for the particular arm to which he belongs for one year at least, on leaving the Academy, where he will be brought in contact with the enlisted men of the Army and at once commence a career of usefulness to his country. Theoretical instruction is but the first step to a great practical operation and hence the advantage of an educated mind at the Academy;"[183]

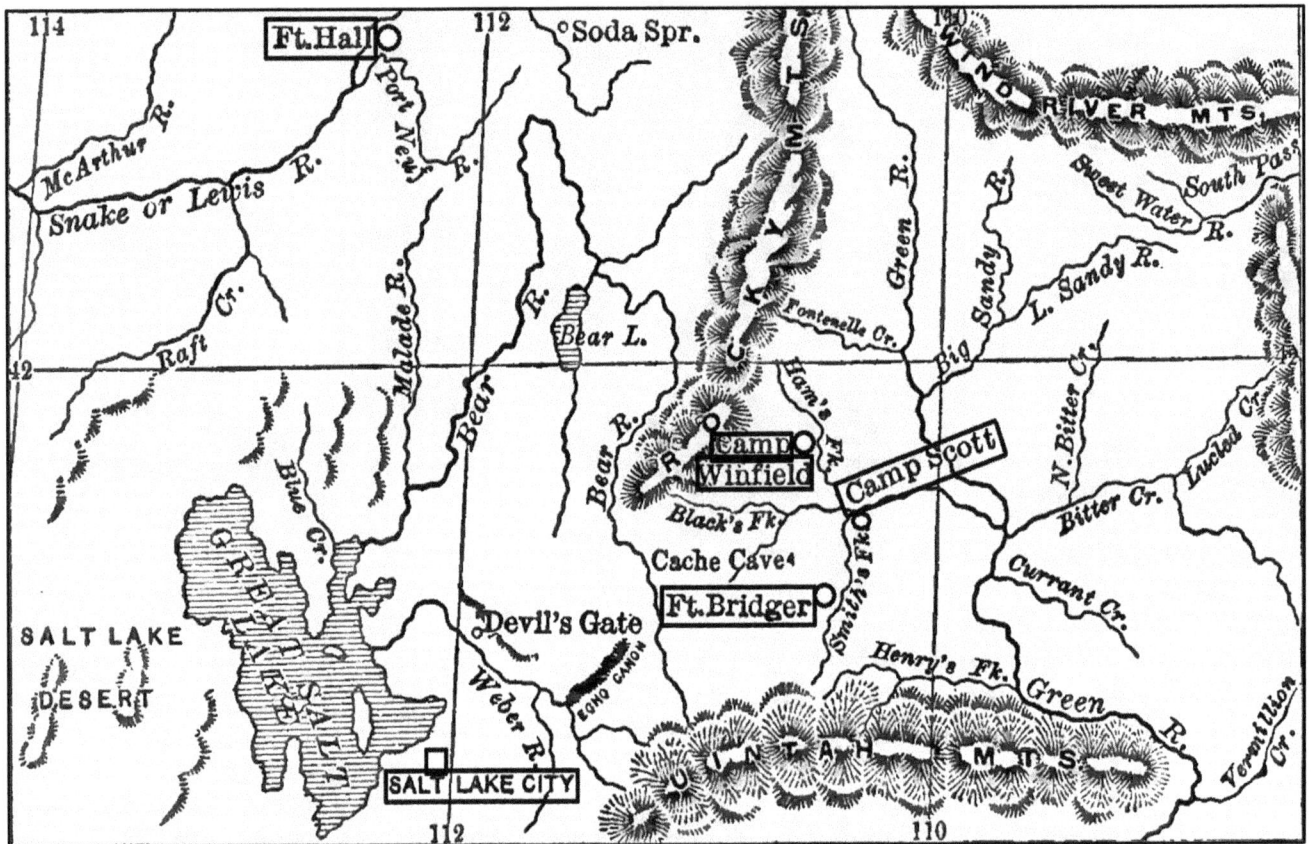

Forts Bridger and Hall shown along with Camps Winfield and Scott. U.S. troops would have had to fight their way through Echo Canyon to the northeast of Salt Lake City had a settlement between the parties not occurred. Map from Bancroft, vol. 26, p. 513.

---

[183] Letters courtesy of the Middlesex County Historical Society. Secretary of War Davis among others was interested in increasing the West Point curriculum to five years. Mansfield was against this even though it took him five years to finish his studies and graduate.

Fort Bridger in 1851, lithograph by Captain Howard Stansbury, Corps of Topographical Engineers, courtesy Wikipedia.

Portrait of Brigadier General Albert S. Johnston, taken at Camp Floyd, Utah Territory, by Samuel C. Mills, during the winter of 1858-59; courtesy Wikipedia from NARA. Johnston was an 1826 West Point graduate who served in the Black Hawk War, but resigned from the Army in 1834 and moved to Texas in 1836. After serving as Secretary of War for the Republic of Texas from 1838 to 1840, he resigned and returned to Kentucky. He returned to Texas in 1843. During the Mexican-American War, he was the colonel of the 1st Texas Rifle Volunteers. He returned to the U.S. Army as a major in 1849. He became the colonel of the 2nd Cavalry 3 March 1855 and was brevetted to brigadier general 18 November 1857 for his command of the Army of Utah. He commanded the Department of the Pacific from 22 November 1860 to 23 February 1861. He resigned 3 May 1861 becoming a general in the Confederate Army in September 1861. He was killed at the Battle of Shiloh 6 April 1862.

Image of Brigadier General William Selby Harney taken by Brady in 1863, courtesy NARA. Harney entered the Army 13 February 1818. He was brevetted to colonel for his actions against Indians in Florida; brigadier general for the Battle of Cerro Gordo during the Mexican-American War, and major general in 1865 for long and faithful service. He retired in 1863 and died in 1889. He received his regular promotion to brigadier general effective 14 June 1858. He commanded the Department of the West at Jefferson Barracks in St. Louis, Missouri, in 1861. Because of his Tennessee birth and difficulties he encountered in Missouri in 1861, he was recalled to Washington, D.C. En route he was captured by Confederates at Harper's Ferry and taken to Richmond, Virginia. He refused a command in the Confederate Army offered by Robert E. Lee and returned to Washington. When he decided that he would never receive another command, one of the hardest fighting generals in the U.S. Army retired.

Departments of California and Oregon 1858–1859

Department of Oregon

Fort Walla Walla	1–11 October 1858
Fort Simcoe	16–20 October 1858
Fort Dalles	22–26 October 1858
Fort Vancouver	28 October 1858
Fort Cascades	27 October 1858
Fort Yamhill	10 November 1858
Fort Hoskins	12 November 1858
Fort Townsend	3–4 December 1858
Fort Bellingham	7–8 December 1858
Northwest Boundary Comm. escort camp at Semi-ah-moo	10–12 December 1858
Fort Steilacoom	14–19 December 1858

On 10 April 1858 Mansfield wrote Assistant Adjutant General Irvin McDowell from Middletown: "I am still too unwell to travel but am slowly recovering, yet do not think I shall be well enough to do any duty in Kansas this month. I shall however report as soon as I am well enough to do duty." He added in a footnote that "My cough is not removed and I have a steady pain in the left side and am now under medical treatment." Obviously although Mansfield was not a sickly man his frequent travels under harsh, primitive, conditions took its toll. Then on 16 April he wrote to McDowell that his convalescence was well enough along to attend a general court martial at Newport Barracks for General David E. Twiggs. The 17 March order he received assigning him to duty in Kansas with which he was unable to comply because of his illness was still on his mind as he was not sure if he would proceed to Kansas after the adjournment of the court martial should a relapse of his illness occur. On 20 April he again wrote McDowell from Middletown about the special orders he received on 15 April relieving him from inspecting reinforcements for the Army of Utah. He noted that his orders of 27 January required him to finish his inspection of the posts in the Department of the West which he began last year but to wait until after inspecting the reinforcements for the Army of Utah. Mansfield presumed that he should now proceed with the post inspections unless he received further orders. He did not return to inspect those posts.[184]

Colonel Lorenzo Thomas wrote Mansfield from Washington on 23 June 1858 and generously allowed him to choose which department he wanted to inspect—"Department of New Mexico or Department of the Pacific—I will take the other." Mansfield replied on 25 June to McDowell that "I have to state that under circumstances I shall prefer that of the Pacific.[185] Mansfield's tour there was his second as he made his first in 1854. He undoubtedly remembered his first journey on the Pacific Coast and the adventures he had which could make this second tour easier. The new Department of the Pacific was created on 31 October 1853, and replaced the older Pacific Division. This new Pacific Department abolished the 10th, California, and 11th Oregon, Departments, consolidating them within this new Department of the Pacific. This large, new department included the country west of the Rocky Mountains--California, Oregon Territory, and Washington Territory, except for the Utah Territory and the Territory of New Mexico east of the 110th meridian west. On 2 September 1854, the headquarters was moved to Benicia Barracks, in Benicia, California. In January 1857, the headquarters again returned to San Francisco from Benicia. On 14 January 1858, the Utah Territory was placed within the Pacific Department but later in 1858 changed to the Department of Utah. The Department of Oregon was one of two Army Departments created 13 September 1858, which replaced Department of the Pacific and was composed

---

[184] Mansfield received a letter from Major Isaac Lynde of the 7th Infantry at Fort Laramie dated 24 April informing him "that a train with the supplies for the Army in Utah which were stored at this place during the last winter left this Post for that Army on the 23rd under the command of Brevet Lieutenant Colonel W. Hoffman 6th Inf. and in good condition." Letters courtesy of the Middlesex County Historical Society.

[185] Letters courtesy of the Middlesex County Historical Society. Both Thomas and his commander, General Scott, performed inspections in addition to the two named Inspectors General, Mansfield and Churchill, as there were so many posts and recruits that only two men could not do all.

of the Territories of Washington and Oregon, except the Rogue River and Umpqua Districts, which were assigned to the Department of California. The Department of Oregon's Headquarters was at Fort Vancouver, in Washington Territory. "The Department of Oregon...embraced all of the Washington Territory and most of Oregon; between September 20, when he entered the Columbia River by steamer, and December 19, 1858, when he completed his inspection of Fort Steilacoom....he visited every post in the department, traveling throughout the Pacific Northwest by land and water something over fifteen hundred miles." Mansfield's Pacific Coast inspections thus bridged the change of the structure of the Departments in 1857-1858.[186]

A letter from the governor of the Oregon Territory, Isaac Stevens, on 14 July 1858, contained news about Colonel Edward Jenner Steptoe's defeat at the Battle of Pine Creek during the Spokane-Coeur d'Alene-Palouse War. Steptoe and 164 men were ambushed by over 1,000 Indian warriors. "S. is a very bad officer." Stevens also wrote that he would go to Washington to get Mansfield put in command. On 14 July Mansfield wrote Colonel Samuel Cooper, Adjutant General of the Army, that he "had just received a telegram from Head Quarters of the Army assigning me to the command of the new Department of Oregon subject to the approval of the Hon. The Secretary of War. If the Secretary approves the same, I have to state agreeably to conversation previously had with the Commanding General that I shall select Captain Seth Williams of the Adjutant General's Department to accompany me as Asst. Adj. General of that Department and have to request he may be ordered at once to get ready to depart in the steamer of the 20th." Mansfield finished with a list of items he wished be given Williams to ensure "he had with all the essentials to enter immediately on our duties." Mansfield on 15 July wrote a similar letter to McDowell that he received on the 14th a telegram which created "the Department of Oregon and assigning me to its command subject to the approval of the Secretary of War. I immediately sent a telegram to the Adj. General selecting Captain Seth Williams Asst. Adj. General to accompany me, and wrote to him by last evening's mail on the subject of Captain William's outpost, and to be ready to start from New York on the 20th in the event of the order being affirmed as there would be no time to lose. In my consequent instructions from the Commanding General I trust I shall be given ample powers to meet any emergency the state of affairs in that quarter might require as the distance from headquarters is too great for consultation on unforeseen circumstances." Next on 16 July Mansfield wrote McDowell that the officer who is chosen to inspect the Department of the Pacific should leave in March because the "months...Nov., Dec., Jan., Feb., and March are the rainy, misty and snowy months and in some parts of this Department in winter it is extremely cold and little can be done in travelling from post to post except at great hardship and exposure to man and beast in consequence of cold and bad state of the roads and the duty of escorts in such seasons will be extremely unpleasant without a corresponding benefit. I have no desire to be excused from this or any duty it may be the wish of the Commanding General to assign me but I fear if I should go out at this season I shall be obliged to lay by all the winter at some one of the posts without benefit to the service."[187]

To Mansfield's surprise, on 17 July, he received very bad news from Governor Stevens: he had visited the President on the 15th and expressed to him his wishes that Mansfield be appointed commander of the new Department of Oregon and Washington but the President demurred. While the President was "most complimentary" and held Mansfield in the highest regard, he preferred not to assign a staff officer to command any departments despite the recommendations of the General-in Chief and the Secretary of War. That was the only objection the President expressed to the governor. The governor was very disappointed that Mansfield was not chosen: "I am very sorry that we are not to have the benefits of your labors in the field for I know no officer of the Army in whom our people would have greater confidence." On 20 July the governor followed up with a letter regarding Mansfield's request for information about

---

[186] Douglas, *Readings in Pacific Northwest History*, 157.

[187] Letters courtesy of the Middlesex County Historical Society. Lieutenant Colonel Edward Jenner Steptoe was an 1837 West Point graduate and was brevetted to major and lieutenant colonel during the Mexican-American War. After he declined the governorship of Utah Territory on 6 May 1858 Colonel Steptoe led 157 soldiers north from Fort Walla Walla across the Snake River and into the Palouse Indian region as a show of force. He planned on marching to Fort Colville and on 15 May, he camped along Pine Creek. The next day as the troops continued marching northward, large numbers of Indians numbering about 1,000 appeared in the surrounding hillsides including members of the Spokane, Palouse, Coeur d'Alene, and Yakama tribes. Steptoe concluded that his troops were outnumbered and decided to retreat. The retreat began on May 17. Battles broke out during the retreat and casualties resulted on both sides; Steptoe recorded 21 officers and men killed, wounded or missing. Indians claimed only nine killed and 40 or 50 wounded but Steptoe was certain that it was an underestimate. That night, Steptoe was surrounded and almost out of ammunition so he decided to escape and head for the Snake River crossing some 85 miles away; he left disabled animals and his two howitzers. The Indians considered this an important victory but later that summer Colonel George Wright returned to the area with 700 troops and crushed the tribes which ended organized Indian resistance there. Courtesy Wikipedia and State of Washington Steptoe Battlefield Park; http://parks.state.wa.us/591/Steptoe-Battlefield; Benjamin F. Manring, *The Conquest of the Coeur d'Alenes, Spokanes and Palouses: The Expeditions of Colonels E.J. Steptoe and George Wright Against the "Northern Indians" in 1858* (Spokane, Washington: John W. Graham & Co., 1912), 127-133.

Indian affairs in the department; the governor closed with "I have not given up the idea that it may yet be done [getting Mansfield appointed]." On 10 August Major William W. Chapman wrote Mansfield and commented on his nonselection for the Oregon Department commander: "General [Joseph] Lane said that some protest or paper was handed in or opposition made from some quarter and I inferred that it must have been from some line officer as the General told me that he came in with you from Washington. I presumed that he had told you more than he said to me and therefor I did not question him as particularly as I now wish I had done. He spoke in the highest terms of your eminent qualification for the command in Oregon and seemed to regret exceedingly that he and Governor Stevens had failed to get you appointed commander of the Oregon Army. He is not alone in such regrets." Assistant Adjutant General Irvin McDowell sent Mansfield another letter supporting him on 13 August. He started his letter by ensuring Mansfield that he would be "supplied with proper escort from post to post on your application." He then continued with his view on the line officer versus staff officer issue: "Chapman is the only person I heard speak of some 'line' officer's having objections to your being put in command because you were in the staff. I cannot tell you who they are (I do not know) nor what argument they addressed to sustain their objections. I know that General Scott did not object to your being a staff officer and in command. As to line officers objecting—of course they will object—and it is of not much moment what their arguments are. Their motives are quite plain. I believe Lieutenant Colonel Henry L. Scott does not admit that staff officers can command or rather that there is a doubt whether they can legally do so."[188]

Isaac Ingalls Stevens was appointed by President Pierce on 7 March 1853 as governor of the newly created Washington Territory. He was an 1839 West Point graduate as first in his class and served as an engineer. He was brevetted to captain and major during the Mexican-American War and was severely wounded; he resigned in 1853 to become governor. He was a friend of Mansfield and he knew Mansfield as he superintended fortifications on the New England coast from 1841 until 1849 including Fort Adams, and was given command of the coast survey office in Washington, D.C., until March 1853. He became colonel of the 79th New York Regiment and a brigadier general but was killed at the Battle of Chantilly 1 September 1862 leading his men. He was posthumously promoted to major general effective 4 July 1862.

---

[188] Letters courtesy of the Middlesex County Historical Society. On 26 July 1858 Henry Hammond wrote Mansfield from Worcester, Massachusetts, asking to be appointed Mansfield's "clerk during your visit to California and that perhaps you would be willing to employ me." Letter courtesy of the Middlesex County Historical Society. Scott was the aide de camp to General Winfield Scott 7 March 1855 to 14 May 1861. He was an 1833 West Point graduate brevetted to major and lieutenant colonel during the Mexican-American War. He resigned in 1862 and died in 1886.

Lieutenant Colonel Edward Jenner Steptoe who commanded the ill-fated expedition which ended up at the Battle of Pine Creek also known as the Steptoe Disaster; Manring, *The Conquest of the Coeur d'Alenes, Spokanes and Palouses*, frontispiece.

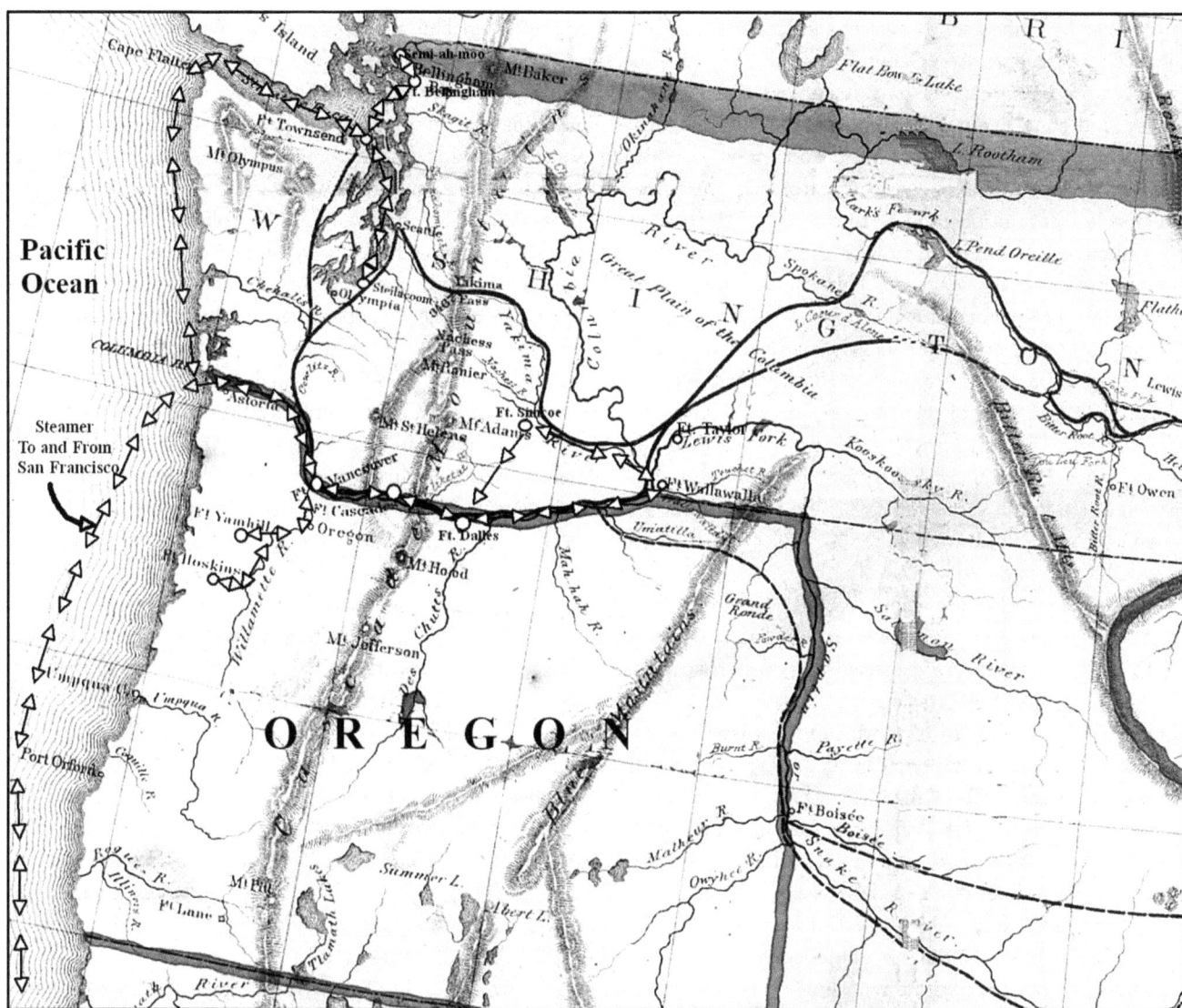

Mansfield's 1858 inspection of Washington Territory and Oregon. He took a steamer north from San Francisco and stopped first at Fort Vancouver and after a few days journeyed to Fort Dalles and after a brief stay journeyed to and inspected Fort Walla-Walla then Fort Simcoe. From Fort Simcoe he travelled to and inspected Fort Dalles, Fort Cascades then continued downriver and inspected Fort Vancouver. He next continued south and inspected Forts Yamhill and Hoskins. He then returned to Fort Vancouver to rest before he continued his inspection tour north. Next on his inspection list were Forts Townsend and Bellingham and then the Escort of the Boundary Commission at Semi-ah-moo. His final inspection was at Fort Steilacoom which he reached travelling through Fort Townsend where he caught a steamer for Fort Steilacoom. He rested at Olympia before boarding a steamer for San Francisco. In his letters he wrote that he travelled from Fort Simcoe to Fort Dalles without mentioning returning to Fort Walla-Walla so he may have ridden on horseback cross country to do so. Map courtesy LOC.

On 7 September 1858, Mansfield wrote his wife from the steamer *Sonora* "200 miles south of Acapulco." Weather was good during his journey but very hot so he had to buy ice to survive. The ship would put into Acapulco for coal and supplies. He informed her of shipboard activities such as messing and religious services then gave her advice for the children and told her to make sure to pay "your meat bills regularly. Do not get in debt and make good calculations." Mansfield's steamer which brought him up the Pacific Coast after he crossed Panama arrived in San Francisco in the middle of September and he quickly boarded another ship to go immediately to Oregon to investigate and report about the recent Indian war. Mansfield wrote to Cooper from Fort Dalles on 14 September 1858 and informed him that he arrived there on the 13th and planned on leaving the 15th for Walla-Walla; he wrote that it would take him "7 days being 172 miles." He reported that he mailed a copy of his report of his inspection of the Department headquarters and summarized: "All matters are well conducted and reflecting thus far to the credit of all parties connected with the service." Mansfield also wrote to McDowell on 24 September from Fort Dalles and reported that on the 21st he spent the day at Fort Vancouver "where General N[ewman]. S. Clarke had temporarily established his headquarters." Mansfield wrote that he inspected "the letters and orders of the Department...and had a familiar official conversation with the General and his Asst. Adj. General who have afforded me all the information desirable, particularly as the war with the Indians now being carried on....it appears that General Clarke adopted the most efficient and prompt means in his power, and concentrated his troops above the Cascades at Forts Simcoe and Walla-Walla by the abandonment of San Bernardino, San Diego, Fort Miller, Fort Jones, Fort Bragg, and the moving of the company from San Francisco, one company from Benicia, one company from the Klamath; 6 mountain howitzers with the rifled muskets and Sharps rifles and ample ammunition ordered to the seat of the war, and Colonel George Wright and Major Robert S. Garnett of the 10th Infantry were ordered to take the field with their respective commands the first with 600 men and punish the enemy and carry the war into their country to its termination....The result is that Major Garnett captured and shot Indians on the 15th August and Colonel Wright reports a decisive battle on the 2nd September in which the Indians were severely whipped and subsequently another battle and the further defeat of the Indians and the capture of a large number of animals and supplies and much has yet to be done before peace." Mansfield noted that General Clarke had asked for cooperation of the troops from Utah "but unhappily the 6th Infantry was ordered by Brevet Brigadier General Johnston via...Benicia instead of direct to Walla Walla" thus costing more in transportation from Benicia to Walla Walla and not having any effect on the morale of the Indians in the lands through which the regiment could have marched. He found all records he inspected in order and "there appears to be no want of troops to which the enemy now in the field and bringing them to subjection. The official records of the Department as far as I have been able to see them are well conducted."[189]

On 20 September Mansfield wrote Louisa from the steamer *Oregon* as he ascended the Columbia River. His trip up from San Francisco was pleasant and Portland and Fort Vancouver were next. He encouraged his wife to be thrifty and spend "as if you would never see me again" perhaps anticipating the difficult journeys he would make during the next few months. Mansfield was at the Cascades on the Columbia River in Washington Territory when he wrote his 22 September 1858 letter to Irvin McDowell. Mansfield reached there on the 22nd on his way to Walla Walla. Mansfield requested the "official reports of Colonel Wright's fights with the Indians." Then on 1 October he wrote to McDowell from Fort Walla Walla, Oregon Territory, that he arrived that day. He reported that apparently Colonel Wright has finished the latest Indian War and is "on the other side of the Snake River." Mansfield planned on leaving the next day for Fort Taylor "to inspect that post and shall there see Colonel Wright and his command. I trust he has closed the war effectually; a number of chiefs have been executed. The Chiefs of the Nez Pierces are here at this time with their camps and are quite friendly." Next on 2 October he wrote Brigadier General Clarke, Commander of the Pacific Department, from Fort Walla Walla, that he would leave for Fort Taylor on 3 October and wrote that "even if peace be made with all the tribes, I would not withdraw a single company to any point below The Dalles this winter." He wrote another letter on 6 October to Clarke and reported that he inspected on the 5th the Army of the Field under Colonel Wright after their march of 15 to 20 miles. "They appeared in fine order as to health and armament and I was much gratified. They halted in column of companies on the Parade of this new fort and in one hour's time I completed my inspection with but little additional fatigue to the Command." The following describes from the troops' point of view what Mansfield saw that day:

> At noon on the 5th they arrived at Walla Walla, having been gone sixty marching days, and were most cordially received. The column reached the fort in the following formation, says Kip: "The four companies of dragoons came first; then our thirty Nez Perces allies; then the hostages, drawn up in two ranks, under the command of Lieutenant Fleming; then the two rifle companies; then Major Wyse's company and battery of six-pounders; then the howitzer battery, under Lieutenant White; and, lastly, the artillery battalion. By far the most conspicuous and distinguished looking person in the command was Cutmouth John. He rode generally by the side of the Nez Perces, dressed in a red blanket, his head surmounted by a large skin cap, and holding in his hand a long pole, from the end of which dangled a scalp he had taken in the battle of the Four Lakes."
>
> The Inspector General, Colonel Mansfield, had arrived a few days before, and it was determined that he should exercise the duties of his office on the spot. As soon, therefore, as we reached the parade ground, the column halted, the ranks opened, and

---

[189] Letters courtesy of the Middlesex County Historical Society. Fort Bragg was established in June 1857 50 miles south of Cape Mendocino within the Mendocino Indian Reservation. It was named after Captain Braxton Bragg, 3rd Artillery. It was abandoned in 1864. It is not clear why Mansfield did not inspect this post unless as Mansfield noted that troops stationed there were sent north to campaign. Brigadier General Newman S. Clarke was a War of 1812 veteran was brevetted to captain in 1814 and brigadier general during the Mexican-American War. He died in 1860. Major Robert Selden Garnett was an 1841 West Point graduate who was brevetted to captain and major during the Mexican-American War. He resigned in 1861 and became a brigadier general in the Confederate Army; he was killed in action 13 July 1861.

Colonel Mansfield, with Colonel Wright and his staff, made a thorough inspection. There was nothing about the command, of the 'pomp and circumstance of glorious war.' During two months no one had slept under a roof, and all were begrimed with mud and rain and dust. The artillery and infantry wore blue flannel shirts drawn over their uniforms and belted at the waist; the dragoons had a similar dress of grey flannel. The officers had adopted the same, with slouched hats. The only marks of their rank were the shoulder straps sewed on the flannel. Yet all this was showing the reality of service. If there was little display of uniforms, the arms were in perfect order, and we believe the troops had never been in a higher state of discipline, or a more efficient condition for action. At all events, Colonel Mansfield expressed himself highly gratified with the result of his inspection.[190]

Fort Walla Walla 1–11 October 1858

In his 11 October 1858 draft report of his inspection at Walla Walla of Wright's troops he wrote that he performed his inspection on the 5th at noon. "These troops were halted in columns of companies as they arrived. The 4 companies of 1st Dragoons and one company of mounted Nez Perce Indians with a company of hostages in the rear, all under the command of Brevet Major W[illiam].N[icholson] Grier, 1st Dragoons in advance, constituted the mounted force. The six companies of 3rd Artillery with two mountain howitzers and two six pounders were under Brevet Major F[rancis]. O. Wyse, 3rd Artillery succeeded by two companies of the 9th Infantry, the whole under the command of Captain E[rasmus].D. Keyes, 3rd Artillery closed the column." He did not have them pass in review as they had just completed an 18 mile march. After they had opened ranks he inspected the Dragoons which he wrote "appeared remarkably well. The men looked healthy and rugged, the horses in good condition. The arms in good serviceable order…the clothing of the men and officers were not in uniform after such a campaign and they exhibited the appearance of hard service being much worn. The troop of mounted Nez Perces with the Harpers Ferry Rifle were a fine looking set of men on Indian horses….as a whole the cavalry presented an imposing appearance very creditable to the gallant commander Brevet Major Grier. The 6 companies of Artillery and 3rd and 9th Infantry appeared remarkably well and the men looked healthy and rugged. The arms and field equipment and Mountain Howitzers in good serviceable order but the clothing and shoes of the men much worn out….The whole command on foot presented a formidable appearance very creditable to the service...under the immediate command of Captain E. D. Keyes." The total command was 28 officers and 631 enlisted men with 30 Nez Perces with only 11 on the sick list. The supply and transportation train had 99 civilian employees and included 465 pack mules and 56 beef cattle. Mansfield described the campaign Colonel Wright's column undertook which thoroughly defeated the hostile Indians in battle and also destroyed foodstuffs, crops, horses, and took hostages, all without the loss of a man. Colonel Wright described the "chastisement which these Indians have received" as "severe but well merited; and absolutely necessary to impress them with our power. For the last eighty miles our route has been marked by slaughter and devastation; 900 horses and a large number of cattle have been killed or appropriated to our own use; many houses, with large quantities of wheat and oats, also many caches of vegetables, camas, and dried berries, have been destroyed. A blow has been struck which they will never forget."[191] Wright also brought back the two howitzers left by the unfortunate Steptoe. All told the troops were 50 days in the field and marched 383 miles. He did note that many pack mules had sore backs but few Dragoon horses did. This was attributed to the poor saddles used on the mules. Based on what he heard from members of the recent expedition against the Indians, he commented on their weapons: "The troops in the field have fully tested the new rifled musket and there is but one opinion and that in their favor. Objection is made to the old musket rifled as it is rendered too weak and has burst in one or two instances. The Harpers Ferry Rifle and Sharps Carbine and Colts pistol have given satisfaction." He

---

190 Manring, 258-260.

191 Manring, 218-219. All the tribes agreed to Colonel Wright's demands: "1st, that they should surrender to me the men who commenced the attack on Lieutenant Colonel Steptoe, contrary to the orders of their chiefs; 2nd, that they should deliver up to me all public or private property in their possession, whether that abandoned by Lieutenant Colonel Steptoe, or received from any other source; 3rd, that they should allow all white persons to travel at all times through their country unmolested; 4th, that as security for their future good behavior, they should deliver to me one chief and four men with their families, as hostages, to be taken to Fort Walla Walla;" Manring, 219-220. Major William Nicholson Grier was an 1835 West Point graduate who was brevetted to major in the Mexican-American War and to colonel and brigadier general during the Civil War. He was also promoted to major general during that war and died in 1867. Major Francis Octavius Wyse was an 1837 West Point graduate who was brevetted to major during the Mexican-American War. He was promoted to lieutenant colonel during the Civil War and retired in 1879; he died in 1893. Erasmus Darwin Keyes was an 1832 West Point graduate who was brevetted to brigadier general during the Civil War. He was an aide-de-camp to General Winfield Scott from 1837 to 1841 and Scott's military secretary from 1860 to 1861. In 1862 he became a major general of volunteers and resigned in 1864; he died in 1895. Camas, of the lily family, had edible bulbs and was a staple of Indian tribes in the Northwest. It could be eaten cooked or dried.

also wrote that the six companies of artillery left down the river to The Dalles on their way to Fort Vancouver and the two companies of the 9ᵗʰ Infantry and four of the 1ˢᵗ Dragoons would winter over at Fort Walla Walla. He noted also that Colonel Wright and Steptoe left for The Dalles. Mansfield opined that the post required two more companies of Dragoons. Mansfield also reported that he was almost finished with the Walla Walla inspection and would leave shortly "in a boat for The Dalles."[192]

Sketch of Old Fort Walla Walla. "Railroad Survey," vol. 12, facing p. 152.

In his two reports about his inspections of both Colonel Wright's column and the fort itself, Mansfield took a written page in each to discuss Indians. Mansfield was convinced that all the tribes would be at peace after Colonel Wright's "chastisement" of them. He found the 2,800 "Nez Pierces the most intelligent and enlightened…in the region" and he noted favorably that they are Christians and most have only one wife. He urged that one chief from each Indian Nation be received in Washington, D.C., to visit "their great father." Fort Walla Walla he declared "is admirably placed to destroy all combinations this side of the Cascade Mountains and west of the Rocky Mountains in this region and should have at least 4 full companies of Infantry and Cavalry to overawe them.…I consider the war ended." Fort Walla Walla was a new post and "there are quarters for 5 companies for both officers and soldiers that will be comfortably covered in before the close of this month and there are more in the old fort one and one half miles off for three companies of Dragoons with their stables, one company of Dragoons are in the new fort and buildings and stables." The artillery troop were in tents as their quarters are not yet ready. It was 170 miles by land from Fort Dalles and 145 by land and water; it was about 600 miles from Salt Lake City and 200 from old Fort Boise. Mansfield described his journey to Walla Walla and found that most of the roads he took required extensive repair and improvement. He also noted the difficulties in going up river with portages involved as well as his descent to Des Chutes which took 44 hours, 20 of which required paddling from his two men. Fort Walla Walla was well situated "in the Valley of the Walla Walla River between two of its tributaries in a fine country for vegetation and with ample grass, wood, and timber all within ten miles of it and vegetables of all kinds in this climate in abundance." The post was "in the midst of the Cayuse and Walla Walla Indians and accessible to other tribes east of the Cascade and Rocky Mountains and should always be strongly occupied by troops.…I look upon it as of the first importance." The post was built by Colonel Steptoe of the 9ᵗʰ Regiment on 23 September 1856 with a command of one company of the 3ʳᵈ Artillery, one of the 1ˢᵗ Dragoons, and one from each of the 4ᵗʰ and 9ᵗʰ Infantry Regiments. They built a temporary post about one and one half miles from the final position leaving the original site which was then occupied by three companies of the 1ˢᵗ Dragoons. New quarters were nearly completed. Mansfield reported that there was "a good and ample hospital, a good quartermasters store, corral, barn and stable, a water-powered saw mill, smith, and carpenters shops. The Dragoon companies were erecting stables." He wrote that "This command occupy three separate reservations of 600 acres, distant some 4 to 6 miles apart. Two of

---

[192] Letters courtesy of the Middlesex County Historical Society.

them, to wit, a reservation for hay in Dry Creek in the route to Fort Taylor and one other on the Walla Walla River for wood. These have been marked out and are indispensable to the post."[193]

Mansfield began his inspection and noted that Colonel Steptoe was in command of the post "with parts of Companies B and E of the 9th Infantry and part of Company H 1st Dragoons, a detachment of the 3rd Artillery....in the aggregate 5 commissioned officers and 164 enlisted men." Company B had two officers and 35 men; Company E had one officer and 35 men; the artillery detachment had one corporal and 22 men; and Company H, 1st Dragoons, one officer and 76 men. Mansfield wrote that all the men were engaged in building quarters. (Note that these company members include noncommissioned officers, sergeants, and corporals; five officers included the surgeon.) Mansfield wrote that most of the enlisted men were recruits. The parts of the three Dragoon companies were located at the old cantonment where the original temporary post was built about a mile and half away. Company C had two officers, two noncommissioned officers and 63 privates of which 27 were recruits. Company E had two officers, two noncommissioned officers, and 61 enlisted of whom 37 were recruits. Company I had two noncommissioned officers and 62 men of whom 40 were recruits. They had mixed uniforms but the companies' books were in order and arms neat. There were good stables and corrals but he noted that two of the companies would probably winter over at the new post since this older one had only log houses. His careful eye noted that "there are many barrels of whiskey here in storage" but made no further note about the "demon." Mansfield continued his post inspection with the Quartermaster Department which he found "extremely well managed with talent and to the interest of the Service." The sawmill produced ample lumber and the costs of transportation for supplies reduced by the efforts of Lieutenant Charles R. Woods. All company, Quartermaster, Commissary, and post funds were correct and "medicines and furniture ample for one year." "All the companies, the hospital, staff, and Quartermaster Department have excellent gardens which yield abundantly all kinds of vegetables and potatoes sufficient for the winter." The post had a good bakery but needed two bakers; the hard bread received from San Francisco was usually spoiled since it was poorly packed—it should have been put up in casks. He also criticized the troops' payments, writing that they are only paid three times a year. But he found that the post had an excellent hospital under Assistant Surgeon Thomas A. McParlin. The ordnance of the post consisted of four 12 pound mountain howitzers. He finished his 22 October 1858 report by making recommendations: "the route from Walla Walla to Fort Benton should be opened at once. There should be a post established at some point along the road between the Spokane River and Colville after a thorough reconnaissance of the country as the mode of supplies, if transported by the river or overland."[194]

Fort Simcoe 16–20 October 1858

From 16 to 20 October 1858 Mansfield inspected Fort Simcoe. He arrived there on 15 October and began his inspection on the 16th. There he found Major Robert S. Garnett in command of three companies of the 9th Infantry: C, G, and I. Garnett had received a 60 day leave of absence and planned on applying for another 60 days to escort the remains of his wife and child who had died on the post. He left the morning Mansfield began his inspection. Garnett had been absent 45 days on an expedition after a band of "Indian murderers taking about 250 troops." Garnett's party had captured two Indian camps and executed 10 Indians, plus one he hanged upon his return to Fort Simcoe. Mansfield commented upon the fort's usefulness unfavorably: "The peculiar strategic position is not apparent to me although it may exercise an influence on the Indians east of the Cascades. It is however in no particular route to any place and the travelling ceases when the post is reached. It is 65 miles from The Dalles over a good mountainous road. It is accessible from Walls Walla via The Dalles with wagons and by trail by crossing the Columbia River at Walla Walla, say 90 miles.

---

[193] Letters courtesy of the Middlesex County Historical Society. Fort Taylor mentioned by Mansfield was a temporary fort used for six weeks as a base of operations against the Spokane, Coeur d'Alene, and Palouse Indians. It was on the left bank of the Snake River at the mouth of the Tucannon. It was established by Colonel Wright on 11 August 1858 named for Lieutenant Oliver Hazard Perry Taylor of the 1st Dragoons who was killed during a fight with Spokane Indians on 17 May 1858. It was abandoned after the campaign ended; Roberts, *Encyclopedia of Historic Forts*, 837.

[194] Letters courtesy of the Middlesex County Historical Society. Mansfield routinely spelled "Chutes" as Chuttes." Fur trappers of the Hudson's Bay Company gave the name Riviere des Chutes (River of the Falls) to the Deschutes River, from which U.S. soldiers derived the name Des Chutes in the 1850's; the name evolved to its current version, Deschutes. Lieutenant Charles Robert Woods was an 1852 West Point graduate who was brevetted from lieutenant colonel to major general during the Civil War. He retired in 1874 and died in 1885. Dr. Thomas Andrew McParlin joined the Army as an assistant surgeon in 1849 and became Medical Director of the Pacific in 1861. During the Civil War he was brevetted to lieutenant colonel, colonel and brigadier general. He held several posts during the war including Medical Director of the Army of the Potomac. He retired in 1889 and died in 1897.

It is, say, 90 miles by trail from Colville and say 100 miles by trail to Fort Vancouver." He did note that it was convenient to three good springs and to mountain pines within 10 miles useful for building purposes. Although there is "a want of rain for vegetation, yet gardens do well except for the attacks of the cricket which are as bad as the grasshopper in other localities." He also noted that the soil is poor so grass is not abundant although enough can be had for fodder within 10 miles for a reasonable number of animals.[195]

The fort was started on a site selected by Colonel Wright on 8 August 1856. Garnett began to erect building to house four companies. Buildings "commenced on 4 sides of a square parade of 400 feet....At the four corners are four blockhouses designed for defense flanking of the whole. The officers and soldiers quarters are relatively well placed and the hospital and quartermasters and commissary store houses also. The soldiers' quarters are built of hewn logs and supplied with kitchens." He did find that the men were too crowded but opined that if the post were reduced to two companies instead of four that would not then be an issue. The officers had four frame buildings and four log buildings ample for three companies. The commanding officer's quarters he saw as not well planned but he saw the hospital in a good building, and adequate as this was a healthy post. He also found a good post bakery and good stables, corral, and hay yard. The mule-powered sawmill was in good order and "As a whole the post is very creditable to Major Garnett who planned and superintended the building of it." The sutler's store was not allowed to sell liquor which Mansfield thought was excellent regulation. But he did note that the sutler here was the same person who was a sutler at The Dalles and Walla Walla which he did not think wise. He found three gardens, one to each company, in addition to a hospital garden "which yield a fair supply of vegetables, melons, etc., of excellent quality notwithstanding the crickets which are so destructive." He noted that the post is almost completed except for a magazine and some painting and liming. He wrote that the planed boards must be painted on the outside to preserve them. Since Garnett left, the senior captain, James J. Archer of the 9th Infantry was in command. Company C had one officer present as a second was on duty at Fort Dalles and the other was killed in battle against Indians; there were four sergeants, two corporals, two buglers, and 55 men for duty with five sick, one corporal and four men in confinement and four men on detached service; and one sick at Benicia; aggregate of 79 men and one officer for duty. Company G had one officer present as the other two were on duty elsewhere. It had four sergeants, four corporals, two buglers, and 55 men for duty; 5 were sick and three confined, six on detached service; aggregate one officer and 79 men for duty. Company I had two officers on post and one on recruiting duty elsewhere; there were four sergeants, four corporals, two buglers, and 59 men for duty, five sick, one confined, five on detached service, aggregate 80 men and two officers for duty. The post ordnance consisted of two brass howitzers and a portable forge. The magazine was not yet built. The hospital was well supplied with nothing lacking on this healthy post. Its books and records were in good order. The Quartermaster Department's and Commissary Department's records and books were also in good order. He found the discipline of the post good and the company books well kept. "The general appearance of the men was neat and their arms, etc., clean on inspection" but they were in the old uniform. Each company drilled separately due to the large number of untrained recruits who did not participate. Target firing was at 200 yards; Companies C and G had one fifth (20%) strike the target but Company I only had one in 20 (5%) do so—"The firing was wild. The drills but fair. There has been no bayonet exercise, nor has the Heth target practice been yet introduced." He excused their lack of practice due to their employment building the post. He heard complaints from soldiers about the infrequent pay which forced them to long accounts with the sutler "and deprived them of funds to purchase little comforts. They also complained of the small and insufficient allowance of flour" although they had a good harvest of potatoes which apparently made up somewhat for this lack.[196]

Fort Dalles 22–26 October 1858

Fort Dalles was next on Mansfield's list; he inspected it from the 22nd to the 26th of October 1858 and wrote a report from Fort Vancouver on 30 October to McDowell. He reached Fort Dalles from Fort Simcoe on the evening of the 21st. He found it situated about 100 miles above Fort Vancouver at the foot of The Dalles of the Columbia River. Mansfield wrote that it was certain that "no navigation can ever be effective through this Dalles and over the Des Chutes falls at

---

[195] Letters courtesy of the Middlesex County Historical Society.
[196] Letters courtesy of the Middlesex County Historical Society. Captain James Jay Archer was appointed directly from civilian life as a captain in 1847 and was brevetted major during the Mexican-American War. He was mustered out in 1848 but rejoined as a captain in 1855. He resigned in 1861 and became a brigadier general in the Confederate Army; he was wounded and captured at Gettysburg in 1863 and he died in 1864.

any stage of the water. Fort Dalles is therefore a place for landing for all persons and articles on the way to Fort Walla Walla. A road on the north bank of the river is impracticable in consequence of the precipitous mountains." He found that supplies for Fort Simcoe about 65 miles away "or any other place in that section of country must come....[here so] it is necessary to keep up this post. Further it exercises a control over several small bands of Indians, and is well established." He also decided that two companies "are ample" here. Fort Dalles was the headquarters of the 9th Infantry, Colonel George Wright commanding. Companies A and K were stationed here. He complimented the post's books: "I find all the Regimental books very neat and handsomely written. I think the best I have ever seen. The post records are also well kept and the Adjutant's office in complete order." He also found the post's discipline good and "The post well commanded." The Medical Department was in excellent order but in "a miserable old work of a building...unfit for the post." The Commissary Department was also "well managed" housed in a good building. He found a good bakery. Company A was commanded by Major Pinkney Lugenbeel with two other officers, enlisted staff, and 71 privates of these four sick, one confined, one absent with leave and 22 on extra duty. "This company was in excellent order and unexceptionable, the books in good order." It had 11 desertions in 1856, eight in 1857, and none in 1858. It was well quartered in a good barrack with messroom and kitchen but the "bunks were quite inferior but others will soon be supplied....They will soon have the rifle musket." Captain Crawford Fletcher commanded Company K and had two other officers, eight enlisted staff, and 70 privates of which there were four sick, four in confinement, and 10 on extra duty. "This company was in tolerable order, many of the rifles defective in parts." It was quartered as well as Company A and the books "were neatly kept." There were 14 desertions in 1856, 26 in 1857, and five in 1858. The guard was in a proper building and the band well housed. He found four good gardens at the post "with ample vegetables." "Each company drilled at the new infantry drill but there were many recruits and they were not able to drill as skirmishers." Target firing at 200 yards showed that Company A had only six shots (15%) on target and K only four (10%). "The firing was bad for want of practice." The post had one six pounder brass field piece and one 12 pounder mountain howitzer both in good order. He found four new quarters for officers but he criticized two of them as "quite showy and handsome and fanciful in external appearance....They however are cheaply built houses of the kind, but not so cheap as plain two story houses of the same size, which would be more appropriate and I doubt not quite as comfortable. The other two buildings are not fanciful in appearance but intended to keep up the same character of edifice." There were also two large, well-built stables with a large corral. Mansfield explained in more detail about his disagreement with Captain Thomas Jordan about the "style of buildings for a garrison in this remote region of country. Such buildings necessarily require much painting to keep up appearances and to keep them in order and must be more expensive in construction." He also noted that the post supplies "are ample except for the item of shoes"--he found too many pair of large sizes, 11 and 12, and too few of smaller sizes. Also, he wrote that "There are 1,000 gutta percha canteens on hand. These should not be manufactured for the service. They do not last and are worthless...they spoil the water." He suggested the tin canteen covered with cloth. Mansfield also recommended against using other gutta percha items such as the knapsack and haversack since in the field they cannot be mended plus they have a poor appearance. He suggested "stout canvas" instead. The 12,000 Indians in the general area he described "peaceable" and he wrote that "The Government should pursue a liberal course toward these Indians, and treat them as well as the Indians on the Brazos Reservation in Texas and there would be no more murders." Mansfield was happy to report that "this post has been regularly paid every two months by paymaster A[braham] B. Ragan."[197]

---

[197] Letter courtesy of the Middlesex County Historical Society. Major Pinkney Lugenbeel was an 1840 West Point graduate who was brevetted to captain and major during the Mexican-American War. He remained in the Army and was finally promoted to colonel in 1880 and retired in 1882. He died in 1886. Captain Crawford Fletcher was appointed directly from civilian life in 1846 and mustered out of the Army in 1847. He reentered as a captain in 1855 and resigned in 1861; he died in 1876. Captain Thomas Jordan was an 1840 West Point graduate and became a quartermaster captain in 1847. He resigned in 1861 and became a brigadier general in the Confederate Army; he died in 1895. Abraham B. Ragan was directly appointed into the Army in 1848 and discharged in 1849. He rejoined as a major and paymaster but resigned in 1861 and became a major and paymaster in the Confederate Army. He died in 1875. Gutta percha became popular in the mid-19th century. It resembled rubber and was easy to mold and made an excellent insulator. It may be that the canteens did impart a peculiar flavor to water although it is biologically inert. The material softened with high temperatures so exposure to fire would be inadvisable. The tin canteen became the standard issue after the Army experimented with gutta-percha and leather canteens.

Fort Dalles Surgeon's Quarters built in a style Mansfield decried as "showy" and "fanciful." Courtesy Wikipedia.

Fort Cascades 27 October 1858

Mansfield wrote to McDowell from Fort Vancouver on 28 October 1858 and gave his report of his inspection of Fort Cascades. He stopped there on his way down the Columbia River from Fort Dalles: "I stopped at the Cascade Falls, the portage on this river of five miles, and inspected the post." He determined that "This is an important locality in the line of communication of supplies to the posts east of the Cascade Range of Mountains. It is 45 miles from Fort Vancouver and 45 miles below The Dalles. It is here the Columbia River rushes through a gap in these mountains and down such a rapid and falls among rocks for about 5 miles that it is impracticable to get a boat up them. In consequence, a portage is necessary, and there are now roads on both sides of the river and a horse rail road on the north side….The horse rail road unfortunately….does not extend down the river to the steamer navigation by about two miles and consequently requires a transshipment into another boat." This meant that Army supplies are "carried in four mule wagons stationed at the steamer landing." He determined that "this post is of the utmost importance in case the Indians should ever feel themselves strong enough to undertake again, as in 1856, the destruction and burning of houses and massacre of the population." The post was well-defended "by the aid of three block houses one at the foot, one at the middle and one at the upper end of the falls pierced with loop holes and embrasures suitable for defense. The one at the upper end is large enough, being two stories high, for the accommodation of a full company and is in a commanding eminence and within musket range of the landing for steamers and well built in the form of a cross. It is armed with one six pounder and is garrisoned by a sergeant and eleven privates." Its supplies and its troops [are] in excellent order. The center block house looks down on the termination of the horse rail road but "miserably built of logs two stories high "yet suitable for defense against Indians under existing circumstances." It was armed with a six pounder and garrisoned "by a corporal and 8 privates and amply supplied" with ammunition and rations with the men in "fine order." The block house at the foot of the falls is built of logs and two stories high also but "of no material value. It is now used as a store house for supplies of ammunition, etc., and constitutes a part of the post. It is here the main body of the command [contains]… the supplies for this locality." On the second story was a 24 pounder howitzer with adequate ammunition. "The officers were well-quartered in frame buildings. The men are comfortable in a log barrack, two stories, but too low. The kitchen and washroom are…entirely too contracted, a good mess room [is] required and the bunks of the men indifferent. A bakery existed but the oven is defective and requires rebuilding." The post hospital was insufficient and a new one desirable; medical supplies ample. Troops on this post consisted of Company H of the 4th Infantry commanded by Captain Henry Davies Wallen with two other officers and 10 staff enlisted, with 69 privates "in excellent order and discipline." He noted that a military road nearby was poorly designed and recommended that "the officers in charge of the construction and laying out of military roads be under the order of...the General Commanding this Department." The Quartermaster papers and accounts were in good order. Company books were "neatly kept and in order and written up." Captain Wallen drilled the company as riflemen and skirmishers apparently acceptably well as Mansfield made no further comment.[198]

Fort Vancouver 28 October 1858

Mansfield wrote again to McDowell from Fort Vancouver on 28 October 1858 and gave his report of his inspection of Fort Vancouver which he accomplished that day; he had reached there on the 27th. He reported that the post is the headquarters of the Department of Oregon "and is beautifully situated on the north bank of the Columbia River in latitude 45 degree 30 minutes and longitude 121 degree 36 minutes, say 6 miles above the mouth of the Willamette River, 100 miles above Astoria at the mouth of the river and 10 miles by land from Portland at the head of navigation for sea steamers up the Willamette. The reservation is 640 acres and has within its limits the buildings of the Hudson Bay Company. Brigadier General W.S. Harney is here in command of the Department with acting assist. Adj. General A[lfred]. Pleasonton." Paymaster Major Benjamin Alvord's books and accounts "are correctly kept....[and is] assigned to pay the troops at this post...7 posts in all." Mansfield found a new hospital which needed more appropriations "before it can be completed" but he found all in order with "the sick well provided for." The Ordnance Department was in a rented old Hudson Bay Company log building but "in good order" but the nearby magazine "in case of fire...is dangerous." He found that all new construction at the post had been suspended because of issues with the Hudson Bay Company. Mansfield recommended "that these buildings be recommenced as they are very much wanted for the security of the public property and a magazine must soon be built somewhere." But overall, Mansfield wrote that "This Department is in good hands."[199]

The post was also the headquarters of the 4th Infantry with Lieutenant Colonel Thompson Morris in command in the absence of Colonel William Whistler; Morris also commanding the post. There were three other officers present along with four staff noncommissioned officers. "Records were neatly kept and all the books of the regiment and post written up and the post well-commanded...and in a good state of discipline and police." Mansfield did note however that "the Adjutant's Office is at the end of a building, a very unsuitable place, now occupied by a company of the 3rd Artillery." He wrote that the total post staff was five officers and 12 enlisted men. He noted that there were five companies of the 3rd Artillery "temporarily at the post....A, B, C, G, K. These companies by an arrangement between Brigadier General Clarke and Brigadier General Harney were stopped here on their route returning to California after having been in the field under Colonel Wright." Company E of the 4th Infantry was also stationed at the post. Company A of the 4th Artillery with four officers on the rolls had only two of them present along with nine staff enlisted men. There were 78 privates "of which 6 are sick, 8 confined, 7 on extra duty and absent...showing an aggregate of 74 privates for duty with 2 officers." Company books were "in good order." He noted that the company "required clothing and many things" since they had been "in the field" for five months. He found however that "their arms and equipments are in good fighting order." But "This company and B Company are crowded into one building formerly the hospital...just large enough for one company with a worthless log kitchen and messroom." He wrote that the commanding officer was accountable for "one brass 6 pounder cannon in good order but no ammunition for it" which he deemed unnecessary as there was an Ordnance Depot on the post. Company B with four officers on the rolls had one present with eight staff enlisted and 80 privates "of whom 9 sick, 10 confined, 1 extra duty, absent 1 sick, 1 with leave, 1 on detached service showing an available force for duty of 1 officer and 85 men." Company B also had bad clothing

---

[198] Letter courtesy of the Middlesex County Historical Society. Captain Henry Davies Wallen was an 1840 West Point graduate who was brevetted to lieutenant colonel, colonel, and brigadier general during the Civil War. He remained in the Army and retired in 1874 as colonel of the 2nd Infantry. He died in 1886.

[199] Letter courtesy of the Middlesex County Historical Society. Adjutant General Alfred Pleasonton was an 1844 West Point graduate who was brevetted to first lieutenant during the Mexican-American War and lieutenant colonel through major general during the Civil War. He resigned in 1868 but an Act of Congress allowed him to retire as a major in 1888. He died in 1897.

because in addition to being in the field for months it had just been burnt out of its barracks but its "arms [were] in a tolerable condition." The company left Fort Umpqua on 20 June and had been in the field since. It was now crowded "into a building with Company A and badly accommodated." Mansfield noted that General Harney ordered "immediately a two story barrack for 2 companies frame building to be put up…and it will be ready for occupation by the 1st December." Company D had its four officers absent so had Lieutenant "Dunbar R. Ransom detailed to command that company temporarily which he did extremely well." It had eight noncommissioned officers and "77 privates, of these 10 sick, 4 confined, 5 on extra duty; absent 2 on detached service, 2 with leave, 3 sick, 3 confined; in the aggregate 0 officers and 75 men." Twenty seven had deserted in the last three years. He found the company's arms "in a serviceable condition" but the clothing incomplete with "all sorts of caps, many without stocks" again attributable to its being in the field for many months without its supplies. Company books were in good order. Company G had four officers, two of which were present and nine noncommissioned officers with 78 privates of which 7 were sick, 8 in confinement, 7 on extra duty; absent 3 sick, 1 on leave, 6 on extra duty, "in the aggregate 77 men and 2 officers for duty." As with D Company its clothing was in poor condition but its books and arms in good order. But its quarters were cramped with bad accommodations with more bunks needed. Company H had its commanding officer, Captain Erasmus D. Keyes, present, but of the remaining three officers, only one was present. It had 12 noncommissioned officers with "76 privates of which 4 sick, 4 confined, 10 on extra duty; absent 3 with leave, 9 on detached service, in the aggregate 2 officers 76 men for duty." Its books were in good order. He found that "this company is better quartered than any of the others and in a few days a good kitchen will be ready….It is better clothed than the others and their arms in good serviceable order." As its sister companies, it had been in the field for months. Company E of the 4th Infantry had one of its three officers present along with 10 staff enlisted and "62 privates of which, 2 sick, 4 confined, 14 on extra duty; absent 3 with leave and 9 on detached service. In the aggregate one officer and 60 men for duty. Arms in good serviceable order and books in order." He found that "This company was burnt out with Company B and has not yet recovered from its effects. It is quartered in the Block House without a kitchen and mess room and no bunks." "These artillery Companies each drilled separately at the Hardee drill and as skirmishers which were tolerable. E Company, 4th Infantry drilled at the Hardee drill but not as skirmishers as it was not sufficiently instructed. They all fired at the target 6' by 22" one round per 40 men at 200 yards and A company struck it 6 times (15%), B, 2 times (5%), D, 5 times (13%), G, 4 times (10%), H, 5 times (13%), and E, 3 times (8%). The firing was quite wild. It only showed the want of practice. General Kearny has issued an order for the Heth target practice and the Hardee drill."[200]

The band was well accommodated in a small building but it had a worthless cooking stove. The Guard House was in an old log building which housed 40 prisoners including an Indian chief of the Des Chutes tribe. The post had a good baker and oven but housed in "a miserable old log building." Mansfield wrote that the Commissary Department was "a very important one as the posts up the river and at Yamhill and Hoskins receive supplies" from it. This Department and the Quartermaster share "a first rate framed store house two stories high at the wharf landing here, and there is nothing wanting in this department in every respect to issue a correct and prompt supply of all the posts in a timely and economical manner." The Pay Department now at the post was to be stationed instead at The Dalles so he could pay the posts of the Cascades, Dalles, Simcoe, and Walla Walla. Paymaster accounts were "all correct." Captain Rufus Ingalls, the Quartermaster, had a difficult job of transporting goods using steam boats, and a five-mile portage system which he devised at "Fort Cascades with 4 teams and 1 agent and 8 men." Mansfield recommended that supplies for this

---

[200] Letter courtesy of the Middlesex County Historical Society. William Joseph Hardee was an 1838 West Point graduate who was brevetted to major and lieutenant colonel during the Mexican-American War in which he was wounded and captured. He was Commandant of Cadets at West Point from 1856 to 1860. He resigned in 1861 and became a lieutenant general in the Confederate Army. He died in 1873. He authored the *Rifle and Light Infantry Tactics for the Exercise and Manoeuvres of Troops When Acting as Light Infantry or Riflemen* in 1855 which became the standard instructional manual for the Army. Henry Heth was an 1847 West Point graduate and resigned in 1861. He became a major general in the Confederate Army and died in 1899. He wrote a 48 page marksmanship manual in 1858 published by the War Department, *A System of Target Practice for the Use of Troops When Armed with the Musket, Rifle-Musket, Rifle, or Carbine*, which was adapted from the French. It contained instructions on firing at targets up to 1,000 yards. The target size Mansfield routinely required at 200 yards was six feet high and 22 inches wide was as required in Heth's manual. Occasionally Mansfield had troops fire at 100 yards likely due to the lack of a longer rifle range. Colonel William Whistler joined the Army in 1801 as a second lieutenant and was promoted to colonel of the 4th Infantry in 1845; he retired in 1861 and died in 1863. Lieutenant Colonel Thompson Morris was an 1822 graduate of West Point, a classmate of Mansfield's, who was brevetted to major and lieutenant colonel during the Mexican-American War. He retired in 1861 and died in 1870. Lieutenant Dunbar Richard Ransom left West Point in 1850 without graduating but graduated from Norwich University in 1851. In 1855 he rejoined the Army and became a second lieutenant in the 3rd Artillery. He was brevetted to major, lieutenant colonel, and colonel during the Civil War. He was dismissed from the Army in 1872 but reinstated in 1894 and retired as a captain in 1895; he died in 1897.

Department be shipped here from New York rather than first to San Francisco as doing that meant that the supplies take longer to reach their final destinations causing more spoilage and also more shipping costs. The supplies "can well be shipped at a convenient time when freights are low, around the Cape without fear of damage and to the saving of many thousands of dollars in freight, and in the original cost it merely requires a little forethought and concert of action." Mansfield highly commended Ingalls: he "has built a first rate wharf and 2 story store house, a frame building at the landing, divided so as to accommodate both the Quartermaster and Commissary. He has put up excellent stables to accommodate say 70 horses and has mule sheds and corrals ample. He has a first rate frame building near the landing for the occupancy of himself with his officer and clerks very suitable." He was "well supplied with everything but shoes and clothing." "His books and accounts are in good order." Mansfield noted large expenses due to the Indian war and the establishment of the posts of Simcoe and Walla Walla as well as the costs of building the wharf and supporting buildings. He ended his report and stated that "there is ample room for a large garden to each of the 6 companies now at this post. Water is supplied by hauling in horse carts from the river."[201]

On 6 November 1858 Mansfield wrote McDowell from Fort Vancouver. He said that he would leave there shortly for Forts Yamhill and Hoskins. He would then go to Puget Sound and inspect the posts there. He would then return to San Francisco and inspect posts in California or go to Humboldt Bay. He wrote Louisa on 16 October from Fort Simcoe and told her that he reached Fort Dalles from Walla Walla on the 14th as he had left Walla Walla on the 11th and rode 30 miles to Old Walla Walla and then he got into a small yawl boat and with four soldiers, Dr. McParlin, his servant, and a pilot to descend the river. They made 15 miles before dark then the next morning they recommenced at 6 a.m. After a few more days on the river they reached Des Chutes Falls after more than 100 river miles. They next got Indian horses with an Indian guide and rode along an Indian trail some 15 miles to The Dalles. The next morning he started early for Fort Simcoe and arrived there that night after riding 65 miles through the mountains. He was happy to find there Major Garnett, an "old companion in arms," but Mansfield was saddened to learn that Garnett's wife and child had recently died. On 6 October he again wrote to her from Fort Walla Walla and told her that he was with Colonel Steptoe "in his quarters and farewell." On 5 October he had inspected the "Army under Colonel Wright just came in from the war. The war is considered at an end and peace is made with the hostile Indians. I invited all the officers here, about 38, to take wine with me at 12 today, as a complement to those particularly who have been out after the Indians." He planned on "leaving within a few days and would take a boat to the Des Chutes Falls then overland." On 8 November he wrote Louisa from Fort Vancouver and noted that "Lieutenant Colonel Thompson Morris my old class mate and roommate at West Point is in command…and I have been staying with him, and have a very comfortable room. I shall however leave today for the Willamette Valley to inspect Forts Yamhill and Hoskins, etc. The trip may occupy me ten or 12 days, when I shall return to this post, and start for Puget Sound. I hope to get through this quarter before the snows and rains set in hard. I have hereto had a very favorable time. I shall mail today the reports for 4 posts up this river. My two trunks and my servant man, Arthur's, will be left here till my return in charge of Colonel Morris. Arthur does very well and I have no trouble with him." Mansfield supplied advice for his son's pig, and the hams which would result. He also cautioned Louisa to "Look out well for Katie's eyes. I don't want any near sighted children about me. If her school room is such as to glare or injure her eyes at all, send her to Miss Payne. The more I see of the world the more I am satisfied we are better off in Middletown than we could be anywhere else. Officers' families are subjected to a great many inconveniences." He added that Samuel's letter showed that he seems to be ambitious and contented but that he hoped to find him at the head of his class. He warned that Livingston "must be active and energetic and not be suffered to slouch in his chair." Finances were on his mind as he reminded her that "You must manage economically. It will cost me much hereafter out here…..I expect to be probably about the 25 December in San Francisco and from that time my expenses at hotels will be large. Here I have been living on my friends at the various posts."[202]

---

[201] Letter courtesy of the Middlesex County Historical Society. Captain Rufus Ingalls was an 1843 West Point graduate and was brevetted to first lieutenant during the Mexican-American War. He became the Chief Quartermaster of the Army of the Potomac in August 1862 and in June 1864, he was put in charge by Ulysses S. Grant to supply all Federal armies operating against Petersburg and Richmond. He was brevetted from lieutenant colonel to major general during the Civil War. He retired from the Army in 1883 as the Quartermaster General of the Army and died in 1893.

[202] On 17 September Mansfield wrote Louisa from San Francisco and told her that the ship arrived safely on the 16th. It took him a total of 27 days to journey from New York to San Francisco. He would start for Portland, Oregon, that day on the steamer *Oregon*. Letters courtesy of the Middlesex County Historical Society.

Fort Yamhill 10 November 1858

Mansfield next wrote McDowell on 18 November from Fort Vancouver and reported that he had arrived at "Fort Yamhill via Portland and Dayton on the evening of the 9th instant, and on the 10th inspected that post." Fort Yamhill, named after a river, was located on the border of an Indian reservation of 900 and "is about two miles from, and in full view of, the Indian Agent's house and the Indian Lodges and cultivated fields." He noted that the fort is about 35 miles from Dayton, 65 miles from Portland and 40 from Fort Hoskins. He further commented on the relationship of the Indians to the fort writing that if the Indians continue to pursue cultivation of land "the necessity of this military post can be dispensed with for the country up to this reservation is all occupied by farmers in prosperous circumstances." He also provided further commentary about the tribe: "These Indians are polygamists. They have from 1 to 3 wives. They are superstitious and will burn down the house in which an Indian dies....They have only about 75 or 80 inferior guns and are contented and peaceful." He gave the history of the fort reporting that it "was commenced by order of Brevet Major General Wool in 1856 by Brevet 2nd Lieutenant W.B. Hazen now of the 8th Infantry which attached to the 4th Infantry and was constructed by Captain Andrew J. Smith of the 1st Dragoons and finally completed by Captain David A. Russell of the 4th Infantry with his company. It was originally designed for two companies but never completed thus far. There are quarters sufficient for one company of soldiers but deficient in the necessary mess room without a modification which is about to be made. There are more than quarters enough for the officers allowing one building to an officer. These buildings however are made without attics." He noted that there was a good block house "which is used as a magazine and ordnance store." He also noted good storehouses for quartermaster and commissary goods as well as for the guardhouse and prison, and a good hospital sufficient for one company. All other buildings including laundress houses, bake house, stables, barn, smith's and carpenter shops, sutler's store, etc., "were economically and well-planned and there appears to be no unnecessary expense in their construction....There is a good garden and vegetables of most kinds can readily be raised." Captain David A. Russell commanded Company K, 4th Infantry with two other officers present including Lieutenant Philip H. Sheridan; eight staff enlisted and 58 privates were present with five sick and five confined. He wrote that the "company was in excellent order and good discipline in the old uniform armed with the smooth bore musket but was soon to receive the new rifled musket." He again noted that it was equipped with the gutta percha canteen "which were of no value." The "company drilled at the new Hardee drill tolerably" but he did not test their target firing "as the smooth bore barrel musket had not suitable sights." Company quarters were in good order as were the company books and the "company had one laundress and a good garden where it raised about 400 bushels of potatoes and other vegetables." The hospital was also in good order as was its books with adequate space as this was a "healthy post." The "sufficient" guard house had a total of 14 prisoners; the commissary department under Lieutenant Sheridan stored its supplies in "a good frame building" and had supplies laid in for the winter. But he found that flour cost one third more than at Fort Hoskins for no good reason and other food items also had high costs—"I shall call the attention of the purchasing officer to these high prices." The Quartermaster Department also under Lieutenant Sheridan had ample supplies well stored. Mansfield concluded that "This post is well commanded by Captain Russell. He had studied the comfort and protection of his command. It is not his fault that the officers' quarters are more than sufficient for the company. He has supplied the post with water as it stands in a side hill by digging a well and constructing a reservoir and filling it by pumping daily and leading it to the quarters thence in pipes underground." The post had one 6 pounder gun and one 12 pounder howitzer. Overall Mansfield found a good post.[203]

Fort Hoskins 12 November 1858

On 19 November 1858 Mansfield wrote McDowell from Fort Vancouver to report his inspection of Fort Hoskins which he began the day he arrived there on the 12th. The fort was in King's Valley "about 35 miles from Salem in a southwest course through the town of Dalles which is 22 miles distant from the fort and it is 40 miles from Fort Yamhill via Dalles." Mansfield could not visit the Indian reservation due to the heavy rain and muddy roads. The post was well sited to provide assistance to the nearby Indian Agent and civilians in case of trouble which he found unlikely but he

---

[203] Letter courtesy of the Middlesex County Historical Society. Lieutenant Philip Henry Sheridan was an 1853 West Point graduate and was promoted from captain to major general during the Civil War. He became a lieutenant general in 1869 and general in 1888 as Commander in Chief of the Army. He died in 1888.

determined it prudent "to preserve this two company station for perhaps two years yet, till the Indians become identified with the soil." Mansfield's only objection to the post was that it was located on leased ground "at 300 dollars per annum but when broken up the U.S. will have the right to all the buildings." The post was begun by Captain Christopher C. Auger of the 4th Infantry on the 26th July 1856 by orders of General Wool and was "calculated for a two company post and is ample." He found three buildings for officers' quarters, a good hospital and stone houses for Quartermaster's and Commissary supplies. There was also a good two story barrack, a good hospital, with kitchens, mess rooms, wash rooms, and a good bakery. "These buildings are all framed and new and judiciously executed, with no unnecessary expense and water is brought into most of them from a spring in the side hill and by means of pipes underground. I regard this post as built with a proper regard to economy and quite creditable to Captain Auger. There are good gardens and a summer and winters supply of vegetable are easily cultivated." Companies G and F of the 4th Infantry comprised the troops at the post with Captain Auger who also led Company G, in command. He had two other officers but one was detached; there were 10 staff enlisted and 68 privates with one sick, two confined, one absent confined and 18 on detached duty. The company was in the old uniform but "very neat and in good order. Knapsacks and haversacks painted canvas." Again he wrote that the gutta percha canteens were of no use. The company had the old smooth bore musket but "The new rifled musket was expected by the next steamer. The rain precluded all drill and target firing." Quarters and company books were in excellent order. He opined that the new double bunks were "very desirable." The company had "a good garden in which it raised 800 bushels of potatoes for winter use." Company F had no officers as two were detailed off post and the third was under arrest. The company had 10 staff enlisted and 66 privates of which three were sick, four confined, and 17 on detached duty. The Company was in "was in the old uniform in excellent order in every respect and equally well accommodated by itself in the left half of the same building [as Company G]." Mansfield noted that there were twice as many deserters in Company F compared to Company G due to lack of officers. He was critical of the dearth of officers: "The want of officers at this post is felt where a company is left in command of a second lieutenant and a detachment of 30 men is kept at the block house say 25 miles distant under the command of 2 sergeants and 2 corporals. Such a detachment should be under an officer. Lieutenant [William Thomas] Gentry was necessarily ordered to take command of the company." The post had one 12 pounder brass gun with one 12 pounder howitzer at the block house. While the surgeon had only a supply for one company that was sufficient as the post is healthy. The guard house was adequate and the bakery which shared the building produced good bread. The Commissary Department had ample supplies and well stored in a building shared with the Quartermasters Department. The Quartermaster Department had ample supplies except for clothing and shoes in sizes seven, eight and nine; accounts were correct. Mansfield reported that "Captain Auger is a good commander, the troops are in good discipline and the comforts of the men attended to."[204]

Mansfield wrote to the Secretary of War, John B. Floyd, from Fort Vancouver on 22 November 1858 "Agreeably to your wishes expressed to me in your office before my departure for this Department." He reported to Floyd that he arrived "at this post in the evening of the 20th September just one month from the day of my departure from New York and commenced the next day the execution of my duties." Mansfield wrote a list of reports he sent to the commanding general: "A report of the measures adopted by Brevet Brigadier General N.S. Clarke in the defeat of Lieutenant Colonel Steptoe; a report of the inspection and doings of the troops in the field under Colonel Wright." Mansfield then listed the reports of inspection he had done for Forts Walla Walla, Simcoe, operations in the field under Major Garrett; Dalles, Cascades, Vancouver and its connection with the headquarters of the Department of Oregon, Yamhill, and Hoskins. He then spent the remaining two pages of this letter discussing Indian affairs and asserted that all treaties made by Governor Isaac Stevens should be "confirmed by the Senate without delay." He also urged that all the now defeated tribes be allowed to return to their reservations: "This will be treating them humanely and opening the country to the American people to pass over and occupy unmolested in spite of a weak nomadic race who have no idea of cultivating the soil themselves and will benefit from our own citizens. This seems to be the opinion of the general commanding this Department....I regard the peace as permanent and would not guarantee it without [keeping the tribes separate on their own reservations]." He ended by earnestly recommending that the "Superintendent of Indian Affairs be required to gather some four or five of the Chiefs and young men to assist them of the different tribes east of the Cascades and take

---

[204] Letter courtesy of the Middlesex County Historical Society. Captain Christopher Colon Auger was an 1843 West Point graduate who received brevets to colonel, brigadier general and major general during the Civil War. He remained in the Army and retired in 1885 as a brigadier general; he died in 1898. Lieutenant William Thomas Gentry was an 1856 West Point graduate who was brevetted to major and lieutenant colonel during the Civil War. He remained in the Army and died as a lieutenant colonel in 1885.

them to Washington City to visit their Great Father the President. The moral effect of such a visit would be felt here among the Indians on their return and result in more respect for the citizens of the U.S. and in future harmony."[205]

On 24 November 1858 Mansfield wrote a letter to his wife from Portland, Oregon Territory, to catch her up on his travels. He stated that he left San Francisco in the morning of the next day after arriving. He sailed from San Francisco to Fort Vancouver on the steamer *Oregon,* and arrived 20 September, one month from the day when he sailed from New York. He continued his travelogue and wrote that the distance from Vancouver to a gap in the Cascade Mountains was 100 miles up the Columbia River; next 45 miles then a five mile stage around rapids, then a steamer 45 miles to Fort Dalles; finally 15 soldiers on mules and a two-horse spring wagon through Indian Country to Fort Walla Walla, about 172 miles—it took seven days. "We then continued our journey to the old Fort Walla Walla on the Columbia River; and myself and Dr. [Thomas Andrew] McParlin who travelled with me, & 4 soldiers, and Arthur,[206] and a pilot; we all got into a boat...and we rowed down the river, stopping for two nights on the river on the shore to sleep, till we reached the falls of the Des Chutes, 100 miles below Walla Walla. Here the whole river pitches over a rocky bottom down some 20 feet. Of course we go out of our boat here, and hired two Indian horses, and an Indian guide, & followed the river down to The Dalles and left our men to come on by the road in a wagon. It was an exciting time in the boat. Sometime we would pass down rapids very fast; and there were many Indians camped on the river, fishing for salmon. And then from The Dalles, went to Fort Simcoe 65 miles north through Indian Country with only two men besides Arthur....I then returned to Fort Vancouver and wrote for several days, when I started for Fort Yamhill, and Fort Hoskins in the Willamette Valley and on my return went through Salem and Oregon City. Waiting for steamer to go up Puget Sound."[207]

Fort Townsend 3–4 December 1858

Mansfield next inspected Fort Townsend on 3 and 4 December 1858. He recorded that it is on the Bay of Port Townsend on Puget Sound "about five miles by land following the beach." He also noted a "smoking volcano," Mount Baker and saw Mount St. Helens both "perpetually covered with snow." He reported that the post is "well selected for a military post as a protection to the Citizens located in this vicinity and to overawe the Indians and to afford aid to the Custom house officer at Port Townsend in case of necessity, and to the Indian Agent of this vicinity who resides in that place." He also remarked that it had good timber, a good spring, and "a good prairie for garden" but he found the bakery "average." The post was established by order of Colonel Silas Casey of the 9th Infantry on 6 October 1856. This post had Company I of the 4th Infantry commanded by Major Granville Owen Haller and consisted of three officers and 71 men including eight staff enlisted. He wrote that "The men were well quartered, and slept in double bunks two tiers high, and the Kitchen and Messroom neat & comfortable. I have never seen soldiers better accommodated....[and the] Company was neat and completely equipped." "The officers' quarters are 3 buildings in a line....These are roomy and simple and frame buildings lathed and plastered. Further in the same line on the left is a block log house, guard house, with prisoners' room and two cells. Further on the right is a block and log house bakery, and soldiers' library, and reading room. Perpendicular to this line on the right stands a fine two story barrack roomy and ample for one company with kitchen, messroom and commissary store room and lounging room for soldiers on the 1st floor." The "company was neat and completely equipped, armed with the new rifled musket." He saw that even though the company drilled well

---

[205] Letter courtesy of the Middlesex County Historical Society. Also on 22 November, he wrote a letter to Major Richard B. Lee and expressed concern with commissary supplies not being forwarded "all of them this season before the winds became uncertain and the rainy season set in....The consequence of such late shipments of supplies is that they get damaged by the long transit, and the rains of this season of the year, and the roads being in a bad state the transportation wagons when resorted to at an extra expense cannot take half a load and the evil is very great and they are now in want....supplies destined for the Department of origin should if practicable be forwarded to reach Fort Vancouver before the 1st September, in order to take the trade winds up the river from the Des Chutes and to escape damage by transportation and landing in the rain." Letter courtesy of the Middlesex County Historical Society.

[206] "Arthur" is probably his personal servant.

[207] Letter courtesy WPL. In a few other letters during this time he wrote to the President, Secretary of War, Secretary of State, etc., and expressed his views on Indian affairs and the boundary dispute with England. Letters found at of the Middlesex County Historical Society, Box 3, File 5. On 4 January 1859 he wrote a confidential letter from San Francisco to one of his senators from Connecticut, L.S. Foster, about his concerns with the boundary with Canada. In that letter he added a P.S. expressing his hope that the senator would support a bill to build a railroad to the Pacific, "without delay," as it would be vital during a war with a sea power to unite the U.S. Pacific coast with the east. Then on 19 January he wrote to his other senator, James Dixon, a letter strongly supporting a Pacific railroad bill which he said was critical should a war happen with Britain or France which, as great sea powers, could isolate the West Coast of the United States. He believed the route should go from the Missouri River to the Northwest. Letters courtesy of the Middlesex County Historical Society.

at the light infantry drill, target shooting was poor as he saw at many other posts with only five of forty shots (13%) hitting a 6 foot by 22 inch target at 200 yards with the rifled musket. He then wrote at length about the problem of desertions—74 in three years--which he linked with poor quality of recruits: "This is to be attributed to 4 causes. 1st The worthless unprincipled character of many recruits. 2nd The want of proper discipline & instructions as soldiers at the General Recruiting Depot before they are sent to join companies; a fatal error in our system. 3rd The vicinity of this post to the British frontier, where the gold diggings are enticing, and where they cannot be seized if discovered; 4th The bad treatment of an orderly sergeant since reduced to the ranks." After describing in detail some of the worthless recruits he saw, he summarized his recommendations: "I would earnestly urge that no recruits be sent from the General Depot, till they have been disciplined & Trained to the performance of military duties. This can be better done at the depot than at the Military Posts. It would prevent much desertion, & the men kept at the depot for 6 months, under strict discipline, & instructions, would not fail to show their defects; such as fits &c, and could be discharged without further expense. I do not think a left handed man should be enlisted. He cannot fire efficiently by the right shoulder in the ranks, & better be out of the service. The pay & compensation of a soldier are ample, and none but good & active men, & men of good habits, should be allowed to enter the service." While he discovered "no want of discipline" he wrote that "there was a want of old soldiers to make noncommissioned officers, and I think it much to be regretted that our service cannot afford American citizens enough to make noncommissioned officers." The hospital, Commissary and Quartermasters Departments were in good order and the post had one 12 pounder brass mountain howitzer. He noted that there were 5,000 Indians scattered about with only 100 "close at hand" but "are peaceable" however they suffered depredations by northern Indians who "should be shut out of these waters entirely…by pursuing them when they enter our waters in their large canoes….by means of a small steamer….one should be built especially for the purpose to navigate the rough waters of the Straits de Fuca….such a Steamer would be of great service in transporting supplies from post to post…and would save a large amount of contingent expenses." He finally reported that "This post is paid once in 4 months" but may be paid oftener. Overall Mansfield found the post in good order.[208]

Fort Bellingham 7–8 December 1858

Mansfield's next inspection was at Fort Bellingham which he accomplished on 7 and 8 December 1858. He wrote his report from San Francisco to the Adjutant General on 10 January 1859. He departed "from Port Townsend in the Revenue Cutter *Jefferson Davis*" which was placed at his disposal "and without which I probably would not have been able, except with much delay and inconvenience, to reach my destination and we sailed for Fort Bellingham where I landed early in the morning of the 7th." The fort was located on the north shore of Bellingham Bay about 50 miles from Port Townsend. He found it "beautifully situated about 80 feet above the sea." He noted that it was cold in winter "with frequent rain and snow…but owing to the proximity to the ocean and southerly winds, the snow seldom fall over 6 inches and goes off quick. One inch of snow was on the ground at the time of this inspection." He noted that the post was established for one company by order of Lieutenant Colonel Silas Casey 16 August 1856 for Company D, 9th Infantry and started on 27 August. It was built on private land and the owner refused the Army's offer and "he with his family was finally forcibly put off the premises by the troops." That site was chosen as it was the only piece of land nearby that had a good spring. Unlike many posts, this one was "within an enclosed square of about 80 yards per side made of palisades set in the ground and loop holed for muskets and flanked by two block houses two stories high placed for mountain howitzers and loop holed and is provided with three gates. All the buildings are one story." He found the

[208] Courtesy of the Middlesex County Historical Society; Douglas, *Readings in Pacific Northwest History*, 157-163. "This report [for Oregon written to Lieutenant General Winfield Scott] was written at San Francisco, where Colonel Mansfield had gone to complete his reports on the Pacific Northwest and to begin an inspection of the Department of California. Fort Townsend was established by Major Granville Owen Haller on 6 October 1856 and buildings were completed for a one-company post. The company there was transferred to San Juan Island in 1859 but reestablished in 1874. In 1895, it was abandoned after it was destroyed by a fire. Interesting to note that he opined that more "American Citizens" were needed to make good noncommissioned officers. Major Haller was a rare non-West Point officer who entered service as a second lieutenant in the 4th Infantry in 1839. He was brevetted to captain and major during the Mexican-American War. He was dismissed from the Union Army in 1863 but rejoined in 1879 as a colonel. He retired in 1882 and died in 1897. Colonel Silas Casey was an 1826 West Point graduate who was brevetted to major and lieutenant colonel during the Mexican-American War and to brigadier and major general during the Civil War. He retired from the Army in 1868 and died in 1882.

officers' and enlisted quarters "ample" as were the store houses, the Quartermaster's and Commissary's buildings. A block house near the shore was used as a prison. The hospital, laundresses' houses, carpenters and smith shops, barn and root house all in good order in frame buildings. "The garden is quite large and affords all the vegetable required....the troops are well quartered and there seems to be nothing wanted of consequence." He did find that the military road between the post and Fort Steilacoom needed "some bridging and alteration ...before it be passible with wagons. This is an important matter as the Bay is quite shoal immediately in from of the post for ½ of a mile off the good anchorage." Flats were used to offload cargo in fair weather however. Captain George E. Pickett was in command of the post but was on leave leaving Lieutenant James W. Forsyth in command of nine staff enlisted and 57 privates of which two were sick, six confined, and 14 on extra duty. He found that "The company was neat on inspection; it passed in review and drilled at the Light Infantry and rifle and as skirmishers and fired at the target 6'x22" at 200 yards distant, one round for 40 men and put only one shot in the target (3%). This only showed the want of instruction and practice; the drills were tolerable. It was armed with the Harpers Ferry rifle and sword bayonet but these arms were old and much out of order, the new musket was expected soon. It was well commanded by Lieutenant Forsyth who is a highly meritorious officer." He also found the quarters neat with the men in two tier bunks. Company books in good order showing 50 desertions in three years. He wrote that "the company raised 1,500 bushels of potatoes for its use besides other vegetables." Post ordnance consisted of one six pounder brass gun and two 12 pounder brass mountain howitzers. The post hospital was in good order and the post was a healthy one. The Quartermaster's and Commissary Departments were in good order but he noted the lack "of shirts, socks, drawers and small sized shoes." Lieutenant Forsyth served as both the Quartermaster and Commissary officers. The 1,000 Indians nearby were peaceable. He concluded by again lauding Lieutenant Forsyth, the only officer on site, "who manifested much ability and zeal and the post was in a good state of discipline but like all posts in this new country the soldiers work more than they drill and they need instruction here as well as at other posts in target firing, rifle drill, and bayonet exercises." Forsyth served Mansfield briefly as an aide during the Battle of Antietam in September 1862.[209]

---

[209] Letters courtesy of the Middlesex County Historical Society. Captain George Edward Pickett was a 1846 West Point graduate who was brevetted to first lieutenant and captain during the Mexican-American War. He resigned in 1861 and became a Confederate major general. He died in 1875. Lieutenant James William Forsyth was an 1856 West point graduate and was brevetted from major through brigadier general during the Civil War. He was an aide to Mansfield during the Battle of Antietam from 15 through 17 September 1862. He retired in 1897 as a major general and died in 1906.

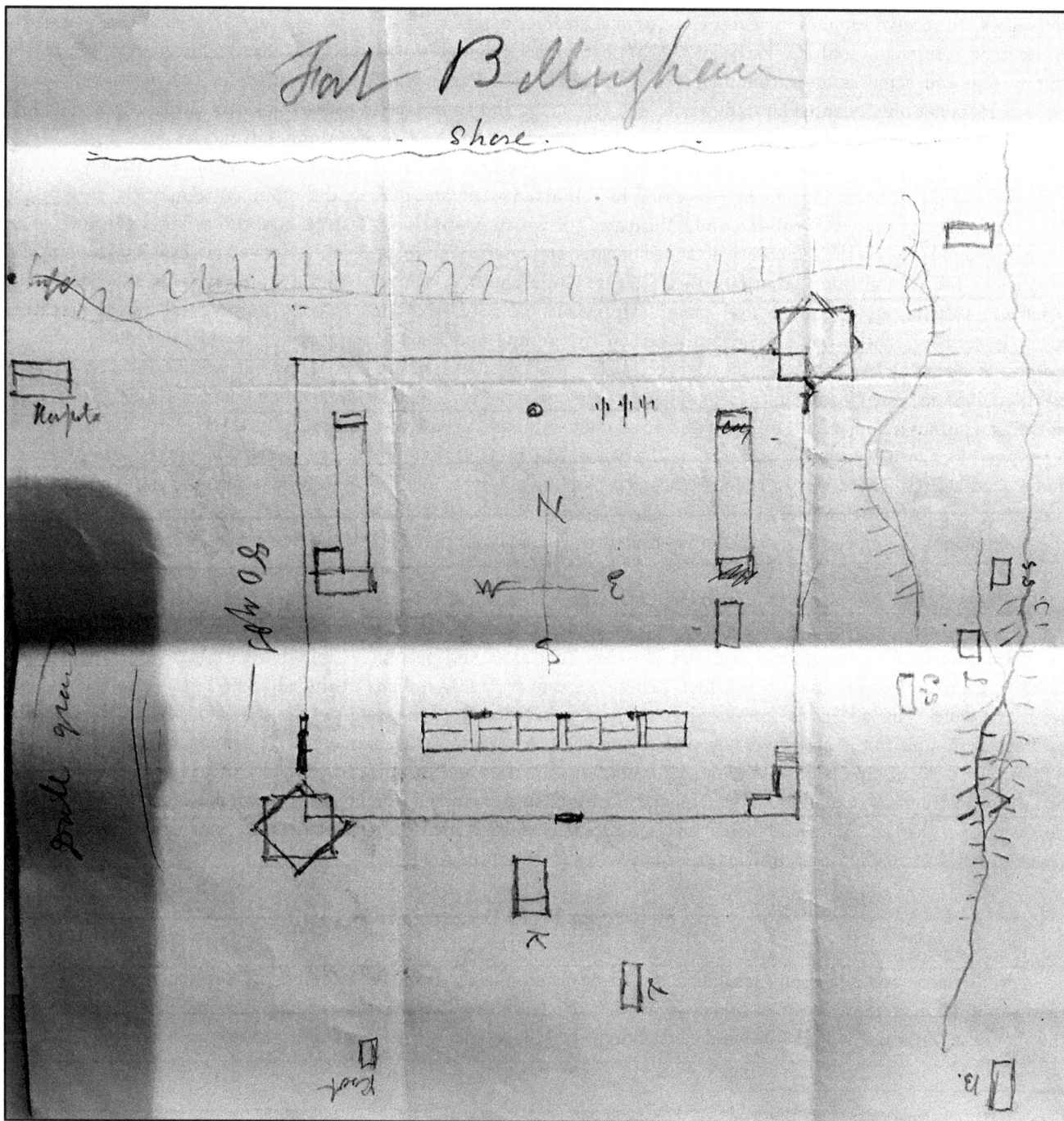

Mansfield's sketch of the plan of Fort Bellingham. Courtesy of the Middlesex County Historical Society.

Northwest Boundary Commission Escort Camp at Semi-ah-moo 10–12 December 1858

Off went the peripatetic inspector again this time into Canada to inspect the Escort of the Boundary Commission at Semi-ah-moo on the 10th through the 12th of December 1858. He reported on 14 January 1859 from San Francisco that he left Fort Bellingham "on the 8th in the Revenue Cutter *Jefferson Davis*...and after much cold and bad weather with rain and snow reached [Semi-ah-moo on] on the 10th and immediately commenced my inspection." That place was located on the beach on the north side of "a fine little bay of that name....It seems to be well selected for the object of the Commissioner, Archibald Campbell, and his astronomers, and is found to be on British soil, a very unimportant matter as it is but a temporary position. It is 2 ½ miles by land from Semi-ah-moo city, a little village growing up in our Territory on the south side of the Bay where there is good anchorage....It is about 55 miles from Port Townsend" and he found it had "a good spring of water" and in a neighborhood "with a thick growth of fir, spruce and cedar....It is convenient to receive supplies by water and the mail steamer makes from Olympia her regular trips to this place." He wrote that Lieutenant John G. Parke of the Topographical Engineers was the only Army officer attached to the commission and acted as an astronomer. Mansfield wrote that Parke was "well qualified for the position in every respect. He is not only talented but industrious and systematic and an ornament to his particular Corps." Parke told him that the commission would probably next winter be quartered near the Cascade Mountains not far from Fort Colville "Hence the necessity of establishing a post in that quarter the next summer." Company F of the 9th Infantry was the commission's escort with Captain D. Woodruff in command with one officer, the other on temporary duty at the Military Academy; nine staff enlisted and 63 privates "of which 5 were sick, 1 sergeant and 6 privates confined, 8 on extra duty and [10]… at the temporary detached depot…on Fraser River about 35 miles above Fort Langley guarding the supplies of the commission." Another officer, Lieutenant August V. Kautz of the 4th Infantry, was attached to the command as acting quartermaster and commissary. Mansfield noted that "It was cold, stormy, and freezing weather when I was here. There was 6 inches of snow on the ground and it was impracticable to turn out the men and I contented myself by inspecting the quarters, etc." The company had Harpers Ferry rifles but were to be soon replaced by rifled muskets. The troops and the Commission were quartered in "rough sheds of rough boards put up to answer the immediate purposes and are all sufficient and answer a very good purpose at a cost to the government of $5,500." There were two blockhouses with one occupied by the guard. The barracks had no bunks but had a messroom and a kitchen and a good bakery. There was an adequate hospital. Among other complaints to Mansfield, a solder stated that he had been shot by a Commission employee because he continued to talk to "a young squaw" who was apparently a friend of the Commission member. Mansfield wrote that the Commission member should have been turned over to civil authorities to be dealt with but that would have been difficult given the remote location of the post. Mansfield stated that he would refer the whole matter to General Harney. Mansfield reported that there was little forage at hand for horses and mules and there was a deficiency of under clothing and shoes sized seven, eight, and nine. Indians numbering about 50 in the immediate vicinity were "harmless and peaceable" but there were "about 100 at Point Roberts, drunken and disposed to mischief." There were over 23,000 Indians in the adjacent British possessions who were "the worst" but "all that is necessary is to keep these Indians out of the waters of the U.S. and this can only be done by steamer suitable to the object as I have before and shall write again." He commented on the command's discipline: "I do not regard the discipline of this command as what it should be and I think this company should have the advantage of further instruction at some post like Steilacoom. I will suggest to the Commanding general of this department the necessity of a change." Mansfield wrote that the company needed its officers so Lieutenant Kautz must remain as its Quartermaster and Commissary officers especially when it was in the field.[210]

Fort Steilacoom 14–19 December 1858

Fort Steilacoom was next on Mansfield's list; his inspection lasted from 14 December 1858 to the 19th. He wrote his report on 8 January 1859 from San Francisco. He left the Boundary Commission camp at 12 noon on 12 December on the *Jefferson Davis* and "with a fair wind, and without making a tack, we reached…Port Townsend at 12 midnight, and

[210] Courtesy of the Middlesex County Historical Society. Semi-ah-moo was the name of an Indian tribe occupying the area; today it is usually spelled Semiahmoo. The name means "half-moon" which describes the crescent shaped land of the bay. Mansfield's comment that the post was in British territory highlights the work of the commission as today the international boundary is about one mile north of this site. Obviously the Boundary Commission was settling the exact location of the boundary and engaged in joint negotiations with British surveyors from 1857-1862. The British commission for the Land Boundary Survey of the 49th Parallel was commanded by Captain John Summerfield Hawkins of the Royal Engineers. Archibald Campbell graduated from West Point in 1835 but resigned in 1836 to pursue a civil engineering career. In 1845 he began what would become a 31 year career with the U.S. government. In 1857 he was appointed the American Commissioner for the land survey of the 49th parallel from the Gulf of Georgia to the summit of the Rocky Mountains and the water boundary through the San Juan Islands and Straits of Juan de Fuca to the Pacific Ocean. Land Surveyors' Association of Washington Historical Society, Denny DeMeyer, "Campbell versus Hawkins: The Sometimes Stormy Relationship between the American & British Commissioners to the 1857-1862 Northwest Boundary Survey;" http://lsawhistorical.org/documents/articles_CampbellvrsHawkinPOB.pdf, accessed 17 August 2018. Lieutenant John Grubb Parke was an 1849 West Point graduate who was brevetted from lieutenant colonel to major general during the Civil War. He retired as a colonel of engineers in 1889 and died in 1900. Captain Dickinson Woodruff was directly appointed as a lieutenant colonel of a New Jersey battalion in 1847 and discharged in 1848. He became a captain of the 9th Infantry in 1855 and remained in the Army and retired as a lieutenant colonel in 1870, and died in 1896. Fort Colville was established by the Hudson's Bay Company in 1826, 10 miles east of the Columbia River and about 30 miles south of the Canadian border. About 14 miles to the west of that fort, Fort Colville (Harney's Depot) was established on 15 June 1859 to provide a base for the Boundary Commission. It was established by Captain Pinkney Lugenbeel of the 9th Infantry. It was abandoned in 1882.

the next night the 13th I was so fortunate as to take passage in the Pacific Mail Steamer *Panama*, and was landed at Steilacoom early in the morning of the 14th." He wrote that the post was "located about one and a half miles from the town of that name on the eastern shore of Puget Sound...in an old Hudson Bay trading post. It is about 25 miles from Olympia both by land and water. It is in direct communication by land say 115 miles to Monticello near the mouth of the Cowlitz River thence by steamer some 50 miles up the Columbia River to Fort Vancouver....It is about 70 miles from Port Townsend by water only." He next recommended that the road to Fort Bellingham which was about 100 miles away should be completed "without delay." He wrote that "this post is of the first importance and one where the gravelly prairie all around it, is such that troops, both horse and foot, can drill and be instructed at all seasons of the year, as the ground is not materially softened by the rains of the wet season which are intermittent and not continuous, and the snows are mostly marginal. Such is the importance of this post, that it should never have less than three companies always highly instructed in the use of their arms, in every particular and commanded by an officer of character and there should be here a first rate small steamer always ready at any time and capable of moving rapidly and calculate for the rough seas, and weather of the waters of Puget Sound and the northern Pacific Ocean. With this boat, supplies could be sent and troops in emergency landed at any spot against the Indians." Mansfield was always worried about Indian tribes located in British territories which he here estimated at 45,000 who are "always ready for murder and plunder. Many of these Indians are Cannibals and are always ready to capture the Indians within our territory and make slaves of them. With a steamer at command there and a system of telegraphs from the tops of the heights of the Islands from Port Townsend and Bellingham Bay to this post, a force could be brought down on these northern intruders within our waters unexpectedly to them and sink their large canoes at once. There is no safety without a steamer and I most urgently recommend one be built expressly for this object and kept subject to the order of the Commanding Officer of this post."[211]

He wrote that the post was "rebuilt on the old spot claimed by the Puget Sound Agricultural Company." Lieutenant A.V. Kautz of the 4th Infantry as acting assistant quartermaster on 30 July 1847 gave to that company $600 for ten years to occupy the land. Mansfield was critical that the contract did not address buildings present at the time the contract was agreed to and did not address buildings remaining at the end of the contract. "I would recommend that Congress make an appropriation of 2 hundred thousand dollars to liquidate all their claims to soil within our Territory north of the Columbia River." He found that quarters were erected "for a post of three companies, and a field officer, and probably is the best arranged post as a whole in this Department and amply provided." The "buildings are all new with but trifling exception and ample for all the command. The soldiers are very well provided for. There seems to be nothing more required for buildings. The Post is supplied by a magnificent spring source 500 yards off and the water thrown into a reservoir within the enclosure." He also found "an excellent garden...4 miles off and is the only suitable spot for that purpose. It yields abundant vegetables for both summer and winter. Each company had 500 bushels of potatoes for the winter." Lieutenant Colonel Silas Casey of the 9th Infantry commanded the post. Company A of the 4th Infantry was commanded by Captain Maurice Maloney but Lieutenant Kautz was on detached service at Semi-ah-moo and Lieutenant Edward J. Conner was the acting post adjutant; there were 10 staff enlisted with 74 privates of which 10 were sick, four confined, 20 on extra duty, seven absent with leave, two absent without leave, and one absent confined. Mansfield noted that this company had the new rifled muskets but "old knapsacks, tin canteens and old caps." The company was well quartered and the men slept in double bunks; there was a good mess room and kitchen and well provided. Company books were in good order; he noted a total of 25 desertions in three years however. Company C of the 4th Infantry had Captain Lewis C. Hunt newly in command but not able to attend inspection due to his recent arrival; Lieutenant Arthur Shaaff was in command on parade. The company had nine staff enlisted with 71 privates, of which there were seven sick, five confined, 14 on extra duty, and four on detached service. The company also had the new rifled musket but old knapsacks and old caps with the execrable gutta percha canteens. He found the company well quartered and its books in order; there were a total of 30 desertions in the last three years. Company H of the 9th Infantry was commanded by Captain Thomas C. English but Lieutenant Edwin J. Harvie was the post's acting quartermaster and commissary officer; also present was Lieutenant Charles A. Reynolds along with 10 staff noncommissioned officers and 49 privates of which there were seven sick, three confined, 14 on extra duty and 10 on detached service. He took notice of its arms: the Harpers Ferry rifles which were "much worn and many out of order." The company was well quartered with a messroom and kitchen with double bunks in their barracks but as he previously

---

[211] Letter courtesy of the Middlesex County Historical Society.

reported, deficient in drawers and properly sized shoes. The company's books were in good order showing 47 desertions in three years.[212]

The post's Guard and Guardhouse was in proper order as was the hospital. He noted that the post was "not sickly" and the hospital had ample room. The post had three twelve pounder mountain howitzers "in excellent order" and the "ordnance is well stored in a good wooden magazine well-constructed for the purpose and a good ordnance sergeant has the charge of the same." The Quartermaster's Department was in good order except Mansfield noted that an extra duty man was working on a bureau; Mansfield reported this to Colonel Casey who had this stopped. Mansfield again noted the dearth of small sized shoes, stocking, and drawers. The Commissary Department was also in good order except for the lack of rice and candles. Mansfield wrote that "This post is extremely well commanded by Lieutenant Colonel Casey an officer of high military attainments and character and in case of a war he is well qualified to command in these waters. The discipline is good and harmony both among the officers and men....the soldiers appear contented and have got up a literary society and some books as a library." Mansfield reported that "Colonel Casey divided the command into 4 companies and took them through the battalion drill of light infantry and the movements were tolerably well performed. It showed however that most of the time had been devoted to labor; rain interrupted the drill at skirmishers. The Companies fired separately at the target of 6' x 22" at 200 yards 40 men each one round and A Company hit in 8 shots (20%), H Company 7 (18%), C. Company 9 (23%). This last company had the best shots in this Department and the 3 Companies together put in more shots than any three Companies at any post in this Department. This is owing to the fact that it was the last post of this Department inspected by me and they had had more time to be instructed since the order of General Harney on this point." Mansfield estimated that there were about 2,500 Indians within 25 miles of the post but they were "all peaceable and there seems to be nothing at present to be apprehended."[213]

---

[212] Letter courtesy of the Middlesex County Historical Society.

[213] Letter courtesy of the Middlesex County Historical Society. Captain Maurice Maloney was a rare officer who had risen from the enlisted ranks. This Irish-born officer enlisted as a private in 1836 and rose through the ranks to sergeant major by 1846. During the Mexican-American War, he was brevetted to first lieutenant and captain. During the Civil War, he was brevetted to lieutenant colonel and colonel. He retired in 1870 as a lieutenant colonel and died in 1872. Captain Lewis Cass Hunt was an 1847 West Point graduate who was brevetted from major to brigadier general during the Civil War. He remained in the Army and died as a colonel in 1886. Lieutenant Edward J. Conner was an 1857 West Point graduate who retired as a captain in 1863 and died in 1868. Lieutenant Arthur Shaaff was a civilian direct appointment as a second lieutenant of the 4th Infantry in 1855. He resigned in 1861 and became a major in 1st Battalion Georgia Sharpshooters during the Civil War. He died in 1874. Captain Thomas Cooper English was an 1849 West Point graduate who was brevetted to lieutenant colonel during the Civil War. He remained in service and died in in 1876 as a lieutenant colonel. Lieutenant Edwin James Harvie was a Virginia Military Institute graduate and a direct civilian appointment as a second lieutenant in the 9th Infantry in 1855. He resigned in 1861 and became a colonel inspector general in the Confederate Army. He died in 1911. Lieutenant Charles Ambrose Reynolds joined as a private in the Mexican-American War and was demobilized in 1848. He was appointed a second lieutenant in the 9th Infantry in 1855 and during the Civil war was brevetted to major and lieutenant colonel. He retired from the Army in 1887 as a lieutenant colonel and died in 1896. Army quartermasters at various Northwest posts sometimes chartered steamers but the Army did not purchase any in the mid 1800's.

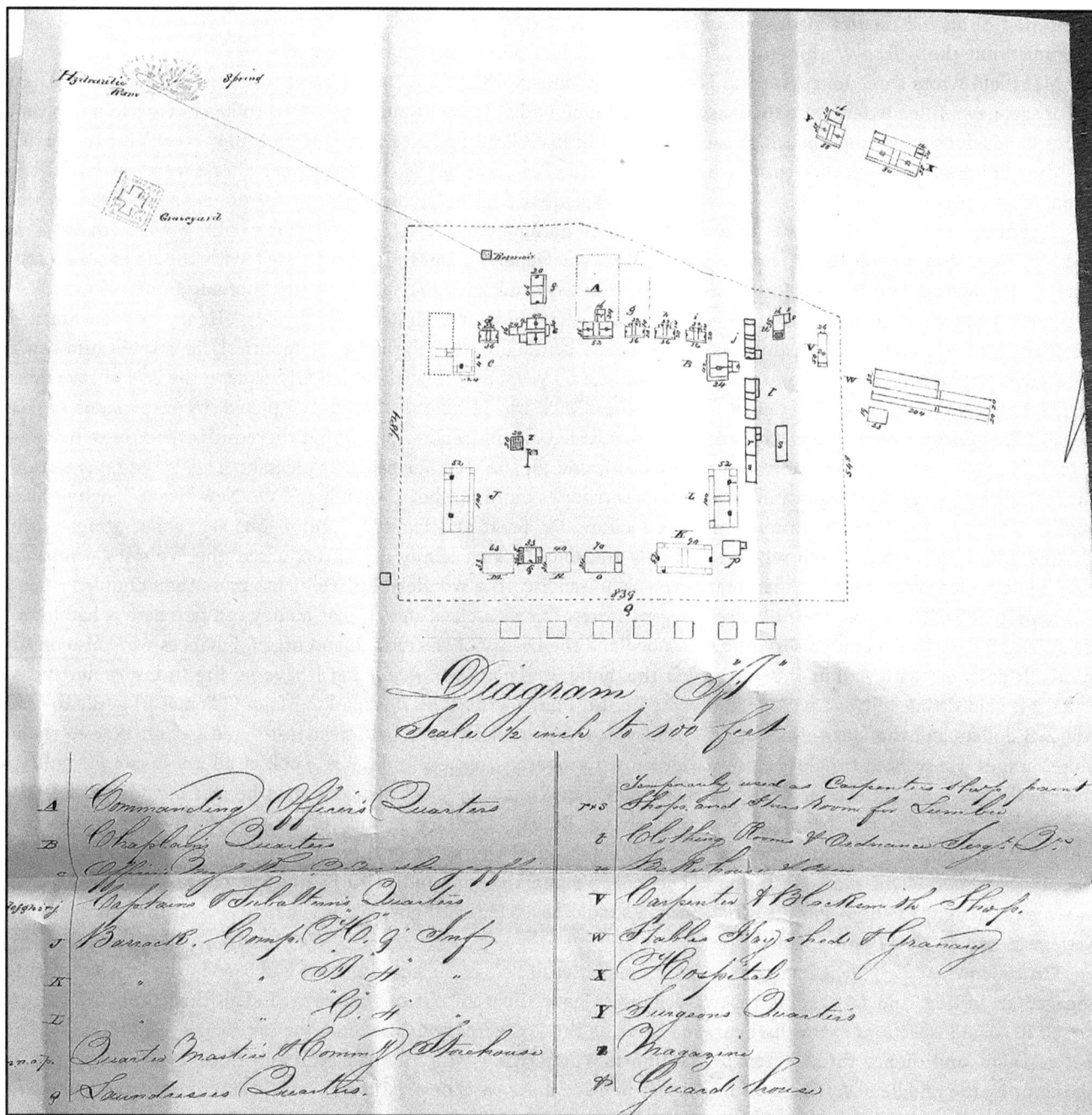

Diagram of Fort Steilacoom drawn for Mansfield by an officer at that post. Mansfield likely obtained it there and included it in his draft files and from which he would have made a copy for his official report. Courtesy of the Middlesex County Historical Society.

Mansfield wrote again to the Secretary of War, John B. Floyd, this time from Olympia, Washington Territory, on 24 December 1858. This follow up was necessary as he "completed the inspection of the four military posts on the waters of Puget Sound to express my views on the treaties made by Governor Stevens with the Indians in this quarter." He stated that there were about 12,000 Indians "in the different localities and on the reservations" and most were peaceable. The majority of those on the reservations took no part in the 1856 uprising and a few who did were punished. He was very critical that the treaties with the tribes on the several reservations were not ratified by the Senate and he had "reason to believe that there is fear of a war if they be not faithfully ratified and kept. The whites are now occupying the land and these [Indian] reserves should be kept sacred for the Indians and the treaties should be ratified as soon as possible and the Indians no longer be kept in doubt. The Indians are now all friendly and wish the treaties ratified. Neglect to do so might bring in this quarter a second Florida war which would be disastrous in the extreme. I therefor urge earnestly the ratification of all the treaties made by Governor Stevens at the present session of Congress." He concluded by again recommending the visit to Washington of Indian chiefs "under the protection of an agent."

Mansfield wrote three long letters to Louisa during January 1859 from the Oriental Hotel in San Francisco. These multipage, news-filled letters were the longest letters found which he had written to Louisa so he clearly had much time on his hands during his long sojourn in San Francisco. In his 3 January letter he wished a Happy New Year to her and his "dear children" and told her that he arrived there the "evening of the 31st December after a very successful trip through the waters of Puget Sound." He wrote that he spent six days in Olympia waiting for the mail and during which the "legislature of the Territory was in session and the Supreme Court also. I visited them both, got acquainted with many of them and all the Judges, and with the Surveyor General [James] Tilton. I dined with the acting Governor [Charles H.] Mason, an old acquaintance, on Christmas day, and with the Judges of the Supreme Court. On the 22nd December I dined on board the Steamer *Constitution* at Olympia at a dinner given by Mr. [Henry W.] Cushman, a merchant from Massachusetts, on the anniversary of the landing of the Pilgrims at Plymouth. I did not tell him it was the anniversary of my own birth and that I was then just 55 years old." Mansfield left Olympia on the 26th of December on the *Panama* but the next day rough seas made him "sick for 24 hours....I have completed my inspections of that Department [Oregon] and in ten days will have forwarded all my reports pertaining thereto. I expect next to move toward the South and leave the northern part of California till the weather becomes pleasant. This is the rainy season, but the rains are worse in Oregon and Washington Territories on the seaboard than here." On New Year's Day he "made several calls....on some of my Army friends also a Rev. Dr. Scott and family." After a long tale about a ragamuffin Mansfield met on the boat south who was actually the son of a rich family in San Francisco, the Walton's, whom he met, he described what he saw in San Francisco: "San Francisco is a wonderful place. It has more than doubled since I was here in 1854. There are elegant houses, elegant stores, fine churches, and all that money can purchase is had here." He at length described a church service he attended and the beauty of the church and organ. Finances were also on his mind: "It costs me with Arthur [his servant] at this hotel 30 dollars per week, and I have no fire in my room, and at times it is cold sitting still, and writing. But write I must. I have written by this mail to Major [Thomas J.] Leslie to send you 298 dollars and the Quartermaster will send you 138.67 dollars more." He next instructed her on how to spend those monies. He wanted to "clear all my Middletown property from encumbrance. Look at all my insurance policies and see that they do not expire." He spent many paragraphs chatting about acquaintances he met including one, "Mr. Carrington's son" who may have lost $1,200 gambling. Perhaps thinking about this wastage, he assured Louisa that while he was obliged to spend a "deal of money...I don't fool any away in wine, cigars, theaters, etc." In a P.S. he warned that "Miss Payne must not fill up her school [the one he sponsored] with babies. She has now got 60 desks all the room is designed to hold and the little children should be excluded." Mansfield was happy to hear that his daughter, Katie, was now in Miss Payne's school.[214]

On 16 January 1859, Mansfield again wrote a long letter to Louisa. He noted that he had been in the city "constantly engaged at writing, and forwarding reports. I hope to have them all out of the way....I shall then probably occupy myself in some inspections in this harbour, and leave on the 3rd February in a steamer for Los Angeles and thence to the fort at Tejon, and thence through San Bernardino to Yuma. After which I shall return to this city say about the 1st March or by the middle of April....I do not expect to leave these parts before June or July." He wrote that he had dined with Colonel Thomas Swords and his wife and also dined with Major Hartman Bache at the Union Club House "where bachelors congregate to dine, read papers, and play billiards." He observed that "people have breakfast before 10 a.m., lunch at one, and dine from 5 to 6 p.m. There is no business done after dinner." He dined with other officers and friends and discovered a distant relative, Mrs. Kife. He visited a gold refinery and wrote that he planned on visiting "all the institutions of the place." He then warned Louisa to guard against incendiaries. The barn must be kept locked at night and "all the fire buckets gathered and put up...where they should be perfectly convenient. I expect Douglas's Carpenter's shop will one day be burnt and then Mrs. Parker's house will have the full benefit of the tin roofs. Tell Liv to say to Mrs. Parker to take all straw and paper out of her garret and...put it my barn." He then gave her his usual

---

[214] Letter courtesy of the Middlesex County Historical Society. James Tilton was the first Surveyor General of the Washington Territory from 1854 to 1861. He entered service as a first lieutenant in 1847, was wounded, and was mustered out in 1848. He died in 1878. Charles H. Mason was the first Secretary of State for Washington Territory, and was acting Governor for two and a half years while the territorial Governor, Isaac Ingalls Stevens, conducted railroad surveys and concluded treaties with Indians. He died in 1859. Major Thomas Jefferson Leslie was an 1815 West Point graduate and was brevetted from lieutenant colonel to brigadier general during the Civil War. He spent his Army career as a paymaster and retired in 1869 as a major; he died in 1874.

domestic advice: "Get the children all up by daylight, otherwise they will be ruined by laziness. Be careful to be as economical as possible." He urged her to keep her bills paid. He maintains his concern with his daughter, Katie's, nearsightedness, so she should not be permitted to hold her book "up to her face." "She better not study much. Educate her physically and Mary too, by jumping, dancing, etc." Here he reflects the cultural view that women need not be highly educated as they were destined to become housewives.[215]

Mansfield wrote again to Louisa on Sunday, 23 January, and noted that he had "just returned from the Congregational church....It was full and the singing excellent." After he recited his religious adventures, he discussed a family which brought out from Virginia three slaves. He told Louisa how all of them disappeared, one taken by force, by a "dozen negroes." He lamented that "this is one of the evils of slavery." He wrote about another incident in which a boarder in his hotel had jumped out of a window and broke his leg—"He was said to be out of his mind." Mansfield told Louisa about Paymaster Colonel Andrew Jackson Coffee who lost $50,000 in speculations. "His brother-in-law helped him into the difficulty." He again was worried about fires: "I trust your kitchen is not filled nights by visitors, and that you have it closed at 9 p.m. without fail, and before you retire to bed, and see that your gate is fastened....I would have a well-regulated kitchen clear of idlers at all time." It seems that Louisa may have operated some sort of a food establishment but this has not been mentioned before. It may be that "idlers" may be deliverymen or other nonfamily members. Mansfield was very upset that his son, Samuel, was not at the head of his class, but was happy to hear that his other children were doing well. "Katie must learn to write a handsome hand, and so must Mary and Livingston. Livingston must practice at his music and all must dance and enjoy themselves and sing." He commented that he wished her to tell him when she received his letters he sent by steamer versus overland mail. He wrote that "The overland mail from Middletown goes to St. Louis, thence to Fort Smith, Arkansas, thence to El Paso, New Mexico, thence to Los Angeles, and thence to this City [San Francisco]. It takes about 25 days but it goes twice a week." He warned Louisa that "Mary is too sedentary and must move about house more....she should read and write elegantly and know the standard poets and read them and know history. Arithmetic is not very essential beyond what she now knows....Humbug women who know nothing about housekeeping are of no use to anybody. People must learn to work if they will advance in life. There is no use in a person sitting still and sucking their fingers."[216]

On 19 January 1859, Mansfield wrote from San Francisco to the Department Commander, Brigadier General William S. Harney, with his views on the recently completed inspections. Mansfield noted that when he began his inspections a war was underway with Indians east of the Cascade Mountains and he was instructed to "proceed to the seat of war" by orders of the Secretary of War. Mansfield began by inspecting Fort Walla-Walla "172 miles by land beyond The Dalles which I had just finished when Colonel Wright returned from the field with the troops under his command and I inspected those troops before they went into camp & quarters. Thence I inspected in succession forts Simcoe, Dalles, Cascades, Vancouver, Yamhill, Hoskins, Townsend, Billingham, escort camp at Semi-ah-moo, and Fort Steilacoom....Walla-Walla should always be a command under an efficient officer of at least 6 companies, so long as the country is not settled. Three of them should be Dragoons, and three light Infantry, & all be completely equipped & instructed in the use of the ball cartridge at all ranges. I look upon this position as the key to the Indian Country, and so long as it is properly commanded, there will be no fear of a combination among the Indians for war against the whites." He also urged that continued good relations remain with the Nez Perce Indians as they lead the Indian council and help with guides and furnishing fighting men. He further recommended that the road leading from The Dalles to Walla-Walla "requires much work...particularly the first 15 miles." Fort Simcoe 65 miles north of The Dalles only guards two mountain passes and does not need three companies but rather two. Fort Dalles has two companies with ample quarters but it needs a small hospital if two companies will remain but he believed one company would suffice. Fort Cascades he believed should also be retained as it was "an important link in the line of communication of troops and supplies...[and] should be retained as a one company post till the country is more completely settled." He found Fort Hoskins with two companies necessary and was Fort Yamhill, both should be retained but one company could be withdrawn as "in an emergency volunteer troops can be put at both." He finally wrote that Forts Townsend, Billingham and Steilacoom "cannot be dispensed with, nor reduced in garrisons with safety. I look upon Fort Steilacoom as an important depot post

---

[215] Letter courtesy of the Middlesex County Historical Society. Colonel Swords was an 1829 West point graduate who was brevetted to lieutenant colonel during the Mexican American War and to brigadier and major general during the Civil War; he died in 1886. Bache was an 1818 West Point graduate and was the great-grandson of Benjamin Franklin. He was promoted to colonel of engineers during the Civil War and was brevetted to brigadier general. He died in 1872.

[216] Letter courtesy of the Middlesex County Historical Society. For more about Coffee, see p. 436 below.

for supernumerary troops for the defense of the water of Puget Sound, and the 3 companies should always be well instructed in the use of the ball cartridge at all ranges, & completely equipped. And the post commanded by an efficient officer, and I know of no better officer under your command than Colonel Casey for this object." Mansfield repeated a request he made in his official report of his inspection of Fort Steilacoom that it was important to have "a small, fast steamer to be kept under the commanding officer…with a view to defend against the northern Indians, who have been disposed to enter our waters, & commit murders & steal our Indians, & make slaves." After numbering Indians in the area, Mansfield recommended that "The military road from Steilacoom to Billingham Bay [is] only partly opened" and the road from Steilacoom to Seattle…" should be finished. He also recommended that the troops at camp at Semi-ah-moo should be sent to another post such as Fort Steilacoom as their time on this escort duty is laborious. But he determined that one company on this duty would not suffice due to the large territory that must be covered so he suggested that a post be established near Colville. He found that drills and target firing needed improvement but Fort Steilacoom stood "first in your Department in target firing and Simcoe next. But I regard both as quite indifferent." Lastly, he reported that all funds for disbursing officers were proper and kept according to regulations.[217]

Department of California

Alcatraz Island	24 January 1859
Fort Point	26 January 1859
San Francisco	26 January–1 February 1859
Fort Tejon	21 February–3 March 1859
Fort Yuma	10–21 March 1859
San Diego	1 April 1859
Benicia Arsenal	11 April 1859
Fort Humboldt	20–25 April 1859
Fort Gaston	29 April–2 May 1859
Fort Ter-Waw	3 May 1859
Fort Umpqua, Oregon	9 May 1859
Presidio, San Francisco	17–19 May 1859
Fort Crook	25 May 1859
San Francisco	4 June 1859

Alcatraz Island 24 January 1859

In a series of 11 letters, Mansfield wrote to McDowell from San Francisco and reported his inspections of headquarters activities for the Department of California as well as for installations in the San Francisco area. The first was dated 24 January 1859 in which he described his inspection of the fortifications on Alcatrazes Island in the San Francisco harbor. It was under the superintendence of Lieutenant James B. McPherson since 1 January 1858 when he relieved Major Zealous Bates Tower who began the work. Mansfield wrote that "This work from the beginning has been extremely well conducted and managed and by the most faithful and meritorious officers. The progress has been great under the difficulties to the encountered in a new country at the time this work was commenced. At first it was difficult to obtain suitable building materials. Now stone is had at various places. Excellent granite comes from Folsom in the American River for both coping and walls. Granite for coping is had at Monterey. Blue calcareous sand stone is had in this harbor from Angel Island, brick in the great abundance and excellent quality form Sacramento; Lime from Diablo Mountain via San Joaquin River, water from Sausalito in the main and cement from New York and all at comparatively reasonable rates. The prices of labor, etc., have very much diminished since my inspection in 1854." Mansfield found all

---

[217] Letter 19 January 1859, NARA, RG 393, Pt. 1, Department of Oregon, 1858-61, Letters Received. Rough draft courtesy of the Middlesex County Historical Society.

books and reports in good order and Mansfield estimated that another $100,000 was needed to finish the works in addition to the $866,666 already appropriated. "Congress should not fail to make any appropriation without delay as this position is of the utmost importance." He found the batteries contemplated by the plan "essentially completed....There are now mounted 54 Columbiads, 4 forty two pounder guns and 15 carronades. In addition there is a battery made for 8 more Columbiads and 8 forty two pounders, in the aggregate 89 guns. There is a fine position for a battery of about 11 guns to front on the Golden Gate, which would make the chain of battery complete and which I think should be added to the present plan." Mansfield also noted that there were five eight inch Navy pattern and one eight inch Columbiad not yet mounted; additionally, he wrote that "there are wanting 8 forty two pounder guns and 2 eight inch Columbiads for the battery already prepared." He reported that the barrack was two stories high, made of brick, well placed on high ground "and calculated for two companies and will be finished in about three months." Mansfield was clearly very pleased with what he saw that his fellow engineer, McPherson, had accomplished: "The workmanship as well as the plans for the defences on this Island are excellent and highly creditable to the officers of the Corps of Engineers who have been engaged in them and the present superintendent, Lieutenant McPherson, is a young officer of high attainments in his Corps."[218]

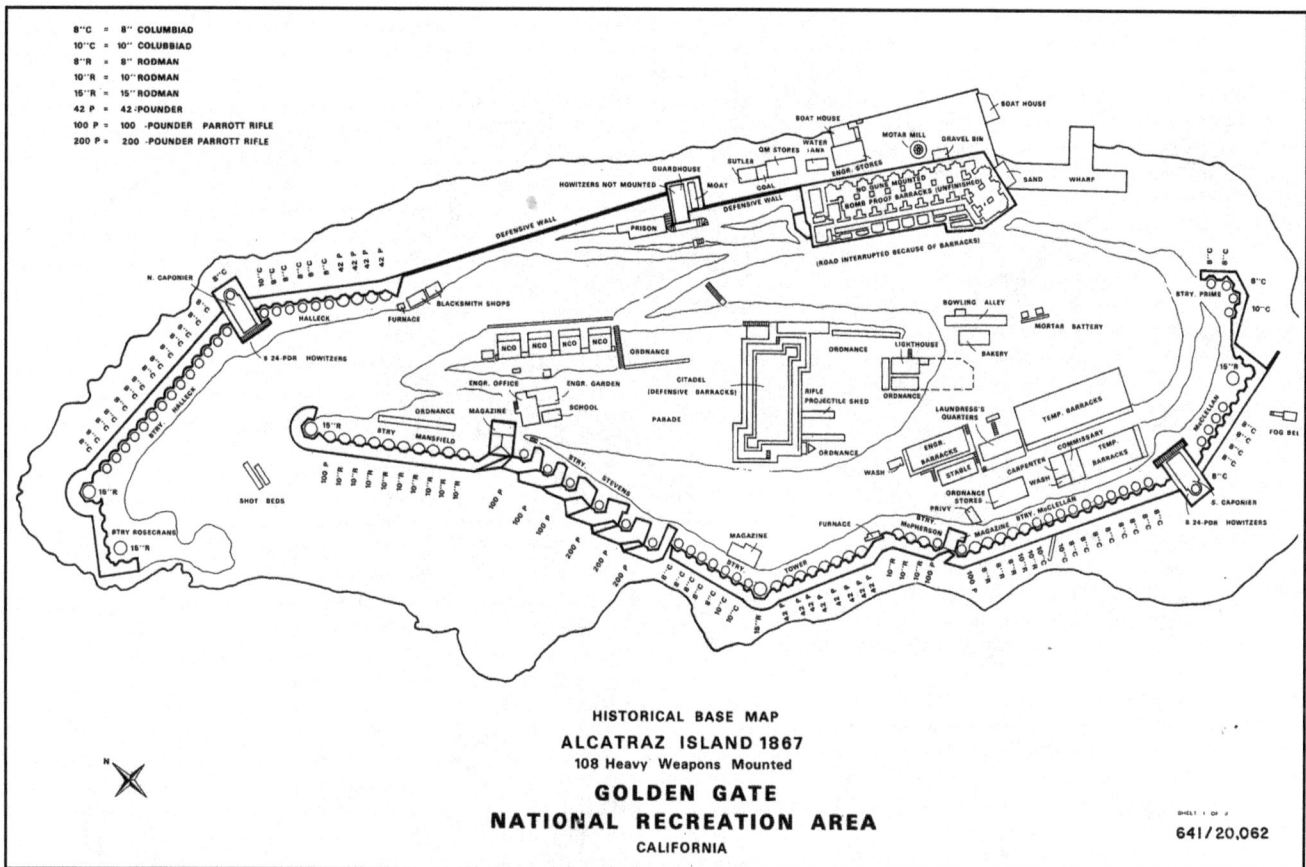

Map of Alcatraz showing 1867 configuration with 108 guns. Courtesy NPS.

---

[218] Letter courtesy of the Middlesex County Historical Society. Mormon Island Quarries, near Folsom, supplied granite for the first tier traverse circles while in 1858, an additional 200,00 bricks from San Quentin State Prison; *Abbreviated Fort Point Historic Structure Report*, Cultural Resources & Museum Management Division, Golden Gate National Recreation Area (Washington, D.C., NPS, 2006), 32. Lieutenant James Birdseye McPherson was an 1853 West Point graduate and was promoted to major general of volunteers in 1862. He was killed in action in 1864 near Atlanta, Georgia.

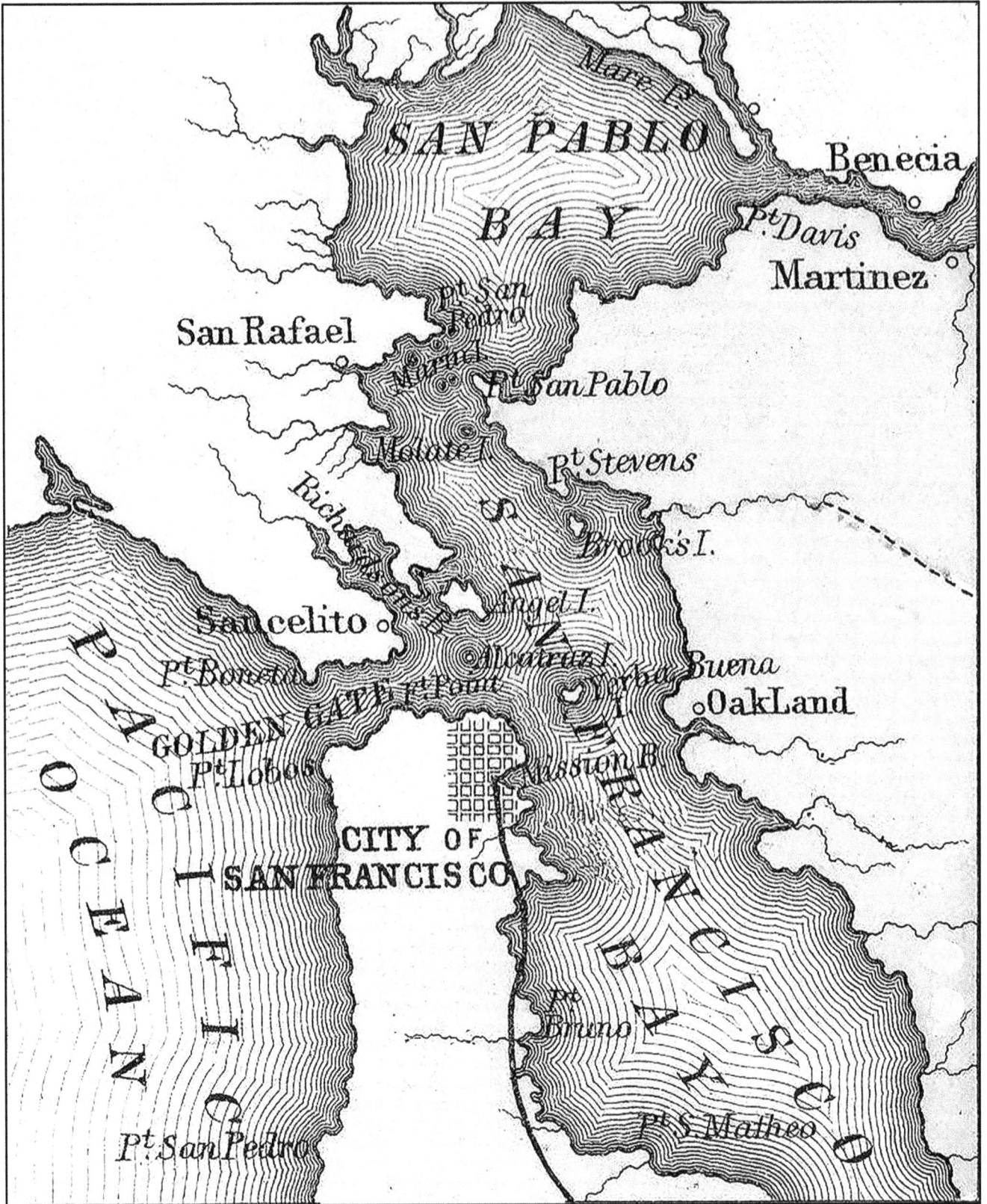

San Francisco Bay area in 1860 showing the City of San Francisco, the Golden Gate, Fort Point, Alcatraz, and Benicia. Courtesy Wikipedia.

Model of Fort Alcatraz on display at NPS, Alcatraz Island, showing the lighthouse and the 200' by 100' Citadel to its left. This model represents Alcatraz during its most heavily armed period when it mounted 108 guns from 1866 to 1868. Model researched, designed and constructed by NPS Ranger Rex Norman. Courtesy Wikipedia.

Fort Point 26 January 1859

Fort Point was next on his San Francisco tour which he inspected on 26 January 1859, the same day he wrote his report letter. The fort which protected the entrance to the harbor through the straits of the Golden Gate consisted of "three tiers of casemate guns high, surmounted by a barbette battery with a closed gorge the first story of which is devoted to guard, storeroom, magazine, etc., the 2nd to the officers' quarters, the 3rd to the soldiers' quarters." He wrote that the first tier was designed for 30 forty two pounders, the second for 30 eight inch Columbiads and the third for 30 eight inch Columbiads. The traverses were not ready for any of them, however. He further noted that the barbette was "well advanced but there will be no funds to complete this battery without further appropriations." It was intended for "36 8 and 10 inch Columbiads." He also found that a battery on a height just in the rear of the fort was completed which was designed for 8 eight inch and 2 ten inch Columbiads. He lamented that at the time of his inspection there were only a total of 10 guns mounted at Fort Point and outside of it. He found a total of 30 guns near the wharf or the fort, but he wrote that "Of course there will be wanted for this work, 106 heavy guns of suitable calibers in addition to those already here and it is important they should be shipped without delay. I will write to the Chief of Ordnance and to the ordnance officer at Benicia on this subject." Overall Mansfield was happy with what he found as far as the fort's construction was concerned: "This work is extremely well built in every particular, its foundation is of granite, its superstructure brick, with granite coins and entrance and cordon....This work has been in the hands of first rate officers of Engineers...[currently Lieutenant George Washington Custis] Lee." He found the books correct and described Lee as "a young officer of high attainment in his Corps." Mansfield again expressed his view of the importance of this post emphasizing that it must be completed as soon as possible "as the safety of this harbor and the Navy Yard in time of an unexpected war depends on these fortifications."[219]

---

[219] Letter courtesy of the Middlesex County Historical Society. This fort he noted had received $1,545,833 in appropriations to 31 December 1858, a significant sum for this vital post but more was needed as he found. The Fort Point works was designed to hold a total of 142 guns; Erwin N. Thompson, *Historic Resource Study: Seacoast Fortifications, San Francisco Harbor, Golden Gate National Recreation Area, California* (NPS, 1979), 40.

Photograph of Fort Point taken in 1869 looking north across the Golden Gate. Courtesy NARA.

San Francisco 26 January–1 February 1859

Also on the 26th the busy Mansfield "inspected the operations of Lieutenant R[obert] S[tockton] Williamson of the Topographical Engineers." Williams was stationed there under the orders of General Clarke and the Topographical Bureau in Washington. He had the superintendence of the military roads from Camp Stewart to Myrtle Creek and from Myrtle Creek to Scottsburg in Oregon. Williams was "also in charge of a Geographical Exploration by order of the Topographical Bureau in Mount Diablo....The services of a Topographical Engineer, under the orders of the Genl. Commanding this Department might be very useful to reconnoitre and report maps of certain locations and waters where information is wanted." Mansfield found his books in order but believed that he paid $15 per month too much rent for his office. Mansfield continued his 26 January inspection marathon by examining Paymaster Samuel Woods. Mansfield found his "accounts...correctly kept and his vouchers and account current to the 30th November" and his December accounts ready to be forwarded. Mansfield determined that Major Woods's "duties appear to be ably and faithfully performed." [220]

The next day on the 27th, Mansfield inspected Paymaster Andrew Jackson Coffee and this provided what must have been something of an unpleasant surprise to the inspector. Mansfield began by reporting that Coffee's accounts were correctly kept but there the good news came to a crashing halt as he wrote: "I regret to have to state that from the 31st last August when he reported $49,985.80 due the U.S. to the present date. He acknowledges to me he is $49,985.80

Lee was the oldest son of Robert. E. Lee and was an 1854 West Point graduate who resigned in 1861 to join the Confederate Army where he attained the rank of major general. He died in 1913. Paymaster Samuel Woods was an 1837 West Point graduate who was brevetted to major and lieutenant colonel during the Mexican-American War and to colonel during the Civil War. He retired in 1881 as a Paymaster Colonel and died in 1887.

[220] Letters courtesy of the Middlesex County Historical Society. Lieutenant Robert Stockton Williamson was an 1848 West Point graduate and was brevetted to major and lieutenant colonel during the Civil War. He retired from the Army due to illness in 1882 as a lieutenant colonel and died in 1882.

deficient which he says he has lost in unofficial and private transactions, but desires to be afforded time till the 1st July next when he hopes to be able to pay about $40,000 of it. A copy of this report I presume should be forwarded to the Paymaster General." Undoubtedly Colonel Coffee would have much explaining to do in short order. The following day the indefatigable Mansfield inspected Major Richard Bland Lee, the Chief Commissary of Subsistence for the Departments of California and Oregon. Unlike poor Colonel Coffee, Lee's books and accounts were in "excellent order....The whole duty is well and satisfactorily performed by Major Lee and his accounts to the close of December have been forwarded." Next on the 28th of January 1859, Mansfield inspected Surgeon Charles McCormick who was the Chief Medical Doctor for the Departments of California and Oregon. The doctor afforded "medical aid to all officers and soldiers that may be at or near these Headquarters. He had no funds and keeps no office and but few medicines in his quarters. His duties are satisfactorily performed." Medical supplies were stored at Benicia and under direct supervision of the Assistant Surgeon stationed there." The next day Mansfield again inspected the office of a Topographical Engineer, Major Hartman Bache. This engineer "was assigned to duty here as General Superintendent of Light Houses on the Pacific Coast and of the military roads and inspector of ...buoys." He also constructed fog bells and a fog whistle. His accounts, records and drawings were found to be correct and creditable. Mansfield noted that Bache was relieved from superintendence of military roads six months previously and from the duty of inspector of light houses and buoys six weeks earlier. Likely his duties of construction in addition to those duties was too onerous. Overall Mansfield was pleased with Major Bache's performance.[221]

Still in San Francisco, Mansfield inspected the Department Quartermaster General, Colonel Thomas Swords, on 29 January 1859. Swords supplied all the posts in the Department of California "and has so far supplied the Department of Oregon wither directly or indirectly with funds and quartermaster stores, etc." Mansfield found his "books and accounts...neatly and correctly kept....The main depot of supplies is at Benicia where there are other employees which I shall notice again in the inspection of that post. The duties are extremely well conducted by Colonel Swords and performed satisfactorily and to the credit of the service." Two days later on the 31st, he inspected Major Robert Allen, Assistant Quartermaster, stationed in San Francisco. Mansfield noted that Allen had been stationed there since his first inspection in 1854. Allen performed the duty of "transporting and forwarding troops and supplies, furnishes quarters and fuel to the Head Quarters of this Department and other officers stationed here, furnishes storehouses for the Chief Commissary, and offices to the Paymasters stationed here." Mansfield found his books "perfectly kept" and "all the duties well performed." Finally on 1 February Mansfield performed his last in this series of inspection by inspecting Paymaster George H. Ringgold. Ringgold was ordered to relieve Lieutenant Colonel Coffee as chief paymaster in the Department and did so on 11 August 1858. Mansfield reported that Coffee "turned over no funds to Major Ringgold." Mansfield noted that Ringgold appeared to perform his duties "faithfully."[222]

On 4 February 1859 Mansfield wrote McDowell from San Francisco informing him that he would leave there on the 8th or 9th of February to inspect Fort Yuma. He planned on sailing with the steamer *Uncle Sam* which would also carry Lieutenant Colonel Hoffman with five companies of the 6th Infantry via the Gulf of California to the mouth of the Colorado River and then by mail steamers and a land march to Fort Yuma. Two companies which marched from Los Angeles would meet the other troops there then the whole force would move up the Colorado River to establish a post at Beale's Crossing. That post was necessary to fight the Mohave and Paiute Indians in the area. But for Mansfield the importance of this trip was that he wanted to see the practicability of the water route from San Francisco to Fort Yuma. Then on 17 February Mansfield wrote McDowell from San Francisco describing an adventurous trip he took on the steamship *Uncle Sam* starting on the 11th. Severe storms and winds cause damage to the ship remedied by repairs and

---

[221] Letters courtesy of the Middlesex County Historical Society. Coffee was born in Tennessee and was the grandnephew of Andrew Jackson; he attended West Point for one year from 1 July 1837 but left to become a civilian engineer. He became a paymaster for volunteers in 1846 and a U.S. Army paymaster in 1847. He was brevetted to lieutenant colonel for Buena Vista in 1847, and resigned 31 July 1859 undoubtedly due to his misappropriation of almost $50,000. He lived in Oakland then moved to San Francisco and became a notary public. He died in 1891 in California. He was involved in land speculation in California near Oakland and perhaps lost the government funds in poor business decisions. "Andrew J. Coffee, Notable Career of an Old Californian," *San Francisco Chronicle*, 13 Mar 1891, p. 8. Major Richard Bland Lee was an 1817 West Point graduate who resigned in 1861 when he was a major in the Commissary Department. He became a colonel in the Confederate army Commissary Department; he died in 1875. Surgeon Charles McCormick became an Army Assistant Surgeon in 1836 and was brevetted to lieutenant colonel during the Civil War. He died in service as a colonel in 1877.

[222] Letters courtesy of the Middlesex County Historical Society. Major George Hay Ringgold was an 1833 West Point graduate who resigned from the Army in 1837 but reentered in 1846; he was promoted to lieutenant colonel in 1862 and died in 1864. Major Robert Allen was an 1836 West Point graduate who was brevetted to major during the Mexican-American War and from lieutenant colonel to major general during the Civil War. He retired in 1878 as a colonel and died in 1886.

lightening the load. It returned for repairs and left on the 12th with a lighter load. Mansfield wrote that he "gave up the trip to Yuma via the Gulf and shall proceed overland." On 5 March he wrote Louisa from Los Angeles and informed her that he left San Francisco on the 12th and arrived at Fort Tejon on the 21st. He told her he was staying at the Lafayette Hotel and had been busy writing up his report which he said he would mail with this letter. His overland trip as he later wrote to Louisa was less than pleasant and he probably was disappointed that he was unable to take steamers from San Francisco to Fort Yuma.[223]

Sketch of Los Angeles, United States, War Department, Reports of Explorations and Surveys, to Ascertain the Most Practicable and Economical Route for a Railroad from the Mississippi River to the Pacific Ocean, vol. 5, facing p. 34.

---

[223] Letters courtesy of the Middlesex County Historical Society. He also cautioned her to "Lock up my letters and do not leave them where Betsy can read them on the mantel piece. It is not proper anybody should know what I write to you about matters." It is not clear to which report he referred when he told her he would mail one with his 5 March letter. It may have been one of his monthly reports or just an update since his final reports were only finished and mailed once he returned to Middletown. Lieutenant Colonel William Hoffman was an 1829 West Point graduate who was brevetted to major and lieutenant colonel during the Mexican-American War and to brigadier and major general during the Civil War. He retired as a colonel in 1870 and died in 1884.

Mansfield's trip to southern California mainly by mail coach starting in San Francisco with his first stop at Fort Tejon. His next inspection was Fort Yuma followed by a mail coach and horseback ride to San Diego for three inspections there. He likely retraced his route using the same methods back to San Francisco but it is possible that he took a steamer to San Francisco from San Diego as he mentioned this plan in a letter to his wife written 26 March from Fort Yuma so both returns are shown here. Map courtesy LOC, Official Atlas, pl. 162.

Fort Tejon 21 February–3 March 1859

Also on 5 March 1859 Mansfield wrote to McDowell from Los Angeles with his inspection of Fort Tejon. He left San Francisco on 18 February on the overland mail coach and reached the fort on the 21st where he completed his inspection on 3 March. The post was designed in 1854 he wrote and "at the time I made an inspection of this Department and General Wool then in command of the Department desired me, in connection with the Indian Agent at that time [Edward F.] Beale, and Asst. Quartermaster Gordon, to select a suitable site for the same. We fixed on a site some 20 miles from this post in the valley near the Indian reservation and at the foot of the mountains which was deemed a strategic as well as a pleasant and comfortable and suitable place. At that time I could see no valid objections to it, and I have since my arrival at Tejon visited it again and am of the same opinion still, and believe it be a much more suitable position than this present site. The road through the canyon there is better and nearer to Los Angeles. Why it was not adopted as originally selected I cannot say." Mansfield was obviously not happy that his original choice was not used. He wrote that in its current location at 2,500 feet in elevation, was "a cold and damp and unpleasant climate for the whole fall, winter and spring and on the 1st and 2nd of this month the ground is white with snow and ice while on the Reservation the peach trees are in bloom." He also noted that there was no garden and no grazing within five miles but there was a good spring and "abundant oak for firewood." He wrote that the post was 374 miles from San Francisco and 100 miles from Los Angeles. He again commented on the post's location: "I think its site unfortunately selected, it should have been either north of this canyon….Yet it has ample drill grounds, and there has been so much expenditure here in the construction of quarters, that it seems now too late to change the location." He then spent many paragraphs describing problems the post had with earthquakes: "It is particularly exposed to earthquakes and every building is cracked by them and on one occasion the gable ends of two buildings were thrown down by an earth quake, and a few miles off I saw an immense crack and crevice in the earth extending for many miles caused recently by them….one person has been killed by the fall of an adobe building and one cow swallowed up." He then listed the dates and severity of the hundreds of shocks during the past few years. He noted that most of the buildings were well made of adobe and were ample—"There seems to be no necessity for any more buildings for the present."[224]

---

[224] Letter courtesy of the Middlesex County Historical Society. Tejon was the name given to the extreme southern portion of the Tulare Valley lying at the base of the mountains.

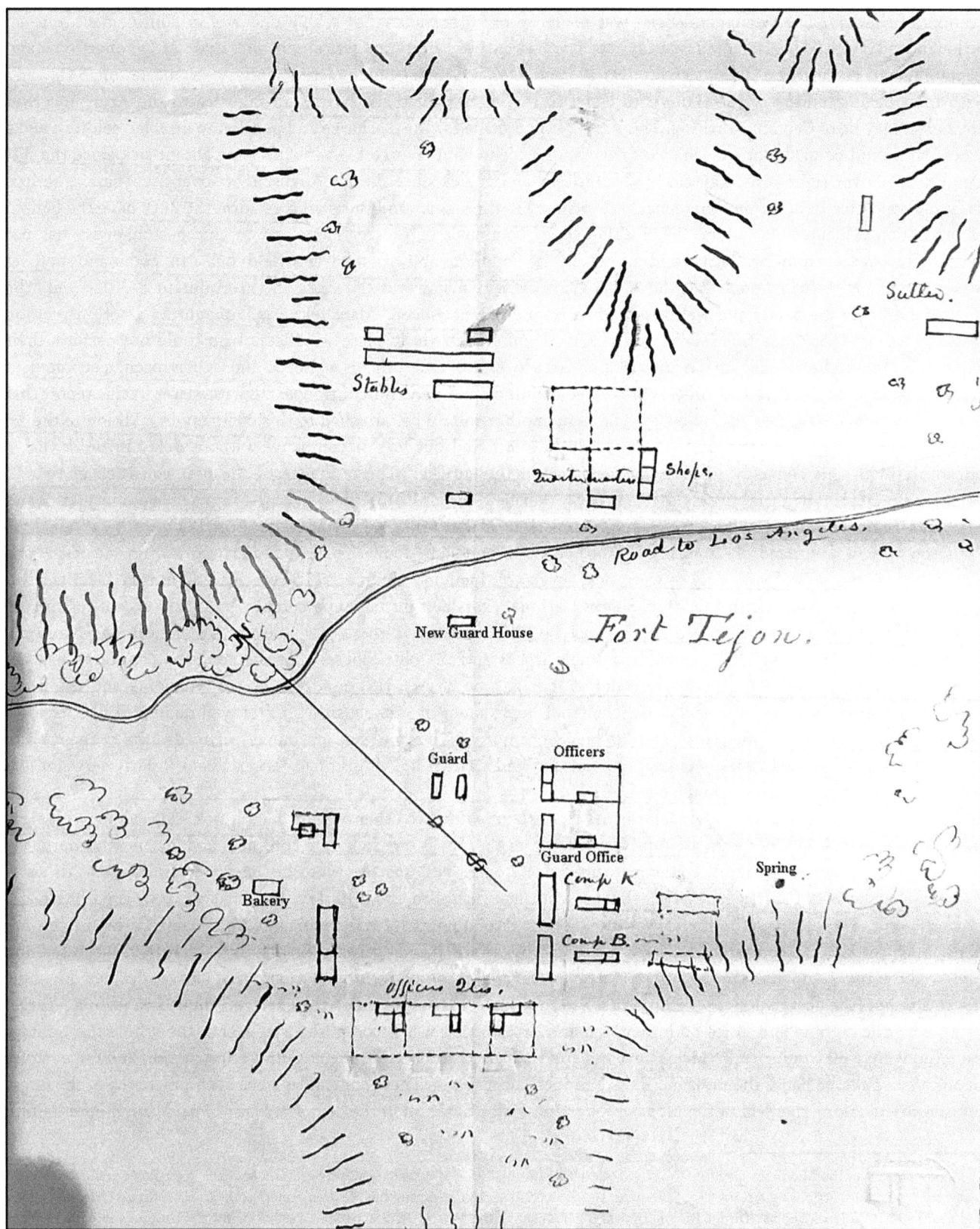

Mansfield's rough sketch map of Fort Tejon. The unlabeled building to the upper left of the officers' quarters at the bottom is likely the commanding officer's office and that of his staff. Above it may be the hospital. Courtesy of the Middlesex County Historical Society.

Mansfield next began his review of the troops at Fort Tejon, the headquarters of the 1st Dragoons, under the command of Lieutenant Colonel Benjamin Lloyd Beall who was temporarily absent at Los Angeles—he returned the evening of the 23rd. The Regimental Band was made up of 10 musicians "of which one was in confinement, one on furlough, and 3 sick." He also noted that Colonel Thomas Turner Fauntleroy was absent sick since 21 October 1857, and Captain Lucius B. Northrop absent sick for over 19 years "and as I understand practicing physic in Charleston, S.C., and I wish to call the attention of the General in Chief to this matter, particularly it is an injustice to the Army however pleasant it may be to Captain Northrop. There is provision made for the discharge and pension to disabled soldiers, and a provision should be made for a disabled officer. Second Lieutenant George F. Evans has been absent sick since the 30th October 1850 over eight years, Captain J.H. Whittlesey absent sick since the 21st August 1856, over 2 ½ years. A retired list is indispensable in order that there may be efficiency in the service and those who perform the duty have the benefit of promotion….Lieutenant Colonel Beall although in command of the regiment and of this post likewise has not entirely recovered from his hurts, and is not in my opinion able to take the field but can command here at headquarters." Mansfield found that the regimental sergeant major was the clerk in the Adjutant's Office and "the Regimental Books are neatly and well-kept and he is an efficient officer." Mansfield was highlighting a not uncommon situation for the U.S. Army since there was no retirement system yet in place so officers who could not perform their duties were nevertheless still on a regiment's books preventing able officers to serve and as has been seen often in Mansfield's reports, the dearth of officers prevented training and instruction of troops. He wrote later in this report that Company K would be losing one of its lieutenants so another should be "attached to this company in addition to the 2nd lieutenant in [A.B.] Chapmans' place [who would be promoted out of this company] without delay in order that 3 officers be with this company to meet the demands of the service." The ordnance of the post consisted of two 12 pounder mountain howitzers "in serviceable order." Mansfield listed the distribution of the regiment's companies: B and K at Fort Tejon; A and F at Fort Crook; C, E, F and H at Walla Walla, and D and G at Fort Buchanan. Captain J.W. Davidson was in command of Company B and had one lieutenant, four sergeants, four corporals, no musician, one farrier, and 48 privates of which three were sick, seven confined and 16 on extra duty; it had 57 horses. Like its sister Company K, it was armed with the sabre, Sharps Carbine, Colts belt pistol, and a complete uniform except for the old pattern cap and the absence of sword knots. And also like Company K, there was a deficiency of clothing—"drawers, stockings, boots, shoes, overalls, jackets, caps, stable frocks and the blue blouse." But the company "appeared neat on inspection and appearance well, arms in order" but it had no stocks. He found the horses "tolerable and the horse equipments generally worn out, [and] a deficiency of horse shoes of suitable size." It was well quartered like its sister company but unlike it the messroom and kitchen were not yet finished "and no bunks yet made." Its ordnance and property were well stored and its books "properly kept and written up." It also had "an excellent orderly sergeant and was in good discipline and well commanded."225

Company K was commanded by Major James H. Carleton with two other officers one on sick leave, along with eight staff enlisted including a farrier, and 46 privates of whom there was one sick, five confined, and 20 on extra duty; the company had 52 horses. Its arms, equipment, uniforms, horses, and quarters were in the same conditions as its sister company but he noted that it had an excellent set of mess furniture and a library. Its books were in good order and properly kept. The company he found was in excellent discipline and "well-commanded by Major Carleton who has done much for it." The company baked its own bread but there was no garden. On the 22nd, Mansfield inspected and reviewed the two companies through all of the cavalry exercises which went well except that "it was deemed advisable not to attempt [the charge due to] the little practice they had." Mansfield called the exercises "quite interesting." Target firing with the carbine and pistol both mounted and dismounted was accomplished well: "On the whole the military exercises were well conducted by Major Carleton and indicate that a better state of military instruction and target firing in our service can be had if the rank and file are properly instructed. These companies have been practicing at the target preparatory to taking the field in the Mohave River and Major Carleton in the day of my arrival paid [for]…ammunition

---

225 Letter courtesy of the Middlesex County Historical Society. Lieutenant Colonel Benjamin Lloyd Beall was an 1818 West Point graduate and was brevetted to major for actions against the Florida Indians, and to lieutenant colonel during the Mexican-American War. He retired as a major in 1862 and died in 1863. Colonel Thomas Turner Fauntleroy was a lieutenant in the War of 1812 appointed a major in the 2nd Dragoons in 1836 rising to colonel in 1850. He resigned in 1861 and became a brigadier general in the Virginia Militia and a major in the Confederate Army. He died in 1883. Captain Lucius Ballinger Northrop was an 1831 West Point graduate who resigned in 1861 and became a commissary general colonel in the Confederate Army. He died in 1894. Second Lieutenant George F. Evans was an 1846 West Point graduate who was brevetted to first lieutenant during the Mexican-American War. He died in 1859. Captain Joseph Hotchkiss Whittlesey was an 1844 West Point graduate who was brevetted to first lieutenant during the Mexican-American War. He retired in 1863 as a major and died in 1886. Lieutenant Alfred Brunson Chapman was an 1854 West Point graduate who resigned in 1861 and became a captain of artillery in the Confederate Army. Captain John Wynn Davidson was an 1845 West Point graduate who was brevetted from lieutenant colonel to major general during the Civil War. He died in service as a colonel in 1881.

out of his company fund for the 3 test shots." Mansfield found that some of the problems Company K had "was in consequence of some of the cartridges of that company not being made with sufficient powder for Sharps Rifles and not cutting off properly some of them hung fire." He found that one box of cartridges sent from Benicia were improperly made so Mansfield wrote that he "shall write to him accordingly to guard against experiments in an arm already sighted for certain ranges." Mansfield found a problem with Paymaster Ringgold and wrote that he was at the post "personally but 4 times in two years. The sutler sometimes pays for him. I regard this a bad practice." The sutler however, he wrote had "ample supplies" and "gives satisfaction." The horses for the two companies "were kept in temporary stables....and are daily herded on the scanty grass in the neighborhood within 8 miles. Barley is had in abundance. If this post had been placed as originally selected the horses could have grazed the whole winter in the Tulare Valley...New stables of adobe had been commenced....These stables should not be erected of adobe. They should be frame buildings to resist the shocks of earthquakes....I shall notify the General Commanding this Department accordingly." Mansfield also complained that the new guard house was "too far off, but work on it has been suspended. The present guard house I think preferable of the two." He found all well in the Adjutant's Office and saw that the band had adequate quarters "with a suitable kitchen and messroom." Mansfield also found the hospital adequate and the books in good order; he described it as a "healthy post." He was also pleased with his inspection of the Commissary Department as he found ample supplies, well stored; "his accounts and records are all properly kept." Similarly, the Quartermasters Department was in good order "with ample supplies except for some clothing items and horseshoes." He also found the books in good order. Mansfield visited the Indian reservation in Tulare Valley some 20 miles away and found about 1,000 on the reserve and "about 10 Rancherias....they have made some progress in civilization since I was here in 1854 but have lessened in numbers....now many of them live in permanent houses of adobe with chimneys—plant a few acres of land—raise most kinds of vegetables—keep fowls, hogs, cattle, horses and will soon have peaches and other fruit....There is no danger of these Indians making war on the White people and I regard them as perfectly peaceable and well disposed. There are no wild Indians here."[226]

Fort Yuma March 10–21 1859

Next came Fort Yuma at which Mansfield wrote his report on 21 March 1859 and reported that his inspection began on the 10th, the day he arrived from Los Angeles where he left three days earlier, and ended on 21 March. He wrote that he "left Los Angeles on the 7th instant via the overland mail and reached [Fort Yuma] on the 10th and immediately commenced the inspection....Fort Yuma is situated on the west bank of the Colorado River in the state of California at the junction of the Gila [River] with that river....it is 282 miles by stage road from Los Angeles, about 225 miles from San Diego, about 100 miles above the mouth of the Colorado River, about 600 miles from El Paso, 340 from Fort Tejon." The post was established by Major Samuel P. Heintzelman with three companies of the 2nd Infantry in 1850. It was located about 80 feet above the surrounding country on a plateau but he found it "isolated in the midst of a desert of 120 miles in every direction....It seldom rains here and the thermometer ranges from 34 degrees to 114 degrees." He found no gardens due to the dry climate and poor soil with no reasonable means of irrigation. The post had no grazing and it was "frequently visited by dry sand storms from over the desert....It is however on the high road for the immigrants, the mail, the trader and there is a stage station and stores and two ferries within a mile of the post....All circumstances conspire to make this a very important military post that cannot be dispensed with for a term of years. And it seems judiciously considered, both as to strength of command (which should never be less than three companies) and position." Lieutenant Colonel George Nauman of the 3rd Artillery commanded the post with three companies of the 3rd—F, H, and I. The commander had an assistant surgeon and an ordnance sergeant on his staff. But on 8 February, Company F commanded by "Captain Butler[?]" was detached up the Colorado River 65 miles to establish a depot of supplies for the command of Lieutenant Colonel Hoffman now here, en route for the 35th parallel, to establish a post, and if need be, punish the Mohave Indians. It is probable this company will be put under the orders of Colonel Hoffman temporarily."[227]

Company H was commanded by Captain Joseph Stewart with three other officers one of which had not yet joined, a second was and aide to General Wool, and the third was Acting Post Adjutant, Assistant Quartermaster, and

---

[226] Letter courtesy of the Middlesex County Historical Society. "Rancheria" is a name given to a collection of Indian huts.
[227] Letter courtesy of the Middlesex County Historical Society.

Commissary Officer. The company also had 8 staff enlisted and 64 privates "of these, 6 sick, one in confinement, one on furlough for 6 months…,one absent at Benicia confined, 13 on extra duty, thus showing an available force of two officers and seventy enlisted men to which must be added 9 recruits just joined and not enumerated above." Mansfield found the company "in excellent order on inspection and in uniform except the old cap, and well-armed with the new rifled musket and well found in every respect. It was quartered in an excellent adobe barrack one story with…a veranda…a good adobe messroom and kitchen also covered with zinc and company store rooms. The men were as comfortable as need be." Its four laundresses were also well-quartered and the company's books "were neatly written up and kept. There were 10 desertions in 1856, 16 in 1857, 16 in 1858….It is in good discipline and well commanded by Captain Stewart and a fine looking set of men." Company I had no captain but had Lieutenant John Hamilton in command; another officer was on recruiting service and a second temporarily assigned to Company F. It had 12 staff enlisted and 59 privates and with those missing due to the usual causes, showed an available force of one officer and 60 enlisted men "to which must be added 10 recruits just arrived. This company also was in excellent order on inspection in every respect as to arms and quarters like Company H and equally comfortable without any essential difference." It also had four laundresses, well-quartered….The books of the company were in good order and written up." It had 17 desertions in the last three years. Since gold had been discovered up the Colorado River it is likely most of the deserters decided to try their luck in the gold fields. Mansfield reported that the company was "in good discipline and well commanded by Lieutenant Hamilton, and it is a first rate set of men in personal appearance and general height." Both companies drilled well "at the heavy infantry and as rifles and as skirmishers." But he found that neither company had "practiced the bayonet exercise….but they had both had some practice at the target under the Heth System to a distance of 150 yards. I however had them both fire one round each at the target 6'x22" and at 200 yards and they made as follows: Company H, 1 of 3 hits (33%) and Company I, 1 of 2 ½ hits (40%), vastly better than any Infantry or Rifle practice I have seen in this Department of Oregon. This is because they have had time to practice and the drills have been properly kept up. I was much pleased with the military and fine appearance of both these Companies." Mansfield found that the post had three 12 pounder mountain howitzers in excellent order and well-housed.[228]

The post guard was well mounted and housed all in good order. The post hospital was also in excellent order, well housed and supplied, and books in good order; he wrote that it was a "healthy post." The bakery had two ovens and two bakers who made excellent bread. The Adjutant's Office was also in a good adobe building with "all the books and records of the post neatly and properly kept." The books and accounts of the Quartermaster and Commissary Departments, both under Lieutenant John Drysdale, Mansfield determined were in good order; he wrote that Drysdale was "an active and energetic officer." But Mansfield found that even though all commissary and quartermaster supplies were ample, they were expensive since they were shipped in from San Francisco (except for hay). Also some of the commissary supplies were damaged in transit and some even not good when shipped. Mansfield wrote that "the Chief Commissary at San Francisco has been at times cheated in the purchases." Both the commissary and quartermaster stores were in good buildings. Two small private steamers bring all supplies from the gulf up the Colorado River after the goods are landed near the mouth of the river by larger ships from San Francisco. Mansfield wrote that this route is the only practicable one as the route across the desert would be much more costly. Mansfield criticized the lack of payment of the troops since May 1858 eight months earlier so all soldiers were out of funds. "this is a pecuniary injury to the soldier as it obliges him to run in debt to the sutler, and others, and to pay exorbitant prices. It is all no doubt occasioned by the misapplication by a paymaster of this department of nearly $50,000 as I have before reported to the General in Chief." Mansfield found the same sutler who was there when he inspected the post in 1854 and found him "a very respectable man….he is very much in advance to the men and money is scarce." The Yuma Indians around the post Mansfield found "peaceable" and not numerous, as were other tribes farther away however the Mohave have committed murders. "It is uncertain how they will act as Colonel Hoffman advances to establish the post of two companies at the 35th parallel." Mansfield concluded that the "Post is very well commanded by Brevet Lieutenant Colonel Nauman, and the duties properly performed by all under him….There seem to be nothing amiss here, and the discipline good." But he also found that although it was a chaplain post, there was none as the last one was dismissed because he could not speak

---

[228] Letter courtesy of the Middlesex County Historical Society. Captain Joseph Stewart was an 1842 West point graduate who retired from the Army as a lieutenant colonel of the 3rd Artillery in 1879. He died in 1904.

English; he wrote that a school was needed so a chaplain should be assigned. But all things considered, Mansfield was well pleased with this inspection.[229]

---

[229] Letter courtesy of the Middlesex County Historical Society. Lieutenant John Drysdale was appointed a second lieutenant in 1855 and became a first lieutenant in 1857. He was dropped from the rolls in 1860. Mansfield wished to travel to Fort Yuma by steamer but was not able to do so due to scheduling problems.

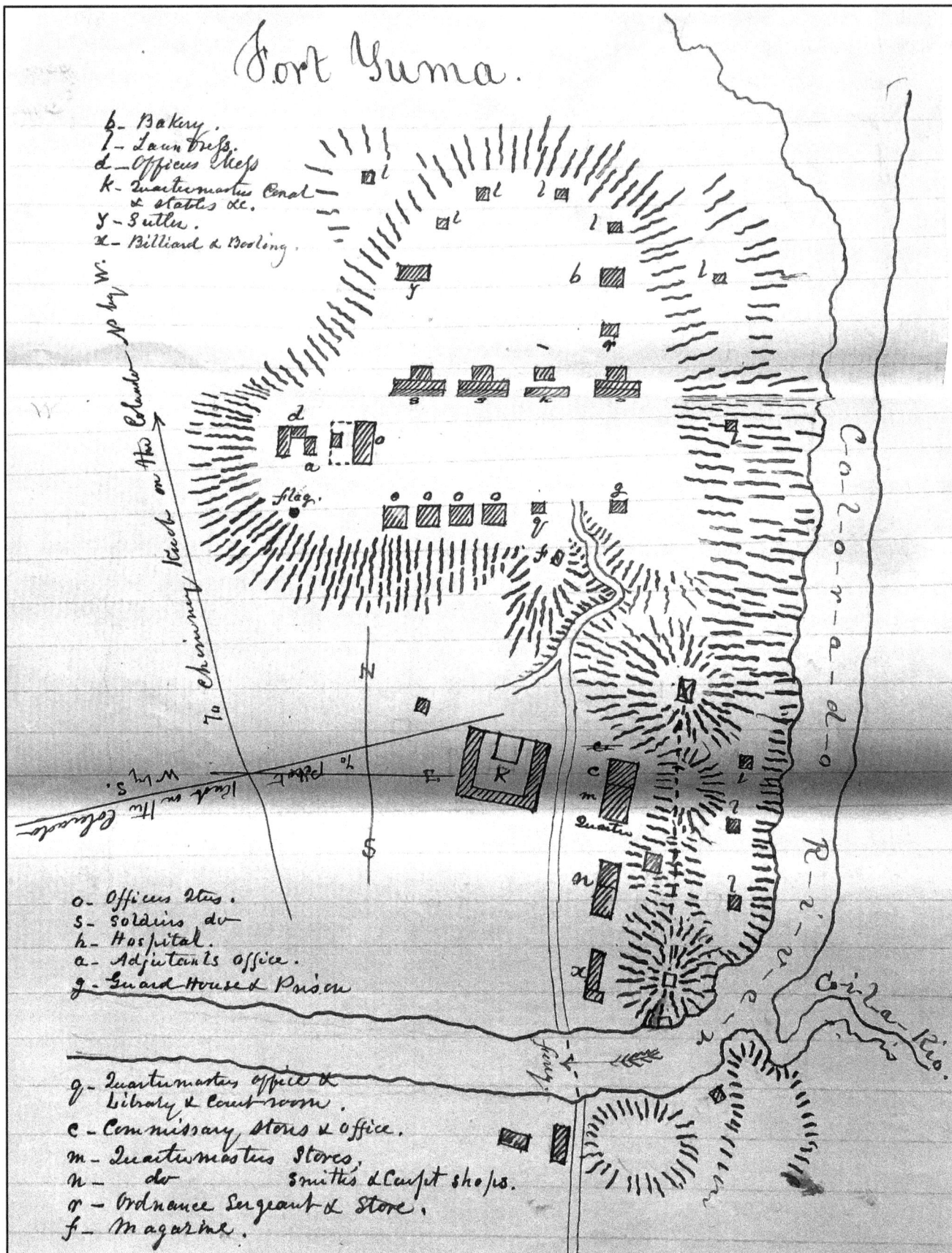

Mansfield's rough sketch of his 1858 inspection of Fort Yuma, California. Courtesy of the Middlesex County Historical Society.

Mansfield wrote his wife on 12 March 1859 from Fort Yuma and complained about the weather and the desert. He had arrived there after "a very fatiguing ride in the stage of 280 miles" and then he had received only two meals. Fortunately he had carried a little food in his bag "so did not suffer." He hoped to get "home in August if God spares my life. If so I shall never again come to this Pacific Coast—I am tired of it, and am too old now for such hardships." On 3 February he had written her From San Francisco and cautioned her that she must be able to live on her income alone since "you know not what a day may bring forth." Later in that letter that "I am getting quite tired of the life I lead. I am not going to live so much longer." Obviously the difficult travelling he endured during his trips from post to post were taking their toll. On 26 March he wrote her that since he was done with his inspection he would leave on the 27th for Warm's Ranch about 160 miles on the stage then 60 miles on mules to San Diego, and finally a steamer to San Francisco.[230]

While Mansfield was at Fort Yuma, he took the opportunity to inspect seven companies of the 6th Infantry under Lieutenant Colonel W. Hoffman which were to gather there and then march up the Colorado River to the 35th parallel to establish a new post. That post became Fort Mojave after Colonel Hoffman initially named it Camp Colorado. It was located on the left bank of the river near the head of the Mojave Valley. Mansfield wrote his report of the inspection of these companies from Fort Yuma on 26 March. Colonel Hoffman along with four companies left San Francisco on 11 February but the next day ran into a terrible storm so had to turn back. The steamer *Uncle Sam* was then refitted and again departed on the 16th and reached San Diego that day. There the ship offloaded 200 mules which were to be driven across the desert to Fort Yuma and loaded another company of the 7th. Finally on February 27th the ship dropped anchor "20 miles below Montague Island off the mouth of the Colorado River whence the troops and supplies were landed by means of the Quartermaster's schooner *Monterey* on a point of the riverbank called the Gridiron." Then two smaller steamers transported the men and supplies to Fort Yuma where the five companies rejoined the two companies, E and K, which had previously marched across the desert.[231]

Colonel Hoffman's command staff consisted of the Regimental Adjutant and Quartermaster, a sergeant major and a Quartermaster sergeant and an Acting Commissary Officer; its companies were C, E, F, G, H, I, and K. Mansfield then inspected each company and not surprisingly found the men's uniforms in bad repair given their long journey by ship, boat and for two of them, over the desert. Company C was commanded by Lieutenant Silas Parsons Higgins since the company commander was on furlough. Higgins had one officer and nine enlisted on the company staff along with 65 privates "of these 12 were sick, 2 in confinement, 1 on detached service at Fort Laramie, 3 in confinement at the Presidio of San Francisco. In the aggregate 2 officers and 70 enlisted men present. If we deduct 6 of the sick to be left in hospital it will have the available strength…2 officers and 64 men for the field. These men looked ragged and were tolerably well drilled at the old light infantry as skirmishers and fired at the target 6'x22" and made 1 of 2 ½ hits (40%), a very good result. They were not in uniform, some coats some shirts, some hats, some caps. They however were provided generally with the requirements for the march and were well armed with the new rifled muskets and some old muskets for ball and buck….The officers are young but ambitious." He noted that the company had only six desertions in three years—"an unusually small number." Company E had only one officer as the company commander who was on detached service, and a second officer was Acting Commissary. Company enlisted staff had nine men and there were 73 privates; available force would be one officer and 78 men. "These men were only tolerable in personal appearance, not all in uniform, old hats, caps, shirts, and pants, and ragged—they could not get clothing.….They drilled at the old light infantry as skirmishers, and fired at the target 6'x22" at 200 yards one round each man and made 1 of 13 ½ hits (7%), a very bad result, the worst I have seen in the Pacific Coast. They were armed with the new rifled musket." The company had 39 desertions in three years. Mansfield wrote that "Lieutenant Clark [the acting company commander] is a meritorious officer and drills his company well. The target practice has been but recently commenced." Company F was commanded by Major Lewis Addison Armistead who had one other officer on his staff as the third was on leave; he had 10 enlisted staff and "69 privates…aggregate 2 officers and 62 men present…if the 5 were left in hospital, there will be 2 officers and 57 men available." The company also had the rifled musket but was "in the old uniform cap and in uniform otherwise all appeared well with good knapsacks, tin canteens, and haversacks and were well found and ready for the field. They drilled well at the old light infantry drill and as skirmishers. They fired at the target 6'x22" at 200 yards and made 1 of three hits (33%) which was satisfactory." It had 43 desertions in the last three years and Mansfield wrote that

---

[230] Letters courtesy of the Middlesex County Historical Society.
[231] Letter courtesy of the Middlesex County Historical Society.

the company was "well commanded and efficient." Company G was commanded by Captain William Scott Ketchum and another officer as the third was absent on detached service; there were nine staff enlisted and 67 privates, in the aggregate two officers and 72 men available. This company also had the rifled musket and "were well provided and in uniform with hats and were in a good condition to take the field. They drilled at the old light infantry and as skirmishers." The company at the firing range made one of three hits "which was satisfactory." It had 45 desertions in the last three years. Mansfield found it "well commanded and efficient." Company H had its captain absent on sick leave and was commanded by Lieutenant Benjamin F. Smith; its third officer was absent as he was the regimental Quartermaster. There were 10 staff enlisted and 69 privates; aggregate one officer and 75 men available. "They were good looking men but not in uniform but mixed with coats and hats and ample clothes and well provided for the march." They also had the rifle muskets. They drilled similarly to their sister companies but did "very good" at target firing making one of two and a half hits (40%) at 200 yards. It had 56 desertions in the last three years. Mansfield found "Lieutenant Smith …a very meritorious young officer but no company should be sent into the field with but one officer." Company I was commanded by Lieutenant E.G. Marshall as its captain was absent sick; in addition to another officer the company had 10 staff enlisted and 56 privates, aggregate two officers and 49 present but only two officers and 46 men available. It also had the rifled musket and the old smooth bore for buck and ball. "They were generally in the uniform coat and they were a good looking set of men and generally well supplied for the march. They drilled similarly to its sister companies and made one of 2 and a half hits "which was very good." It had 39 desertions in three years. Company K was commanded by Captain Richard B. Garnett, a second officer serving as Acting Assistant Quartermaster, and the third on a leave of absence. It had nine staff enlisted and 74 privates, in the aggregate one officer and 67 men available. "These were inferior looking men, out of clothes with hats, caps, shirts and pants very ragged. Clothes could be had." It also had the rifled musket and drilled as its sister companies. The men fired poorly making only one of five and one third hits. It had 47 desertions in three years. Mansfield summarized that "of these 7 companies to take the field, three of them have but one officer each and 4 two officers each, say 11 officers, and 463 rank and file available; an average of one officer to every 42 men."[232]

The Quartermasters and Commissary Department were unremarkable and Mansfield noted that there were sufficient supplies of food for the regiment. The Medical Department was also adequate. The Fort Yuma command had "detailed a detachment of one officer and two noncommissioned officers and 16 privates with two mountain howitzers to accompany Colonel Hoffman. He also put under his order F Company Captain H.S. Burton of the 3rd Artillery which he had established at an advance position by General Clarke's order some 65 miles up the [Colorado] river since the 8th February." This temporary post named Camp Gaston, was located on the west bank of the Colorado River about 45 miles above Fort Yuma by trail. It was abandoned when Colonel Hoffman established Fort Mojave and served only as an outpost of Fort Yuma. On the 26th, the regiment left heading upriver on the west bank and then would change to the east bank when it reached Captain Burton's camp. It had to use pack mules as "transportation by wagon is wholly impracticable if the reports be true." Mansfield ended and expressed concern that Colonel Hoffman and his large regiment would need supplies so he urged that a direct road west to San Bernardino be built "or there will be no use in this new post as a protection to travelers."[233]

San Diego 1 April 1859

On 4 April Mansfield updated his wife from San Diego and told her that at Warm's Ranch he hired three horses and an Indian guide and left for San Diego. Also on the 4th he wrote his draft report to McDowell for the post at San Diego. He reported that he left Fort Yuma "by the overland mail stage on the morning of the 27th March, I reached Warm's Ranch 158 miles from Yuma and there took an Indian guide and animals and proceeded some 70 miles to San Diego over

[232] Letter courtesy of the Middlesex County Historical Society. Lieutenant Silas Parsons Higgins was an 1853 West Point graduate and died in service as a first lieutenant in 1860. Lieutenant Darius D. Clark was an 1849 West Point graduate who died as a first lieutenant in 1859. Major Lewis Addison Armistead resigned from West Point in 1836. He was appointed a second lieutenant in the 6th Infantry in 1839 and was brevetted to captain and major during the Mexican-American War. He resigned in 1861 and became a Confederate brigadier general; he was killed at Gettysburg in 1863. Captain William Scott Ketchum was an 1834 West Point graduate who was brevetted from colonel to major general during the Civil War. He retired as a colonel in 1870. Lieutenant Benjamin Franklin Smith was an 1853 West Point graduate who was brevetted from major to brigadier general during the Civil War. He died in service as a major of the 27th Infantry in 1868. Lieutenant Elisha Gaylord Marshall was an 1850 West Point graduate who received brevets from major to major general during the Civil War. He retired as a colonel in 1867 and died in 1883.
[233] Letter courtesy of the Middlesex County Historical Society.

a trail and arrived there on the evening of the 31st March." He wrote that the "military post at the Old Mission of San Diego [is] situated some 6 miles up the Valley of the San Diego River which at this season of the year is dry ...and was abandoned in 1858, [when] Brevet Major [Francis Octavius] Wyse with his company was ordered into the Department of Oregon after the defeat of Brevet Lieutenant Colonel Steptoe, and I am informed by Colonel Swords Chief Quartermaster that he, by letter, had turned it over to the Catholic Bishop. As I passed by the post I dismounted and inspected the premises." There he found it vandalized and plundered "without restriction....I presume it will never be used as a mission as there seems to be no population in this quarter." Mansfield then wrote about the "so called" New San Diego about three miles south on the harbour at which Company G of the 6th Infantry was stationed. "This company occupied part of a large two story frame building which belonged to the Quartermaster's Department which answered the triple purpose of Quartermaster's store and Commissary also. When the company left to join Colonel Hoffman the post was abandoned "and the public property left in the charge of an Ordnance Sergeant, Hospital Steward and a soldier of Captain Ketchum's Company. There is here also a stable and sundry small buildings as sheds on the government land. And there was an amount of Commissary and medical and Quartermaster's stores well cared for....This New San Diego post, is deficient in many respects by nature. Water here has to be brought 3 miles from Old San Diego where it is obtained out of a well dug in the dry bed of San Diego River. There is no grazing about here for animals, and wood is hauled 20 miles. If it be designed to occupy this locality again, of course new San Diego is the only spot where there is a public building and of course it will be reoccupied." He ended by noting that "There has been no improvement in this country since I was here in 1854, and there can be none as there is no back country of value, for 125 miles in any direction except for grazing...for 120 miles farther eastward of this nothing but a sandy desert void of grass to Fort Yuma."[234]

---

[234] Letter courtesy of the Middlesex County Historical Society.

Mansfield's journeys from San Francisco north to Forts Crook, Humboldt, Gaston, Ter-Waw and Umpqua. Map courtesy LOC.

Benicia Arsenal 11 April 1859

Mansfield penned his next report from San Francisco on 16 April where he arrived by using again the overland mail coach from San Diego or a steamboat from San Diego. He reported that on the 11th he "proceeded to Benicia and inspected there the Head Quarters of the 3rd Artillery, the military post, the Depot of Quartermaster and Commissary and Medical Purveying Department, [and] the Arsenal." The 3rd Artillery headquarters at Benicia was commanded by Lieutenant Colonel Charles Spencer Merchant since Colonel William Gates was absent...stationed at Fort Yuma; and Major John Benjamin Scott was stationed at Umpqua. There were 17 staff enlisted including the sergeant major. He noted that there were five companies stationed at Fort Vancouver, three at Fort Yuma, one at Umpqua, one at Old Point Comfort, Light Company E at Fort Ridgely, and Company C at Camp Floyd. He found "The books and records of the Regiment are neatly and well written up by the Sergeant Major and the band and staff on parade were neat and in good order with the old uniform. Colonel Merchant, although advanced in age, performs the duty of commanding at this Headquarters well, all seems to be harmonious and in order there. He exercises no particular control over the Depots and the Hospital is common to the whole post and ample and well attended to and supplied." Mansfield noted the absence from the regiment of five officers and wrote that there is only one line officer at the post for daily duty who alternated with Lieutenant John Gorham Chandler as officer of the day who also performed the duty of Adjutant. Mansfield noted also that "At this post was stationed, for the present, Company A, 6th Infantry commanded by Captain Franklin Foster Flint" with its two other officers not present; it had 10 staff noncommissioned officers and 62 privates with eight sick, three confined, four on extra duty and one on detached service. "This company was in excellent order armed with the new rifled musket, and accoutrements, and in the old uniform. It drilled at the heavy infantry well, but did not attempt the light infantry nor as skirmishers on account of the number of recruits. It fired at the target 6'x22" at 200 yards and made 1 5/7 hits (4%), but had never before fired at that distance. It was comfortably quartered in the principal barrack and had mess room and kitchen in tolerable order." Its books were in order with 41 deserters in three years. He found the company in "good discipline and well commanded by Captain Flint who is a very promising officer. But it is not for the good of the service that both his subordinates should be absent at the same time." Mansfield also objected to a group of 38 enlisted men at the post who belonged to absent companies of the 3rd Artillery—"These men [should be] sent to their respective companies." He found that the guard had two prisoners awaiting trial one for seven months and the other for eight months which Mansfield believed was an excessive time to be held without trial. The Hospital at Benicia served all stationed at the post which he found to be well staffed and in very good order. The assistant surgeon in charge had "also to supply both Departments of California and Oregon with medicines." Mansfield reported that this was a healthy post "and well suited as a depot for medical supplies to be put up and forwarded." Unfortunately the post had "no good baker among the enlisted men and the oven has worked badly. The bread has been baked in the village and returned pound for pound for the flour....The oven has been rebuilt and as soon as a good baker is had they will bake their bread in the garrison. There is no sutler here." The officers' and enlisted men's quarters were ample, two stories high; enlisted men had mess rooms and kitchens on the 2nd story. But he did comment that the barracks badly needed painting on the inside.[235]

Mansfield spent many pages devoted to the Quartermaster's Depot. He noted that it "is well located here, out of the influences of the City of San Francisco and so in time of war, wagons, ambulances, and stores can accumulate here ready for war service." The Depot was in temporary charge of Major George Pearce Andrews of the 3rd Artillery. He had some two dozen civilians working for him at the Depot. There were two schooners used to transport supplies and troops; there were many buildings used by the Depot including those for storage, workshops, stables, corrals, etc., all in good order and made of wood. Teamsters transported goods from the coast to the Depot and also hauled wood and water. The Depot's books were in good order. Mansfield suggested that the large stock of old uniforms at the Depot be disposed of as they had no value as most were badly moth-eaten. He suggested that these thousands of articles of clothing should be

---

[235] Letter courtesy of the Middlesex County Historical Society. Lieutenant Colonel Charles Spencer Merchant was an 1814 West Point graduate who retired as a colonel of the 4th Artillery in 1863. He was brevetted to brigadier general in 1865 and died in 1879. Colonel William Gates was an 1806 West Point graduate who retired as a colonel of the 3rd Artillery in 1863. He was brevetted to brigadier general in 1865 and died in 1868. Major John Benjamin Scott was an 1821 West Point graduate who Mansfield likely knew there as both were from Connecticut. He was brevetted to major during the Mexican-American War. He died in 1860. Lieutenant John Gorham Chandler was an 1853 West Point graduate who was brevetted from major to colonel during the Civil War. He retired as a quartermaster colonel in 1894. He died in 1915. Captain Franklin Foster Flint was an 1841 West Point graduate who retired in 1882 as colonel of the 4th Infantry. He died in 1891.

distributed to the Indians on the coast as those tribes would be the only people who could use them as "they cannot be sold at all." The Commissary Department was under Major Andrews who "issues to the garrison, Arsenal, etc., and ships supplies to different posts in the Pacific Departments." His accounts and books were correct. All supplies were well stored and in order. The Arsenal of Benicia was under the command of Captain Franklin Dyer Callender who Mansfield wrote was "a highly meritorious officer and takes great interest in the duties of his station." Callender was authorized 40 enlisted men but had only 37 of which eight were absent without leave. Mansfield opined that "The men absent without leave are old soldiers….They make the worst kind of men as artisans and should not be enlisted in the ordnance. The man confined was for drunkenness, the great evil of this whiskey drinking community." Callender also employed 65 civilians. Ordnance was stored in two large frame buildings the second floors of which he decided were overloaded and "one quarter of the weight should be taken out of them, which will be done as soon as the new store house is completed. There are two full large first rate store magazines separated by a hill which in case of accident to one would protect the other." As Mansfield had noted in the past, San Francisco was the most important port on the Pacific Coast and should be heavily defended. Here he wrote again of this need: "There is a great deficiency of heavy and sea coast artillery on this coast. About 100 guns of the largest class are required now for the fortifications at Fort Point which I understand have been in part shipped. There should be a large shipment for guns to lay in this Depot to meet the emergency of an unexpected war for it is clear they could not be shipped in time for war and there are no foundries on this coast for such purpose." In his conclusion he reported that Benicia "labored under a great disadvantage for want of suitable gardens. It is impossible to raise summer vegetables here. The soil is good but there is a want of seasonable rains and there are no means of irrigation. Hence troops and workmen must depend on the market for…vegetables."[236]

On 18 April Mansfield wrote to Secretary of War Floyd that the Navy Department was going to send a large steamer to Puget Sound to help pursue Indians in that region. He urged that this ship not be sent as it was much too large and slow to be of much use, plus it would be extremely costly to keep it fueled; he urged instead a small, faster, more agile ship for the purpose.[237]

Fort Humboldt 20-25 April 1859

On 23 April 1859, Mansfield wrote his rough draft of his visit to Fort Humboldt. He arrived there on the 20th aboard the steamer *Columbia* after leaving San Francisco on the 18th. He reported that the fort was "on the mesa land of this [Humboldt] bay directly east of the town of Bucksport….Bucksport has not improved any in business since I was here in 1854. It is directly east of the light house and commands a full view of the bar and Pacific Ocean ….It is about 3 miles south of the flourishing little town of Eureka of 500 population." Mansfield continued his history of the post and wrote that it "was established in 1852 by Brevet Lieutenant Colonel R[obert] C[hristie] Buchanan of the 4th Infantry. It seems to be well located to accomplish much good in the protection of both the white man and the Indian….There are no wagon roads leading into the interior but there are trails which can be passed over with pack mules and mounted and foot troops in any direction desirable." The two-company post was commanded by Major Gabriel Jones Rains of the 4th Infantry. His officers in addition to the post surgeon were one lieutenant who was both acting Assistant Quartermaster and Commissary, and another who was the post adjutant. The post's two companies were Company B of the 4th Infantry and Company B of the 6th Infantry. Company B of the 4th Infantry had two officers and 59 men who were assigned to the company but were absent on detached duty in Hoopa Valley leaving one officer and 21 men at the post. Eighteen men were available for inspection and Mansfield noted that they were armed with the rifled musket and were "neat on inspection but were in mixed uniforms with a deficiency of clothing and haversacks and canteens." He next inspected Company B of the 6th Infantry which was commanded by Captain Charles Swain Lovell who had only one of his two lieutenants present; he had nine staff enlisted and 60 privates with 10 absent. He wrote that "They were fine looking men and young in the old uniform cap, without pompons with frock coat and light and dark blue pants with a deficiency of canteens and haversacks and some with old knapsacks. They drilled at the heavy infantry and not as light infantry and skirmishers as they did not know it; a squad of about 12 went through a part of the bayonet exercise and

---

[236] Letter courtesy of the Middlesex County Historical Society. Major George Pearce Andrews was an 1845 West Point graduate who was brevetted to captain and major during the Mexican-American War He retired in 1885 as colonel of the 1st Artillery and died in 1887. Captain Franklin Dyer Callender was an 1839 West Point graduate who was brevetted to first lieutenant during the Florida War against the Indians, captain during the Mexican-American War, and from major to brigadier general during the Civil war. He retired as a colonel in 1879 and died in 1882.

[237] Letter courtesy of the Middlesex County Historical Society.

they fired at a target 6'x22" at 200 yards and made 1 of 39 hits (3%), the worst firing I have ever seen. But most of the men were recruits." This company also had rifled muskets which obviously did not help their target firing given their lack of practice. Company books were in good order and it had 17 desertions in three years. He saw that the company barracks would be finished in a few weeks and "will afford it ample accommodations." He also noted that Company B 4th Infantry were quartered in old barracks but would join its sister company in the new one when finished; it will have mess rooms and kitchens for the men. Mansfield found the hospital in "excellent order as to books, records, etc." with ample medicines, but he found the guard house located in an "inferior" log building. The post's one baker produced "excellent" bread. He found the magazine located in "a very inferior little wooden building not 50 feet from the barn and wholly unsuited and dangerously located in case of fire....A new one in a suitable place should be built." The Quartermaster's Department Mansfield found was in very good order with all accounts and records "properly kept." He did write however that the Quartermaster required "bricks, cooking stoves for the soldiers' kitchens and wood stoves for the soldiers' quarters." The Commissary Department was also under the same officer who performed "this duty well also. His records and accounts are all properly and well kept." Mansfield later noted that this officer was also the Recruiting Officer—a very busy young officer but not unusual in a small post with a limited number of officers present for duty.[238]

But Mansfield was not pleased with many of the buildings he inspected at Fort Humboldt. Those buildings were erected early in the history of the post when the cost of lumber and workmen's wages were very high so they were not sturdily constructed—many needed new underpinnings and brick for chimneys. Other than these two issues, they were adequate for this two-company post. He noted that stoves were needed for "warming and cooking and should be supplied. It is better to put a good cooking stove into the soldiers' kitchen than a range and they cost no more in the end." He also noted that the "storehouse answers all the purposes required for a temporary building for commissary and quartermaster but if it should take fire caused by the burning of the little adjacent buildings of course the supplies will be lost. This building also requires more underpinning as it is settling down." Another problem which he noted on visits to other posts was that the soldiers were not paid timely, some not for six months. This was due to Colonel Coffee's misappropriation of some $50,000 previously reported. Mansfield wrote that soldiers complained to him about the pay issue. He was apparently pleased to find "a fine large garden attached to the post and many valuable vegetable can be raised for the comfort of the men." He also wrote that "there is no sutler here and none necessary" but did not mention that without regular pay men were not able to borrow from a sutler to buy goods in town. He saw a "large number of children at this post just the age to commence to go to school and it is to be regretted there is no school." Otherwise he was pleased with what he saw: "The discipline of this post is good and there appears to be ...harmony among the officers and families present....The post is supplied with excellent water by a well and force pump at the foot of the mesa and the water is delivered near the flag staff on the Parade." Mansfield wrote favorably that "Major Rains has issued order for the troops to be instructed in the Hardie Light Infantry and skirmish drill which they so much need." He wrote that within 50 miles there are "several thousand [Indians] and generally peaceable and unoffending yet they have so little to subsist on that whenever they by stealth kill a beef belonging to the whites, they are hunted down like so many wild beasts. I myself saw a drunken white man in 1854 in the Town of Union go into a tavern after a rifle to shoot an Indian in the street. I motioned the Indian to run off and caused the rifle to be taken from the man." Mansfield was clearly not pleased with the attitude some whites had about the Indians and arbitrary actions they took against them but when he brought this up to Major Rains he had no remedy for these atrocities. Mansfield believed in law and order so actions like this rankled him.[239]

---

[238] Letter courtesy of the Middlesex County Historical Society. Captain Charles Swain Lovell was one of the few officers in the Army who began as a private soldier. He became a sergeant major in 1832, a second lieutenant in 1837 and by 1846 was a captain in the 6th Infantry. During the Civil War he was brevetted from lieutenant colonel to brigadier general. He retired in 1870 as colonel of the 14th Infantry and died in 1871.

[239] Letter courtesy of the Middlesex County Historical Society.

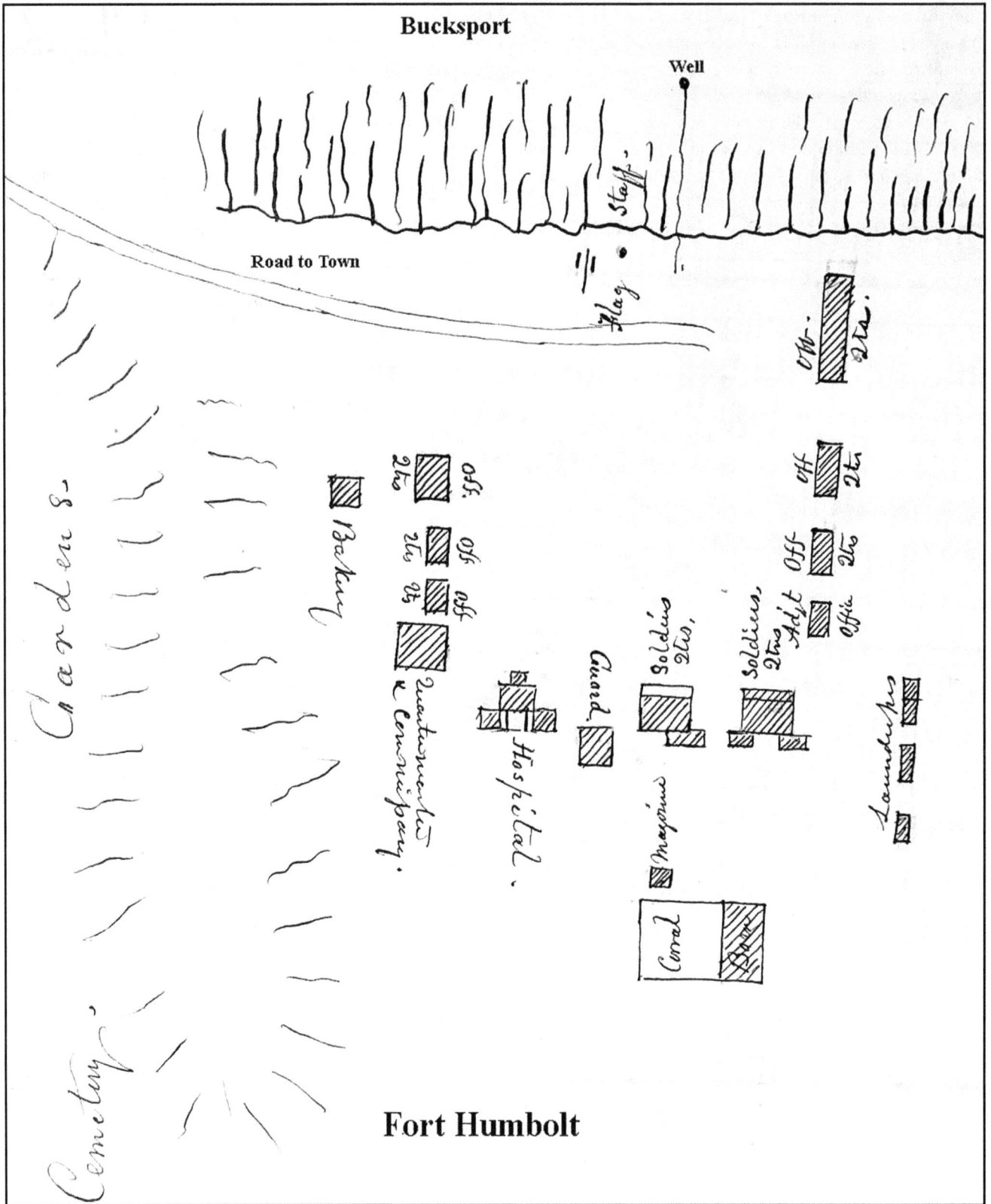

Mansfield's sketch of Fort Humboldt in April 1859 with clarifications added by the author. Courtesy of the Middlesex County Historical Society.

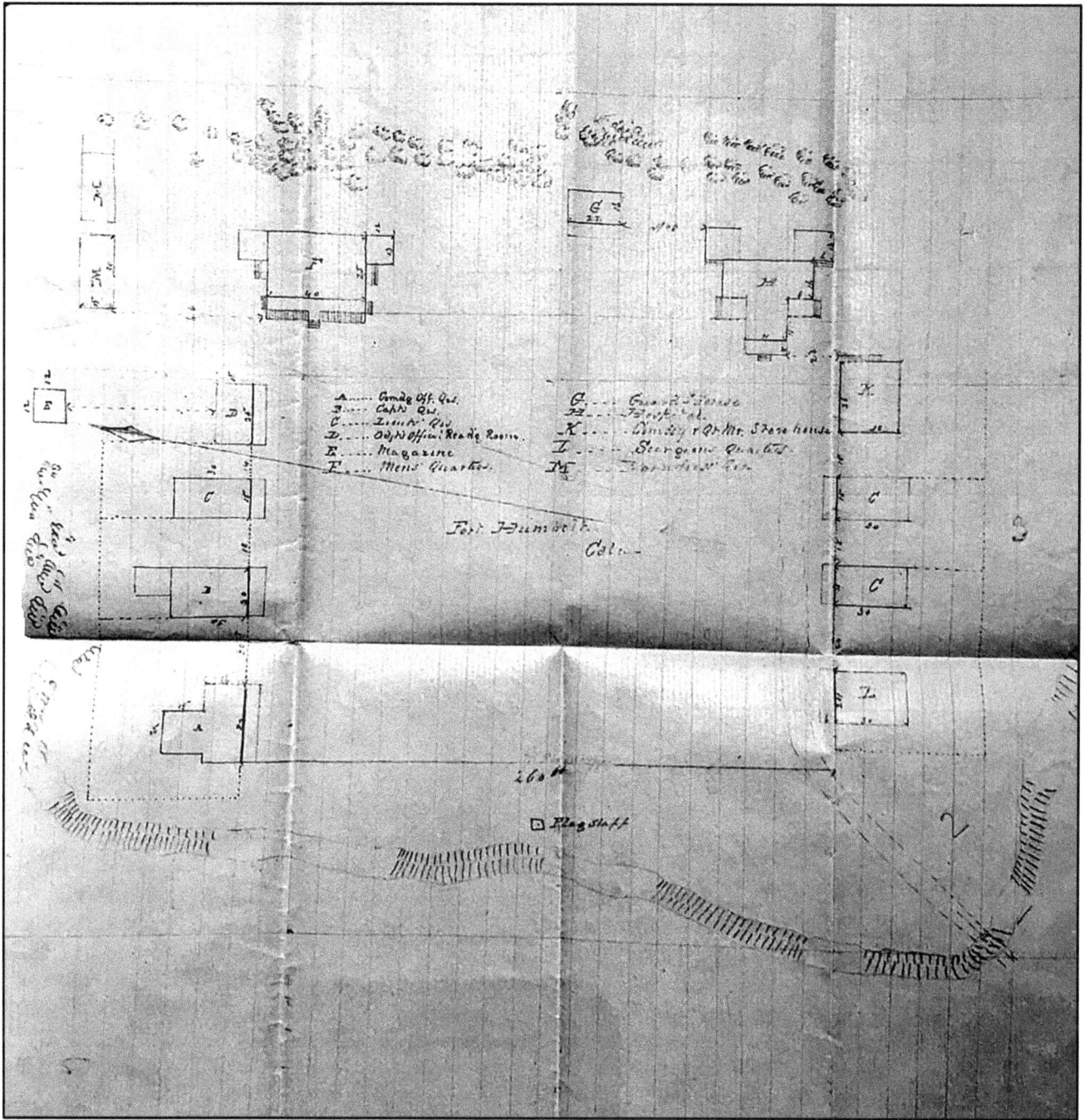

Another sketch of Fort Humboldt found in Mansfield's personal file probably not drawn by him. Courtesy of the Middlesex County Historical Society.

Fort Gaston 29 April–2 May 1859

On 2 May 1859 from Hoopa Valley, California, Mansfield wrote to Lieutenant Colonel Lorenzo Thomas, Assistant Adjutant General at Headquarters of the Army, with his inspection of Fort Gaston. "On the 25th April I left Fort Humboldt and reached the Town of Union at the head of the bay en route for Fort Ter-Waw. At Union I was detained procuring animals and waiting the opening of the trail over the mountains through the snow till 28th when we took our departure for this Valley, where most of a company of the 4th Infantry left under Captain E. Underwood was stationed, and on the 29th after a very fatiguing ride over a bad trail and for 2 miles through the snow reached here. This post called Fort Gaston is situated in the little valley known as Hoopa on the Trinity River about 14 miles long and say 13 miles below the south fork of the Trinity and 9 miles following the river from its junction with the Klamath. It is a beautiful little valley, well-timbered and watered and susceptible of great improvement. It is occupied by about 20 settlers planting wheat and farming. There is no mining done here and there is a flouring and a saw mill." He then continued with his remarks concerning the difficulties involved to reach this post: "It is 40 miles from Union, about 40 miles from Trinidad, about 80 miles from Weaverville, whence there is a stage line via Shasta City to Sacramento City. It is in direct communication over the mountains with the Salmon River and other mining regions….It is in direct water communication by canoe down the rapid currents of the Trinity and the Klamath, with Ter-Waw say 40 miles." He noted that "The climate was congenial being low down between the mountains and it is very agreeable in winter…and in summer it is warm and suited to vegetation." Because of the some 5,000 Indians in the county and the post being in the center of them, Mansfield wrote that it was "clear the white population here are isolated in winter and cut off from communication by trail over the mountains….all the inhabitants might be destroyed before it [help] could reach here….I think a one company post indispensable here, till such time as the means of obtaining aid from neighboring towns are certain, easy, and prompt. This can only be when a wagon road will be opened to Union say 35 miles….Such a road would never be blocked by snows in winter and could be made in six months by 30 men under proper direction. This road would add to the military resources of this Department and in due time would be continued to Weaverville and thus a wagon road and steamboat route opened via the Sacramento Valley to San Francisco; one 6 mule team would supply this post if this road were opened. Hence it would be economical for the Government to open this road at once and I advised it in a letter to General Clarke."[240]

The post was established by Captain Edmund Underwood under order of Major Rains; Underwood and his company reached the current valley on 4 December 1858 "just before the trails were closed by snow. He had his tents and a limited supply for Quartermaster and Commissary. Captain Snyder, the pioneer settler here, gave him the use of a log building for a store house and a small log house and he went into camp. This spring he has selected a reservation of about 640 acres on the River's west bank mostly gravelly prairie with fine, clean streams of water and wood, and shade and garden, ample fine bathing for the men in the Trinity and he has just erected a small stone house on it and a frame building at a small expense….the selection is judicious; he called the post Fort Gaston. I think all his arrangements very satisfactory. He has opened a wagon road to communicate freely up and down the valley and will change his camp to it in a few days." Captain Underwood was in command of B Company of the 4th Infantry at this small post except for a small detachment of 22 men who "were retained at Fort Humboldt…." Underwood had one officer, five staff enlisted and 52 privates of which five were absent sick or confined. Underwood's men "were mostly recruits sent out here soon after their arrival without instruction and arrived with 12 rifles, the ammunition amounted to 400 musket rifle cartridges, and the …old worn out smooth barrel muskets. It is fortunate they were never called into action. They could hardly go through the manual of arms together, had never drilled in movements, and of course could not. They had however fired at the target, and they fired one round the man at the target 6'x22" at 200 yards. Ten rifles made 1 hit of ten (10%) and 37 muskets made 4 hits or say one of nine (11%)….This company was deficient in clothes, and shoes, and caps and knapsacks worn out, haversacks and canteens deficient and worn out and accoutrements worn. It requires an entire new outfit. It was improbable to get these articles over the mountain trail in mid-winter. And the men suffered much and had to purchase boots and shoes at heavy cost to themselves." He did note that items the men required including rifled muskets were at Fort Humboldt awaiting shipment to the post. The men lived in tents and cooked in the open but had an oven which furnished "excellent bread." The company's books were in order; desertions were 51 in two years most of which were caused by "a detachment left at Fort Humboldt under Major Rains's orders without a company officer." The four-man guard detachment used a log prison which had three occupants. The very healthy locality meant that the one hospital steward had little work but Mansfield noted that "This man was an educated physician in Germany and command the confidence of the men and people." The Acting Quartermaster and Commissary Officer, Lieutenant Joseph Benson Collins, "performed the duties well and all his papers and returns properly kept." The poor results Mansfield found during his inspection of the troops prompted these remarks: "No blame can be attached to the officers here for want of instruction of the rank and file. It is true these officers are not graduates of the Academy, yet they are competent, whenever time and opportunity will be offered them to instruct the men in the various military exercises. Hitherto they have had enough to do on account of the rainy season and bad accommodations…. The rank and file are rather inferior looking men as to height yet their countenances were good and they were young and promising."

---

[240] Letter courtesy of the Middlesex County Historical Society. Captain Edmund Underwood was a direct civilian appointment as a second lieutenant in the 4th Infantry in 1848. He was promoted to major in 1861, retired in 1862, and died in 1863.

Mansfield's assessment of this small, new post was as positive as the old inspector could make it given the mess he found.[241]

Fort Ter-Waw 3 May 1859

Now at Crescent City, California, Mansfield wrote to Thomas on 6 May 1859, and gave details of his harrowing journey to Fort Ter-Waw. "On Tuesday the 3rd instant I hired a canoe and four Indians and left Hoopa Valley at 7 a.m. following the current of the Trinity River through the canyon of the mountains 9 miles to its junction with the Klamath. Thence we continued down the river in a rapid current till we reached the 1st rapid say about 10 miles below the Trinity when the canoe struck a rock and was instantly capsized, and I lost my sword, rifle and all my baggage except a small carpet bag containing my uniform. Fortunately I had got out to walk round the rapids. The next rapid about two miles further down the river was too dangerous for the Indians and the canoe was hauled over the rocks. The residue of the distance was readily got over and we reached Fort Ter-Waw about 5 p.m., a distance by water of about 50 miles." The fort was situated on the north bank of the Klamath River about six miles above its mouth. He found that "It is well located being about 40 miles below the mouth of the Trinity and 35 miles by trail from Crescent City and in the middle of the Indian Reservation." Mansfield estimated that there were about 2,000 Indians within 40 miles of the post. "At present they are peaceable and as there is no gold here and no good land for cultivation it is quite probable they will not be molested by the whites for years." The post was garrisoned by Company D of the 4th Infantry commanded by Lieutenant George Crook who had one officer on site as Lieutenant Colonel Henry Lee Scott was absent serving as an aide to the General in Chief. The company had 10 staff enlisted and 70 privates of which six were absent as sick or confined. "This company passed in review and on inspection the men appeared well but the most of them were recruits. They were armed with the old musket rifled and with rifles and some smooth barrel muskets. The new rifle musket and equipments were expected soon. They were in the old forage cap and the old uniform pants and coat and neat. They were deficient in knapsacks and canteens. The continued wet weather for the past 6 months prevented the drill by movements and they accordingly could not drill as Light Infantry and skirmishers but Lieutenant Crook had divided his company into 6 squads for the bayonet exercise and they went through that drill handsomely and they had been practiced at the target and fired at 200 yards at the target 6'x22" and made 1 of 3 ½ hits (29%) which was quite creditable considering the number of recruits. The command was in a good state of discipline and Lieutenant Crook is a highly meritorious officer." Mansfield found the company books in good order; there were 23 desertions in the last three years. He found the men "comfortably quartered in a log barrack shingled and slept in double bunks two tiers high and had a good mess room and kitchen...they appeared cheerful and contented." But he found that the guard house "was inadequate as there was no prisoners' room and a new one required." The medical officer was a civilian and while young, was apparently well qualified. Hospital supplies were adequate but lacked a few items...."there was no hospital furniture, no sheets, blankets, coverlets, mattresses, pillow cases, etc., and no cooking utensils." But he opined that "in due time the proper supplies will be furnished." The Quartermaster and Commissary Departments, both run by Lieutenant Thomas E. Turner, were in good order but "He is deficient in shoes, coats, stockings, stocks, scales, drawers, and flannel shirts." Commissary supplies were good "and came from San Francisco via Crescent City over trails, and by Indian canoes." Buildings he found were constructed of logs with shingled roofs and mud chimneys. He identified "A fine, large garden just planted and the post is surrounded by a heavy growth of red wood and other timber. This post seems to occupy the only prairie spot. It is on a bend of the river and it is quite probable in extraordinary freshets the parade will be covered with water and the river will take a short cut across this bend. Yet there can be no danger to the post from this cause as the log house and other places afford abundant refuge." As at the last post he inspected, Mansfield found the troops' pay in arrears, here for six months. Mansfield concluded that "This post is very creditable to Lieutenant Crook who established it and it is well commanded and he is a highly meritorious young officer. He understands the Indian character and he is feared and respected by them. Lieutenant Turner is quite a young officer, but

---

[241] Letter courtesy of the Middlesex County Historical Society. Lieutenant Joseph Benson Collins began his Army career as a private in 1846. He became a second lieutenant in the 4th Infantry in 1848. He was brevetted to major, lieutenant colonel and colonel during the Civil War. He retired in 1871 as a major.

meritorious and attentive to his duties. This post owing to the large number of Indians when viewed in conjunction with the post at Hoopa Valley is very well placed and it must be kept up for a number of years to come."[242]

Fort Umpqua, Oregon 9 May 1859

On 16 May 1859, Mansfield wrote his rough draft from San Francisco of his inspection of Fort Umpqua. He wrote that he left Fort Ter-Waw on the 5th "in an Indian canoe with two Indians and proceeded down the Klamath River 6 miles to its mouth where I took mules and Indian guides and passed over the trail 30 miles to Crescent City which place I reached at 5 p.m. [I]…remained there till the evening of the 6th when on the arrival of the steamer *Columbia* I went on board and on the evening of the 8th instant crossed Umpqua bar and landed at Fort Umpqua." The post was "situated some two miles up the Umpqua River on the north shore….It was established by order of Brevet Major General Wool in 1856 after the Rogue River War….It is 5 miles below Gardenia City, the landing of the Pacific Mail steamer, which pass over the bar where there is 20 feet of water at high tide without difficulty." The post was about "22 miles below Scottsburg, the head of navigation by the two small steamers on this river. There is a mule trail along the coast over the mountains connecting it with Crescent City." The site was selected by Major John Fulton Reynolds of the 3rd Artillery. Mansfield was not pleased with the fort's location: "This post is very badly placed as to site. To the west and northwest to the Pacific Ocean is nothing but an ocean of sand for two miles and high sand bluffs are thrown up encircling the post and are only stayed temporarily by the pine and fir trees immediately around the buildings. They are being covered in rapidly and the northwest winds which blow all summer will in less than 5 years cover this post up entirely unless timely removed and the sand bank's advance will only be stopped in its progress by the river which will wash the sand into the ocean as fast as it is blown into the water." Mansfield was also upset that the post was on private property of one Amos E. Rogers "and was once the site of a town but for good reasons was abandoned. He claims rent and desires the Government to purchase it. It might be proper to pay him a small rent for it is of no value otherwise to him, but I would not advise a purchase as the post must be removed in less than 5 years. If a post on this river be desirable after two or three years it would be well to move it some 5 or 6 miles further up the river if a suitable point could be fixed upon." He wrote that it rained at the post "every month of the year. But the rainy season when it rains from 14 to 31 days in the months…[of] October through April and as much as six feet of rain falls in the year." He observed that the 600 Indians within 70 miles "have never been engaged in war against the whites and are peaceable and harmless." Major John Benjamin Scott of the 3rd Artillery commanded the post which contained Company L. Major Scott also had a post surgeon along with a hospital steward. Company L was commanded by Captain Henry Bethel Judd who was absent sick and left Lieutenant Alexander Piper in command with one of the two remaining officers sick. The second officer acted as the Quartermaster and Commissary Officer. The company had 10 staff enlisted and 49 privates with six absent. "This company is very small, many recruits among them. It passed in review, but the musicians were young and played badly and evidently had no ear for music. It was armed with the new rifled musket and accoutrements, in the old uniform cap and pants. It had never practiced at the target or bayonet exercise, but went through with some of the movements of the Light Infantry drill. The rainy weather for half the year, and the want of suitable drill ground operates to the disadvantage of this company combined with the absence of 2 of its officers." Company books were in order; there were 16 desertions during the last three years. He noted that the company "was comfortably quartered in a one-story frame building with piazza with a good mess room and kitchen." "This company should be filled up by recruits and will be soon." He found the guard adequate and the building suitable for the post. The post hospital was also in a good building with four staff plus the doctor; it had ample medicines and was well organized and complete. The post's magazine was adequate and the three guns—a 6 pounder bronze gun, a 12 pounder bronze howitzer, and one mountain howitzer, were "on the parade in good serviceable order." The post's Quartermaster and Commissary Officer, Lieutenant Lorenzo Lorain, performed all his duties well and his books were in good order and supplies ample and well stored. All his

---

[242] Letter courtesy of the Middlesex County Historical Society. Ter-Waw was the Indian name for the flat on which the fort was placed. It was destroyed by floods in 1861 and 1862 and then abandoned. Lieutenant George Crook was an 1852 West Point graduate and was brevetted from major to major general during the Civil War. He was in command of the Division of the Missouri from 1880 to his death in 1890. Lieutenant Colonel Henry Lee Scott was an 1833 West Point graduate who was brevetted to major and lieutenant colonel during the Mexican-American War and served as an aide to Lieutenant General Scott, his father-in-law, from 1855 to 1861. He retired in 1861 and died in 1886. Lieutenant Thomas Elwyn Turner was a civilian appointment as a second lieutenant in the 2nd Artillery and transferred to the 4th Infantry in 1858. He was brevetted to major in 1862 for Gaines's Mill and died that year.

supplies and funds came from San Francisco. The post had a "good bakery and the bread excellent." The troops' pay was only four months in arrears. Overall, Mansfield was happy with what he saw: "The discipline of the post is good and it is well commanded by Major Scott and harmony prevails."[243]

Presidio, San Francisco 17–19 May 1859

Three days later on 19 May 1859, Mansfield wrote his rough draft from San Francisco and reported his inspection of the 17th of the Presidio of San Francisco. He wrote that he boarded an omnibus and rode three miles to the Presidio. Mansfield noted that the post was temporarily commanded by Lieutenant Horatio Gates Gibson of the 3rd Artillery since Company C of the 6th Infantry had just returned from Fort Yuma conducting an "expedition against the Mohave Indians and which I did not inspect again as I had previously inspected it at Fort Yuma, and it had not had time to get into quarters comfortably." Mansfield took stock of the men he found at the post: "Assistant Surgeon C[harles] C[arter] Keeney, an hospital steward, an ordnance sergeant, a quartermaster sergeant, a principal musician, and 15 of the 6th Infantry band in the aggregate of Staff and Band, 1 officer and 19 men, six recruits of the 1st Dragoons, 41 recruits of the general service, 43 casually at the post, in the total 2 officers and 109 men. Of these men, there were under guard and in the guard house, 24 awaiting sentence, 3 confined for desertion, 2 for serious offences, and 9 for minor offenses, in the aggregate 39." Unfortunately for the prisoners, he found the guard house "a miserable old adobe building...not in good police....some allowance must be made for the peculiarly unsettled state of the command." He found the hospital in a better condition housed in a frame building: "It answered all the immediate demands of the post and was better in proportion than any other department here." As he found in his 1854 inspection, most of the buildings were constructed of adobe by the Mexican government many years before and now were in need of replacement. At best a few of them were "only tolerable" but most were "worthless and not fit for such objects in any purpose and should be levelled." He recommended to the commanding general that there were only two frame buildings of any value "and it is idle to think of repairing and patching up and adding to ...[adobe] buildings. I would therefore urge...that all the adobe buildings here be leveled to the ground, and the post remodeled in a plan to provide for four companies and that permanent stone and brick, fire proof outside buildings be erected." Lieutenant Gibson was both the Acting Assistant Quartermaster and Commissary Officer; all his books and accounts were in order and up to date—his "duty well performed." Mansfield was concerned when he inspected the ordnance at the post and wrote that "There is but little pertaining to the department here of value. There are 4 six pounder brass guns in serviceable order....It is well there is no more as there is no fit place for ordnance here." He vented his concerns about this post in the rest of his report. The post was about one mile from both Forts Point and Alcatraz and "it is convenient for supernumerary troops as reserves and reliefs to the garrisons of these forts. It is perfectly healthy and water abundant....Hence there is no objections to it as a depot for troops to move wherever ordered by land and water. I regard a depot of troops here as indispensable to meet any emergency as to war whether with savage or civilized foes, and have come to the conclusion there should be here at all times at least two supernumerary companies of troops to meet any emergency and if practicable four companies....It may be said that Benicia will answer the same purpose, to which I reply that Benicia is an indispensable post to meet the immediate demands for defence through and at the Navy Yard only 8 miles off by land. But Benicia is 30 miles from the Presidio and besides has accommodations for one company comfortably. It may be necessary at one hour's notice to throw troops into the newly built batteries here and no place is so convenient as the Presidio for that purpose. I look upon the defences of San Francisco and the Navy Yard as extremely weak at present in proportion to their importance."[244]

---

[243] Letter courtesy of the Middlesex County Historical Society. Major John Fulton Reynolds was an 1841 West Point graduate who was brevetted to captain and major during the Mexican-American War. He became a colonel of the 5th Infantry in 1862 and a major general of volunteers also in 1862. He was killed in action at Gettysburg, PA, 1 July 1863. Captain Henry Bethel Judd was an 1839 West Point graduate and was brevetted to captain during the Mexican-American War, and to lieutenant colonel and colonel during the Civil War. He died in 1892. Lieutenant Alexander Piper was an 1851 West Point graduate who was brevetted to major and lieutenant colonel during the Civil War. He remained in the Army and retired as the colonel of the 5th Artillery in 1891. He died in 1902. Lieutenant Lorenzo Lorain was an 1856 West Point graduate who was brevetted to captain and major during the Civil War. He remained in the Army and died as a major of the 1st Artillery in 1882.

[244] Letter courtesy of the Middlesex County Historical Society. Omnibuses ran regularly from downtown San Francisco to outlying points, usually pulled by a four horse team. In 1857, a newspaper reporter took such a trip: "At the corner of Washington and Pacific streets, he boarded one of Bowman & Gardner's four-horse omnibuses. A 40-minute ride through Spring Valley, past the tollgate, along the marge of Washerwoman's Bay, and by a number of ranches, brought the conveyance to the end of its route to Presidio House [a place of refreshment just outside the reservation boundary near the Lombard Street gate]. Disembarking, the reporter continued on foot, passing to the north of the Presidio. Only a few of the old adobe

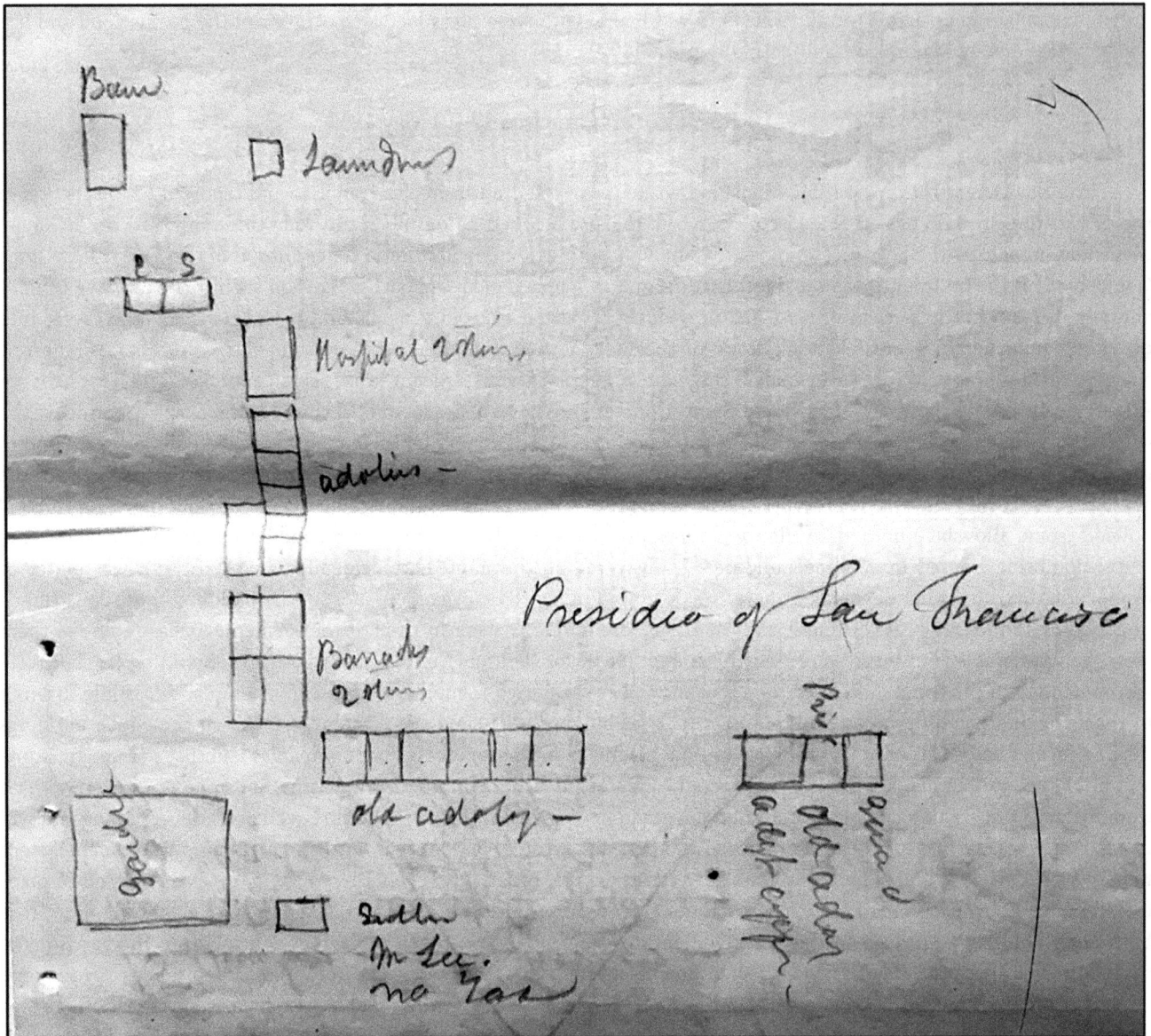

Mansfield's 1859 rough sketch of the Presidio at San Francisco, a post he heavily criticized as inadequate in most respects. Courtesy of the Middlesex County Historical Society.

Fort Crook 25 May 1859

Fort Crook was next on Mansfield's list and he wrote his draft of its inspection from San Francisco on 2 June 1859. He reported that "On the 20th May I left this City in the steamer for Sacramento, on the 21st left Sacramento for Red Bluff in a steamer, on the 23rd left Red Bluff in a two horse buggy and with a driver and reached Fort Crook via Pit River on the 25th." The fort was "situated on the north bank of Fall River 7 miles above its junction with Pit River and on the wagon road between Red Bluff or Shasta City, and Yreka, and thence into Oregon. It is 115 miles from Red Bluff and on

structures were occupied by the army. Nearby were the new wooden buildings….A 20-minute walk along a "fair road" built by the military brought the reporter to the [engineer] wharf [at Fort Point]." Edwin C. Bearrs, *Fort Point, Historic Structure Report, Historic Data Section* (Denver: National Park Service, 1973), 103; quotation from Erwin N. Thompson, *Defender of the Gate: The Presidio of San Francisco, A History from 1846 to 1995* (Historic Resource Study Golden Gate National Recreation Area National Park Service, 1994), 57. Lieutenant Horatio Gates Gibson was an 1847 West Point graduate who was brevetted from major to brigadier general during the Civil War. He remained in the Army and retired in 1891 as the colonel of the 3rd Artillery. He died in 1904.

the emigrant trail from Utah into California and in the midst of a race of wild Pit River Indians, numbering about 700 souls. It is about 60 miles from the nearest white settlement except some few settlers in the vicinity of the post on the Pit River Valley who rely on the protection of the troops. The situation is picturesque with Mount Shasta which is perpetually covered with snow in full view bearing west northwest say 75 miles distant. The river water is excellent and wood and grazing convenient and abundant. It is however cold in winter and the snow falls to a great depth at times, so much so, as to interdict any communication over the mountains with Red Bluff…my buggy could just get along over the snow on the mountain canyon late in May." He found the post "well located to overawe the Indians and protect the emigrant and transportation travel between the eastern states and Oregon and California and should be maintained and garrisoned with not less than two companies." Mansfield noted that the fort substituted for old Fort Reading in the Sacramento Valley "which I recommended to be abandoned in 1854 on account of sickness." Fort Crook was established on 1 July 1854 and Mansfield found the site "well-suited." Captain John Adams was in command of the post which was garrisoned by Companies A and F of the 1st Dragoons. Lieutenant Milton T. Carr was in command of Company A as its commander was absent sick. Carr was also the Acting Quartermaster and Commissary of the post. The company's second officer was also absent sick; it had 10 staff noncommissioned officers, but no farrier, and 44 privates of whom three were sick, and five on detached service. On review Mansfield found the company "neat in the old uniform with pompons. It had no valises; the spurs were deficient in number. The horses were old but in good condition not having been on any long scout recently. Their feet were not in proper order as many shoes should be removed and hoofs trimmed, etc." While he noted their arms in good order, the horse equipments were worn. But he found the "company…very deficient in the drill. They went through some of the movements of the platoon drill on the walk; did not attempt the sabre exercise and could not drill as skirmishers dismounted. It had practiced some at the target; …one round each man at a target 200 yards and 6'x22" made 1 of 3½ hits which will compare favorably with other troops in this Department." He attributed the lack of drill competence only "to circumstances—1st They have been laborers and mechanics building log houses for the post two years….[the company had] no officer at all to assist [Lieutenant Carr] and the company is now in exactly the same condition as to want of officers; an additional lieutenant, a graduate of the Academy, should be attached to this company immediately. It is in good discipline and the men look well and of good habits." The company was well quartered with a mess room and kitchen "but it had no bunks and should be supplied with them without delay." While he found the corral and stable ample, the men had "no stable frocks…an indispensable article to preserve cleanliness in the soldiers' person and dress while grooming horses and should be furnished." The company books were in order and showed 38 desertions in three years. Mansfield was concerned about the company fund of $1,542 "of which $1,387 was a commissary check….The company fund book was not balanced when I inspected the company book and it was handed to me the evening before I left and I did not examine it as closely as I now wish I had as this fund is so large." But he was happy with the company's "fine library with 600 dollars of well selected books. Of course this company can have all the vegetables etc., they need by purchase out of their own savings of rations."[245]

Mansfield inspected Company A next and found it commanded by Captain John Adams but wrote that Lieutenant William Thomas Magruder absent on recruiting service. A second officer, Lieutenant John Thomas Mercer, was acting post Adjutant. The company had 11 staff noncommissioned officers including one farrier and 40 privates of whom one was absent sick, five on detached duty, and one absent confined. The company "passed in review at a walk and trot, was neat and in good order in the old uniform, with pompons. The horses were old but in good condition not having been on a scout lately. Their hoofs however wanted trimming and their shoes should be occasionally removed for that purpose…..the arms in good order. The horse equipments and valises much worn, It went through the movements of the drill of platoon at the walk and trot, and the sabre exercise and some of the movements of the drill dismounted and fired at the target; [it] made at 200 yards on a target 6'x22" 1 of 5 (20%) and 1/3 hits (33%), not so good as the other company and not so bad as in many other companies on this Department and that of Oregon….It is impossible to have well instructed troops without officers at their posts qualified for that duty. It was in good discipline and the men good looking." It was quartered in the same manner as its sister company and its books in order which showed 47 desertions in two years; company fund books correct. Again he noted that stable frocks were absent. The post's guard house was in order with only "one Indian confined for murder….It was an unusual circumstance to find no soldiers confined and creditable to the men." The hospital was ample, well housed, with ample medicines, and the books and records well

245 Letter courtesy of the Middlesex County Historical Society. Captain John Adams was an 1846 West Point graduate who was brevetted to first lieutenant during the Mexican-American War. He resigned from the Army in 1861 and became a brigadier general in the Confederate Army. He was killed at the Battle of Franklin 30 November 1864.

kept. The post's Adjutant's office was well-housed and the "records are well and properly kept." The bakery had an adobe oven which he noted required a few bricks for repair. He found however, that the companies' attempts at gardening were "not very promising." As at prior posts, he reported that the troops' pay was in arrears, here for six months. The Quartermaster's Department under Lieutenant Carr had its supplies "in a good state of preservation….[but] his accounts and papers are behind times….Lieutenant Carr is not prompt enough in his returns and accounts and does not seem to have any taste for the keeping of accounts." Unfortunately Lieutenant Carr was also the Commissary Officer and had similar problems with keeping his accounts correct and accurate as he did with the Quartermaster's. "As I before remarked I do not think Lieutenant Carr has a taste for accounts and in addition he has too much duty to perform and I recommended verbally to General Clarke to attach another officer to this post and to let that officer perform this duty." Mansfield was pleased with the post's log buildings, shingle roofs, and adobe hearths and chimneys although some of these latter needed a few bricks for repairs. Unfortunately bricks were "not to be had short of Red Bluff 115 miles distant." He found Indians in the vicinity "to be hostile. It is only the fear of the consequences that deters them from murders and the extermination of the frontier settlers. They are cowardly, are armed with the bow and arrow, have no guns except there be some among them taken from the murdered white men from time to time. They had committed a number of murders which have come to light and I suppose a great many that have never come to light." He detailed some 18 murders in recent years and ended by estimating their number at 1,000 "within 100 miles of this post." He concluded by again showing his unease with too few officers: "This post has but three officers at it for two companies and when I arrived Captain Adams was just recovering from severe sickness; Lieutenant Carr is performing the heavy duty of commanding his company and the only officer with it and acting Quartermaster and Commissary, and Lieutenant Mercer has a leave of absence in his pocket. I would now ask how is an expedition after Indians to be commanded, the post protected in the absence of such an expedition, and the troops instructed. There certainly should be more officers at this post and officers who have graduated at the Academy and of experience in the service. It is no easy task to make efficient Dragoons out of recruits some of whom have never fired a pistol from a horse's back and who know but little about riding."[246]

San Francisco 4 June 1859

On 4 June 1859, Mansfield wrote from San Francisco of another inspection of the Department's Commissary Office as it was under a new officer, Captain Marcus De Lafayette Simpson. Mansfield had previously inspected the Commissary Department in January 1859 when commanded by Major Richard Bland Lee. Mansfield was now pleased to find that Simpson had done away with the "expense of the depot at Benicia as unnecessary" and rented a large brick store house in San Francisco….I think his arrangements all good and judicious….He keeps a suitable safe and all his books and records are systematic….Captain Simpson is industrious, energetic, and well qualified for this department and takes a pride in performing his duty well. I doubt not the duties here will be properly performed to the interest of the service."[247]

Again on 4 June, Mansfield wrote a draft report from San Francisco and reported his inspection of the "Office of Headquarters of the Department of California which closed my labors here." Brigadier General Clarke of the 6th Infantry was in command of the Department of California and resided in San Francisco, his headquarters. His office on Bush Street was located with the Department's Chief Quartermaster. Mansfield noted that he had found General Clarke at Fort Vancouver when the inspector arrived in the Washington Territory last September. The office's records he found to be well kept and neat with all head of department's records correct and the officers' duties well performed except for Colonel Coffee. Mansfield wrote that the department needed another paymaster and that General Clarke was not aware

---

[246] Letter courtesy of the Middlesex County Historical Society. The one Company A soldier Mansfield noted confined was apparently confined elsewhere. Lieutenant William Thomas Magruder was an 1850 West Point graduate who resigned in 1862 and became a captain in the Confederate Army. He was killed 3 July 1863 at the Battle of Gettysburg. Lieutenant John Thomas Mercer was an 1854 West Point graduate who resigned in 1861 and became the colonel of the 21st Georgia Infantry. He was killed 19 April 1864 in the attack on Plymouth, North Carolina.

[247] Letter courtesy of the Middlesex County Historical Society. Captain Marcus De Lafayette Simpson was an 1846 West Point graduate who was brevetted to first lieutenant and captain during the Mexican-American War and from colonel to major general during the Civil War. He retired from the Army as a colonel in 1888 and died in 1909.

of Coffee's misappropriations. Mansfield did write somewhat critically that after he asked "for the reports of the officers in charge of public funds....no such reports were on file."[248]

Finally on 4 June 1859, Mansfield wrote Brigadier General Newman S. Clarke from San Francisco and announced his completion of his inspection of the Department of California. When Mansfield arrived, Clarke commanded the Department of the Pacific which was divided into the Departments of California and Oregon. After congratulating him on his successful war against the Indians, he give the commander a brief summary of what he found—"I have seen nothing to which I should particularly call your attention unless it be the site of Fort Umpqua" which Mansfield thought would be covered in sand in a few years. Accounts were in order except for Colonel Andrew J. Coffee about whom Mansfield had already informed Clarke. Another major problem was desertions—he described them as "enormous." He also faulted the instruction of the troops and noted that there "was a very great difference" from post to post although all were deficient. He attributed this problem to the great amount of time taken to construct posts as well as an inadequate number of officers to supply instruction. Bad weather with heavy snows at some posts also prevented more troop instruction. On 1 July 1859, Mansfield wrote Colonel Samuel Cooper from Middletown and reported that he had left San Francisco on 6 June and on the 27th "reported at Headquarters of the Army and received orders to repair to my post [Middletown] and complete my report." His August report showed that he remained in Middletown during July "completing my reports of inspection on the Pacific Coast." His August report revealed that he was in Middletown except for 14 days spent in New York "on the General Court Martial for...Major Osborne Cross." Mansfield remained in Middletown except for a seven-day leave during which he visited Norwich, Connecticut. Then during October he remained in Middletown except for the 18th to the 21st when he went to New York and inspected recruits and transport who were heading for the Department of Oregon. He described the ship, the *Atlantic*, as "splendid" and "well-conditioned to proceed to sea." He found "nothing wanting to ensure a safe and pleasant trip." He noted that "provision was made in crossing the Isthmus on the Panama Railroad of 2nd class cars for the enlisted men and 1st class for the officers to Panama whence they were to leave for San Francisco in the splendid steamer *Golden Gate*." He inspected 266 enlisted men "on the whole were fine looking and well provided for the trip. They had been more instructed than usual with recruits and some of them had been drilled at the company drill....they marched well for recruits. Attached to this body of men were 12 or 13 laundresses, a class of women very much wanted on the Pacific Coast." His November and December monthly reports show that he remained at his post in Middletown. He also spent January 1860 in Middletown except that he left on the 23rd to attend a General Court Martial of some cadets at West Point. He was on that duty until he returned to Middletown on the 13th. During the months of March and April he remained at his post in Middletown except for six days he spent in New York inspecting Texas bound recruits and transport. Similarly in May he remained in Middletown except for three days when he journeyed to Fort Columbus, New York, to inspect recruits bound for Utah. For the months of June, July, and August, he remained at his home except for seven days in August when he was on leave. The next month would begin his final major inspection—the Department of Texas.[249]

---

[248] Letter courtesy of the Middlesex County Historical Society.

[249] Letters courtesy of the Middlesex County Historical Society. Major Osborne Cross was an 1825 West Point graduate who was brevetted to brigadier general during the Civil War. He retired as a colonel in 1866 and died in 1876.

1860-1861 Department of Texas (24 September 1860 – 23 January 1861)

Galveston	24 September 1860
Indianola	25–26 September 1860
Fort Inge	6–7 October 1860
Camp Wood	12 October 1860
Fort Davis	29 October 1860
Fort Quitman	5 November 1860
Fort Stockton	15–16 November 1860
Fort Lancaster	20 November 1860
Fort Hudson	24 November 1860
Fort Clark	29–30 November 1860
Fort Duncan (Eagle Pass)	3–5 December 1860
Fort McIntosh	10–11 December 1860
Ringgold Barracks	17–18 December 1860
Fort Brown	2–3 January 1861
Paymaster Cunningham	3 January 1861
Captain George Stoneman's Cavalry	4–5 January 1861
San Antonio, Department HQ	21–23 January 1861

This, Mansfield's last inspection tour, was similar to his Pacific Coast tour as he revisited posts he had inspected in an earlier tour in 1856. He received Special Order No. 23 of 5 March 1860 to inspect the Department of Texas and also inspect recruits at Carlisle Barracks, Pennsylvania. Mansfield acknowledged the order in a letter from Middletown to Lorenzo Thomas 8 March 1860.[250] Mansfield may have wisely decided to inspect Texas this time during the cooler months based on the heat he encountered during his March to September 1856 inspection but, as will be seen, he was not able to finish his inspections as he became ill.

---

[250] Letters courtesy of the Middlesex County Historical Society.

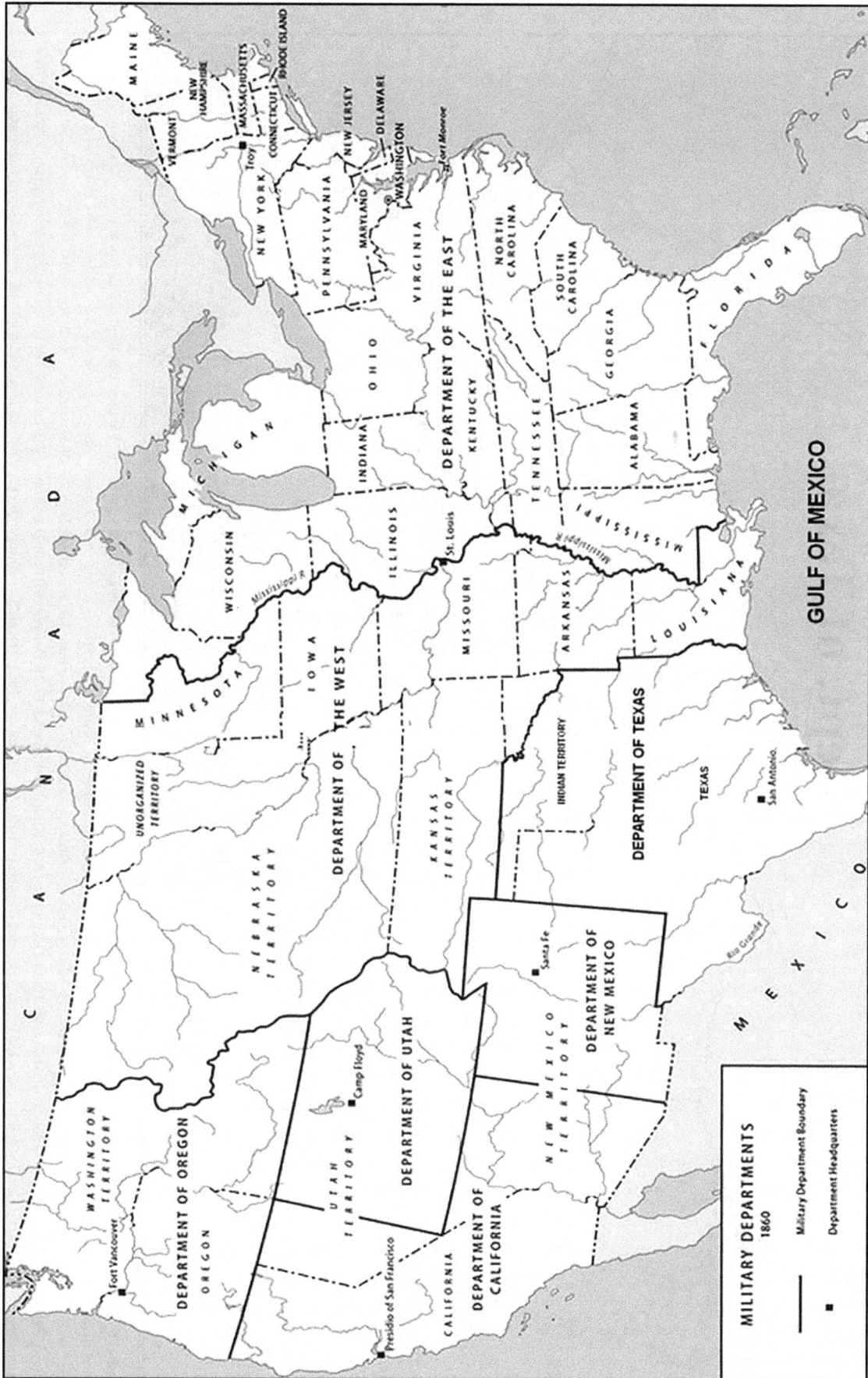

Department map showing the 1860 configuration with Department headquarters depicted by squares. Courtesy USACMH.

Mansfield's 1860-1861 Department of Texas inspection which began in Galveston and ended in San Antonio. He began in Galveston on 24 September 1860 so like his previous Texas inspection he arrived there by steamer from New Orleans. He then proceeded by water to Indianola 25-26 September 1860; Fort Inge 6-7 October 1860; Camp Wood 12 October 1860; Fort Davis 29 October 1860; Fort Quitman 5 November 1860; Fort Stockton 15-16 November 1860; Fort Lancaster 20 November 1860; Fort Clark 29-30 November 1860; Fort Duncan (Eagle Pass) 3-5 December 1860; Fort McIntosh 10-11 December 1860; Ringgold Barracks 17-18 December 1860; Fort Brown 2-3 January 1861; Paymaster Cunningham 3 January 1861; Captain George Stoneman's Cavalry 4-5 January 1861; San Antonio, Department HQ 21-23 January 1861. From San Antonio he probably rode to Indianola then by water to Galveston, then by Steamer to New Orleans. Map courtesy LOC.

Galveston 24 September 1860

Mansfield arrived at Galveston on 24 September 1860 at 7 a.m., by steamer from New Orleans and decided to inspect Lieutenant Walter H. Stevens of the Corps of Engineers who was still stationed there as Mansfield recalled from his 1856 visit. Lieutenant Stevens was under orders "to turn over all the works in Louisiana to Brevet Major Beauregard of the Corps of Engineers." Mansfield reported that all of Stevens's accounts were in order and he was "a highly meritorious officer and has been steadily employed since my last report in constructing and raising 16 lighthouses and beacons, and in commencing the customhouse and the accumulating of materials for the fortifications of Galveston Bay."[251]

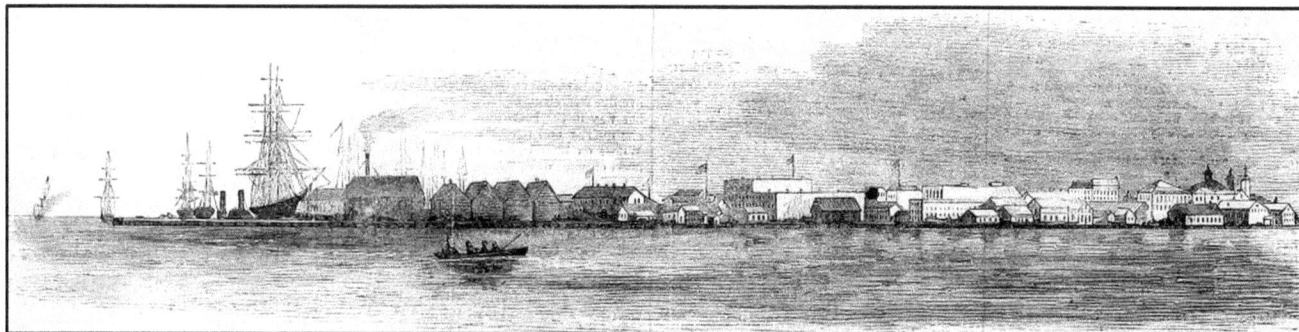

Sketch of Galveston by Theodore R. Davis, *Harper's Weekly*, 27 Oct. 1866, 684.

Sketch of Custom House in Galveston by Theodore R. Davis, *Harper's Weekly*, 27 Oct. 1866, 684. This structure was designed and constructed by Lieutenant Walter H. Stevens from 1857 to 1859.

From his camp on Rio Frio, Texas, on 6 October 1860, Mansfield wrote to Cooper and summarized his trip there from Middletown. Mansfield left on 14 September and reached Washington on the 15th and remained there "on duty" until the 18th when he "took his departure for Memphis thence to New Orleans, and left that place…on the 22nd, and on Monday the 24th arrived at Galveston where I was kept by the steamer till 5 p.m. of that day, and in that time inspected Lieutenant Walter H. Stevens of the Corps of Engineers. On the 26th at 10 a.m., landed at Indianola and in the afternoon commenced the inspection of that depot and completed my inspection on the 26th, and on the 27th forwarded to Head Quarters my reports from Indianola of the inspections at Galveston and Indianola. On the 28th, took a stage and on the

---

[251] Joseph K.F. Mansfield, *Texas & New Mexico on the Eve of the Civil War: The Mansfield & Johnston Inspections, 1859-1861,* Jerry Thompson, ed. (Albuquerque, NM: University of New Mexico Press, 2001), 85-86. Pierre Gustave Toutant Beauregard was an 1838 West Point graduate and brevetted to captain and major during the Mexican-American War. He resigned in 1861 becoming a general in the Confederate Army. He died in 1893.

30th reached San Antonio, and I was engaged in that place to the 3rd instant, in making my preparations to move toward the South Western Posts and left that place on the 4th. I purposely omitted the inspections of the Heads of Departments at San Antonio till my return to that place some time in December, as this advanced state of the season made it necessary for me so to do. My report too of that inspection will be made more complete after first having inspected most of the subordinate posts."[252]

Indianola 25–26 September 1860

Mansfield had journeyed by steamer to Indianola arriving on the 25th for a two-day inspection at this important U.S. Army supply depot. Mansfield noted that as a result of his 1856 recommendation, the depot was placed four miles closer to the water, now at the general steamer landing, Powder Horn. The depot was commanded by Lieutenant James Patrick Major who "performs [his] duty very well & creditably to the service." Mansfield was satisfied with what he found here.[253]

Sketch of Indianola taken from the bay on board the barque *Texana*, Sept. 1860, by Helmuth Holtz. Courtesy LOC.

Fort Inge 6–7 October 1860

Mansfield rode to San Antonio, the department headquarters, but did not begin inspecting there as he wished to inspect the posts to the south and west to take advantage of good weather. He "left that place [San Antonio on 4 October] in the spring wagon drawn by four mules accompanied by an escort of ten privates & a sergeant of Company I, of the 1st Infantry, Captain [John Haskell] King with three baggage wagons of 6 mules each, which transported, in addition to the baggage, forage, the escort above named & my servant. We reached Fort Inge on the morning of the 7th, and on the following day commenced and completed the inspection of that post." They travelled on the El Paso Road there. Fort Inge on the Leona River is 80 miles from San Antonio, 45 miles from Fort Clark and 45 miles from Camp Wood. The post was commanded by Captain James Oakes and garrisoned by Company C of the 2nd Cavalry. The aggregate force was three officers and 25 men, which size Mansfield found too small to inspect for drill as only 13 men

---

[252] Letter courtesy of the Middlesex County Historical Society.
[253] Mansfield, *Texas & New Mexico on the Eve of the Civil War*, 87-89. Lieutenant James Patrick Major was an 1856 West Point graduate who resigned in 1861 becoming a Confederate brigadier general. He died in 1877.

were present: "With so small a force & mostly recruits, there will be no military drills to test the instruction of the men. Recruits to fill up this company should be forwarded at once and [an] additional officer, a [West Point] graduate, to drill them. The large number of horses & mules & arms at this post are of no use without men to use them." Buildings including the soldiers' quarters were poor and the bakery was "a worthless building of logs on end with a poor oven;" only the hospital was in good condition. He found that Captain Oakes and Lieutenant [James Bonaparte] Witherell were "highly meritorious & gallant officers except that Oakes suffered illness when on horseback." Discipline at this post was good. Mansfield wrote that "It is questionable whether this post is now of any importance so near the high road to El Paso, where the passing is now quite frequent, and where the Indians would be very careful not to expose themselves in this section of the country." The post had no garden due to the very dry climate; Mansfield suggested that due to the poor climate and lack of Indian depredation that the post was unnecessary.[254] Mansfield wrote to his wife from Fort Inge on the Leona River on 8 Oct 1860. "[He was] about 83 miles from San Antonio. From San Antonio furnished one spring wagon with a top and 4 mules carrying his light things and small arms. Also 3 baggage wagons drawn by 6 mules each for baggage and to transport 10 soldiers, a sergeant with their baggage, provisions and corn for the mules. Canvas covered wagons. He hired a servant man, a discharged soldier for this trip--Irishman by birth in country 10 years. Left San Antonio on 4th and got to Castroville, a Dutch settlement on the San Antonio River, 24 miles that day. Next day 23 miles to the River Saco. Camped River Frio 26 miles; 8 miles to here. Leave tomorrow morning for Camp Wood 45 miles from here; 2 day trip."[255]

Camp Wood 12 October 1860

Mansfield wrote that he left Fort Inge "at the head waters of the Nueces and arrived at that place [Camp Wood] on the 11th ...and on the 12th commenced the inspection." Mansfield noted that Camp Wood was well-sited and was "about 40 miles by trail from Fort Clark & about 90 miles by trail from Fort Chadbourne, & 60 miles by trail from Fort Mason. It is 45 miles from Fort Inge and 80 miles from Fort Clark by wagon road." This small, one company post, was garrisoned by Company K of the 2nd Cavalry commanded by Captain Charles J. Whiting. The company had two officers and 50 enlisted men as one officer, Lieutenant John Bell Hood, had been ordered to duty at West Point. Despite the large number of recruits present, Mansfield observed that the company drill was adequate as far as it could be performed. Dismounted target practice gave one in three hits (33%) with the rifle and slightly worse with the pistol. He remarked that the company's Sharps carbines and Colt Navy Revolvers were in serviceable order but holsters for the pistols were lacking but on order. The company's quarters and most other buildings were in Sibley tents but adequate for the men and stores. He observed a good bakery but due to the lack of seasonal rains, a garden was not possible. He found discipline good but having only one officer present made it "impossible...to perform all duties of this post & drill the men & command the scouts."[256]

---

[254] Mansfield, *Texas & New Mexico on the Eve of the Civil War*, 91-96. Captain John Haskell King entered the Army as a second lieutenant in 1837 and brevetted three times during the Civil War to major general. He retired in 1882 and died in 1888. Captain James Oakes was an 1846 graduate of West Point and received two brevets during the Mexican-American War to lieutenant and captain, and during the Civil War to colonel and brigadier general. He retired in 1879 and died in 1910. Lieutenant James Bonaparte Witherell entered the Army directly as a 2nd lieutenant; he drowned 20 March 1861.

[255] Letter courtesy of the Middlesex County Historical Society.

[256] Mansfield, *Texas & New Mexico on the Eve of the Civil War*, 96-101. Camp Wood was established by Lieutenant Edwin D. Philips and a company of the 1st Infantry in May 1857 near the site of a 1762 Spanish mission, San Lorenzo de la Santa Cruz. It was named for Bvt. Major George W. F. Wood of the 1st Infantry who died in 1854. The camp was deserted in March 1861.

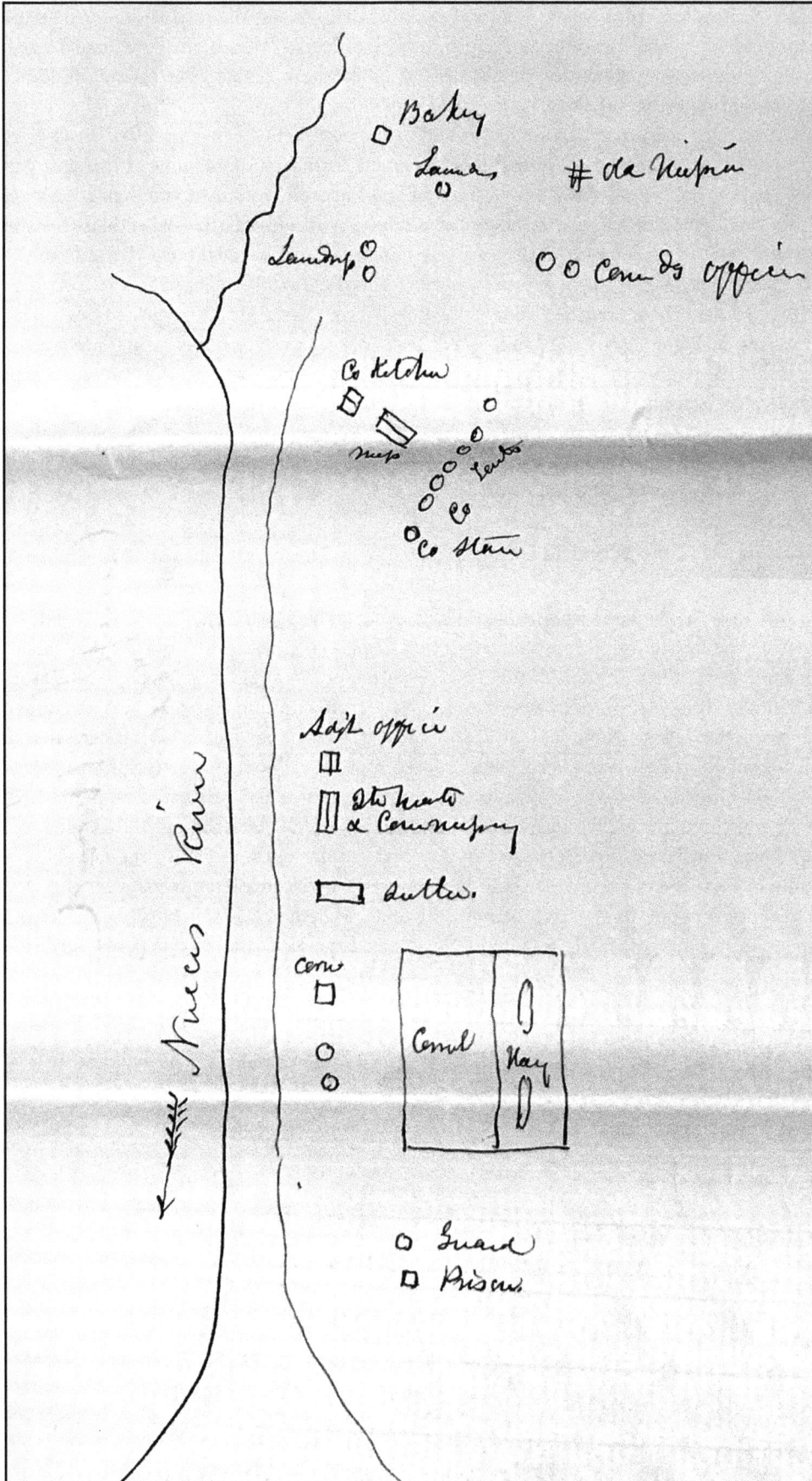

Mansfield's rough sketch of Camp Wood. Courtesy of the Middlesex County Historical Society.

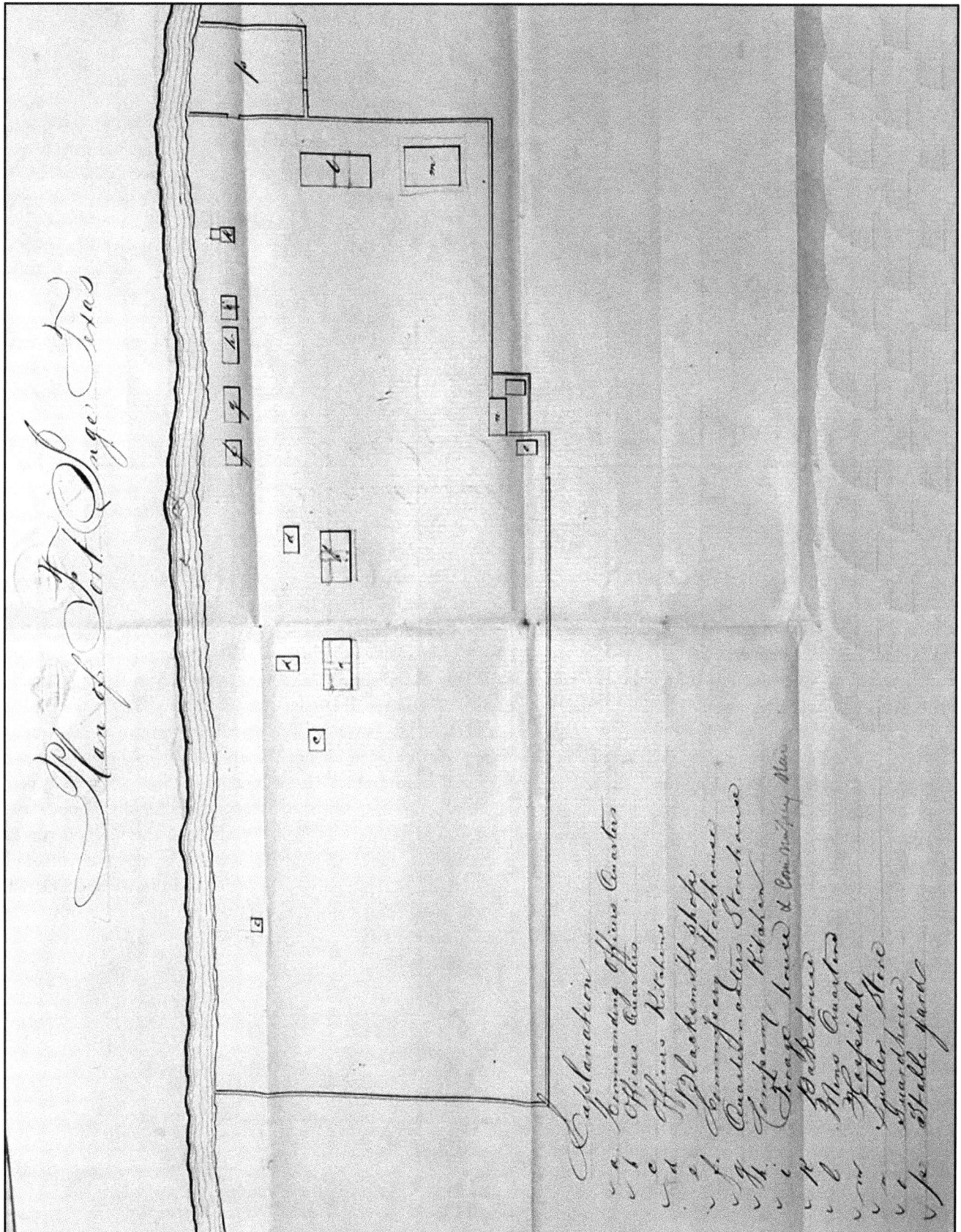

Sketch of Fort Inge not drawn by Mansfield but kept by him in his rough draft notes to use for his final report. Courtesy of the Middlesex County Historical Society.

Sketch of Fort Inge in 1867 drawn by Leon Trousset. Courtesy Wikipedia.

Fort Davis 29 October 1860

Mansfield inspected Fort Davis on 29 October, the day after he arrived there. To get there he stayed at Forts Clark, Hudson, Lancaster and Stockton which he planned on inspecting on his return from the forts farthest west--Davis and Quitman. At his last inspection of this post in 1856 there were six companies present from the 8th Infantry, while on this visit he found one, Company H, 8th Infantry, commanded by Colonel James V. Bomford. The commander was absent on court martial duty at Fort Bliss so the post was under temporary command of Lieutenant James J. Van Horn; company aggregate total was three officers and 59 enlisted. Lieutenant Van Horn was detailed from Company G, 8th Infantry. As he found at Fort Inge, so many officers and men were detailed on other duties that there were only 10 men at inspection, too few to attempt any drill. Discipline was inadequate due to the lack of officers as Mansfield noted that "on one occasion recently the corporal and almost the entire guard were drunk." He recommended that this should be a two-company post as it was "a very important post to hold in connection with the overland mail and emigrants as a resting place, unmolested by Indians." He determined that the magazine was "very unsafe" and the hospital was "a worthless building of posts set on end, and chinked in, and rotten ...[and] will soon fall down or be blown down." The stone enlisted quarters had thatched roofs which he wrote should be replaced with shingles and the windows glazed. The baker produced "indifferent bread" as that was not his trade before entering service and the post garden was "tolerable" thanks to efforts made to supply it with water. While Lieutenant Van Horn did his best, having only one officer at the post meant that discipline and military readiness suffered.[257]

---

[257] Mansfield, *Texas & New Mexico on the Eve of the Civil War*, 101-106. In his report, Mansfield recorded that it was located about 455 miles from San Antonio, 80 miles from Fort Stockton and 121 from Fort Quitman. Interesting to note Inspector Johnston's inspection of this post one year earlier found none of the problems which Mansfield detailed; Mansfield, *Texas & New Mexico on the Eve of the Civil War*, 71-73. It may be that Mansfield was much more thorough in his inspection or that the post suffered in the time since Johnston's report. Colonel James Voty Bomford was an 1832 West Point graduate who was brevetted to major and lieutenant colonel during the Mexican-American War and to colonel and brigadier general during the Civil War. He retired in 1874 as colonel of the 8th Infantry. He died in 1892. Lieutenant James Judson Van Horn was an 1858 West Point graduate who was brevetted to major during the Civil War. He remained in the Army and was promoted to colonel in 1891; he died in 1898. Mansfield summarized his October inspections in his November monthly report and noted that on the night of the 31st, they "encamped at Dead Man's Hole." Letter courtesy of the Middlesex County Historical Society.

Fort Quitman 5 November 1860

Mansfield arrived at Fort Quitman on the 3rd from Fort Davis and began his inspection on the 5th. There was one company at this post, Company F, 8th Infantry, commanded by Lieutenant Edward D. Blake with an aggregate of one officer and 63 enlisted men. Thirty-eight men turned out for inspection parade and were in excellent order. Drill went well except for the bayonet as they had not yet been taught it. Target firing went better than Mansfield thought it would with 60 percent hits at 100 yards and 24 percent at 200. The company had good adobe quarters but no bunks and the mess hall had no benches due to the lack of wood. Mansfield recommended that wood be immediately supplied for these purposes. Mansfield thought that the post should have been established "where the road first strikes the Rio Grande from the east" but now that it was already built it should stay, but he suggested that a road be built to shorten the route to El Paso and gave easier passage to travelers. He found the bread to be "ordinary" and there was no garden due to lack of rain and no possibility of irrigation. Overall the discipline was good.[258]

Fort Stockton 15–16 November 1860

Mansfield turned back east as he left on the 7th and reprised his route through Fort Davis to Fort Stockton which he inspected on 15-16 November 1860. Here he found Company H of the 1st Infantry commanded by Captain Stephen D. Carpenter with an aggregate of three officers and 69 enlisted men. Mansfield was pleased with the excellent inspection and drill of the company. He noted that target firing was very good with over 62 percent hitting at 100 yards; 40 percent at 200 yards, and over 14 percent at 300 yards. He wrote that the fort was "one of the best built and arranged company posts I have seen in the service and made essentially out of the mud, water, and grass on the spot, and is highly creditable to Captain Carpenter and his company." There was an excellent garden thanks to the efforts of Captain Carpenter and the bakery produced excellent bread due to its "first rate baker." The post is very well-sited and is healthy. Mansfield recommended that 16 extra horses at the post "be withdrawn" as infantrymen cannot use them. "Captain Carpenter commands with ability and zeal and does justice to the service and the country." Mansfield found the location of this post essential. Mansfield left on the 17th.[259]

Fort Lancaster 20 November 1860

Fort Lancaster was Mansfield's next stop. He arrived on 19 November and inspected the post the next day. He previously inspected it in 1856. Captain Robert S. Granger was in command with his Company K, 1st Infantry; two officers and 66 enlisted men in the aggregate. The men did very well at inspection and drill and Mansfield noted that their target firing was "the best ball practice I have seen": at 100 yards over 62 percent; 200 yards over 56 percent, and 300 yards 28 percent. Quarters were comfortable and adequate with adobe buildings--half shingled and the remainder thatched. Mansfield wrote that the Turnley Cottages which he found on his earlier inspection were a failure as he anticipated. He recommended that since the hospital building was in poor condition an extra soldiers' quarters could be used instead. He found the bread "of the first quality" and a successful garden which had to be hand-watered. "Captain Granger commands with ability and satisfactorily and is untiring in his effort in the performance of his duties....The discipline of the post is good." He left on the 21st for Fort Hudson.[260]

---

[258] Mansfield, *Texas & New Mexico on the Eve of the Civil War*, 106-111. Fort Quitman was the farthest west for Mansfield on this tour. It was on the Rio Grande about 85 miles below El Paso and 116 miles from Fort Davis. It was established in September 1858 by Captain Arthur T. Lee with Company C, 8th Infantry. Lieutenant Edward D. Blake was an 1847 West Point graduate who resigned in 1861 and became a lieutenant colonel in the Confederate Army. He died in 1882.

[259] Mansfield, *Texas & New Mexico on the Eve of the Civil War*, 112-117. Fort Stockton was established by Lieutenant John P. Sherburne of Company H, 1st Infantry, in March 1859. It was named after Commodore Robert Field Stockton, a naval officer who commanded the U.S. Pacific Fleet during the Mexican-American War. It was located at Comanche Springs at the meeting of the Overland Mails via Fort Chadbourne, and mail from San Antonio. It was 87 miles from Fort Lancaster and 80 miles from Fort Davis. The post was abandoned in 1886. Captain Stephen Decatur Carpenter was an 1840 West Point graduate who received two brevets during the Civil War to lieutenant colonel and colonel; he was killed in action at Murfreesboro, Tennessee, 31 Dec. 1862.

[260] Mansfield, *Texas & New Mexico on the Eve of the Civil War*, 117-121. Fort Lancaster was 97 miles from Fort Hudson and 87 from Fort Stockton.

Sketch of Fort Lancaster, *Harper's Weekly*, 23 March 1861, 185. The post is located on the San Antonio and San Diego mail route and is important for the protection it afforded for the ford of the Pecos River, a few miles away, where all the trains from Texas to California crossed.

Fort Hudson 24 November 1860

Mansfield then rode southeast and arrived next at Fort Hudson on 23 November, inspecting the post on the 24th. Only Company A of the 8th Infantry garrisoned the post with Major Larkin Smith commanding; aggregate of three officers and 41 enlisted men. Located on San Pedro Creek, a tributary of the Devil's River near the road from Fort Clark to El Paso, Mansfield noted that it had "abundant wood and good water, but little grazing." He believed that the fort was located on "probably the very best point to occupy on this river." The company drilled well although one of the three squads was not well advanced in the bayonet drill. He complemented the company's target firing with 46 percent hitting the target at 100 yards and 23 percent at 200: "This firing shows great progress in target shooting in our service" even though it was very windy and cold. The troops were adequately housed in adobe buildings with shingled roofs but with some missing windows covered only with canvas. Mansfield was critical of an 11-year-old drummer boy who was "too young and will not drum well for several years." There was a good bakery but no garden because of lack of rain. Mansfield was pleased overall: "Major Smith commands the post well, is a good drill officer and the command in a good state of discipline." However Mansfield did note that "Captain G. Stoneman of the 2nd Cavalry with his company has been reported on the returns of this post. But as he has been scouting all the season in the lower Rio Grande and no part of his company, etc., is here. I have not noticed him as belonging to the post at all....this is no station for cavalry, as there is no grain, and all the supplies of hay and corn are brought a great distance." He left on the 26th for Fort Clark.[261]

Fort Clark 29–30 November 1860

Mansfield continued to ride southeast and arrived at Fort Clark on 28 November 1860 and inspected the post the following two days. Mansfield had previously inspected this post in 1856 and it was again inspected by Colonel Joseph E. Johnston in November 1859. This large post served as the headquarters of the 3rd Infantry commanded by Colonel Benjamin L.E. Bonneville. The companies at this post were B, D, H, K, and G; Companies A, C and E were at Ringgold Barracks, and Companies F and I at Fort McIntosh. Companies B and G were on their way to this post but not yet present. Mansfield wrote that this important post "has improved less in accommodations for the military command than any post I have hitherto seen. While other posts have been built and rebuilt, this post has hardly progressed at all." Companies D, H, and K along with the staff passed "in review in quick and double quick time imperfectly." Company D did well except for the bayonet exercise and did acceptably well at target firing, with Companies H and K doing comparably. He believed that the reason for lack of performance in some drills and target shooting was due to the units being in the field too long "scouting and marching"—in the case of Company D for 12 months. "I will also remark that

---

[261] Mansfield, *Texas & New Mexico on the Eve of the Civil War*, 121-126; letter of the Middlesex County Historical Society. Fort Hudson was 78 miles from Fort Clark and 97 miles from Fort Lancaster. It was established 4 October 1857 by Captain James N. Caldwell with two companies of the 1st Infantry and one from the 8th Infantry. It was permanently abandoned in 1877. Note that it was properly named a "camp" rather than a "fort" according to modern authorities. It was named for Lieutenant Walter W. Hudson who was killed by Indians in April 1850. Major Larkin Smith was an 1835 West Point graduate and was brevetted to major during the Mexican-American War. He resigned in 1861 to become a colonel in the Confederate States Army. He died in 1884. For Mansfield's discussion of Stoneman's cavalry, see below.

every company should occasionally be withdrawn from the field to recruit and be instructed, especially as recruits cannot be instructed in the field." Mansfield noted that the quarters for the men were poor as were most other buildings used by the companies: "since 1856 two stone buildings have been erected…for officers. These are good buildings but there is not a soldier properly quartered.…It is to my mind clear that the rank and file have been too long neglected in providing quarters for them when the officers are comparatively comfortable.…There will be 5 companies here soon and no quarters for the soldiers at all. I have therefore to recommend that an appropriation be made for the soldiers' quarters of Fort Clark…of 15,000 dollars." He also recommended a plan for the location of the new quarters. He did find the bakery good and the garden productive depending on the commanding officer. Discipline for the companies was good as were books and records. He left Fort Clark on the 1st of December and took two days to reach Fort Duncan.[262]

Fort Duncan 3–5 December 1860

Mansfield rode south to Fort Duncan on the Rio Grande at Eagle Pass, arriving there on 2 December 1860, and inspected the post on 3 through 5 December. Here Major William H. French was in command with his Light Battery K and Companies F and L of the 1st Artillery. The aggregate for these three units was 12 officers and 194 enlisted. The companies "passed in review at quick and double quick time very well." The Light Company K had "carriages, caissons, guns, and harness in excellent order and the company…made a fine appearance.…the drill of the battery…was handsomely done,…and the firing was efficient, well done, and very satisfactory.…[and] the manual of the sabre…showed they were well instructed in this arm." Obviously the artillery company was, in Mansfield's opinion, in excellent order. Companies F and L performed well at drill but target firing was not very good. Note that these companies had no cannon as they were foot companies. The artillerymen were well-quartered in stone buildings but Company F was in tents and Company L in adobe buildings, however all were clean and in good order. He found a good bakery but the fort did not have a garden because "The Mexicans bring over corn, onions, sweet potatoes, and oranges, to the great accommodation of the garrison, as there is no garrison garden here." He found that the post was essential and in a good location despite the "excessive heat and the want of seasonable rains. This is peculiar to this latitude and the frontier of Texas and cannot be avoided." He opined that this post "is probably the best in southwestern Texas…for the present school of the light battery." He recommended $800 be spent to put Company F into buildings and that the post remain an artillery school. He also reported that "In my opinion it is time our soldiers were relieved from this business of building posts and then abandoning them and that their time should be employed [in]…military instructions." He lamented that battery horses and mules must be restored to their full rations of corn and hay as he wrote that "My own mule teams on the road are failing [on the reduced ration] and I shall have to purchase grain for them out of my own private means or they will be left on the road." He finally recommended that "I think it would be better for the service if none [no enlisted men] were employed.…as servants to officers. He left Fort Duncan on the 6th and reached Fort McIntosh in four days.[263]

Fort McIntosh 10–11 December 1860

Off again down the Rio Grande Mansfield rode to Fort McIntosh where he arrived on 9 December 1860, inspecting the post on the following two days. It is located about 116 miles from Fort Duncan and 120 from Ringgold Barracks, near the town of Laredo. He reported that the buildings he now found were in worse condition than he found in his previous inspection. He also wrote (perhaps adding uncharacteristic irony) that the main reason for this post is to protect the frontier against "another nation and another race, who do not like us and perhaps with good reason." Major Caleb C. Sibley was in command with Companies F and I of the 3rd Infantry present with four officers and 89 enlisted men at the command. The companies did well in passing in review at quick and double quick time and satisfactorily in

[262] Mansfield, *Texas & New Mexico on the Eve of the Civil War*, 126-134. Colonel Benjamin Louis Eulalie Bonneville was an 1815 West Point graduate who was wounded and brevetted to lieutenant colonel during the Mexican-American War and to brigadier general during the Civil War after he retired in 1861; he died in 1878.

[263] Mansfield, *Texas & New Mexico on the Eve of the Civil War*, 134-143. Fort Duncan was ordered abandoned by General Order 2 dated 16 May 1859. The post was 45 miles from Fort Clark and 118 from Fort McIntosh. Major William Henry French was an 1837 West Point graduate who was brevetted to captain and major during the Mexican-American War and to lieutenant colonel through major general during the Civil War. He remained in the service and retired as a colonel in 1880 and died in 1881. Mansfield's personal servants were never active military men.

the light infantry drill "as far as it went." Bayonet drill was executed well as far as the men were trained. Target firing was acceptable but Mansfield noted that he found "Four of the muskets…had sights different from the standard and were arranged for 100, 300 and 500 yards only. This is a disadvantageous innovation. The great benefit of the rifle musket is the long and certain range and why cut off its range and efficiency [at] 600 yards." Here Mansfield's opinion of long-range target practice was influenced by the orders of the Army Headquarters as shown here in General Orders No. 8 16 December 1854:

GENERAL ORDERS.⎫
No. 8.   ⎬   HEAD QUARTERS OF THE ARMY,
              ⎭   *New York, Dec. 16th,* 1854.

The following extract from the letter of the Colonel of Ordnance is printed for the information and government of the troops supplied with rifles and ammunition prepared for long ranges :—

" In giving orders for the practice firing with these arms, I would suggest the following general instructions :—The sights are marked for ranges 200, 300, 400, 500, 600 and 700 yards, (calculated for taking a fine sight,) and the practice should be at these distances. The cartridges issued with the arms, may be used with the best advantage in the following proportion for each man :—Five shots at 200 yards ; seven at 300 ; nine, each, at 400 and 500 ; and ten, each, at 600 and 700 yards. The targets should be placed at these distances carefully measured ; but the men should be instructed and practised in measuring distances by the eye. The ranges may be increased or diminished, and intermediate distances obtained by placing the sliding sights between the marks, or when varying but little, by taking coarser or finer sights, which each man will learn as he becomes more familiar with his arm. In loading, the outer wrapper of the cartridge must be torn, as usual, and the powder poured from the inner paper cylinder into the bore, taking care to pour in the whole of it; the charge of powder being reduced. none of it should be lost, and there is no danger from excessive recoil. The ball is then to be taken from the inner cylinder, reversed, and inserted into the muzzle. It must be set down on the powder charge by pressure with the ramrod, and must not be struck or rammed hard. No part of the paper of the cartridge must be put into the rifle."

BY COMMAND OF MAJOR GENERAL SCOTT.

Optimistic target shooting criteria promulgated by General Scott. Copy courtesy of the Middlesex County Historical Society.

He found that the Harpers Ferry Rifle had a screw for the rear sight which "penetrates in many instances the bore of the barrel, thereby creating a lump, or impediment to the ball and sometimes to the ramrod. This is a gross oversight of the inspection of the Harpers Ferry armory. My attention was also called to another evil, either the flange of the cap is too large or the nipple sits too close to the Maynard magazine, and the cap cannot be readily put on….Tap primer springs did not feed well. Many failed to bring out the primer and many of the caps also failed." The companies were quartered in frame buildings and tents and were clean but "The buildings occupied by the officers are in a very bad condition. They leak, the plastering is fallen down in part. The doors have been robbed of their locks, they want kitchens, etc., and….There should be about 8,000 dollars appropriated for these objects." He found that the bakery produced good bread despite poor conditions but no garden as "There can be but little produce from planting the soil as there is but little land suitable for that purpose." Mansfield wrote that "The officers at this post are all highly meritorious and the command in a good state of discipline." He recommended two enlisted men for promotion to recruiting duty and commented on their background and fitness for more responsible duties. He left Fort McIntosh on the 12th and reached Ringgold Barracks in six days.[264]

Ringgold Barracks 17-18 December 1860

Ringgold Barracks was next on Mansfield's tour; he arrived there on 17 December 1860 and on that day and the next he completed his inspection. It was located on the Rio Grande 121 miles downstream from Fort McIntosh and 115 above Fort Brown. Lieutenant Colonel Electus Backus commanded the post with Company D 8th Infantry and Company A 3rd Infantry. Company D had one officer and 50 privates at the post, two other officers were absent. The two companies passed in review "ordinarily well." Company D was not able to drill as skirmishers or bayonet although the light infantry drill went well. Target firing was adequate and the troops "were neat and in excellent order." Mansfield found that the company's quarters were the same as he found in 1856 "but much dilapidated" as the frame building had 12 windows without glass or sashes and there were no stoves or bunks. The company's bread he found "ordinary." Company A had two of its three officers at the post along with 46 enlisted men. The company did "tolerably well" at the light infantry drill and skirmishing but did not know the bayonet drill. Its target shooting was "quite poor" even though its "arms were in good order." The company was in quarters similar to Company D "but not quite as well" and the company bread was apparently unremarkable. Mansfield also reviewed 138 recruits who "were a good looking set of men....very much crowded in two old frame buildings." They had no arms. Mansfield reported that "They are temporarily crowded here. It is to be regretted that the first impressions a recruit gets in entering the service are to come from such accommodations. I am not surprised at the many desertions in our service." And, as in his 1856 report, he considered the post as "not healthy." Mansfield concluded that the post needed "an appropriation of 6,000 dollars to erect and repair suitable buildings for a garrison of at least 3 companies for the soldiers, and 2,000 dollars for the repair of the officers' quarters." He ended his report with a recommendation that Sgt. Duncan McIntyre receive a previously recommended certificate of merit and an appointment to ordnance sergeant. Mansfield left on the 19th and five days later reached Fort Brown.[265]

Fort Brown 2–3 January 1861

Mansfield's return to Fort Brown on 23 December 1860 must have again brought back memories of his time there as Chief Engineer for General Taylor during the Mexican-American War. He wrote that due to bad weather, the Christmas and New Year's Holidays, and "the necessity of resting my mules till the 4th inst., [4 January 1861]" he could not leave sooner. He inspected the post on 2 through 3 January which was "about 600 yards to the northward of Fort Brown of the Mexican War, and is close adjoining the town of Brownsville....The old fort is grown over with bushes and trees and the outline of its grandeur recalls to mind its intrusive value. It is a lovely place where the past can be rehearsed by those living who took part in the exciting scenes of the war, and the patriot can silently mourn for those brave and honored officers, and soldiers, who have done their duty for their country, and are now no more." Clearly the veteran soldier was touched by walking the grounds of the old fort which 14 years before he planned, helped build, defend, and in which he saw Major Brown killed as he stood next to him. Fort Brown was 116 miles downriver from Ringgold Barracks on a good road directly across the Rio Grande from the Mexican town of Matamoros, and 300 miles from San Antonio via a wagon road "which can be travelled in from 10 to 16 days. It has a steamer communication with Ringgold Barracks and with the Brazos, and thence to New Orleans." He also noted that the post is 30 miles from Point Isabel which was established during the Mexican-American War as a port, and became an important shipping point since the war. He further wrote that the post could be made healthier by filling in areas where stagnant water sat and paying better attention to latrines (sinks) by freer use of lime, and repairing cisterns. Captain Bennett H. Hill commanded the post with his Company M 1st Artillery and Light Battery M of the 2nd Artillery. Company M 1st Artillery had at the post

[264] Mansfield, *Texas & New Mexico on the Eve of the Civil War*, 143-150. For comments on effective range fire, see Paddy Griffith, *Battle Tactics of the Civil War* (New Haven, CT: Yale University Press, 1989), 145-150. Accurate firing at extreme ranges was very difficult as relatively untrained Civil War soldiers learned. Major Caleb Chase Sibley was an 1829 West Point graduate who was brevetted to brigadier general at the end of the Civil War, retired in 1869 as a colonel, and died in 1875. Soldiers did fire their rifle muskets at long ranges often up to 650 or more yards; reports to the Adjutant General from posts in Oregon and Washington, RG 94, Letters to the Adjutant General, NARA.

[265] Mansfield, *Texas & New Mexico on the Eve of the Civil War*, 150-157.

two officers and 76 enlisted men available for duty. The company was performing duty as infantry. It passed in review at the quick and double quick time imperfectly due to the large number of recruits and could not perform the bayonet exercise not having learned it yet. Its light infantry drill was tolerable but could not drill as skirmishers; target firing was adequate. The company's quarters were in a frame building and were neat but the double-tier bunks made by the men were "very inferior and not suitable." Light Company M 2nd Artillery commanded by Major Henry J. Hunt, who was on leave, left Lieutenant Edward R. Platt in command of three officers and 69 enlisted men (Platt was the only officer present who was not sick). The company had four light 12-pounders and passed in review well. Its equipment and men were in very good order. The horses were on half forage and the hay supplied was worthless plus the horses had no feed troughs and were housed in a building 600 yards from a muddy corral. The men were quartered similarly to its sister company. He noted that the post bakery was well-housed and produced good bread. Mansfield was somewhat exercised about the prisoners he found and he wrote that some had been released by order of the Department commander, General Twiggs. "And here I must remark, that when a soldier has been condemned to be indelibly marked, and shaved, and drummed out of camp or dishonorably discharged, he should never be permitted to enter the ranks again and stand by the side of a soldier....There is no use in retaining such a fellow in the service to lower the standard of the private soldier. There were several such cases here and I think three of them belonged to Captain Stoneman's Company 2nd Cavalry." He finally recommended that "an appropriation of 3,000 dollars for repairs of soldiers quarters and bunks and corral, and 2,000 dollars for repairs of officers' quarters and cisterns and store houses....one company is ample at this post and that it should be relieved every year [to reduce chances of illnesses]."[266]

Sketch of Fort Brown on the Rio Grande, *Harper's Weekly*, 23 March 1861, 185. The fort is located about 30 airline miles from The Gulf of Mexico coast and 70 miles along the river. This is not the fort Mansfield designed but the later one.

Paymaster Francis A. Cunningham 3 January 1861

While he was inspecting Fort Brown, Mansfield also inspected the operations of Paymaster Francis A. Cunningham who was stationed there. Mansfield wrote that Cunningham pays his posts every two months and to do so takes a steamer to Ringgold Barracks then with "4 mules to his own spring wagon, and with an escort of 10 men and two wagons and a wagon for his specie [monies]." Mansfield wrote that the paymaster needed a stove in his quarters and that a large safe previously here had been sent to San Antonio and never returned, so the paymaster had only a travelling safe which Mansfield evidently believed inadequate. Although Mansfield found that the major performed his duties well, the amount of monies he had on hand of over $11,000 should be paid out before more is sent him.[267]

---

[266] Mansfield, *Texas & New Mexico on the Eve of the Civil War*, 157-164. Captain Bennett Hoskin Hill was an 1837 West Point graduate who was brevetted to colonel and brigadier general during the Civil War. He retired as a lieutenant colonel in 1870 and died in 1886. Major Henry Jackson Hunt was an 1839 West Point graduate who was brevetted to captain and major for his actions during the Mexican-American War and from colonel to major general during the Civil War. He retired as a colonel in 1883 and died in 1889.

[267] Mansfield, *Texas & New Mexico on the Eve of the Civil War*, 165. Paymaster (Major) Francis A. Cunningham joined the Army as a volunteer in 1847 and retired in 1863; he died in 1864.

Captain George Stoneman's Companies E and G 2nd Cavalry 4–5 January 1861

Mansfield took the opportunity to inspect Captain George Stoneman's nearby camp with Companies E and G 2nd Cavalry on 4 January, the day he left Fort Brown. Mansfield wrote that Stoneman's camp was "on the open prairie some 5 miles from the Rio Grande." Stoneman was apparently employed occupying positions between Fort Brown and Ringgold Barracks due to raids by the Mexican Bandit Juan Cortina in 1859. Mansfield thought that the cavalry would be more effective if it were stationed at two of the current posts on the Rio Grande relieving "two companies of the artillery [at those posts] for sea coast service." Company E had two officers present along with 47 enlisted men and 57 serviceable horses. "This company passed in review at a walk and a trot, tolerably." He noted that the new Sharps Carbines had some of the rear sights broken as they were "too delicate for mounted men. The leaf sight is much more durable." He also found that through the fault of the ordnance department that balls for the carbine were too small so no target firing was done for the rifle or pistol. He also saw that the company platoon and sabre drill was "indifferent." Much equipment was missing and the steel bridle bit for the horses was too narrow. Several types of saddles were in use--the troopers liked the Hope Tree the best. Mansfield wrote that "there is yet nothing yet fixed or settled as to the saddle and bridle belts, and it is well to try all kinds for the experiment." The company was housed in tents. Mansfield observed that the company "was not sufficiently instructed in the drill" due to Captain Stoneman being ill and another officer away on recruiting duty. Company G, commanded by Captain William R. Bradfute, had one officer and 69 men available at the post but suffered problems similar to its sister company. One major difference was that the troopers used Harpers Ferry Rifles which Mansfield judged "old and inferior, same old carbines with the swivel-ram-rod....It is folly to put the Harpers Ferry Rifle and that worthless carbine into the hands of cavalry." The drills were poorly done and there was no target shooting. Mansfield clearly found that the lack of training and of good equipment and firearms produced two cavalry companies which were not up to acceptable standards. As in most of his inspections over the previous years, lack of officers at their posts meant that training suffered. On 31 December in his monthly report he noted that at Fort Brown he was "engaged in completing my reports and detained by bad weather to the close of the month. In a few days I shall start for San Antonio." He finally left for San Antonio on 4 January and reached the camp of Captain Stoneman with two companies of the 2nd Cavalry on the 5th when he inspected that command. Then on the 6th, he resumed his march to San Antonio and reached there on the 19th.[268]

Department of Texas Headquarters at San Antonio 21-23 January 1861

Mansfield, because of illness, finished his Texas tour with his final trip to, and inspection of, the Department of Texas Headquarters at San Antonio. He arrived there on 19 January 1861 and his inspection lasted from 21 through 23 January. Major General Daniel E. Twiggs was in command as of 27 November 1860 having relieved Colonel Robert E. Lee of the 2nd Cavalry who was in temporary command. His inspections of the Commissary, Medical, Pay,

---

[268] Mansfield, *Texas & New Mexico on the Eve of the Civil War*, 166-168; letter courtesy of the Middlesex County Historical Society. Captain George Stoneman, Jr. was an 1846 West Point graduate who was brevetted to colonel, brigadier general and major general during the Civil War. At the beginning of the Civil War, he was at Fort Brown and refused General Twiggs order to surrender to Confederate authorities and escaped to the north with most of his men. He retired initially in 1871 then was reinstated in 1891 then retired again that year and died in 1894. He had a varied and eventful Civil War career including being a prisoner of war for three months and he also became governor of California for one term. See above for Bradfute's opinion on a revolving rifle firearm. Captain William R. Bradfute joined the Army in 1846 as a lieutenant in the 1st Tennessee Infantry then a captain in the 3rd Tennessee Infantry. He then became a captain in the 2nd Cavalry in 1855 and resigned in 1861 becoming a colonel of cavalry in the Confederate Army and had a checkered career. He died in 1906. Note that the Grimsley saddle was the regulation saddle for U.S. mounted troops from 1847 up to the adoption of the McClellan saddle in 1859; Randy Steffen, *United States Military Saddles, 1812-1943* (Norman, OK: University of Oklahoma Press, 1973), 38-47. In 1855, the Adjutant General's Office gave instructions for equipping two new cavalry regiments having one squadron equipped with the new Campbell saddle as an experiment. It did not survive field trials. The Hope saddle was tried in 1856 but was not officially adopted although it proved a good saddle; Steffen, *United States Military Saddles,* 57. Mansfield was aware that the Ordnance Department in 1857 put types of saddles such as the Campbell, Hope, and Jones, in addition to the Grimsley "in actual service ...[to] afford the means of comparing their actual merits....In 1858, Colonel [Henry Knox] Craig of the Ordnance Department wrote that "there is no regularly prescribed pattern for cavalry or dragoon horse equipments, the various pattern in use, viz: Grimsley's, McClellan's, Jones, and Hope's, being all experimental....It seems proper that the pattern should be selected by a board of officers of rank and experience representing each of the five mounted regiments;, " Randy Steffen, *The Horse Soldier, 1776-1943: The United States Cavalryman: His Uniforms, Arms, Accoutrements, and Equipments,* vol. II, *The Frontier, the Mexican War, the Civil War, the Indian Wars, 1851-1880* (Norman, OK: University of Oklahoma Press, 1978), 58-59.

Topographical, and Quartermaster Departments, showed all was in order except that the two Topographical officers had completed their mapping assignments there and were now unemployed so should be reassigned "to some place where they can be of service to the country." Mansfield also suggested that some rents paid were too high and should be reduced, and that a new post for a school of artillery near Fort Inge should not be built as "This I consider a superfluity." He then inspected Company I 1st Infantry, Captain John H. King commanding, stationed in San Antonio on duty as escorts to paymasters in their journeys to the various posts and to guard the public stores in the city. Due to bad weather, he did not have the company's three officers and 53 privates turn out for drill or inspection but found its books in good order. He also inspected the headquarters of the 8th Infantry in the city, Major Larkin Smith in command, who had just arrived from Fort Hudson with his company. The company was assigned to guard the buildings of the Ordnance Department. Mansfield found all in order. He inspected lastly the Arsenal of San Antonio which had Captain Robert H.K. Whitely in charge. A new facility for this department was almost completed and Mansfield found all in good order. He stated that "Captain Whitely is a highly meritorious and distinguished officer...and performs his duty well." Thus Mansfield's final Texas inspection showed that the Department Headquarters was in excellent order but unknown to him this post, and the others he inspected on this tour, would be taken by Confederate forces within one month.[269]

Mansfield took advantage of his sojourn in San Antonio to consult the Medical Director of the Department of Texas. Mansfield felt the effects of his long, arduous trek across hundreds of miles of mostly desert and suffered from "an attack of Rheumatism contracted by him whilst on a tour of inspection in this Department" The doctor also wrote that Mansfield should not complete "his tour to the Northern Posts which would necessitate his travelling over the wildest and most exposed portion of the State to inclement weather" which could exacerbate if not render "incurable" his rheumatism. The northern posts Mansfield had not yet inspected were Camp Cooper, and Forts Belknap, Chadbourne, McKavett, and Mason. During his 1856 inspection tour, he had visited all these posts. Mansfield must have felt some embarrassment being unable to complete his assignment but his illness obviously forced him to immediately journey home.[270]

---

[269] Mansfield, *Texas & New Mexico on the Eve of the Civil War*, 179-169. Captain Robert Henry Kirkwood Whiteley was an 1830 West Point graduate and was brevetted to captain for the Florida Indian War and to colonel and brigadier general during the Civil War. He retired as a colonel in 1875 and died in 1896.

[270] "Rheumatism" was a general term used for many medical conditions related to inflammation or pain in joints or muscles. One might conjecture that Mansfield foresaw the events which would result in the loss of U.S. military posts in Texas so he contrived a quasi-legitimate way to escape without controversy.

Having been called upon to attend professionally Col. J. H. Mansfield, U. S. Army, for an attack of Rheumatism, contracted by him whilst on a tour of Inspection in this Dept. I do hereby certify, that I have carefully examined this Officer and have advised him, in consequence of the natural tendency of his desease to be aggravated if not rendered incurable by exposure to the vicissitudes of the weather, to deffer until entirely restored to health, the completion of his Tour to the Northern Post, which would necessitate his travelling over the wildest and most exposed portion of the State to inclement weather.

Given at San-Antonio, Texas, this 23ᵈ day of January 1861.

E. H. Abadie,
Surg. U. S. A. &
Med. Director, Dept.
of Texas.

Letter by the Medical Director of the Department of Texas 23 January 1861 which certified that Mansfield was ill. Courtesy of the Middlesex County Historical Society.

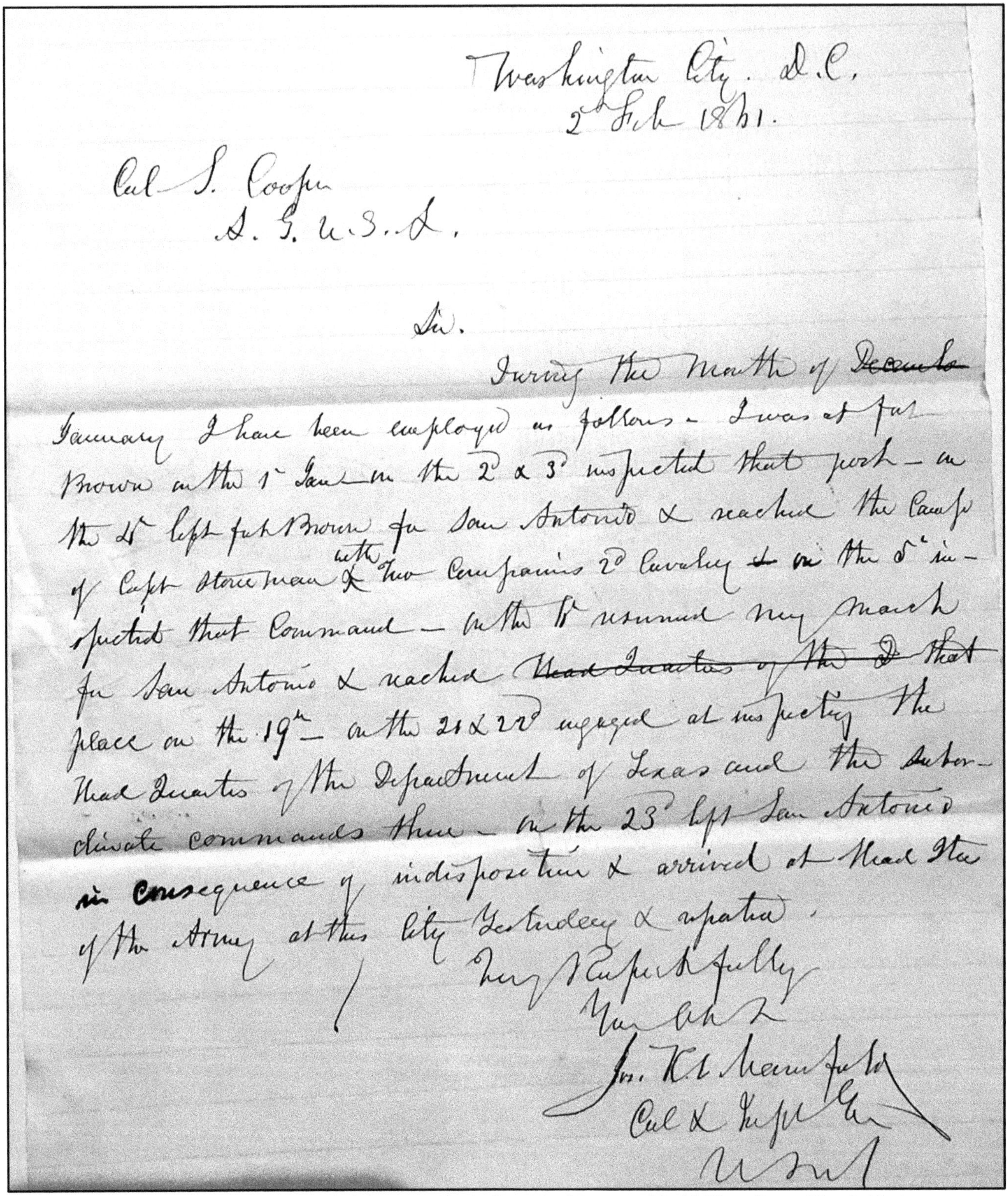

Washington City, D.C.
2ᵈ Feb 1861.

Col S. Cooper
    A. G. U.S.A.

        Sir.

            During the month of ~~December~~
January I have been employed as follows – I was at ~~fort~~
Brown on the 1ˢᵗ Jan on the 2ᵈ & 3ᵈ inspected that post – on
the 4ᵗʰ left fort Brown for San Antonio & reached the Camp
of Capt Stoneman with two Companies 2ᵈ Cavalry & on the 5ᵗʰ inspected that Command – on the 6ᵗʰ resumed my march
for San Antonio & reached ~~Head Quarters of the D~~ that
place on the 19ᵗʰ – on the 21 & 22ᵈ engaged at inspecting the
Head Quarters of the Department of Texas and the subordinate commands there – on the 23ᵈ left San Antonio
in consequence of indisposition & arrived at Head Qtr
of the Army at this City Yesterday & reported.

            Very Respectfully
            Your obt

            Jos. K. F. Mansfield
            Col & Insp Genl
            U.S.A

Mansfield's 2 February 1861 letter to Cooper in which he wrote of his "indisposition." Courtesy of the Middlesex County Historical Society.

Surrender of General Twiggs in the Gran Plaza, San Antonio, Texas 16 February 1861, to Texas Ranger Ben McCulloch under authority of the Texas Convention Committee. *Harper's Weekly,* 23 March 1861, 184.

Major General David Emanuel Twiggs was born in Georgia in 1790 and served in the War of 1812 and in the Seminole Wars. During the Mexican-American War, he led a brigade in Taylor's Army at the battles of Palo Alto and Resaca de la Palma and was promoted to brigadier general in 1846. He next commanded a division at the Battle of Monterrey. He joined Winfield Scott's expedition in command of the 2nd Division of Regulars. He was wounded at Chapultepec. After Mexico City surrendered, he was appointed military governor of Veracruz. He received a promotion to major general for the Battle of Monterrey in 1846 and was awarded a ceremonial sword by Congress 2 March 1847. As commander of the Department of Texas, he surrendered his entire command including the Federal Arsenal at the Alamo to the Confederacy: 20 military installations, 44 cannons, 400 pistols, 1,900 muskets, 500 wagons, and 950 horses, valued at a total of $1.6 million. He insisted that all Federals retain personal arms and all artillery as well as flags and standards. After being dismissed from the Army effective 1 March 1861 he accepted a commission as a Confederate major general. Due to ill health, he resigned his commission, retired 11 October 1861, and died on 15 July 1862. Courtesy Wikipedia.

Colonel Mansfield returned home to Middletown to await his next assignment. "At length an order came, assigning him duties in the north-west. But he had scarcely reached his destination, when his presence was demanded immediately in the metropolis. Washington was in danger; and to him the authorities looked as the proper person to secure its defense. In the meantime, there were occurring those startling scenes of the ever memorable nineteenth of April....Colonel Mansfield, coming from the west, in hopes of reaching Washington via Baltimore, found himself shut off from the railroad, and was obliged to make his way on foot and alone, as best he could. Those were hours when no one could tell who were the friends or the foes of the country. Several days were passed before he worked his way through, and his rations were not at all times very liberal for a private soldier. A dry biscuit or cracker was all the food he could obtain for one day. But the end came at last. He reports himself at headquarters, ready for duty, and is immediately placed in command of the forces detailed for the defense of the Capitol, April 30, 1861, the journals of the day announced."[271] See Chapter 7 below for the beginning of his Civil War adventures.

---

[271] H. Mansfield, *The Descendants of Richard and Gillian Mansfield Who Settled in New Haven, 1639 With Sketches of Some of the Most Distinguished. Also, of Connections of Other Names* (New Haven, CT: Hoggson & Robinson, Printers, 1885), 92.

Attachment 1
History of the Inspector General's Department 1777-1868[272]

The office of Inspector General dates from Dec. 13, 1777, although Lieutenant-Colonel Mottin de la Balme, a French cavalry officer, was appointed by Congress July 8, 1777, Inspector General of cavalry; and on Aug. 11, M. du Coudray, a French artillery officer, was appointed Inspector General of ordnance and military manufactures with the rank of major general. It is not probable that either of these officers performed much service as inspectors, for the entire cavalry force consisted of but four regiments, used chiefly as escorts, messengers and orderlies, while the ordnance and military manufactures were as yet unorganized. De la Balme resigned three months and three days after his appointment, and Du Coudray held his position about one month. He was drowned September 15, while attempting to cross the Schuylkill en route to Army headquarters as a volunteer.

On December 12, 1777, the Board of War reported to Congress that they had considered the letters from Brigadier General Thomas Conway, and that it was expedient to the promotion of discipline and to the reformation of the various abuses which prevailed in the different departments, that an appointment should be made of an Inspector General, whose duties should be to determine, with the consent of the Commander-in-Chief, the instruction, discipline, strength, and condition of all organizations, their accounts, rations, arms and equipment, and the capacity of all officers; his reports to go to the board of war, and a copy to the majors of regiments, and all complaints and grievances to Congress. It was further resolved that two inspectors general be appointed, which resulted in the election of Brigadier General Thomas Conway with the rank of major general; the other was not chosen. Conway held the office of Inspector General until April 28, 1778, when he resigned.

Lieutenant-General Baron von Steuben, a German soldier, received the brevet rank of captain and joined General George Washington's Army at Valley Forge on 23 February 1778, accepting the appointment of temporary inspector on March 28, about a month after he had reported to General Washington, the latter issued an order announcing that the Baron had "obligingly undertaken the exercise of the office of Inspector General of the Army," and appointed Lieutenant-Colonels William Davies, John Brooks, Barber and Mr. Ternant, as sub-inspectors. This order was followed by others requiring colonels and regimental commanders to review and inspect their regiments weekly, brigadiers their brigades fortnightly, and major generals their divisions. The inspectors were held responsible for the discipline of the troops, and that all instruction conformed strictly to that given by the Baron to the model company, and issued by him with the consent of the general-in-chief. Washington proposed a plan under which the business of the office was to form a system of manual and maneuvers; to prepare all necessary regulations for the government, discipline and arrangement of the Army in all its branches; and to see that they were strictly observed. For this purpose the inspectors were to be considered "the instructors and censors of the Army in everything connected with its discipline and management." The Inspector General to be under the direction of the general in-chief, his deputies to have charge of the wings or divisions under the major generals commanding, and the inspectors the brigades. He recommended Steuben for Inspector General, also General John Cadwalader, "of a decisive and independent spirit," Colonel Fleming and the Barons Arendt and Holtzendorf, as assistants. As a result of this correspondence, Congress on May 5, 1778, approved the plan and appointed Baron von Steuben Inspector General with the rank and pay of major general. It was also resolved, "that there be two ranks of inspectors under the direction of the Inspector General, the first to superintend two or more brigades, and the other to be charged with the inspection of only one brigade."

Steuben's appointment as major general, however, caused much ill feeling among those who were below him in rank, and those of the same grade now objected to the privileges and authority previously exercised by him. Washington also, while fully appreciating the benefits to the Army that had resulted from his efforts, thought that too much authority might be prejudicial to the inspectorship as well as to discipline, and accordingly issued an order, June 15, 1778, specifying the duties of the inspectors, and requiring all rules and regulations to be first approved by him, and then either published in orders or communicated by his direction. All exercises and maneuvers were to be executed under the immediate orders of the several commanders, the inspectors acting as assistants, and the maneuvers, which the Baron had practiced, were only to take place after orders specially issued, in each case, by the general-in-chief.

February 18th 1779, Congress approved the following plan of organization and management for the department of the Inspector General: There should be an Inspector General, who, in all future appointments, should be taken from the line of major generals, and whose principal duty should be to form a system of regulations for drill and maneuver, service of guards and detachments, and for camp and garrison duty. Together with his assistants he was to review and inspect the troops and receive such returns as the Commander-in-Chief or officers in command might direct, reporting all defects and deficiencies to the officers ordering the inspection and to the board of war; all regulations whatsoever to be finally established by Congress, but the exigencies of the service requiring it, temporary regulations might be introduced by the Inspector General, with the approval of the Commander-in-Chief, such regulations to be communicated to the Army by the adjutant general, and transmitted at once to the board of war for the action

---

[272] Abridged and Adapted from J.P. Sanger, "Inspector General's Department," in *The Army of the United States, Historical Sketches of Staff and Line*, ed. by Theophilus F. Rodenbough and William L. Haskin (New York, NY: Maynard, Merrill, & Co., 1896), 12-32 *passim*. Only internal quotes will be used. See also Thomas H.S. Hamersly, ed., *Complete Regular Army Register of the United States: for One Hundred Years, (1779 to 1879)* (Washington, DC: T.H.S. Hamersly, 1881), 269-271. For the definitive study of the inspector generals department see David A. Clary and Joseph W.A. Whitehorne, *The Inspectors Generals of the United States Army 1777-1903* (Washington, DC: U.S. Government Printing Office, 1987).

of Congress; to be as many sub-inspectors as the Commander-in-Chief or commander of a detachment, in view of the strength and situation of the Army, might deem necessary, to be taken from the line of lieutenant-colonels and to receive their instructions relative to the department from the Inspector General ; one inspector to each brigade to be taken from among the majors and the office to be annexed to that of brigade major; that all the officers of the inspectorship having appointments in the line should retain their rights of command, succession, and promotion, but they should not exercise command except on particular occasions and by special assignment of the Commander-in-Chief; to be exempt from all duties except those of their office; the Inspector General to be subject to Congress and the Commander-in-Chief only; and the sub-inspectors to be also subject to the orders of the division and brigade commanders on whose staff they were serving.

On the surrender of Cornwallis, Steuben recommended a reduction in the number of inspectors and proposed some other changes. Accordingly, on January 10, Congress authorized one Inspector General, to be appointed from the general officers, with one secretary and two aides to be taken from the line; one field officer of the line to be inspector of each separate Army, with $80 per month additional pay, and to be allowed to select a captain or subaltern to assist him in the duties of his office, with $10 per month additional pay. The inspectors in the execution of their offices were made subject only to the orders of Congress, the Secretary of War, the Commander-in-Chief, or commanding officer of a separate Army. The authority and duties of the Inspector General and his assistants continued unchanged. Congress on May 7, 1782, provided for the appointment of inspectors of contracts and supplies for the two American armies, who were to report any fraud, neglect of duty, or other misconduct by which the public property was wasted or expense unnecessarily incurred. Under these resolutions Colonel Ezekiel Cornell of Rhode Island, was made inspector of contracts for the main Army, and Colonel Francis Mentges of the 5th Pennsylvania regiment, the inspector of the southern Army. When the Army was disbanded it was divided into a northern and southern force. The main body of the northern Army was stationed along the Hudson River from Newburg to West Point. On the 19th of March, 1784, Steuben appointed Major William North, his aide-de-camp, inspector of these troops, and the appointment was confirmed by Congress April 15, when he was made "inspector to the troops remaining in the service and pay of the United States," which consisted at the end of April, of 433 infantry and 80 artillery. On the 2nd of June Congress ordered all the troops in service to be mustered out, except 25 privates to guard the stores at Fort Pitt, and 55 at West Point. From this date to July 31, 1787, the Army was increased and reduced several times; at the latter date it consisted of one regiment of infantry and four companies of artillery. On June 25, 1788, it was resolved in Congress, "That the office of inspector of troops in the service of the United States immediately cease, and be discontinued, and that the Secretary of War report what mode may be most eligible for having the troops inspected in the future."

Under the act of April 12, 1808, the Army was increased to 9,921 aggregate, and two inspectors to be taken from the line were authorized. On April 2, Colonel Thomas H. Cushing was succeeded by Major Abimael Nicoll of the artillery. From the close of the Revolution to the year 1808, the Army was subjected to many changes. There were no printed regulations other than those prepared by Steuben. The systems which prevailed at the close of the Revolution continued, modified by such regulations and orders as circumstances suggested. In February, 1810, Colonel Alexander Smyth of the regiment of riflemen, compiled a system of infantry exercises and maneuvers, chiefly from French sources, which he was directed to test with the troops in camp near Washington, "there being," so says the order, "no established system for the Army of the United States." Owing to the difficulties growing out of the Napoleonic wars, the refusal of the British to evacuate the posts surrendered by the Treaty of Paris, and the depredations and insults of her cruisers, Congress, on December 24, 1811, increased the Army. The staff included one Inspector General with rank of brigadier general, with two assistants to be taken from the line of lieutenant colonels. On May 4, 1812, the following regulations defining the duties of the Inspector General were issued by the Secretary of War: It will be the duty of the Inspector General to organize the Army; to superintend and enforce discipline; to visit and inspect camps, cantonments, quarters, prisons, places of arms and hospitals; to make stated and unexpected inspections of troops, arms, equipments, clothing, ammunition and horses; to make inspections, returns, and confidential reports relative to the state and discipline of the Army; to designate men and horses unfit for service or the fatigues of war, that the former may be discharged or sent to garrisons and the latter sold; to examine the books of quartermasters, paymasters and companies, and ascertain the balances; and to prescribe forms of returns exhibiting all the wants of the Army.

By the act of July 6, 1812, the president was authorized to appoint to any Army of the United States other than that in which the Inspector General was serving, one deputy Inspector General to be taken from the line with increased pay, and such number of assistant deputies as the service might require. On July 6 Colonel Alexander Smyth was appointed Inspector General, and on July 14 the Secretary of War issued instructions merging, temporarily, the offices of adjutant and Inspector General with the adjutant general's department, the duties of both to be performed under the direction of the adjutant general, to whom Major Abimael Y. Nicoll was appointed assistant. Captain William King of the 15th infantry was made assistant to the Inspector General. On the reduction of the Army in 1815 the 8 inspectors general and 16 assistant inspectors general were discharged and four brigade inspectors, to be taken from the line of the Army, substituted. By the act of April 14, 1818, the pay of division inspectors was made equal to the pay of division adjutants general. The administration of inspectors continued unchanged until October, 1820, when, by orders, all assistant inspectors general were placed under the division commanders acting through the division inspectors.

By the act of March 2, 1821, the Army was reduced and reorganized. The office of adjutant and Inspector General was abolished, and but two inspectors general, with the rank, pay and emoluments of colonels of cavalry, authorized. Colonels Wool and Gadsden (the latter appointed October 1, 1820, but not confirmed) were continued as inspectors. It was their duty to make a complete annual inspection of the Army under the orders of the general commanding, the troops, posts and other establishments, being equitably divided between them.

On May 17, 1821, an order was issued by the president substituting an eastern and western department for the two divisions into which the country was divided in 1815. In August Colonel James Gadsden was appointed adjutant general, and in November, Major Samuel B. Archer of the artillery was appointed to succeed him.

In December the inspections were specialized, the infantry being assigned to Colonel John E. Wool, and the artillery, arsenals, foundries and manufactories of arms, to Colonel Archer. This was a departure from the practice previously observed, under which there was no division of inspections according to the previous service of inspectors.

During the years 1823 and 1824 additional duties were imposed on inspectors in reference to returns, reports, accounts, statements and inventories of public property, and they were held responsible for all estimates for supplies, which were to be made on consultation with post commander. When not engaged inspecting, they were required to take station at Army headquarters.

On March 2 the order specializing the inspections was revoked, and the two inspectors were directed to alternate in the annual inspections which were to be made under the orders of the commanding general. No reasons for this change are given in the order, which was doubtless issued to more perfectly equalize the duties. The commandant of engineers was made inspector of the military academy.

By the act of March 3, 1825, authorizing the sale of unserviceable ordnance, arms and military supplies, Congress designated inspectors general as primarily the proper officers to inspect public property with a view to its elimination from service. By Par. 4 of G.O. 58, series of 1825, such inspections were to be "made by an Inspector General when practicable."

On December 11, 1825, Colonel Archer died and was succeeded, December 31, by George Croghan, of Kentucky, formerly lieutenant colonel of the 15th infantry and renowned for the defense of Fort Sandusky, Ohio, in 1813, against the British and Indians. In April, 1829, inspectors general were authorized to discharge soldiers on certificates of disability, a power previously exercised by them.

On May 19, 1837, the two great departments were changed into divisions with different limits, and divided into seven geographical departments. To each division one of the inspectors general was assigned as chief of staff, and to perform the duties of adjutant and Inspector General. The act of July 5, 1838, having added two assistant adjutants general with brevet rank of major, and four with rank of captain, and required them to perform the duties of assistant inspectors, the two inspectors general were returned to the headquarters of the Army, December 13. On June 25 Brevet Brigadier General Wool was appointed full brigadier, and in December, 1839, was succeeded by Major Sylvester Churchill of the artillery.

In May, 1842, the following important addition to the duties of inspectors was made by the Secretary of War, Mr. John C. Spencer: "It is made the duty of the inspectors general, or officers acting as inspectors, carefully to examine and inspect all supplies and materials procured for the construction of forts, or for harbor and river improvements, and all the means applicable thereto, and the number and description of vessels, boats, machinery and instruments, etc., and they will inquire into all contracts for supplies and materials of all kinds, in the different departments, and whether the articles furnished conform to such contracts, and also into contracts made by the quartermaster's department for the transportation of troops and stores. The results of these inspections will be forthwith reported as provided in Par. 835."

On August 23, 1842, an act of Congress abolished one of the inspectors general, but on January 12, 1846, this act was repealed thus fixing them at two. During this period both inspectors continued in office, and were, for a time, on duty with the Army in Mexico.

In August, 1848, G.O. 49 divided the country into two military divisions, the eastern consisting of four departments and the western of five departments. There were in addition two separate departments, Nos. 10 and 11, from which, in October, was formed the third, or Pacific division. This arrangement of the country continued until October 31, 1853, when seven military departments were substituted for it. Colonel Croghan died January 8, 1849, and was succeeded, January 26, by Captain James Duncan, 2nd artillery, who died July 3, and was followed June 10, 1850, by Major George A. McCall, 3rd Infantry. In May, on the accession of General Scott to the command of the Army the inspectors general were ordered to report to him by letter.[273]

On October 16, 1850, General Churchill was assigned as inspector of the eastern division; Colonel George A. McCall of the Pacific division; and Brevet Colonel Samuel S. Cooper, assistant Inspector General, to the western division. On December 17 the order was revoked and the inspectors were again attached to Army headquarters, but ordered to inspect the three divisions in regular rotation, after which they were to report in person to the commanding general. Colonel McCall resigned 29 April 1853, and was succeeded by Captain J. K. Mansfield of the Engineers, May 28.

No change in the number of inspectors took place between 1842 and 1861, but on March 6, 1860, Brevet Colonel Joseph E. Johnston of the 1st cavalry was assigned to duty as acting Inspector General of the Army according to his brevet rank. On May 14, 1861, Colonel Mansfield was appointed brigadier general and was succeeded on the same date by Captain and Brevet Lieutenant Colonel Henry L. Scott of the 4th infantry. On August 3, 1861, five assistant inspectors general with rank of major, and on August 6 two inspectors general with the rank of colonel, were added by Congress.

---

[273] While Mansfield was an inspector general, Colonel Sylvester Churchill was the designated Army inspector general according to Heitman, *Historical Register and Dictionary of the United States Army*, 39.

No change in the number of regular inspectors occurred until 1864, but by the act of July 17, 1862, an Inspector General with the provisional rank and pay of lieutenant colonel was provided for each Army corps. The names of those appointed under the act will be found in G.O. 181 of 1862. No change in the organization of the department occurred during the war. In 1861 Colonel Randolph B. Marcy was appointed brigadier general and chief of staff to the Army of the Potomac, and so served to November, 1862. Colonel Delos B. Sacket was Inspector General of that Army to 1863, when he was succeeded by Colonel Edmund Schriver. Armies, Army corps, divisions, brigades, geographical divisions and departments, had inspectors general, assistant or acting assistant inspectors general, usually selected by the several commanders; and all parts of the Army were subject to frequent inspections. The number of geographical departments increased, until, in 1865, there were 29 departments forming five divisions, and also a number of districts nearly all of which had inspectors.

On January 22, 1866, the war department published in G.O. No. 5, regulations relating to the inspection service, which prescribed the ordinary subjects of inspection and the general principles to be observed. This order, based on the wide experience of the department up to date, defined the "ordinary duties of inspection" to be "the condition as to efficiency, discipline, supplies, etc., of bodies of troops, and the resources, geographical features, lines of communication and supply, the military wants, etc., of any section of the country; the military status in any field of operations; the condition and supply of military materials of various classes; the condition of the administrative or disbursing departments of the service; the efficiency and conduct of military commanders and agents; the cause of failure or delay in movements or operations; of losses by accidents, disasters, etc., and in general, all matters pertaining to the military art or having interest in a military point of view." In the ordinary discharge of the duties, the sphere of inquiry was thus made to include every branch of military affairs, being defined and limited only in specific cases by the orders issued. This order and the circular of November 2, 1868, are fundamental, and have been the basis of all subsequent regulations and orders affecting the department. The act of July 28, 1866, fixed the number of inspectors general with rank of colonel at four; assistant inspectors general with rank of lieutenant colonel at three, and the number with rank of major at two.

Attachment 2
Inspector General's Department Instructions in the *General Regulations for the Army of the United States, 1847*[274]

969--It is through this department that the Secretary of War and the Commanding General are to be made acquainted with the actual state and condition of the Army, and, more especially, the character and proficiency of the officers.

970--It is therefore made the duty of the Inspector-General critically to inspect, as often as the Secretary of War or the Commanding General may direct, every branch connected with the military service, including the armories, arsenals, military posts, the departments of the staff, the department of the Commissary-General of Purchases, and the troops in general. At the conclusion of an inspection of any armory, arsenal, or military post, &c, the Inspector General will forthwith make a report of the same to the Commanding General; and at the end of a tour, or by the 15th of November of each year, the Inspectors General will make and transmit to the Commanding General, to be laid before the Secretary of War, reports of all that may have passed under their observation during their inspections. These reports will embrace the information required, under the following heads, viz:

OFFICERS IN COMMAND OF BRIGADES, REGIMENTS, CORPS, OR MILITARY POSTS.

971--What officers have been in command since last inspection; whether the officers in command appear to discharge their duties with zeal and ability; what degree of attention has been paid by them to the instruction and training of the officers, cadets, or men, placed under their command, in field exercises, and such other duties as are required by regulations. To ascertain whether the troops have been properly instructed in the exercises and evolutions of the field, the Inspectors will cause them to be exercised and maneuvered as prescribed by regulations; and all officers in command of troops, though superior in rank to the Inspector General present, will direct in person the evolutions. This is not, however, to preclude junior officers from maneuvering the troops, if required by the Inspector.

OFFICERS OF THE ARMY IN GENERAL.

972--Whether the officers in general appear to understand their duties, and are intelligent and zealous in the performance of them. Whether the company and staff-officers are sober, active, and afford their superior officers that support which they are entitled to require from them. Whether that unanimity and respect for each other, which are essential to good order and discipline, prevail among them. Whether any of the officers appear, from infirmity, or any other cause, to be unfit for the service, or have been absent from their regiments, corps, or posts, for any unusual length of time.

973--If it should be discovered that an officer is not qualified to perform his duty in the regiment or corps to which he may belong, a special report of his incapacity will be made; and when any officer has been absent for an unusual period, the circumstances which may have occasioned his absence will be fully stated, and also the probable time of his return.

NON-COMMISSIONED OFFICERS, MUSICIANS, AND PRIVATES.

974--Whether they are obedient and well instructed in the prescribed drill; and attentive to personal appearance; and particularly whether the non-commissioned officers perform their duty correctly, and with promptitude. Whether the numbers actually in the ranks correspond with the returns, and whether any men are kept on the rolls of the regiment or corps, who are not clothed and equipped, and who do not do their duty as soldiers.

OFFICERS, NON-COMMISSIONED OFFICERS, MUSICIANS, AND PRIVATES OF CAVALRY.

975--Whether the officers, non-commissioned officers, musicians, and privates of cavalry, are properly instructed in their duties. Whether they are expert in the exercise of the sword, carbine, and pistol; and perform with accuracy and promptitude the evolutions prescribed by regulations. Whether the officers have attained that knowledge of horsemanship which is requisite for a due performance of their duty.

REGIMENTAL AND COMPANY BOOKS.

---

[274] *General Regulations for the Army of the United States, 1847*, 179-185. Mansfield would have had a copy of these regulations as well as those promulgated in 1855 and 1857 so he would have had an excellent idea of what was expected of him. His papers at the of the Middlesex County Historical Society show that he had copies of the 1851 and 1861 Regulations for the Uniforms and Dress of the Army of the United States.

976--Whether the regimental and company books are regularly and accurately kept, and in the form and manner prescribed by regulations.

QUARTERMASTERS, PAYMASTERS, AND COMMISSARIES OF SUBSISTENCE, AND ALL DISBURSING OFFICERS OF THE ARMY.

977--Whether the Quartermasters, Paymasters, and Commissaries of Subsistence, and other disbursing officers of the Army, discharge their duties faithfully, and in a satisfactory manner; and whether their books and accounts are kept with accuracy and regularity; and whether their accounts are transmitted to the proper departments within
the time required by regulations. Whether they are engaged in any commerce or traffic; and whether the funds placed in their hands are always at command, and appropriated to their proper use; and where, or in what banks, they are deposited.

ORDNANCE DEPARTMENT.

978--Whether the officers of this department are intelligent, active, and industrious, and competent to the duties required of them; whether they keep the arsenals, magazines, store-houses, ordnance, and ordnance-stores, in their charge, in a state of preservation. Whether the carriages, guns, implements, and equipments, are made according to prescribed models and patterns; and whether the system pursued is calculated to establish uniformity in the Ordnance Department. If any neglect of duty, waste, or destruction of property, should be discovered in this department, a special report of the same will be made, in order that measures may be taken for a prompt correction.

ARMORIES.

979--Whether the superintendents and under officers of the armories are attentive, industrious, and capable of performing the services required of them. Whether the arms are well made, and according to the patterns prescribed by the Ordnance Department. Whether the books and accounts are regularly and accurately kept, as well those of the paymasters, as of the superintendents. Whether due attention is paid to the purchase of materials for the manufacture of arms; and whether the system pursued in the manufacture is calculated to ensure the best quality of arms; and whether payment for all purchases is regularly made.

MEDICAL DEPARTMENT.

980--Whether the officers of this department are faithful in the discharge of their duties. Whether suitable hospitals are furnished and well supplied with medicines and hospital stores, of good quality; and whether the sick are well attended.

VETERINARY DEPARTMENT OF CAVALRY.

981--Whether the Veterinary Surgeon is competent to the duties of his station. Whether, according to prescribed regulations, the registry of the veterinary practice be regularly kept. Whether the Farriers are properly instructed, and expert in their business. Whether the horses are shod in a proper manner, and on the most approved principle. Whether the stables are properly ventilated. Whether any diseases, more especially the glanders [a destructive and contagious disease], have prevailed among the horses, and what remedies have been adopted, and with what success.

COMMISSARY-GENERAL OF PURCHASES.

982--Whether the Commissary-General of Purchases discharges his duty with efficiency and promptitude; and whether the clothing in store is of good quality, well made, and according to prescribed patterns.

REPAIRS OF FORTS, QUARTERS, BARRACKS, MAGAZINES, ETC.

983--Whether any repairs are necessary for the better security or preservation of forts, quarters, barracks, magazines, or other public buildings. If any should be required, a special report of the same will be made.

984--In all cases it is made the duty of commanding officers to inform the Inspectors-General, at the time of their visits, of the extent of the repairs necessary, with an estimate in detail of such repairs for the preservation of forts, barracks, quarters, magazines, and other public buildings and works. The estimates, with the remarks of the Inspector, will be transmitted to the chief of the proper department, in order that means may be provided for such repairs in due season.

ARMS.

985--Whether in a serviceable state, and cleaned and preserved in a proper manner.

CLOTHING AND EQUIPMENTS.

986--Whether the officers, non-commissioned officers, musicians, and privates, strictly conform to regulations. Whether the clothing is regularly furnished, of good quality, and made according to prescribed patterns.

CAVALRY HORSES.

987--Whether of sufficient size, strength, and activity; and whether they are generally of a description adapted to the particular service for which they are designed. Whether well trained and in good condition.

FORAGE

988 Whether regularly furnished in sufficient quantity, and of good quality.

SUBSISTENCE DEPARTMENT.

989--Whether the supplies of this department are regularly furnished, and of good quality; and whether the meat, bread, and other articles allowed to the men for their subsistence, are sufficient for their proper wants.

QUARTERS AND BARRACKS.

990--Whether preserved in a state of cleanliness; and whether the interior arrangements are according to prescribed regulations.

ADDITIONAL DUTIES OP INSPECTORS GENERAL, WHEN WITH AN ARMY, INCLUDING MILITIA AND VOLUNTEERS, ON ACTIVE SERVICE AND IN THE FIELD.

991--The Inspectors-General will muster and inspect the militia and volunteers, as well as the regular troops, as often as the Commanding-General of the Army may direct. The object of which shall be to ascertain the exact state of the arms, equipments, and clothing, and any other circumstance tending to show the actual state and condition of the troops. Whether the militia and volunteers are organized according to law; and whether the officers are duly proportioned to the men, in rank and number. It will be their duty, under the direction of the General-in-chief, to designate all guards for the security and good order of the camp; to review and inspect them previous to their being detached for the service of the day.—To take charge of all prisoners; to examine and report their several cases to the Commanding General for his orders in relation to their future disposal.—To inspect the state of the tents and other camp-equipage, and barracks, and hospitals, and to report any want of care and cleanliness.—To regulate all sutlers and markets within any camp, cantonment, or garrison; and to inspect and enforce the order of march.—To ascertain whether there has been any irregularity in the proceedings of courts-martial, or in the execution of sentences pronounced by them.—To inspect quarterly, dragoon, artillery, and all other horses belonging to the public, employed by the Army in the field. Those unfit for service will be branded with the letter C, and turned over to the quartermaster's department for public sale.

992--The Inspectors-General will report separately under the heads pointed out in these regulations, and not blend the whole together, with one general remark. Each inspection report should be complete in itself, and contain a full and faithful representation, with such suggestions as they may consider necessary for the improvement of all the objects to which their attention may be directed.

Attachment 3
Mansfield's 19 September 1853 Letter to Adjutant General Samuel Cooper[275]

[Handwritten letter, transcribed as follows:]

Fort Defiance New Mexico
19 Sept 1853.

Col Saml Cooper.
Adjt Genl U.S.A
Washington City.

Sir.

I have just completed the inspection of this post, and shall leave here tomorrow morning for Los Lunes: and as it will be impracticable for me to forward my report of the inspection of this Department till my return to the states, say early in December, I have thought it best to recommend certain matters which will be embodied in my final report, to the consideration of the Hon the Secretary of War before he makes his annual report prior to the next session of Congress.

1st The road from Fort Union across the Moro Mountain to the valley of Taos, is impracticable for loaded wagons, on account of the steep ascents & descents, but it is believed a good road can be made that will be made perfectly practicable at a small expense & at a saving of 20 to 30 miles in the distance.

2d The road from fort Burguin via Don Fernandez

---

275 Photocopy of letter courtesy of the Middlesex County Historical Society. Note that the copy found in the National Archives shows very different cursive writing than this one so possibly his servant or another person helped him with this task. Copy of letter courtesy NARA.

de Taos to fort Massachusetts is impracticable for loaded wagons on account of six very steep & long ascents & descents between Don Fernandez de Taos and Rio Colorado. These objections can be remidied by a change in the road or by grading the inclinations

3rd The only road between the valley of Taos and Santa Fé over the mountain between fort Burguin and Rio Ribra, on the Rio del Norte, is impractica- ble for loaded wagons on account of steep grades which can be remidied.

4th The wagon road from Albuquerque to fort Defiance altho' comparatively a good road requires great im- provement to make it suitable for loaded wagons at all seasons.

All these roads I have travelled over myself with a light wagon & a 6 mule team, & am an eye witness of their condition, and accordingly recom- mend the following amounts to be appropriated to their repair as Military Roads of great importance : and which cannot be done properly otherwise than by the funds of the Government, under the direction of the commanding officer of this Department, by the em- ployment of soldiers or otherwise. — accordingly I would ask that 2000 dollars be appropriated for the road from fort Union to Taos valley — 1000 dolls for the road from Don Fernandez de Taos to Rio Colorado — 4000 dolls for the road from fort Burguin to the Rio Ribra and 1000 dolls for the road from Albuquerque to fort Defiance : and from Los. Lunes to fort Defiance.

in addition to the foregoing I am informed by Officers acquainted with the Subject, that the road from Fort Union to Santa Fé, via Las Vegas, requires an appropriation of 2000 dollars; and I doubt not the necessity of the Same.

—. At the close of my duties in this Department I may find it necessary to extend this recommendation for Military Roads which of course will appear in due time.

I have one other subject to recommend to the favourable consideration of the Hon the Secretary of War at this time. It is the renewal by law of the additional per diem of one dollar per day to the Officers & of an increase of half pay to soldiers in this Department which expired last march by limitation. Flour & every article that is purchased of the Sutlers & retail Merchant in this Territory is from one to three hundred per cent higher than in any of the Western & Atlantic States of the Union. It is the very natural result of the transportation to this Department of 800 miles & risk attending the same across the Indian Territory & a consequent want of competition in trade. There are no other Military posts probably so peculiarly situated, and so excluded from intercourse with their friends, & at the same time subjected to the treacherous dealings of the Indians, & I will add jealousy of a different race.

I have the honor to be very Respectfully &c

Jos. K.F. Mansfield
Col & Inspector Genl

Attachment 4

General Scott's 18 March 1854 Letter to Mansfield Describing His Wishes for Mansfield's Inspection[276]

Head-Quarters of the Army
New York. March 18. 1854.

Colonel:

In your Inspection of the Department of the Pacific, as directed in Special Orders N° 45, besides what is required of you by the Army Regulations — "Inspector Genl's Dept." — the General in Chief directs you make a minute inspection into every branch of the military service connected with the Department, and to exhibit in your report the true state and condition of the commands at the time of the inspection; as well as the location of the several posts and stations, the objects they were designed to accomplish, and to what extent, thus far, the purposes in view have been attained; their distance from each other, the practicability of the routes leading to them, the nature of the country in which they are situated and to what extent it may be relied on in obtaining supplies; specifying also the nearest settlements, and the number of the population capable of bearing arms; what Indian tribes reside in the vicinity, and the number of warriors they could bring into the field; with such other general information, as, in a military view, may be deemed

General in Chief Scott's letter to the new Inspector General reminding him of what he should inspect and report. Courtesy of the Middlesex County Historical Society.

---

[276] Photocopy of letter courtesy of the Middlesex County Historical Society.

important to be communicated.

I have the honor tobe,
Very respectfully,
Your, obdt servt.
L. Thomas
Asst. Adj. Genl.

Col. Jos. K. F. Mansfield,
Inspr Genl,
Middletown.
Conn.

Attachment 5

General Wool's 12 May 1854 Letter to Mansfield Describing His Wishes for Mansfield's Inspection and Expressing Wool's Plans for His Department and Special Order to the Department for Mansfield's Tour[277]

Head Quarters Dept. of the Pacific,
San Francisco, May 12, 1854.

Colonel,

In making your official tour through the Pacific Department I would ask your particular attention to the Posts as now established, whether their location is such as to give the best protection to the white inhabitants and restrain the Indians; whether the Posts should be temporary or otherwise; whether the buildings and improvements have been made with reference to the comfort of the troops and the preservation of the public property, and lastly whether any changes can be made for the better protection of the whites and Indians.

Lieut. Beale who possesses the confidence of the Administration has established a Reserve for the location of the Indian tribes at the Tejon Pass. This measure appears to meet the approbation of the Secretary of War, and from the success which Lieutenant Beale has met with, the happiest results are anticipated. He proposes to add to his present Reserves, two more, making four in all. If we can get the Indians to settle on these Reserves and to cultivate the soil, it will not only preserve these people who are fast disappearing by disease and other

277 Copies of letters courtesy of the Middlesex County Historical Society.

causes from the face of the land of their fathers but relieve us of much trouble and a great expense of maintaining Military Posts in the interior. So far as California is concerned, if the plan can be carried out, and I think it practicable, it would reduce the Military Posts in the Interior to two, at most three. Forts Miller, Reading and Jones could be dispensed with, which are now kept up at a very heavy extra expense. The estimate for two months amounts to more than $21,000.

Lieut. Beale thinks that within a very few years he will be able to concentrate the greater part of the Indians in California at the Tejon Pass. If this can be done, it would reduce the Interior Posts to the Tejon Pass and Yuma.

The latter Post, Yuma, is considered an important position at the present time, and will continue so unless by treaty, the Mexican boundary should be carried farther South, when it may become a question whether or not it ought to be given up. I propose to station at this Post two full companies of Artillery, and at the Tejon Pass a company of Artillery and a company of Dragoons.

To all which I would be much pleased with your opinion after your inspection and examination.

My Aide-de-Camp, Lieut. Moore will accompany you to assist you in the discharge of your arduous duties.

I am Very Respectfully
Yr ob. Servt.
John E Wool
Major General

To/
Colonel J. K. F. Mansfield
Inspector General
U. S. Army
San Francisco
Cala

Head Quarters Dept. of the Pacific,
San Francisco, May 12, 1854.

Special Orders
no. 46.

1... Colonel J. K. F. Mansfield,
Inspector General, having arrived in this
Department pursuant to Special Orders, no. 45,
from Army Head Quarters, Commanding
Officers of Posts and Officers of the Quarter
master Department are hereby required to
afford him every facility in transportation,
in escorts and otherwise, which he may desire
to accomplish his tour of inspection.

2... 1st. Lieut. T. Moore, Aide
de Camp, will report to Colonel Mansfield
to accompany him on his tour.

By command of Major General Wool:

E D Townsend
Asst. Adjt. Genl.

Chapter 8

The Civil War Begins—Mansfield in Washington

THE AGING COLONEL ARRIVED IN WASHINGTON in February 1861 finding a city in even more turmoil than that transpiring in the Department of Texas he had just left. He took leave to visit Middletown before receiving new orders. He knew that Washington was just across the Potomac River from Virginia which, although not yet out of the Union, would quickly follow its sister states.[1] Washington must be protected. But unlike most U.S. Army officers and Federal government officials, he did not underestimate the strength of secessionist feelings not only in the Deep South but in the northern tier states like Virginia and Tennessee. He would do his duty as he had done for 44 years and did not consider leaving the Army. He wrote his daughter Mary, from his Headquarters of the Department of Washington 17 June 1861: "I feel that I am right, and I shall do my duty to the full extent of my ability and power."[2] As a senior colonel albeit in a staff position, Mansfield hoped to be appointed to a command position rather than remain a staff officer. Having seen rapid brevet promotions for himself in the Mexican-American War, and knowing that an enlarged Army meant more regular promotions as well, he was undoubtedly encouraged that this new war would mean that his long and faithful service would be rewarded. In Texas, he had been well aware of secessionist feelings among southern-born officers. Mansfield wrote a letter to his cousin Edward, in which the veteran officer stated that he believed, unlike many in the United States, "that the whole South would go out of the Union, and the war was inevitable."[3]

Mansfield was in the Department of Texas in 1860 and 1861 on inspection duty before being summoned to Washington.[4] Major General David E. Twiggs commanded that department from 7 November 1860 to 18 February 1861, and was an old acquaintance of Mansfield's from the Mexican-American War. During that war, Twiggs had led a brigade in Taylor's Army of Occupation at the battles of Palo Alto and Resaca de la Palma. He was promoted to brigadier general

---

[1] Seven states had seceded by the time Lincoln was inaugurated 4 March 1861: South Carolina, December 1860; Mississippi, Florida, Alabama, Georgia, and Louisiana, in January 1861; Texas, February 1861. After Fort Sumter was fired on 12 April, and Lincoln's call up of 75,000 militia on 15 April, four more states followed suit: Arkansas and North Carolina, May; Virginia, April with a confirming referendum in May; and Tennessee, May, with a confirming referendum in June. Mansfield first reported to Washington 1 February 1861.

[2] Courtesy of the Middlesex County Historical Society. Most northerners, including Lincoln, overestimated Unionist feelings in the South.

[3] Jeremiah Taylor, *Memorial of General J.K.F. Mansfield,* 66. Edward D. Mansfield wrote a three-page tribute which appeared in the *Cincinnati Gazette,* containing this quotation.

[4] "Mansfield…. 'In consequence of indisposition,' but in reality because of the growing secessionists crisis, Mansfield departed San Antonio on January 23, 1861, and arrived in Washington on February 1," Samuel Peter Heintzelman, *Samuel Peter Heintzelman's Journal of Texas and the Cortina War,* ed. by Jerry Thompson (Austin, TX: Texas State Historical Association, 1998), 281-282. Heintzelman served with General Scott during the Mexican-American War so did not run across Mansfield who remained with Taylor.

in 1846 and commanded a division at the Battle of Monterey. Twiggs then joined Winfield Scott in command of the Second Division of Regulars and led the division in all the battles from Veracruz through Mexico City. He was wounded at Chapultepec. After the fall of Mexico City, he was appointed military governor of Veracruz.[5] Mansfield and Twiggs were not friends, however.

Colonel Mansfield was in Middletown when the Rebels fired on Fort Sumter on 12 April 1861 and received orders in April to report to Columbus, Ohio, to supervise the enlistment and recruiting activities there.[6] He was engaged there from 19 to 27 April when he received further orders to report to Washington. Mansfield returned to Washington in April 1861 via Baltimore, eager to do anything he was asked, to thwart the secessionist movements in the south. He may have thought of his chances as he walked part of the way as train service from Baltimore to Washington was interrupted.[7] Veteran regular officers were quickly needed at the capital to organize the defense of the city. Newspapers announced on 30 April that "Colonel Mansfield is now in command of the troops at Washington. He is an officer of high attainments and great experience."[8] Mansfield wrote a letter to Lorenzo Thomas 6 May 1861 after he was appointed a brevet brigadier general on that date: "It affords me pleasure to accept the same with the hope that in so doing I can better serve my country in the trying circumstances in which it is placed."[9]

---

[5] *ORA*, vol. 1, 197, 579-597. Jeanne Twiggs Heidler, "The Military Career of David Emanuel Twiggs," unpublished PhD dissertation, Texas Christian University, 1976; 198-203. Twiggs was born in 1790 and was a veteran of the War of 1812, the Seminole Wars, the Black Hawk War, and the Mexican-American War. He was awarded a ceremonial sword by the Congress on 2 March 1847. Under Twiggs's command in 1860 was almost twenty percent of the regular U.S. Army posted mainly in small posts and forts watching the Mexican border. Southern states began to secede in December 1861 and Twiggs became concerned as he knew that Texas forces coveted Federal arms and equipment. Despite several requests to U.S. Army headquarters in Washington asking what course he should pursue, he did not receive concrete instructions until it was too late. Even his letters to General Scott were fruitless undoubtedly due to the fact that Texas had not yet seceded and the politicians in the Buchanan administration were uncertain of the course to take with the seceding states and the Federal property within them. The Georgia-born Twiggs was almost frantic as he did not wish to shed American blood in his efforts to retain arms and supplies but did not want to surrender to Texas forces. Twiggs did tell Scott that he would follow Georgia if his state seceded. But after Twiggs wrote to Adjutant General Samuel Cooper that he would surrender all Federal property if Texas seceded and state officials asked for it, Twiggs was relieved from command of the Department of Texas 28 January 1861; he was replaced by New York-born Colonel Carlos A. Waite, a reliable Unionist, who was the next senior officer in the department. He was dismissed from the U.S. Army in an order dated 1 March 1861 by the president "for his treachery to the flag of his country, in having surrendered, on the 18th of February 1861, on the demand of the authorities of Texas, the military posts and other property of the United States." Twiggs subsequently accepted a commission as a major general from the Confederate States and was appointed to command the Department of Louisiana, but because of his age (he was past his 70th birthday) and poor health, wasn't able to pursue an active command; he retired 11 October 1861 and died 15 July 1862. Waite was captured at San Antonio, Texas, 23 April 1861 by armed Texans and along with other Union officers made a prisoner of war, *AOR*, vol. 1, 552.

[6] Thompson, 196. Mansfield was stationed at Columbus, Franklin County, Ohio, between 19 and 27 April 1861.

[7] Jeremiah Taylor, *Memorial of General J.K.F. Mansfield, United States Army, Who Fell in Battle at Sharpsburg, Md., Sept. 17, 1862* (Boston, MA: Press of T.R. Marvin & Son, 1862), 35. According to Taylor, his journey took Mansfield several days and his rations were meager.

[8] Jeremiah Taylor, *Memorial of General J.K.F. Mansfield*, 35. He was in command of the Department of Washington 27 April 1861 to 25 July 1861. He was appointed brevet brigadier general in the U.S. Army 6 May 1861, and brigadier general, U.S. Army, 14 May 1861. He was in command of the City of Washington 25 July 1861 to 2 October 1861, Cullum, 221-222.

[9] Courtesy of the Middlesex County Historical Society. Major General Robert E. Patterson was previously in command from 19 April 1861, House of Representatives, *Report of the Joint Committee on the Conduct of the War*, pt. 2 (Washington, DC: U.S. Government Printing Office, 1863), 114. Lincoln in a memorandum 17 May 1861 asked Scott and Mansfield to cease military arrests unless the necessity for them are "manifest, and urgent." U.S. Attorney Edward C. Carrington's had complained that military authorities were arresting, trying, and imprisoning citizens in Washington. Mansfield's remarks on it state that he had ordered only two men into confinement, Abraham Lincoln, *The Collected Works of Lincoln*, vol. 5, Roy P. Basler, ed. (New Brunswick, NJ: Rutgers University Press, 1953), vol. 4, 372.

Mansfield shown as a colonel in his dress uniform with his model 1850 Staff and Field officer's sword, taken in the Brady studios, Washington, D.C. His dress frock is wrinkled which may show that he recently arrived in Washington and did not have time to have it pressed. Note that his sash is buff colored general's sash, rather than crimson. Perhaps he viewed his title as inspector general meriting buff vice a field officer's crimson sash or that red sometimes appears as white in period photographs. Courtesy NARA.

Mansfield spoke of his time in Texas over a year later on 8 September 1862, when he met with Secretary of the Treasury Chase in Washington after his duty in Southeastern Virginia. He told Chase that he was in Texas the winter before the Rebellion broke out and saw Twiggs who hated him because he was on court-martial duty. Mansfield was then told by an officer there about a council of war of the Knights of the Golden Circle (K.G.C.) which revealed that John Buchanan Floyd and Howell Cobb in President James Buchanan's cabinet, and Senator Jefferson Davis and Vice President John Cabell Breckinridge, Jr., were members. In this council of war, orders were given to seize Federal navy yards, forts, etc., while its members were still cabinet officers and senators. The K.G.C. planned to seize Washington and inaugurate Breckinridge but the plot failed because Union troops began to arrive in Washington.[10] Mansfield clearly knew that secession and armed strife were likely well before he left Texas.

Mansfield would have been familiar with the unfinished Capitol dome shown in this photograph taken 4 March 1861 during Lincoln's inauguration. The dome was not finished until 1863. Courtesy LOC.

---

[10] Salmon P. Chase, *Annual Report of the American Historical Association for the Year 1902*, vol. 2, Diary and Correspondence of Salmon P. Chase (Washington, DC: Government Printing Office, 1903), 69-72. Knights of the Golden Circle was a group established in 1854 to engage in filibustering to expand slavery south into Mexico and around the Caribbean. It proved of little consequence except to inflame northern public opinion against the Democratic Party, Heidler, *Encyclopedia*, 1129. Floyd was U.S. Secretary of War 6 March 1857 to 29 December 1860, was indicted for treason, and became a major general in the Confederacy, Eicher, 237. Jefferson Davis and Mansfield were comrades and friends during the Mexican-American War, and Davis appointed Mansfield as a colonel and Inspector General as already seen. Davis was U.S. Secretary of War 7 March 1853 to 3 March 1857, then U.S. Senator from Mississippi from 4 March 1857 to 21 January 1861, becoming President of the Confederacy, Eicher, 202. Cobb was U.S. Secretary of the Treasury 6 March 1857 to 10 December 1860, and became a major general in the Confederacy, Eicher, 178. Breckinridge was vice president of the U.S. 4 March 1857 to 4 March 1861 and became a major general and secretary of war in the Confederacy, Eicher, 143-144.

During his visits to the White House and perambulations around Washington, he would also have seen this southern view of the White House. Courtesy LOC.

North side of the White House taken during the Civil War. Mansfield saw this view from a more southerly direction across Pennsylvania Avenue at the northeast corner of Pennsylvania Avenue and Madison Place. Courtesy LOC.

Mansfield was assigned command the Department of Washington on 27 April which he retained to 17 August 1861. He established his headquarters at the northeast corner of Pennsylvania Avenue and Madison Place, a few steps from the White House, and found this Southern city in turmoil.[11] Rebel flags were sighted on the heights across the Potomac River to the south and spies and southern sympathizers abounded both within and without the government.[12] Volunteer units had begun arriving in the capital to supplement the 600 District of Columbia militia and 600 regular troops plus 200 Marines guarding government offices. "Some Pennsylvania militia and regulars from Minnesota arrived in the capital on April 18, to join these troops. The Sixth Massachusetts Infantry Regiment arrived the next day, after experiencing problems and violence in Baltimore....On April 21, word reached Washington that the First Rhode Island Infantry Regiment, the Seventh New York Infantry Regiment, and a force of Massachusetts troops under the command of Major General Benjamin Butler, were offshore at Annapolis. These troops would land and rebuild the railroad line to proceed to Washington. The Seventh New York Infantry Regiment arrived in Washington on the 25th and the First Rhode Island Infantry Regiment began arriving on the 26th....Within five days of the Seventh New York Infantry Regiment's arrival in the Union capital, 7,500 volunteers were quartered in the city and by the end of the month, the number had grown to nearly 11,000. Some resided in the Treasury Building, Patent Office, City Hall, Navy Yard and even in the Capitol. As more and more men arrived, troops encamped and drilled wherever unused land was found."[13]

---

[11] Some sources show the address as 15½ Street vice Madison Place; it is now named Madison Place NW. Mansfield's headquarters on Madison Place on the east side of Lafayette Square was built in 1831 by a dentist named James S. Gunnell on a lot owned by Senator Henry Clay of Kentucky. He became the Postmaster General under President Martin Van Buren and later returned to his practice. He then sold his house to a naval officer, Lafayette Maynard. At the beginning of the war, the house belonged to the former Secretary of War under President Buchanan, John B. Floyd, but taken over to serve as the Headquarters of the Commanding General of the Washington area. The McClellans lived in a house on H Street and 15th Street; McClellan had his headquarters at the Wilkes-Madison House at H and Madison Place in 1861. Seward's residence was on Madison Place. The house was torn down in 1919 to build the Treasury Annex. After Mansfield went to Fort Monroe, McClellan occupied the house as his headquarters, Generals Heintzelman and Auger followed McClellan making the house their headquarters. George E. Hutchinson, *The History of Madison Place, Lafayette Square, Washington, DC* (Washington, DC: The Federal Circuit Historical Society, n.d.), 107-111; Richard M. Lee, *Mr. Lincoln's City: An Illustrated Guide to the Civil War Sites of Washington* (McLean, VA: EPM Publications, Inc., 1981), 15, 101-103. The Department of Washington was constituted 9 April 1861 and consisted of the District of Columbia to its original boundaries, and the State of Maryland as far as Bladensburg. The department was enlarged to include the states of Delaware and Pennsylvania 19 April 1861 under command of Brig. General Robert Patterson. Then on 27 April it was reduced to its prior size but included Fort Washington. It was merged into Military Division of the Potomac 25 July 25 1861. On that date, the department added Prince George's, Montgomery, and Frederick, Maryland. But also on 25 July, the Military Division of the Potomac was formed which consisted of the Department of Washington and the Department of Northeastern Virginia, with McClellan in command effective 27 July 1861. Finally on 17 August 1861, the Department of Washington was discontinued when the Department of the Potomac was constituted to include the departments of Washington, the Shenandoah, and Northeastern Virginia, Welcher, vol. 1, 159-160. Lieutenant Colonel Charles F. Smith, was in command 9 April to 19 April 1861; Robert Patterson 19 April to 27 April; Mansfield, 27 April 1861, to 17 August 1861, G.O. no. 12, 27 April 1861; Eicher, 850; Welcher, vol. 1, 159-160; Dyer, 254.

[12] Even Lincoln was aware of Rebel sympathizers: "Their sympathizers pervaded all departments of the government and nearly all communities of the people;" *Abraham Lincoln: His Speeches and Writings*, ed. by Roy P. Basler (Cleveland, OH: The World Publishing Company, 1946), 701.

[13] *Civil War Defenses of Washington, Historic Resource Study*, Pt. I, Chap. IV: "The Civil War Years," United States Department of the Interior, National Park Service, National Capital Region, Washington, D.C.; http://www.cr.nps.gov/history/online_books/civilwar/hrs1-4.htm, accessed 5 Jan. 2014.

Willard's Hotel at 14ᵗʰ and E Streets, photograph taken during the Civil War. Mansfield stayed here when he visited Washington. Courtesy LOC.

Samuel P. Heintzelman's headquarters in Washington D.C., drawn January 1863, was previously occupied by Mansfield. Lafayette Park is to the left and Pennsylvania Avenue in the front; Riggs's Bank is partially shown on the far right of the picture. The frame addition to the house was added by the Quartermaster Corps for offices for the pass officer and clerks; to the right rear is the house of Secretary of State Seward. The frame addition was likely done after Mansfield departed. Note the stables in the rear and the fence surrounding Lafayette Park; the fence is now at the Gettysburg National Cemetery, Gettysburg, Pennsylvania. The iron fence had been donated to the Gettysburg Battlefield Memorial Association by Congress in 1888 through the efforts of Major General Daniel Sickles. From the Robert Knox Sneden scrapbook, vol. 4, watercolor, courtesy Virginia Historical Society.

Washington celebrated the 4th of July 1861 under the watchful eyes of the general. At the end of the festivities, he was presented with flowers accompanied with this testimonial but unfortunately the wish expressed in the last sentence was not fulfilled:

FOR GENERAL MANSFIELD

Beloved by his friends;
Esteemed and trusted by his acquaintances;
Honored by all, as the good man, the noble and efficient officer,
The just and loyal citizen,--
May his life measure many years.[14]

Washington's *National Tribune* newspaper reported on 8 July 1861 speeches given on the Fourth of July celebration on the occasion of the Review of the New York Regiments: "Speeches by Lincoln, Lieutenant General Scott, Seward, Sec. of the Interior Smith, Atty. Gen Bates, General Sandford of NY, then Mansfield: Introduced by Seward: 'I think you would have no objection to seeing the man under whose care we have slept safely here during the last three months, surrounded by enemies.' Mansfield: 'Fellow-citizens and countrymen: I was not called here by my distinguished chief, Lieut. General Scott to make speeches, but from the very fact that speeches were at an end. I would say to you, as a distinguished Governor remarked on a certain occasion, 'Having exhausted the argument, we now resort to our arms.' I can only say to you that I am here in obedience to orders, and not to receiving the plaudits of my fellow-citizens, but simply to perform my duty, and fight for that Constitution which has been handed down to us from our sires.' Followed by General Dix of NY and Lincoln again."[15]

At dawn on Independence Day, the small fusillades in the Washington streets mimicked the rumble of artillery from the entrenchments across the river and the Rhode Island battery north of the city. Major General Sandford had ordered a parade of the New York regiments which remained on the District side of the river. Over twenty thousand soldiers marched the broiling length of the Avenue that morning. It was the first grand Army that Washington had ever seen....

Holidaymakers filled Lafayette Square and the President's grounds, and were massed along the Avenue. On a platform, canopied with flags, in front of the White House, the President and the General-in-Chief were stationed with Cabinet members and staff officers to receive the marching salute of the regiments. As the Garibaldi Guard passed by, each man tossed a spray of flowers or evergreens toward the platform, while a bouquet was thrown from the head of each company. A pretty carpet was spread before the dignitaries, and the old General was garlanded with blossoms. The graceful ceremony, with its foreign flavor, evoked the admiration of all but the owners of the ravaged gardens in the neighborhood of the Garibaldians' encampment.[16]

Mansfield's fellow Nutmegger, Navy Secretary Gideon Welles however, did not find Mansfield to be more aggressive or creative than fellow West Pointers as he expressed in his diary on 17 August 1862:

A difficulty has existed from the beginning in the military, and I may say general management of the War.... General Scott was for a defensive policy, and the same causes which influenced him in that matter, [reinforcement of Norfolk, Virginia, which Welles championed and Scott denied] and the line of policy which he marked out, have governed the educated officers of the Army and to a great extend shaped the war measures of the Government. "We must erect our batteries on the eminences in the vicinity of Washington," said General Mansfield to me, "and establish our military lines; frontiers between the belligerents, as between the countries of Continental Europe, are requisite." They were necessary in order to adapt and reconcile the theory and instruction of West Point to the war that was being prosecuted. We should, however, by this process become rapidly two hostile nations.... Instead of halting on the borders, building intrenchments, and repelling indiscriminately and treating as Rebels—enemies—all, Union as well as disunion, men in the insurrectionary region, we should, I thought, penetrate their territory, nourish and protect the Union sentiment, and create and strengthen a national feeling counter to Secession.[17]

---

[14] Jeremiah Taylor, *Memorial of General J.K.F. Mansfield*, 37.
[15] *National Tribune*, 8 July 1861.
[16] Margaret Leech, *Reveille in Washington 1860-1865* (New York: Harper; reprint, Alexandria, VA: Time-Life Books, Inc., 1980), (page citations are to the reprint edition), 109.
[17] Gideon Welles, *The Diary of Gideon Welles*, vol. 1 (Boston, MA: Houghton Mifflin Co., 1911), 83-84.

Welles continued lamenting the quality of leadership of West Point graduates with which many civilians held:

> The best material for commanders in this civil strife may have never seen West Point. There is something in the remark that a good general is "born to command." We have experienced that some of our best-educated officers have no faculty to govern, control, and direct an Army in offensive warfare. We have many talented and capable engineers, good officers in some respects, but without audacity, desire for fierce encounter, and in that respect almost utterly deficient as commanders. Courage and leaning are essential, but something more is wanted for a good general,--talent, intuition, magnetic power, which West Point cannot give.[18]

Mansfield's staff in Washington was composed of officers who were mostly Old Army men such as Lieutenant Colonel Delos Bennett Sacket, Colonel Samuel Peter Heintzelman, Major Daniel Henry Rucker, 1st Lieutenant Amos Beckwith, and Major John Gross Barnard. Sacket served as acting inspector general under Mansfield from June 1861 to August when he was assigned to New York City as a mustering and disbursing officer. Colonel John Sedgwick from the 1st Cavalry was appointed in his stead.[19] Heintzelman was under Mansfield briefly as assistant inspector general of the Department of Washington in May 1861 before he received command of the 17th U.S. Infantry a few days later, and then promotion to brigadier general 17 May 1861.[20] Rucker was quartermaster general for Mansfield from 29 April 1861.[21] Barnard was Mansfield's chief engineer from 28 April 1861 to 2 July 1861.[22]

---

[18] Welles, *Diary*, 85. Welles is entirely correct in that many, including the author, believe that a good leader is born, rather than trained, at least to a certain degree. A perceptive officer's personality although set, can be modified by himself, but not easily. One may speculate that Welles's opinion of West Pointers affected the enthusiasm with which he lobbied for Mansfield's higher level commands. It seems that he included Mansfield as lacking in audacity and deficient as a commander. However, not all West Pointers were conservative, plodding, defensive-minded engineers as Robert E. Lee, Stonewall Jackson, Ulysses S. Grant, William T. Sherman, and many others demonstrated.

[19] George Frederic Price, *Across the Continent with the Fifth Cavalry* (New York, NY: D. Van Nostrand, 1883), 247-248. Sacket graduated from West Point in 1845 32nd out of a class of 41 and served in the First and Second Dragoons. Mansfield knew him from the Mexican-American War where he was in the battles of Palo Alto, Resaca de la Palma, and Monterey. He was promoted to first lieutenant for gallant and meritorious services at the battles of Palo Alto and Resaca de la Palma. He had various duties including a tour at West Point as a cavalry instructor. He was promoted to lieutenant colonel of the 5th Cavalry 3 May 1861. After his duty with Mansfield in Washington, he was assigned to New York City as a mustering and disbursing officer. On 1 October 1861, "he was appointed an inspector general with the rank of colonel, and served as inspector-general of the Army of the Potomac from December 1861 to January 1863. He participated in the Virginia Peninsular, Maryland, and Rappahannock campaigns, and was engaged in the battles of Gaines's Mill, Glendale, Malvern Hill, South Mountain, Antietam, and Fredericksburg…Sacket was then placed in charge of the inspector general's office in the War Department….In April 1864,…he began a tour of inspection which embraced the Departments of the Tennessee, the Cumberland, Arkansas, and New Mexico, and occupied his time until August, 1865, when he returned to New York City, and awaited orders until April, 1866. He was made a brevet brigadier-general and a brevet major general, to date from March 13, 1865, for gallant, faithful, and meritorious services in the field during the war of the Rebellion," Price, 247-249. Amos Beckwith from the 1st Artillery was an 1850 West Point graduate becoming a brigadier general in March 1865. Sedgwick was appointed 3 August 1861, *AOR*, vol. 51, pt. 1, 434.

[20] *AOR*, vol. 51, pt. 1, 372. Eicher, 293. Heintzelman entered West Point in 1822, the year Mansfield graduated; he had an undistinguished academic record and graduated four years later 17th in his class of 41. He served in the 2nd and 3rd U.S. Regiments on the frontier and fought in the Mexican-American War under Scott where he received a brevet to major for Huamantla, Mexico, 9 October 1847. He received another brevet promotion to lieutenant colonel 19 December 1851. He was in command of the Union forces which took Alexandria and Arlington Heights in Northern Virginia in May 1861. He continued in brigade, division and corps command positions in the Army of the Potomac. The twice-wounded officer became a brevet major general in 1865. Eicher 293; Jerry Thompson, *Civil War to the Bloody End: The Life and Times of Major General Samuel P. Heintzelman* (College Station, TX: Texas A&M University Press, 2006), 3-30, passim.

[21] Rucker was Philip H. Sheridan's father-in-law and an Old Army officer who enlisted 13 October 1837. He fought at Buena Vista and received a brevet to major there so knew Mansfield from the Mexican-American War. He served in the quartermaster corps and retired as a brigadier general as the Quartermaster General in 1882, Eicher, 464. Mansfield assigned two Regular Army officers to Rucker as "acting assistant quartermasters": 2nd Lieutenant Elisha Ely Camp from the 9th Infantry and 2nd Lieutenant Edward Ross, from the 7th Infantry; *AOR*, vol. 51, pt. 1, 341-342.

[22] Barnard graduated from West Point in 1833 second in his class and entered the engineer corps. He served in the Mexican-American War and superintended the construction of defenses at Tampico and made surveys around Mexico City. He became the Superintendent at West Point from May 1855 to September 1856, succeeding Robert E. Lee, and was promoted to major in December 1858. After his service with Mansfield designing fortifications around Washington, he was on the Navy Blockade Strategy Board, then the engineer for the Department of the Northeast followed by the engineer for McDowell at First Bull Run and then the Army of the Potomac from August 1861 to August 1862. Lincoln promoted him to brigadier general of volunteers which was confirmed in March 1862. He continued to serve in important engineering posts such as chief engineer of the Military District of Washington, Chief Engineer XXII Corps, Department of Washington, between February 1863 and May 1864, and from May 1864 to June 1864, Chief Engineer for the Army of the Potomac. He was chief engineer under General Grant. He received honorary promotions to major general in the U.S. Volunteers and finally in 1866 to honorary grade of brevet major general, U.S.A. to rank from 13 March 1865; Eicher 116. "General Barnard was nominated by the President, on the death of General Totten, to succeed him as brigadier general and chief of engineers, April 22, 1864; but the nomination was withdrawn, at the request of General Barnard, before any action was taken," Henry L. Abbot, *National Academy of Sciences, Biographical Memoirs*, vol. 5, "Biographical Memoir of John Gross Barnard, 1815–1882" (Washington, DC: Press of Judd & Detweiler, 1905), 228. The promotion went to 65-year old Colonel Richard Delafield instead; it is likely that Barnard deferred to Delafield as Delafield was senior to him, 227.

Major General Charles W. Sandford who Scott sent to Virginia allowing Mansfield to remain in command in Washington. Courtesy LOC.

Mansfield appointed Surg. (Major) Adam Neill McLaren, U.S. Army medical staff, as his medical director, and Surgeon Charles H. Lamb, U.S. Army medical staff, as medical purveyor, *AOR*, vol. 51, pt. 1, 377. McLaren had been in the army almost 30 years 1833 and Lamb over 10 years.

Colonel Delos Barnard Sacket, Mansfield's acting inspector general. Courtesy LOC.

Colonel Samuel Peter Heintzelman served briefly as Mansfield's assistant inspector general. Courtesy NARA.

Mansfield did not hesitate to use troops in his command as needed. The 11th New York Volunteer Infantry Regiment, popularly known as Ellsworth Zouaves or First Fire Zouaves, was recruited from volunteer fire companies in New York City. The Zouaves were quartered in the Capitol where they enjoyed themselves by holding informal sessions of Congress in the chamber of the House of Representatives but were ordered to change camp to heights overlooking the Navy Yard. They were a rowdy bunch but proved to be very effective and athletic firemen:

The boys had a taste of their former calling this morning [9 May], which was highly relished. About 3 o'clock word was sent to Colonel Ellsworth that a large building on Pennsylvania-avenue, occupied as a clothing store, adjoining Willard's Hotel, was on fire, and the assistance of his men would be grateful. No sooner was a call made for volunteers, than the lads were ready. About 300 of them started off for the various engine-houses to get the machines, which was done, in many instances, by breaking open the doors, as the Fire Department of the city were not particularly energetic in responding to the alarm. How the boys astonished the natives when they rushed up the avenue to the scene of the fire, by the celerity of their movements and the confident manner in which measures were adopted for putting out the flames! But considerable difficulty was experienced in obtaining water; so much so, in fact, that very little doubt exists that a design was entertained, by the rebels here, to burn the block and thus destroy Willard's Hotel, which has so often sheltered good and loyal Republicans. It was discovered that the water had been turned off at the aqueduct at Georgetown, and the quantity which came through the pipes scarcely passed faster than a trickle. The boys made an effort, however, and conquered. Captain [William] Hackett, assistant engineer, directed operations on the street, while Captain [John] Wildey, of Company I, with pipe in hand, led his cohorts on the roof. Colonel Ellsworth was present also. A brass trumpet was taken from the hand of a man who did not know how to use it according to the practice obtaining in New York, and thrust into the colonel's hand. With this he marshaled his forces after the fire was over, and marched them back to quarters, none looking in any manner fatigued after two hours of as hard labor as ever, probably, fell to their lot....The Messrs. Willard, and, indeed, all Washington, is loud in praise of the gallant fellows for their heroism and public spirit, and the fact of its exhibition will be to retrieve the character of the regiment from the disgrace cast upon by the excesses of the few rogues who have been turned out of its ranks -- disgrace, however, which was very unjustly cast upon it in consequence of the habit some newspapers have of exaggerating and magnifying small offences into grave outrages. The Washington Fire Department took no part whatever in subduing the flames. Indeed, only a few straggling members had reached the place when the whole thing was over. No one questions that Willard's would now be a heap of ruins had they had the fire been left to their puny efforts at resisting it. Refreshments were abundantly provided for the boys after they had accomplished their work, partaken of in the large dining hall of the hotel. Messrs. Willard felt in duty bound to give a repast to the generous fellows who had saved his property from destruction, and in expressing his gratitude to Colonel Ellsworth was almost affected to tears.[23]

---

[23] *New York Times*, 11 May 1861. A collection was taken up and the regiment was given $500 to reward its efforts; Leech, 91-92.

Zouaves fighting the Willard's Hotel fire. Note Colonel Ellsworth with trumpet at center right or upper right directing operations and the depiction of the extraordinary athletic abilities of his New York City firemen. *Harper's Weekly*, 25 May 1861. Author's collection.

Mansfield did not number among his concerns policing the city of Washington as his jurisdiction was confined to military matters and for which he employed his Provost Marshal.[24] However the line between civilian and military concerns merged in the case of spies and Southern sympathizers, as well as espionage. Washington had many Southerners in administrative positions in the government and not all left to go south when southern states began to secede. Many of the capital's militia numbered secessionists in their ranks, too.[25] In April, he put a fellow Nutmegger, William C. Parsons, a lawyer, in charge of a group of mostly unpaid agents recruited from the Washington area. Parson's operatives were primarily concerned with local security and counterespionage rather than spying on Rebels across the Potomac in Virginia. He relied on his experience serving in a local militia unit to help track down arms caches and signals supposedly being sent from Washington to Northern Virginia. He was also tasked with certifying the trustworthiness of people crossing into Virginia. His services to Mansfield ended when he became seriously ill in August 1861 and his group disbanded. Mansfield paid him off in November but did not believe that the War Department would fully pay him even though Parsons "works for the cause & I doubt not will receive the amount I award without a word." Surprisingly, Parsons received the full amount Mansfield requested.[26]

Allan Pinkerton took over spying duties in November 1861 when McClellan arrived in Washington, and after McClellan's departure for the Peninsula in April 1862, Lafayette Baker became the chief agent for the administration, working under General Scott, then eventually for Stanton.[27] Lincoln however, in a memorandum 17 May 1861, asked

---

[24] The Washington Metropolitan Police Board had $92,000 in Federal funds and was authorized to employ 150 patrolmen, 10 sergeants, and a superintendent, but found itself overwhelmed with policing the District given the rapid wartime population increase, Green, 250-251. Before this increase, the police force was inadequate. "The municipality supported a day force of fifty patrolmen; while the fifty members of the night force were paid by the [Federal] Government. The chief duty of the latter, however, was the protection of the public buildings; while the city's appointments were made as a reward for services in the local elections," Leech 13. The day police and the Federal night guard were abolished; Leech 135.

[25] John Bakeless, *Spies of the Confederacy* (Mineola, NY: Dover Publications, Inc., 1970), 2-6. The National Rifles was the name of one of the volunteer company of militia in Washington, D.C., noted for its excellent drill maneuvers and for having a large number of members. The Inspector General of the District of Columbia, Colonel Charles P. Stone, learned that its commander, Captain Schaffer, had Southern sympathies and had amassed a large amount of ordnance unsuited to a rifle company. An operative Stone placed in the company learned that Schaffer was planning to create a unit having infantry, cavalry and artillery and that many in the unit had Southern sympathies. Stone was able to remove Schaffer and the Southern sympathizers left with him so the company became a valuable addition to the early, reliable units in Washington. Another unit, the National Volunteers, was mostly composed of secessionists led by Dr. Cornelius Boyle. Stone placed a spy in the unit and learned that it was planning an active role in taking parts of the Union government by force. Stone tricked the doctor into giving him the company's roster as a necessity prior to giving it uniforms and arms. The doctor later gave up his house in Washington and joined the Confederate Army becoming the provost marshal at Manassas. Thomas Nelson Conrad, one of the Confederacy's best spies, was active in the Washington, D.C., area since he was very familiar with that territory having been a schoolmaster of a boy's school there. He was initially arrested and sent South in June 1861 after apparently sending messages by having his students raise and lower shades in their rooms and for giving an inflammatory speech on his school's graduation day. He then joined Jeb Stuart as chaplain of the 3rd Virginia and became a cavalry scout as one of a group of young, intelligent men who worked for General Robert E. Lee and Stuart. He then returned to Washington and disguised his appearance becoming a resident Confederate spy. He used "secession clerks" in the War Department to which he had unfettered access to collect information which he passed south. He even placed an operative in Lafayette Baker's group. One of his more ambitious plans, the assassination of Winfield Scott, was turned down by the Richmond administration. In 1861, more than 100 civilians left government service as most refused to take the new loyalty oath of allegiance to the Constitution and the government of the United States both then and thereafter; they joined the 313 Army officers out of 727 who resigned, Constance McLaughlin Green, *Washington: Village and Capital, 1800-1878* (Princeton, NJ: Princeton University Press, 1962), 248. Government clerks were investigated and hundreds were suspected of disloyalty including some in the War Department, Leech, 178-179.

[26] Edwin C. Fishel, *The Secret War for the Union: The Untold Story of Military Intelligence in the Civil War* (Boston, MA: Houghton Mifflin Company, 1996), 14, 21, 56-57.

[27] Ibid., 26-27. Allan Pinkerton was born on 25 August 1819 in Glasgow, Scotland, and died on 1 July 1884. He, along with Baker, was one of the two best known Union agents in the Civil War. He was a barrel maker in Scotland and in Illinois but quickly began his detective career after organizing a citizen's group to capture a gang of counterfeiters. Becoming sheriff of Kane County, Illinois, then Cook County, he relocated to Chicago and formed his own detective agency in 1850, the Pinkerton National Detective Agency. He guarded President-elect Lincoln from Philadelphia on his way to Washington, D.C., after one of his detectives had accidentally discovered a plot against Lincoln. He then did spying for McClellan and was next put in charge of McClellan's Department of the Ohio secret service activities. When McClellan was called to Washington, Pinkerton moved his operations with him as a private contractor working for the Union government. His operations were limited to counter intelligence, which responsibility he shared with Baker's group, espionage and interrogations. He concentrated too much on sending spies to Richmond and using few for less strategic purposes; his men were not trained well for military spying. He worked solely for McClellan and transmitted his reports only to him. His most famous exploit was his pursuit and jailing of Rose O'Neal Greenhow while his most notorious were his overestimated numbers of Confederate troops during the Peninsular Campaign and the Seven Days followed by similar problems during the Antietam Campaign. He left government service with McClellan's departure. Lafayette Curry Baker was born in Stafford, N.Y., on 13 October 1826 and died on 3 July 1868 in Philadelphia. He traveled around the country as a handyman and may have taken part in vigilante activities in San Francisco before the Civil War. He was first employed as a detective in Washington, D.C., and then was employed by Winfield Scott in the summer of 1861. He was sent to Richmond but was captured near Manassas and interrogated by General P.G.T. Beauregard. In Richmond, he said he was interviewed three times by President Jefferson Davis. He next organized what he called his "National Detective Police" and he later named himself as "Chief of the United States Secret Service" which also had no

Scott and Mansfield to cease military arrests unless the necessity for them are "manifest, and urgent." United States Attorney Edward C. Carrington had complained that military authorities were arresting, trying, and imprisoning citizens in Washington. Mansfield's remarks on it state that he had ordered only two men into confinement.[28]

Before Mansfield hired Samuel Parsons, he employed another agent, Abel Huntingdon Lee. Mansfield used Lee mainly for learning about routes used by Confederate sympathizers between Washington and Virginia as well as the lower counties of Maryland. Lee was unfortunately arrested by Confederates in Maryland on one of his missions and was held by them in Virginia for 16 months. He died soon after he returned home to Washington.[29] Mansfield again demonstrated his practical experience of many years in the U.S. Army and in the Mexican-American War by knowing the value of information about the enemy. A New Yorker, Kirk R. Mason, journeyed to Harper's Ferry in May and June 1861 under Mansfield's orders, where he had an eventful time. He was arrested but did not confess and left for Washington, narrowly escaping recapture on the Washington-bound train. The leading Civil War military intelligence historian, Edwin C. Fishel, described his efforts as "the earliest known purely military espionage mission" in the Eastern Theater. Mason's report was delivered personally to Secretary of War Cameron and President Lincoln. Mason then scouted Rebel positions at Arlington and Alexandria before returning to Harper's Ferry. During that brief visit, he was almost captured by two Confederate cavalrymen but talked his way out of being arrested again. He was more careful on his third trip only venturing to Knoxville, Maryland, two miles below Harper's Ferry. His services were apparently not seen as particularly valuable and he was soon paid off.[30]

Mansfield apparently raised the ire of one of the most famous Washington, D.C., civilian Confederate spies, Rose O'Neal Greenhow. She wrote at least two letters to Mansfield; on 1 and 3 August 1861; her first letter asked him to grant her an audience and issue her a pass to permit her to visit prisoners of war held in the Old Capitol Prison. She wrote that Mansfield's aide, Drake DeKay, was very offensive and insolent when he demanded that she tell him first why she wanted to see Mansfield. Apparently she never met with Mansfield. She may have had as a motive to ply Mansfield with her feminine charms as she had other Union officers and officials but despite her beauty, Mansfield would not have succumbed given his religious beliefs and absolute faithfulness to his wife. She had antebellum access to government officials and military officers at the highest levels and continued many of these relationships after the war began and successfully established a spy network, the Greenhow Group. She was credited with warning Rebels of the impending Union movements prior to First Bull Run. But she allowed her cipher and incriminating letters and reports to fall into Union hands. Some believe that the myth-making around her persona created by Greenhow and perpetuated by the books of Allan Pinkerton and Lafayette Baker overshadowed her real contributions to the South. She and her daughter were under house arrest and other women arrested for spying joined them there; her home became known as "Fort Greenhow." Her house arrest was not effective in stopping the flow of information, so she was sent to the Old Capitol Prison, but even there she managed to send messages out, aided by the fact that it was in the same building her aunt had previously run as a boarding house.[31]

foundation in law. He primarily had police authority in the general Washington, D.C., area but did send agents to Canada as well as to Union field armies. He seemed to have unlimited authority and investigated virtually all areas in addition to chasing spies and saboteurs almost leading a reign of terror. Since there was so much to do, his activities usually did not overlap those of Pinkerton. He started as a civilian employee and then received a colonelcy. He did most of his work under the aegis of Secretary of War Stanton but was directly under Stanton's former legal associate, Levi C. Turner. His group was successful in arresting spies and disloyal citizens but he was apparently not above accepting bribes to let accused persons go free. He was in charge of the party which captured John Wilkes Booth on 26 April 1865 for which he was promoted to brigadier general and given a reward. But his reputation was fatally tarnished after the war due to his spying on President Andrew Johnson and his lying at Johnson's impeachment trial. His memoirs published in 1867 have been found to be in many areas full of creative fiction and selective memory thus his exploits described therein are mostly untrustworthy.

[28] Basler, *Collected Works of Lincoln*, vol. 4, 372.

[29] Fishel, 22; *ORA*, ser. 2, vol. 2, 1427; vol. 4, 528; vol. 5, 483.

[30] Fishel, 23-24. It is likely that Mansfield received Mason's report first and was present when Mason reported to Lincoln and Cameron.

[31] Letters courtesy NARA, ARC Identifier 1634028; RG 59. Rose O'Neal Greenhow was born in 1817 and died in 1864. She and her daughter were exchanged for Union prisoners in June 1862 and exiled to the South ending up in Richmond where she was met by President Davis. She received $2,500 out of secret service funds as a reward. Davis sent her to Europe to help secure financial and political support in addition to operating as a courier in France and Britain. While in Europe, she wrote and published a book of her exploits and returned to the Confederacy in September 1864. The ship she was on was pursued by a Union warship and it ran aground near Wilmington, North Carolina. She got in a rowboat which capsized and due to the heavy surf and the $2,000 worth of gold sewn in her dress from her book royalties weighed her down so she went to the bottom and drowned 1 October 1864. Her body was found washed up on shore and President Davis honored her with a military funeral.

Rose O'Neal Greenhow with her youngest daughter, "Little" Rose, at the Old Capitol Prison, Washington, D.C., after she was transferred there on orders of Allan Pinkerton, 18 January 1862. Mansfield refused to meet with her while he was in command in Washington. Courtesy LOC.

Old Capitol Prison, Washington, DC, located behind the Capitol building at 1ˢᵗ and A Streets, NE. Rose Greenhow was imprisoned there but continued her spying activities by dropping notes from its windows. Photograph taken in 1866 by Alexander Gardner. Courtesy LOC.

Mansfield's Troops Secure Northern Virginia May 1861

As an experienced Regular Army officer, and a highly capable engineer, Mansfield was able to quickly assume the oversight of the construction of defenses for Washington, D.C. And with his experience in the Mexican-American War, he saw that the heights in Arlington, Virginia, made the low-lying City of Washington vulnerable to artillery fire--they must be secured by Union troops, and with volunteers at that, as Regular Army units were mostly unavailable.[32] Additionally, he recommended fortifying southern approaches to the bridges linking Washington with Virginia and seizing the port of Alexandria, Virginia.

Mansfield sent this letter to Scott on 3 May outlining his plans for taking sites in Northern Virginia:

Agreeably to the deliberations of last evening I now submit to you the following on the defenses of this city:

1st. On the side of the navy-yard and bounded by the Anacostia River, I have simply to say that with ample troops in the city at command there can be no difficulty in crowning the heights on the opposite shore, and affording a complete defense from an enemy approaching from that quarter to attack the city or the navy-yard.

2d. That part of the city between the Anacostia River and the Potomac can readily be fortified at any time by a system of redoubts encircling the city. This is always in our power.

3d. We now come to the city and Georgetown and arsenal, exposed to the Virginia shore. Here I must remark that the Presidents House and Department buildings in its vicinity are but two and a half miles across the river from Arlington high ground, where a battery of bombs and heavy guns, if established, could destroy the city with comparatively a small force after destroying the bridges. The Capitol is only three and a half miles from the same height at Arlington, and at the Aqueduct the summits of the heights on the opposite shore are not over one mile from Georgetown.

With this view of the condition of our position, it is clear to my mind that the city is liable to be bombarded at the will of an enemy, unless we occupy the ground which he certainly would occupy if he had any such intention. I therefore recommend that the heights above mentioned be seized and secured by at least two strong redoubts, one commanding the Long Bridge and the other the Aqueduct, and that a body of men be there encamped to sustain the redoubts and give battle to the enemy if necessary. I have engineers maturing plans and reconnoitering further. It is quite probable that our troops assembled at Arlington would create much excitement in Virginia, yet, at the same time, if the enemy were to occupy the ground there a greater excitement would take place on our side, and it might be necessary to fight a battle to disadvantage.

I know not exactly how many troops we have at command. I presume the enemy might bring 10,000 troops into the field in a short time on such an occasion. I would not urge any premature movement in this quarter, yet one taken too late might cause much bloodshed....

P. S.: I should have said in the body of this report that I have been in consultation with my chief engineer, Major Barnard, in all these views, and his services have been and are very valuable to me.[33]

All his recommendations were followed once Virginia seceded from the Union.[34] Finally on 23 May 1861, the public referendum in Virginia held on the Ordinance of Secession was three to one in favor of leaving the Union—the Union advance could now begin.

Lincoln was ready to begin as he wrote to Winfield Scott on 24 May 1861 concerning the seizure of Alexandria and Arlington:

What think you of the propriety of yourself, or the more immediate commander—Genl. Mansfield, as I understand—taking the occasion of occupying Alexandria & Arlington Heights, to make a proclamation to the citizens of those places, and vicinity,

---

[32] "With an actual strength of 1,080 officers and 14,926 enlisted men on June 30, 1860, the Regular Army was based on five-year enlistments. Recruited heavily from men of foreign birth, the U.S. Army consisted of 10 regiments of infantry, 4 of artillery, 2 of cavalry, 2 of dragoons, and 1 of mounted riflemen....The Regular Army was deployed within seven departments, six of them west of the Mississippi. Of 198 line companies, 183 were scattered in 79 isolated posts in the territories. The remaining 15 were in garrisons along the Canadian border and on the Atlantic coast." Regulars would be of little use to Mansfield although its officers would prove essential on his staff; *American Military History, The United States Army and the Forging of a Nation, 1775-1917*, vol. 1, Richard W. Stewart, ed. (Washington, DC: GPO, 2009), 200. Volunteer troops saved the Union.

[33] *AOR*, vol. 2, 618-619.

[34] Leech, 99. Lincoln likely heard of Mansfield's letter to Scott but knew he must wait for the Virginia secession vote. Lincoln could see Rebel flags on the heights across the Potomac and probably mentioned that to Scott. The 2 May meeting with Scott is not of record so it is not known who put forth the idea for an attack across the river. Likely both Scott and Mansfield were of one mind.

assuring them that they are not to be despoiled, but can have your protection, if they will accept it, and inviting such as may have left their homes, and business to return?[35]

Edward Burgin Knox who was a first lieutenant in the 11th New York State Volunteer Militia (the New York Fire Zouaves), and an observant participant, recorded the subsequent crossing and fight in Northern Virginia:

On May 23d, General Mansfield ordered preparations for an advance into Virginia. Instructions to the respective leaders were given with great secrecy, and before midnight the various commands were in readiness near the points of crossing to the Virginia side. The troops moved in three columns, as follows:

By the Aqueduct: The Fifth, Twenty-eighth, and Sixty-ninth New York State Militia, one company of cavalry, and a section of artillery; Major W.H. Wood, U.S. Army, commanding.

By Long Bridge: District of Columbia Volunteers, a regiment of New Jersey troops, one company of cavalry, the Seventh, Twelfth, and Twenty-fifth New York State Militia, and a section of artillery; Colonel Heintzelman, U.S. Army, commanding. Also, the First Michigan infantry, one company of cavalry, and a section of artillery; Colonel O[rlando] B[olivar] Willcox commanding.

By Steamer: The New York Fire Zouaves (Eleventh New York State Volunteer Militia); Colonel O.E. Ellsworth commanding. The whole under Major General Charles W. Sandford, of the New York State Militia, who, however, did not assume command until the troops had crossed the river.

At two o'clock A.M. on the 24th the crossing began. The enemy had held possession of the Virginia end of Long Bridge for several days, but our advance guard surprised and drove them away before they could set fire to it. The troops crossed rapidly, and before daylight were in position, the right resting near the Aqueduct, the left at Alexandria, with long intervals unguarded. Colonel Willcox, immediately upon crossing, proceeded by the Washington turnpike toward Alexandria.

Colonel Ellsworth's orders were to act in concert with Willcox, the two commands to enter Alexandria simultaneously, — Willcox from the north of the town, and Ellsworth by the river front. They were to cut the telegraph wires, tear up the railroad tracks, and take military possession of the place.

Ellsworth's regiment was organized in the city of New York, and was recruited wholly, or nearly so, from the fire department of that city. Nearly every fire company was represented….It was the first volunteer regiment to reach Washington, where it arrived on the 2d of May, *via* Annapolis (no troops at that time being allowed to pass through Baltimore), and a week later it marched into Maryland and encamped on the "Eastern branch," about a mile below the navy yard, near Poolsville.

At "retreat," on the 23d, orders were given the regiment to prepare to move. Immediately all was bustle and confusion. At eleven o'clock, everything being in readiness, the regiment was formed in column of division *en masse;* and the Colonel, mounted and at the head of the column, addressed the men at some length regarding their duties on the morrow.

I shall never forget that scene. The night was peculiarly still and clear, not a leaf stirring, and the moon so full and lustrous that objects were visible at a great distance. The men stood immovable as statues, listening attentively to the words that fell from the lips of their commander, who, in a low, clear voice, explained to them, so far as he could consistently with instructions, the nature of the service they were expected to perform. He endeavored to impress upon their minds the great necessity of obedience. I can call to mind but little of what he said, but I remember distinctly these words: "I will never order one of you to go where I fear to lead;" also, "Don't fire without orders." And he added, "Now go to your tents, and remain quiet until called."

At two o'clock the "Baltimore" and "Mount Vernon" (the steamers chartered to take the regiment to Alexandria) appeared off the shore, under charge of Captain [John Adolph Bernard] Dahlgren, of the navy, who announced their arrival, whereupon the men were marched by company to the river bank, and the embarkation began. Owing to the absence of wharf or landing-place, and the shallowness of the river at that point, the men were conveyed to the steamers in small boats, which consumed nearly two hours' time. At length all was in readiness, and just before dawn we slowly and silently steamed down the river, the "Mount Vernon" leading.

As we approached the place of landing, the United States steamer "Pawnee" was discovered at anchor off the town, the ship being "cleared for action." At the same time a boat was seen to leave the vessel for the shore, filled with men, and bearing a flag of truce. This boat reached the wharf a few minutes before us. As we drew nearer, several Rebel sentinels were observed on shore, quietly walking their posts, apparently ignorant of our approach. Suddenly they discharged their pieces in the air and started away on the run, when some half-dozen men on our upper deck, in violation of orders, began a fusillade upon the retreating sentinels, which was promptly checked. The boat soon touched the wharf, and the regiment hastily landed and formed on Cameron Street in column of companies, my company (A) at the head, which rested at the intersection of Lee Street. During the formation, two companies were dispatched to the Orange & Alexandria Railroad depot to take possession, cut off the retreat of the Rebels if possible, and tear up the track. These dispositions being made, the next matter of importance, it seems, was to cut off telegraphic communication with the interior. Leaving the regiment standing in the street, the Colonel,

---

[35] Abraham Lincoln, *The Collected Works of Abraham Lincoln*, ed. By Roy P. Basler, vol. 4 (New Brunswick, NJ: Rutgers University Press, 1953), 385.

accompanied by two officers, a New York "Tribune" reporter, and a squad of four men under a sergeant, taken from the right of my company, started for the telegraph office, some two blocks distant.

Meanwhile Willcox's command had entered the town, marching along Washington Street. As the head of the column neared the railroad depot, a company of cavalry was discovered in front of the "Slave Pen," nearly opposite the depot, some of the men mounted, and others preparing to mount. The artillery was placed in position, and the cavalry, finding their retreat cut off by a company of Zouaves approaching from the river front (one of the companies that had been sent to destroy the railroad tracks), obeyed the summons to surrender. They were confined in the "Slave Pen," under guard as prisoners of war. This company was known as the "Fairfax Cavalry," numbering thirty-five men, and commanded by Captain [Mottrom Dulany] Ball. These, I believe, were the only prisoners captured.[36]

---

[36] Charles W. Davis, *Military Essays and Recollections: Papers Read Before the Commandery of the State of Illinois, Military Order of the Loyal Legion of the United States*, vol. 2, Edward B. Knox, "The Capture of Alexandria and Death of Ellsworth" (Chicago, IL: A.C. McClurg and Company, 1894), 10-14. Colonel Ellsworth took a squad of men and headed for the telegraph office in Alexandria but just before they arrived, the colonel saw a large Rebel flag above the roof of a small hotel, the Marshall House. He decided that it must be taken down and quickly entered the hotel and ran up the stairs tearing the banner down. As he was leaving, he was shot dead by the hotel owner who was then shot by one of Ellsworth's men. The twenty-four old Ellsworth lay in state at the Navy Yard and then his body was taken to the White House for the funeral service before he was sent to Mechanicsville, New York, for burial; 15-16. The "Sunday Bulletin," Middletown, Connecticut, 26 May 1861, wrote that General Mansfield and staff led the advancing troops from Washington [on 25 May]; article courtesy of West Point Library Research Library. Note that "Poolsville" is not "Poolesville," Maryland, which is some 30 miles northwest of Washington. If "Poolsville" is correctly written then then the author was mistaken or that this Poolsville was a local name now forgotten.

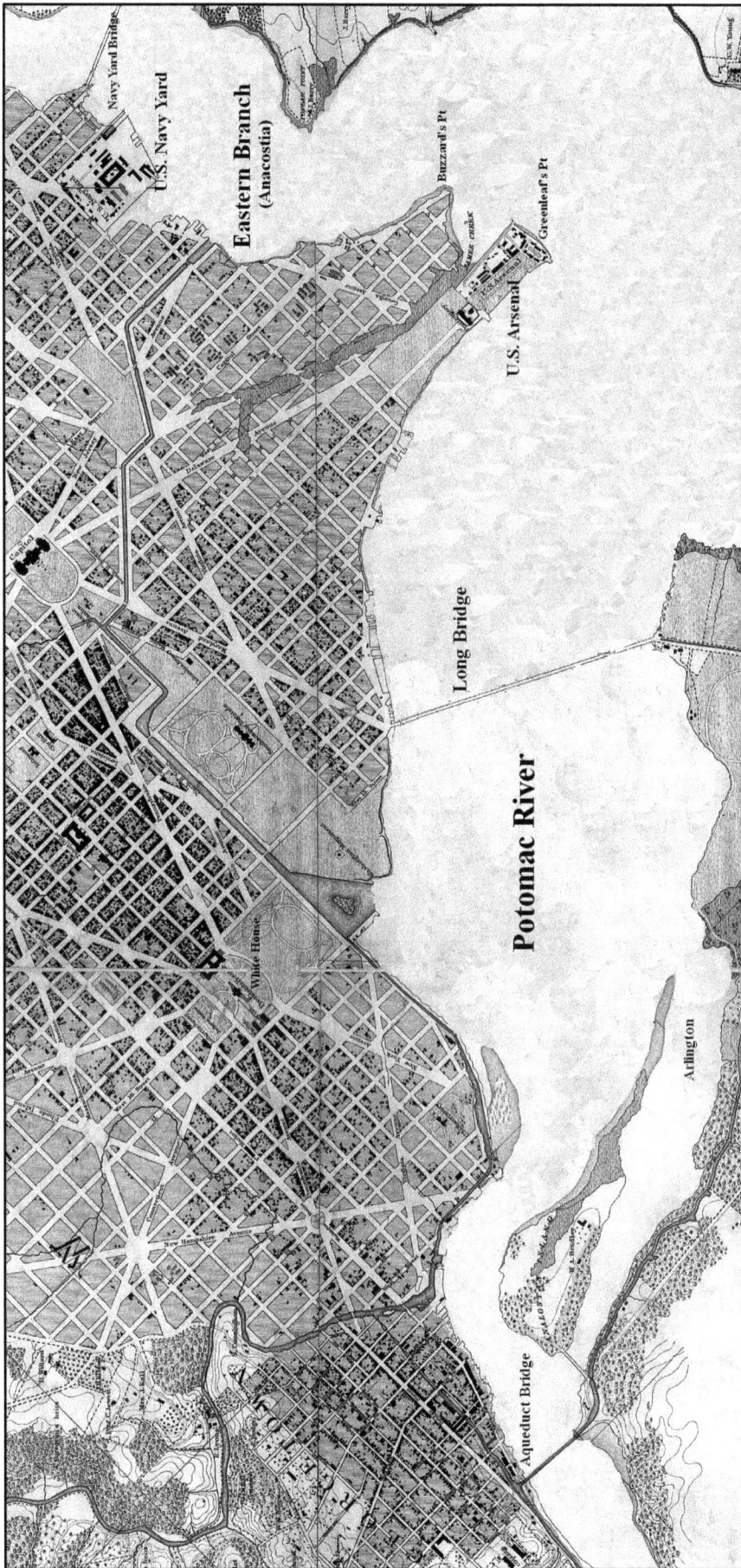

Map of the Union attack on 24 May 1861 across the Aqueduct Bridge, Long Bridge, and by steamer from the Navy Yard. Ellsworth Zouaves boarded the steamers *Baltimore* and *Mount Vernon* and was transported across the Potomac, landing at the Alexandria wharves under the guard of the gunboat *Pawnee*. Long Bridge is now the 14th Street Bridge; the Aqueduct Bridge is now the Francis Scott Key Bridge, and the Navy Yard Bridge is the 11th Street Bridge/Officer Kevin J. Welsh Memorial Bridge. Courtesy NPS.

Aqueduct Bridge as it would have appeared in 1862, Virginia in the distance. Note Long Bridge downstream in the distance, Mason's Island in the middle distance, and the unfinished Washington Monument to the upper left. Drawn by F. Dielman; lithograph by E. Sachse & Co. Courtesy LOC.

The 7th New York marches across Long Bridge to attack Arlington and Alexandria. William Swinton, *History of the Seventh Regiment, National Guard, State of New York during the War of the Rebellion* (New York, NY: Fields, Osgood, & Co., 1870), facing 199.

Colonel Marshall Lefferts, commander of the 7th New York during the attack on Arlington. Courtesy NARA.

After the 7th New York spent two days in Virginia, Mansfield desired their return as the regiment was apparently one of the best available to defend the capital as he noted in this missive to Colonel Lefferts: "Your regiment has accomplished all that was intended, in crossing over to Arlington to take possession of the Heights, having labored in the intrenchments manfully also. The security of this city makes it imperative you should resume your encampment on this side, and you will, this afternoon, march over accordingly, and hold your regiment here ready to turn out when called upon. I would recommend that you afford your command an opportunity to bathe in the canal, if desirable, before you march."[37] At the end of May, the regiment was to be mustered out and festivities included serenading President Lincoln at the White House, Secretary of State Seward's residence, and then to Willard's Hotel where the band and men serenaded General [Irvin] McDowell, Major [Adam Jacoby] Slemmer, and "General Mansfield, the latter of whom made a short speech, as did his adjutant, Drake de Kay."[38]

On 2 May 1861, Mansfield sent another message to Colonel Marshall Lefferts: "Lieutenant General Scott desires me to say to you, that, in case of an alarm of attack at night, you will march your regiment directly to the President's house." Mansfield was again giving detailed instructions to the 7th on 14 May such as "There will be no serenading by bands after tattoo (half past nine, P.M.), except by written permit from these head-quarters."[39]

A reporter for the New York Herald described in riveting prose the Union advance on the 24th into Virginia:

> There can be no more complaints of inactivity of the government. The forward march movement into Virginia, indicated in my dispatches last night, took place at the precise time this morning that I named, but in much more imposing and powerful numbers.
>
> About ten o'clock last night four companies of picked men moved over the Long Bridge, as an advance guard. They were sent to reconnoitre, and if assailed were ordered to signal, when they would have been reinforced by a corps of regular infantry and a battery.
>
> At twelve o'clock Colonel Ellsworth's regiment of Zouaves embarked in steamers from the Navy Yard for Alexandria, and must have reached there about one o'clock this morning. They landed under the cover of the *Pawnee's* guns. An attack would have been signalized. No attack was made.
>
> At twelve o'clock the infantry regiment, artillery and cavalry corps began to muster and assume marching order. As fast as the several regiments were ready they proceeded to the Long Bridge, those in Washington being directed to take that route.
>
> The troops quartered at Georgetown, the Sixty-ninth, Fifth, Eighth and Twenty-eighth New York regiments, proceeded across what is known as the chain bridge, above the mouth of the Potomac Aqueduct, under the command of General McDowell. They took possession of the heights in that direction.
>
> The imposing scene was at the Long Bridge, where the main body of the troops crossed. Eight thousand infantry, two regular cavalry companies and two sections of Sherman's artillery battalion, consisting of two batteries, were in line this side of the Long Bridge at two o'clock…. last came the New York Seventh, the liveliest party, and with more men than any other regiment. They seemed delighted at the idea that they were to have a show at something that looked like service before returning home. Following them was a long train of wagons filled with wheelbarrows, shovels, &c.
>
> Altogether there were at least thirteen thousand troops in the advancing Army. This includes the Zouaves who went by steamer, the forces that moved from Georgetown, as well as the main body that proceeded over the Long Bridge.
>
> General Mansfield commanded the movement of the troops until the last corps left the district. The first regiment of the main body that crossed the Long Bridge started at twenty minutes past two, and the last corps left the district at about a quarter to four o'clock.
>
> At four o'clock Major General Sandford and staff left Willard's, and proceeded to Virginia to take command of the advancing forces. He informed me that he should establish his headquarters on Arlington Heights, and should take possession of the Arlington mansion.
>
> Two thousand troops, the New York Zouaves and New York Twelfth, are to occupy Alexandria; the remainder the heights by regiments from the chain bridge to Alexandria.
>
> General Mansfield took the greatest care to instruct the troops just before entering the bridge to take the route step-that is, to avoid marching together, as the solid step together might injure the bridge….
>
> The sun of the 24th of May has risen and exposed to our gratifying gaze the Stars and Stripes floating over Alexandria, where the secession flag has been haunting the sight for weeks past. Truly the past has been a great night's work for the Union.

---

[37] Swinton, 205-206. According to the regimental history, a drenching rain shower substituted for a canal bath.

[38] Ibid., 214. Slemmer was an 1850 West Point graduate and a major in the 16th Infantry at this time and became a volunteer brigadier general in 1862. He received brevets to lieutenant colonel, colonel and brigadier general during the Civil War, and died in 1868.

[39] Swinton, 167, 172.

Secession is suddenly doomed, and nothing but an ignominious doom awaits the leading traitors in this great wrong against popular government and free institutions.[40]

1862 photograph of the Navy Yard Bridge which connected Washington, D.C., with Uniontown across the Anacostia River. Courtesy Wikipedia.

Federal forces had now secured Alexandria and Arlington which allowed the beginning of fortifying the capital to the south. Washington rapidly became the best-defended capital in the world. The chief architect of that task, Major John Gross Barnard, discussed the beginnings:

Previous to this movement [Battle of First Bull Run] the Army of Washington, yet weak in numbers and imperfectly organized, under General Mansfield, had crossed the Potomac and occupied the south bank from opposite Georgetown to Alexandria. The first operations of field engineering were, necessarily, the securing of our debouches to the other shore and establishing of a strong point to strengthen our hold of Alexandria. The works required for these limited objects (though being really little towards constructing a defensive line) were nevertheless, considering the small number of troops available, arduous undertakings. Fort Corcoran, with its auxiliary works, Forts Bennett and Haggerty, and the block-houses and infantry parapets around the head of the Aqueduct, Forts Runyon, Jackson, and Albany (covering our debouches from the Long Bridge), and Fort Ellsworth, on Shooter's Hill, Alexandria, were mostly works of large dimensions. During the seven weeks which elapsed between the crossing of the Potomac and the advance of General McDowell's Army the engineer officers under my command were so exclusively occupied with these works (all of which were nearly completed at the latter date), to make impracticable the more general reconnaissances and studies necessary for locating a line of defensive works around the city and preparing plans and estimates of the same.

The works just mentioned on the south of the Potomac, necessary for the operations of an Army on that shore, were far from constituting a defensive system which would enable an inferior force to hold the long line from Alexandria to Georgetown or even to secure the heights of Arlington.[41]

---

[40] *The New York Herald*, 25 May 1861, "The Insurrection. Advance of the Federal Troops into Virginia, May 24, 1861."
[41] *ORA*, vol. 5, 678-679.

Major John Gross Barnard, Mansfield's gifted chief engineer in Washington, taken before the Civil War. He was the chief architect of the defenses of Washington. Courtesy NARA.

Mansfield issued practical orders as he saw were needed such as one noted by Captain John Mead Gould of the 1st Maine on 14 June 1861: "Tomorrow, by order of Gen'l Mansfield, the non-commissioned officers and privates will have their pistols taken from them. There have been cases of injury in other reg'ts. from the careless use of them and thus the whole suffer."[42]

---

[42] John Mead Gould, *The Civil War Journals of John Mead Gould 1861-1866*, ed. William B. Jordan, Jr. (Baltimore, MD: Butternut and Blue, 1997), 27.

Map of Arlington and Alexandria drawn 31 May 1861, found in Mansfield's papers, courtesy WPL.

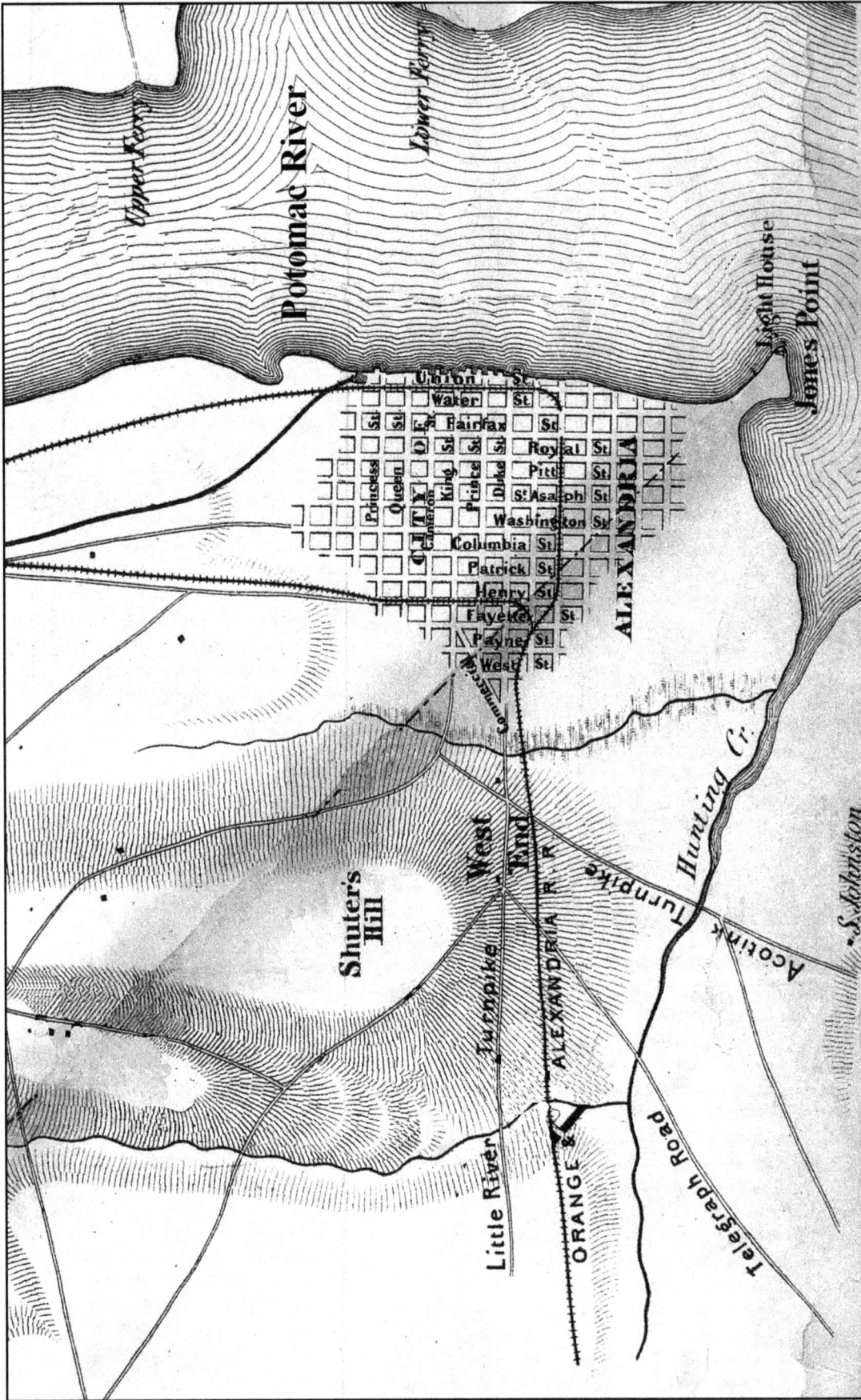

Alexandria in 1861 when Union forces took it and other sites in Northern Virginia to secure the high ground preventing Confederates from using artillery or launching attacks on Washington. The Marshall House was located on the southeast corner (bottom of "g" in King) of King Street and South Pitt Street and was the site of the killing of Colonel Elmer E. Ellsworth 24 May 1861. North is to the left. Courtesy NPS.

Mansfield and the Battle of First Bull Run

Mansfield was angry that Lincoln wanted Brigadier General Irvin McDowell in command of the Union Army of Northeastern Virginia instead of him. It was very likely that there would be a confrontation with the Rebel Army under Confederate General Pierre Gustave Toutant Beauregard near Manassas, Virginia, and Mansfield wanted to be in command. It is unfortunate that the old general's disappointment may have led to his not being enthusiastic or punctilious about helping McDowell's efforts in the summer of 1861 prior to the battle.[43]

Irvin McDowell, shown here as a major general, was in command of the Union forces at the Battle of First Bull Run. Courtesy NARA.

Brevet Lieutenant General Winfield Scott, "Old Fuss and Feathers," the senior officer in the Army from 5 July 1841 until his resignation on 1 November 1861. McClellan succeeded him as general-in-chief. Courtesy NARA.

---

[43] James B. Fry, *McDowell and Tyler in the Campaign of Bull Run 1861* (New York, NY: D. Van Nostrand, Publisher, 1884), 9-11.

Secretary of the Treasury Chase clearly favored Ohioans for positions as generals in the Army. Lieutenant Colonel Irwin McDowell, assistant Adjutant General of the Army, was an early favorite of his, perhaps helped by a plan he submitted to Chase describing a Union deployment toward Manassas Junction. With Chase's support, McDowell was put in command of the new Department of Northeastern Virginia.[44] McDowell also had support of Gov. William Dennison of Ohio and Winfield Scott as McDowell was adjutant general on Scott's staff during the Mexican-American War. McDowell was assigned to mustering and organizing the district militia in Washington, and was in command of the Capital during part of April and May. Lincoln called out 10 companies of the District militia to furnish guards for public buildings but many did not report or take the oath; McDowell swore in about a half dozen companies for three-month's duty.[45] At a cabinet meeting in May 1861, Chase ensured that McDowell received a brigadier generals star although Chase wanted him to be a major general. But Scott was not happy with McDowell's elevation over another friend, Mansfield, who, among other senior officers, would be unhappy at being passed over. Outside of the cabinet meeting, Chase spoke to McDowell who was surprised and chagrined that he might be made a major general ahead of senior officers, but acquiesced in accepting a single star.[46]

Mansfield was senior to McDowell; McDowell graduated from West Point in 1838, long after Mansfield in 1822. More importantly, even though both were appointed brigadier generals on 14 May 1861, Mansfield was senior to McDowell: Mansfield was a colonel before his promotion but McDowell was only a major. Both were in staff departments however, McDowell in the Adjutant General's department and Mansfield in the Office of Inspector General. McDowell was 43 years old in early 1861 while Mansfield was 58. As photographs taken during 1861 reveal, Mansfield appeared grizzled and tired compared to his younger rival. McDowell had more political support also.

General Scott had plans for Mansfield and McDowell but McDowell did not cooperate. Scott wanted Mansfield to remain in charge at Washington but did not want McDowell to command in northern Virginia. Scott tried unsuccessfully to get McDowell to refuse the command of the new Department of Northeastern Virginia, so on 27 May 1861, the War Department placed McDowell in command. In fact, both Scott and Mansfield were not happy with McDowell's decision and thereafter neither was as cooperative as they might have been in McDowell's trials before First Bull Run: "Regiments were slow in coming across the river to take their assigned places with the Army of Northeastern Virginia. Scott or Mansfield had to approve each such assignment, and they took their time about it. When McDowell went personally to Mansfield to ask for more men, and more speedily, Mansfield just shook his head and replied, 'I have no transportation.'"[47]

As Union forces arrived in Washington from the north they necessarily reported to Mansfield, and became for the time a part of his command. He attended diligently to the duty of equipping and preparing the troops for the field, but every officer and enlisted man who was sent across the Potomac changed the relative importance of Mansfield and McDowell by reducing the command of the former and increasing that of the latter. When McDowell appealed to Mansfield to hurry forward the troops, the excuse was they were not supplied with baggage wagons. When this was reported to the Quartermaster General, his answer was that he could furnish the transportation, but Mansfield did not want it till the troops should move. The result was that the troops which McDowell was to lead had not all been sent to him by Mansfield before the day fixed by General Scott for McDowell's advance. Some of them did not join until the Sunday before he advanced, and some not until the very Tuesday on which he marched to the front. It was only by great exertion that he succeeded in having his wants partially supplied. He failed to secure transportation to carry rations with his army, and had to march trusting that wagon-trains would be made up, loaded with provisions and sent to follow him.[48]

[44] John Niven, *Salmon P. Chase: A Biography* (New York, NY: Oxford University Press, 1995), 254.

[45] Fry, 8; Leech, *Reveille in Washington*, 65-66, 71.

[46] William C. Davis, *Battle at Bull Run: A History of the First Major Campaign of the Civil War* (Mechanicsburg, PA: Stackpole Books, 1977), 10-11; Benjamin Franklin Cooling, III, *Symbol, Sword, and Shield: Defending Washington during the Civil War* (Shippensburg, PA: White Mane Publishing Company, Inc., 1991), 39.

[47] Davis, *Bull Run*, 35. It is not clear who Scott wanted in command in Northern Virginia as he wanted Mansfield to remain in command of Washington. Perhaps Scott wanted Mansfield's command extended to cover that area. Scott showed his trust in Mansfield in his reply to Major General Charles W. Sandford that he could command New York troops in Washington but told him that there would be a disadvantage: "We are in critical circumstances, and it would take you weeks to make you as well acquainted with localities, officers, and men as Brevet Brigadier-General Mansfield, whom you would supersede as the commander of the department," *AOR*, vol. 51, pt. 1, 372. Scott solved the seniority issue by having Sandford in charge of the Dept. of Northeast Virginia from 9 April to 27 May 1861. Sandford commanded when troops crossed the Potomac.

[48] Fry, McDowell and Tyler, 10-11.

McDowell testified before the Committee on the Conduct of the War on 26 December 1861 about the Battle of First Bull Run. He said that General Scott did not want to advance into Virginia but Scott told McDowell that he was told to put either McDowell or Mansfield in command "on the other side of the river" but since Scott wanted Mansfield to remain in command in Washington, McDowell by default commanded over the river in Virginia. Scott thought that McDowell's promotion over Mansfield would do a "hurt" to him so Scott wanted Mansfield's promotion backdated a week to give Mansfield seniority. But McDowell did not say that even with the same promotion date, Mansfield's prior rank as colonel trumped his as major. McDowell refused Scott's requests to turn down the command in Virginia as McDowell stated:

> Just appointed a general officer, it was not for me to make a personal request not to take the command which I had been ordered upon....So I went to the other side [of the Potomac], and the general [Scott] was cool for a while....I was on the other side a long while without anything. No additions were made to the force at all....General Mansfield felt hurt, I have no doubt, in seeing the command he had divided in two and a portion sent over there. I got everything with great difficulty....I had difficulty in getting transportation....If I went to General Mansfield for troops, he said: "'I have no transportation.'" I went to General Meigs and he said he had transportation, but General Mansfield did not want any to be given until the troops should move. I said: "I agree to that, but between you two I get nothing."[49]

McDowell also testified that he attended a conference during which he was instructed to submit a plan of operations for the Manassas operation. After Scott read and approved it, the plan was submitted to Lincoln's cabinet at which meeting Mansfield and other generals attended, including Brigadier General Montgomery Meigs, Major General Charles W. Sanford, and Brigadier General Daniel Tyler. McDowell said that only Mansfield had any comments or questions. McDowell testified that Mansfield "made some remarks, but said he had not thought about the matter, and did not know anything about it, and was not prepared to say anything in relation to it. And the plan was all approved of, without any alteration, and, I think, without any suggestion, except a slight one from General Mansfield, I then called the engineers to assist me...."[50] Mansfield apparently was not going to offer any helpful suggestions to aide McDowell or it may be that he had not been asked by Scott to review the plan before the cabinet meeting. McDowell's testimony about the cabinet meeting immediately preceded his testimony noted above about Scott favoring Mansfield over himself. General Sanford who testified after McDowell said he objected at the cabinet meeting to moving against Beauregard at Manassas unless General Patterson were able to prevent General Joseph E. Johnston from uniting with Beauregard. So apparently others in addition to Mansfield commented on McDowell's plans.[51]

Among his other duties, Mansfield attended ordnance presentations by those inventors who wished to impress Lincoln and other high government officials with their inventions. In September 1861, Mansfield along with Lincoln, three cabinet members, the Prince de Joinville, McClellan and McDowell, attended a demonstration of marksmanship by Colonel Hiram Berdan at the Berdan camp. Berdan and his breechloader reportedly shot out the right eye of a Jefferson Davis target at six hundred yards from the standing position—an extraordinary feat. Lincoln was taken with Berdan and his abilities telling the colonel that "I will give you the order for the breechloaders."[52] Mansfield had previously seen a demonstration of one of the first of what are now called machine guns—a repeating gun—at the Washington Arsenal grounds with Lincoln, three cabinet members and the governor of Connecticut, William A. Buckingham. Mansfield was very impressed and asked Secretary Cameron to "get a number of coffee-mill guns for the city's fortifications. 'I think it an excellent rampart gun...a good field gun against cavalry & horse Artillery, an excellent gun to defend the passage of the bridge and should be thoroughly tested in the field at once.'"[53]

---

[49] House of Representatives, *Report of the Joint Committee on the Conduct of the War*, pt. 2 (Washington, DC: U.S. Government Printing Office, 1863), 37-38.

[50] Committee on the Conduct of the War, 35-36.

[51] Ibid., 55. Sanford joined Patterson but was not allowed to move on Johnston at Winchester.

[52] Robert V. Bruce, *Lincoln and the Tools of War* (Indianapolis, IN: The Bobbs-Merrill Company, Inc., 1956), 110-111.

[53] Bruce, 119-120. Mansfield's experience in the Mexican-American War undoubtedly showed him the value of the machine gun in the defense. While Mansfield was in Washington on various administrative duties after he left command of the department, he still had Lincoln's ear: he asked Lincoln for a favor for Charles Hawes Hosmer and was granted his request: "To Simon Cameron. General Mansfield wishes Charles H. Hosmer to be a 2nd. Lieut.; and so let it be done. A. LINCOLN, Aug. 1, 1861." Hosmer of Illinois was nominated to the Senate as second lieutenant in the First Infantry on 1 August and confirmed 5 August 1861. He was brevetted captain 4 October 1862 for gallant and meritorious service at the Battle of Corinth, Mississippi, and to major for the siege of Vicksburg, and promoted to captain 19 April 1866; Lincoln, *Collected Works*, vol. 4, 467. He took leave to visit Middletown in August 1861 during an hiatus in his command assignments but stayed less than two weeks. Samuel Russell there feted him even though informally during his stay. This was his last trip home.[53]

Mansfield and his staff joined McClellan and his staff along with several other generals and 5,000 spectators reviewing the Army of the Potomac's cavalry under Brigadier General George Stoneman. The spectacle took place one mile east of the Capitol on the parade grounds. Some 2,000 cavalry and eight batteries of artillery participated in this grand review on 24 September 1861. *Harper's Weekly*, 12 October 1861, 652, author's collection.

As already seen, Mansfield described General John Pope in unfriendly terms although there is nothing of record to show Pope personally disliked Mansfield. Mansfield complained to his wife about him: "Pope who has command of the Army of Virginia was a Second Lieutenant, and my aide at the storming of Monterey. A man of no sound moral principles and kept for a week at Monterey under arrest by General Taylor for bad conduct disgraceful to the service."[54] But Pope's memoirs do not show similar hatred although not totally complementary of his Old Army comrade--the subtitle of Pope's article in the *National Tribune* was "General Mansfield—Fussy in Camp, but a Lion in Battle."[55] Pope's article gives a first-person account even though written many decades later:

Another officer, very different in all possible respects from General Twiggs, who was famous in the Mexican war and occupied a prominent position in the early days of the civil war, was General J.K. Mansfield, who was for some months in the Fall of 1861 in command at Washington. He will, perhaps, be more generally remembered by the sign manual of his Aide-de-Camp Captain Drake DeKay. Everybody who was about Washington even for a short time in those last days of 1861, and especially every soldier, will remember that gigantic signature, without which no man was safe from arrest and confinement who wore the uniform of the United States, or indeed who ventured to cross the Potomac in any costume whatever. The writer of that autograph was a large-hearted and valiant soldier, and as loyal a man, not only to his country but to his comrades, as ever wore the uniform of the United States. I had occasion to know him well during the time I was in Washington, and I not only bear my testimony thus to his character and his conduct, but I give the evidence with the deepest and warmest feeling personally for him. At the time to which I am now referring, however, the Captain's signature was about THE BIGGEST THING OUT, bigger even than the Captain and the General put together.[56] General Mansfield himself was a peculiar man, combining in his

---

[54] Courtesy of the Middlesex County Historical Society.

[55] John Pope, *National Tribune,* 19 March 1891, "War Reminiscences."

[56] Joseph Rodman Drake de Kay (Drake DeKay) was born in New York City 21 October 1836. His father was a seaman who rose to the rank of commodore in the Argentine Navy before the age of 25. His mother was the only child of poet, Joseph Rodman Drake. His father died while Drake was attending West Point so he left school and became a merchant in New York City dealing with the West India trade. After the Confederates fired on Fort Sumter, he closed his office and pinned this notice on its door: "Return at the end of the war," and left for Washington, D.C. He joined Mansfield's staff there. He stayed with Mansfield in Southeastern Virginia but left when Mansfield's son Samuel was assigned to his father's staff. His duties as Mansfield's gatekeeper rankled one who likely encountered him: "Who is DRAKE DE KAY, of autographic notoriety? The people are gradually becoming alive to the fact that none but true and tried men should now be placed in positions of influence, and I simply wish to ask if it can be possible that one who was known to many here six months since as a noisy and profane young brawler, of strong Southern sympathies and antecedents, is to-day a Captain in the U.S. Army, and the confidential aide of an officer to whom the defence of Washington is specially intrusted?" Signed "A Friend of the Union," this letter appeared in the 29 July 1861 edition of the *New York Times.* The next day a reply in the newspaper took DeKay's side lauding his volunteering to go to Washington to serve: "If General MANSFIELD retains him on his staff, I, for one, shall feel satisfied that he does so solely because from a three months experience of his courage, conduct and tact, the General knows the Lieutenant deserves the honor and the place." DeKay subsequently served on the staffs of Generals Pope and Hooker before he was appointed by Lincoln to the Regular Army. He became a captain in the 14th Infantry and was brevetted to major and lieutenant colonel. He was wounded during the Battle of the Wilderness when

own person two quite distinct characters, almost the precise opposite of each other. In ordinary times and circumstances he was a sort of fussy, particular man, very much given to pry into all manner of details and to meddle with other people's work, especially that of his subordinates. His manner, too, was a querulous faultfinding, and altogether he was an uncomfortable person to have anything to do with, and was far from popular. Place this same man on a field of battle, amidst the roar and the fury of the fight, and a transformation as complete as that between Dr. Jekyll and Mr. Hyde at once appeared. It was magnificent to see General Mansfield in battle. He visibly swelled before your eyes; his face flamed out with fiery ardor, and his whole figure and his every movement seemed filled with a sort of terrible passion. He pervaded all places of danger, and everywhere put himself in the forefront of the battle. He was like a lion, and no man could look on him at such a time without a thrill of admiration and wonder. I never yet have seen a man so regardless of his personal safety or so eager to imperil it. The wonder with me has always been how he could have survived any battle with his uncontrolled inclination to thrust himself where the danger was greatest. I first saw him in action at the storming of Monterey. He was the Chief Engineer on General Taylor's staff, and I was one of the junior officers under him. We led the advance of the column which attacked and carried some of the fortifications on the lower part of the city. Of course Mansfield was wounded, shot through the calf of the leg; but he had it bound up, and the next I saw of him he was stretched out in a partly-reclining position behind a piece of artillery of Webster's battery, within open sight of the enemy's intrenchments, not 200 yards distant, and from which A TERRIFIC FIRE FROM ARTILLERY and small-arms was being poured upon the spot until the dust and dirt were flying in every direction. The place was too hot even for the gunners, and this one gun was served in person by Lieut. J.L. Donaldson, the First Lieutenant of the battery, who seemed as careless of his life as Mansfield. The latter was unable to walk on his wounded leg but was lying in the midst of this tremendous fire, in which it seemed impossible to live, with his field-glass to his eye, directing Donaldson where to aim his gun. Absolutely he seemed as unconscious of danger or as indifferent to it as if he had been walking the streets of Washington. I saw him again in battle under somewhat different circumstances at Buena Vista. Although still on General Taylor's staff, he did not go back with the General that night to Saltillo, but remained on the field with General Wool to help him select positions and post the troops for the next day's work. When we rode up on the plateau in the midst of a lost battle, as I have described, one of the first men I saw was General Mansfield. He rode a gray horse, which made him very conspicuous, and was charging furiously back and forth across the field, trying to rally the broken columns, but without success. He was beside himself with shame and humiliation, and the tears poured down his face. He was not tranquilized until the effects from Bragg's and Sherman's batteries became apparent. Mansfield had a keen military eye and most excellent military judgment, but he never afterward had the opportunity to exhibit them until the civil war, and he was killed, as it was almost certain he would be, in the first battle in which he was engaged.

General Mansfield was of middle height and robust figure. He had a broad and rather ruddy face, with a thick shock of white hair and beard. He was A MAN OF KINDLY DISPOSITION, and very just; but, as I have said before, he was rather fussy and fond of meddling with his subordinates, so that, although all of his officers exulted in his behavior in battle, and were immensely proud of him for some time after the battle was over, he soon reduced them to their old feeling that he tormented and persecuted them unwarrantably. He was still a comparatively young man when he was killed at Antietam, but I think it may be said of him that his complete recklessness, and his apparently irresistible inclination to seek the most exposed and most dangerous places on a field of battle, of necessity deprived him of the power to use his great military abilities and acquirements to the best advantage for the Army or the Government. He was a gallant soldier and a true and loyal man, and will always be remembered with pride and respect by these who knew him in those old days.[57]

---

he was injured by a falling tree hit by artillery fire; he resigned at the end of the war and resumed his New York business. He was an ardent Republican and became a well-known figure in the business and social life of New York City. He died 9 June 1886. "In the civil war he was idolized by the rank and file of his regiment. He had a talent for language and often wrote comic verses for the amusement of his friends." *The National Cyclopaedia of American Biography*, vol. 9 (New York: James T. White & Company, 1899), 206. As will be seen in the next chapter, Mansfield asked DeKay to depart from his staff apparently to make way for his son to whom Mansfield was in constant contact. Mansfield wrote to Samuel, then a student at West Point, 30 June 1861 from Washington: "Be patient in all your duties. Submit cheerfully to all the requirements of your superiors....Your chances are great for 2d or 3d in your class next year;" letter courtesy West Point Library. Mansfield encouraged Samuel to be near the top of his class so he would be appointed to the engineers. The general did eventually have Samuel on his staff. His father's constant badgering Samuel at West Point to do well resulted in a testy reply from West Point to Colonel Mansfield: "I have tried to please you in every way; I am completely discouraged and tired of life. Instead of receiving pleasant letters from home to encourage and cheer me up, your letters have had just the contrary effect and sometimes almost drive me crazy," courtesy West Point Library. Note discussion of Mansfield's letters to his wife during the Mexican-American War which were similar in dictatorial tone to those he sent to Samuel.

[57] John Pope, *National Tribune*, 19 March 1891, "War Reminiscences." Mansfield's height: Pope wrote that he was of "middle height" and "robust figure." Average height would have been 5'7" to 5'9", but upper classes were taller thanks to better nutrition so Mansfield was likely about 5'10" and weighed about 170-180 pounds.

Famous signature of DeKay on a 21 July 1861 pass for General Rufus King to travel to the "Grand Army of N.E. Virginia & back." Rufus and Charles King Collection, courtesy Carroll University Digital Collections, http://content-dm.carrollu.edu (accessed 23 January 2014).

Brigadier General John Pope. Courtesy LOC.

In the least charitable review of Pope's comments, Mansfield was insufferable during peacetime, and careless of his life during war. Pope's description of Mansfield written in 1891 for the newspaper was likely more generous to the hero Mansfield than if Pope had written about him privately during the war. But overall, Pope's article showed that Mansfield was at his best in battle and, as will be seen in the following chapter, he was revered by his enlisted men.

Attachment 1
Lincoln's Letter to Brigadier General Carl Christian Schurz[58]

Executive Mansion,
Washington, Nov. 24, 1862.

General Carl Schurz:

My Dear Sir

I have just received, and read, your letter of the 20th. The purport of it is that we lost the late elections, and the Administration is failing, because the war is unsuccessful; and that I must not flatter myself that I am not justly to blame for it. I certainly know that if the war fails, the Administration fails, and that I *will* be blamed for it, whether I deserve it or not. And I ought to be blamed, if I could do better. You think I could do better; therefore you blame me already. I think I could not do better; therefore I blame you for blaming me. I understand you *now* to be willing to accept the help of men who are not republicans, provided they have "heart in it." Agreed. I want no others. But who is to be the judge of hearts, or of "heart in it"? If I must discard my own judgment, and take yours, I must also take that of others; and by the time I should reject all I should be advised to reject, I should have none left, republicans or others—not even yourself. For be assured, my dear sir, there are men who have "heart in it" and think you are performing your part as poorly as you think I am performing mine. I certainly have been dissatisfied with the slowness of Buell and McClellan; but before I relieved them I had great fears I should not find successors to them who would do better; and I am sorry to add that I have seen little since to relieve those fears. I do not clearly see the prospect of any more rapid movements. I fear we shall at last find out that the difficulty is in our case rather than in particular generals. I wish to disparage no one—certainly not those who sympathize with me; but I must say I need success more than I need sympathy, and that I have not seen the so much greater evidence of getting success from my sympathizers than from those who are denounced as the contrary. It does seem to me that in the field the two classes have been very much alike, in what they have done, and what they have failed to do. In sealing their faith with their blood, [Edward D.] Baker, and [Nathaniel] Lyon, and [Henry] Bohlen, and [Israel B.] Richardson, republicans, did all that men could do; but did they any more than [Philip] Kearney, and [Isaac I.] Stevens, and [Jessie L.] Reno, and [Joseph K.F.] Mansfield, none of whom were republicans, and some at least of whom have been bitterly and repeatedly denounced to me as secession sympathizers? I will not perform the ungrateful task of comparing cases of failure.

In answer to your question, "Has it not been publicly stated in the newspapers, and apparently proved as a fact, that from the commencement of the war the enemy was continually supplied with information by some of the confidential subordinates of as important an officer as Adjutant General Thomas?" I must say "no," as far as my knowledge extends. And I add that if you can give any tangible evidence upon the subject, I will thank you to come to the City and do so.

Very truly your friend,

A. Lincoln"[59]

---

[58] Schurz was a vocal Republican Abolitionist who Lincoln appointed as one of his "political generals" as a favor to the German community as well as Abolitionists. Prussian-born expatriate Schurz left Germany after the failed 1849 revolution eventually moving to Wisconsin. He supported Lincoln in Illinois in 1858 and made speeches to German-Americans supporting Lincoln. He was first appointed by Lincoln as Minister to Spain and then brigadier general in April 1862. Schurz did not hesitate in giving his advice and opinions to Lincoln. His most quoted saying: "My country, right or wrong; if right, to be kept right; and if wrong, to be set right," "The Congressional Globe," 42nd Congress, 2nd Session, 29 February 1872, 1287. While Lincoln included Mansfield's name with other Democrat generals, he did so to demonstrate that they sacrificed the same as Republicans. Nothing has been found showing Mansfield was anti-Lincoln.

[59] Basler, *Collected Works of Lincoln*, vol. 5, 509-510.

Attachment 2
Mansfield's Troops in the Department of Washington 30 April 1861[60]
Regulars

Posts	Garrisons	Commanders	Present for duty/ Aggregate present & absent	Arrived 1861	Field Arty
Washington	Dept. Staff	J.K.F. Mansfield	9/9	--	0
Washington	Co.'s D & H, 2nd U.S. Cav.	Captain Innis N. Palmer	117/137	14 April	0
Washington	Lieutenant Co. I, 1st U.S. Arty	Lieutenant Absalom Baird	72/80	29 Jan.	6
Washington	Co. E, 2nd U.S. Arty	Captain J. Howard Carlisle	64/79	7 Feb.	0
Washington Arsenal	Co. F, 4th U.S. Arty	Lieutenant Nathaniel H. McLean	38/47	18 April	0
Washington	West Point Bty	Lieutenant Charles Griffin	72/86	1 Feb.	6
Washington	Co. I, 1st U.S. Infantry	Captain John H. King	63/83	14 April	0

Volunteers

Posts	Garrisons	Commanders	Present for duty/ Aggregate present & absent	Arrived 1861
Capitol	6th Mass. Inf.	Colonel Edward F. Jones	593/633	19 April
Capitol	7th New York Inf.	Colonel Marshall Lefferts	811/837	25 April
Capitol	8th Mass. Inf.	Colonel Timothy Munroe	507/696	26 April
Navy Yard	71st New York Inf.	Colonel Abram S. Vosburgh	702/806	27 April
Inauguration Hall	5th Penn. Inf.	Colonel Robert P. McDowell	645/752	27 April
Treasury	5th Mass. Inf.	Colonel Samuel C. Lawrence	765/787	28 April
Patent Office	1st R.I. Inf.	Colonel Ambrose E. Burnside	1,072/1,112	26/28 April
Assembly Rooms/ 6th St. & Penn	12th N.Y. Inf.	Colonel Daniel Butterfield	858/898	28 April
Caspari's House, Capitol Hill[61]	25th N.Y. Inf.	Colonel Michael K. Bryan	451/488	29 April
Capitol	Penn. Vols. 5 Cos.[62]	--	490/503	18 April
Capitol	Dist. of Colonel Vols.	Colonel Charles P. Stone	489/547	--
Various	Dist. of Colonel Vols.	Colonel Charles P. Stone	2,145/2,356	--

---

[60] *AOR*, vol. 51, pt. 1, 343-344.

[61] Caspari's House was a hotel just south of the Capitol at South A Street between New Jersey Avenue and First Street East. From July 1862 to 26 February 1863 it was used as a hospital.

[62] Colonel Mansfield on 1 May ordered two companies from the Pennsylvania Volunteers to guard the Washington Arsenal as Lincoln had found it virtually unguarded during a personal inspection, *AOR*, vol. 51, pt. 1, 345; Leech, 80.

Chapter 9

Fort Monroe, Hatteras, Suffolk, and Camp Butler

Brigadier General Mansfield returned to Washington on 10 September 1861 after a brief visit to his home in Middletown, Connecticut, fervently hoping for a combat command. He wrote to his wife on the day he arrived in the capital: "I arrived here at 7½ a.m. General [Benjamin F.] Butler came in with me. I only remained in N.Y. long enough to pay for my pantaloons and send you three drafts....I called to report to General Scott who was very friendly indeed and invited me to dine with him at 4½ which I did very pleasantly....In the morning I went out in a carriage with General Butler some 4 miles to see a review of General [George A.] McCall's Brigade by the Governor of Pennsylvania. The Little Napoleon [McClellan] was there and it was quite interesting to see. I saw the President and Secretary of War and others....I am not yet assigned to duty. I shall probably have a division assigned to me tomorrow or next day."[1]

Mansfield was not certain of his next position and noted in a 12 September letter to his son, Samuel, who was attending West Point, that he was staying at Willard's and Mr. [Drake] DeKay was his only aide. "I want a West Point graduate for my second aide." He asked Samuel if any recent graduates he knows were good. He wrote again to his son on the 19th giving him advice no doubt remembered from his years at the Academy when Samuel commands the battalion: "Give your words plain and distinct....I was much pleased with your drawings." The general also mentioned that he was on a Retiring Board in the capitol as President--"All old and worthless officers are put on the shelf."[2]

He wrote of his frustration at not receiving orders in a letter to his daughter Mary, on 22 September 1861: "If my country in this unnatural civil war did not require my services, I would certainly retire to my home, and leave it no more. But alas! It is otherwise, I am bound by all the love I have to my country and its free and noble institutions to

---

[1] Mansfield to Louisa Mansfield, September 1861, Mansfield Papers, of the Middlesex County Historical Society. McCall was a classmate of Mansfield's at West Point and also served with him in the Mexican-American War. He was also an Inspector General, Mansfield's immediate predecessor, from 10 June 1850 to 29 April 1853.

[2] Ibid.

fight its battles as far as in me lies till this foul rebellion be put down and peace be restored."[3] Mansfield also wrote Louisa from Willard's on 28 September informing her that he was still president of retiring board. Good news was that "I have had Mr. Dyer's son appointed assistant adjutant general to my staff with the rank of captain. I like his appearance much and think will do well."[4]

He finally received orders to report to Fort Monroe on 1 October 1861. He left Willard's on 2 October and arrived at the fort by steamer a day later. He reported to Major General John E. Wool, an Old Army regular, with whom he served in the Mexican-American War, and who was also an Inspector General before Mansfield.[5] Mansfield wrote to his wife from Fort Monroe, Old Point Comfort, on 3 October stating that he left Washington in "quite in a hurry yesterday. I had just attended the funeral of General [George] Gibson as a pall bearer and then immediately left Washington under orders for this place to relieve General Wool for the present and my orders for California have been revoked....I don't feel exactly right about the manner I have been used. I should have been given a separate command in the place others assigned. I shall not forget this soon. They have allowed politics to interfere with my matters, and deprive me of my just position."[6] The old veteran was happy to get out of Washington and into the field but angered that he did not receive a major command.[7]

Mansfield's son, Samuel Mather Mansfield, was born 23 September 1839, in Middletown, Connecticut. He graduated from West Point on 17 June 1862, sixth in his class and was appointed a second lieutenant of engineers. Shown here in full dress uniform, stripes showing he was a captain, photograph taken in 1862. He received a brevet promotion to captain 14 June 1863 for gallant and meritorious service and brevet major and lieutenant colonel 13 March 1865 for gallant and meritorious service during the war. General Mansfield had pressured Samuel to finish high in his class to ensure an engineer assignment. Courtesy of the Middlesex County Historical Society.

---

[3] Mansfield Papers, courtesy of the Middlesex County Historical Society.

[4] Ibid. His new aide was Clarence Hopkins Dyer.

[5] Wool was Inspector General from 1 June 1821 to 25 June 1841. He was appointed to command of the Department of Southeastern Virginia on 17 August 1861 replacing Major General Benjamin F. Butler; Wool placed Butler in command of volunteer forces other than those at Fort Monroe, *ORA*, vol. 4, 601–602. He ordered Butler to capture the Confederate batteries at Hatteras Inlet. Butler was in command of the Department of Virginia from 22 May 1861; Wool was in command to 2 June 1862 when he reassumed command of the Middle Department headquartered in Baltimore, Maryland, taking over from Major General John Adams Dix, who assumed command of the Department of Virginia; Eicher, 363.

[6] Major General Gibson was an Old Army general who first joined as an infantry captain in 1805 and served in the Mexican-American War; he died on 29 September 1861. Mansfield letter courtesy of the Middlesex County Historical Society.

[7] Mansfield's commands for this period: Hatteras Inlet, N.C., 5 October 1861 to 13 October 1861; Command of brigade at Camp Hamilton near Fort Monroe 13 (14) October to 24 November 1861; turned over command at Hamilton to Max Weber 23 November and relieved John W. Phelps in command at Newport News; First Brigade, First Division, Dept. of Virginia, 3 March 1862 to 22 June 1862; Suffolk Division, VII Corps, Dept. of Virginia 22 July 1862 to 8 September 1862. Mansfield wrote that he assumed command at Suffolk on 12 June 1862, *ORA*, ser. 2, vol. 4, 409. Mansfield wrote to Louisa from Fort Monroe, Old Point Comfort, 24 November 1861: "I am now about to start for Camp Butler Newport News where I am to command for the present," courtesy of the Middlesex County Historical Society.

Taken at Camp Butler, Newport News, Virginia. Courtesy LOC.

Hatteras Inlet

Wool quickly sent Mansfield to Hatteras Inlet to bring order out of chaos at Union outposts on the North Carolina coast. Union military activities had begun in August 1861 on North Carolina's Outer Banks soon after the disaster at First Bull Run. North Carolina Sounds occupied the coast from Cape Lookout, North Carolina, to the Virginia border. The sounds were bounded on the east by the Outer Banks, and were well located for raiding Northern ships heading north from the Caribbean, taking advantage of the north-flowing Gulf Stream. Rebel Raiders waited in the many hiding places in the sounds and pounced on Yankee ships. Rebels took advantage of the Hatteras Lighthouse as a vantage point to target unsuspecting Union vessels.

North Carolina quickly began building forts at the inlets through which vessels had to pass to and from the sounds. Of the four inlets which were deep enough for large vessels to pass, Hatteras Inlet was the most important. Confederates built two forts, Fort Hatteras and Fort Clark—Fort Hatteras was adjacent to the inlet, on the sound side of Hatteras Island, while Fort Clark was about half a mile southeast closer to the Atlantic Ocean. Fort Hatteras had ten guns mounted by the end of August 1861, with another five guns not mounted; Fort Clark had only five. Most of the guns were rather light 32-pounders or smaller, so were inadequate for coastal defense.[8]

---

[8] *ORN*, vol. 6, 140-145; *ORA*, vol. 4, 584.

Union Secretary of the Navy Gideon Welles took action to capture the under-gunned and undermanned Confederate forts to reduce the Rebel privateers opportunities to attack passing cargo ships. In a joint Navy-Army attack, Major General Benjamin F. Butler with about 900 troops, and the Atlantic Blockading Squadron under Captain Silas H. Stringham with six ships, began operations on 28 August 1861. While warships bombarded Fort Clark, troops landed three miles to the east, and easily took the fort after the defenders fled when ammunition ran out. Fort Hatteras was a tougher nut to crack. Union troops which landed later ran into problems as heavy surf swamped boats. The Union infantry commander, Colonel Max Weber, had only about 300 troops available, along with two pieces of field artillery. The Confederate defenders of Fort Hatteras held the fort that night as Butler suspended the attack due to bad weather and heavy surf.

That night however, Confederate reinforcements arrived at Fort Hatteras bolstering their numbers to 700. But the next day, Union warships pounded the fort mercilessly as they were able to stay out of range of the smaller Rebel guns. About 11 a.m., the fort surrendered and the prisoners were taken to New York City. Union forces were instructed to maintain control of Hatteras Inlet; early the next year Major General Ambrose E. Burnside began his North Carolina Expedition to establish Union hegemony on the Outer Banks and the North Carolina coast.[9]

Mansfield's commander at Fort Monroe, Major General John Ellis Wool. Wool left for Baltimore to become the commander of the Middle Department on 9 June 1862 replacing Major General John A. Dix, who then took over at Fort Monroe. See Attachment 2 below for Wool's biography. Even though he is almost 20 years older than Mansfield, he looks younger, perhaps thanks to his closely cropped hair and lack of facial hair. Photograph by Southworth and Hawes, courtesy Wikipedia.

---

[9] *ORA*, vol. 4, 581-586; 592-594.

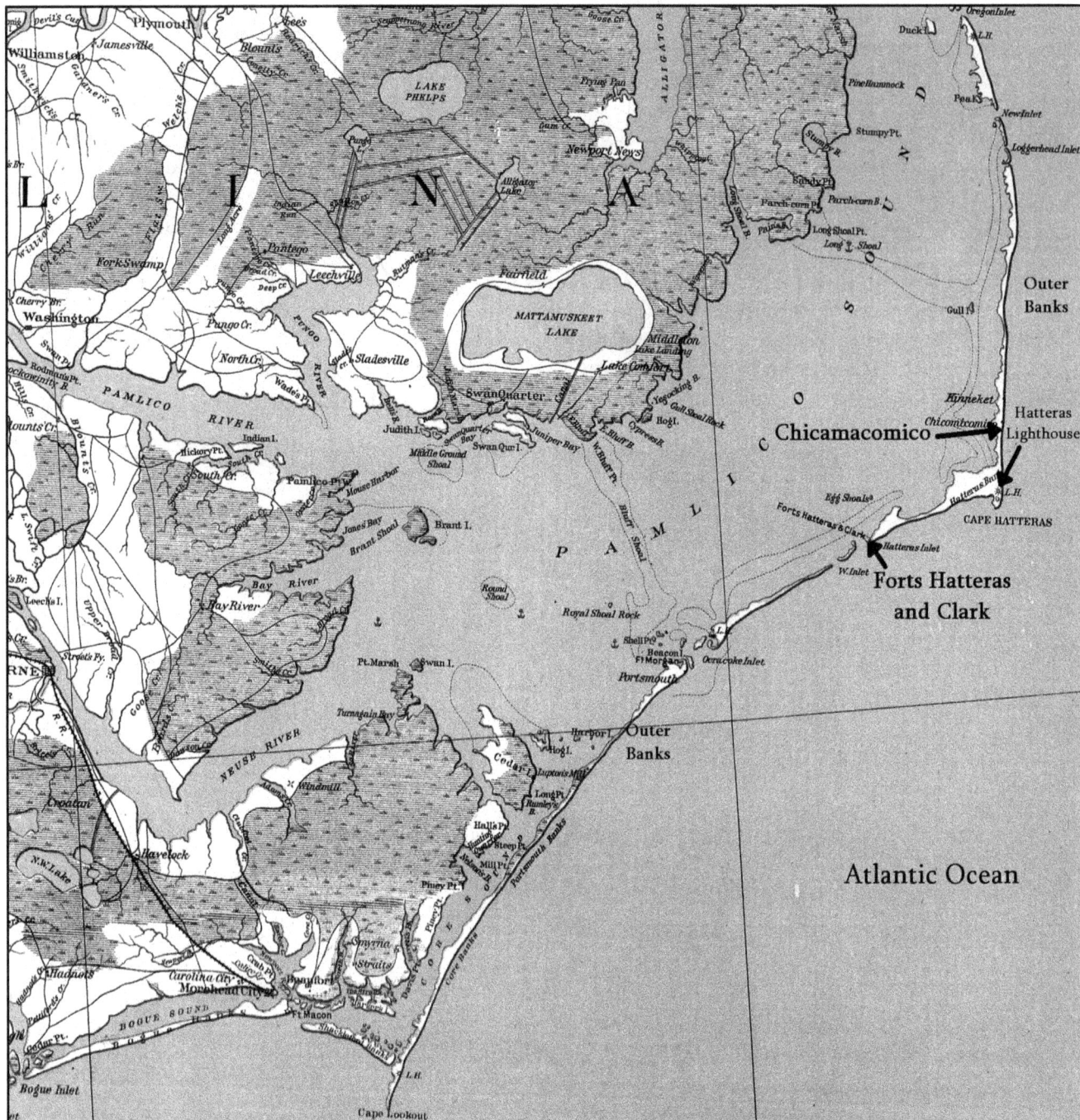

Hatteras Inlet and Fort Hatteras, North Carolina, the area of operations for Mansfield in October 1861. *OA*, pl. 138.

Mansfield was ordered to take command at Hatteras Inlet 5 October 1861 by General Orders No. 21, from the Headquarters of the Department of Virginia: "Mansfield will proceed to Hatteras Inlet in the steamer *Spaulding*... [and] will assume command and make such disposition of the forces as may be necessary for the defense of the place."[10] The previous officer in charge, Colonel Rush C. Hawkins, commanding the 9th N.Y. Infantry, was relieved as General Wool held him responsible for the debacle in which the Union steam tug *Fanny* was surrendered, and for the "Chicamacomico Races" a few days later: "Apprehensive that Colonel Hawkins had committed a great error in placing his troops at so great a distance from his batteries, I regretted extremely the withdrawal of Brigadier-General [John F.] Reynolds." Wool

---

[10] *ORA*, vol. 4, 621.

also sent 500 men as reinforcements with Mansfield bringing the total number of troops at Hatteras Inlet to 2,000.[11] Obviously Wool sent Mansfield since he was a veteran soldier known to Wool and who was available at Fort Monroe on short notice; three days later on 8 October, Wool sent Brigadier General Thomas Williams to Hatteras Inlet to relieve Mansfield who returned to Fort Monroe on 14 October.[12]

Mansfield wrote reports to Wool and Lieutenant General Winfield Scott on 5, 8, 10, and 14 October. His 5 October report, written before he departed for Hatteras Inlet, was based on his interviews with the captain, mate, engineer and a deck hand of the *Fanny* who were transported to Fort Monroe on the steamer *Pawnee*; it did not reflect well on the conduct of the soldiers aboard:

It appears that the steamer *Fanny* left Fort Hatteras about 6 a.m. on the 1st instant, with ammunition and supplies for the Twentieth Indiana Regiment, stationed some 40 miles on the beach northward, at a locality called Chicamacomico, or Loggerhead Inlet. She had on board Captain I.W. Hart, Sergeant-Major Peacock, and about 23 men of the Twentieth Indiana and Ninth New York Regiments, with a Sawyer gun and a large supply of ammunition and stores for the troops. When within 5 miles of her destination she met the U.S. naval steamer *Putnam*, which turned round and convoyed her to anchorage in 6 feet of water off the landing some 3 miles. The *Putnam* put on board the *Fanny* a rifled cannon and ammunition therefor, and then started for Fort Hatteras. At the same time stated she had seen a rebel steamer westward, and gave as reason for returning that she was short of coal. In about an hour and a half after, say at 2.30, a large flat from the shore came alongside the *Fanny* and received a load of supplies, such as tents, bread, etc. In about two hours after, three steamers approached from the westward, and at a long range commenced an attack. Not a shot struck the *Fanny*, and some eight or nine shots were fired at the enemy, one of which took effect. Then the cable was slipped and the *Fanny* was run ashore some 2¾ miles still from the beach, and the crew abandoned her in a boat, and the officer in charge, Captain Hart, hoisted a white flag, and surrendered before a gun was fired on either side. The captain of the *Fanny*, John M. Morrison, left in a small boat with his sick son. The mate, George K. Ridgely, and engineer and others of the crew remained until the white flag was hoisted. Some ammunition was thrown overboard, but the guns were not thrown overboard nor the boat sunk, as was recommended by the mate and engineer.[13]

Capture of steam tug *Fanny* by Rebel gunboats. The steamer was originally operated by the United States Army Quartermaster Corps and on 3 August 1861 on the James River, balloonist John La Mountain made an ascent from its deck to observe Confederate positions. After its capture on 1 October 1861, it was salvaged and taken by the Confederate States Navy. It was used four days after its capture to participate in the capture of the Union forces at Chicamacomico. The *Fanny* spent the next four months patrolling Pamlico Sound, Hatteras Inlet, towing supply schooners to Roanoke Island. In February 1862, it fought against the Union invasion force in the battle of Roanoke Island. It retreated to Elizabeth City and on 10 February, it was attacked by Federal gunboats advancing from Roanoke Island. During the battle, it ran aground and was blown up by her captain. *Harper's Weekly*, 19 Oct. 1861, courtesy Wikipedia.

---

[11] *ORA*, vol. 4, 621. John F. Reynolds was ordered to take command at Hatteras Inlet but before he could do so he was ordered to join the Army of the Potomac; Mansfield replaced him at Hatteras Inlet, Welcher, 132. Rush C. Hawkins had taken command at Fort Clark as senior colonel and Colonel Max Weber was stationed at Fort Hatteras.

[12] *ORA*, vol. 4, 622, 626. Williams was a West Point graduate and a Mexican-American War veteran, who was killed at Baton Rouge 5 August 1862 while he was a brigade commander in the Dept. of the Gulf. The men of the 9th New York resented him, Matthew J. Graham, *The Ninth Regiment New York Volunteers (Hawkins' Zouaves)* (New York, NY: E.P. Coby & Co., 1900), 97-98.

[13] *ORA*, vol. 4, 595. Mansfield's reports and those made by Navy participants are congruent, *ORN*, vol. 6, 275-277. The premature departure of the accompanying steamship, *Putnam*, ostensibly to re-coal, was an error on its captain's part.

Mansfield's follow-up report on 8 October was sent to Wool the day after Mansfield arrived at Fort Hatteras. It described the retreat of Colonel [William L.] Brown from Chicamacomico at the north end of Hatteras Island on 4 October to Fort Clark, after the *Fanny's* capture, better known as the Chicamacomico Races. The Yankees had a difficult time as they struggled for miles retreating through heavy sand, shedding equipment as they ran, enduring hot weather. The weary troops finally reached the Cape Hatteras Lighthouse where they camped. Union reinforcements from Fort Hatteras and Union Navy ships chased away the Confederates whose turn it was to race north back to Chicamacomico:

> I learned on my arrival that the Twentieth Indiana Regiment had fallen back before the enemy from Chicamacomico to this inlet. The circumstances were as follows:
> The day after the loss of the steamer *Fanny*, Colonel Brown sent to Fort Hatteras his sick and extra baggage. On the 3d instant (Thursday last) the steam-tugs *Putnam* and *Ceres* arrived at Chicamacomico with five days' supply of provisions, which they landed immediately and returned to Fort Hatteras. On Friday the camp was approached by a fleet of some nine steamers and sail vessels, besides flats, with the intent to land south of the camp and cut off the command from Hatteras. The command of Colonel W.L. Brown, being but seven companies--say 500 strong--and the enemy supposed to be at least 2,000 strong, Colonel Brown immediately, by orders received from Colonel R.C. Hawkins at that moment, took up his line of march on the east beach for Hatteras light-house, when he was met by Colonel Hawkins, with his command, and finally the whole command fell back to this station, with a loss on the part of Colonel Brown of 3 sergeants, 2 corporals, and 24 men, stragglers. He sent back a party to burn and destroy his camp, which was supposed to be partially done, and fell into the hands of the enemy.[14]

Colonel Hawkins was responsible for sending the *Fanny* and troops north so as a consequence was severely criticized. He defended himself at that time in a report to Wool which Wool characterized as "highly insubordinate, and ought not to pass unnoticed."[15] His 8 October report was ill-advised at best and certainly did not improve his standing in Wool's eyes or in those of other Old Army regulars:

> It is evident to me, from the tone of your letter of the 6th instant, that a change in your feelings towards me has taken place. I do not wish to know the reason for the change nor do I ask it. I suppose that I shall be blamed for the recent disaster at this post. If such is the case, I have only to say that I am ready, eager, and willing to go before the country and give all the particulars in relation to my course since I have been in command at this post, and then let the people judge between me and the criminal neglect of the Government in not heeding my suggestions
> If I have within me any part of my nature which is good, it has all been brought to bear in this cause. I entered it because I wished to punish those people who were trying to destroy our Government. I was willing to sacrifice life and everything else, if necessary, in the performance of my duty, without honor or reward. I was willing to work without pay and to undergo any hardships which the service could impose upon me. But how different is the feeling now. I feel that I have an ungrateful and unappreciating Government at my back, which cannot or cares not to discern the difference between those of its servants who have its interests truly at heart and those who work for pay only.
> Sending a new commanding officer here to step into my shoes, after all the dirty work has been done, to supersede me, indicates that all confidence in my ability has been lost. This touches my pride. Next to doubting my integrity this is the most tender point in my nature, and now I have only to say that if by return mail you should inform me that you will accept my resignation, I will send it at once. One word more and I have done. I do not seek promotion. Brigadier-generals are made of such queer stuff nowadays, that I should not esteem it any very great honor to be made one. I had supposed, when I entered the service, that, if I should live to the end of my term, I might come out a very respectable colonel, but nothing more.[16]

Mansfield Returns to Fort Monroe

Mansfield returned to Fort Monroe on 14 October, and was in command of Camp Hamilton near Fort Monroe from 13 October to 24 November 1861, when he turned over command to Colonel Max Weber, and was ordered to relieve Brigadier General John W. Phelps at Newport News 24 November 1861. On 3 March 1862, Mansfield's command was

---

[14] *ORA*, vol. 4, 625. Chicamacomico is near modern-day Rodanthe.

[15] *ORA*, vol. 4, 624.

[16] *ORA*, vol. 4 623-624. Colonel Hawkins did not join the ranks of brigadier generals until 1865, so his rant apparently was not quickly forgotten. What may have saved him from Wool kicking him out of the Army was his apparently successful visit in early November 1861 to Washington and meetings with Lincoln and his cabinet, and General McClellan, He was mustered out of service in 1863. Rush C. Hawkins, "Early Coast Operations in North Carolina," *Battles and Leaders of the Civil War: Being for the Most Part Contributions by Union and Confederate Officers Based upon "The Century War Series,* vol. 1, 632-640.

designated the First Brigade, First Division, Department of Virginia. Dix sent Mansfield to Suffolk with three regiments on 13 June 1862.[17]

Mansfield wrote letters to Louisa on 18 and 22 October after he returned to Fort Monroe, Old Point Comfort. He told her that he has taken his quarters with his aides Lieutenant DeKay and Captain Dyer. Next he said that he wanted more aides: "General Wool is very friendly and all things are harmonious here. I have applied for another aide a graduate. I want two—say nothing to Mr. Parsons about it, as he made application for the husband of a Mrs. Kir (?). At the McDonough House quite a modest request to make for a person I had never seen." In his next letter on the 27th of October, he was still was happy with General Wool: "Yesterday General Wool had a review of my troops here, 4 regiments and it went off well. We are very friendly in all matters and I have his confidence of course. I have had a deal to do here, and the troops one half are very green....Halleck should never have had a preference over me. It is all Scott's doings. He married the daughter of Mr. Hamilton of N.Y. and Schuyler Hamilton General Scott's aide is his brother in law....The interest of the service is not considered when favorites are to be advanced."[18] Mansfield was still smarting over men junior to him such as General Halleck who were promoted over him. On 8 November in his letter to Louisa, he wrote that "Halleck is soon to be provided for" implying that Halleck's star was about to rise? Mansfield also disparaged Secretary of War Cameron: "I see through the whole of Cameron's acts and will trust him no more He has not the capacity for his position. I wish you would say so to Mrs. Douglas and Mr. also when you see them." In his 22 December 1861 letter to Mary from Camp Butler he wrote that he rides a lot but is "tired;" he also notes that it is his birthday: he was 58.[19]

Private William H. Osborne, historian of the 29th Massachusetts Infantry, stationed at Camp Butler in November 1861, compared Mansfield to their previous commander, the veteran Brigadier General John W. Phelps: "Phelps was a superior drill-master, and it was to the rigid system of drill inaugurated by him, and continued by his worthy successor, General Mansfield, that the troops constituting the garrison at Newport News owe much of the proficiency which they displayed in the battles and campaigns of a later date."[20] Mansfield obviously knew from his Mexican-American War experience what was most important to soldiers in the field as Osborne explained in detail:

> The same stern sense of duty which the General manifested while in the field was daily impressed by him upon the men under his command at Newport News. He was not a preacher nor a martinet; he was a plain, shrewd, well-educated gentleman, with a fine sense of humor, great practical talent, inexhaustible tact, and had an intimate knowledge of human nature. He was familiar with the men, always had a kind word for the sentinel at headquarters, and when the sentinel had once properly saluted him, he would say, "You will oblige me by not saluting me again to-day, as I have to be constantly going out and coming in, and I don't care for it."
>
> One of the first orders issued by him, after taking command of this post, was to institute target practice, at ranges of 200, 400, 600, and 1,000 yards. By this order, a record of shots was to be kept; each company was to shoot three times a week, and the ten best marksmen of the regiment, every week, were to be selected and allowed a day's liberty at Fortress Monroe; and as this included a sail on the steamer of some twenty miles (both ways) and a visit to one of the most interesting places in the department, being, as it were, a sort of metropolis, the reward thus offered was highly prized and eagerly sought for by all the men. By the same order, officers were encouraged to compete with the men in this exercise. No man was to fire less than ten shots each week; guards, on relief, were to discharge their pieces at a target, and be marked for it; and the best marksman in the guard got a day's liberty. The targets used were pieces of old tents, stretched on frames six feet high and two feet wide, with a black cross four inches wide on them, the horizontal arm at a height of four and a half feet....
>
> One of General Mansfield's drills was a march in campaign order, and he was very particular to describe what things a soldier should carry in campaign, permitting what was forbidden in the Army of the Potomac at one time, — photographs and letters, — and not encouraging a superfluity of blacking brushes. Upon the first marching drill, the staff-officers were sent round to say, that at route-step it was usual to allow the men to smoke and talk in campaign; and he desired the officers to encourage it

---

[17] *ORA*, vol. 51, pt. 1, 507. Phelps was a West Point graduate and a fervent Abolitionist. After his transfer to the Dept. of the Gulf, he resigned 21 August 1862 after an argument with General Benjamin F. Butler over employment of black Americans in the army—Phelps wanted immediate emancipation for these men but Butler refused, Eicher, 427; *ORA*, vol. 51, pt. 1, 547: Mansfield's Brigade had the 1st, 2nd, 7th, 11th New York Regiments, 20th Indiana, and the 29th Massachusetts along with Captain Howard's light Company L, Fourth Artillery, ibid., 674; *ORA*, vol. 5, 755. Dix wrote to Mansfield on 9 June 1862 and put him in command at Suffolk telling him that he has five infantry regiments there. On 9 June 1862 Mansfield telegraphed to Dix that he was ready to leave tomorrow--10 June, courtesy of the Middlesex County Historical Society.

[18] Courtesy of the Middlesex County Historical Society.

[19] Letters courtesy of the Middlesex County Historical Society.

[20] William H. Osborne, *The History of the Twenty-Ninth Regiment of Massachusetts Volunteer Infantry, in the Late War of the Rebellion* (Boston, MA: Albert J. Wright, 1877), 85.

then, as it would be necessary to allow it in the future. The drills thus inaugurated were continued as long as the weather would permit, and were all chosen with special reference to active service in the field.

The following anecdote shows the dry humor of General Mansfield and his efficient tact in the management of citizen soldiery. One day a soldier neglected to salute him. He stopped his horse, and said, "My man, did you know it was my duty, by the Army regulations, to touch my hat to you every time I meet you?" "No, sir; I am sure I never thought of such a thing." "Yes; but it is yours to touch your hat to me first. I hope you will never allow me again to fail in my duty to you." Civility at Newport News, after that, was not so often forgotten.[21]

Mansfield's quarters at Camp Butler were Spartan, similar to those in which he lived some 40 years earlier at West Point, but adequate, as he told Louisa in his letter 3 December 1861: "I live in a little room 15 feet square door opening outdoors. My cot bedstead and blankets in one corner, a ___ table in another a pile of wood and a fire place. Captain Dyer and my aide sleep in a room of a small house where we take our meals for $5 per week. The soldiers are in tents and in log huts and are doing the best they can....I am on horseback about half my time....My two Black servant men cost me 50 dollars per month for wages and board. So that my current expenses here are all told not less than 100 dollars per month. You know that my life is quite precarious now and you must make your calculations accordingly."[22]

He added some details in a 24 January 1862 letter to Mary from Camp Butler: "Bad weather. But men have good log huts enough to eat and good clothes. We allow no grog but when the picket guards come in in the morning wet and cold I order a half gill of whiskey to each man who wishes it." Mansfield had a one-story, one-room house with fireplace, and room and restaurant, costs he shows as $6 per week. He had two fine horses and two black servants, one free and other a contraband. "I think all the slaves of Virginia should be set free as fast as they come into our lines." He mentioned to Louisa in a letter from Camp Butler 15 January 1862 that a famous Connecticut firearms maker sent him weapons: "Colt Manufactory sent me 2 handsome holster pistols, a belt pistol and a pocket pistol, with my name engraved on them. I have now seven pistols here, quite enough to supply my boys when I am done with them." He updated Samuel 24 May to tell him that he has 7 pistols, and Colt had presented him with two holsters.[23]

---

[21] Osborne, 97-100.
[22] Courtesy of the Middlesex County Historical Society.
[23] Courtesy of the Middlesex County Historical Society.

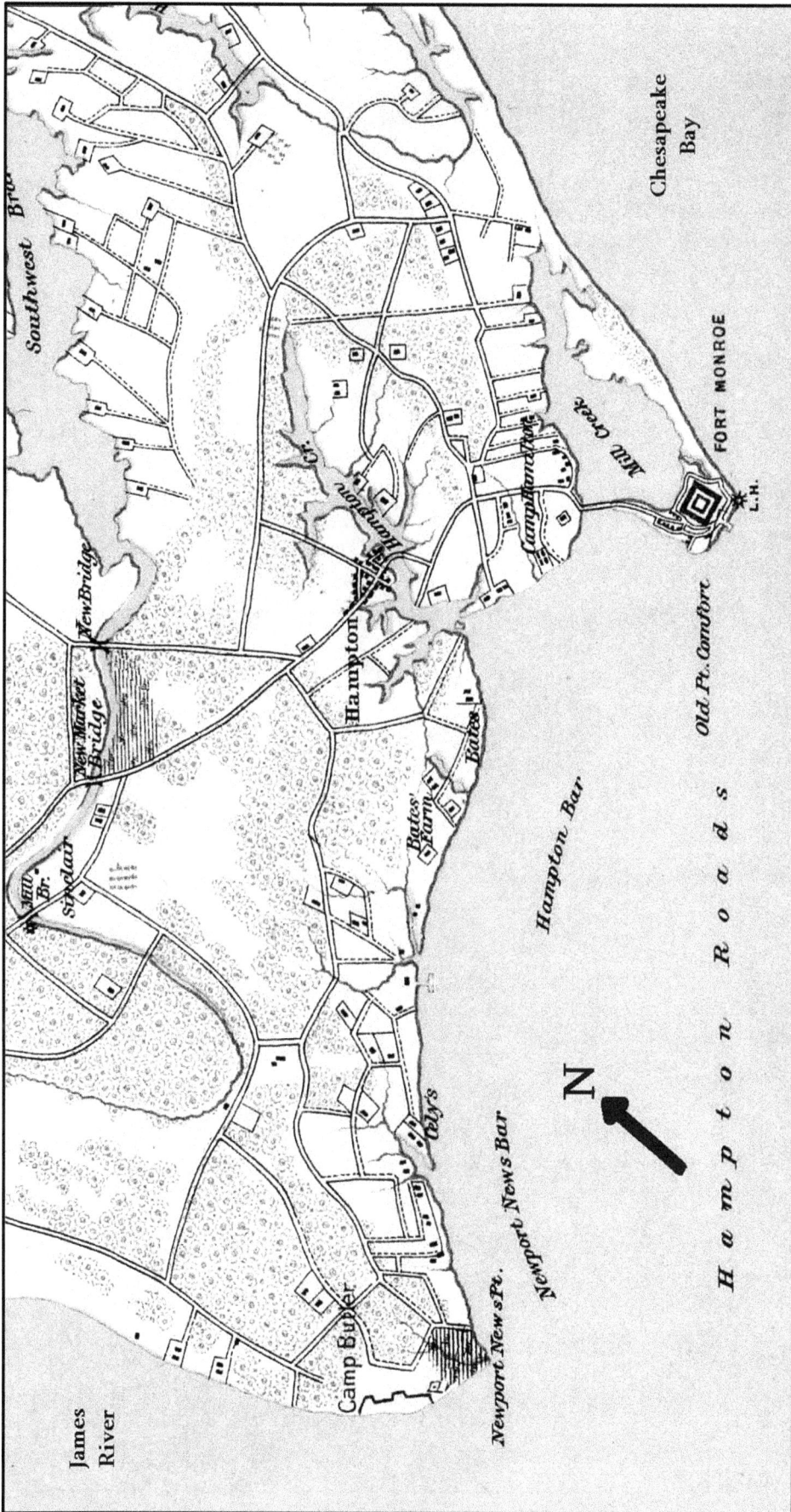

Fort Monroe, Camp Butler, and vicinity showing Mansfield's stations. *OA*, pl. 18.

J.Wells.del.

R.Hinshelwood.sc.

Entered according to act of Congress in 1862 by Virtue & Co. in the Clerks office of the District court of the United States for the southern district of New York.

1. Old Point Comfort.
2. Fortress Monroe.
3. Water Battery.
4. Hampton Roads.
5. Rip Raps.
6. Chesapeake Bay.
7. Sewall's Point.
8. Craney Island.
9. Elizabeth River.
10. Norfolk.
11. Portsmouth.
12. Dismal Swamp.
13. Atlantic Ocean.
14. Cape Hatteras, NC.
15. Nansemond River.
16. James River.
17. Newport News.
18. Hampton.
19. Mill Creek.
20. Land approach to Fortress.

General Wool reported on 31 January 1862: Mansfield at Camp Butler, Newport News, with the 1st, 2nd, 7th, and 11th New York Regiments along with the 29th Massachusetts.[24] At the end of August 1862, Mansfield was in command at Suffolk with Weber's Brigade, VII Corps, and Ferry's Third Brigade, Second Division, IV Corps. One of the regiments of volunteers which served under Mansfield in late 1861 was the 48th Pennsylvania Regiment. It arrived at Fort Monroe 24 September 1861, and served there until 11 November when it was assigned to Fort Clark at Hatteras Inlet. One of its men, Charles H. Hazzard from Company G, was appointed as a clerk to Mansfield.[25]

The 48th left Harrisburg, Pennsylvania, on 24 September and wound up at Camp Hamilton via steamer from Baltimore. The green regiment began training in earnest "At Camp Hamilton…strict attention was given to squad, company and regimental drills, and the regiment was soon considered the best-drilled organization of the volunteers at this camp." Unlike some new regiments, the soldiers found living conditions not onerous: "We enjoyed every minute we spent at this place. We were pleasantly situated, having plenty of Army rations and luxuries in lavish abundance. Fish, oysters, clams and crabs could be had with little effort, and despite a few rain-storms, accompanied by wind, which blew our tents down, and obliged some of us to sleep in a few inches of water, we were comfortable and happy."[26]

But according to the regimental historian, the old Regular Army veteran Mansfield did not let the 48th rest easy perhaps knowing that the war was not going to be easy or short:

> Mansfield… walked into the camp of the 48th, night after night, going to the Colonel's tent to let him know of his presence in camp and his manner of entry. Day after day, while on regimental drill, Colonel [James] Nagle formed the regiment in "hollow square" and told of Mansfield's nocturnal visit to his quarters. He was greatly displeased at this seeming lack of vigilance on the part of the guards, and demanded greater care by officers and men; but the nightly invasions continued, though not so frequently.
>
> On one night, however, the guards, instead of meeting at intervals to exchange remarks and pause a moment before marching away from each other, only to repeat the trick with the next sentinel, kept about equidistant, and General Mansfield found so much difficulty in trying to get through the line, that his entry was under the escort of the Officer of the Guard, who conducted him to the Colonel's quarters, to whom he admitted the danger of further trying to "run the guard." Congratulations followed, and that officer never again tried to get into the 48th camp, so far as known, except in the regular way, and by daylight. This episode occurring just in the formative period of the regiment, the impression remained, and vigilance on camp and picket guard became a marked characteristic of the command….[27]

A member of the regiment, Lieutenant Oliver Christian Bosbyshell, reiterated the journey and arrival of the 48th Pennsylvania:

> On the morning of the twenty-sixth the command disembarked at Fortress Monroe, just as the Twentieth Indiana was leaving for Hatteras, a region destined to be full of events for the Forty eighth. Passing around the walls of the fortress over the long, narrow road and bridge connecting with Hampton, the command reached a camping ground within the confines of "Camp Hamilton," in charge of dear old General Mansfield. His mild disposition and benevolent heart, that caused him to be ever on the lookout for the welfare of his soldiers, combined, however, with a firm, just discipline, endeared him to all with whom he came in contact.

Bosbyshell gave added detail about Mansfield's nighttime prowling:

> One dark, blustery night, and this camp was prolific of such kind of nights, Jake Haines let General Mansfield slip through the camp guard without challenge. Jake was as deaf as a post, and besides was walking away from him when the General entered. The General notified the officer of the guard to have the offender reprimanded the next morning at guard-mount, and then attempted to pass out of camp on the opposite side, but Rogers was there, and his "halt, or I'll prog ye" brought him up a-standing. Colonel Nagle reprimanded Haines next morning, but it was done in the low squeaking voice which the Colonel sometimes adopted, so that when it was over Haines inquired "What did he say?"[28]

---

[24] *ORA*, vol. 9, 15. Total officers and men present for duty, 3,451; total aggregate present and absent, 4,376.

[25] Joseph Gould, *The Story of The Forty-Eighth: A Record of the Campaigns of the Forty-Eighth Regiment Pennsylvania Veteran Volunteer Infantry during the four eventful years of its service in the war for the preservation of the Union* (Philadelphia, PA: Alfred M. Slocum Co., 1908), 28.

[26] Ibid., 37.

[27] Ibid., 37-38.

[28] Oliver Christian Bosbyshell, *The 48th In The War, Being a Narrative of the Campaigns of the 48th Regiment, Infantry, Pennsylvania Veteran Volunteers During the War of the Rebellion* (Philadelphia: PA, Avil Printing Company, 1895), 19-20.

Mansfield's aide-de-camp, Lieutenant Drake DeKay, made his mark on the men of the 48th perhaps to provide amusement for himself if not the troops: "The passes required for visiting Fortress Monroe or other points of interest were prescribed by orders to be written on a quarter-sheet of foolscap paper, with an allowance of at least four lines for the assistant adjutant general's signature, and what a wonderful signature; "Drake DeKay," written with a paint brush!"[29]

Another regiment, the 1st Delaware, arrived at Fort Monroe and trekked to Camp Hamilton as described in its regimental history by its adjutant, Captain William P. Seville:

> The morning of October 21, 1861, when the command disembarked at Fort Monroe, was chilly and rendered dismal by a fine drizzle of rain (which sort of weather, by the way, continued for several days thereafter), and the regiment stood upon the wharf while Colonel [John W.] Andrews went to report to General Wool. Very soon an aide was sent to conduct us to our camping-ground at Camp Hamilton, about a mile from the fort, whither we soon arrived, and all hands set to work to lay out the ground and pitch tents. Notwithstanding the inclemency of the weather, dress-parade was gone through with, much to the surprise of other regiments situated near us.
>
> We found ourselves to be a portion of General Mansfield's brigade of General Wool's division, and were associated with the following-named regiments, viz.: Twentieth New York (German Turners), Colonel Max Weber; Sixteenth Massachusetts, Colonel [Powell T.] Wyman; Ninety-ninth New York (Union Coast Guard), Colonel [David W.] Wardrop; and Forty-eighth Pennsylvania, Colonel [James] Nagle....
>
> Our dress-parades had become a fine military pageant to the other regiments of the brigade, some of which changed the time for their own evening parade to a later hour that they might have the opportunity to witness ours. Frequently among the spectators that honored our parades were seen Generals Wool and Mansfield, with their staff-officers, and these commanders paid us many compliments on the appearance and discipline of the regiment and the fine military bearing of officers and men.[30]

General Mansfield was out and about as noted by Captain Seville:

> On the 1st of November it fell to the lot of Captain [John B.] Tanner and his company to go out on a scout to Fox Hill Station, the extreme outpost, and to receive a flag of truce accompanied by seven rebel officers,—they had brought the usual summons from General Magruder "to get out."...
>
> It was quite evident that the main object of this strong delegation of rebel officers was to gain information, for they desired to go into Hampton on the pretext of wanting to find a colored woman; but Captain Tanner detained them at the outpost and sent word to General Mansfield, who was at the time near the picket-line. The general came to meet the flag of truce, sent the rebel officers back, and commended Captain Tanner for his discretion.[31]

Then three weeks later, Mansfield was again in the field, desiring to see some action:

> Quite a furor of excitement was raised on the 21st of November by the arrival in camp of a messenger from Captain [Evan S.] Watson, who had been sent out with his company scouting. It appeared that the enemy had been of the same mind, and had also dispatched a scouting-party, or, rather, a reconnaissance in force, consisting of infantry, cavalry, and two guns. This was the force that Company A encountered, and at once availing themselves of their lately-acquired knowledge of skirmishing, deployed, and kept the enemy amused at long range for several hours, until word was brought to camp, and reinforcements in the shape of three companies of the Twentieth New York, under the command of no less a personage than General Mansfield himself, with about forty staff-officers, volunteers from the other regiments, came to their relief, and the enemy was bluffed.[32]

Mansfield did not spend his time huddled in his camp as he noted in a letter to his wife from Camp Butler on 3 January 1862: "I have just returned from a trip of 10 miles up the James River with a flag of truce and we received 240 prisoners that were taken at Bull Run."[33]

Wool started to annoy Mansfield perhaps commencing with Wool's disapproval of Mansfield firing Rebel buildings. In his 6 January 1862 letter to Louisa from Camp Butler, he wrote that "General Wool's abominable order is in the *Tribune* of the 3rd instant. I am glad it is published as it shows the grounds of my application to leave. I was right in the burning of buildings in a true military sense. The enemy were using them and I deprived them of their use."[34]

---

[29] Bosbyshell, 20.

[30] William P. Seville, *History of the First Regiment, Delaware Volunteers* (Wilmington, DE: The Historical Society of Delaware, 1884), 34.

[31] Ibid.

[32] Seville, 35. Seville obviously appreciated the likely few staff officers who rode with Mansfield.

[33] Courtesy of the Middlesex County Historical Society.

[34] Courtesy of the Middlesex County Historical Society.

The Battle of the Ironclads: Monitor versus the Merrimack 8-9 March 1862

The most noteworthy adventure Mansfield had while in command at Newport News was related to the remarkable naval battle of the Civil War, the U.S.S. *Monitor* versus the C.S.S. *Virginia* (U.S.S. *Merrimack*). While the battle between the two ironclads took place on 9 March, Mansfield's involvement was primarily the day before, when the *Virginia* attacked Union blockaders in Hampton Roads, attempting to break the blockade which had stopped Confederate naval access to the Chesapeake Bay. Mansfield ordered Union shore batteries and infantry to fire at Rebel ships and sailors as they approached the helpless U.S.S. *Congress* which had run aground, and after the ship had run up white flags. As will be seen, controversy ensued.

At the beginning of the war, Confederates, with little effort, had seized the navy yard at Portsmouth, Virginia, with the Union drydock, over 1,000 heavy guns, gun carriages, stores, and powder, plus the remains of the U.S.S. *Merrimack* which was burned to the water line. One estimate of the value of items seized exceeded $4,000,000.[35] The Rebels resurrected the *Merrimack* into a large ironclad renamed the C.S.S. *Virginia*. The Confederacy now controlled the area to the south of Hampton Roads and next set up batteries at Sewell's Point and Craney Island. Fortunately, Union commanders were more resolute than the navy yard commander and held onto Fort Monroe, and the small, man-made island opposite the fort known as the Rip Raps on which they built Fort Wool. The two forts meant that the Union controlled the entrance to Hampton Roads and the blockade which was instituted in April 1861, stopped access to the sea for Confederates in Norfolk and Richmond.

---

[35] *Southern Historical Society Papers*, ed. by R.A. Brock (Richmond, VA: Published by the Society, 1892), vol. 20, January-December 1892, Virginius Newton, "The Ram Merrimac," 1.

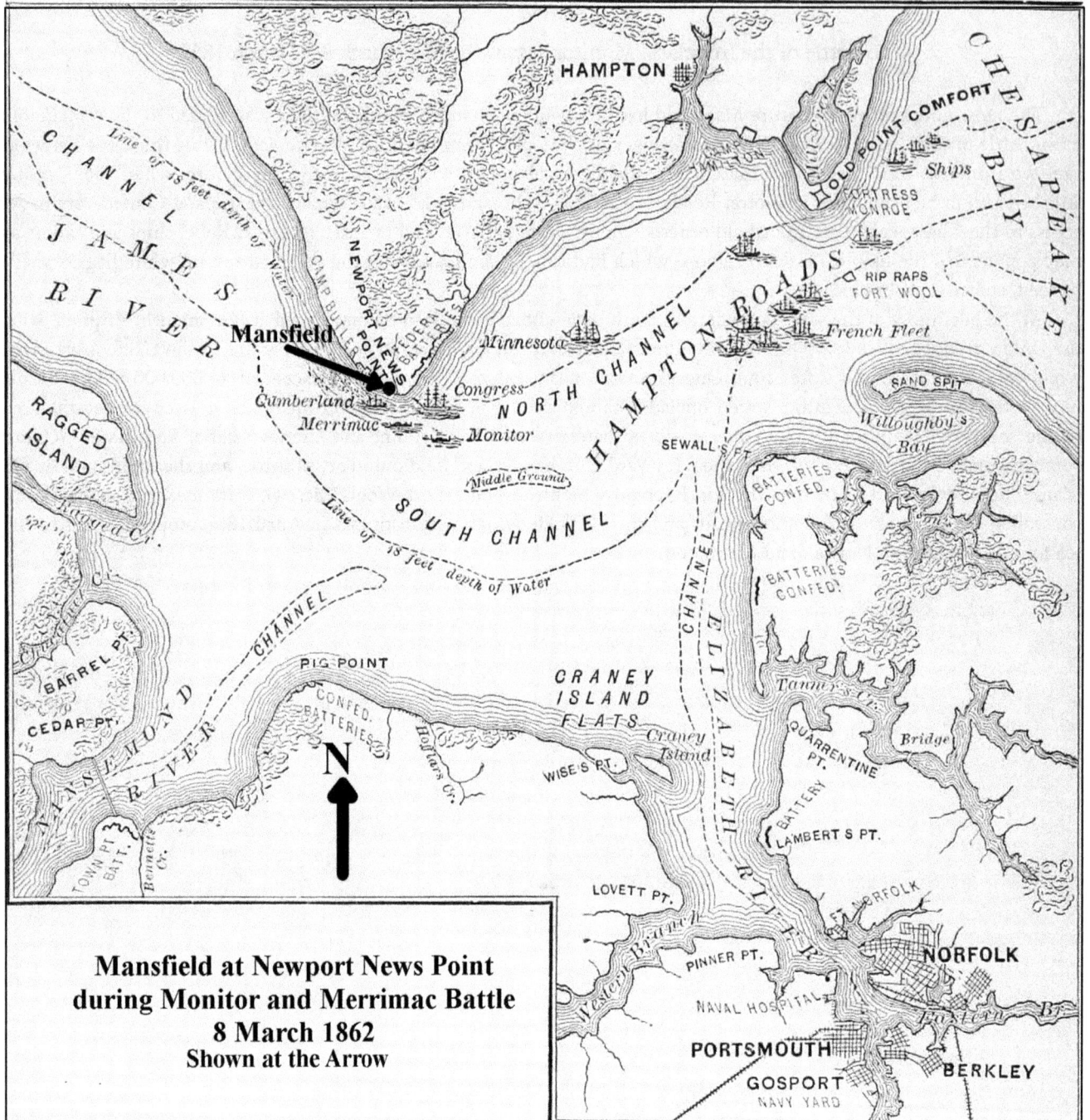

Map showing the famous clash of the ironclads on 8 and 9 March with Mansfield's position at Newport News Point. *A Comprehensive Sketch of the Merrimac and Monitor Naval Battle* (New York, NY: Merrimac and Monitor Panorama Company, 1886), 4.

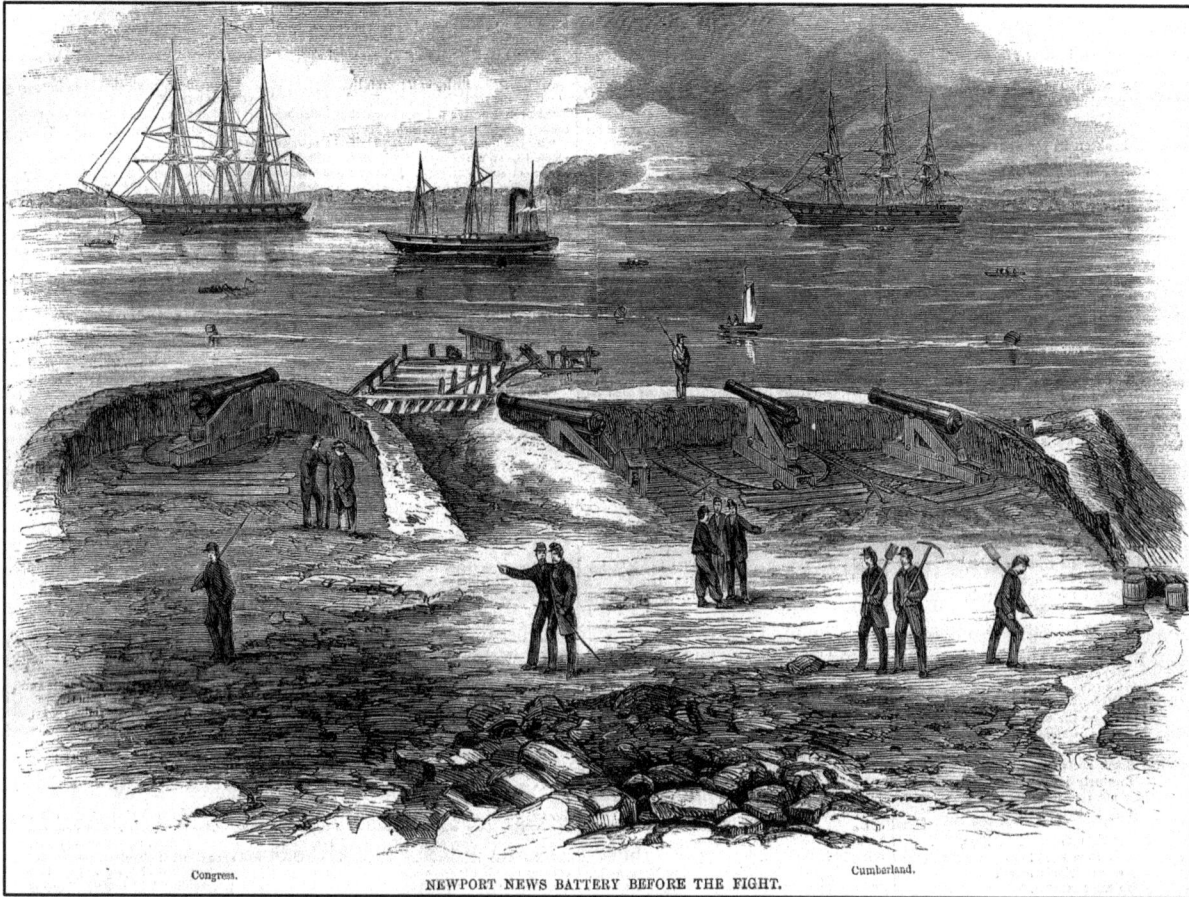

Battery at Newport News before 8 March 1862 prior to the battle between Rebel warship C.S.S. *Virginia* and the Union ship *Cumberland*; the *Cumberland* is the large vessel on the right and the *Congress* is on the left. *Harpers Weekly*, 22 August 1862, 181, author's collection.

Heavy guns in the fort at Newport News Point at Camp Butler which fired at Confederate gunboats. The camp and town are shown in the rear. *A Comprehensive Sketch of the Merrimac and Monitor Naval Battle* (New York, NY: Merrimac and Monitor Panorama Company, 1886), 7.

Lieutenant Israel N. Stiles was an officer in the 20th Indiana Infantry watching from Newport News, and witnessed the attack of the C.S.S. *Virginia* on 8 March.[36] His vivid account is the best Union account viewed from the shore which includes Mansfield's famous order and depicts the gruesome aftermath as Union sailors from the damaged ships reached shore:

My...narrative will be confined to such incidents as came under my own observation from on shore at Newport News....On the 8th of March, at about one o'clock P.M., the long-roll sounded, and the cry ran through the camp, "The 'Merrimac' is coming." She was now about five or six miles away, and looked very like a house submerged to the eaves, borne onward by a flood....Our position was strongly fortified; we had heavy guns commanding our front; and we thought we were ready to receive her becomingly should she come within our range. Nearby and at anchor were two of our largest sailing frigates, the "Congress" and "Cumberland," carrying fifty and thirty guns respectively....A few miles away were also the Union frigates "Minnesota," "Roanoke," and "St. Lawrence," and several gun-boats.

The "Merrimac" moved very slowly, accompanied by the "Beaufort" and "Raleigh," two small boats carrying one gun each....She moved directly for the "Cumberland" which had cleared for action when the enemy was first sighted, and for the last half-hour had been ready with every man at his post. On her way she passed the "Congress" on her starboard side, and within easy range. The latter greeted her with a terrific broadside, to which the "Merrimac" responded, but kept on her course. Soon she came within range of the shore batteries, which opened upon her, and a minute or two later the thirty guns of the "Cumberland" were doing their duty. Many of the shots struck her, but they rebounded from her sides like marbles thrown by boys against a brick wall. Approaching the "Cumberland," she fired her bow gun, and struck her at full speed on her port bow, delivering another shot at the same time. The blow opened an immense hole in the frigate, and the force of it was so great that the "Merrimac's" iron prow, or beak, was wrenched off as she withdrew, and was left sticking in the side of the ship. The two shots which had been delivered from her bow gun had been terribly destructive. One entered the "Cumberland's" port, killing or wounding every man at one of her guns; the other raked her gun-deck from one end to the other....

Meantime the shore batteries had kept up their fire, while the "Congress" had been towed up into position, and with her thirty guns pounded away at the iron monster. It was plain to us on shore that all combined were not a match for her. This must have been plain to the officers and men of the "Cumberland" as well; yet with their ship sinking under them, they continued the fight with a courage and desperation which is recorded of no other naval battle. It was stated at the time that while her bow guns were under water, those in the after part of the ship were made to do double duty. Her commander was called upon to surrender; he refused, and his men cheered him. Still she sank, and the men were ordered to save themselves by swimming ashore. The water closed over her with her flag still flying....

While the "Merrimac" was occupied with the "Cumberland," three Confederate steamers, the "Patrick Henry," "Jamestown," and "Teaser," had come down the James River, and with the two gun-boats "Beaufort" and "Raleigh" had already engaged the "Congress." On our side, the screw frigate "Minnesota" had worked her way from the fort, but had grounded a mile and a half away. The "Roanoke," which was disabled by a broken shaft, was towed up by a couple of tugs, but from her great draught failed to get into position; and the "St. Lawrence" was unable to use her fifty guns, for like reasons. For half an hour or more the "Merrimac" alternated her attentions between the "Congress" and the "Minnesota." Owing to her great draught of water, she could not get near enough to the latter to do much damage, although the other gun-boats worried her exceedingly. She chose her own position with regard to the "Congress," and the utter destruction of the frigate became only a question of time. She had repeatedly been set on fire; her decks were covered with the dead and wounded; and the loss of life (including that of her commander) had been very great. She was run ashore, head on, and not long after hoisted the white flag. Two tugs were sent by the enemy alongside the "Congress" to take possession and to remove the prisoners, but a sharp fire of artillery and small arms from the shore drove them off. General Mansfield had directed the Twentieth Indiana to deploy along the beach and behind a sand ridge; and a couple of field-guns under command of Lieutenant Sanger were also wheeled into position to prevent the enemy from hauling away their prize. Captain Reed, of the Twentieth, — who had been as good a lawyer as he was now a good soldier, — raised a question of military law: "Since the ship has surrendered, has not the enemy the right to take possession of her?" The question was answered by General Mansfield (Judge Mansfield in this instance), in one of the shortest and most conclusive opinions on record. "I know the damned ship has surrendered," said he, "but we haven't." That settled it. During the firing which was kept up by the infantry, Commander Buchanan, of the "Merrimac," received a wound which disabled him from further participation in the fight. Being unable to take possession of the frigate, the ironclad again opened fire upon her, — this time with incendiary shot, — and the ship was soon on fire in several places....

The "Congress" continued to burn, her loaded guns discharging as the fire reached them, until about one o'clock A.M., when the fire reached her magazine, and she blew up with a tremendous noise, and with a shock so great that many of us on shore

---

[36] Stiles was born in Suffield, Connecticut, moved to Indiana and became a lawyer. He was a first lieutenant in the 20th Indiana Infantry 22 July 1861. He was subsequently captured at Malvern Hill, Virginia, 30 June 1862. After his exchange, he was a major in the 63rd Indiana, then lieutenant colonel and colonel; he was finally a brevet brigadier general 31 January 1865, and mustered out 21 June 1865, Eicher, 511.

were prostrated, although we had retired to what we considered a perfectly safe distance. We were not sleepy that night, and before morning we heard of the arrival at the fort of "Ericsson's Battery [U.S.S. *Monitor*]."[37]

Another perhaps more dramatized version of Mansfield's orders to fire on the Rebels boarding the *Congress* was in the pamphlet describing the panorama done by a commercial company portraying the actions on the 8th and 9th:

> The 20th Indiana Regiment and the 1st and 2nd Volunteers and the 11th Fire Zouaves Regiments of New York, with several other detachments, were lined along the shore, and sharp-shooters from their rifle-pits on the banks picked off officers and men on the decks and in the rigging. Confederate officers cried to General Mansfield to cease firing, and pointed to the white flag of the *Congress*. "The ship may float the white flag," shouted the General in return, "but we don't."[38]

The morning of 8 March at 11 a.m. had begun the drama with the banks of the river lined with spectators, both civilian and military.[39] The Rebel flotilla's commander, Flag Officer Franklin Buchanan, reported the actions of that fateful day first listing his vessels, commanders, and armament:

> Steamer *Virginia*, flagship, 10 guns; steamer *Patrick Henry*, 12 guns, Commander John R. Tucker; steamer *Jamestown*, Lieutenant Commanding J. N. Barney, 2 guns; and gunboats *Teaser*, Lieutenant Commanding W. A. Webb, *Beaufort*, Lieutenant Commanding W. H. Parker, and *Raleigh*, Lieutenant Commanding J. W. Alexander, each 1 gun; total, 27 guns....
>
> The *Virginia* left....Norfolk, accompanied by the *Raleigh* and *Beaufort*, and proceeded to Newport News to engage the enemy's frigates *Cumberland* and *Congress*, gunboats, and shore batteries. When within less than a mile of the *Cumberland*, the *Virginia* commenced the engagement with that ship with her bow gun, and the action soon became general, the *Cumberland*, *Congress*, gunboats, and shore batteries concentrating upon us their heavy fire, which was returned with great spirit and determination. The *Virginia* stood rapidly on toward the *Cumberland*, which ship I had determined to sink with our prow, if possible. In about fifteen minutes after the action commenced we ran into her on starboard bow; the crash below the water was distinctly heard, and she commenced sinking, gallantly fighting her guns as long as they were above water. She went down with her colors flying....
>
> Having sunk the *Cumberland*, I turned our attention to the *Congress*. We were some time in getting our proper position, in consequence of the shoalness of the water and the great difficulty of managing the ship when in or near the mud.... we were subjected twice to the heavy guns of all the batteries in passing up and down the river, but it could not be avoided. We silenced several of the batteries and did much injury on shore. A large transport steamer alongside of the wharf was blown up, one schooner sunk, and another captured and sent to Norfolk. The loss of life on shore we have no means of ascertaining.
>
> While the *Virginia* was thus engaged in getting her position for attacking the *Congress*, the prisoners state it was believed on board that ship that we had hauled off; the men left their guns and gave three cheers. They were soon sadly undeceived, for a few minutes after we opened on her again, she having run on shore in shoal water. The carnage, havoc, and dismay caused by our fire compelled them to haul down their colors and to hoist a white flag at their gaff and half-mast another at the main. The crew instantly took to their boats and landed. Our fire immediately ceased, and a signal was made for the *Beaufort* to come within hail. I then ordered Lieutenant Commanding Parker to take possession of the *Congress*, secure the officers as prisoners, allow the crew to land, and burn the ship....While the *Beaufort* and *Raleigh* were alongside the *Congress*, and the surrender of that vessel had been received from the commander, she having two white flags flying hoisted by her own people, a heavy fire was opened on them from the shore and from the *Congress*, killing some valuable officers and men....During this delay we were still subjected to the heavy fire from the batteries, which was always promptly returned....

---

[37] Israel N. Stiles, "The Monitor and the Merrimac," read 5 April 1885, *Military Essays and Recollections: Papers Read Before the Commandery of the State of Illinois, Military Order of the Loyal Legion of the United States* (Chicago, IL: A.C. McClurg and Company, 1891), 125-129. Stiles obviously made use of statements and other sources in the 20 years since the naval action in addition to his personal observations. His descriptions of the heroic sufferings of the sailors were in keeping with the 19th century style of effusive praise for men wounded and dying in combat.

[38] *A Comprehensive Sketch of the Merrimac and Monitor Naval Battle*, 12. Given the distance Mansfield was from the *Congress*, combined with the smoke and noise, this conversation seems improbable.

[39] The Capital and the Bay: Narratives of Washington and the Chesapeake Bay Region, ca. 1600-1925, "A record of events in Norfolk County, Virginia, from April 19th, 1861, to May 10th, 1862, with a history of the soldiers and sailors of Norfolk County, Norfolk City and Portsmouth, who served in the Confederate States army or navy," 358-361. The Capital and the Bay: Narratives of Washington and the Chesapeake Bay Region, ca. 1600-1925, comprises 139 books selected from the Library of Congress's General Collections and two books from its Rare Book and Special Collections Division. The collection includes first-person narratives, early histories, historical biographies, promotional brochures, and books of photographs that capture in words and pictures a distinctive region as it developed between the onset of European settlement and the first quarter of the twentieth century.

The ships from Old Point opened their fire upon us. The *Minnesota* grounded in the north channel, where, unfortunately, the shoalness of the channel prevented our near approach. We continued, however, to fire upon her until the pilots declared that it was no longer safe to remain in that position, and we accordingly returned by the south channel (the middle ground being necessarily between the *Virginia* and *Minnesota*, and *St. Lawrence* and the *Roanoke* having retreated under the guns of Old Point), and again had an opportunity of opening upon the *Minnesota*, receiving her heavy fire in return, and shortly afterwards upon the *St. Lawrence*, from which vessel we also received several broadsides. It had by this time become dark and we soon after anchored off Sewell's Point....The *Congress*, having been set on fire by our hot shot and incendiary shell, continued to burn, her loaded guns being successively discharged as the flames reached them, until a few minutes past midnight, when her magazine exploded with a tremendous report.[40]

C.S.S. *Virginia* rams U.S.S. *Cumberland* off Newport News 8 March 1862. Cannon fire from Union ships had little effect on the Rebel ironclad whereas the wooden ships suffered immensely and were defenseless. If the Union ironclad, the *Monitor*, had not appeared the next day, 9 March, the *Virginia* would have returned to finish off remaining Union wooden ships. *Harper's Weekly*, 22 March 1862, author's collection.

---

[40] *ORN*, vol. 7, 44-48.

Fanciful depiction of Mansfield witnessing the battle of the *Monitor* and *Merrimack* 9 March 1862. Union field cannon firing on the left in the open and on the right in an earthwork fort at Newport News Point. While it shows the *Congress* still burning, by this time it had blown up and was sunk; the print concatenated the two-day battle. Kurtz and Allison 1889 chromolithograph. Courtesy LOC.

Mansfield on his white horse directing field artillery fire on Rebel gunboats firing on Union vessels during the battle at Hampton Roads, 8 March 1862. Mansfield and his staff were near the earthwork fort depicted at the white mass to the left of the picture. This view is inland from the shore, facing north. With Mansfield in addition to his staff are Colonel William Brown and Adjutant Israel Stiles of the 20th Indiana. To the upper left are tents and houses; stretchers are shown at the center left. Detail of print *Monitor* and *Merrimac* Panorama. Courtesy USMA Library.

BRIGADIER-GENERAL MANSFIELD AND STAFF AT NEWPORT NEWS DURING THE ENGAGEMENT.

Mansfield at Newport News during battle between Rebel warship C.S.S. *Virginia* and the Union ship *Cumberland*. *Harpers Weekly*, 22 August 1862, 181, author's collection.

Detail of cyclorama showing Mansfield directing the action. Courtesy of the Middlesex County Historical Society.

Casualties from the naval battle on 8 March being rescued from the water. Total Union casualties on all ships were about 300, *ORN*, vol. 7, 87. *A Comprehensive Sketch of the Merrimac and Monitor Naval Battle*, 10.

Mansfield's first report about his firing on Rebel vessels near the *Congress* was a telegram to Wool on 8 March: "The *Congress* has surrendered, but aground at Signal Point. I expect to see her in flames soon. We had driven off from her the gunboats. We want ammunition for all our guns at once by land."[41] This request followed four prior telegrams on 8 March notifying Wool of the progress of the *Merrimack* as it approached Union ships. Mansfield continued to send terse telegrams to Wool asking for "powder by the barrel. We want blankets sent up tonight for the crews of the *Cumberland* and the *Congress*....We have no more ammunition and the *Merrimack* and *Yorktown* are off Signal Point. Send us cartridges and shells fort 8 inch columbiads and howitzers by land."[42] The old general clearly had desire to fight the Rebels at sea and on land as he also asked for another light battery "to resist attack by land if they come."

In his official report to Wool he described his actions mentioning that his guns and infantry were firing on the Rebels after the *Congress* ran up a white flag. He justified his actions as doing everything he could to save the Union ships which included firing on Confederate vessels after the *Congress* hoisted the white flag:

Hdqrs., First Brigadier, First Div., Dept. of Virginia.
Newport News, Va., March 10, 1862.

I have the honor to report that in the forenoon of Saturday, the 8th instant, the commanders of the *Congress* and *Cumberland*, at anchor in the stream, notified me that the iron-clad *Merrimac* steamer of the enemy was approaching from Norfolk to attack them, and I immediately telegraphed you to that effect. At about 2 o'clock p.m. she approached very near these vessels slowly, engaged first the *Congress* and passed on to the *Cumberland* and ran into her, and all within a mile of our batteries. I immediately ordered Lieut. Colonel G. Nauman, chief of artillery, to open our batteries of four columbiads and one 42-pounder James gun to fire on her. It was done with alacrity, and kept up continuously with spirit as long as she was in range, and although our shot often struck her, they made no impression on her at all. I also ordered three of our 8-inch siege howitzers from the land batteries hauled by hand and brought to bear on her from the bank of the river and two of Howards light battery rifled guns, but no visible serious damage to her from our guns was done, such was the strength of her mail.

---

[41] *ORN*, vol. 3, 4. Wilbur F. Holloway opened the Norfolk office of the military telegraph at Mansfield's headquarters in May 1862, connecting Newport News, Portsmouth, Suffolk, and Fort Monroe, etc., William R. Plum, *The Military Telegraph During the Civil War in the United States*, vol. 1 (Chicago, IL: Jansen, McClurg & Company, 1882, 146.
[42] *ORN*, vol. 3, 4.

As soon as the *Cumberland* was sunk three steamers, supposed to be the *Yorktown*, *Jamestown*, and a tug, came down the river from Day's Point under full head of steam. Our guns were then turned on them, but they kept at a distance and moved rapidly past, and received but little damage from us.

During the sinking of the *Cumberland* the *Congress* slipped her cable and hoisted sail and ran ashore just above Signal Point, where many of her men escaped to the shore, and was there followed by the *Merrimac*, and after two raking shots she hauled down her flag and hoisted a white flag and ceased action. The enemy then sent two steamers with Confederate flags flying and made fast on either side of her, with a view to haul her off or burn her. As soon as I saw this I ordered Colonel Brown, of the Twentieth Indiana Regiment, then close at hand, to send two rifle companies (A and K) to the beach. The two rifled guns, under Captain Howard, and a rifled Dahlgren howitzer, manned by Master Stuyvesant and 14 sailors of the *Cumberland*, went into action from a raking position on the beach, covered by sand banks and trees, against these steamers.

We here had them at about 800 yards to advantage, and immediately they let go their hold on the *Congress* and moved out of range with much loss. They endeavored to approach her again with a steamer and row-boat, but were beaten off with loss, till finally the *Merrimac*, finding her prize retaken, approached and fired three shots into her and set her on fire. The remaining men escaped from the *Congress* over the bows of the ship to the shore, assisted by our boats, and the wounded were removed by dark.

Thus closed the tragedy of the day. The enemy retired at dark toward the opposite shore, and the *Congress* illuminated the heavens and varied the scene by the firing of her own guns and the flight of her balls through the air till about 2 o'clock in the morning, when her magazine exploded and a column of burning matter appeared high in the air, to be followed by the stillness of death. Through the whole day our troops were under arms, and the officers and men engaged at the batteries and as riflemen on the beach performed their duty well, and the enemy were beaten off wherever we could penetrate them. All was done that it was possible to do under the circumstances to save these ships from the enemy. Some officers and men from the *Cumberland*, as they escaped to the shore, came forward and volunteered their services at our guns and afforded aid. Toward the close of the day the enemy must have experienced considerable loss. There were none killed of my command, and but one man, private of the Seventh New York Volunteers, severely wounded by a shell from the *Merrimac*, resulting in the loss of his leg.

The loss on the part of our Navy must have been great by the bursting of shells and the drowning by the sinking of the *Cumberland*, although our best efforts were made to save them. Our ships were perfectly helpless against the *Merrimac*, as their broadsides produced no material effect on her.[43]

On 8 March Mansfield sent two telegrams to Wool requesting immediate assistance to replenish ammunition and blankets for the wounded from the Union ships destroyed or damaged by the Rebel attack: "The *Congress* has surrendered but aground at Signal Point....To see her in flames ___ so we have driven off from her the small boats. The want of ammunition for all our guns at once by land....We want powder by the barrel. We want blankets sent up tonight for the crews of the *Cumberland* and the *Congress*. The *Merrimack* has it all her own way this side of the Signal Point and will probably burn the *Congress* now aground with white flag flying and our sailors swimming ashore."[44]

Mansfield's questionable decision to fire on Confederate sailors boarding the *Congress* as well as the Rebel ships around the sinking Union ship resulted in a few Rebel casualties but did drive off boarders as reported by the executive officer of the *Congress*:

A sharp fire with muskets and artillery was maintained from our troops ashore upon the tug, having the effect of driving her off. The *Merrimack* again opened on us, although we had a white flag at the peak to show that we were out of action. After having fired several shells into us she left us and engaged the *Minnesota* and the shore batteries. We took the opportunity to man the boats and send the wounded ashore. We then ourselves left, the ship being on fire near the after magazine and in the sick bay. In fact, the ship was on fire from the commencement to the end of the action, three times in the sick bay and wardroom and twice in the main hold, produced by hot shot thrown from the *Merrimack*.[45]

Southern reaction to Mansfield's firing on the Rebels was predictable as written in the *Southern Historical Society Papers* by Virginius Newton, who was a member of the Confederate Navy on board the C.S.S. *Beaufort* and witnessed the action. His history of the Confederate ironclad is instructive in its comments about Mansfield. He wrote about the commander of the U.S.S. *Congress* running "up a white flag at the fore and main masts in token of surrender." The C.S.S. *Beaufort* closed in to the *Congress* and made fast to her port side. Captain Parker of the *Beaufort* told the *Congress's*

---

[43] *ORA*, vol. 9, 4-5.

[44] Courtesy WPL.

[45] *ORN*, ser. 1, vol. 7, 24. The executive officer of the *Virginia*, confirmed that the *Congress* had raised the white flag but then continued to fire, a fact not confirmed by U.S. Navy sources, *ORN*, ser. 1, vol. 7, 42. In the confusion and smoke it may not have been apparent from where the cannon fire emanated.

commanding officer to come aboard and also sent some Confederate sailors to board the *Congress* and help evacuate the wounded. Newton recalled the horrible carnage aboard the *Congress* while the commander of the ship had boarded the *Beaufort* to surrender his sword. He was sent back to his ship to help unload his wounded sailors.

> We quickly descended the sides of the ship and landed on the decks of the *Beaufort*, to find that the enemy on shore, disregarding our errand of mercy and the white flags on the *Congress*, had opened fire upon us with infantry. We were within two hundred yards of the shore, so near that I could plainly see the faces of the men. The fire was most destructive, the first discharge killing Midshipman Hutter and mortally wounding Lieutenant Taylor, acting as volunteers on the *Raleigh*, besides killing some eight or ten of the men of the *Congress* on the decks of the *Beaufort* and wounding many others. The forward cabin of the *Beaufort* was riddled with balls and her smoke-stack was perforated through and through so as to look somewhat like a sieve. Why every man on her decks was not slain or wounded is one of those phenomena which battles alone reveal. Finding no cessation to this fire, but rather an augmentation, the *Beaufort* and *Raleigh* having taken some thirty prisoners and stands of arms, backed off from the *Congress* and opened fire upon the shore, but with little or no damage, as the enemy were protected by breastworks.[46]

The Rebel fleet commander, Buchanan saw that the *Congress* was not burning so he sent a boat to the more protected starboard side of the *Congress*. But again, Mansfield opened fire: "choosing the starboard side of the *Congress* as more protected, Minor, with a boat's crew, started to execute the order, but had hardly gotten within fifty yards of the vessel, when fire was again opened upon him both from the shore and the vessel, wounding him severely and several of his men. Commodore Buchanan observing the failure of the attempt, recalled the boat and gave orders to set the *Congress* on fire with hot shot and shell."[47]

Newton next focused in on Mansfield as "The Responsible Party":

> It is undoubtedly permissible in war to make recapture, but it can never be justifiable when the sacrifice of life which it requires must be borne alike by friend and foe. A moment's reflection on the part of the officer in command at Newport News would have convinced him of this fact, so that the responsibility for the men of the *Congress* killed on the decks of the *Beaufort*, and the further loss of life on this vessel occasioned by our firing upon her with hot shot and shell must be upon him. I find that Brigadier General Joseph K. F. Mansfield, United States Army, then in command at Newport News, is responsible for the execution of this order.[48]

Another Confederate sailor who participated in this incident, Lieutenant Robert D. Minor, was on board the *Virginia*, and volunteered to Buchanan to burn the *Congress*. As he approached the Yankee ship, Mansfield fired and Minor described the action:

> I did not think the Yankees on shore would fire at me on my errand to the *Congress*, but when in about two hundred and fifty yards of her they opened on me from the shore with muskets and artillery; and the way the balls danced around my little boat and crew was lively beyond all measure. Soon two of my men were knocked over, and, while cheering them on I got a clip through the side which keeled me up for a second or two; but I was soon onboard the *Teaser*...seeing what the scoundrels were doing...the *Virginia*...poured gun after gun, hot shot and incendiary shells into her stern and quarter, setting her on fire; but while doing his he [Buchanan] was knocked over by a minnie ball through his left thigh.[49]

Mansfield never apologized for his actions and there was no investigation into his involvement on that day defending the U.S.S. *Congress* in its death throes.

The historian of the 29th Massachusetts Infantry was another observer of the fight on 8 March describing in dramatic detail the events that day, obviously aided by studying accounts written after the fight:

> The Federal naval force present in Hampton Roads and James River, on the 8th of March 1862, consisted of the "Minnesota," a steam-frigate, commanded by Captain [Como Gershom] Van Brunt, carrying fifty guns; the frigate "Congress," a sailing vessel of fifty guns, commanded by Captain [Joseph B.] Smith; the "Roanoke," a steam-frigate of the same class of the "Minnesota,"

---

[46] Newton, 9-10.

[47] Newton, 10-11 .

[48] Newton, 11.

[49] *Southern Historical Society Papers*, ed. by R.A. Brock (Richmond, VA: Published by the Society, 1891), vol. 19, January 1891, John M. Brooke, "The Virginia, or Merrimac," 6-7.

carrying fifty guns, commanded by Captain [John] Marston; the "St. Lawrence," a sailing-frigate, twelve guns; the sloop-of-war "Cumberland," twenty-four guns. Beside these were two armed tugs, the "Whilden" and "Zouave," and a small gunboat called the "Dragon."

The "Minnesota," "St. Lawrence," "Roanoke," and the tugs and gunboat lay off Fortress Monroe, while the "Congress" and the "Cumberland" were anchored in the James; the former nearest the mouth of the river, and the latter about three-fourths of a mile from the shore, and directly opposite the camp at Newport News....

At about two o'clock in the afternoon of the 8th of March, the long roll startled the garrison at Newport News. The men were quickly in line, and in a few minutes the cry of, "The 'Merrimack'! The 'Merrimack'!" resounded throughout the camp. A dense volume of black smoke was now seen at the mouth of the Elizabeth River, and in the course of fifteen minutes the dark form of the foe was distinctly seen. The day was bright and warm; not a breeze rippled the surface of the river. The "Congress" being nearest the enemy, began making preparations for the battle. Her masts and spars soon whitened with her sails, and the four thousand soldiers in Camp Butler stood mute, but with intense anxiety, waiting the opening of the contest. The painful silence that brooded over that strange scene was at last suddenly broken by a sharp, angry "bang!" from one of the larboard ports of the "Cumberland." The shot struck within a few yards of the "Merrimack," sending the water in silvery spray high into the air. The signal for the assault thus given was quickly followed by a whole broadside from the "Congress." For a short time both "Congress" and "Merrimack" were veiled from sight by the clouds of curling smoke. To the surprise and alarm of the garrison, the cloud rose, revealing the "Merrimack" still afloat and apparently unharmed, still approaching. The "Congress" now began a rapid and continuous fire upon the enemy. The "Merrimack," without replying to this fire, passed close alongside the frigate, and when within a few hundred yards of her, across her bows, opened on her with a rifled gun. The shot entered the frigate, raking her from stem to stern, dismounting several of her guns, and killing and wounding many of her crew, among them her brave commander.

The "Congress" was fairly disabled by this shot; her commander was killed, confusion reigned supreme, and now the Stars and Stripes were hauled down, and the white flag of truce run up to masthead. The frigate slipped her cables and floated helplessly away, the "Merrimack" continuing on her course toward the "Cumberland."

It was reserved for the latter vessel to make the bravest fight of that terrible and eventful day. As soon as the "Merrimack" was within easy range, the sloop-of-war opened with a whole broadside; but the shot glanced harmlessly from the mailed sides of the foe; and now, with full head of steam, the enemy made a desperate and angry plunge toward his plucky antagonist, sending his ugly prow crashing through her timbers. The prow struck the "Cumberland" under her starboard fore-channels, making an enormous hole. For a few minutes, both vessels seemed to be sinking. The prow had wedged itself so firmly in the timbers as to render it difficult for the enemy to withdraw and save himself from the same fate he had designed for the ship. After a few trials, he succeeded, however, and backing off, took up a position directly across the bows of the "Cumberland," and opened on her at very close range, the two vessels almost touching each other. In this position the "Cumberland" could only use her bow guns (some three or four); but these were worked with great energy, sending their heavy shot directly at the enemy's ports.

The shell and canister of the "Merrimack" were sweeping the gun-decks of the "Cumberland" with fearful slaughter. At times, nearly every gun was unmanned, but other brave sailors came upon the bloody deck and renewed the unequal contest. The flag of the "Cumberland" was still flying defiantly from her mizzen-mast; the shouts and cries of friend and foe, the angry and excited commands of the officers, could be distinctly heard on shore....she was now rapidly sinking....the sloop-of-war trembled and creaked, her bows plunged into the dark water, her stern mounted high into the air, and down she went, with a roaring, rushing sound of the waves.

The water was now filled with struggling men striking for the shore. The beach was lined with enraged and pitying soldiers. Logs and planks were seized by them and thrown into the water, to aid the swimmers, and others rushing into the water to their arm-pits, seized the half-drowned sailors and brought them to the land. Others of the sailors were rescued by the steam-propeller "Whilden," Captain William Riggins, which put off to the scene of the disaster in the midst of the fire of the "Merrimack," and thus saved the lives of many who would otherwise have found a watery grave. About one hundred of the dead and wounded of the "Cumberland" went down with the ship, and among them the Chaplain, the Rev. J. Lenhart.

The land-battery in Camp Butler, which was chiefly manned by members of the Twenty-ninth, and which mounted some five guns, — among them two 42-pounder James rifles,— was very active during the entire contest between the "Merrimack" and "Cumberland." When the "Cumberland" sunk, the Confederate ram was a fair target for our men, but their shots were wholly powerless to do her harm. The "Merrimack" replied to several of our shots, one of her shells striking the parapet, and throwing the earth in clouds of dust over the gunners.

The river now presented a scene of great interest. The "Jamestown" and "Patrick Henry," two Confederate steamers, had arrived, and taking up a position about two miles from our camp, began shelling it with great vigor. One of these missiles passed through a barrack of the First New York, while others cut off the tops of the pines about the camp. These two steamers divided their attentions about equally between the camp and the floating "Congress," firing at the latter with murderous effect, and in shameful and savage violation of the rules of civilized warfare, the "Congress" displaying all the while her flag of truce.

An attempt was now made to capture our frigate, and tow her off, a prize of war. The steam-tug "Zouave" (Union) immediately ran down to her and towed her to our shore, fairly beaching her, before the Confederate steamers "Beaufort" and

"Raleigh" arrived. Upon reaching the "Congress," these steamers immediately hauled alongside. General Mansfield, observing this movement, ordered Captain Howard, with a section of his light battery, and Colonel Brown, with two companies of the Twentieth Indiana Regiment, to open fire upon these steamers. The order was promptly obeyed, and in a few moments our shot were striking the Confederate steamers, and whistling about the ears of their men, as they were attempting to clamber up the sides and into the ports of our ship, causing them to withdraw, and killing and wounding several of their number. Among the wounded were Buchanan, the commander of the "Merrimack," who received a severe gunshot wound in the thigh, and Lieutenant Minot of the "Beaufort."...

By this time the day was far spent, the sun having already set; and when everybody on shore had begun to consider the sad day's work ended, the huge monster, the "Merrimack," was again observed approaching Camp Butler. This time she took the inner channel, and as she came along, her immense chimney towering up among the branches of the trees that overhung the river bank, belching forth volumes of smoke and sparks, her appearance was simply appalling. Arriving at a point where the channel winds in nearest to the shore, the camp was fairly within range of her bow gun. A sudden burst of light, a dismal, deafening roar, and the crashing of boards and timbers were heard almost simultaneously. The large shot passed entirely through the post hospital and the headquarters' building of General Mansfield, tearing down the chimney of the latter, and nearly burying that venerable officer in the ruins. He was, fortunately, but little hurt, and soon emerged from the house white with plaster. This ended the hostilities of the 8th of March. The "Merrimack" now withdrew, and darkness soon settled down upon both land and water....

At twelve o'clock, the magazines blew up with a terrific noise. This event had been anticipated by the garrison, and the shores and adjacent camps were crowded with awe-struck gazers. The whole upper works of the frigate had, hours before, been reduced to ashes by the devouring flames; the masts and spars, blackened and charred, had fallen into and across the burning hull; these were sent high into the air with other *debris,* and as blast succeeded blast, were suddenly arrested in their descent and again sent heavenward. The spectacle thus presented was awfully grand; a column of fire and sulphurous smoke, fifty feet in diameter at its base and not less than two hundred feet high, dividing in its centre into thousands of smaller jets, and falling in myriads of bunches and grains of fire, like the sprays of a gigantic fountain, lighted up the camp and bay for miles....

During much of the time that the two iron-clads were actively engaged [next day on the 9th], they were scarcely visible from the shore, being enveloped in clouds of smoke; but occasionally the garrison were disagreeably reminded of what was going on by a huge shot from one or the other of the vessels missing its mark and reaching the land. Several of these huge missiles went bounding over the long plain, casting the dust high into the air, and plowing up the earth in deep, irregular furrows....

The excitement in Camp Butler was not to end just here. The men had hardly swallowed their dinner, before a number of horsemen came riding into camp, their horses flecked with foam and themselves covered with dust. They had come from the outposts to inform General Mansfield that the enemy in large numbers were advancing, and that an attack was imminent....Things looked very much like a fight at that moment; the entire garrison was under arms, and General Mansfield, mounted, was moving briskly about the camp, speaking cheering words to the troops. This was his speech to the Twenty ninth: "My men, Magruder is up the river with ten thousand troops. I have in camp six thousand men with muskets and a million rounds of cartridges; and so long as there is left me a man, a musket, or a cartridge, I'll keep that flag flying!" pointing to the post flag flying near his quarters....

The repose and quiet which had reigned so constantly during the long winter of 1861-62, in Camp Butler, were ended by the tragic occurrences of these two days. As long as the regiment thereafter continued to remain at Newport News, scarcely a day passed without its exciting incident; and not infrequently the slumbers of the men at night were rudely broken by the ominous sound of the long roll and the sudden screech of a shell thrown from the "Teaser," an insolent little nondescript of the enemy's fleet, which sailed down the river occasionally, and amused herself by firing into our camp....[50]

Mansfield wrote about his house being hit by a Rebel shell in a letter from Newport News to Samuel dated 16 March 1862: He had just taken his seat "when the rifled shell smashed through and passed 4 feet behind me as I sat in my chair....It knocked a wardrobe all to pieces and threw the pieces against my back. On Sunday the fight was beautiful between the *Erickson* (Monitor) and the *Merrimack. The Monitor* only got here at 10 o'clock in the night of Saturday and on Sunday the *Merrimack* advanced fearlessly on the *Minnesota* then aground and expected to make an easy prey of her. But the *Monitor* happened to be laying very quietly near the *Minnesota* and advanced on the *Merrimac* and handled her beautifully and coolly."[51]

---

[50] Osborne, 111-126.
[51] Courtesy of the Middlesex County Historical Society.

Events of this nature, and the daring exploits of Captain Drake DeKay, a very gallant young officer of General Mansfield's staff, furnished abundant material for camp talk, and kept up a constant excitement. DeKay formed a crew from among the members of companies A and B of the Twenty-ninth Regiment, manned one of the large barges of the *Cumberland*, saved from the battle, and made nightly excursions up the river, capturing on one occasion a schooner, and setting her on fire; and at another time landed on the opposite shore, and reconnoitered the enemy's position."[52]

Union casualties on 8 March totaled 300 sailors killed and wounded with only two Confederates killed and 12 wounded. The U.S.S. *Monitor* arrived before daylight the next day and the battle of the ironclads began and ended with a draw as neither ship had ammunition which could pierce the other's armor. Neither ship fought the other again nor other ships. The C.S.S. *Virginia* was destroyed by its crew after Confederate Major General Benjamin Huger abandoned Norfolk 12 May 1862 as noted below. The ship's draft was too great so she could not be taken up the James River to Richmond. The U.S.S. *Monitor* sunk in heavy weather as she was being towed to Beaufort, North Carolina, to become part of the Union blockade. She went down on 31 December 1862 along with 16 of her crew.

Some of Mansfield's artillery which fired at the Rebel ships included the 4th U.S. Light Artillery. He was well acquainted with these artillerists from its duty in the Mexican-American War with Taylor's Army. Battery L of the 4th was mounted as a light battery at Fort Monroe, in July 1861, with six 12-pdr. Napoleons, and remained as such throughout the Civil War. Its first engagement was 8 March 1862, at Newport News, against the *Merrimac*. It was then sent to Suffolk in July 1862 to form part of Mansfield's force, and remained there until it joined the Army of the James, Ferry's Brigade, in September 1862.[53]

Battery L of the 4th U.S. Artillery firing at the pilot house of the Rebel *Merrimac* from Newport News Point at Camp Butler. Wounded sailors are shown struggling ashore. *Sketch of the Merrimac and Monitor Naval Battle*, 13.

A few days after the *Monitor* and *Merrimac* battle, McClellan, who did not get along well with Wool, asked Stanton on 14 March to create a new division from troops around Fort Monroe with Mansfield in command. This division would

---

[52] Osborne, 126-128.
[53] Alexander B. Dyer, "The Fourth Regiment of Artillery," *The Army of the United States, Historical Sketches of Staff and Line with Portraits of Generals-in-Chief*, ed. by Theophilus F. Rodenbough and William L. Haskin (New York, NY: Maynard, Merrill, & Co., 1896), 355-356, 370.

be annexed to the I Corps "as soon as McDowell is confirmed as major-general."[54] Then on 16 March, he again asked Stanton to have Mansfield take command at Fort Monroe and its dependencies until McClellan's Army of the Potomac arrived there. McClellan wanted to merge the Department of Virginia with the Department of the Potomac and have its present commander, Wool, "assigned to some other command."[55] For the third time, McClellan on 19 March asked Stanton to have Mansfield given command of troops around Fort Monroe formed into a division under McClellan's command. McClellan was doing all he could to squeeze Wool out of the picture to have a less senior general in command of Fort Monroe and its troops and one who was subordinate to Little Mac.[56] And McClellan knew that the veteran Mansfield would be a valuable commander. The feud between Wool and McClellan died down after Wool agreed to work with his junior, McClellan, and allow Mansfield to organize a division out of the troops around Fort Monroe: "It would afford me great pleasure to aid and assist General McClellan in organizing any force which our President may think proper to place under his [McClellan's] command and any force you may deem proper to place under the command of Brigadier-General Mansfield to constitute a part of General McClellan's forces."[57] McClellan was now satisfied that Wool would be forced to work with him without squabbling over rank and on 31 March, he notified Edwin Vose Sumner he would replace Louis Blenker's division which was being sent to General John C. Fremont by a division under Mansfield.[58] Mansfield was praised for helping Brigadier General Erasmus D. Keyes, IV Corps commander, for providing him with forage and provisions from Newport News when Keyes had difficulties obtaining them from Ship Point.[59] The practical Mansfield did not stand on ceremony when he saw a need he could fulfill. As the dust settled between McClellan and Wool due to Stanton's intervention, the Department of the Army finally notified the two major generals on 3 April that clarified the jurisdictions of the two: "General Wool will continue in command of Fort Monroe and the troops heretofore assigned to the Department of Virginia, and General McClellan will command the troops constituting the Army of the Potomac."[60] So by early April, Mansfield realized that his hopes to command a division in active operations against the Rebels vanished. His dislike for Wool and McClellan must have intensified and he likely perceived that the administration in Washington was not favorably disposed to him.[61]

Wool and Mansfield were Old Army veterans and Mansfield liked serving under Wool when he first transferred to Fort Monroe. Seemingly Wool and Mansfield had some disagreements starting in early 1862. McClellan shared Mansfield's dislike as noted in a letter from Mansfield to his wife on 7 April 1862: "there is not that admiration of him [McClellan] here that there was nor anywhere else. I have not heard from him. But General Wool is not a man of large views and does not see far ahead. Yet he is as cunning as a fox. He told the reporter for the *Herald* at Fort Monroe if he published anything in my favor he would send him off. He is small potatoes....I send you an article that Henry can give to John Douglas after copying it and let John have it published as his <u>own</u>. Or John Douglas can do it, but it must be kept a secret...I find it necessary to take care of myself."[62]

Mansfield again wrote to Louisa about Wool and McClellan this time on 22 April 62: "I have seen many of the officers [with McClellan], being old acquaintances of mine, all of whom have large commands although I rank them. This was accomplished by Little Mac the 2nd Napoleon. My time has not yet come....The more I see of the Old General

---

[54] *ORA*, vol. 5, 755. In Lincoln's private letter to McClellan 1 November 1861, Lincoln placed McClellan in command of the whole Army except "For the present, let General Wool's command be excepted," Lincoln, *Collected Works*, vol. 5, 9-10.

[55] *ORA*, vol. 11, pt. 3, 8-9.

[56] *ORA*, vol. 11, pt. 3, 18.

[57] *ORA*, vol. 11, pt. 3, 25, 27-28.

[58] *ORA*, vol. 11, pt. 3, 53.

[59] *ORA*, vol. 11, pt. 3, 83-84.

[60] *ORA*, vol. 11, pt. 3 65.

[61] Wool's return shows that as of 31 March 1862, Mansfield at Camp Butler had seven regiments: 20th Indiana, 5th Maryland, 29th Massachusetts, 1st, 2nd, 7th, 11th New York, and the 4th U.S. Artillery, Battery L, *ORA*, vol. 11, pt. 3, 54. As of 30 June 1862, Mansfield had 46 companies with 2,678 officers and men present for duty; Mansfield had taken command of Suffolk as a separate command 14 June 1862. The 13th and 25th New York State Militia had arrived from New York in early June, and the 3rd and 4th New York had arrived from Baltimore also in early June. Mansfield reported five officers on his staff along with a detachment of the 11th Pennsylvania cavalry, two companies 130 men; and the 4th U.S. Artillery, Battery L, one company with 119 men. Brigadier General Weber had four officers on his staff, with the following units: 13th New York State Militia, 10 companies, 618 men; 25th New York State Militia, 10 companies, 482 men; 3rd New York, 10 companies, 665 men; 4th New York, 10 companies, 581 men; and a detachment of the 11th Pennsylvania cavalry, three companies, and 217 troopers, Leon Walter Tenney, "Seven Days in 1862: Numbers in Union and Confederate Armies Before Richmond, master's thesis, George Mason University, 1992, 271.

[62] Courtesy of the Middlesex County Historical Society. The article Mansfield mentioned has not been found but since he did not want his name connected with it, it probably had some negative comments about Wool, McClellan, or the course of the war. John Douglas was a friend and neighbor from Middletown, Connecticut, brother to William Douglas.

Wool my commander the less I like him. He is cunning close and mean." As an aside, he notes that he has six good regiments under his command.[63]

Mansfield still very much wanted to have active service in the field in a combat command. In his 26 May 1862 letter to Samuel he told his son that he had asked Washington to go to Harper's Ferry to command troops in the field. Two days later, the general told his wife that he had telegraphed the Secretary of War expressing that desire, this in addition to writing him and Connecticut Republican Senator Lafayette Sabine Foster. Indeed, on the 27th, he sent a telegram to Stanton from Newport News: "I wish to be ordered to the Army at Harpers Ferry where I can be of service to my country and not kept here doing nothing of importance." Mansfield did ask Wool's permission before sending the missive.[64]

His letter to Secretary of War Stanton 27 May 1862 from Newport News: "I have to request you will order me to the neighborhood of Harpers Ferry to a command where I can be of service to my country. I am of no use here. I have also two regiments at this port of no use here and which want to be of good service there, to wit, the 1st New York and the 7th N.Y., the last mostly foreigners but well officered. You will excuse my writing this private letter as I have just telegraphed General Wool to telegraph you in substance the same as above and he has given me no answer and I hasten to send this by mail."[65]

The War Department responded quickly, but negatively on the 28th: "The Secretary of War directs me to acknowledge the receipt of your letter of the 27th instant and your telegram of the same date, and to state in reply that the President deems it inexpedient to reduce the force of General Wool's command, except on the recommendation of General Wool himself, in the present posture of affairs. Your patriotic and soldierly ardor to engage the enemy do you great honor, which the Secretary and the President both appreciate."[66]

No major combat occurred but Mansfield kept his troops busy scouting and passing on reports about enemy activity, but the information he gleaned was not always accurate as in shown by a telegram he sent to General Henry Halleck 17 August 1862 from Suffolk: "Stonewall Jackson has 125,000 men at least. He is fortifying between Louisa Court House & Gordonsville. They knew a week ago the movements of McClellan's movements on the Peninsula. It is their intention to whip Pope and move on to Washington. I have from good authority."[67] And he was also concerned with maintaining good order and discipline while in command judging from his telegram to General Dix 27 June 1862: "From New Port News: parties of negroes & soldiers cross to the opposite shore & demand keys & rob families of bacon, chickens, & even furniture. This should be stopped & no boat allowed to cross over except by order."[68]

General Mansfield also was keen on ensuring that his son, Samuel, would enter the Engineer Corps and also be on his father's staff. Because Samuel did not graduate in the top five, he would not automatically be assigned to the prestigious Engineers. Mansfield wrote to his son on 13 May 1862 urging him to get into the engineers; he restated this in every letter to him and mentioned as an aside that he thought the war would end when Richmond and Corinth were taken. The general solicited help from high-level governmental officials and likely everyone else he knew to ensure that his son would be his aide and in the Engineers. In a letter to Stanton from Suffolk on 16 June 1862, he asked help telling him that Samuel just graduated from West Point sixth in his class in general merit and second in engineering and wants him to enter the Corps of Engineers. "Having done this I wish you would have him ordered to join my staff as I have but one aide and want another and an engineer officer very much and which he will supply. I rely on you to effect his for me and I trust you will not disappoint me. My son has excellent physical ability is active and well qualified to serve his country." The general also told Samuel on 17 June 1862 that he had written to General Totten, the secretary of war, and the president to get Samuel into the engineers.[69]

Mansfield finally succeeded in having Samuel placed in the Engineer Corps. He wrote to his wife on 18 July 1862 from Suffolk: "Samuel is here, he arrived yesterday [17 July] at noon and ordered to report to me. I have made him my

[63] Courtesy of the Middlesex County Historical Society.

[64] Courtesy of the Middlesex County Historical Society.

[65] Courtesy of the Middlesex County Historical Society.

[66] Courtesy of the Middlesex County Historical Society.

[67] Telegram courtesy of USMA West Point Library.

[68] Telegram courtesy of USMA West Point Library.

[69] Courtesy of the Middlesex County Historical Society. Mansfield wrote a letter to Stanton from Newport News 20 May 62 telling him that all the troops McClellan and Halleck had would be able to crush rebels at Richmond and Corinth. Mansfield mentioned to his wife that Samuel has been ill although there is nothing of record which shows that he suffered from chronic illness.

chief engineer and aide, also being aide gives him 20 dollars more per month...." Three days later he added news about their son:

> "Samuel has been with me for several days. He was quite unwell yesterday but is better today and has taken a pill and eaten his breakfast. He does not seem to be as rugged as I would wish. I enclose the order making him a member of my staff....I am waiting very quietly the course of events. McClellan has run aground—Pope who has command of the Army of Virginia was a Second Lieutenant, and my aide at the storming of Monterey. A man of no sound moral principles and kept for week at Monterey under arrest by General Taylor for bad conduct disgraceful to the service. This is not for you to make public as he is now connected with the Alsops, etc., and would not look well coming from us.
>
> This war is extremely irksome to me as I now am. I do not wish to go home on a leave till I can go for good. The administration have no claim on me, but my country has and I mean to serve till no fault can be found at my leaving, and till I see the means of a support—taxes will soon be enormous. Here am I over 58 years of age, been at work all my life, and now cannot find repose."[70]

There is an interesting but isolated note the General wrote to his aide, DeKay, on 8 Aug 1862, which recommends he resign as Mansfield is dissatisfied with his staff. There is no record of problems with DeKay or others, although as seen, DeKay was something of a gadabout and may not have been as steady as the old General would have liked. Perhaps also he was making sure that his son would hold a more important role on his staff. The general apparently had a backup plan for Samuel—a commission from the governor of Connecticut to put his son in command of a Connecticut regiment. Mansfield received a military telegraph on 15 August 1862 from Hartford, Connecticut, from the governor, William A Buckingham: "I will give your son a lieutenant colonel and possibly a command advise me if he will accept and have him come on at once as the men are assembling." The General reacted quickly as the next day, 16 August 1862, he wrote to Stanton: "Will you authorize my aide Lieutenant Samuel M. Mansfield to take a colonel or Lieutenant Colonel commission from the State of Connecticut in one of the new regiments of volunteers?"[71] It took some months however before Samuel became the colonel of the 24th Connecticut Infantry effective 18 November 1862.

Mansfield had another son, Henry Livingston, who entered the Naval Academy but resigned before graduation. President Lincoln wrote to Gideon Welles on 21 August 1862 with a list of candidates for the Naval Academy "from the Sons of officers or soldiers who distinguished themselves in the service of the United States" with the first on the list being H. Livingston Mansfield.[72] Legislation had been passed on 14 July 1862 which accorded sons of distinguished officers in the U.S. Army for appointment to the military service academies at West Point and Annapolis.

Mansfield at Norfolk
The Capture of Norfolk, Virginia, 8-11 May 1862

The Norfolk Navy Yard commander, veteran Captain Charles Stewart McCauley, ordered the burning of the shipyard and the evacuation of its personnel to Fort Monroe 20 April 1861 after Virginia joined the Confederacy. The Rebels captured vast quantities of cannon and other arms in addition to capturing valuable parts of the shipyard. Importantly, they captured the remains of the U.S.S. *Merrimac* which they rebuilt into an ironclad renamed the C.S.S. *Virginia*. As noted above, during the Battle of Hampton Roads 8-9 March, the U.S.S. *Monitor* fought the *Virginia* to a draw. Subsequently, the *Virginia* did not meet again in battle since the *Monitor* was ordered by Lincoln on 10 March not to fight unless absolutely necessary.[73] Norfolk was still in the hands of the Rebels as McClellan was pushing up the Peninsula toward Richmond and no attempt had been made to capture it. Union forces at Fort Monroe were not aware that it was not heavily defended.

On 6 May, President Abraham Lincoln visited Fort Monroe across Hampton Roads from Norfolk. Recognizing the value of Norfolk, he decided on a plan to capture the city and thus eliminate the base for the C.S.S. *Virginia*. On May 8, Union ships, including the U.S.S. *Monitor*, and batteries on Fort Wool opened fire on the Confederate batteries on Sewell's Point. Only the approach of the C.S.S. *Virginia* drove the Union ships back to the protection of Fort Monroe. At

---

[70] Courtesy of the Middlesex County Historical Society.

[71] Courtesy of the Middlesex County Historical Society.

[72] Abraham Lincoln, *The Collected Works of Abraham Lincoln*, ed. By Roy P. Basler, vol. 5 (New Brunswick, NJ: Rutgers University Press, 1953), 387-388.

[73] *ORN*, vol. 7, 83, 85.

this point, Lincoln directed the invasion to be on Willoughby Spit, away from the Confederate batteries, postponed to the next day. On the morning of 10 May, Wool landed 6,000 Union soldiers on Willoughby Spit. Within hours, the Union troops arrived at Norfolk. Mayor William Lamb surrendered the city without firing a shot. For the remainder of the war, the city was held under martial law.

As accounts above pertaining to the Battle of the Ironclads demonstrate, the best are those of witnesses written at the time. The most complete first-person report was written by Secretary of the Treasury Salmon P. Chase to his daughter Nettie. He, along with President Lincoln and Secretary Chase, were involved in the activities surrounding the recapture of Norfolk from the Rebels and supplied many details to his daughter:

Revenue Steamer *Miami*, off Fortress Monroe, 7 May 1862

My Darling Nettie: I write to you from the cabin of the steamer *Miami*, just outside of the steam transports loaded with troops, embarked for a proposed attack on Norfolk.

We came here night before last, having left Washington on Monday evening. Our party consisted of the President, Secretary Stanton, and General Vielé, who had just returned from Port Royal, where he had commanded a brigade charged with the most important duties in the reduction of Fort Pulaski. Our staunch little steamer bore us rapidly and pleasantly down the river until we were some ten or fifteen miles below Alexandria, when the night, which had come on with a drizzling rain, became so thick and dark that the pilot found himself unable to discern the right course. We were, therefore, obliged to cast anchor and wait for a clearer sky.

By 3 o'clock of Tuesday morning, we were again on our way. We passed Aquia about day, and found ourselves about noon tossing on the Chesapeake. It would have amused you to see us take our luncheon. The President gave it up almost as soon as he began, and, declaring himself too uncomfortable to eat, stretched himself at length on the locker. The rest of us persisted; but the plates slipped this way and that, the glasses tumbled over and slid and rolled about, and the whole table scorned as topsy-turvy as if some spiritualist was operating upon it. But we got through, and then the Secretary of War followed the example of the President, and General Vielé and I went on deck and chatted.

Between 8 and 9 o'clock we reached our destination. Mr. Stanton at once sent a message to General Wool, notifying our arrival, and, after a while the General and a number of his staff came on board. It was near 10 o'clock; but after a short conference it was determined that the President, Mr. S.[tanton], General W.[ool], and myself, with General V.[ielé], should visit Commodore [John R.] Goldsborough [on the *Minnesota*], and talk with him about the condition of things and the things to be done....

The next morning—yesterday, Wednesday—we of the *Miami* were up pretty early, for it isn't easy, somehow, to sleep on shipboard. We were to breakfast at 9 o'clock with General Wool, and Mr. Stanton....We sailed round the *Monitor* and *Stevens*, and then back to the wharf; but I must omit in this letter the breakfast, the visit to the *Monitor* and *Stevens*; to the Rip Raps, Commodore G.[oldsborough]'s coming, and discussion, the appearance of the *Merrimac* and disappearance, the review, the visit to ruined Hampton, the determination to direct Commodore Goldsborough to send the *Galena* and two gunboats up the river; how it was determined to attempt the reduction of the batteries at Sewell's Point next morning; how we went to the Rip Raps; how the fleet moved to the attack; how the great guns of the Rip Raps joined in the fray, throwing shot and shell more than three miles; how the *Merrimac* came down and out; how the *Monitor* moved up and quietly waited for her; how the big wooden ships got out of the way, that the *Minnesota* and *Vanderbilt* might have fair sweep at her and run her down; how she wouldn't come where they could; how she finally retreated to where the *Monitor* alone could follow her—all this, and much more, I must leave untold this evening; for, since I wrote the first half and more of this letter, a night is past and the sun of the 8th of May has risen splendidly over Fortress Monroe.

Headquarters Department of Virginia, Fortress Monroe, Va., May 8, 1862

....I will now give you a little better idea of what took place yesterday.

Yesterday morning we came ashore early. Commodore G. came at the same time, on a summons from the President, and it was then that the attack on Sewell's Point Batteries was determined on. After the orders had been given, the President, Mr. Stanton, and myself, went over to the Rip Raps in a tug to observe its execution. It was not a great while before the great ships were in motion. The *Seminole* took the lead, the *San Jacinto* and the *Dakota*, and, finally, the *Susquehanna* followed, whose captain, Lardner, was the commanding officer of the vessels engaged. With these ships were the *Monitor* and little gunboat *Stevens*, which Commodore Stevens presented to the Treasury Department, and which I christened "Stevens," in honor of him.

By and by, the *Seminole* reached her position, and a belch of smoke, followed in a few seconds by a report like distant thunder, announced the beginning of the cannonade. Then came the guns from the Rip Raps where we were, and soon the *Monitor* and the *Stevens* joined. In a little while, the small battery at the extreme point was silenced, and the cannonade was directed on a battery inside the point, a half mile or a mile nearer Norfolk. While this was going on a smoke curled up over the woods on Sewell's Point, five or six miles from its termination, and each man, almost, said to the other, "There comes the *Merrimac*;" and, sure enough, it was the *Merrimac*. But, before she made her appearance, we had left the Rip Raps, and had reached the landing on our way to head-quarters....

This was the end of the battle. Its results were, on our side, nobody and nothing hurt, with the certainty that the battery at the extreme point was useless to the rebels, and the battery on the inside much less strong and much less strongly manned than had been supposed. The results on the rebel side we can't tell, but only know that their barracks were burnt by our shells. Another certainty is that the rebel monster don't want to fight, and won't fight if she can help it, except with more advantage than she is likely to have. Enough for one day.

Steamer Baltimore, May 11, 1862

I believe I closed my letter to you with an account of the bombardment. That was thought to have shown the inability of an attempt to land at Sewell's Point while the *Merrimac* lay watching it; it at once became a question, what should now be done? Three plans only seemed feasible: to send all the troops that could be spared around to Burnside, and let him come on Norfolk from behind—that is, from the south; to send them up James River to aid McClellan; or to seek another landing place out of reach of the *Merrimac*. I offered to take the *Miami*, if a tug of less draught, and capable, therefore, of getting nearer shore, could accompany me, and make an examination, in company with an officer, of the coast east of the Point. Colonel [Thomas Jefferson] Cram offered to go, and General Wool said he would accompany us. We started accordingly, and being arrived...sent a boat's crew on shore to find the depths of water. We had already approached within some five hundred yards in the *Miami*, and the tug had approached within perhaps one hundred, of the shore. The boats went very near the shore, and then pulled off, somewhat to my surprise. But when they returned to the boat, the mystery was explained. They had seen an enemy's picket, and a soldier standing up and beckoning to his companions to close, and they had inferred the existence of an ambush, and had pulled off to avoid being fired upon. When the officer of the boat and Colonel Cram came on board, they could still see the picket on horseback, and pointed his position out to me; but I, being near-sighted, could not see. It was plain enough that there was no use in landing men to be fired upon and overcome by a superior force, and so the order was given to get under way to return to Fortress Monroe. We had indeed, accomplished our main purpose, having found the water sufficiently deep to admit of landing without any serious difficulty.... [Colored] women were the soldiers who had alarmed our folks....

Next morning (yesterday [10 May]) I was up early, and we got off as soon as possible. As soon as we reached the place, I took the tug which brought us down, and went up the shore to where the President's boat had attempted to land the evening before. I found the distance to be only three-quarters of a mile, and returned to the *Miami*, where I had left the General. He had gone ashore, and I at once followed. On shore I found General Vielé, with an orderly behind. He asked if I would like a horse, and I said yes. He thereupon directed his orderly to dismount, and I mounted. I then proposed to ride up to where the pickets had been seen the night before. He complied. We found a shed where the pickets had stayed, and fresh horse tracks in many places, showing that the enemy had only withdrawn a few hours. Meantime, Mr. Stanton had come down, and on my return to General Wool, asked me to go with the expedition, and I finally determined to do so.

Accordingly, I asked General W. for a squad of dragoons and for permission to ride on with General Vielé ahead of him. He granted both requests. After going about five miles, General V. and myself came up with the rear of the advance (which had preceded us three or four hours), and soon heard firing of artillery in front. We soon heard that the bridge which we expected to cross was burnt, that the enemy's artillery was posted on the other side, and that Generals Mansfield and Weber were returning.

About one-half or three-quarters of a mile from the burning bridge, we met them, and of course turned back. Returning, we met General Wool, who determined to leave a guard on that route and take another to Norfolk.

There was now a good deal of confusion, to remedy which and provide for contingencies General Wool sent General M.[ansfield] to Newport News to bring forward his brigade, and brigaded the troops with him, assigning General Vielé to the command of one and General Weber to the command of the other. The cavalry and Major [Charles C.] Dodge were in advance, General Wool and staff next, then a body of sharpshooting skirmishers, then the main body of Vielé's brigade, and then Weber's. We stopped everybody from whom we could obtain information, and it was not long before we were informed that the entrenched camp, where we expected the rebels would fight, if anywhere, had just been evacuated, and that the barracks were fired. This pleasant intelligence was soon confirmed by the arrival of one of Dodge's dragoons, who told us that the cavalry were already within it.

We kept on, and were soon within the work—a very strong one, defended by many heavy guns, of which twenty-one still remained in position. The troops, as they entered, gave cheer after cheer, and were immediately formed into line for the farther march, now only two miles to Norfolk. General Wool now invited General Vielé, General Weber, and Major Dodge to ride with us in front, and so we proceeded until we met a deputation of the city authorities, who surrendered the city in form. General Wool and myself entered one carriage with two of the deputation, and General Vielé another, with others, and so we drove into town and to the City Hall, where the General completed his arrangements for taking possession of the city. These completed, and General Vielé being left in charge as military governor, General Wool and myself set out on our return to Ocean View, our landing-place, in the carriage which had brought us to the City Hall; which carriage, by the way, was that used by the rebel General [Benjamin] Huger, and he had, perhaps, been riding in it that very morning.

It was sundown when we left Norfolk—about ten when we reached Ocean View—and near twelve when we reached Fortress Monroe. The President had been greatly alarmed for our safety by the report of General M.[ansfield], as he went by to Newport News; and you can imagine his delight when we told him Norfolk was ours. He fairly hugged General Wool.

For my part, I was very tired, and glad to get to bed.

This morning, as the President had determined to leave for Washington at seven, I rose at six, and just before seven came into the parlor, where Commodore Goldsborough astonished and gratified us that the rebels had set fire to the *Merrimac*, and had blown her up. It was determined that, before leaving, we would go up in the *Baltimore*, which was to convey us to Washington, to the point where the suicide had been performed, and above the obstructions in the channel, if possible, so as to be sure of the access to Norfolk by water, which had been defended by the exploded ship. This was done; but the voyage was longer than we anticipated, taking us up the wharves of Norfolk, where, in the Elizabeth River, were already lying the *Monitor*, the *Stevens*, the *Susquehanna*, and one or two other vessels. General Wool and Commodore Goldsborough had come up with us on the *Baltimore*; and, as soon as they were transferred to the *Susquehanna*, our prow was turned down stream, and touching for a moment at the Fortress, we kept on our way toward Washington, where we hope to be at breakfast to-morrow.

So has ended a brilliant week's campaign of the President; for I think it quite certain that if he had not come down, Norfolk would still have been in possession of the enemy, and the *Merrimac* as grim and defiant, and as much a terror as ever. The whole coast is now virtually ours. There is no port which the *Monitor* and *Stevens* cannot enter and take.[74]

---

[74] Robert B. Warden, *An Account of the Private Life and Public Services of Salmon Portland Chase* (Cincinnati, OH: Wilstach, Baldwin & Co., 1874), 426-432. Brigadier General Egbert Ludovicus Vielé was born in Waterford, New York, in 1825 and graduated from West Point in 1847. He served in the Mexican-American War but resigned in 1853 to become a civil engineer. He was instrumental in designing Central Park in New York. He was a captain in the 7th New York and appointed a brigadier general in 1861. He commanded Union forces during the siege of Fort Pulaski. He resigned in 1863 to pursue his engineering career.

Salmon Portland Chase, Secretary of the Treasury, who participated in the capture of Norfolk and wrote a detailed account. Courtesy LOC.

Secretary of War Edwin Stanton, who accompanied Lincoln and Chase on the Norfolk expedition. Courtesy LOC.

Brigadier General Egbert Ludovicus Vielé. Courtesy LOC.

Lincoln was anxious for the Norfolk expedition to succeed as noted by Vielé when he and Mansfield along with Colonel [Joseph B.] Carr were summoned to Fort Monroe on 10 May. The President asked Mansfield why he was at the fort and not on the other side of the bay aiding the attack. Mansfield replied that "'I am ordered to the fort by General Wool.'" Then as Vielé wrote "'President Lincoln with vehement action threw his tall hat on the floor, and, uttering strongly his disapproval and disappointment, he said finally, 'Send me someone who can write'" and Lincoln dictated an order to Wool that troops at Camp Hamilton be ordered to Norfolk and that troops there be pushed forward to prevent the Rebels from burning the navy yard and ships at Portsmouth.[75] Lincoln wanted forceful, decisive, and fast action; Wool, he perceived, was not providing that.

Mansfield's aide, De Kay, was mentioned by the correspondent of the *New York Times* as he participated in a humorous but brave engagement with the enemy:

One of the neatest little exploits of the campaign was performed by Captain Drake De Kay, of General Mansfield's Staff, while awaiting the General's arrival at a house called Moore's Ranche, a kind of Summer hotel kept by a man named Moore, at Ocean View, the place of debarkation. All the white men, and most of the women of this vicinity had fled -- it was said by those they had left behind, to the woods, to prevent being forced into the rebel service. Captain De Kay, while supper was being prepared, mounted his horse and determined to explore the country, followed only by his negro servant. As he was passing a swamp toward evening, he came suddenly upon seven of the secession troops, who were lurking by the roadside, and were armed with double-barreled guns. The Captain turned and shouted to his (imaginary) company to prepare to charge -- and then riding forward rapidly, revolver in hand, told the men they were his prisoners, as his cavalry would soon be upon them, ordered them to discharge their pieces and deliver them to him, which they did without delay. He then informed them that his only "company" was his negro servant, and directed them to follow him into camp. An hour later, just after General Wool had returned from Norfolk, the Captain rode to the beach and informed Colonel Cram, as Chief of the General's Staff, that the seven prisoners, whom he had marched to the beach, were at his disposal. Their arms were taken away, and on promising to take the oath of allegiance, the men were at once dismissed. One of them proved to be Moore himself, who came over to his house, where he found half-a-dozen of us in full possession, and just preparing to discuss a very comfortable supper which his colored cook had got ready for us. Like nearly all the rebel soldiers in this section, he said that he had been forced into the service, and was only awaiting a chance to run away; but his statements on this point did not obtain, to say the least, any more credit than they

---

75 Carl Sandburg, *Abraham Lincoln: The War Years*, vol. 1 (New York, NY: Harcourt, Brace & Company, 1939), 488. Sandburg noted that Lincoln's friends had never seen him before or later throw his silk hat on the floor in anger, 489.

deserved. The guns of this little squad, who were probably one of the rebel pickets scattered through the woods, were all handsome and effective double-barreled fowling-pieces.[76]

Dispatches by reporters for the Associated Press provide some highlights of the taking of Norfolk:

Willoughby's Point, Saturday Morning, May 10.

[The correspondent] obtained a permit to accompany General Wool and General Mansfield to Willoughby's Point, on the steamer *Kansas*, and ...arrived about eight miles from Norfolk at Point Pleasant.

The first regiment landed was the Twentieth New-York, known as Max Weber's regiment, which pushed on immediately, under command of General Weber, and were at 8 A. M., picketed within five miles of Norfolk. The First Delaware, Colonel Andrews, was pushed forward at 9 o'clock, accompanied by Gens. Mansfield and Vielé and Staff. They were soon followed by the Sixteenth Massachusetts, Colonel Wyman. The balance of the expedition consists of the Tenth New-York, Colonel Bendix, the Forty-eighth Pennsylvania, Colonel Bailey, the Ninety-ninth New-York, (Coast Guards,) Major Dodges' Battalion of Mounted Rifles, and Captain Follett's Co. D of Fourth (regular) Artillery. General Wool and staff remained to superintend the landing of the balance of the force, all of whom were landed and off before noon.

Tuesday, May 13, 1862.

Ocean View, Opposite Fortress Monroe, Saturday evening, 8 o'clock.

One leading object of pushing forward the infantry rapidly was to secure, if possible, the bridge across Tanner's Creek, by which the route to Norfolk would be shortened by several miles. The route lay through pine woods and over roads in only tolerable condition. At about 1 o'clock the leading regiment, under Max Weber, came to the bridge and found it burning, having just been set on fire by a body of men who had planted a couple of small guns on the opposite bank, which they opened upon our advance. General Mansfield, who had come over from Newport News, at General Wool's request, to join the expedition, thought this indicated an intention to resist the further progress of our troops, and that nothing could be done without artillery and a larger force. He accordingly started back to hurry up the batteries and to provide for bringing over a portion of his command as reinforcement. General Wool, however, meantime decided to push forward. The column marched back about two miles and a half to a point where a diverging road led around the head of Tanner's Creek, and took that route to Norfolk. Nothing further was heard from the party that had fired upon our column, and it was evident that the demonstration was merely intended to protect them in the destruction of the bridge. They fired about a dozen shots, none of which took effect.[77]

Wool's report details his official view of the events:

Fort Monroe, Va., May 12, 1862. On the 9th of May (Friday afternoon) I organized a force to march against Norfolk.

On Saturday morning, the 10th of May, the troops were landed, under the direction of Colonel Cram, at Ocean View, and commenced the march toward Norfolk, under the direction of Brigadier-Generals Mansfield and Weber, who proceeded on the direct route by way of Tanner's Creek Bridge, but finding it on fire, they returned to the cross-roads, where I joined them and took the direction of the column.

I arrived by the old road and entered the entrenchments in front of the city at 20 minutes before 5 p.m. I immediately proceeded toward Norfolk, accompanied by the Hon. Secretary Chase, and met the mayor and a select committee of the common council of Norfolk at the limits of the city, when they surrendered the city, agreeably to the terms set forth in the resolutions of the common council, presented by the mayor W.W. Lamb, which were accepted by me so far as related to the civil rights of the citizens.

A copy of the resolutions have been already furnished you.

I immediately took possession of the city, and appointed Brigadier General Egbert L. Vielé military governor of Norfolk, with directions to see that the citizens were protected in all their civil rights. Soon after I took possession of Gosport and Portsmouth.

The taking of Norfolk caused the destruction of the iron-clad steamer *Merrimac*, which was blown up by the rebels about 5 o'clock on the morning of the 11th of May, which was soon after communicated to you and the President of the United States. On the 11th I visited the navy-yard, and found all the work-shops, store-houses, and other buildings in ruins, having been set on fire by the rebels, who at the same time partially blew up the dry-dock.

---

[76] *New York Times*, 13 May 1862.
[77] Ibid.

I also visited Craney Island, where I found thirty-nine guns of large caliber, most of which were spiked; also a large number of shot and shells, with about 5,000 pounds of powder, all of which, with the buildings, were in good order. So far as I have been able to ascertain we have taken about two hundred cannon, including those at Sewell's Point batteries, with a large number of shot and shells, as well as many other articles of value to the Government.[78]

Mansfield's sojourn in North Carolina and around Fort Monroe was eventful but ultimately unsatisfying to the old general. He longed to be in command of a division at least and in action against the Rebels. Even though McClellan wished him to be given a division and to join his army, that event did not occur. Mansfield's disappointment seeing officers much junior to him not only be promoted over him but then given combat assignments infuriated him. He wrote to his daughter Mary on 10 November 1861 that "I am tired of this war, and they now have generals as thick as blackberries and it is of little use for me now to remain in the field."[79] He fervently wanted and asked for an assignment to get into the fighting happening all around him in Virginia and North Carolina but to no avail until September 1862. He would be sent to the Army of the Potomac to command a corps seeking General Lee's Army. Both the Army of the Potomac and Mansfield were successful both in finding and fighting Lee but while the Union Army won the Battle of Antietam, Mansfield's first battle command ended all too quickly.[80]

---

[78] *ORA*, vol. 11, 634-635.

[79] Letter courtesy of the Middlesex County Historical Society.

[80] Mansfield was in command of Camp Hamilton near Fort Monroe from 13 October to 24 November 1861, Newport News from 24 November 1861 to 12 June 1862, and Suffolk from 27 June to 8 September 1862.

Attachment 1
General Mansfield on Contrabands and Prisoners

A commission having been appointed to inquire into the condition of the numerous contrabands at Fortress Monroe, who are now held by the government under partial control, General Mansfield wrote a letter to the commission, stating his views on the subject. He divides the negroes into four classes, comprising those abandoned by their owners; those who have run away from their masters to obtain freedom; those who have been put at work on rebel entrenchments and made their escape; and free negroes seeking employment. He then argues the point whether the United States is bound to hold them as slaves, on which he said:

It is clear they are not prisoners of war, for they have never been found in arms, and have made their escape to avoid taking part against the United States, or have been abandoned to the United States, as the rebels have abandoned lands, houses, cattle, &c., and are human beings cast on the world with nothing but their hands to obtain a livelihood. Some of them having worked on rebel fortifications, &c., are released (under the 4th section of the act of Congress of the 6th August, 1861, to confiscate property) from further service to their masters—and in such cases what is their position? Why, simply that of any person in the country released by law from the payment of an obligation—a free person."

After stating that if the claim of the rebels to the negroes as property be valid, they are therefore confiscated, he said:

But they are not property, but persons held to labor under the constitution in certain states, and nowhere else; and are not bound or held to labor for the United States, consequently they are not slaves to the United States. It is clear the condition of slaves with them was coexistent with the obligations of the confederate slave states to the constitution and laws of the United States, against which they are in open armed rebellion.

Now what are these negroes? Are they not freemen by this state of rebellion? By the act of secession, the confederate states have voluntarily broken the constitution and laws of the Union, and have taken up arms against that constitution and those laws, and the United States are thereby absolved from the enforcement of the fugitive slave law, even if so absurd a claim were put forth. If this statement be true, they are entitled as laborers, to all the wages they can earn, and to go where they please, and I would recommend that all their earnings be paid to them while in the United States employ, and that all officers and others who employ them in this department be required to pay them a just compensation, and that they be allowed to improve their condition if opportunity should admit."[81]

Mansfield also wrote a letter to Louisa from Camp Butler 24 January 1862 about slavery and reflected many white northern sentiments including returning them to Africa. Mansfield was a longtime member of the American Colonization Society. Early in the war, Lincoln held similar beliefs although he had a softer view of punishing slave-holding states for their transgressions:

Mr. Douglas is right about slavery, it has cost us this war, and these arrogant slaveholders…must now pay the forfeit. I hope to see Virginia reduced under the sword to submission to the laws and if need be to be made a territory. And as to South Carolina she should never again show forth her share through her public men in Congress. Let the negroes cultivate the soil there for a period of years till they can be all transported to Africa. I am no abolitionist in that sense but I regard slavery a curse on the face of the earth and I believe that God has hardened the hearts of these slave holders….No man on earth has a right to require the labor of another without an equivalent."[82]

Earlier in 1862 while Mansfield was commanding at Suffolk, he had some exchanges with his new commander at Fort Monroe, Major General John Adams Dix, concerning Rebel prisoners and contrabands. Mansfield, in Dix's eyes, had been a bit too zealous in detaining white southern citizens. Mansfield had been sending some prisoners to be held at Camp Wool on the Rip-Raps and Dix chastised Mansfield for not supplying paperwork supporting detention for some of

---

[81] Middletown *Constitution*, 5 March 1862, courtesy of the Middlesex County Historical Society, and from Mansfield's letter to a Congressional commission studying contrabands.

[82] Courtesy of the Middlesex County Historical Society. Douglas was probably Senator Stephen A. Douglas made famous by the Lincoln-Douglas debates..

the prisoners. Mansfield comes across as more of an Abolitionist than the Democrat Dix and more willing to detain southern citizens on what Dix thought were insufficient grounds.[83] At this period in the war, Dix may have had beliefs similar to McClellan's regarding the course of the war--that its purpose should be to wage war against the southern armies and not southern civilians, and to not adopt Abolitionist views.

The correspondence between Mansfield and Dix was not acrimonious but both old generals were not going to back down to the other—Mansfield maintained the correctness of his actions and Dix asserted that he was following orders and regulations more closely. In a letter to Mansfield 12 August 1862, Dix began the dispute:

> I was yesterday at Fort Wool and discharged a large number of prisoners on parole. I found quite a number from Nansemond and Giles Counties and retain them for the purpose of communicating with you. I examined several of them and am satisfied that they have committed no act of hostility against the United States. That they sympathize with the insurgents there is no doubt, but if we undertake to arrest all such persons our forts and prisons would not contain a tithe of them. So long as they continue quietly about their business they should not be molested.

> The exercise of this power of arrest is at the same time the most arbitrary and the most delicate which a state of war devolves on a military commander, and it is one which should not be delegated to a subordinate. I find that many of the persons imprisoned at Fort Wool were arrested by Colonel Dodge and some of them on suspicion. This must not be repeated. Your subordinates may arrest persons detected in open acts of hostility to the Government but in every other instance and in every case the order for arrest should come from you, or if an arrest is made in an emergency without your order the case should be brought directly before you and the evidence taken before the party is sent here for imprisonment. Two of the persons sent to Fort Wool by you have died within the last three days, one of them, Mr. Jordan, the most respectable of all in standing. His body goes to his friends in Norfolk today. Imprisonment at Fort Wool is a most severe punishment at this season. The water is bad and the heat is intense, and no citizen should be sent there for a light cause and without pretty clear evidence of guilt. If parties in your neighborhood need temporary restraint you must find some place of safe-keeping there unless the case is very marked.

> My inclination is to discharge all these prisoners on a stringent parole, but before doing so I await your reply with your views on any particular case or cases.[84]

Mansfield was not going to let this pass and answered his commander in detail rebutting all points, in his 14 August reply:

> It is very natural that these prisoners should make an effort to excite your sympathy. No man has been arrested on suspicion. There has always been good reasons for apprehending certain persons, and my officers have not been allowed to exercise any arbitrary acts beyond the performance of their duty and instructions received by me. There are always two sides to the picture. These chivalric gentlemen find it quite hard to be confined themselves but do not hesitate to shoot negroes for bringing chickens and berries to sell to the damned Yankees, as they call them. A free negro on the road with his little cart and horse was shot with a ball and buck load by Charles Sumner, and he is now moving about on crutches and I have been obliged to give his family bread and meat. Another negro has been in my hospital covered with shot in his body. Two negroes were shot at or near Smithfield. Out of four in a boat, one dead, fell into the water and the other dying of his wounds, and the remaining two were sent to Richmond and sold. Whole families of negroes, free and slaves, are run across the Blackwater to Richmond to work in the fortifications against their will by these kind rebels who don't like to be restrained themselves. Only a few days since a respectable farmer had to abandon his land and property and came in to me with his wife, and I gave him a pass to go to the North. The man had been taken to Richmond on suspicion of disloyalty and imprisoned forty days and only set at liberty after taking the oath of allegiance to the Confederate Government which he would not live under. Another respectable farmer they were going to hang on suspicion and escaped by no man coming forward to swear against him. I sent you the other day a man, a magistrate in North Carolina, who went to a Union poor man and with pistol in hand said he would shoot him if he joined the Union home guard. Are we not to curtail the liberty of such rebels? My own opinion is they will all be fortunate to escape the

---

[83] Dix was a native of New Hampshire born 24 July 1798. He was not a West Point graduate although he did serve in the Old Army beginning in 1813 serving in the War of 1812. He resigned in 1828 as a captain, and was a lawyer, publisher, Secretary of the State of New York, New York State legislator, U.S. Senator, Postmaster of New York City, railroad president, and U.S. Secretary of the Treasury. He then became a major general in the New York Militia then major general of volunteers commanding the departments of Maryland, Pennsylvania, Potomac, and then the Middle Department, before commanding the Department of Virginia. While Dix had been a veteran wounded in 1814, he had not served in the Mexican-American War, and was an officer in the infantry and artillery, never in the engineers. He became more of a politician than a soldier. In 1861 however, he did prevent the Maryland legislature from meeting by arresting them, so Maryland did not secede from the Union. Dix's patriotism was unquestioned. When Dix was Treasury Secretary, he instructed his treasury agent he sent to New Orleans that "If anyone attempts to haul down the American Flag, shoot him on the spot." Even though he was a Democrat, he certainly did not treat all Rebels with kid gloves.
[84] ORA, ser. 2, vol. 4, 377.

just retribution of taking up arms against our country. All the Union people I have seen in Virginia say we are too easy with these secessionists and that is my opinion.

As to the death of prisoners at Fort Wool the proportion is small compared with the death and hanging of our own prisoners and Union men at the South. If they do not get proper treatment there they should have it and a reform take place. I have in most instances ordered a military commission to examine and try such cases of arrests as are made. The proceedings of these boards are on record and I have always put on such boards officers of the soundest principles of honor and justice I have at command. I cannot examine such cases myself for want of time. I inclose you a list of the persons brought before the military commissions, most of whom I presume you have at Fort Wool. A written statement of the circumstances has always been sent with the prisoners to your provost-marshal.[85]

The former lawyer Dix now had his back up so sent a lengthy reply to Mansfield two days later:

I have received your letter of the 14ᵗʰ instant with a list of prisoners sent by you to Fort Wool and a brief statement of the charges against them. This is the first specification of their offenses I have seen and I know that several citizens have been sent here without any memorandum of the causes for which they were imprisoned. The crimes specified by you as having been committed by secessionists in general deserve any punishment we may think proper to inflict. But the first question is in every case of imprisonment whether the party has actually been guilty of any offense, and this is a question to be decided upon proper evidence. If the guilt is not clearly shown the accused should be released. There is nothing in your position or mine which can excuse either of us for depriving any man of his liberty without a full and impartial examination. My duties are at least as arduous as yours and I have never shrunk from the labor of a personal examination of every case of imprisonment for which I am responsible.

In regard to arrests in your command there was at least one and I think more for which there was not in my judgment the slightest cause. I speak from a personal examination of them. The arrests were made without your order as I understood, but acquiesced in by you subsequently. The parties referred to were released nearly a month ago. Had I not looked into their cases they would no doubt have been in prison at this moment. When Judge Pierrepont and I examined the cases of the political prisoners in the various places of custody from Washington to Fort Warren we found persons arrested by military officers who had been overlooked and who had been lying in prison for months without any just cause. For this reason as well as on general principles of justice and humanity I must insist that every person arrested shall have a prompt examination, and if it is considered as proper case for imprisonment that the testimony shall be taken under oath and the record sent with the accused to the officer who is to have the custody of him. This is especially necessary when the commitment is made by a military commission and the party accused is sent to a distance and placed like the prisoners at Fort Wool under the immediate supervision of the commanding officer of the department or Army corps. The only proper exception to the rule is where prisoners are temporarily detained during military movements in order that they may not give information to the enemy.

I consider it my duty to go once in three or four weeks to the places of imprisonment within my command, inquire into the causes of arrest and discharge all persons against whom charges sustained by satisfactory proof are not on file. I did not enter into a minute examination of the persons sent here by your order nor did I release any one of them, but referred the whole matter to you for explanation; and it is proper to suggest that an imputation of undue susceptibility on my part or the general reprobation of the guilt of faithless citizens for whom when their guilt is clearly shown I have quite as little sympathy as yourself is not an answer to the question of culpability in special cases. The paper you sent me is all very well as far as it goes, but it is no more complete without a transcript of the evidence on which the allegations are founded than a memorandum of the crime and the sentence of a military prisoner would be without the record of the proceedings of the court. You will please therefore send to me the testimony taken by the military commission before whom the examination was made.

It is proper to remark here that a military commission not appointed by the commanding general of the Army or the Army corps is a mere court of inquiry, and its proceedings can only be regarded in the light of information for the guidance of the officer who instituted it and on whom the whole responsibility of any action under them must from the necessity of the case devolve.

In regard to persons whom you think right to arrest and detain under your immediate direction I have nothing to say. You are personally responsible for them, and as your attention will be frequently called to them the duration of their imprisonment will be likely to be influenced by considerations which might be overlooked if they were at a distance. I am therefore quite willing to leave them in your hands. But when a prisoner is sent here and comes under my immediate observation and care I wish the whole case to be presented to me.

---

[85] *ORA*, ser. 2, vol. 4, 388.

The engineer department has called on me to remove the prisoners from Fort Wool that the work may not be interrupted. I have sent away all the military prisoners and wish to dispose of those who are confined for political causes. When I have received from you a full report of the cases which arose under your command I will dispose of them and send to you all the prisoners whom I do not release, or if you prefer it (and it would be much more satisfactory to me) I would send them all to you without going into any examination myself and leave it to you to dispose of them as you think right. If you have no suitable guard-house there is a jail near your headquarters where they may be securely confined.[86]

Mansfield took Dix's suggestion which ended the acrimonious exchange as Mansfield agreed to keep his own prisoners as he replied on 19 August:

I hardly know how to recapitulate the subject of prisoners. I send you the proceedings of the military commissions marked A, B, C, H, E, and copies of the letters numbered 1, 2, 3, 4, 5, agreeably to your instructions. In forwarding prisoners to provost marshal, Lieutenant Weber, aide to General Weber, may have omitted to send to the provost marshal at Fort Monroe the proper documents on the subject. He is now sick and I have in his place a very competent officer and the records of his office will hereafter show transactions of this kind more minutely. The papers I send are from my own office. It is difficult to judge of what should be done with individuals in certain cases. I am not aware of intentional injustice to any citizen. I assumed command here on the 12th of June, and the person to whom you allude a month ago as having been discharged without fault against him I don't think could have been confined by my orders. You sent me some papers about some prisoners some time ago before Colonel Dodge was ordered to this post and I was obliged to refer you to him at Norfolk. The persons examined by the commission as you will see all had a prompt hearing and the commissioners were sworn. This commission was duly ordered to relieve me from the duty of personal examination which I cannot find time to do properly. In short it was nothing more than a board of examination to aid my judgment in disposing of offenders temporarily. I am aware I have no power to order a military commission for the final trial of a prisoner of war and never entertained such an idea. I regret you should suppose for a moment I could impute to you "undue susceptibility and that my warm criticism of the bad conduct of the rebels in certain cases should have been thought out of place when taken in connection with the subject. Certainly it was dictated by my best feelings for my distracted country.

In reference to my letter of the 14th instant I have to explain that I have not yet apprehended the man who shot the negroes near Smithfield in a boat. I only know the facts and the parties. It has not been thought judicious to take such a step at this moment so far off. I have to request you will act on all the cases now at Fort Wool. Some are prisoners of war and should be exchanged for our own officers and soldiers. In future I will endeavor to keep the prisoners and relieve you from a troublesome and unpleasant duty as you suggest and which I can do without difficulty.[87]

---

[86] *ORA*, ser. 2, vol. 4, 398-399.
[87] *ORA*, ser. 2, vol. 4, 409.

Attachment 2
Major General John Ellis Wool Biography

Courtesy LOC.

John Ellis Wool was born in Newburgh, New York, 20 February 1784. He was orphaned at a young age but attended local schools. Working as a bookseller in Troy, New York, he drilled with the militia, the Troy Invincibles, read the law and was admitted to the bar. At the outbreak of the War of 1812, he was a practicing attorney, and raised a company. He was commissioned as its captain in the 13ᵗʰ U.S. Infantry Regiment and fought at the Battle of Queenstown Heights, Canada, 13 October 1812, where he was shot through both thighs. He fought well although the Americans eventually lost the battle. For his bravery, he was promoted to major in the 29ᵗʰ U.S. Infantry, which he led with distinction at the Battle of Plattsburgh 11 September 1814. He was brevetted lieutenant colonel for his gallantry there. Following the war in April 1816, he was promoted to colonel and inspector-general of the Northern Division and later as a member of the Army General Staff which office he held until 1841. The Army appointed Colonel Wool one of the two Inspectors General of the United States Army in 1821. He was appointed a brevet brigadier general in April 1826 for 10 years in grade, and a regular brigadier general in June 1841.

He was sent to Europe in 1832 to procure models of the latest French and British artillery and observe foreign military organizations; he was entertained by the Kings of France and Belgium. He observed French artillery in action against Antwerp, Belgium, in December 1832. He also negotiated the difficult and politically charged transfer of the Cherokee Indians to west of the Mississippi in 1836. In 1841, he was made commander of the Department of the East resolving border disputes with Canada.

In the Mexican-American War, he participated in the organization of western regiments and commanded 3,400 men on the march from San Antonio to Saltillo, some 900 miles, where he joined General Taylor as second in command. Taylor placed Wool in command at Saltillo. Wool was in command at the Battle of Buena Vista before Taylor arrived and did well stemming General Santa Anna's attacks. Wool remained in command of the U.S. Army in northern Mexico after Taylor left and assumed command in November 1847. Wool's leadership was recognized by Congress when it presented him with a sword and a vote of thanks in 1854; he was also promoted to brevet major general. After the battle, he commanded the occupation forces of northern Mexico. He commanded the Eastern Military Division from 1848 to 1843 and the Department of the East from 1853 to 1854, then the Department of the Pacific from 1854 to 1857. He was heavily involved in damping down the filibustering efforts in the southwest. Wool appreciated Mansfield's arrival in 1854 which relieved Wool from having to travel to distant posts in his department. Wool was kept busy with Indian versus settler hostilities traveling to many posts in California and Oregon and Washington Territories. He departed San Francisco in February 1856.

He was in command of the Eastern Department to 1860 after his return from the Pacific. As the Civil war began, Wool believed that he should be the one to command the Union Army, but Lieutenant General Winfield Scott stood in his way. Scott ordered Wool to take command at Fort Monroe after the Union debacle at First Bull Run and Butler's defeat at Big Bethel, about nine miles north of Fort Monroe. On the morning of 17 August, Wool and his staff reached the fort which became headquarters for the Department of Virginia. The next day, Butler turned over command to Wool.

President Lincoln appointed McClellan to general-in-chief in November 1861, deeply offending Wool, who was senior to McClellan and comparable to Scott in rank and experience. Wool contemplated resigning but some of his friends and political allies convinced him to continue his service. Wool and McClellan reached an uneasy truce after McClellan soothed Wool's feathers by seeking his advice concerning Union military actions around Fort Monroe. McClellan used Fort Monroe as his base for his Peninsular Campaign moving between the York and James Rivers to attack Richmond. But the prickly Wool objected to McClellan's appointment and telegraphed McClellan and Stanton that he would not be subordinated to a junior officer. Wool wanted McClellan to report to him, upon his arrival at the fort and told a staff officer that he would arrest McClellan if he did not pay him this courtesy. McClellan urged Stanton to remove Wool but the Secretary sustained the veteran general. On 3 April 1862, McClellan reported to Wool, had breakfast, and agreed to cooperate fully on the forthcoming campaign.

In early May, Wool participated in the capture of Norfolk and later that month took Suffolk. Stanton placed McClellan in charge of the Department of Virginia on 1 June, and ordered Wool to Baltimore to command the Middle Department. There, he was active in moving troops to aid McClellan in his campaign against General Robert E. Lee's invasion of Maryland. Wool who was 78, likely suffered a stroke in November 1862 and was bedridden. In December, he gave up command to Major General Robert C. Schenck, and returned to Troy, New York, to convalesce. He was next assigned command of the Department of the East in January 1863 with his headquarters in New York City. Wool was in his headquarters when, after the Union victory at Gettysburg, riots broke out in protest over the draft. Wool had only a few hundred soldiers on hand to face mobs totaling over 10,000 so he order a gunboat stationed on the Hudson River to provide cannon fire if needed. But the rioters continued to rampage until the 7th New York Infantry arrived from Gettysburg to bolster troops in the city; Wool also used artillery at key intersections to further intimidate the mobs. Order was restored by 16 July, and then on 18 July, Wool turned over command to Major General John A. Dix but requested another assignment. He learned to his dismay in Troy that the army had retired him effective 1 August 1863 after more than 50 years of service. He died at Troy 10 November 1869.[88]

---

[88] Harwood P. Hinton, "The Military Career of John Ellis Wool, 1812-1863," unpublished PhD dissertation, Univ. of Wisconsin, 1960, passim; Nathaniel Bartlett Sylvester, *History of Rensselaer Co., New York* (Philadelphia, PA: Everts & Peck, 1880), 261; Eicher, 581. Inspector General Wool's military jurisdiction was vast. The Northern Division stretched from northern Maine to eastern Wisconsin and encompassed five military departments, the First Department, with headquarters at Brownville [New York], covered western New York and Vermont; Second (Boston), Connecticut, Rhode Island, Massachusetts, and New Hampshire; Third (New York City) , eastern New York and New Jersey; Fourth (Philadelphia), Pennsylvania, Maryland and Delaware; and Fifth (Detroit), the country north of the Ohio and east of the Mississippi," Hinton, 43-44. Wool accompanied the Board of Visitors at West Point in 1819 at the behest of the Secretary of War, John C. Calhoun, based on Wool's success in his inspection duties. He likely met or at least was acquainted with Mansfield who was a student there.

Chapter 10

To Antietam Creek and Glory

Mansfield returned to Washington, D.C., on 5 September 1862 from Suffolk, Virginia, and took a room at Willard's Hotel eagerly hoping to be assigned to a combat command.[1] Three days later on 8 September, he called on Secretary of the Treasury Salmon P. Chase, who recorded the visit in his diary of Mansfield's gossip-filled news:

Genl. Mansfield came in, and talked very earnestly about the necessity of ordering up, from Suffolk, 1st Delaware and 3 and 4 New York, trained and disciplined now 14 months, each 800 strong, say 2,400 men; and from Norfolk 19th Wisconsin and 48th Pennsylvania, say 1,600 men; leaving at Suffolk, Forey's Brigade of four diminished Regiments, say 1,800 men in all, late of [Brigadier General James] Shield's division,—11th Pennsylvania Cavalry (a full and good Regiment) say 900 men;—and [Col. Charles Cleveland] Dodge's Regiment of mounted Rifles except one Company; and at Norfolk, 99th New York, and one Company of Dodge's, sufficient for military police. He favored leaving [Major General Erasmus Darwin] Keyes and [Major General John James] Peck at Yorktown. — He said the defences of the city [Washington] were weak on the Eastern side; and that there ought to be at least 65,000 good men to hold it if McClellan is defeated—to improve victory if he is successful—He referred to old times. Was in Texas the Winter before the Rebellion broke out. Saw [Major General David Emanuel] Twiggs who hated him because he was on Court-Martial. Was then told by officer in Council of War of K.G.C. [Knights of the Golden Circle] that [John Buchanan] Floyd and [Howell, II] Cobb in Cabinet and Jeff. [Jefferson Finis] Davis and [John Cabell, Jr.] Breckinridge, were

---

[1] *ORA*, ser. 2, vol. 4, 496.

members. In this Council of War, Orders were given to seize Navy Yards, Forts, etc. while its members were yet Cabinet officers and Senators. The Order of the K. G. C. ramified throughout the South. First offered services to [Mexican President Benito Pablo] Juarez, who refused them because too dangerous. They then plotted the invasion of Cuba, which failed. Then declared themselves Protectors of Southern Rights and levied a contribution upon all planters and slaveholders—some giving $5 and some $10, and some more or less. In this way they got large sums and commenced operations. They designed to seize Washington and inaugurate Breckinridge; and in reference to this [James Murray] Mason wrote Faulkner advising him not to resign—this letter being now in Seward's possession. This plot only failed through the bringing of troops to Washington, and the unwillingness of leaders to make a bloody issue so early. He spoke of Genl. Scott. Said he had not treated him well—had placed McDowell in command over the river last year, superseding himself, and when he had asked for explanation he simply replied that his orders had been given. He felt himself wronged, but did his duty to the best of his ability. He was afterwards treated badly by Genl. Wool who did not like him, though he treated him civilly. Had lately been in command at Suffolk (an insignificant post) until summoned here to Court of Inquiry. Wanted active employment but was unable to get any. Had sent for his horses, and proposed to visit all the fortifications around the city on his own account.—I was a good deal affected by the manifest patriotism and desire to do something for his country manifested by the old General; and could not help wishing that he was younger and thinking that, perhaps, after all, it would have been better to trust him.[2]

Mansfield's meeting with Chase in which the old general discussed troops at Suffolk and points around Southeastern Virginia reiterated Mansfield's opinions which he had already expressed in a private letter to Major General Halleck on 5 September:

The enemy will never attack this place [Suffolk], which is naturally strong, so long as pressed on the [northern] side of Richmond. I repeat, there are three old regiments here--the First Delaware and Third and Fourth New York Volunteers--well drilled, and been in service for about fourteen mouths and have never fired a gun at the enemy. They will average 800 men, and many men and officers have been in the Mexican war. Three green regiments could readily take their places here, and these could, by return boats, proceed up the Potomac to the Army of Virginia.

I am ready at all times myself to take any command you will think it to the interest of the country to give me, and believe I can do more than I can here.

You will excuse this private letter; an official one on this subject might by some be thought out of place.[3]

---

[2] Salmon P. Chase, *Annual Report of the American Historical Association for the Year 1902*, vol. 2, "Diary and Correspondence of Salmon P. Chase" (Washington, DC: Government Printing Office, 1903), 69-72. Knights of the Golden Circle was a group established in 1854 to engage in filibustering to expand slavery south into Mexico and around the Caribbean. It proved of little consequence except to inflame northern public opinion against the Democratic Party, Heidler, 1129. Juarez was president of Mexico for five terms from 1858 to 1872. Floyd was U.S. Secretary of War 6 March 1857 to 29 December 1860, was indicted for treason, and became a major general in the Confederacy, Eicher, 237. Davis and Mansfield were comrades during the Mexican-American War and Davis appointed Mansfield as a colonel and Inspector General as already seen. Davis was U.S. Secretary of War 7 March 1853 to 3 March 1857, then U.S. Senator from Mississippi from 4 March 1857 to 21 January 1861, becoming President of the Confederacy, Eicher, 202. Cobb was U.S. Secretary of the Treasury 6 March 1857 to 10 December 1860, and became a major general in the Confederacy, Eicher, 178. Breckinridge was vice president of the U.S. 4 March 1857 to 4 March 1861 and became a major general and secretary of war in the Confederacy, Eicher, 143-144. Mason was a member of the U.S. Senate from 1847 to 1861 when he was expelled. He was captured by the U.S. Navy while travelling to Britain as a Confederate envoy on 8 November 1861 in the famous Trent Affair. Charles James Faulkner was a U.S. Congressman from Virginia and minister to France from 1859-1861. He was arrested in August 1861 on charges of negotiating sales of arms for the Confederacy while in France and was imprisoned at Fort Warren in Boston. After his exchange, he enlisted in the Confederate Army and was assistant adjutant general on Stonewall Jackson's staff. "Forey's Brigade" should read "Ferry's Brigade." He was a Congressman from Connecticut; born in Bethel, 15 August 1823, entered the Union Army in 1861 as colonel of the 5th Connecticut and brigadier general March 1862. He likely was a friend of Mansfield while they were in Suffolk as they were fellow Nutmeggers.

[3] *ORA*, vol. 18, 376-377; 385-386. At Suffolk in August 1862, Mansfield had 7,178 men present and absent:

Brig. Gen. Max Weber
    1st Delaware
    3rd New York
    4th New York
    13th New York
    25th New York

    1st New York Mounted Rifles
    11th Penn. Cavalry
    4th U.S. Artillery, Battery L

Brig. Gen. Orris S. Ferry
    39th Illinois

Mansfield wanted to get into action at least as a brigade commander with regiments and officers he knew--he would get his wish shortly, but not with the troops he requested. Halleck thought Mansfield had a wise suggestion so on 7 September the general in chief of the Army ordered Major General John Dix to "Send to Washington as promptly as possible the First Delaware and the Third and Fourth New York Regiments, now at Suffolk." Dix quickly demurred the next day after agreeing to send the order to Suffolk that "You [Halleck] are perhaps not aware that these regiments are the flower of command, and my main reliance if Suffolk is to be defended." Dix suggested that he would send the regiments but wished to substitute the 5th Maryland for the 3rd New York—Halleck agreed. The 4th New York, 1st Delaware, and 5th Maryland left for Washington on 9 September. It may be that Halleck was contemplating forming a brigade with these units with Mansfield commanding but Mansfield's orders for 8 September were to report to McClellan and there is no further record of Mansfield becoming a brigade commander.[4]

Salmon Portland Chase, Secretary of the Treasury under Lincoln from 1861 to 1864, and an acquaintance of Mansfield, with whom the general visited just before departing to join the Army of the Potomac near Frederick, Maryland. Chase had served as U.S. Senator from Ohio, its governor, and as the sixth Chief Justice of the United States after resigning from Lincoln's cabinet. He had not championed Mansfield's promotion earlier in the war rather favoring Ohio natives. Courtesy LOC.

Major General Samuel Peter Heintzelman also wrote about Mansfield's assignment in Washington. His journal entry for 5 September 1862 relates that he met Generals Joseph Hooker and Washington Lafayette Elliott at Willard's Hotel. Heintzelman learned that Hooker was given Irvin McDowell's corps and that John Pope was relieved and would be sent to Minnesota. Also, Generals William Buell Franklin and Fitz John Porter had gone before a Court of Inquiry for disobedience of orders in not marching promptly during Second Bull Run, and Brigadier General Charles Griffin for disrespect to General Pope. Generals Mansfield and George Cadwalader were on their court with Judge Advocate

---

13th Indiana
62nd Ohio
67th Ohio

[4] *ORA*, vol. 18, 386-387. Dix continued his requests for replacement troops fearing Rebel attacks but as new regiments arrived his fears diminished even though he complained that "The One hundred and thirtieth New York has just arrived and will go to Suffolk. It is very raw, not even knowing the manual of arms...The loss of my three best regiments at that point is unfortunate," ibid., 392.

General Joseph Holt as recorder, but then the cases were suspended due to General Lee's invasion of Maryland.[5] Not only was the trial suspended, but McClellan convinced Lincoln, Stanton, and Halleck, to reinstate Franklin, Porter, and Griffin.[6]

The chaplain of the 124th Pennsylvania, Robert M. Green, also met Mansfield in Washington on 12 September at Willard's Hotel finding time to comment on the venerable general's appearance: "I had the pleasure and privilege to see, for the first time, Major-General Mansfield, who had recently been appointed Commander of the corps of which our regiment formed a part. He was a fine specimen of the true soldier; his hair was snowy white, his bearing that of the true and noble man."[7]

It would not be unusual for Mansfield to be appointed to a Court of Inquiry given his long service plus having been an inspector general for eight years; he had sat on many courts-martial during his career. But one might speculate why he was chosen by Halleck possibly in consultation with Lincoln for this assignment. At this time, Lincoln was angry over the conduct of McClellan and his generals upon the arrival of units of the Army of the Potomac from the Peninsula. McClellan and his generals did not rush to the aid of McDowell who was being pummeled by Lee and his Army of Northern Virginia at Manassas. Lincoln was casting about for generals in the east who were not part of McClellan's coterie, who had faithful and unblemished military service, and were available. It was also very likely that Mansfield had come to Lincoln's attention again when Lincoln was at Fort Monroe and Norfolk and of course Lincoln knew Mansfield well when he was in command of Washington in 1861. Mansfield's recent letters to generals and politicians ardently requesting combat service likely reminded Lincoln that Mansfield should be a general pushed forward as others fell away due to poor performance or for political reasons. And it may be that finally his entreaties to friends such as Welles, Chase, Thayer, Totten, etc., bore fruit. But it mattered not the reasons for being finally chosen for a combat command, the old general was thrilled.

---

[5] *ORA Supp.*, pt. 1, vol. 3, 437. Telegram from Sec. Stanton in Washington to Mansfield dated 5 September 1862: "Most speedy" conveyance to report to the War Department to sit on a court of inquiry which was ordered by the Pres.; telegram courtesy WPL.

[6] *ORA*, vol. 19, pt. 2, 189-190. The Court of Inquiry appointed on 5 September had Major General George Cadwalader, Brigadier General Silas Casey, Mansfield, and Colonel Joseph Holt as Judge Advocate. The commission met on 6 and 8 September but adjourned and dissolved without taking action, Richard B. Irwin, "The Case of Fitz John Porter," In *Battles and Leaders of the Civil War: Being for the Most Part Contributions by Union and Confederate Officers Based upon "The Century War Series."* Vol. 2, vol. 2, 695.

[7] Robert M. Green, *History of the One Hundred and Twenty-fourth Regiment Pennsylvania Volunteers in the War of the Rebellion—1862-1863* (Philadelphia, PA: Ware Bros. Company, Printers, 1907), 148. Note that Mansfield was only posthumously appointed a major general.

Photograph taken after May 1861 showing Mansfield as a brigadier general. Courtesy WPL.

Mansfield was not high on the administration's lists for appointment to important field command. He had spent most of his long career as an engineer or staff officer and had spent no time in direct command of troops until the Civil War. Certainly his age, fifty seven at the war's beginning, was not in his favor, although he was not the oldest regular Army corps commander on active field service--that honor belonged to sixty-five-year-old Major General Edwin Sumner, Mansfield's wing commander at Antietam. "Bull Head" Sumner, Sr., was 65 years old, born 30 January 1797. Brigadier General George Sears Greene, Mansfield's Second Division commander, was over two and one-half years older than Mansfield, born 6 May 1801. Mansfield's commander at Norfolk, Major General John E. Wool, 78 years old, was the oldest Union soldier on active duty. Although he had friends in Washington, like Secretary of the Navy Gideon Welles, Mansfield may not have cultivated enough proper connections. His obituary notice which appeared in the *Cincinnati Gazette* was written by his cousin, Edward Deering Mansfield, to render honors to the fallen general, but given the general's difficulty in gaining field commands during the Civil War, there may be more than a grain of truth in it: "It might have been supposed that an officer of so much experience, skill and courage, would, when military capacity was so much needed, have been placed in important commands, now filled by his inferiors. It is sufficient to say, that he was not one of those who are constantly demanding place and reward at the hands of the Government. He pleaded no political influence, and left place to follow his work, not to be sought after. These are not times when silent merit takes precedence, or fit men are always put in fit places."[8] As has been seen above, Mansfield was well acquainted with Lincoln and had known Scott for decades, so it may be that Mansfield's lack of field command plus his age, when combined with only adequate performance in command in Washington, did not place him high on Lincoln's watch list for future high commands. Lincoln promoted aggressive generals who brought him important victories or those men who were forced on him for political reasons.

Mansfield wrote his wife, Louisa, on 3 November 1861 from Fort Monroe decrying his treatment by General Scott and the administration:

> I am myself disgusted with the management of the Military Affairs of the country at Washington. Our Secretary of War [Simon Cameron] should be changed. He has not the necessary talent and General Scott is too old to effect anything.
>
> If things go on in this way much longer I shall next year retire. I cannot stand it much longer. They have put men over my head, that I used to rank in the Mexican War—McClellan, Fremont, Halleck, were all 2nd lieutenants in the Regular Army under me.
>
> General Scott appointed the 1st two Major Generals, at the same time he appointed me Brigadier General, dated 15 May. Where is the justice of this? And he has invariably removed me from every place where I could act efficiently, and yet he professes the greatest regard and I have always done good service.
>
> They must soon see something done or the whole people will cry out. Since I left Washington the Potomac has been closed by batteries. This should not be tolerated any longer.
>
> I am now determined to do all in my power to put the country right.[9]

Mansfield was eager to have his son, Samuel, recently graduated from West Point, join him as soon as possible. In a letter to his wife on 13 September 1862 from Willard's Hotel he reiterated his wishes:

> I got orders last evening to join General McClellan. I shall leave today. Tell Samuel as soon as he is well enough to come to me and bring no useless baggage.

---

[8][Rev. Jeremiah Taylor], *Memorial of Gen. J. K. F. Mansfield, United States Army, Who Fell in Battle at Sharpsburg, Md. Sept. 17, 1862* (Boston: Press of T.R. Marvin & Son, 1862), 29., 67. Edward Deering Mansfield (17 August 1801- 27 October 1880), was the son of Lieutenant Colonel Jared Mansfield, General Mansfield's uncle, and first professor of Natural and Experimental Philosophy at West Point. Edward was an American author, born in New Haven, Connecticut. He entered West Point 1 August 1815 and graduated fourth in his class, but declined a commission as second lieutenant of engineers 1 July 1819. He studied at Princeton, from which he graduated in 1822. In 1825 he was admitted to the Connecticut bar. He moved to Cincinnati and in 1836 became professor of constitutional law at Cincinnati College (now the University of Cincinnati). Shortly afterward he abandoned the legal profession to enter journalism, and edited the *Cincinnati Chronicle, Atlas*, and *Railroad Record*. He was Commissioner of Statistics for the State of Ohio from 1859 to 1868. He published several books including the following: *Political Grammar of the United States* (1835); *Life of Gen. Winfield Scott* (1848); *History of the Mexican War* (1849); *American Education* (1851); *Memoirs of Daniel Drake* (1855); *A Popular Life of Ulysses S. Grant* (1868); and *Personal Memories* (1870); courtesy Wikipedia; *Cullum's Register*, vol. 1, 184. As has been seen in letters General Mansfield wrote to his wife, Mansfield was certainly not apolitical.

[9] Letter from Mansfield to Louisa 3 November 1861 from Fort Monroe, courtesy of the Middlesex County Historical Society. Mansfield likely recalled a letter he had received a few years earlier dated 30 December 1857, from West Point from Captain G.W. Smith. Smith asked Mansfield for his help for himself and McClellan to rejoin service "pretty high amongst the field officers of the new regiments" courtesy of the Middlesex County Historical Society. This was probably George Washington Smith from New York who had only became a captain of the 88th Illinois Infantry in August 1862.

I am in great haste and have only time today....I shall leave all my extra baggage in the charge of some officer here in one of the departments....

Tell Samuel to call at the Engineer Office and get a bundle of two shirts and a pair of pantaloons. He will purchase a horse of the quartermaster Col. [Daniel H.] Rucker by telling who he is and then join me after filling his saddlebags with something to eat.[10]

Willard's Hotel at 14th and E Streets, photograph taken during the Civil War. Mansfield would have seen this on his last journey from Washington to report to McClellan at Frederick, Maryland. Courtesy LOC.

[10] Mansfield to wife, 13 September 1862, courtesy of the Middlesex County Historical Society. Rucker was likely known to Mansfield as Rucker was captain in the 1st Dragoons and was brevetted to major for his actions at the Battle of Buena Vista, Mexico.

Interior room at Willard's Hotel showing the "Gentlemen's Parlor" used for "reading and sitting" drawn during Lincoln's inauguration week in 1861, by Thomas Nast. In the foreground Nast depicted a "United States Army Officer" and a "Southern member of Congress" and a tired-looking Lincoln sitting before the fire reading a newspaper. This room at Willard's would have been very familiar to Mansfield during his many sojourns in Washington. The writer Nathaniel Hawthorne, visited Washington in 1863, observed that "Willard's Hotel could more justly be called the center of Washington and the Union than either the Capitol, the White House, or the State Department....Everybody may be seen there....You are mixed up here with office seekers, wire pullers, inventors, artists, poets, editors, Army correspondents, attachés of foreign journals, long-winded talkers, clerks, diplomatists, mail contractors, railway directors—until your identity is lost among them," Carl Sandburg, *Abraham Lincoln: The War Years* (New York: Harcourt, Brace & Company, 1939), vol. 2, 274. Drawing courtesy LOC.

Mansfield was a very happy man as he rode out of Washington, D.C., at about 4 p.m. on Saturday, 13 September 1862. He on his strawberry roan along with his two companions turned their horses heads away from Willard's Hotel heading northwest on the Georgetown Pike to Frederick. This would be the first time in his long U.S. Army career that he would be in command of a large body of men almost certainly heading into combat. The previous April he had written to his commanding officer, Brigadier General John Wool, "I am ready to march with any force from a company to ten thousand men," voicing his desire to do more active service.[11] Upon learning of his assignment to McClellan's Army, he wrote to his son, Samuel, who graduated from West Point 17 June 1862, to "[f]ill your pockets with sandwiches and follow me," then headed west.[12] But Mansfield certainly did not think that his ride to the front would take him past a spot a mile to the west where a fort would be built just a few months later named in his memory. Had he known, he likely would have wanted to inspect his namesake fort to ensure its worth.[13] He had seen death firsthand

---

[11] Mansfield to John Wool, 24 April 1862, Mansfield Papers, USMA Library.

[12] Mansfield and Johnston, 198; John Mead Gould, *Joseph K.F. Mansfield, Brigadier General of the U.S. Army. A Narrative of Events Connected with His Mortal Wounding at Antietam, Sharpsburg, Maryland, September 17, 1862* (Portland, ME: Stephen Berry, Printer, 1895), hereafter *A Narrative of Events*, states that Mansfield's son was not with him when he was wounded and the general's two aides, Captain Clarence H. Dyer and Captain James W. Forsyth were apparently kept busy by Mansfield so Gould never saw them, 12.

[13] Benjamin Franklin Cooling,, III and Walton H. Owen, II., *Mr. Lincoln's Forts: A Guide to the Civil War Defenses of Washington* (Lanham, MD: The Scarecrow Press, Inc., 2010),149-152.

during his Mexican-American War experience and had been seriously wounded, but his thoughts were likely focused on what his new command might be with McClellan and how quickly he could get to his headquarters. Mansfield reported to McClellan's headquarters on the Koogle Farm west of Middletown, Maryland, about 9 a.m. the morning of the 15th. Since he departed Washington late afternoon on the 13th, he spent two nights somewhere between the beginning and ending points of his trek. It is not of record where those overnight halts were spent. Sunset was just after 6 p.m. so his ride from Willard's could not have been long—less than three hours. And given that once he was on the Georgetown Pike, the road would have been clogged with troops, artillery, and wagons heading for Frederick, it is unlikely he made more than several miles on his first day. Since no Union commanders wrote that Mansfield stayed with them, and it is not likely he camped by the side of the road, he probably found accommodations in a hotel or house next to the pike. The first sizable town leaving Washington is Rockville, Maryland, about 17 road miles from Willard's, a good first day's start. On the 14th, he could have then ridden to Frederick believing that McClellan was still there or, if not, learning his whereabouts. The ride from Rockville to Frederick would have been almost 30 miles but given the congested roads that might have taken much of the day. Plus, Mansfield would have been seeking information of the location of McClellan's headquarters as McClellan had moved west along the National Pike the day before. Mansfield could have started west following McClellan and perhaps stayed at Hagan's Tavern on Catoctin Mountain west of Frederick. Regardless, Mansfield and his two riding companions spent over 40 hours journeying from Willard's to Middletown, a total distance of less than 60 miles. Of those 40 hours, available daylight riding was only about 17 hours giving a slow pace of less than four miles an hour. Mansfield must have been frustrated and anxious at not being able to get to McClellan more quickly to learn about his new command.

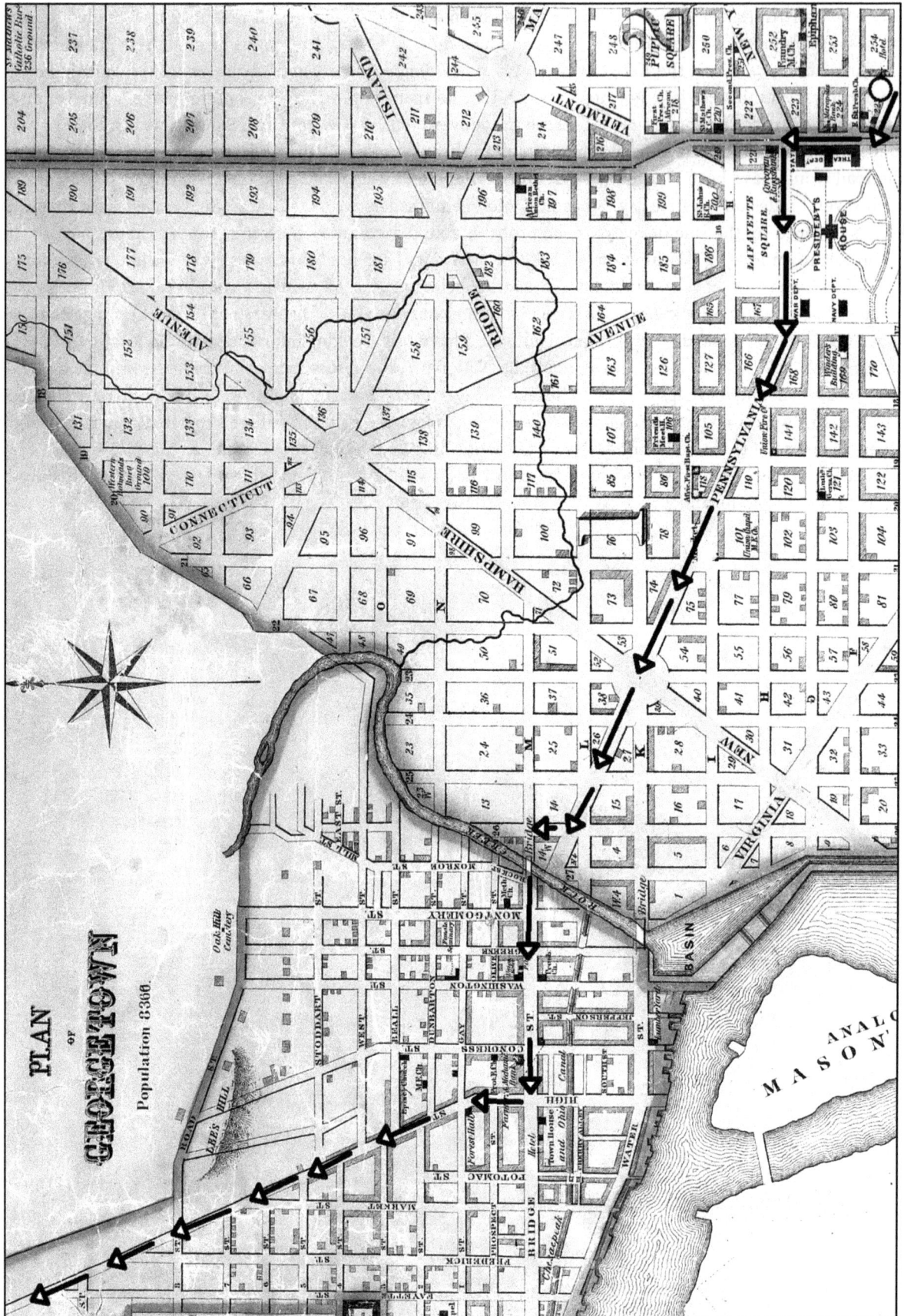

Most likely route Mansfield took as he rode from Washington on 13 September from Willard's Hotel on the northwest corner of 14th Street and Pennsylvania Avenue at the white dot. His most direct route would have been up Pennsylvania Avenue to Bridge Street then up High Street to the Rockville (Georgetown) Pike to Frederick. Detail from 1851 map of Washington, DC, courtesy NPS.

Mansfield did not like serving under McClellan in 1861, perhaps because of McClellan's rapid rise to high command or due to McClellan's age and relative few years of active service. Mansfield had entered West Point in 1817, nine years before McClellan's birth in 1826, and the old general had stayed in the U.S. Army serving with distinction for over 40 years. When the "Young Napoleon" found out that some senior generals resented his meteoric ascent to power, he wrote in a letter to his wife, Mary Ellen, on 27 July 1861, from Washington: "I have been assigned to the command of a Division [of the Potomac]—composed of Depts. of N.E. Va (that under [Brigadier General] McDowell) & that of Washington (now under Mansfield) – neither of them like it much—especially Mansfield, but I think they must ere long become accustomed to it, as there is no help for it."[14]

McClellan's vanity and treatment of long-serving officers likely rankled many. Mansfield at age 57 was now under the command of a 34-year-old major general who was a second lieutenant during the Mexican-American War, thrice brevetted to captain, while Mansfield, who began as a captain there, received brevets to major, lieutenant colonel, and then colonel, and had been seriously wounded. Mansfield was likely aware of McClellan's shabby treatment of Lieutenant General Winfield Scott which resulted in Scott's retirement on 1 November 1861.[15] During the Mexican-American War, even Henry W. Halleck was a first lieutenant, brevetted only to captain, and Irvin W. McDowell was a first lieutenant also brevetted to captain.[16] McClellan had seen Mansfield in the Mexican-American War and wrote to his wife then about that encounter:

> When we got to Victoria [Texas], we were attached to the 1st Division, Regulars, under Genl. Twiggs. Here we saw all the "heroes" and other big bugs, such as Old Zack, Major Mansfield, Bliss, Charley May, etc., etc. You can form no idea of the pleasure it gave us to meet the Regulars after having been so long with the cursed volunteers."[17]

It may be that Mansfield had somehow learned through his Washington connections that Lincoln wrote a memorandum around 14 May 1861 which listed McClellan and Mansfield as appointments to major generals in the Regular Army and Butler as a major general in the "3 year corps." Mansfield's name was crossed out, presumably by Lincoln, and Mansfield's appointment as a brigadier general was sent to the Senate on 13 July. No evidence has been found to show that Lincoln was ever displeased with Mansfield's conduct while he served in Washington or at Fort Monroe. One may speculate that Mansfield's lack of field command experience in the Old Army combined with perhaps

---

[14] George B. McClellan, *McClellan's Own Story. New York: Charles L. Webster & Company, 1887, Reprint, Scituate, MA: Digital Scanning, Inc., 1998*. 82; George B. McClellan, *The Civil War Papers of George B. McClellan: Selected Correspondence, 1860-1865*, edited by Stephen W. Sears (New York: Ticknor & Fields, 1989. Reprint, Cambridge, MA: Da Capo Press, 1992), 70. McClellan may have heard second-hand discussion or rumors of what Mansfield and other generals had said of him.

[15] McClellan, *Own Story*, "Gen. Scott is the great obstacle....I have to fight my way against him. Tomorrow the question will probably be decided by giving me absolute control independently of him....[he] is the most dangerous antagonist I have. Our ideas are so widely different that it is impossible for us to work together much longer....Gen. Scott proposes to retire in favor of Halleck. The President and cabinet have determined to accept his retirement, but not in favor of Halleck....Senators Wade, Trumbull, and Chandler....will make a desperate effort tomorrow to have Gen. Scott retired at once; until that is accomplished I can effect but little good. He is ever in my way, and I am sure does not desire effective action...I presume the Scott war will culminate this week...," 85-86, 136, 170-172. See *ORA*, vol. 51, pt. 1, 491-493, for Scott's complaints about McClellan addressed to Secretary Cameron. During the Mexican-American War, Mansfield was among only a few officers thrice brevetted; the others were Robert E. Lee, Zelous B. Tower, Joseph E. Johnston, Joseph Hooker, and Benjamin Huger; William Hugh Robarts, *Mexican War Veterans: A Complete Roster of the Regular and Volunteer Troops in the War Between the United States and Mexico, from 1846-1848* (Washington, DC: Brentano's, 1887), 5-9.

[16] Cadmus M. Wilcox, *History of the Mexican War* (Washington, DC: The Church News Publishing Company, 1892), 610, 614.

[17] George B. McClellan, *The Mexican War Diary and Correspondence of George B. McClellan*, ed. By Thomas W. Cutrer (Baton Rouge, LA: Louisiana State University Press, 2009), 67. The term "big bugs" was not at all derogatory but meant important people. Victoria, Texas, was an old Spanish city, located on the Guadalupe River, about 30 miles from the Gulf of Mexico and 70 airline miles northeast of Corpus Christie. Victoria, established in 1824, was originally named in honor of Guadalupe Victoria who had just become the first president of Mexico. Victoria was incorporated under the Republic of Texas in 1839, and was becoming an important trade center when McClellan was there; Robert W. Shook, "Victoria, TX (Victoria County)" *Handbook of Texas Online* (http://www.tshaonline.org/handbook/online/articles/hdv01), accessed March 18, 2013. Published by the Texas State Historical Association. McClellan did however, recognize that Mansfield was a general he wanted in his army as he telegraphed to Sec. Stanton 14 March 1862 that he desired "to form another division, under Mansfield, from the troops now in the vicinity of Fort Monroe, and to annex that division to the First Army Corps as soon as McDowell [its commander] is confirmed as major-general," *ORA*, vol. 5, 755. Stanton agreed on 20 March and Wool agreed, *ORA*, vol. 11, pt. 3, 24, 28; on 31 March, McClellan told Sumner that a division under Mansfield would replace Blenker's, 53. It is not shown why McClellan left Mansfield at Suffolk rather than joining McDowell's or Sumner's Corps.

an average performance while in Washington put other candidates ahead of him. Lincoln may have been waiting to see how the old general would perform once he had been given a large field command in an active theater.[18]

Mansfield was understandably jealous of McClellan and others who were his juniors as he wrote his wife again from Suffolk on 22 April 1862: "I have seen many of the officers [with McClellan], being old acquaintances of mine, all of whom have large commands although I rank them. This was accomplished by Little Mac the 2nd Napoleon. My time has not yet come."[19] Even an old acquaintance from his past, Scott, angered Mansfield almost as much as McClellan as he wrote in a vitriolic January 1862 letter to his wife: "I am a deal put out about my neglected position [at Camp Butler]. It is General Scott and McClellan who I regard as Little in every sense of the word. He [McClellan] is awfully conceited and will probably burst up out of sheer self-esteem. He has done nothing as yet. As to the other man, he is as much overgrown and spoiled by the flattery of people as a man can possibly be without stinking, and it has been his study under the garb of friendship to keep me back. The day of reckoning will come at last. I feel quite independent of them all."[20]

While one cannot say that Mansfield had any premonition of death upon being granted his first major command, he visited with Secretary of the Navy Gideon Welles, an old Connecticut friend, before he departed Washington. Welles wrote that "Mansfield…was from my State and almost a neighbor. He called on me last week, on his way from Norfolk to join the Army….When parting he once shook hands, there then was a farther brief conversation and he came back from the door after he left and again shook hands. 'Farewell,' said I, 'success attend you.' He remarked, with emphasis, and some feeling, 'We may never meet again.'"[21] Mansfield also "wrote an ominous and nostalgic letter 'in great haste' to his old West Point professor and friend, Colonel Sylvanus Thayer. 'This is only to say if I never see you again, that I have not forgotten your inestimable favors to me. May God bless you in your old age & finally receive you into his glorious Kingdom of Heavenly Peace.'"[22] Mansfield might have realized that McClellan's upcoming battles with General Robert E. Lee's Army were likely to be intense in the Union effort to halt Lee's invasion of the north. He would have also recalled the battles he was in almost 20 years before in Mexico where he was seriously wounded while in heavy combat. This old soldier did not begin his journey to join the Army of the Potomac without some trepidation but mostly the thrill of gaining his first field command during an active campaign after over 40 years of U.S. Army service. But there was no question in his mind that he could and would do his duty well as he had since he first entered West Point at age 13 in 1817.

[18] Abraham Lincoln, *The Collected Works of Abraham Lincoln*, ed. by Roy P. Basler, vol. 4 (New Brunswick, NJ: Rutgers University Press, 1953), 370. Note that Lincoln did ask Mansfield on 19 June 1861 his opinion of Joseph Hooker regarding a command of a regiment. Mansfield replied that he "would be highly gratified to see Col. Hooker a Col. In the Regular Army" but that General Scott was unwilling since Hooker and Scott had a falling out at the end of the Mexican-American War, ibid., 412-413. Lincoln did accept Mansfield's wish to have Charles H. Hosmer of Illinois appointed a second lieutenant in the Regular Army; he was nominated 1 August 1861, ibid., 467. Lincoln again acquiesced in Mansfield's personal appearance to request the appointment of Horatio G. Wright, of the Topographical Engineers to be a brigadier general of volunteers as a Connecticut appointment, in which General Totten concurred, ibid., 517. But Mansfield had no success in his attempt to have Lieutenant Col. Samuel W. Owen of the 1st Kentucky Cavalry appointed its colonel since Simon Cameron wrote "that Le Prince Felix de Salm Salm has been appointed the Colonel of this Regiment." Apparently this information was incorrect as the Prince never commanded that regiment, ibid., 524.

[19] Letter to wife 22 April 62, courtesy of the Middlesex County Historical Society. And Mansfield clearly thought even less of Pope: "Pope who has command of the Army of Virginia was a Second Lieutenant, and my aide at the storming of Monterey. A man of no sound moral principles and kept for a week at Monterey under arrest by General Taylor for bad conduct disgraceful to the service," letter to his wife 21 July 1862, courtesy of the Middlesex County Historical Society.

[20] Letter to wife, 24 January 1862, courtesy of the Middlesex County Historical Society. Perhaps it still rankled Scott that Mansfield was a friend of Jefferson Davis who appointed him an inspector general in 1853.

[21] Mansfield and Johnston, 198; Gideon Welles, *The Diary of Gideon Welles*, vol. 1 (Boston, MA: Houghton Mifflin Co., 1911), 140. Welles was born in Glastonbury, Connecticut, the center of which is about 10 airline miles across the Connecticut River from Mansfield's home in downtown Middletown, Connecticut.

[22] Mansfield to Sylvanus Thayer, 11 September 1862, Mansfield Papers, of the Middlesex County Historical Society. Today, these expressions to Thayer and Welles seem overly dramatic but were not so during the Victorian Era. See copy of this letter in an appendix below.

Major General George Brinton McClellan, commander of the Army of the Potomac. He knew and appreciated Mansfield's experience and abilities as an Old Army officer having served with him in the Mexican-American War. Courtesy NARA.

Honorable Gideon Welles, Secretary of the Navy under Lincoln and a friend of General Mansfield, was from Glastonbury, Connecticut. He was a favorite of Pres. Lincoln who called him "Father Neptune." Reportedly, he always wore a wig. He served as Secretary of the Navy from 5 March 1861 to 3 March 1869. He was a lawyer, journalist and politician, well-known in Connecticut. He became one of Lincoln's most trusted and reliable cabinet members although he clashed with others in that group. Photograph courtesy NARA.

Mansfield's son, Samuel Mather Mansfield, shown as a colonel. He became colonel of the 24ᵗʰ Connecticut Infantry 18 November 1862, and mustered out of volunteer service 30 September 1863, then rose through the Regular Army ranks retiring as a brigadier general in 1903. He was brevetted in the Regular Army to captain, major, and lieutenant colonel, for meritorious service during the Civil War. He was born 23 September 1839, in Middletown, Connecticut. He graduated from West Point on 17 June 1862, sixth in his class and was appointed a second lieutenant of engineers. Photograph courtesy WPL.

The Maryland Campaign of September 1862 was noteworthy for many reasons, but arguably the most important one was that its outcome was a Union victory, the first major victory in the Eastern Theater, a victory which allowed President Lincoln to issue his Preliminary Emancipation Proclamation. The Union victory, in addition to driving the best army that the South possessed back to Virginia, also meant that European powers, mainly England, would postpone any type of recognition of the Confederacy. The issuance of the Emancipation Proclamation changed the meaning of the war for the North and South. Lincoln sensed that it was time, both politically and militarily, to take the first major step to free the slaves. Admittedly, it only did so in a limited number of areas in the South, but it was a needed, first small step giving an official imprimatur to the administration's growing anti-slavery stance. This step also made it easier to enlist African Americans in the U.S. Army and to legitimize their employment in the armed forces.[23]

---

[23] Historians have argued whether the Battle of Antietam was a "draw" or a victory for McClellan. The general public at the time believed that the key factor to decide a victor was which army held the field after the battle. Here, both McClellan and Lee held the field, but Lee for only a day before his retreat. McClellan had pushed the Army of Northern Virginia back on all points of the battlefield on 17 September so many would argue that since

While no one battle in the Civil War determined its outcome, some historians argue the Battle of Antietam on 17 September 1862 was the key battle of the war. Historian James M. McPherson believes that the battle "changed the course of the war...[because it] arrested Southern military momentum, forestalled foreign recognition of the Confederacy, reversed a disastrous decline in the morale of Northern soldiers and civilians, and offered Lincoln the opportunity to issue a proclamation of emancipation."[24] Another remarkable aspect of the campaign was General Lee's saving his army from a crushing defeat after he divided it into four and then five parts during the campaign. It reveals how the best general in the Confederacy and arguably the best on either side, commanding the foremost army in the South, dealt with superior numbers and the loss of his operational plan to McClellan. The South's best army and its most victorious army commander were finally halted after an unbroken string of victories in the East which drove Union forces from the Confederate capitol's front door at Richmond, Virginia, back to the Potomac River. Lee and his Army had been victorious in the Peninsular Campaign against superior numbers but an inferior Union commander, Major General George B. McClellan. McClellan had victory in his grasp but in an overly cautious and poorly conducted campaign found himself just outside of Richmond but unable to take the city believing that he was heavily outnumbered. His opponent, General Joseph E. Johnston, also an unaggressive general, was finally forced to attack and, at the Battle of Seven Pines, was severely wounded, opening the door for Confederate President Jefferson Davis to appoint Robert E. Lee as the Southern Army's new commander. Lee soon began fighting ferociously to push McClellan away from Richmond, and succeeded, but at a higher cost to himself than to Union forces. McClellan, surprised and dismayed, retreated, ostensibly merely "changing his base" to ensure his continuing ability to maintain his supply line and to consolidate his lines.[25]

Lee retreated back into Virginia on the 18th/19th, McClellan was the victor. Modern interpretations of who was the "victor" sometimes address numbers of casualties on either side as absolute numbers or as percentages of numbers engaged. At Antietam, Carman shows Union strength as 55,956, Confederate as 37,351. Union casualties at Antietam were 12,401, or 22.16%; Confederate 19,316, or 27.62%. Thus the Union was victorious using both absolute and percentage calculations. Another measure is how the result contributed to national or military strategy, and here, since the battle gave Lincoln the opportunity to issue the Preliminary Emancipation Proclamation, as well as stopping Lee's move north, the Union's military and national strategies prevail. Often the Battle of Antietam is not viewed alone but in combination with the Union debacle at Harper's Ferry especially by the Confederacy as this perspective supported its appraisal that it was not a failure but an overall success. Total Maryland Campaign casualty data support this view: total Union losses 27,979 versus Confederate 13,922 as 12,737 were added due to the Harper's Ferry Union debacle. The author's opinion is that the Battle of Antietam was a Union victory as was McClellan's entire Maryland Campaign. Data from Ezra A. Carman, *The Maryland Campaign of September 1862. Vol. 2: South Mountain*, ed. Thomas G. Clemens (New York, NY: Savas Beatie LLC, 2010), 584-585, 601-602, 611; and Ezra A. Carman, *The Maryland Campaign of September 1862: Ezra A. Carman's Definitive Study of the Union and Confederate Armies at Antietam*, edited by Joseph Pierro (New York: Routledge Taylor & Francis Group, 2008), 478-479.

[24] James M. McPherson, *Crossroads of Freedom: Antietam*, (New York: Oxford University Press, 2002), 8-9; xvi. McPherson's book is the best single volume summarizing the totality of the Antietam Campaign discussing the events, political and military, leading up to the campaign as well as briefly talking about the battles themselves, and their aftermath. See also Joseph L. Harsh, *Sounding the Shallows: A Confederate Companion for the Maryland Campaign of 1862* (Kent, OH: The Kent State University Press, 2000), 73. This book is one of the companions to Harsh's *Taken at the Flood: Robert E. Lee and Confederate Strategy and the Maryland Campaign of 1862* (Kent, OH: The Kent State University Press, 1999). The former will hereafter be cited as "*Shallows*" and the latter as "*Flood.*" The proem to *Flood* is *Confederate Tide Rising: Robert E. Lee and the Making of Southern Strategy, 1861-1862* (Kent, OH: The Kent State University Press, 1998), hereafter cited as "*Rising.*" Harsh's books are the preeminent works on the Army of Northern Virginia and Lee during the campaign and before, and must be read by any serious student of the Maryland Campaign. Unless otherwise stated, all text references to "Harsh" pertain to *Taken at the Flood*. For British government opinions see Allan Nevins, *The War for the Union*, Vol. 1 (New York: Charles Scribner's Sons, 1959), 388-394, and vol. 2, 242-274 *passim*, showing that it would have been difficult for Britain to intervene especially due to the South's adamant position on slavery. Compare Howard Jones, *Blue & Gray Diplomacy: A History of Union and Confederate Foreign Relations* (Chapel Hill, NC: The University of North Carolina Press, 2010), 203-251, in which he argues that there was a very good chance of British intervention in the fall of 1862 in the form of mediation especially after the Union defeat at Second Bull Run, but the British decided to wait for the outcome of Lee's excursion north of the Potomac. After Lee returned to Virginia, there was still talk of mediation between the Union and Confederacy but given the Union strategic victory, the belief in England was that the Union was unlikely to agree. The desire for mediation remained in England because the war now seemed headed for a stalemate and the Emancipation Proclamation was not generally viewed with favor: "Contrary to the traditional story, the battle of Antietam and the Emancipation Proclamation did not stop the British movement toward intervention; rather, they only slowed down a process that once again had gotten under way," 235. See also James A. Rawley, *Turning Points of the Civil War* (Lincoln, NE: University of Nebraska Press, 1966), 101-104, where Rawley believes that a Confederate victory at Antietam might have led to mediation by Britain and France. James V. Murfin agreeing with McPherson wrote that "Tactically, Antietam was a draw. Strategically, politically, diplomatically and morally, it was a Union victory of high magnitude," *The Gleam of Bayonets: The Battle of Antietam and the Maryland Campaign of 1862* (Baton Rouge: Louisiana State University Press, 1965), 26.

[25] One of the best accounts of the Peninsular Campaign is found in Stephen W. Sears, *To the Gates of Richmond: The Peninsula Campaign* (New York: Ticknor & Fields, 1992). Sears, like most other historians, found McClellan the primary culprit in turning an arguably certain Union victory culminating in the capture of Richmond, to a resounding failure. Clearly, the replacement of Johnston by Lee materially aided in McClellan's defeat but it must be left to conjecture the outcome of the campaign had Johnston remained in command of the Confederate Army. The debate about McClellan being outnumbered continues, with modern research showing that later in the Peninsular Campaign, Lee's total forces facing McClellan

On the Peninsula, once Lee was certain that McClellan was no longer a threat to Richmond, he rapidly moved to confront the other major Union Army in Virginia, John Pope's Army of Virginia. Lee knew that he could not allow McClellan's Army of the Potomac to unite with Pope, so he moved to attack Pope quickly, soundly thrashing him at the Battle of Second Manassas on 30 August 1862. After failing to destroy major portions of the Federal Army there, or two days later just east of that battlefield at Chantilly, Lee decided that his best strategic move would be to enter Maryland. Just as he undoubtedly knew when he took over from Johnston at Richmond, neither he nor the South could afford to be passive; the overwhelming industrial and manpower advantages the North possessed would, if given time, overwhelm the Confederacy. But the recent campaigns in which his army had fought so hard resulted in major deficiencies in the material, munitions, food, and fodder, needed for further campaigning. Lee had to remain aggressive but take time to resupply, recruit, and rest his men.

The Union Army high command and the Lincoln government were alarmed and confused by Lee's movement north. It was feared that Lee might surround and attack the capitol and then move on Baltimore. Alternatively, he could continue north from his crossing point some thirty miles up the Potomac River near Leesburg, Virginia, and move into Pennsylvania attacking railroad links to the west and its capitol, Harrisburg, possibly then moving on New York City. Pope's Army was in disarray after its defeat at Second Bull Run while McClellan's relatively intact army was still recovering from its trials during the Peninsular Campaign and its return to Washington. Lincoln was forced to put McClellan in charge of the defense of Washington since he had no better choice and by default, McClellan became the commander of the Union pursuit of Lee. McClellan, an excellent administrator and organizer, quickly put units together and resupplied them even sending them out to find Lee in the middle of doing so. Confused by the conflicting and contradicting information being received about Confederate movements, McClellan was forced to cover a broad front as his units moved west and northwest to cover both Washington and Baltimore. McClellan performed well in Maryland during this campaign, as he confounded Lee by moving relatively rapidly from Washington. He reorganized his troops on the move, which included the majority from his Army of the Potomac, as well as parts of Pope's recently defeated Army of Virginia, leavened with regiments of raw recruits. The best of all the generals Lincoln had in the east shone brightly here in his finest campaign, and carried with him Lincoln's best wishes.

Ezra Carman, the premier historian of the Maryland Campaign, listed the various units McClellan commanded when he began chasing Lee exclusive of the forces left for the defense of Washington:

> The First Corps (Hooker), the Second Corps (Sumner), a division of the Fourth Corps, under Couch, the Sixth Corps (Franklin), the Ninth Corps (Burnside), and the Twelfth Corps (Williams). Brigadier General George Sykes's division was an independent command at the beginning of the campaign; it was joined on the march near Frederick by Major General George W. Morell's division—the two comprising the Fifth Corps, under Porter. In addition to this infantry force there was the cavalry division led by Pleasonton and an artillery reserve of seven batteries. Including the two divisions (Sykes's and Morell's) of the Fifth Corps, and excluding Brigadier General Andrew A. Humphrey's division of the same (which did not leave Washington until September 14), the Army of the Potomac in the field numbered 75,800 infantry and artillery and 4,300 cavalry. The artillery had sixty batteries aggregating 326 guns. Nearly 30,000 men were new recruits, fresh from the stores, workshops, and farms of the North. Over 48,000 were tried, seasoned veterans who had seen service on the Peninsula, in the Shenandoah Valley, in North Carolina, in West Virginia, and in front of Washington.[26]

While this was going on, Lee spent several days in bivouac near Frederick, Maryland, some forty miles northwest of Washington, resting and resupplying his troops, utilizing everything Frederick County's farms, fields and shops had to offer. Lee knew that the Union forces were sure to pursue but he did not anticipate their speed, nor did he know that McClellan would soon be in possession of an order Lee sent to his chief commanders detailing his campaign plans. His cavalry chief, Brigadier General James Ewell Brown (Jeb) Stuart, like Lee, did not show much concern. He did not conduct an aggressive scouting mission as he held Parr's Ridge and Sugar Loaf Mountain picketing Lee's Army's eastern flank. Lee was forced to divide his army because the Union garrisons at Harper's Ferry, and Martinsburg, Virginia, did not, as good military sense dictated, flee, as word reached them that the Confederate Army was in their rear cutting

---

were comparable, and perhaps during the Seven Days' Battles, Lee's forces outnumbered McClellan's, Leon Tenney, "Seven Days in 1862: Numbers in Union and Confederate Armies before Richmond," Master's thesis, George Mason University, 1992, vi, 51, 128; Tenney shows Lee with 113,000 and McClellan with 101,000. McClellan would have needed at least two to one odds to take a fortified city so had Johnston or Lee conducted a good defense, taking Richmond would have been difficult as Lieutenant Gen. Ulysses S. Grant learned two years later.

[26] Carman, Clemens, vol. 1, 149. Clemens opined that McClellan did not have 30,000 new recruits but closer to 18,000, 149 n. 68.

their lines of communication with Washington. Lee was forced to dispose of them since they posed a threat to his supply line from the Shenandoah Valley north into the Cumberland Valley in Pennsylvania. Lee's original plan, to move to Hagerstown, Maryland, and then through Chambersburg, Pennsylvania, further drawing the Union Army from its supply bases, was put on hold while he dealt with the two Union garrisons.[27]

Mansfield arrived at McClellan's headquarters near Middletown, Maryland, on Monday, the 15th, at 9 a.m., where he was assigned to temporary command of the XII Corps. Brigadier General John Gibbon wrote that two days earlier, he was in McClellan's tent late in the day on the 13th in the outskirts of Frederick. There he had witnessed an exchange between the army commander and one of his aides, Assistant Adjutant General Lieutenant Colonel Albert V. Colburn, about the command of the XII Corps: "McClellan, turning to Colburn, said 'Some one must be designated to command [Banks's] corps; get the list and read over the names of the general officers.' .... 'John Sedgwick,' read Colburn. 'He will do. Publish an order assigning Sedgwick to command that corps.' 'I don't think General Sedgwick wants it, General, I think he would rather command his present division,' said Colburn. 'I can't help that. He *must* take it. Issue the order.'"[28] McClellan's order was Special Order No. 254, 13 September 1862:

> II. Major General J. Sedgwick is assigned, temporarily, to the command of the II (Banks') Corps, late Army of Virginia, and will immediately enter upon duty accordingly. Brigadier General O.O. Howard will relieve Major-General Sedgwick in the command of his division.[29]

Perhaps the main reason Sedgwick refused was because "he 'felt he could do better service with the troops which he knew and which knew him'; he placed this consideration above advancement."[30] Sedgwick wrote in a letter to his sister on 4 September 1862: "I have worked hard and incessantly in bringing up my division, and it is now equal to any in the service, I hope."[31] Sedgwick was also obviously depressed, tired after many months of combat on the Peninsula, and unhappy with volunteers--his malaise is reflected in a letter written to his sister on 4 September 1862: "The Army are now around Washington, occupying nearly the same positions they did last winter. The enemy have outgeneralled us. Their hearts are in the cause; our men are perfectly indifferent, think of nothing but marauding and plundering, and the officers are worse than the men. The few officers that are disposed to do their duty, from a sense of doing it, are so outnumbered by the vicious that they can do but little. You cannot imagine how perfectly shameless people who are decent when at home become out here....Our men's hearts are not in the fight, and theirs [Confederates'] are."[32] Despite his depression, he did well at Antietam as he kept his head and seemed to be everywhere rallying his men. He was then wounded in a leg and a wrist but ignored these wounds as he tried to get his men out of the slaughter pen. Next, his horse was shot and disabled; a surgeon examined the general's two wounds and advised him to go to the rear. Sedgwick refused to do so and attempted to mount the surgeon's horse but had difficulty riding with the broken wrist. Finally, a third shoulder wound caused him to leave the field semiconscious, an hour after receiving his first wound.[33]

---

[27] Harsh, 252. Harsh is in the minority asserting that McClellan, given all the circumstances, did well in his pursuit of Lee even before the famous "Lost Order" was found. This order, Special Order 191, showed McClellan the disposition of Lee's forces and allowed the Union commander to hasten his pursuit even though he still was concerned about the strength of Lee's Army—the order had no information about strength. Here, as on the Peninsula, McClellan was convinced he was heavily outnumbered thus constraining, in his mind, his options. Harsh argues that given the abilities of his army, McClellan could not have done much more than he did after finding the order, 241. Most information McClellan received from Washington, his cavalry, civilians, and state government officials showed that General Lee had at least 120,000 men in Maryland, *ORA*, vol. 19, pt. 2, 281. For details surrounding the Lost Order see Wilbur D. Jones, "Who Lost the Lost Order?," *Civil War Regiments: A Journal of the American Civil War*, vol. 5, no. 3, (1997). Jones argues that the most likely culprit was Henry Kyd Douglas, one of Stonewall Jackson's staff, although some Antietam historians such as Dr. Thomas Clemens disagree with Jones's conclusions.

[28] John Gibbon, *Personal Recollections of the Civil War* (New York, NY: G.P. Putnam's Sons, 1928; reprint, Dayton, OH: Morningside House, Inc., 1988), 72-73, emphasis in original. *ORA*, vol. 19, pt. 2, 283. Sumner wrote to McClellan on 13 September recommending Sedgwick to command the XII Corps and O.O. Howard taking command of his division, Sumner to Marcy, 13 September 1862, A79, Reel 31.

[29] *ORA*, vol. 19, pt. 2, 283.

[30] Richard Elliot Winslow III, *General John Sedgwick: The Story of a Union Corps Commander* (Novato, CA: Presidio Press, 1982), 43.

[31] John Sedgwick, *Correspondence of John Sedgwick, Major General*, vol. 2 (n.p.: Carl and Ellen Battelle Stoeckel, 1903), 81.

[32] Ibid., 80-81.

[33] Winslow, 47.

Brigadier General John Gibbon was in McClellan's tent late in the day on the 13th in the outskirts of Frederick and wrote that he had witnessed an exchange between the army commander and one of his aides, Assistant Adjutant General Lieutenant Colonel Albert V. Colburn, about the command of the XII Corps. McClellan told Colburn to assign Sedgwick even though Colburn said that he did not want it and would rather command his present division.[34] Courtesy LOC.

Photograph taken at Harrison's Landing, Virginia, August 1862, showing McClellan's Assistant Adjutant General Lieutenant Colonel Albert V. Colburn on the far left, Inspector General Colonel Delos B. Sacket in the center, and Brigadier General John Sedgwick.[35] Courtesy LOC and Brian Downey, *Antietam on the Web.*

---

[34] Gibbon was an 1847 West Point graduate, commanded the Fourth Brigade, First Division, III Corps, in the Army of Virginia, and the Fourth Brigade, First Division, I Corps, at Antietam. His brigade was known as the "Black Hat Brigade," one of a few in the Union Army with that name, and the most famous. He was a fighting general twice wounded during the war becoming a division and then corps commander; he was promoted to major general of volunteers 7 June 1864 and brigadier general in the Regular Army 10 July 1885.

[35] Colburn graduated from West Point in the class of 1855 and was commissioned into the cavalry. He led two companies from his 4th U.S. Cavalry at First Bull Run and was appointed to McClellan's staff remaining there until November 1862, travelling with McClellan to New Jersey after his commander was relieved on 5 November 1862. In December, he was assigned to Major General John Schofield's staff as Adjutant General of the Department of the Missouri. Quartered in St. Louis, Colburn died of illness there six months later on 17 June 1863.

Clarence Hopkins Dyer after the Civil War. Captain Dyer was born at Harwinton, Connecticut, 21 July 1832, and was appointed Captain and Assistant Adjutant General, U.S.V., 25 September 1861, Heitman, vol. 1, 392. "His first service was with Major General Mansfield, in command at Camp Hamilton, Virginia, and Newport News, at the time of the fight between the Monitor and the Merrimac off that point." After Antietam, "He then reported to Major General Banks for temporary duty at Washington City, after which he served with Major General E.A. Carr," then Canby, and Merritt; William Eliot Furness, Chmn., *Memorials of Deceased Companions of the Commandery of the State of Illinois, Military Order of the Loyal Legion of the United States*, vol. 1 (Chicago, IL: n.p., 1901), 192-193. Dyer became a major and adjutant of the First Regiment Chicago Volunteers 2 August 1865. *Companions of the Commandery*, 192.[36] Photograph courtesy Nicholas Picerno Collection.

---

[36] Clarence was the son of Thomas Dyer, who was born in Canton, Connecticut, 13 January 1805. At about age 30, he moved with his family, including two-year-old Clarence, to Chicago, Illinois. There he was a successful businessman as a director of the Galena & Chicago Union road, a state legislator, and Mayor of Chicago in 1856. He died in Middletown on 6 June 1862. Clarence apparently found himself in Washington, D.C. in 1861, there met with his friend, Cassius M. Clay. As there were few Federal troops in Washington at that time, Clay organized a group of 300 volunteers to protect the White House and U.S. Naval Yard from a possible Confederate attack. These men became known as Cassius M. Clay's Washington Guards. After a brief service, the Guards were disbanded when Federal troops arrived. Clarence probably came to the attention of Lincoln and his administration, and likely to Mansfield, during Mansfield's tenure in Washington in 1861, and from their Middletown connections. A.T. Andreas, *History of Chicago from the Earliest Period to the Present Time* (Chicago, IL: A.T. Andreas, Publisher, 1884), 622.

McClellan assigned Captain James William Forsyth from his staff as a temporary aide to Mansfield. Photograph taken when Forsyth was Provost Marshall of the Army of the Potomac, sitting atop a crate of hardtack at Aquia Creek Landing, Virginia, February 1863.[37] Courtesy LOC.

There is no record why McClellan replaced his first selection, Sedgwick, with Mansfield. Possibly he learned from Washington that Mansfield was soon to arrive and receive a command so if Mansfield's fellow Nutmegger, Sedgwick, did not wish to leave his division, McClellan was not going to force the issue--Mansfield would command his smallest

---

[37] Forsyth was born in Ohio, and graduated from West Point 1 July 1856 receiving a commission as second lieutenant in the 9th Infantry. He helped finish the fort at San Juan Island, Washington Territory, and served as acting commander when Captain George E. Pickett was away. Forsyth was promoted to first lieutenant in 1861 and returned east. He was appointed colonel of the 64th Ohio Infantry on 9 November 1861, and was temporarily in command of a brigade during Don Carlos Buell's march to the relief of Major General U.S. Grant at Shiloh but did not participate in the battle. Forsyth transferred to the Army of the Potomac where he served as the assistant inspector general during the Peninsular Campaign. After Mansfield's death, Forsyth became provost marshal to the Army of the Potomac. In 1863, he transferred back to the Western Theater to serve as adjutant to Sheridan at Chickamauga and was brevetted to major in the Regular Army for his service. He followed Sheridan to the Army of the Potomac's Cavalry Corps when Sheridan went east, as his chief of staff. He received brevets to lieutenant colonel, colonel, and brigadier general. He remained in the Army after the war rejoining Sheridan and taking part in campaigns against Indians in 1868-69. Forsyth went to Europe in 1870 as an official observer of the Franco-Prussian War. He was promoted to major general 11 May 1897, retiring three days later. He died 24 October 1906 in Columbus, Ohio. *Cullum's Register*, vol. 2, 434-435; courtesy Wikipedia.

corps. These Old Army men, all Mexican-American War veterans--McClellan, Mansfield and Sedgwick--were not going to squabble at this time when combat was imminent. McClellan was obviously too busy to spend much time on what he probably wound up seeing as a relatively minor matter. Because Mansfield had been in charge of the Washington, D.C., area in 1861, he was well known to Lincoln and Stanton so the old general's lobbying for a combat command was effective as he had done his job well enough early in the war. He was ordered to report in person to McClellan by Special Orders No. 229 dated 8 September 1862 from the Army's Adjutant General's Office by command of Major General Halleck: "IV. Brigadier General J.K.F. Mansfield, U.S. Volunteers, is relieved from duty in the Army of Virginia, and will report in person to Major-General McClellan."[38] McClellan issued an unnumbered Special Order on 15 September 1862 "temporarily" assigning Mansfield to command of Banks's corps the day after assigning it to Sumner:

Special Orders,   Headquarters Army of the Potomac
No. —.   In the Field, September 14, 1862

Major General A. E. Burnside is assigned to the command of the right wing of this Army, which will be composed of his own and Hooker's corps.

The Second Corps (Banks'), late Army of Virginia [Twelfth Corps] is placed, until further orders, under the command of Major General E. V. Sumner, commanding Second Corps, Army of the Potomac.

By command of Major-General McClellan:
      S[eth] Williams,
      Assistant Adjutant-General

The first part of these orders was never implemented as before the advance resumed on the morning of the fifteenth, new orders were issued as Mansfield had caught up with McClellan's headquarters:

Special Orders,   Headquarters Army of the Potomac
No. —.   In the Field, September 15, 1862

I. The operation of the Special Orders of yesterday's date, assigning General Burnside to the command of the right wing, owing to the necessary separation of the Third [First] Corps, is temporarily suspended. General Hooker will report direct to these headquarters.

II. Brigadier General J. K. F. Mansfield is temporarily assigned to the command of Banks' corps.

By command of Major-General McClellan: S. Williams,   Assistant Adjutant-General.[39]

McClellan did not leave Brigadier General Alpheus S. Williams in command of the XII Corps. Perhaps he preferred Mansfield over Williams as Williams was a volunteer officer who did not attend West Point and was never in the Old Army. Williams did however, have prior military experience, was a businessman, and held civic offices. He never received any officer rank in the Regular Army although after the war he was brevetted as a major general in the volunteer army. In the final analysis, Williams was never in contention as the permanent commander of the XII Corps as he had several strikes against him: first, he never graduated from, or attended West Point; second, he was not in the Old Army; third, he was associated with General Banks's failures, and finally, he had no strong political connections nor did he cultivate favor with newspaper reporters.

Williams was not angered over being relegated to division command and did not take it as a personal affront perhaps because he liked McClellan more than Pope or Banks: "'I went back to my division rather pleased that I had got rid of an onerous responsibility."[40] He also was very fatigued from the battle at Cedar Mountain. He had lost his adjutant who had been captured there while Banks had taken his with him so Williams had few aides to help with paperwork while dealing with the crippling losses his corps suffered at Cedar Mountain. He wrote to his daughter on

---

[38] *ORA*, vol. 19, pt. 2, 214.

[39] *ORA*, vol. 19, pt. 2, 290, 297. Mansfield's official date of command of the XII Corps was 12 September, McClellan did not receive notice of this on that date however. The XII Corps was also officially created that date, Frederick H. Dyer, *A Compendium of the War of the Rebellion* (Des Moines, IA: The Dyer Publishing Company, 1908), 320.

[40] Williams, 123; Jeffrey Gordon Charnley, "'Neglected Honor,' The Life of General A.S. Williams of Michigan (1810-1878)," (Ph.D. dissertation, University of Michigan, 1983), 135, 137-138.

26 August that he had not changed clothes in 10 days. He, like Sedgwick, was dismayed that he and his men were back where they started with Pope.[41]

Howard Mather Burnham applied to his uncle, Brigadier General Mansfield, to become an aide. Mansfield wrote to Secretary Stanton on 12 September 1862 requesting that he "may be ordered to report to me on my staff as Aide." Unfortunately, Second Lieutenant Burnham was unable to join his uncle before Antietam. Burnham was killed at the Battle of Chickamauga 19 September 1863 at the age of 21, commanding Battery H, 5th U.S. Light Artillery. Frontispiece, Anon., *Memorial of Lieutenant Howard M. Burnham* (Springfield, MA: Samuel Bowles and Company, Printers, 1864).

---

[41] Ibid., 134; Williams, *From the Cannon's Mouth*, 119-120.

Brigadier General Alpheus Starkey "Pap" Williams, senior division commander in the XII Corps, with his wig well in place. See Attachment 2 below for his biography. Courtesy LOC.

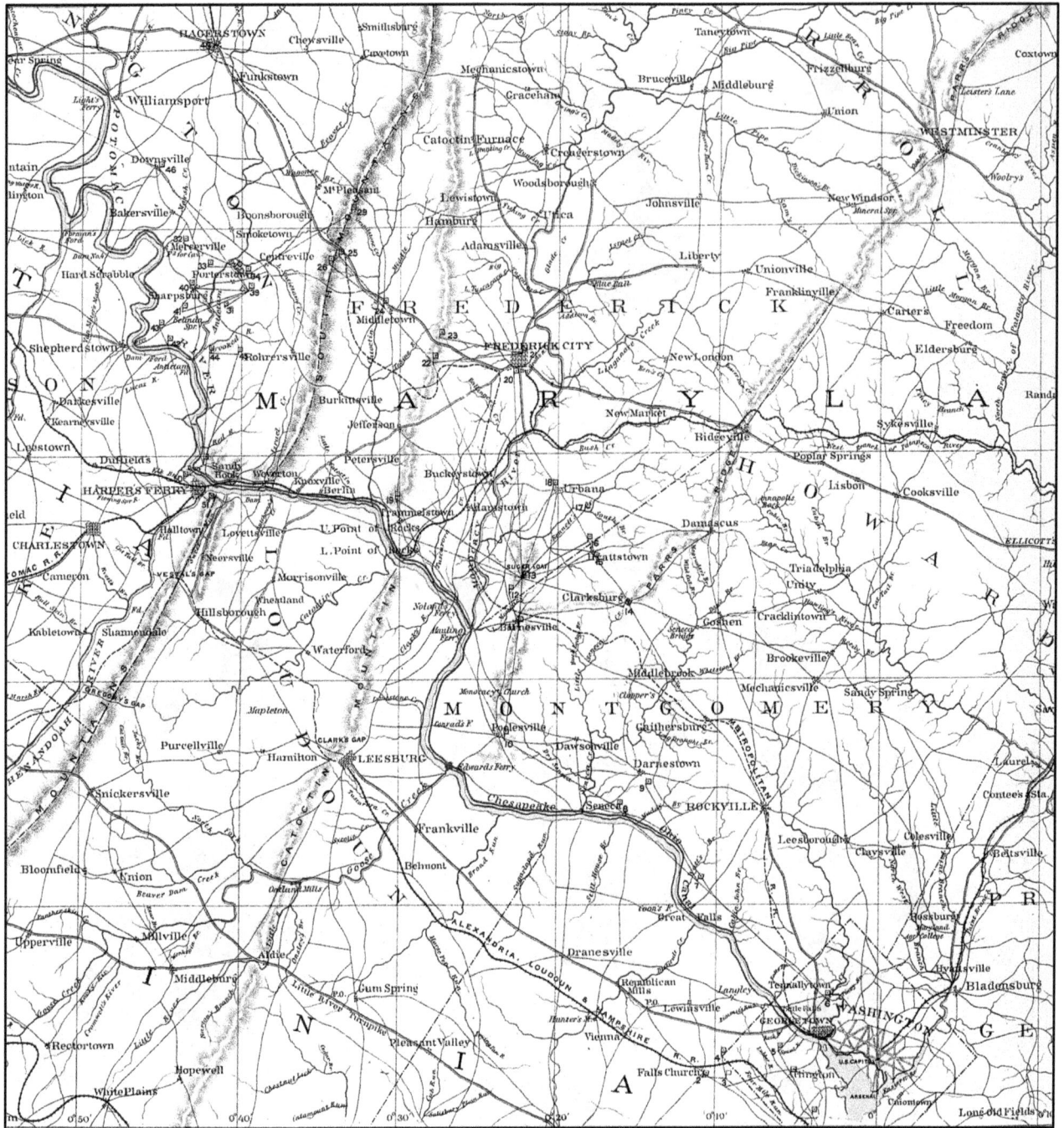

Area of operations of the II/XII Corps in September 1862. General Lee's goal was to form his Army around Frederick, Maryland, at the upper center behind the Monocacy River and Parr Ridge barriers. The main road from Washington to Frederick was called the Georgetown Pike; Frederick was on the National Pike from Baltimore. Sugarloaf Mountain is to the Northeast of Poolesville next to Barnesville; White's Ford is almost due west of Barnesville northwest of Poolesville. Conrad's Ferry below White's Ford is today White's Ferry. White's Ferry is about three river miles below White's Ford. Parr's Ridge is the ridge farthest to the right which runs through Damascus, Maryland. The valley between the Catoctin Mountains and Parr's Ridge is sometimes called Monocacy Valley. The Catoctin Mountains, the Maryland extension of the Bull Run Mountains in Virginia, are just west of Frederick and to their west is the South Mountain Range. Between them is the Middletown (or Catoctin) Valley. West of South Mountain near Harper's Ferry is Elk Mountain or Elk Ridge which terminates at Harper's Ferry and is called Maryland Heights at that point; Elk Ridge is the Maryland extension of the Virginia Blue Ridge Mountains located near Sandy Hook just above Harper's Ferry. Pleasant Valley lies between South Mountain and Elk Ridge. Rebel pickets were initially located at Clarksburg, Hyattstown, Damascus, Ridgeville, Barnesville, Poolesville, and around Sugarloaf. Harper's Ferry is about fifty airline miles from Washington while Frederick is about forty miles. Note that this map shows Keedysville erroneously as Centerville. On 4 September, McClellan reported his disposition as follows: First Corps at Upton's Hill, the Ninth Corps on the 7th Street Road, the II and XII Corps at Tenallytown, the Sixth Corps at the Alexandria Seminary, and Couch's division at Tenallytown, George B. McClellan, *Report on the Organization and Campaigns of the Army of the Potomac* (New York: Sheldon & Company, 1864) · 349. *Official Atlas*, Plate 27. Courtesy LOC.

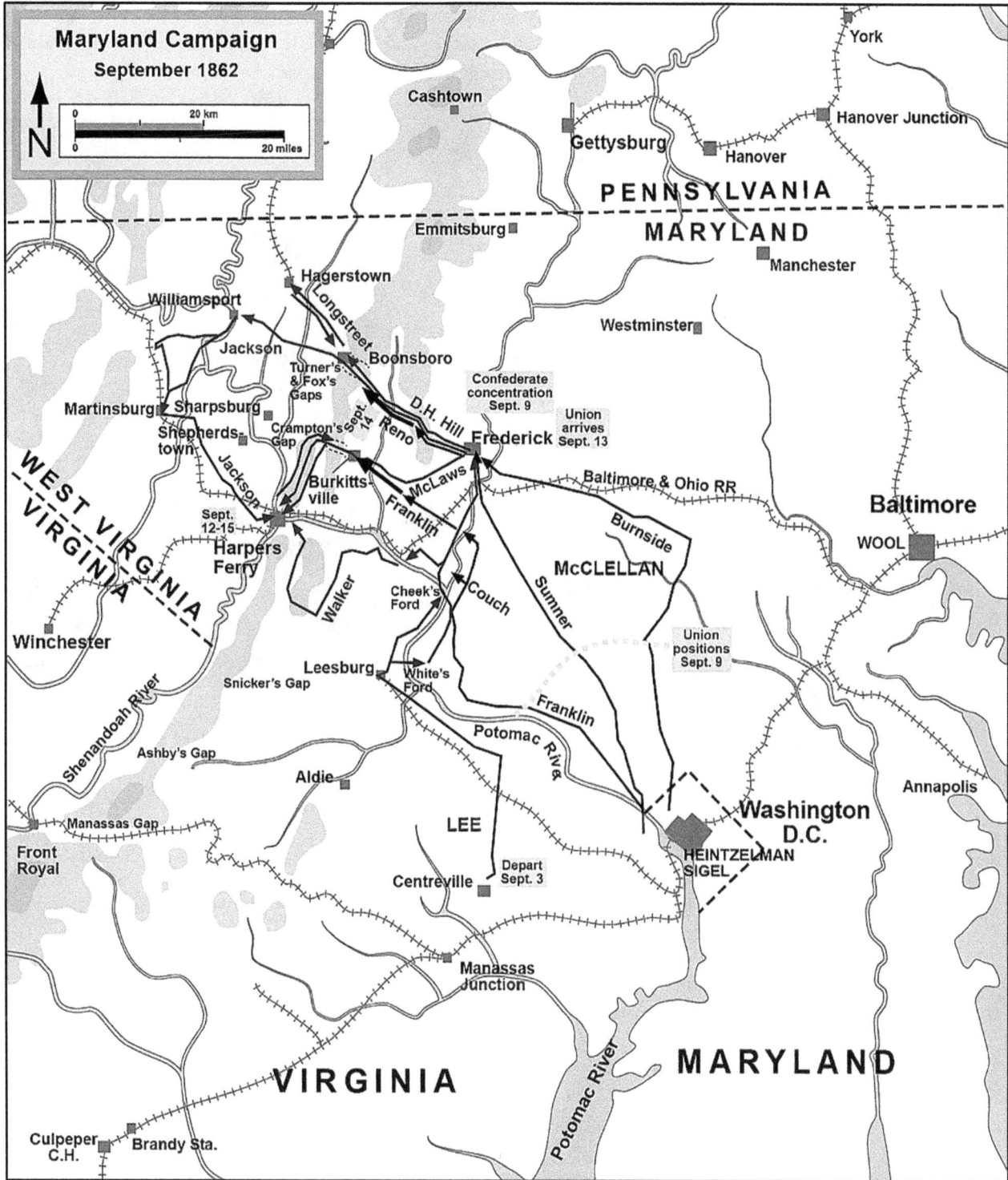

General map of Maryland Campaign to 15 September 1862 showing troop movements. Courtesy Hal Jespersen from Wikipedia.

The XII Corps from Frederick to Antietam

The XII Corps continued its trek westward from camps around Frederick. Its troops counted themselves fortunate as they heard the thunder of artillery from the Battle of South Mountain on the 14th from a safe distance. Their comrades in Burnside's Wing in the van battled furiously with determined Rebel defenders at the gaps along the impressive mountain: Turner's Gap on the National Pike, and Fox's Gap just one mile south of there on the Old Sharpsburg Road. Just seven miles south of Turner's Gap, the Union VI Corps commander, Major General William B. Franklin, at Crampton's Gap, pushed his greatly outnumbered foe west over the crest of South Mountain but decided that the Confederate defenders in Pleasant Valley were too strong to continue on the offense. With his lack of aggression, he allowed the successful escape of his Confederate foes which were then left to reinforce General Lee at Sharpsburg during the following two days, as well as ensuring the fall of the Harper's Ferry garrison.[42]

Many troopers in the XII Corps toiling uphill on 14 September would have passed Hagan's Tavern at Hagan's (Braddock's, or Fairview) Gap on the National Pike, up the eastern slope of Catoctin Mountain just west of Frederick. In this area nearer the crest, Rebel cavalry under Wade Hampton stopped Union cavalry pursuit commanded by Alfred Pleasonton. The front porch is a 1914 addition to the original building which was built in the late 1700's. Hagan operated the tavern in 1830. Mansfield may have spent the night of 14 September here. Courtesy Craig Swain HMdb.org.

Lieutenant John Mead Gould of the 10th Maine wrote in his diary that on the 14th, the XII Corps packed three-days rations and moved out about 8 a.m. from near Frederick: "Everyone was out dressed in their Sunday clothes....women and children were waving handkerchiefs and giving water to our soldiers...." The march was difficult due to "poking through cornfields and ploughed lots till at length we struck a road and marched along that. Then came a halt every three minutes and halt after halt the most tedious and aggravating as well as tiresome...." He welcomed their bivouac but found that their marching was not finished. Gould went to sleep then got up, made supper, then "marched, halted, marched, halted, filed right, filed left, and at length off into a field and stacked arms." He found only about 100 men had kept up when he finally went to bed after midnight.[43]

Captain William F. Fox, of the 107th New York, also described the move west from Frederick:

On...the fourteenth...the Twelfth Corps moved forward also, and marching through Frederick the troops pushed on towards the front, where the fighting had already commenced. Behind them the Sabbath bells were ringing in the Frederick steeples, their peaceful sound mingling with the sullen boom of the artillery at South Mountain and Harper's Ferry. The

---

[42] Turner's Gap on the National Pike was the most important pass in South Mountain. The crest of the mountain is some 600 feet higher than the floor of Middletown Valley to the east and Cumberland Valley to the west. Fox's Gap is about one mile south of Turner's Gap through which passes the Old Sharpsburg Road. It branches off to the northwest from the National Pike just west of Middletown; Crampton's Gap, six miles south of Fox's Gap, was the location of a road which joined the Arnoldstown Road and the extension of Burkittsville's main street.

[43] John M. Gould, *The Civil War Journals of John Mead Gould 1861-1865*, ed. by William B. Jordan, Jr. (Baltimore, MD: Butternut & Blue, 1997), 190-191.

march this day, though not a long one, was wearisome in the extreme. The roads were occupied by cavalry, artillery and ammunition trains. The infantry moved across fields and through tall standing corn, where the still, close air intensified the suffocating heat. Up and over the Catoctin Range they climbed and then marched down into the beautiful valley of the Catoctin Creek [Catoctin or Middletown Valley], wading this stream long after dark. It was past midnight when the head of the column reached the field, and went into position ready to begin the fighting at daylight if necessary. But the enemy retreated during the night, leaving his dead unburied on the field.[44]

Lieutenant Julian Wisner Hinckley of the 3rd Wisconsin wrote of this march: "We were ready to march by four o'clock on the morning of the 14th. But we might as well have stayed in camp until seven. The road west from Frederick was a fine, broad turnpike, wide enough for two or three wagons abreast, but it was now completely choked with the ammunition and provision wagons of the troops in advance. Even after we did finally get started, and were clear of the town, we had to march through the fields and woods on either side of the road."[45]

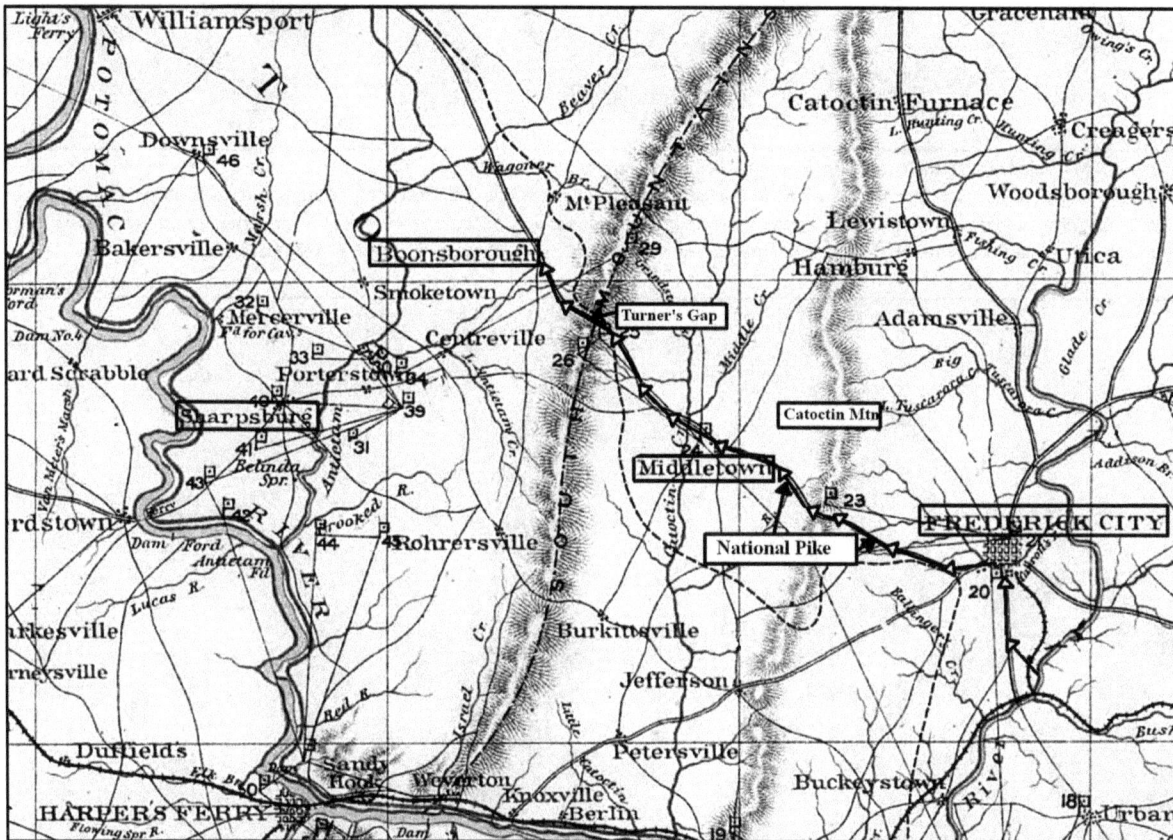

XII Corps march from near Frederick to Boonsboro along the National Pike through the Catoctin Mountains, Middletown Valley, Middletown, Turner's Gap through South Mountain to Boonsboro, 13 September to 15 September. "September 13, Hooker's First Corps moved from Lisbon to Cooksville, by the National Road [Pike], to the Monocacy, the average march of the divisions being about sixteen miles; no other divisions covered half this distance. Sumner's Second Corps marched from Urbana to Frederick, about six miles; Williams's Twelfth Corps from Ijamsville Cross Roads to Frederick, about six miles; Sykes's Division from Urbana to Frederick, about six miles; Franklin's Sixth Corps from Licksville to Buckeystown, about six miles, and Couch's Division from Barnesville to Licksville, about five miles. Farnsworth's cavalry brigade marched out of Frederick by the National Road on the morning of the 13th, drove Hampton's cavalry from Fairview [Hagan's] Gap of the Catoctins, followed through Middletown, overtook Hampton's rear-guard on Catoctin Creek, brushed it away, and pursued nearly to the foot of Turner's Gap of South Mountain....Cox's Kanawha Division of the Ninth Corps moved from Frederick to Middletown and thence a mile beyond (a total of seven miles), and Sturgis's and Willcox's divisions of the same corps marched to within one mile of Middletown;" Carman, Clemens, vol. 1, 288-289. *OA*, pl. 27.

[44] William F. Fox, *In Memoriam, Henry Warner Slocum, 1826-1894* (Albany, NY: J.B. Lyon Company, 1904), 139.
[45] Julian Wisner Hinckley, *A Narrative of Service with the Third Wisconsin Infantry* (Democrat Printing Co., State Printer, Wisconsin History Commission, 1912), 49.

Boonsboro, Maryland, 15 September; South Mountain is in the distance looking southeast, Turner's Gap to the left upper center through which the National Pike passes on its way from Frederick to Hagerstown. Fox's Gap is one mile south of Turner's Gap to the right. Note smoke showing where the fight was. It may also be that the artist mislabeled the scene as it may be looking west from Middletown so the wagons would be moving west on the National Pike. Alfred R. Waud, Drawing done for *Harper's Weekly*, October 25, 1862, p. 677. Author's collection.

Union troops marching west through Middletown, Maryland, 14 September, on the National Pike, pursuing the Confederate Army. Note telegraph wire on poles to the left. Drawing from *Harper's Weekly*, October 25, 1862, p. 677. Author's collection.

Gould wrote in his 10th Maine regimental history of the detritus and horror of the South Mountain battlefield near Turner's Gap his regiment viewed early on the 16th:

We for the first time saw a battle field from which we had not been driven....The [Rebel] wounded were those who had been able to help themselves a little, and were not suffering very much. Passing up the "Old Sharpsburg road" on the left side of the ravine (the [National] pike is on the right [north] side), we met a train of ambulances and a party of men with stretchers, all bringing down the dead and wounded—principally the first, for the wounded had been taken off during the night. The few houses were full of the wounded and the medical officers. The adjoining yards were also full of wounded men, with now and then a dead one, all laid in good order and all very quiet. The shade trees had scores under them. Passing up farther we found the 46ᵗʰ Penn. burying the dead; they were all union soldiers and had been brought down from the field. They were buried in their clothes and wrapped in blankets or tents, and each corpse had a grave to itself, and a head board made of a cracker box.

Still farther up was the principal battle ground. Here the enemy had a position behind a stone wall and sunken road, and the woods were about sixty yards off, so they had the benefit of shelter while our men had little. The rebel dead literally lined this road for nearly half a mile, for the union dead had been taken out and buried, and those who had fallen in the road itself had been thrown up one side. All the dead had been robbed of their valuables, their pockets were turned, and the accoutrements were thrown about and haversacks emptied. So don't let us accuse rebels alone of robbing the dead. The rebel dead looked unlike ours, which were swollen and so appeared hale and hearty. Theirs were mere skeletons, and had an ashy skin against which the ash colored dust hardly showed. There were many old men and boys among them. We saw one little child of scarcely fourteen years; his face showed a sprightly look not seen on the others.[46]

Fox wrote glowingly of Mansfield's first appearance and subsequent encounters with his troops:

Major General Joseph K. F. Mansfield, an old officer of the Regular Army, had been assigned to the command of the Twelfth Corps, and he joined it on the morning of the fifteenth, the day after the battle of South Mountain, General Williams resuming charge of the First Division. Mansfield was a white-bearded veteran of advanced years, who had served in the Mexican war with many honors, and wounds as well. Prior to joining the Twelfth Corps he had held important commands at Fort Monroe, Norfolk and Suffolk. His dignified, soldierly demeanor created a favorable impression, and withal he had a kindly manner that appealed strongly to the men in the ranks....

The march this day [15ᵗʰ] led through the little hamlet of Boonsborough, where the church and several houses had been converted into hospitals for the Confederate wounded, while along the roadside lay many of their dead. General Mansfield was sitting on his horse near a dead Confederate who was covered with a blanket, when a sergeant in one of the new regiments stepped out of the ranks and pulled aside the covering to look at the dead man's face. Mansfield spoke up quickly— "There, there, Sergeant! No idle curiosity! Don't uncover the face of the dead. You will soon have a chance to see all you want of them." And the first man shot that the sergeant saw was Mansfield himself.[47]

That night [15ᵗʰ] the corps bivouacked in the fields near Keedysville, not far from the Antietam Creek. The next morning — the sixteenth— brought orders to move, and line of battle was formed. Just over the low ridge of hills that skirted the stream a lively cannonade was in progress that sounded as if it were close by. Hooker was shelling the enemy's lines on the farther side of the creek; at times a brisk skirmish fire was heard. The gray-haired corps commander as he rode along his line announced that they were going into battle immediately; but his troops did no fighting that day....The hours passed quickly, and, in the fading light of a gorgeous sunset the men prepared their evening meal. Then, while the bugles were sounding sweet and clear from distant camps, they made their simple bivouac under the starlight and lay down to sleep.[48]

Gould described meeting Mansfield anew as many in his regiment had done in its first iteration as the 1ˢᵗ Maine while in Washington, DC:

Brigadier General Joseph K. F. Mansfield, of the regular Army, took command of our corps this morning [15ᵗʰ]. He was the old commanding general over the 1st Maine, and was much respected by our 1st Maine officers. We never saw another like him; venerable, but not old; white haired, yet fresh and vigorous, his face showed that intelligent courage which a soldier admires rather than that which by distinction may be called brute courage. There was nothing pretentious about him, though his dress and horse equipments were new and beautiful. Nor did he have either aide or orderly when he visited us. Our first sight of him gave us the impression that he was a fine old gentleman, an able soldier and our father.[49]

---

[46] John M. Gould, *History of the First-Tenth-Twenty-ninth Maine Regiment in Service of the United States from May 3, 1861, to June 21, 1866* (Portland, ME: Stephen Berry, 1871), 227.

[47] Fox, *In Memoriam*, 140.

[48] Fox, *In Memoriam*, 140.

[49] Gould, *History of the First-Tenth-Twenty-ninth Maine Regiment*, 227-228.

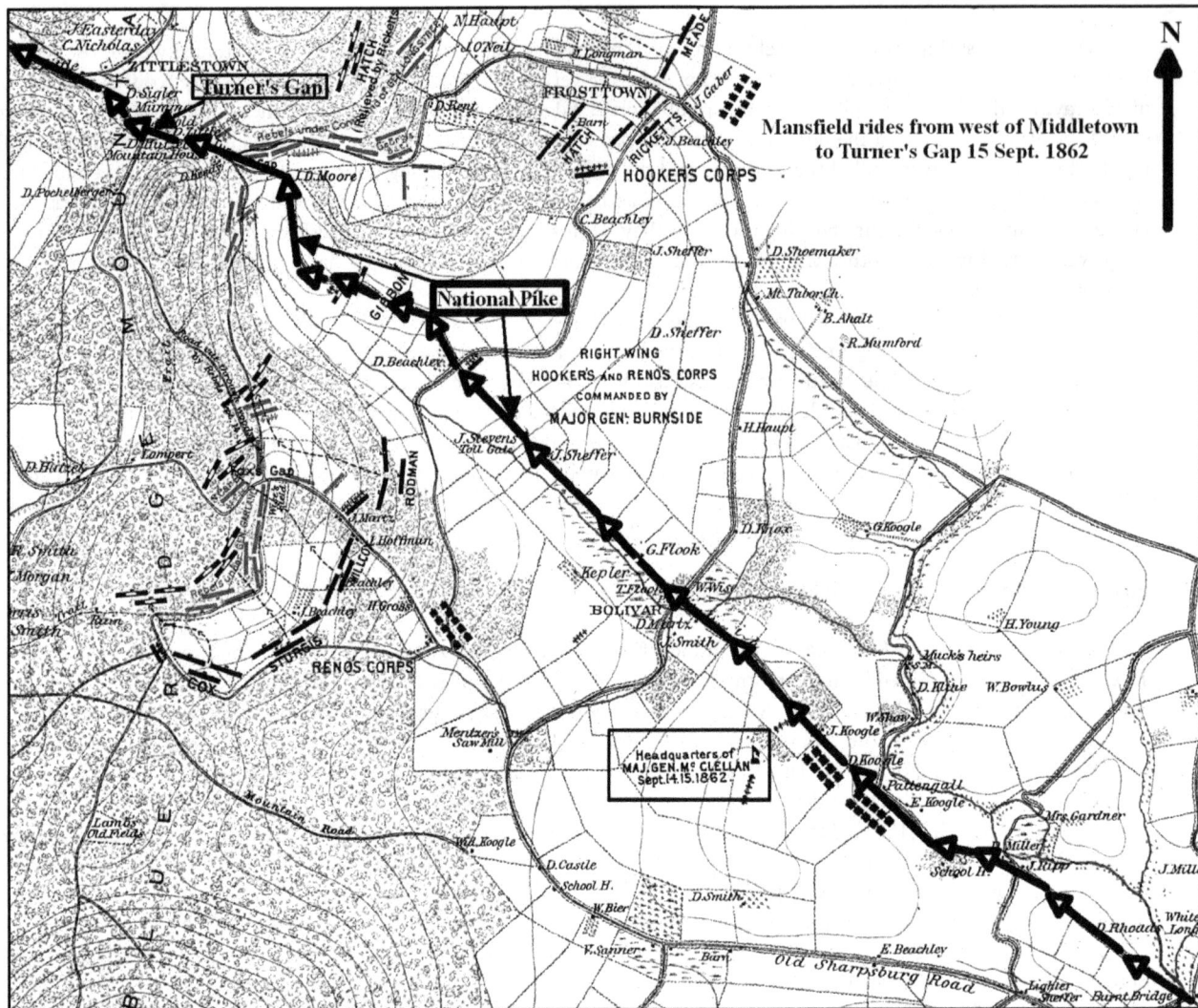

Mansfield rode from Middletown to McClellan's Headquarters on the David Koogle Farm to the west of the National Pike on the morning of 15 September about 9 a.m. He then continued on to join his corps near Boonsboro around noon. *OA*, pl. 27, courtesy LOC.

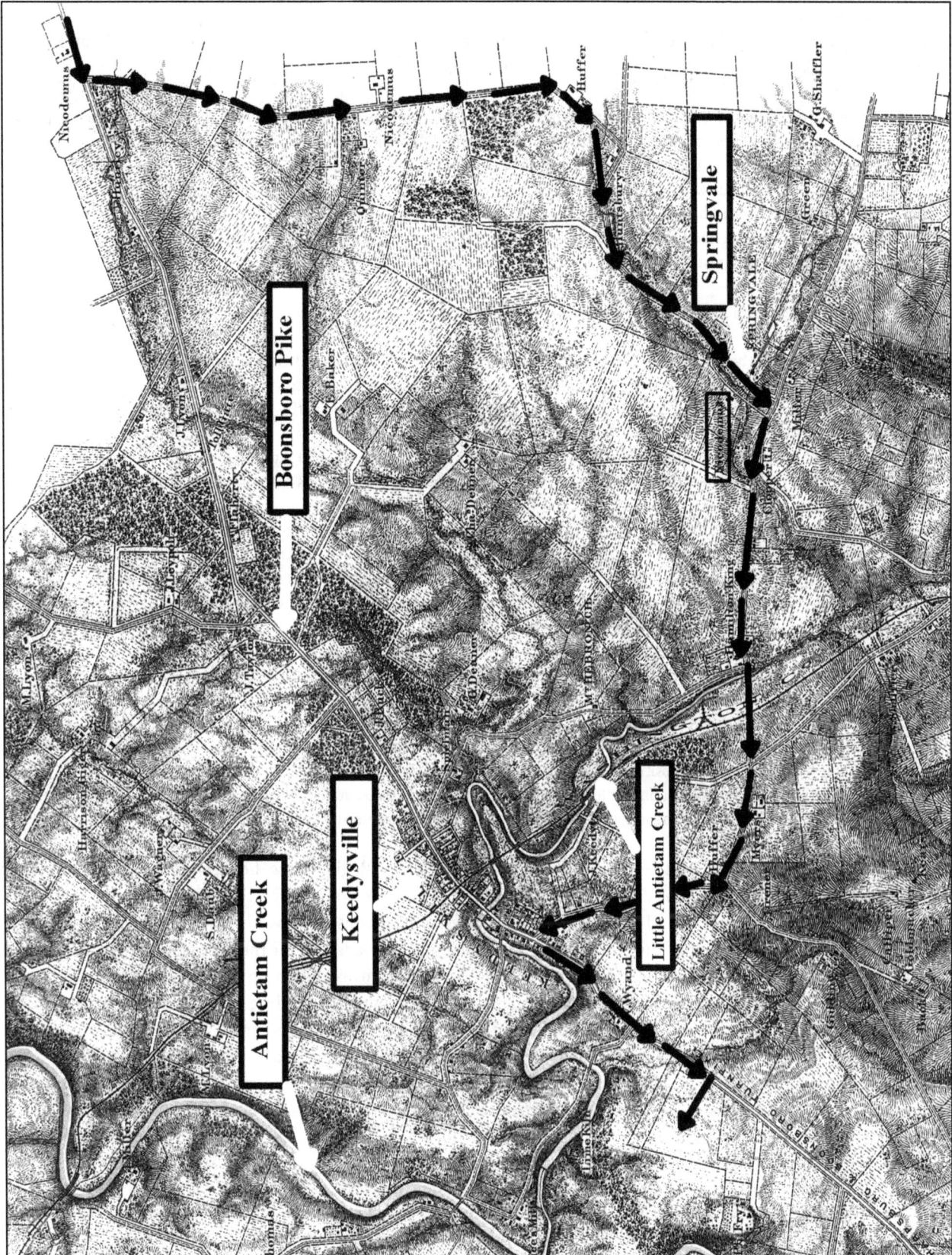

Detail of Michler map showing most likely route taken by the XII Corps from Boonsboro on 15 September, to Springvale, and finally to Keedysville on the 16th. Note that the railroad shown going through Keedysville did not exist in 1862. Courtesy LOC.

The exact route of the XII Corps once it crossed South Mountain at Turner's Gap, and its route to Antietam Creek is not certain. Most likely it followed the National Pike to Boonsboro as Williams wrote of the journey ending at the Antietam on 16 September:

> Citizens [in Boonsboro] met us on horseback and the whole population seemed rejoiced that we were chasing the Rebels from the state. At Boonsboro we passed south towards Sharpsburg, taking across lots and in all sorts of out of the ways. We encamped at a crossroads and for the first time for weeks I slept in a house, the home of a Mr. Nicodemus....The next morning [16th] we were ordered hurriedly to the front, General Mansfield, in an excited and fussy way, announcing that we should be in a general engagement in half an hour. Over we went across lots till we struck a road and after a three-mile march we were massed close column in a small space where the shells of the enemy's guns fell close to us....We lay here all day, and at night fancied we were going to rest.[50]

Carman described the movements of the XII Corps on the 15th and 16th:

> At 8:45 a.m. [on the 15th] McClellan ordered Sumner to move with the Second Corps (Sedgwick's and French's divisions) and the Twelfth Corps from Bolivar, on the National Road, to Boonsboro, following Pleasonton and Richardson....McClellan directed Sumner, should Boonsboro be abandoned, to take a strong position in the vicinity. Before sending this order, he heard from citizens and from Hooker that Lee was making a demoralized retreat for the Potomac, whereupon he gave additional orders that, should such be the case, Sumner was to pursue the enemy as rapidly as possible. Hooker was ordered to get rations from his train and, if Sumner was closed up when he reached Turner's Gap, to allow him to pass. Hooker would then follow Sumner.
> Sumner and Hooker moved as ordered, the advance of the column reaching Keedysville about 3:00 p.m. Instead of massing the brigades and divisions on either side of the road as they came up, the entire column was halted in the road and remained there. Consequently, the road was congested for miles back. Some of the troops did not get up until midnight, some not until next morning. The Twelfth Corps, starting from Bolivar late in the forenoon, after marching through Boonsboro and a short distance beyond, turned into the fields and bivouacked at Nicodemus's Mill, nearly two miles southeast of Keedysville, on the Old Sharpsburg Road.
> During the forenoon [of the 16th] the Twelfth Corps advanced from its bivouac near Nicodemus's Mill and massed in a field west of Keedysville and in the rear of French's Division....
> Under McClellan's direction, placing the troops in bivouac, the First Corps marched to the right, crossed the Little Antietam by a stone bridge and bivouacked in the forks of the Big and Little Antietam. The divisions of French and Sedgwick of the Second Corps went into position, after dark, in the rear of Richardson and on either side of the Sharpsburg turnpike, Sedgwick on the right and French on the left. The Twelfth Corps remained at Nicodemus's Mills until next day. Burnside was directed to move still further to the left, and McClellan sought headquarters at Keedysville.[51]

Carman was in the XII Corps leading his new 13th New Jersey Regiment so he very likely knew or certainly learned in later years that his corps did bivouac at Springvale before moving to the rear of French's Division west of the Boonsboro Pike. How did the XII Corps get to that point from Boonsboro? Williams wrote of his corps' "taking across lots and in all sorts of out of the ways. We encamped at a crossroads and for the first time for weeks I slept in a house, the home of a Mr. Nicodemus." There are several Nicodemus farms shown on the 1867 Michler map but only one close to an intersection near Springvale. This map shows a Nicodemus building or mill to the northwest of the intersection of Dogstreet Road and a road leading from the northeast, today's Nicodemus Mill Road. As it is extremely unlikely that Carman was in error about Springvale, the route taken by Mansfield to Springvale most likely was on a road south from the Boonsboro Pike about ½ mile west of Boonsboro turning onto today's King Street which continues to Springvale today as Nicodemus Mill Road.[52] The distance today along this route from the intersection of

---

[50] Williams, *From the Cannon's Mouth*, 124. Williams's twice-used description in his memoirs of Mansfield as "fussy" appears to have been used in a mildly derogatory manner not employed by anyone else; it was not meant to complement Mansfield. Williams likely meant "fussy" as defined for "fuss" in the *OED*: "A bustle or commotion out of proportion to the occasion; a needless or excessive display of concern about anything; ostentatious or officious activity." It could be argued that Mansfield's activities given the circumstances of his new command were justified.

[51] Carman, Clemens, vol. 1, 403-404, 411; vol. 2, 24.

[52] The LOC map is prepared by Nathaniel Michler, 1867, courtesy LOC. Both the 1859 Taggart Washington County map and the 1877 Atlas of Washington County show that modern roads are on the same roadbeds. The Taggart Map shows a mill to the northeast of the intersection of Nicodemus Mill and Dogstreet Roads.

the Boonsboro Pike to the intersection of today's Dogstreet Road which leads to Keedysville most of which existed at the time of the battle is about 2.4 miles. The distance from Springvale to the Boonsboro Pike in Keedysville is about 1.75 miles. Williams's description may be hyperbole or just acknowledging the fact that usually the infantry marches along the sides of a road while the artillery, wagons, and cavalry use the hard surfaced part which in the case of the Boonsboro Pike, was in good, if dusty, condition, due to its limestone surface.

An aide on McClellan's staff, Lieutenant Colonel David Hunter Strother, was sent ahead to fetch the XII Corps which had apparently continued on the National Pike toward Hagerstown: "I found the head of the column had already passed the Sharpsburg road, and so closely packed was the street with troops and supply trains that it was impossible to turn it. Not finding Mansfield immediately, I got General Williams to halt the corps until the proper order could be given for changing its direction. General Mansfield presently came up, and a way was made across lots by tearing down some fences. Strother further wrote that I "ordered them to turn down the Sharpsburg road, flanking Cedarville [Keedysville] and entering Sharpsburg through Porterstown. As Porterstown is located to the southwest of Keedysville just east of the Boonsboro Pike and south of the Pry House, this observation lends support to the march of the XII Corps to a bivouac east of Keedysville. Porterstown is on a road to the southwest of Springvale, today's Geeting Road, which leads southwest from Dogstreet Road. Mansfield wrote a note to McClellan on 16 September from "Spring Mills one & half miles from Porters Town." He wrote that "I am within a mile and ¾ of Portersville with my whole Corps <u>together</u> except my Baggage Train which is not up and my rations are exhausted tonight. I shall send back for my train of supplies. I would have reached Portersville after dark yesterday had I not met a party of your command directly from there. I have lost Genl Sumner and wait your orders as to the direction I shall move in." Sumner apparently replied in a note written by his chief of staff, Captain Taylor that "If General Mansfield had followed the 2nd Corps as directed on the march of yesterday he would not have lost General Sumner."[53] It is obvious that Mansfield was not familiar with the area he was traversing and needed help after he lost the track of the 2nd Corps. It is not clear why Mansfield wrote that some of McClellan's staff somehow delayed Mansfield's arrival at Porterstown. After the Battle of South Mountain on the 15th, there was confusion about the order of pursuit of Lee's army but Mansfield's tardy arrival on the 16th did not materially affect the course of the battle on the 17th.

---

[53] David Hunter Strother, *A Virginia Yankee in the Civil War: The Diaries of David Hunter Strother*, ed. By Cecil D. Eby, Jr. (Chapel Hill, NC: The University of North Carolina Press, 1961), 108; David Hunter Strother, "Personal Recollections of the War," *Harper's New Monthly Magazine*, vol. 35, Feb. 1868, 280; D. Scott Hartwig, *To Antietam Creek: The Maryland Campaign of September 1862* (Baltimore, MD: The Johns Hopkins University Press, 2012), 506. The regimental historian of the 27th Indiana wrote however, that "towards evening [on the 15th the regiment] went in to bivouac above the Pry House....While we were here we used water from the spring used by the Pry house....To one standing facing this house the position of the Twenty-seventh would be a short distance (not much over one hundred yards) to [the left]....We remained at this point throughout the night of the 15th, also all day, and part of the night, of the 16th," Edmund Randolph Brown, *The Twenty-Seventh Indiana Volunteer Infantry in the War of the rebellion 1861 to 1865* (Monticello, IN, n.p.,1899), 235-236. While it is possible only his regiment was near the Pry House the night of the 15th, that is unlikely. His regimental history is not the most reliable for other details so his account must be dismissed as it is unsupported. Letters courtesy of the Middlesex County Historical Society.

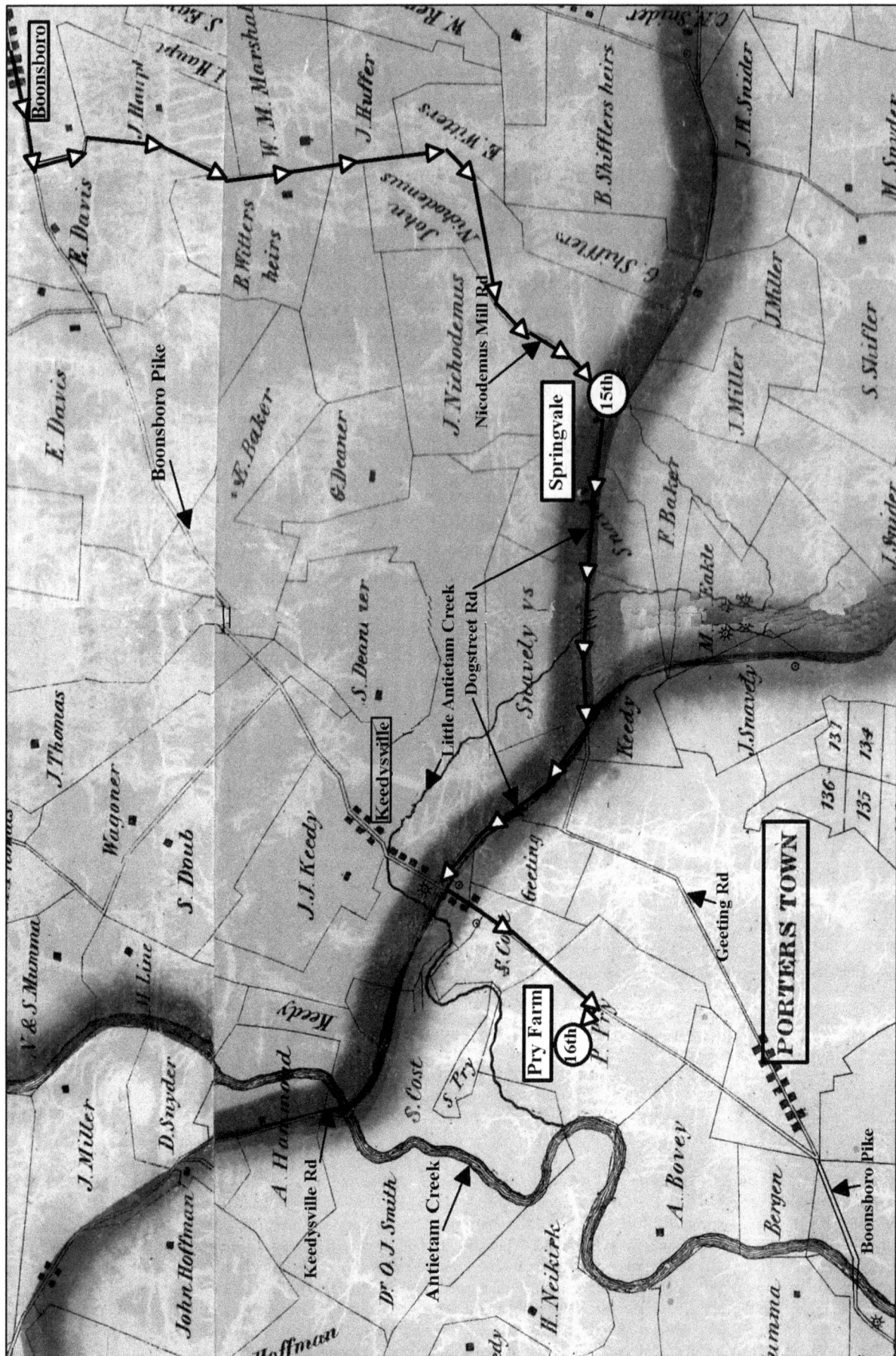

XII Corps March on the 15th from Boonsboro to Springvale, and the 16th to the Pry Farm. Taggart Map courtesy LOC.

Mansfield ate his last supper here at the Cost or Hitt House near the Keedysville Road on the evening of 16 September. It was also used as a hospital after the battle. It is private property. Courtesy LOC.

On the eve of the battle, 16 September, Mansfield dined at the Cost house. Although it is not recorded with whom he supped, it is likely that his aides joined him. The Cost or Hitt House is located on the east side of the Keedysville Road just east of Antietam Creek. Samuel Cost owned this farm during the Battle of Antietam. In addition to having numerous Federal troops stationed in the area and being at a major crossing point of Antietam Creek, the Cost house and barn were also used as hospitals during and after the Battle on the 17th. After the battle the farm also served briefly as headquarters for General Meade.[54]

---

[54] Historic American Buildings Survey, National Park Service, HABS NO. MD-957, Martha Wagner, 1991. Mansfield must have eaten with the Cost family had they not already evacuated and likely with other officers, at least his aide, Dyer, although none wrote of the event.

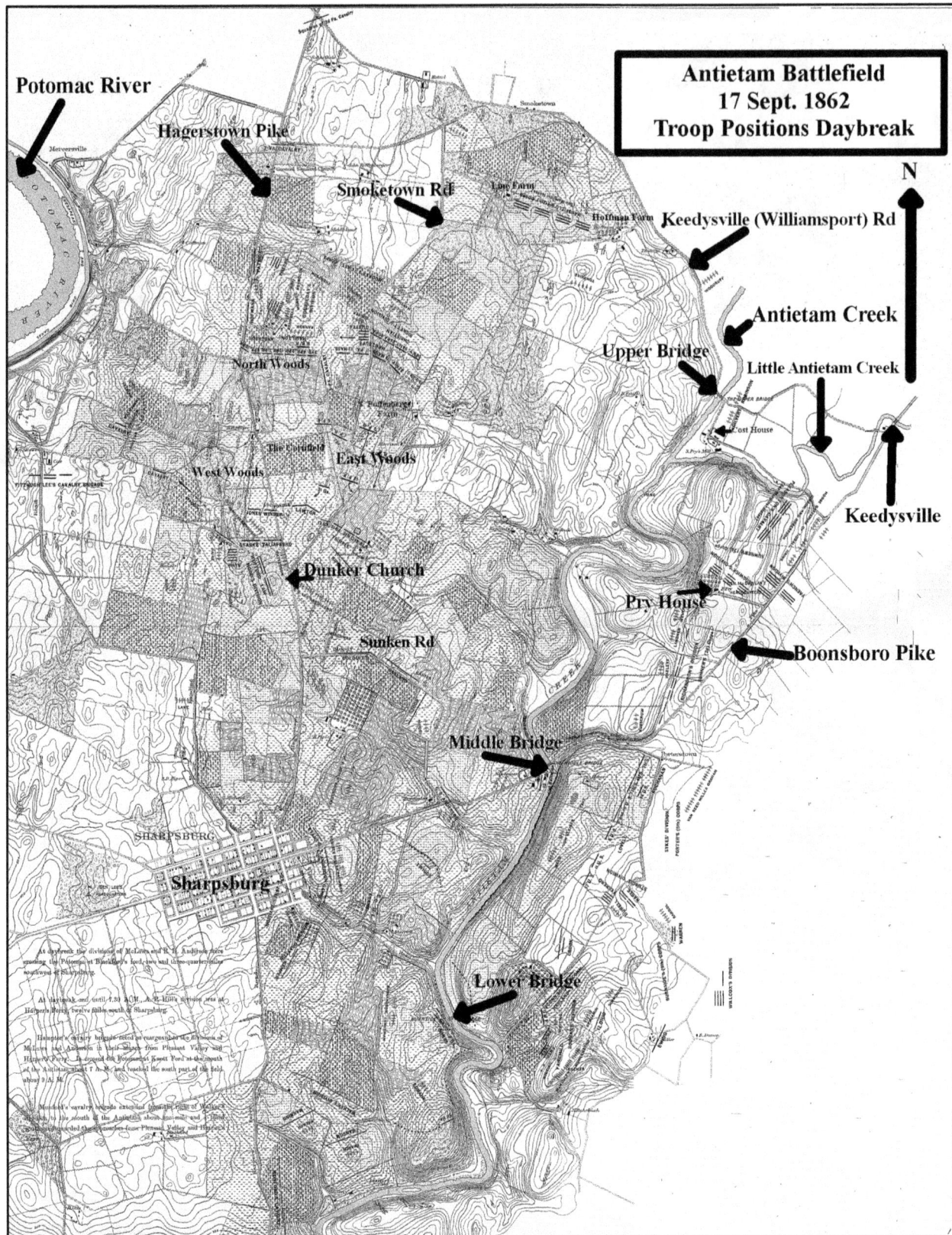

Map showing main features on the Antietam battlefield. Bibliographic information taken from the LOC "Atlas of the battlefield of Antietam, prepared under the direction of the Antietam Battlefield Board, lieut. col. Geo. W. Davis, U.S.A., president, General E.A. Carman, U.S.V., General H. Heth, C.S.A. Surveyed by Lieut. Col. E.B. Cope, engineer, H.W. Mattern, assistant engineer, of the Gettysburg National Park. Drawn by Charles H. Ourand, 1899. Position of troops by General E. A. Carman. Published by authority of the Secretary of War, under the direction of the Chief of Engineers, U.S. Army, 1908." This series of 14 maps for 17 September are invaluable for the study of the battle and are the most accurate ever published.

General Robert E. Lee, with his excellent engineering eye, experience in the Old Army, and service in the Confederate Army, chose his ground well at Sharpsburg. He formed his line, anchored at both ends on the Potomac River, just west of Antietam Creek. Antietam Creek, like the Potomac a few miles further west, runs generally north to south but with fewer large and more small perturbations than the meandering Potomac. He established his units conforming to the mostly gentle hills and ridges which also run north to south. The rolling hills composed of farmland with a few woodlots, did provide cover and concealment in many areas which became of great importance during parts of the battle. While Antietam Creek was not deep, it had few good fords due to its steep banks. These fords were inadequately scouted by McClellan's cavalry and engineers leading to major flaws in the execution of Union attacks primarily for Burnside on the Union left flank. The Upper Bridge (also known as the Hitt Bridge), or the Hooker Bridge after the battle, was about .8 mile in a straight line above McClellan's field headquarters at the Pry House and about .3 mile above Pry's Ford. The other important ford across the Antietam was Snavely's Ford, downstream some 1.5 miles from the Lower Bridge (also known as the Rohrbach Bridge), and after the battle as Burnside's Bridge. It was less than two airline miles from Snavely's Ford to the mouth of the Antietam at the Potomac, and about 3.5 miles along the creek. McClellan's field headquarters at the Pry House was about one airline mile from the Middle Bridge. (McClellan had his main headquarters in Keedysville and only used the Pry House as a forward headquarters to take advantage of the view from its roof.)[55] The Antietam can be crossed at other smaller fords such as cattle fords but none were suitable for large-scale, quick crossings of cavalry or infantry. Lee did not contest Pry Ford and at Snavely's Ford, Confederate forces were withdrawn after Rodman's men finally pushed the Confederates away from the area west of the ford. Of the three bridges crossing the creek on the battlefield, Lee decided to only defend one, the Lower Bridge on the Union left flank; McClellan assigned Burnside's Ninth Corps to that flank. While the Middle Bridge was in defilade from the Confederate cannon on Cemetery Hill, ridges to the west were visible. The Middle Bridge was about one airline mile from the Confederate cannon on Cemetery Hill. Safely enclosed within one of the Potomac's meanderings, Lee's Army had one major geographical problem: there was only one good ford available across the Potomac which was about 1.3 river miles below the burned bridge which had connected Sharpsburg with Shepherdstown, Virginia. Boteler's Ford, heavily used by the Confederates, was not taken by Union forces until 19 September, when Lee's Army had already retreated across it and was never seriously threatened until then.[56]

McClellan finally decided to attack Lee at Sharpsburg and his plan on the evening of 16 September was not a bad one considering that he firmly believed he still faced a numerically superior enemy, behind the hills surrounding the town. If McClellan knew that he greatly outnumbered Lee, and that in fact virtually none of Lee's troops were

---

[55] For a thorough discussion of McClellan's two headquarters during the battle see Thomas G. Clemens, "In Search of McClellan's Headquarters," *Civil War Times*, June 2016, 26-33.

[56] Timothy R. Snyder, "Civil War Fords of the Potomac River," Unpublished Manuscript, 12. He describes the various fords used during the Civil War giving some supplementary information on each. See also A.D. Kenamond, "Potomac Crossings," in *Magazine of the Jefferson County Historical Society*, vol. XXIV, December 1958; in Shepherdstown, this ford was generally best known as Pack Horse Ford; in Virginia, it was called Boteler's Ford after Boteler's cement mill close to the ford; in Maryland, it was known as Blackford's Ford as the Maryland side was owned by the Blackford family; 38. It was sometimes called the Shepherdstown Ford. Antietam Ford was near the mouth of Antietam Creek and was of good low water use according to a 10 June 1861 correspondent of the Baltimore *American and Commercial Advertiser*. "Five fords have recently been discovered near the mouth of the Antietam, seven miles above Harper's Ferry. They are not more than three feet deep anywhere in low water. There is a perfect rock bed the whole way." Historian Timothy R. Snyder wrote the following succinctly describing a desirable Civil War ford: All nineteenth century river fords were not the same. Those that served local citizens may not have been sufficient to pass an army. In addition, a ford that permitted the passage of cavalry may not have been sufficient to pass infantry... [and] a ford that allowed the passage of infantry may not have been sufficient to pass artillery and wagon trains. The conditions of fords also varied greatly during a year. During high water, typically in the spring, a ford that previously permitted infantry to cross might only allow cavalry to pass. In addition, high water might carry obstructions to a ford that was previously passable. During periods of low water the river was usually fordable in dozens of additional locations....The ideal river ford, sufficient to allow passage of all three branches of the army and wagon trains, required three primary features: Low water was the obvious feature; no more than three feet is ideal since the water would not extend to the men's waists and therefore would not require the soldiers to take special precautions to prevent their cartridge boxes from getting wet. The second important characteristic of a ford was a good river bottom over which to cross. An ideal ford had a bedrock bottom with a minimum of silt over it. This prevented wagons from getting mired in the mud and the men from getting their shoes pulled off by the thick muck....The bottom of a good ford was also free of pits and obstructions, such as sink holes, crevices, large rocks, fallen trees or sunken boats that could trip up men and horses and snag passing wagons. The third significant feature of a good ford was the approaches. An otherwise fine ford was of little value if an Army could get into the river, but only with great difficulty get out of it. This condition not only slowed the passage of the army, but put it at risk of attack in a vulnerable position. A gentle grade to and from a ford was especially important for artillery and wagon trains since their weight made it difficult for mules and horses to pull them up a steep and slippery bank. Snyder, "Civil War Fords of the Potomac River," 4.

entrenched, he would have had a more aggressive battle plan. As it was, he initially desired to attack the enemy's left flank to see if Lee would stand and fight, as well as to learn if Lee's flank was in the air. McClellan chose Major General Joseph Hooker for the early morning attack, knowing the aggressive spirit he possessed would be necessary. McClellan planned a follow-up attack on the other flank which he believed Lee would have weakened to support the opposite flank. Finally, McClellan would throw his best reserves at the now much weakened center of Lee's line, perhaps using Pleasonton's cavalry division as shock troops, completing the rout of the enemy through the streets of Sharpsburg, cutting Lee off from Boteler's [Blackford's] Ford. The Federal commander knew he could not surprise Lee, nor did he initially plan on using more than one corps for each flank attack. The attack would begin on the Rebel left early on the morning of 17 September. McClellan realized that neither attack might be able to get in Lee's rear since both Lee's flanks were probably anchored on the Potomac, but the first attack on the left early in the morning could advance far enough to enfilade Lee's entire line to the south toward Sharpsburg, making it untenable. Had Union troops taken Nicodemus Heights and the northern part of Hauser's Ridge, and planted artillery on those points and to the high ground west of Dunker Church, the Army of Northern Virginia would have been in serious trouble.

Carman, however, believed that McClellan's tactics were flawed:

> The first step in McClellan's plan was the transfer of Hooker's First Corps to the west bank of the Antietam. If this movement was not in itself a reconnaissance in force, it should have been preceded by such an examination of the ground as would have sufficed to determine where Lee's left was with some approach to accuracy….This first step was a blunder, in that the movement was made in the afternoon of the sixteenth at an hour too late to accomplish anything before dark and serving no purpose, save to inform Lee where he was to be attacked.
>
> It was 2:00 p.m. when McClellan gave Hooker orders to cross the Antietam by the Upper Bridge and the ford below to attack and, if possible, turn Lee's left…. It was nearly 4:00 p.m. when Hooker put his troops in motion, Meade's division in advance. He then rode to McClellan's headquarters…and was informed by McClellan that he was at liberty to call for reinforcements should he need them and that on their arrival they would be placed under his command, upon which he rode off and joined his troops on the march. His direction lay nearly perpendicular to the Antietam, his object being to gain the high ground or divide between the Antietam and the Potomac and then incline to the left (following the elevation toward Sharpsburg), feeling for Lee's flank, which it was believed would be found somewhere on the divide—its exact or even approximate position being unknown to either McClellan or Hooker that day or early on the next.
>
> ….Hooker, as was his custom, rode in advance, close to the skirmishers, and had not proceeded over half a mile when he was joined by McClellan and his staff, apparently to see how Hooker was progressing. "Among other subjects of conversation," reports Hooker, "I said to the general that he had ordered my small corps, now numbering between 12,000 and 13,000 (as I had just lost nearly 1,000 men in the battle of South Mountain), across the river to attack the whole rebel Army, and that if re-enforcements were not forwarded promptly, or if another attack was not made on the enemy's right, the rebels would eat me up." Soon after this conversation, McClellan recrossed the Antietam and rode to the Pry house, from which he could see across the Antietam and observe the effect of Hooker's march or any movement made to meet it….Ricketts's division followed Meade's over the bridge and on the Williamsport [Keedysville] Road, and most of the artillery and all the ammunition train followed Ricketts.[57]

McClellan was impressed by Hooker's entreaties and took action:

> [A]fter his march with Hooker…he ordered Sumner to send the Twelfth Corps to Hooker's support that evening and to hold his own Second Corps in readiness to march for the same purpose an hour before daylight. Sumner, who was anxious to have his command of two corps act as a unit under his own eye (in so far as this was possible), asked permission to follow Mansfield's corps that night, but McClellan would not consent. He would give Sumner no authority to move till next morning….Sumner sent the order to Mansfield…late in the night. The Twelfth Corps crossed the Little Antietam and the main Antietam by the stone bridges, went up the Williamsport [Keedysville] Road nearly a mile, then turned to the left, and about 2:30 a.m. went into bivouac on the Hoffman and Line farms, a mile in Hooker's rear. Sumner, anticipating the movement of his own corps, and impressed with the importance of having everything at the front at the earliest hour, sent five of his batteries across the Antietam during the night. They parked near the Twelfth Corps.

The exact location of the XII Corps' bivouac early evening on the 16th is uncertain but Carman wrote that on its night march 16-17, it crossed both the Little and Big Antietam Creeks so it could not have camped at the Cost House as its location is well west of the Little Antietam Bridge. Its bivouac could have been near where the

---

[57] Carman, Pierro, 205-206.

Carman-Cope map shows Pleasonton's Cavalry as notes to the map state that the cavalry location is "approximate." The march from the XII Corps bivouac to the Line Farm was about three miles, and two and one-half miles to the Hoffman Farm. Modern-day roads such as the Keedysville and Smoketown Roads are almost the same as those in 1862. A 27th Indiana soldier wrote that his regiment spent the night of the 15th and all of the 16th in bivouac near the Pry House and that the men used the Pry House spring.[58]

---

[58] Carman, Pierro, 210-211. Edmund Randolph Brown, *The Twenty-Seventh Indiana*, 235. Note that Antietam historian Tom Clemens believes that McClellan had only his field headquarters at the Pry House and his main, administrative headquarters was in Keedysville.

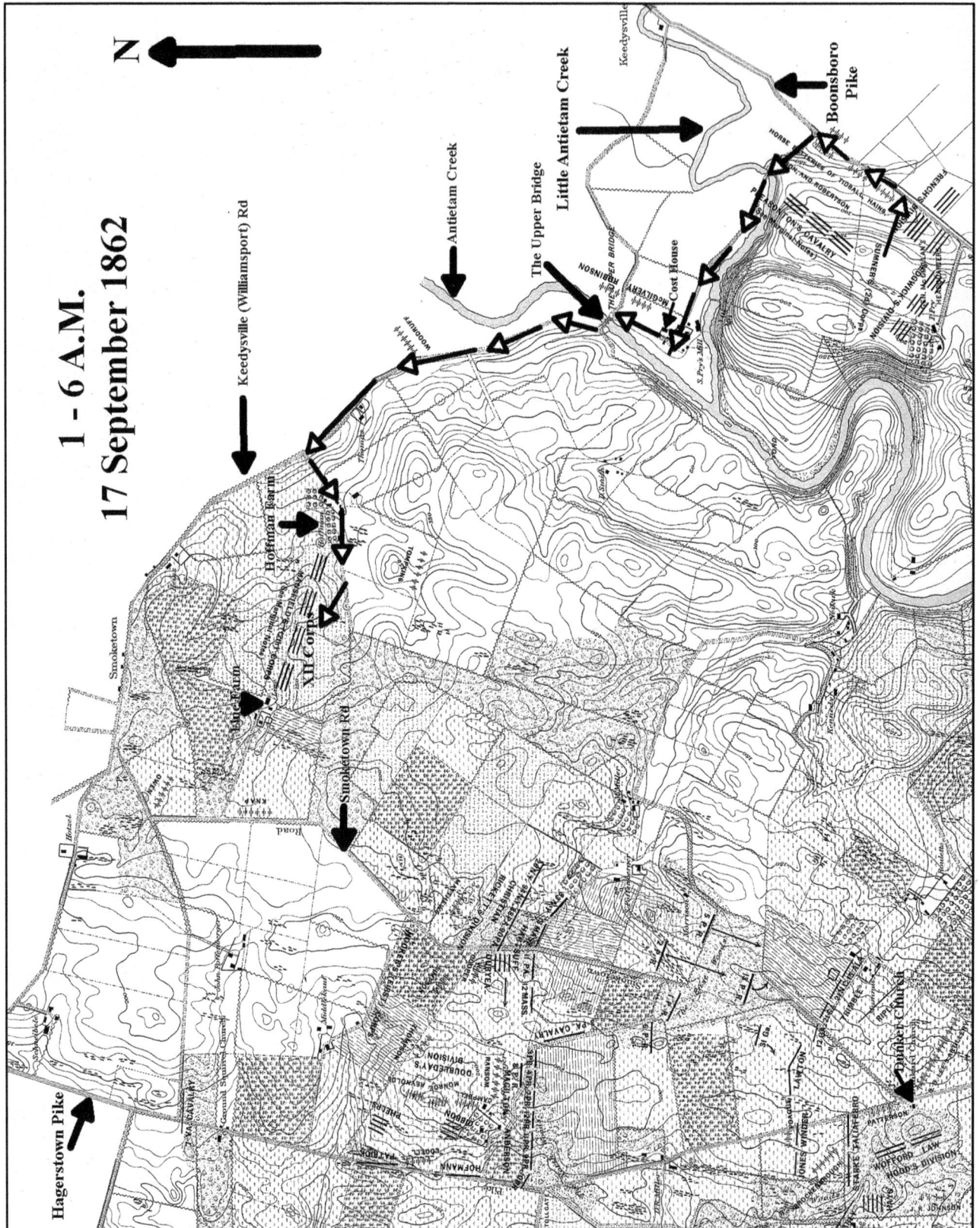

"About two o'clock on the morning of the seventeenth, Joseph Mansfield and the Twelfth Army Corps, after crossing the Antietam at the upper bridge, lay down to rest on the Hoffman and Line farms, a short mile in rear of Hooker's left. In the darkness a regular line was not formed. The men were informed that the enemy was in their immediate front and were ordered to rest on their arms....The veteran commander spread his blankets in a fence corner near the Line house and had a fitful sleep." Carman, Pierro, 235. Carman-Cope map, courtesy LOC.

That night, Mansfield moved his 10,000-man corps across the Antietam Creek and bedded them down after 2 a.m. for a few hours rest.[59] Mansfield had reason to not sleep well that night since he was virtually brand new to command of this corps having joined the day before, and therefore knew little about its commanders or the qualities of its regiments. What he did know seriously worried him: many of his men were new recruits untested in battle while a few veteran regiments were shells of their former strength having been severely mauled at the Battle of Cedar Mountain.[60] The five green regiments in the XII Corps were its largest, strengths taken from mustering-in rolls: 124th Pennsylvania, 974; 125th Pennsylvania 963; and 128th Pennsylvania, 950. The 13th New Jersey mustered in 899, and the 107th New York, 1,031. The total mustering in strength of these five regiments was 4,817. The estimated number in the XII Corps actually on the firing line on the day of the battle was 3,936 out of 7,631, 52% of the Corps.[61] Since his men were virtually all volunteers, he had the Old Army suspicion, formed during the Mexican-American War, which held that volunteers were best used behind fortifications and were unreliable in the attack. Mansfield had commented on his interactions with volunteers during the Mexican-American War finding them wanting as already noted in the chapter detailing his experiences with Taylor in Northern Mexico.[62]

Mansfield took time to post his corps' artillery that night according to the artillery commander of the XII Corps, Captain Clermont Livingston Best:

> At 2 a.m. on the morning of the 17th, the corps being then near the battle-ground, I was ordered by General Mansfield to proceed in person to the rear to post two batteries of the corps on some hills adjacent to the headquarters of General McClellan, to be pointed out by a staff officer. After performing this service, posting the Fourth Maine Battery and the Sixth Maine Battery.[63]

Mansfield's troops thought well of him despite his brief role as their corps commander. Captain Robert Gould Shaw of the 2nd Massachusetts wrote when he heard the news of Mansfield's wounding: "He had been with us only three days, but everyone liked him; he took more personal interest in the comfort and welfare of the men than any commander the Corps has had. He has died since, to the great regret of all."[64] Sergeant Henry Newton Comey also of the 2nd, wrote that Mansfield "came to us with an excellent reputation as a brave and conscientious veteran of many battles, and we had confidence that he would lead us well."[65] But another 2nd Massachusetts soldier wrote that after Mansfield joined on the 15th, "It was not without regret that the Corps thus finally parted with General Banks. It had been made a corps, it had won its historic glory, under him….The white-haired, brave, conscientious veteran who succeeded, had, alas! but three days of further service, before he fell."[66] The 125th Pennsylvania Regimental history stated that "This morning [15th] General Mansfield took command of the Twelfth Corps, and all were pleased with his

---

[59] The 12th Corps strength, like all numbers given for units on the firing line, varies according to how one counts men available to carry a rifle: Sears states only 7,200 men were on the line, half of whom never fired a rifle in anger, *Landscape Turned Red: The Battle of Antietam* (New York, NY: Houghton Mifflin Company, 1993), 203; McClellan shows 10,126 fit for duty for the 12th Corps but not the actual number on the firing line the morning of the 17th; however many were there, 1,743 became casualties, *ORA*, pt. 1, 67; for numbers of casualties see *ORA*, vol. 19, pt. 1, 36. See Attachment 1below.

[60] Sears, *Landscape Turned Red*, 203; three Ohio regiments, when combined, could barely comprise one regiment.

[61] *ORA*, series 3, vol. 3, 749, 760, 775. The mustering in strength is not the number appearing on the firing line; for firing line strength see OOB, Attachment 1. See also D. Scott Hartwig, "The Volunteers of '62," in *The Antietam Campaign*, ed. By Gary W. Gallagher (Chapel Hill, NC: The University of North Carolina Press, 1999), 143-168, in which Hartwig discusses McClellan's problem with such large numbers of green troops and how it affected his strategic thinking for the campaign. Carman, Clemens, vol. 2, 583-584.

[62] Paddy Griffith, *Battle Tactics of the Civil War* (New Haven, Connecticut: Yale University Press, 2001), where he argues that the Mexican War showed many Regular Army officers that militia and volunteer troops were best suited for a defensive role since they were insufficiently trained to undertake more complicated maneuvers especially during the attack, 125. Similarly, Archer Jones, *Civil War Command and Strategy: The Process of Victory and Defeat* (New York: The Free Press, 1992), argues that the Mexican War taught regular officers that untrained militia and volunteers were best on the defense, 269.

[63] *ORA*, vol. 19, pt. 1, 482.

[64] Robert Gould Shaw, *Blue-Eyed Child of Fortune: The Civil War Letters of Colonel Robert Gould Shaw*, ed. by Russell Duncan (New York: NY: Avon Books, 1994), 240. Shaw had previously seen Mansfield in Washington in March 1861 when his regiment marched in review for Mansfield, Sec. of War Simon Cameron, and Major Robert Anderson of Fort Sumter fame, 97. No record has been found of any troops under Mansfield voicing a complaint, rather all comments are laudatory.

[65] Henry Newton Comey, *A Legacy of Valor: The Memoirs and Letters of Captain Henry Newton Comey, 2nd Massachusetts Infantry* (Knoxville, TN: The University of Tennessee Press, 2004), 74-75.

[66] Quint, *Record of the Second Massachusetts Infantry*, 133.

fatherly appearance and the interest he took in us."[67] This history also commented upon Mansfield's concern for his troops: "[Mansfield] had only been assigned to the command of our corps, and my first sight of him was on Monday's march, September 15th. We had been halted and kept standing for some time exposed to a sweltering sun, when a venerable, white-haired officer came galloping along the line, and, noticing this oversight, exclaimed, 'Why are the men kept standing in the sun?' and immediately directed us to be moved to the welcome shade of a woods close by. This was Mansfield, and the incident revealed his considerate care for his men."[68] Even back in October 1861, at Camp Hamilton, near Fort Monroe, a member of the 48th Pennsylvania commented about that "dear old General Mansfield. His mild disposition and benevolent heart, that caused him to be ever on the lookout for the welfare of his soldiers, combined, however, with a firm, just discipline, endeared him to all with whom he came in contact."[69]

Other XII Corps soldiers who had seen him or heard reports of him during the battle commented favorably; a member of the 28th New York in the First Brigade of the First Division wrote: "General Mansfield in command, was a conspicuous figure as he rode his horse rapidly about the field. His actions were nervous and excited like those of a young man rather than one far advanced in life. He wore a bright new uniform, and his long white hair was streaming behind as he fearlessly reconnoitered the position of the Confederates."[70] A member of the 27th Indiana also described Mansfield before the march to Hooker's aide began on the 17th:

> The old general had much of the courtly, but not offensive dignity which seems to have characterized the officers of the old Army, before the war. His bearing that morning as he rode around among his troops, his long white hair streaming in the wind, elicited great admiration. He sat erect and graceful in his saddle and gave his orders quietly but firmly; withal, he was so kind and fatherly.
>
> Before the order "Fall in" is given the boys run to their places, ready at the word to seize their muskets. As they stand thus in ranks they greet the old general with cheers. He removes his hat in acknowledgment, and shouts: "That's right, boys; you may well cheer. We are going to whip them to-day." These statements are received with still more cheering, especially the allusion to a victory.[71]

Gould wrote in his regimental history of that evening:

> At half past ten P.M. the noise from the other regiments woke us up, and immediately the Colonel received the order to march forthwith. So down came our tents and off we marched—where we came from and where we went to, I have not the remotest idea, and cannot find out, but we went around "Robin Hood's barn," stopped on plowed land, dropped at once, stowed ourselves away between the furrows, and slept soundly, with General Mansfield and an orderly on the other side of a fence. We heard picket firing, and just as we were going off to sleep we heard volleys, and these seemed to disturb our distinguished neighbor on the other side of the fence. If I am not mistaken we have marched four miles on the outer circumference of a crescent whose horns point toward the rebellious....It was after midnight when we settled in the furrows and slept. We had marched...from the left of the Army to the right, and our corps, as will be seen, reinforced Hooker's, which was the extreme right of the infantry forces,—and also partly filled a gap between Hooker's corps and the Antietam river.[72]

Captain Fox of the 107th New York wrote of their short rest on the night of the 16th:

> At eleven o'clock the men were awakened and ordered to fall in quietly; they were instructed to make no noise. Silently and half asleep the column moved off in the darkness, and crossing the Antietam on one of the upper bridges arrived at their designated position after a three hours' march. The corps was now on the farm of J. Poffenberger [George Line], at the right of the Union Army, and in rear and partly to the left of Hooker's Corps. Heavy dew was falling, but the men threw themselves down in the wet grass for a few hours of sleep. They were soon startled from their heavy slumbers by a volley of musketry that rang out noisily on the night air from a piece of woods close by. It was an accidental collision between the Confederate pickets of Hood's Division and a regiment of the Pennsylvania Reserves. Nothing came of it, and soon all was quiet again.

---

[67] William W. Wallace (Chmn.), *History of the One Hundred and Twenty-fifth Regiment Pennsylvania Volunteers 1862—1863* (Philadelphia, PA: J.B. Lippincott Company, 1906), 229.

[68] Ibid., 171.

[69] Bosbyshell, *The 48th in the War*, 19.

[70] C.W. Boyce, *A Brief History of the Twenty-Eighth Regiment New York State Volunteers, First Brigade, First Division, Twelfth Corps, Army of the Potomac* (Buffalo, NY: The Matthews-Northrup Co., 1896), 46.

[71] Edmund Randolph Brown, *The Twenty-Seventh Indiana*, 241-242.

[72] Gould, *History of the First*, 229-230. Interesting that Gould did not make an effort to learn the route of the XII Corps as his regimental history was written in 1871. He did make heroic efforts otherwise in writing of Mansfield's wounding.

Wednesday, September 17, 1862 — the day of the battle of Antietam. No bugle in the Twelfth Corps sounded reveille that morning; the call had already been sounded by the rifles of the skirmishers as they rang out sharp and clear on the morning air. This firing commenced at daylight — so early that the musketry showed a red flash in the dim mist that overhung the fields and woods. The dropping fire of the skirmish line was soon followed by heavy volleys intermingled with a rapid, continuous discharge of light artillery. Hooker, with his First Corps, had opened the battle by making a vigorous attack on the enemy's left.

Aroused by this heavy firing in its immediate front the Twelfth Corps fell into line. By Mansfield's orders the regiments were formed in column by division, closed en masse, with the exception of some of the new ones, which, on account of their full ranks, were formed in close column by companies. In this formation the troops moved forward up onto the plateau, where the First Corps was battling hard to retain possession of the ground which it had gained in its opening attack, and halted in close support of Hooker's line. It was now about six o'clock in the morning.[73]

The 2nd Massachusetts historian and Chaplain, Alonzo H. Quint, wrote that at "about ten o'clock, P.M., [16th] came low, quiet orders to make ready to move instantly. Not ten minutes afterwards, General Mansfield came along. 'When *will* you be ready?" said he. 'Ready now, sir.' 'You are! Well, I like that: but you are the only brigade ready.' 'Fall in.' The regiment soon reached a macadamized road, or what seemed like it [Boonsboro Pike]; went through a village guessed to be Keedysville, and across the Antietam; got a little wet in the rain; turned into somebody's field, and lay down in the darkness."[74]

Another regiment in the 2nd Massachusetts's Third Brigade was the 3rd Wisconsin whose historian corroborated the Bay Staters' historian: "At about 9 o'clock at night, orders in an undertone were given to be ready to move. Soon General Mansfield—the old veteran was full of energy—came to the Third brigade and asked, 'When will you be ready?' 'Ready now, sir,' was the reply of the commander. 'That's right,' said he, 'but you are the only brigade ready."' Soon the corps was in motion, moved to the northwest, in the darkness and through a field, across Antietam creek, and lay down in a low piece of ground....near Hoffman's house.[75]

---

[73] Fox, *In Memoriam,* 140-141. The XII Corps was bivouacked to the northeast of the Joseph Poffenberger Farm.

[74] Alonzo H. Quint, *The Record of the Second Massachusetts Infantry, 1861-65* (Boston, MA: 1867), 134. Emphasis in the original. The 2nd Massachusetts was known by Historian Edwin Bearss as the "Democratic Harvard Regiment" so nicknamed because many junior officers of the 20th were Harvard graduates from Massachusetts's most elite families. The 20th Massachusetts was known as the "Harvard Regiment."

[75] Edwin E. Bryant, *History of the Third Regiment of Wisconsin Veteran Volunteer Infantry 1861-1865* (Cleveland, OH: The Arthur H. Clark Company, 1891), 122-123.

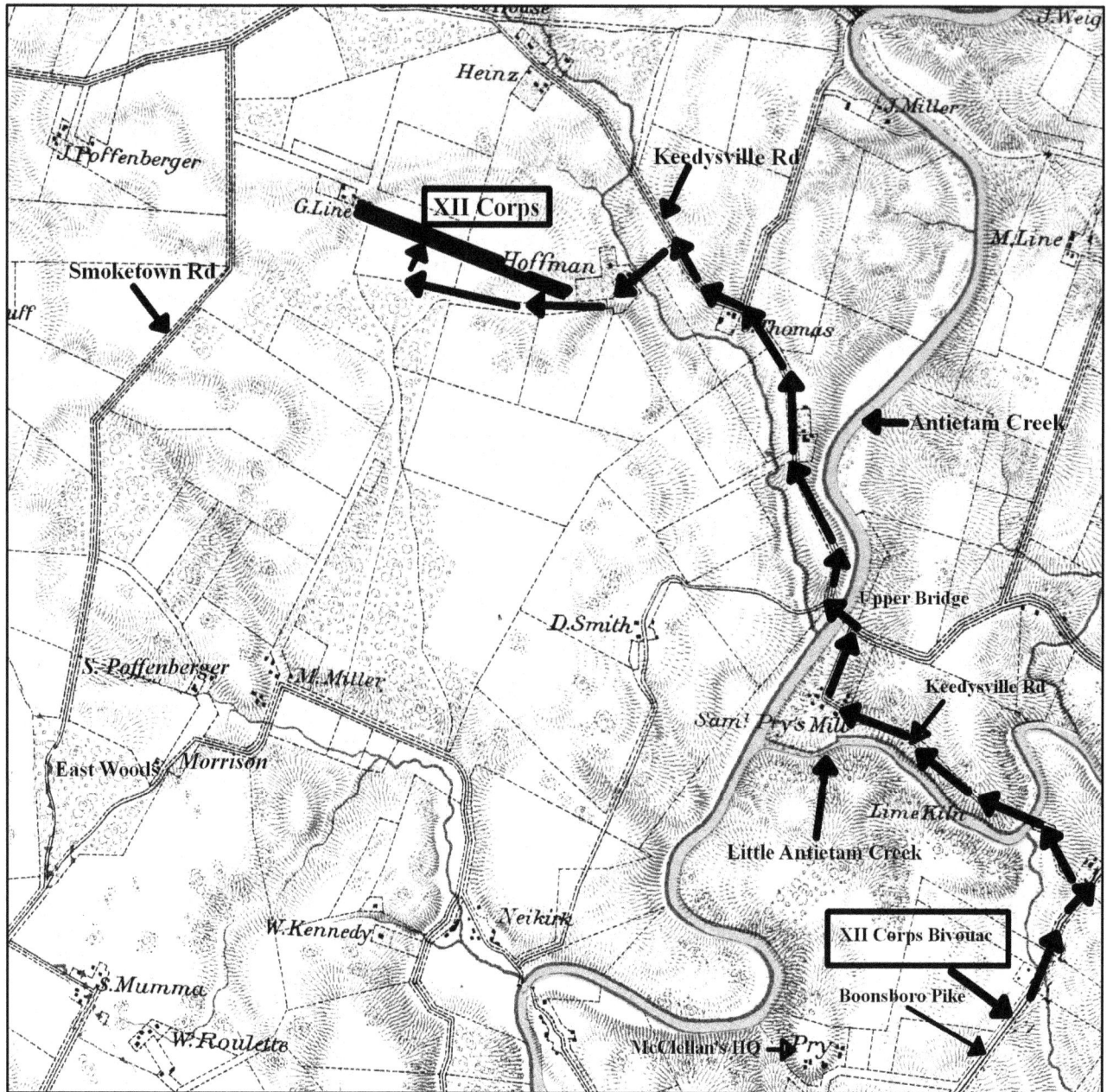

Another map representation of the march of XII Corps, 16-17 September, from its bivouac near the Pry House. *OA*, pl. 29. Carman-Cope map, courtesy LOC.

Modern view of Hoffman Farm, main house on Keedysville Road, facing northeast. Keedysville Road is to the right of this photograph about 240 yards. The Hoffman Farm is private property. Courtesy LOC.

Modern view of Hoffman Farm, Spring House, likely the oldest dwelling on the farm, from the west and south side. Both buildings existed during the battle. Courtesy LOC.

Hooker's attacks drive the Confederates back. Mansfield begins marching his troops from their bivouac at the Line and Hoffman Farms to assist Hooker, Williams's Division in the lead, the column guiding between the East and North Woods to confront Confederates facing north. The 13th New Jersey from Gordon's Brigade is sent west to the edge of a wood to be held in reserve.[76] Carman-Cope map, courtesy LOC.

[76] *ORA*, vol. 19, pt. 1, 494.

The Battle of Antietam, thanks to its chief historian, Ezra A. Carman, has traditionally been studied as three separate battles: the Union right from day break to 10:30 a.m., the center from 9:30 a.m. to 1 p.m., and the left at 10 a.m. to sundown. Carman added that while Union commands did not fight on different parts of the line, General Lee was forced to maneuver outnumbered Confederate troops all day from one part of his line to the other to stave off heavy Union attacks.[77]

Hooker with his I Corps began his attack heading south along the Hagerstown Pike aiming for the flat, high ground to the east of the Dunker Church, and southwest along the Smoketown Road, but in heavy fighting was thrown back sustaining severe losses. Hooker had sent an order to Mansfield around 5:30 a.m. that morning to form up his corps and advance. In hindsight, Hooker may have wished to urge Mansfield to do so in all haste at 5:30 as the I Corps was wrecked by the time Mansfield was able to provide useful support almost two hours later: "On a 500-yard front, 5,000 Confederates and 8,700 Federals delivered and stood to endure withering volleys of musketry, while each suffered heavily under the cross fire of the other's artillery. Of the 13,682 men engaged, 4,386 were casualties by seven o'clock, a staggering 32 percent....the skeleton that remained of the First Corps had not only lost all offensive punch, but it was incapable of withstanding another serious attack."[78] Had Mansfield arrived earlier and provided effective support to the I Corps, General Lee probably would have lost permanently the area around the Dunker Church and then the Sunken Road as the road would have been enfiladed by artillery fire from Hauser's Ridge and Nicodemus Heights to the west of the Dunker Church. In hindsight, Hooker should have met with Mansfield as soon as he arrived at the Line Farm to coordinate the XII Corps movements in the morning. The two hours it took Mansfield to get his corps moving was reasonable under the circumstances of its late arrival on the Line and Hoffman Farms and the early hour but doomed Hooker's I Corps.

---

[77] Carman, Clemens, vol. 2, 49. Clemens notes that these important time overlaps are often forgotten by modern studies, n.1.
[78] Harsh, *Flood*, 373.

By 7 a.m., Hooker's troops are succeeding in driving back the Confederate defenders of Jackson's and Ewell's Divisions. Mansfield is moving up his corps west of the Smoketown Road to assist Hooker, with Williams's Division leading; Crawford's First Brigade in the van is beginning to deploy. Carman-Cope map, courtesy LOC.

Mansfield rode ahead to assess the situation and while he was gone, Williams saw that his division's regiments were not deployed into line to meet the close-by enemy. Williams ordered his leading brigade, Crawford's, to deploy, but Mansfield, upon returning, disagreed. The new corps commander was adamant about marching his troops to Hooker's aid in formation of columns to maintain better control of his inexperienced troops, however, Williams did not agree:

I had five new regiments without drill or discipline. General Mansfield was greatly excited. Though an officer of acknowledged gallantry, he had a very nervous temperament and a very impatient manner. Feeling that our heavy masses of raw troops were sadly exposed, I begged him to let me deploy them in line of battle, in which the men present but *two* ranks or rows instead of *twenty*, as we were marching, but I could not move him. He was positive that all the new regiments would run away (emphasis in original).[79]

Hooker had ordered Mansfield to form an arc behind the disintegrating I Corps. Since the new XII Corps regiments were unused to changing formation under battle conditions, this took much personal attention from both Mansfield and Williams. "Directing Williams to lead the [new] 124th and 125th Pennsylvania to the right as far as the Hagerstown Road, Mansfield advanced with the three old regiments and the 128th Pennsylvania, all still in column of divisions. It was then about 7:15 a.m."[80] Williams said that he got the 124th Pennsylvania into line by having a fence to align on while Mansfield guided the 10th Maine to a point then rode off.[81] Advancing his regiments in a column gave the enemy artillery an excellent target as it fired into the masses of troops presenting a company front.

Ezra Carman commanded the 13th New Jersey, in the Third Brigade, First Division, of the XII Corps. He was proud of his regiment and the units and men of the XII Corps, perhaps to the point of favoring them over others.[82] His description of the advance of his Corps is an accurate portrayal of its morning fight and is similar to the other regiments in the corps:

> It went into action without coffee or food and after an almost sleepless night. At the first sound of cannon at daybreak of the "misty, moisty morning," it was put in motion, crossed the Smoketown Road, moved west a short distance, swung to the left, and marched south in column of battalions in mass: the First Division under Alpheus Williams in advance (Samuel Crawford's brigade leading, Brigadier General George H. Gordon's following Crawford) and George Greene's Second Division bringing up the rear. From the moment of leaving the bivouac, the column marched directly in the line of fire of S.D. Lee's guns [near the Dunker Church]. The advance was slow and cautious, and the haltings (by Mansfield's orders) very frequent, but of sufficient time to allow the men to boil coffee. Regiments were detached to occupy woods on the flanks, brought back, and again detached. At 6:30 a.m. the head of the column was halted near the middle of an open field west of and adjoining the Samuel Poffenberger woods, and Mansfield rode forward to survey the ground and consult with Hooker. At the time of the halt, the old regiments of Crawford's [leading] brigade—the 10th Maine, 28th New York, and 46th Pennsylvania—were on the right, and the new regiments— the 124th, 125th, and 128th Pennsylvania—on the left. "It was the understanding," one regimental commander reports, "that the latter three regiments should move to the front when wanted, and the old ones (the Forty-sixth Pennsylvania, Tenth Maine, and Twenty-eighth New York) should follow at a proper distance in the rear, constituting, as it were, a reserve for the brigade."[83]

---

[79] Williams, 125. Williams later describes Mansfield as "an excellent gentleman, but a most fussy, obstinate officer," 133. Clearly, Williams's and Mansfield's disagreements about how to employ the corps were the primary controversy. Untrained troops are more easily to direct while in column until battle is imminent so the question for Mansfield and Williams was a matter of judgment as to where and when battle would be joined. Perhaps Williams felt that Mansfield should have consulted him as Williams was more familiar with the units in the corps.

[80] Carman, Pierro, 236.

[81] Sears, *Landscape Turned Red*, 204; Gould, *A Narrative of Events*, 9.

[82] Carman, Clemens, vol. 2, 113, n. 3

[83] Carman, Pierro, 235. The final quotation is from Colonel Joseph F. Knipe, commander of the First Brigade, First Division, *ORA*, vol. 19, pt. 1, 487. Sears describes the weather as the rain having stopped but a patchy ground fog was evident, *Landscape Turned Red*, 183-184; Thompson also describes the morning as "foggy and misty," 198. Many other veterans' accounts mention light rain during the night. See also Carman, Clemens, vol. 2, 113, n. 4.

Advance of the 10th Maine from its bivouac at the Line Farm. Gould's map shows where Mansfield slept the night of the 16th/17th near a fence on the Line Farm at the black arrow; Gould's annotation "620" at the left center is the time when the 10th Maine was at that location. "D" shows Croasdale Knoll near where Colonel Croasdale, commander of the 128th Pennsylvania, was killed. The 10th Maine marched across the Smoketown Road and one of Sam Poffenberger's fields to a fence where they held position.

Gould's regimental history described the beginning of that fateful day for the 10ᵗʰ Maine, a senior regiment in the First Brigade, First Division:

We slept quietly in the furrows [of the Line Farm] till about 5 o'clock in the morning, and then a sharp rattle of musketry precisely like that which had served as a "good-night" to us, brought every man to his feet. Without so much as peeping into our haversacks we broke [our rifle] stacks and waited for orders. In a few minutes General Crawford rode down and commanded Col. Beal to move us forward. It was a relief to do something; the leading division ["regimental division" = two companies] under Capt. Furbish, knocked over two or three lengths of fence in a flash and we marched through the gap into the open field beyond. The volley which had been our reveille was followed by others and by cannonading, and even before we had marched the sounds told us that the enemy had given battle.

We had slept with our left toward the enemy; hence we faced toward the rear of Hooker's center, though we knew nothing of that fact then—and we were now marching so as to be where we could more promptly reinforce him; hence we did not move directly toward the sounds, but looked over to our left with anxious eyes, though the tactics says "Guide right!" for double columns. We soon came to a post and rail fence, and pulled that all down by order, then fell in and moved again squarely to our left, that is, toward the firing. We passed through Best's battery, which stood halted across our path, exchanged grins with the lucky rascals and went straight on. Then came the order to halt and lie down; we did it well!—and willingly! We remained here an hour by the watch, under the crest of a little knoll which sheltered us from a wonderfully wild and meaningless fire of artillery.

General Mansfield remarked very quietly to Col. Beal, "We are in reserve to-day, sir," and every man heard it or says he did. It was a dreary hour; we were not allowed to leave our places, save one or two who filled the canteens for all. And though the command was to "lie down" we could not help rising a little to peep over the crest and notice what was going on ahead. We looked up to the right, toward Joseph Poffenberger's mansion on the turnpike, and saw wagons and ambulances, and then to the front and saw only the woods with the shot from the artillery sizzling and whirring through and over them toward us—poor shooting we called it. But at the left front there was activity; here the woods swarmed with troops moving sullenly away from the battle; these were the skulks and the wounded. This day was in the grand old times for sneaks, when a gang of men could leave the battle to carry off a dead or wounded comrade; so out of these woods there poured a current of disabled and unfaithful ones.[84]

Modern photograph of the Joseph Poffenberger Farm about 250 yards east of the Hagerstown Pike and 625 yards west of the Smoketown Road. The farm has been renovated by the National Park Service and resembles what some troops in Mansfield's Corp would have seen. Photograph by author, September 2013.

---

[84] Gould, *History of the First*, 232-233. Mansfield's remark was obviously made before Hooker's urgent calls for help as Gould noted that they halted an hour laying down in defilade.

Modern view of the west front of the Samuel Poffenberger Farmhouse, looking north. XII Corps troops on the left flank would have seen this view to their left and rear. The property is privately owned. Courtesy LOC.

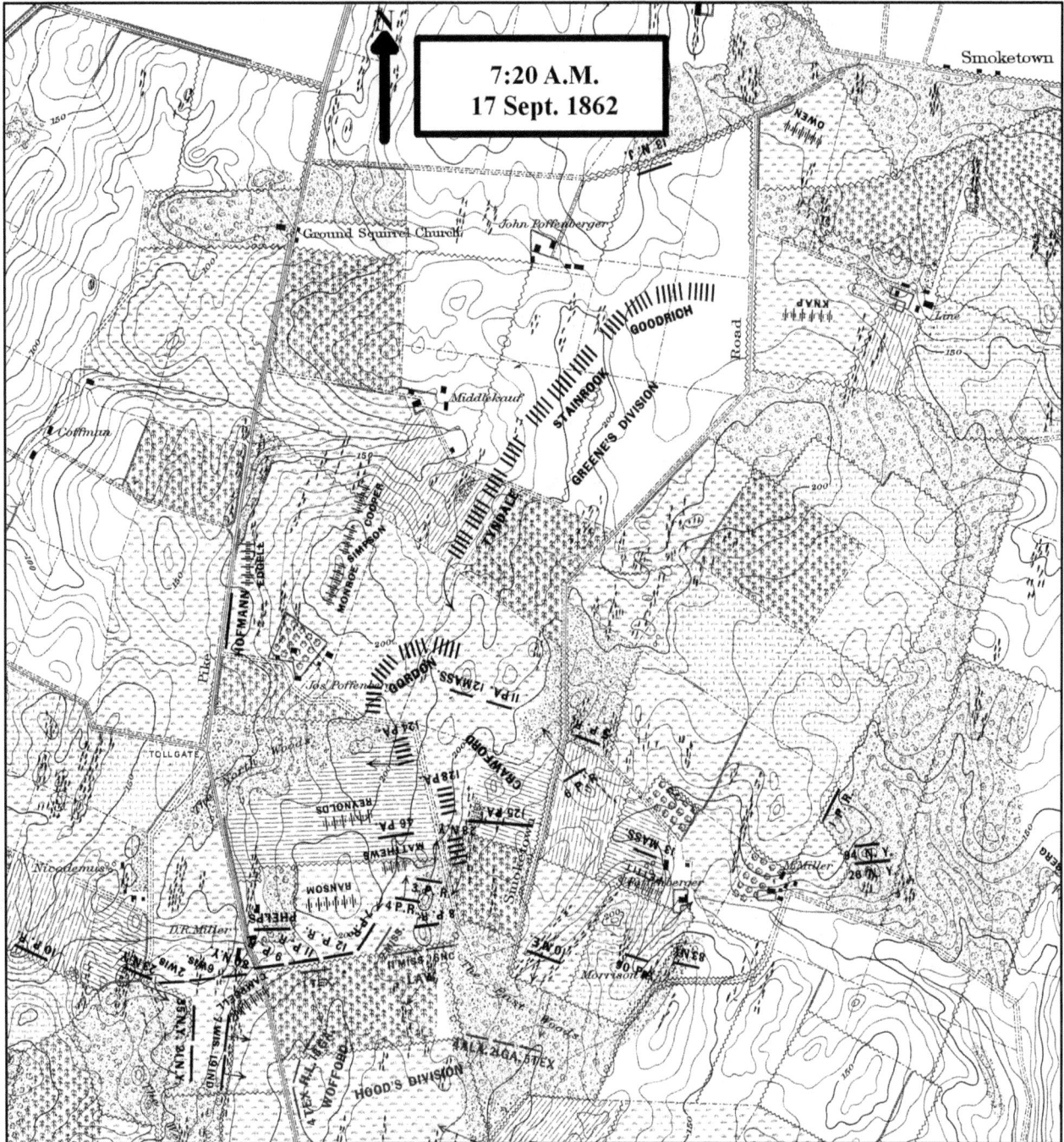

Confederate General Hood's counterattack pushed the Federals back through the East Woods and out of farmer Miller's cornfield but by 7:20 a.m., he is being hit from front and flank taking serious losses so began falling back. The 10th Maine is moving just east of the Smoketown Road toward The East Woods through a field on Samuel Poffenberger's Farm at the lower center. Other XII Corps units are deployed to the south and west to stop the Rebel advance. Carman-Cope map, courtesy LOC.

The historian of the 3rd Wisconsin, Third Brigade, First Division, Edwin Bryant, wrote about Mansfield being a conspicuous target as indeed all men on horseback were riding near the front lines:

As the Third Wisconsin formed its line the field of battle was open before it. Far to the left our lines could be seen. The right view was obstructed by the buildings of Miller's house and the orchard trees. In front, about one hundred yards and on the right of the regiment, was Battery B, Fourth United States artillery, with twelve-pounder brass guns, which had evidently been in action for some time. Their horses were killed or crippled and many of their men had been killed or wounded, and the Confederate sharpshooters were making serious havoc with them....As soon as Gordon's brigade completed its deployment it moved forward as far as the battery. The gunners, thus supported, opened with a will upon the advancing Confederates.

While this deployment was going on the brave old Mansfield, as full of ardor as any young man, rode forward to reconnoiter the position, and fair mark as he sat his horse in open view, he fell mortally wounded.[85]

Modern view of front of Miller Farm looking northwest. The farm is east of the Samuel Poffenberger Farm and is privately owned. Courtesy LOC.

Samuel Poffenberger Farm looking slightly east of north. The fence line where the 10th Maine formed was to the right of this photograph but not in view here. Courtesy LOC.

[85] Bryant, *Third Wisconsin*, 126-127.

Brigadier General Samuel Wylie Crawford, commander of the First Brigade, First Division, XII Corps, entered the army in 1851 as a surgeon, but transferred to the infantry in 1861. He replaced Williams as the First Division commander but was wounded in the right thigh and replaced by Brigadier General George H. Gordon, commander of the Third Brigade. He was brevetted successively from colonel, in 1863, up to major general in 1865, for conspicuous gallantry in the battles of the Wilderness, Spotsylvania, Petersburg, Five Forks, and other engagements. General Crawford was mustered out of the volunteer service in 1866, and then served with his regiment in the south, becoming colonel of the 16th infantry in February 1869 then the 2nd Infantry. He was retired with the rank of brigadier general in February 1873 due to disability from wounds. Courtesy LOC.

General Crawford's report relates his brigade's actions that morning:

My brigade led the march of the corps, when, leaving the main road [Smoketown Road], before daylight we took up a position on [Samuel] Poffenberger's farm, to the rear and left of General Hooker's force. At early dawn on the 17th my command was moved forward in column of companies, still leading the corps. Passing through strips of woods, and open ground and cornfields, we were suddenly halted, and a deployment ordered without delay. While in the act of executing the order I received orders from General Mansfield, in person, to suspend the deployment and again to mass my command, although the command was then exposed to an artillery fire. A third order to again deploy was brought to me by one of the officers of the division staff, and I at once deployed, my command being on the right of the line, which rested on a turnpike, and moved forward through the woods and open space, driving before us a thin line of the enemy's skirmishers. The new regiments from Pennsylvania (One hundred and twenty-fourth, One hundred and twenty-fifth, and One hundred and twenty-eighth) moved with great promptness and with the coolness of old troops, although they had not before been under fire. During this movement the One hundred and twenty-fourth Pennsylvania, Colonel Hawley, was detached from my brigade by some superior order unknown to me, and sent in advance through the woods on our right to Miller's farm, to hold that position.[86]

The struggle for the skirt of the woods to which the enemy clung, and the open space and corn-fields opposite and along the turnpike on the right, was long and determined. Finally the enemy was driven out of the woods across the fields, and into the opposite woods beyond the rocky ridges, to his supports. There he rallied, and bringing up fresh troops, our lines were exposed not only to a severe fire of his infantry, but also to an effective fire of his artillery on our right. While engaged in the struggle for the corn-field, Colonel Croasdale, of the One hundred and twenty-eighth Pennsylvania, was killed, and Lieutenant-Colonel Hammersly, of the same regiment, severely wounded. The One hundred and twenty-fifth Pennsylvania, Colonel Higgins, in the general movement had pushed on into the woods beyond our lines, and had become seriously engaged with the enemy while much exposed, but returned in good order with great loss to our lines.

---

[86] The general officer who ordered Hawley up has never been identified but certainly from Hooker's I Corps as Hawley would have known the general officers in the XII Corps and the II Corps had not yet arrived.

Shortly before our movement, Major-General Hooker had come to examine my position, and I received orders from him to hold the woods (Miller's) at all hazards, as otherwise the right of the army would be seriously imperiled. General Mansfield, the corps commander, had been mortally wounded, and was borne past my position to the rear. Shortly afterward I received an order from a staff officer of Brigadier General Williams to assume command of the First Division, he having assumed command of the corps. Sending orders to Colonel Knipe, of the Forty-sixth Pennsylvania, the senior colonel of my brigade to assume command at once of the brigade, I rode forward to find the Third Brigade (Gordon's), which had moved into action on the center of our line, and had been gallantly pushing the enemy before it. Our line had driven the enemy from Miller's woods across the wheat-fields into the [West] woods beyond the Dunkard Church and Hagerstown road. A fine wooden fence which skirted the road had proved a very serious obstacle to our farther advance. The regiments of the Third Brigade had become separated. In the absence of the brigade commander, I ordered Lieutenant-Colonel Andrews, commanding the Second Massachusetts, to maintain his position until the line could be formed.[87]

Colonel Jacob C. Higgins, commanded the 125th Pennsylvania Regiment, First Brigade, First Division, XII Corps. He had served in the Mexican-American War under Scott and was severely wounded in Mexico City. At the beginning of the Civil War, Higgins enlisted as a captain in the 1st Pennsylvania Cavalry, and was promoted to lieutenant colonel. He resigned in October 1861. In July 1862, he recruited a regiment and became colonel of the 125th Pennsylvania 16 August 1862. He mustered out with his regiment 18 May 1863. Courtesy Wikipedia.

Colonel Jacob C. Higgins, commanded the new 125th Pennsylvania in Crawford's Brigade, supplied details of his regiment's trials that morning as the brigade led the XII Corps' advance; Crawford led the 125th regiment's advance in person:

I was ordered by General Crawford to advance in close column, at daylight, through some fields to a piece of woods where there was heavy firing at that time going on. I was then ordered into the woods and then back again by General Crawford, then to throw out skirmishers and again advance through the woods until I reached the other side of the timber, and then deploy in line of battle and advance through the fields and there halt. At this place my command was exposed to a most terrific fire of musketry, shot, and shell. I then fell back a few rods [one rod equals 5½ yards/16½ feet], by order of General Crawford, where I remained some minutes, and was again ordered forward to the crest of a hill, which I was to hold.

At this time some colonel, whose name I do not know, told me that his troops were falling back for want of ammunition, and asked me to advance to his support. I immediately reported this to General Crawford, who ordered me to advance at once. I gave the command, and my men started forward with a yell, driving the enemy before them and gaining possession of the woods….Again I was ordered to advance and halt in line with a battery….At the battery I gave the command for my men to lie down whilst awaiting further orders. About this time the fire of the enemy slackened somewhat, only some shots from their sharpshooters being fired, and these at mounted officers and the artillery horses. Previous to this General Mansfield fell, some of my men carrying him off the field on their muskets until a blanket was procured. General Hooker here came up to me and inquired if any troops were in the woods in front. I replied, "None but rebels, and that my command was in the front." While talking to me, his horse was shot by some of the enemy's sharpshooters. I remarked to him that his horse was shot. He replied, "I see," turned and went away.

---

[87] *ORA*, vol. 19, pt. 1, 484-485.

In a short time I received an order to advance into the woods. I gave the order, "Forward," my regiment advancing in splendid style, and driving some South Carolina and Georgia troops back into the woods. I halted at the edge of the woods, and ordered Captain McKeage, of Company G, to deploy his company as skirmishers. This done, I again advanced a short distance in the woods, and halted again to examine the enemy's position. I found him in force in my front and on my right. On looking around I discovered myself without support either in my rear or right, and, being the only mounted officer present, I gave my horse to Lieutenant Higgins, and instructed him to ride back to the general, inform him of my situation, and ask him to send me support immediately, or I would be unable to hold my position, and that the enemy would certainly flank me and cut me off, my command being at this time in advance of the whole corps.[88]

---

[88] *ORA*, vol. 19, pt. 1, 491-492.

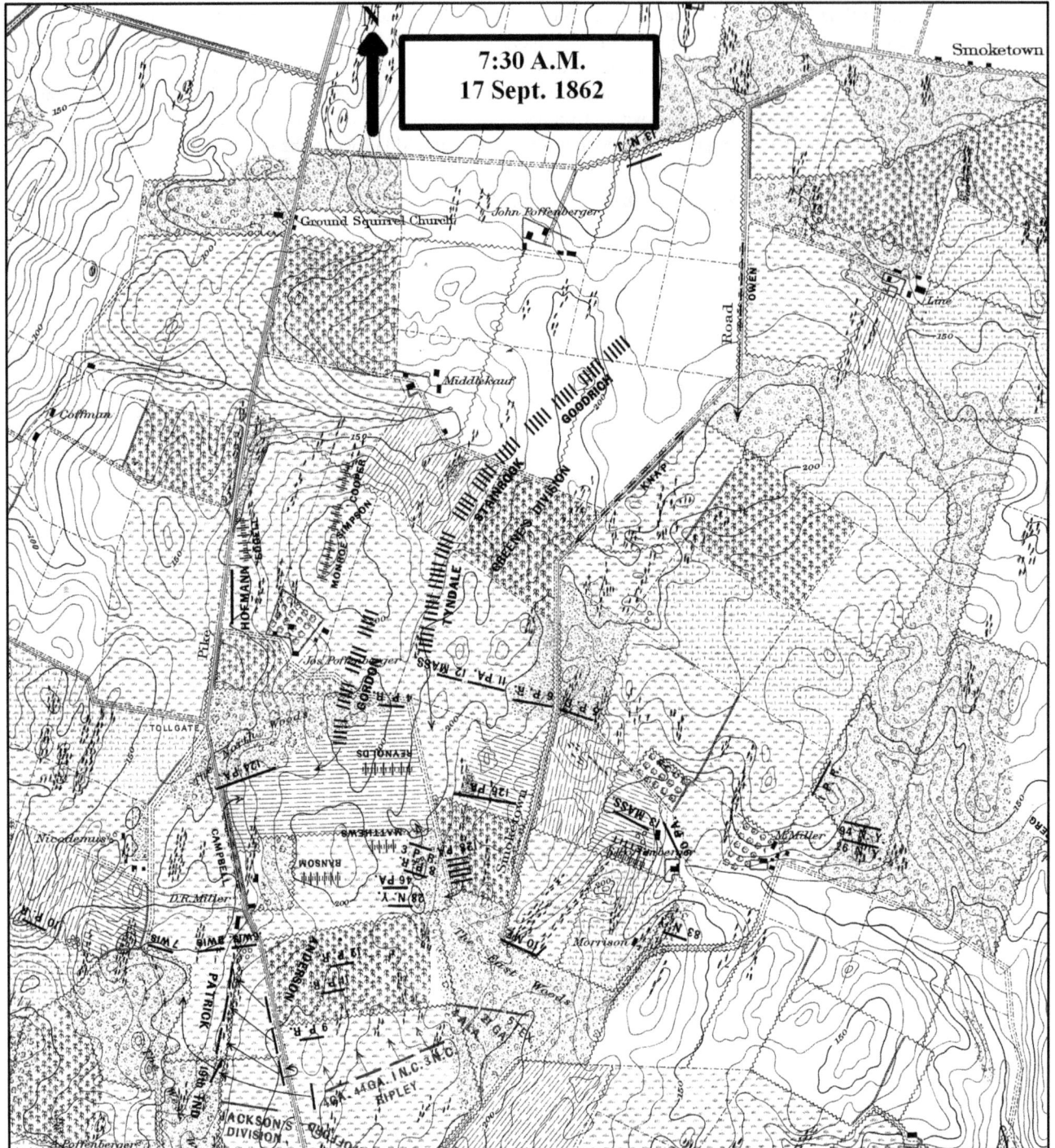

The 124th Pennsylvania, led by General Williams, has moved west to a blocking position on the Hagerstown Pike, while Williams rode off to find more regiments to put into line. Greene's Division continued south while Gordon's Brigade moved to the southwest. The 10th Maine has taken its position along the fence line near the East Woods at the lower center. Carman-Cope map, courtesy LOC.

John Mead Gould shown as a major in 1865. Gould was the 10ᵗʰ Maine's regiment's historian and a participant at Antietam as a first lieutenant in Co. E, and the Adjutant of 10ᵗʰ Maine. He became an authority for the 10ᵗʰ Maine's activities and collaborated with Carman for details of actions on that part of the field especially concerning Mansfield. In addition to the regiment's history, Gould wrote *The Civil War Journals of John Mead Gould 1861-1866*, ed. William B. Jordan, Jr. (Baltimore: Butternut & Blue, 1997), based on his letters and diary he wrote during the war; and, *Joseph K. F. Mansfield, Brigadier General of The U.S. Army: A Narrative of Events Connected with His Mortal Wounding at Antietam, Sharpsburg, Maryland, September 17, 1862* (Portland, ME: Stephen Berry, Printer, 1895). See Gould's biography below. Photograph courtesy Nicholas Picerno Collection.

John Mead Gould's regimental history described in rich detail and with effusive praise Mansfield's activities as the general led some of the regiments in person deploying them under fire:

> We all saw General Mansfield riding about the field in his new, untarnished uniform, with his long, silvery hair flowing out behind, and we loved him. It never fell to our lot to have such a commander as he. Very few of us had ever seen him till three days before this, but he found a way to our hearts at once. It would be saying too much to affirm that in three days he impressed us with the belief that he was a great warrior, for the time and opportunities were too limited for this, but he made us feel that he was our father and would care for us, and you remember we needed someone high in rank to care for us then. We never had a corps commander like Mansfield in this respect, and I doubt if the Army at that time could have furnished us another general like him.
>
> The General had been watching the battle from a knoll in our front, but soon after the change of affairs, he rode rapidly toward his command, and if we noticed correctly, he set all of his regiments in motion. For ourselves, we were the extreme right regiment of the corps, and were considerably in advance of and removed from all the others that we saw. The order was given to "ADVANCE!"
>
> Col. Beal at once commanded "Attention!" and "Forward!" We then moved a few steps straight for the battle, but the General ordered the Colonel to oblique to the left; whereupon the Colonel shouted "Left oblique!" and we obeyed, but did not

gain sufficiently to the left even then to suit General Mansfield, who still beckoned to the left, and we went hustling or sidling into a small cornfield, and should have been badly confused had not Col. Beal ordered "Left flank," etc. The men then found their places, and we moved through the corn into a plowed field [Samuel Poffenberger's], crossing a road [Smoketown Road], to do so, which leads from Hoffman's house to the Dunker church.

It was almost exactly 7.30 o'clock, by my watch, when we went through the gap in the fences of this road. Just then Asst. Surgeon A.A. Kendall, of the 12th Mass., was being carried out mortally wounded, and General Hooker himself rode down and inquired of our field officers what regiment ours was, and told them that the rebels were breaking through his lines, and "You must hold those woods!" An order like this may not be the one most desired, but it is a great relief to a commander to be assigned to some special duty, and to have the great burden of suspense thereby removed.

When a few rods inside of the field the order "Right flank!" etc., brought us to the front, and we advanced to the position which had been pointed out to the Colonel. General Mansfield had followed us through part of these movements—in truth he was placing us in what was just then the vital point of the battle. He forbade our being deployed into one line, remarking to Col. Beal that the men could be handled better in mass, and less straggling would result.

A few stray bullets whizzed around us as we crossed the road. After this our march toward the enemy was down and up a very gentle slope. Once in sight of the woods again, our leading companies saw a picket line of rebels behind the fence which skirted the union edge of the woods. These fired at us but their bullets fell short or went over, and we pressed on, many of us not noticing them.

I have stated that when the corps was put in motion we were on its right, but our march to the left had brought us now to be the left regiment of our brigade. We saw no Union troops except one of the new Penn. regiments, the 128th, which was on the right side of the road, also advancing and in mass.

And now came the moment of battle that tried us severely, not that there was a sign of hesitancy, or show of poor behavior, but it is terrible to march slowly into danger, and see and feel that each second your chance for death is surer than it was the second before. The desire to break loose, to run, to fire, to do something, no matter what, rather than to walk, is almost irresistible. Men who pray, pray then; men who never pray nerve themselves as best they can, but it is said that those who have been praying men and are not, suffer an agony that neither of the other class can know.

The mention of the position of our regiment at this stage of the battle is enough to horrify a military man. We were under fire and advancing at a brisk walk closed in mass, that is ten ranks deep (or fifteen ranks counting the file closers). We were almost as good a target as a barn.

The fire of the enemy became more galling every step we took, and one man after another fell, so that at length Col. Beal could not endure to see his command so uselessly butchered, and without obtaining consent of the General he ordered us to deploy into one line, which was done at double quick and without halting. Possibly a sixth of our loss occurred before we halted.

After deploying, the right companies met an obstacle in the road fence and a clump of bushes, and the left ones ran on a ragged ledge, but the men kept together finely, and we soon reached the rail fence from which the rebel pickets had just retired, and here we halted to deliver our fire at the men of the enemy who were running around in the woods in front of us.

It made a good impression upon them; one by one they dodged back till they reached the farther part of the woods, where they staid a while and fired back at us.

Our general position was the fence, and [Co.] F with a part of C was behind it. Co. F was further sheltered by the ledge. The right companies, with the instinct which prompts a man to face the fire rather than to take it in his side, jumped over the fence and then broke their lines by rushing behind the logs and trees; thus the regiment made a left quarter-wheel, and thereby unknowingly conformed itself to the general alignment of the Union forces at this moment. A great many of the men worked far ahead of the colors, and as a consequence a very few may have been hit by the wild shooting of our own men in the rear.

We were on low land, and although so many troops were engaged around us we could see only the 128th Penn. on our side. When we first went into the battle, and before we had fired a musket, we saw in the open field away through the woods a group of forty or fifty men around the stars and stripes, quite near an abandoned gun or limber. They were falling to the rear inch by inch, the color sergeant waving his flag, and the officers shouting and beckoning for the men who had gone to the rear to return, which some of them did [105th New York of Duryée's Brigade—Gould]. This waving of the Union flag upon what appeared to be rebel ground has been supposed by some of us to be a device of the enemy to steal upon us without being fired at.

On the rebel side we saw the men we were firing into, dodging from tree to tree, aiming at us, yelling, shaking their fists sometimes, and saucy generally. As well as we could tell, they were about as numerous as we, and it was a desperate fight we made of it. Indeed, as far as we and our immediate enemies were concerned, it partook of the character of a heavy skirmish, every man fighting for himself, and so it happened that the advanced men of friend and foe were sometimes within ten or fifteen yards of each other.[89]

[89] Gould, *History of the First*, 235-238.

Lieutenant Colonel James S. Fillebrown wrote the 10th Maine's brief official report as its colonel, Beal, was recovering from wounds, and Fillebrown himself was seriously injured by Beal's horse early in the morning:

> The regiment went on to the field in column by division, closed in mass on first division, right in front, and was ordered to deploy while under fire, by General Mansfield, the only general officer present, to the left of the Forty-sixth Pennsylvania Volunteers, and, before we were in line, had some few men killed or wounded. Before we received orders to commence firing, we were obliged to oblique to the left the length of our regiment, and at once commenced the engagement with a regiment of the enemy, which afterward proved to be the Twentieth Georgia. The men went into the woods some few rods, when I was knocked from my horse by Colonel Beal's horse, which had been twice mortally wounded, and, returning, gave me a severe kick in the stomach, entirely disabling me for three days. Colonel Beal received a shot, after his horse was twice wounded, in the legs, passing through one and entering the other slightly.[90]

---

[90] *ORA*, vol. 19, pt. 1, 489. Note the differences with Gould's account. Gould had the benefit of writing the regimental history many years later and after discussing the events with other 10th Maine men as well as other veterans of the battle including Ezra Carman. The 20th Georgia was at Burnside Bridge, so the unit here was likely the 21st Georgia according to Thomas Clemens.

Captain George H. Nye, captain of Co. K, 10ᵗʰ Maine, courtesy Nicholas Picerno Collection.

Captain William P. Jordan of the 10ᵗʰ Maine, Co. C, courtesy Nicholas Picerno Collection.

Colonel George L. Beal, commander of the 10ᵗʰ Maine regiment, courtesy Nicholas Picerno Collection.

Lieutenant Colonel James S. Fillebrown of the 10ᵗʰ Maine, courtesy Nicholas Picerno Collection.

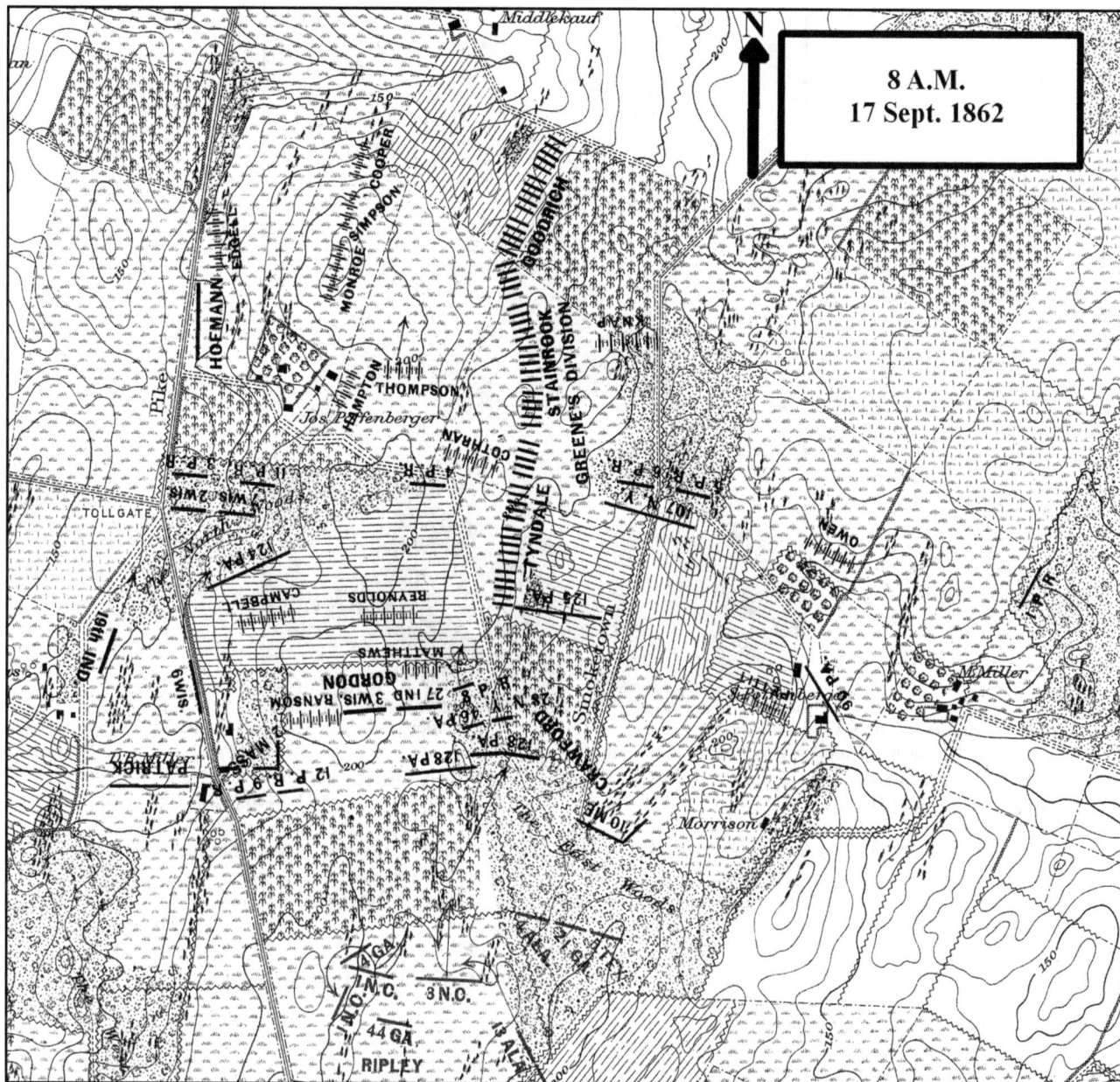

Mansfield by this time was shot and on his way to the Line Farmhouse along the Smoketown Road. Carman-Cope map, courtesy LOC.

Brigadier General George Henry Gordon, commander of the Third Brigade, First Division, was an 1846 West Point graduate who had served with Scott in Mexico. He was in the siege of Vera Cruz in 1847, in the battle of Cerro Gordo, where he was wounded and brevetted 1st lieutenant, took part in the battles of Contreras and Chapultepec, and in the assault and capture of Mexico City. In a hand-to-hand encounter with two guerillas near the San Juan Bridge on 21 December 1847, he was severely wounded. He resigned from the Army in 1854 to practice law in Boston. In 1861, he organized and became colonel of the 2nd Massachusetts Volunteer Infantry which served guarding the upper Potomac River and near Frederick, Maryland. In the spring of 1862, Gordon served under Major General Nathaniel P. Banks in the unsuccessful fight against Major General Stonewall Jackson in the Shenandoah Valley. In June 1862 he was appointed brigadier general of volunteers, and then commanded the Third Brigade, First Division of the Army of Virginia II Corps at Cedar Mountain and Chantilly. At Antietam, he relieved the wounded Crawford to command the First Division. He was brevetted major general of volunteers on 9 April 1865. Courtesy LOC.

General Gordon reported his actions on that day to Brigadier General Williams, the new XII Corps commander:

Just after the break of day we were aroused from a brief slumber by sharp firing of musketry in front of General Hooker's position. The corps, then commanded by the lamented General Mansfield, was by that officer immediately put in motion. My brigade, formed in columns of battalions closed in mass, I directed toward a battery which I was ordered to support, but before reaching the same I received a countermanding order to move forward with all possible dispatch to the support of General Hooker, then severely pressed. I moved accordingly my ployed ["ployed": troops formed in columns] masses by the flank at double-quick, gradually gaining deployment distance, thus throwing forward in line of battle on the right the Second Massachusetts Regiment, Colonel Andrews; in the center the Third Wisconsin, Colonel Ruger; on the left the Twenty-seventh Indiana, Colonel Colgrove. The One hundred and seventh New York Regiment, Colonel Van Valkenburgh, I held in reserve, throwing them into the edge of a piece of woods on the left, which I was informed by an aide of General Hooker, who met me advancing, was to be held at all hazards. The only remaining regiment of my brigade, the Thirteenth New Jersey, I had, by direction of General Mansfield, thrown into the edge of a piece of woods behind my first position as a reserve. This regiment remained as posted during the deployment of my line and the posting of the One hundred and seventh New York.

While moving forward the three regiments referred to, an aide of General Hooker's, galloping rapidly toward my command, begged me to hurry forward. It was apparent, from the steady approach of the sound of musketry, that the enemy were advancing. Their shouts of exultation could be distinctly heard as the line of my deployed battalion, sustained on the right by Crawford's brigade and on the left by Greene's division, both of our own corps, advanced boldly to the front. Before the impetuous charge and the withering fire of our line, the enemy halted, wavered, fled in confusion, and sought shelter in the woods opposite from whence he had emerged. I immediately ordered the One hundred and seventh New York to support the movement of my advance line, at the same time sending my aide, Captain Wheaton, to bring up the Thirteenth New Jersey.

We now held possession of the field, had driven the enemy into the concealment of the woods, and, by a partial change of front forward on our left, were advancing toward the center of the general line of battle.

General Mansfield had been mortally wounded at the commencement of the action while making a bold reconnaissance of the woods through which we had just dashed. The command of the corps here devolved upon you [General Williams].

My brigade was now drawn up in two lines. In the first, the Second Massachusetts and the One hundred and seventh New York Regiments; in the rear, the Third Wisconsin and Twenty-seventh Indiana. These latter regiments had suffered considerably. In the others the casualties had been unusually light. We were at this time re-enforced by General Sumner's corps, who, coming with shouts to the field, pushed across into the woods containing the enemy, and engaged him with ardor....

About this time, in the order of events as narrated, I received an urgent call from General Greene, commanding the Second Division of our corps, to send him any re-enforcements I might have and could spare.

General Greene at this time was gallantly holding a portion of the woods to the left, the right of which was held by the enemy in force. I directed the Thirteenth New Jersey, Colonel Carman, to support him. This regiment, also for the first time this day under fire, moved boldly and in an orderly manner toward General Greene's position, and I am much gratified to report that the general has spoken to me of their conduct in terms of high commendation. The services of my brigade during a portion of the remainder of the day were confined to forming a supporting line to fresher troops in our front.[91]

---

[91] *ORA*, vol. 19, pt. 1, 494-496.

**8:30 – 8:40 A.M.
17 Sept. 1862**

The 10th Maine moves north away from Samuel Poffenberger's fence as Stainrook with his brigade moves toward the East Woods. Sumner's two divisions begin to move from the east with Sedgwick's Division leading. Confederates are in retreat. Carman-Cope map, courtesy LOC.

A fanciful but inaccurate depiction of the Battle of Sharpsburg on the right drawn by Alfred Waud. It shows Mansfield, Williams, Greene, and Col. Knipe. Bests Battery, 4th Maine is on the far left; 27th Indiana Infantry on the left, the 3rd Wisconsin is in the center and right; Col. Ruger wounded; 43rd N.Y. lying on the ground. Col. Joseph F. Knipe commander of the 46th Pennsylvania Infantry was put in command of the First Brigade of the First Division of the XII Corps after Mansfield was wounded and Brig. Gen. Samuel W. Crawford was moved up to command the First Division. Waud's notes for units and commanders portrayed here require interpretation. He noted the 16th Indiana on the extreme left but that regiment was not at Antietam so if he is correct that the 5th Wisconsin is in the center, then the unit to its left is the 27th Indiana. He shows the 43rd New York laying down to the left foreground but that regiment was in the VI Corps under Franklin and not on the field when Mansfield was wounded; it may have been the 107th New York. He also shows Col. Ruger of the 3rd Wisconsin wounded in the right center foreground but Ruger was only slightly wounded and not incapacitated. If the wounded officer was not Ruger, there were no other wounded officers in Ruger's Third Brigade, First Division, so Waud may be depicting another colonel from the First Brigade. The 4th Maine battery never left the area of the Upper Bridge. Obviously Waud is trying to show this part of the line as best he could to represent scenes he witnessed. If he is depicting action at 8 a.m., then Mansfield would already be on his way to the Line Farm hospital. Alfred Waud's sketch, *Harper's Weekly*, 16 October 1862, 648-649. Author's collection.

Photograph of Mansfield taken in 1861 or 1862 at Union Photographic Gallery, Camp Butler, Newport News, Virginia, according to the photograph's back stamp. Even though he is only **58** years old, his appearance shows that life in the U.S. Army since his entry to West Point in 1817 took its toll, showing a man who has endured much during his 40-year career. The arduous inspections involving much travel to frontier posts in the west for several years while he was in his 50's were reflected in his careworn face. His hirsute appearance with an unkempt mane of white hair and large, unruly beard certainly did not help portray an image of a vigorous man capable of strenuous active service in the field as an army commander as Secretary Chase noted after an interview. But many of his soldiers commented on his long white hair flowing in the wind as he vigorously rode about the field. He was not the oldest soldier on the field as his wing commander at Antietam, Major General Edwin Vose "Bull Head" Sumner, Sr., was 65 years old, born 30 January 1797. Brigadier General George Sears Greene, Mansfield's Second Division commander, was over two and one-half years older than Mansfield, born 6 May 1801. Mansfield's commander at Norfolk, Major General John E. Wool, 78 years old, was the oldest Union soldier on active duty. All except Greene had served in the Mexican-American War. Courtesy LOC.

General Williams's report of the battle for the XII Corps is vital to understand the corps' actions that terrible morning and reflects the chaos as the I Corps fell apart under heavy Confederate attacks:

About 2 o'clock the night before the action, the corps took up position about 1½ miles in rear of General Hooker's corps, near the farm of J. Poffenberger, bivouacking in columns of companies. At the first sound of cannon at daylight on the morning of the 17th instant, the command was put in movement, each regiment, by order of General Mansfield, marching in column of companies, closed in mass. In this order the corps moved to the front by battalions in mass, the First Brigade, First Division, leading, over ground of intermingled woods, plowed fields, and corn-fields. Before reaching the position of General Hooker's corps, information was brought that his reserves were all engaged and that he was hard pressed by the enemy. The columns were hastened up and deployed in line of battle with all the rapidity that circumstances would permit. Five of the regiments of the First Division were new and wholly without drill.

The massed battalions had been moved with such haste that the proper intervals for deployment had not been carefully attended to. The old regiments, however, deployed promptly, and the new regiments (both officers and men of which behaved with marked coolness) soon got into line of battle, with more promptitude than could have been expected.

While the deployment was going on, and before the leading regiments were fairly engaged, it was reported to me that the veteran and distinguished commander of the corps was mortally wounded. I at once reported to Major-General Hooker on the field, took from him such directions as the pressing exigencies would permit, and hastened to make a disposition of the corps to meet them. Crawford's brigade was directed to deploy to the right, its right regiment extending to the Williamsport [Hagerstown] and Sharpsburg stone pike. Gordon held the center, while Brigadier-General Greene's division, following the first division in column, was directed to the ridge on the left, extending its line from the lane on Gordon's left to the burned buildings [Mumma Farm], a few rods northerly of the brick church.

While General Greene was moving into position, I was strongly solicited by Brigadier-General Gibbon to send re-enforcements to the right to support General Doubleday's position. I accordingly detached the Third Brigade of General Greene's division, with orders to report to any general officer found on the field indicated. At the same time I ordered the One hundred and twenty-fourth Pennsylvania Volunteers (Crawford's brigade) to push forward past the farm-house of Mr. [David R.] Miller, cross the pike into the woods beyond, and hold the ridge as long as practicable.

In the meantime the whole line had formed in good order, and were pushing the enemy from the woods and open fields. The requisitions made upon the corps would permit of no reserves, and it may be truly stated that, to cover the points threatened or pressed, every regiment (save Thirteenth New Jersey, held in reserve for a while by General Gordon) was, as early as 6:30 to 7 o'clock a. m., engaged with the enemy.

The enemy at this time had pushed his columns into the open fields in advance of a strip of woods, a few hundred yards wide, which extended along a gentle ridge from the brick church, on the Sharpsburg road, to the farm-house of J. [D.R.?] Miller, and extending beyond in the same direction to a distance not discernible from my position.[92]

---

[92] *ORA*, vol. 19, pt. 1, 475-476.

David R. Miller farmhouse taken shortly after the battle with family members on the porch. Note the apparent battle damage on the house's siding. The farmhouse was located on the eastern side of the Hagerstown Pike just south of the Joseph Poffenberger farm and the North Woods; in its fields heavy fighting took place on the morning of the 17th. The stucco exterior was applied over the original logs. Courtesy LOC.

Colonel Joseph Farmer Knipe, commander of the First Brigade after Crawford was bumped up to division command after Williams took over for Mansfield. Knipe was a shoemaker who enlisted as a private in the Old Army in 1842, and served in the Mexican-American War, discharged in 1848, becoming a Pennsylvania Railroad employee. In 1861, he was brigade inspector of Pennsylvania militia, and in October 1861 commissioned Colonel of the 46th Pennsylvania Regiment. He led them in the Shenandoah Valley campaign and at Cedar Mountain, where he was captured. He was wounded both at Winchester and Cedar Mountain. At Antietam, he was initially in command of the 46th Pennsylvania but succeeded to the command of the First Brigade of the First Division. Courtesy LOC.

Colonel Joseph F. Knipe who commanded Crawford's First Brigade in the First Division was in the van of the XII Corps on the morning of the 17th. In his official report he described his actions:

At an early hour of the morning of the 17th September the different regiments were set in motion. The Forty-sixth Pennsylvania, Tenth Maine, Twenty-eighth New York, One hundred and twenty-fourth, One hundred and twenty-fifth, and One hundred and twenty-eighth Pennsylvania took position in the rear of a belt of woods, the other side of which our troops were engaged with the enemy; the Tenth Maine, the Forty-sixth Pennsylvania, and Twenty-eighth New York constituting the right, with the new regiments (One hundred and twenty-eighth, One hundred and twenty-fifth, and One hundred and twenty-fourth) on the left. It was the understanding that the latter three regiments should move to the front when wanted, and the old ones (the Forty-sixth Pennsylvania, Tenth Maine, and Twenty-eighth New York) should follow at a proper distance in the rear, constituting, as it were, a reserve for the brigade. This plan was not carried out, and after remaining for upward of thirty minutes in the position described, the entire brigade was marched to the front, in column of division, to relieve the troops of General Hooker, who had up to this time borne the brunt of battle on the right. In this march of half a mile, the Tenth Maine, which had been on the right of the Forty-sixth Pennsylvania, by some means for which I cannot account got on the left of it, and both, with the Twenty-eighth New York, in advance of the One hundred and twenty-fourth, One hundred and twenty-fifth, and One hundred and twenty-eighth Pennsylvania. On emerging from the woods, the columns of the three advance regiments were deployed, and immediately opened upon the enemy, who were in strong force in a corn-field about 250 yards from our front.

While in this position, the One hundred and twenty-eighth Pennsylvania came up and took position on the right of the Forty-sixth Pennsylvania Volunteers, still massed in column of company. Colonel Croasdale, its commander, fell dead while endeavoring to deploy it into line of battle, and Lieutenant-Colonel Hammersly was so severely wounded in the arm at the same time as to be obliged to leave the field. At this moment, seeing the uselessness of a regiment in that position, I took the responsibility of getting it into line of battle the best way circumstances would admit. When this was accomplished, I returned to my own regiment and ordered an advance, which was gallantly made as far as the fence of the corn-field. This position would have been held, and the advance continued in face of the leaden hail which was fast decimating our ranks had it not been for the Twenty-seventh Indiana forming in our rear and exposing us to a fire from a quarter unexpected. I immediately ordered my command to fall back to the woods, when I met General Williams, then in command of the corps (General Mansfield having been carried to the rear mortally wounded), who ordered the regiments to retire to the rear of the woods and then reform. On our march to the position designated, we were met by re-enforcements of General Sumner's command, I think, hastening to the front. My regiments (what was left of them) formed in their immediate rear, and, with them, went into and through the corn-field and into the one lying beyond it. Having by this movement completely driven the enemy out of the open fields into the woods beyond, it was deemed inexpedient to proceed farther, and the whole force reclined upon the ground to avoid the fire of the enemy's artillery.

While in this position, I noticed that the One hundred and twenty-fifth Pennsylvania Volunteers had advanced into the field beyond our position and into the woods occupied by the enemy. At the same time a brigade came out of them to our rear, and, passing us, joined the One hundred and twenty-fifth, and engaged the enemy, who had been reinforced to such an extent as to compel our troops to retrace their steps in confusion if not in panic. At this juncture a battery was placed in position to cover the retreat of our forces, and poured in the advancing and dense masses of the enemy a tremendous fire of grape and canister. Notwithstanding the huge gaps made in their ranks, the rebels continued to advance, and threatened the capture of the battery. I was in the immediate rear of the battery at the time with my colors and a few more men than its guard, when I was requested by some general, to me unknown, to form a rallying point for our retreating regiments. I was successful so far as to get the One hundred and seventh New York to form on my flag, and believe that it was this show of front that saved the guns from the enemy's hands. Fresh troops having arrived on the ground, I ordered my men to retire to the position they marched from in the morning, where they were joined by the Twenty-eighth New York, Tenth Maine, and One hundred and twenty-eighth Pennsylvania Volunteers.

It was shortly after this and late in the afternoon that I was advised of the wounding of Brigadier-General Crawford, and ordered, in consequence, to take command of the brigade. Ordering my own and the three regiments last named to remain where they were, I hastened to the front to look out the whereabouts of the One hundred and twenty-fourth and One hundred and twenty-fifth Pennsylvania regiments. I found them in the woods where our first line of battle had been formed, and, by order of Major-General Franklin, whose corps then formed our advance line, placed the two regiments to the rear of his center, where they bivouacked for the night.[93]

Colonel Thomas Howard Ruger, commander of the Third Brigade, First Division, was appointed to West Point from Wisconsin in 1850, graduating third in the class of 1854. He served as an engineer in New Orleans, but resigned in 1855. Until the war, he practiced law in Wisconsin. He was commissioned Lieutenant Colonel of the 3rd Wisconsin on 29 June 1861, and its Colonel on 1 September 1861. He led it in the Shenandoah Valley and in Northern Virginia in the campaigns of spring and summer 1862. Commissioned brigadier general of volunteers in November 1862, he led his brigade of the XII Corps, Army of the Potomac, in the Battle of Chancellorsville, and commanded the division of Brigadier General Alpheus Williams temporarily at Gettysburg....In the summer of 1863, Ruger was in New York City, where he aided in suppressing draft riots. Ruger led a brigade of XX Corps in Major General William T. Sherman's Atlanta Campaign until November 1864, and with a division of XXIII Corps took part in the campaign against General John B. Hood's Army in Tennessee. He was appointed a brevet major general of volunteers, 30 November 1864, for the Battle of Franklin. Ruger organized a division at Nashville and led his command to North Carolina in June 1865, and then had charge of the department of that state until June 1866. He accepted a regular army commission as colonel, 28 July 1866, and on 2 March 1867, was brevetted brigadier general, for Gettysburg. During Reconstruction, he was the military governor of Georgia and in the Freedmen's Bureau in Alabama in 1868. He was the superintendent of the United States Military Academy from 1871 to 1876, and retired in 1897, as a major general in the Regular Army. William H. Powell, *Officers of the Army and Navy (Volunteer) Who Served in the Civil War* (Philadelphia, PA: L.R. Hamersly & Co., 1893), 104.

---

[93] *ORA*, vol. 19, pt. 1, 486-488.

Colonel Thomas H. Ruger, 3rd Wisconsin, who took over command of the Third Brigade, First Division, from Gordon when he was moved up to command of the First Division, was slightly wounded on the 17th when a bullet creased his skull. His after-action report was written by Captain Charles Wheaton, Jr., Acting Assistant Adjutant-General, Third Brigade:

The regiment arrived at the position assigned it, in company with other regiments of the brigade, between the hours of 6 and 7 a.m. The particular place occupied by the regiment was a knoll overlooking a cornfield, from which, as the brigade arrived, the enemy were driving our troops, belonging to some other brigade. The regiment suffered somewhat before the corn-field was sufficiently clear of our own troops to render it safe to fire. The fire of the enemy was returned with steadiness and spirit for a long time, until the ammunition in the boxes became nearly exhausted, and in some cases quite so. At one time the enemy had succeeded in advancing to within about 100 yards, at which point he became exposed to a cross-fire from the Second Massachusetts Volunteers, on my right. The combined fire of the regiments of the brigade particularly engaged at the point referred to - the Second Massachusetts, Twenty-seventh Indiana, and Third Wisconsin - drove the enemy rapidly out of the corn-field and into the woods. At this time an advance was ordered, and was being executed, with bayonets fixed, for the purpose of charging. Before any considerable distance was made, however, the corps of General Sumner came upon the field in two or three lines, which were perpendicular, or nearly so, to our line, which compelled a halt of our line. Very soon the troops, or some portion of them, that had passed and gone into the woods into which the enemy had been driven from the corn-field, come back in some disorder.

The regiment, with others of the brigade, was now placed by a change of front in position to support a battery, covering the retreat of the troops driven back from the woods. During the remainder of the day the regiment, with others of the brigade, continued in position as support to batteries, being exposed at times to the fire of the enemy's shells.[94]

---

[94] *ORA*, vol. 19, pt. 1, 503-504.

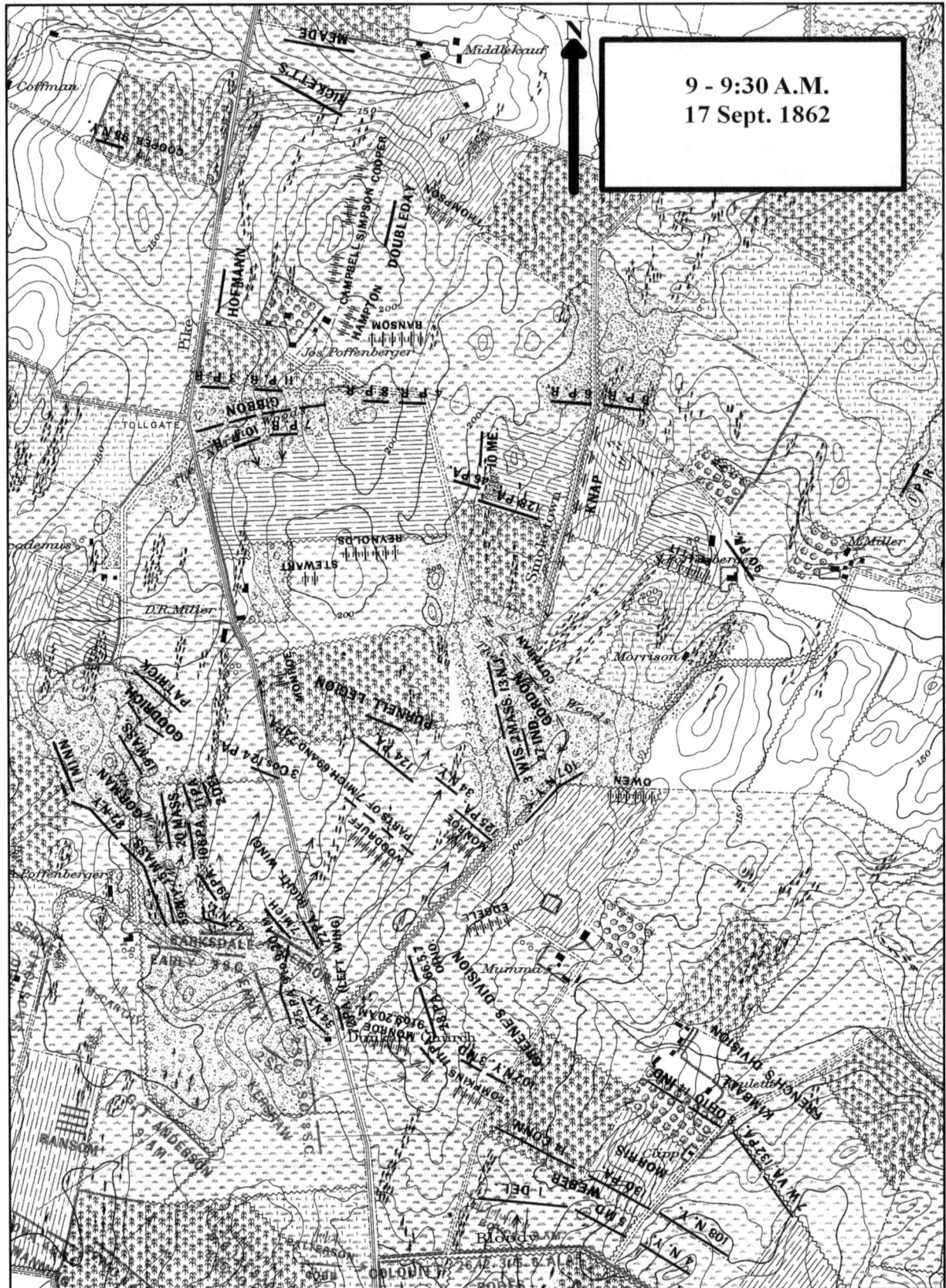

Major General Sumner led Sedgwick's 1st Division across the Antietam and directly west across the battlefield starting at about 9 a.m. He was hit by strong Confederate attacks on his front, left flank, and rear in the West Woods which routed his men with heavy casualties. Meanwhile, Brigadier General French led his 3rd Division of the II Corps to the battlefield about 9:00 a.m. Angling slightly left (south) of the path of Sedgwick's Division, he marched into part of Major General D.H. Hill's Division, posted in a sunken road at the center of the Confederate line.

Brigadier General George Sears "Pop" Greene, commanded Mansfield's Second Division. He was a Rhode Island native and well-educated before he entered West Point graduating in 1823, second in his class. Instead of joining the Engineers, he chose artillery but remained at West Point as an instructor until 1827. He likely knew Mansfield who had graduated the year before. He resigned in 1836 becoming a successful civil engineer. After the Civil War began, the 60-year-old was appointed colonel of the 60th New York, 18 January 1862. After Antietam, he was involved in the Battle of Chancellorsville and then in his famous defense of Culp's Hill at Gettysburg. After the XII Corps was transferred to reinforce Union troops at Chattanooga, he was wounded in the face from which he never fully recovered. He was assigned to court-martial duty until January 1865, when he was sent to join Major General William T. Sherman's Army in North Carolina. Greene voluntarily served on the staff of Major General Jacob D. Cox participating in the battle at Kinston, where he had his horse shot out from under him. At the end of the war, he was in command of the 3rd Brigade in the 3rd Division, XIV Corps, and participated in the capture of Raleigh and the pursuit of General Joseph E. Johnston's Army until it surrendered. He gained further distinction when, in an effort to obtain a death pension for his family, he took the oath of office as a first lieutenant of artillery and became, at 93, the oldest lieutenant in the U.S. Army, *In Memoriam, George Sears Greene, Brevet Major-General, United States Volunteers, 1801-1899* (Albany, NY: J.B. Lyon Company, 1909. Photograph courtesy LOC.

General Greene reported his command's actions on the 17th:

The division was carried into action about 6.30 a.m., under the orders of Brigadier-General Mansfield. As we were going into action, the Third Brigade was detached to the right, leaving under my command the First and Second Brigades, with an aggregate of 1,727. The division encountering the enemy in the first [East] woods in our front drove them before it, and, entering the open ground partly covered with corn, moved to the left and took position on the right of the post and rail fence inclosing the field on the right of the burned house [Mumma's]. There was a battery of brass guns at our left, which we protected. This battery getting out of ammunition for long range was replaced by another.

While in this position the enemy formed in strong force in the woods to the right of the white brick church and advanced on our line. The line was advanced to the axle-trees of the guns, and delivered their fire when the enemy were within 70 yards. They immediately fell back, having suffered immense loss. The division advanced, driving the enemy from the woods near the church and occupying the woods. The Purnell Legion joined us during the action. The Twenty-seventh Indiana was sent to our support, and, after doing good service, retired in consequence of their ammunition being exhausted. The Thirteenth New Jersey then joined the division, and assisted in holding the woods. The position of the division in the advanced woods was very critical. We were in advance of our line on the right and left of us. Sumner's corps, which had advanced on our left, had retired, as had also the troops on our right. Guns were sent for, and a section of Knaps battery arrived, and were ordered to take position on our left. The ground on our left and front was broken and wooded, and concealed the movements of the enemy. I placed the division in line, with the right thrown back, and sent forward skirmishers and sought re-enforcements from General Williams. None were at the time available, and the enemy advancing in large force, threatening to envelop the small command, they were forced to retire. They rallied in the second line of woods. They held the woods by the church nearly two hours, in advance of any other troops in their vicinity. They were in action from 6.30 a.m. to 1.30 p. m.

....Colonel Goodrich, of the Sixtieth New York, commanding Third Brigade, was killed early in the day while gallantly leading his command into action, the command of the brigade devolving upon Lieutenant-Colonel Austin, Seventy-eighth New York Volunteers, who remained in command during the remainder of the day.[95]

Greene's Division pushes Confederates to the Hagerstown Pike and past the Dunker Church. Carman-Cope map, courtesy LOC.

[95] *ORA*, vol. 19, pt. 1, 505.

Major Orrin J. Crane, commander of the First Brigade, Second Division, born in Troy, New York in 1829, moved to Ohio in 1852, becoming a ship carpenter in Cleveland. At the beginning of the Civil War, he joined Capt. Creighton's company in the 7th Ohio as first lieutenant becoming captain when Creighton was promoted. He served in Western Virginia, up to Winchester, and was at Port Republic and Cedar Mountain, where he was slightly wounded in the foot. He was promoted to major 25 May 1862. He was promoted to lieutenant colonel then moved west with his regiment. At Missionary Ridge on 27 November 1863, he was killed leading his regiment during a charge. AOTW; *Cleveland, Past and Present* (Cleveland, OH: Fairbanks, Benedict & Co., printers, 1869), 481-482.

Major Orrin J. Crane submitted his report for the First Brigade of Greene's Second Division in place of Lieutenant Colonel Hector Tyndale who was seriously wounded during the battle on the 17th:

> The brigade, under command of Lieut. Col. H. Tyndale, Twenty-eighth Pennsylvania Volunteers, was formed at 5.30 a. m. in column of division, right in front. It was then marched in column about 1 mile to a point of woods, where the enemy were in force and had engaged our right, holding them in check.
>
> At this point the order came to deploy column into line of battle, which was promptly executed. We then advanced a short distance into the woods, where the enemy were formed under cover of a fence. The action commenced. After exchanging a few shots the engagement became general, which continued for an hour and a half of severe fighting, with great slaughter to the enemy, when the enemy gave way in confusion and disorder before the furious onset of our troops. We pursued them rapidly, capturing many prisoners, and strewing the ground with their dead and wounded. After pressing them closely for a distance of one-half mile, we were obliged to slacken our fire, as our ammunition had given out, when, receiving a supply, we changed our line by the right flank, and marched to an elevation, where we awaited the advance of the enemy, who was advancing in column of regiments. We then received orders to fall back under cover of the hill, and awaited the advance of the enemy; when within a short range our troops were quickly thrown forward to the top of the hill, where we poured into their advancing columns volley after volley. So terrific was the fire of our men that the enemy fell like grass before the mower; so deadly was the fire that the enemy retired in great disorder, they not being able to rally their retreating forces....We gained the woods, and held our position for two hours. We were then ordered to retire, and be relieved by other troops, under the command of General [William F.] Smith.[96]

---

[96] *ORA*, vol. 19, pt. 1, 506.

Lieutenant Colonel Hector Tyndale commanded the First Brigade, Second Division. He was born in Philadelphia, and was an importer of china and glassware. He returned from Europe when he heard the news of Fort Sumter, and offered his services to the Union. He was commissioned major of the 28th Pennsylvania in June 1861, and in August was put in command of Sandy Hook, opposite Harper's Ferry. He was promoted to lieutenant colonel in April 1862, and served in General Nathaniel P. Banks's corps in the Shenandoah Valley, under General John Pope at Chantilly, and the Second Battle of Bull Run. Early in the day, he received a wound in the hip, but he kept the field until the afternoon, when he was struck in the head by a musket ball and carried off the field, thought mortally wounded. For "conspicuous gallantry, self-possession, and good judgment at Antietam" he was promoted to brigadier general of volunteers, 29 November 1862. In March 1865, he was brevetted major general of volunteers for gallant and meritorious services during the war. Image from his book: Hector Tyndale, *A Memoir of Hector Tyndale* (Philadelphia, PA, MOLLUS, 1882), frontispiece.

Lieutenant Colonel James Crandall Lane, commanded the Second Brigade, Second Division. Lane had been an architect and civil engineer. He worked on construction of the Illinois Central Railroad, the U.S. Coast Survey, and on mining surveys of Cuba and Puerto Rico. On the organization of the 102nd New York Volunteers in March 1862, Lane was appointed major. He was promoted to lieutenant colonel just before the Antietam Campaign. He was promoted to colonel 14 December 1862. He was wounded 2 July 1863 on Culp's Hill at Gettysburg. He resigned from the service on 12 July 1864 due to illness. AOTW; image courtesy Tom Shay, Frederick Hill Meserve's Historical portraits, ca.1850-1915, vol. 17, 41.

Lieutenant Colonel James C. Lane, commanded the Second Brigade, Second Division, reported in place of Colonel Stainrook:

I have the honor to report that the Second Brigade of this division entered the field of battle on September 17, 1862, under command of Col. H. J. Stainrook, at about 6.30 am, the regiments marching in column of divisions. The brigade consisted of the One hundred and second New York Regiment, One hundred and eleventh Pennsylvania Regiment, and Third Maryland Regiment, the One hundred and ninth Pennsylvania Regiment being on detached service. Line of battle was formed in face of the enemy, and under fire, when the order was given to charge, and the enemy was driven back over half a mile, and batteries placed in position in front of the line gained. Soon after, the right and center of brigade rose from behind the battery and again drove the enemy some 500 yards through another piece of woods, with great slaughter, the regiment on the left being ordered by General Sumner to remain behind the battery as a support.

At about 12 m. the brigade fell back, from lack of support and want of ammunition, and at about 1 p. m. was drawn up in line about half a mile to rear of line of battle and allowed to rest.[97]

Colonel Henry J. Stainrook commanded the Second Brigade, Second Division. He had served in the Mexican-American War, and enlisted on 23 April 1861 in the Union Army as the captain of Company C of the 22nd Pennsylvania Infantry, a three-month regiment. He was honorably mustered out following the expiration of his term of enlistment. Stainrook was involved in organizing the 109th Pennsylvania Infantry and was commissioned its colonel in November 1861. The 109th Pennsylvania served in the brigade of Brigadier General Henry Prince in the Second Division, II Corps at the Battle of Cedar Mountain on 9 August 1862. In their first battle, the 109th advanced under Confederate fire and Colonel Stainrook was wounded in the abdomen by Confederate artillery, but he refused to leave the field. At the Battle of Chancellorsville 3 May 1863, Stainrook was killed. Courtesy USAMHI.

---

[97] *ORA*, vol. 19, pt. 1, 510.

Greene's Division retreats from woods west of Dunker Church. The XII Corps' fighting is done for the day except near the Dunker Church. Carman-Cope map, courtesy LOC.

Colonel William Bingham Goodrich, commander of the Third Brigade, Second Division, was killed at Antietam. Goodrich was born in New York and entered Wesleyan Seminary in 1835 and became a teacher. He moved to Wisconsin where he started a mercantile business. With the outbreak of the Mexican-American War, Goodrich traveled to St. Louis, enlisted, and was mustered into service as an adjutant for the Missouri battalion of infantry. Following the end of the war, Goodrich settled briefly in California but returned to New York to study law. He became involved in the state militia system and was mustered into service as the lieutenant colonel of the 60th New York when the war began. In May 1862, Goodrich was promoted to colonel. Then he was elevated to command of the Third Brigade, Second Division, XII Corps, on 16 September 1862. On the morning of 17 September, Goodrich's men were sent toward the Hagerstown Pike to reinforce Brigadier General Abner Doubleday's I Corps division. Goodrich went into action near the Miller Farm and the northern edge of the West Woods. On horseback, Goodrich led his men into the West Woods, but a bullet entered his chest and traveled down into his stomach, severing an artery along the way. He was helped up and exclaimed: "My God! I am hit!" and then fell unconscious. When Goodrich was hit, Lieutenant Colonel Jonathan Austin of the 78th New York assumed command of the Third Brigade. Biographical sketch written by John David Hoptak from AOTW. Photograph courtesy the William B. Goodrich Papers, MSS 56, Special Collections, St. Lawrence University Libraries, Canton, NY.

Lieutenant Colonel Charles R. Brundage, commanding the 60th New York, took over command of the Third Brigade, Second Division, after Colonel Goodrich was killed. He was born in Vermont in 1822 and moved to Clifton, New York, at the age of 21. He served in public offices for many years. He had been colonel of the 33rd New York State Militia when he was authorized in July 1861 to raise a regiment for Federal service which became the 60th New York. He was commissioned its major 2 November 1861, and was promoted to Lieutenant Colonel 13 May 1862. He was honorably discharged due to illness 6 November 1862. Biography courtesy AOTW, photograph courtesy LOC.

Lieutenant Colonel Charles R. Brundage reported the activities of the Third Brigade of the Second Division as its colonel commanding, William B. Goodrich, was killed in action that morning, and Lieutenant Colonel Austin was not available:

I have the honor to report that, on the morning of September 17, 1862, the late Col. William B. Goodrich, of the Sixtieth Regiment New York Volunteers, being in command of this brigade, was ordered to take the brigade, then composed of the Sixtieth and Seventy-eighth Regiments New York Volunteers, Third Delaware, and Purnell Legion; into the field on the right of the line of battle. Before getting into position, the Purnell Legion was ordered to some other portion of the field, which reduced the line of this brigade to the three first-named regiments. On getting into position, skirmishers were thrown out on the right and left, who cleared the woods of the enemy's sharpshooters. While thus engaged, and about an hour after the commencement, the colonel commanding was mortally wounded and borne from the field. The command then devolved upon Lieutenant-Colonel Austin, of the Seventy-eighth New York, who remained in command during the remainder of the day. In about an hour and a half from this time orders were received to withdraw the brigade from the field. This was done and the line shortly after reformed about half a mile to the rear of its former position.[98]

---

[98] *ORA*, vol.19, pt. 1, 513-514.

Modern photograph of Samuel Poffenberger Farm east of where Mansfield was wounded. View looking northwest from Mansfield Road, which did not exist at the time of the battle. Photograph by author, August 2013.

General Williams continued his narrative of that morning's fight:

At nearly 9 o'clock a. m., it being reported that a portion of the Second Corps (Major-General Sumner's) was advancing to our support, I dispatched a staff officer to apprise him of our position and the situation of affairs. Soon after, the firing on both sides wholly ceased. Some of the old regiments had emptied their boxes of ammunition, and all were greatly exhausted by the labors of the day and of the preceding night. As the line of General Sedgwick's division appeared, the regiments of the First Division of this corps were withdrawn to the first line of woods in the rear, within supporting distance of several batteries, and directed to replenish their cartridge-boxes and to rest the men. A portion of the One hundred and twenty-fourth Pennsylvania Volunteers continued, however, to hold the woods near Millers house until it was ordered, without my knowledge, to withdraw, by some officer unknown to the commanding officer of the regiment. Greene's command had also the possession of the woods at the other end near the church....I was ordered, through a staff officer, to send to the front all of my command immediately available. As General Gordon held his brigade in line most convenient for a movement to the point indicated, he was ordered to advance at once.... The troops which the support was intended for had; however, withdrawn, or changed position toward the right. The regiments of Gordon's brigade brought into action this second time, I regret to add, suffered severely, and were obliged to retire after a stubborn contest. The enemy did not follow, and Gordon's regiments again took position, in good order, behind our batteries.

The enemy, gathering his strongest columns in the woods, made several efforts to dislodge General Greene's command in the left extremity of the woods, as well as to seize upon our batteries in front. All were unsuccessful until about 1:30 p.m., when, by a desperate effort, they forced our wearied forces to retire from the woods, making, at the same time, a rapid dash for our batteries. They met with terrible slaughter by canister at point-blank range, as well as by musketry from the supports, fell back in confusion, and gave up all further efforts to advance beyond their stronghold. Soon after this, General William F. Smith arrived with his division, and, moving through our lines to the front, gave me an opportunity to withdraw those of this corps which had been most engaged a few rods to the rear, where they could find refreshment and rest. Several of the new regiments were left in support of batteries....

General Greene's division and Gordon's brigade were subsequently sent to the front in support of a portion of General Franklin's corps, and remained in that position through the night. Of the batteries of this corps, two (Fourth and Sixth Maine) were posted by Captain Best, U.S. Army, chief of artillery, under orders of General Mansfield, on hills adjacent to general headquarters [Pry House]. Knap's Pennsylvania, Cothran's New York, and Hampton's Pittsburg batteries were ordered to the front as soon as the command of the corps devolved on me. Knap and Cothran took post in front of the woods occupied by the enemy, Hampton farther to the left, near General Greene's position. These batteries were bravely and excellently served from morning till late in the afternoon. The enemy repeatedly attempted to seize them, but always met with bloody punishment. One section of Knap's, temporarily detached for the aid of General Greene, unfortunately was ordered into the woods, where it fell under a heavy infantry fire, by which men and horses were lost and one piece necessarily abandoned. This battery subsequently brought from the field a 12-pounder howitzer of the enemy.[99]

General Mansfield saw nothing of the heroic fight of the XII Corps after he was wounded around 7:45 a.m. but would have been proud of his Corps' efforts.

---

[99] *ORA*, vol. 19, pt. 1, 475-477.

Federal attack near the Dunker Church which may portray the attack by Tyndale's brigade in Greene's division about 10 a.m. But in the 125th Pennsylvania Regimental history, it is claimed that this depicts the 125th Pennsylvania, 70. This lithograph by L. Prang from a painting by Thure de Thulstrup has been compared to an engraving from a sketch portraying a similar scene with the charge of Colonel William H. Irwin's brigade in Major General William F. Smith's division. Franklin's VI Corps. in *Battles and Leaders of the Civil War*, vol. 2, 646. Courtesy LOC.

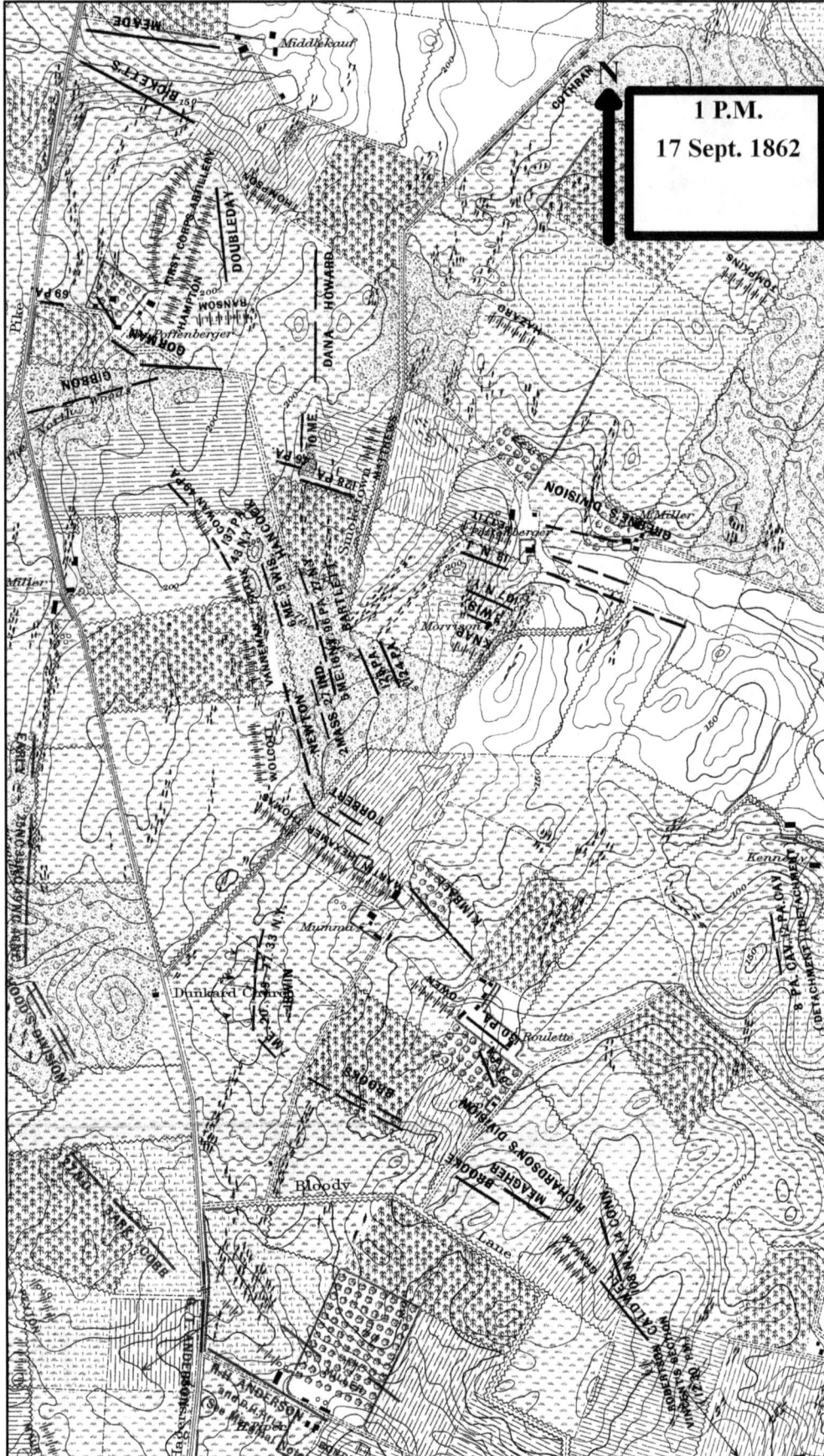

At the Dunker Church, Greene held on about four hours of desperate fighting. Two divisions of Sumner's corps came up on his left and drove the Confederates across the turnpike but was attacked in the flank and forced back. Greene was reinforced by two regiments from Gordon's brigade, the 13th New Jersey and the 2nd Massachusetts along with the Purnell Legion, which had been helping Gibbon. But Jackson brought up fresh troops, and this overwhelming force was concentrated on Greene at the church. With ammunition running low, Greene, at 1:30, was forced to retreat across the turnpike to the East Woods. The heaviest fighting is now over on the northern portion of the battlefield as Williams's Division retreats to reform near the Samuel Poffenberger and Michael Miller Farms. Carman-Cope map, courtesy LOC.

The XII Corps slept on its arms the night of 17 September expecting a renewed battle in the morning while Mansfield fought for his life. He would soon join the 275 who died in his XII Corps; total casualties for the corps were 1,746 out of about 9,500 engaged, a loss of over 18%. Carman-Cope map, courtesy LOC.

Even before McClellan learned that most of the three corps he sent to his right flank were decimated, he ordered Major General Burnside to immediately open his attack on his left flank. Burnside's ineptly managed attacks took three hours to cross the Lower Bridge over the Antietam but by early afternoon, he had a foothold on the opposite bank. Burnside then paused to resupply and rest his troops, which turned out to be a critical tactical mistake. The end finally came to the day's fighting when Burnside's restarted attack on the Union left which was driving the Confederates into the outskirts of Sharpsburg, ran head on into Major General Ambrose Powell Hill's men who had just arrived after a forced march from Harper's Ferry. Burnside's men were quickly pushed back to the vicinity of the Lower Bridge finally drawing the curtain on a day of horror: "For both sides, Sharpsburg was a compact field of concentrated fury. In twelve hours, 82,000 men fought over less than 1,000 acres. Nearly 23,000 (27.1 percent) fell casualty" by sunset, a day none of the participants would ever forget.[100]

Neither opponent desired to resume the battle the next day although Lee expected McClellan to attack as did most of McClellan's troops; the Union commander did make plans to attack on the 18th but suspended them after realizing that the "fresh" troops he was gathering would not be sufficient in quality or quantity to drive Lee into the Potomac. Too, his army was short of ammunition; then McClellan fell ill with severe dysentery.[101] Lee, on the other hand, was not ready to give up his Maryland adventure. On the morning of the 18th, Lee conferred with Stonewall Jackson and Jeb Stuart to examine the possibility of attacking the Union right flank and slipping his army to Hagerstown. After learning of the strength of the Federal units there, even Lee now realized that he must return to Virginia. Again, not wishing to completely give up on his fall campaign, he wanted to try to return to Maryland crossing the Potomac at Williamsport, about ten miles to the northwest, by way of Martinsburg, a total trip of about twenty-five miles. Lee sent Stuart's cavalry and along with infantry and artillery to chase away Federal troops holding the crossing for the remainder of Lee's army.

But Lee soon learned that his army had less fight left in it than he believed: a small Federal attack over the Potomac at Shepherdstown on 20 September showed him that he had run the wheels off his army after he had difficulty finding units to push the Federals back over the river. This, combined with the news that Stuart had been pushed out of Williamsport, was the final straw Lee needed to end his Maryland Campaign.[102]

Mansfield was one of six generals killed or mortally wounded at Antietam, three Federal: Mansfield, Brigadier General Isaac Peace Rodman, Brigadier (posthumous Major) General Israel Bush Richardson; and three Confederate: Brigadier Generals George Burgwyn Anderson, Lawrence O'Bryan Branch, and William Edwin Starke. All of the Federal generals were mortally wounded, Mansfield dying on 18 September, Rodman on 30 September, and Richardson on 3 November; only Confederate general Anderson was mortally wounded dying on 16 October 1862, as both Branch and Starke died on the field on 17 September. Two other generals were killed at the Battle of South Mountain on 15 September at Fox's Gap: Union Brigadier (posthumous Major) General Jesse Lee Reno and Confederate Brigadier General Samuel Garland, Jr.

---

[100] Harsh, *Flood*, 423.

[101] Harsh, *Flood*, 437–440, 453. Harsh finds less fault with McClellan's decision not to attack than most other historians after reviewing what McClellan likely knew about his army's status and what he reasonably could have known about Lee's.

[102] Harsh, *Flood*, 466–467. For a complete account of the abortive Union attempt at Boteler's Ford south of Shepherdstown, see Thomas A. McGrath, *Shepherdstown: Last Clash of the Antietam Campaign September 19-20, 1862* (Lynchburg, VA: Schroeder Publications, 2007).

Circumstances of Mansfield's Mortal Wounding and Death

The question of the exact location on the battlefield where General Mansfield 1862 was wounded was a matter of controversy for years after the battle and is not wholly settled today. Many who said they observed the site of his wounding came forward to offer evidence but most of these accounts were relatively easily dismissed since they reported his wounding at locations or times where Mansfield could not have been. Carman detailed the salient claims:

> At least seven places have been indicated on the field where it occurred. Colonel William F. Rogers of the 21st New York states that he saw him killed beyond the D.R. Miller barn in the West Woods. As Mansfield never crossed the Hagerstown Road, Rogers is in error, probably mistaking Colonel William B. Goodrich for Mansfield. Another statement is that he was shot in the D.R. Miller orchard, but he was not on that part of the field after he had led his corps forward. Two places have been indicated that, at the time, were 250 yards inside the Confederate lines. Brigadier General George H. Gordon reports that Mansfield was wounded "while making a bold reconnaissance of the woods through which we had just dashed." If Gordon refers to the North Woods, through which his own brigade advanced, he is in error; if he refers to the East Woods, through which a part of Crawford's brigade deployed, he is nearer the fact. Colonel Jacob Higgins of the 125th Pennsylvania, whose regiment was in line fronting the East Woods and north of the Smoketown Road, reports that some of his men carried the general "off the field on their muskets until a blanket was procured," and these men say that where they saw him wounded was at a point in front of and to the left of the 128th Pennsylvania in the edge of the East Woods and about 120 yards west of the Smoketown Road. John M. Gould, adjutant of the 10th Maine, says Mansfield was wounded about 35 yards east of the Smoketown Road.[103]

John Mead Gould, adjutant of the 10th Maine, first recorded in his diary the circumstances of Mansfield's wounding and later spent much time and effort to ensure that his recollection prevailed over all the others. His diary entry for 17 September 1862, his 1871 history of the 1st, 10th, and 29th [same regiment, different designations],[104] and an 1895 pamphlet he published, recount more or less the same story. This account is from his 17 September diary entry:

> We deployed and at length reached a rail fence over which a few men jumped and some got behind and fired through. Gen'ls. Mansfield and Crawford were on the right, over the fence and in rear of one of the new reg'ts. and saw us firing at what he took to be Union forces and rode down in front of us and yelled "cease firing." With great difficulty he succeeded in making himself heard....I noticed Gen'l. Mansfield and couldn't keep my eyes off him. He rode in front of us and beckoned us not to fire. He at length came clear to the left [of my regiment], within 20 yards of the rebels and as his horse was hurt in the leg he dismounted and helped him over the fence. He passed through our line and with his orderly went down along the ledge where I was. A gust of wind blew his coat skirt aside and showed to me that he was wounded as well as his horse. ran to him at once and told him his horse was shot, he was trying to mount him. I beckoned for a man to help me carry the Gen'l. away. No one seemed to notice us and I waited some time till Joe Merrill of [Co.] F came up and dropping his gun we took the Gen'l. along. Two others were shortly after pressed into the service and a nigger. I got a gun and put it under his shoulder and at length having got quite a crowd I let go my hold and ran for a doctor.

---

[103] Carman, Pierro, 467; Gould quote: John M. Gould, *History of the First-Tenth-Twenty-ninth Maine Regiment, in Service of the United States from May 3, 1861, to June 21, 1866* (Portland: Stephen Berry, 1871), 240–41. Gould discussed the mistaken location identifications in his pamphlet, *A Narrative of Events*, 3-5. According to the leading Carman historian, Dr. Thomas Clemens, Carman accepted Gould's analysis, Carman, Clemens, vol. 2, 167, n. 95. Not all modern historians, however, are convinced of Gould's recollections. John Michael Priest, *Antietam: The Soldiers' Battle* (Shippensburg, PA: White Mane Publishing Company, Inc., 1989), opined that "In all likelihood, the historian of the 125th [Pennsylvania] is more accurate. It seems highly unlikely that a regiment under fire, such as the 10th Maine, would have allowed three file closers to leave the ranks to care for anyone. Gould also wrote two very contradictory accounts of Mansfield's wounding and death, whereas the historian of the 125th Pennsylvania was more succinct and less melodramatic," 357 n.32. The majority of historians however find Gould's narratives sufficiently convincing; the author agrees since Carman supported Gould's version. Bruce Catton, *The Army of the Potomac: Mr. Lincoln's Army* (Garden City, NY: Doubleday & Company, Inc., 1951), wrote that the 125th Pennsylvania men picked Mansfield up and carried him back into the wood, where men from the 10th Maine took over, 278-279. His account is taken from Carman who gives both the 125th and Gould's account, Carman, Clemens, vol. 2, 167. Clemens writes that Gould's persistence eventually won out, 167, n.95. It is probable that Carman accepted Gould's research.

[104] "The 1st [Maine Volunteer Infantry] Regiment, after serving three months in 1861, re-organized as the 10th to serve till May 1863, when it was again recruited and re-organized as the 29th to serve three years more. The 10th Battalion was that portion of the 10th Regiment which was not discharged in 1863," Gould, *A Narrative of Events*, 6.

I came across Gen'l. Gordon and asked him to send off an orderly for help but he was short of orderlies and paid no attention to me. About ¾ mile we came to a surgeon and ambulance and finding everything was likely to go right now I left the Gen'l. and turned back.[105]

Gould mentioned an orderly with Mansfield when he was shot, but there was not one with Mansfield at this time according to all other reports, including Gould's later regimental history and pamphlet. In his regimental history, he clarified his regiment's position at the fence: "Our general position was the fence, and [Co.] F with a part of C was behind it. Co. F was further sheltered by the ledge. The right companies, with the instinct which prompts a man to face the fire rather than to take it in his side, jumped over the fence and then broke their lines by rushing behind the logs and trees."[106] In his hand-drawn map, Gould shows that the eight companies of his regiment were aligned along the fence but in front of it toward the enemy while the Carman-Cope maps show it behind the fence. Both Gould's and the Carman-Cope maps do show the left-most companies, part of C and all of F behind the fence.

Gould recounted a similar history in his 1895 pamphlet with some elaboration:

The 10th Maine was guided by General Mansfield in person. We had all seen him for some time previous sitting on his horse at the northwest corner of the East Wood, marked W on the map. He hurried us [Crawford's brigade, 46th Penn., Col. Knipe; 10th Maine, Col. Beal; 28th N.Y., fragment, Capt. Mapes; 124th Penn., Col. Hawley; 125th Penn., Col. Higgins; 128th Penn., Col. Samuel Croasdale (killed.)], first to the front, downhill through a field where several piles of stone lay, the Smoketown road still being on our left. We barely entered the "ten acre cornfield" when Mansfield beckoned us to move to our left. We then marched a few steps by what the tactics call "Left oblique," but did not gain ground to the left sufficiently to suit the General, so Col. Beal commanded "Left flank," whereupon each man faced east, and we presently knocked over the two fences of the Smoketown road and marched into Sam Poffenberger's field. While going across the Smoketown road General Hooker rode from the woods (M) and told Col. Beal "The enemy are breaking through my lines; you must hold these woods," (meaning East Woods.)

After crossing the road, bullets from the enemy began to whiz over and around us. When well into Sam Poffenberger's field the Colonel commanded "Right flank," then each man again faced south (or west of south to be more exact) and we all marched straight for the enemy, whom some of us could see in the woods, close to where our Mansfield marker is now standing, marked M on the map....

Apparently fifty to a hundred Confederates were strung along the fence (M) firing at us. They had the immense advantage that they could rest their rifles on the fence and fire into us, massed ten ranks deep, while we could only march and "take it."

It was high time to deploy, and Col. Beal proposed to do so, but General Mansfield said "No," and remarked that a regiment can be easier handled "in mass" than "in line"; which is very true in the abstract. General Mansfield then rode away, and Col. Beal, hardly waiting for him to get out of sight, ordered the regiment to deploy in double quick time. Everybody felt the need of haste.

In the execution of this order Companies I and G, with the color guard, continued marching straight ahead at the ordinary step, just as if no order had been given. The men of Co.'s F, C, D and B turned to their left and ran east—toward Sam Poffenberger's. Co.'s H, A, K and E turned to the right and ran west —toward the Smoketown road. As fast as the respective companies "uncovered," they came to "Front" and advanced to the front, still running. In other words, after Co. B had run east and Co. E west, the length of their company, each man turned to the front (or the woods) and the company ran till B was left of G, and E was right of I, which being done B and E quit running and took up the ordinary step....

I have been so circumstantial in describing all this for two reasons. First, because standing today on the battle line of the 10th Maine (which is the position the enemy occupied at the time the 10th was deploying), and looking over the fence northeast into Sam Poffenberger's field, as the Confederates did, one will see how it was that when the 10th Me., with about 300 men, came to deploy and to advance afterward, the Smoketown fence, and the trees of [George L.] Beal and [Almon S.] Goss, with "the bushes," were an obstacle to the right companies, and the ledge would have been somewhat so to the left companies if Capt. Jordan had not halted his division [regimental "division" = two companies] behind it. He did this for shelter as the first reason, and because, perceiving there was no Union force on our left, he knew it was better to have our left "refused" and hence not so easily "flanked" by the enemy....

The enemy fell back as we approached. On arriving at the fence, we opened fire, and then rushed into the woods for such cover as the trees, &c, offered. The enemy also was well scattered through the woods, behind numerous ledges, logs, trees and piles of cord wood, a few men only being east of the Smoketown road, which at that time was not fenced.

---

[105] John Mead Gould, *The Civil War Journals of John Mead Gould 1861-1866*, ed. William B. Jordan, Jr., (Baltimore: Butternut & Blue, 1997), 194-195.

[106] Gould, *History of the First – Tenth - Twenty-ninth Maine Regiment*, 237.

The fire of the enemy was exceedingly well aimed; and as the distance between us was only about one hundred yards we had a bloody time of it.

We had fired only a few rounds, before some of us noticed Gens. Mansfield and Crawford, and other mounted officers, over on the Croasdale Knoll, which, with the intervening ground, was open woods. Mansfield at once came galloping down the hill and passed through the scattered men of the right companies, shouting "Cease firing, you are firing into our own men!" He rode very rapidly and fearlessly till he reached the place where our line bent to the rear (behind the fence). Captain Jordan now ran forward as far as the fence, along the top of the ledge behind which his division was sheltered, and insisted that General Mansfield should "Look and see." He and Sergt. Burnham pointed out particular men of the enemy, who were not 50 yards away, that were then aiming their rifles at us and at him. Doubtless the General was wounded while talking with Jordan; at all events he was convinced, and remarked, "Yes, you are right." He then turned his horse and passed along to the lower land where the fence was down, and attempted to go through, but the horse, which also appeared to be wounded, refused to step into the traplike mass of rails and rubbish, or to jump over. The General thereupon promptly dismounted and led the horse into Sam Poffenberger's field. I had noticed the General when he was with Crawford on the Croasdale Knoll, and had followed him with my eye in all his ride. Col. Beal was having a great deal of trouble with his horse, which was wounded and appeared to be trying to throw the Colonel, and I was slow in starting from the Colonel to see what Mansfield's gestures meant. I met him at the gap in the fence. As he dismounted his coat blew open, and I saw that blood was streaming down the right side of his vest.

The General was very quick in all his motions and attempted to mount as soon as the horse had got through the fence; but his strength was evidently failing, and he yielded to the suggestion that we should take him to a surgeon. What became of the orderly and the horse none of us noticed. Sergt. Joe Merrill, of Co. F, helped carry the General off; a young black man, who had just come up the ravine from the direction of Sam Poffenberger's, was pressed into service. He was very unwilling to come with us, as he was hunting for Capt. Somebody's frying-pan, the loss of which disturbed him more than the National calamity. Joe Merrill was so incensed at the Contraband's sauciness, his indifference to the danger, and his slovenly way of handling the General, that he begged me to put down the General and "fix things." It turned out that Joe's intention was to "fix" the darkey, whom he cuffed and kicked most unmercifully. We then got a blanket and other men, and I started off ahead of the re-formed squad [Sergt. Joseph S. Merrill, Co. F; Private Storer S. Knight, Co. B; Private James Sheridan, Co. C] to find a Surgeon.

The road had appeared to be full of ambulances a half hour before, but all were gone now and we carried the General clear to Sam Poffenberger's woods. Here I saw General Geo. H. Gordon, commanding the 3rd brigade of our division, told him the story and asked him to send an orderly or aide for a surgeon, but he said he could not as he had neither with him. He was moving the 107th N. Y., a new, large regiment; an ambulance was found and two medical officers, just inside the woods, a few steps north of where Sam Poffenberger's gate now hangs, marked K on the map. The younger doctor put a flask to the General's mouth. The whiskey, or whatever it was, choked the General and added greatly to his distress. We put the General into the ambulance and that was the last I saw of him. Lieut. Edw. R. Witman, 46th Penn., an aide to General Crawford, had been sent back by General Crawford, who evidently saw Mansfield in his fatal ride. I turned over ambulance and all to him and returned to the regiment; but when I arrived I found that Tyndale's and Stainrook's brigades of Greene's division had swept the woods a little while after I had gone, carrying a dozen or two of the 10th with them, and that General Gordon had followed later with the 107th New York. Only twenty or thirty men of the 10th Maine were left on the ground; the colors and the others had gone out and taken position somewhere back of the Croasdale Knoll.

Doctor Francis B. Davison, of the 125th Penn., met the ambulance near Line's house and turned it in there, and there the General was treated and died....[107]

---

[107] Gould, *A Narrative of Events*, 9-17. Thomas McCamant of the 25th Pennsylvania wrote that "Col. Hawley of the 124th P.V. says it was the ambulance of his regiment in which Genl. Mansfield was conveyed to the hospital where he died," copy 27 June 1895 of letter to Gould courtesy Tom Clemens.

Sergeant Almon L. Goss of the 10th Maine, Co. K, courtesy Nicholas Picerno Collection.

Doctor Davison wrote a letter to Gould on 5 March 1894 describing in detail what he remembered seeing on 17 September 1862. Davison, assistant surgeon of the 125th Pennsylvania, was acting surgeon in charge for his regiment during September 1862 as he was the only doctor available—the surgeon-in-charge had not yet arrived and the other assistant surgeon was sick in hospital in Georgetown. On the 16th when Davison was southwest of Keedysville, he was ordered to go back toward Turner's Gap to Nicodemus's barn where his regiment had sick men and ambulances; he was to send them to Frederick. As it was dark by the time he finished, he stayed there and started out the next morning, the 17th, to find his regiment. As he was searching, he met the ambulance carrying Mansfield:

> This meeting was in the oblong square field northeast of George Lyon's [Line's] house as shown on your son's map—only the fences had been demolished. I should have passed the ambulance with little thought only that the driver appeared bewildered and expressed great agitation by his demeanor, so I was induced to inquire as to the cause of his trouble. He answered me that he had General Mansfield in the ambulance wounded and did not know where to drive him. (He was driving north and appeared to have driven a hundred yards east of George Line's house, and probably left the Smoketown road at the "East Woods" to drive down Sam. Poffenberger's lane as this would be the least dangerous way to drive.) I replied to the driver turn your ambulance about and follow me to this house, which proved to be George Line's, and I will see that he has proper care. About the first man I met at Mr. Line's house was James King, M.D., an eminent surgeon of Pittsburg Pa, (I think he was Division Surgeon) who was afterwards Surgeon General of the State of Pennsylvania. I told him of the approach of the wounded General Mansfield, and we had a bed and bedding brought from the chamber and laid on a bedstead then standing in a rear room, first story. The first sheet was being spread on the bed as the men brought the General through the door and laid him thereon. All this was done very rapidly and carefully, and the General was attended and his wounds dressed by Surgeon James King associated with Surgeon Cox whom I never saw except that day.
>
> General Mansfield was wounded by a minie ball entering about two inches below and a little to the right of the right nipple and passing straight through the chest from front to rear. It is supposed General M. was shot by a sharp shooter from D.R. Miller's barn—I think he died next day at 8 a.m.
>
> I was in Mr. Line's from 9 or 10 a.m. to 4 or 5 P.M. Sept. 17 helping Dr. King before going to my regiment, and was not in Line's house much, if any, afterwards till the day I saw you [Gould] 29 years later. Col. Higgins of the 125th Penn. located the ground where General M. received his wound as about the extreme Southeast corner of the Great cornfield as shown on your map or perhaps a little north of this point and near the woods.
>
> The above is a mixture of narrative history facts and guesswork, and I reckon you know many points where I am at sea, if so it may be valuable to you as amusement and you have a right to laugh at my theories and hearsay.[108]

---

[108] Photo copy of letter courtesy Thomas Clemens. Note that the doctors who attended Mansfield at least on the 17th were Davison, King, and Cox; compare these names with the doctors Antisell, Porter, and Weeks, shown in Dyer's letter below. As the surgeon of the XII Corps, Dr. Antisell very likely at least consulted with doctors attending Mansfield, but the identities of Porter and Weeks remain unknown. Since Davison left the Line Farm by 5 p.m. on the 17th, there was time for other surgeons to have attended the dying general.

Battlefield of
ANTIETAM.
~ North West section ~

- Scale -
Three inches to
one mile.

North

Harpers town Road

John Poffenberger
of the Tenth
Maine

Geo. Line
Mansf... 10 ft
Bivouack
morning of 17th

John Middlekauf.

Route.

Smoketown Road

Joseph Poffenberger

620

Sam. Poffen.
Woods

Michael Miller

Toll Ho.
NORTH WOODS

Joe Poff.

Sam!
Poffenberger

Jacob Hofsdman

W

C 10 acr.
Cornfield
Grassdale
Knoll

Stone
fence

Bushes
HOME
Log cabin

David R Miller
grass

B

A East Wood
D

Simon
Morrison

The great
cornfield

Confed.
Robbins

Sam. Poff.

Confeds.

reinforcing

Cemetery

W. Kennedy

West

Clover

Clover

Smoketown

E Smoketown

Cherry Lane
Stacks

S. Mumma
(burned)

Woods

Dunker
Church

Wm Roulette.

Clipp's
Log cabin

Sharpsburg Turnpike.

Bloody Lane

Henry Piper

Gould's map detailing his locations of places related to Mansfield's wounding. "The spot marked 'A' on the map is said to have been vouched for by a 'New York officer of Mansfield's staff.' 'B' is where the late David R. Miller understood the General was wounded by a sharpshooter stationed in Miller's barn, west of the pike. 'C' is where Capt. Gardiner and Lieut. Dunegan [Dunigan], of Co. K, 125th Penn. Vols., assured me that the General fell from his horse in front of their company. 'D' is where, in November, 1894, I found a marker, that had been placed there the October previous, by someone unknown to me. These are the four principal places which have been pointed out to visitors. Still another spot was shown to our party when the 1-10-29th Maine Regiment Association made its first visit to the field, Oct. 4, 1889; it is south of A, but I did not note exactly where. There has also been published in the National Tribune, which has an immense circulation among the soldiers, the statement of Col. John H. Keatley, now Commandant of the Soldier's Home, Marshalltown, Iowa, who locates the place near the Dunker Church [at "E"]." "K" under "M" in "Sam" is the gate near which Gould placed Mansfield in an ambulance. "M" is about where Mansfield was shot; "W" shows where Mansfield watched the battle, Gould, *A Narrative of Events* (Portland, ME: Stephen Berry, Printer, 1895), 3–4, 10, 29, 33.

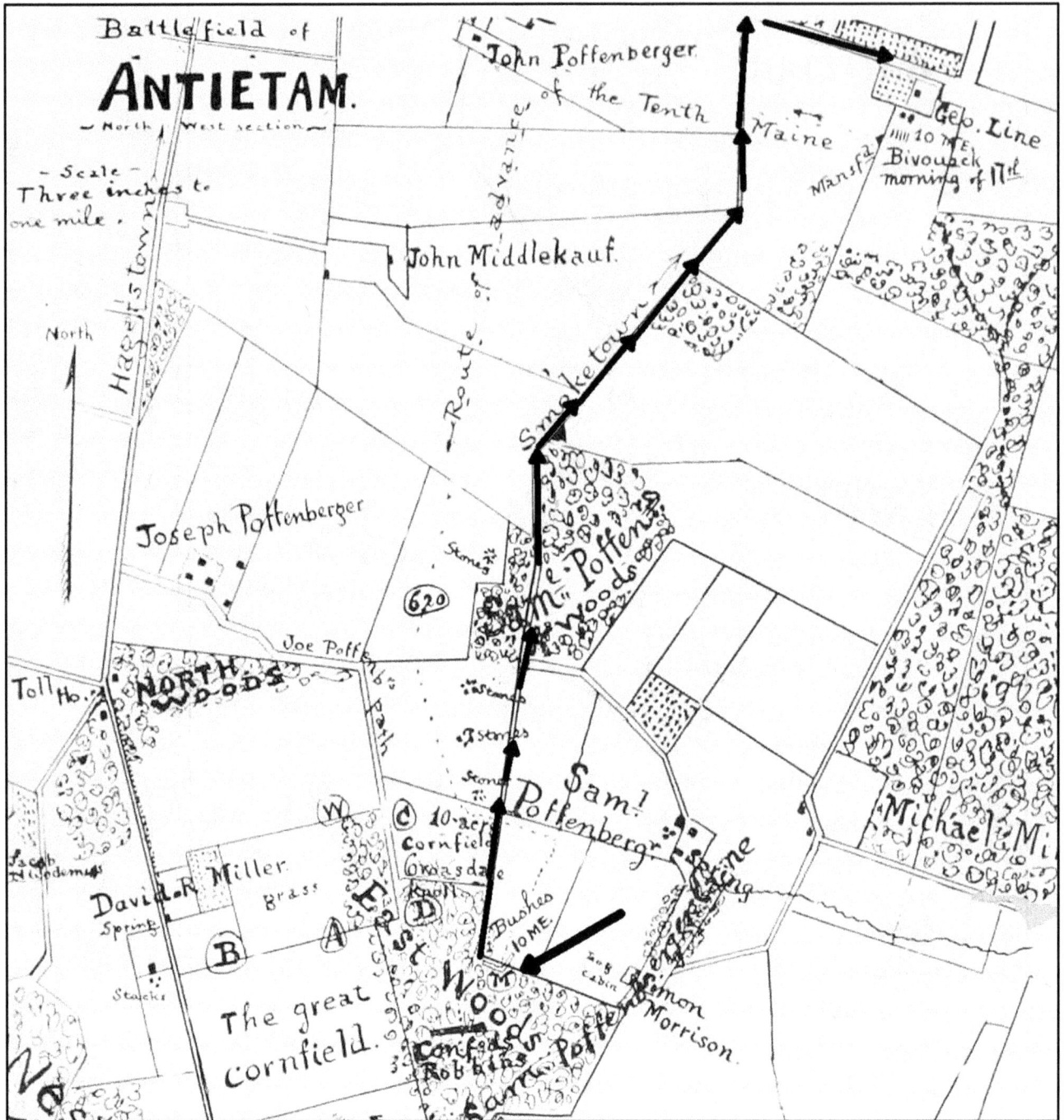

Detail of Gould map on preceding page showing where Mansfield was mortally wounded and the route over which he was carried to the Line Farm. The distance from the site of the wounding to the Line Farm is just under 1½ road miles. Note that Gould's map shows that the 10th Maine had refused its line near the fence where Mansfield was shot with most of the regiment in from of the fence.

Doctor Davison's report repeats the 125th Pennsylvania's effort to show that Mansfield was wounded near its regiment, an effort that Gould successfully refutes. Also, there is no evidence that Mansfield was shot by a sharpshooter but rather by troops from the 21st Georgia as Gould finally determined. The doctor's conjecture that the ambulance driver left the Smoketown Road at the East Woods and drove down Samuel Poffenberger's lane seems implausible based on the Carman-Cope and Gould maps. There is no apparent connection with any shown roads or lanes which could possibly have made such a connection. He may have heard the stories that Mansfield was loaded into an ambulance on the Smoketown Road at Samuel Poffenberger's gate which was on his farm lane which led to his house. But there is to the northeast of Line's house a very large cornfield with what appears to be a lane leading northwest from the house. The driver may have been on this lane after turning onto Line's farm road leading east-southeast from the Smoketown Road. But his statement about meeting the ambulance and escorting it to the Line Farm must be taken seriously as he was an eyewitness although writing almost 32 years after the event.

Lieutenant Edward R. Dunigan of Company K, 125th Pennsylvania, wrote in a newspaper article that attempted to refute Gould's assertions posted in *The National Tribune* article 3 November 1892:

> To the right and beyond S. Poffenberger's farm, there is, or was, a strip of the so called East Woods that extended partly across an old field to the right—mind you, not the left—of the Smoketown Road. It was right here during the deployment of General Williams's Division that our corps commander, General Mansfield, fell mortally wounded while examining the ground in front of the 125th Pa., and was carried to the rear a short distance by Serg't John Kohoe and Private Samuel Edminson [Edmonson], of Co. K of said regiment. After carrying him to the road they were relieved by men of the 10th Me. They carried him down the road a short distance and placed him in an ambulance, and he was then taken to the farmhouse of Mr. G. Lyon, where our gallant old General died that night.
>
> This all occurred on the right of the road, and the spot where Mansfield fell is at least 400 yards to the right of said road. The 10th Me. were on the left of the road all this time, but Comrade Gould still insists that it was in front of the 10th Me. That General Mansfield fell, and has this date a tablet marking the spot.
>
> Now there are dozens of other witnesses, as well as myself, who know that the General was on horseback, riding a medium-sized roan horse, when he was shot, and he reeled and partly fell from the saddle. The horse was caught by some men—I think they were of Co. A of our regiment; and all this occurred on the right [west] of the Smoketown Road, in front of the 125th Pa., and the 10th Me. Were all this time on the left of the road, at a distance of at least 500 yards to the left of where the General fell.[109]

Dunigan's arguments were addressed in a following article by a member of the 10th Maine, Pvt. A.H. Hutchinson, Co. D, apparently a sober man as he "had taken no commissary [liquor] that morning, and therefore could see straight":

> General Mansfield was right in front of Co. D of my regiment, and was mortally wounded just after entering the woods, and while on horseback. He was not over a rod from me when he wheeled his horse, which I think was also wounded, and tried to get him back over the wall; then he reeled in his saddle, and some men, I don't know who, helped him from his horse.
>
> General Mansfield was a very conspicuous figure, and could not be mistaken for anyone else. I am positive I was there. I am positive I saw him taken from his horse, and I am positive it was in front of the 10th Me....
>
> I was myself wounded soon after, and made my way to the rear, and to the same place where General Mansfield was taken. Our Orderly Serg't Braskett and privates Easty, Waddell, Carson, and Corp'l Baker, were also in the yard adjoining the house.[110]

Hutchinson's telling of the tale was quickly challenged by a member of the 125th Pennsylvania, Private R. Hobart, who tells a different story after first contending that Hutchinson's telling conflicts with Gould's:

> I was a private in Co. K, 125th Pa., and was in the fight that morning; saw General Mansfield ride down between our regiment and the woods, and when he was opposite our company, near the right of the regiment, he was struck and reeled and partly fell from his horse. Two of our men, Kohoe and Edmonson, ran to his assistance and carried him down to the road, where they were relieved by some men, some of whom were stragglers, who took the General and placed him in an ambulance. Kohoe and Edmonson came back to their company and saw no more of Mansfield....
>
> Where the General fell is a considerable distance to the right of the [Smoketown] road, and the 10th Me. Were on the left of the road....I say he [Mansfield] was in an open field between the woods and our troops when shot, and more than 20 rods in advance of our (the advance) line.[111]

Another report stated that Mansfield was involved in bringing up the 128th Pennsylvania among other regiments.[112] The 124th Pennsylvania veterans recalled the incident upon their return to the battlefield during the 17 September 1900 reunion of the regiment:

[109] Edward R. Dunigan, *The National Tribune*, "Battle of Antietam," 3 November 1892, 4. The Samuel Poffenberger Farmhouse was the location at which Clara Barton nursed wounded soldiers.

[110] A.H. Hutchinson, *The National Tribune*, "Gen. Mansfield's Death," 1 December 1892, 4.

[111] R. Hobart, *The National Tribune*, "Battle of Antietam," 16 February 1893, 4.

[112] Oliver C. Bosbyshell, *Pennsylvania at Antietam: Report of the Antietam Battlefield Memorial Commission of Pennsylvania* (Harrisburg, PA: Harrisburg Publishing Company, State Printer, 1906), 136-137.

The Dr. Joe Smith (now Bovey) farm extends down to the [Pry] Ford. The old buildings which were used as a hospital have been torn down. The brick house that stands near the Hooker Bridge, on the southwest side, is the old log house that formerly belonged to George Line and was purchased by Mr. Bovey, removed, rebuilt and brick-cased, and was the house in which General Mansfield died. Mr. George Line built a new house on the site of the old one. The road to the left (southwest) of the Hooker Bridge was, during war times, only a private farm road, but now is a county road. The road to the right is the old road running through Bakersville to Williamsport; a portion of the Army took this road before the battle to get on the right. All the buildings as you pass along were, for a short while, filled with wounded soldiers until they could be placed in the regular hospitals. The Hoffman farm buildings were quite well known among the soldiers, the Smoketown Hospital being on a part of the farm. In the edge of Smoketown Woods hundreds lay and died, and the old log school-house that stood about a quarter of a mile farther on, where a number had wounds dressed, has been torn away. We pass on through the remaining woods to the George Line farm, where the First Brigade (Crawford's) lay on the morning of the 17th, having moved there during the night. It consisted of the 10th Maine, 28th New York, 46th, 124th,125th and 128th Pennsylvania Regiments, extending from the Line house across the Smoketown road—the road south through the East Woods, to the Dunkard Church. Before entering East Woods we take Mansfield Avenue to the right of where Colonel Croasdale, of 128th Pennsylvania, was killed. It is now called Croasdale Knob [Knoll].

Just as you leave the Smoketown road, the 10th Maine crossed the road near this point, and in entering East Woods they met the enemy. General Mansfield received his mortal wound at this point, near where his monument stands, and was carried back to the old George Line house, where he died the same day, the 10th Maine being on the left of the advance of Crawford's Brigade and the 124th Pennsylvania on the right, extending across the Hagerstown pike by the Miller house, with the other named regiments between; the 125th Pennsylvania reaching the Dunkard Church Woods."[113]

The 124th Pennsylvania recollection about the Line Farmhouse is actually from a pamphlet written by Antietam guide O.T. Reilly to accompany their visit to Antietam, but he was not given credit in their history:

General Jos. K.F. Mansfield, who commanded the 12th corps, Union, came onto the Line farm about midnight of the 16th, and at daybreak on the morning of the 17th, before his men had time to get something to eat, a message was sent to come to the relief of General Hooker, then hotly engaged in and near the East Woods. Just as General Mansfield was entering the woods near where his monument stands he received his mortal wound, in the breast, by a minnie ball. He was carried back to the George Line house, where they had advanced from and died the same day. The house that General Mansfield died in isn't the house standing there now. Mr. Line sold the old house which was log, rough-casted, to Mr. Daniel R. Bovey, who removed it and rebuilt it for his dwelling on the hill near the Hooker Bridge and it is now cased with brick.[114]

---

113 Green, 124th Pennsylvania, 285-286.
114 Reilly information courtesy Stephen Recker, from the USAMHI.

Map shows the most likely sequence of events at 7:45 a.m. 17 September when Mansfield was wounded, accepting Gould's version. Mansfield along with Brigadier General Crawford and other officers were on Croasdale Koll observing the battle, at the lower left of the map. Mansfield rode down from the knoll shown by the black-headed arrows to the front of the 10th Maine yelling to stop firing. The white circle shows where he was wounded; the white-headed arrows show the route on which he was carried about ½ mile up the Smoketown Road to Poffenberger's Wood where he was placed in an ambulance at the white rectangle. He was next taken on the Smoketown Road to the Line Farm shown on the next map. Carman-Cope map courtesy LOC.

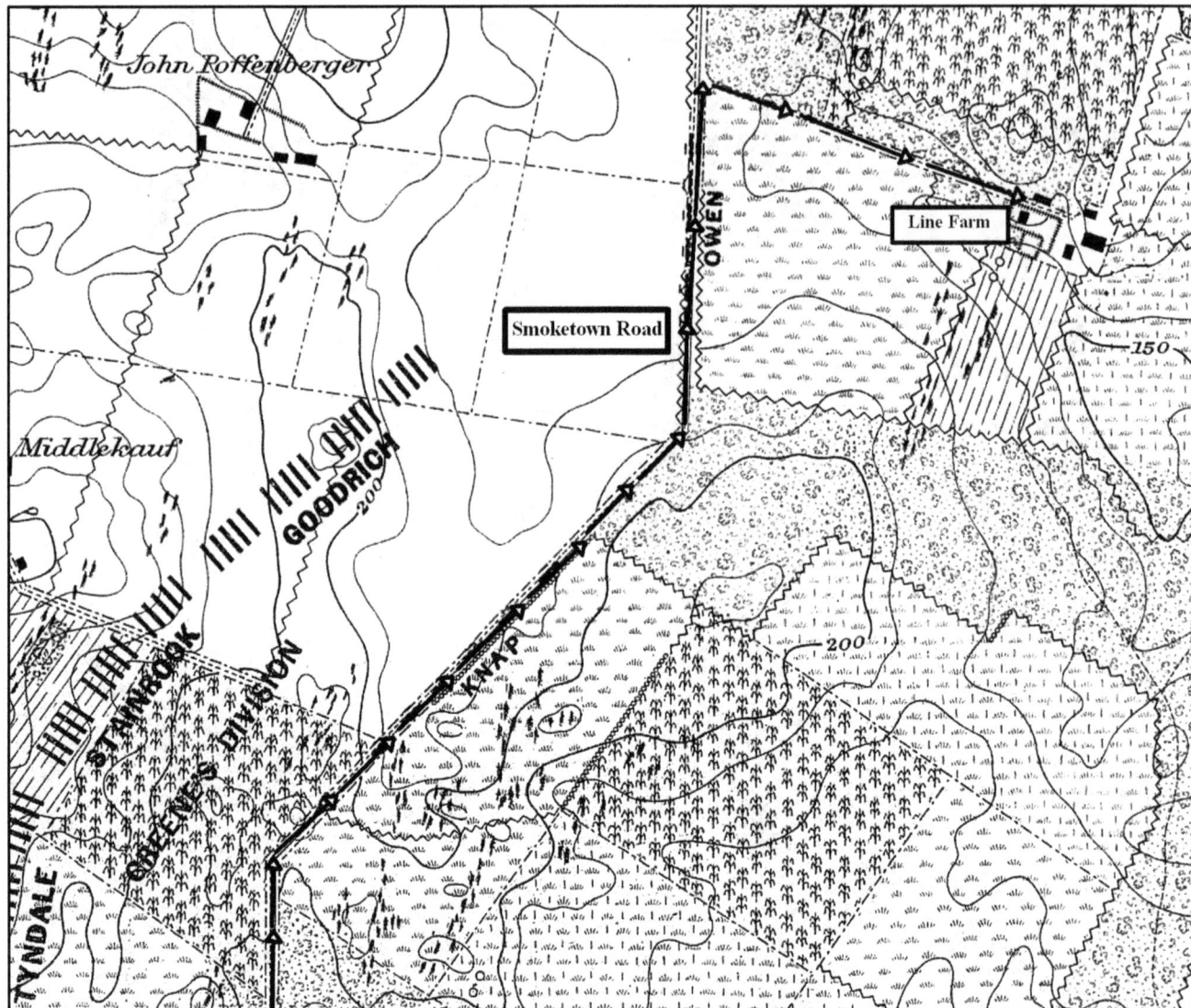

Map showing Mansfield's ambulance route from Poffenberger's Woods to the Line Farm house along the Smoketown Road, just under a mile. The farm lane leading to the Line Farm from Smoketown Road still exists. Carman-Cope map courtesy LOC.

Even the color of the horse Mansfield was riding when he was shot caused controversy. Gould maintained Mansfield rode a chestnut-colored steed while Private John Bresnahan of Company A of the 27th Indiana was certain it was white or "a very light grey." Captain Dyer wrote to Mansfield's widow in June 1863 and gave details about the horse which was killed and its equipment for which Mrs. Mansfield would be reimbursed. He wrote that "the horse was purchased from Lieutenant Colonel Charles G. Sawtelle, Asst. Qr. Ms., at, or near Perryville, Penn., in January or February 1862....The horse was a strawberry roan, between 15 and 16 hands high, six years old, dark mane and tail." Bresnahan also strongly protested Gould's recollection of the site of Mansfield's wounding writing that according to D.R. Miller, who lived in a farm east of the Hagerstown Pike, the general was wounded by a sharpshooter in Mr. Miller's barn. Gould never considered any other location as valid based on his personal knowledge. It is very unlikely that Mansfield ventured west of the Hagerstown Pike or close to it from the east.[115] Bresnahan wrote of Mansfield's early-morning actions when Mansfield rode toward Gordon's Brigade: "When the men saw the gallant old General, with his flowing white beard and hair, approaching them, they sprang to their stacked arms, expecting the order to

---

[115] Letters from John Bresnahan to Gould, 16 and 29 December 1892. Bresnahan wrote an article which appeared in the 21 February 1889 of the *National Tribune* describing Mansfield's mortal wounding. Private Hugh A. Jameson in a letter to Gould dated 5 February 1892 described "a colonel who was mounted on a big grey when he was shot," letter courtesy Thomas Clemens. This was about the time Mansfield was shot so maybe Bresnahan confused the colonel with Mansfield. Dyer did not remember the exact cost of the horse but believed it was about $105 to $115. Letter courtesy of the Middlesex County Historical Society.

advance; but the old General told the men to rest, and said, with a smile that inspired us: "'BOYS, WE WILL GIVE THEM HELL TODAY.' These words enthused every man with the old General's spirit. We felt for the first time that we had a corps commander capable of leading us to victory. About 6:30 o'clock Mansfield gave the order to advance."[116] He repeated this story in a letter dated 10 December 1892 to Pvt. A.H. Hutchinson of the 10th Maine: "[Mansfield] rode at a full gallop back to our brigade. When our men saw him coming they commenced taking their guns from the stacks for they expected the order to move forward. The General observed this and he said, as near as I can remember his words: 'Rest boys we will give them hell today.' I have a very vivid recollection of him as he sat on his grey horse in front of our regiment, with his hat in hand, long grey beard and hair."[117]

Another soldier, A.S. Fitch of the 107th New York, wrote about seeing Mansfield that morning: "At dawn of the 17th [we] were put in motion. We soon came in sight of the contending forces, and advanced in line of battle and awaited orders to 'go in.' General Mansfield and staff rode along the front of our regiment and as he passed our company (B) he smiled and said 'ah boys we shall do a fine thing today. We have got them where we want them; they cannot escape by the skin of their teeth.' A half hour later we saw him carried to the rear in a blanket." He also described what the 107th NY did earlier that morning: "Early on 17th, at 6 or 6:30, the 107 NY moved in a N.W. [S.W. is correct] direction from the Line house, through Sam Poffenberger's woods, turning slightly toward the west as it advanced, halting where it stood when Mansfield was carried to the rear, then advancing into the East Wood, the right companies crossing a corner of the cornfield, the left extending down the slope in the woods." He later describes his position which allowed him to see Mansfield being carried off which jibes with Gould's description; the 107th was to the south of Samuel Poffenberger's woods where they were "ordered to hold the woods at all hazards. While here, Mansfield went back wounded."[118]

To bolster his argument that Mansfield was wounded in front of the 10th Maine, Gould recounted the locations for Mansfield's uniform which were lost when he was shot: "When General Mansfield was swinging his hat at our left companies, his hat cord came off. It was picked up, and Major Jordan has it now in his possession here in Portland [Maine]. The General's hat fell off at the fence, and General George H. Nye, of South Natick, Mass., (then Captain of Co. K,) secured that. In 1864, after Major Knowlton, of our regiment (29th Me. then), was killed at the battle of Opequon (Winchester), a pair of fine gauntlets, with stains of blood on them, were found among his effects at home, marked 'General Mansfield's.'"[119]

Private Osborne, in his history of the 29th Massachusetts Infantry, was mistaken in his description of Mansfield on that morning likely in an effort to honor his old brigade commander from their time together in Newport News:

> Our line wavered a little; the fire was frightfully destructive. The field-officers perceiving this, ran through the ranks to the front. Instantly the line stiffened. And now for the fence. "Tear it down!" Immediately two thousand strong hands seize it, and it is flat upon the ground. "Forward!" Everything moves like clock-work. Without firing a shot, the Brigade moved in perfect line toward the sunken road, the enemy all the while firing deadly volleys. "Look at the perfect line of the Irish Brigade as it moves on the enemy!" said General McClellan to his generals, as he sat on his horse, near the creek. "Yes," says the brave old General Mansfield, who was present and watching the movement with intense interest, "I claim the credit of having drilled the Twenty-ninth Massachusetts Regiment of that Brigade."[120]

There is no likelihood that Mansfield watched The Irish Brigade assault the Sunken Road that morning as by that time, about 10 a.m., Mansfield had been shot and carried from the field.[121]

Mansfield's staff was small as he had no time to organize a larger one before he reported to McClellan in the less than two days before the Battle of Antietam. Gould commented on this lack of staff related to Mansfield's wounding:

---

[116] John Bresnahan, *National Tribune*, 21 February 1889, "Battle of Antietam."

[117] Bresnahan letter courtesy of Thomas Clemens.

[118] A.S. Fitch diary, courtesy Thomas Clemens.

[119] Gould, *National Tribune*, "Fighting Them Over," 17 November 1892, 4. Nicholas Picerno owns a letter from the Mansfield family thanking Captain Nye for returning the General's hat after he fell. The letter adds that they enclose a light cavalry sword of their manufacture as a token of their appreciation, see Chapter 11, Attachment 1. Mr. Picerno owns that inscribed Mansfield and Lamb sword. Mr. Picerno asserts that the possession of these items adds credible evidence that Mansfield was in fact wounded with the 10th Maine as Gould states.

[120] Osborne, 186.

[121] The 29th Massachusetts, although a part of The Irish Brigade, was not like the other regiments in the brigade as it had few Irish soldiers, Carman, Clemens, vol. 1, 264-272. Even if Mansfield were still on the field, the battlefield topography and battle smoke would not have allowed Mansfield to easily view the Sunken Road assault even from Croasdale Knoll.

A singular phase in this case is the fact that none of General Mansfield's subordinate commanders excepting General Crawford, and none of Mansfield's staff, witnessed the wounding. In the three days he was our commander, none of us saw a staff officer with him. It was only a vague memory of a lost and forgotten general order, and the reference to "Captain Dyer" in the General's memorial volume, that suggested the possibility there was a staff. In 1890 to '94 I made a special and persistent effort to learn who his staff were; also who was the orderly and who the colored servant that we saw with him. The orderly and servant we have not found. After much writing I learned that Samuel M. Mansfield, a son of the General, had been appointed an Aide but had not been able to join his father. Major Clarence H. Dyer, at that time Captain and A.A.G., had accompanied the General from Washington and was on duty with him till his death.

Furthermore, General James W. Forsyth, then a Captain, (familiarly known as "Toney") was temporarily assigned as aide-de-camp to Mansfield by General McClellan [on the 15th], at whose headquarters Forsyth was then serving. These two were "present"; but General Mansfield kept them flying so constantly that none of us recognized them as his staff.[122]

In an article published in the *The National Tribune* 25 August 1892, Gould wrote about the Confederate regiment against which he and the 10th Maine fought on 17 September. He called them the "best marksmen we ever met" as they fought on the extreme left of the Union position. He also explained in great detail his research not only for identifying that unit but also in reaffirming the location where he saw Mansfield shot. Gould wrote to many veterans including Confederate officers and men as well as attending the 125th Pennsylvania reunion at Antietam in 1891. After staying seven days "on the field" he did "not think there will be any more dispute where or how Mansfield fell." He and Major Jordan "easily found the rock where he stood when remonstrating with Mansfield about the character of the men in our front." Gould ended his article stating that although it was not the 20th Georgia the 10th Maine fought but rather "one company from each of the 6th, 23rd, 27th, and 28th Ga., and 13th Ala., with about an equal number from the 5th Tex. and 4th Ala., the very best, it proves now, of Lee's army."[123]

Gould, having convinced Carman and most other veterans that Mansfield was wounded in front of the 10th Maine, determined after corresponding with Confederate veterans that the 21st Georgia were the ones most likely to have shot Mansfield although he admitted that units of the 5th Texas and 4th Alabama were mixed in.[124]

[122] Gould, *A Narrative of Events*, 27. John Mead Gould, *The Civil War Journals of John Mead Gould 1861-1865*, ed. by William B. Jordan, Jr. (Baltimore, MD: Butternut & Blue, 1997), i-iii; "enfilading lines" blog by Randy Buchman, http://enfiladinglines.com; and a John M. Gould website: http://www.johnmeadgould.com.

[123] Gould, *The National Tribune*, 25 August 1892, 4, courtesy LOC.

[124] Gould, *A Narrative of His Wounding*, 22-23. He also admitted that initially he wrote that it was the 20th Georgia which did the deed: "The Confederate force opposed to the 10th Maine at Antietam appears to have been mainly the skirmish battalion of Colquitt's brigade of D.H. Hill's division, under Captain W.M. Arnold of the 6th Georgia, with scattered parts of the 4th Alabama (Law's brigade) and 5th Texas (Wofford's brigade), of Hood's division. Arnold's battalion was composed of the rifle company (generally Co. A) from the 6th Georgia, 23rd Georgia, 27th Georgia, 28th Georgia and 13th Alabama regiments. This conclusion has been reached after correspondence with one or more representatives from every regiment, Union and Confederate, that fought in or near East Wood," Gould, Regimental history, "Additions and Corrections," 4.

Modern-day George Line Farm is not the original but built in the late 1800's. It stands on the site of the original farm, however. See the description of the Line Farm in the 124ᵗʰ Pennsylvania Regiment's history of the 1900 reunion above. The original Line house was moved and "The brick house that stands near the Hooker Bridge, on the southwest side, is the old log house that formerly belonged to George Line and was purchased by Mr. Bovey, removed, rebuilt and brick-cased." Green, 124ᵗʰ Pennsylvania, 285. Historians Stephen Recker and John Banks concur about the new site. The old farmhouse was renovated in recent years removing the newer brick siding.

The regimental history of the 125ᵗʰ Pennsylvania contains its version of events surrounding Mansfield's wounding and is the only one of the many recollections other than Gould's which could be considered as likely:

General Mansfield rode forward, to reconnoiter, and very soon came back, and not far from the right front of the 125ᵗʰ Regiment, it was noticed that his body bent forward on the saddle of his horse and his head appeared to drop on his breast. Then Captain Gardner, of Company "K," near the right of the regiment (as we were at this time in reverse order), ordered Sergeant John Kehoe and Private Samuel Edmundson, of said company, to go to the assistance of the General, and as they did so, Lieutenant Ziegler says, Private E.S. Rudy, of Company "H," joined them, also two other men, not of the 125ᵗʰ Regiment. One of them took hold of the bridle reins of his horse, whilst two others removed him from the horse, and all then reversed their muskets, placed him on the same, carried him to a tree a few steps to the rear, where a surgeon appeared, and where he was delivered to a second party, believed to be of the 10th Maine Regiment, who carried him still further to the rear in a blanket....

The 10ᵗʰ Maine were no doubt battling near the point where General Mansfield was wounded, and we admit he was wounded near them, and we detract nothing from their record as a regiment or the good work they did on the 17ᵗʰ day of September, 1862, but we say again, that the General was wounded west of the Smoketown road and much further to the right front than the spot marked by Major Gould, and the men of the 125th Pennsylvania were the first to come to his assistance after he was wounded. The writer is positive that he spoke to two men of the 10th Maine on our halt west of the Smoketown road, and further to the front than the Gould marker, who said they were engaged at our right front close to the cornfield, and furthermore he was on the battlefield on May 29ᵗʰ, 1897, with General Knipe, who commanded the first brigade, first division, Twelfth Corps, and who said without hesitation, after looking at the spot marked by Major Gould, that it was much too far to the left rear. He pointed out the stone fence over which the 46ᵗʰ Pennsylvania climbed to cross the Smoketown road when they moved to the cornfield, also the mound where Colonel Croasdale was killed, and then remarked, "Out there, I think, in front of the mound, Mansfield was killed."[125]

---

[125] *History of the 125ᵗʰ Pennsylvania Volunteers*, 95-96.

Regardless of the identity of the regiment from which Mansfield's stretcher bearers were formed, his loss was felt by all the men of his corps. Historian Bruce Catton wrote a fitting summary for the old general's efforts that day: "He had had the corps only two days, but he had already made the soldiers like and respect him; it seems likely that he might have made quite a name if he had been spared."[126]

[126] Catton, *Mr. Lincoln's Army*, 279.

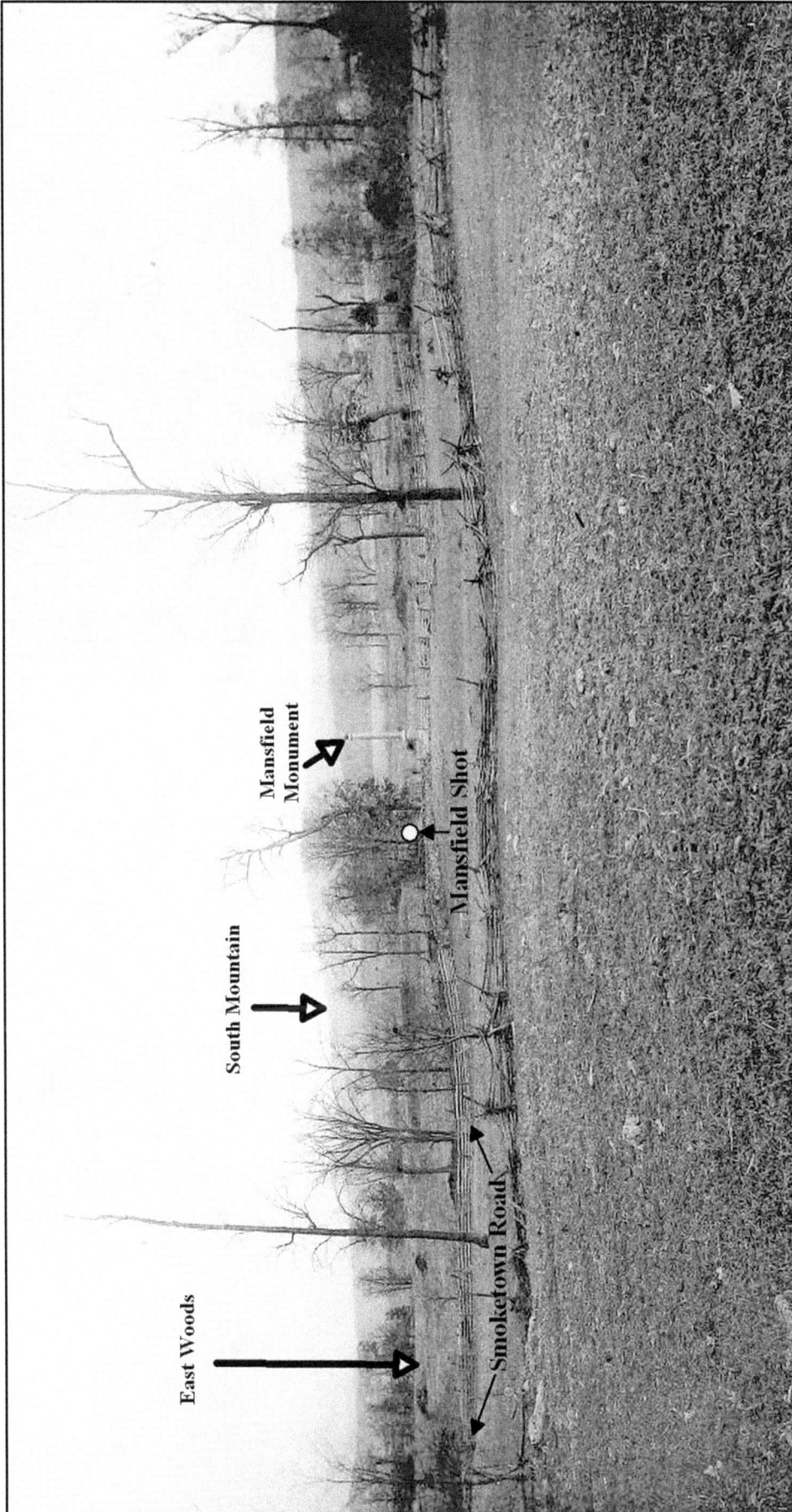

East Woods

South Mountain

Mansfield Monument

Mansfield Shot

Smoketown Road

View looking east showing monument to Mansfield marking place near where he was mortally wounded, at the intersection of Mansfield Road and the Smoketown Road. The 10th Maine and the 107th New York of Williams's Division charged across the field on which the monument stands and drove the Confederates out of the East Woods, which at that time covered the higher ground at the left of the photograph as well as to the right of the monument. Photograph from In Memoriam Henry Warner Slocum, facing p. 140, taken about 1904.

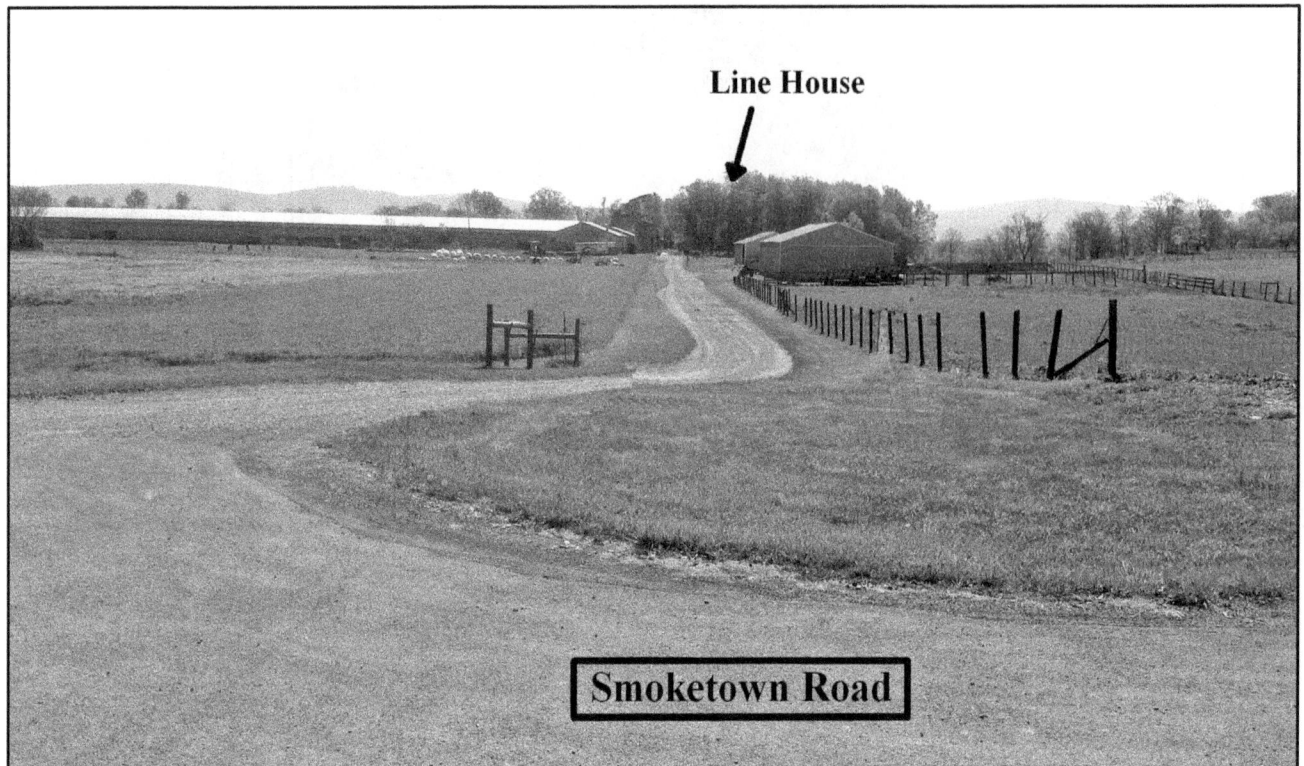

Modern-day entrance to George Line Farm from the Smoketown Road, view looking east. The house is located in the grove of trees in the background. All of the buildings seen here were constructed after the battle. The original Line house was moved to near the Hooker Bridge, on the southwest side by Mr. Bovey; it was rebuilt and brick-cased. Photograph by author April 2013.

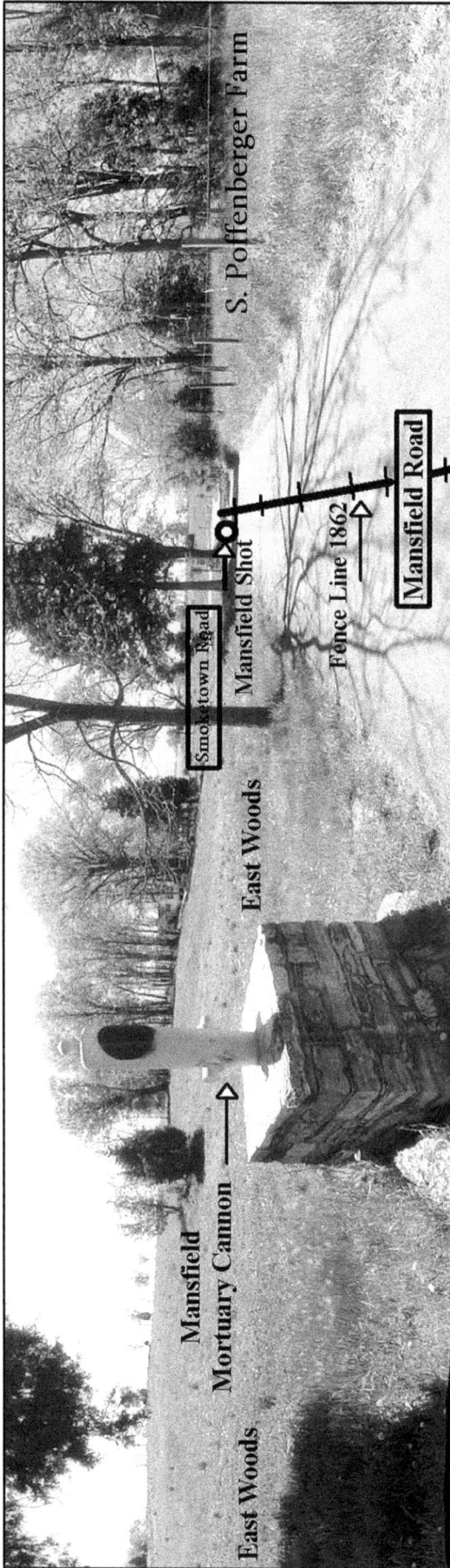

Modern-day photograph of the Mansfield mortuary cannon at Antietam looking southwest on Mansfield Road. Mansfield Road did not exist at that time. The Smoketown Road became a farm lane continuing on to the left where the fence line stopped in the distance. Carman-Cope maps show that the Smoketown Road became less defined as it continued south from today's Mansfield Road. Mansfield was shot about 100 feet west of the cannon just outside of the fence line which existed at the center of today's road. The East Woods were on the left and at the far end of Mansfield Road. None of the buildings seen here existed in 1862. Courtesy John Banks.

Photograph looking west showing where Mansfield was wounded. Note that the road on which the sign appears on its south side, Mansfield Road, did not exist during the battle. The sign was placed there by Gould and Leonard G. Jordan on 17 September1891. The sign reads: "MANSFIELD mortally wounded here IN FRONT OF 10th MAINE REG'T." The sign was made and painted by William Delauney of Sharpsburg. Courtesy Nicholas Picerno Collection and Stephen Recker. Photograph by Bascom William Tell Phreaner c. 1895, courtesy of the Middlesex County Historical Society.

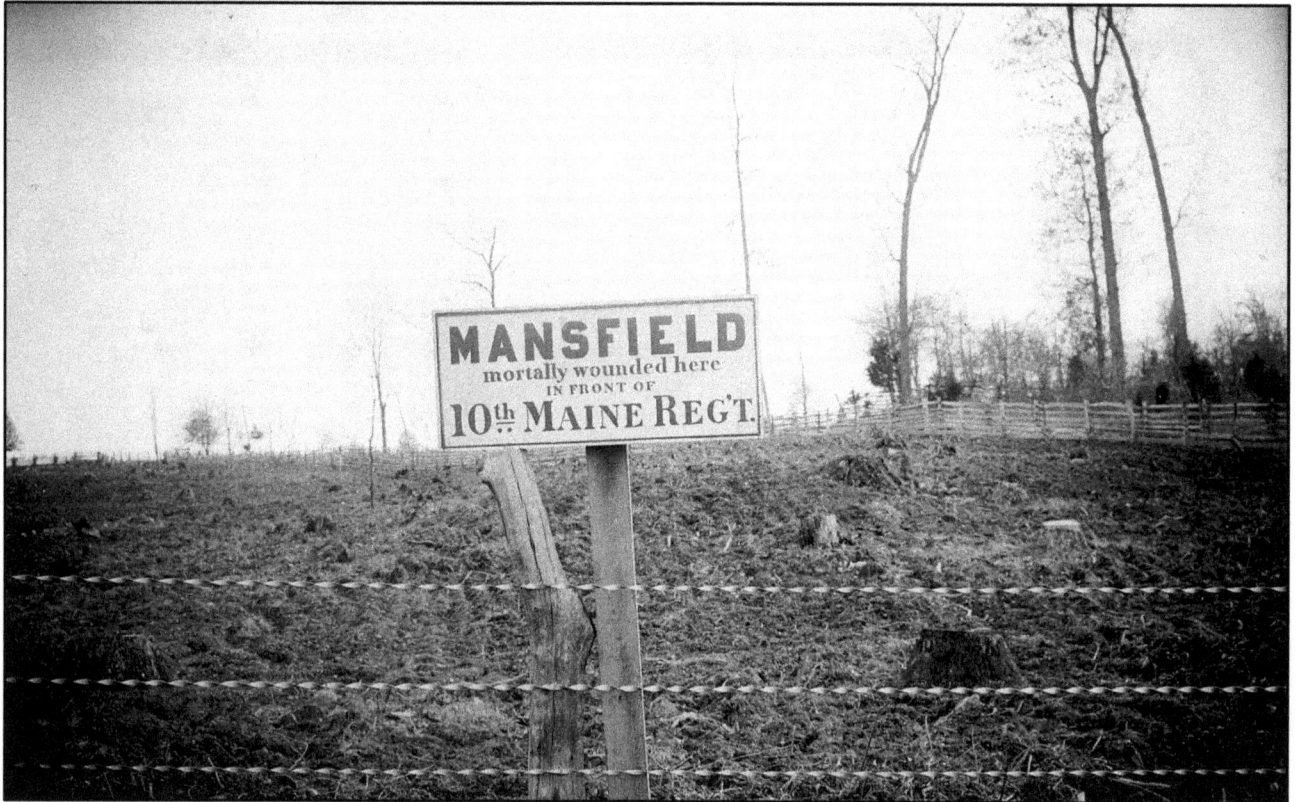

Sign placed by John M. Gould and Leonard G. Jordan on Mansfield Avenue, the East Woods is in the background but here mostly devoid of trees unlike in 1862. Neither of the two modern Mansfield markers is on this spot. Courtesy Nicholas Picerno Collection and Stephen Recker, *Rare Images of Antietam and the Photographers Who Took Them* (Sharpsburg, MD: Another Software Miracle, LLC, 2012), 59.

Gould photograph taken in 1891 showing where Mansfield was wounded along the fence line, facing north. The typed annotation: "Sept. 21 1891 Antietam Position of the 10th Maine. This view from Confederate lines. It was at this location that General Mansfield was mortally wounded" Courtesy John Banks Collection.

Attachment 1
XII Corps Army of the Potomac
Order of Battle, Strength, and Casualties at Antietam 17 September 1862[127]

Brigadier General Joseph K. F. Mansfield (mw)
Staff (2) [0]
Brigadier General Alpheus S. Williams
Staff (3) [0]
Escort: Co. L, 1ˢᵗ Michigan Cavalry, Capt. Melvin Brewer (54)

First Division
Brigadier General Alpheus S. Williams
Staff (5) [0]
Brigadier General Samuel W. Crawford (w)
Brigadier General George H. Gordon

First Brigade (4)
Brigadier General Samuel W. Crawford (w)
Col. Joseph F. Knipe
Staff (4) [0]
5ᵗʰ Conn., Capt. Henry W. Daboll[128] (287) [0]
10ᵗʰ Maine, Col. George L. Beal, Lt. Col. James S. Fillebrown, Major Charles Walker (w) (297)[129] [72]
28ᵗʰ New York, Capt. William H.H. Mapes (68)[130] [12]
46ᵗʰ Penn., Col. Joseph F. Knipe, Lt. Col. James L. Selfridge (150)[131] [19]
124ᵗʰ Penn., Col. Joseph W. Hawley (w), Major Isaac L. Haldeman (670)[132] [64]
125ᵗʰ Penn., Col. Jacob C. Higgins (670)[133] [145][134]
128ᵗʰ Penn., Col. Samuel Croasdale (k), Lt. Col. William W. Hammersly (w), Major Joel B. Wanner (670)[118]

Third Brigade (4)
Brigadier General George H. Gordon
Staff (4) [0]
Col. Thomas H. Ruger (w)

---

[127] Casualty data basically from *ORA*, vol. 19, pt. 1, 198-199, unless other data is available such as from regimental histories. Carman, Clemens, vol. 2, 538-540. Numbers in parentheses show strength, brackets show casualties when data available. Those shown wounded (w) or killed (k) were injured on 17 Sept. Mansfield died on 18 Sept. Staff numbers taken from Allen as of 2 September; all Allen numbers as of 2 September; John Owen Allen, "The Strength of the Union and Confederate Forces at Second Manassas, master's thesis, George Mason Univ., 1993.

[128] The 5ᵗʰ Connecticut was not involved in the Battle of Antietam as it was detached 15 September to be part of the provost guard in Frederick, Maryland, just prior the Battle of South Mountain, *ORA*, vol. 19, pt. 1, 179. They watched as the 16ᵗʰ Connecticut marched through Frederick on its way to Antietam and later considered themselves fortunate not to have joined its sister regiments in the slaughterhouse there, Edwin E. Marvin, *The Fifth Regiment Connecticut Volunteers* (Hartford, CT: Press of Wiley, Waterman & Eaton, 1889), 237. The 5ᵗʰ Connecticut remained in Frederick until 10 December 1862 when it entrained for Harper's Ferry.

[129] Gould, *A Narrative of Events,* 12. Allen shows 491 on 2 September, 117. Gould's regimental history shows 298 carried into battle and 71 casualties, 258, 261.

[130] Carman, Clemens, vol. 2, 583, n. 97. Clemens infers that this is an estimate; Allen shows 231, 117.

[131] Carman, Clemens, vol. 2, 583; Allen shows 346, 117.

[132] Carman, Clemens, vol. 2, 583, n. 99. A "green" Union regiment as was its sister regiments, the 125ᵗʰ and 128ᵗʰ Pennsylvania. All mustered in within four weeks of the Battle of Antietam. Mustering in rolls for the green regiments: 124ᵗʰ Pennsylvania, 974; 125ᵗʰ Pennsylvania 963; and 128ᵗʰ Pennsylvania, 950. The 13ᵗʰ New Jersey mustered in 899, and the 107ᵗʰ New York, 1,031. The total mustering in strength of these five regiment was 4,817, *ORA*, series 3, vol. 3, 749, 760, 775.

[133] Carman, Clemens, vol. 2, 583; Wallace wrote that "it is doubtful if we left our bivouac on the Lines farm with a full seven hundred men," 85.

[134] Total killed, mortally wounded, seriously wounded, and "slightly wounded and not reported" total 229 according to William W. Wallace, (Chmn.), *History of the One Hundred and Twenty-fifth Regiment Pennsylvania Volunteers 1862—1863* (Philadelphia, PA: J.B. Lippincott Company, 1906), 245, 251.

27th Indiana, Col. Silas Colgrove (443)[135] [209]
2nd Mass., Col. George L. Andrews (551)[136] [73]
13th New Jersey, Col. Ezra A. Carman (937)[137] [101]
107th New York, Col. Robert B. Van Valkenburgh (1,016)[138] [63]
Zouaves d'Afrique (Penn.)[139] [3][140]
3rd Wisconsin, Col. Thomas H. Ruger (w) (300)[141] [198]

Second Division
Brigadier General George S. Greene[142]
Staff (3) [0]

First Brigade
Lt. Col. Hector Tyndale (w)
Major Orrin J. Crane
Staff (3) [0]
29th Ohio, Lt. Theron S. Winship[143] (253)[144] [0]
5th Ohio, Major John Collins (100)[145] [48]
7th Ohio, Major Orrin J. Crane, Capt. Frederick A. Seymour (317)[146] [38]
66th Ohio, Lt. Col. Eugene Powell (w) (120)[147] [24]
28th Penn., Major Ario Pardee, Jr. (795)[148] [266]

Second Brigade
Col. Henry J. Stainrook
Staff (3) [0]
3rd Maryland, Lt. Col. Joseph H. Sudsburg (148)[149] [29]
102nd New York, Lt. Col. James C. Lane (279)[150] [37]
109th Penn., Capt. George E. Seymour[151] (305)[152] [0]
111th Penn., Major Thomas M. Walker (243)[153] [110]

---

[135] Allen shows 464, 117.

[136] Allen, 117.

[137] Mustering in strength 25 August 1862, William S. Stryker, *Record of Officers and Men of New Jersey in the Civil War, 1861—1865* (Trenton, NJ: John L. Murphy, Steam Book and Job Printer, 1876), 628. This was one of the "green" regiments.

[138] This is the mustering in strength, Towner, *Our Country and Its People*, 225. Another "green" Union regiment.

[139] No officer present, enlisted men of company attached to 2nd Mass. Regiment.

[140] Bryant, *Third Regiment Wisconsin Veteran Volunteer*, 133.

[141] Lieutenant Julian Wisner Hinckley wrote that less than 300 enlisted were taken into battle plus 12 officers. Hard marching reduced the number on the firing line, *A Narrative of Service with the 3rd Wisconsin Infantry*, 60. Colonel Ruger stated that about 340 were carried into battle, Fox in *In Memoriam: Henry Warner Slocum*, 143; *ORA*, vol. 19, pt. 1, 504. Allen shows 530, 117.

[142] Taken into battle number: 3rd Maryland, 148; 111th Pennsylvania, 243; 3rd Delaware, 126; 60th New York, 226; 78th New York, 221, Fox in *In Memoriam: Henry Warner Slocum*, 146.

[143] Regiment detached 9 Sept.

[144] Allen, 117.

[145] Carman, Clemens, vol. 2, 135 and n. 39; Allen shows 286, 117.

[146] Ibid.

[147] *ORA*, vol. 19, pt. 1, 509; Allen shows 292 for 10 companies, 117.

[148] Carman, Clemens, vol. 2, 135 and n. 39, Carman, Clemens, vol. 2, 308 and n. 12, shows 300 at noon at the Dunker Church; Allen shows 1,104; 117. Tyndale estimates about 650 muskets present that morning with about 250 casualties, Hector Tyndale, *A Memoir of Hector Tyndale* (Philadelphia, PA, MOLLUS, 1882), 101-102, 104.

[149] *ORA*, vol. 19, pt. 1, 511. Allen shows 392 in 9 companies, 117.

[150] Allen, 117.

[151] Regiment detached 13 Sept.

[152] Allen, 9 companies, 117.

[153] *ORA*, vol. 19, pt. 1, 513.

Third Brigade
Col. William Bingham Goodrich (k), Lt. Col. Jonathan Austin
Staff (4) [0]
3rd Delaware, Major Arthur Maginnis (w), Capt. William J. McKaig (126)[154] [17]
Purnell (Maryland) Legion, Lt. Col. Benjamin L. Simpson (200)[155] [26]
60th New York, Lt. Col. Charles H. Brundage (226)[156] [22]
78th New York, Lt. Col. Jonathan Austin, Capt. Henry R. Stagg (221)[157] [34][158]

Artillery[159]
Capt. Clermont L. Best

4th Maine Light, Capt. O'Neil W. Robinson, Jr.[160] (104)[161] [0]
6th Maine Light, Capt. Freeman McGilvery[162] (85)[163] [0]
Bty. M, 1st New York, Capt. George W. Cothran (124)[164] [6]
10th Bty. N.Y. Light, Capt. John T. Bruen (117)[165] [0]
Bty. E, Penn. Light, Capt. Joseph M. Knap (101)[166] [8]
Bty. F, Penn. Light, Capt. Robert B. Hampton (79)[167] [3]
Bty. F, 4th U.S., Lt. Edward D. Muhlenberg (98)[168] [0]

---

[154] Ibid., 514.

[155] Carman, Clemens, vol. 2, 308 and n. 12; Allen shows 347 in 9 companies, 118.

[156] *ORA*, vol. 19, pt. 1, 515. Allen shows 343 in 10 companies, 118.

[157] *ORA*, vol. 19, pt. 1, 516. Allen shows 379 in 10 companies, 118.

[158] Capt. Stagg reported 28 casualties, *ORA*, vol. 19, pt. 1, 516.

[159] All batteries have six guns except for Bty. F, Penn. Light, with four guns, Curt Johnson and Richard C. Anderson, Jr., *Artillery Hell: The Employment of Artillery at Antietam* (College Station, TX: Texas A&M University Press, 1995), 81-82.

[160] Posted near McClellan's headquarters on the 17th, *ORA*, vol. 19, pt. 1, 477, 482.

[161] Strength as of 22 September, also show casualties for each unit, Anderson, *Artillery Hell,* 81; Allen shows 102, 118.

[162] Posted near McClellan's headquarters on the 17th, *ORA*, vol. 19, pt. 1, 477, 482.

[163] Anderson, *Artillery Hell,* 82; Allen shows 42, 118.

[164] Anderson, *Artillery Hell,* 82; Allen shows 74, 118.

[165] Anderson, *Artillery Hell,* 82; Allen shows 76, 118.

[166] Anderson, *Artillery Hell,* 82; Allen shows 66, 118.

[167] Anderson, *Artillery Hell,* 82; Allen shows 36, 118.

[168] Anderson, *Artillery Hell,* 82; Allen shows 94, 118.

Attachment 2
Brigadier General Alpheus Starkey Williams

Brigadier General Alpheus Starkey Williams was a volunteer officer whose nom-de-guerre was "Pops" or "Pap." He was a fellow Nutmegger with Mansfield born in Saybrook (now Deep River), Connecticut, 20 September 1810, just a few miles away from Mansfield's birthplace in New Haven. He graduated from Yale in 1831 and began reading law in New York City. Not enjoying his studies, he took breaks during which he traveled in the United States, attended the theater and reading. He then visited Mexico for two months with a brother followed by a trip through the southern states. After returning to New Haven, he attended classes at Yale Law School but in May 1834, he and a friend decided to take a trip to the mid-west traveling through Pennsylvania, down the Ohio River and then the Mississippi to St. Louis. They returned to New Haven by way of Kentucky, Virginia, and Pennsylvania, but Williams did not feel inclined to return to studying law. He and his friend next determined to do a "Grand Tour" of Europe and he set out in October 1834 with the first stop in Paris. After four months in and around Paris, visiting museums, manufacturing sites, and meeting royalty, they toured Italy for 10 weeks. After returning to England, the recrossed the English Channel to the Continent continuing their adventure. Williams "toured various battlefields, visited arsenals and military museums, and proved to have a considerable knowledge of weaponry. He thought he could distinguish between good and bad soldiers on sight and he placed great stock in appearances and military bearing."[169] Williams returned to the United States in late April 1836 and somewhat surprisingly, moved to Michigan in 1836. His biographer found nothing in Williams's papers to show why he did so but it was perhaps to seek a better life in a less settled part of the country which was experiencing a "great boom." He finally became a lawyer in 1838 and was active in Whig politics, however, by 1859, he ran as a Democrat for city alderman but lost. He was elected Probate Judge of Wayne County, became president of the Bank of St. Clair and bought the Detroit *Daily Advertiser* which he owned until January 1848. He began a four-year term as postmaster of Detroit and held other civic offices: volunteer of the night watch in 1849, recorder (Detroit's city judge), 1845-1848, and member of the Board of Education from 1856-1857.

His military activities began early in his Detroit years, when he enlisted as a private in the local militia, the Brady Guards, on 26 November 1836. His company was mustered in for three months as U.S. troops served on active Army duty during Canada's Patriot War of 1838 – 1839 doing patrol and guard duty. He was among a contingent of the guards who met with Lt. General Winfield Scott who was visiting Detroit. Williams was elected first lieutenant of the company in 1839, captain in 1843, and major then colonel in 1846. Williams also served during the Mexican-American War, but lost out the colonelcy of the 1st Michigan infantry regiment to a West Pointer, Colonel Thomas B.W. Stockton. He was appointed lieutenant colonel and departed for Mexico in February 1848 after most of the regiment left in December 1847. It arrived too late to participate in the fighting. The regiment was engaged in garrison and guard duties but 200 men died of disease out of 1,103. The regiment returned to Detroit and then was mustered out in July 1848. In November 1855, he became captain of a company named the Detroit Light Guard. He next became major of the Guard in 1859 when it became a battalion of two companies. He became Major General of the Michigan Militia in March 1859.

Michigan governor Austin Blair appointed Williams brigadier general of Michigan Volunteers 24 April 1861 then President Lincoln gave him a commission as a brigadier general U.S. Volunteers retroactive to 17 May 1861. He trained Michigan troops at the camp of instruction at Fort Wayne until he was ordered to Washington in October and placed in command of the First Brigade in Major General Nathaniel P. Banks's division, Army of the Potomac. He was stationed near Darnestown, Maryland, until he was moved to the extreme right wing of the Army of the Potomac at Hancock, Maryland, where he remained from January to March of 1862. Put in motion March 1, he departed for Williamsport, Maryland, where he joined the main body of Banks's command, crossed the Potomac, and marched into the Shenandoah Valley. He was in command of the First Division of the V Corps, Army of the Potomac, 13 March 1862 to 4 April 1862, then in command of the First Division of the Dept. of the Shenandoah, to 26 June 1862. Driven out of Winchester by Jackson on 25 May to Williamsport, he reentered the Valley in early June and camped at Front Royal until ordered to cross the Blue Ridge Mountain and concentrate with Pope's command at Culpeper, Virginia. Arriving there on the eighth, his command was placed near Cedar Mountain. On the ninth, his command encountered the elements of Jackson's command opening the Second Bull Run campaign. Banks ordered Williams to attack and

---

[169] Charnley, 28.

Williams at first did well against Jackson but then encountered Jackson's main body. Williams lost about a third of his command and most of his officers but retired in good order, his efforts slowing Jackson's movement. Due to Banks's being injured by his horse, Williams assumed corps command as of 10 August 1862. Williams did not participate further in Second Bull Run battles and joined Banks's retreat into the Washington defenses.

In Washington, he had a number of recently recruited regiments added to his command and then was promptly sent to join McClellan.[170] On 13 September, troops from his corps, the 27th Indiana, found what became General Lee's famous Lost Order detailing the positions and objectives of Lee's Army. After Antietam, his command crossed to Virginia near Harper's Ferry, marched through Fairfax, and into winter quarters near Stafford, Virginia and participated in Burnside's famous Mud March. On 20 October 1862, Major General Henry W. Slocum took command of the XII Corps and William's resumed command of its first Division. In early May 1863 he marched west with Hooker crossing Germana Ford to occupy Chancellorsville stealing a march on General Lee in Fredericksburg. When Hooker's command was rolled up by Jackson's march around the Union' right flank, it was Williams who hastily entrenched his troops and halted the Rebels in the night battle of 3-4 May. By June he was marching north into Union territory with the Army of the Potomac in search of General Lee. Williams arrived at Gettysburg on the evening of the first day and took over command of Slocum's corps. He recognized the importance of Culp's Hill and had his troops fortify it withstanding repeated Rebel attacks on Meade's right flank. After Gettysburg, he followed Lee's retreat into Virginia, until 24 September 1863, when Slocum's XII Corps was ordered west to join Major General William S. Rosecrans's Army of the Cumberland besieged in Chattanooga. He was in Sherman's advance on Atlanta and fought in the battles at Resaca, (New Hope Church where he was wounded in the arm), Kolb's Farm, and Peach Tree Creek, and with the Twentieth Corps joined Sherman's march to the sea across Georgia; he took over command of the Twentieth Corps, Slocum having been promoted to Army command, then marched north into South and North Carolina. Williams was relieved from command of the XX Corps when Slocum became commander of the Army of Georgia as a major general, Joseph A. Mower, took over command.

Williams received a brevet promotion 12 January 1865 to major general in the volunteers. After the war, he served as military administrator of the Ouachita District in Southern Arkansas until he resigned his commission in early 1866. He returned to Michigan only to face financial difficulties that forced him to take a post as minister resident to San Salvador (now El Salvador). Returning to Michigan he made an unsuccessful run for Governor in 1870, but was elected to Congress in 1874 and 1876. He died on December 21, 1878 in Washington, D.C.[171]

Colonel Ezra A. Carman, commanding the 13th New Jersey in Williams's Division, wrote an encomium for his general; likely he was personally familiar with him and apparently developed a friendship:

> Alpheus S. Williams....was appointed brigadier general of volunteers and joined the Army of the Potomac. He was assigned to the command of a brigade in Banks's division on the upper Potomac. In March 1862 he was given command of a division in Banks's corps and in the operations in the Shenandoah Valley displayed great skill and courage. When Jackson's aggressive movement on Banks's flank compelled him to fall back from Strasburg, Virginia, Williams had full charge of covering the retreat and did so skillfully, retiring on May 24 and, in a series of brilliant engagements, checking Jackson's advance at Newtown, Kernstown, and Winchester long enough to save a part of the trains. The retreat was a disastrous and humiliating one; it would have been much more so had Williams not shown greater skill and judgment as a soldier than his immediate superior. At Cedar Mountain he handled his division admirably and in the subsequent campaign around Manassas was active and unsparing in

---

[170] The new regiments in the XII Corps were as follows: 13th New Jersey, 107th New York, and 124th, 125th, and 128th Pennsylvania, adding about 3,000 men, Charnley, 275 n. 38; D. Scott Hartwig, "Who Would Not Be a Soldier: The Volunteers of '62 in the Maryland Campaign," in The Antietam Campaign, ed. Gary W. Gallagher (Chapel Hill, NC: The University of North Carolina Press, 1999). Hartwig estimates that about twenty percent of McClellan's strength was composed of raw recruits with little or no training and therefore "significantly affected its mobility and combat effectiveness....McClellan's new regiments lacked discipline; most of their company and many of their field officers were unfamiliar or uncomfortable with their duties and responsibilities... [and] exhibited incredible ignorance of elementary commands and duties" 147. These regiments would find themselves fighting against Lee's veterans and would be severely tried despite their best efforts, 162.

[171] Eicher, 571; Alpheus S. Williams, The Civil War Letters of General Alpheus S. Williams: From the Cannon's Mouth, ed. Milo M. Quaife (Detroit: Wayne State University Press and Detroit Historical Society, 1959; reprint, Lincoln: Bison Books, Univ. of Nebraska Press, 1995), 3-11 (page citations are to the reprint edition); Robert B. Ross, The Early Bench and Bar of Detroit from 1805 to the End of 1850 (Detroit, MI: Richard P. Joy and Clarence M. Burton, 1907), 224-230; Heidler, "Williams, Alpheus Starkey," 2115-2116; Lowell Boileau, http://bhere.com/plugugly/williams/williamsbio.html#return; "Michigan's General A.S. Williams and Civil War Historians: A Century of Neglect", (Michigan Historical Review 12 [Spring 1986], Central Michigan University 1986); Welcher, 465-472.

effort. When Banks assumed command of the defenses of Washington on September 8, Williams succeeded to the command of the corps in which he had served as a brigade and division commander.

Throughout his long and arduous service, which began with the beginning of the war and ended only when the final surrender was made, he never was taken by surprise and when in action was cool and quick to see a faulty disposition or movement in his own Army or in that of the enemy. He was not a brilliant soldier, but a safe one; he never sacrificed his men for the mere sake of winning to himself the attention of the newspaper correspondents and the plaudits of the public, but whenever hard work was to be done or hard knocks to be received he was ready. He was social in his habits, kind and considerate to officers and men, ever alive to their needs and comforts, and always with them from the beginning to the end. He never received a furlough; his life was in camp with his men. He never received the promotion to which his long and faithful service entitled him, but this did not lessen his honesty of purpose or diminish the energy with which he performed duty. His ambition was more concerned in the welfare of his country and the triumph of her armies than his own promotion and advancement, and he was never above the work to which he was assigned, whether commanding a corps, a division, or a brigade. It has been truly said of him, 'He was content that he did his duty, and in the satisfaction that he never committed an error, never misrepresented an order, never relaxed his careful watchfulness and disinterested devotion to his country.' Although this devotion to duty was not recognized by the government, he never complained; 'he never said ought in derogation of a fellow soldier; he was charitable even toward those who supplanted him or when advanced when seemingly he justly was entitled to the promotion. He was a noble man as well as a gallant solder.'[172]

---

[172] Carman, Pierro, 78-79; included quotes are from Memorial Addresses on the Life and Character of Alpheus S. Williams, A representative from Michigan, delivered in the House of Representatives and Senate. 45th Cong. 3d sess., 1878–1879 (Washington DC: Government Printing Office, 1880), Mr. Willits of MI, 30.

Attachment 3
Mansfield's Letter from Willard's Hotel to Sylvanus Thayer 11 September 1862
Courtesy Middlesex County Historical Society[173]

---

[173] Mansfield rode from Washington on 13 September so the 11 September date shown, appears incorrect, as his official orders did not assign him the XII Corps until 12 September. It is likely that he was not sure exactly when he would leave and was getting his final good-byes done.

into his glorious Kingdom
of Heavenly Peace.

Your friend

Jno. K. L. Mansfield.

Col Sylvanus Thayer
South Braintree.
Massachusetts.

Attachment 4
Secretary Stanton's Telegram to Benjamin Douglas 18 September 1862 Reporting Mansfield's Death
Courtesy Middlesex County Historical Society

THE AMERICAN TELEGRAPH COMPANY.
NORTH, SOUTH, EAST AND WEST,
Connecting with all the Southern, Western, Eastern and Northern Lines of Telegraph.

TERMS AND CONDITIONS ON WHICH THIS AND ALL MESSAGES ARE RECEIVED BY THIS COMPANY FOR TRANSMISSION.

In order to guard against errors or delays in the transmission or delivery of messages, every message of importance ought to be REPEATED by being sent back from the station at which it is to be received to the station from which it is originally sent. Half the usual price for transmission will be charged for repeating the message, and while this Company will, as heretofore, use every precaution to ensure correctness, it will not be responsible for errors or delays in the transmission or delivery of repeated messages beyond FIFTY dollars, unless a special agreement for insurance be made and paid for at the time of sending the message, and the amount of risk specified on this agreement; nor is the Company to be responsible for any error or delay in the transmission or delivery or non-delivery of any unrepeated message, BEYOND FIVE DOLLARS, unless in like manner specially insured and amount of risk paid for at the time. No liability is assumed for any error or neglect by any other Company over whose lines this message may be sent to reach its destination. No liability for any errors in cipher messages.

CAMBRIDGE LIVINGSTON, Sec'y,
145 BROADWAY, N. Y.

E. S. SANFORD, Pres't,
145 BROADWAY, N. Y.

.No.   COMPLAINTS SHOULD BE SENT TO THE SECRETARY.

Dated Washington Sept 18 1862.

Rec'd, Sept 18th 1862 6 o'clock 30 min. PM.
5.45 P.M.

To Benj Douglas

Your telegram just recd. I regret to say that the sad inteligence of the death of Gen'l Mansfield is true. He fell in the battle of yesterday. Gallantly leading a charge. The particulars have not reached here. His remains will be taken in charge by friends

Edwin M. Stanton
Secy of War

Attachment 5
Letter from Samuel Mansfield to Sylvanus Thayer[174]

FROM Samuel M. Mansfield*

Middletown Conn.
26th Sept. 1862.

Dear Colonel,
    Mother desires me to write and express to you her
gratification for your tender sympathy in her behalf.
    We have met with a great loss and cannot realize our
situation at present as we could had he been more at home.
In our future troubles we shall not have him to look to for
help and advice. Then we shall miss him.
    I regret exceedingly I could not have been with him in
his last hours. Sickness had kept me from him for about five
weeks and upon my arrival in Washington on Tuesday while
making my preparations to join him and seeking his whereabouts the sad news of Wednesday that General (Joseph K. F.)
Mansfield* was mortally wounded sent a chill through me.
I immediately made every endeavour to learn the truth of it.
I saw the President (Abraham Lincoln)* and Secy. of War
(Edwin M. Stanton)* but neither could give me further
information. Lieut. Norton who had just arrived from Suffolk
and was about to join Father was with me and went immediately
to the Battle ground in search of him, while I remained,
fearing that, should I leave I might miss him as it happened
Lieut. Norton did.
    Friday morning I intercepted at the War Dept. a dispatch
from Capt (Clarence Hopkins) Dyer* his Aid, dated Frederick,
to Mother saying that he should leave that morning with the
remains of the Genl.
    I left Washington in the afternoon and met Capt. Dyer
with the remains at the Relay House. Also Mr. (Benjamin?)
Douglas* of Middletown who had come on upon learning the
news of his death.
    I enclose to you a copy of notes made by Mr Douglas on
the cars taken fresh from Capt Dyer's memory.
    Mother is quite uneasy to think that he should say
nothing special of his family, after being informed by his
Surgeon that he could not live. That he should leave no
message. I tell her that his mind was fixed upon the Battle,
that he gave up family and all that could be dear to him
even his life, for his Country - I feel proud to think
that I had such a Father. and his life has been an example
that I shall not feel ashamed to imitate.
    It would be gratifying to Mother and myself if you
would write an Obituary notice We feel that you (who have
know him so long and intimately) can best give to the public
his character as a Soldier and Friend.   Very Respectfully
Your Obt. Servt.   SAMUEL M. MANSFIELD
Col. Sylvanus Thayer
South Braintree Mass.

---

[174] Typescripts courtesy West Point Library online: http://digital-library.usma.edu/libmedia/archives/thayer/THAPAP10.pdf.

```
FROM (Benjamin?) Douglas*
                                      (26 Sept. 1862)
General (Joseph K. F.) Mansfield* left Washington accom-
panied by his Aid Capt Dyer* and body Servant, on Saturday
the 13th of Sept. 1862, At about 4 o'clock P.M. on horse
back.  arrived at Middletown Maryland on Monday the 15h at
9 o'clock A.M. and reported here to Genl (George B.)
M.Clellan* as ordered, and was then assigned to the Command
of Genl (Nathaniel P.) Banks* Corps of 11,000 men of two
Divisions (Genls (Alpheus S.) Williams* and (Stearns)*
(James Shields?)* and on the morning of Wednesday the 17th
he lead them forth to action, at about 7. o'clock and had
been out an hour or so engaged when at the head of his troops,
urging on one of the new or "raw" regiments, which needed
some encouragement, as they were timid, being under their
first fire, and the firing of the enemy was very heavy of
both Infantry and Artillery.
     He was shot with a minie ball thro. the right lung,
passing clear through him, so that he literally bled to
death.  His horse was shot dead at the same time, three
balls passing through him.  The General lived 24 hours, he
conversed freely most of the time, was under the influence
of opiates some of the time.  Was constantly inquiring how
the Action was going, and after the other officers, as to
their safety etc.  Having it reported to him at one time that
Genls (Ambrose E.) Burnside* & (Joseph) Hooker* both were
killed he lifted up his hands and exclaimed "Too bad"
"Too bad".  "Poor Fellows" "Poor Fellows".  Being afterward
told it was not so he seemed much gratified and relieved.
Enquired several times how the Battle was going, and when
told in our favor was much pleased.  He gradually grew
weaker and weaker and sent love to all his friends wished to
be remembered to all, and to have his remains taken home.
Wanted Capt Dyer to stay by him all the time until his death.
     Doct. (Anselum) Surgeon of the Corps, and Docts Porter
and Weeks (the latter of the Navy) were all very attentive
to him.  He had the best of care and attention and went off
quietly as one going to sleep.
     He expired on Thursday morning at 8 o'clock and ten
minutes.  His remains were immediately taken by Capt Dyer
and put into a rough box and carried in an ambulance from
the place (which was between Cadysville and Sharpsburg) to
Monocacy Station near Frederick where they took the Cars
for Baltimore.
     He seemed impressed with the idea that he should be
killed as he had expressed to several persons that he should
never come out of the fight alive.  He told Hon Ely Thayer*
in Washington just as he was leaving there that he was going
into the field and did not expect to come back alive and
desired him to have his body recovered and sent home to his
friends in Middletown.
```
175

---

[175] "Ely Thayer" was Sylvanus Thayer. "Doctor Anselum" was Dr. Thomas Antisell XII Corps surgeon. "Thomas Antisell graduated in medicine from the Royal College of Surgeons, London, and subsequently studied chemistry in Paris and Berlin. He practiced medicine in Dublin until 1848, when he became a political exile on account of his connection with the young Ireland party. He then came to this country and settled in the city of New York, where he pursued his profession until 1854, when he accepted the position of geologist to the Park expedition in the railroad survey of southern California and Arizona. In 1856, he returned from the expedition and accepted the position of chief examiner in the chemical department of the patent office. At the breaking out of the war he entered the volunteer service as brigade surgeon, and at its close was mustered out with the rank of brevet lieutenant colonel," The Washington *Evening Star*, 2 February 1919.

Capt Dyer was not with the General at the moment he fell, he having been ordered back by the General to bring on Genl (George Henry) Gordon's* Brigade to their support. Genl Mansfield was at the time he fell at the head of Genl. (Samuel Wylie) Crawfords* Brigade. As he fell he was immediately caught up in the arms of five of the privates (from one of our Regiments next to him) also by the Surgeon of one of the Penn. Regiments and carried back about ¼ of a mile to the rear, where he was put into an ambulance and carried back about 1½ mile further to a hospital (made from a old Farm House) where he was attended to by the Chief Surgeon of the Corps and had the best of care. Capt. Dyer his aid was with him in about 20 minutes after he fell and remained over him constantly until he expired. He required opiates to quiet his pains. His last moments after he could no longer talk audibly from loss of blood, seemed spent in Prayer as occasional expressions could be understood such as "My Lord," and "Father in Heaven" into thy hands" etc. seeming perfectly resigned to God's Will.

He was conscious from near the first that he could not live. But as he expressed it when told by his Surgeon, he could not survive, "It is God's Will it is all right"

Arriving in Baltimore at about 8o'clock in the evening of Friday Sept 19th with the Generals remains we were met by Genl. (John Ellis) Wools* Aid with a detachment of Cavalry to perform Escort duty to the remains taking them into a hearse drawn by a fine team they escorted them to the Embalmer's Room a mile or so from the Depot and offered another escort when the remains were ready to leave the next day. The Rail Road to Philadelphia was thrown open to the remains free, as well as to those who accompanied the same.

The body was found by the Embalmer to be too far gone (decomposition having commenced) to admit of being embalmed, and was put in an air tight metalic case. At Phila the Agent of the Camden & Amboy line to New York, with tears in his eyes gave us a whole car for the remains free to N. Y. and offered to do all in his power to assist in forwarding the remains and said he felt it as a personal loss. We the Country had but few such men to lose as Mansfield. Arriving in N. Y. we were met by Col. J. H. Almy* the Connect State Ag. tendering most kindly an escort, Hearse, Carriages etc to convey the remains to the Governors Room at the City Hall there to lay in State for a day, that the Son's of Connecticut and other citizens of N. Y. might have the honor of paying their respects to the noble dead, but we could only thank them and decline stopping as we had arranged to be home.

Col. Almy accompanied the remains and friends to the New Haven Depot (taking them in a fine hearse drawn by four horses furnished by Col. Almy) arrived at New Haven Depot at 7½ o'clock in the evening of Saturday where we were met by two Gentlemen a committee from the Board of Aldermen of the City of New York, requesting that the remains of Genl. Mansfield might be taken

back to the City Hall to lay in State there that the Citizens of New York might have an opportunity of paying some proper tribute of respect to his remains. We had to decline yet they were very urgent and said that General Mansfield was not Connecticut's man alone but the Country's man, and they wished to show to the country that they loved him.

The N. Y. N. H. & Hartford R. Roads opened free to our passage with remains to Meriden where we arrived at about 12 o'clock Saturday night the 20th and took carriages for Middletown with the remains arriving here at half past 3 o'clock on Sabbath morning, Sept. 21st. depositing the remains in the Town Hall, placing them under guard of a detachment from the 24th Regt Conn. Militia in Camp here.

Compare this transcription with the following handwritten account in the West Point Library. The envelope containing the account shows this: "General Mansfield's last hours—Capt. Dyer's report [likely Benjamin Douglas's report].

General Mansfield left Washington accompanied by his aide Capt. Dyer and body servant on Saturday 13th Sept. 1862 at about 4 o'clock P.M. on horseback, arrived at Middletown Md., on Monday the 15th at 9 o'clock a.m. and reported there to General McClellan as ordered and was then assigned to the command of Genl Banks Corps of about 11,000 men the two divisions of Generals Williams and Sterns and on the morning of Wednesday the 17th he lead them forth to action at about 7 o'clock and had been but an hour or so engaged when at the head of his troops urging on one of the new or 'raw' regiments which needed some encouragement as they were timid being under their first fire and tho firing of the enemy was very heavy of both Infantry and Artillery. He was shot by a minie ball through the right lung passing clear through him so that he literally bled to death. His horse was shot dead at the same time three balls passing through him.

The General lived 24 hours and conversed freely most of the time was under the influence of opiates some of the time. He was constantly inquiring how the action was going on and after the other officers as to their safety etc. Having it reported to him at one time that Generals Burnside and Hooker both were killed he lifted up his hands and exclaimed 'Too bad, 'Too bad.' 'Poor Fellows.' 'Poor Fellows.'

Being afterward told it was not so he seemed much gratified and relieved. Enquired several times how the Battle was going and when told in our favor was much pleased.

He gradually grew weaker and weaker and sent love to all his friends wished to be remembered to all and to have his remains taken home. Wanted Captain Dyer to stay by him all the time until his death.

Doctor Anselum surgeon of the Corps and Docts Porter and Weeks (the latter of the Navy) were all very attentive to him. He had the best of care and attention and went off quietly as one going to sleep. He expired on Thursday morning at 8 o'clock and 10 minutes. His remains were immediately taken by Capt. Dyer and put into a rough box and carried in an ambulance from the place which was between Cadysville [Keedysville] and Sharpsburgh to Monocacy Station near Frederick, where they took the cars for Baltimore.

He seemed impressed with the idea that he should be killed, as he had expressed to several persons that he should never come out of the fight alive. He told Hon. Ely Thayer in Washington just as he was leaving there, that he was going into the field and did not expect to come back alive and desired him to have his body recovered and sent home to his friends in Middletown Ct.

Capt. Dyer was not with the General at the moment he fell, he having been ordered back by the General to bring on Gens Gordon's Brigade to their support.

The General was at the time he fell at the head of Genl Crawford's Brigade. As he fell he was immediately caught up in the arms of five of the privates (from one of our regiments next to him) also by the surgeon of one of the Pennsylvania regiments and carried back about ¼ mile further to a hospital (made of an old farm house) where he was attended to by the chief surgeon of the Corps and had the best of care. Capt. Dyer his aide was with him in about 20 minutes after he fell and remained over him constantly until he expired. Opiates were used to quiet his pains.

His last moments after he could no longer talk audibly from loss of blood, served spent in prayer as occasional expressions could be understood, such as: 'My Lord' 'Father in Heaven' 'into thy hands' he seeming perfectly resigned to God's will.

He was conscious from near the first that he could not live. But as he expressed it when told by his surgeon he could not survive, 'It is God's will it is all right.'

October 10th 1862[176]

---

[176] Courtesy WPL. As Samuel relates, Capt. Dyer related the story to Benjamin Douglas who then added information he witnessed after meeting Dyer in New York City. The New York City Aldermen's request to have Mansfield lie in state had a precedent when Connecticut's Brig. Gen. Nathaniel Lyon was so honored for three days in August and September 1861, Ashbel Woodward, *Life of General Nathaniel Lyon* (Hartford, CT: Case, Lockwood & Co., 1862), 339-340.

Attachment 6
Dr. Patrick H. Flood Letter to General Mansfield's Wife, Louisa[177]

Camp 107th Regt. N.Y. Vols.   Hope Landing, Va.   April 28-1863

Mrs. Genl. Mansfield,

Madam.

I received a letter some few days since from Col. S.M. Mansfield, asking of me the particulars of the death of his father Genl. Mansfield, who fell at the battle of Antietam on the 17th day of Sept. last, and wishing me to communicate the same to you. I cheerfully comply with your son's request, for if you have for so long a period remained without that detail, it is time that the same was put in your possession. What I know of that melancholy catastrophe, fell under my own observation, as a Surgeon on that sanguinary day, in which our Country lost a brave and gallant soldier, and yourself a husband.

The first time I met with Genl. Mansfield, was on the 16th. A member of our Regt. had become overpowered by the heat, and on being summoned by his side I found the Genl. giving him some stimulus, and he requested me to bathe his head with water. I did not meet with him again, until I was summoned to his assistance on the battle field; word having been sent "that Genl. Mansfield was wounded."

To give you the detail in full of that sad event, I must necessarily digress and speak of connecting circumstances. Our Regt. the 107th N.Y., was engaged soon after daylight, and was near the "center" a little to the right, and about 1000 rods on the right and front opposite the "Duncard Church". We had driven the rebels back, out of a piece of wood, and a field that was very stony, and slightly sprinkled with locust trees, to a road that ran parallel with a long piece of wood, where they made a stand. As our Regt. advanced to the edge of the locust field, they succeeded in getting a "cross fire" on us, which was terrible and very destructive. We were obliged to halt for many of our men were falling, and to proceed were madness. I was in the rear of the Regt. attending to our own wounded, as they were carried back, and was so engaged, when Col. Diven [colonel of the 107th NY was Robert B. Van Valkenburgh—there was no colonel of that name on the field] at about Eight & a half o'clock A M, called to me and said that "our Genl. was shot." I left my position quickly, and went forward, taking with me a man named McGovern, who volunteered to do so and found the Genl. by seeing his horse running & following the course from whence he came. He was about 100 yards in front of our Regt. and the woods, a most perilous position where the bullets and missiles were flying like hail, and where no one upon horse could survive the position. It seemed as if the very depths of Pandemonia, had here sent her furies, and such a tornado of deadly missiles screaming through the air, baffles all description – Add to this, the press of Rebel Sharpshooters, and you may conceive somewhat the deadly work that was in progress. I am satisfied that the Genl. was shot by one of these, as the wound was inflicted by a "minnie ball". When I came up, some men were trying to carry him in a blanket, but the jolting motion, made him bleed so fast, they were afraid to move. I found the clothing around his chest saturated with blood, and upon opening them, found he was wounded in the right breast, the ball penetrating about two inches from the nipple, and passing out of the back, near the edge of the shoulder blade. He inquired if I was Surgeon, & on replying in the affirmative – "then", said he "for God's sake, do all you can for me, and stop the bleeding, and get me to some house." I placed a compress on each orifice, and bandaged his body, which stopped the hemorage, and conveyed him as fast as possible towards a white house the Regt. had passed when going into the battle.- It was about ¾ of a mile distant.- He was carried in a blanket about 1/3 of the way, and the balance in an ambulance – When we arrived at the house, I found it well filled already with the wounded, but fortunately I found one room, with a good bed vacant, in which I had him placed. Here the Medical Director of our Division came to my assistance. I removed his clothing, belt, watch and guard which were about his neck, flask, and I think pistols, which

[177] From copy of original at the Middlesex County Historical Society courtesy of John Banks: http://bunkfoss.com/i/banks_letter.pdf. "In 1862, at age 50, Elmira physician Dr. Patrick Flood went off to war as the surgeon of the 107th New York Infantry. The more than 1,000 men of the 107th were about one month into their time of service at the Battle of Antietam. Dr. Flood served throughout the war, finishing as the surgeon of the First Division of the 20th Corps. He returned to Elmira and to civilian medical practice. He was also a two-term mayor of the city, and one of his four sons was a U.S. Republican Congressman," Randy Buchman http://enfiladinglines.com. For a biography of Flood, see Ausburn Towner, *Our Country and Its People: A History of the Valley and County of Chemung From the Closing Years of the Eighteenth Century* (Syracuse, NY: D. Mason & Co., Publishers, 1892), 225-227.

were given to an officer present, at his instance, who said that they would be cared for. The Doctor and myself examined the wound, which at this time was not bleeding, and I saw that a small portion of the lung protruded from an orafice, which convinced me, as before stated, a "Minnie ball" had occasioned it. The lung was much torn, and I saw at a glance the wound must prove fatal.

He was very pallid, almost as white as paper as I approached him – his pulse was small and quick. He seemed excited, and was very talkative, relating the position he was in when he was shot, and that he was going to stop our men firing, as they were firing at each other. In this the Genl. was mistaken for I afterwards learned, that our forces occupied one piece of wood – the rebels the opposite, and the position of the Genl. was between the two. He had his senses, until about 12 o'clock midnight, when he would mutter, and his lips move as if talking, but could not be understood. On our way to the hospital he repeated many times "Oh my God, am I to die thus!" – "Get me a house". "Oh my poor family" – "We are driving them thank God." McGovern had a canteen full of fresh cool water, and I one, filled with Brandy. His thirst was very great, and he would ask for water every minute.- I mixed the two, but he did not like it, but I urged it, as he was growing very weak & required stimulus, & I feared he would expire before a house could be reached.

After I had dressed his wound, I left him in charge of the medical director, but called to see him often, and saw him one hour before he expired. On entering the room, he heard me, and turning his head towards the door recognized me, and asked the officer (the same his effects were given to) "If I was the Doctor that took him off the field – He answered "yes" – The Genl. then turned his head back and closed his eyes. I saw he must soon expire – He lived about 24 hours after he was shot. Had the very best of care and attention. One of my nurses, Geo. W. Beers, took charge of him during the night. He died about 8½ o'clock on the morning of the 18th. From Beers I learn he inquired "if the news had been sent to his family", and on being told it had probably not been sent, he "asked the reason"- The battle was expected to be renewed the following morning and the difficulty attending it explained. Nothing further of importance transpired worthy of being related.

Thus Madam, I have endeavored to give you a faithful detail of all that transpired in my relations with your lamented husband. I cannot tell you the anguish of heart I experienced in being called to attend one, who only a few hours before I had met with in health, and leading our armies into Victory. The Country has suffered an irreparable loss in his death. It was the adding of another of those brave noble spirits, to the list of Martyrs who have died for our Country, and a Nation will never forget him, but treasure his memory with the most heroic tenderness.-

I am Very Respectfully
P.H. Flood, Surgeon 107th Regt. N.Y.V.

Attachment 7
John Mead Gould Letter 29 November 1862[178]

Headquarters Fourth Maine Regiment

Berlin, Maryland
November 29, 1862

It is now more than two months since the battle of Antietam, yet I have never seen in print a single item relating to the death of our General, Mansfield. The circumstances are so peculiar and were witnessed by so few that I deem it important to make a brief statement of the facts coming under my observations.

General Mansfield, on ordering forward the First Brigade ([Samuel Wylie] Crawford's) of Williams' Division, which brigade was the first one of our Corps to enter the fight, he personally attended to its deployment and, having got the new regiments, which formed the center, in line, came down to the left and rear where the Tenth Maine Reg't in attempting to follow his orders were opposed by an equal force of the enemy, posted behind trees, logs and a ledge. This small force of the enemy was far in advance of any other of theirs and the General imagined them to be Union troops into which we had commenced firing by mistake. He immediately ordered "Cease firing" – "They are our own men" which was enforced with great difficulty by the company officers, as the men had become satisfied of the character of the troops in their front.

The General now took out his glass, but immediately his horse was shot in the right hind leg and became unruly. Then the General was shot, I am told—by an officer who stood near him, a few seconds afterwards, but it was not observed by the men, who thought only the horse was wounded. Passing, still in front of our line and nearer the enemy, he attempted to ride over the rail fence which separated a lane from the ploughed land, where most of our regiment were posted. The horse would not jump it and the General, dismounting led him over. He passed to the rear of the Regimental line, when a gust of wind blew aside his coat and I discovered that his whole front was covered with blood.

I had watched the General for more than five minutes, expecting every moment to see him shot but this was the first knowledge I had of the accident. I ran to him and asked if he was hurt badly. He said "Yes. I shall not live – shall not live – I am shot by one of our own men."

He was attempting to mount his horse again but I informed him that the horse was wounded and suggested his taking the orderly's (the orderly was the only person who was with him during the perilous passage). He turned to do so but his strength now failed him and he said, "No! Take me off. I am shot. I shall not live." He directed the orderly to look out for his horse. Sergeant Merrill of Company F, happened also to discover the General's condition and caught him as he was falling in the attempt to mount the horse. A third person, whom I cannot recollect, also came up shortly after as we were bearing him off, but being now in the rear, I had much difficulty in getting the fourth [assistant]. I had to send off a wounded man to find the nearest surgeon, and after having borne him some distance and got relief for the first four, I ran myself to find a spot to carry him to. Lieutenant [Edward L.] Witman of General Crawford's staff, who was sent by that officer to assist General Mansfield off, found a surgeon and cared for him otherwise. I saw the General put into an ambulance and then started forward to my regiment.

The General was shot by the enemy, whom he took to be the Union forces, from their nearness to our lines and distance from all other Rebels. It is now learned to have been the Twentieth [Twenty First] Georgia Regiment.

Sergeant Merrill went with him to the hospital and made him as comfortable as possible, but I did not see the General again.

John M. Gould
Lieut + Actg. Adjutant 10th Maine

---

[178] Transcript from "enfilading lines" blog by Randy Buchman http://enfiladinglines.com from Antietam National Battlefield Library, Mansfield Folder; original at the Middlesex County Historical Society; and from a copy of Gould's draft courtesy Nicholas Picerno Collection. There are slight, immaterial, differences between the two; from John Mead Gould Letters, 1853-1864, Box 1, Duke University in *ORA Supp.*, pt. 1, vol. 3, 562-564; http://www.johnmeadgould.com. Gould's letter at of the Middlesex County Historical Society is dated 2 December 1862 written from Berlin, Maryland.

Attachment 8
John Mead Gould's Biography[179]

John Mead Gould was born on 15 December 1839 in Portland, Maine, son of a banker. He attended two private academies and then worked in the Merchants' and Traders' Bank with his father in 1856. The twenty-one-year old Gould enlisted for two years in a local militia company, the Portland Light Guards, on 23 April 1861, answering President Lincoln's call for 75,000 volunteers. His company, along with nine others, became the 1st Maine Volunteer Infantry Regiment on 9 May 1861. The 1st Maine arrived in Washington on 3 June and camped there during the Battle of First Bull Run on 21 July. They could hear the rumble of artillery, but on 31 July, with their time of commitment served, they left Washington and returned home and mustered out.

Gould soon joined most of the rest of the 1st Maine men to form the 10th Maine on 9 September 1861 and was promoted to Sergeant Major.[180] His regiment was finally assigned to the Railroad Brigade in November 1861 guarding the Baltimore and Ohio Railroad (B&O) at Relay House, and it was next transferred to Harper's Ferry in April 1862 joining Brigadier General Alpheus's division. Effective 29 March 1862, Gould was promoted to second lieutenant in Co. E, but spent most of his time as acting adjutant of the regiment. On 9 May, the regiment moved south and was assigned as provost guards in Winchester. His regiment participated in the skedaddle from there as Stonewall Jackson approached on the 25th. In June, the 10th was reassigned to the 1st Brigade, 1st Division of the II Corps of the Army of the Potomac and chased Stonewall Jackson through July 1862.

The 10th suffered very heavy losses which approached 37% in the Battle of Cedar Mountain, Virginia, 9 August 1862. Gould was promoted to first lieutenant effective 9 August 1862 becoming his regiment's permanent adjutant general.[181] Like most of its sister regiments in the II Corps, the Mainers spent the Battle of Second Bull Run picketing and guarding supply trains.

On the morning of 17 September, as part of Mansfield's XII Corps, the 10th Maine and Gould were engaged in fierce fighting when Gould witnessed Mansfield's mortal wounding. After the battle on 25 October, the regiment was sent to Brunswick (now Berlin), Maryland, on the Potomac River, to guard a newly-reconstructed pontoon bridge there. His regiment moved into Northern Virginia on 10 December remaining there until April 1863, missing the Army of the Potomac's bloodletting at Fredericksburg. Most of the regiment's two-year enlistments expired in April as did Gould's, a nd he returned to Portland, Maine, for eight months, missing the Battle of Gettysburg, Pennsylvania in July 1863. The remaining part of the 10th Maine had reorganized into the 10th Maine Battalion but was not engaged in combat at Gettysburg. His sojourn in Portland was eventful as he took part in the pursuit and capture of a Confederate crew from the Rebel commerce raider *Tacony* which had entered the harbor and pirated the Revenue Cutter *Caleb Cushing*. The Rebels were captured after they abandoned the *Cushing* with Gould witnessing the event.

Gould reenlisted on 16 September 1863, joining the 29th Maine Veteran Volunteer Infantry Regiment in Portland. He was commissioned Regimental Adjutant with the rank of first lieutenant. The 29th was mustered into Federal service on 17 December as a three-year regiment. It took several months to recruit a sufficient number of men so 29th did not ship out until 31 January 1864, heading for New Orleans to serve in the Department of the Gulf. He and his regiment joined their old commander, Major General Nathaniel P. Banks, in his ill-fated Red River Campaign in Louisiana. His regiment shipped back north on 2 July rejoining the Army of the Potomac guarding the Harper's Ferry and Washington, D.C., area as Major General Jubal A. Early menaced the capitol. His regiment was with Major General Philip Sheridan during the battles near Winchester finally forcing Early up the Shenandoah Valley destroying his Army at Cedar Creek on 19 October 1864.

Gould was promoted to major 20 December 1864, as his regiment went into winter quarters near Stephenson's Depot north of Winchester. It remained there until the war ended. He was not with his men as he was seriously ill in hospital at Harper's Ferry. Gould and the 29th Maine marched in the Grand Review in Washington, D.C., on 23 May 1865, but the war was not over for him. He and his regiment would up in Darlington, S.C., for an unpleasant tour of occupation duty. Gould became Provost Judge of part of the state. He abhorred his duty there finally resigning

---

[179] John Mead Gould, *The Civil War Journals of John Mead Gould 1861-1865*, ed. By William B. Jordan, Jr. (Baltimore, MD: Butternut & Blue, 1997), i-ii; "enfilading lines" blog by Randy Buchman http://enfiladinglines.com/2012/01/25/john-mead-gould-report-on-the-mortal-wounding-of-general-mansfield/; and a website dedicated to John Mead Gould created by his great-great-great grandson, which contains much information about Gould and his life, especially during the Civil War, http://www.johnmeadgould.com.

[180] Joining Gould were 698 1st Maine veterans bringing the new regiment to 881, Gould, *Journals*, i.

[181] His regiment reported 173 killed, wounded and missing out of 461 men engaged at Cedar Mountain, *ORA*, vol. 12, pt. 2, 136-138.

effective 18 March 1866, and moved to northeastern South Carolina to make his fortune in the lumber and turpentine industry. His business failed and he returned to Portland in July 1867, leaving unpaid debts behind.

Gould joined the Grand Army of the Republic and became active in veterans' organizations eventually writing the regimental history based on his extensive diaries. He became deeply interested in events surrounding Mansfield's mortal wounding at Antietam and Gould sent many letters and other documents to the Antietam Battlefield Board and Ezra Carman. Most historians have accepted Gould's account, as did Carman, of the events of that day. Gould published a short book in 1895 titled *Joseph K. F. Mansfield, Brigadier General of The U.S. Army: A Narrative of Events Connected With His Mortal Wounding at Antietam, Sharpsburg, Maryland, September 17, 1862.* He was heavily involved in the controversy with the 125th Pennsylvania which claimed that Mansfield had been wounded near that regiment vice the 10th Maine; Gould addressed this controversy at the beginning of his book: "It was bad enough and sad enough that General Mansfield should be mortally wounded once, but to be wounded six, seven or eight times in as many localities is too much of a story to let go unchallenged."[182] Carman generally accepted Gould's accounts and this is of import as Carman was a member of the Antietam National Battlefield Site Board as an historical expert from 12 October 1894 to 17 August 1895, and from 1 August 1897 to 1 December 1897. Carman was the author of a 1,800 page manuscript describing in detail the Maryland Campaign which is regarded as the most authoritative account extant.

Gould was never a wealthy man but did well in banking in Portland, becoming a prominent citizen and raising a family there. He died on 1 January 1930 at his home in Portland at the age of 90, and was buried with his relatives in the Riverside Cemetery, Bethel, Maine.

---

[182] Gould, *Wounding*, 3.

Attachment 9
Telegram from Lieutenant Samuel Mansfield to Benjamin Douglas Relating His Father's Death[183]

THE AMERICAN TELEGRAPH COMPANY.
NORTH, SOUTH, EAST AND WEST,

Connecting with all the Southern, Western, Eastern and Northern Lines of Telegraph.

TERMS AND CONDITIONS ON WHICH THIS AND ALL MESSAGES ARE RECEIVED BY THIS COMPANY FOR TRANSMISSION.

In order to guard against errors or delays in the transmission or delivery of messages, every message of importance ought to be REPEATED by being sent back from the station at which it is to be received to the station from which it is originally sent. Half the usual price for transmission will be charged for repeating the message, and while this Company will, as heretofore, use every precaution to ensure correctness, it will not be responsible for errors or delays in the transmission or delivery of repeated messages beyond FIFTY dollars, unless a special agreement for insurance be made and paid for at the time of sending the message, and the amount of risk specified on this agreement; nor is the Company to be responsible for any error or delay in the transmission or delivery or non-delivery of any unrepeated message, BEYOND FIVE DOLLARS, unless in like manner specially insured and amount of risk paid for at the time. No liability is assumed for any error or neglect by any other Company over whose lines this message may be sent to reach its destination. No liability for any errors in cipher messages.

CAMBRIDGE LIVINGSTON, Sec'y,
145 BROADWAY, N. Y.

E. S. SANFORD, Pres't,
145 BROADWAY, N. Y.

.No.   COMPLAINTS SHOULD BE SENT TO THE SECRETARY.

Dated Washington Sept. 18 1862.

Rec'd, Sept. 18 1862 8 o'clock 35 min. P. M.

To Benj Douglas.

Gen'l Mansfield is dead. He fell Mortally wounded in the charge of yesterday. His body will be sent to Baltimore to be Embalmed.

Lieut Mansfield

---

[183] Image courtesy John Banks's Blog from of the Middlesex County Historical Society.

Attachment 10
Telegram from Captain Clarence Dyer to Mrs. Louisa Mansfield Announcing his Departure from Frederick, MD, with General Mansfield's Remains[184]

THE AMERICAN TELEGRAPH COMPANY.
NORTH, SOUTH, EAST AND WEST,
Connecting with all the Southern, Western, Eastern and Northern Lines of Telegraph.

TERMS AND CONDITIONS ON WHICH THIS AND ALL MESSAGES ARE RECEIVED BY THIS COMPANY FOR TRANSMISSION.

In order to guard against errors or delays in the transmission or delivery of messages, every message of importance ought to be REPEATED by being sent back from the station at which it is to be received to the station from which it is originally sent. Half the usual price for transmission will be charged for repeating the message, and while this Company will, as heretofore, use every precaution to ensure correctness, it will not be responsible for errors or delays in the transmission or delivery of repeated messages beyond FIFTY dollars, unless a special agreement for insurance be made and paid for at the time of sending the message, and the amount of risk specified on this agreement; nor is the Company to be responsible for any error or delay in the transmission or delivery or non-delivery of any unrepeated message, BEYOND FIVE DOLLARS, unless in like manner specially insured and amount of risk paid for at the time. No liability is assumed for any error or neglect by any other Company over whose lines this message may be sent to reach its destination. No liability for any errors in cipher messages.

CAMBRIDGE LIVINGSTON, Sec'y,
145 BROADWAY, N. Y.

E. S. SANFORD, Pres't,
145 BROADWAY, N. Y.

.Vo.   COMPLAINTS SHOULD BE SENT TO THE SECRETARY.

Dated *Frederick Md Sept 19* 1862.

Rec'D, *Sept 19th* 1862 o'clock. *10* min. *A.*M.

To *Mrs. Mansfield*

I leave here today with the remains of the General.

Capt C. H. Dyer.

---

[184] Image courtesy John Banks's Blog from of the Middlesex County Historical Society.

Attachment 11
Receipt from John Weaver to Lieutenant Samuel Mansfield for General Mansfield's Coffin[185]

[185] Image courtesy John Banks's Blog from the Middlesex County Historical Society.

Attachment 12
Letter from Captain Dyer certifying to the Army Mansfield's horse and equipment losses at Antietam.

In Camp in Rear of Vicksburg, Miss.
June 7th 1863.

I certify, on honor, that at the battle of Antietam, Md., September 17th 1862, Brig. General J. K. F. Mansfield, had a horse killed.

The horse was purchased from Lieut. Col. Charles G. Sawtelle, Asst. Qr. Mr., at, or near Perryville, Penn, in January or February, 1862. price paid $, transportation to Newport News, $10⁹⁰.

I also certify that the following equipments were lost at same time, viz: One Saddle $18⁰⁰, One Bridle $4⁵⁰, one Blanket $2³⁵, One Halter $2¹²/₁₀, One Field Glass $20; Making a total loss, horse and equipments, $

The horse was a strawberry roan; between 15 and 16 hands high; six years old, dark mane and tail.

The above is the nearest and best evidence of which the case is susceptible, as Brig. Gen. Mansfield, was mortally wounded in said battle, and died the next day, and Maj. Gen. E. V. Sumner, his immediate commanding officer, is since dead.

I certify on honor that the above statement is correct in all its particulars to my personal knowledge.

C. H. Dyer
Capt. & A. A. Genl. U.S.V.

Courtesy of the Middlesex County Historical Society from John Banks Civil War Blog, Monday, Jan. 16, 2012, used with permission. Banks wrote that the amount for the horse was $105 or $115 as found in another letter.

Chapter 11

Mansfield Goes Home

Do you know the story well?
How the dauntless Mansfield fell.
With his reverend locks of snow,
Flowing round his warrior brow.

Where the famous East Woods stood.
Where the ground was drenched with blood;
There the gallant Mansfield lay,
On that fair autumnal day.

See, his life blood's ebbing fast!
Now his soul has breathed its last!
Far above you starry height.
That brave spirit winged its flight.[1]

THE OLD WARRIOR RETURNED TO REST IN HIS HOMETOWN, 45 years after leaving at age 13 in 1817, to put on the uniform of a West Point cadet. Had he scripted his death, he could not have done better than what fate provided: dying in battle leading his troops in a desperate fight, in the most important battle of the Civil War. Augustus Woodbury wrote: "Among our losses [at Antietam] were those of officers whom we could ill afford to lose. Major

---

[1] John P. Smith, "Reminiscences of Antietam Field," *Hagerstown Morning Herald*, 29 March 1901.

General Joseph K.F. Mansfield, the commander of the twelfth corps, was....unsurpassed for his skill and thoroughness as an engineer, and was remarkable for the manly simplicity and the bravery of his character. Highly esteemed by the army, his death was deeply lamented. But he died, as he would have desired, in the full possession of all his military faculties, and in the course of the faithful discharge of his duty."[2] Of the many encomiums given at his funeral, perhaps none could surpass the one sentence in the 27 September 1862 diary entry of a participant of the Battle of Antietam who had witnessed Mansfield's mortal wounding: "Had general Mansfield survived we would have followed him into the jaws of death."[3]

Shortly after 8 a.m. on Thursday, September 18, the veteran general died. His body was placed in a "rough box," loaded into an ambulance, and was probably taken from the Line Farm via the Smoketown and Keedysville Roads to the Boonsboro Pike, and then on the National Pike to Monocacy Junction near Frederick, Maryland. Soldiers of Major General Andrew A. Humphreys' V Corps, who were hurriedly marching through Boonsboro to reinforce McClellan at Sharpsburg on that day, remarked on the numbers of ambulances carrying wounded to the rear. Then they saw one carrying Mansfield's body halted by the roadside.[4] At Monocacy Junction, it was put into a casket to be carried by the Baltimore and Ohio Railroad to Baltimore. There, his son, Samuel, joined Mansfield's faithful aide, Dyer for the trip home to Middletown, Connecticut.[5]

---

[2] Augustus Woodbury, *Major General Ambrose E. Burnside and the Ninth Army Corps: A Narrative of Campaigns in North Carolina, Maryland, Virginia, Ohio, Kentucky, Mississippi and Tennessee, During the War for the Preservation of the Republic* (Providence, RI: Sidney S. Rider & Brother, 1867), 151.

[3] John Mead Gould, *Joseph K.F. Mansfield, Brigadier General of the U.S. Army. A Narrative of Events Connected with His Mortal Wounding at Antietam, Sharpsburg, Maryland, September 17, 1862* (Portland, ME: Stephen Berry, Printer, 1895), 204.

[4] Charles F. McKenna, *Under the Maltese Cross: Antietam to Appomattox* (Pittsburg, PA: The 155th Regimental Association, 1910), 73.

[5] *Memorial of General J.K.F. Mansfield, United States Army, Who Fell in Battle at Sharpsburg, Md., Sept. 17, 1862* (Boston, MA: Press of T.R. Marvin & Son,1862), 16, 56. This 67-page booklet contains primarily addresses given at Mansfield's funeral, 23 September, at the North Church. The addresses, in order, are by Jeremiah Taylor, Ebenezer Jackson, Dixon, and then lastly, Taylor's 34-page oration. Governor Buckingham's address was impromptu, and not recorded. An appendix contains two items, the first, an account of the funeral from the *Hartford Courant*, 24 September 1862, and a tribute from Edward D. Mansfield, the General's cousin, which appeared in the *Cincinnati Gazette*. There is an engraving of General Mansfield in the frontispiece of an original printing of this book which shows him in dress uniform as a brigadier general, but later printings show him as a major general; he was posthumously promoted to that higher rank 12 March 1863 which explains the difference in rank shown in later printings, 53

Benjamin Douglas, Mansfield's nephew, accompanied Mansfield's body from Maryland to Connecticut. Douglas, between 1850 and 1862, served as Mayor of Middletown, a member of the General Assembly, a presidential elector, and as lieutenant governor. In Middletown, he and his brother, William, formed a successful pump manufacturing company; he was a neighbor and friend, as well as a relative of General Mansfield. He married Mary Adeline Parker, General Mansfield's niece, 3 April 1838. *History of Middlesex County, Connecticut, With Biographical Sketches of Its Prominent Men* (New York, NY: J.B. Beers & Co., 1884), 164.

Mansfield's remains arrived in Baltimore about 8 p.m. on Friday, 19 September. There, the casket and attendants were met by an aide to Major General John Ellis Wool with a cavalry detachment, and escorted to an embalmer about a mile from the station. The embalmer found that the body was too decomposed to embalm, so it was placed in an airtight metal casket. Put back on a train, it journeyed to Philadelphia where it was transferred to the Camden & Amboy Railroad to New York City. In New York, Samuel Mansfield, Captain Dyer, and Benjamin Douglas, were met by Colonel John H. Almy, the Connecticut Assistant Quartermaster General, along with an escort, hearse, and carriages, to convey them to the Governor's Room at City Hall, where Mansfield could lie in state for a day to allow New Yorkers to pay last respects. Mansfield's escorts declined this offer because they had already made arrangements to journey to Middletown. Colonel Almy accompanied the remains and friends to New Haven Depot in New York arriving at 7:30 p.m. on Saturday, 20 September. There, they met two men from the Board of Aldermen of New York City who asked that Mansfield's remains be returned to New York's City Hall to lie in state; the offer was again refused. The entourage and Mansfield boarded the New York, New Haven, and Hartford Railroads and journeyed to Meriden arriving at midnight, Sunday, September 21. Finally, the group took carriages to Middletown and arrived there at 3:30 a.m., then placed the coffin in the Town Hall, under guard of a detachment of the Mansfield Guards.[6]

At a special meeting of the Middletown Common Council "called to take action in relation to the death of J.K.F. Mansfield, it was voted: That the following gentlemen be appointed a committee to proceed to New York, and escort the remains of General Mansfield to this city, viz., Hon. E. [Ebenezer] Jackson, His Honor the Mayor [Samuel L. Warner], Alderman [William G.] Hackstaff, and Henry G. Hubbard, Esq. Voted: That Messrs. [Bartlett] Bent, [Benjamin] Douglas,

[6] Courtesy WPL.

G. T. Hubbard, [Edward] Russell, [John N.] Camp, S. [Samuel] C. Hubbard, and E.W.N. Starr be a committee with power to make all necessary and proper arrangements for the funeral of General Mansfield."[7]

In his hometown, he laid in state in the town hall for two days, as Middletown was in mourning for its proudest son. All of the town's prominent citizens as well as thousands of others attended his funeral on 23 September. His funeral was very impressive, unlike the other more than 200 Connecticut burials of Antietam dead, due to its being only the second battle death of a general officer from the small state.[8] Reverend Ebenezer Jackson gave this encomium at the general's funeral: "In social life, modest and unpretending; in all its relations, just and truthful; a brave, accomplished soldier; an earnest patriot, and an humble Christian; his memory will ever be dear to this community, and his name enrolled among those who have most honored their native land." Jackson ended his long speech with a fitting epitaph: "The end of earth, to General Mansfield, has in all respects been worthy of the patriotic, Christian soldier. He died at his post, with all his honors on, his eyes not dimmed, nor his natural force abated."[9]

He was posthumously promoted to major general of volunteers on 12 March 1863, retroactive to 18 July 1862, after being recommended by Lincoln on 5 March 1863. In 1900, the State of Connecticut and the Grand Army of the Republic, a Union Civil War veterans' organization, erected a monument to Mansfield at the East Woods on Mansfield Road, near the intersection of the Smoketown Road near where he fell. His home on Main Street in Middletown, the General Mansfield House, now appropriately hosts the Middlesex County Historical Society which possesses many of his papers and artifacts. He is buried in the Indian Hill Cemetery in Middletown (corner of Washington and Vine streets) having been moved in 1867 after his initial burial in the Mortimer Cemetery.[10]

A Middletown newspaper, *The Constitution*, published a lengthy article about the hometown hero and his funeral:

DEATH OF GENERAL MANSFIELD[11]

General Mansfield is dead. He fell at the battle of Sharpsburg, on Wednesday morning last, while fighting bravely at the head of his corps.

Connecticut has lost one of her noblest sons and Middletown one of her most honored citizens. We know of no one whose death would cause a wider or deeper sorrow than that of General Mansfield. It is not so much on account of his high standing in his profession and the honors which the country have heaped upon him, as on account of his pre-eminent social and domestic virtues that he commanded the confidence and love of this whole community. Munificent in his charities, ready to every good work, unsuspicious in his character, kind and sympathetic towards the humblest, he was a man whom hundreds in this place have blest for his goodness, and who in his death will feel that they have lost a friend and father. For very many years we have been intimately acquainted with General Mansfield, and have never ceased to admire him for his true nobility of character, which made him always forgetful of himself and aiming to do good to those around him. No man in Middletown has interested himself more than he in visiting the poor and personally attending to their wants. We hazard nothing in saying that no citizen of this place has contributed so much for the education of youth as he. Objects of charity abroad as well as at home always engaged his interest and received from him a liberal support. He was a consistent and valued member of the North Church, which has in him sustained an incalculable loss.

Of his eminence in his profession it is not necessary that we should here speak. We can add nothing to his high reputation. His name will hold a distinguished place in the history of the country, and will go down to future generations among those of prominent actors in the Mexican war and of the brave chieftains in this momentous struggle. Mansfield will henceforth have a place among the honored heroes of our land.

---

[7] *The History of Middlesex County*, 83. Names verified by Debby Shapiro, Director, Middlesex County Historical Society.

[8] Niven, 322. Mansfield was not the first general officer from Connecticut killed in the Civil War, that honor belonged to Brigadier General Nathaniel Lyon, born in Ashford, who graduated from West Point in 1841. A veteran of the Mexican-American War, he was killed at the Battle of Wilson's Creek, 10 August 1861, the first Union general killed in the war. He lay in state for a day in Cincinnati and three days in New York where 15,000 people visited his coffin; then his remains lay in state in Hartford in the State House Senate Chamber before being transported to Eastford. There, another 15,000 attended his funeral on 5 September 1861, Ashbel Woodward, *Life of General Nathaniel Lyon* (Hartford, CT: Case, Lockwood & Co., 1862), 338-343.

[9] *Memorial of General J.K.F. Mansfield*, 16, 56.

[10] The Mortimer Cemetery was a small cemetery established in 1778, and even though enlarged a few times, was eventually cut off by North Pearl Street, *The History of Middlesex County*, 150.

[11] "Death of Mansfield and His Funeral," *The Constitution*, Wednesday, 24 September 1862, vol. 25, no. 1291, Courtesy of the Middlesex County Historical Society.

Intelligence that he was severely wounded reached here first by the newspapers on Thursday noon. In the course of the afternoon the report was confirmed by a telegraphic dispatch. About five o'clock another dispatch announced that he was dead. His wife and children are thus at once thrown into a state of the deepest affliction. His son, Lieut. Mansfield, had left for Washington the week previous.

The body of General Mansfield reached this city on Sunday morning having come to Meriden by the midnight train. It was in charge of Ex-Lieut. Gov. Douglas, nephew of the General, Lieut. Mansfield his son, and Captain Dyer his Aid. The several railroad companies passed the body and all having charge of it free of expense. It was at first taken to his late residence, but soon after removed to the Town Hall where it remained during Sunday, the Home Guard having been detailed to guard the remains. The body had not been embalmed, and was not exposed to view. It was enclosed in a handsome metallic case. On Sunday evening it was removed to the North Church, and placed at the east end of the centre aisle. The church was draped in black, and the family pew was covered with black cloth. Around the body the National Flag hung in festoons. On the coffin were two beautiful bouquets of white flowers. In front of the church were hung two life-like pictures of the honored dead. One was taken within a year and the other some time previous to the war. Here the body has remained in state, until the present time just previous to the funeral. It is in charge of the Home Guard.

It appears that General Mansfield did not die immediately after he was wounded, but lived several hours. He was wounded early in the battle, and was taken to the rear, where he remained perfectly conscious until he died. At first he did not think his wound mortal; and when finally told that he could not live long, he received the announcement with the utmost composure, saying—"It is God's will." Tidings were brought to him from time to time of the progress of the battle, in which he felt a great interest. He lived long enough to know that a victory had been gained by the national arms.

General Mansfield had spent nearly his whole life in the public service. He was a native of this city. His age was 58 years. He entered West Point Academy, having been appointed from this state, in October 1817, and passed through the regular course of studies in that institution. He entered the service of the Government on the 1st of July 1822, as a second lieutenant of engineers, and afterwards rose to higher position, as his merits became appreciated. In March 1832, he was made first lieutenant, and in July 1832, became captain. During the Mexican war (in 1846-7) he rose to the position of chief engineer of the army under General Taylor. He was brevetted major for gallant and distinguished services in defense of Fort Brown, May 9, 1846. In the storming of Monterey he received no less than seven wounds, several of which were most severe; and for gallant and meritorious conduct in those conflicts he was honored with the rank of lieutenant colonel. His gallantry at Buena Vista won him his colonelcy.

In the war for the Union his services, however, have been equally conspicuous, and they are still so fresh in the public memory that it is needless to recount them here. On the 14th of May 1861, he was commissioned a brigadier general in the regular army, in recognition of his distinguished worth, and his subsequent career, down to the day when he sacrificed his life to his zeal for the cause, is a noble testimony that the trust reposed in him by the Government was not misplaced. The death of General Mansfield is a serious loss not to his immediate command alone, but to the war bureau, and to the whole country.

THE FUNERAL

Is attended this afternoon at half past two o'clock. Business in the city is suspended, and all unite in honoring the memory of the lamented dead. The military display exceeds anything ever before seen here. The following is the order of exercises.

The funeral exercises of the lamented General Mansfield, will take place in this city, on Tuesday, Sept. 23d inst., by a prayer at the late residence of the deceased at 2 o'clock, P. M., after which the family and relatives will proceed to the North Church, where the principal exercises will take place. The procession will be formed in the following order:

Putnam Phalanx of Hartford, Major Stillman.

Governor's Foot Guard of New Haven, Major Norton.

City Guard of Hartford, Captain Prentiss.

Governor's Horse Guard of New Haven, Major Ingersoll.

Governor's Horse Guard of Hartford, Major Watrous.

BAND

The Hearse escorted by the Mansfield Guard.

Aides of General Mansfield.

Body Servant and Horse.

Family and Relatives in carriages.

Committee of Arrangements.

Mayor, Aldermen and Common Council.

Town Authorities.

Gov. Buckingham and Staff.

Major General Russell and Staff.

Officers of the Army and Navy.

Military Officers off duty.

Mayors and Common Councils of the several cities.

Strangers.

Reverend Clergy.

Members of the Bar.

Medical Faculty.

Faculty and Students Wesleyan University.

Professors and Students Berkley Divinity School.

Board of Education.

Public Schools.

Private Schools.

Odd Fellows Society.

St. John's Society.

Fire Department.

Citizens generally.

The military will be formed with the right resting up Main street, the left opposite the church. The Body will be received by the "Mansfield Guard," acting as a Guard of honor and escorted up the line to the right and countermarched. The Military will then be broken into column, left in front, and move down Main street, the rear halting at the intersection of College street, when the family, relatives and remainder of the procession will be assigned their places as above stated. The several bells will be tolled and minute guns fired when the procession moves. The procession will pass around Union Park and up Main street to the Mortimer Cemetery. Three vollies will be fired over the grave after the concluding exercises. All stores are requested to be closed after 9 o'clock, A.M.

By order of the

COMMITTEE OF ARRANGEMENTS

Postscript—Wednesday morning.

We have delayed a part of our edition on account of the funeral. The military companies from abroad came in on a special train and reached here about one o'clock. All the companies mentioned in the programme above were present. The Mansfield Guard of this city, Captain J.N. Camp, was on duty. The Military display was of the most magnificent kind, rank and file numbering not less than 500 men. After brief exercises at the late residence of the deceased, the friends proceeded in carriages to the North Church. Seats were arranged for them in the porch of the church, around the coffin. The metallic burial case had been enclosed in a handsome wood coffin, on the top of which were laid wreaths of flowers. The sword, sash, and the hat worn by the General in the battle were placed on the coffin. The services at the church consisted of music by the choir, and an address and prayer by the pastor, Rev. Mr. Taylor, after which short addresses were given commemorative of the virtues of the deceased by Hon. Ebenezer Jackson, Senator [James] Dixon and Gov. Buckingham. The body was then placed in the hearse, the Mansfield Guard acting as a guard of honor. The procession was formed according to the published programme under the direction of General Starr, and proceeded around Union Park up Main street to Mortimer Cemetery. It was very long, and reached from Mortimer Cemetery to William street. At the grave the services were brief. A few remarks were made and a prayer offered by the Rev. Mr. Dudley, when three vollies were fired over the grave, and the remains of the honored and lamented Mansfield were left to their last repose.

Besides Gov. Buckingham and Senator Dixon already mentioned, there were present from abroad Major General Russell, the Mayor and Common Council of Hartford, and many other gentlemen of note in this and other states. The wife of General McClellan was present at the funeral.

There was a dense crowd in Main street during the afternoon, and every available window fronting the street, and the tops of the houses were occupied by interested spectators. Flags were displayed at half mast. Many of the stores, the public buildings, and some private dwellings were appropriately draped for the occasion. The Young Ladies' Seminary in Broad street, which was under the especial patronage of General Mansfield and was founded by his liberality, was dressed in the most beautiful and becoming manner.[12] During the passage of the procession the bells were tolled, and minute guns were fired. The funeral services at the grave were concluded at sundown.

Refreshment tables were spread in McDonough Hall for the accommodation of those from abroad. Three hundred could partake of refreshments at a time. Hundreds resorted to the hall during the afternoon. It is proof of the liberality of our citizens, and especially of the ladies, that at night large quantities of provisions yet remained untouched.

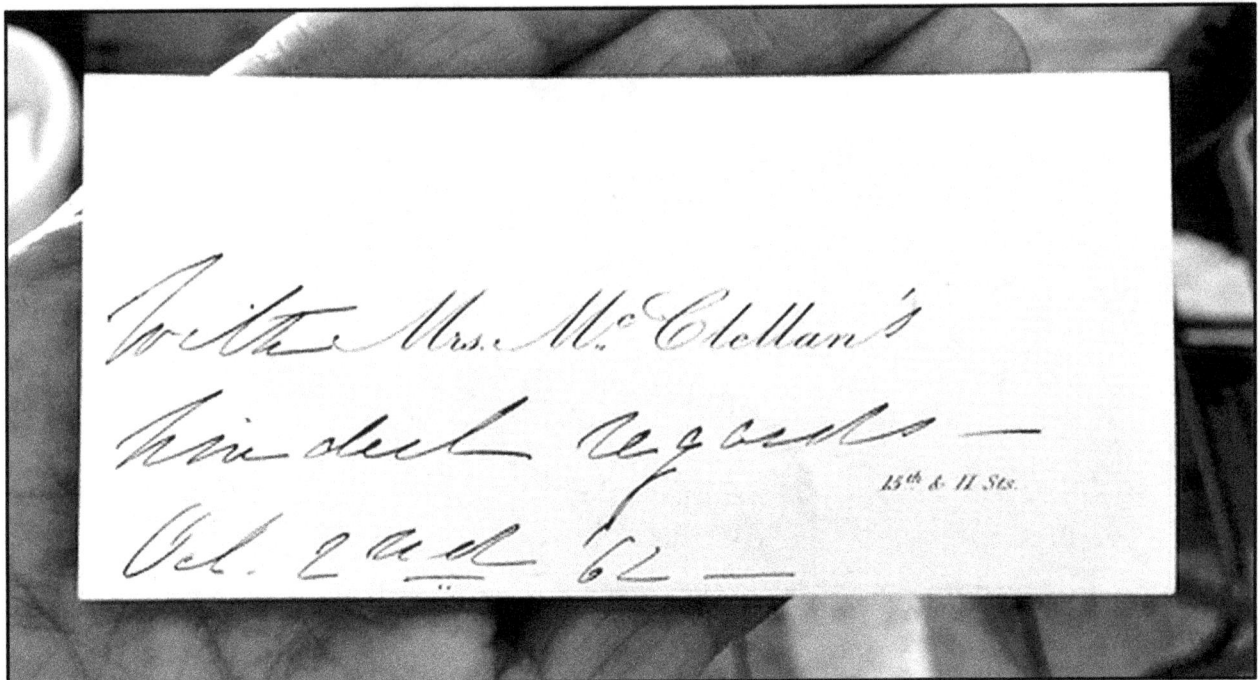

Calling card from Mrs. George B. McClellan. Courtesy of the Middlesex County Historical Society.

---

[12] The Young Ladies' Seminary was successor to The Middletown Female Seminary. The Seminary began in 1840 opened by Dr. Daniel H. Chase; it continued to 1848. Then in 1850, it reopened then operated by Rev. Josiah Brewer and was described as "a school of more than ordinary facilities for furnishing a complete education for young ladies. It was discontinued in 1856. Soon afterward, a similar school was opened by Miss Maria Payne in "a new brick building erected on Broad Street near William [Street] by General J.K.F. Mansfield." It closed about 1870, Beers, *History of Middlesex County*, 132. Mansfield's house was near the intersection of William Street and Main Street, one block from Broad and William Street.

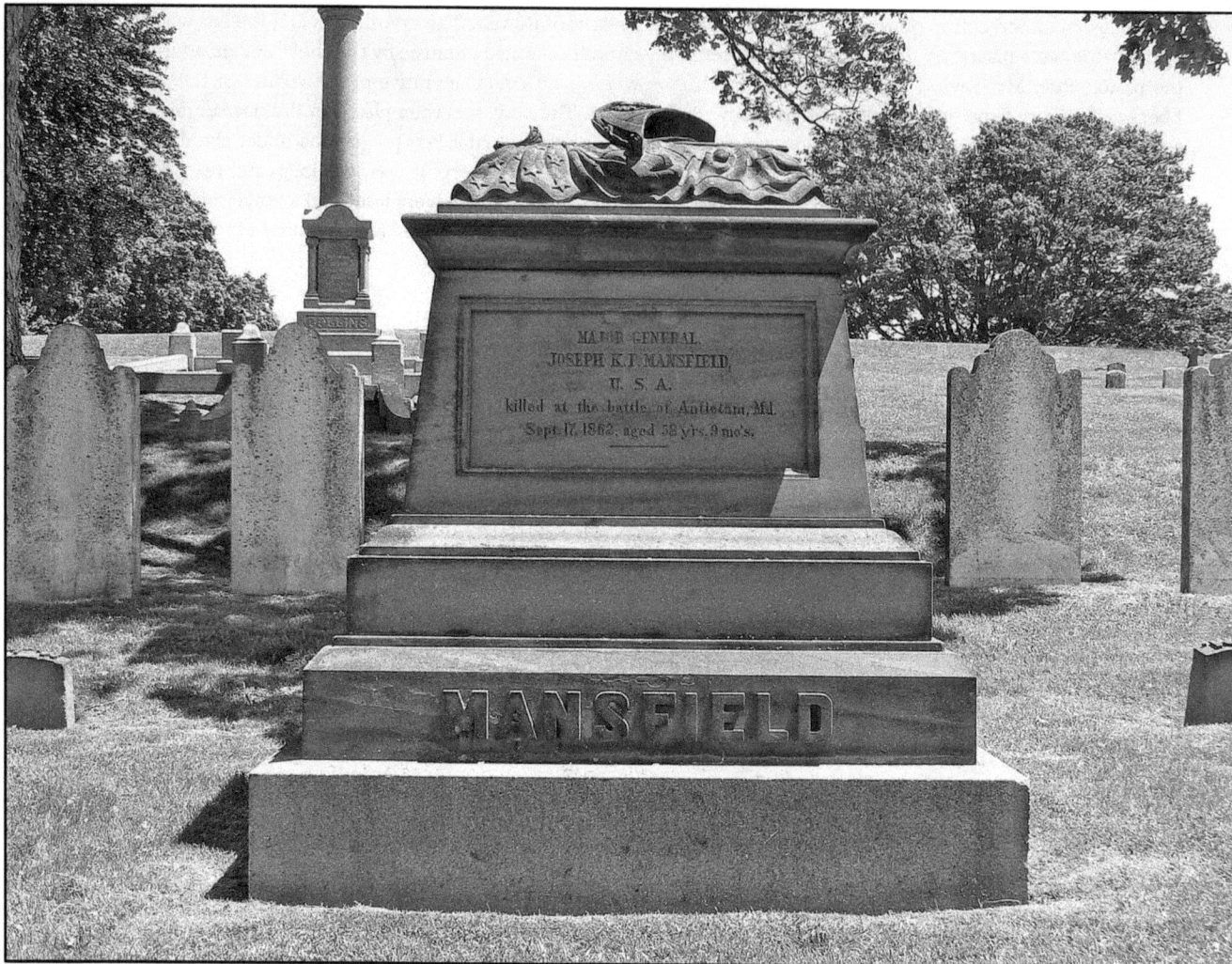

Mansfield's tombstone in Indian Hills Cemetery, Middletown, Connecticut. It is topped by a carving of a U.S. flag, a sword, and a dress hat. Unfortunately, the sword blade is broken off. Courtesy Dave Pelland.

Another view of Mansfield's tombstone. Courtesy Dave Pelland.

Inscriptions on the tombstone panels:

MAJOR GENERAL
JOSEPH K.F. MANSFIELD,
U.S.A.
killed at the battle of Antietam, Md.
Sept. 17, 1862; aged 58 y'rs. 9 mo's.

South:

MARY LOUISA,
daughter of
Jos. K.F. and Louisa M.
Mansfield,
died June 22, 1863:
aged 22 y'rs. & 3 mo's

East:

LOUISA MATHER,
WIFE OF
JOSEPH K.F. MANSFIELD
Born June 14, 1808,

Died Feb. 22, 1880
Blessed are the dead which die in the Lord.
North:

JOSEPH TOTTEN, son of
Jos. K.F. and Louisa M.
Mansfield,
died July 15, 1844;
aged 9 mo's. & 11 days.

"The Mansfield Monument"
"Final Report of the Committee in Charge of the Memorial"[13]

The committee on the monument to General J.K.F. Mansfield, which was dedicated on the battlefield of Antietam, May 24, 1900, has presented its final report to those interested in the project and to Mansfield Post No. 53, G.A. R. of Middletown. The report gives in detail the work performed by the committee and contains a description of the monument and an account of the dedicatory exercise on the battlefield. The cost of the site was $105, and as $150 was received for that purpose, a balance of $45 was left over for the improvement of the lot.

The cost of the monument was $1,000, which sum was appropriated for the purpose by the State of Connecticut. After the monument had been dedicated it was found that it had been placed several feet away from the spot where it should have been. Later it was decided to relocate and that has been done. The monument now stands back of a ledge of rocks which rises a little above the surface of the ground and forms a natural barrier, protecting the memorial against the encroachments of passing teams.

The total cost of making the change and of improving the location was $137.74. This sum was raised by the balance of $45 from the monument fund; $49.74 from the excursion fund and by subscriptions of $43 from members of the excursion party. In its location the monument is conspicuous from that portion of Antietam battlefield which was the scene of operations of the Twelfth Army Corps.

The report of the committee closes with a brief account of the excursion to Antietam and with an expression of thanks to Quartermaster General George B. Newton for assistance given by him. The members of the committee from Mansfield Post were Major John C. Broatch and A.R. Crittenden of the Fourteenth Regiment and R.W. Burke of the Eighth Regiment.

---

[13] *Hartford Courant* 22 July 1901, courtesy of the Middlesex County Society Historical Society.

Mansfield Post
No. 53,
Dept. of Conn., G. A. R.

DEDICATION
OF THE
GENERAL MANSFIELD
MONUMENT,
Antietam, May 24th,
1900.

There were several G.A.R posts apparently named after Mansfield in addition to Middletown, Connecticut: Mansfield, Arkansas, Post 100; Red Bluff, California, Post 75; Keedysville, Maryland, Post 75; Brooklyn, New York, Post 35; Mansfield, Illinois, Post 357; Hawarden, Iowa, Post 159; Ayersville, Missouri, Post 181; Palmyra, Nebraska, Post 54; Bayonne, New Jersey, Post 22; Mansfield, Pennsylvania, Post 48; and Hermosa, South Dakota, Post 129. Albert E. Smith, Jr., "The Grand Army of the Republic and Kindred Societies: A Guide to Resources in the General Collections of the Library of Congress." Item courtesy WPL.

Mansfield monument at Antietam, east corner of Smoketown Road and Mansfield Road, photograph looking northwest. Mansfield Road did not exist at the time of the battle. Of the six generals on both sides who were killed or mortally wounded on 17 September, Mansfield is the only one honored with a monument in addition to a mortuary cannon. Mansfield was shot about 150 yards northwest of this location. The monument was dedicated on 23 May 1900. "A 5' square limestone base supports a smooth, square, granite pedestal decorated with swags, text, a bronze star on the west elevation and a bronze plaque Connecticut State Seal on its east elevation. A smooth granite column topped with a capital and sphere extends from the pedestal. The entire monument stands approximately 30 feet tall. The text on the south side of the pedestal reads: "MANSFIELD MONUMENT/ ERECTED BY THE/ STATE OF CONNECTICUT/ A.D. – 1900/ UNDER THE AUSPICES OF/ MANSFIELD POST NO. 53/ DEPARTMENT OF CONNECTICUT." The text on the north elevation of the pedestal reads: "THE SPOT WHERE/ GEN. MANSFIELD FELL IS A FEW YARDS/ EASTERLY FROM THIS MONUMENT/ BORN DECEMBER 22, 1803/ KILLED SEPTEMBER 17, 1862. The west side is inscribed with: "MAJOR GENERAL/ JOSEPH K. F. MANSFIELD/ COMMANDING THE 12TH CORPS/ARMY OF THE POTOMAC/ MORTALLY WOUNDED NEAR THIS SPOT/ SEPTEMBER 17, 1862/ ABOUT 7:35 A.M./ WHILE DEPLOYING HIS CORPS/IN ACTION/ MANSFIELD." NPS, List of Classified Structures.

Most sources show it was dedicated on 24 May 1900. The original bronze State Seal of Connecticut plaque was replaced on 13 September 2002, as the original had been stolen. A reenactment and historic preservation organization, Company G, 14th Regiment, Connecticut Volunteer Infantry, 1862-1865, Inc., led the effort to design and replace the plaque. Samuel Poffenberger's fields are to the rear of this photograph which was taken facing north. Note the street signs showing the intersection of Mansfield Road and Smoketown Road. Courtesy Dave Pelland.

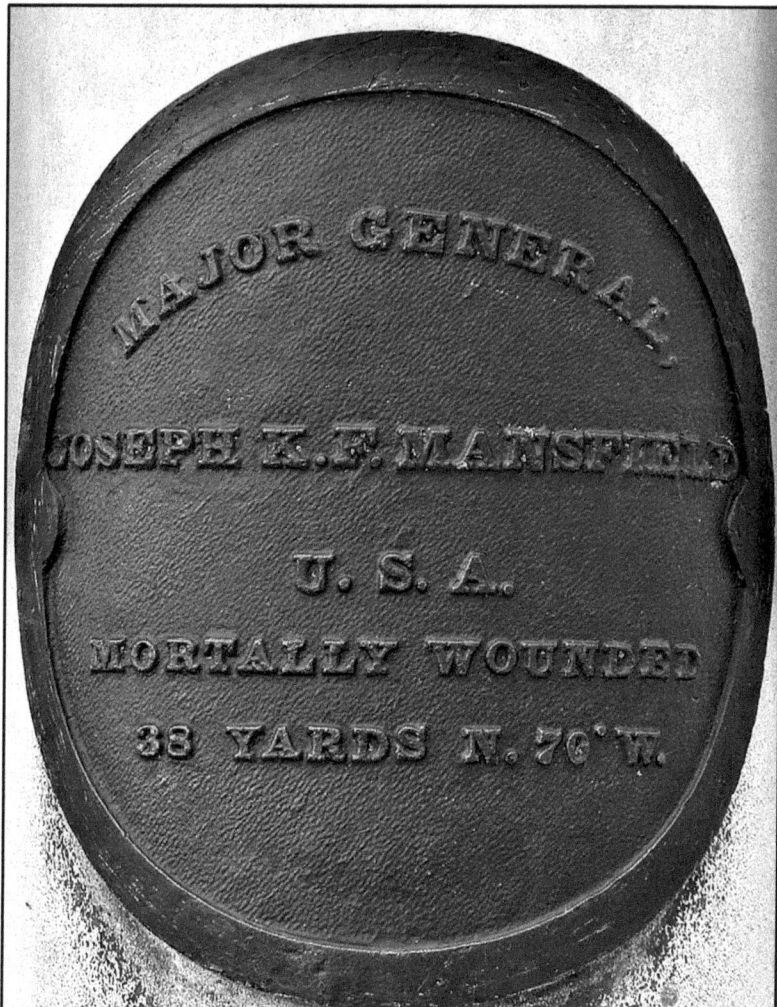

Detail of plaque on Mansfield's mortuary cannon on Mansfield Road, Sharpsburg, Maryland. Courtesy Dave Pelland.

Mansfield monuments at Antietam, photograph facing east. Mansfield Road did not exist during the battle. The East Woods behind and to the right of the monuments have not been replanted as this area is privately owned. Courtesy Dave Pelland.

Mansfield monuments at Antietam, photograph facing west. Courtesy Dave Pelland.

Attachment 1
Henry Mansfield Letter to Captain George Nye of the 10th Maine

Letter to Captain George Nye of the 10th Maine who sent General Mansfield's hat to his nephew, Henry, in 1863. Henry sent a new Mansfield & Lamb sword to Nye as a thank you gift. It is curious that Nye did not return it to General Mansfield's son, Samuel, who was still in the army except that it was easier to send it to a fixed address instead of to an officer in the field. Letter courtesy Nicholas Picerno Collection.

Attachment 2
Tributes to Mansfield

A town in Texas was named for him after the Mexican-American War. A trader, John Young, moved to the north side of the Rio Grande to avoid high Mexican tariffs. Young founded a town he named in honor of Mansfield upstream from Brownsville, Texas, at Magnolia Bend. It was near a ford across from the Mexican ranches of Ramireno and Las Rucias, one mile west of Brownsville by land, and three miles by river. The town was originally planned by Asa Wheeler who was the owner of the Washington House grocery and restaurant in Matamoros. He built a warehouse but the little town never developed because of competition from nearby small towns and from Brownsville. Brownsville replaced Matamoros as the leading trade center for this area of northern Mexico when merchants on both sides of the border recognized the advantage of shipping goods to Brownsville and then smuggling them south across the Rio Grande to avoid paying high Mexican tariffs.[14]

Fort Mansfield, Washington, D.C., was a connector fort, now vanished, and built as part of an advanced line of forts to the northeast of Washington, protecting the Receiving Reservoir to its south. It was built in in late 1862 and mounted one 8" siege howitzer, four 4½" rifles, two 12-pounder howitzers, and four 12-pounder James rifles; it had two vacant positions. Mansfield Battery was built in 1864 in response to General Jubal Early's raid on Washington but its two-gun battery was never mounted.[15]

---

[14] Mary Margaret McAllen Amberson, James A. McAllen, Margaret H. McAllen, *I Would Rather Sleep in Texas: A History of the Lower Rio Grande Valley and the People of the Santa Anita Land Grant* (Austin, TX: Texas State Historical Assn., 2003), 128-129. The current Mansfield, Texas, is not the one which was established on the Rio Grande, but is located near Fort Worth; it grew up around the Ralph S. Man and Julian Feild mill, and took on the name of "Mansfeild", a combination of the names of the founders. Repeated misspellings over the years resulted in the acceptance of the conventional spelling of "Mansfield." The town incorporated in 1909. Mansfield wrote to his wife on 20 August 1847 about the town: "I understand they have laid out a city on the American side opposite Matamoros and called it Mansfield after me;" courtesy WPL.

[15] Benjamin Franklin Cooling, III and Walton H. Owen, II, *Mr. Lincoln's Forts: A Guide to the Civil War Defenses of Washington* (Lanham, MD: The Scarecrow Press, Inc., 2010), 149-150. Batteries were built between forts along with lunettes and redoubts to provide better coverage of the intervening space between the forts.

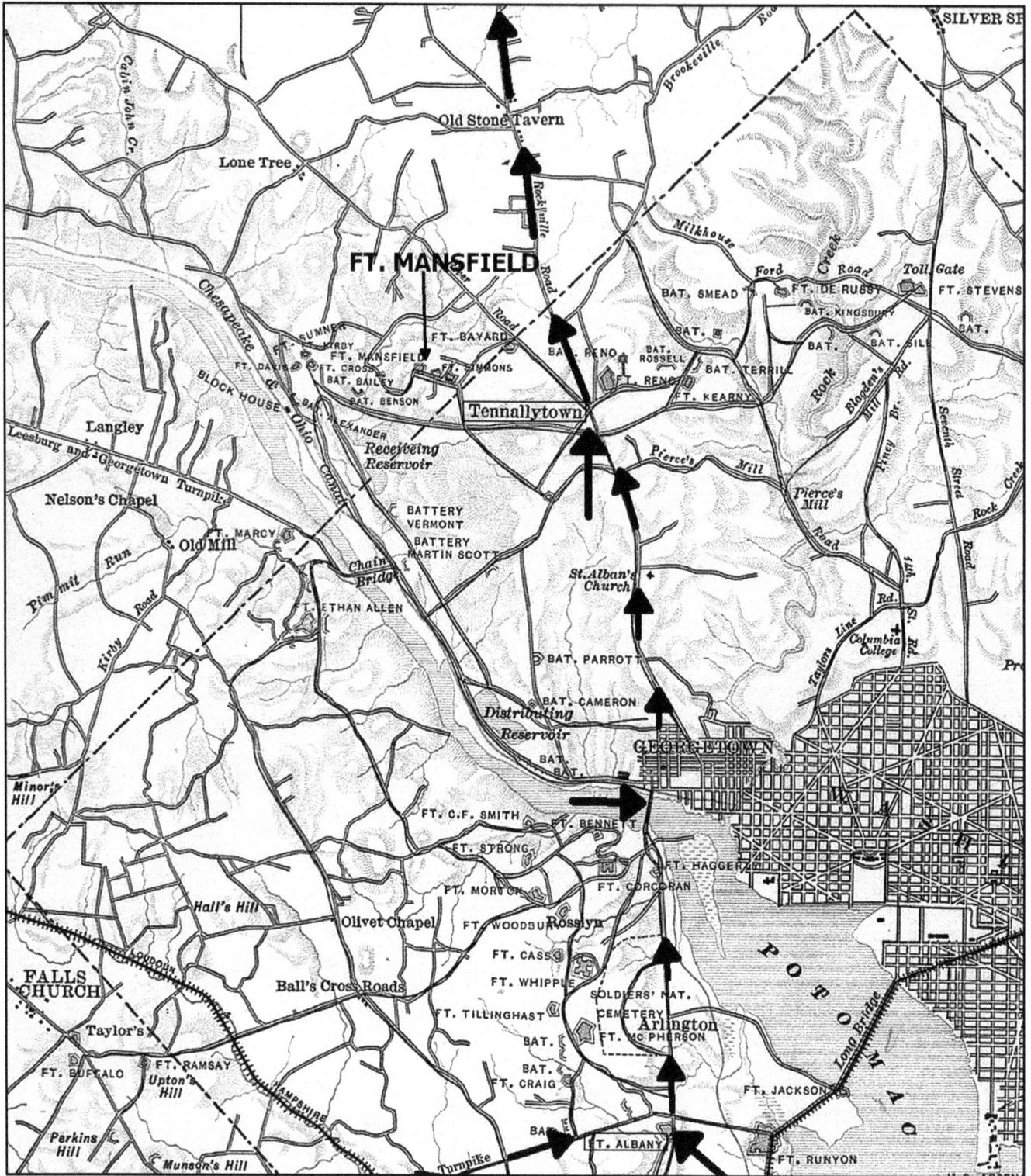

Location of Fort Mansfield on 1865 map also showing the route Mansfield took on his last ride 13 September 1862 from Washington to join the Army of the Potomac near Frederick, Maryland. Courtesy NPS.

Camp Mansfield in Apache County, Arizona, was named after Mansfield. It was about seven miles south of Fort Defiance and was a temporary camp apparently used during Colonel Kit Carson's Navajo Campaign in the summer of 1863.[16]

---

[16] Robert B. Roberts, *Encyclopedia of Historic Forts: The Military, Pioneer, and Trading Posts of the United States* (New York, NY: Macmillan Publishing Company, 1988), 42.

Union troops occupied Suffolk, Virginia, in 1862 and built a ring of earthworks around the city which were then destroyed when they relocated to Portsmouth in June 1863. They included several forts named after famous Union generals including Battery Mansfield, a smaller work, on the Nansemond River. There was also a Mansfield Camp, Virginia, located at Deep Creek, about 10 miles from Norfolk, at which Union forces were stationed in 1862 and 1863. [17]

Ruins of Battery Wooster at Fort Mansfield, an Endicott Period coastal artillery fort, located at the end of Napatree Point, a long barrier beach, in the village of Watch Hill in Westerly, Rhode Island. Construction of the fort began in 1898 and finally consisted of 27 buildings. When the fort was first manned in 1901, it was considered a sub-post of Fort Trumbull in New London, Connecticut, but when fully manned in 1902, its status changed to an independent battery. The fort's armaments consisted of two Crozier 8-inch disappearing guns, plus several rapid-fire 5-inch cannon, and were divided among three batteries, manned by one company of about 140 men. War games held in 1907 proved the fort had a fatal flaw: an attacking vessel could approach the fort from a "dead angle" along the Rhode Island coast which its cannon did not cover. Because of this, the fort was removed from the list of active coastal artillery posts in 1909, and early in WWI, all guns were removed and sent to other installations. By 1916, only six men manned the post. In 1926, the land was put up for sale, and was sold in 1928. Napatree Point is now a wildlife preserve and public beach protected by the Watch Hill Conservancy and Fire District. Courtesy Wikipedia.

---

[17] Heitman, vol. 2, 522; Ron Field, *American Civil War Fortifications (2): Land and Field Fortifications* (New York: NY: Osprey Publishing, 2005), 37.

Courtesy NARA.

Attachment 3
Connecticut Mansfield Guards

In 1847, Elihu William Nathan Starr organized and commanded the 7th Light Infantry Company of the 6th Regiment, named for then Colonel Joseph Mansfield, Starr's friend. Starr had joined the state militia in 1830. Starr was elected colonel of the regiment in 1853. In 1861, the state legislature deactivated the old guard units and created a new state militia of one division. The old militia units became ceremonial organizations and no longer underwent military training.

The Guards became Company A of the 2nd Regiment Connecticut Volunteers, and on 9 May 1861, with the other companies of the regiment, the 79 men and officers left for Washington, D.C. Captain David Dickerson was in command of the Middletown men in Company A. Colonel Alfred H. Terry was the regimental commander. Most of the company enlisted on 20 April 1861 and were mustered in on 7 May 1861, in Brewster Park, New Haven. These 90-day-men were mustered out on 7 August 1861. Subsequently, 31of these reenlisted for active duty.

Their short period of service was eventful. The regiment boarded the steamer *Cahawba* and reached Washington, D.C., on 14 May, after first stopping at Fort Monroe. It camped at Meridian Hill, Camp Corcoran, until it crossed Long Bridge over the Potomac on 16 June. It was initially attached to Mansfield's Department of Washington command to June 1861. The next day, it was ordered to support Colonel McCook's Ohio regiment which had been attacked at Vienna Station. Arriving too late to help, it continued to march to Taylor's Tavern on Oak Hill, near Falls Church. There, along with other Connecticut 90-day men, it formed a camp of instruction. It was brigaded with the 1st and 3rd Connecticut Regiments, the 8th New York, 2nd Maine, and with Tompkin's New York Cavalry and Berrian's New York Battery; Brigadier General Daniel Tyler was in command, in McDowell's Army of Northeastern Virginia. After Tyler was moved up to division command, General E.D. Keyes took over the brigade.

The 2nd Connecticut took part in the Battle of First Bull Run on 21 July and did well despite being green. It lost two killed, 5 wounded, and nine prisoners. In late afternoon, it was ordered to retreat to Centerville Heights and then to the camp at Oak Hill. There it packed up the brigades camps as well those of other brigades which failed to do so, loading much material into wagons and escorted them into Washington. It returned to New Haven and mustered out on 7 August 1861.[18]

Middletown Mansfields Baseball Team

The "Middletown Mansfields" baseball team was organized by Benjamin Douglas Jr., who named the team after his great-uncle General Mansfield. They began playing in 1866, improving steadily until in 1870, the team was voted amateur champions of the state. The club joined the National Association, forerunner to today's National League, for one year in 1872. Going up against the best teams and players in the country, the team was not successful, and folded that year.

---

[18] *Record of Service of Connecticut Men in the Army and Navy of the United States during the War of the Rebellion* (Hartford, CT: Press of The Case, Lockwood & Brainard Company, 1889), 18-21; *ORA*, vol. 2, 354.

Attachment 4
Miscellaneous

Mansfield on U.S. Treasury note

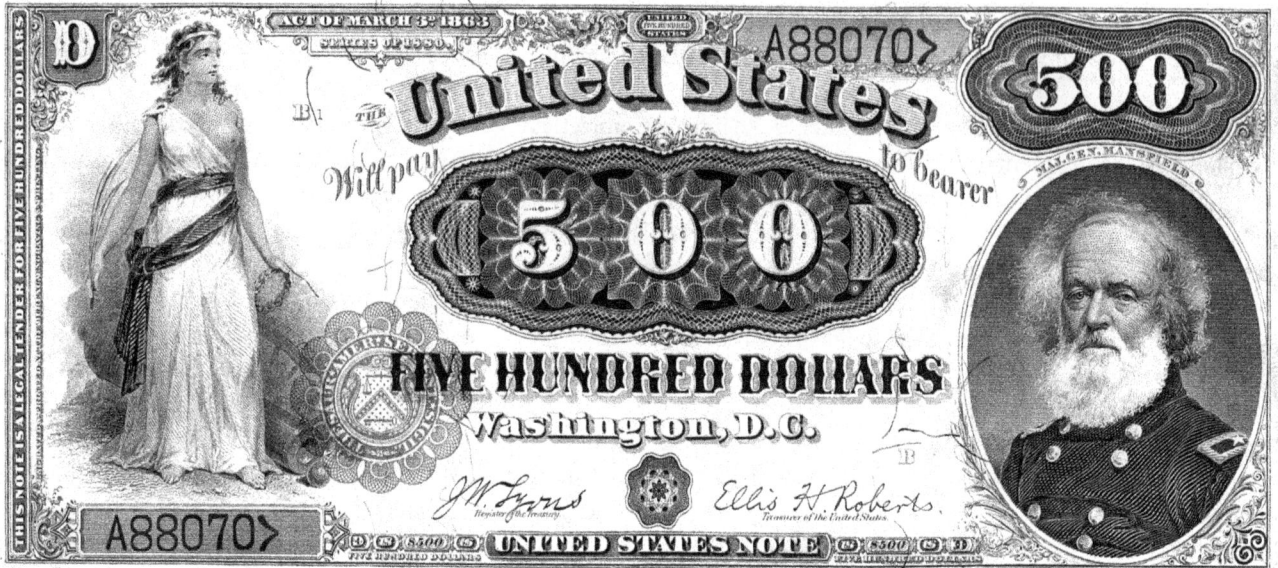

Mansfield honored on an 1880 U.S. Treasury note. Image courtesy Wikipedia.

Mansfield on an Envelope

Envelope showing both McClellan as general in chief and Mansfield as a major general. Courtesy WPL.

Appendix
The II/XII Corps from Cedar Mountain to Frederick
"The corps that never lost a color or a gun."
and
Lee and Pope at Second Bull Run

The XII Corps was the smallest of McClellan's corps at Antietam as it had been decimated at the Battle of Cedar Mountain on 9 August 1862, its only major action before Antietam. After Cedar Mountain, Army of Virginia commander, Major General John Pope, assigned the corps to picket and guard duties so it missed the bloodletting at the Battle of Second Bull Run and Chantilly. Its genesis was as the II Corps of the Army of Virginia, with Major General Nathaniel Prentiss Banks in command.[1] Who were these troops who Mansfield would command for a few short days in September 1862? As will be seen, they were a mixture of veteran troops and several newly-raised regiments which performed better than could have been expected on 17 September at Antietam.

The II Corps was created in the new Army of Virginia 26 June 1862, commanded by Major General John Pope. His new corps was composed of troops from the Mountain, Rappahannock, and Shenandoah Departments; from Banks's Department of the Shenandoah: Brigadier General Alpheus Starkey Williams in command of the First Division which had only two brigades: the First Brigade under Brigadier General Samuel Wylie Crawford and the Third Brigade commanded by Brigadier General George Henry Gordon, because the Second Brigade, under Brigadier General George Lucas Hartsuff, was assigned to the Department of the Rappahannock and was part of Major General Irvin McDowell's III Corps; Hartsuff fought at Cedar Mountain under McDowell in his Second Division as its Third Brigade.

The II Corps' Second Division was initially commanded by Brigadier General James Cooper to 11 July 1862 then by Brigadier General Christopher Columbus Auger. After some reorganization, it ended with its three brigades as follows: First Brigade, Brigadier General John White Geary; Second Brigade, Brigadier General Henry Prince; and the Third Brigade by Brigadier General George Sears Greene.[2]

II Corps
(Major General John Pope)

1st Div. (Brigadier General Alpheus S. Williams)

    1st **Brigade** (Brigadier General Samuel W. Crawford)
    [2nd **Brigade** (Brigadier General George L. Hartsuff)]*
    3rd **Brigade** (Brigadier General George H. Gordon)

2nd Div. (Brigadier General Christopher C. Auger)

    1st **Brigade** (Brigadier General John W. Geary)
    2nd **Brigade** (Brigadier General Henry Prince)
    3rd **Brigade** (Brigadier General George S. Greene)

* Assigned to Major General Irvin McDowell's III Corps

---

[1] Williams was in command of the First Division of the II Corps, Army of Virginia, from 26 June 1862 to 4 Sept; the Corps was changed to the II Corps of the Army of the Potomac and finally to the XII Corps in that army on 12 September, Eicher, 571; Welcher, 342-343.

[2] The First Brigade was organized from the First Brigade, First Division, Dept. of the Shenandoah, and the Third Brigade from the same division's Third Brigade. The First Division had no Second Brigade as it was transferred to the Dept. of the Rappahannock. The Second Division's First Brigade came from the First Brigade, Sigel's Division, Dept. of the Shenandoah. The Second Brigade, initially commanded by Brigadier General John P. Slough to 7 July 1862, was taken over by Brigadier General Gustavus A. Scroggs, then Brigadier General Henry Prince. It was organized from the Second Brigade, Sigel's Division, Department of the Shenandoah. On 2 August 1862, the Second Division underwent extensive reorganization. Brigadier General Erastus B. Tyler's Brigade had arrived and was consolidated with Geary's Brigade and redesignated as the First Brigade commanded by Geary. Cooper's First Brigade became the Second Brigade led by Prince, and a new Third Brigade was organized from the former Second Brigade and assigned to Greene, Welcher, 342, 917. McDowell's III Corps became the I Corps in the Army of the Potomac 12 September 1862 under command of Brigadier General Joseph Hooker who had taken command on 7 September. Hartsuff's brigade became the Third Brigade, Second Division, I Corps, never rejoining its parent division.

Major General John Pope, Army of Virginia commander, shown here as a brigadier general. Courtesy LOC.

This new II Corps under Banks had a tough baptism of fire as it met Major General Thomas J. "Stonewall" Jackson at the Battle of Cedar Mountain, Virginia. Pope had a sound strategic plan to trap Lee's army between himself and McClellan, but General Lee began to receive information as early as 13 August that McClellan was not going to move again on Richmond, so he could turn his attention to the growing Union threat to the north as Pope probed south. Lee moved towards Pope's army which was strung out from Fredericksburg to the Blue Ridge; he first sent Jackson in mid-July to the northwest to Gordonsville with about 14,000 men to guard against a Union incursion on that important railroad junction. In late July, Jackson was reinforced by Major General Ambrose Powell Hill with 10,000 more troops. On the morning of 9 August, Jackson's army crossed the Rapidan River into Culpeper County, led by Major General Richard Stoddard Ewell's division, followed by Brigadier General Charles Sidney Winder's division, with Brigadier General Ambrose P. Hill's division in the rear. Around noon, Brigadier General Jubal Anderson Early's brigade, leading Ewell's division, encountered Federal cavalry and artillery occupying the ridge above Cedar Run, just to the northwest of Cedar Mountain. Early brought up his guns and began an artillery duel. The rest of Ewell's division formed on Early's right, anchored against the northern slope of the mountain and deployed six guns on its ridge. Winder's division formed to Early's left, with Brigadier General William Booth Taliaferro's brigade closest to Early and Colonel Thomas S. Garnett's on the far Confederate left in a wheat field.

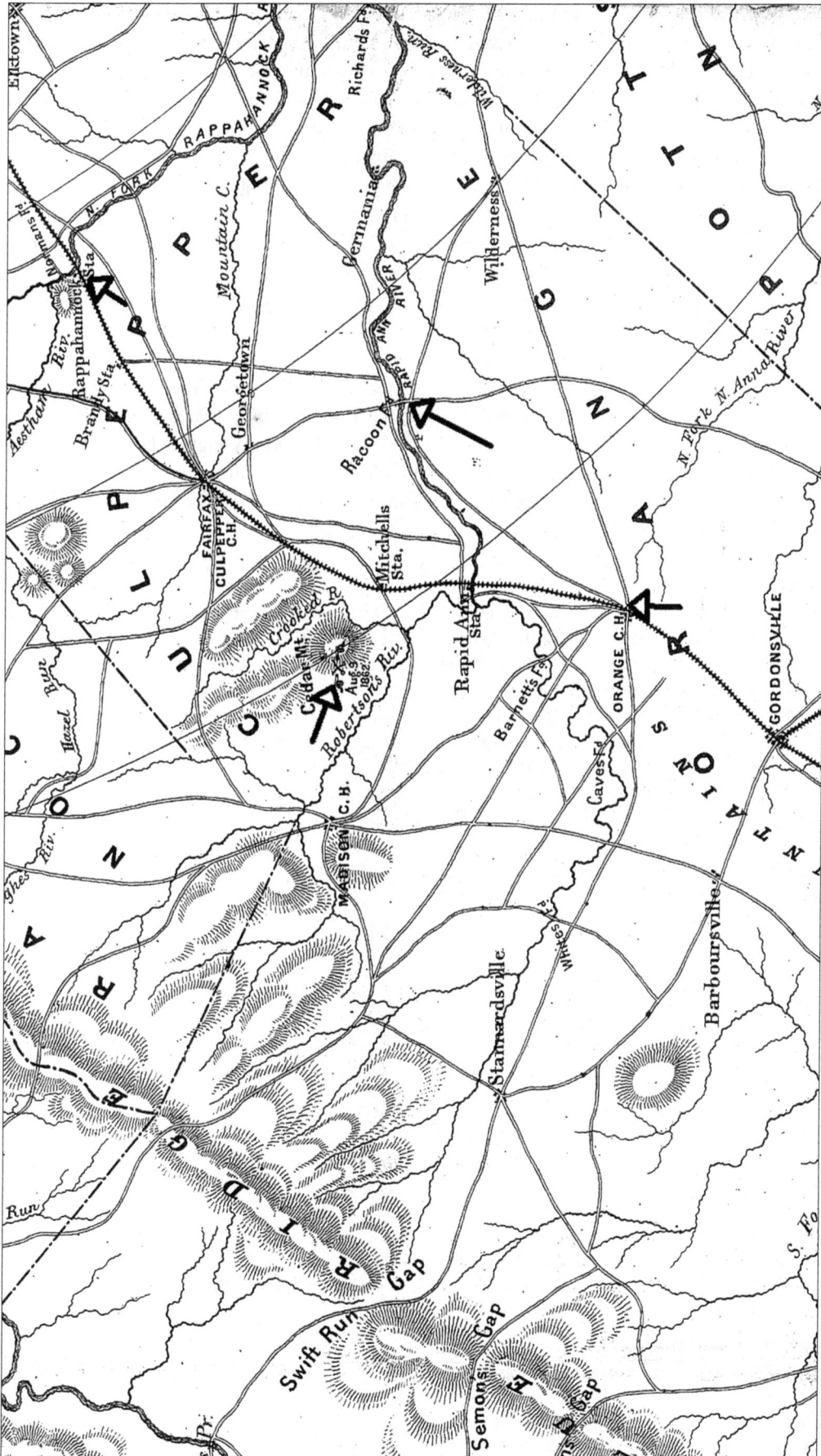

Battle at Cedar (Run) Mountain shown at the upper center at arrow. Orange Court House is at the upper center at arrow. Rappahannock Station at arrow at top right. The Blue Ridge Mountains are to the west. Detail from "New map of the seat of war in Virginia and Maryland" by J. G. Bruff. 1863. Robertson River below and to the left of Cedar Mountain, and Brandy Station is at the upper right. Courtesy LOC. Map following shows details of troop positions. OA, pl. 22, courtesy LOC.

[Side caption, rotated:] Battle at Cedar (Run) Mountain shown at the upper center at arrow. Orange Court House is at the lower center with Gordonsville below it. Raccoon Ford is to the east of Cedar Mountain to the right of Mitchell Station;

The Federals formed a line on a ridge above Cedar Run, with Brigadier General Samuel W. Crawford's brigade on the Union right in a field across from Garnett, and Brigadier General Christopher C. Auger's division on the Union left. Brigadier General John W. Geary's brigade was anchored on the Culpeper-Orange Turnpike opposing Taliaferro, while Brigadier General Henry Prince's brigade formed the far left opposite Ewell. Brigadier General George S. Greene's two regiments were kept in reserve. The Union attack began about 5 p.m. when Geary and Prince were sent against the Confederate right. This bold attack was halted when Early came up to command Rebels on the right. But on the left, Crawford's attack pushed Confederate troops back until Crawford's men were threatening Rebel artillery. Even the famed Stonewall Brigade was pushed aside. Jackson rode up and saved the day for the Rebels as he grabbed a battle flag and rallied the Stonewall Brigade driving back the onrushing Yankees. The Confederate line reformed and General Ambrose P. Hill's troops came up to bolster the line. The Union line collapsed under the weight of these fresh troops and even Greene's reserve brigade could not prevent a rout. Jackson stopped his pursuit at dark as he was unsure about the location of the remainder of Pope's troops. Fighting stopped about 10 p.m.[3]

Banks's corps paid dearly for the gallant fight they made at Cedar Mountain. Total Union casualties were very high: 2,222 for the II Corps of about 7,000 engaged, giving a 32% casualty rate.[4] General Williams reported that "of the three remaining regiments which continued the charge (Twenty-eighth New York, Forty-sixth Pennsylvania, and Fifth Connecticut) every field officer and every adjutant was killed or disabled. In the Twenty-eighth New York every company officer was killed or wounded; in the Forty-sixth Pennsylvania all but 5; in the Fifth Connecticut all but 8." Three regiments of General Crawford's brigade lost every company officer.[5] General Crawford who commanded the First Brigade of the First Division added details:

In the Twenty-eighth New York its colonel (Donnelly) had fallen mortally wounded, and was borne from the field. Lieutenant-Colonel Brown had his arm shattered. Major Cook, after being wounded, was made prisoner by the enemy. Out of the 14 company officers in action there is not one remaining able to do duty. All are either wounded or prisoners. Of the Forty-sixth Pennsylvania its Colonel (Knipe) was twice wounded and carried from the field, Lieutenant Colonel Selfridge had his horse shot under him, and Major Mathews fell dangerously wounded. Of its 20 company officers who went into action 17 were killed, wounded, or missing, and 226 of its rank and file. Of the Fifth Connecticut, Colonel [George] Chapman, Lieutenant-Colonel [Henry] Stone, and Major [Edward] Blake are gone. The first is reported a prisoner in the hands of the enemy. The latter two were seen to fall, and have not since been heard from. Out of 18 company officers who went into action 10 are killed, wounded, or missing, amid 224 of the rank and file. Out of 88 officers and 1,679 men taken by me into action 56 officers and 811 men are killed, wounded, and prisoners.[6]

---

[3] Freiheit, *Boots and Saddles*, 90, 96. Cedar Mountain was also known as Slaughter's Mountain or Cedar Run Mountain. Cedar Run was a small stream on the battlefield while the alternate name, Slaughter's Mountain was named for a nearby family.

[4] Krick's total casualties are 2,222 for II Corps only; total Federal 2,403, Robert K. Krick, *Stonewall Jackson at Cedar Mountain*, hereafter cited as *Stonewall* (Chapel Hill, NC: The University of North Carolina Press, 1990), 372, 376. Casualties include killed, wounded, and missing/captured. See Appendix for the order of battle for the II Corps and casualties at Cedar Mountain. Compare casualties with those shown in *ORA*, vol. 12, pt. 2, 136-139, showing 2,218 compared to Krick's 2,222. Allen shows 9,420 total present for duty in the II Corps at Cedar Mountain including artillery and cavalry escorts, 64. Total brought into battle from Federal *ORA* reports 6,914 which include general officers.

[5] *ORA*, vol. 12, pt. 2, 147.

[6] *ORA*, vol. 12, pt. 2, 151-152. Chapman and Stone were captured, Blake was killed. One historian wrote that only three officers were available in the 5th Connecticut's eight companies. Of about 380 of the 5th who began the battle, 35 were killed, Matthew Warshauer, *Connecticut in the American Civil War: Slavery, Sacrifice, and Survival* (Middletown, CT: Wesleyan University Press, 2011), 81.

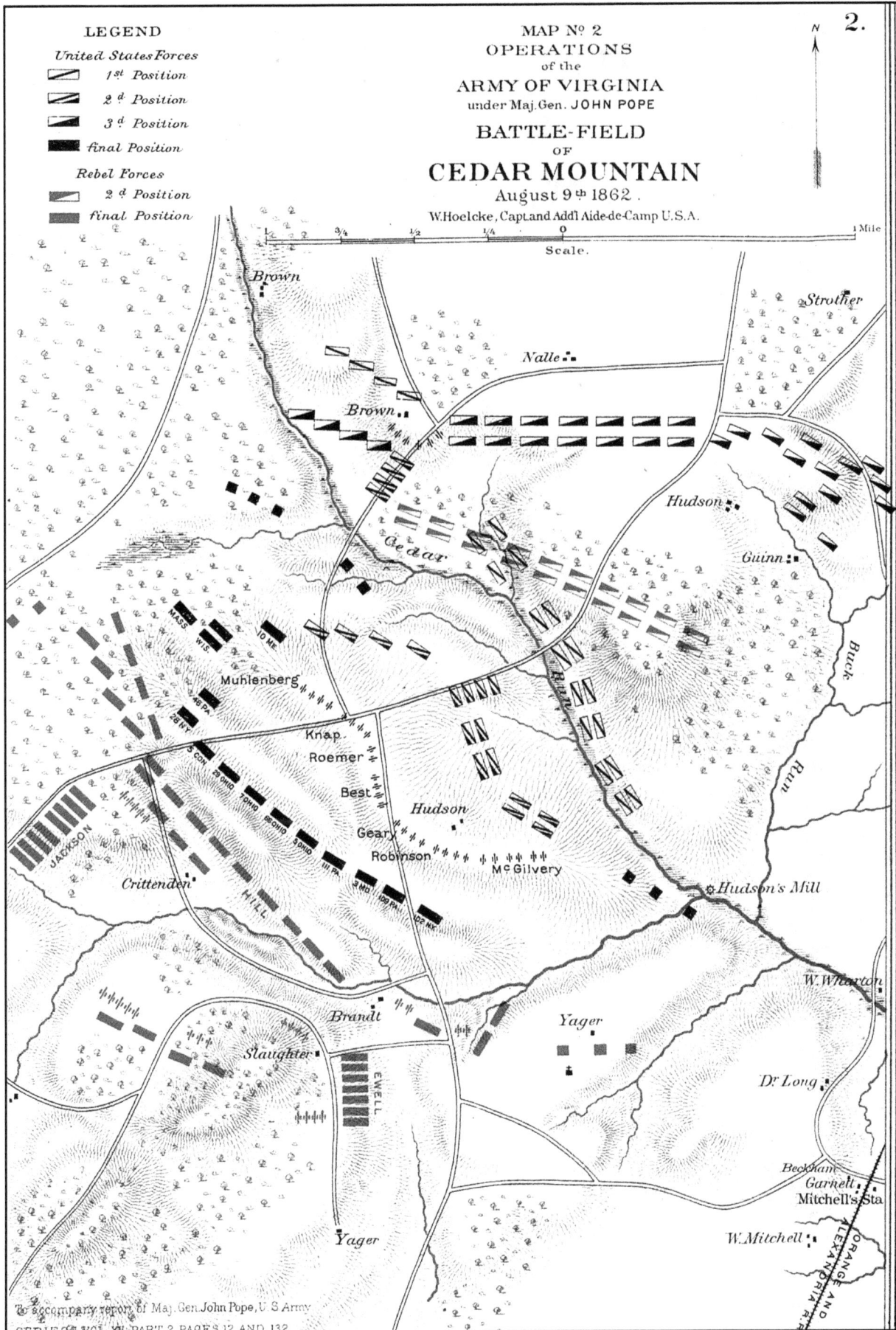

2.

LEGEND

United States Forces

- 1st Position
- 2d Position
- 3d Position
- final Position

Rebel Forces

- 2d Position
- final Position

MAP N⁰ 2

OPERATIONS
of the
ARMY OF VIRGINIA
under Maj. Gen. JOHN POPE

BATTLE-FIELD
OF
CEDAR MOUNTAIN
August 9th 1862.

W. Hoelcke, Capt. and Add'l Aide-de-Camp U.S.A.

Scale.

1   3/4   1/2   1/4   0   1 Mile

N

Brown

Strother

Nalle

Brown

Hudson

Cedar

Guinn

MASS
WIS
10 ME
Muhlenberg
28 N.Y.
5 PA.
Knap
Roemer
Best
5 CON.
29 OHIO
7 OHIO
3 MD
Geary
III PA.
Robinson
3 Md.
McGilvery
109 ME.
102 N.Y.

HILL

JACKSON

Crittenden

Hudson

Hudson's Mill

W. Wharton

Brandt

Yager

Slaughter

EWELL

Dr Long

Yager

Beckham
Garnett
Mitchell's Sta

W. Mitchell

Buck Run

ORANGE AND ALEXANDRIA R.R.

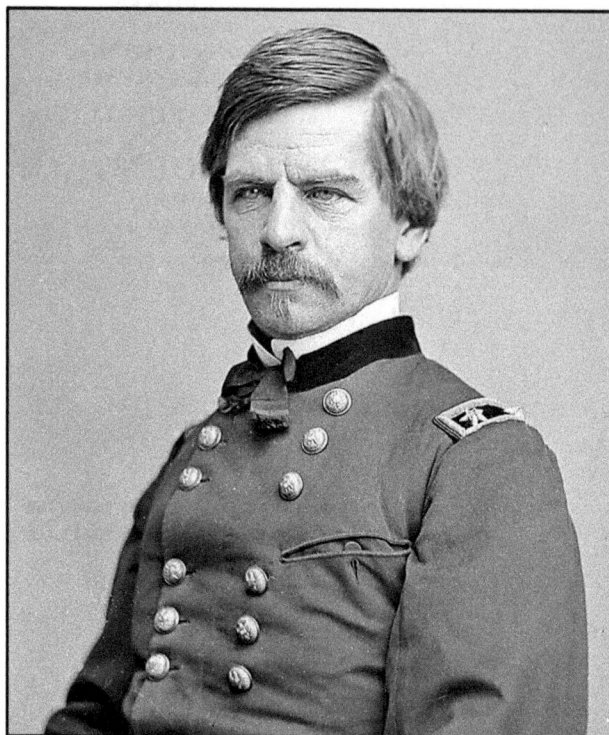

Major General Nathaniel Prentiss Banks, one of President Lincoln's political appointees, a former governor of Massachusetts, was commander of the II Corps, Army of Virginia, from 26 June 1862 to 23 September 1862, but assumed command of the Defenses of Washington, Army of the Potomac, under McClellan's command, on 8 September 1862. Courtesy LOC.

Banks had the best battle of his career. He was very aggressive at Cedar Mountain fighting with almost all his troops, but was faulted by Pope for not waiting for additional Union forces under Major General Franz Sigel to arrive. "The fight of Saturday was precipitated by Banks, who attacked instead of waiting, as I directed him, until the corps of Sigel was rested after its forced march....General Banks was instructed to take up his position on the ground occupied by Crawford's brigade, of his command, which had been thrown out the day previous to observe the enemy's movements. He was directed not to advance beyond that point, and if attacked by the enemy to defend his position and send back timely notice. It was my desire to have time to give the corps of Sigel all the rest possible after their forced march and to bring forward all the forces at my disposal."[7] But in the same report, Pope praised Banks and his corps: "The behavior of Banks' corps during the action was very fine. No greater gallantry and daring could be exhibited by any troops. I cannot speak too highly of the intrepidity and coolness of General Banks himself during the whole of the engagement. He was in the front and exposed as much as any man in his command. His example was of the greatest benefit to his troops, and he merits and should receive the commendation of his Government."[8] Perhaps Pope realized that Banks's political connections were worth considering before further condemning the former Massachusetts governor. Banks's later service would serve to demonstrate that Banks was not the best political general President Lincoln appointed during the Civil War.[9]

In addition to all this carnage, Union officers at the highest levels also found themselves in serious trouble at Cedar Mountain thanks to an aggressive Rebel cavalry commander. Colonel William E. "Grumble" Jones leading the 7th Virginia Cavalry returned during the evening of the 9th from an expedition toward Madison Court House. He then led a cavalry probing action after the Union retreat on the Rebel right, with part of his 7th Virginia Cavalry going through the Confederate front line into Union lines. Jones was totally unaware of the presence of Pope, his staff, and other generals,

---

[7] *ORA*, vol. 12, pt. 2, 133.

[8] Ibid., 133-134.

[9] Stonewall Jackson defeated Banks during Jackson's famous Valley Campaign in the spring of 1862 then Banks was sent to direct the Dept. of the Gulf; he failed miserably in the famous Red River Campaign in the spring of 1864 in Louisiana, effectively ending his career as a field commander.

when he charged a group of mounted men. The fleeing generals and their staffs also had to run the gauntlet of fire from a nearby Union regiment, bruising General Banks in the melee when he was run over by a horse; friendly fire also killed two enlisted men. Yankee artillery joined in sending Jones galloping away to shelter behind a nearby hill. Brigadier General Alpheus S. Williams described what he saw of this brou-ha-ha:

> I was riding towards a road in front of which I had been directed to mass my division, or what was left of it. When but a few rods off, a spirited fire of infantry was opened upon us. Just in front of me was General Gordon and an escort of cavalry. Fortunately we were in a small hollow and the balls passed over us. There was, however, a general stampede of officers and dragoons. Just behind us Gens. Pope and Banks were sitting dismounted with a good many staff officers and escorts. This was a hurrying time with them and all together the skedaddle became laughable in spite of its danger. In front of the wood not over 500 yards off was an infantry regiment just come up, which opened fire with very little regard to friend or foe."[10]

Lieutenant Colonel David Hunter Strother one of Pope's staff also witnessed this event which occurred just after sunset on 9 August:

> General Pope rode immediately to the front where he met General Banks. They and their staffs and escorts gathered on an eminence near a wood where it was supposed we had pickets....we heard some trampling in the wood and presently a body of cavalry issued from the forest and passed along until their flank entirely covered our position. Turning suddenly, they yelled and poured in upon us a rapid and continuous volley from carbines and pistols. We mounted in hot haste, as the enemy were not more than fifty paces from us. In attempting to mount, General Banks was overthrown and his hip badly hurt by the horse of a dragoon, the rider of which was killed. By the time we had started across the field, the fire in our rear became more furious. The balls struck around us so rapidly that I thought it impossible for anyone to escape....General Pope stuck his head down and, striking spur, led off at full speed. I gave my mare the reins and, as we crossed a hollow, a regiment of our own infantry seeing a dark mass of cavalry advancing opened fire....I swerved to the left to avoid the fire of the U.S. troops and with the body of the staff pushed on toward a fence....Several horses without riders galloped with us; among the missing were General Pope and Major [James F.] Meline....the batteries had been keeping up the most furious fire I ever heard. It was a steady roar, and the blazing of the guns, the bursting of shells, and the vast columns of white smoke obscuring the woods and piling up like snow mountains in the moonlight was a scene so dramatic and grand that it will not be soon forgotten....Riding forward we found Generals Pope, Banks, McDowell, and Sigel sitting on a pile of fence rails under a tree....The Generals had again been doing picket duty for the army.[11]

"Grumble" Jones captured 15 prisoners including three lieutenants and a black Union Army servant. This officer's servant said that the Union's General Sigel was advancing to the front confirming information Jackson had already obtained from one of Stuart's scouts, thus stalling any further movement north for his depleted troops.[12]

---

[10] Alpheus S. Williams, *From the Cannon's Mouth: The Civil War Letters of General Alpheus S. Williams*, ed. Milo M. Quaife (Detroit, MI: Wayne State University Press, 1959; reprint, Lincoln, NE: University of Nebraska Press, 1995), 101.

[11] Strother, 77-78.

[12] Krick, *Stonewall*, 315-318; *ORA*, vol. 12, pt. 2, 184, 239; Brown, *Stringfellow*, 155-156. During the Battle of Cedar Mountain, the Union II Corps had Company L of the 1st Michigan Cavalry as an escort under Capt. Melvin Brewer, Company M of the 5th New York cavalry under Lt. Eugene Dimmick, and Company H of the 1st West Virginia Cavalry led by Capt. Isaac P. Kerr. The First Division had Company M of the 1st Michigan Cavalry under Capt. R. C. Dennison as an escort. The escort loss for the II Corps was five killed, five wounded and six missing. The II Army Corps' cavalry brigade led by Brigadier General John Buford consisted of the 1st Michigan cavalry led by Col. Thornton F. Brodhead, 9 companies, 490 men; 5th New York cavalry commanded by Col. Othneil De Forest, 10 companies, 365 troopers; the 1st Vermont cavalry led by Col. Charles H. Tompkins, 10 companies, 504 men; and the 1st West Virginia Cavalry commanded by Lt. Col. Nathaniel P. Richmond, seven companies, 540 horsemen. Bayard's cavalry, not Buford's, was involved at the Battle of Cedar Mountain suffering 61 casualties in its four regiments, Krick, 376.

William Edmonson "Grumble" Jones photographed while a colonel with the 7th Virginia Cavalry in the Army of the Valley in 1862. This veteran cavalry commander, despite being one of the best General Lee had, was not one of Jeb Stuart's favorites. From *Photographic History of the Civil War: Cavalry*. Courtesy Wikipedia.

General Robert E. Lee knew he could not cross the Rappahannock River to assault Pope since Pope was well sited on higher ground, so Lee moved to his left, upstream, sending Stuart to scout ahead. As Stuart reached each ford, he met Union troopers placed by Pope on the opposite bank lively defending the ford; turning Pope's right flank was becoming more difficult than Lee had anticipated. Lee gave permission to Stuart to raid Catlett's Station well in Pope's rear hoping to break Pope's concentration. Catlett's Station is near the junction of the Warrenton Railroad, and the Orange and Alexandria Railroad, and was Pope's headquarters. On the stormy night of 22-23 August, Stuart crossed the Rappahannock with Robertson's and Lee's Brigades minus two regiments and headed to Warrenton. From there he journeyed to Catlett's Station and planned an attack. After careful scouting, he learned that the station was lightly guarded by invalids and about 160 men from the Bucktails--the 13th Pennsylvania Reserves. Stuart detailed Rosser and some of his men to capture the Yankee pickets and then had Rooney Lee and his 9th Virginia Cavalry lead the charge into the camp. Rosser would then head for the Union camp south of the railroad while the 4th Virginia cavalry under Colonel Wickham were assigned to burn the vital railroad bridge over Cedar Run. The Rebel attack at the station completely surprised and overwhelmed the Yankees allowing the Confederate troopers to set wagons and tents ablaze, steal horses, mules, money chests, and most importantly, find Pope's dispatch book, which was among his uniforms. This critical find contained valuable information for General Lee about the numbers and disposition of Pope's army and also showed that Porter's Corps, from McClellan's Army of the Potomac, was approaching. Of additional help to Lee, was Pope's talkative field quartermaster, Major Charles Goulding. Lee now knew he must move quickly to defeat Pope before Porter and more of McClellan's troops reached Pope's Army of Virginia. Lee and Pope were now destined to meet at Bull Run.[13]

---

[13] Freeman, 296-300; John J. Hennessy, *Return to Bull Run: The Campaign and Battle of Second Manassas* (New York: Simon & Schuster, 1993), 53-54; see Blackford, 99-108 for a detailed and entertaining account of the raid; *ORA*, vol. 12, pt. 2, 333, 730-732; *ORA*, pt. 3, 657.

The II/XII Corps Moves to Frederick

The II Corps of the Army of Virginia, moved into the defenses of Washington after the Battle of Second Bull Run and Chantilly. It was a shadow of the corps which had appeared on the field before the Battle of Cedar Mountain 9 August, and it desperately needed rest, refitting, and replacements. After Cedar Mountain, the corps saw only minor skirmishing as its two divisions moved up and down the Rappahannock River, separately supporting other units. Its commander, General Banks, moved his headquarters to Culpeper on 11 August and remained there until 18 August. On the 18th, Banks moved to Sulphur Springs and on the 19th to Rappahannock Station. Then the divisions reunited on 26 August marching from Fayetteville and guarded the army trains taking over that duty from Porter's corps on the 27th. They marched with the trains from Warrenton toward Bristoe Station. Pope, on the 28th, ordered Banks to march to Kettle Run Bridge, between Catlett's Station and Bristoe Station, to repair the Orange and Alexandria Railroad tracks. Banks returned to Bristoe Station and remained there on the 29th and 30th. On the night of the 30th into the 31[st,] they burned the stores at Bristoe Station including seven locomotives and 150 cars, and marched to Centerville, and then on 1 September, marched on the Old Braddock Road coming into the Little River Turnpike east of Fairfax Court House.[14]

Captain William F. Fox, of the 107th New York, described this peripatetic period:

> During the operations that followed Cedar Mountain — the Manassas or Second Bull Run campaign — the corps did not participate in the actual fighting to any great extent. Its artillery was engaged at times with creditable success in some of the contests at the fords of the upper Rappahannock, and in the battle of Chantilly, it moved up in close support of the firing line. Its principal duties were confined to guarding the lines of communication and the protection of the supply trains, an important but inglorious task. In the course of this duty there were long, fatiguing marches, over dusty roads and under an August sun. There was much of hurrying to and fro under orders from army headquarters, some of which were useless and ill-advised; and, at times, the men suffered from lack of food and water.[15]

A member of the 5th Connecticut described the attempted destruction of Pope's trains his unit was guarding comparing it to Jackson's capture of Pope's trains at Manassas Junction:

> Our whole force commenced to destroy the trains of stores and provisions which we were guarding. There was more than a solid mile of the trains of provisions, ammunition and stores, with from ten to fifteen locomotives, which we undertook to destroy. Immense bon-fires were started for the destruction of all stores and property serviceable to the rebels. Boxes and cars were broken to pieces, hay and forage stuffed inside and under the cars, everywhere, to make the destruction of the fire complete. It is said there was more than a million of value of stores, etc., caught here by the burning of the railroad bridges at Broad Run, by Jackson, on the 27th, and so were entirely lost to us. Doubtless much was saved from the fires after we left them for the benefit of the Confederates. Everything was so saturated with the rain, that the destruction of stores by fires was not complete.
> At 9 A.M. we had the work as well under way as possible, and we marched off south rapidly for several miles, then east and through the village of Brentsville, where the people jeered at us a little as to the time we were making; then we pushed on north again about as fast as we could go all day long, and by night we reached Centerville and were once more with Pope's army.[16]

---

[14] William F. Fox in *In Memoriam: Henry Warner Slocum, 1826-1894* (Albany, NY: J.B. Lyon, Co., 1904), 136; *ORA*, vol. 19, pt. 1, 478-479. Fox wrote in his *Regimental Losses in the American Civil War 1861-1865* (Albany, NY: Brandow Printing Company, 1898), 87, of the XII: "The corps that never lost a color or a gun." Fox was wounded by a shell explosion at Antietam and wounded again at Chancellorsville and Resaca. He was discharged for disability as a lieutenant colonel.

[15] Fox in *In Memoriam: Henry Warner Slocum*, 136.

[16] Edwin E. Marvin, *The Fifth Regiment Connecticut Volunteers, a History* (Hartford, CT: Press of Wiley, Waterman & Eaton, 1889), 233. Marvin refers to the vast quantity of booty Jackson captured at Manassas Junction on the evening of 26 August. After Jackson reached the Orange & Alexandria Railroad at Bristoe Station, he and his men derailed two Federal supply trains and destroyed a quarter mile of track. Jackson learned that Manassas Junction, located four miles north of Bristoe, was lightly guarded, and selected two regiments under the command of Isaac Trimble to capture the junction. Trimble's two regiments quickly seized the depot and 300 prisoners. Private John H. Worsham described the scene: "The Federal depot was "vast storehouses filled with . . . all the delicacies, potted ham, lobster, tongue, candy, cakes, nuts, oranges, lemons, pickles, catsup, mustard, etc. It makes an old soldier's mouth water now just to think of the good things captured there. . . . Some filled their haversacks with cakes, some with candy, others with oranges, lemons, canned goods etc. I know one that took nothing but French mustard," John H. Worsham, *One of Jackson's Foot Cavalry, His Experience and What He Saw During the War 1861-1865* (New York, NY: The Neale Publishing Company, 1912), 120-121.

The march of some units in the II Corps on 1 September was eventful as Stonewall Jackson's troops were hunting Pope's army. The 5th Connecticut was not directly involved and was fortunate to be south of Jackson's attack having only spent bullets fall near them:

> The next day, September 1st, we remained pretty much stationary through the forenoon and until about 3 o'clock in the afternoon, when the army moved toward Fairfax in parallel lines, about a quarter of a mile apart. When abreast a side road running from the Little River pike from a point near the village of Chantilly, the outside or west line was attacked by the rebels. The line was then moving along an old worn, washed-out road across a pine barren, and the men were fairly entrenched till the rebels appeared near at hand above them. Troops were hurried forward and back in the line to the position attacked, and the parallel line next to the outside line was advanced in support, and a short and terrible struggle was waged till darkness ended it....Shells were constantly screeching and bullets hissing just over our heads, and the thunder of artillery and of the heavens was, for a long time, entirely continuous, without an instant's intermission. The spent bullets of the struggle but just reached us, but to those participating and close at and it was terribly deadly.[17]

The next day, 2 September, the 5th Connecticut Nutmeggers "moved on to and above Alexandria and encamped. Sutlers and peddlers, who came out to meet this hungry, ragged and lousy army, were cleaned out in a twinkling and went back empty handed."[18]

---

[17] Marvin, 234.
[18] Ibid., 235.

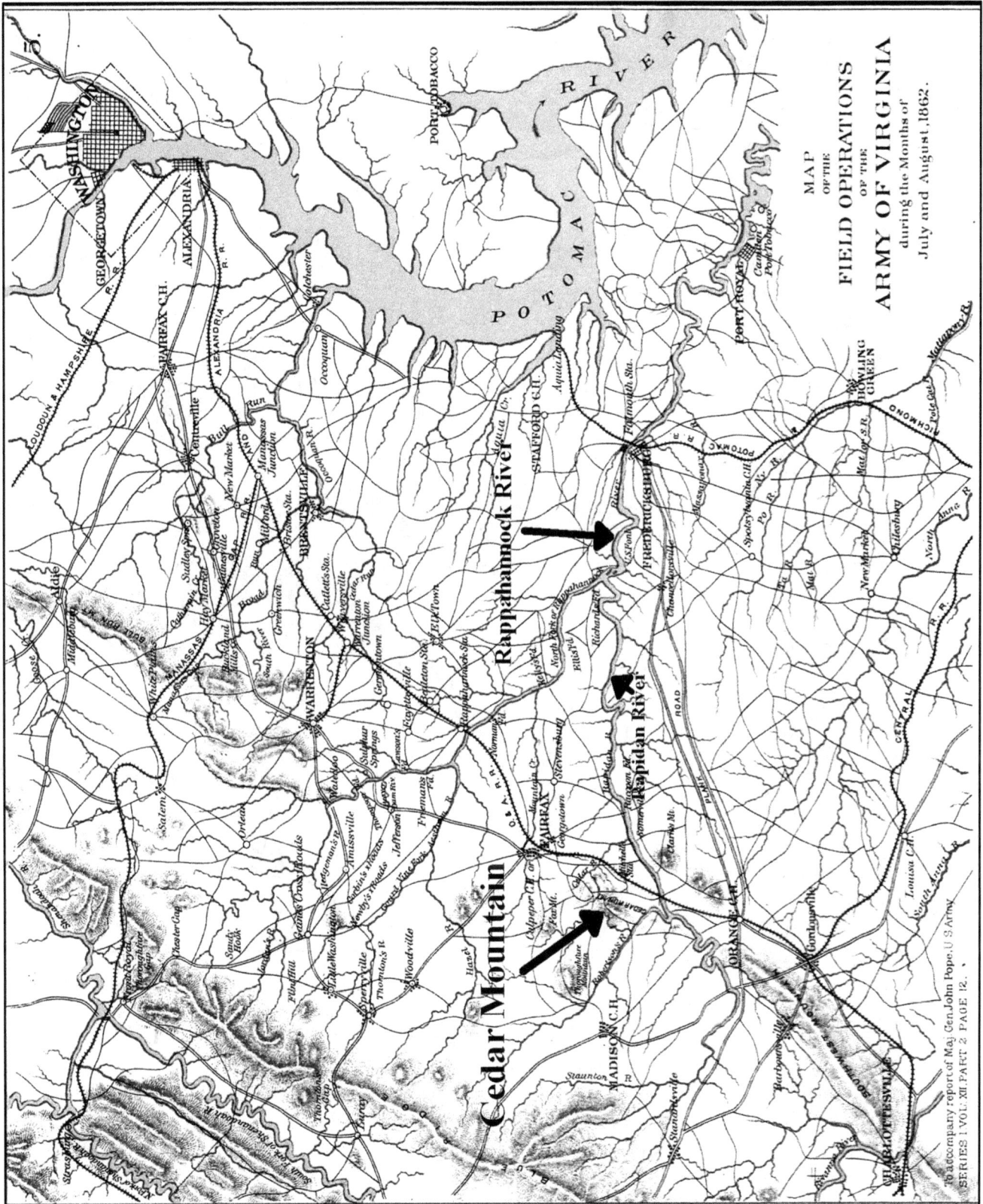

Map of area of operations after the Battle of Cedar Mountain. *OA*, pl. 22, courtesy LOC.

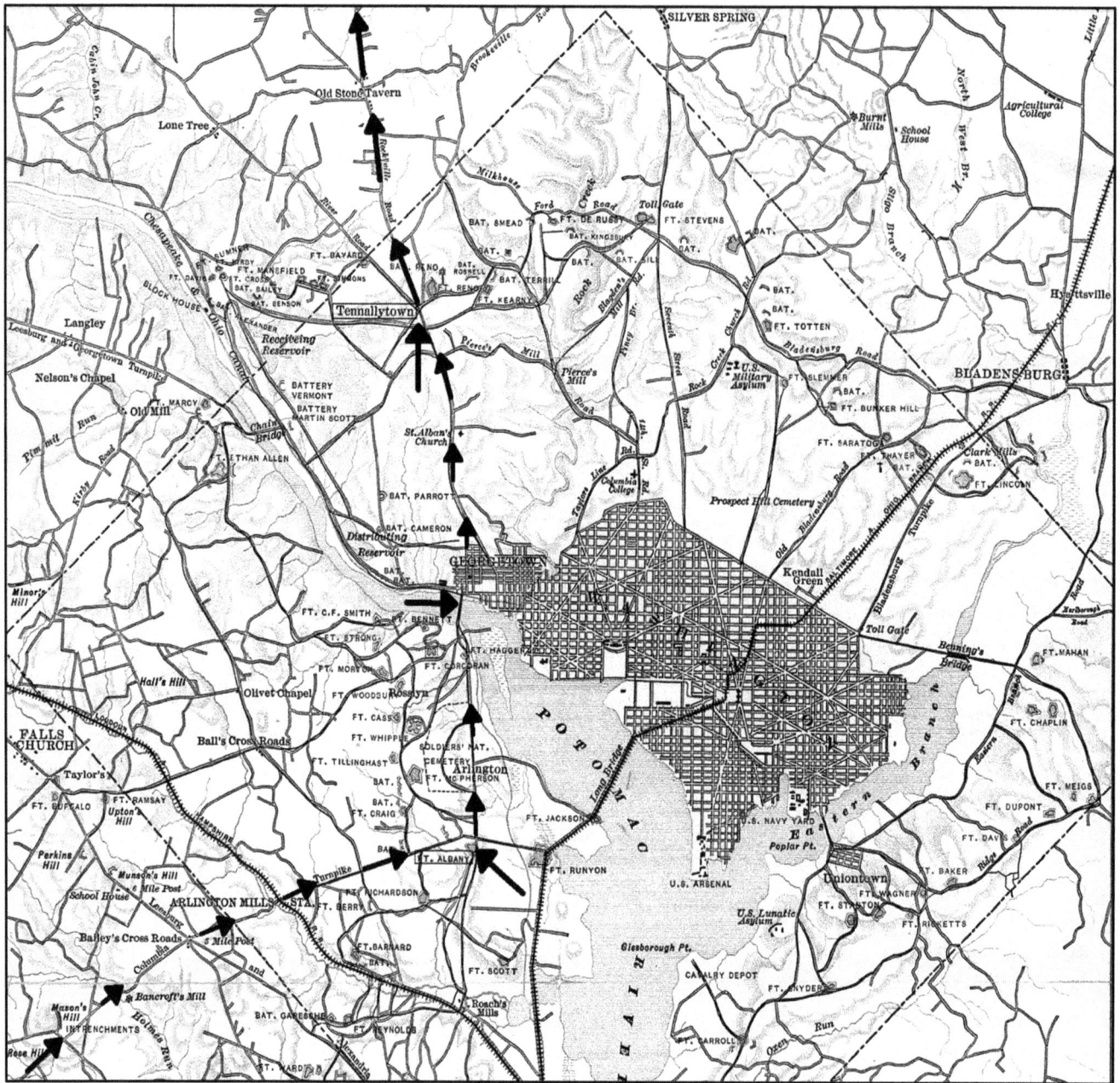

An 1865 map of the Washington, DC, area showing forts and the route of the II/XII Corps. On 1 September, it marched on the Old Braddock Road coming into the Little River Turnpike east of Fairfax Court House, then along the Columbia Pike; on 3 September the corps was near Fort Albany at Fort Richardson just to the southwest, and the next day it marched up the Georgetown-Alexandria Road, across the Potomac on the Aqueduct Bridge, and moved through Georgetown to camp near Tennallytown. Note that this map also shows forts constructed after the 1862 Maryland Campaign such as Fort Mansfield to the upper left of Tennallytown named to commemorate Mansfield after his death. Courtesy NPS: http://www.nps.gov/cwdw/historyculture/upload/cw0684000.pdf. For an excellent history of the forts in and near Washington and Fort Mansfield, see Benjamin Franklin Cooling III and Walton H. Owen II, *Mr. Lincoln's Forts: A Guide to the Civil War Defenses of Washington* (Lanham, MD: The Scarecrow Press, Inc., 2010), 149-152.

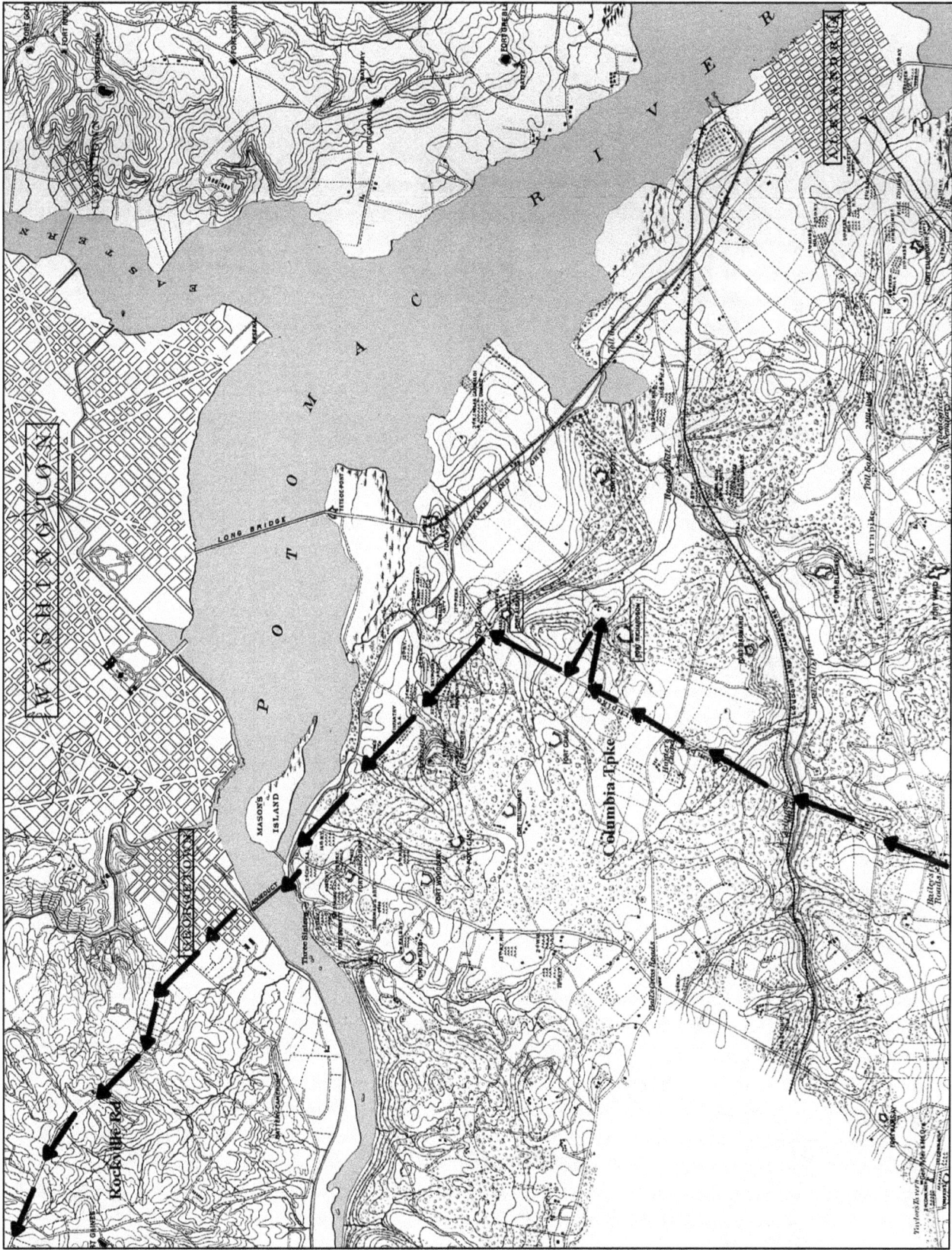

An 1861 map showing likely route of II/XII Corps. The deviation near the center shows that troops reportedly bivouacked to the rear of Fort Richardson to the southwest of Fort Albany. *OA*, Plate 6. Courtesy LOC.

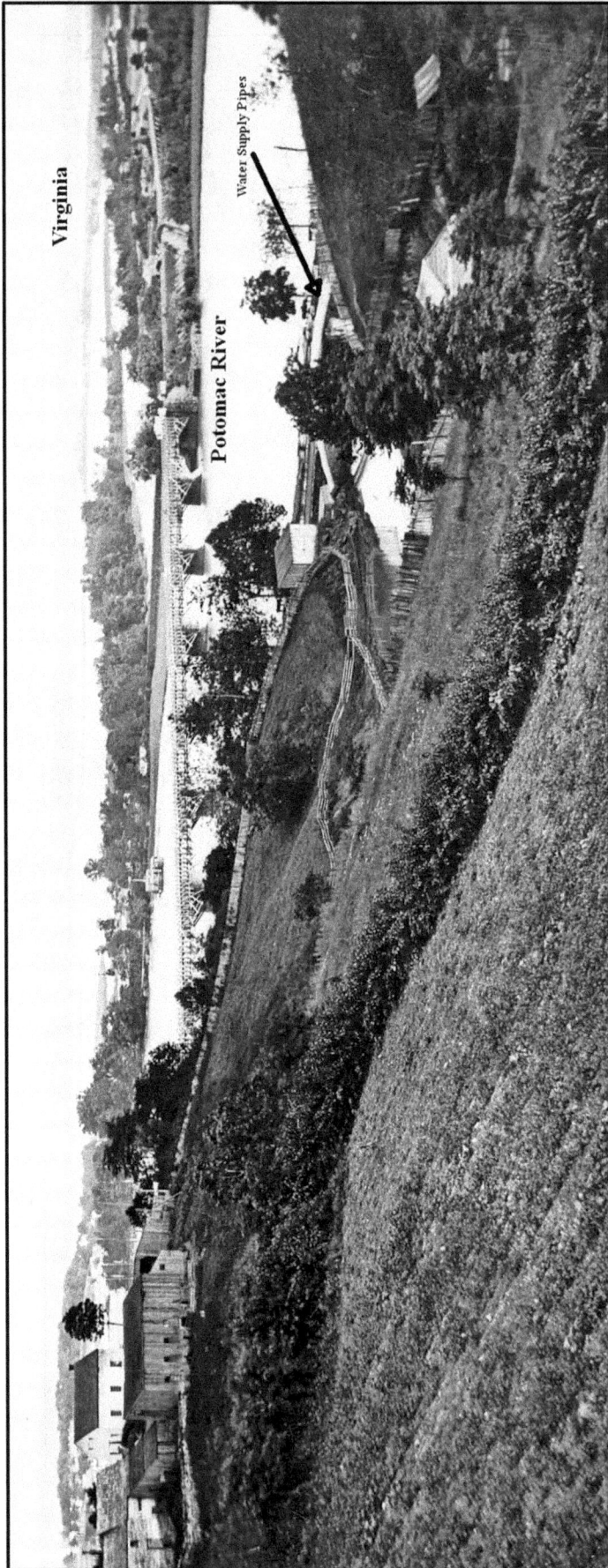

Photograph of the Aqueduct Bridge/Potomac Aqueduct. Georgetown in the foreground and Virginia in the distance, taken c. 1860. The II/XII Corps crossed 4 September 1862. Note the white-arched pipes at the right center which carry water downstream to Washington. In 1830, merchants from Alexandria, Virginia, still part of the District of Columbia, proposed linking their city to Georgetown to capitalize on the new Chesapeake and Ohio Canal. Congress granted a charter to the Alexandria Canal Company in 1830, and construction soon began on the Aqueduct Bridge that would carry canal boats across the Potomac River and downriver on the south side in the Alexandria Canal without unloading in Georgetown. The bridge was designed by Maj. William Turnbull; construction of the bridge and Alexandria Canal began in 1833, and both were completed in 1843. The water-filled bridge was a weatherproofed-timber, queen-post truss construction. The bridge was 110 feet wide across the top and 1,600 feet long including its approaches. During the Civil War, the canal was drained to allow a wider roadway. Charles J. Allen, *Annual Reports of the War Department for the Fiscal Year Ended June 30, 1901,* Part 5 (Washington, DC: Government Printing Office, War Department, 1901), 3641. Photograph courtesy LOC.

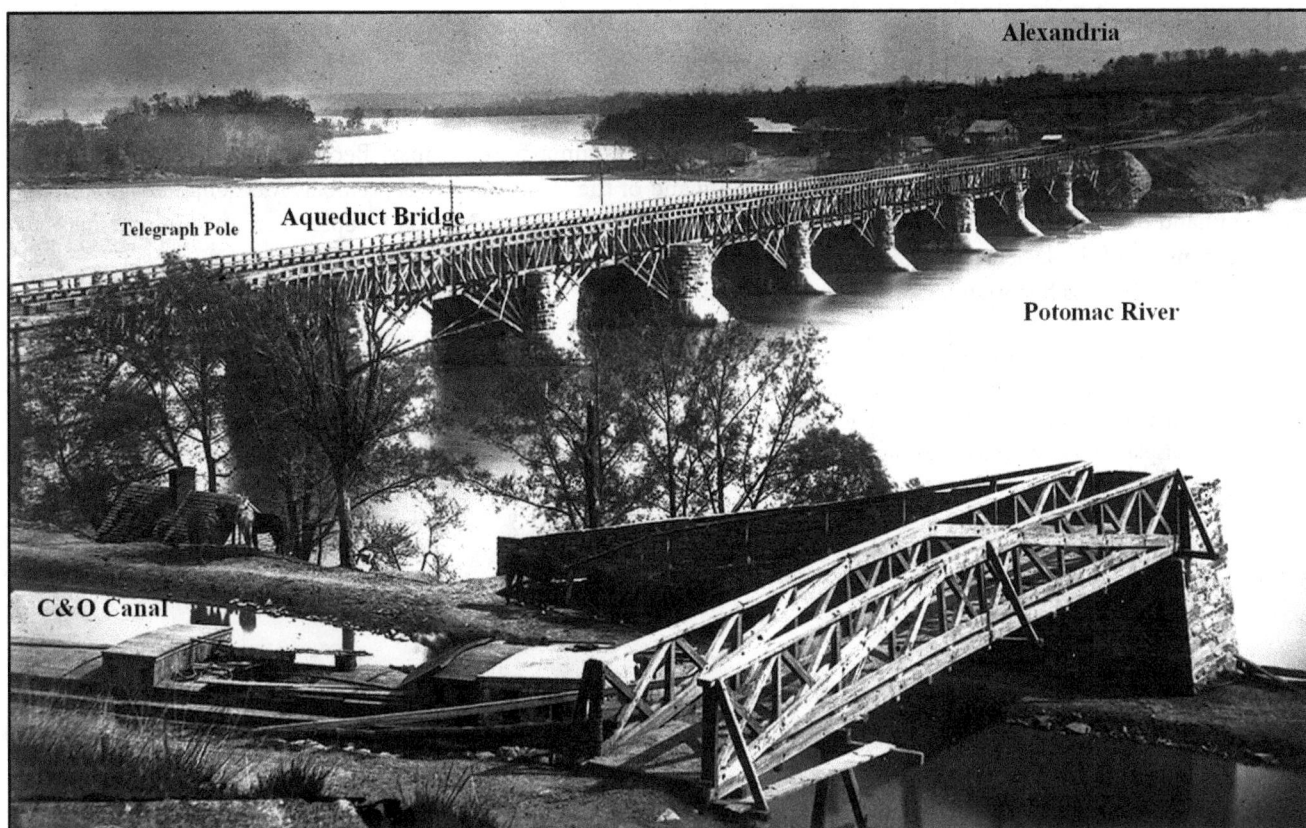

Another view of Aqueduct Bridge taken from Georgetown. Note the canal boat to the left of the bridge over the C&O Canal in the foreground and the telegraph poles on the bridge. Photograph taken during the war as the bed appears dry on the Virginia shore; it was emptied in 1861 after the Federal government took it over for use as a bridge. Courtesy LOC.

On 3 September, the corps was near Fort Albany, camping in the rear of Fort Richardson; the next day, 4 September, it marched across the Potomac on the Aqueduct Bridge and moved through Georgetown, three miles to camp near Tenallytown, a village within the northwestern boundary of the District of Columbia. There, they found the wagon train awaiting their arrival. Their sojourn there allowed them to sleep in their tents, have a hearty meal, get clean, read mail, and refit. A member of the 10th Maine recalled the 4 September march:

> Hot and pleasant. Fell in at nine, waited till ten, performed strategy a half hour and finally, at 10:30, we marched with the corps up the [Potomac] river to the aqueduct bridge, and crossed, some one singing, "Oh! Ain't you glad to get out the wilderness?"….We made a few halts in Georgetown, and the women and young ladies opened their doors and windows to give us bread and butter, meat, apples, peaches and preserves!...The rush upon the sutler wagons is frightful; reminding us of our swarming upon the cherry trees last July. We marched to Tennallytown and camped two miles beyond—eight miles. Next day, Sept. 5th, after sweltering all the morning, we marched at 2 p.m., across the fields to the right, (east) till we reached the Rockville turnpike, and then traveled slowly along it, making more exertion in one mile than was needed for three. We passed through Rockville after dark and camped two miles beyond, and were exceedingly fatigued.[19]

The chronicler of the 5th Connecticut approved of Marylanders' hospitality undoubtedly comparing it with the less than welcoming Virginians':

---

[19] John Mead Gould, *History of the First – Tenth - Twenty-ninth Maine Regiment* (Portland, ME: Stephen Berry, 1871), 222-223. In addition to the regiment's history, Gould wrote *The Civil War Journals of John Mead Gould 1861-1866*, ed. William B. Jordan, Jr., (Baltimore: Butternut & Blue, 1997); and, *Joseph K. F. Mansfield, Brigadier General of The U.S. Army: A Narrative of Events Connected with His Mortal Wounding at Antietam, Sharpsburg, Maryland, September 17, 1862* (Portland, ME: Stephen Berry, Printer, 1895). A photograph and biography is above in a Chapter 10 appendix.

September 5th. Moved across country and encamped near Rockville....The Maryland people are growing in loyalty since we left them in March last, for today they furnish us with substantial lunches as we pass, and at one place in Rockville they served the men with whiskey from buckets and tubs; each man an ordinary tumbler full if he would take it.[20]

Pope was relieved from command of the Army of Virginia 5 September. Because Banks was ill, Brigadier General Williams had already assumed temporary command of the II Corps on 3 September. McClellan assigned Banks the command of the District of the Defenses of Washington replacing Little Mac on 8 September, and Heintzelman was put in command of the Defenses South of the Potomac under Banks's orders.

Fox, the XII Corps historian, described warmly Banks's service:

Banks took a final leave of the war-worn troops that had served so faithfully under him during the arduous campaigns of the past year. Though it does not appear that the men were ever enthusiastic in his favor, he had gained their respect, and when he left he carried with him their best wishes for his future welfare. Entering the service without any military training or experience, he had displayed a courageous bearing in action and shown an ability of no mean order in the management of affairs. Sadly hampered at times by interference with his plans, he was patient and uncomplaining, and in this respect the records of his official correspondence with the authorities at Washington contrast favorably with that of the other generals at the time.[21]

---

[20] Marvin, *The Fifth Regiment Connecticut Volunteers*, 236.

[21] Fox, *In Memoriam*, 136-137. Bryant, *History of the Third Regiment of Wisconsin Veteran Volunteer Infantry 1861-1865*, 118. This well-written regimental history by Lieutenant Bryant and Fox's *In Memoriam*, were the sources of much relevant information for the march from Washington to Antietam. But note that many histories of units and commanders written after the war become encomiums versus critical analyses of events.

XII Corps march from Rockville to Damascus 9 September to 12 September. The corps marched about 10 miles to Middlebrook on the 9th. The following day, it moved to near Damascus marching eight miles, and the 10th one mile to the outskirts of Damascus where it rested two days. On September 12, it marched to Ijamsville on the B&O Railroad. Martenet and Bond 1865 map Montgomery County, MD. Courtesy LOC.

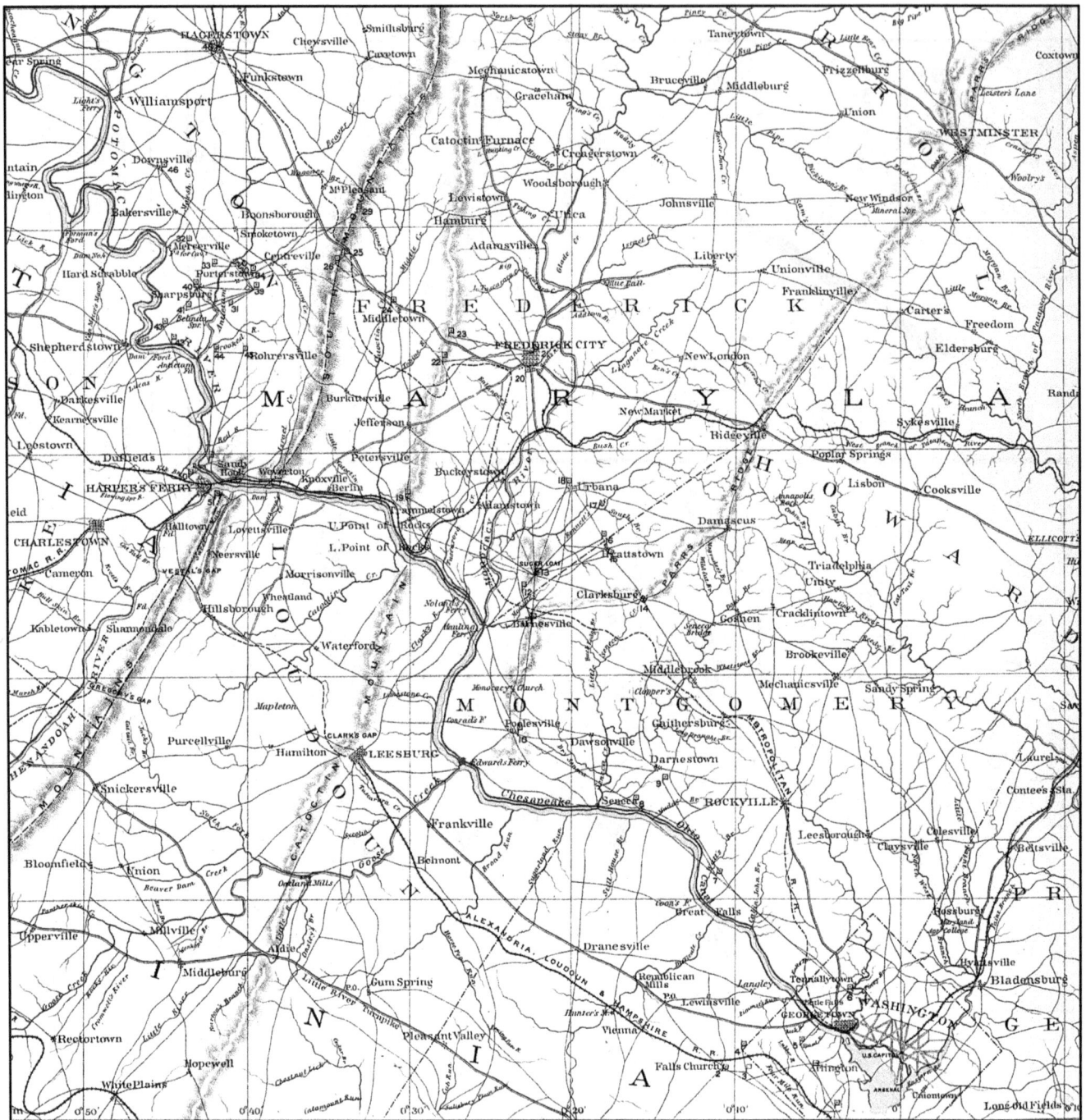

Area of operations of the II/XII Corps in September 1862. General Lee's goal was to form his army around Frederick, Maryland, at the upper center, behind the Monocacy River and Parr's Ridge barriers. The main road from Washington to Frederick was called the Georgetown Pike; Frederick was also on the National Pike from Baltimore. Sugarloaf Mountain is to the Northeast of Poolesville next to Barnesville and was eagerly sought by McClellan; White's Ford is almost due west of Barnesville northwest of Poolesville. Conrad's Ferry below White's Ford is today White's Ferry. White's Ferry is about three river miles below White's Ford. Parr's Ridge is the ridge farthest to the right which runs through Damascus, Maryland. The valley between the Catoctin Mountains and Parr's Ridge is sometimes called Monocacy Valley. The Catoctin Mountains, the Maryland extension of the Bull Run Mountains in Virginia, are just west of Frederick and further to the west is the South Mountain Range. Between them is the Middletown (or Catoctin) Valley. West of South Mountain near Harper's Ferry is Elk Mountain or Elk Ridge which terminates at Harper's Ferry and is called Maryland Heights at that point; Elk Ridge is the Maryland extension of the Virginia Blue Ridge Mountains located near Sandy Hook just above Harper's Ferry. Pleasant Valley lies between South Mountain and Elk Ridge. Harper's Ferry is about fifty airline miles from Washington while Frederick is about forty miles. On 4 September, McClellan reported his disposition as follows: I Corps at Upton's Hill, the IX Corps on the 7th Street Road, the II and XII Corps at Tenallytown, the VI Corps at the Alexandria Seminary, and Couch's division at Tenallytown, *Report on the Organization and Campaigns of the Army of the Potomac*, 349. *OA*, Plate 27. Courtesy LOC.

On 5 September, Williams moved his corps to Rockville, about 10 airline miles from Tennallytown. His sadly depleted corps finally received reinforcement gaining five new regiments: the 13th New Jersey and 107th New York, three-year men, assigned to Gordon's Brigade; and three regiments of the nine-months levy: 124th, 125th, and 128th Pennsylvania, which were placed in Crawford's Brigade, in the First Division.[22]

> These men, with their full ranks, clean uniforms and bright, new flags, were viewed with wonder and curiosity by the old campaigners. Each one of these regiments at dress parade showed a longer line than that of some veteran brigades. They still had some of the characteristics pertaining to raw recruits, having been in service but a month or so. They had attained, however, a commendable proficiency in drill, and in the great battle which soon followed it was noticed that they deployed under fire with steadiness, and faced the enemy with a cool courage that elicited praise in the official reports. Though the sound of their good-byes was still lingering in their northern homes, they were destined to fill scores of bloody graves before many days had passed.[23]

Private Edmund Randolph Brown, a member of the 27th Indiana and its historian, recalled seeing two new regiments assigned to his Third Brigade:

> Their appearance when they first came to us was in striking contrast to that of the older regiments. There seemed to be a countless number of them. We had not realized before how large a regiment really was. Their new uniforms, their enormous knapsacks, and their seeming excess of equipments of all kinds, attracting more attention by their inexperienced way of bundling them up and caring for them, we shall not soon forget. No less in contrast with ours were their bleached faces and soft, white hands...."[24]

His 27th Indiana also received some reinforcements: "...a considerable squad of recruits [were received] at this time...this was the largest number of recruits that came to us at any one time" but "Several of these recruits were killed at Antietam, less than two weeks after reaching us."[25]

Also on 5 September, the two major Union armies in Virginia, the Army of Virginia and the Army of the Potomac, were consolidated: the II Corps of the Army of Virginia and the II Corps of the Army of the Potomac were organized into McClellan's center wing under command of the venerable Major General Edwin Vose Sumner, at Rockville, Maryland. On 6 September, the corps was formed in line of battle a short distance from Rockville: "The preparations indicated that an attack was expected. But not a shot was heard; in fact, there was no enemy within many miles. The cause of this alarm was unknown at the time, and has remained so ever since; at least it does not appear in any record. It may have been ordered merely for the purposes of drill — perhaps to give the new regiments an opportunity to acquaint themselves with an important part of their tactical duties."[26] The II Corps marched about 10 miles to Middlebrook on the 9th. The following day, it moved to near Damascus marching eight miles, and the 10th one mile to the outskirts of Damascus where it rested two days. On September 12, it marched about eight miles to Ijamsville located on the B&O Railroad.

A soldier in the 5th Connecticut described with understated Nutmegger humor the serendipitous arrival of knapsacks on 8 September: "Regiment obtained again their knapsacks from baggage train, and to get a change of

---

[22] *ORA*, series 3, vol. 3, 749, 760, 775. The mustering in strength is not the number appearing on the firing line; for firing line strength see OOB in Appendix. See also D. Scott Hartwig, "The Volunteers of '62," in *The Antietam Campaign*, ed. By Gary W. Gallagher (Chapel Hill, NC: The University of North Carolina Press, 1999), 143-168, in which Hartwig discusses McClellan's problem with such large numbers of green troops and how it affected his strategic thinking for the campaign. Carman, Clemens, vol. 2, 583-584. The five green regiments in the XII Corps were its largest, strengths taken from mustering-in rolls: 124th Pennsylvania, 974; 125th Pennsylvania 963; and 128th Pennsylvania, 950. The 13th New Jersey mustered in 899, and the 107th New York, 1,031. The total mustering in strength of these five regiments was 4,817. The estimated number actually on the firing line on the day of the battle of Antietam was 3,936 out of 7,631, 52% of the Corps.

[23] Fox, *In Memoriam: Henry Warner Slocum, 1826-1894*, 136-137; *ORA*, vol. 12, pt. 2, 324-325; *ORA Supp.*, pt. 1, vol. 2, 524-525, 538; vol. 3467-468; Welcher, 768-771, 918-932. Edwin E. Bryant, *History of the Third Regiment of Wisconsin Veteran Volunteer Infantry 1861-1865* (Madison, WI: Democrat Printing Co., 1891), 119-120. This well-written regimental history by Lt. Bryant was the source of much relevant information for the march from Washington to Antietam," Julian Wisner Hinckley, *A Narrative of Service with the Third Wisconsin Infantry* (Madison, WI: Democrat Printing Co., 1912), 46.

[24] Edmund Randolph Brown, *The Twenty-Seventh Indiana Volunteer Infantry in the War of the Rebellion 1861to1865* (Monticello, IN: n.p.), 225-226.

[25] Edmund Randolph Brown, *The Twenty-Seventh Indiana*, 226-227.

[26] Fox, *In Memoriam: Henry Warner Slocum, 1826-1894*, 138; *ORA*, vol. 19, pt. 1, 478-479.

underwear, after four weeks sweltering in the same set of rags, was a new joy. We shall wash and change now every day until the inhabitants [lice] emigrate. We can, perhaps, make it too lively for them to form local attachments."[27]

On 6 September, volunteer regiments' evening serenades ended when they lost their bands due to War Department orders. The 10th Maine and its sister regiments rested until 9 September "when orders came to march at noon....The 124th, 125th and 128th Pennsylvania regiments of nine months men marched with us today, and are now a part of our brigade; either of them have more men on duty than all the old brigade, and I noticed that they kept closed up better than we did, but they are hurrahing or yelling all the time, and on the march they try to out run each other as all green troops will!"[28]

Williams with his two-division corps left Rockville on the ninth, marching to Middlebrook, then on the 10th, to Damascus, for a two-day rest. On the twelfth, the corps moved to near Ijamsville, a station on the B&O Railroad. The XII Corps received its official designation as such on 12 September 1862 in General Orders No. 129 from the Adjutant-General's Office, when Lincoln directed that the II Corps of the Army of Virginia should become the XII Corps Army of the Potomac.[29] The 10th Maine marched at 9 a.m. on 10 September about eight miles to camp near Damascus, and the next day after receiving rations, it moved twice, only marching about one mile. "[These marches] were anything but easy marches to us, by reason of the delay and uncertainty that characterized every move....Our rations were not bountiful, but we were not starved, and then the cornfields and orchards of the Maryland farmers helped us.[30]

But not all marches were grueling for some regiments as a veteran of the 29th Massachusetts in the II Corps wrote: "The marches were not at this time very long [through 9 September] nor forced; the country through which the army moved was very picturesque and fruitful; the fields were filled with corn, and from these the soldiers had many delicious meals--roasting the milky corn, gathering peaches and apples from the well-laden orchards, and not seldom supping upon fresh pork (purchased of course of the country people)."[31] But the regimental history of the 125th Pennsylvania complained that on and after 9 September, the roads were so crowded "that our supply train could not reach us, and we were obliged to live from that time until September 19th on green corn and green apples and what we could beg or buy."[32]

---

[27] Marvin, *Fifth Regiment Connecticut Volunteers*, 237.

[28] Gould, *History of the First*, 223.

[29] Fox, *In Memoriam*, 137; *ORA*, vol. 19, pt. 1, 479.

[30] Gould, *History of the First*, 223-224.

[31] William H. Osborne, *The History of the Twenty-Ninth Regiment of Massachusetts Volunteer Infantry in the Late War of the Rebellion* (Boston, MA: Albert J. Wright, 1877), 181. Perhaps a tough of humor when he wrote "purchased of course."

[32] Wallace, *History of the One Hundred and Twenty-fifth Regiment Pennsylvania*, 228. Clearly experiences of the various regiments differed based on their experience, ingenuity of their troops, and the indulgence of their officers. Note that "green corn" did not mean raw corn but rather not ground into corn meal or otherwise processed. Usually ears were roasted on open fires and if not eaten could be carried. Certainly soldiers did eat raw corn but only in emergencies. Green corn also meant ears not fully ripened. Green apples could refer to the apples' color, that they were eaten raw, or just unripe. There were many recipes for using apples as well as corn during the Civil War but exigencies often outweighed demands of gourmet soldiers. For an excellent discussion of soldier rations, see William C. Davis, *A Taste for War: The Culinary History of the Blue and Gray* (Mechanicsburg, PA: Stackpole Books, 2003).

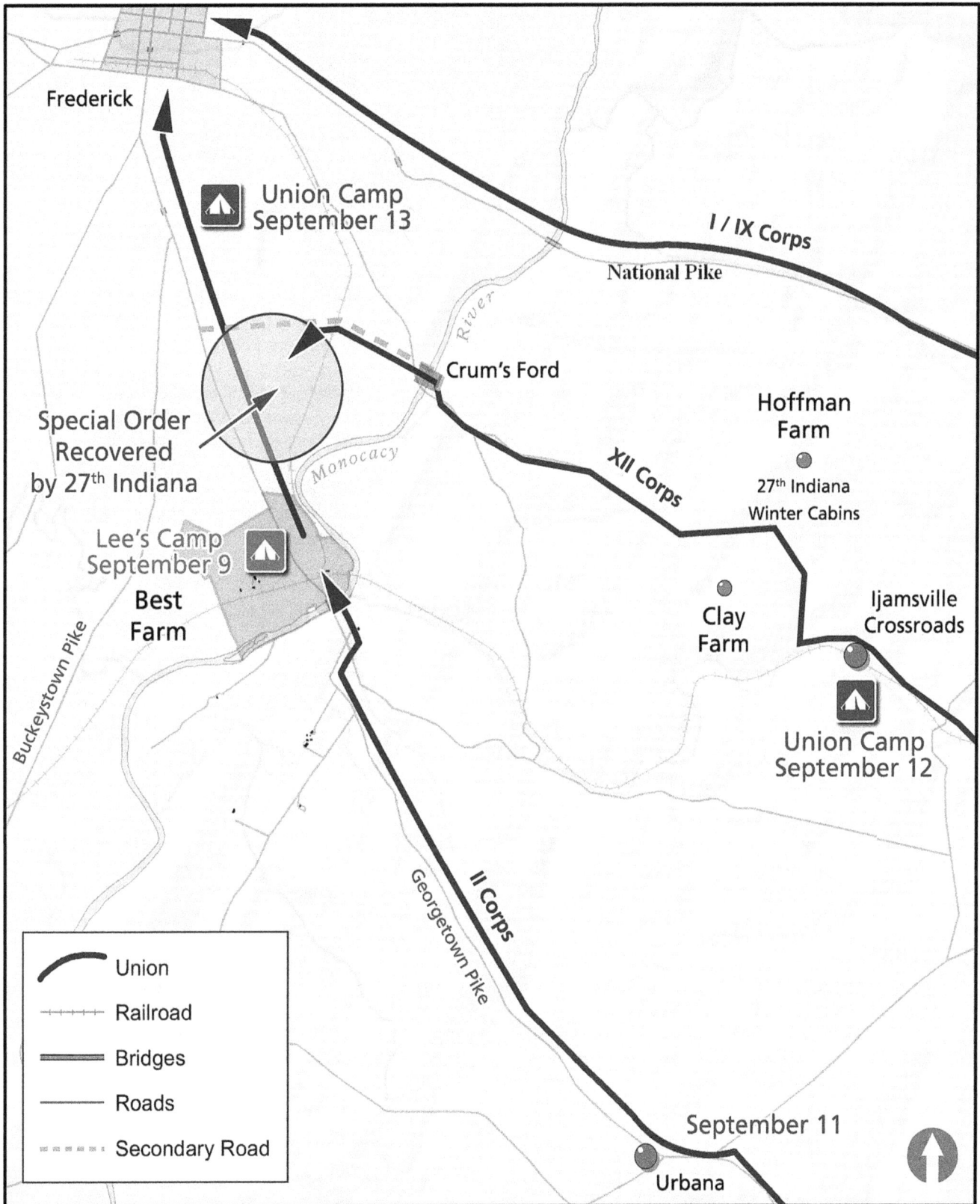

The 27th Indiana and the XII Corps marched from Ijamsville on the Ijamsville Road past the Clay Farm where they camped the previous December; north of the road was the Hoffman Farm where they had wintered 1861-1862. There was no bridge at Crum's Ford. General Daniel H. Hill destroyed both the B&O Railroad Bridge and covered wooden bridge on September 8-9. During the Civil War, a secondary road ran from Crum's Ford across farm fields to the Georgetown Pike; it is conceivable that the soldiers used this secondary road to cut south toward the Georgetown Pike. Description and map courtesy of Tracy Evans, NPS Monocacy Battlefield. Antietam expert Thomas Clemens believes that the order was found just south of Frederick on the map to the right of the south arrow just above the Union Camp September 13 label.

Brown, in his history of the 27th Indiana, described its travels to Frederick from the 9th to the 13th:

> On the 9th we moved to Middlebrook, northward; on the 10th, to Damascus, and, remaining in camp there on day, moved, on the 12th, to Ijamsville. This village is on the main line of the Baltimore & Ohio railroad, eight or ten miles east of Frederick. Our route this time carried us east of Old Sugar Loaf mountain, though it was in sight for a day or more. The summit was occupied by a signal station....
>
> On the 13th we moved by the direct road to Frederick. This took us immediately past Mr. Clay's house, in whose orchard we had camped the previous December. Looking northward, we could plainly see our deserted cabins of the previous winter....
>
> The bulk of Lee's army had been at Frederick up to a very recent period. We were likely at any time to encounter rebel scouts or outposts. The Twenty-seventh led the column, expecting at any moment to sight an enemy, though passing over this ground, where we had formerly felt so secure, and which, indeed, almost seemed like home to us, the sudden and violent changes which the fortunes of war may bring about were forcibly impressed upon us.
>
> There being no bridge over the Monocacy, on this road, we forded that stream. The water was only knee-deep, and warm, so it was no hardship, except to our badly-worn shoes and tattered pants. Some of our officers had put on their best boots and pants when we came up with our wagons at Washington. To plunge into the water in the river, and then into the dust, shoe-mouth deep, on the other side, caused them to make wry faces, but they did not flinch.
>
> When we emerged from the timber east of the Monocacy, we saw smoke rising from several pieces of artillery, engaged in the open country west of Frederick. It was now clear that no enemy would be encountered short of that point. But, with skirmishers still deployed in our front, we moved on and finally halted in a clover field, adjoining the city on the south....The weather was very beautiful.[33]

A sad report from Brigadier General Samuel W. Crawford camped near Rockville, Maryland, shows the status of his brigade on 9 September was typical of those units which fought hard at Cedar Mountain:

> Since the engagement at Cedar Mountain, on the 9th of August, and in which my brigade was well-nigh destroyed, the service required has been of such a character as to threaten, in its reduced and shattered condition, the very existence of its organization.
>
> No time or opportunity has been allowed, from the necessities of the service, either to rest the men or to reorganize the companies and regiments, which have lost field and staff and company officers, both commissioned and non-commissioned, and I am now in command of a brigade which, consisting nominally of four regiments, numbers at this moment, in the rank drawn up in the advance line to meet the enemy, but 629 effective men.
>
> Every day adds to the report of the medical officers of these regiments, and they unanimously show that it is owing to the nature of the service to which we have lately been subjected, the great exposure they have suffered, the deprivation of proper food, and the want of absolute rest that the present condition has been induced. Depression of spirit adds greatly to the induction of camp diseases, and this exists to a certain extent among the men.
>
> Most of our marches have been made during the heat of the day, and we arrived in camp almost invariably at night, when the men, worn out, throw themselves upon the ground to seek rest, regardless of the dews and indifferent to hunger.
>
> There are many men belonging to the command who cannot, from absolute want of muscular tone, follow in its marches. Men never known to fall behind, upon previous marches, do so now. Three of the regiments are without one field or staff officer; company officers are few, and non-commissioned officers either wholly or partially wanting in all the companies.
>
> The organization, the very existence, of these regiments trembles in the balance. Captains, inexperienced in the service, are commanding the Twenty-eighth New York, the Fifth Connecticut, and the Forty-sixth Pennsylvania. Corporals are commanding companies, reduced almost to their proper guards....
>
> My men need rest, and I respectfully urge upon the general commanding that he will use his influence, after the present exigency, to send this brigade to some point where, while they may be useful, they at the same time will have an opportunity to reorganize and recruit both the health and spirits as well as men.[34]

---

[33] Edmund R. Brown, *The Twenty Seventh Indiana Volunteer Infantry in the War of the Rebellion, 1861-1865* (n.p., c. 1899) 227-228. Thomas Clemens emphasizes that this camp was not the Best Farm.

[34] *ORA*, vol. 19, pt. 2, 223-224.

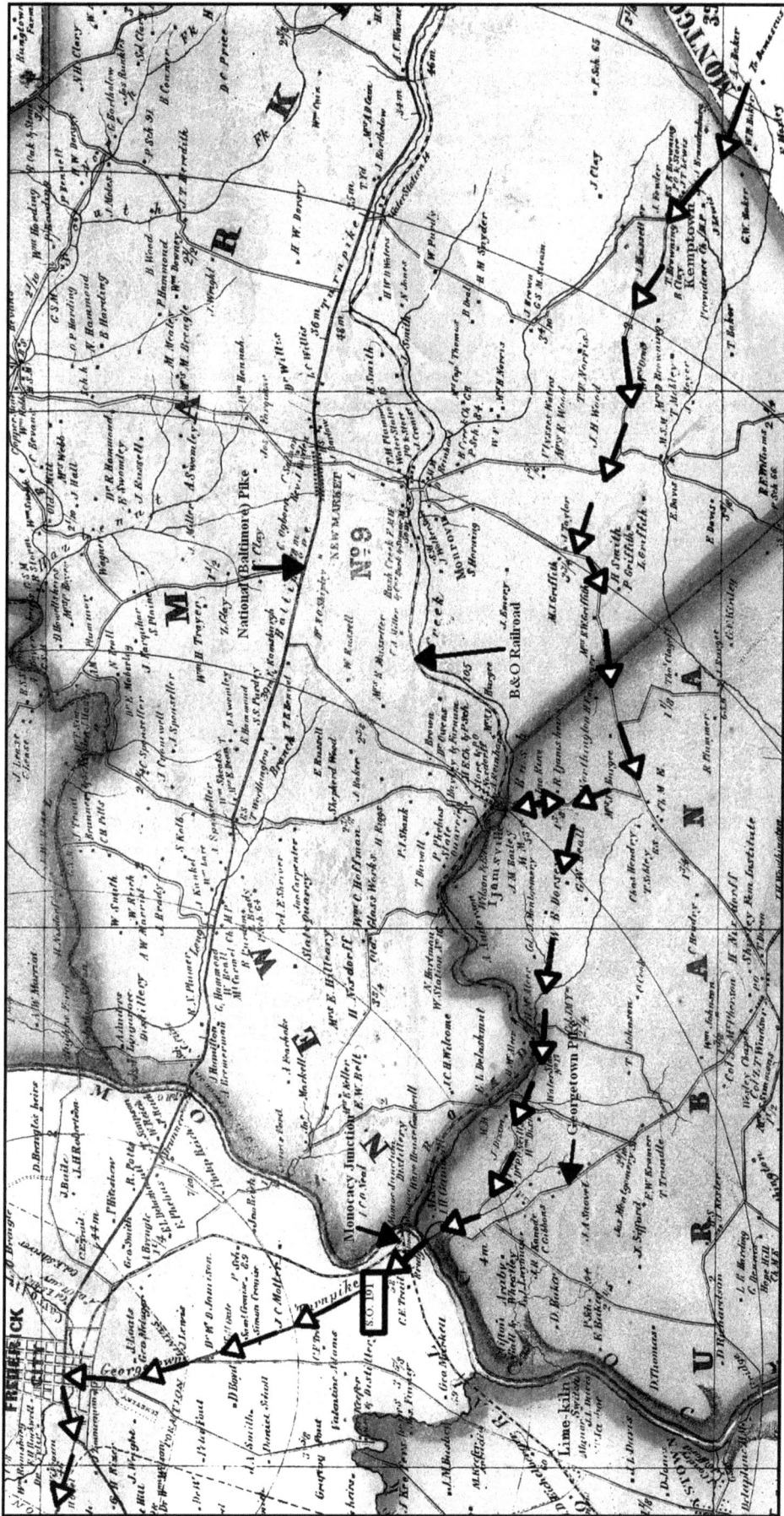

XII Corps march from 11 to 14 September. The road from Damascus is at the starting arrow at the lower right corner on the landscape map. Ijamsville is on the B&O Railroad at the lower center of the map. General Lee's S.O. 191 was found by a XII Corps unit, the 27th Indiana, near Monocacy Junction 13 September. Bond 1858 Map. Courtesy LOC.

Lee and Pope at Second Bull Run

Lee sent Jackson with his three divisions west with orders to cut the Orange and Alexandria Railroad, Pope's supply line. Lee assumed that Pope would retreat towards Washington when he found Jackson in his rear. Stuart would follow Jackson and Longstreet would bring up the rear. Jackson was to march through Thoroughfare Gap in the Bull Run Mountains and get in the rear of Pope's army; Longstreet was to follow thirty-six hours later and unite the army. Jackson marched some 25 miles in severely hot weather on the first day arriving in Salem.[35] On August 28, Jackson observed a Federal column just outside of Gainesville, near the farm of John Brawner, moving east along the Warrenton Turnpike. It consisted of the brigades of Brigadier Generals John P. Hatch, John Gibbon, Abner Doubleday, and Marsena R. Patrick, marching eastward to join the rest of Pope's army at Centreville.

Jackson tried to draw the Yankee's attention but failed so he decided to attack to help spoil any attempt Pope might be making to withdraw behind Bull Run creek and await reinforcement by McClellan. After intense fighting which lasted well into the night, Union forces withdrew ending the costly stalemate. Jackson achieved his intent of drawing Pope's attention and Pope now thought Jackson was retreating and sent forces to bag him.

General Lee, who had joined Longstreet west of the Bull Run Mountains, had to fight at Thoroughfare Gap. Sir Percy Wyndham's 1st New Jersey Cavalry brought Brigadier General Ricketts the first warning of Longstreet's approach to the western side of the gap. Wyndham's troopers had been busy felling trees to block the road from the gap and began the fight with Longstreet troops. In addition to warning Ricketts, he sent word to McDowell on the Warrenton Turnpike. Buford's dispatch to Brigadier General James Ricketts on the morning of 29 August reported the Rebel movement.[36] Unfortunately, after Ricketts' commander, General McDowell, received this report and passed it on to Porter, McDowell did not inform Pope, to whom he gave this news only late that evening. Ricketts' division held Longstreet's infantry back until evening and then was forced back after being flanked on both ends of his line thus allowing clear passage for Longstreet's men for an early start the next morning, 29 August.

That morning, Jackson, believing Union forces would attack, adjusted his line, ensuring that he could escape north if needed. Union forces attacked Jackson piecemeal starting in the morning of the 29th. Shortly after noon, Longstreet's men arrived and were substantially deployed on Jackson's right flank relieving the fears of Lee, as well as Jackson, of the army being defeated in detail. Jackson had an eventful day repelling several attacks.

Pope, on 30 August, based on erroneous reports, believed Jackson was retreating and acted on that belief, wanting to defeat him before he got away. Pope did not heed warnings of Longstreet's troops on Jackson's right which had extended the Confederate lines. Pope did little to have the left of his line reconnoitered to confirm his beliefs. His attacks were repulsed quickly on Jackson's left by the 1st Virginia Cavalry as elements of Kearney's Division crossed Bull Run to threaten Jackson's rear. Pope finally realized that the Confederates were not retreating but still there in force and full of fight. But Pope dismissed a report brought to him in person by Brigadier General John F. Reynolds that the Rebels were massing for an attack on Pope's left; he did, however, deign to send Buford with some cavalry to confirm it.

Pope next received a report from Sigel that the 4th New York Cavalry, which performed a reconnaissance around the Rebel right, and found that the Confederates were moving against the Union left; Pope also dismissed this report.[37] He decided to attack Jackson's right not understanding that his men were charging into the center of the Confederate line. Longstreet, instead of sending a division to reinforce Jackson's weakened line, had several batteries of artillery enfilade the long Union lines decimating Pope's attack and he followed up with an infantry charge of some 25,000 men, sending the Federal troops reeling. Federal artillery, usually the master of the Confederate batteries, suffered one of its rare failures; it was parceled out to brigades and divisions so was unable to concentrate its fire as Rebel artillery did.[38] The Federal's retreat was not a rout as at First Bull Run but by nightfall, Pope was in full flight to Centerville with the Confederate pursuit stopped only by darkness.[39] Union casualties at Second Bull Run were 16,054 while Lee reported 9,197.[40]

---

[35] Harsh wrote that General Lee's strategy may not have been to just chase Pope towards Washington but away from Gordonsville and Richmond and then lure him into the Shenandoah Valley where Lee would have room to maneuver and hope to seriously damage Pope's army. Too, Harsh observed that "Washington was most vulnerable on its western flank on a line that menaced the upper Potomac and the Baltimore and Ohio Railroad and threatened both Pennsylvania and the capital's tenuous communications with the North through Baltimore," *Rising*, 145-146, 151.

[36] *ORA*, vol. 12, pt. 3, 730.

[37] Hennessy, 328-330.

[38] Hennessy, 351, 462.

[39] Ibid., 431.

[40] David J. Eicher, *The Longest Night: A Military History of the Civil War* (New York, NY: Simon & Schuster, 2001), 334.

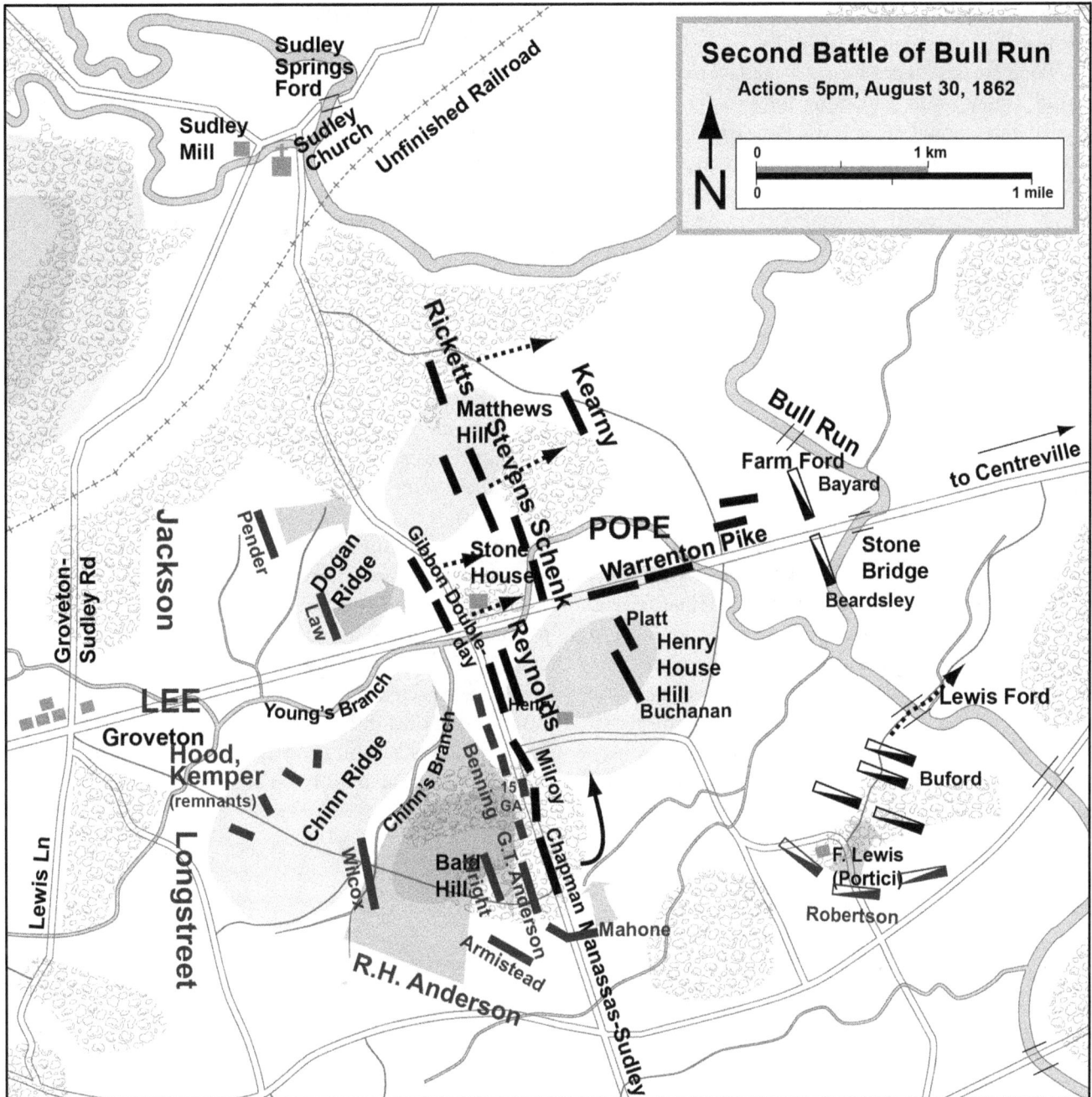

Situation 30 August at 5 p.m. Courtesy Hal Jespersen from Wikipedia.

General Lee had Stuart pursue the retreating Federals early on 31 August in the middle of a heavy rainstorm. Stuart found strong Union forces near Cub Run and was halted. Stuart scouted Union lines near Centreville on the 31st and reported to Lee that Pope's flank was secure, except perhaps to the north, which was a better approach anyway, as it had better roads. Lee sent Jackson around Pope's right flank, east on Little River Turnpike, with Stuart's cavalry in the van. Longstreet would follow Jackson after demonstrating in Pope's front at Centreville. Lee hoped to cut Pope off from Washington and gain the destruction of the Union army which he had missed accomplishing the day before.

On 1 September, Jackson had Stuart send a cavalry brigade under Fitzhugh Lee, east along the Little River Turnpike, and Robertson's Brigade south on Walney Road. Jackson had posted infantry and artillery about one mile south of the intersection of Little River Turnpike and Stringfellow Road at Chantilly, which held off an advance by some of Union Brigadier General Oliver O. Howard's brigade. Under orders not to bring on a general engagement, Howard withdrew, but ordered up two of Bayard's depleted cavalry regiments, the 1st New Jersey and the 1st Maine, to picket the road.

These two regiments traded shots with Rebel infantry for the remainder of the afternoon.[41] Jackson continued marching east past the intersection at Chantilly.

Pope quickly understood that he had to send forces to strengthen his defenses at Germantown and Fairfax Court House. He also sent a blocking force under Brigadier General Stevens north near West Ox Road to ensure that the Confederates would not surprise Pope's men by heading south, before Union forces reached Germantown. Meanwhile, Hooker on his way to Germantown to take command of the defenses there, had gathered up the 1st Rhode Island Cavalry and sent the troopers west on the Little River Turnpike searching for the Rebel column. Rosser was riding with the 5th Virginia cavalry when it came under fire from the dismounted 1st Rhode Island troopers. The Virginians retreated, but Fitzhugh Lee decided to hold the road as he formed a dismounted line on a ridge overlooking Difficult Run, along with two cannon. The Rhode Islanders retreated when supporting Union infantry, Duryée's 1st Rhode Island Brigade, came up to replace them. As Hooker's line was strengthened by troops coming from Fairfax Court House, Beardsley's cavalry brigade, including the 6th Ohio Cavalry, the 9th New York cavalry, and a squadron from the 1st Connecticut cavalry, kept the Warrenton Pike open to the retreating Federal units.[42]

Jackson was stalled at Germantown at 4 p.m., so had sent two brigades south of Little River Turnpike west of West Ox Road to protect his right flank. Brigadier General Isaac I. Stevens' and Major General Jesse L. Reno's divisions confronted them at 4:30 p.m. just as a fierce thunderstorm broke. Stevens was killed leading his men in desperate fighting as they pushed back some Confederate units near the center of the Rebel line. Strong Confederate reinforcements quickly arrived routing the charging Unionists. Stevens' request for help finally found a commander willing to come to his aid: Major General Philip Kearney, who rushed north from the Warrenton Pike. Jackson adjusted his lines to meet the Union attacks he expected would continue. As Kearney was bringing up and aligning his troops in the semidarkness, he was killed. A short time later at 6:45 p.m., Longstreet appeared with his command and found Jackson, but the fighting was over. The cost to Pope to keep General Lee away from the Union line of retreat was 655 Federal casualties, including the deaths of two promising Union brigadier generals, Isaac Stevens and Philip Kearny. Lee lost about 500. Jackson and Longstreet placed their troops to face the expected Union morning attack. Pope's men were not seen the next day as he decided to retreat to Fairfax Court House and then into the Washington defenses. He had his fill of battling and losing to General Lee on all fronts, but although he was beaten, many of his troops felt chagrined at continuing to run from the Rebels.[43] Lee was now satisfied that Pope was beyond his reach and surely lamented that too much of the Union army survived the battles of the prior three days.

[41] David A. Welker, *Tempest at Ox Hill: The Battle of Chantilly* (Cambridge, MA: Da Capo Press, 2002), 118-119; *ORA*, vol. 12, pt. 2, 744.
[42] Welker, 129-136; Frederic Denison, *Sabres and Spurs: The First Regiment Rhode Island Cavalry in the Civil War, 1861-1865* (Central Falls, RI: The First Rhode Island Cavalry Veteran Association, The Press of E. L. Freeman, and Co., 1876), 148-149. The Ocean Staters lost two men holding the pike.
[43] Welker, 204.

II Corps Army of Virginia
Order of Battle and Casualties at Cedar Mountain 9 August 1862[44]

Major General Nathaniel P. Banks (w)[45]
Staff (12) [0]
Escort: Co. L, 1st Michigan Cavalry, Capt. Melvin Brewer (54) [9]
Co. M, 5th New York Cavalry, Lt. Eugene Dimmick (50)[46] [1]
Co. H, 1st West Virginia Cavalry, Capt. Isaac P. Kerr (50)[47] [6]

First Division
Brigadier General Alpheus S. Williams
Staff (6) [1]
Escort: Co. M, 1st Michigan Cavalry, Capt. R.C. Dennison (50)[48] [0]
Brigadier General Samuel W. Crawford (w)
Brigadier General George H. Gordon

First Brigade
Brigadier General Samuel W. Crawford
Staff (4) [0]
5th Conn., Colonel George D. Chapman (w), Lt. Colonel Henry B. Stone (mw) (445)[49] [237]
10th Maine, Colonel George L. Beal (461)[50] [173][51]
28th New York, Colonel Dudley Donnelly (mw), Lt. Colonel Edwin F. Brown (w) (357)[52] [213]
46th Penn., Colonel Joseph F. Knipe (w), Lt. Colonel James L. Selfridge (w) (504)[53] [244]

Third Brigade[54]
Brigadier General George H. Gordon
Staff (4) [0]
27th Indiana, Colonel Silas Colgrove (453)[55] [50]
2nd Mass., Colonel George L. Andrews (446)[56] [173]
3rd Wisconsin, Colonel Thomas H. Ruger (476)[57] [108]
Zouaves d'Afrique (Penn.)[58] (50) [13]

---

[44] Numbers in parentheses show strength, brackets show casualties when data available. Numbers taken into battle are shown for the First Brigade of the First Division and the First Brigade of the Second Division from the *ORA*. Present for duty numbers in the Third Brigade of the First Division are adjusted downward by 25% to estimate those taken into battle based on numbers given for the First Brigade. Present for duty numbers for the Second and Third Brigades of the Second Division are reduced by 35% based on numbers given for the First Brigade to estimate taken into battle numbers. Commanders described much straggling due to heat. John O. Allen, "The Strength of the Union and Confederate Forces at Second Manassas," master's thesis, George Mason University, 1993, 64-65; Krick, Cedar Mountain, 365-367, 373-376. *ORA*, vol. 12, pt. 2, 136-138; *ORA*, vol. 12, pt. 3, 583. Casualties include killed, wounded, missing/captured. The data listing unit numbers show present for duty taken from primarily from Allen's, "The Strength of the Union and Confederate Forces at Second Manassas." This thesis provides the basis for the comparison of the II Corps AOV numbers at Cedar Mountain to the XII Corps AOP numbers at Antietam. The Cedar Run numbers as calculated based on Allen's data for 9 August 1862 with supplementary numbers from his 1 August data as he did not break down the Cedar Mountain number to the regiment level.

[45] Banks was struck by a runaway horse 9 August 1862, Eicher, 115; Strother, 77-78.

[46] Estimate based on strengths for comparable companies at this time.

[47] Estimate based on strengths for comparable companies at this time.

[48] Estimate based on strengths for comparable companies at this time.

[49] Allen shows 576 present for duty 1 August while Crawford reported 445 taken into battle, *ORA*, vol. 12, pt. 2, 153.

[50] Allen shows 623 present for duty 1 August while Crawford reported 461 taken into battle, Ibid., 153.

[51] Gould's regimental history reports 179 total casualties, 196.

[52] Allen shows 500 present for duty 1 August while Crawford reported 357 taken into battle, Ibid., 153.

[53] Allen shows 633 present for duty 1 August while Crawford reported 504 taken into battle, Ibid., 153.

[54] 29th Penn. in the brigade on detached service and not in the battle at Cedar Mountain; *ORA*, pt. 2, 145.

[55] Allen shows 604 present for duty 1 August, 59.

[56] Allen shows 595 present for duty 1 August, Ibid.

[57] Allen shows 635 present for duty 1 August, Ibid.

[58] No officer present, enlisted men of company attached to 2nd Mass. Regiment; company strength 50 estimated and not reduced 25%.

Second Division

Brigadier General C.C. Auger (w)

Brigadier General Henry Prince (c)

Brigadier General George S. Greene

Staff (6) [3]

First Brigade

Brigadier General John W. Geary (w)

Colonel Charles Candy

Staff (4) [1]

5th Ohio, Colonel John H. Patrick (275)[59] [122]

7th Ohio, Colonel William R. Creighton (w) (307)[60] [182]

29th Ohio, Capt. Wilbur F. Stevens (189)[61] [66]

66th Ohio, Lt. Colonel Eugene Powell (250)[62] [94]

28th Pennsylvania, Lt. Colonel Hector Tyndale (1,035)[63] [2]

Second Brigade

Brigadier General Henry Prince (c)

Colonel David P. De Witt

Staff (4) [3]

3rd Maryland, Lt. Colonel Joseph H. Sudsburg (275)[64] [70]

102nd New York, Major James C. Lane (267)[65] [115]

109th Penn., Colonel Henry J. Stainrook, (w) (272)[66] [114]

111th Penn., Major Thomas M. Walker (252)[67] [90]

8th and 12th U.S. Infantry Battalion Capt. Thomas G. Pitcher (w) (126)[68] [60]

Third Brigade[69]

Brigadier General George S. Greene

Colonel James A. Tait

Staff (4)

1st Dist. Of Columbia, Colonel James A. Tait (166)[70] [4]

78th New York, Lt. Colonel Jonathan Austin (261)[71] [22]

Artillery

Captain Clermont L. Best

---

[59] Allen shows 434 present for duty 1 August while Patrick reported about 275 taken into battle, *ORA*, vol. 12, pt. 2, 163. He previously reported about 300 taken into battle, Ibid., 162.

[60] Allen shows 492 present for duty 1 August while Creighton reported 307 taken into battle, Ibid., 164.

[61] Allen shows 346 present for duty 1 August while Stevens reported 189 taken into battle 189, Ibid.

[62] Allen shows 353 present for duty 1 August while Colonel Candy reported about 250 taken into battle, Ibid., 166.

[63] Allen shows 1,231 as of 18 August 1862; Tyndale reported 1,035, Ibid., 167; not at Cedar Mountain—reconnaissance to take the signal station on Thoroughfare Mountain 9 August; Samuel P. Bates, *History of Pennsylvania Volunteers, 1861-1865*, vol. 1 (Harrisburg, PA: B. Singerly, State Printer, 1869), 426.

[64] Allen shows 423 present for duty 1 August, 60.

[65] Allen shows 410 present for duty 1 August, 60.

[66] Allen shows 419 present for duty 1 August, 60.

[67] Allen shows 388 present for duty 1 August, 60.

[68] Allen shows 194 present for duty as of 18 August, 68.

[69] Augur reported that the 3rd Delaware was detached at Front Royal; the Purnell Legion, Maryland Volunteers, detached at Warrenton and Warrenton Junction; and the 60th New York detached at Warrenton Springs, *ORA*, vol. 12, pt. 2, 157. He reported that the number remaining for Greene's brigade at Cedar Mountain was 457 enlisted men, with a total of about 3,013 from his division on the field. The 3rd Delaware rejoined the division on 21 August, the 60th New York on 24 August, and the Purnell Legion on 27 August, *ORA*, vol. 12, pt. 2, 325.

[70] Allen shows 256 present for duty 1 August, 60.

[71] Allen shows 401 present for duty 1 August, 60.

4th Maine Light, Capt. O'Neil W. Robinson, Jr. (109) [8]

6th Maine Light, Capt. Freeman McGilvery (96) [18]
Bty. K, 1st New York Light, Capt. Lorenzo Crounse (87) [0]
Bty. L, 1st New York Light, Capt. John A. Reynolds (86) [0]
Bty. M, 1st New York Light, Capt. George W. Cothran (85) [0]
Bty. L, 2nd New York Light, Capt. Jacob Roemer (108) [1]
10th Bty. N.Y. Light, Capt. John T. Bruen (78) [0]
Bty. E, Penn. Light, Capt. Joseph M. Knap (73) [8]
Bty. F, 4th U.S., Lt. Edward D. Muhlenberg[72] (99) [5]

---

[72] Lieutenant Muhlenberg is described as the battery commander by Brigadier General Crawford, *ORA*, vol. 12, pt. 2, 150-152, but Krick shows Lieutenant Hiram B. Howard, 366, 374. Knap wrote that Howard commanded a section, *ORA*, vol. 12, pt. 2, 162.

Brigadier General Alpheus S. Williams's XII Corps Itinerary
1 September to 30 September 1862[73]

First Division

September 1, division moved from Bull Run and encamped near Fairfax

September 2, moved toward Alexandria, Va., arriving on the morning of the 3d instant, and halted outside the city

September 3, moved to Georgetown, D.C., and bivouacked in rear of Fort Richardson

September 4, crossed the Potomac at Georgetown, and moved to near Tennallytown, and encamped

September 5, the division moved to near Rockville, Md., and encamped

September 6, moved a short distance, formed in line of battle, and lay upon the field

September 7, lay upon the field

September 8, the One hundred and twenty-fourth, One hundred and twenty-fifth, and One hundred and twenty-eighth Regiments Pennsylvania Volunteers assigned to First Brigade

September 9, moved to Middlebrook and bivouacked

September 10, moved to Damascus, Md.

September 11, remained in camp

September 12, moved to near Ijamsville and bivouacked

September 13 moved to near Frederick and encamped

September 14, division moved to South Mountain and bivouacked

September 15, moved to Keedysville and bivouacked

September 16, lay in line of battle

September 17, battle of Antietam, in which the division took an active part, under General Mansfield, on the right

September 18, division lay upon the field in line of battle

September 19, moved, via Sharpsburg, to Brownsville

September 20, moved over Maryland Heights, down the mountain, and to near Sandy Hook, and encamped

September 22, moved upon Maryland Heights

September 28, moved down the mountain, and again encamped near Sandy Hook, Md., where the division remained until the end of the month

Second Division

September 1, division left Bull Run, and took up the line of march for Fairfax, encamping at the forks of the road

September 2, marched toward Alexandria, halting near Fort Worth

September 3, marched beyond Alexandria, and halted in the rear of Fort Richardson

September 4, marched through Georgetown, and encamped near Tennallytown

September 5, marched through Tennallytown, and encamped near Rockville

September 6, moved up and took position in line which had been formed about 2½ miles from Rockville

September 9, marched to Middlebrook

September 10, marched toward Damascus, and encamped within 2 miles of that place

September 11, moved on to Damascus

September 12, took up line of march toward Frederick, gaining 7 miles, and encamped

September 13, crossed the Monocacy River and encamped near Frederick

September 14 marched toward the South Mountain, encamping near there

September 15, passed through Boonsborough and halted near Sharpsburg, encamping

September 16, at night, moved up and took position on the left of General Mansfield's corps, on the right of the line of battle

September 17, engaged in the battle of Antietam

September 19, marched in the direction of Harper's Ferry, Va., being on the road all night, and arrived near Sandy Hook, Md., at 3 p.m., on the 20th

September 22, took position on Loudoun Heights, Va., where the division lay until the end of the month

---

[73] *ORA*, vol. 19, pt. 1, 478–480.

John Mead Gould
Record of Principal Events for the 10ᵗʰ Maine Regiment from 6 July 1862 to 25 September 1862[74]

July 6. The brigade marched through Chester Gap to Sandy Hook, 8 miles

7. Marched past Flint Hill to near Amissville, 10 miles

11. The army, now under Gen Pope, concentrates. Marched to near Warrenton, 12 miles

16. Returned toward Amissville, 6 miles

17. Through Amissville and Gaines's Cross Roads, to Washington C.H., 12 miles.

22. Paid by Major W.C.H. Sherman for May and June

23. Marched through Sperryville and Woodville, 13 miles

24. Through Boston and Griffinsburg to Culpeper C.H., 13 miles

25. Co. A, Capt. Adams, was sent to Rixleyville, ten miles, to guard a bridge

28-30. Shelter-tents given to the men

Aug. 6. Co. A returned from Rixleyville. Railroad opened and McDowell's troops arrived. Jackson marching north

8. 1st brigade marched toward Orange C. H., 7 miles

9. Battle Of Cedar Mountain. Aggregate loss 179

11. Enemy retiring. 10th Me. and 5th Conn, ordered to guard Culpeper C.H.

13. Review of the brigade by General Crawford

15. Review of Division by General Williams

16. Inspection by Major Perkins. Muskets condemned

18. Muster for the purpose of learning who were absent. All the trains moved north

Pope's Retreat

19. Marched to Rappahannock Station, Fauquier Co., 11 miles.

21. At night marched down the river to a ford, 2 miles

22. Returned and went up river to support Sigel, about 8 miles

23. To near Sulphur Springs, about 6 miles

24. Countermarched and went past the springs under artillery fire. No injuries in the regiment, about 8 miles.

25. Marched up Piney Mountain. Returned and went toward Warrenton, and finally toward Bealeton Station, 10 miles.

26. Marched toward Bealeton, 4 or 5 miles

27. Marched past Bealeton to Warrenton Junction, 10 or 12 miles

28. To Kettle Run. Capt. Knowlton here assisted in repairing the railroad bridge, 7 miles

29. Remained near the battlefield where Hooker whipped Ewell

30. Marched to Manassas Junction and returned to Broad Run, 10 miles

31. Went on picket with 5th Conn. on Gainesville road, 4 A.M. Withdrawn hastily at 9 A.M., and marched through Brentsville to Blackburn's Ford. Cars and wagons burned before starting, 11 miles. The infantry of Banks's corps took no part in the battles and skirmishes on Pope's retreat

Sept. 1. Marched near Centerville and Fairfax C.H., Halted while the battle of Chantilly was pending. 6 miles

2. Struck the pike at Annandale; halted while the main army retreated past us, marched all the evening, and at 2 A.M. of the 3d reached Fort Ward, 14 miles

3. Changed camp to Fort Albany, 2 miles

Maryland Campaign--Antietam

4. Crossed the Potomac and marched beyond Tennallytown, 8 miles

5. Marched beyond Rockville, 10 miles

6. The regimental band was ordered to Washington for muster out. Our wagons, with knapsacks aboard, arrived. Changed camp—half mile

9. Marched with Sumner's corps (2d) to Middlebrook, 10 miles

10. Marched to near Damascus, 8 miles

11. Moved to the outskirts of Damascus, 1 mile

12. To within a mile of the railroad at Ijamsville, 12 miles

13. Forded the Monocacy and camped outside of Frederick, 9 miles

---

[74] Gould, *History of the First*, 662-663. Gould was his regiment's historian and a participant in the Battle as a first lieutenant in Co. E, 10ᵗʰ Maine. He became an authority for the 10ᵗʰ Maine's activities and collaborated with Ezra Carman for details of actions on that part of the field especially concerning Mansfield. See, Carman, Clemens, vol. 2, 111, n. 1.

14. Marched through Middletown and up South Mountain, 13 miles

15. Through Turner's Gap and Boonsboro to Nicodemus's mills, 7 miles

16. Long roll in morning. Advanced toward enemy one mile, and remained under cover all day. At 11 p.m. our corps marched to right of the army, 4 miles

17. Battle of Antietam. At 6.10 A. M. moved. Halted an hour and were shelled. Went to support Ricketts at 7.30 A.M. Loss 31 killed and mortally wounded, and 40 wounded

18. Moved to the front. Picket firing only, to-day

19. The enemy having retreated we marched through Sharpsburg and Rohrersville to Brownsville, 13 miles

20. Marched to the Potomac near Sandy Hook, 5 miles

23. Marched up Maryland Heights, 3 miles

25. Co. K marched to Knoxville to do provost duty, 4 miles

SELECT BIBLIOGRAPHY

Abbot, Henry L. *National Academy of Sciences, Biographical Memoirs*, vol. 5. "Biographical Memoir of John Gross Barnard, 1815–1882." Washington, DC: Press of Judd & Detweiler, 1905.

_____. "The Corps of Engineers," in *The Army of the United States, Historical Sketches of Staff and Line*. Ed. by Theophilus F. Rodenbough and William L. Haskin. New York, NY: Maynard, Merrill, & Co., 1896.

Adams, Anton. *The War in Mexico*. Chicago, IL: The Emperor's Press, 1998.

Alcaraz, Ramon. *The Other Side: Or, Notes for the History of the War Between Mexico and the United States*. Trans. by Albert C. Ramsey. New York, NY: John Wiley, 1850.

Allen, John Owen. "The Strength of the Union and Confederate Forces at Second Manassas." Master's thesis. George Mason University, 1993.

Amberson, Mary Margaret McAllen; McAllen, James A.; McAllen, Margaret H. *I Would Rather Sleep in Texas: A History of the Lower Rio Grande Valley and the People of the Santa Anita Land Grant*. Austin, TX: Texas State Historical Assn., 2003.

Ambrose, Stephen E. *Duty, Honor Country: A History of West Point*. Baltimore, MD: The Johns Hopkins University Press, 1999.

American Phrenological Journal and Life Illustrated 36, no. 5, November 1862. "General Mansfield, Phrenological Character and Biography."

Andreas, A.T. *History of Chicago from the Earliest Period to the Present Time*. Chicago, IL: A.T. Andreas, Publisher, 1884.

Andrews, Henry Franklin. *The Hamlin Family: A Genealogy of Capt. Giles Hamlin of Middletown, Connecticut 1654-1900*. Henry Franklin Andrews: Exira, IA, 1900.

Anderson, Robert. *An Artillery Officer in The Mexican War, 1846-7: Letters of Robert Anderson, Captain 3rd Artillery, U.S.A.* New York, NY: G.P. Putnam's Sons, 1911.

Backus, Electus. "A Brief Sketch of the Battle of Monterrey." The Historical Magazine, X, July 1866.

Bacon, Edwin M. *Boston Illustrated*. Boston, MA: Houghton, Mifflin and Co., 1886.

Bakeless, John. *Spies of the Confederacy*. Philadelphia: J. B. Lippincott Company, 1970. Reprint, Mineola, NY: Dover Publications, Inc. 1997.

Ball, Durwood. *Army Regulars on the Western Frontier, 1848-1861*. Norman, OK: University of Oklahoma Press, 2001.

Bancroft, Hubert Howe. *The Works of Hubert Howe Bancroft: the History of Utah*, vol. 26. San Francisco, CA: The History Company, 1889.

Bandel, Eugene. *Frontier Life in the Army, 1854-1861*. Ed. by Ralph B. Bieber. Glendale, CA: The Arthur H. Clark Company, 1932.

Barbour, Philip Norbourne. *Journals of the Late Brevet Major Philip Norbourne Barbour and His Wife Martha Isabella Hopkins Barbour*. Ed. by Rhoda van Bibber Tanner Doubleday. New York, NY: G.P. Putnam's Sons, 1936.

Barnard, John Gross. "Memoir of Joseph Gilbert Totten 1788-1864." *National Academy of Sciences Biographical Memoirs,* vol. 1. Philadelphia, PA: Collins, Printer, 1877.

_____. *Eulogy on the Late Brevet Major-General Joseph G. Totten*. New York, NY: D. Van Nostrand, 1866.

Bauer, K. Jack. *The Mexican War 1846-1848*. Lincoln NE, Univ. of Nebraska Press, 1974.

_____. *Surfboats and Horse Marines: U.S. Naval Operations in the Mexican War, 1846-48*. Annapolis, MD: U.S. Naval Institute Press, 1969.

_____. *Zachary Taylor: Soldier, Planter, Statesman of the Old Southwest.* Baton Rouge, LA: Louisiana State University Press, 1985.

Bearss, Edwin C. *Fort Point, Historic Structure Report, Historic Data Section.* Denver: National Park Service, 1973.

Bender, Averam B. *The March of Empire: Frontier Defense in the Southwest 1848-1860.* New York: NY: Greenwood Press, 1968.

Benham, Henry W. "Recollections of Mexico and the Battle of Buena Vista, Feb. 22 and 23, 1847," in *Old and New,* June and July, 1871, Boston, MA.

Bennett, James A. *Forts and Forays: A Dragoon in New Mexico, 1850-1856.* Ed. by Clinton E. Brooks and Frank D. Reeve. Albuquerque, NM: The University of New Mexico Press, 1948.

Berard, Augusta Blanche. *Reminiscences of West Point in the Olden Time.* East Saginaw, MI: Evening News Printing and Binding House, 1886.

Bigler David L. and Bagley, Will. *The Mormon Rebellion: America's First Civil War, 1857-1858.* Norman OK: University of Oklahoma Press, 2011.

Black, William M. "Pamphlet on The Evolution of the Art of Fortification." Washington, DC: GPO, 1919.

Bodge, George Madison. *Soldiers in King Philip's War.* Leominster, MA: Rockwell and Churchill Press, 1896.

"The Bostonian, An Illustrated Monthly Magazine of Local Interest," vol. II, April-Sept. 1895. N.A. The Bostonian Publishing Company, 1895.

Bosbyshell, Oliver Christian. *The 48th In The War, Being a Narrative of the Campaigns of the 48th Regiment, Infantry, Pennsylvania Veteran Volunteers During the War of the Rebellion.* Philadelphia: PA, Avil Printing Company, 1895.

Boynton, Edward C. *History of West Point.* New York, NY: D. Van Nostrand, 1871.

Bresnahan, John. "Battle of Antietam." *National Tribune,* 21 February 1889.

Breth, Bruce R. *An Historical Analysis and Comparison of the Military Retirement System and the Federal Employee Retirement System.* Master's thesis. Naval Postgraduate School, Monterey, CA, 1998.

Brooke, John M. "The Virginia, or Merrimac.," *Southern Historical Society Papers,* vol. 19, January 1891. Ed. by R.A. Brock. Richmond, VA: Published by the Society, 1891.

Brooks, Nathan C. *A Complete History of the Mexican War: Its Causes, Conduct, and Consequences; Comprising an Account of the Various Military and Naval Operations, from Its Commencement to the Treaty of Peace.* Philadelphia, PA: Grigg, Elliot & Co., 1851.

Brown, Edmund Randolph. *The Twenty-Seventh Indiana Volunteer Infantry in the War of the rebellion 1861 to 1865.* Monticello, IN, n.p.,1899.

Brown, William E. *The Santa Fe Trail.* St. Louis, MO: The Patrice Press, 1988.

Bruce, Robert V. *Lincoln and the Tools of War.* Indianapolis, IN: The Bobbs-Merrill Company, Inc., 1956.

Bryant, Edwin E. *History of the Third Regiment of Wisconsin Veteran Volunteer Infantry 1861-1865.* Cleveland, OH: The Arthur H. Clark Company, 1891.

Buker, George E. *Sun, Sand and Water: A History of the Jacksonville District U.S. Army Corps of Engineers, 1821-1975.* Washington, DC: U.S. Government Printing Office, 1981.

Butler, Gerald W. *The Guns of Boston Harbor (From the Bay Colony through the Present)*. Ed. by Mary and Richard Shaner. 1st Books Library, 1999.

Butler, Steven R., ed. *A Documentary History of the Mexican War*. Richardson, Texas: Descendants of Mexican War Veterans, 1995.

Carleton, James Henry. *The Battle of Buena Vista with the Operations of the Army of Occupation for One Month*. New York, NY: Harper and Brothers, 1848.

Carman, Ezra A. *The Maryland Campaign of September 1862: Ezra A. Carman's Definitive Study of the Union and Confederate Armies at Antietam*. Ed. by Joseph Pierro. New York, NY: Routledge Taylor & Francis Group, 2008.

_____. *The Maryland Campaign of September 1862. Vol. 1: South Mountain*. Ed. by Thomas G. Clemens. New York, NY: Savas Beatie LLC, 2010.

_____. *The Maryland Campaign of September 1862. Vol. 2: Antietam*. Ed. by Thomas G. Clemens. New York, NY: Savas Beatie LLC, 2012.

Carney, Stephen A. "Gateway South, The Campaign for Monterrey," in *The U.S. Army Campaigns of the Mexican War Series*, U.S. Army Center of Military History, Pub. 73-1.

_____. U.S. Army Center of Military History, "The Occupation of Mexico, May 1846-July 1848.

Chamberlain, Samuel E. *My Confession*. New York, NY: Harper and Brothers, 1956.

_____. *My Confession: Recollections of a Rogue*. Ed. by William H. Goetzmann. Austin, TX: Texas State Historical Association, 1996.

Chance, Joseph E. "Walnut Springs." *The United States and Mexico at War: Nineteenth-Century Expansionism and Conflict*. Donald S. Frazier, ed. New York, NY: Macmillan Reference USA, 1998.

Charnley, Jeffrey Gordon. "'Neglected Honor,' The Life of General A.S. Williams of Michigan (1810-1878)." Ph.D. dissertation, University of Michigan, 1983.

Chase, Salmon P. *Annual Report of the American Historical Association for the Year 1902*, vol. 2. Diary and Correspondence of Salmon P. Chase. Washington, DC: Government Printing Office, 1903.

Churchill, Franklin Hunter. *Sketch of the Life of Bvt. Brig. Gen. Sylvester Churchill, Inspector General U.S. Army*. New York, NY: Willis McDonald & Co., 1888.

Clary, David A. and Whitehorne, Joseph W.A. *The Inspectors Generals of the United States Army 1777-1903*. Washington, DC: U.S. Government Printing Office, 1987.

Clemens, Thomas G. *Corps Commanders in Blue: Union Major Generals in the Civil War*. Edited by Ethan Rafuse; Clemens, Thomas G., "'Too Bad, Poor Fellows', Joseph K.F. Mansfield and the XII Corps at Antietam" Baton Rouge, LA: Louisiana University Press, 2014.

_____. "In Search of McClellan's Headquarters." *Civil War Times*, June 2016.

Comey, Henry Newton. *A Legacy of Valor: The Memoirs and Letters of Captain Henry Newton Comey, 2nd Massachusetts Infantry*. Knoxville, TN: The University of Tennessee Press, 2004.

Cooling, Benjamin Franklin, III and Owen, Walton H., II. *Mr. Lincoln's Forts: A Guide to the Civil War Defenses of Washington*. Lanham, MD: The Scarecrow Press, Inc., 2010.

_____. *Symbol, Sword, and Shield: Defending Washington during the Civil War*. Shippensburg, PA: White Mane Publishing Company, Inc., 1991.

County Atlas of Middlesex Connecticut. F.W. Beers & Co., NY, NY, 1874.

The Colonial Records of Connecticut, 1678-1689 and 1689-1706. Hartford: Case, Lockwood and Brainard, 1868.

Crackel, Theodore J. *The Illustrated History of West Point.* New York, NY: Harry N. Abrams, Inc., 1991.

Crane, Ellery Bicknell. *Historic homes and institutions and genealogical and personal memoirs of Worcester County, Massachusetts,* vol. 2. Lewis Pub., 1907.

Crimmins, Martin Lalor. "Colonel J.K.F. Mansfield's Report of the Inspection of the Department of Texas in 1856." *The Southwestern Historical Quarterly*, vol. 42, July 1938-April 1939.

Croghan, George. *Army Life on the Western Frontier.* Ed. by Francis Paul Prucha. Norman, OK: University of Oklahoma Press, 1958.

Cullum, George W. *Biographical Register of the Officers and Graduates of the U.S. Military Academy at West Point, New York Since Its Establishment in 1802*, suppl., vol. 5, 1900-1910. Ed. by Charles Braden. Saginaw, MI: Seemann & Peters, Printers, 1910.

Dana, Napoleon Jackson Tecumseh. *MONTEREY IS OURS! The Mexican War Letters of Lieutenant Dana 1845-1847.* Ed. by Robert H. Ferrell. Lexington, KY: The University Press of Kentucky, 1990.

Dary, David. *The Santa Fe Trail: Its History, Legends, and Lore.* New York, NY: Alfred A. Knopf, 2000.

Davis, William C. *Battle at Bull Run: A History of the First Major Campaign of the Civil War.* Mechanicsburg, PA: Stackpole Books, 1977.

_____. *A Taste for War: The Culinary History of the Blue and Gray.* Mechanicsburg, PA: Stackpole Books, 2003.

Davis, William Watts Hart. *El Gringo: New Mexico and Her People.* New York, NY: Harper, 1857.

Denison, Frederic. *Sabres and Spurs: The First Regiment Rhode Island Cavalry in the Civil War, 1861-1865*, Central Falls, RI: The First Rhode Island Cavalry Veteran Association, The Press of E. L. Freeman, and Co., 1876.

DePalo, William A., Jr. *The Mexican National Army, 1822-1852.* College Station, TX: Texas A&M University Press, 1997.

DeVoto, Bernard. *The Year of Decision—1846.* Boston, MA: Houghton-Mifflin Co., 1943.

Dexter, Franklin Bowditch. *Biographical Sketches of the Graduates of Yale College with Annals of the College History*, vol. V, June, 1792-September, 1805. New York, NY: Henry Holt and Company, 1911.

Dishman, Christopher D. *A Perfect Gibraltar: The Battle for Monterrey, Mexico, 1846.* Norman, OK: University of Oklahoma Press, 2010.

Doubleday, Abner. *My Life in the Old Army: The Reminiscences of Abner Doubleday from the Collections of the New York Historical Society.* Ed. by Joseph E. Chance. Fort Worth, TX: Texas Christian University Press, 1998.

Dugard, Martin. *The Training Ground: Grant, Lee, Sherman, and Davis in the Mexican War, 1846-1848.* New York, NY: Little Brown and company, 2008.

Dunigan, Edward R. *The National Tribune.* "Battle of Antietam," 3 November 1892.

Dupuy, R. Ernest. *Where They Have Trod: The West Point Tradition in American Life.* New York, NY: Frederick A. Stokes Company, 1940.

Dyer, Alexander B. "The Fourth Regiment of Artillery." *The Army of the United States, Historical Sketches of Staff and Line with Portraits of Generals-in-Chief.* Ed. by Theophilus F. Rodenbough and William L. Haskin. New York, NY: Maynard, Merrill, & Co., 1896.

Dyer, Brainerd. *Zachary Taylor*. New York, NY: Barnes & Noble, Inc., 1967.

Dyer, Frederick H. *A Compendium of the War of the Rebellion*. Three volumes. Cedar Rapids, IA: 1909. Reprint, New York, NY: Thomas Yoseloff, 1959.

Eicher, David J. *The Longest Night: A Military History of the Civil War*. New York, NY: Simon & Schuster, 2001.

Eicher, John H. and Eicher, David J. *Civil War High Commands*. Stanford, CA: Stanford University Press, 2001.

Eisenhower, John S.D. *So Far from God: The U.S. War with Mexico, 1846-1848*. Norman OK: University of Oklahoma Press, 1989.

Eldridge, David P. "Brick Versus Earth: The Construction and Destruction of Confederate Seacoast Forts Pulaski and McAllister, Georgia." Master's thesis. University of North Florida, 1996.

Encyclopedia of Connecticut Biography, vol. 1. Boston, MA: The American Historical Society, Inc., 1917.

Field, Ron. *American Civil War Fortifications (2): Land and Field Fortifications*. New York, NY: Osprey Publishing, 2005.

Fishel, Edwin C. *The Secret War for the Union: The Untold Story of Military Intelligence in the Civil War*. Boston, MA: Houghton Mifflin Company, 1996.

Fletcher, David M. *Diplomacy of Annexation: Texas, Oregon, and the Mexican War*. Columbia Missouri: University of Missouri Press, 1973.

Foos, Paul. *A Short, Offhand, Killing Affair: Soldiers and Social Conflict during the Mexican-American War*. Chapel Hill, NC: The University of North Carolina Press, 2002.

Foreman, Grant, ed. *A Traveler In Indian Territory - The Journal of Ethan Allen Hitchcock*. Cedar Rapids, IA: Torch Press, 1930.

Fox, William F. *In Memoriam, Henry Warner Slocum, 1826-1894*. Albany, NY: J.B. Lyon Company, 1904.

_____. *Regimental Losses in the American Civil War 1861-1865*. Albany, NY: Brandow Printing Company, 1898. Reprint, Dayton, OH: Press of Morningside Bookshop, 1985.

Frazer, Robert W. *Forts and Supplies: The Role of the Army in the Economy of the Southwest 1846-1861*. Albuquerque, NM: University of New Mexico Press, 1983.

_____. *Forts of the West, Military Forts and Presidios and Posts Commonly Called Forts West of the Mississippi River to 1898*. Norman, OK: University of Oklahoma Press, 1965.

Frazier, Donald S., ed. *The United States and Mexico at War: Nineteenth-Century Expansionism and Conflict*. New York, NY: Simon & Schuster Macmillan, 1998.

Freeman, Douglas Southall. *R. E. Lee: A Biography*. Vol. 1. New York, NY: Charles Scribner's Sons, 1936.

Freiheit, Laurence H. *Boots and Saddles: Cavalry During the Maryland Campaign of September 1862*, 2nd ed. Iowa City, Iowa: Camp Pope Publishing, 2013.

French, Samuel G. *Two Wars: an Autobiography of Gen. Samuel G. French*. Nashville, TN: Confederate Veteran, 1901.

Frost, John. *Pictorial History of Mexico and the Mexican War*. Philadelphia, PA: Charles Desilver, 1862.

Fry, James B. *The History and Legal Effect of Brevets in the Armies of Great Britain and the United States from Their Origin in 1692 to the Present Time*. New York, NY: D. Van Nostrand, 1877.

Furber, George C. *The Twelve Months Volunteer or, Journal of a Private in the Tennessee Regiment of Cavalry*. Cincinnati, OH: J.A. & U.P. James, 1849.

Furness, William Eliot, Chmn. *Memorials of Deceased Companions of the Commandery of the State of Illinois, Military Order of the Loyal Legion of the United States*, vol. 1. Chicago, IL: n.p., 1901.

Gamble, Richard Dalzell. "Garrison Life at Frontier Military Posts, 1830-1860," unpub. PhD thesis, The University of Oklahoma, Norman, K, 1956.

Ganoe, William A. *History of the United States Army*. New York, NY: D. Appleton and Company, 1924.

General Regulations for the Army; or, Military Institutes. Washington, DC: Davis & Force, 1825.

General Regulation for the Army of the United States, 1841. Washington, DC: J. and G.S. Gideon, Printers, 1841.

General Regulations for the Army of the United States, 1847. Washington, DC: J. and G.S. Gideon, 1847.

General Taylor and His Staff. Philadelphia, PA: Grigg, Elliot & Co., 1848.

Gibbon, John. *Personal Recollections of the Civil War*. New York, NY: G.P. Putnam's Sons, 1928. Reprint, Dayton, OH: Morningside House, Inc., 1988.

Giddings, Luther. *Sketches of the Campaign in Northern Mexico in Eighteen Hundred Forty-Six and Seven*. New York, NY: George P. Putnam & Co., 1853.

Gillmore, Quincy A. *Official Report to the United States Engineer Department, of the Siege and Reduction of Fort Pulaski, Georgia, February, March, and April, 1862*. New York, NY: D. Van Nostrand, 1862.

Goetzmann, William H. *Army Exploration in the American West, 1803-1863*. Austin, TX: Texas State historical Association, 1991.

Gould, John Mead. *The Civil War Journals of John Mead Gould 1861-1866*. Ed. by William B. Jordan, Jr. Baltimore: Butternut & Blue, 1997.

_____. *History of the First-Tenth-Twenty-ninth Maine Regiment in Service of the United States from May 3, 1861, to June 21, 1866*. Portland, ME: Stephen Berry, Printer, 1871.

_____. *Joseph K.F. Mansfield, Brigadier General of the U.S. Army. A Narrative of Events Connected with His Mortal Wounding at Antietam, Sharpsburg, Maryland, September 17, 1862*. Portland, ME: Stephen Barry, Printer, 1895.

Gould, Joseph. *The Story of The Forty-Eighth: A Record of the Campaigns of the Forty-Eighth Regiment Pennsylvania Veteran Volunteer Infantry during the four eventful years of its service in the war for the preservation of the Union*. Philadelphia, PA: Alfred M. Slocum Co., 1908.

Graham, Matthew J. *The Ninth Regiment, New York Volunteers (Hawkins' Zouaves)*. New York, NY: E.P. Coby & Co., 1900.

Grant, Ulysses S. *Personal Memoirs*. New York, NY: The Modern Library, 1999.

Grau, Lester W. "The Delafield Commission: Forerunner of the Foreign Area Officers Program." "The FAO Journal," vol. XIV, no. 4, Dec. 2011.

Green, Constance McLaughlin. *Washington: Village and Capital, 1800-1878*. Princeton, NJ: Princeton University Press, 1962.

Green, Robert M. *History of the One Hundred and Twenty-fourth Regiment Pennsylvania Volunteers in the War of the Rebellion—1862-1863*. Philadelphia, PA: Ware Bros. Company, Printers, 1907.

Greene, George S. "Address," *Annual Reunion, June 11th, 1888*, Annual Report by the United States Military Academy Association of Graduates. East Saginaw, MI: Evening News, Printers and Binders, 1885.

Griffith, Paddy. *Battle Tactics of the Civil War*. New Haven, CT: Yale University Press, 2001.

_____. *The Vauban Fortifications of France*. New York, NY: Osprey Publishing, 2006.

Haecker, Charles M and Mauck, Jeffrey G. *On the Prairie of Palo Alto: Historical Archaeology of the U.S.-Mexican War Battlefield*. College Station, TX: Texas A&M University Press, 1997.

Hafen, LeRoy Reuben. *The Overland Mail, 1849-1869: Promoter of Settlement, Precursor of Railroads*. Norman, OK: University of Oklahoma Press, 2004.

Hamersly, Thomas H.S. *Complete Army Register of the United States for 100 Years (1789 to 1879)*. Washington, DC: T.H.S. Hamersly, 1881.

Hamilton, Holman. *Zachary Taylor: Soldier of the Republic*. Indianapolis, IN: The Bobbs-Merrill Company, 1944.

_____. *The Three Kentucky Presidents: Lincoln, Taylor, Davis*. Lexington, KY: The Univ. Press of Kentucky, 1978.

Hannings, Bud. *Forts of the United States: A Historical Dictionary, 16ᵗʰ through 19ᵗʰ Centuries*. Jefferson, NC: McFarland & Co., 2006.

Harlow, Neal. California Conquered: The Annexation of a Mexican Province 1846-1850. Berkeley, CA: University of California Press, 1982.

Harsh, Joseph L. *Taken at the Flood: Robert E. Lee and Confederate Strategy and the Maryland Campaign of 1862*. Kent, OH: The Kent State University Press, 1999.

_____. *Confederate Tide Rising: Robert E. Lee and the Making of Southern Strategy, 1861 – 1862*. Kent, OH: The Kent State University Press, 1998.

_____. *Sounding the Shallows: A Confederate Companion for the Maryland Campaign of 1862*. Kent, OH: The Kent State University Press, 2000.

Hart, Herbert M. *Old Forts of the Southwest*. New York, NY: Bonanza Books, 1964.

_____. *Tour Guide to Old Western Forts*. Boulder, CO: Pruett Publishing Co., 1980.

Hartwig, D. Scott. *To Antietam Creek: The Maryland Campaign of September 1862*. Baltimore, MD: The Johns Hopkins University Press, 2012.

_____. "The Volunteers of '62." *The Antietam Campaign*. Ed. by Gary W. Gallagher. Chapel Hill, NC: The University of North Carolina Press, 1999.

_____. "Who Would Not Be a Soldier: The Volunteers of '62." *The Antietam Campaign*. Ed. by Gary W. Gallagher. Chapel Hill, NC: The University of North Carolina Press, 1999.

Hasluck, ed. Paul N. *Cassell's Cyclopaedia of Mechanics*, New York, NY: Cassell and Company, 1900.

Hauptman, Laurence M. and Dixon, Heriberto. "Cadet David Moniac: A Creek Indian's Schooling at West Point, 1817-1822." *Proceedings of the American Philosophical Society*, vol. 152 no. 3, September 2008.

Hawkins, Rush C. "With the Cavalry on the Peninsula." In *Battles and Leaders of the Civil War: Being   for the Most Part Contributions by Union and Confederate Officers Based upon "The Century War Series."* Vol. 1. Johnson, Robert U. and Buel, Clarence C. eds. New York, NY: Thomas Yoseloff, 1956.

Hawkins, Vince. "The U.S. Army's 'Camel Corps' Experiment,'" 16 July 2014, National Museum of the United States Army, https://Armyhistory.org/the-u-s-Armys-camel-corps-experiment/.

Hazen, Azel Washburn. *A Brief History of the First Church of Christ in Middletown Connecticut for Two Centuries and a Half*. n.p., 1920.

Heidler, Jeanne Twiggs. "The Military Career of David Emanuel Twiggs." PhD dissertation. Texas Christian University, 1976.

Heintzelman, Samuel Peter. *Samuel Peter Heintzelman's Journal of Texas and the Cortina War.* Ed. by Jerry Thompson. Austin, TX: Texas State Historical Association, 1998.

Heitman, Francis B. *Historical Register and Dictionary of the United States Army, from Its Organization, September 29, 1789, to March 2, 1902.* Vol. 1. Washington, D.C.: GPO, 1903.   Reprint, University of Illinois Press, Urbana, IL: 1965.

Hennessy, John J. *Return to Bull Run: The Campaign and Battle of Second Manassas.* New York, NY: Simon   & Schuster, 1993.

Henry, Robert Selph. *The Story of the Mexican War.* New York, NY: Frederick Ungar Publishing Co., 1961.

Henry, William Seaton. *Campaign Sketches of the War with Mexico.* New York, NY: Harper & Brothers, 1847.

Henshaw, John Cory. *Recollections of the War with Mexico.* Ed. by Gary F. Kurutz. Univ. of Missouri Press, Columbia, MO., 2008.

Heyman, Max L., Jr. *Prudent Soldier: A Biography of Major General E.R.S. Canby 1817-1873.* Glendale, CA: The Arthur H. Clark Company, 1959.

Hinckley, Julian Wisner. *A Narrative of Service with the Third Wisconsin Infantry.* Democrat Printing Co., State Printer, Wisconsin History Commission, 1912.

Hines, Blaikie, *Civil War Volunteer Sons of Connecticut.* Thomaston, ME: American Patriot Press, 2002.

Hinton, Harwood P. "The Military Career of John Ellis Wool, 1812-1863." PhD dissertation, Univ. of Wisconsin, 1960.

History of Middlesex County, Connecticut with Biographical Sketches of Its Prominent Men. New York, NY: J.B. Beers & Co., 1884.

Hitchcock, Ethan Allen. *Fifty Years in Camp and Field: Diary of Major General Ethan Allen Hitchcock.* Ed. by W.A. Croffut. New York, NY: G.P. Putnam's Sons, 1909.

Hobart, R. *The National Tribune.* "Battle of Antietam," 16 February 1893.

Horsman, Reginald. *Race and Manifest Destiny: The Origins of American Racial Anglo-Saxonism.* Cambridge, MA: Harvard University Press, 1981.

Howard, Oliver Otis. *Autobiography of Oliver Otis Howard,* vol. 1. New York, NY: The Baker & Taylor Company, 1907.

Hull, William. *Memoirs of the Campaign of the North Western Army of the United States, A.D. 1812.* Boston, MA: True & Greene, 1824.

Hutchinson, A.H. *The National Tribune.* "Gen. Mansfield's Death," 1 December 1892.

Hutchinson, George E. *The History of Madison Place, Lafayette Square, Washington, DC.* Washington, DC: The Federal Circuit Historical Society, n.d.

Inman, Henry. *The Old Santa Fe Trail: The Story of a Great Highway.* Topeka, KS: Crane & Company, 1916.

Irwin, Richard B. "The Case of Fitz John Porter." In *Battles and Leaders of the Civil War: Being for the Most Part Contributions by Union and Confederate Officers Based upon "The Century War Series."* Vol. 2. Johnson, Robert U. and Buel, Clarence C. eds. New York: Thomas Yoseloff, 1956.

Jenkins, John S. *History of the War Between the United States and Mexico.* New York, NY: C.M. Saxton, 1859.

Johnson, Curt, and Anderson, Richard C., Jr. *Artillery Hell: The Employment of Artillery at Antietam.*   College Station, TX: Texas A&M University Press, 1995.

Johnson, Forrest Bryant. *The Last Camel Charge: The Untold Story of America's Desert Military Experiment.* New York, NY: Berkley Caliber, 2012.

Jones, Archer. *Civil War Command and Strategy: The Process of Victory and Defeat.* New York: The Free Press, 1992.

Jones, Charles C., Jr. "The Seizure and Reduction of Fort Pulaski." *The Magazine of American History Illustrated,* vol. 14, July 1885.

Jones, Howard. *Blue & Gray Diplomacy: A History of Union and Confederate Foreign Relations.* Chapel Hill, NC: The University of North Carolina Press, 2010.

Jones, Wilbur D. "Who Lost the Lost Order?" *Civil War Regiments: A Journal of the American Civil War.* Vol. 5, no. 3, (1997).

Kanarek, Harold. *The Mid-Atlantic Engineers: A History of the Baltimore District, U.S. Army Corps of Engineers, 1774-1974.* Washington, DC: U.S. Government Printing Office, 1976.

Kaufmann, J.E. and H.W. *Fortress America: The Forts that Defended America, 1600 to the Present.* Cambridge, MA: Da Capo Press, 2004.

Kelley, Brooks Mather. *Yale: A History.* New Haven, CT: Yale University Press, 1974.

Knox, Edward B. "The Capture of Alexandria and Death of Ellsworth." Ed. by Charles W. Davis. *Military Essays and Recollections: Papers Read Before the Commandery of the State of Illinois, Military Order of the Loyal Legion of the United States,* vol. 2. Chicago, IL: A.C. McClurg and Company, 1894.

Krick, Robert K. *Stonewall Jackson at Cedar Mountain.* Chapel Hill, NC: The University of North Carolina Press, 1990.

Ladd, Horatio O. *History of the War with Mexico.* New York, NY: Dodd, Mead & Company, 1883.

Lane, Walter P. *The Adventures and Recollections of General Walter P. Lane, a San Jacinto Veteran.* Austin, TX: Pemberton Press, Jenkins Publishing Company, 1970.

Larkin, Jack. *The Reshaping of Everyday Life 1790-1840.* New York, NY: Harper & Row, 1988.

Latrobe, John Hazlehurst Boneval. *Reminiscences of West Point from September 1818 to March 1882.* East Saginaw, MI: Evening News, Printers and Binders, 1887.

Lattimore, Ralston B. *Fort Pulaski National Monument, Georgia*; National Park Service Historical Handbook Series No. 18. Washington, DC: GPO, 1954; reprint 1961.

Lavender, David. *Climax at Buena Vista: The Decisive Battle of the Mexican-American War.* Philadelphia, PA: University of Pennsylvania Press, 2003.

Lee, Richard M. *Mr. Lincoln's City: An Illustrated Guide to the Civil War Sites of Washington.* McLean, VA: EPM Publications, Inc., 1981.

Levinson, Irving. *Wars Within War: Mexican Guerrillas, Domestic Elites, and the United States of America, 1846-1848.* Fort Worth, TX: Christian University Press, 2005.

Lewis, Emanuel Raymond. *Seacoast Fortifications of the United States, An Introductory History.* Annapolis, MD: Naval Institute Press, 1970.

Lincoln, Abraham. *The Collected Works of Lincoln.* Ed. by Roy P. Basler. New Brunswick, NJ: Rutgers University Press, 1953.

_____. *Abraham Lincoln: His Speeches and Writings.* Ed. by Roy P. Basler. Cleveland, OH: The World Publishing Company, 1946.

Longstreet, James. *From Manassas to Appomattox: Memoirs of the Civil War in America*. Philadelphia, PA: J.B. Lippincott Company, 1895.

Mahon, John K. *History of the Second Seminole War 1835-1842*. Gainesville, FL: University of Florida Press, 1967.

Manring, Benjamin F. *The Conquest of the Coeur d'Alenes, Spokanes and Palouses: The Expeditions of Colonels E.J. Steptoe and George Wright Against the "Northern Indians" in 1858*. Spokane, WA: John W. Graham & Co., 1912.

Mansfield, Edward D. *Personal Memories, Social, Political, and Literary with Sketches of Many Noted People, 1803-1843*. Cincinnati, OH: Robert Clarke & Co., 1879.

_____. *The Mexican War: A History of Its Origin*. New York, NY: A.S. Barnes and Co., 1873.

Mansfield, H. *The Descendants of Richard and Gillian Mansfield Who Settled in New Haven, 1639 With Sketches of Some of the Most Distinguished. Also, of Connections of Other Names*. New Haven, CT: Hoggson & Robinson, Printers, 1885.

Mansfield, Joseph K. F. "Colonel Joseph K.F. Mansfield Visits Fort Townsend, 1858." Ed. by Jesse S. Douglas. *Readings in Pacific Northwest History, Washington, 1790-1895*. Ed. by Charles Marvin Gates. Seattle, WA: The University Bookstore, 1941.

Mansfield, Joseph K. F. *Mansfield on the Condition of the Western Forts, 1853-4*. Robert W. Frazer, ed. Norman, OK: University of Oklahoma Press, 1963.

Mansfield, Joseph K. F. and Johnston, Joseph E. *Texas and New Mexico on the Eve of the Civil War: The Mansfield & Johnston Inspections, 1859-1861*. Jerry Thompson, ed. Albuquerque, NM: University of New Mexico Press, 2001.

Marcum, Richard T. "Fort Brown, Texas: The History of a Border Post." PhD dissertation, 1964. Texas Technological College.

Marcy, Randolph B. *The Prairie Traveler: A Hand-Book for Overland Expeditions*. New York, NY: Harper & Brothers, 1861.

Marvin, Edwin E. *The Fifth Regiment Connecticut Volunteers*. Hartford, CT: Press of Wiley, Waterman & Eaton, 1889.

McCaffrey, James M. *Army of Manifest Destiny: The American Soldier in the Mexican War, 1846-1848*. New York, NY: New York University Press, 1992.

McCall, George Archibald. *Letters from the Frontiers*. Philadelphia, PA: J.B. Lippincott & Co., 1868.

McClellan, George B. *The Civil War Papers of George B. McClellan: Selected Correspondence, 1860-1865*. Ed. by Stephen W. Sears. New York, NY: Ticknor & Fields, 1989. Reprint, Cambridge, MA: Da Capo Press, 1992.

_____. *McClellan's Own Story*. New York: Charles L. Webster & Company, 1887. Reprint, Scituate,   MA: Digital Scanning, Inc., 1998.

_____. *The Mexican War Diary and Correspondence of George B. McClellan*. Ed. by Thomas W. Cutrer. Baton Rouge, LA: Louisiana State University Press, 2009.

_____. *Report on the Organization and Campaigns of the Army of the Potomac*. New York, NY: Sheldon & Company, 1864.

McGrath, Thomas A. *Shepherdstown: Last Clash of the Antietam Campaign September 19-20, 1862* (Lynchburg, VA: Schroeder Publications, 2007.

McKenna, Charles F. *Under the Maltese Cross: Antietam to Appomattox*. Pittsburg, PA: The 155th Regimental Association, 1910.

McPherson, James M. *Crossroads of Freedom: Antietam*. New York, NY: Oxford University Press, 2002.

Meade, George Gordon. *The Life and Letters of George Gordon Meade*. Ed. by George Meade. New York, NY: Charles Scribner's Sons, 1913.

Memorial of Gen. J.K.F. Mansfield, United States Army, Who Fell in Battle at Sharpsburg, Md., Sept. 17, 1862. Boston, MA: Press of T.R. Marvin & Son, 1862.

Memorial of Lieutenant Howard M. Burnham. Springfield, MA: Samuel Bowles and Company, Printers, 1864.

The Mexican War and Its Heroes: Being a Complete History of the Mexican War. Philadelphia, PA: J.B. Lippincott & Co., 1860.

Meyers, Augustus. *Ten Years in the Ranks U.S. Army.* New York, NY: The Sterling Press, 1914.

Miller, Ray. *Texas Forts: A History and Guide.* Houston, TX: Cordovan Press, 1985.

Montgomery, Henry. *The Life of Major General Zachary Taylor.* Auburn, NY: J.C. Derby & Co., 1847.

Moten, Matthew. *The Delafield Commission and the American Military Profession.* College Station, TX: Texas A&M University Press, 2000.

Murfin, James A. *The Gleam of Bayonets: The Battle of Antietam and the Maryland Campaign of 1862.* Baton Rouge: Louisiana State University Press, 1965.

Murphy, Douglas A. *Two Armies on the Rio Grande: The First Campaign of the US-Mexican War.* College Station, TX: Texas A&M University Press, 2015.

Ness, George T., Jr. *The Regular Army on the Eve of the Civil War.* Baltimore, MD: Toomey Press, 1990.

Nevins, Allan. *The War for the Union*, Vols. 1, 2. New York, NY: Charles Scribner's Sons, 1959.

Newell, Clayton R. *The Regular Army before the Civil War 1845-1860.* Washington, DC: The Center of Military History, 1975.

Newton, Virginius. "The Ram Merrimac." *Southern Historical Society Papers*, vol. 20. Ed. by R.A. Brock, vol. 20, January-December 1892. Richmond, VA: Published by the Society, 1892.

Nichols, Edward J. *Zach Taylor's Little Army.* Garden City, NY: Doubleday & Company, Inc., 1963.

Niven, John. *Salmon P. Chase: A Biography.* New York, NY: Oxford University Press, 1995.

Oliva, Leo E. *Fort Union and the Frontier Army in the Southwest.* Southwest Cultural Resources Center Professional Papers No. 41. National Park Service, Dept. of the Interior, 1993.

Olmstead, Charles H. "Fort Pulaski." *The Georgia Historical Quarterly*, vol. 1, no. 2, June 1917.

Osborne, William H. *The History of the Twenty-Ninth Regiment of Massachusetts Volunteer Infantry, in the Late War of the Rebellion.* Boston, MA: Albert J. Wright, 1877.

O'Sullivan, John. "Annexation," *United States Magazine and Democratic Review 17,* no. 1, July-August 1845.

Our Georgia History: The Capture of Fort Pulaski. Woodstock, GA: Golden Ink, Inc., copyright 2001, http://www.ourgeorgiahistory.com/wars/Civil_War/ftpulaski.html; Internet; accessed 21 December 2006.

Owen, Tom. *The Taylor Anecdote Book: Anecdotes and Letters of Zachary Taylor.* New York, NY: D. Appleton & Company, 1847.

Pappas, George S. *To The Point: The United States Military Academy, 1802-1902*. Westport, CT: Praeger Publishers, 1993.

Parker, William Harwar. *Recollections of a Naval Officer 1841-1865.* New York, NY: Charles Scribner's Sons, 1883. Reprint, Annapolis, MD: Naval Institute Press, 1985.

Parkman, Aubrey. *Army Engineers in New England: The Military and Civil Work of the Corps of Engineers in New England 1775-1975.* Waltham, MA: U.S. Army Corps of Engineers, New England Division, 1978.

Payne, Darwin. "Camp Life in the Army of Occupation: Corpus Christi, July 1845 to March 1846," *The Southwestern Historical Quarterly*, vol. 73, no. 3, Jan. 1970.

Phelps, John Wolcott. "Diary of Captain Phelps," *Mormon Resistance: A Documentary Account of the Utah Expedition, 1857-1858*. Ed. by Leroy R. Hafen and Ann W. Hafen. Lincoln, NE: University of Nebraska Press, 2005.

Philips, John and Rider, Alfred. *Mexico Illustrated in Twenty-six Views*. London: E. Atchley, Library of Fine Arts, 1848.

Plum, William R. *The Military Telegraph during the Civil War in the United States*, vol. 1. Chicago, IL: Jansen, McClurg & Company, 1882.

Pope, John. *National Tribune*, 19 March 1891, "War Reminiscences."

Price, George Frederic. *Across the Continent with the Fifth Cavalry*. New York, NY: D. Van Nostrand, 1883.

Prucha, Francis Paul. *A Guide to the Military Posts of the United States*. Madison, WI: The State Historical Society of Wisconsin, 1964.

Quint, Alonzo H. *The Record of the Second Massachusetts Infantry, 1861-65*. Boston, MA: 1867.

Rafuse, Ethan S. "Jefferson Finis Davis." *The Encyclopedia of the Mexican-American War*. Ed. by Spencer C. Tucker. Santa Barbara, CA: ABC-CLIO, 2013.

Rawley, James A. *Turning Points of the Civil War*. Lincoln, NE: University of Nebraska Press, 1966.

Recker, Stephen. *Rare Images of Antietam and the Photographers Who Took Them*. Sharpsburg, MD: Another Software Miracle, LLC, 2012.

Regulations for the Army of the United States, 1857. New York, NY: Harper & Brothers, 1857.

Remini, Robert V. *John Quincy Adams*. New York, NY: Henry Holt and Company, 2002.

Ripley, Roswell Sabine. *The War with Mexico*, vol. 1. New York, NY: Harper & Brothers, 1849.

Risch, Erna. *Quartermaster Support of the Army: A History of the Corps, 1775-1939*. Washington, DC: Dept. of the Army, 1962.

Robarts, William Hugh. *Mexican War Veterans: A Complete Roster*. Brentano's: Washington, DC, 1887.

Roberts, Robert B. An *Encyclopedia of Historic Forts: The Military, Pioneer, and Trading Posts of the United States*. New York, NY: Macmillan Publishing Company, 1988.

Robinson, Fayette. *An Account of the Organization of the Army of the United States*, vol. 1. Philadelphia, PA: E.H. Butler, 1848.

Rockey, J.L., et al., ed. *History of New Haven County, Connecticut*, vol. 1. New York, NY: W.W. Preston & Co., 1892.

Rodenbough, T.F. *From Everglade to Canon with the Second Dragoons*. New York, NY: D. Van Nostrand, 1875.

Ross, Robert B. *The Early Bench and Bar of Detroit from 1805 to the End of 1850*. Detroit, MI: Richard P. Joy and Clarence M. Burton, 1907.

Sandburg, Carl. *Abraham Lincoln: The War Years*, vol. 1. New York, NY: Harcourt, Brace & Company, 1939.

Sandweiss, Martha A.; Stewart, Rick; Huseman, Ben W. *Eyewitness to War: Prints and Daguerreotypes of the Mexican War, 1846-1848*. Fort Worth, TX: Amon Carter Museum, 1989.

Sanger, J.P. "Inspector General's Department," in *The Army of the United States, Historical Sketches of Staff and Line*. Ed. by Theophilus F. Rodenbough and William L. Haskin. New York, NY: Maynard, Merrill, & Co., 1896.

Scott, H.L. *Military Dictionary*. New York, NY: D. Van Nostrand, 1861.

Sears, Stephen W. *Landscape Turned Red: The Battle of Antietam*. New York, NY: Houghton Mifflin Company, 1993.

_____. *To the Gates of Richmond: The Peninsula Campaign*. New York: Ticknor & Fields, 1992.

Sedgwick, John. *Correspondence of John Sedgwick, Major General,* vol. 2. Carl and Ellen Battelle Stoeckel, 1903.

Semmes, John E. *John H.B. Latrobe and His times, 1803-1891*. Baltimore, MD: The Waverly Press, 1917.

Seville, William P. *History of the First Regiment, Delaware Volunteers*. Wilmington, DE: The Historical Society of Delaware, 1884.

Sexton, Jay. "Steam Transport, Sovereignty, and Empire in North America, circa 1850-1885." *The Journal of the Civil War Era*, vol. 7, no. 4, Dec. 2017. Chapel Hill, NC: Univ. of North Carolina Press, 2017.

Shaw, Robert Gould. *Blue-Eyed Child of Fortune: The Civil War Letters of Colonel Robert Gould Shaw*. Ed. by Russell Duncan. New York: NY: Avon Books, 1994.

Shook, Robert W. "Victoria, TX (Victoria County)" *Handbook of Texas Online* (http://www.tshaonline.org/handbook/online/articles/hdv01), accessed March 18, 2013. Published by the Texas State Historical Association.

Skelton, William B. *An American Profession of Arms: The Army Officer Corps, 1784-1861*. Lawrence, KS: University Press of Kansas, 1992.

Smith, George Winston, and Charles B. Judah. *Chronicles of the Gringos: The U.S. Army in the Mexican War, 1846-1848; Accounts of Eyewitnesses & Combatants*. Albuquerque: University of New Mexico Press: 1968.

Smith, John P. "Reminiscences of Antietam Field," *Hagerstown Morning Herald*, 29 March 1901.

Smith, Justin H. *The War with Mexico*, vols. 1 and 2. New York, NY: The Macmillan Co., 1919.

Smith, S. Compton. *Chile Con Carne; Or, The Camp and the Field*. New York, NY: Miller & Curtis, 1857.

Smith, Stephen R., et al. *Record of Service of Connecticut Men in the Army and Navy of the United States During the War of the Rebellion*. Hartford, CT: Press of The Case, Lockwood & Brainard Company, 1889.

Snyder, Timothy R. "Civil War Fords of the Potomac River." Unpublished Manuscript.

Spurlin, Charles D. *Texas Volunteers in the Mexican War*. Austin, TX: Eakin Press, 1998.

Steere, Thomas. *History of the Town of Smithfield from Its Organization, in 1730-1 to Its Division, in 1871*. Providence, RI: E.L. Freeman & Co., 1881.

Steffen, Randy. *United States Military Saddles, 1812-1943*. Norman, OK: University of Oklahoma Press, 1973.

_____. *The Horse Soldier, 1776-1943: The United States Cavalryman: His Uniforms, Arms, Accoutrements, and Equipments,* vol. II, *The Frontier, the Mexican War, the Civil War, the Indian Wars, 1851-1880*. Norman, OK: University of Oklahoma Press, 1978.

Stephenson, Charles, ed. *Castles: A History of Fortified Structures, Ancient, Medieval & Modern*. New York, NY: St. Martin's Griffin, 2011.

Stephenson, Nathaniel W. *Texas and the War with Mexico: A Chronicle of the Winning of the Southwest*. New Haven, CT: Yale University Press, 1921.

Stevens, Peter F. *The Rogue's March: John Riley and the St. Patrick's Battalion, 1846-48*. Washington, DC: Potomac Books, Inc., 1999.

Stewart, Richard W., ed. *American Military History, The United States Army and the Forging of a Nation, 1775-1917*, vol. 1. Washington, DC: GPO, 2009.

Stiles, Israel N. "The Monitor and the Merrimac," read 5 April 1885, *Military Essays and Recollections: Papers Read Before the Commandery of the State of Illinois, Military Order of the Loyal Legion of the United States*. Chicago, IL: A.C. McClurg and Company, 1891.

Strother, David Hunter. *A Virginia Yankee in the Civil War: The Diaries of David Hunter Strother*. Ed. by Cecil D. Eby, Jr. Chapel Hill, NC: The University of North Carolina Press, 1961.

_____. "Personal Recollections of the War." *Harper's New Monthly Magazine*, vol. 35, Feb. 1868.

Stryker, William S. *Record of Officers and Men of New Jersey in the Civil War, 1861—1865*. Trenton, NJ: John L. Murphy, Steam Book and Job Printer, 1876.

Swinton, William. *History of the Seventh Regiment, National Guard, State of New York during the War of the Rebellion*. New York, NY: Fields, Osgood, & Co., 1870.

Sylvester, Nathaniel Bartlett. *History of Rensselaer Co., New York*. Philadelphia, PA: Everts & Peck, 1880.

Symonds, Craig L. *Joseph E. Johnston: A Civil War Biography*. New York, NY: W.W. Norton & Company, 1992.

Tate, Michael L. *The Frontier Army in the Settlement of the West*. Norman, OK: University of Oklahoma Press, 1999.

Taylor, Jeremiah. *Memorial of Gen. J. K. F. Mansfield, United States Army, Who Fell in Battle at Sharpsburg, Md. Sept. 17, 1862*. Boston: Press of T.R. Marvin & Son, 1862.

Taylor, Zachary. *Letters of Zachary Taylor from the Battlefields of the Mexican War*. Ed. William K. Bixby. Rochester, NY: The Genesee Press, 1908.

Tenney, Leon. "Seven Days in 1862: Numbers in Union and Confederate Armies before Richmond." Master's thesis. George Mason University, 1992.

Thompson, Erwin N. *Historic Resource Study: Seacoast Fortifications, San Francisco Harbor, Golden Gate National Recreation Area, California*. NPS, 1979.

Thompson, Jerry. *Civil War to the Bloody End: The Life and Times of Major General Samuel P. Heintzelman*. College Station, TX: Texas A&M University Press, 2006.

Thonhoff, Robert H. "Taylor's Trail in Texas." *The Southwestern Historical Quarterly*, vol. 70, no. 1, July 1966.

Thorpe, Thomas Bangs; (pseud. Tom Owen). *Our Army on the Rio Grande*. Philadelphia, PA: Carey and Hart, 1846.

_____. *The Taylor Anecdote Book: Anecdotes and Letters of Zachary Taylor*. New York, NY: D. Appleton & Company, 1848.

Ticknor, George. *Life, Letters, and Journals of George Ticknor*, vol. 1. Edited by George S. Hillard. Boston, MA: Houghton Mifflin Company, 1909.

Tillman, Samuel E. *The Centennial of the United States Military Academy at West Point, New York*, vol. 1: Addresses and Histories, "The Academic History of the Military Academy, 1802-1902. Washington, D. C.: Government Printing Office, 1904.

Towner, Ausburn. *Our Country and Its People: A History of the Valley and County of Chemung From the Closing Years of the Eighteenth Century.* Syracuse, NY: D. Mason & Co., Publishers, 1892.

Trass, Adrian G. *From the Golden Gate to Mexico City: The U.S. Topographical Engineers in the Mexican War, 1846-1848.* Washington, DC: GPO, 1993.

Turnley, Parmenas Taylor. *Reminiscences of Parmenas Taylor Turnley: From the Cradle to Three-Score and Ten.* Chicago, IL: Donohue & Henneberry, 1892.

Tyler, Ronnie C. *The Mexican War: A Lithographic Record.* Austin, TX: Texas State Historical Association, 1973.

Tyndale, Hector. *A Memoir of Hector Tyndale.* Philadelphia, PA, MOLLUS, 1882.

The U.S. Army Corps of Engineers: A History. Washington, DC: Headquarters, U.S. Army Corps of Engineers, Office of History, Alexandria, Va., 2008.

U.S. Congress, *Report of the Joint Committee on the Conduct of the War.* Washington, DC: GPO, 1863. Reprint, Wilmington, NC: Broadfoot Publishing Company, 1998.

U.S. War Department. *The War of the Rebellion: A Compilation of the Official Records of the Union and Confederate Armies.* 128 vols. Washington, D.C.: GPO, 1880-1901. Reprint, Harrisburg: Broadfoot Publishing Company, 1985.

U.S. War Department. *The War of the Rebellion: A Compilation of the Official Records of the Union and Confederate Navies.* 31 vols. Washington, D.C.: GPO, 1897. Reprint, Harrisburg, PA: The National Historical Society, 1987.

_____. *The Official Military Atlas of the Civil War: Atlas to Accompany the Official Records of the Union and Confederate Armies.* Washington, DC: GPO, 1891-1895. Reprint, New York, NY: Arno Press, Inc., 1978.

Upton, Emory. *Military Policy of the United States.* Washington, DC: GPO, 1904.

Utley, Robert M. *Fort Union and the Santa Fe Trail.* El Paso, TX: Texas Western Press, 1989.

_____. *Frontiersmen in Blue: The United States Army and the Indian, 1848-1865.* New York, NY: The Macmillan Company, 1967.

Wagner, Martha. Historic American Buildings Survey, National Park Service, HABS NO. MD-957, 1991.

Walker, Dale L. *Bear Flag Rising: The Conquest of California, 1846.* New York, NY: Forge Books, 1999.

Walkley, Stephen. *History of the Seventh Connecticut Volunteer Infantry.* Hartford, CT: n.p., 1905.

Wallace, Lew. *Lew Wallace: An Autobiography.* Vol. 1. New York, NY: Harper & Brothers, 1906.

Wallace, William W. (Chmn.). *History of the One Hundred and Twenty-fifth Regiment Pennsylvania Volunteers 1862—1863.* Philadelphia, PA: J.B. Lippincott Company, 1906.

Warden, Robert B. *An Account of the Private Life and Public Services of Salmon Portland Chase.* Cincinnati, OH: Wilstach, Baldwin & Co., 1874.

Warshauer, Matthew. *Connecticut in the American Civil War: Slavery, Sacrifice, and Survival.* Middletown, CT: Wesleyan University Press, 2011.

Watson, Samuel J. "Manifest Destiny and Military Professionalism: Junior U.S. Army Officers' Attitudes Toward War with Mexico, 1844-1846." *The Southwestern Historical Quarterly*, vol. 99, July 1995 - April, 1996.

Weaver, John R., II. *A Legacy in Brick and Stone: American Coastal Defense Forts of the Third System, 1816-1867.* McLean, VA: Redoubt Press, 2001.

Weems, John Edward. *+.* Garden City, NY: Doubleday & Company, Inc., 1974.

Weigley, Russell F. *History of the United States Army.* New York, NY: Macmillan Publishing Co., Inc., 1967.

Weinert, Richard P., Jr., and Arthur, Robert. *Defender of the Chesapeake: The Story of Fort Monroe*, third revised edition. Shippensburg, PA: White Mane Publishing Company, Inc., 1989.

Welker, David A. *Tempest at Ox Hill: The Battle of Chantilly.* Cambridge, MA: Da Capo Press, 2002.

Welles, Gideon. *The Diary of Gideon Welles*, vol. 1. Boston, MA: Houghton Mifflin Co., 1911.

The Western Reserve Historical Society, Tract No. 96, Oct. 1916, Annual Report for 1915-1916. Cleveland, OH, 1916.

Whittemore, Henry, et al, eds. *History of Middlesex County, Connecticut, with Biographical Sketches of Its Prominent Men.* New York, NY: J.B. Beers and Company 1884.

Wilcox, Cadmus M. *History of the Mexican War.* Washington, DC: The Church News Publishing Co., 1892.

Wilkins, Frederick. *The Highly Irregular Irregulars: Texas Rangers in the Mexican War.* Austin, TX: Eakin Press, 1990.

Williams, Alpheus S. *From the Cannon's Mouth: The Civil War Letters of General Alpheus S. Williams.* Ed. by Milo M. Quaife. Detroit, MI: Wayne State University Press, 1959. Reprint, Lincoln, NE: University of Nebraska Press, 1995.

Winders, Richard Bruce. *Mr. Polk's Army: The American Military Experience in the Mexican War.* College Station, TX: Texas A&M University Press, 1997.

Winslow, Richard Elliot, III. *General John Sedgwick: The Story of a Union Corps Commander.* Novato, CA: Presidio Press, 1982.

Woodbury, Augustus. *Major General Ambrose E. Burnside and the Ninth Army Corps: A Narrative of Campaigns in North Carolina, Maryland, Virginia, Ohio, Kentucky, Mississippi and Tennessee, During the War for the Preservation of the Republic.* Providence, RI: Sidney S. Rider & Brother, 1867.

Woodward, Ashbel. *Life of General Nathaniel Lyon.* Hartford, CT: Case, Lockwood & Co., 1862.

Worsham, John H. *One of Jackson's Foot Cavalry, His Experience and What He Saw During the War 1861-1865.* New York, NY: The Neale Publishing Company, 1912.

Young, Rogers W. "Story of Gen. Mansfield, the Builder of Fort Pulaski During the Years 1831-45." *Savannah Morning News.*

_____. "A Connecticut Yankee on the Georgia Coast: The Engineering Epic of Fort Pulaski, 1821-1861: Being The Story of the Trials and Triumphs of Lieutenant, later Captain, Joseph K.F. Mansfield, United States Corps of Engineers, in the building of Fort Pulaski, on Cockspur Island, Savannah River, Georgia." NPS, Branch of Historic Sites and Buildings, Manuscript, 1938.

_____. *The Georgia Historical Quarterly*, vol. 20, no. 1, 1936.

Zhu, Liping. "Fort Union National Monument: An Administrative History." NPS, Santa Fe, NM, 1992.

Index

Page numbers in bold italics refer to location in illustration captions.